DON'T THROW THIS CARD AWAY!
THIS MAY BE REQUIRED FOR YOUR COURSE!

6 MONTHS ACCESS FREE WITH THIS TEXT!

THOMSON ONE | Business School Edition

Congratulations!

Your purchase of this NEW textbook includes complimentary access to Thomson ONE – Business School Edition for Finance. Thomson ONE – Business School Edition is a Web-based portal product that provides integrated access to Thomson Financial content for the purpose of financial analysis. This is an educational version of the same financial resources used by Wall Street analysts on a daily basis!

For hundreds of companies, this online resource provides seamless access to:

- **Current and Past Company Data:** Worldscope which includes company profiles, financials and accounting results, market per-share data, annual information, and monthly prices going back to 1980.

- **Financial Analyst Data and Forecasts:** I/B/E/S Consensus Estimates which provides consensus estimates, analyst-by-analyst earnings coverage, and analysts' forecasts.

- **SEC Disclosure Statements:** Disclosure SEC Database which includes company profiles, annual and quarterly company financials, pricing information, and earnings.

- **And More!**

SOUTH-WESTERN
CENGAGE Learning

THOMSON ONE
Business School Edition

ACCESS CODE

PS65ZCBPPSZ7SW

HOW TO REGISTER YOUR ACCESS CODE

1. Launch a web browser and go to **http://tobsefin.swlearning.com**

2. Click the "Register" button to enter your access code.

3. Enter your access code **exactly** as it appears here and create a unique User ID, or enter an existing User ID if you have previously registered for a different South-Western product via an access code.

4. When prompted, create a password (or enter an existing password, if you have previously registered for a different product via an access code.) Submit the necessary information when prompted. **Record your User ID and password in a secure location.**

5. Once registered, return to the URL above and select the "Enter" button; have your User ID and password handy.

Note: The duration of your access to the product begins when registration is complete.

For technical support, contact **1-800-423-0563** or email **support@cengage.com**

Investments: 10e
An Introduction

Herbert B. Mayo

The College of New Jersey

SOUTH-WESTERN
CENGAGE Learning™

Australia • Brazil • Japan • Korea • Mexico • Singapore • Spain • United Kingdom • United States

**Investments: An Introduction,
Tenth Edition**

Herbert B. Mayo

Vice President of Editorial, Business:
   Jack W. Calhoun

Publisher: Joe Sabatino

Executive Editor: Michael R. Reynolds

Developmental Editor:
   Michael Guendelsberger

Marketing Manager: Nathan Anderson

Sr. Marketing Communications Manager:
   Jim Overly

Sr. Media Editor: Scott Fidler

Marketing Coordinator: Suellen Ruttkay

Sr. Editorial Assistant: Adele Scholtz

Sr. Content Project Manager:
   Tamborah Moore

Sr. Frontlist Buyer: Kevin Kluck

Production Service: MPS Limited,
   A Macmillan Company

Compositor: MPS Limited,
   A Macmillan Company

Sr. Art Director: Michelle Kunkler

Cover and Internal Designer: Mike Stratton

Cover Image: © iStockphoto

Sr. Rights Acquisitions Account Manager,
   Images: Deanna Ettinger

Sr. Rights Acquisitions Account Manager,
   Text Permissions: Mardell Glinski Schultz

Permissions Researcher: Sue C. Howard

For product information and technology assistance, contact us at
Cengage Learning Customer & Sales Support, 1-800-354-9706

For permission to use material from this text or product,
submit all requests online at **www.cengage.com/permissions**
Further permissions questions can be emailed to
permissionrequest@cengage.com

Library of Congress Control Number: 2010921486

Package ISBN 13: 978-0-538-45209-0

Package ISBN 10: 0-538-45209-9

Book only ISBN 13: 978-0-538-45210-6

Book only ISBN 10: 0-538-45210-2

South-Western Cengage Learning
5191 Natorp Boulevard
Mason, OH 45040
USA

Cengage Learning products are represented in Canada by Nelson Education, Ltd.

For your course and learning solutions, visit **www.cengage.com**

Purchase any of our products at your local college store or at our preferred online store **www.CengageBrain.com**

Printed in the United States of America
1 2 3 4 5 6 7 14 13 12 11 10

Brief Contents

Contents

Preface

Many individuals find investments to be fascinating because they can actively participate in the decision-making process and see the results of their choices. Of course, not all investments will be profitable because you will not always make correct investment decisions. Over a period of years, however, you should earn a positive return on a diversified portfolio. In addition, there is the thrill from a major success, along with the agony associated with the stock that dramatically rose after you sold or did not buy. Both the big fish you catch and the big fish that got away can make wonderful stories.

Investing, of course, is not a game, but a serious subject that can have a major impact on your future well-being. Virtually everyone makes investments. Even if the individual does not select specific assets such as the stock of AT&T or federal government Series EE bonds, investments are still made through participation in pension plans and employee savings programs or through the purchase of whole-life insurance or a home. Each of these investments has common characteristics, such as the potential return and the risk you must bear. The future is uncertain, and you must determine how much risk you are willing to bear, since a higher return is associated with accepting more risk.

You may find investing daunting because of specialized jargon or having to work with sophisticated professionals. A primary aim of this textbook is to make investing less difficult by explaining the terms, by elucidating the possible alternatives, and by discussing many of the techniques professionals use to value assets and to construct portfolios. Although this textbook cannot show you a shortcut to financial wealth, it can reduce your chances of making uninformed investment decisions.

This textbook uses a substantial number of examples and illustrations employing data that are generally available to the investing public. This information is believed to be accurate; however, you should not assume that mention of a specific firm and its securities is a recommendation to buy or sell those securities. The examples have been chosen to illustrate specific points, not to pass judgment on individual investments.

Many textbooks on investments are written for students with considerable background in accounting, finance, and economics. Not every student who takes a course in investments has such a background. These students cannot cope with (or be expected to cope with) the material in advanced textbooks on investments. *Investments: An Introduction* is directed at these students and covers investments from descriptive material to the theory of portfolio construction and efficient markets. Some of the concepts (for example, portfolio theory) and some of the investment alternatives (for example, derivatives) are difficult to understand. There is no shortcut to learning this material, but this text does assume that you have has a desire to tackle a fascinating subject and to devote real energy to the learning process.

CHANGES FROM THE PREVIOUS EDITION

This edition of *Investments: An Introduction* is a major effort to make the book more concise by combining chapters, tightening others, and removing specific sections. While the basic structure of six parts has been retained, the result has been to reduce the number of chapters from 24 to 20. Part 1, Chapters 1 through 5, is devoted to the investment process and fundamental financial concepts such as the time value of money and the measurement of risk. Part 2, Chapters 6 and 7, covers investment companies. References to investment companies such as exchange-traded funds occur throughout the text. Part 3, Chapters 8 through 12, is devoted to investing in stock while Part 4, Chapters 13 through 16, is devoted to fixed-income securities. Chapters 17 through 19 (Part 5) cover those fascinating speculative and financial assets referred to as derivatives. The text ends with one chapter (Part 6) that serves as a summing up of the process of financial planning, the management of risk, and the role of the individual's belief in the efficiency of financial markets. Specific changes to the individual chapters are as follows.

Chapter 1 serves as an introduction to the text, so material on specific topics has been removed. The chapter sets several themes such as planning, risk versus return, and the efficient market hypothesis that appear throughout the text. Chapter 2 combines material from Chapters 2 (secondary markets) and 3 (primary markets) in the previous edition into a single chapter on securities markets. The various types of financial intermediaries have been deleted and the material on money market instruments has been transferred to the section on money market mutual funds in Chapter 6.

Chapters 3 and 5 on the time value of money and the measurement of risk are essentially unchanged. Although these topics may be covered in other courses in finance, the material is crucial to an understanding of investments. The individual instructor can determine the extent to which these chapters are appropriate for a specific course. Many of the problems in Chapters 3 and 5 illustrate essential concepts such as valuation, retirement accounts, the computation of returns, correlation, and the dispersion around averages (the standard deviation). Chapter 4 in Part 1 combines financial planning, taxation and tax shelters, and the efficiency of financial markets. While some textbooks exclude much of this material, I believe that investments should not be made independently of the determination of financial goals and the consideration of impact of taxation. Both are part of the process of selecting assets and constructing a portfolio.

Chapters 6 and 7 cover investment companies. Chapter 6 on mutual funds is unchanged, but Chapter 7 on other types of investment companies has been expanded with additional coverage of ETFs, REITs, private equity funds, and hedge funds. The use of investment companies as a means to make foreign investments has been moved to this chapter.

Part 3 on investing in common stock has been reorganized. After a brief description of stock, Chapter 8 now includes cash dividends, dividend reinvestment plans, stock dividends and splits, stock repurchases, and the analysis of financial statements. Previously this material was spread over three chapters, so the current approach tightens the coverage. Since preferred stock is legally equity, it is now covered in Chapter 8. In the previous edition, preferred stock was covered in the chapter describing various types of debt instruments. The valuation of preferred stock, however, remains in Chapter 14 on the pricing of debt instruments.

Chapters 9 and 10 are devoted to common stock valuation and selection (Chapter 9) and the computation of returns, stock indexes, and the historical returns investors have earned (Chapter 10). Prior to 2000–2009, returns on stock investments over ten-year time horizons had not been negative since the 1930s. This general conclusion no longer holds, and one important question facing the investor is whether the historical pattern of returns will be restored. Chapter 11 on the macroeconomy has been recast with less emphasis on historical information. More emphasis is placed on the target federal funds rate, the recent expansion in the money supply and its possible implication for future inflation, and investments for an inflationary environment.

The last chapter in Part 3 is an introduction to behavioral finance and technical analysis. Behavioral finance places emphasis on human traits that affect investment decisions and often lead to lower returns. Technical analysis places emphasis on the analysis of trends and tendencies of stock prices to move in identifiable patterns. The large decline in stock prices experienced during 2008–2009 has increased interest in both of these topics. The expanded coverage in Chapter 12 includes several behavioral characteristics that affect investment decisions and technical indicators that may forecast price changes.

Part 4 on fixed-income securities and Part 5 on derivatives are the least-changed sections of this new edition. Chapter 13, which describes the features of debt securities, has new material on yield differentials and the taxation of accrued interest. Chapter 14 provides a detailed discussion of bond valuation and, with the exception of the deletion of the equation for the approximation of the yield to maturity, is virtually unchanged. Chapter 15 on government securities has new material on taxable municipal and state government securities (Build America Bonds), and Chapter 16 on convertibles has expanded coverage of contingent convertible bonds.

Part 5 on derivatives begins with an introduction to puts and calls (Chapter 17) and continues with option valuation (the Black-Scholes model) and option strategies in Chapter 18. Chapter 19 is devoted to futures contracts. With the exception of new material on the Volatility Index (VIX), additional problems and selective rewriting, these chapters are virtually unchanged.

The text ends with a synthesis (Chapter 20 in Part 6) that places emphasis on the need for financial planning prior to portfolio construction. This chapter has been completely rewritten and stresses that investments are made to serve a purpose. Making investments requires the individual to bear risk. Diversification reduces risk but does not erase it. Higher returns require the investor to bear more risk, and the investor should not expect that over an extended period the return will beat the market on a risk-adjusted basis.

PEDAGOGICAL FEATURES

This textbook has a variety of features designed to assist the individual in the learning process. Chapters begin with a set of learning objectives that emphasize topics to be covered as the chapter develops. Terms to remember are defined in the marginal glossary entry that appears as each term is introduced. Chapters also include questions and, where appropriate, problems. The questions and problems are straightforward and designed to review and apply the material in the chapter. Answers to selected problems are provided in Appendix B.

In addition to problems, most of the chapters have short cases. These are not cases in the general usage of the term, in which a situation is presented and the student is required to determine the appropriate questions and formulate an answer or strategy. Instead, the cases are essentially problems that are cast in real-world situations. Their primary purpose is to illustrate how the material may apply in the context of real investment decisions.

Many instructors have students construct a paper portfolio. A project, referred to as "Investment Assignment," is included. It is essentially a buy-and-hold strategy, and as the semester proceeds more parts are added to the assignment. The text also includes interesting side points that may not fit neatly into a particular chapter. These appear in boxed Point of Interest features and may amplify the text material or present supplemental material. The tone of the Point of Interest features is often lighter than the text and is designed to increase reader interest in the chapter as a whole.

SUPPLEMENTARY MATERIALS

A number of supplements are included in the Investments package and are available to instructors and students using the textbook.

Instructor's Manual and Test Bank (found on the IRCD-ROM and on the Instructor's companion website)

The Instructor's Manual includes points to consider when answering the questions as well as complete solutions to the problems. In addition, suggestions are given for using the Investment Assignment feature in the classroom; teaching notes are provided for the cases; and instructions are provided for the Investment Analysis Calculator, which can be found on the book's website. The Test Bank section of the manual includes approximately 1,000 true/false and multiple-choice questions. It is available on the text website in Word format for simple word-processing purposes. The Test Bank can also be found in ExamView. This edition's Test Bank answers include tagging with AACSB Standards.

ExamView

This computerized testing software contains all of the questions in the printed Test Bank. ExamView is easy-to-use test creation software that is compatible with both Microsoft Windows and Macintosh. Instructors can add or edit questions, instructions, and answers and select questions by previewing them on the screen, selecting them randomly, or selecting them by number.

CengageNOW: A New Web-Based Course Management Platform

CengageNOW is a Web-based course management system. CengageNOW includes the following features:

Homework Assignments with Automatic Grading

CengageNOW includes select end-of-chapter and Test Bank problems. With just a few clicks, an instructor can create a Web-based homework assignment that contains unique problems and answers for each student. The assignment is automatically graded, and the scores are posted to a gradesheet that can be exported into Excel or into the gradesheets of Blackboard and WebCT. Similarly, an instructor can create sets of practice problems (based on the end-of-chapter problems and Test Bank problems). In Finance, practice makes perfect, so CengageNOW's ability to quickly and easily create practice problems and grade homework assignments can have a dramatic impact on a student's progress and knowledge.

e-Book

CengageNOW also contains the full e-book. In addition, the end-of-chapter homework problems contain links to the relevant sections of the e-book, so that students can read the text and work problems without ever leaving the computer.

Investment Analysis Calculator

This browser-based tool found on the book's website is designed to accompany the book and is free to adopters of the text. It includes numerous routines that may be used to help solve end-of-chapter problems. The software is menu driven and is a useful tool for solving complex problems. Please note that it is not designed as a substitute for understanding the mechanics of problem analysis and solution. Thus, while the Investment Analysis Calculator may help determine a stock's value, it cannot answer the question of whether or not the stock should be bought or sold; such a judgment must come from the user of the Investment Analysis Calculator.

PowerPoint™ Slides

These are available on the website and on the Instructor's Resource CD-ROM for use by instructors for enhancing their lectures. These slides bring out the most important points in the chapter. They also include important charts and graphs from the text, which will aid students in the comprehension of significant concepts. This edition's slide package has been revised by Anne Piotrowski.

Instructor's Resource CD-ROM

Get quick access to all instructor ancillaries from your desktop. This easy-to-use CD-ROM lets you review, edit, and copy exactly what you need in the format you want. The Instructor's Resource CD-ROM contains electronic versions of the Instructor's Manual, the Test Bank, the resource PowerPoint presentation, and the ExamView files.

Website

The support website for *Investments: An Introduction*, Tenth Edition (**www.cengage .com/finance/mayo**) includes the following features:

- Instructor Resources
- CaseNet

- Investment Analysis Calculator
- About the Product

POSSIBLE ORGANIZATIONS OF INVESTMENT COURSES

This textbook has 20 chapters, but few instructors are able to complete the entire book in a semester course. Many of the chapters are self-contained units, so individual chapters may be omitted (or transposed) without loss of continuity. There are, however, exceptions. For example, the pricing of bonds uses the material on the time value of money. The valuation of common stock employs statistical concepts covered in the chapter on risk.

Individual course coverage also depends on the background of the students or how much they have retained from prior courses. Time value of money (Chapter 3), measurement of risk (Chapter 5), and the analysis of financial statements in Chapter 8 may have been covered in other finance or accounting courses. These chapters may be quickly reviewed or omitted. Other chapters are not easily omitted. Securities markets (Chapter 2), the analysis, valuation, and selection of common stock (Part 3), and fixed-income securities (Chapters 13 and 14) are the backbone of investments and need to be covered. Since investment companies (Part 2) have become such a large part of savings programs such as retirement plans, they should also be included in an introduction to investments.

The remaining chapters offer individual instructors considerable choice. My preference is to include an introduction to options (Chapter 17), which many students find both difficult and exciting. I also have a personal bias toward the material on financial planning and taxation, since I believe they play an important role in portfolio construction and asset selection.

ACKNOWLEDGMENTS

A textbook requires the input and assistance of many individuals. Over the years, my publisher has provided a variety of reviews from individuals who sincerely offered suggestions. Unfortunately, suggestions from different reviewers are sometimes contradictory. Since I cannot please all the reviewers at the same time, I trust that individuals whose advice was not or could not be taken will not be offended.

In addition to academic reviewers, I have received help from Andy Carver (The College of New Jersey), George A. Jouganatos (University of California–Davis), and Leo Kelly III (Merrill Lynch). Several of my students have done projects on topics that I have used in this edition; these include the following individuals (in alphabetical order with their current employers): Agnieszka Baczyk (Merrill Lynch), Stephanie Joyce (Management Planning Inc.), and Shane Mullin (Moody's).

Anne Piotrowski created the PowerPoint slides. Her willingness to work through various styles and possible presentations greatly enhanced the final product. Suzanne Davidson and Margaret Trejo served as a copy editor and proofreader. Anne, Suzanne, and Margaret deserve a special "thank you" for their efforts.

At this point, it is traditional for the author to thank members of the editorial and production staff for their help in bringing the book to fruition. I wish to thank Mike Reynolds, my editor; Mike Guendelsberger, the development editor; Tamborah Moore, Content Project Manager; Nathan Anderson, Marketing Manager; Scott Fidler, Senior Media Editor; Adele Scholtz, Senior Editorial Assistant; and Michelle Kunkler, Senior Art Director.

These individuals deserve warm thanks for their efforts toward facilitating the completion of this text.

PART
One

The Investment Process and Financial Concepts

Investing is a process by which individuals construct a portfolio of assets designed to meet specified financial goals. These goals range from financing retirement or paying for a child's education to starting a business and having funds to meet financial emergencies. The specification of financial goals is important, for they help determine the appropriateness of the assets acquired for the portfolio.

Part 1 of this text covers the mechanics of buying and selling financial assets, the legal and tax environment in which investment decisions are made, and crucial financial concepts that apply to asset allocation and portfolio management. Chapter 1 introduces important definitions and concepts that appear throughout the text. Chapter 2 is devoted to the mechanics of investing. These include the process by which securities are issued and subsequently bought and sold. Next follows one of the most important concepts in finance, the time value of money (Chapter 3). All investments are made in the present but returns occur in the future. Linking the future and the present is the essence of the time value of money.

Chapter 4 combines several disparate topics. It begins with financial planning and the importance of asset allocation. However, you execute your financial plan in a world of taxation and efficient financial markets. Tax rates differ on long-term and short-term capital gains; some investments defer tax obligations and others avoid taxation. These differences in taxation affect the amount of your return that you *get to keep*. In addition, some facet of the tax law changes each year, complicating investments decision making and affecting investment strategy.

Since the future is not known, all investments involve risk. Chapter 5 is devoted to sources of risk, how risk may be measured, and how it may be managed. The allocation of your assets and the construction of a diversified portfolio may be the most important financial concept you must face. Failure to diversify subjects the investor to additional risk without generating additional return. Your objective should be to construct a portfolio that maximizes your return for a given level of risk. Of course, this requires that you determine how much risk you are willing to bear. Individuals with different financial resources and disparate financial goals may be willing to accept different levels of risk, but in each case the goal is to maximize the return for the amount of risk the investor bears.

One final caveat before you start Part 1. Chapter 4 introduces the concept that investments are made in exceedingly competitive markets. Rapid dissemination of information and stiff competition among investors produce efficient markets. Efficient markets imply that you cannot expect to earn abnormally high returns over an extended period of time. Although you may outperform the market, such performance on a consistent basis is rare. Perhaps you will do exceptionally well, but then there is also the chance of doing exceptionally poorly. The emphasis in this text will be not how to outperform but how to use financial assets to meet financial goals. That is, you should emphasize constructing a diversified portfolio that meets your financial objectives and earns a return that compensates you for the risk you take.

CHAPTER 1

An Introduction to Investments

LEARNING OBJECTIVES

After completing this chapter you should be able to:

1. Explain why individuals should specify investment goals.
2. Distinguish between primary and secondary markets, risk and speculation, liquidity and marketability.
3. Identify the sources of risk and the sources of return.
4. Differentiate between efficient and inefficient markets.

In 1986, Microsoft first sold its stock to the general public. Within ten years, the stock's value had increased by over 5,000 percent. A $10,000 investment was worth over $500,000. In the same year, Worlds of Wonder also sold its stock to the public. Ten years later, the company was defunct. A $10,000 investment was worth nothing. These are two examples of emerging firms that could do well or could fail. Would investing in large, well-established companies generate more consistent returns? The answer depends, of course, on which stocks were purchased and when. In 1972, Xerox stock reached a high of $171.87 a share. The price subsequently declined and did not exceed the old high for the next 26 years. Now it languishes way below that historic high.

Today the investment environment is even more dynamic. World events can rapidly alter the values of specific assets. There are so many assets from which to choose. The amount of information available to investors is staggering and grows continually. The accessibility of personal computers and the dissemination of information on the Internet increase an individual's ability to track investments and to perform investment analysis. Furthermore, the recessions of 1990–1991 and 2008–2009, the large decline in stock prices during 2007–2009, the historic decline in interest rates during 2001–2003 and 2008–2009, and the frequent changes in the tax laws have increased investor awareness of the importance of financial planning, asset selection and allocation, and portfolio construction.

This text will describe and explain many investment alternatives and strategies. But a textbook cannot make investment decisions for you; it can only provide information about your choices. This text explains techniques for analyzing and valuing financial assets, their sources of risk, and how these risks may be managed, if not eliminated. It is your obligation to learn the material, determine which parts are most relevant, and then apply them to your financial situation.

PORTFOLIO CONSTRUCTION AND PLANNING

Investment decisions are about making choices: Will income be spent or saved? If you choose to save, you face a second decision: What should be done with the savings? Each saver must decide where to invest this command over resources (goods and services)

portfolio

An accumulation of assets owned by the investor and designed to transfer purchasing power to the future.

that is currently not being used. This is an important decision because these assets are the means by which investors transfer today's purchasing power to the future. In effect, you must decide on a **portfolio** of assets to own. (Terms will be in boldface and defined in the margin.) A portfolio is a combination of assets designed to serve as a store of value. Poor management of these assets may destroy the portfolio's value, and you will then not achieve your financial goals.

There are many assets (e.g., stocks, bonds, derivatives) that you may include in the portfolio. This textbook will discuss many of them, but the stress will be on long-term financial assets. While you may hold a portion of the portfolio in short-term assets, such as savings accounts, these assets do not present the problem of valuation and choice that accompanies the decision to purchase a stock or a bond. Understanding how long-term securities are bought and sold, how they are valued, and how they may be used in portfolio construction is the primary focus of this text.

Several factors affect the construction of a portfolio. These include the goals of the investor, the risks involved, the taxes that will be imposed on any gain, and a knowledge of investment alternatives. This text describes these alternative investments, their use in a portfolio, the risks associated with owning them, and their valuation.

The investor's goals should largely determine the construction and management of the portfolio. Investing must have a purpose, for without a goal a portfolio is like a boat without a rudder. Some objective must guide the composition of the portfolio.

There are many reasons for saving and accumulating assets. Individuals may postpone current consumption to accumulate funds to make the down payment on a house, finance a child's education, start a business, meet financial emergencies, finance retirement, leave a sizable estate, or even accumulate for the sake of accumulating. For any or all of these reasons, people construct portfolios rather than spend all their current income.

The motives for saving should dictate, or at least affect, the composition of the portfolio. Not all assets are appropriate to meet specific financial goals. For example, savings that are held to meet emergencies, such as an extended illness or unemployment, should not be invested in assets whose return and safety of principal are uncertain. Instead, emphasis should be placed on safety of principal and assets that may be readily converted into cash, such as savings accounts or shares in money market mutual funds. The emphasis should not be on growth and high returns. However, the funds should not sit idle but should be invested in safe assets that offer a modest return.

Other goals, such as financing retirement or a child's education, have a longer and more certain time horizon. The investor knows approximately when the funds will be needed and so can construct a portfolio with a long-term horizon. Bonds that mature when the funds will be needed or common stocks that offer the potential for growth would be more appropriate than savings accounts or certificates of deposit with a bank. The longer time period suggests the individual can acquire long-term assets that may offer a higher yield.

Most investors have several financial goals that must be met simultaneously. Thus, it is not surprising to learn that their portfolios contain a variety of assets. Of course, priorities and needs differ. The individual who is employed in a cyclical industry and may be laid off during a recession may place more stress on funds to cover unemployment than would the tenured professor. An individual with a poor medical history may seek to have more short-term investments than the person with good health. Medical coverage or disability insurance will also affect the individual's need for funds to cover a short-term emergency. If the investor has this coverage, more of the portfolio may be directed toward other financial goals.

In addition to the individual's goals, willingness to bear risk plays an important role in constructing the portfolio. Some individuals are more able to bear (that is, assume) risk. For example, if the saver wants to build a retirement fund, he or she can choose from a variety of possible investments. However, not all investments are equal with regard to risk and potential return. Those investors who are more willing to accept risk may construct portfolios with assets involving greater risk that may earn higher returns.

Taxes also affect the composition of an individual's portfolio. Income such as interest and realized capital gains are taxed. When a person dies, the federal government taxes the value of the estate, and many states levy a tax on an individual's inheritance. Such taxes and the desire to reduce them affect the composition of each investor's portfolio.

Portfolio decisions are obviously important. They set a general framework for the asset allocation of the portfolio among various types of investments. Individuals, however, rarely construct a portfolio all at once but acquire assets one at a time. The decision revolves around which specific asset to purchase: Which mutual fund? Which bond? or Which stock? Security analysis considers the merits of the individual asset. Portfolio management determines the impact that the specific asset has on the portfolio.

A large portion of this text is devoted to descriptions and analysis of individual securities, because it is impossible to know an asset's effect on the portfolio without first knowing its characteristics. Stocks and bonds differ with regard to risk, potential return, and valuation. Even within a type of asset such as bonds there can be considerable variation. For example, a corporate bond is different from a municipal bond, and a convertible bond differs from a straight bond that lacks the conversion feature. You need to know and to understand these differences as well as the relative merits and risks associated with each of the assets. After understanding how individual assets are valued, you may then construct a portfolio that will aid in the realization of your financial goals.

PRELIMINARY DEFINITIONS

I went to the doctor and he said, "You have a contusion." I asked, "What is a contusion?" and he said, "A bruise." I thought: "A bruise by another name is still a bruise" and immediately wanted to ask (but did not), "Why not call it a bruise?"

**investment
(in economics)**

The purchase of plant, equipment, or inventory.

**investment
(in lay terms)**

Acquisition of an asset such as a stock or a bond.

Every discipline or profession has its own terminology. The field of investments is no different. Some of the jargon is colorful (e.g., *bull* and *bear*); some is descriptive (e.g., *primary* and *secondary markets*); and some, like *contusion*, seems to confuse or muddy the waters (e.g., *purchasing power risk*, which is the risk associated with loss from inflation). In order to proceed, it is desirable to know some initial definitions concerning investments, and the best time to learn them and to start using them is now.

The term **investment** can have more than one meaning. In economics, it refers to the purchase of a physical asset, such as a firm's acquisition of a plant, equipment, or inventory or an individual's purchase of a new home. To the layperson the word denotes buying stocks or bonds (or maybe even a house), but it probably does not mean purchasing a plant, equipment, or inventory.

In either case, the firm or the individual wants a productive asset. The difference in definition rests upon the aggregate change in productive assets that results from the investment. When firms invest in plant and equipment, there is a net increase in productive assets. This increase generally does not occur when individuals purchase stocks and bonds. Instead, for every investment by the buyer there is an equal *dis*investment by the seller. These buyers and sellers are trading one asset for another: The seller trades the security for cash, and the buyer trades cash for the security. These transactions occur in secondhand markets, and for that reason securities markets are often referred to as **secondary markets**. Only when the securities are initially issued and sold in the **primary market** is there an investment in an economic sense. Then and only then does the firm receive the money that it, in turn, may use to purchase a plant, equipment, or inventory.

In this text, the word *investment* is used in the layperson's sense. Purchase of an asset for the purpose of storing value (and, it is hoped, increasing that value over time) will be called an investment, even if in the aggregate there is only a transfer of ownership from a seller to a buyer. The purchases of stocks, bonds, options, commodity contracts, and even antiques, stamps, and real estate are all considered to be investments if the individual's intent is to transfer purchasing power to the future. If these assets are acting as stores of value, they are investments for that individual.

Assets have **value** because of the future benefits they offer. The process of determining what an asset is worth today is called **valuation**. An investor appraises the asset and assigns a current value to it based on the belief that the asset will generate cash flows (e.g., interest) or will appreciate in price. After computing this value, the individual compares it with the current market price to determine if the asset is currently overpriced or underpriced.

In some cases this valuation is relatively easy. For example, the bonds of the federal government pay a fixed amount of interest each year and mature at a specified date. Thus, the future cash flows are known. However, the future cash flows of other assets are not so readily identified. For example, although you may anticipate future dividends, neither their payment nor their amount can be known with certainty. Forecasting future benefits is difficult but crucial to the *process of valuation*. Without forecasts and an evaluation of the asset, you cannot know if the asset should be purchased or sold.

Because the valuation of some assets is complicated and the future is uncertain, people may have different estimates of the future cash flows. It is therefore easy to understand why two individuals may have completely divergent views on the worth of a particular asset. One person may believe that an asset is overvalued and hence seek to sell it, while another may seek to buy it in the belief that it is undervalued. Valuation may be subjective, which leads to one person's buying while the other is selling. That does not mean that one person is necessarily irrational or incompetent. People's perceptions or estimates of an asset's potential may change, affecting their valuation of the specific asset.

An investment is made because the investor anticipates a **return**. The total return on an investment is what the investor earns. This may be in the form of **income**, such as dividends and interest, or in the form of **capital gains**, or appreciation if the asset's price rises. Not all assets offer both income and capital appreciation. Some stocks pay no

secondary market
A market for buying and selling previously issued securities.

primary market
The initial sale of securities.

value
What something is worth; the present value of future benefits.

valuation
The process of determining the current worth of an asset.

return
The sum of income plus capital gains earned on an investment in an asset.

income
The flow of money or its equivalent produced by an asset; dividends and interest.

capital gain
An increase in the value of a capital asset, such as a stock.

current dividends but may appreciate in value. Other assets, including savings accounts, do not appreciate in value. The return is solely the interest income.

Return is frequently expressed in percentages, such as the **rate of return**, which is the annualized return that is earned by the investment relative to its cost. Before purchasing an asset, the investor anticipates that the return will be greater than that of other assets of similar risk. Without this anticipation, the purchase would not be made. The *realized* return may, of course, be quite different from the *anticipated* rate of return. That is the element of risk.

Risk is the uncertainty that the anticipated return will be achieved. As Chapter 5 discusses, there are many sources of risk. The investor must be willing to bear these risks to achieve the expected return. Even relatively safe investments involve some risk; there is no completely safe investment. For example, savings accounts that are insured still involve some element of risk of loss. If the rate of inflation exceeds the rate of interest that is earned on these insured accounts, the investor suffers a loss of purchasing power.

While the term *risk* has a negative connotation, uncertainty works both ways. For example, events may occur that cause the value of an asset to rise more than anticipated. Certainly the stockholders of Rubbermaid reaped larger-than-anticipated returns when it was announced the firm would merge with Newell. The price paid for the stock was considerably higher than the price the security commanded before the announcement of the merger.

A term that is frequently used in conjunction with risk is **speculation**. Many years ago virtually all investments were called "speculations." Today the word implies a high degree of risk. However, risk is not synonymous with speculation. Speculation has the connotation of gambling, in which the odds are against the player. Many securities are risky, but over a period of years the investor should earn a positive return. The odds are not really against the investor, and such investments are not speculations.

The term *speculation* is rarely used in this text, and when it is employed, the implication is that the individual runs a good chance of losing the funds invested in the speculative asset. Although a particular speculation may pay off handsomely, the investor should not expect that many such gambles will reap large returns. After the investor adjusts for the larger amount of risk that must be borne to own such speculative investments, the anticipated return may not justify the risk involved.

Besides involving risk and offering an expected return, stores of value have marketability or liquidity. These terms are sometimes used interchangeably, but they may also have different definitions. **Marketability** implies that the asset can be bought and sold. Many financial assets, such as the stock of AT&T, are readily marketable.

The ease with which an asset may be converted into money is its **liquidity**. Unfortunately, the word *liquidity* is ambiguous. In academic writings on investments liquidity usually means ease of converting an asset into cash *without loss*. A savings account with a commercial bank is liquid, but shares of IBM would not be liquid, since you could sustain a loss. In professional writings, liquidity usually means ability to sell an asset without affecting its price. In that context, liquidity refers to the *depth* of the market for the asset. You may be able to buy or sell 1,000 shares of IBM stock without affecting its price, in which case the stock is liquid. The context in which the word is used often indicates the specific meaning.

rate of return
The annual percentage return realized on an investment.

risk
The possibility of loss; the uncertainty of future returns.

speculation
An investment that offers a potentially large return but is also very risky; a reasonable probability that the investment will produce a loss.

marketability
The ease with which an asset may be bought and sold.

liquidity
Moneyness; the ease with which assets can be converted into cash.

All assets that serve as stores of value possess some combination of marketability, liquidity, and the potential to generate future cash flow or appreciate in price. These features, along with the risk associated with each asset, should be considered when including the asset in an individual's portfolio. Since assets differ with regard to their features, you need to know the characteristics of each asset. Much of the balance of this text describes each asset's features as well as its sources of risk and return and how it may be used in a well-diversified portfolio.

DIVERSIFICATION AND ASSET ALLOCATION

Chapter 5 indicates that the impact of asset-specific risk may be diversified away. As that chapter explains in detail, to achieve diversification the returns on your investments must not be highly correlated. Factors that negatively affect one security must have a positive impact on others. For example, higher oil prices may be good for ExxonMobil but bad for Delta Air Lines. By combining a variety of disparate assets, you achieve diversification and reduce risk.

Asset allocation refers to acquiring a wide spectrum of assets. Individuals use their finite resources to acquire various types of assets that include stocks, bonds, precious metals, collectibles, and real estate. Even within a class such as stocks, the portfolio is allocated to different sectors or geographic regions. For example, you may own domestic stocks and stocks of companies in emerging nations. It would appear that "asset allocation" and "diversification" are synonymous, and to some extent they are. By allocating your assets over different types of assets you contribute to the diversification of the portfolio. But asset allocation and diversification are often used in different contexts. For example, you may tilt your allocation toward energy stocks and away from airlines if you anticipate high gas prices. Your allocation between stocks, bonds, and other assets remains the same, but the allocation between two sectors is altered.

The words *diversification* and *asset allocation* are often used in this text. Diversification is important because it reduces your risk exposure. Asset allocation is important because it has a major impact on the return your portfolio earns. Whenever you make an investment decision, you need to consider its impact on the diversification of your portfolio and the allocation of your assets. Both are crucial components of portfolio management.

EFFICIENT AND COMPETITIVE MARKETS

Have you ever been fishing? (If not, substitute playing golf or some similar activity.) Did you catch any fish? Which fish did you talk about? The answer to that question is probably the "big one" or the "big one that got away." What is more important, of course, is the size of the average fish (or average golf score). If you go fishing several times, you will not catch a "big one" every time or even frequently. The average size of the fish you catch becomes the norm. And other individuals who fish in the same waters will have comparable results. Unless they have special skills or knowledge, most individuals' catch should be similar to and approach the average size of fish that is caught.

In many ways, the fishing analogy applies to investing in stock. Individuals tend to talk about the big return ("I bought X and it doubled within a week") or the lost opportunity ("I bought Plain and Fancy Doughnuts of America. It rose 80 percent within an hour and I did not sell"). But what matters is the return you earn after making many investments over an extended period of time. Unless you have special skills or knowledge, that return should tend to be comparable to the return earned by other investors in comparable investments.

Why is this so? The answer lies in the reality that investors participate in efficient and competitive financial markets. Economics teaches that markets with many participants (i.e., buyers and sellers) who may enter and exit freely will be competitive. That certainly describes financial markets. Investors may participate freely in the purchase and sale of stocks and bonds. Virtually anyone, from a child to a grandmother, may own a financial asset, even if it is just a savings account. Many firms, including banks, insurance companies, and mutual funds, compete for the funds of investors. The financial markets are among the most (and perhaps *the* most) competitive of all markets.

Financial markets tend to be efficient. As is explained throughout this text, securities prices depend on future cash flows, such as interest or dividend payments. If new information suggests that these flows will be altered, the market rapidly adjusts the asset's price. Thus, an efficient financial market implies that a security's current price embodies all the known information concerning the potential return and risk associated with the particular asset. If an asset, such as a stock, were undervalued and offered an excessive return, investors would seek to buy it, which would drive the price up and reduce the return that subsequent investors would earn. Conversely, if the asset were overvalued and offered an inferior return, investors would seek to sell it, which would drive down its price and increase the return to subsequent investors. The fact that there are sufficient informed investors means that a security's price will reflect the investment community's consensus regarding the asset's true value and also that the expected return will be consistent with the amount of risk the investor must bear to earn the return.

The concept of an efficient financial market has an important and sobering corollary. Efficient markets imply that investors (or at least the vast majority of investors) cannot expect on average to beat the market *consistently*. Of course, that does not mean an individual will never select an asset that does exceedingly well. Individuals can earn large returns on particular assets, as the stockholders of many firms know. Certainly the investor who bought Gold Kist stock on Friday, August 18, 2006, for $12.93 and sold it one trading day later on Monday, August 21, 2006, for $19.02 made a large return on that investment. (After trading closed on August 18, it was announced that Pilgrim's Pride would buy Gold Kist for $20 per share.) The concept of efficient markets implies that this investor will not consistently select those individual securities that earn abnormally large returns.

If investors cannot expect to outperform the market consistently, they also should not consistently underperform the market. (That is, you would not always be the investor who *sold* Gold Kist just prior to the large increase in its price.) Of course, some securities may decline in price and inflict large losses on their owners, but efficient markets imply that the individual who constructs a well-diversified portfolio will not always select the stocks and bonds of firms that fail. If such individuals do exist, they will soon lose their resources and will no longer be able to participate in the financial markets.

While the concept of efficient financial markets permeates investments, the question remains: How efficient? Do exceptions to the efficient market hypothesis exist? Many of the various investment techniques and methods of analysis covered in later chapters are designed to help identify possible anomalies and increase investment returns. You, of course, will have to decide for yourself how efficient you believe financial markets are, because that belief should determine which of the many investment strategies to follow. A stronger belief in efficiency argues for a more passive strategy. If you think markets are inefficient or that there are pockets of inefficiency that you can exploit, then you will want to follow a more aggressive, active strategy.

PORTFOLIO ASSESSMENT

Much of the popular press places emphasis on returns without considering risk. Mutual funds are often ranked on the basis of return. Statements such as "portfolio manager of growth fund X earned the highest return for the last three months" often appear in the popular financial press. The portfolio managers of the best-performing funds appear on *Bloomberg* (http://www.bloomberg.com) or CNBC. Obviously, some fund manager had to earn the highest return for the last quarter. (Some student also earned the highest grade on my last test.)

⊕ Point of Interest

PROFESSIONAL DESIGNATIONS AND CERTIFICATIONS

Do you know what "CPA" or "DVM" stand for? You probably do know that CPA stands for certified public accountant. While you can do accounting work without passing the CPA exam, becoming a CPA is the minimum standard for working as a public accountant. (There is also a CMA for management accounting.) DVM is doctor of veterinary medicine. Earning that degree is a minimum requirement if you plan to become a practicing veterinarian.

Careers in financial planning, portfolio management, and investments also have professional certifications and license requirements. For example, passing the NASD Stockbroker Series 7 Exam given by the National Association of Securities Dealers (http://www.nasd.com) is required for you to become a registered representative (broker) who acts as an account executive for clients. To become an investment advisor and provide research and opinions on securities and the securities market, you must pass the Series 66 (or comparable) exam. (For information on the Series 66 exam, see the North American Securities Administrators Association [NASAA] webpage at http://www.nasaa.org.)

While professional designations are not required for you to buy and sell securities and to construct a portfolio, you should consider pursuing one if you plan on a career in some facet of investments. The following list, in alphabetical order, provides several financial professional designations and where you may obtain information concerning them.

CAIA   Chartered Alternative Investment Analyst, granted by the CAIA Association (http://www.caia.org)

CFA   Chartered Financial Analyst, granted by the CFA Institute (http://www.cfainstitute.org)

CFP   Certified Financial Planner, granted by the Certified Financial Planner Board of Standards (http://www.cfp.net)

ChFC   Chartered Financial Consultant, granted by the American College (http://www.chfc-clu.com)

CIPM (CGIPS)   Certification in Performance Management (Certification in Global Investment Performance Standards), granted by the CFA Institute (http://www.cfainstitute.org)

While it can be useful to rank and compare returns, investments involve risk. You certainly will not read in *Money* or see on TV the portfolio manager of fund X who achieved the highest level of risk! But it could also be useful to rank and compare risk as well as returns. Throughout this text, risk and return are often related. You make an investment in order to earn an expected return and have to bear the risk associated with that investment. After investments are sold (or redeemed), both the realized returns and the variability of those returns may be calculated. While particular sections of this text may discuss only risk or return, the fusion of the two cannot be far away.

You should start now to think of return in a risk context. How does this investment decision affect my risk exposure? Can I reduce risk without reducing my return? How may I compare returns on a risk-adjusted basis? Chapter 6 on investment companies presents several methods for ranking returns on a risk-adjusted basis. In both the professional and academic investment environments, these risk adjustments are important. As an informed investor, you too should want to compare returns and portfolio performance on a risk-adjusted basis.

THE INTERNET

Web addresses appear throughout this text. Much information can be obtained through the Internet free of charge, but some vendors do charge a fee for the material. While many of the websites provided in the text are free, fee sites are included. Some of these fee sites have complimentary information that you may find useful.

With the existence of the Internet, you face several important problems. First, too much information may be available, or you may obtain contradictory information from different sites. A defined topic, such as growth mutual funds, will generate more facts and data than you could possibly assimilate. The information problem is compounded because growth mutual funds are tied to other areas of investments, such as taxation or financial planning. Selecting a growth mutual fund (or any investment) may be tied to psychology, which can help explain why some investors prefer a particular fund or have a particular financial strategy. A developing area of finance, behavioral finance, would argue that you will select the information that justifies or supports your preconceived investment ideas.

The second problem with information received through the Internet concerns its accuracy. You may not know the provider's motivation! If you access a company's or government agency's webpage, the information should be accurate. If you make a general search for information on a company, the data, analysis, and recommendations you find may be inaccurate or even purposefully misleading. In addition, misleading information can be sent directly to you through the Internet. The *Wall Street Journal* (August 17, 1998, p. C22) reported a story concerning individuals who had received an e-mail stock tip promoting a company called Maxnet Inc. The stock was selling for $3 but an unnamed analyst believed the stock could reach $50. After the bogus e-mail generated buying, the price of Maxnet Inc. stock quickly rose but just as quickly declined when the scam was discovered.

Buying stock based on such unsolicited recommendations is a recipe for disaster. Unscrupulous individuals can create stories designed to persuade people to buy a stock and inflate its price so the creators of the stories can unload the security. Such actions are not new. Touting a stock to unsuspecting investors has probably occurred since trading in stocks began. The Internet, however, creates the possibility of such fraud on a large scale. My broker has told me that he often receives stock recommendations through e-mail. While some of these recommendations may come from legitimate financial analysts, others appear to be scams.

There is probably little you (or anyone else) can do to stop the dissemination of inaccurate information through the Internet, but you do not have to act on it. If you limit your search to reliable sources, then the Internet (or any other source of data or advice) can help you make investment decisions. If you indiscriminately use the Internet (or any other source) to make investment decisions, then you too can become a victim of a scheme to drive up prices so those perpetrating the scam can sell securities at inflated prices.

THE AUTHOR'S PERSPECTIVE AND INVESTMENT PHILOSOPHY

Financial textbooks present material that is factual (e.g., the features of bonds), theoretical (e.g., the theory of portfolio construction and diversification), and the results of empirical studies. This text is no exception. Effort is made to avoid the author's bias or perspective. In reality, however, an author's viewpoint cannot be completely disregarded. It affects the space devoted to a topic and how the topic is covered.

The first tenet that affects my perspective is a belief that investment decisions are made in exceedingly competitive financial markets (the efficient markets referred to earlier). Information is disseminated so rapidly that few individual investors are able to take advantage of new information. This theme of efficient markets reappears throughout the book. You could conclude that the reality of efficient markets ends your chances of making good investments, but that is the wrong conclusion. The presence of efficient markets ensures that you can make investments on a level playing field. In other words, the return you earn does not have to be inferior to the returns generated by more seasoned or professional investors.

A second tenet that affects my perspective is my investment philosophy. I began the first edition of this text during the 1970s, so it is possible to infer how long I have been investing. Over the years I have developed my personal investment strategy that stresses patience and long-term wealth accumulation. Additional considerations are taxation and transaction costs. The philosophy and strategies of other individuals and portfolio managers may be the exact opposite. They may have a shorter time horizon and may be less concerned with current taxes or the costs of buying and selling securities.

Understanding yourself and specifying financial goals is important when developing an investment philosophy and making investment decisions. If your investments cause you to worry (frequently expressed as causing you to lose sleep), you need to look inside yourself to determine why. If I had to buy and sell securities frequently, I would have a conflict with my personality and long-term financial goals. As a graduate student, I would often buy and sell for small gains. I found such trading to be fun and stimulating, but I observed that stocks I sold always seemed to rise and those I did not sell always seemed to decline. In effect, I violated one of investing's cardinal rules: "Let your winners run but cut your losses." It was many years before I realized that a buy-and-sell strategy (a trading strategy) did not work for me. Part of the reason was my inability to sell the losers. (Behavioral finance might suggest that I had a problem with "letting go" or that I wanted to avoid the "pain of regret" in which I refused to face the reality that I had made a bad investment decision.) I also had failed to specify why I was investing. I was treating investment as a game and not a means to reach a financial goal.

Your background also affects your investment strategies. I grew up in a family of homebuilders. As would be expected, family members had a bias, which I continue to have, for companies related to real estate (e.g., the real estate investment trusts discussed in Chapter 7). Natural resources for building (e.g., trees for lumber), building materials (e.g., plumbing supplies), and appliances for homes were often the topic of discussion at dinner. Such companies as Georgia-Pacific (lumber) or Maytag (appliances) I remember from childhood. The same applies to such companies as the local gas and electric (Dominion Resources) or phone (AT&T) companies, because I grew up with their names.

In addition to efficient markets, financial goals, and your background, the time you have to devote to investing affects your decisions. I teach courses in finance, have contact with former students who work in the area, and know investment professionals. Daily news coverage, programs like *The Nightly Business Report* on public TV, and materials I have retained, such as annual reports, mean I can obtain information even when I am away from my personal computer and the Internet! I think about some topic in finance and investments every day, holidays and vacations included.

Most individuals do not have such continuous contact with investments. Their jobs and family obligations preclude it. These individuals may not develop financial goals and investment strategies, but their need for financial planning does not disappear. When individuals lack time or believe they do not have expertise, they may use professional financial planners or other professionals, such as brokers, to facilitate the construction of a diversified portfolio. The growth in the popularity of mutual funds and exchange-traded funds is partially explained by individuals who do not want to select specific securities and who turn over that process to portfolio managers. These investors, however, continue to need specific investment goals and strategies.

Your background, time available to devote to investments, and financial goals may produce an investment philosophy and strategy different from mine. The material in this text presents alternative investments and strategies, some of which I have not used (and would not use). I will, however, try to present all the material in an unbiased manner so that you may draw your own conclusions and develop your own financial goals, investment philosophy, and strategy.

THE PLAN AND PURPOSE OF THIS TEXT

Because you participate in efficient financial markets and compete with informed investors, including professional securities analysts and portfolio managers, you need fundamental information concerning investments. This text helps you to increase your knowledge of the risks and returns from various investment alternatives. Perhaps because investing deals with individuals' money and the potential for large gains or losses, it seems more mysterious than it should. By introducing the various investments and the methods of their analysis, valuation, and acquisition, this text removes the mystery associated with investing.

The number of possible investment alternatives is virtually unlimited. Shares in thousands of corporations are actively traded, and if an investor does not want to select individual stocks, he or she still has over 8,000 mutual funds from which to choose. Corporations, the federal government, and state and local governments issue a variety of debt instruments that range in maturity from a few days to 30 or 40 years. More than 10,000 commercial banks and thrift institutions (e.g., savings banks) offer a variety of savings accounts and certificates of deposit. Real estate, futures, options, and collectibles further increase the available alternatives, and, as if there were insufficient domestic choices, the investor may purchase foreign securities. The problem is not one of availability but of choice. You cannot own every asset but must choose among the alternatives.

Frequently, investment alternatives are classified as short-term (one year) or long-term (greater than one year), variable-income or fixed-income, or defensive or aggressive (even speculative). Short-term assets, such as savings accounts and shares in money market mutual funds, are readily converted into cash and offer modest returns. Bonds and stocks have a longer time horizon and are referred to as long-term investments. Common stock is also referred to as a variable-income security because the dividends and capital gains may fluctuate from year to year. Bonds illustrate a fixed-income security. While the investor's return from such investments can vary, the flow of income generated by bonds and preferred stock is fixed, so these securities are referred to as fixed-income securities. Options, convertible bonds, and futures may be considered aggressive investments because they may offer high returns but require the investor to bear substantial risk. Other possible investments include nonfinancial assets (tangible or real assets) such as real estate, gold, and collectibles.

The subject of investments is sometimes viewed as complex, but the approach in this text is to isolate each type of asset. The sources of return, the risks, and the features that differentiate each are described. Techniques for analyzing and valuing the assets are explained. Most of the material is essential information for all investors, whether they have large or small portfolios.

This text is divided into parts. The first lays the foundation on which security selection and portfolio management are based. This encompasses how securities come into existence and are subsequently bought and sold (Chapter 2). Chapter 3 covers the process of compounding and discounting. Since valuation is the process of determining the present value of future cash flows and financial planning involves projecting future cash needs, no topic is more important to the study of investments than the time value of money. (If you already know this material, you may move on to the next chapter, but you do so at your own risk!) Financial planning, the allocation of assets, and the impact of taxation are covered in Chapter 4. The analysis and measurement of risk constitute the bulk of Chapter 5. Because calculating and interpreting measures of risk require knowledge of selected statistics, Chapter 5 has an appendix on statistical methods that apply to risk measurement.

The second part of the text is devoted to investment companies. Chapter 6 covers mutual funds, their portfolios, returns, buying and redeeming their shares, and measures to standardize returns for risk. Chapter 7 is devoted to alternatives to the traditional mutual fund: closed-end funds, exchange-traded funds (ETFs), and real estate investment trusts (REITs).

Parts 3 through 5 concern specific types of financial assets. Part 3 is devoted to investments in equity. Chapters 8 and 9 discuss the analysis and valuation of common stock. The next two chapters cover measures of the stock market and historic returns (Chapter 10) and the macroeconomic environment (Chapter 11). The last chapter (Chapter 12) adds behavioral finance and the use of technical analysis to aid in the selection of securities.

Part 4 covers fixed-income securities. Chapter 13 describes the features common to all debt instruments and the variety of corporate bonds. Chapter 14 covers bond pricing, yields, the impact of changing interest rates, and the management of risk. Chapter 15 adds the various types of federal, state, and local government bonds. The last chapter in Part 4 (Chapter 16) is devoted to fixed-income securities that may be exchanged for the issuing firm's common stock.

Part 5 considers derivatives, whose value is related to (derived from) another asset. Chapter 17 provides a general introduction to options (puts and calls), and Chapter 18 expands the material to include option valuation and option strategies. Chapter 19 covers futures, which are perhaps the riskiest of all the investment alternatives covered in this text.

Chapter 20 returns to the themes of financial planning and the allocation of assets to achieve the individual investor's financial goals. This chapter serves both as a capstone and a review as it encompasses the construction of a diversified portfolio, the allocation of investment resources, and active and passive management of an individual's portfolio in an efficient market context.

SUMMARY

This chapter has introduced important financial concepts that apply to investments and investment decision making. These concepts are the following:

- the importance of setting financial goals
- asset valuation as the present value of future cash flows
- the trade-off between risk and return
- the management of risk through asset allocation and the construction of a diversified portfolio
- the efficiency of financial markets
- the need to assess performance on a risk-adjusted basis.

Each of these themes reappears at various places throughout this text. Even though a chapter may be devoted to a specific topic such as mutual funds or convertible securities, these specific assets ultimately must fit into a portfolio. It is important to know the features, risks, and returns of a specific security, but you need to remember that each individual asset is only a part of your portfolio. While a particular investment may do exceptionally well or exceptionally poorly, it is the aggregate portfolio that helps you achieve your financial objectives.

The Financial Advisor's Investment Case
Investment Assignment (Part 1)

1. You have $100,000 to invest in ten stocks, $10,000 in each (no mutual funds). You may not alter your selections during the semester, and cash is not an option. (Sorry; the purpose of this assignment is not to teach trading. Additional material will be added as the semester progresses.) Select an Internet source and set up a "watch account." Possible websites with information on companies include the following:

   Bloomberg: http://www.bloomberg.com
   CNN/Money: http://money.cnn.com
   Forbes: http://www.forbes.com
   Google: http:///www.google.com/finance
   MarketWatch: http://www.marketwatch.com
   Morningstar: http://www.morningstar.com
   MSN Money: http://moneycentral.msn.com/ investor
   Reuters: http://www.investor.reuters.com
   Yahoo! Finance: http://finance.yahoo.com

   The watch account will help you follow the stocks over time and keep track of your gains or losses.

2. One successful portfolio manager, Peter Lynch, has suggested that you should buy stock in companies that you know or whose products you use. Since this strategy may be as good a starting point as any to learn about investing, I have selected five stocks I know or whose products I use. You should select five and track your five against mine. Using the information in the previous assignment, set up a watch account that includes both sets.

   My stocks and their ticker symbols are

   Coca-Cola (KO)
   ExxonMobil (XOM)
   Merck (MRK)
   Tupperware (TUP)
   Washington Real Estate Investment Trust (WRE)

   Since disclosure is important in investments, you should know that I had a position in each stock at the time this text went to press.

CHAPTER

2

Securities Markets

LEARNING OBJECTIVES

After completing this chapter you should be able to:

1. Explain the role of market makers and distinguish between securities exchanges and over-the-counter markets.
2. Differentiate between the types of security orders and identify the costs of investing in securities.
3. Contrast cash and margin accounts.
4. Contrast long and short positions and explain the source of profit from each.
5. Define American depository receipts (ADRs) and explain their advantages.
6. State the purpose of the Securities and Exchange Commission (SEC) and the Securities Investor Protection Corporation (SIPC) and the role of regulation in securities markets.
7. Identify the components necessary for the sale of securities to the general public.
8. Examine the price volatility of new issues (IPOs).

On January 7, 2010, 5.8 million shares of IBM traded on the New York Stock Exchange. In all, over 4 billion shares of stock traded that day on the New York Stock Exchange. Not one penny of the proceeds of those sales went to the firms whose stocks were exchanged. Instead, all these transactions were among investors. Obviously, many individuals were altering their portfolios through either buying or selling these existing securities.

This buying and selling of securities has a certain mystique or fascination both for the novice and for the seasoned investor. Investors may be drawn to securities by the jargon used in the stock market or the excitement generated by trading securities. Perhaps the investor's fascination is the result of the fact that many dollars can be earned or lost through investments in stocks and bonds. For whatever reason, investors who are drawn to Wall Street must understand both how securities markets work and the mechanics of buying and selling securities.

The purpose of this chapter is to explain the sale of securities to the general public and the mechanics of buying and selling securities. The initial section covers securities dealers and the role of secondary markets such as the New York Stock Exchange. Next follows descriptions of how the individual trades securities, the role of brokers, the variety of orders, margin versus cash accounts, and the cost of buying and selling securities. Although you make money by buying low and selling high, either the purchase or the sale may come first. The third section is devoted to the short sale, which is a sale for future delivery. The investor initially sells the stock in anticipation of buying it back at a lower price.

Securities markets, like many financial markets, are subject to regulation. The federal regulation of the securities markets and the role of the Securities and Exchange Commission (SEC) are covered next. The chapter concludes with a discussion of initial public offerings (IPOs), in which funds are transferred from investors to firms. The emphasis is on the process of the initial sale, the role of investment bankers, and the subsequent volatility of the securities' prices in the secondary markets.

SECONDARY MARKETS AND THE ROLE OF MARKET MAKERS

Although securities are issued in the primary market, all subsequent transactions are in the secondary markets. If an investor buys a stock, it is highly unlikely that the purchase is part of the IPO. Instead, the individual buys the stock in one of the secondary markets.

This section covers securities dealers (market makers) and their role in secondary markets. Securities are bought and sold every day by investors who never meet each other. The market transfers stocks and bonds from individuals who are selling to those who are buying. This transfer may occur on an organized exchange located in one geographical area, such as the New York Stock Exchange (http://www.nyse.com), which is sometimes referred to as the "Big Board," or the American Stock Exchange, the AMEX or "the curb." Trading on either exchange is not automatic. A company must apply to have its securities accepted for trading. If the company meets the conditions set by the exchange, the securities are "listed" and may be bought and sold through the exchange.[1]

over-the-counter (OTC) market
The informal secondary market for unlisted securities.

Securities of public companies with shares that are not listed on an exchange are traded **over-the-counter (OTC)**. The most important OTC market is the Nasdaq stock market (http://www.nasdaq.com). Nasdaq is an acronym for National Association of Securities Dealers Automated Quotation system, which is the system of communication for over-the-counter price quotations. (Some companies such as Microsoft and Intel choose not to have their shares traded on one of the exchanges.) All major unlisted stocks are included in the Nasdaq stock market. Investors may readily obtain bid and ask prices for many OTC stocks and bonds by simply entering the security's symbol into the system.

dealers
Market makers who buy and sell securities for their own accounts.

In either case, a listed or an unlisted security, professional securities dealers make markets in stocks and bonds and facilitate their transfer from sellers to buyers. The Securities and Exchange Act of 1934 defines a **dealer** as anyone who engages in the "business of buying and selling for his *own account*." Buying and selling for your own account has the effect of making a market in the security. Dealers in the OTC markets are referred to as "market makers," and dealers in listed securities on the NYSE or AMEX are referred to as **specialists**. All of these dealers offer to buy securities from any seller and to sell securities to any purchaser. In effect, they make markets in securities.

specialist
A market maker on the New York Stock Exchange who maintains an orderly market in the security.

round lot
The general unit of trading in a security, such as 100 shares.

Transactions are made in either round lots or odd lots. A **round lot** is the normal unit of trading and for stocks that is usually 100 shares. Smaller transactions such as 37 shares are called **odd lots**. The vast majority of trades are round lots or multiples of rounds lots. The volume and value of transactions for many stocks is substantial. For example, on June 6, 2009, some 3.6 million shares of Google (GOOG) traded. At the closing price of \$444, the total value of those trades was approximately \$1.6 billion (\$444 × 3.6 million). There are, however, stocks that are inactively traded. Such issues are referred to as "thin" and are generally the stock of small companies with a modest number of shares outstanding.

odd lot
A unit of trading, such as 22 shares, that is smaller than the general unit of sale.

[1]Delistings do occur. In June 2009, GM was delisted as it went through bankruptcy and reorganization. Over time the number of listed securities has increased. In 1973, over 1,500 stocks were traded on the NYSE. By 2009, the NYSE Annual Report stated that the number of companies traded on the NYSE exceeded 2,400 and that over 900 closed-end and exchange-traded funds were traded on the exchange. The annual report is available at the NYSE's website: **http://www.nyse.com**.

bid and ask

Prices at which a securities dealer offers to buy and sell stock.

Securities dealers quote prices on a **bid and ask** basis; they buy at one price (the bid) and sell at the other price (the ask). For example, a market maker may be willing to purchase a specific stock for $20 and sell for $21. The security is then quoted "20–21," which are the bid and ask prices. For example, if the quote for National Retail Properties is 23.56–23.61, I can currently buy the stock for $23.61 and sell it for $23.56.

spread

The difference between the bid and the ask prices.

The difference between the bid and the ask is the **spread** (i.e., the $0.05 difference between $23.61 and $23.56 for National Retail Properties). The spread, like brokerage commissions, is part of the cost of investing. These two costs should not be confused. The spread is one source of compensation for maintaining a market in the security. The broker's commission is compensation for executing your purchase or sell orders.

While the spread is a primary source of compensation for market makers, it is not their only source. Market makers also earn income when they receive dividends and interest from the securities they own. Another source of profit is an increase in securities prices, for the value of the dealers' portfolios rises. These profits are a necessary element of securities markets because they induce the market makers to serve the crucial function of buying and selling securities. These market makers guarantee to buy and sell at the prices they announce. Thus, an investor knows what the securities are worth at any given time and is assured that there is a place to sell current securities holdings or to purchase additional securities.

Determination of Prices

equilibrium price

A price that equates supply and demand.

Although the bid and ask prices are quoted by market makers, securities prices are set by the demand from all buyers and the supply from all sellers of securities. Market makers try to quote an **equilibrium price** that equates the supply with the demand. If market makers bid too low a price, too few shares will be offered to satisfy the demand. If they ask too high a price, too few shares will be purchased, which will result in a glut, or excess shares, in their portfolios.

Could market makers set a security's equilibrium price? For large companies the answer is probably no. If the market makers tried to establish a price above the equilibrium price that is set by supply and demand, they would have to absorb all of the excess supply of securities that would be offered at the artificially higher price. Conversely, if the market makers attempted to establish a price below the equilibrium price, they would have to sell a sufficient number of securities to meet the excess demand that would exist at the artificially lower price. The buying of securities requires the delivery of the securities sold. Market makers do not have an infinite well of money with which to purchase the securities nor an unlimited supply of securities to deliver. They may increase or decrease their inventory, but they cannot support the price indefinitely by buying securities, nor can they prevent a price increase by selling them.

Although market makers cannot set the market price, they perform an extremely important role: They maintain an orderly market in securities so that buyers and sellers will have an established market in which to trade. To establish this orderly market, the market makers offer to buy and sell at the quoted bid and ask prices but guarantee only one round-lot transaction at these prices. If a market maker sets too low a price for a certain stock, a large quantity will be demanded by investors. The market maker is required to sell only one round lot at this price and then may increase the bid and ask prices. The increase in the price of the stock will (1) induce some holders of the stock

---

⊕ Point of Interest

THE "BUY SIDE" AND THE "SELL SIDE" OF THE STREET

Investors buy stock at the asking price and sell at the bid. The purchases and sales are executed by brokers and are made through securities dealers. Are these participants the "buy side" and "sell side" of Wall Street? If a financial analyst works the "buy side" or the "sell side" of Wall Street, does that mean he or she is buying or selling stocks and bonds?

The answer is no. A *financial analyst* (or *securities analyst* or *investment analyst*—all three names are used) is an individual who analyzes financial statements, interviews corporate management, and uses other sources of information to construct earnings estimates and buy or sell recommendations for individual securities. These analysts are not brokers and are not securities dealers, and they are not buying and selling for their own accounts. They are (very well) paid employees who work for money management firms and brokerage houses.

A buy-side analyst works for a nonbrokerage firm that manages mutual funds, pension plans, or trust services for corporate clients or individual investors. The buy-side analyst provides recommendations, which are given to the firm's portfolio managers, who buy and sell securities. Since these analysts are developing recommendations for possible purchases by their employers, they work the "buy side" of the Street.

A sell-side analyst does the same type of work but is employed by a brokerage firm. The sell-side analyst's recommendations are provided to the brokers who, in turn, give the recommendations to investors. The purpose of a sell-side analyst's reports is to generate sales, hence the name "sell side."

Since buy-side analysts' reports are solely for their employers' use, the recommendations may remain private. Sell-side analysts' reports, however, become public, and this creates a potential conflict of interest or at least a potential bias in the analysis. There are several possible reasons for this bias. First, analysts may issue favorable reports to maintain good relationships with corporate management, since executives are one source of an analyst's information. Second, the corporation may employ an underwriter to issue new securities. Analysts do not want to lose this future business for their brokerage firms. Third, analysts' reports are designed to encourage transactions, especially purchases, by the brokerage firm's customers. Any of these reasons could cause an analyst to issue a favorable report concerning a firm and its securities. Since more favorable reports are issued than negative reports, one could easily draw that conclusion.

---

to sell their shares and (2) induce some investors who wanted to purchase the stock to drop out of the market.

If the market maker sets too high a price for the stock, a large quantity of shares will be offered for sale, but these shares will remain unsold. If the market maker is unable to or does not want to absorb all these shares, the securities dealer may purchase a round lot and then lower the bid and ask prices. The decline in the price of the stock will (1) induce some potential sellers to hold their stock and (2) induce some investors to enter the market by purchasing the shares, thereby reducing any of the market maker's surplus inventory.

Composite Transactions

With the development of the Nasdaq stock market, the distinction between the various exchanges and the over-the-counter market is being erased. (The distinction between exchanges and over-the-counter markets was reduced by the merger of the AMEX and Nasdaq in November 1998.) Since New York Stock Exchange securities trade on other exchanges, the actual reporting of New York Stock Exchange listings includes all the trades and is reported as the NYSE-Composite transactions.

third market

Over-the-counter market for securities listed on an exchange.

In addition to the primary market (the initial sale of the security) and the secondary market (subsequent trading in the security), there is also the **third market**, which is over-the-counter trading in listed securities. While any trades in listed securities off the exchange may be referred to as the third market, the bulk of these trades are large transactions. Such large trades (i.e., 10,000 shares or more) are called *blocks*, and the market makers who organize and execute the trades are referred to as *block positioners*.

The participants in the third market are usually institutional investors, such as pension plans, mutual funds, or insurance companies, who want to buy or sell large amounts of stocks in listed securities, such as the stock of IBM, which trades on the NYSE. The institutional investor works through a large brokerage firm that completes the transaction. If the investor desires to buy a large position, the brokerage firm (or securities dealer) seeks potential sellers. After the required seller (or sellers, for a sufficiently large block) is found, the securities are traded off the floor of the exchange.

In the *fourth market*, the financial institutions do not use brokerage firms or securities dealers but may trade securities through a computerized system, such as *Instinet* (**http://www.instinet.com**), which provides bid and ask price quotations and executes orders. This system is limited to those financial institutions that subscribe to the service. Transactions through Instinet are reported in the financial press through the composite transactions just like trades on the various exchanges.

Block trades, the third market, and the fourth market offer financial institutions two advantages: lower commissions and quicker executions. Competition among brokerage firms for this business has reduced the commission fees. In addition, the effort and time required to put together a block to purchase or to find buyers for a sale is reduced through the development of block trading and over-the-counter trading of listed securities. The effect of this trading and the change in the regulatory environment for financial institutions has led to a computerized market for the execution of security orders.

THE MECHANICS OF INVESTING IN SECURITIES

broker

An agent who handles buy and sell orders for an investor.

Individual investors usually purchase stocks and bonds through **brokers**, who buy and sell securities for their customers' accounts. (Some brokerage firms use different titles, such as "account executive" or "assistant vice president." These individuals perform the traditional functions of "brokers.") While a few companies (e.g., ExxonMobil) offer investors the option to purchase shares directly from the corporation, the majority of purchases are made through brokerage firms, such as Merrill Lynch or Charles Schwab. Many brokerage firms also act as market makers and may be referred to as "broker-dealers" since different divisions within the firm perform both functions. The firm has individuals who buy and sell for the firm's account (i.e., are securities dealers) and other individuals who buy and sell for customers' accounts (i.e., are brokers).

registered representative

A person who buys and sells securities for customers; a broker.

The broker services an individual's account and is the *investor's agent* who executes buy and sell orders. To be permitted to buy and sell securities, brokers must pass a proficiency examination administered by the National Association of Securities Dealers. Once the individual has passed the test, he or she is referred to as a **registered representative** and can buy and sell securities for customers' accounts.

Although registered representatives must pass this proficiency examination, the investor should not assume that the broker is an expert. There are many aspects of

⊕ Point of Interest

PINK SHEETS

When Mirant went bankrupt and the NYSE suspended the stock, the security continued to trade and quotes could be found in the "pink sheets." This occurrence is common; the shares of companies that fall on hard times trade after being delisted through the pink sheets.

Originally printed on pink paper, the pink sheets are a daily listing of over-the-counter stocks not included in the daily OTC bulletin board. Most of the stocks traded through the pink sheets are small companies. (The exceptions are large companies such as Mirant whose value has plunged because of the firm's financial difficulties.) The volume of transactions is small and the total value of a particular stock traded on a given day is often less than $1 million. Such securities are of interest only to speculators, but if you are curious, information and quotes may be found at **http://www.pinksheets.com**.

investing, and even an individual who spends a considerable portion of the working day servicing accounts cannot be an expert on all the aspects of investing. Thus, many recommendations are based on research that is done by analysts employed by the brokerage firm rather than by individual salespersons.

The investor should realize that brokers make their living through transactions (i.e., buying and selling for their customers' accounts). There are essentially two types of working relationships between the brokerage firm and the salesperson. In one case, the firm pays a basic salary, but the salesperson must bring in a specified amount in commissions, which go to the firm. After the minimum amount of sales has been met, the registered representative's salary is increased in proportion to the amount of additional commissions generated. In the second type of relationship, the salesperson's income is entirely related to the commissions generated. In either case, the investor should realize that the broker's livelihood depends on the sale of securities. Thus, the broker's advice on investing may be colored by the desire to secure commissions. However, the investor is ultimately responsible for the investment decisions. Although advice may be requested from the broker, and it is sometimes offered even though unsolicited, the investor must weigh the impact of a specific investment decision in terms of fulfilling his or her financial goals.

Selecting a brokerage firm can be a difficult task. Various firms offer different services; for example, some may specialize in bonds. Other brokerage firms offer a full range of services, including estate planning and life insurance, as well as trading of stocks and bonds. Still other firms offer virtually no services other than executing orders at discount (i.e., lower) commissions. Each investor therefore needs to identify his or her personal investment goals and decide on the strategies to attain those goals in order to select the firm that is best suited to that individual's needs.

Choosing a registered representative or financial advisor is a more difficult task than selecting a brokerage firm. This individual will need to know specific information, including the investor's income, other assets and outstanding debt, and financial goals, in order to give the best service to the account. People are reluctant to discuss this information, so trust and confidence in the registered representative are probably the most important considerations in selecting a broker or financial advisor. Good rapport between the broker and the investor is particularly important if the relationship is going to be mutually successful.

The Long and Short Positions

long position

Owning assets for their income and possible price appreciation.

bullish

Expecting that prices will rise.

short position

Selling borrowed assets for possible price deterioration; being short in a security or a commodity.

bearish

Expecting that prices will decline.

market order

An order to buy or sell at the current market price or quote.

limit order

An order placed with a broker to buy or sell at a specified price.

day order

An order placed with a broker that is canceled at the end of the day if it is not executed.

good-till-canceled order

An order placed with a broker that remains in effect until it is executed by the broker or canceled by the investor.

stop order

A purchase or sell order designed to limit an investor's loss or to assure a profit on a position in a security.

Essentially, an investor has only two courses of action, which involve opposite positions. They are frequently referred to as the *bull* and *bear* positions and are symbolized by a statue, which is located outside the NYSE, of a bull and a bear locked in mortal combat.[2]

If an investor expects a security's price to rise, the security is purchased. The investor takes a **long position** in the security in anticipation of the price increase. The investor is **bullish** because he or she believes that the price will rise. The long position earns profits for the investor if the price rises after the security has been purchased. For example, if an investor buys 100 shares of AB&C for $55 (i.e., $5,500 plus brokerage fees) and the price rises to $60, the profit on the long position is $5 per share (i.e., $500 on 100 shares before commissions).

Opposite the long position is the **short position (bearish)**, in which the investor anticipates that the security's price will fall. The investor sells the security and holds cash or places the funds in interest-bearing short-term securities, such as Treasury bills or a savings account. Some investors who are particularly bearish or who are willing to speculate on the decline in prices may even "sell short," which is a sale for future delivery. (The process of selling short is discussed in the next section.)

Types of Orders

After an investor decides to purchase a security, a buy order is placed with the broker. The investor may ask the broker to buy the security at the best price currently available, which is the asking price set by the market maker. Such a request is a **market order.** The investor is not assured of receiving the security at the currently quoted price, since that price may change by the time the order is executed. However, the order is generally executed at or very near the asking price.

The investor may enter a **limit order** and specify a price below the current asking price and wait until the price declines to the specified level. Such an order may be placed for one day (i.e., a **day order**), or the order may remain in effect indefinitely (i.e., a **good-till-canceled order**). Such an order remains on the books of the broker until it is either executed or canceled. If the price of the security does not decline to the specified level, the purchase is never made. While a good-till-canceled order may remain in effect indefinitely, brokerage firms generally have a time limit (e.g., one month or three months) that specifies when the order will be canceled if it has not been executed.

After purchasing the security an investor may place a **stop order** to sell, which may be at a higher or lower price. Once the stock reaches that price, the stop order becomes a market order. An investor who desires to limit potential losses may place a stop-loss order, which specifies the price below the cost of the security at which the broker is authorized to sell. For example, if an investor buys a stock for $50 a share, a stop-loss order at $45 limits the loss to $5 a share, plus the commission fees for the purchase and the sale. If the price of the stock should fall to $45, the stop-loss order becomes

---

[2]The derivations of "bull" and "bear" are lost in time. "Bearish" may originate from trading in pelts when bearskins were sold before the bears were caught. Bullbaiting and bearbaiting were also sports in the eighteenth century. See Steele Commager, "Watch Your Language," *Forbes* (October 27, 1980): 113–116.

⊕ Point of Interest

OBTAINING QUOTES

Before establishing a position, the investor should have an indication of the stock's current price. Prior to the formation of the Internet, individuals obtained price quotes for specific stocks by calling their broker. When the investor asked the broker for a quote, the answer was often a price like $75, which was probably the last trade. An investor generally had to ask to obtain the bid and ask prices. It is, of course, the bid and ask prices that are relevant when considering making a trade.

Today, quotes are considerably easier to obtain, since they are readily available on the Internet. Many of the sites given throughout this text provide quotes, but the actual prices may differ. To write this section, I typed in NOR (NorthWestern Corporation) at Schwab's site and received the following information:

	Last	Change	Bid	Ask	Volume	Time
NOR	1.62	−0.02	1.61	1.64	9,300	9:36:57.

These data indicate that the stock was marginally lower from the previous day.

Fifteen minutes later, I typed in NOR at MSN Money and received the following:

Last	1.62
Change	−0.02
Percent change	−1.22%
Volume	5,500
Day's high	1.62
Day's low	1.62
Bid	NA
Asked	NA

Notice that the two sources did not give me the same information. For example, MSN Money did not provide the bid/ask prices, and the information such as the volume of transactions differed. The volume data from MSN Money was less even though the information was requested later. The reason for the difference is that the Schwab information was in "real time" and the MSN Money data was delayed 20 minutes. Since investments are made in real time, it is important to obtain real-time data.

MSN Money also provides real-time data, and when I went to that source, I received the following:

Last	1.68
Change	0.04
Volume	33,200
Bid	1.65
Ask	1.68
Bid/Ask size	5500/3600

Once again the information was different. The price of the stock was higher, and this source added the bid/ask size. The bid/ask size is important because it indicates how many shares the market maker is willing to buy and sell at the quote. In this case the market maker was willing to buy 5,500 shares at 1.65 but sell only 3,600 share at the ask. If you want to buy 4,000 shares at $1.68, you should not assume the market maker will accommodate the request. The market maker may sell 3,600 shares at $1.68 and the remaining 400 shares at a higher price. You may avoid the higher price by putting in an order for "all or nothing" at the specified price, but then you are not assured of having the order executed. In effect you must decide to accept the going price and buy the desired number of shares or specify the number and price but then run the risk that the order will not be executed.

a market order, and the stock is sold. (Since the order is now a market order, there is no assurance that the investor will get $45. If there is an influx of sell orders, the sale may occur at less than $45.) Such a sale protects the investor from riding the price of the stock down to $40 or lower. Of course, if the stock rebounds from $45 to $50, the investor has sold out at the bottom price.

The investor may also place an order above the purchase price. For example, the investor who purchases a stock at $50 may place a sell order at $60. Should the price of the stock reach $60, the order becomes a market order, and the stock is sold. Such an order limits the potential profit, for if the stock's price continues to rise, the investor who has already sold the stock does not continue to gain. However, the investor has protected the profit that resulted as the price increased from $50 to $60. In many cases the investor watches the stock's price rise, decides not to sell, and then watches the price subsequently decline. Sell orders are designed to reduce this possibility.

The placing of sell orders can be an important part of an investor's strategy. For example, in the previous case the investor who purchased a stock at $50 may place sell orders at $45 and $60. If the price of the stock subsequently rises, this investor may change these sell orders. For example, if the price rises to $56 per share, the investor may change the sell orders to $52 and $64. This will preserve the capital invested, for the price of the stock cannot fall below $52 without triggering the sell order, but the price can now rise above $60, which was the previous upper limit for the sell order. By continuously raising the prices for the sell orders as the stock's price rises, the investor can continue to profit from any price increase and at the same time protect the funds invested in the security against price declines.

Because both limit orders and stop orders specify a price, they are easy to confuse. The limit order specifies a price at which a stock is to be bought or sold. (The purchase could be made at a lower price, and the sale could occur at a higher price.) Limits orders are filled in order of receipt. A limit order to buy stock at $10 may not be executed if other investors have previously entered purchase orders at that price. (Since individuals tend to think in terms of simple numbers such as $10 or $15, it may be a wise strategy to enter the buy order at $10.05, so that the order would be executed before all orders placed at $10. The same applies to sell orders. A limit to sell at $13 is executed once the stock price rises to $13 and prior sell orders are executed. A sell order at $12.90 stands before all sell orders at $13.)

A stop order also specifies a price. Once the price is reached, the order becomes a market order and is executed. Since the stop becomes a market order, the actual price at which it is executed may not necessarily be the specified price. For example, an investor buys a stock for $25 and enters a "stop-loss order" to sell at $20 to limit the possible loss on the stock. If the price declines to $20, the stop loss becomes a market order and stock is sold. As mentioned before, the investor may anticipate receiving $20, but there is no guarantee that the stock will be sold at that price. If, for example, the stock reported lower earnings and the price immediately dropped from $25 to $19, the stop-loss order would be executed at $19 instead of the specified $20.

If the investor were unwilling to accept a price less than $20, the individual could enter the sale order as a "stop-limit" order that combines a stop-loss with a limit order. However, the stock would not be sold if the price declined through the specified price before the limit order was executed. If, after the earnings announcement the price immediately dropped from $22 to $19, a stop-limit order at $20 would not be executed unless the stock subsequently rose to $20. With any limit order there is no assurance that the order will be executed. In other words, investors cannot have their cake and eat it too. Once the specified price is reached, a stop order guarantees an execution but not the price, whereas a limit order guarantees the price but not an execution.

confirmation statement

A statement received from a brokerage firm detailing the sale or purchase of a security and specifying a settlement date.

Once the purchase has been made, the broker sends the investor a **confirmation statement**, an example of which is shown in Exhibit 2.1. This confirmation statement gives the number of shares and name of the security purchased (100 shares of Clevepak Corporation), the unit price ($12.13) and the total amount that is due

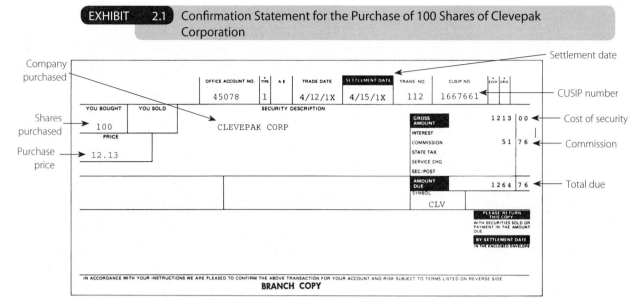

EXHIBIT 2.1 Confirmation Statement for the Purchase of 100 Shares of Clevepak Corporation

Company purchased

Shares purchased

Purchase price

Settlement date

CUSIP number

Cost of security

Commission

Total due

Source: Adapted from Scott & Stringfellow, Inc.

($1,264.76). The amount that is due includes both the price of the securities and the transaction fees. The major transaction fee is the brokerage firm's commission, but there may also be state transfer fees and other miscellaneous fees. The investor has three business days after the trade date (the day the security is purchased—April 12, 201X) to pay the amount that is due. The settlement date (the day the payment is due—April 15, 201X) is three business days after the trade date, and this time difference is frequently referred to as $T + 3$. The CUSIP in the confirmation statement (1667661) refers to the Committee for Uniform Securities Identification Procedures, which assigns a unique number for each security issue.

Cash and Margin Accounts

The investor must pay for the securities as they are purchased. This can be done either with cash or with a combination of cash and borrowed funds. The latter is called buying on **margin**. The investor then has either a cash account or a margin account. A cash account is what the name implies: The investor pays the entire cost of the securities (i.e., $1,264.76 in Exhibit 2.1) in cash.

When an investor uses margin—that is, purchases the security partially with cash and partially with credit supplied by the broker—he or she makes an initial payment that is similar to a down payment on a house and borrows the remaining funds necessary to make the purchase. To open a margin account, the investor signs an agreement with the broker that gives the use of the securities and some control over the account to the broker. The securities serve as collateral for the loan. Should the amount of collateral on the account fall below a specified level, the broker can require that the investor

margin
The amount that an investor must put down to buy securities on credit.

⊕ Point of Interest

DETERMINING THE PERCENTAGE RETURN ON A MARGIN PURCHASE, INCLUDING COMMISSIONS, INTEREST PAID, AND DIVIDENDS RECEIVED

The body of the text illustrated the potential magnification of the percentage return on a margin purchase versus a cash purchase. The example was an oversimplification because it excluded commissions, interest on any borrowed funds, and dividends received (if any). The following is a more complete illustration.

Assume the investor buys 100 shares of stock for $10 a share and sells it for $14. Also assume the margin requirement is 60 percent, the commission rate is 5 percent of the purchase or sale price, the interest rate is 10 percent, and the stock pays a dividend of $1.00 a share. The following illustrates the two positions:

	Cash	Margin
Sale price	$1,400	$1,400
Commission	70	70
Proceeds of sale	1,330	1,330
Loan repayment	0	420
Cash received	1,330	910
Dividends received	$100	$100
Interest paid	0	42

Percentage earned on the cash purchase:

$$\frac{\$1,330 + \$100 - \$1,050}{\$1,050} = 36.2\%$$

Percentage earned on the margin purchase:

$$\frac{\$1,330 - \$1,050 + \$100 - \$42}{\$630} = 53.7\%$$

Notice that the profit on the purchase and sale ($1,330 − $1,050) and the dividend payment are the same in both cases. The difference in the percentage earned is the result of having to pay interest ($42) and the fact that the investor only put up 60 percent of the funds ($630) and borrowed $420. It is the commitment of less than the full purchase price plus commissions and borrowing the balance that is the source of the magnification of the percentage return.

The percentage returns are also different from those in the simple illustration in the body of the text. When commissions, interest, and dividends are included, the return on the all-cash investment is 36.2 percent versus 30 percent in the simplified illustration. The return on the margin investment is 53.7 percent instead of 67 percent because the commissions and interest consume part of the return.

---

put more assets in the account. This is called a *margin call*, and it may be satisfied by cash or additional securities. If the investor fails to meet a margin call, the broker will sell some securities in the account to raise the cash needed to protect the loan.

The **margin requirement** is the minimum percentage of the total price that the investor must pay and is set by the Federal Reserve Board. Individual brokers, however, may require more margin. The minimum payment required of the investor is the value of the securities times the margin requirement. Thus, if the margin requirement is 60 percent and the price of 100 shares is $1,000, the investor must supply $600 in cash and borrow $400 from the broker, who in turn borrows the funds from a commercial bank. The investor pays interest to the broker on $400. The interest rate will depend on the rate that the broker must pay to the lending institution.

Investors use margin to increase the potential return on the investment. When they expect the price of the security to rise, some investors pay for part of their purchases with borrowed funds. If the price rises from $10 to $14, the profit is $400. If the investor pays the entire $1,000, the percentage return is 40 percent ($400/$1,000). However, if the investor uses margin and pays for the stock with $600 in equity and

$400 in borrowed funds, the investor's percentage return is increased to 67 percent ($400/$600). In this case, the use of margin is favorable because it increases the investor's return on the invested funds. (This illustration is an oversimplification since it does not consider the impact of commissions, interest on the borrowed funds, and any dividends. For a more complete illustration, see the accompanying Point of Interest.)

Of course, *if the price of the stock falls*, the reverse occurs—that is, *the percentage loss is greater*. If the price falls to $7, the investor loses $300 before commissions on the sale. The percentage loss is 30 percent. However, if the investor uses margin, the percentage loss is increased to 50 percent. Because the investor has borrowed money and thus reduced the amount of funds that he or she has committed to the investment, the percentage loss is greater. The use of margin magnifies both the potential return and potential percentage loss. Because the potential loss is increased, buying securities on credit increases the element of risk.

Maintenance Margin

The margin requirement establishes the minimum amount the investor must deposit (and the maximum amount the investor may borrow) when purchasing a security. If the price of the stock subsequently rises, the investor's position improves because the amount borrowed as a proportion of the total value of the stock declines. If, however, the value of the stock falls, the investor's position deteriorates and the amount owed becomes a larger proportion of the value of the stock.

maintenance margin

The minimum equity required for a margin account. (The minimum level of funds required before a margin call.)

In order to protect the broker from the investor's default (not repaying the loan), a second margin requirement is established. This **maintenance margin** sets the minimum equity the investor must have in the position. If the stock's price declines sufficiently so that the investor violates the maintenance margin requirement, the investor receives a margin call and must advance additional funds or the broker will sell the stock and close the position. (Maintenance margin applies to the account as a whole. The investor receives a margin call when the value of the portfolio does not meet the maintenance margin requirement.)

Assume the maintenance margin requirement is 35 percent in the previous illustration. The initial margin requirement was 60 percent, so the investor paid $600 in cash (the investor's equity in the position) and borrowed $400 through the broker. If the investor's equity falls to below 35 percent, additional cash will be required. Suppose the price of the stock declines to $7, and the value of the stock is $700. Since $400 is owed, the investor's equity is $300, which is 42.9 percent of the value of the stock ($300/$700). Since 42.9 exceeds 35 percent, the investor is meeting the maintenance margin requirement. If, however, the price of the stock is $6, the investor's equity is $200—only 33.3 percent ($200/$600 = 33.3%) of the value of the stock. Since the maintenance margin requirement is 35 percent, the required margin is $210 (0.35 × $600). The investor will receive a margin call and be required to commit an additional $10 to raise the equity to $210 and meet the maintenance margin requirement.

The price of the stock (P) that triggers a margin call is determined by Equation 2.1, in which B is the amount borrowed per share and MM is the maintenance margin requirement. In this illustration, the price that produces a margin call is

2.1

$$P = B/(1 - MM)$$
$$= \$4/(1 - 0.35) = \$6.15.$$

At $6.15 the investor's equity is $215 ($615 × $400) which is 35 percent of the value of the stock ($215/$615 = 0.35 = 35%). As long as the price of the stock remains above $6.15, the investor will not receive a margin call to commit additional cash to meet the maintenance margin requirement.

Delivery of Securities

street name

The registration of securities in a brokerage firm's name instead of in the buyer's name.

Once the shares have been purchased and paid for, the investor must decide whether to leave the securities with the broker or to take delivery. (In the case of a margin account, the investor *must* leave the securities with the broker.) If the shares are left with the broker, they will be registered in the brokerage firm's name (i.e., in the **street name**). The brokerage firm then becomes custodian of the securities, is responsible for them, and sends a statement of the securities that are being held in the street name to the investor. The statement (usually monthly) also includes transactions and dividends and interest received. Some statements sent by brokerage firms include additional information such as the portfolio's asset allocation, year-to-date performance, cost basis of securities in the account, unrealized gains and losses, and dividends to be received.

The primary advantage of leaving securities with the brokerage firm is convenience, and the vast majority of investors (probably in excess of 95 percent) have their securities registered in street name. The investor does not have to store the securities and can readily sell them, since they are in the brokerage firm's possession. The accrued interest and dividends may be viewed as a kind of forced savings program, for they may be immediately reinvested before the investor has an opportunity to spend the money elsewhere. The statements are a readily accessible source of information for tax purposes.

The requirement that securities be paid for within three days after purchase or delivered within three days after sale is often used by brokerage firms as an argument for registering securities in street name. Many brokerage firms require investors to have the securities or cash in their accounts before executing sales or purchases. As an additional deterrent, some brokerage firms charge for the delivery of securities.

Brokerage firms, however, cannot require the investor to leave the securities in the street name (Some debt instruments, such as municipal bonds, are issued only as "book" entries. No certificates are created, so the "securities" must be registered in the street name.) There is an important disadvantage to leaving the securities in the brokerage firm's name. If the brokerage firm fails or becomes insolvent, the investor may encounter difficulty in transferring the securities to his or her name and even greater difficulty in collecting any accrued dividends and interest. (The Securities Investor Protection Corporation [SIPC] has reduced the investor's risk of loss from the failure of a brokerage firm. SIPC is discussed later in this chapter.)

trader

An investor who frequently buys and sells.

If the investor frequently buys and sells stock, the shares need to be registered with the broker to facilitate the transactions. Such investors may be referred to as **traders**. The term *trade* is often used concerning investments. Although trading implies frequent buying and selling, any securities transaction may be referred to as a "trade." A market maker may also be referred to as a trader. The buying and selling of stocks that brokers and financial advisors do for clients is often referred to as "trading." A variation on the term, *proprietary trading*, is used to apply to individuals who buy and sell stock for their own accounts using their own funds.

MARGIN ACCOUNTS

As the body of the text explains, margin accounts can increase the percentage returns on your investments. By borrowing some of the cost of an investment, you are able to leverage your returns. However, here are some realities that anyone who buys stock on margin should know.

1. The interest on the borrowed funds is a short-term rate that your broker sets, and the rate will increase with a general increase in interest rates.

2. While the Federal Reserve sets the minimum margin requirement, your broker can set a higher minimum rate and can raise that minimum rate without giving you advance written notice.

3. If you receive a margin call, the brokerage firm can determine which assets in your account will be sold to meet the margin call.

4. If you receive a margin call, you are not entitled to an extension of time.

5. It is possible to lose more funds than you deposit with the broker, and you are responsible for that additional loss.

Yes, the use of margin can magnify your return, but as the above points indicate, the use of margin increases your personal risk. Use margin wisely.

If the investor chooses to take delivery of the securities, that individual receives the stock certificates or bonds. Because the certificates may become negotiable, the investor may suffer a loss if they are stolen. Therefore, care should be taken to store them in a safe place such as a lock box or safe-deposit box in a bank. If the certificates are lost or destroyed, they can be replaced, but only at considerable expense in terms of money and effort. For example, the financial statements of Dominion Resources direct stockholders who lose certificates to write the transfer agent for instructions on how to obtain replacements. Bond is required to protect the stockholder and the transfer agent should the lost certificates return to circulation. The cost of the bond is 2 percent of the current market value (not the investor's cost) of the stock plus a processing fee.

The Cost of Investing

commissions

Fees charged by brokers for executing orders.

Investing, like everything else, is not free. The individual must pay certain costs, the most obvious of which are **commission** fees. There may also be transfer fees, and while these last expenses tend to be trivial, they can add up as the dollar value or the number of trades increases.

Commission costs are not trivial, and for small investors they may constitute a substantial portion of the total amount spent on the investment. Commission rates are supposed to be set by supply and demand, but in reality only large investors (e.g., financial institutions such as insurance companies or mutual funds) are able to negotiate commissions with brokerage firms. These institutions do such a large dollar volume that they are able to negotiate lower rates. For these institutions, the commission rates (as a percentage of the dollar amount of the transaction) may be small. Individuals, however, do not have this influence and generally have to accept the rate that is offered by the brokerage firm.

In general, commission rates are quoted in terms of round lots of 100 shares. Most firms also set a minimum commission fee (e.g., $50) that may cover all transactions involving $1,000 or less. Then, as the value of the 100 shares increases to greater than $1,000, the fee also increases. However, this commission fee as a percentage of the dollar value of the transaction will usually fall.

discount broker

A broker who charges lower commissions on security purchases and sales.

Some brokerage firms, known as **discount brokers**, offer lower commissions. (Full-service brokers may offer discounts, but the investor must ask for them. Receiving the requested discount will depend on such factors as the volume of trades generated by the investor.) Discount brokerage firms do not offer the range of services available through the full-service brokerage houses, but if the individual does not need these services, discount brokers help to reduce the cost of investing by decreasing commissions.

Investors may further reduce commission costs by trading online. Firms that offer this service initially charged substantially lower commissions than were assessed by discount brokers. Even discount brokerage firms like Charles Schwab offer customers discounts from regular commissions if these investors use their electronic trading system. Obviously, individuals who feel comfortable using online trading and who do not need regular brokerage services may be able to obtain substantial reductions in the cost of buying and selling securities.

Impact of the Spread on the Cost of Investing

Whereas commissions and other fees are explicit costs, there is also an important implicit cost of investing. This cost is the spread between the bid and the ask prices of the security. As was explained earlier in this chapter, the investor pays the ask price but receives only the bid price when the securities are sold. This spread should be viewed as a cost of investing. Thus, if an investor wants to buy 100 shares of a stock quoted 20–21, he or she will have to pay $2,100 plus commissions to buy stock that is currently worth (if it were to be sold) only $2,000. If the commission rate is 2.5 percent on purchases and sales, the cost of a round trip in the security (i.e., a purchase and a subsequent sale) is substantial. The total cost is illustrated in Exhibit 2.2. First, the investor pays $61.80 to buy the stock, for a total cost of $2,161.80 ($2,100 + $61.80). If the stock is then sold, the investor receives $1,939. Although the investor paid $2,161.80, only $1,939 is received if the stock is sold at the bid price. The total cost of this purchase and the subsequent sale exceeds $220. Thus, the bid price of the security must rise sufficiently to cover both the commission fees and the spread before the investor realizes any capital appreciation.

Another possible cost of investing is any impact on the price of the stock. If the portfolio manager of a mutual fund wants to buy (or sell) 50,000 shares of a stock, it is highly unlikely that this order can be filled without it affecting the stock's price. To fill the buy order, the market makers may have to raise the price to induce other investors to sell. This price effect may even apply to stocks that trade over a million shares daily. For stocks with only a modest number of shares outstanding, filling the order can

---

EXHIBIT 2.2 Effect of the Spread on the Cost of Investing

Purchase price	Brokerage commission	Total cost
$2,100.00	$61.80	$2,161.80
Sale price	Commission	Total received
$2,000.00	$61.00	$1,939.00
Net loss (total cost minus total received = net loss)		
$2,161.80 − $1,939.00 = $222.80		

certainly increase (or decrease in the case of a sale) the price. Any impact on the price of the security should be considered as a cost of investing.

To understand this potential cost, consider a market order to buy 600 shares of a small OTC stock with an asking price of $12. The total anticipated outlay is $7,200 (before commissions). The dealer, however, fills the order with 350 shares at $12 and 250 shares at $12.10 for a total outlay of $7,225. The $25 is an additional cost of buying the stock. The market was insufficiently deep to accept the market order without affecting the stock's price.

This illustration also points out the risk associated with a market order. Since the asking price was $12, the investor might assume that he or she can buy any number of shares, but that is not the case. To avoid the possibility of two transactions (and possibly two commission fees), the investor may ask the broker how many shares are being offered at the asking price. If the answer is 350 shares, there is no reason to expect that a market order for 600 shares will be filled at $12.

The investor could place an "all-or-nothing order" at the specified price, in which case he or she buys the entire 600 shares if they become available at the asking price. Once again, there is no assurance the order will be fulfilled. Thus, the investor may specify the complete order (i.e., price and all-or-nothing) and accept the risk that the order will not be filled. Or the investor may place a market order with the assurance that the order will be filled but accept the risk that the price may be affected by the size of the order.

THE SHORT SALE

How does an investor make money in the securities markets? The obvious answer is to buy low and sell high. For most people this implies that the investor first buys the security and then sells it at some later date. Can the investor sell the security first and buy it back later at a lower price? The answer is yes, for a **short sale** reverses the order. The investor sells the security first with the intention of purchasing it in the future at a lower price.

short sale

The sale of borrowed securities in anticipation of a price decline; a contract for future delivery.

Because the sale precedes the purchase, the investor does not own the securities that are being sold short. Selling something that a person does not own may sound illegal, but there are many examples of such short selling in normal business relationships. A magazine publisher who sells a subscription, a professional such as a lawyer, engineer, or author who signs a contract for future services and receives an advance, or a manufacturer who signs a contract for future delivery are all making short sales. When your school collected the semester's tuition, it established a short position; it contracted for the future delivery of educational services. If the cost of fulfilling the contract increases, the short seller loses. If the cost declines, the short seller profits. Selling securities short is essentially no different: It is a current sale with a contract for future delivery. If the securities are subsequently purchased at a lower price, the short seller will profit. However, if the cost of the securities rises in the future, the short seller will suffer a loss.

The mechanics of the short sale can be illustrated by a simple example employing the stock of XYZ, Inc. If the current price of the stock is $50 per share, the investor may buy 100 shares at $50 per share for a total cost of $5,000. Such a purchase represents taking a long position in the stock. If the price subsequently rises to $75 per share and the stock is sold, the investor will earn a profit of $2,500 ($7,500 − $5,000).

The short position reverses this procedure: The investor sells the stock first and buys it back at some time in the future. For example, an investor sells 100 shares of XYZ short at $50 ($5,000). Such a sale is made because the investor believes that the stock is *overpriced* and that the price of the stock will *fall*. In a short sale the investor does not own the 100 shares sold. The buyer of the shares, however, certainly expects delivery of the stock certificate. (Actually, the buyer does not know if the shares come from an investor who is selling short or an investor who is liquidating a position in the security.) The short seller has to *borrow* 100 shares to deliver to the buyer. The shares are usually borrowed from a broker, who in turn probably borrows them from clients who have left their securities with the broker. (Shares held in a margin account may be used by the broker, and one such possible use is to lend the shares to a short seller. However, shares left with the broker in a cash account cannot be lent to a short seller.)

covering the short sale

The purchase of securities to close a short position.

Although the investor has sold the securities, the proceeds of the sale are not delivered to the seller but are held by the broker. These proceeds will be subsequently used to repurchase the shares. (In the jargon of securities markets such repurchases are referred to as **covering the short sale.**) In addition, the short seller must deposit with the broker an amount of money equal to the margin requirement for the purchase of the stock. Thus, if the margin requirement is 60 percent, the short seller in the illustration must deposit $3,000 ($5,000 × 0.6) with the broker. This money protects the broker (i.e., it is the short seller's collateral) and is returned to the short seller plus any profits or minus any losses when he or she buys the shares and returns them to the broker. This flow of certificates and money is illustrated in Figure 2.1. The broker receives the money from the short seller (the $3,000 collateral) and from the buyer of the stock (the $5,000 in proceeds from the sale). The investor who sells the stock short receives nothing, but the borrowed securities flow through this investor's account en route to the buyer. The buyer then receives the securities and remits the funds to pay for them.

If the price of a share declines to $40, the short seller can buy the stock for $4,000. This purchase is no different from any purchase made on an exchange or in the over-the-counter market. The stock is then returned to the broker, and the loan of the stock is repaid. The short seller will have made a profit of $1,000 because the shares were purchased for $4,000 and sold for $5,000. The investor's collateral is then returned by the broker plus the $1,000 profit. These events are illustrated in Figure 2.2. The 100 shares of XYZ stock are purchased for $4,000 by the short seller. When the certificate for the 100 shares is received, it is returned by the short seller to the broker (who, in

FIGURE 2.1 The Flow of Money and Certificates in Short Sale

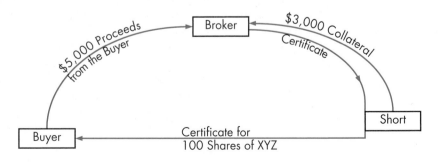

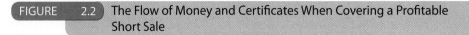

FIGURE 2.2   The Flow of Money and Certificates When Covering a Profitable Short Sale

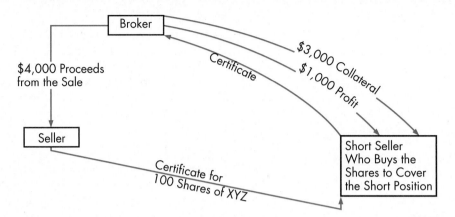

turn, returns the shares to whomever they were borrowed from). The broker returns the investor's $3,000 that was put up for collateral. Since the investor uses only $4,000 of the $5,000 in proceeds from the short sale to purchase the stock, the broker sends the investor the remainder of the proceeds (the $1,000 profit).

If the price of the stock had risen to $60 per share and the short seller had purchased the shares and returned them to the broker, the short position would have resulted in a $1,000 loss. The proceeds from the short sale would have been insufficient to purchase the shares. The short seller would have to use $1,000 of the collateral in addition to the proceeds to buy the stock and cover the short position. The broker would owe the short seller only what was left of the collateral ($2,000) after the transactions had been completed.

Although the previous transactions may sound complicated, they really are not. All that has occurred is that an investor has bought and sold a security. Instead of first purchasing the security and then selling it, the investor initially sold the security and subsequently purchased the shares to cover the short position. Because the sale occurred first, there is additional bookkeeping to account for the borrowed securities, but the transaction itself is not complicated.

Unfortunately, many individuals believe that short selling is gambling. They believe that if investors sell short and the price of the stock rises substantially, the losses could result in financial ruin. However, short sellers can protect themselves by placing stop-loss purchase orders to cover the short position if the stock's price rises to a particular level. Furthermore, if these investors fail to place stop-loss orders, the brokers will cover the position for them once their collateral has shrunk and can no longer support the short position. In effect, the short seller receives a margin call. Thus, the amount that an investor can lose is limited to the required amount of margin.

While selling short generally involves no greater risk than purchasing stock, the possibility does exist that the price of the stock could rise dramatically and inflict large losses. Suppose an investor sold a stock short at $50 and the company subsequently became a takeover target with a price of $75. The price of the stock immediately jumps from $50 to $72.67 and sells for a small discount from the $75 takeover price. Since there were no trades between $50 and $72.67, the short seller is unable to cover until

---

⊕ Point of Interest

THE SHORT SALE AND DIVIDENDS

You sell 100 shares of Southern Company short and the company subsequently pays a $0.35 quarterly dividend. The $35 dividend is sent to the individual who bought the 100 Southern shares, because that investor is the owner of record. However, the investor from whom you borrowed the Southern shares expects to receive the $35 dividend. Where does the money come from?

The answer is the short seller. The company is certainly not going to make two payments, so the short seller makes a payment equal to the dividend to the lender. The process is automatic. Your broker debits $35 from your account and credits the $35 to the account of the lender. While this transfer appears to be detrimental to the short seller, it is not. As is explained in Chapter 9 on dividends, the price of the stock adjusts downward for the dividend. You lose the $35 that you must pay but the value of the stock declines by $35. That's a wash and the short seller is neither better nor worse off as a result of the dividend payment.

---

trading resumes at $72.67. In this possible scenario, the short seller could sustain a loss that exceeds the collateral necessary to meet the margin requirement.

Although the possibility exists for a large loss, short selling is basically consistent with a rational approach to the selection of securities. If an investor analyzes a company and finds that its securities are overpriced, the investor will certainly not buy the securities, and any that are currently owned should be sold. In addition, if the individual has confidence in the analysis and believes that the price will decline, the investor may sell short. The short sale, then, is the logical strategy given the basic analysis. Securities that are overpriced should be considered for short sales, just as securities that the investor believes are undervalued are the logical choice for purchase.

Short selling is not limited to individual investors; market makers may also sell short. If there is an influx of orders to buy, the market makers may satisfy this demand by selling short. They will then repurchase the shares in the future to cover the short position after the influx of orders has subsided. Frequently, this transaction can be profitable. After the speculative increase in price that results from the increased demand, the price of the security may decline. When this occurs, the market makers profit because they sell short when the price rises but cover their positions after the price subsequently falls.

Short-Interest Ratio

The short selling of a stock requires that the shares must eventually be repurchased. Such repurchases imply future demand for the stock, which may increase its price. Of course, the argument could be expressed in reverse. Increased short selling suggests that those in the know are anticipating lower stock prices. For either reason, some investors track short sales as a means to forecast price changes.

Such tracking requires obtaining data on short sales. The number of shares that have been sold short is referred to as the *short interest*. Since companies have differing amounts of stock outstanding, the absolute number of shares sold short may be meaningless. Instead, the number of shares short is often divided by the number of shares outstanding and expressed as the *short-interest* ratio. An alternative ratio considers the number of shares sold short relative to the average daily trading. If this ratio exceeds 1.0, that means more than one day's volume has been sold short. A ratio of less than 1.0 suggests the opposite: The average daily volume exceeds the number of shares sold short.

The numerical value of the short-interest ratio is easy to interpret. A ratio of 2.5 indicates that it will take 2.5 days of trading to cover (on the average) existing shorts. The implication of the ratio, however, is ambiguous. Does a higher ratio suggest that a stock's price will rise or fall? The answer to that question can be argued either way. A high numerical value implies that it will take several days for all the existing short positions to be covered. This future buying of the shares by the short sellers will drive up the price of the stock, so a high short-interest ratio is bullish. There is, however, an exact opposite interpretation. A high short-interest ratio indicates that knowledgeable investors are shorting the stock in anticipation of a price decline. Thus, the high short-interest ratio is bearish and forecasts a declining stock price.

The number of shares sold short and the short-interest ratio are readily available; they are published monthly in financial publications such as the *Wall Street Journal* or national newspapers such as the *New York Times*. Data on the short interest may be found through Bloomberg (http://bloomberg.com). Enter the company's ticker symbol. You may also obtain the short interest and the short ratio through Yahoo!. Go to *yahoo.finance.com*, enter the ticker symbol, and click on key statistics for the individual firm. Depending on the investor's interpretation, an increase in the short-interest ratio suggests that short sellers will ultimately have to repurchase the shares or it suggests that investors are becoming more bearish and are selling the stock in anticipation of a price decline.

If an investor does sell short, there is always the possibility of being unable to repurchase the shares. Such a situation is referred to as a *short squeeze*. A short squeeze occurs when short sellers are unable to buy the stock to close their positions. This results in their bidding up the price as they frantically seek to buy the stock before its price rises further. Such a short squeeze is unlikely in a stock for which there are many shares outstanding and that actively trades. If, however, the stock has only a few shares publicly traded, the possibility does exist that short sellers will be unable to buy shares, which pushes up the price as the short sellers panic and bid increasingly higher prices to close their positions. (The short squeeze essentially applies to commodity markets. If the long positions can control the supply of the commodity, that is, obtain a monopoly or a "corner on the market" for the commodity, they can demand virtually any price from the shorts, who must pay in order to cover their positions.)

FOREIGN SECURITIES

Foreign companies, like U.S. companies, issue a variety of securities as a means to acquire funds. These securities subsequently trade on foreign exchanges or foreign over-the-counter markets. For example, there are stock exchanges in London, Paris, Tokyo, and other foreign financial centers. Unless Americans and other foreigners are forbidden to acquire these securities, Americans can buy and sell stocks through these exchanges in much the same way that they purchase domestic U.S. stocks and bonds. Thus, foreign securities may be purchased through the use of U.S. brokers who have access to trading on these exchanges. In many cases this access is obtained through a correspondent relationship with foreign securities dealers and brokerage firms.

The easiest way for American investors to acquire foreign stocks is to purchase companies such as Canon or Sony, whose shares are traded on a U.S. exchange or Nasdaq. (Foreign stock exchanges also list U.S. securities; the London Stock Exchange is the most liberal and actually encourages foreign listings.) American securities markets do not actually trade the foreign shares but trade receipts for the stock, called **American Depository Receipts (ADRs)** or American Depository Shares. These receipts are created by large financial institutions such as commercial banks. The ADRs are sold to the public and continue to trade in the United States. (Information concerning foreign securities, such as financial data, earnings estimates, price, and linkages to the company, may be found at http://www.adr.com, a website that is a joint project of J. P. Morgan and Thomson Financial.)

There are two types of ADRs. *Sponsored* ADRs are created when the firm wants the securities to trade in the United States. The firm employs a bank to perform the paperwork to create the ADRs and to act as transfer agent. In this case the costs are absorbed by the firm. All ADRs listed on the NYSE and AMEX are sponsored ADRs. *Unsponsored* ADRs are created when a brokerage firm believes there will be sufficient interest in a stock or bond to make a market in the security. The brokerage firm buys a block of securities and hires a commercial bank to create the ADRs and to act as transfer agent. However, fees for this service and for converting dividend payments from the foreign currency into U.S. dollars will be paid by the stockholders, not the issuing firm.

If there are no ADRs issued for the stock the investor wants to purchase, then the actual foreign securities will have to be acquired. The individual instructs the broker to purchase the foreign stock in the appropriate foreign market. As with any other security purchase, the shares or bonds are acquired through exchanges or over the counter from dealers who make a market in the security. The trading practices followed by foreign exchanges need not coincide with U.S. practices. For example, after a stock is purchased, a settlement date is established at which time payment is due. This settlement date may not coincide with the U.S. practice of payment due after three business days. However, such differences are more a matter of detail than substance and are diminishing with increased global investing.

REGULATION

Like many industries, the securities industry is subject to a substantial degree of regulation from both the federal and state governments. Since the majority of securities are traded across state lines, most regulation is at the federal level.

The purpose of these laws is to protect the investor by ensuring honest and fair practices. The laws require that the investor be provided with information upon which to base decisions. Hence, these acts are frequently referred to as the **full disclosure laws**, because publicly owned companies must inform the public of certain facts relating to their firms. The regulations also attempt to prevent fraud and the manipulation of stock prices. However, they do not try to protect investors from their own folly and greed. The purpose of legislation governing the securities industry is not to ensure that

---

American Depository Receipts (ADRs)

Receipts issued for foreign securities held by a trustee.

full disclosure laws

The federal and state laws requiring publicly held firms to disclose financial and other information that may affect the value of their securities.

investors will profit from their investments; instead, the laws try to provide fair market practices while allowing investors to make their own mistakes.

Although current federal regulation developed during the 1930s as a direct result of the debacle in the securities markets during the early part of that decade, state regulations started in 1911 with the pioneering legislation in the state of Kansas. These state laws are frequently called *blue sky laws* because fraudulent securities were referred to as pieces of blue sky. Although there are differences among the state laws, they generally require that (1) security firms and brokers be licensed, (2) financial information concerning issues of new securities be filed with state regulatory bodies, (3) new securities meet specific standards before they are sold, and (4) regulatory bodies be established to enforce the laws.

The Federal Securities Laws

The first modern federal legislation governing the securities industry was the Securities Act of 1933, which primarily concerns the issuing of new securities. It requires that new securities be "registered" with the Securities and Exchange Commission (SEC). As discussed previously, registration consists of supplying the SEC with information concerning the firm, the nature of its business and competition, and its financial position. This information is then summarized in the prospectus (refer to Exhibit 2.4 later in this chapter), which makes the formal offer to sell the securities to the public.

Once the SEC has determined that all material facts that may affect the value of the firm have been disclosed, the securities are released for sale. If the investor incurs a loss on an investment in a new issue of securities, a suit may be filed to recover the loss if the prospectus or the registration statement that was filed with the SEC contained false or misleading information. Liability for this loss may rest on the firm, its executives and directors, the brokerage firm selling the securities, and any experts (e.g., accountants, appraisers) who were employed in preparing the documents. Owing to this legal accountability, those involved exercise caution and diligence in the preparation of the prospectus and the registration statement.

Although the Securities Act of 1933 applies only to new issues, the Securities Exchange Act of 1934 (and subsequent amendments) extends the regulation to existing securities. This act forbids market manipulation, deception and misrepresentation of facts, and fraudulent practices. The SEC was also created by this act to enforce the laws pertaining to the securities industry. A summary of the SEC's objectives is provided in Exhibit 2.3.

Under the Securities Exchange Act of 1934, publicly held companies are required to keep current the information on file with the SEC. This is achieved by having the firm file timely reports with the SEC. Perhaps the most important is the **10-K report**, which is the firm's annual report to the SEC. Because it gives detailed statements of the firm's financial position, the 10-K is the basic source of data for the professional financial analyst. The content of the 10-K includes audited financial statements, breakdowns of sales and expenses by product line, information concerning legal proceedings, and management compensation including deferred compensation and incentive options. Although the 10-K is not automatically sent to stockholders, a company must supply stockholders this document upon written request, and it is

10-K report

Required annual report filed with the SEC by publicly held firms.

EXHIBIT 2.3	Summary of the Objectives of the SEC

1. To ensure that individuals have sufficient information to make informed investment decisions.
2. To provide the public with information by the registration of corporate securities prior to their sale to the general public, and to require timely and regular disclosure of corporate information and financial statements.
3. To prevent manipulation of security prices by regulating trading in the securities markets; by requiring insiders to register the buying and selling of securities; and by regulating the activities of corporate officers and directors.
4. To regulate investment companies (e.g., mutual funds) and investment advisors.
5. To work in conjunction with the Federal Reserve to limit the use of credit to acquire securities.
6. To supervise the regulation of member firms, brokers, and securities dealers by working with the National Association of Securities Dealers, which is the self-regulatory association of brokers and dealers.

10-Q report

A required quarterly report filed with the SEC by publicly held firms.

8-K report

A document filed with the SEC that describes a change in a firm that may affect the value of its securities.

13-D report

Document filed with the SEC by an individual who acquires 5 percent of a publicly held firm's stock.

generally available through the company's website. (Some firms send stockholders the 10-K as the firm's annual report.)

The **10-Q report** is the firm's quarterly report to the SEC. Like the 10-K, it is a detailed report of the firm's financial condition. The quarterly report the firm sends to its stockholders is basically a summary of the 10-Q. (Most firms have ceased sending stockholders quarterly reports; instead these firms provide access to the 10-Q report through their websites.) The **8-K report** provides specific information and must be filed with the SEC within 15 days after an event that may materially affect the value of the firm's securities. This document often details materials previously announced through a press release.

Individuals as well as firms may have to file forms with the SEC. Any stockholder who acquires 5 percent of a publicly held corporation's stock must submit a **13-D report**. This document requires crucial information, such as the intentions of the stockholder acquiring the large stake. Many takeover attempts start with the acquiring stockholder accumulating a substantial stake in the corporation. The required filling of the 13-D means that once the position reaches 5 percent of the outstanding shares, the buyer's intentions can no longer be hidden.

All the forms that are filed with the SEC are readily available through EDGAR, which is an acronym for Electronic Data-Gathering, Analysis, and Retrieval. All publicly held firms (and mutual funds) are required to file information electronically. Investors (and other interested parties) may readily download a firm's 10-K or 10-Q by accessing EDGAR from the SEC's website, http://www.sec.gov. (You should realize that you are obtaining a copy of the document. Making the data useful is a different issue. Several firms process the data into more useful forms and sell their services by subscription. See, for instance, EDGAR Online at http://www.edgar-online.com.)

Firms are also required to release during the year any information that may materially affect the value of their securities. Information concerning new discoveries, lawsuits, or a merger must be disseminated to the general public. The SEC has the power to suspend trading in a company's securities for up to ten days if, in its opinion, the public interest and the protection of investors necessitate such a ban on trading. If a firm fails to keep investors informed, the SEC can suspend trading pending the release of the required information. Such a suspension is a drastic act and is seldom used, for most companies frequently issue news releases that inform the investing public of significant changes affecting the firm. Sometimes the company itself asks to have trading in its securities halted until a news release can be prepared and disseminated.

The disclosure laws do not require that the company tell everything about its operations. All firms have trade secrets that they do not want known by their competitors. The purpose of the full disclosure laws is not to restrict the corporation but (1) to inform the investors so that they can make intelligent decisions and (2) to prevent a firm's employees from using privileged information for personal gain.

It should be obvious that employees, ranging from the CEO to the mailroom clerk, may have access to information before it reaches the general public. Such information (called *inside information*) may significantly enhance the employees' ability to make profits by buying or selling the company's securities before the announcement is made. Such profiteering from inside information is illegal. Officers and directors of the company must report their holdings and any changes in their holdings of the firm's securities to the SEC. Thus, it is possible for the SEC to determine if transactions have been made prior to any public announcement that affected the value of the securities. If insiders do profit illegally from the use of such information, they may be prosecuted under criminal law and their gains may have to be surrendered to the firm. (The use of reports of insider transactions to forecast stock prices is discussed in Chapter 4 in the section on the efficient market hypothesis.)

 Point of Interest

ILLEGAL USE OF INSIDE INFORMATION

The use of inside (privileged) information for personal gain is illegal. Management cannot buy a stock, make an announcement that causes the value of the stock to rise, and then sell the stock for a profit. If insiders do this, the corporation or its stockholders may sue, and if the defendants are found guilty, any profits must be returned to the corporation.

The law does not forbid insiders from buying and subsequently selling the stock. However, the Securities Exchange Act of 1934 requires that each officer, director, and major stockholder (i.e., any individual who owns more than 5 percent of the stock) of a publicly held corporation must file a report with the SEC disclosing the amount of stock held. These individuals must also file a monthly report if there are any changes in the holdings. This information is subsequently published by the SEC. If these insiders make a profit on a transaction that is completed (i.e., the stock is bought and sold) within six months, it is assumed the profit is the result of illegally using confidential corporate information.

Individuals who may be considered insiders are not limited to the corporation's officers and directors. An insider is any individual with "material information" not yet disclosed to the public. Material information implies information that could reasonably be expected to affect the value of the firm's securities. The individual need not necessarily be employed by the firm but could have access to inside information through business relationships, family ties, or being informed (tipped off) by insiders. Use of such privileged information even by nonemployees is also illegal. In one of the most famous cases concerning the illegal use of inside information, several officers and directors of Texas Gulf Sulfur became aware of new mineral discoveries. Their stock purchases, along with purchases made by individuals they had informed, were ruled illegal. Thus, an insider who may not directly profit through the use of inside information cannot pass that information to another party who profits from using that knowledge.

Sarbanes-Oxley Act of 2002

The large increase in stock prices experienced during 1998 and into 2000 and the sub-sequent decline in prices may be partially attributed to fraudulent (or at least question-able) accounting practices and securities analysts' touting of stocks. These scandals led to the creation of the Sarbanes-Oxley Act, which was intended to restore public confidence in the securities markets. While it is too early to determine the ramifications of Sarbanes-Oxley, its range and coverage are extensive. The main provisions encompass

- the independence of auditors and the creation of the Public Company Accounting Oversight Board
- corporate responsibility and financial disclosure
- conflicts of interest and corporate fraud and accountability

Sarbanes-Oxley created the Public Company Accounting Oversight Board, whose purpose is to oversee the auditing of the financial statements of publicly held companies. The board has the power to establish audit reporting rules and standards and to enforce compliance by public accounting firms. Firms and individuals who conduct audits are prohibited from performing nonaudit services for clients that they audit.

Corporate responsibility and financial disclosure require a publicly held firm's chief executive officer (CEO) and chief financial officer (CFO) to certify that the financial statements do not contain untrue statements or material omissions. These officers are also responsible for internal controls to ensure that they receive accurate information upon which to base their certifications of the financial statements. Corporate personnel cannot exert improper influence on auditors to accept misleading financial statements. Directors and executive officers are also banned from trading in the firm's securities during blackout periods when the firm's pensions are not permitted to trade the securities. Personal loans to executives and directors are prohibited, and senior management must disclose purchases and sales of the firm's securities within two business days. (The previous requirement for disclosure was ten days after the close of the calendar month.)

Conflicts of interest revolve around the roles played by securities analysts and by investment bankers. Investment bankers facilitate a firm's raising funds. Analysts determine if securities are under- or overvalued. Both are employed by financial firms such as Merrill Lynch. If a securities analyst determines that a stock is overvalued, this will damage the relationship between the investment bankers and the firm wishing to sell the securities. Hence, there is an obvious conflict of interest between the securities analysts and the investment bankers working for the same financial firm.

These two divisions need to be independent of each other. While the financial firms asserted that a "firewall" did exist between the investment bankers and the securities analysts, the actions of the securities analysts often implied the opposite. Sarbanes-Oxley seeks to strengthen the firewall. An investment banker's ability to preapprove a securities analyst's research report is restricted. Individuals concerned with investment banking activities cannot supervise securities analysts. Retaliation against securities analysts for negative reports is prohibited. An analyst must disclose whether he or she owns securities or received compensation from the companies covered by the analyst. Penalties for violating Sarbanes-Oxley and existing corporate fraud laws, which prohibit destroying documents and impeding or obstructing investigations, were increased, with penalties including fines and imprisonment of up to 20 years.

Other Regulations

Although the Securities Act of 1933, the Securities Exchange Act of 1934, and the Sarbanes-Oxley Act of 2002 are the backbone of securities regulation, other laws pertaining to specific areas of investments have been enacted. These include the Public Holding Company Act of 1935, which reorganized the utility industry by requiring better methods of financial accounting and more thorough reporting and by constraining the use of debt financing. The Investment Company Act of 1940 extended the regulations to include mutual funds and other investment companies. The Securities Investor Protection Act of 1970, is designed to protect investors from brokerage firm failures and bankruptcies. The act also created the Securities Investor Protection Corporation, which is discussed in the following section.

In addition to the laws affecting the issuing of securities and their subsequent trading, laws require disclosure by investment advisors (the Investment Advisers Act of 1940). Investment advisory services and individuals who "engage for compensation in the business of advising others about securities shall register" with the SEC. This

---

⊕ Point of Interest

ANALYSTS' RECOMMENDATION AND SARBANES-OXLEY

One service that some brokerage firms offer clients is research on specific stocks. These analysts' recommendations take the general form of "buy," "hold," or "sell." There are often gradients with the recommendations such as "strong buy" or "OK to buy" or "short-term hold/strong long-term buy." It is easy to accept these recommendations at face value. That is, "buy" means the stock should be acquired and "hold" means maintain current positions but do not add to them.

Unfortunately, analysts' recommendations should not necessarily be taken at face value. In most cases brokerage firm research reports tend to recommend purchases. Rarely do such recommendations suggest the outright sale of securities. There are two obvious reasons for the purchase recommendations. First, brokerage firms and brokers profit from commissions, and initial commissions are made through purchases of securities by investors. Second, brokerage firms make large fees through underwriting securities for firms and providing consulting services such as valuations and opinions in merger negotiations. If the firm's financial analysts are recommending the sale of the stock, that will not endear the firm to the company whose stock is being recommended for sale.

Prior to the passage of Sarbanes-Oxley, brokerage firms did assert that their investment banking and brokerage operations were independent of each other and that their financial analysts were free to make recommendations based on their analysis. However, during the market decline of 2000 through 2002, many financial analysts continued to recommend the purchase of stocks whose prices were dramatically declining and continuing to decline.

Sarbanes-Oxley requires brokerage firms to maintain a firewall between their investment banking and brokerage operations. Today the number of sell recommendations has increased, but the number of buys continues to exceed the number of sells. (As of July 2006, Yahoo! Finance reported 8 strong buy, 3 moderate buy, 7 hold, 1 moderate sell, and 0 strong sell for Hershey.) Perhaps individual investors should continue to reinterpret recommendations such as "hold" to really mean "sell" or "avoid." At the very least the individual should not make investment decisions solely on the basis of analysts' recommendations.[*]

*For a fascinating discussion of the conflict of interest between financial analysis and investment banking and other means by which financial analysts "sell the investor down the river," see Benjamin Mark Cole, *The Pied Pipers of Wall Street* (Princeton, NJ: Bloomberg Press, 2000).

registration brings investment advisors within the regulation of the SEC. Under this law, investment advisors must disclose their backgrounds, business affiliations, and the compensation charged for their services. Failure to register with the SEC can lead to an injunction against supplying the service or to prosecution for violating securities laws.

Besides the state and federal securities laws, the industry itself regulates its members. The stock exchanges and the trade association, the National Association of Securities Dealers (NASD), have established codes of behavior for their members. These include relationships between brokers and customers, the auditing of members' accounts, and proficiency tests for brokers. While such rules may not have the force of law, they can have a significant impact on the quality and credibility of the industry and its representatives.

SECURITIES INVESTOR PROTECTION CORPORATION

Most investors are aware that accounts in virtually all commercial banks are insured by the Federal Deposit Insurance Corporation (FDIC—http://www.fdic.gov). As of 2010, if an insured commercial bank were to fail, the FDIC reimburses the depositor for any losses up to $250,000. If a depositor has more than $250,000 on account at the time of the commercial bank's failure, the depositor becomes a general creditor for the additional funds.

This insurance has greatly increased the stability of the commercial banking system. Small depositors know that their funds are safe and therefore do not panic if a commercial bank fails (as one occasionally does). This stability simply did not exist before the formation of the FDIC. When panicky depositors tried to make withdrawals, some commercial banks could not meet the sudden requests for cash. Many had to close, which only increased the panic that had caused the initial withdrawals. Since the advent of the FDIC, however, such panic and withdrawals should not occur because the FDIC reimburses depositors (up to the limit) for any losses they sustain.

Securities Investor Protection Corporation (SIPC)

The agency that insures investors against failures by brokerage firms.

Like commercial banks, brokerage firms are also insured by an agency that was created by the federal government—the Securities Investor Protection Corporation (SIPC). The SIPC (http://www.sipc.org) is managed by a seven-member board of directors. Five members are appointed by the president of the United States, and their appointments must be confirmed by the Senate. Two of the five represent the general public, and three represent the securities industry. The remaining two members are selected by the secretary of the treasury and the Federal Reserve board of governors.

The SIPC performs a role similar to that of the FDIC. Its objective is to preserve public confidence in the securities markets and industry. Although the SIPC does not protect investors from losses resulting from fluctuations in security prices, it does insure investors against losses arising from the failure of a brokerage firm. The insurance provided by the SIPC protects a customer's cash and securities up to $500,000. (Only $100,000 of the $500,000 insurance applies to cash balances on an account.) If a brokerage firm fails, the SIPC reimburses the firm's customers up to this specified limit. If a customer's claims exceed the $500,000 limit, that customer becomes a general creditor for the remainder of the funds.

The cost of this insurance is paid for by the brokerage firms that are members of the SIPC. All brokers and dealers that are registered with the Securities and Exchange Commission (SEC) and all members of national securities exchanges must be members of the SIPC. Most securities dealers are thus covered by the SIPC insurance. Some firms have even chosen to supplement this coverage by purchasing additional insurance from private insurance firms.

INITIAL PUBLIC OFFERINGS

Securities and other financial assets facilitate the transfers of savings from those with funds to those who need funds. Two methods exist to facilitate this transfer. The first is the direct investment that occurs when individuals start their own businesses and invest their savings in the operations. A direct transfer also occurs when securities are initially sold to investors in the primary market through investment bankers. As was explained earlier in this chapter, these securities may be subsequently bought and sold in the secondary markets.

financial intermediary

A financial institution, such as a commercial bank, that borrows from one group and lends to another.

The alternative to the direct transfer of savings into investments is an indirect transfer through a **financial intermediary** such as a bank. Individuals lend funds to the bank (e.g., deposit money in a savings account). The bank in turn lends the funds to the ultimate borrower. The financial intermediary stands between the ultimate supplier and the ultimate user of the funds, and it facilitates the flow of money and credit between the suppliers and the users. Through this process, the borrower is able to acquire the funds because the financial intermediary issues a claim on itself (e.g., the account) that the saver will accept.

private placement

The nonpublic sale of securities.

The direct sale of an entire issue of bonds or stock to an investor or to a financial institution, such as a pension fund or a life insurance company, is called a **private placement**. The primary advantages of a private placement to the issuing firm are the elimination of the cost of selling securities to the general public and the ready availability of large amounts of cash. In addition, the firm does not have to meet the disclosure requirements that are necessary to sell securities to the general public. This disclosure of information is for the protection of the investing public; it is presumed that the financial institution can protect itself by requiring information as a precondition for granting a loan. The disclosure requirements are both a cost to the firm when securities are issued to the public and a possible source of information to its competitors that the firm may wish to avoid divulging. An additional advantage of a private placement to both the firm and the financial institution is that the terms of securities may be tailored to meet both parties' needs.

A private placement has similar advantages for the firm that is investing the funds. A substantial amount of money may be invested at one time, and the maturity date can be set to meet the lender's needs. In addition, brokerage fees associated with purchasing securities are avoided. The financial intermediary can gain more control over the firm that receives the funds by building restrictive covenants into the agreement. These covenants may restrict the firm from issuing additional securities without the prior permission of the lender and may limit the firm's dividends, its merger activity, and the types of investments that it may make. All these restrictive covenants are designed to protect the lender from risk of loss and are part of any private sale of securities from a firm to a financial institution. Because each sale is separately negotiated, the individual terms vary with the bargaining powers of the parties and the economic conditions at the time of the agreement.

Private placements are especially important for small, emerging firms. The size of these firms or the risk associated with them often precludes their raising funds from traditional sources such as commercial banks. Firms that do make private placements of securities issued by emerging firms are called **venture capitalists**. Venture capital is a major source of finance for small firms or firms developing new technologies. The venture capitalists thus fill a void by acquiring securities issued by small firms with exceptional growth potential.

Of course, many small firms do not realize this potential, and venture capitalists often sustain large losses on their investments. Success, however, can generate a very large return. In a sense, it is a numbers game. If a venture capitalist invests in five projects and four fail, the one large gain can more than offset the investments in the four losers.

Once the emerging firm does grow, the securities purchased by the venture capitalist may be sold to the general public through a public offering. (The process of selling new securities to the general public is covered in the next section.) Many initial public offerings combine the sale of new securities to raise additional funds for the firm and a sale of securities by current shareholders. These current holdings often include the shares originally purchased by the venture capitalists, who are using the initial public sale as a means to realize the profits on their investments.

Investment Banking

Firms, in addition to acquiring funds through private placements, may issue new securities and sell them to the general public, usually through **investment bankers**. If this sale is the first sale of common stock to the general public, it is referred to as an **initial public offering (IPO)**. Firms sell securities when internally generated funds are insufficient to finance the desired level of investment spending and when the firm believes it to be advantageous to obtain outside funding from the general public instead of from a financial intermediary. Such outside funding may increase public interest in the firm and its securities and may also bypass some of the restrictive covenants that are required by financial institutions.

The following section addresses the sale of new securities to the general public through an investment banker. It covers the role played by the investment banker, the mechanics of selling new securities, and the potential volatility of the new-issue market. Exhibit 2.4, which is the title page for the prospectus of a new issue of Yahoo! Inc. common stock, is used to illustrate the process of an initial public offering. Although the discussion is limited to the sale of stock, the process also applies to new issues of corporate bonds sold to the general public.

A corporation can market its securities directly to the public, but direct plans to sell securities to the general public involve expenses, so many firms employ investment bankers to market new securities. In effect, an investment banker serves as a middleman to channel money from investors to firms that need the capital. Although investment bankers are conduits through which the money flows, they are not financial intermediaries, since they do not create claims on themselves. With a financial intermediary, the investor has a claim on the intermediary. With an investment banker, however,

venture capitalist

Firm specializing in investing in the securities of small, emerging companies.

investment bankers

An underwriter, a firm that sells new issues of securities to the general public.

initial public offering (IPO)

The first sale of common stock to the general public.

> **EXHIBIT   2.4**   Title Page for the Prospectus of an Issue of Common Stock of Yahoo! Inc.

Issuing company →

Number of shares sold →

2,600,000 Shares

Yahoo! Inc.

Type of security →

Common Stock
(par value $0.001 per share)

YAHOO!

All of the shares of Common Stock offered hereby are being offered by Yahoo! Inc. Prior to this offering, there has been no public market for the Common Stock of the Company. For factors considered in determining the initial public offering price, see "Underwriting".

In connection with this offering, the Underwriters have reserved approximately 200,000 shares of Common Stock for sale at the initial public offering price to persons associated with the Company.

See "Risk Factors" commencing on page 6 for certain considerations relevant to an investment in the Common Stock.

The Common Stock has been approved for quotation on the Nasdaq National Market under the symbol "YHOO".

THESE SECURITIES HAVE NOT BEEN APPROVED OR DISAPPROVED BY THE SECURITIES AND EXCHANGE COMMISSION OR ANY STATE SECURITIES COMMISSION NOR HAS THE SECURITIES AND EXCHANGE COMMISSION OR ANY STATE SECURITIES COMMISSION PASSED UPON THE ACCURACY OR ADEQUACY OF THIS PROSPECTUS. ANY REPRESENTATION TO THE CONTRARY IS A CRIMINAL OFFENSE.

Price of the stock to the public and total proceeds →

Underwriting discount →

Proceeds to the company →

	Initial Public Offering Price	Underwriting Discount(1)	Proceeds to Company(2)
Per Share	$13.00	$0.91	$12.09
Total(3)	$33,800,000	$2,366,000	$31,434,000

(1) The Company has agreed to indemnify the Underwriters against certain liabilities, including liabilities under the Securities Act of 1933. See "Underwriting".

(2) Before deducting estimated offering expenses of $700,000 payable by the Company.

(3) The Company has granted the Underwriters an option for 30 days to purchase up to an additional 390,000 shares at the initial public offering price per share, less the underwriting discount, solely to cover over-allotments. If such option is exercised in full, the total initial public offering price, underwriting discount and proceeds to the Company will be $38,870,000, $2,720,900 and $36,149,100, respectively. See "Underwriting". ← The overallotment

The shares offered hereby are offered severally by the Underwriters, as specified herein, subject to receipt and acceptance by them and subject to their right to reject any order in whole or in part. It is expected that certificates for the shares will be ready for delivery in New York, New York, on or about April 17, 1996, against payment therefor in immediately available funds.

Lead underwriters →

Goldman, Sachs & Co.

Donaldson, Lufkin & Jenrette
Securities Corporation

Montgomery Securities

The date of this Prospectus is April 12, 1996.

the investor's claim is on the firm that issues the securities and not on the investment banker who facilitated the initial sale.

Investment banking is an important but often confusing financial practice, partly because of the misnomer. An *investment banker* is often not a banker and generally does not invest. The investment bankers do not buy and hold the newly issued securities on their own account for investment purposes. (When an investment bank does commit its own funds and buys the securities as an investment, it is referred to as a *merchant bank* and its activity as *merchant banking*.)

The Mechanics of Underwriting

underwriting

The process by which securities are sold to the general public and in which the investment banker buys the securities from the issuing firm.

If a firm needs funds from an external source, it can approach an investment banker to discuss an underwriting. The term **underwriting** refers to the process of selling new securities. In an underwriting the firm that is selling the securities, and not the firm that is issuing the shares, bears the risk associated with the sale. The investment banker buys the securities with the intention of reselling them. If it fails to sell the securities, the investment banker must still pay the agreed-upon sum to the firm at the time of the offering (i.e., the sale) of the securities. Failure to sell the securities imposes losses on the underwriter, who must remit funds for securities that have not been sold.

The firm in need of financing and the investment banker discuss the amount of funds needed, the type of security to be issued, the price and any special features of the security, and the cost to the firm of issuing the securities. All these factors are negotiated by the firm seeking capital and the investment banker. If mutually acceptable terms are reached, the investment banker will be the intermediary through which the securities are sold by the firm to the general public.

originating house

An investment banker who makes an agreement with a firm to sell a new issue of securities and forms the syndicate to market them.

Because an underwriting starts with a particular firm that manages the underwriting, that firm is called the **originating house**. The originating house need not be a single firm if the negotiation involves several investment bankers. In this case, several firms can jointly underwrite and sell the securities to the general public.

⊕ Point of Interest

GREEN SHOES

When a firm and an investment banker agree to an underwriting, only the approximate number of shares and their approximate price can be established. Obviously, conditions can change, and underwriters need flexibility when selling the securities. If market conditions worsen, the underwriters may seek to sell a smaller issue at a lower price. If conditions improve, the issue may be increased. Firms often grant the underwriters an option (an "overallotment") to increase the size of the issue. This option is sometimes referred to as a *green shoe* after the first company that gave the option to its underwriters.

How the option works is simple. Suppose the initial agreement calls for the sale of 1,000,000 shares at approximately $10 a share. The issuing firm grants the underwriter an option to purchase up to 10 percent additional shares. If the issue is well received, the underwriter can sell up to an additional 100,000 shares. Of course, the underwriters do not have to sell any additional shares, nor do they have to sell all 100,000 shares if they do exercise the option. They may accept, for example, only an additional 45,600 shares if that number is needed to balance the market's initial demand for the stock.

syndicate

A selling group assembled to market an issue of securities.

The originating house does not usually sell all the securities by itself but instead forms a **syndicate** to market them. The syndicate is a group of brokerage houses that join together to underwrite a specific sale of securities. The members of the syndicate may bring in additional brokerage firms to help distribute the securities. The firm that manages the sale is frequently referred to as the *lead underwriter*. It is the lead underwriter that allocates the specific number of securities each member of the syndicate is responsible for selling. In the Yahoo! illustration, 17 additional firms joined the three lead underwriters to sell the securities.

The use of a syndicate has several advantages. First, the syndicate may have access to more potential buyers for the securities. Second, by using a syndicate the number of securities that each brokerage firm must sell is reduced. The increase in the number of potential customers and the decrease in the amount that each broker must sell increases the probability that the entire issue of securities will be sold. Thus, syndication makes possible both the sale of a large offering of securities and a reduction in the risk borne by each member.

In some cases, the firm seeking funds may not choose to negotiate the terms of the securities with an underwriter. Instead, the firm designs the issue and auctions the securities to the investment banker making the highest bid. In preparation for bidding, the investment banker will form a syndicate as well as determine the price it is willing to pay. The underwriter and its syndicate that wins the auction and purchases the securities marks up the price of the securities and sells them to the general public. Obviously, if the investment banker bids too high, it will be unable to sell the securities for a profit. Then the underwriter may sustain a loss when it lowers the securities' price in order to sell them.

Types of Agreements

best-efforts agreement

Agreement with an investment banker who does not guarantee the sale of a security but who agrees to make the best effort to sell it.

firm commitment

Agreement with an investment banker who guarantees a sale of securities by agreeing to purchase the entire issue at a specified price.

The agreement between the investment bankers and the firm may be one of two types. The investment bankers may make a **best-efforts agreement** in which they agree to make their best effort to sell the securities but do not guarantee that a specified amount of money will be raised. The risk of selling the securities rests with the firm issuing the securities. If the investment bankers are unable to find buyers, the firm does not receive the desired amount of money.

The alternative is a **firm commitment**, an underwriting in which the investment bankers purchase (i.e., underwrite) the entire issue of securities at a specified price and subsequently sell them to the general public. Most sales of new securities are made through firm commitments, and best-effort sales are generally limited to small securities issues by less well known firms. In an underwriting, the investment bankers pay the expenses with the anticipation of recouping these costs through the sale. Because the underwriters have agreed to purchase the entire issue, they must pay the firm for all the securities even if the syndicate is unable to sell them. Thus, the risk of the sale rests with the underwriters.

It is for this reason that the pricing of the underwritten securities is crucial. If the initial offer price is too high, the syndicate will be unable to sell the securities. When this occurs, the investment bankers have two choices: (1) to maintain the offer price and hold the securities in inventory until they are sold or (2) to let the market find a lower price level that will induce investors to purchase the securities. Neither choice benefits the investment bankers. If the underwriters purchase the securities and hold them in inventory, they either must tie up their own funds, which could be earning a return elsewhere, or must borrow funds to pay for the securities. Like any other firm, the investment bankers pay interest on these borrowed funds. Thus, the decision to support the offer price of the securities requires the investment bankers to invest their own capital or, more likely, to borrow substantial amounts of capital. In either case, the profit margins on the underwriting are substantially decreased, and the investment bankers may even experience a loss on the underwriting.

Instead of supporting the price, the underwriters may choose to let the price of the securities fall. The inventory of unsold securities can then be sold, and the underwriters will not tie up capital or have to borrow money from their sources of credit. If the underwriters make this choice, they take losses when the securities are sold at less than cost. But they also cause the customers who bought the securities at the initial offer price to sustain a loss. The underwriters certainly do not want to inflict losses on these customers, because if they experience losses continually, the underwriters' market for future security issues will vanish. Therefore, the investment banks try not to overprice a new issue of securities, for overpricing will ultimately result in their suffering losses.

There is also an incentive to avoid underpricing new securities. If the issue is underpriced, all the securities will be readily sold and their price will rise because demand will have exceeded supply. The buyers of the securities will be satisfied, for the price of the securities will have increased as a result of the underpricing. The initial purchasers of the securities reap windfall profits, but these gains are really at the expense of the company whose securities were underpriced. If the underwriters had assigned a higher price to the securities, the company would have raised more capital. Underwriting is a competitive business, and each security issue is negotiated individually; hence, if one investment banker consistently underprices securities, firms will choose competitors to underwrite their securities.

Although there are reasons for the underwriters to avoid either underpricing or overpricing, there is a greater incentive to underprice the securities. Underpricing facilitates the sale and generates immediate profits for the initial buyers. Studies have found that *initial* purchases earned higher returns as the buyers were given a price incentive to buy the new offering. Subsequent buyers, however, did not fare as well, and any initial underpricing appears to disappear soon after the original offering. In addition, many initial public offerings subsequently underperform the market during the first years after the original sale.[3]

The Prospectus

Once the terms of the sale have been agreed upon, the managing house may issue a **preliminary prospectus**. The preliminary prospectus is often referred to as a *red herring*, a term that connotes the document should be read with caution as it is not final and complete. (The phrase "red herring" is derived from British fugitives' rubbing herring across their trails to confuse pursuing bloodhounds.) The preliminary prospectus informs potential buyers that the securities are being registered with the **Securities and Exchange Commission (SEC)** and may subsequently be offered for sale. **Registration**

preliminary prospectus

Initial document detailing the financial condition of a firm that must be filed with the SEC to register a new issue of securities.

Securities and Exchange Commission (SEC)

Government agency that enforces the federal securities laws.

registration

Process of filing information with the SEC concerning a proposed sale of securities to the general public.

[3]Information on current IPOs may be found at Hoover's IPO Central (**http://www.hoovers.com/global/ipoc/**).

refers to the disclosure of information concerning the firm, the securities being offered for sale, and the use of the proceeds from the sale.[4]

The cost of printing the red herring is borne by the issuing firm. This preliminary prospectus describes the company and the securities to be issued; it includes the firm's income statement and balance sheets, its current activities (such as a pending merger or labor negotiation), the regulatory bodies to which it is subject, and the nature of its competition. The preliminary prospectus is thus a detailed document concerning the company and is, unfortunately, usually tedious reading.

The preliminary prospectus does not include the price of the securities. That will be determined on the day that the securities are issued. If securities prices decline or rise, the price of the new securities may be adjusted for the change in market conditions. In fact, if prices decline sufficiently, the firm has the option of postponing or even canceling the underwriting.

After the SEC accepts the registration statement, a final prospectus is published.[5] (Exhibit 2.4 is the title page to the final prospectus.) The SEC does not approve the issue as to its investment worth but rather sees that all information has been provided and the prospectus is complete in format and content. Except for changes that are required by the SEC, it is virtually identical to the preliminary prospectus. Information regarding the price of the security, the underwriting discount, and the proceeds to the company, along with any more recent financial data is added. As may be seen in Exhibit 2.4, Yahoo! Inc. issued 2,600,000 shares of common stock at a price of $13.00 to raise a total of $33,800,000. The issuing company frequently grants the underwriter an overallotment to cover the sale of additional shares if there is sufficient demand. In this illustration, Yahoo! granted the underwriters the option to purchase an additional 390,000 shares, which would raise the total proceeds received by Yahoo! to $36,149,100.

The cost of the underwriting (also called *flotation costs* or *underwriting discount*) is the difference between the price of the securities to the public and the proceeds to the firm. In this example, the cost is $0.91 per share, which is 7.5 percent of the proceeds received by the firm for each share. The total cost is $2,366,000 for the sale of these shares. Underwriting fees tend to vary with the dollar value of the securities being underwritten and the type of securities being sold. Some of the expenses are fixed (e.g., preparation of the prospectus), so the unit cost for a large underwriting is smaller. Also, because it may be more difficult to sell speculative bonds than high-quality bonds, underwriting fees for speculative issues tend to be higher.

In addition to the fee, the underwriter may receive indirect compensation, which may be in the form of an option (called a "warrant") to buy additional securities.[6] Such indirect compensation may be as important as the monetary fee because it unites the underwriter and the firm. After the initial sale, the underwriter often becomes a market

[4]While there are exceptions, generally unregistered corporate securities may not be sold to the general public. The debt of governments (e.g., state and municipal bonds), however, is *not* registered with the SEC and may be sold to the general public. Information concerning the SEC may be obtained from **http://www.sec.gov**, the Securities and Exchange Commission's home page.

[5]Because corporate securities cannot be sold to the general public before the registration statement becomes effective, information concerning the proposed sale is accompanied by statements such as "orders to buy may not be accepted prior to the registration becoming effective" or "this information concerning the securities is not a solicitation to buy or sell."

[6]This warrant is similar to the options discussed in Chapter 17 except there is no *public trading* in these warrants granted the underwriters.

maker for the securities, which is particularly important to the investing public. Without a secondary market in which to sell the security, investors would be less interested in buying the securities initially. By maintaining a market in the security, the brokerage firm eases the task of selling the securities originally.

Volatility of Initial Public Offerings

The new-issue market (especially for common stock) is extremely volatile. There have been times when the investing public seemed willing to purchase virtually any new security that was being sold on the market. There have also been periods during which new companies were simply unable to raise money, and large, well-known companies did so only under onerous terms.

The market for initial public offerings is volatile regarding not only the number of securities that are offered but also the price changes of new issues. It is not unusual for prices to rise dramatically. In April 1996, Yahoo!'s stock was initially offered at $13 and closed at $33 after reaching a high of $43 during the first day of trading. Two years later the stock was trading in excess of $180.

Few new issues perform as well as Yahoo!, and many that initially do well subsequently fall on hard times. Boston Chicken went public at $20 a share and rose to $48.50 by the end of the first day of trading. However, the company's rapid expansion overextended the firm's ability to sustain profitable operations. Boston Chicken declared bankruptcy, and the stock traded for less than $1 a share.

The late 1990s saw a large increase in the number of IPOs, many of which were very speculative at best. Many companies, especially those related to technology in

---

⊕ Point of Interest

RISK FACTORS

One component of the prospectus is an enumeration of "Risk Factors." For example, Pacer, a logistics provider that facilitates the movement of freight by trailer and containers, devoted ten pages in its 2003 prospectus to risk factors. Here is a sample:

We are dependent upon third parties for equipment and services essential to operate our business.

Work stoppage or other disruptions at sea ports could adversely affect our operating results.

Our revenues could be reduced by the loss of major customers.

Competition in our industry causes downward pressure on freight rates . . .

Our customers . . . could transfer their business . . .

Service instability in the railroad industry would increase costs . . .

If we lose key personnel and qualified technical staff . . .

. . . changes in government regulation . . .

We may not have sufficient cash to service our indebtedness.

Our operating results are subject to cyclical fluctuations . . .

If the markets in which we operate do not grow . . .

Unfortunately, many of these risk factors should be self-evident, and the list may be so encompassing and general that it is of minimal use for investors. However, the enumeration of these factors is a legal necessity. By making the material available to investors to read and digest, the company transfers the burden of the analysis of risk to the potential buyers of the securities.

general and the Internet in particular, raised large amounts of capital. Their stock prices rose dramatically and just as dramatically fell. Ask Jeeves went public in July 1999 at a price of $14. It closed after the first day of trading at $64.94 and reached almost $200 in September. In July 2001, the stock was trading for about $2. Another highflyer, Ariba, saw its stock decline from $242 to $4 in less than a year.

While the late 1990s may be considered an aberration, they were not unique. In a sense, it was a repeat of the late 1960s when stocks of franchising and nursing home companies went public, rose dramatically, and subsequently declined. For example, Four Seasons Nursing Homes went public on May 10, 1968, at $11 a share. The stock rose to $102, but within two years the company was bankrupt and the stock sold for $0.16. In retrospect, a price of $102 seems absurd. The company had 3.4 million shares outstanding, so at a price of $102, the value of the company was $346.8 million ($102 × 3.4). The firm had revenues of only $19.3 million and earnings of less than $2 million, so it made no sense in terms of earnings capacity to value the firm in excess of $300 million.

The new-issue market in the late 1990s, however, was different in one very important respect. Ask Jeeves and Ariba *didn't have earnings*, and even at the collapsed price of $4 a share, the total market value of Ariba exceeded $1 billion. When the price of that stock reached $242, the total value of the company exceeded $60 billion! So if it made little sense to value Four Seasons Nursing Homes, which actually had earnings, at $300 million, it would make even less sense to value Ariba at $60 billion when it was operating at a loss. (This question of valuation is an essential question, perhaps the most important question, in finance. The process of valuation and techniques used to analyze a stock are covered in Chapters 9 and 12. Subsequent material also considers a growth strategy that might justify purchasing an Ariba versus a value strategy that would never consider such a stock.)

The lure of large gains is, of course, what attracts speculative investors. All firms were small at one time, and each one had to go public to have a market for its shares. Someone bought the shares of IBM, Microsoft, and Johnson & Johnson when these firms went public. The new-issue market has offered and continues to offer the opportunity to invest in emerging firms, some of which may produce substantial returns for those investors or speculators who are willing to accept the risk. It is the possibility of such large rewards that makes the new-issue market so exciting. However, if the past is an indicator of the future, many small, emerging firms that go public will fail and will inflict significant losses on those investors who have accepted this risk by purchasing their securities.

Lock-ups

In addition to price volatility caused by speculative buying of an initial public offering, the possibility exists that insiders could use a new public issue of securities as a means to sell their stock. Such sales may also lead to price volatility, although in this case it would be price declines and not increases. (There is an additional ethical question concerning insiders profiting at the expense of the general investing public.) To understand the possible source of the price volatility, consider a privately held company that is considering going public. Before the initial public offering, managers and other employees are allowed to purchase the stock in a "nonpublic" or "private" transaction (e.g., $1 a share) or are granted options to buy the stock at a low price. Because there is no market in the stock, the price cannot be determined, so the sale price to insiders could be artificially low. (Such stock sales and the granting of options prior to the initial public offering are often viewed as "compensation" for those privileged employees.)

Private sales of securities are not illegal, but SEC guidelines indicate that stock acquired through a nonpublic transaction cannot be publicly sold unless it is held for at least one year. If the initial public offering were to occur after a year, the shares could be sold as part of the underwriting or immediately in the secondary market after the completion of the underwriting. For example, insiders who purchased the shares at $1 could sell the stock for a large profit, if the initial offering price to the general public were $10 a share. Such sales may destabilize the market and cause the price of the stock to fall.

To avoid this possible source of price volatility (and also the conflict of interest), the insiders may be forbidden by an agreement with the underwriter to sell their holdings for a period of time. Since the insiders are locked into the shares, the process is referred to as a *lock-up*. Obviously the lock-up cannot remain in effect indefinitely, and once it expires, the employees may sell their holdings.[7] This suggests there may be selling pressure on the stock once the lock-up period has expired.[8]

While lock-ups are not required by the SEC and are negotiated by the issuing firm and the underwriter, the full disclosure laws do require that issuing firms disclose potential sales by insiders. Because large sales may destabilize the market and cause the stock's price to fall, underwriters prefer long lock-ups. The period can range from 90 to 365 days, but 180 days is the most common. If there were no lock-up agreement, insiders could sell shares immediately provided they had met the SEC requirement to disclose the possible sale of previously restricted stock.

Shelf Registrations

The preceding discussion was cast in terms of firms initially selling their stock to the general public (i.e., the "initial public offering" or "going public"). Firms that have previously issued securities and are currently public also raise funds by selling new securities. If the sales are to the general public, the same basic procedure applies. The new securities must be registered with and approved by the SEC before they may be sold to the public, and the firm often uses the services of an investment banker to facilitate the sale.

There are, however, differences between an initial public offering and the sale of additional securities by a publicly held firm. The first major difference concerns the price of the securities. Because a market already exists for the firm's stock, the problem of an appropriate price for the additional shares is virtually eliminated. This price will approximate the market price on the date of issue. Second, because the firm must periodically publish information (for instance, the annual report) and file documents with the SEC, there is less need for a detailed prospectus. Many publicly held firms construct a prospectus describing a proposed issue of new securities and file it with the SEC. This

---

[7]Once insiders have bought stock that they cannot sell, the possibility exists that the stock's price will decline after the underwriting. For strategies using derivatives to protect an insider from losses, see the discussions of protective puts and collars in Chapters 17 and 18. If such hedging strategies are in effect, they must be disclosed on SEC Form 144.
[8]One empirical analysis of lock-ups and their impact on stock values found that prices do decline prior to the release of restricted shares. This suggests that unrestricted investors are selling their shares prior to the release date. See Terrill R. Keasler, "Underwriter Lock-up Release and After-Market Performance," *The Financial Review* (May 2001): 1–20.

⊕ **Point of Interest**

SCOR

Small firms often have difficulty raising money (especially equity funds), but changes in selected state securities laws have eased the process of selling new stock to the general public. Companies seeking to raise up to $1million may complete a Small Company Offering Registration (SCOR) instead of the traditional prospectus. This disclosure statement uses a question-and-answer format and is less complicated than the traditional registration statement. A SCOR may be completed by a lawyer and/or an accountant who need not be an expert in public securities offerings.

SCORs also permit the issuing firm to sell securities directly to individual investors and bypass the use of investment bankers. Stocks issued through the use of SCORs may be traded through brokerage firms who make a market in the securities. Because the dollar value of the offerings and the number of investors participating in these markets are small, these securities tend to be inactively traded. Increased use of SCORs, however, may expand trading in the securities. For information on additional means for small companies to raise funds, see Bruce G. Posner, "How to Finance Anything," *Inc.* (April 1992): 50–62.

document is called a *shelf registration*. After the shelf registration has been accepted by the SEC, the firm may sell the securities whenever the need for funds arises. For example, UDR Inc. (UDR) filed a shelf registration for $1.5 billion in debt securities, preferred stock, and common stock. This shelf registration offers the issuing firm flexibility. The securities do not have to be issued but can be quickly sold if the management deems that the conditions are optimal for the sale. In addition, the firm does not have to sell all the securities. The management of UDR Inc. may choose to sell the debt but not the stock or to sell only the common stock (up to the limit covered by the registration). The remaining securities may be subsequently issued when conditions warrant their sale.

SUMMARY

This chapter has covered securities markets and the mechanics of buying securities. Securities are traded on organized exchanges, such as the NYSE, or in the informal over-the-counter markets, including the Nasdaq stock market. Securities are primarily bought through brokers, who buy and sell for their customers' accounts. The brokers obtain the securities from dealers, who make markets in them. These dealers offer to buy and sell at specified prices (quotes), which are called the bid and the ask. Brokers and investors obtain these prices through a sophisticated electronic system that transmits the quotes from the various dealers.

After securities are purchased, the investor must pay for them with either cash or a combination of cash and borrowed funds. When the investor uses borrowed funds, that individual is buying on margin. Buying on margin increases both the potential percentage return and the potential risk of loss for the investor.

Investors may take delivery of their securities or leave them with the brokerage firm. Leaving securities registered in the street name offers the advantage of convenience because the brokerage firm becomes the custodian of the certificates. Since the advent of the SIPC and its insurance protection, there is little risk of loss to the investor from leaving securities with the brokerage firm.

Investors establish long or short positions. With a long position, the investor purchases stock in anticipation of its price rising. If the price of the stock rises, the individual may sell it for a profit. With a short position, the individual sells borrowed stock in anticipation of its price declining. If the price of the stock falls, the individual may repurchase it at the lower price and return it to the lender. The position generates a profit because the selling price exceeds the purchase price.

Both the long and short positions are the logical outcomes of security analysis. If the investor thinks a stock is underpriced, a long position (i.e., purchase of the stock) should be established. If the investor thinks a stock is overvalued, a short position would be sensible. If the investor is correct in either case, the position will generate a profit. Either position may, however, generate a loss if prices move against the investor's prediction.

Investors living in the United States may assume a global view and acquire stocks and bonds issued in foreign countries. These securities may be bought and sold through U.S. brokers in much the same way that investors acquire domestic securities. American Depository Receipts (ADRs) representing foreign securities have been created to facilitate trading in foreign stocks. These ADRs are denominated in dollars, their prices are quoted in dollars, and their units of trading are consistent with those in the United States.

The federal laws governing the securities industry are enforced by the Securities and Exchange Commission (SEC). The purpose of these laws is to ensure that individual investors have access to information upon which to base investment decisions. Publicly owned firms must supply investors with financial statements and make timely disclosure of information that may affect the value of the firms' securities.

Investors' accounts with brokerage firms are insured by the Securities Investor Protection Corporation (SIPC). This insurance covers up to $500,000 worth of securities held by the broker for the investor. The intent of SIPC is to increase public confidence in the securities industry by reducing the risk of loss to investors from failure by brokerage firms.

A firm may acquire funds indirectly through a financial intermediary such as a commercial bank. Financial intermediaries issue liabilities (e.g., deposits) to acquire funds and subsequently lend the funds to firms, governments, and individuals who need the money. Firms may also acquire funds directly by selling securities to the general public.

When a firm issues new securities, it usually employs the services of an investment banker to facilitate the sale through an initial public offering (IPO). The investment banker acts as a middleman between the firm and the investors. In many cases, the investment bankers underwrite the issue of new securities; they buy the securities and then sell them to the general public, guaranteeing the issuing firm a specified amount of money. Because the underwriters are obliged to remit the specified amount of money, they bear the risk of the sale. The market for IPOs has been volatile. The prices of some new issues rise dramatically but subsequently fall.

QUESTIONS

1. What is the difference between each pair of items?
    a) listed and unlisted securities
    b) brokers and market makers
    c) full-service and discount brokerage firms

    d) primary and secondary markets

    e) market order and good-till-canceled order

    f) cash account and margin account

2. When would you use a stop-loss order?

3. Why is it riskier to buy stock on margin?

4. The following questions concern short selling:

    a) When should an investor sell short?

    b) How can investors sell stock they do not own?

    c) How is a short position closed?

    d) How does the investor profit from a short sale?

    e) What is the risk associated with a short position?

5. How are the SIPC and FDIC similar? Why are securities laws frequently referred to as "full disclosure laws," and what is the role of the SEC?

6. In an underwriting, what role does each of the following play?

    a) the investment banker

    b) the syndicate

    c) the preliminary and final prospectus

    d) the SEC

7. What is the difference between an underwriting and a "best-efforts" sale of securities? Who bears the risk associated with each sale? If the investment banker overprices a new issue of securities, who sustains the losses?

8. The text used Ariba (ARBA) and Ask Jeeves as illustrations of stocks that soared after the IPO, only to decline dramatically in subsequent trading. Suppose investor A bought 100 shares of Ariba at the IPO price of $28.24, investor B bought 100 shares on the first day of trading at $69, and investor C bought 100 shares three months later at $151. What are those shares worth today? If investors A, B, and C sustained losses, who profited? One means to answer these questions is to locate historical stock prices by using an Internet source such as Yahoo! Finance: http://finance.yahoo.com.

9. In May 2006, Vonage (VG) went public at $17 but did not rise in price. What subsequently happened to the price of the stock one month, six months, one year, and three years after the IPO?

10. You may find information on pending IPOs at sites such as Hoover's IPO Central (http://www.hoovers.com/global/ipoc) or IPO Monitor (http://www.ipomonitor .com). Go to a calendar of new offerings and select a company that just went public or is just about to go public. Did the price of the stock increase by more than 10 percent after one day, one week, or one month? If no stocks were going public when you visited the site, what may explain the inactivity?

PROBLEMS

1. A stock sells for $10 per share. You purchase 100 shares for $10 a share (i.e., for $1,000), and after a year the price rises to $17.50. What will be the percentage return on your investment if you bought the stock on margin and the margin requirement was (a) 25 percent, (b) 50 percent, and (c) 75 percent? (Ignore commissions, dividends, and interest expense.)

2. Repeat Problem 1 to determine the percentage return on your investment but in this case suppose the price of the stock falls to $7.50 per share. What generalization can be inferred from your answers to Problems 1 and 2?

3. You purchase 100 shares of stock at $100 ($10,000); the margin requirement is 40 percent. What are the dollar and percentage returns if
    a) you sell the stock for $112 and buy the stock for cash?
    b) you sell the stock for $90 and buy the stock on margin?
    c) you sell the stock for $60 and buy the stock on margin?

4. Investor A buys 100 shares of SLM Inc. at $35 a share and holds the stock for a year. Investor B buys 100 shares on margin. The margin requirement is 60 percent, and the interest rate on borrowed funds is 8 percent.
    a) What is the interest cost for investor A?
    b) What is the interest cost for investor B?
    c) If they both sell the stock for $40 after a year, what percentage return does each investor earn?
    d) In both cases, the value of the stock has risen the same. Why are the percentage returns different?

5. Investor A makes a cash purchase of 100 shares of AB&C common stock for $55 a share. Investor B also buys 100 shares of AB&C but uses margin. Each holds the stock for one year, during which dividends of $5 a share are distributed. Commissions are 2 percent of the value of a purchase or sale; the margin requirement is 60 percent, and the interest rate is 10 percent annually on borrowed funds. What is the percentage earned by each investor if he or she sells the stock after one year for (a) $40, (b) $55, (c) $60, and (d) $70? If the margin requirement had been 40 percent, what would have been the annual percentage returns? What conclusion do these percentage returns imply?

6. Ms. Tejal Gandhi has decided that the stock of SmallCap Inc is overvalued at $4 a share and wants to sell it short. Since the price is relatively low, short sales cannot be executed on margin, so Ms. Gandhi must put up the entire value of the stock when it is sold short.
    a) What is the percentage loss if the price of the stock rises to $8?
    b) What is the percentage loss if the price of the stock rises to $10?
    c) What is the percentage gain if the company goes bankrupt and is dissolved?
    d) What are the maximum percentage gain the short seller can earn and the largest percentage loss the short seller can sustain?
    e) From the short seller's perspective, what are the best and worst case scenarios?

7. An investor sells a stock short for $36 a share. A year later, the investor covers the position at $30 a share. If the margin requirement is 60 percent, what is the percentage return earned on the investment? Redo the calculations, assuming the price of the stock is $42 when the investor closes the position.

8. A speculator sells a stock short for $50 a share. The company pays a $2 annual cash dividend. After a year has passed, the seller covers the short position at $42. What is the percentage return on the position (excluding the impact of any interest expense and commissions)? See the Point of Interest titled "The Short Sale and Dividends."

The Financial Advisor's Investment Case
Investing an Inheritance

The Kelleher brothers, Victor and Darin, could not be more different. Victor is assertive and enjoys taking risks, while Darin is reserved and is exceedingly risk averse. Both have jobs that pay well and provide fringe benefits, including medical insurance and pension plans. You are the executor for their grandfather's estate and know that each brother will soon inherit $85,000 from the estate. Neither has an immediate need for the cash, which could be invested to meet some long-term financial goal.

Once the funds have been received, you expect Victor to acquire some exceedingly risky investment (if he does not immediately squander the money). You would be surprised, however, if Darin chose to do anything other than place the funds in a low-yielding savings account. Neither alternative makes financial sense to you, so before the distribution of the funds you decide to offer financial suggestions that would reduce Victor's risk exposure and increase Darin's potential return.

Given the brothers' ages and financial condition, you believe that equity investments are appropriate. Such investments may satisfy Victor's propensity to take risks and increase Darin's potential return without excessively increasing his risk exposure (willingness to assume risk). Currently, the stock of Choice Juicy Fruit is selling for $60 and pays an annual dividend of $1.50 a share. The company's line of low-to-no-sugar juice offers considerable potential. The margin requirement set by the Federal Reserve is 60 percent, and brokerage firms are charging 7 percent on funds used to purchase stock on margin. While commissions vary among brokers, you decide that $70 for a 100-share purchase or sale is a reasonable amount to use for illustrative purposes. Currently, commercial banks are paying only 3 percent on savings accounts.

To give the presentation focus, you decide to answer the following questions:

1. What is the percentage return earned by Darin if he acquires 100 shares, holds the stock for a year, and sells the stock for $80?
2. What is the percentage return earned by Victor if he acquires 100 shares on margin, holds the stock for a year, and sells the stock for $80? What advantage does buying stock on margin offer Victor?
3. What would be the percentage returns if the sale prices had been $50 or $100?
4. Must the two brothers leave the stock registered in street name? If not, what would be the advantage of leaving the stock with the broker? Does leaving the stock increase their risk exposure?
5. What would be the impact on the brothers' returns if the rate of interest charged by the broker increases to 10 percent?
6. If the maintenance margin requirement were 30 percent and the price of the stock declined to $50, what impact would that have on each brother's position? At what price of the stock would they receive a margin call?
7. Why would buying the stock be more advantageous to both brothers than the alternatives you anticipate them to select?

CHAPTER 3

The Time Value of Money

LEARNING OBJECTIVES

After completing this chapter you should be able to:

1. Explain why a dollar received tomorrow is not equal in value to a dollar received today.
2. Differentiate between compounding and discounting.
3. Distinguish among the future value of $1, the future value of an annuity of $1, the present value of $1, and the present value of an annuity of $1.
4. Solve problems concerning the time value of money.

For 40 years, you diligently put $2,000 in your retirement account at the local bank. The bank pays you 4 percent interest. If, however, you had placed that money in a mutual fund that earned twice as much (8 percent), you would have accumulated $391,062 more in the mutual fund. The account at the bank will be worth $190,051, but the mutual fund will be worth $581,113. Ben Franklin said: "Money makes money. And the money that money makes makes more money." Mr. Franklin, however, did not point out the importance of the rate at which money makes more money.

The time value of money is one of the most crucial concepts in finance. An investment decision is made today. You buy stock in IBM now, but the sale and the return on the investment will be in the future. You believe you need $50,000 to make the down payment on a house. You want to know how much you must save each year. Or if you are able to save $4,000 annually, how long will it take to accumulate the $50,000? You save $50,000 and buy a $300,000 home; now you have a $250,000 mortgage. What will be your periodic payments required by the loan? There has to be a way to express these future amounts in the present. The process of expressing the future in the present and of expressing the present in the future is the essence of the time value of money.

This chapter covers four concepts: (1) the future value of $1, (2) the present value of $1, (3) the future sum of an annuity, and (4) the present value of an annuity. Examples apply these concepts to investments.

You may use financial calculators or computer programs such as Excel to solve these problems. Computer programs may facilitate the calculations, but only if you can properly set up the problem. Even then the specific question being asked may not be answered. You may have to work with the numbers or interpret them.

The purpose of understanding the time value of money is to facilitate understanding investments and to solve problems that pertain to valuation of assets and financial planning. If you already know the topic, you may proceed to the next chapter. If you do not understand the time value of money, careful attention to this chapter is critical because knowledge of the topic and the ability to work problems are essential for comprehending important concepts in investments.

THE FUTURE VALUE OF $1

If $100 is deposited in a savings account that pays 5 percent annually, how much money will be in the account at the end of the year? The answer is easy to determine: $100 plus $5 interest, for a total of $105. This answer is derived by multiplying $100 by 5 percent, which gives the interest earned during the year, and then by adding this interest to the initial principal. That is,

Initial principal + (Interest rate × Initial principal) = Principal after one year.

How much will be in the account after two years? This answer is obtained in the same manner by adding the interest earned during the second year to the principal at the beginning of the second year—that is, $105 plus 0.05 times $105 equals $110.25. After two years the initial deposit of $100 will have grown to $110.25; the savings account will have earned $10.25 in interest. This total interest is composed of $10 representing interest on the initial principal and $0.25 representing interest that has accrued during the second year on the $5 in interest earned during the first year. This earning of interest on interest is called **compounding**. Money that is deposited in savings accounts is frequently referred to as being compounded, for interest is earned on both the principal and the previously earned interest.

compounding

The process by which interest is paid on interest that has been previously earned.

The words *interest* and *compounded* are frequently used together. For example, banks may advertise that interest is compounded daily for savings accounts, or the cost of a loan may be expressed as 8 percent compounded quarterly. In the previous example, interest was earned only once during the year; thus it is an example of interest that is compounded annually. In many cases, interest is not compounded annually but quarterly, semiannually, or even daily. The more frequently it is compounded (i.e., the more frequently the interest is added to the principal), the more rapidly the interest is put to work to earn even more interest.

How much will be in the account at the end of 25 years? By continuing with the above method, it is possible to determine the amount that will be in the account at the end of 25 or more years, but doing so is obviously a lot of work. Fortunately, there are easier ways to ascertain how much will be in the account after any given number of years. The first is to use an interest table called the future value of $1 table.

The first table in Appendix A gives the interest factors for the future value of $1. The interest rates at which $1 is compounded periodically are read horizontally at the top of the table. The number of periods (e.g., years) is read vertically along the left-hand margin. To determine the amount to which $100 will grow after 25 years at 5 percent interest compounded annually, multiply $100 by the interest factor, 3.386, to obtain the answer $338.60. Thus, if $100 were placed in a savings account that paid 5 percent interest annually, there would be $338.60 in the account after 25 years.

Interest tables for the future value of $1 are based on a simple equation. The general formula for finding the amount to which $1 will grow in n number of years, if it is compounded annually, is

3.1
$$P_0(1 + i)^n = P_n.$$

Thus, the general formula for finding the future value of $1 for any number of years consists of (1) the initial dollar (P_0), (2) the interest $(1 + i)$, and (3) the number of years (n). Taken together, $(1 + i)^n$, the interest rate and time, are referred to as the *interest factor*.

This interest factor for selected interest rates and time periods is given in the interest tables in Appendix A.

As may be seen in the first table in Appendix A, the value of $1 grows with increases in the length of time and in the rate of interest. These relationships are illustrated in Figure 3.1. If $1 is compounded at 5 percent interest (*AB* in the figure), it will grow to $1.28 after five years and to $1.63 after ten years. However, if $1 is compounded at 10 percent interest (*AC* on the graph), it will grow to $2.59 in ten years. These cases illustrate the basic nature of compounding: The longer the funds continue to grow and the higher the interest rate, the higher will be the terminal value.

You should also notice that doubling the interest rate more than doubles the amount of interest that is earned over a number of years. In the example just given, the interest rate doubled from 5 percent to 10 percent; however, the amount of interest that will have accumulated in ten years rises from $0.63 at 5 percent to $1.59 at 10 percent. This is the result of the fact that compounding involves a geometric progression. The interest $(1 + i)$ has been raised to some power (n).

Time value problems may be illustrated using time lines, which place time period and payment on a horizontal line. For the previous example, the time line would be

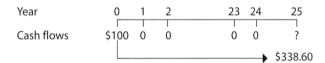

The initial cash outflow of $100 invested at 5 percent grows to $338.60 at the end of 25 years. Notice that the arrow represents the direction of time. When the process is reversed and the future is being brought back to the present, the arrow would point to the left.

The above example illustrates compounding. It is important not to confuse "simple interest" and "compound interest." Simple interest is the result of multiplying an

FIGURE 3.1 Future Value of $1.00

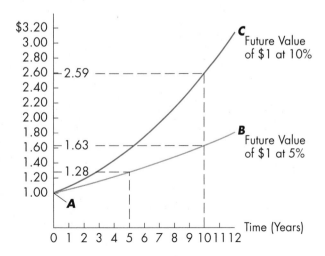

amount, the interest rate, and time. In the previous illustration, if simple interest is applied, the amount earned is

$$\$100 \times .05 \times 25 = \$125,$$

and the total in the account would be

$$\$100 + \$125 = \$225.$$

That future value is perceptibly less than the $338.60 determined using compound interest. When the interest is compounded, the amount earned is $228.60 and not $125.

Simple interest is appropriate only if the interest is withdrawn each period so there is no compounding, or if there is only one period. Obviously, there can be situations when interest is withdrawn each period and when payments are made only once. However, in most of the examples and problems used in this text, funds are withdrawn and payments are made over a number of periods. Thus, compounding is appropriate and is used throughout the text.

Future value problems may also be easily solved with the use of a financial calculator designed for business applications. These calculators have been programmed to solve time value problems. (Some financial calculators also have other business applications, such as determining depreciation expense and statistical analysis. Many employers expect new hires to be able to use financial calculators, so an inability to use them may put you at a disadvantage.)

Although there are differences among models, financial calculators generally have five special function keys:

N   I or %   PV   PMT   FV

These keys represent the time period (N), the interest rate (I or %), the amount in the present (PV for *present value*), the periodic payment (PMT for *annuity*, which will be discussed later in this chapter), and the amount in the future (FV for *future value*).

To illustrate how easy financial calculators are to use, consider the preceding illustration of the future value of $1 in which $100 grew to $338.60 after 25 years when the annual interest rate was 5 percent. Using a financial calculator, enter the present amount (PV = −100), the interest rate (I = 5), and time (N = 25). Since there are no annual payments, be certain that PMT is set equal to zero (PMT = 0). Then instruct the calculator to determine the future value (FV = ?). The calculator should arrive at a future value of $338.64, which is almost the same amount derived using the interest table for the future value of $1. (The difference is the result of the interest tables being rounded to three places.)

You may wonder why the present value was entered as a negative number. Financial calculators consider payments as either cash inflows or cash outflows. Cash inflows are entered as positive numbers, and cash outflows are entered as negative numbers. In the example, the initial amount is an outflow because the individual invests the $100. The resulting future amount is a cash inflow because the investor receives the terminal amount. That is, the investor gives up the $100 (the outflow) and after 25 years receives the $338.64 (the inflow).

Problems involving time value permeate this text and are illustrated with the use of interest tables and with financial calculators. Illustrations using interest tables clarify the basic concept, while the illustrations that employ the financial calculator indicate how easily the answer may be derived. The financial calculator illustrations use the following general form:

PV = ?
FV = ?
PMT = ?
N = ?
I = ?

followed by the answer. When applied to the preceding illustration, the form is

PV = $-100
FV = ?
PMT = 0
N = 25
I = 5
FV = $338.64

The final answer is separated from the data that is entered. Except for the first illustrations in this chapter, each example is placed in the margin so that it does not break the flow of the written material.

THE PRESENT VALUE OF $1

In the preceding section, $1 grew, or compounded, over time. This section considers the reverse. How much is $1 that will be received in the future worth today? For example, how much will a $1,000 payment 20 years hence be worth today if the funds earn 10 percent annually? This question incorporates the time value of money, but instead of asking how much $1 will be worth at some future date, it asks how much that future $1 is worth today. This is a question of **present value**. The process by which this question is answered is called **discounting**. Discounting determines the worth of funds that are to be received in the future in terms of their present value.

present value

The current worth of an amount to be received in the future.

discounting

The process of determining present value.

In the earlier section, the future value of $1 was calculated by Equation 3.1:

3.1
$$P_0(1 + i)^n = P_n.$$

Discounting reverses this equation. The present value (P_0) is determined by dividing the future value (P_n) by the interest factor $(1 + i)^n$. This is expressed in Equation 3.2:

3.2
$$P_0 = \frac{P_n}{(1 + i)^n}.$$

The future is discounted by the appropriate interest factor to determine the present value. For example, if the interest rate is 10 percent, the present value of $100 to be received five years from today is

$$P_0 = \frac{\$100}{(1 + 0.1)^5}$$

$$= \frac{\$100}{1.611}$$

$$= \$62.07.$$

Timeline:

Year 0 1 4   5
Cash   0 0 $100
 flows | | |
$62.07◄──┘

As with the future value of $1, interest tables and financial calculators ease the calculation of present values. The second table in Appendix A gives the interest factors for the present value of $1 for selected interest rates and time periods. The interest rates are read horizontally at the top, and time is read vertically along the left-hand side. To determine the present value of $1 that will be received in five years if the current interest rate is 10 percent, multiply $1 by the interest factor, which is found in the table under the vertical column for 10 percent and in the horizontal column for five years. The present value of $100 is

$$\$100 \times 0.621 = \$62.10.$$

Thus, $100 that will be received after five years is currently worth only $62.10 if the interest rate is 10 percent. This is the same answer that was determined with Equation 3.2 (except for rounding).

To solve this problem using a financial calculator, enter the future amount (FV = 100), the interest rate (I = 10), and the number of years (N = 5). Set the payments equal to zero (PMT = 0), and instruct the calculator to compute the present value (PV = ?). The calculator should determine the present value to be −62.09; once again the answer is virtually the same as that derived from the interest tables. Notice that the calculator expresses the present value as a negative number. If you receive a $100 cash inflow after ten years, that will require a current outflow of $62.09 if the rate of interest is 10 percent.

As may be seen in Equation 3.2, the present value of $1 depends on (1) the length of time before it will be received and (2) the interest rate. The farther into the future the dollar will be received and the higher the interest rate, the lower the present value of the dollar. This is illustrated by Figure 3.2, which gives the relationship between the present

FIGURE   3.2   Present Value of $1 to Be Received in the Future

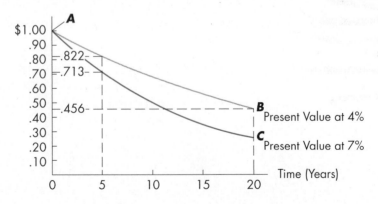

value of $1 and the length of time at various interest rates. Lines *AB* and *AC* give the present value of $1 at 4 percent and 7 percent, respectively. As may be seen in this graph, $1 to be received after 20 years is worth considerably less than $1 to be received after five years when both are discounted at the same percentage rate. At 4 percent (line *AB*) the current value of $1 to be received after 20 years is only $0.456, whereas $1 to be received after five years is worth $0.822. Also, the higher the interest rate (i.e., discount factor), the lower the present value of $1. For example, the present value of $1 to be received after five years is $0.822 at 4 percent, but it is only $0.713 at 7 percent.

THE FUTURE SUM OF AN ANNUITY

annuity

A series of equal annual payments.

future sum of an annuity

Compound value of a series of equal annual payments.

annuity due

A series of equal annual payments with the payments made at the beginning of the year.

ordinary annuity

A series of equal annual payments in which the payments are made at the end of each year.

How much will be in a savings account after three years if $100 is deposited annually and the account pays 5 percent interest? This is similar to the future value of $1 except that the payment is not one lump sum but a series of payments. If the payments are equal, the series is called an **annuity**. The question is an illustration of the **future sum of an annuity**.

To determine how much will be in the account we must consider not only the interest rate earned but also whether deposits are made at the beginning of the year or the end of the year. If each payment is made at the beginning of the year, the series is called an **annuity due**. If the payments are made at the end of the year, the series is an **ordinary annuity**. What is the future sum of an annuity if $100 is deposited in an account for three years starting right now? What is the future sum of an annuity if $100 is placed in an account for three years starting at the end of the first year? The first question concerns an annuity due, while the second question illustrates an ordinary annuity.

The flow of payments for these two types of annuities is illustrated in Exhibit 3.1. In both cases, the $100 is deposited for three years in a savings account that pays 5 percent interest. The top half of the figure shows the annuity due, while the bottom

EXHIBIT 3.1   The Flow of Payments for the Future Value of an Annuity Due and an Ordinary Annuity

Annuity Due				
1/1/×0	1/1/×1	1/1/×2	1/1/×3	Sum
$100.00	5.00	5.25	5.51	$115.76
	100.00	5.00	5.25	110.25
		100.00	5.00	105.00
Amount in the account				
$100.00	205.00	315.25	331.01	$331.01

Ordinary Annuity				
1/1/×0	1/1/×1	1/1/×2	1/1/×3	Sum
—	$100.00	5.00	5.25	$110.25
		100.00	5.00	105.00
			100.00	100.00
Amount in the account				
—	$100.00	205.00	315.25	$315.25

half illustrates the ordinary annuity. In both cases, three years elapse from the present to when the final amount is determined and three payments are made. The difference in the timing of the payment results in a difference in the interest earned. Because in an annuity due the payments are made at the beginning of each year, the annuity due earns more interest ($31.01 versus $15.25) and thus has the higher terminal value ($331.01 versus $315.25). As will be illustrated later in the chapter, the greater the interest rate and the longer the time period, the greater will be this difference in terminal values.

The procedures for determining the future sum of an annuity due (FSAD) and the future sum of an ordinary annuity (FSOA) are stated formally in Equations 3.3 and 3.4, respectively. In each equation, PMT represents the equal, periodic payment, i represents the rate of interest, and n represents the number of years that elapse from the present until the end of the time period. For the annuity due, the equation is

3.3 $$\text{FSAD} = PMT(1 + i)^1 + PMT(1 + i)^2 + \cdots + PMT(1 + i)^n.$$

When this equation is applied to the previous example in which $i = 0.05$, $n = 3$, and the annual payment $PMT = \$100$, the accumulated sum is

$$
\begin{aligned}
\text{FSAD} &= \$100(1 + 0.05)^1 + 100(1 + 0.05)^2 + 100(1 + 0.05)^3 \\
&= \$105 + 110.25 + 115.76 \\
&= \$331.01.
\end{aligned}
$$

For the ordinary annuity the equation is

3.4 $$\text{FSOA} = PMT(1 + i)^0 + PMT(1 + i)^1 + \cdots + PMT(1 + i)^{n-1}.$$

When this equation is applied to the preceding example, the accumulated sum is

$$
\begin{aligned}
\text{FSOA} &= \$100(1 + 0.05)^0 + 100(1 + 0.05)^1 + 100(1 + 0.05)^{3-1} \\
&= \$100 + 105 + 110.25 \\
&= \$315.25.
\end{aligned}
$$

Although it is possible to derive the sum of an annuity in this manner, it is very cumbersome. Fortunately, interest tables and financial calculators facilitate these calculations.[1] In the third table in Appendix A we find the interest factors for the future sum of an ordinary annuity for selected time periods and selected interest rates. (Interest tables are usually presented only for ordinary annuities. How these tables may be used for annuities due is discussed later.) The number of periods is read vertically at the left, and the interest rates are read horizontally at the top. To calculate the future sum of the ordinary annuity in the previous example, this table is used as follows. The FSOA at 5 percent interest for three years (three annual $100 payments with interest being earned for two years) is $100 times the interest factor found in Table 3 of Appendix A for three periods at 5 percent. This interest factor is 3.153; therefore, the future value of this ordinary annuity is $100 times 3.153, which equals $315.30. This is the same answer that was derived by determining the future value of each $100 deposit and totaling them. (The slight difference in the two answers is the result of rounding.)

To use the financial calculator to solve for the ordinary annuity, enter the number of years (N = 3) the rate of interest (I = 5), and the amount of each payment (PMT = −100). Because there is no single initial payment, enter zero for the present

---

[1] The equations for the interest factors for the future value of an ordinary annuity and for the present value of an ordinary annuity are provided in the section on electronic calculators. See Equations 3.8 and 3.9, respectively.

value (PV = 0), and instruct the calculator to solve for the future value (FV = ?). When these data are entered, the calculator determines that the future value is $315.25. (The calculator requires you to express the $100 payment as a negative number because it is assuming you are making a cash outflow of $100 each period and receiving a $315.25 cash inflow at the end of the three years.)

The value of an ordinary annuity of $1 compounded annually depends on the number of payments (i.e., the number of periods over which deposits are made) and the interest rate. The longer the time period and the higher the interest rate, the greater will be the sum that will have accumulated in the future. This is illustrated by Figure 3.3. Lines *AB* and *AC* show the value of the $1 annuity at 4 percent and 8 percent, respectively. After five years the value of the annuity will grow to $5.87 at 8 percent but to only $5.42 at 4 percent. If these annuities are continued for another five years, they will be worth $14.49 and $12.01, respectively. Thus, both the rate at which the annuity compounds and the length of time affect the annuity's value.

While Table 3 in Appendix A is constructed for an ordinary annuity, it may be converted into a table for an annuity due by multiplying the interest factor given in the table by (1 + *i*). For example, in the illustration of the $100 deposited annually in the savings account for three years, the interest factor for the ordinary annuity was 3.153. This interest factor may be converted for an annuity due at 5 percent for three years by multiplying 3.153 by 1 + 0.05. That is,

$$3.153(1 + 0.05) = 3.3107.$$

When this interest factor is applied to the example of $100 deposited in the bank at 5 percent for three years with the deposits starting immediately, the resulting terminal value is

$$\$100(3.3107) = \$331.07.$$

This is the same answer as derived by making each calculation individually and summing them. (Once again the small difference in the two answers is the result of rounding.)

FIGURE **3.3** Future Sum of an Ordinary Annuity of $1

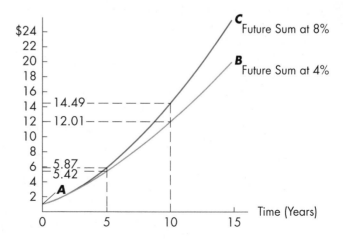

To use a financial calculator to solve for the future value of an annuity due, use the key that informs the calculator that the payments are to be made at the beginning rather than the end of each time period. Enter the amount of the payment (PMT = −100), the rate of interest (I = 5), and the number of years (N = 3). Set the present value equal to zero (PV = 0) and instruct the calculator to solve for the future value.

The difference between the terminal value of the two kinds of annuity payments can be quite substantial as the number of years increases or the interest rate rises. Consider a retirement account in which the saver places $2,000 annually for 20 years. If the deposits are made at the end of the year (an ordinary annuity) and the rate of interest is 7 percent, the terminal amount will be

$$\$2,000(40.995) = \$81,990.$$

However, if the deposits had been made at the beginning of each year (an annuity due), the terminal amount would be

$$\$2,000(40.995)(1 + 0.07) = \$87,729.30.$$

The difference is $5,739.30! Almost $6,000 in additional interest is earned if the deposits are made at the beginning, not at the end, of each year.

The difference between the ordinary annuity and the annuity due becomes even more dramatic if the interest rate rises. Suppose the account offered 12 percent instead of 7 percent. If the deposits are made at the end of each year, the terminal value is

$$\$2,000(72.052) = \$144,104.$$

If the payments are at the beginning of the year, the terminal value will be

$$\$2,000(72.052)(1 + 0.12) = \$161,396.48.$$

The difference is now $17,292.48.

THE PRESENT VALUE OF AN ANNUITY

present value of an annuity

The present worth of a series of equal payments.

In investment analysis, the investor is often not concerned with the future value but with the **present value of an annuity**. The investor who receives periodic payments often wishes to know the current (i.e., present) value. As with the future sum of an annuity, this value depends on whether the payments are made at the beginning of each year (an annuity due) or at the end of each period (an ordinary annuity).

The present value of an annuity is simply the sum of the present value of each individual cash flow. Each cash inflow is discounted back to the present at the appropriate discount factor and the amounts summed. Suppose you expect to receive $100 at the end of each year for three years and want to know how much this series of payments is worth if you can earn 8 percent in an alternative investment. To answer the question, you discount each payment at 8 percent:

Payment	Year	Interest Factor	Present Value
$100	1	0.926	$92.60
100	2	0.857	85.70
100	3	0.794	79.40
			$257.70

The process determines the present value to be $257.70. That is, if you invest $257.70 now and earn 8 percent annually, you can withdraw $100 at the end of each year for the next three years.

This process is expressed in more general terms by Equation 3.5. The present value (PV) of the annual payments (PMT) is then found by discounting these payments at the appropriate interest rate (i) for n time periods.

3.5
$$PV = \frac{PMT}{(1 + i)^1} + \cdots + \frac{PMT}{(1 + i)^n}$$

$$= \sum_{t=1}^{n} \frac{PMT}{(1 + i)^t}.$$

When the values from the previous example are inserted into the equation, it reads

Timeline:
Year 0   1   2   3
Cash ? $100 100 100
flows
$257.70

$$PV = \frac{\$100}{(1 + 0.08)} + \frac{\$100}{(1 + 0.08)^2} + \frac{\$100}{(1 + 0.08)^3}$$

$$= \frac{\$100}{1.080} + \frac{\$100}{1.166} + \frac{\$100}{1.260}$$

$$= \$257.70.$$

Since the payments are equal and made annually, this example is an annuity, and the present value is simply the product of the payment and the interest factor. Interest tables have been developed for the interest factors for the present value of an annuity (see the fourth table in Appendix A). Selected interest rates are read horizontally along the top, and the number of periods is read vertically at the left. To determine the present value of an annuity of $100 that is to be received for three years when interest rates are 8 percent, find the interest factor for three years at 8 percent (2.577) and then multiply $100 by this interest factor. The present value of this annuity is $257.70, which is the same value that was derived by obtaining each of the individual present values and summing them. The price that one would be willing to pay at the present time in exchange for three future annual payments of $100 when the rate of return on alternative investments is 8 percent is $257.70.

To use the financial calculator to solve for the present value of the ordinary annuity, enter the number of years (N = 3), the rate of interest (I = 8), and the amount of each payment (PMT = 100). Since there is no single future payment, enter zero for the future value (FV = 0), and instruct the calculator to solve for the present value (PV = ?). When these data are entered, the calculator determines that the present value is −257.71. (Once again the calculator expresses the $257.71 as a negative number because it is assuming you make an initial cash outflow of $257.71 and receive a $100 cash inflow each period. If you enter the $100 payment as a negative number, the present value will be a positive number. The calculator will then assume you initially received a $257.71 cash inflow through a loan and are making a $100 cash repayment or outflow each period.)

As with the present value of $1, the present value of an annuity is related to the interest rate and the length of time over which the annuity payments are made. The lower the interest rate and the longer the duration of the annuity, the greater the present value

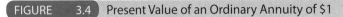

FIGURE   3.4   Present Value of an Ordinary Annuity of $1

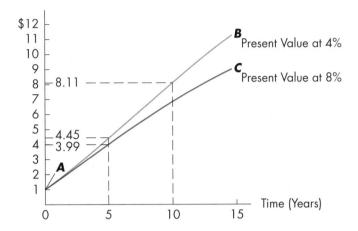

of the annuity. Figure 3.4 illustrates these relationships. As may be seen by comparing lines *AB* and *AC,* the lower the interest rate, the higher the present dollar value. For example, if payments are to be made over five years, the present value of an annuity of $1 is $4.45 at 4 percent but only $3.99 at 8 percent. The longer the duration of the annuity, the higher the present value; hence, the present value of an annuity of $1 at 4 percent is $4.45 for five years, whereas it is $8.11 for ten years.

Many payments to be received in investments occur at the end of a time period and not at the beginning and thus are illustrative of ordinary annuities. For example, the annual interest payment made by a bond occurs after the bond is held for a while, and distributions from earnings (e.g., dividends from stock) are made after, not at the beginning of, a period of time. There are, however, payments that may occur at the beginning of the time period, such as the annual distribution from a retirement plan; these would be illustrative of annuities due.

The difference in the flow of payments and the determination of the present values of an ordinary annuity and an annuity due are illustrated in Exhibit 3.2. In each case, the annuity is for $2,000 a year for three years and the interest rate is 10 percent. In the top half of the exhibit, the payments are made at the end of the year (an ordinary annuity), while in the bottom half of the exhibit, the payments are made at the beginning of the year (an annuity due). As may be seen by the totals, the present value of the annuity due is higher ($5,470 versus $4,972). This is because the payments are received sooner and, hence, are more valuable. As may also be seen in the illustration, because the first payment of the annuity due is made immediately, its present value is the actual amount received. Because the first payment of the ordinary annuity is made at the end of the first year, that amount is discounted, and, hence, its present value is less than the actual amount received.

The interest tables for the present value of an annuity presented in this text (and in other finance and investment texts) apply to ordinary annuities. These interest factors may be converted into annuity due factors by multiplying them by $(1 + i)$. Thus the interest factor for the present value of an ordinary annuity for $1 at 10 percent for

EXHIBIT 3.2	Flow of Payments and Determination of the Present Value of an Ordinary Annuity and an Annuity Due at 10 Percent for Three Years

Ordinary Annuity

1/1/✕0	1/1/✕1	1/1/✕2	1/1/✕3
$1,818 ◄――――(0.909) 2,000			
1,652 ◄―――――――――――(0.826) 2,000			
1,505 ◄――――――――――――――――――(0.751) 2,000			
$4,972			

Annuity Due

1/1/✕0	1/1/✕1	1/1/✕2	1/1/✕3
$2,000			
1,818 ◄――――(0.909) 2,000			
1,652 ◄―――――――――――(0.826) 2,000			
$5,470			

three years (2.487) may be converted into the interest factor for an annuity due of $1 at 10 percent for three years as follows:

$$2.487(1 + i) = 2.487(1 + 0.1) = 2.736.$$

When this interest factor is used to determine the present value of an annuity due of $2,000 for three years at 10 percent, the present value is

$$\$2,000(2.736) = \$5,472.$$

The present value of an ordinary annuity of $2,000 at 10 percent for three years is

$$\$2,000(2.487) = \$4,974.$$

These are essentially the same answers given in Exhibit 3.2; the small differences result from rounding.

To use a financial calculator to solve for the present value of the annuity due, use the key that informs the calculator that the payments are to be received at the beginning rather than the end of each time period. Enter the amount of the payment to be received (PMT = 2,000), the rate of interest (I = 10), and the number of years (N = 3). Set the future value equal to 0 (FV = 0), and instruct the calculator to solve for the present value.

ILLUSTRATIONS OF COMPOUNDING AND DISCOUNTING

The previous sections have explained the various computations involving time value, and this section will illustrate them in a series of problems that you may encounter. These illustrations are similar to examples that are used throughout the text. Understanding

⊕ Point of Interest

PRESENT VALUE AND THE VALUATION OF STOCKS AND BONDS

The valuation of assets is a major theme of this text. Investors and financial analysts must be able to analyze securities to determine their current value. This process requires forecasting future cash inflows and discounting them back to the present. The present value of an investment, then, is related to future benefits, in the form of either future income or capital appreciation. For example, stocks are purchased for their *future* dividends and potential capital gains but *not* for their previous dividends and price performance. Bonds are purchased for *future* income. Real estate is bought for the *future* use of the property and for the potential price appreciation. The concept of discounting future cash inflows back to the present applies to all investments: It is the future and not the past that matters. The past is relevant only to the extent that it may be used to predict the future.

Some types of analysis (including the technical approach to selecting investments that is discussed in Chapter 12) use the past in the belief that it forecasts the future. Technical analysts employ such information as the past price movements of a stock to determine the most profitable times to buy and sell a security. However, most of the analytical methods that are discussed in this text use some form of discounting future cash flows to value an asset. Prices are the present value of anticipated future cash inflows, such as dividends.

For debt, the current price is related to the series of interest payments and the repayment of the principal, both of which are discounted at the current market interest rate. The current price of a stock is related to the firm's future earnings and dividends and the individual's alternative investment opportunities. Cash flows are discounted back to the present at the appropriate discount factor. For these reasons it is important to start to view current prices as the present value of future cash inflows. The various features of the different investments, including stocks and bonds, will be discussed, and their prices will be analyzed in terms of present value. If you do not understand the material on the time value of money presented in this chapter, the analytical sections of subsequent chapters may be incomprehensible.

---

these examples will make comprehending the rest of the text material much easier, because the emphasis can then be placed on the analysis of the value of specific assets instead of on the mechanics of the valuation.

 You may locate additional time value of money explanations, problems, and applications by doing an Internet search using "time value of money calculators." For example, http://www.TeachMeFinance.com has illustrations of using uneven cash flows.

1. An investor buys a stock for $10 per share and expects the value of the stock to grow annually at 9 percent for ten years, at which time the individual plans to sell it. What is the anticipated sale price? This is an example of the future value of $1 growing at 9 percent for ten years. The future value is

$$P_n = P_0(1 + i)^n$$
$$P_{10} = \$10(1 + 0.09)^{10}$$
$$= \$10(2.367) = \$23.67,$$

in which 2.367 is the interest factor for the future sum of $1 at 9 percent for ten years. The investor anticipates selling the stock for $23.67.

2. An investor sells for $23.67 a stock that was purchased ten years ago. A return of 9 percent was earned. What was the original cost of the investment? This is an

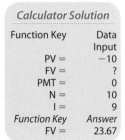

Calculator Solution	
Function Key	Data Input
PV =	−10
FV =	?
PMT =	0
N =	10
I =	9
Function Key	*Answer*
FV =	23.67

example of the present value of $1 discounted back at 9 percent for ten years. The initial value is

$$P_0 = \frac{P_n}{(1 + i)^n}$$

$$= \frac{\$23.67}{(1 + 0.09)^{10}}$$

$$= \$23.67(0.4224) = \$10,$$

in which 0.4224 is the interest factor for the present value of $1 discounted at 9 percent for ten years. The investment cost $10 when it was purchased ten years ago.

You should realize that Questions 1 and 2 are two views of the same investment. In Question 1 the $10 investment grew to $23.67. In Question 2 the value at the time the stock was sold was brought back to the value of the initial investment. Another variation of this question would be as follows. If an investor bought stock for $10, held it for ten years, and then sold it for $23.67, what was the return on the investment? In this case the values of the stock at the time it was bought and sold are known, but the rate of growth (the rate of return) is unknown. The answer can be found by using *either* the future value of $1 table or the present value of $1 table.

If the future value table is used, the question is at what rate (x) will $10 grow in ten years to equal $23.67. The answer is

$$P_0(1 + x)^n = P_n$$
$$\$10(1 + x)^{10} = \$23.67$$
$$(1 + x)^{10} = 2.367.$$

The interest factor is 2.367, which, according to the future value of $1 table for ten years, makes the growth rate 9 percent. This interest factor is located under the vertical column for 9 percent and in the horizontal column for ten years.

If the present value table is used, the question asks what discount factor (x) at ten years will bring $23.67 back to $10. The answer is

$$P_0 = \frac{P_n}{(1 + x)^n}$$

$$\$10 = \frac{\$23.67}{(1 + x)^{10}}$$

$$0.4224 = \frac{1}{(1 + x)^{10}}.$$

The interest factor is 0.4224, which may be found in the present value of $1 table for ten years in the 9 percent column (i.e., the growth rate is 9 percent). Thus, this problem may be solved by the proper application of either the future value or present value table.

3. An employer starts a pension plan for a 45-year-old employee. The plan requires the employer to invest $1,000 at the end of each year. If that investment earns 8 percent annually, how much will be accumulated by retirement at age 65?

This is an example of the future value of an ordinary annuity. The payment is $1,000 annually and grows at 8 percent for 20 years. The fund will be

$$FV = PMT(1 + i)^0 + \cdots + PMT(1 + i)^{n-1}$$
$$= \$1,000(1 + 0.08)^0 + \cdots + \$1,000(1 + 0.08)^{19}$$
$$= \$1,000(45.762) = \$45,762.$$

(45.762 is the interest factor for the future sum of an ordinary annuity of $1 compounded annually at 8 percent for 20 years.)

4. The same employer decides to place a lump sum in an investment that earns 8 percent and to draw on the funds to make the annual payments of $1,000. After 20 years all the funds in the account will be depleted. How much must be deposited initially in the account?

This is an example of the present value of an ordinary annuity. The annuity is $1,000 per year at 8 percent for 20 years. Thus, the present value (i.e., the amount of the initial investment) is

$$PV = \sum_{t=1}^{n}\frac{PMT}{(1 + i)} + \cdots + \frac{PMT}{(1 + i)^n}$$
$$= \frac{\$1,000}{1 + 0.08} + \cdots + \frac{\$1,000}{(1 + 0.08)^{20}}$$
$$= \$1,000(9.818) = \$9,818,$$

in which 9.818 is the interest factor for the present value of an ordinary annuity of $1 at 8 percent for 20 years. Thus, the employer need invest only $9,818 in an account now that earns 8 percent to meet the $1,000 annual pension payment for the next 20 years.

Notice the difference between the answers in Examples 3 and 4. In Example 3, a set of payments earns interest, and thus the future value is larger than just the sum of the 20 payments of $1,000. In Example 4, a future set of payments is valued in present terms. Since future payments are worth less today, the current value is less than the sum of the 20 payments of $1,000.

Also notice that if the employer sets aside $9,818 today and earns 8 percent annually for 20 years, the terminal value is $45,761.28, which is essentially the same amount derived in the third illustration. From the employer's viewpoint, the $9,818 may be used to cover a required $1,000 annual payment or used to accumulate a required $45,762 future value. Essentially, either approach achieves the required terminal value.

5. An investment pays $50 per year for ten years, after which $1,000 is returned to the investor. If the investor can earn 9 percent, how much should this investment cost? This question really contains two questions: What is the present value of an ordinary annuity of $50 at 9 percent for ten years, and what is the present value of $1,000 after ten years at 9 percent? The answer is

$$PV = \sum_{t=1}^{n}\frac{PMT_1}{(1 + i)^1} + \cdots + \frac{PMT_n}{(1 + i)^n} + \frac{FV_n}{(1 + i)^n}$$
$$= \frac{\$50}{(1 + 0.09)} + \cdots + \frac{\$50}{(1 + 0.09)^{10}} + \frac{\$1,000}{(1 + 0.09)^{10}}$$
$$= \$50(6.418) = \$1,000(0.422) = \$742.90.$$

Calculator Solution

Function Key	Data Input
PV =	0
FV =	?
PMT =	−1000
N =	20
I =	8
Function Key	Answer
FV =	45,761.96

Calculator Solution

Function Key	Data Input
PV =	?
FV =	0
PMT =	1000
N =	20
I =	8
Function Key	Answer
PV =	−9,818.15

Calculator Solution

Function Key	Data Input
PV =	?
FV =	1000
PMT =	50
N =	10
I =	9
Function Key	Answer
PV =	−743.29

(6.418 and 0.422 are the interest factors for the present value of an ordinary annuity of $1 and the present value of $1, respectively, both at 9 percent for ten years.)

This example illustrates that an investment may involve both a series of payments (an annuity component) and a lump-sum payment. This particular investment is similar to a bond, the valuation of which is discussed in Chapter 14. Other examples of valuation and the computation of rates of return are given in Chapters 8 and 9, which consider investments in common stock.

6. A corporation's dividend has grown annually at the rate of 5 percent. If this rate is maintained and the current dividend is $5.40, what will the dividend be after ten years? This is a simple future value of $1 problem. The dividend will grow to

$$P_n = P_0(1 + i)^n$$
$$= \$5.40(1 + 0.05)^{10}$$
$$= \$5.40(1.629) = \$8.80.$$

(1.629 is the interest factor for the future value of $1 at 5 percent for ten years.) Although such a growth rate in future dividends may not be achieved, this problem illustrates how modest annual increments can result in a substantial increase in an investor's dividend income over a number of years. (In the calculator solution, if you enter the 5.40 as a positive number, the answer is a negative 8.80. Either is acceptable as long as you interpret the answer correctly.)

7. You borrow $80,000 to purchase a town house. The loan is for 25 years, and the annual payment is $7,494.30, which covers the interest and annual principal repayment. What is the rate of interest on the loan? Notice that both the present amount and the future payments are known. (The future value is also known; it is $0 because the loan is completely paid off at the end of the time period.) To answer the question, use the equation for the present value of an annuity:

$$PV = \frac{PMT}{(1 + i)} + \cdots + \frac{PMT}{(1 + i)^n}$$

$$\$80,000 = \frac{\$7,494.30}{(1 + i)} + \cdots + \frac{\$7,494.30}{(1 + i)^{25}}.$$

Solving for the interest factor gives

$$PV = PMT(PVAIF)$$
$$IFPVA = \$80,000/\$7,494.30 = 10.675.$$

Locate this value in the interest table for the present value of an annuity of $1 for 25 years, where the rate of interest is 8 percent. You use the present value of the annuity because the *loan is taken out in the present.*

This is one of the most crucial problems you will face throughout this text. It appears in many guises; in this illustration the problem is the determination of the interest rate on a loan. For example, in Chapter 10 on stock indexes and returns, the problem determines the annual return on a stock or on the market as measured by an index. In Chapter 14 on bond valuation it appears as the yield to maturity or the yield to call on a bond.

The previous examples illustrate the use of interest tables and the financial calculator. These problems can also be done without the tables or a financial calculator if

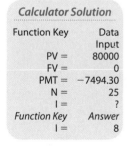

Calculator Solution

Function Key	Data Input
PV =	−5.40
FV =	?
PMT =	0
N =	10
I =	5
Function Key	Answer
FV =	8.80

Calculator Solution

Function Key	Data Input
PV =	80000
FV =	0
PMT =	−7494.30
N =	25
I =	?
Function Key	Answer
I =	8

you have access to an electronic calculator with a y^x key and/or logs. Also, computer programs and spreadsheets such as Excel may be used as substitutes for interest tables or financial calculators to solve the problems. (The use of nonfinancial calculators to determine interest factors that are not in the tables is discussed in the next section.)

EQUATIONS FOR THE INTEREST FACTORS

All time value problems consist of a combination of present value, future value, or series of payments plus an interest factor. All interest factors consist of the rate of interest and number of periods. Financial calculators and spreadsheets greatly facilitate solving time value problems. There may be situations, however, in which you need the equation for the interest factor. For example, a scientific calculator is not preprogrammed for interest factors but may be used to derive a desired factor. What follows are the actual equations (3.6 through 3.9) and an illustration for each of the interest factors.

The equation for the interest factor for the future value of $1 (FVIF) is

3.6 $$\text{FVIF} = (1 + i)^n.$$

To find the interest factor for 6 percent for three years [i.e., $(1 + 0.06)^3$], first enter 1 plus the interest rate: 1.06. The display should read 1.06. Next, raise this amount to the third power, which is achieved by striking the y^x key and the number 3. Press "equal," and the display should read 1.191, which is the interest factor that may be found in the first table of Appendix A under the column for 6 percent and three years.

The equation for the interest factor of the present value of $1 (PVIF) is

3.7 $$\text{PVIF} = \frac{1}{(1 + i)^n}.$$

The interest factor for the present value is the reciprocal of the interest factor for the future value of $1. To derive the interest factor for the present value of $1 at 6 percent for three years, do the preceding steps used to determine the future value of $1 and then take the reciprocal. If the calculator has the $1/x$ key, press this key, and the reciprocal is automatically determined. If the calculator lacks this key, the reciprocal is found by dividing 1 by the number just derived. In the illustration, the reciprocal for 1.191 is 0.8396 (1/1.191), which is the interest factor for the present value of $1 at 6 percent for three years. You may verify this number by looking under the column for the present value of $1 at 6 percent for three years in the second table in Appendix A, which gives the interest factor as 0.840. The difference is, of course, the result of rounding.

The equation for the interest factor for the future sum of an annuity (FVAIF) is

3.8 $$\text{FVAIF} = \frac{(1 + i)^n - 1}{i}.$$

Thus, if the interest rate is 5 percent and the number of years is four, then the interest factor is

$$\text{FVAIF} = \frac{(1 + 0.05)^4 - 1}{0.05} = \frac{1.2155 - 1}{0.05} = 4.310,$$

which is the same number found in the table for the future value of an annuity for four years at 5 percent.

The equation for the interest factor for the present value of an annuity (PVAIF) is

3.9
$$PVAIF = \frac{1 - \dfrac{1}{(1 + i)^n}}{i}.$$

If the interest rate is 6 percent and the number of years is three, then the interest factor is

$$PVAIF = \frac{1 - \dfrac{1}{(1 + 0.06)^3}}{0.06} = \frac{1 - 0.8396}{0.06} = 2.673,$$

which is the interest factor found in the table for the present value of an annuity at 6 percent for three years.

In addition to facilitating the calculation of interest factors, electronic calculators and spreadsheets also offer a major advantage over the use of interest tables. Interest tables are limited to exact rates (e.g., 5 percent) and whole years (e.g., six years). Unless the individual interpolates between the given interest factors, the tables cannot provide the interest factor for 6.7 percent for five years and three months. However, this interest factor can be determined by using the electronic calculator or a spreadsheet. The interest factor for the future value of $1 at 6.7 percent for five years and three months may be found as follows:

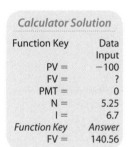

1. Enter 1.067.
2. Raise 1.067 by 5.25 (i.e., $y^x = 1.067^{5.25}$).
3. Press "equal" to derive the interest factor: 1.4056.

Thus, if $100 is invested at 6.7 percent, compounded annually for five years and three months, the future value is $140.56.

Although financial calculators and spreadsheets may ease the burden of the arithmetic, they cannot set up the problems to be solved. You must still determine if the problem concerns future value or present value and whether the problem deals with a lump sum or an annuity. Failure to set up the problem correctly will only lead to incorrect results, so it is imperative that you be able to determine what is being used and which of the various cases applies to the particular problem.

NONANNUAL COMPOUNDING

semiannual compounding

The payment of interest twice a year.

You should have noticed that in the previous examples compounding occurred only once a year. Since compounding can and often does occur more frequently—for example, **semiannually**—the equations that were presented earlier must be adjusted. This section extends the discussion of the compound value of $1 to include compounding for time periods other than a year.

Converting annual compounding to other time periods necessitates two adjustments. First, a year is divided into the same number of time periods that the funds are being compounded. For semiannual compounding a year consists of two time periods, whereas for quarterly compounding the year comprises four time periods.

After adjusting for the number of time periods, the individual adjusts the interest rate to find the rate per time period. This is done by dividing the stated interest rate by the number of time periods. If the interest rate is 8 percent compounded semiannually, then 8 percent is divided by 2, giving an interest rate of 4 percent earned in *each* time period. If the annual rate of interest is 8 percent compounded quarterly, the interest rate is 2 percent (8% ÷ 4) in each of the four time periods. These adjustments may be expressed in more formal terms by modifying Equation 3.1 as follows:

3.10
$$P_0\left(1 + \frac{i}{c}\right)^{n\times c} = P_n.$$

The only new symbol is c, which represents the frequency of compounding. The interest rate (i) is divided by the frequency of compounding (c) to determine the interest rate in each period. The number of years (n) is multiplied by the frequency of compounding to determine the number of time periods.

The application of this equation may be illustrated in a simple example. An individual invests $100 in an asset that pays 8 percent compounded quarterly. What will the future value of this asset be after five years—that is, $100 will grow to what amount after five years if it is compounded quarterly at 8 percent? Algebraically, this is

$$P_n = P_0\left(1 + \frac{i}{c}\right)^{n\times c}$$
$$= \$100\left(1 + \frac{0.08}{4}\right)^{5\times4}$$
$$= \$100(1 + 0.02)^{20}.$$

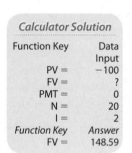

Calculator Solution

Function Key	Data Input
PV =	−100
FV =	?
PMT =	0
N =	20
I =	2
Function Key	*Answer*
FV =	148.59

In this formulation the investor is earning 2 percent for 20 time periods. To solve this equation, the interest factor for the future value of $1 at 2 percent for 20 years (1.486) is multiplied by $100. Thus, the future value is

$$P_5 = \$100(1.486) = \$148.60.$$

The difference between compounding annually and compounding more frequently can be seen by comparing this problem with one in which the values are identical except that the interest is compounded annually. The question is, then, to what amount will $100 grow after five years at 8 percent compounded annually? The answer is

$$P_5 = \$100(1 + 0.08)^5$$
$$= \$100(1.469)$$
$$= \$146.90.$$

Calculator Solution

Function Key	Data Input
PV =	−100
FV =	?
PMT =	0
N =	5
I =	8
Function Key	*Answer*
FV =	146.93

This sum, $146.90, is less than the amount that was earned when the funds were compounded quarterly, which suggests the general conclusion that the more frequently interest is compounded, the greater will be the future amount.

The discussion throughout this text is generally limited to annual compounding. There is, however, one important exception: the valuation of bonds. Bonds pay interest semiannually, and this affects their value. Therefore, semiannual compounding is incorporated in the bond valuation model that is presented in Chapter 14.

⊕ Point of Interest

THE RULE OF 72

Do you want a shortcut method that answers the question, "How long will it take to double my money if I earn a specified percentage?" The rule of 72 does just that! Divide 72 by the rate earned, and the answer is an approximation of how long it takes for the initial amount to double. For example, if the rate is 6 percent, funds double in 72/6 = 12 years. At 10 percent, funds double in 7.2 years.

How accurate is this shortcut? As may be seen from this table, the rule of 72 gives a rather accurate approximation of the time necessary to double one's funds at a specific rate of growth.

Rate (%)	Years for Funds to Double Using the Rule of 72	Actual Years for Funds to Double
5	14.4	14.2
7	10.3	10.2
10	7.2	7.3
12	6.0	6.1
16	4.5	4.7
20	3.6	3.8

UNEVEN CASH FLOWS

With the exception of Example 5 under illustrations, the problems and examples in this chapter involve either single payments or a series of equal payments. In reality, cash flows are often not equal. Dividends may grow over time. The rents from an apartment building vary each year with the occupancy rate and the rates charged the occupants. Individuals may commit different amounts each year to their children's education fund or retirement accounts.

Certainly it is easier to illustrate time value problems when using single payments or equal cash flows. The primary reason is that interest tables assume single payments or equal payments. Using interest factors for multiple unequal single payments requires a large number of calculations. Since the purpose is to illustrate time value and its applications, single or annuity payments are sufficient for pedagogical purposes.

What follows is a series of problems illustrating situations that an investor may encounter involving unequal payments. You may solve these problems using Excel. See this chapter's appendix on spreadsheets if you need help using Excel to solve time value problems.

1. You make the following investments at the end of each year and earn 7 percent. How much will be in the account at the end of the five years?

Year	Annual Contribution
1	$2,000
2	2,500
3	3,000
4	3,000
5	3,500

2. You make the following investments at the beginning of each year and earn 7 percent. How much will be in the account at the end of the five years?

Year	Annual Contribution
1	$2,000
2	2,500
3	3,000
4	3,000
5	3,500

Examples 1 and 2 illustrate an investment such as contributing to your child's education account or your retirement account. The terminal values are $15,829 and $16,937, respectively.

3. You expect the following cash inflows from an investment. If you want to earn 10 percent on your funds, what is the maximum you should pay for the asset?

Year	Cash Inflows
1	$25,000
2	37,500
3	43,000
4	33,000
5	37,500

4. You make an investment that costs $100,000. What is the return if the annual cash inflows are as follows?

Year	Cash Inflows
1	$25,000
2	37,500
3	43,000
4	33,000
5	37,500

Examples 3 and 4 use the same investment (e.g., a building). Example 3 illustrates the maximum you should pay (it is a valuation problem), and Example 4 illustrates the return you will earn given the initial cash outflow and the estimated cash inflows. The answers are $131,850 and 21.2 percent, respectively.

5. You periodically buy a stock for five years starting now and sell the stock at the end of five years for $100,000. What is the return on the investment? The cash flows are as follows.

Year	Cash Outflows	Cash Inflow
now	$15,000	
end of year 1		
beginning of year 2	17,500	

end of year 2	
beginning of year 3	23,000
end of year 3	
beginning of year 4	13,000
end of year 4	
beginning of year 5	7,500
end of year 5	$100,000

The return on the investment is 8.6 percent. This answer is a dollar-weighted return. As is explained in Chapter 10 on returns, an alternative technique calculates time-weighted returns. The results of the two calculations need not be the same.

As these five examples illustrate, there may be situations in which cash flows are not single payments or equal annual payments. Time value principles, however, remain the same. The present may be compounded into the future and the future may be discounted back to the present. Most of the examples and problems in this text are single payments or annuities.

SUMMARY

Money has time value. A dollar to be received in the future is worth less than a dollar received today. People will forgo current consumption only if future growth in their funds is possible. Invested funds earn interest, and the interest in turn earns more interest—a process called compounding. The longer funds compound and the higher the rate at which they compound, the greater will be the final amount in the future.

Discounting, the opposite of compounding, determines the present value of funds to be received in the future. The present value of a future sum depends on how far into the future the funds are to be received and on the discount rate. The farther into the future or the higher the discount factor, the lower will be the present value of the sum.

Compounding and discounting may apply to a single payment (lump sum) or to a series of payments. If the payments are equal, the series is called an annuity. When the payments start at the beginning of each time period, the series is called an annuity due; when the payments are made at the end of each time period, the series is called an ordinary annuity.

Although an investment is made in the present, returns are earned in the future. These returns (e.g., the future flows of interest and dividends) must be discounted by the appropriate discount factor to determine the investment's present value. It is this process of discounting by which an investment's value is determined. As is developed throughout this text, valuation of assets is a crucial step in the selection of assets to acquire and hold in an investor's portfolio.

QUESTIONS

1. What is the difference between a lump-sum payment and an annuity? What is the difference between an ordinary annuity and an annuity due? Are all series of payments annuities?

2. What is the difference between compounding (the determination of future value) and discounting (the determination of present value)?
3. For a given interest rate, what happens to the following as time increases?
    a) future value of $1
    b) future value of an annuity
    c) present value of $1
    d) present value of an annuity
4. For a given time period, what happens to the following as the interest rate increases?
    a) future value of $1
    b) future value of an annuity
    c) present value of $1
    d) present value of an annuity
5. As is explained in subsequent chapters, increases in interest rates cause the value of assets to decline. Why would you expect this relationship?

PROBLEMS

1. A saver places $1,000 in a certificate of deposit that matures after 20 years and that each year pays 4 percent interest, which is compounded annually until the certificate matures.
    a) How much interest will the saver earn if the interest is left to accumulate?
    b) How much interest will the saver earn if the interest is withdrawn each year?
    c) Why are the answers to (a) and (b) different?
2. At the end of each year a self-employed person deposits $1,500 in a retirement account that earns 10 percent annually.
    a) How much will be in the account when the individual retires at the age of 65 if the contributions start when the person is 45 years old?
    b) How much additional money will be in the account if the individual stops making the contribution at age 65 but defers retirement until age 70?
    c) How much additional money will be in the account if the individual continues making the contribution but defers retirement until age 70?
    d) Compare the answers to (b) and (c). What is the effect of continuing the contributions? How much is the difference between the two answers?
3. A saver wants $100,000 after ten years and believes that it is possible to earn an annual rate of 8 percent on invested funds.
    a) What amount must be invested each year to accumulate $100,000 if (1) the payments are made at the beginning of each year or (2) if they are made at the end of each year?
    b) How much must be invested annually if the expected yield is only 5 percent?
4. An investment offers $10,000 per year for 20 years. If an investor can earn 8 percent annually on other investments, what is the current value of this investment? If its current price is $120,000, should the investor buy it?

5. Graduating seniors may earn $45,000 each year. If the annual rate of inflation is 2 percent, what must these graduates earn after 20 years to maintain their current purchasing power? If the rate of inflation rises to 4 percent, will they be maintaining their standard of living if they earn $100,000 after 20 years?

6. A person who is retiring at age 65 and who has $200,000 wants to leave an estate of at least $30,000. How much can the individual draw annually on the $200,000 (starting at the end of the year) if the funds earn 8 percent and the person's life expectancy is 85 years?

7. A 40-year-old individual establishes a retirement account that is expected to earn 7 percent annually. Contributions will be $2,000 annually at the beginning of each year. Initially, the saver expects to start drawing on the account at age 60.
   a) How much will be in the account when the saver is age 60?
   b) If this investor found a riskier investment that offered 10 percent, how much in additional funds would be earned?
   c) The investor selects the 10 percent investment and retires at the age of 60. How much can be drawn from the account at the beginning of each year if life expectancy is 85 and the funds continue to earn 10 percent?

8. You are offered $900 five years from now or $150 at the end of each year for the next five years. If you can earn 6 percent on your funds, which offer will you accept? If you can earn 14 percent on your funds, which offer will you accept? Why are your answers different?

9. The following questions illustrate nonannual compounding.
   a) One hundred dollars is placed in an account that pays 12 percent. How much will be in the account after one year if interest is compounded annually, semiannually, or monthly?
   b) One hundred dollars is to be received after one year. What is the present value of this amount if you can earn 12 percent compounded annually, semiannually, or monthly?

10. At the end of each year, Tom invests $2,000 in a retirement account. Joan also invests $2,000 in a retirement account but makes her deposits at the beginning of each year. They both earn 9 percent on their funds. How much will each have in his or her account at the end of 20 years?

11. You purchase a $100,000 life insurance policy for a single payment of $35,000. If you want to earn 9 percent on invested funds, how soon must you die for the policy to have been the superior alternative? If you die within ten years, what is the return on the investment in life insurance? (Morbid questions, but you might want to view life insurance as an investment alternative. As one financial planner told the author: "Always look at the numbers; analyze life insurance as an investment.")

12. You are offered an annuity of $12,000 a year for 15 years. The annuity payments start after five years have elapsed. If the annuity costs $75,000, is the annuity a good purchase if you can earn 9 percent on invested funds?

13. You purchase a $1,000 asset for $800. It pays $60 a year for seven years at which time you receive the $1,000 principal. Prove that the annual return on this investment is not 9 percent.

14. You invest $1,000 a year for ten years at 10 percent and then invest $2,000 a year for an additional ten years at 10 percent. How much will you have accumulated at the end of the 20 years?

15. You are promised $10,000 a year for six years after which you will receive $5,000 a year for six years. If you can earn 8 percent annually, what is the present value of this stream of payments?

16. A township expects its population of 5,000 to grow annually at the rate of 5 percent. The township currently spends $300 per inhabitant, but, as the result of inflation and wage increments, expects the per capita expenditure to grow annually by 7 percent. How much will the township's budget be after 10, 15, and 20 years?

17. Suppose you purchase a home for $350,000. After making a down payment of $50,000, you borrow the balance through a mortgage loan at 8 percent for 20 years. What is the annual payment required by the mortgage? If you could get a loan for 25 years but had to pay 9 percent annually, what is the difference in the annual payment?

18. You have an elderly aunt, Aunt Kitty, who has just sold her house for $165,000 and entered a retirement community that charges $30,000 annually. If she can earn 6 percent on her funds, how long will the funds from the sale of the house cover the cost of the retirement community?

19. A widower currently has $107,500 yielding 8 percent annually. Can he withdraw $18,234 a year for the next 10 years? If he cannot, what return must he earn in order to withdraw $18,234 annually?

20. You want $100,000 after eight years in order to start a business. Currently you have $26,000, which may be invested to earn 7 percent annually. How much additional money must you set aside each year if these funds also earn 7 percent in order to meet your goal of $100,000 at the end of eight years? By how much would your answer differ if you invested the additional funds at the beginning of each year instead of at the end of each year?

21. You have accumulated $325,000 in a retirement account and continue to earn 8 percent on invested funds.
    a) What amount may you withdraw annually starting today based on a life expectancy of 20 years? How much will be in the account at the end of the first year?
    b) Suppose you take only out 1/20 of the funds today and the remainder continues to earn 8 percent. How much will be in the account at the end of the first year? Compare your answer to (a). Why are they different?

22. Your first child is now a 1-year-old. Tuition currently costs $60,000 to attend a public college for four years. If these costs rise 5 percent annually, how much must you invest each year to cover the expenses after 18 years if you are able to earn 10 percent annually?

23. Which is the better choice when purchasing a $20,000 car:
    a) a four-year loan at 4 percent,
    b) an immediate rebate of $2,000 and a four-year loan at 10 percent?

24. The preceding problems can be solved using the interest tables supplied in Appendix A. To test your ability to construct your own interest factors or to use a financial calculator, solve the following problems.

    a) You place $1,300 in a savings account that pays 5.3 percent annually. How much will you have in the account at the end of six years and three months?

    b) You invest $1,000 annually for seven years and earn 7.65 percent annually. How much interest will you have accumulated at the end of the seventh year?

    c) An investment promises to pay you $10,000 each year for ten years. If you want to earn 8.42 percent on your investments, what is the maximum price you should pay for this asset?

    d) You bought a stock for $10 a share and sold it for $25.60 after 5½ years. What was your annual return (rate of growth) on the investment?

    e) You can earn 7.2 percent annually; how much must you invest annually to accumulate $50,000 after five years?

The Financial Advisor's Investment Case
Funding a Pension Plan

Erin O'Reilly was recently employed by the human resources department of a moderate-sized engineering firm. Management is considering the adoption of a defined-benefit pension plan in which the firm will pay 75 percent of an individual's last annual salary if the employee has worked for the firm for 25 years. The amount of the pension is to be reduced by 3 percent for every year less than 25, so that an individual who has been employed for 15 years will receive a pension of 45 percent of the last year's salary [75 percent – (10 × 3%)]. Pension payments will start at age 65, provided the individual has retired. There is no provision for early retirement. Continuing to work after age 65 may increase the individual's pension if the person has worked for less than 25 years or if the salary were to increase.

One of the first tasks given O'Reilly is to estimate the amount that the firm must set aside today to fund pensions. While management plans to hire actuaries to make the final determination, the managers believe the exercise may highlight some problems that they will want to be able to discuss with the actuaries. O'Reilly was instructed to select two representative employees and estimate their annual pensions and the annual contributions necessary to fund the pensions.

O'Reilly decided to select Arnold Berg and Vanessa Barber. Berg is 58 years old, has been with the firm for 27 years, and is earning $34,000. Barber is 47, has been with the firm for 3 years, and earns $42,000 annually. O'Reilly believes that Berg will be with the firm until he retires; he is a competent worker whose salary will not increase by more than 4 percent annually, and it is anticipated he will retire at age 65. Barber is a more valuable employee, and O'Reilly expects Barber's salary to rise at least 7 percent annually in order to retain her until retirement at age 65.

To determine the amount that must be invested annually to fund each pension, O'Reilly needs (in addition to an estimate of the amount of the pension) an estimate of how long the pension will be distributed (i.e., life expectancy) and how much the invested funds will earn. Since the firm must pay an interest rate of 8 percent to borrow money, she decides that the invested funds should be able to earn at least that amount.

While O'Reilly believes she is able to perform the assignment, she has come to you for assistance to help answer the following questions.

1. If each individual retires at age 65, how much will his or her estimated pension be?
2. Life expectancy for both employees is 15 years at age 65. If the firm buys an annuity from an insurance company to fund each pension and the insurance company asserts it is able to earn 9 percent on the funds invested in the annuity, what is the cost or the amount required to purchase the annuity contracts?
3. If the firm can earn 8 percent on the money it must invest annually to fund the pension, how much will the firm have to invest annually to have the funds necessary to purchase the annuities?
4. What would be the impact of each of the following on the amount that the firm must invest annually to fund the pension?
   a) Life expectancy is increased to 20 years.
   b) The rate of interest on the annuity contract with the insurance company is reduced to 7 percent.
   c) Barber retires at age 62 instead of 65.

Appendix 3

USING EXCEL TO SOLVE TIME VALUE PROBLEMS

Time value problems may also be solved using a spreadsheet such as Excel. In Excel, time value problems may be solved by using the *fx* function under *insert*. Go to the "financial" function category and for a particular problem enter the appropriate data. Excel then determines the answer. The format is similar to that employed by a financial calculator. Amounts are entered as cash inflows or outflows, with outflows being negative numbers. The data to be entered are

Rate	Interest per period (%)
Nper	Number of periods
Pmt	Periodic payment
FV or PV	Future value or Present value
Type	Ordinary annuity or annuity due

(Set type = 0 for an ordinary annuity and = 1 for an annuity due.)

Excel also solves time value problems in which data and the appropriate instructions are entered into cells in a spreadsheet. The unknown is entered first, followed by Rate, Nper, PMT, PV or FV, and type. For example, to answer the question "$1,000 grows to how much in ten years at 10 percent?" use the following form: FV(Rate, Nper, PMT, PV, Type). The unknown (FV) is outside the parentheses and the knowns are inside.

The process for solving this problem is illustrated as follows:

Columns	A	B	C	etc
Rows				
1	FV(Rate,Nper,PMT,PV,Type)			
2	% per period	10%		
3	N of periods	10		
4	Payment	0		
5	Present value	1000		
6	Type	0		

To solve the problem, enter the cells or the actual data. That is, type =FV(b2,b3,b4, −b5,b6) or type =FV(10%,10,0,−1000,0) in an open cell such as B7. The present value is a negative number because it is assumed the $1,000 investment is a cash outflow that will grow into the future amount. This future value will then be received (cash inflow) at the end of the ten years. Once the data are entered in cells B2 through B6 and the instruction is placed in cell B7, the answer $2,593.74 is determined.

What follows is a series of examples that illustrate using Excel. In each case, a simple problem is stated first. The Excel format is given, followed by the data in the order in which each number will be entered. The Excel instructions are given using the individual cells and using the numbers, cells B7 and B8, respectively. (It is not necessary to do both.) The final entry is the numerical answer.

This basic format is employed by Excel to solve time value of money problems. Preference for spreadsheets over financial calculators may depend on convenience and potential usage. For example, material in a spreadsheet may be copied to other documents; this is not possible using a financial calculator.

Case 1: Determine FV of $1

($1,000 grows to how much in ten years at 10%?)

FV(Rate, Nper, PMT, PV, Type)

% per period	10%
N of periods	10
PMT	0
PV	1000
Type	0

Excel instruction:
in cells   =FV(b2,b3,b4,−b5,b6)
or numbers   =FV(10%,10,0,−1000,0)
Answer: $2,593.74

Case 2: Determine PV of $1

($1,000 received after ten years is worth how much today at 10%?)

PV(Rate, Nper, PMT, FV, Type)

% per period	10%
N of periods	10
PMT	0
FV	1000
Type	0

Excel instruction:
in cells   =PV(b2,b3,b4,−b5,b6)
or numbers   =PV(10%,10,0,−1000,0)
Answer: $385.54

Case 3: Determine FV of an ordinary annuity and an annuity due of $1

($2,000 received each year grows to how much in ten years at 10%?)

FV(Rate, Nper, PMT, PV, Type)
Ordinary Annuity

% per period	10%
N of periods	10
PMT	2000
PV	0
Type	0

Excel instruction:
in cells   =FV(b2,b3,−b4,b5,b6)
or numbers   =FV(10%,10,−2000,0,0)
Answer: $31,874.85

FV(Rate, Nper, PMT, PV, Type)
Annuity Due

% per period	10%
N of periods	10
PMT	2000
PV	0
Type	1

Excel instruction:
in cells   =FV(b2,b3,−b4,b5,b6)
or numbers   =FV(10%,10,−2000,0,1)
Answer: $35,062.33

Case 4: Determine PV of an ordinary annuity and an annuity due of $1

($2,000 received each year for ten years is worth how much today at 10%?)

PV(Rate, Nper, PMT, FV, Type)		PV(Rate, Nper, PMT, FV, Type)	
Ordinary Annuity		Annuity Due	
% per period	10%	% per period	10%
N of periods	10	N of periods	10
PMT	2000	PMT	2000
FV	0	FV	0
Type	0	Type	1

Excel instruction:		Excel instruction:	
in cells	=PV(b2,b3,−b4,b5,b6)	in cells	=PV(b2,b3,−b4,b5,b6)
or numbers	=PV(10%,10,−2000,0,0)	or numbers	=PV(10%,10,−2000,0,1)
Answer:	$12,289.13	Answer:	$13,518.05

Case 5: Determine FV of a single payment and an annuity

($1,000 today plus $2,000 each year grows to how much in ten years at 10%?)

FV(Rate, Nper, PMT, PV, Type)		FV(Rate, Nper, PMT, PV, Type)	
Ordinary Annuity		Annuity Due	
% per period	10%	% per period	10%
N of periods	10	N of periods	10
PMT	2000	PMT	2000
PV	1000	PV	1000
Type	0	Type	1

Excel instruction:		Excel instruction:	
in cells	=FV(b2,b3,−b4,−b5,b6)	in cells	=FV(b2,b3,−b4,−b5,b6)
or numbers	=FV(10%,10,−2000, −1000,0)	or numbers	=FV(10%,10,−2000, −1000,1)
Answer:	$34,468.59	Answer:	$37,656.08

Case 6: Determine PV of a single payment and an annuity

($2,000 each year plus $1,000 after ten years is currently worth how much at 10%?)

PV(Rate, Nper, PMT, FV, Type)		PV(Rate, Nper, PMT, FV, Type)	
Ordinary Annuity		Annuity Due	
% per period	10%	% per period	10%
N of periods	10	N of periods	10
PMT	2000	PMT	2000
FV	1000	FV	1000
Type	0	Type	1

Excel instruction:		Excel instruction:	
in cells	=PV(b2,b3,−b4,−b5,b6)	in cells	=PV(b2,b3,−b4,−b5,b6)
or numbers	=PV(10%,10,−2000, −1000,0)	or numbers	=PV(10%,10,−2000, −1000,1)
Answer:	$12,674.68	Answer:	$13,903.59

Case 7: Determine I given PV, FV, and N

a. Single payment
(What is the rate if you invest $500
and receive $1,000 after ten years?)

Rate (Nper, PMT, PV, FV, Type)

N of periods	10
PMT	0
PV	500
FV	1000
Type	0

Excel instruction:
in cells   =RATE(b2,b3,−b4,b5,b6)
or numbers   =RATE(10,0,−500,
                1000,0)
Answer: 7.18%

b. An Ordinary Annuity
(What is the rate if you invest
$10,000 and receive $2,000 a year
for ten years?)

Rate (Nper, PMT, PV, FV, Type)
Ordinary Annuity

N of periods	10
PMT	2000
PV	10000
FV	0
Type	0

Excel instruction:
in cells   =RATE(b2,b3,−b4,b5,b6)
or numbers =RATE(10,2000,
                −10000,0,0)
Answer: 15.10%

c. An Annuity Due
(What is the rate if you invest $10,000 and receive $2,000 at the beginning of each year
for ten years?)

Rate (Nper, PMT, PV, FV, Type)
Annuity Due

N of periods	10
PMT	2000
PV	10000
FV	0
Type	1

Excel instruction:
in cells   =RATE(b2,b3,−b4,b5,b6)
or numbers   =RATE(10,2000,−10000,0,1)
Answer: 20.24%

d. Single payment and Ordinary Annuity
(What is the rate if you invest $10,000 and receive $1,000 after ten years and $2,000
a year for ten years?)

Rate (Nper, PMT, PV, FV, Type)

N of periods	10
PMT	2000
PV	10000
FV	1000
Type	0

Excel instruction:
in cells   =RATE(b2,b3,−b4,b5,b6)
or numbers   =RATE(10,2000,−10000,1000,0)
Answer: 15.72%

e. Single payment and Annuity Due
(What is the rate if you invest $10,000 and receive $1,000 after ten years and $2,000 at the beginning of each year?)

Rate (Nper, PMT, PV, FV, Type)
N of periods   10
PMT   2000
PV   10000
FV   1000
Type   1

Excel instruction:
in cells   =RATE(b2,b3,−b4,b5,b6)
or numbers   =RATE(10,2000,−10000,0,1)
Answer: 20.84%

Case 8: Determine N given PV, FV, and I

a. Single payment
(How long does it take for $500 to grow to $1,000 at 8 percent?)

NPER(I, PMT, PV, FV, Type)
I   8%
PMT   0
PV   500
FV   1000
Type   0

Excel instruction:
in cells   =NPER(b2,b3,−b4,b5,b6)
or numbers   =NPER(8%,0,−500,1000,0)
Answer: 9.01

b. An Ordinary Annuity
(How long will $10,000 last if you withdraw $2,000 a year and earn 8 percent?)

NPER(I, PMT, PV, FV, Type)
Ordinary Annuity
I   8%
PMT   2000
PV   10000
FV   0
Type   0

Excel instruction:
in cells   =NPER(b2,b3,–b4,b5,b6)
or numbers   =NPER(8%,2000,–10000,0,0)
Answer: 6.64

c. An Annuity Due
(How long will $10,000 last if you withdraw $2,000 at the beginning of each year and earn 8 percent?)

NPER(I, PMT, PV, FV, Type)
Ordinary Annuity

I	8%
PMT	2000
PV	10000
FV	0
Type	1

Excel instruction:
in cells   =NPER(b2,b3,−b4,b5,b6)
or numbers   =NPER(8%,2000,−10000,0,1)
Answer: 6.01

d. Single payment and Ordinary Annuity
(How long will $10,000 last if you withdraw $2,000 a year, $1,000 at the end, and earn 8 percent?)

NPER(I, PMT, PV, FV, Type)
Ordinary Annuity

I	8%
PMT	2000
PV	10000
FV	1000
Type	0

Excel instruction:
in cells   =NPER(b2,b3,−b4,b5,b6)
or numbers   =NPER(8%,2000,−10000,1000,0)
Answer: 6.11

e. Single payment and Annuity Due
(How long will $10,000 last if you withdraw $2,000 at the beginning of each year, $1,000 at the end and earn 8 percent?)

NPER(I, PMT, PV, FV, Type)
Ordinary Annuity

I	8%
PMT	2000
PV	10000
FV	1000
Type	1

Excel instruction:
in cells   =NPER(b2,b3,−b4,b5,b6)
or numbers   =NPER(8%,2000,−1000,10000,1)
Answer: 5.52

CHAPTER  4

Financial Planning, Taxation, and the Efficiency of Financial Markets

LEARNING OBJECTIVES

After completing this chapter you should be able to:

1. Identify possible financial goals.
2. Construct an individual's balance sheet and cash budget.
3. Explain the importance of asset allocation to a portfolio's return.
4. Identify the taxes that affect investment decisions.
5. Illustrate how capital losses are used to offset capital gains and ordinary income.
6. Explain how pension plans, IRAs, Keogh accounts, and 401(k) accounts are tax shelters.
7. Explain the importance of the speed of price changes to efficient markets.
8. Differentiate among the three forms of the efficient market hypothesis.
9. Describe several anomalies that are inconsistent with the efficient market hypothesis.
10. Differentiate between active and passive portfolio management strategies and the investor's belief in the efficiency of financial markets.

A portfolio is not an end but a means to achieve financial goals. An investor needs a purpose or financial goal (or goals) that require the individual to save and not spend. After saving, the individual is faced with an important decision: what to do with the savings. The answer to that question guides the selection of specific assets the investor acquires. Financial planning and the construction of the portfolio should not be done in a vacuum. The portfolio should be designed to meet the individual's specified financial goals.

Financial planning is a process by which the individual specifies financial goals, identifies financial resources and obligations, and allocates the assets into a diversified portfolio to meet the goals. Of course, this process is affected by external considerations such as the expectation of inflation and taxation. In addition, changes in the individual's economic or family environment may also have an important impact on financial planning. These changes can and often do require altering the portfolio and its allocation among various assets.

This chapter is concerned with financial planning. Initially, the chapter briefly covers determining financial goals and identifying the individual's assets, liabilities, and cash flows. The second section introduces the importance of asset allocation to financial planning and portfolio construction. The third section is devoted to selected topics in taxation that affect investment decisions. This section emphasizes capital gains and tax shelters, pension plans, and retirement accounts. The chapter ends with the efficient market hypothesis. Portfolios designed to meet specified financial goals are constructed in efficient financial markets. Investors need to be aware that outperforming the market on a consistent basis is rare and that taking excessive risk will, in all likelihood, result in the individual's failure to meet the specified financial goals.

THE PROCESS OF FINANCIAL PLANNING

To construct a portfolio, the investor starts by defining its purpose. There must be some goal (or goals) to guide the selection of the assets that should be included. After specifying realistic financial objectives, the next step is determining which assets are appropriate to meet the goals. After establishing investment goals and identifying assets that may meet the goals, the investor should determine the resources and sources of income with which he or she has to work. The investor then can construct a financial plan designed to fulfill the investment goals within the constraints.

The Specification of Investment Goals

The purpose of investing is to transfer purchasing power from the present to the future. A portfolio is a store of value designed to meet the investor's reasons for postponing the consumption of goods and services from the present to the future. Possible goals include the following:

1. The capacity to meet financial emergencies
2. The financing of specific future purchases, such as the down payment for a home
3. The provision for income at retirement
4. The ability to leave a sizable estate to heirs or to charity
5. The ability to speculate or receive enjoyment from accumulating and managing wealth

financial life cycle

The stages of life during which individuals accumulate and subsequently use financial assets.

In addition to these specific investment goals, many individuals have general financial objectives that are related to their age, income, and wealth. Individuals go through phases, often referred to as a **financial life cycle**. The cycle has three stages: (1) a period of accumulation, (2) a period of preservation, and (3) a period of the use or depletion of the investor's assets.

During the period of accumulation, the individual generates income but expenditures on housing, transportation, and education often exceed cash inflows, which increases debt. Yet individuals with debt (e.g., a mortgage, car payments, or student loans) often start the process of accumulating assets, especially by participating in tax-deferred pension plans. Such participation, especially if the employee's contributions are matched by the employer, may be one of the best investment strategies any individual can follow.

During the period of preservation, income often exceeds expenditures. Individuals reduce debt (e.g., pay off the mortgages on their homes) and continue to accumulate assets. The emphasis, however, may change to preservation of existing assets in addition to the continued accumulation of wealth. Since investors will need a substantial amount of wealth upon reaching retirement, they must continue to take moderate or prudent risk to earn a sufficient return to finance their retirement.

During the period when assets are consumed, most individuals will no longer have salary or wage income. Even though a pension and Social Security replace lost income, many individuals must draw down their assets to meet expenditures. While the assets that are retained continue to earn a return, the amount of both risk and return are reduced as safety of principal becomes increasingly important. These individuals, however, continue to need some growth. A married couple, both age 65, have a combined life expectancy of at least 20 years. Such a long time horizon argues for the inclusion of equities in their portfolio.

An Analysis of the Individual's Environment and Financial Resources

Financial planning requires an analysis of the individual's environment and financial resources. One's environment includes such factors as age, health, employment, and family. In addition to environment, the investor should take an accurate account of financial resources. This may be done by constructing two financial statements. The first one enumerates what is owned and owed, and the other enumerates cash receipts and disbursements. The former is, of course, a balance sheet, whereas the latter is a cash budget.

The entries for a balance sheet are given in Exhibit 4.1, which considers the individual's financial position currently and for some time in the future, such as at anticipated retirement or when a child will attend college. For the purposes of financial planning, individuals should both construct their current financial position and project what that position may be in the future. The projected balance sheet requires assumptions such as (1) the ability to retire debt and accumulate assets and (2) the return that will be earned by the assets. Although the projections will depend on the assumptions, they often bring the individual's financial needs into sharp focus and can help establish investment strategies.

The balance sheets in Exhibit 4.1 are less detailed than is necessary for financial planning, but they do illustrate the concept. The mechanics of constructing a balance sheet are relatively easy. The difficult part is enumerating the assets and placing values on them. Such valuation is easy for publicly traded securities, such as stocks and bonds. The difficulty concerns placing value on tangible personal assets such as collectibles and real estate. Since the purpose of constructing a balance sheet is to determine the individual's financial condition, it may be advisable to be conservative in estimating the value of such assets. If, for example, the individual had to sell antiques to finance living expenses, it would be better to underestimate than to overestimate the prices for which these assets may be sold.

cash budget

A financial statement enumerating cash receipts and cash disbursements.

After listing what is owned and what is owed, the next step is to construct a **cash budget**. A cash budget enumerates receipts and disbursements and may cover a period such as a month or a year. Exhibit 4.2 illustrates the entries needed for the construction of a simplified cash budget. It lists the individual's sources of receipts (e.g., salary, interest income, and dividends) and the individual's disbursements (e.g., mortgage payments, living expenses, and taxes). Like the balance sheet, the cash budget may be constructed for the present and projected to a specified time in the future.

If the individual's receipts exceed disbursements, the excess becomes a source of funds that may be invested to finance future needs. If disbursements exceed receipts, more funds are spent than are received. This implies that the individual's outstanding debts are increasing or assets are being consumed. Constructing the cash budget thus determines where funds are coming from and where they are going. This information should help the individual perceive ways to increase receipts and decrease disbursements, thus generating additional funds for investments.

EXHIBIT 4.1	A Simplified Balance Sheet for an Individual	Present	Future
ASSETS			
1. Bank deposits			
a. Checking accounts		____	____
b. Savings accounts		____	____
c. Certificates of deposit		____	____
	Subtotal	____	____
2. Liquid financial assets			
a. Money market mutual funds		____	____
b. Treasury bills		____	____
c. Tax refunds and other payments owed		____	____
	Subtotal	____	____
3. Retirement and savings plans			
a. IRA accounts		____	____
b. Employee retirement accounts		____	____
c. Employee savings plans		____	____
d. Deferred compensation		____	____
e. Company options		____	____
	Subtotal	____	____
4. Long-term financial assets			
a. Treasury bonds		____	____
b. Corporate bonds		____	____
c. Municipal bonds		____	____
d. Corporate stock		____	____
e. Mutual funds		____	____
	Subtotal	____	____
5. Tangible assets			
a. Real estate: home		____	____
b. Real estate investment properties		____	____
c. Automobiles		____	____
d. Collectibles		____	____
e. Personal tangible property		____	____
	Subtotal	____	____
Total Assets		____	____
LIABILITIES			
1. Short-term			
a. Credit card balances		____	____
b. Current portion of car loan		____	____
c. Current portion of mortgage		____	____
d. Other		____	____
	Subtotal	____	____
2. Long-term			
a. Balance on car loan		____	____
b. Balance on mortgage		____	____
c. Other long-term debts		____	____
	Subtotal	____	____
Total Liabilities		____	____
SUMMARY			
Total assets		____	____
Total liabilities		____	____
NET Worth (value of estate; assets minus liabilities)		____	____

EXHIBIT 4.2	A Simplified Cash Budget for an Individual		

		Present	Future
CASH RECEIPTS			
1. Salary (after deductions)		_____	_____
2. Social Security		_____	_____
3. Pension		_____	_____
4. Interest		_____	_____
5. Dividends		_____	_____
6. Distributions from retirement accounts		_____	_____
7. Annuities		_____	_____
8. Other receipts		_____	_____
Total receipts		_____	_____

		Present	Future
CASH DISBURSEMENTS			
1. Housing			
a. Mortgage payments		_____	_____
b. Rent		_____	_____
c. Maintenance		_____	_____
d. Utilities		_____	_____
e. Operating expenses		_____	_____
f. Property taxes		_____	_____
g. Insurance		_____	_____
2. Personal expenses			
a. Dining		_____	_____
b. Personal care		_____	_____
c. Automobile		_____	_____
d. Clothing		_____	_____
e. Recreation		_____	_____
f. Hobbies		_____	_____
g. Other		_____	_____
3. Medical expenses			
1. Insurance		_____	_____
2. Doctors		_____	_____
3. Other		_____	_____
4. Other cash disbursements			
a. Gifts		_____	_____
b. Contributions		_____	_____
c. Estimated taxes		_____	_____
d. Other		_____	_____

SUMMARY			
Total receipts		_____	_____
Total disbursements		_____	_____
Difference between receipts and disbursements		_____	_____

ASSET ALLOCATION

Once the individual has established financial goals and identified resources to invest, he or she constructs a portfolio to meet those goals. The individual's funds are allocated to various assets in order to achieve both risk reduction through diversification and a portfolio designed to reach the financial goals. This process is often referred to as *asset allocation*. Asset allocation is the process of determining what proportion of the portfolio should be invested in various classes of assets; that is, what percentage of the portfolio should be invested in equities, what proportion should be invested in debt securities, and what proportion should be held in cash or accounts that may be readily converted into cash, such as the money market mutual funds covered in Chapter 6.

This process of asset allocation may be further refined to cover the distribution of the equity component into various sectors. For example, a financial planner may recommend that a client invest (allocate) 60 percent of the portfolio to equities, 30 percent to bonds, and 10 percent to cash. The 60 percent to be held in equities could then be allocated to various sectors of the economy. If, however, the investor favors a specific sector such as consumer staples or technology, the equity component of the asset allocation could be tilted in favor of the preferred sectors and less could be invested in the remaining sectors.

Once the desired asset allocation is determined and the portfolio is constructed, changes in securities prices will alter the asset allocation. For example, an increase in stock prices may alter the allocation to 70 percent equities, 23 percent bonds, and 7 percent cash. The original asset allocation of 60/30/10 no longer holds, so the individual rebalances the portfolio by selling some of the stocks to invest the proceeds in bonds and increase cash. A reduction in stock prices would lead to the opposite rebalancing with the investor selling some of the bonds and using the proceeds and cash to purchase stocks.

The initial asset allocation, however, is not set in stone and maintained indefinitely. As the investor's situation changes and as the investor ages, the asset allocation should change. The birth of a child or the approach of retirement may suggest that the previous allocation is no longer appropriate and a new asset allocation should be determined. Of course, the new allocation may require altering the portfolio. This dynamic process of determining the appropriate asset allocation and then adjusting the portfolio increases the likelihood that the individual's financial objectives will be met.

The importance of asset allocation took on an entirely new dimension with the publication in 1986 of an article by Brinson, Hood, and Beebower. Essentially, the authors decomposed the return by a portfolio into three components: (1) investment policy, (2) market timing, and (3) asset selection.[1] The decomposition then determined the portfolio manager's contribution, since the components could be compared to a passive benchmark such as the S&P 500 stock index. The results startled the investment community; 93.6 percent of the observed variation in returns was attributed to the investment policy and the portfolio's asset allocation. The impact of market timing and specific asset selection was minor. These results are consistent with the efficient market hypothesis (covered later in this chapter), which asserts that on a risk-adjusted basis, active investment management will not lead to superior results.

---

[1]Gary P. Brinson, L. Randolph Hood, and Gilbert L. Beebower, "Determinants of Portfolio Performance," *Financial Analysts Journal* (July-August 1986): 39–44.

As much of this text explains and illustrates, there are many ways to achieve asset allocation. The existence of mutual funds, index funds, exchange-traded funds, and stocks and bonds, and the ease with which these assets may be bought and sold, facilitate the construction of a portfolio that meets a particular asset allocation. If the values of particular assets change and the portfolio deviates from the specified allocation, the funds are easily shifted from one asset to another to restore the desired balance.

A large portion of this text is devoted to those specific assets, since you need to know their features and characteristics in order to make informed investment decisions. Stocks and bonds differ with regard to risk, potential returns, and valuation. Even within a type of security such as bonds, there can be considerable variation. A corporate bond is different from a municipal bond, and a convertible bond differs from a straight bond that lacks the conversion feature. You need to know and understand these differences in order to know the asset's potential impact on the portfolio. When you understand how individual assets are valued, their potential sources of return, and the risks associated with each asset, then you may allocate your resources to construct a portfolio designed to realize specified financial goals.

TAXATION

The remainder of this chapter is devoted to taxation and the efficient market hypothesis. Taxation occurs at many levels: federal, state, and local. This discussion applies only to federal taxation and is limited to taxes that affect investment decisions: the taxation of capital gains and losses from the sale of securities and the tax shelters associated with pension and retirement plans. As the subsequent discussion will highlight, there are important differences between long-term and short-term gains. These taxes alter your net return on an investment. There are also tax shelters associated with pension planning that may affect your decision about how to allocate your assets among various accounts. Knowledge of these tax laws may not make you a better investor, but it should make you aware of the tax implications of your investment decisions.

Capital Gains and Losses

capital gain

The increase in the value of an asset such as a stock or a bond.

capital loss

A decrease in the value of an asset such as a stock or a bond.

Many investments are purchased and subsequently sold. If the sale results in a profit, that profit is considered a **capital gain**; if the sale results in a loss, that is a **capital loss**. If the gain or loss is realized within a year, it is a short-term capital gain or loss. If the sale occurs after a year from the date of purchase, it is a long-term gain or loss.

Short-term capital gains are taxed at the individual's marginal tax rate. Thus, if an investor buys a stock for $10,000 and sells it for $13,000 after nine months, the $3,000 short-term capital gain is taxed as any other source of taxable income. If the stock had been held for 15 months, the $3,000 long-term capital gain would be taxed at no more than 15 percent, depending on the individual's marginal tax rate. Thus, for individuals in the 33 percent marginal tax bracket, long-term capital gains are taxed at 15 percent. An individual in the 33 percent tax bracket would pay $990 on a $3,000 short-term capital gain, while a $3,000 long-term capital gain generates $450 in taxes, a reduction of $540. (These rates applied as of January 2010 and are subject to changes in the tax laws.)

The investor may use capital losses to offset capital gains. If the investor bought a second stock for $15,000 and sold it for $12,000, the $3,000 loss would offset the $3,000 capital gain. This offsetting of capital gains by capital losses applies to both short- and long-term gains. However, there is a specified order in which losses offset gains.

Initially short-term losses are used to offset short-term gains, and long-term losses are used to offset long-term gains. If there is a net short-term loss (i.e., short-term losses exceed short-term gains), it is used to offset long-term gains. For example, if an investor has realized net short-term losses of $3,000, that short-term loss may be used to offset up to $3,000 in long-term capital gains. If net short-term losses are less than long-term gains, the resulting net capital gain is taxed as long-term.

If there is a net long-term loss (i.e., long-term losses exceed long-term gains), the loss is used to offset short-term gains. For example, $3,000 in net long-term capital losses is used to offset up to $3,000 in short-term capital gains. If a married couple files separate returns, the limitation is $1,500 per return. Filing separately cannot double the deductible loss to $6,000. If net long-term losses are less than short-term gains, the resulting net capital gain is taxed as short-term.

If the investor has a net short- or long-term capital loss after subtracting short- or long-term capital gains, that net capital loss is used to offset income from other sources, such as dividends or interest. However, *only $3,000 in capital losses may be used in a given year to offset income from other sources*. If the loss is larger (e.g., $5,000), only $3,000 may be used in the current year. The remainder ($2,000) is carried forward to offset capital gains or income received in future years. Under this system of carry-forward, a current capital loss of $10,000 offsets only $3,000 in current income and the remaining $7,000 is carried forward to offset capital gains and income in subsequent years. If there are no capital gains in the second year, only $3,000 of the remaining loss offsets income in the second year and the balance ($4,000) is carried forward to the third year. In the case of a large capital loss, this $3,000 limitation may be an incentive for the investor to take gains in the current year rather than carry forward the loss.

Even if capital gains are taxed at the same rate as ordinary income, they are still illustrative of a tax shelter. The taxes on capital gains may be deferred indefinitely, because investment profits are taxed only after they have been realized. Many profits on security positions are only **paper profits**, because some investors do not sell the securities and realize the gains. The tax laws encourage such retention of securities by taxing the gains only when they are realized.

Capital gains taxes can be avoided entirely if the individual holds the securities until he or she dies. The value of securities is taxed as part of the deceased's estate. The securities are then transferred through the deceased's will to other individuals, such as children or grandchildren, and the cost basis becomes the security's value as of the date of death. For example, suppose an individual owns shares of IBM that were purchased in the 1960s. The current value of the shares is probably many times their cost. If the investor were to sell these shares, he or she would incur a large capital gain. However, if the shares are held until the investor dies, their new cost basis becomes the current value of the shares, and the capital gains tax on the appreciation is avoided.

paper profits
Price appreciation that has not been realized.

The Wash Sale

Suppose an investor had purchased Merck for $50 a share and it is currently selling for $30. The investor has a paper loss. Can the investor sell a stock for the loss and immediately repurchase it? The answer is yes, but the investor cannot take a tax loss on the sale. The sale of a stock for a loss and an immediate repurchase is a "wash sale," and the loss is not allowed for tax purposes. While the federal tax code does not prohibit the investor from repurchasing the stock, the laws disallow the loss if the taxpayer buys the stock within 30 days prior to or 30 days after the date of the sale.

What other options are available? First, the investor could sell the stock and repurchase it after the 30 days have lapsed. Of course, the stock's price could rise during the 30 days, in which case the individual forgoes the potential gain. Second, the investor could buy an additional 100 shares of Merck, hold the 200 shares for the required 30 days, and then sell the initial 100 shares. The risk associated with this strategy is a continued price decline, in which case the investor would sustain a loss on both the original shares *and* the second purchase. Third, the investor could buy a stock in a similar company (e.g., sell Merck and purchase Johnson & Johnson). This strategy's risk is that Merck and Johnson & Johnson may not be perfect substitutes for each other; Merck stock could rise while Johnson & Johnson stock declines.

The wash sale rule applies not only to sales of stock but also to other financial assets, such as bonds and shares in mutual funds. The basic principle is that the individual cannot purchase "substantially identical" securities within the 30 days before or after the sale. Selling Merck and immediately repurchasing it is obviously a trade in substantially identical securities. Selling Merck and immediately repurchasing Johnson & Johnson is obviously *not* a substantially identical security trade. However, selling AT&T 6 percent bonds due in 2025 and repurchasing AT&T 5.8 percent bonds due in

⊕ Point of Interest

THE SPECIFIC SHARE METHOD FOR IDENTIFYING SHARES SOLD OR REDEEMED

When shares are sold, the gains are subject to capital gains taxation. When the investor sells only part of the holdings, the general rule is first-in, first-out. That is, the first shares purchased are the first to be sold. Since share values tend to rise, first-in, first-out usually generates more taxes. This potential difference in taxes is illustrated in a simple example in which the investor makes the following three purchases of 100 shares:

	Cost Basis	Holding Period
100 shares	$1,000	4 years
100 shares	$2,000	3 years
100 shares	$3,000	2 years

The cost basis rises with the more recent purchases.

The current price of a share is $40 and the investor sells 100 shares for $4,000. Under first-in, first-out, the shares bought four years ago were sold; the long-term capital gain is $3,000. Obviously the tax will be larger than if the last shares were sold and the long-term capital gain is only $1,000. Can the investor sell the shares acquired more recently and retain the first shares? If the investor can sell the last shares instead of the first shares, the capital gains tax owed is obviously less. (If the last shares were held for less than a year and are subject to short-term capital gains tax rates—that is, the investor's marginal income tax rate—it may be more advantageous to use first-in, first-out. Depending on the amount of the gain, the long-term capital gains tax may be lower.)

The answer to the question is yes. The investor uses the "specific share method," which identifies the particular shares that were sold. The IRS, however, will not accept the investor's claim that the last shares were sold. The investor must notify the broker in writing of which shares were sold and receive written confirmation of the sale. Brokers will, of course, provide the written confirmation, but the investor must take the initiative and request it. Without the written confirmation from the fund or the broker, the first-in, first-out rule applies. Investors in mutual funds have an additional alternative. They can average the cost of a fund's shares and use that amount for the cost basis. Averaging to determine the cost basis is not available for investors in stock, who must use first-in, first-out or the specific share method.

2024 is ambiguous. The bonds are so similar that they may be considered "substantially identical." If the 5.8 percent bonds had been issued by Verizon, or were even issued by AT&T but due in 2015, then the securities would not be substantially identical.

An investor in mutual funds may encounter a problem if the dividend distributions are reinvested. If an investor sells part of his or her holdings for a loss on December 10 and the mutual fund pays a dividend that is reinvested (used to purchase additional shares) on December 20, then 30 days have not elapsed. This is a wash sale and the tax loss will be disallowed. This scenario will be avoided if individuals accumulate but do not sell the shares. For individuals, such as retirees, who reinvest dividend payments while systematically withdrawing cash from the mutual fund, the possibility exists that the wash sale rule will disallow the tax benefits of selling the shares for a loss.

PENSION PLANS

One tax shelter that also eases the financial burden of retirement is the pension plan. The company specifies the worker's annual pension, such as 75 percent of the last year's salary, provided that the employee had been with the company for 25 years. If the employee had worked for the company 20 years, the annual pension would be 50 percent of the last year's salary. Since the company determines the amount and the conditions, such pensions are referred to as *defined benefit*.

Defined benefit pension plans have some obvious advantages to both the employer and the employee. To maximize the benefit, individuals need to remain with the company, which reduces employee turnover. Defined benefit plans require no contributions by the employee. Of course, these individuals can save and accumulate additional assets, but they do not have to contribute to the employer's pension plan.

Defined benefit plans, however, have major disadvantages. Remaining with the company to receive the maximum benefit reduces the worker's ability to change jobs. This is a major disadvantage in today's work environment, since most individuals change jobs with some degree of frequency. Defined benefit plans also require firms to set aside the money to "fund" the pension. Not all firms have done this. They have "unfunded" pension liabilities, implying that the promised pension may not be paid. In addition, some firms do fail and have few, if any, assets to cover the promised pensions.

The alternative corporate pension is the *401(k)*, which is a *defined contribution* plan. These plans permit the employee to contribute a portion of earned income, up to a specified limit, to a savings plan. In many cases, the company will match a percentage of the contribution. The employee's contribution is deducted from earnings before determining taxable income, which reduces the individual's federal taxes. The funds are taxed when the individual withdraws the money; this deferral of income taxes means that 401(k) plans illustrate a tax shelter. The contributed funds may be invested in one or several alternatives offered by the company, such as a stock fund, bond fund, or money market fund. The employee can choose how to distribute the contribution among the choices, and the plans permit the employee to shift funds among the alternatives at periodic intervals.

Nonprofit organizations, such as hospitals, religious organizations, public and private schools, and foundations may also offer similar salary reduction plans, referred to as *403(b)* plans. They work essentially in the same way as 401(k) plans. In both cases, the employee's income is reduced by the contribution so that federal income tax is deferred until the funds are withdrawn. The contributions are invested, and the tax on the investment earnings and gains is also deferred until the funds are withdrawn.

Individual Retirement Plans (IRAs)

One criticism of employer-sponsored pension plans was that they were not available to all workers. However, Congress passed legislation that enables all employees as well as the self-employed to establish their own pension plans; thus, the tax shelter that was previously provided only through employer-sponsored pension plans is now available to all workers. An employee who is not covered by a pension plan may set up an **individual retirement account (IRA)**. In 1981 Congress passed additional legislation that extended IRAs to all employees, even if they are already participating in an employer-sponsored pension plan.

individual retirement account (IRA)

An individual retirement plan that is available to workers.

As of January 2009, an individual worker may open an account with a financial institution, such as a commercial bank, savings and loan association (S&L), brokerage firm, or mutual fund company, and may deposit up to $5,000 per year. The funds must be earned, which means that any employee who earns $5,000 or more may place as much as $5,000 in an IRA account. However, if the individual's source of income is dividends or interest, these funds cannot be placed in an IRA.

The amount invested in the IRA is deducted from the individual's taxable income. Income earned by the funds in the account is also not taxed. All taxes are deferred until the funds are withdrawn from the IRA, and then they are taxed as ordinary income. If the individual prematurely withdraws the funds (before age 59½), the money is taxed as ordinary income and a penalty tax is added.

IRA accounts soon became one of the most popular tax shelters, but Congress placed important restrictions on the deductibility of the IRA contribution. For workers *covered by a pension plan*, full deductibility is applicable only for couples filing a joint return with adjusted gross income (in 2010) of *less than* $89,000. (For single workers covered by a pension plan the limit is $55,000.) Note that adjusted gross income is used and not earned income. If an individual earns a modest salary but has significant amounts of interest or dividend income, this additional income counts when determining the deductibility of IRA contributions. Once the cutoff level of income is reached, the deductibility of the contribution is reduced, so that it is completely phased out once the couple reaches adjusted gross income of $109,000 ($65,000 for individuals).

It is important to emphasize that the complete loss of deductibility of the IRA contribution applies only to workers filing a joint return who earn more than $109,000 ($65,000 filing a single return). For the majority of workers, the deductibility of the IRA contribution still applies. And the deductibility still applies to any individual, no matter what the level of income, who is not covered by an employer-sponsored pension plan.

Initially, the deductible IRA required the individual to be working in order to set up the account. For married couples, this meant that both had to be working for both to take advantage of a tax-deductible IRA. Under current tax laws, both spouses may have a tax-deductible IRA provided that at least one of them has earned income equal to the retirement contributions. A question now arises: In whose account, the husband's or the wife's, should the funds be placed? From a tax perspective, the answer is whoever is younger, which is probably the wife. Since withdrawals do not have to start until the individual is 70½, the funds may remain in the account for a longer period of time, continuing to

⊕ **Point of Interest**

WHEN TO START AN IRA

Although an individual worker's ability to establish an IRA is constrained by the availability of funds, the earlier the account is started, the better. Since many young workers often have other priorities for which they are saving (e.g., a down payment on a house) and are not contemplating retirement, they may delay opening an IRA. This is unfortunate, because the final amount in the account is greatly enhanced if the deposits are made at an early age.

This difference in the terminal value is illustrated by the following examples. An individual deposits $1,000 in an IRA starting at age 25 and continues the contribution

for 40 years (i.e., until age 65). If the funds earn 8 percent annually, the account grows to $259,050. If the same individual started the account at age 45 and contributed $2,000 annually until age 65, the account would have $91,524. Even though total contributions in both cases are $40,000, the final amounts are considerably different. When the funds are deposited earlier, they earn more interest, which produces the larger terminal value. Thus it is to the individual's benefit to start IRA contributions as soon as possible, even if the amount of the contributions is modest.

compound tax-deferred. In addition, the wife may have a greater need for the funds during her old age, since the probability is higher that she will be the surviving spouse. Of course, once the funds are in the wife's name, she is the owner and controls the account.

Keogh Accounts

Keogh account (HR-10 plan)

A retirement plan that is available to self-employed individuals.

Self-employed persons may establish a pension plan called a **Keogh account** or **HR-10 plan**. The account is named after the congressman who sponsored the enabling legislation. A Keogh is similar to an IRA or a company-sponsored pension plan. The individual places funds in the account and deducts the amount from taxable income. The funds placed in the account earn a return that (like the initial contributions) will not be taxed until the funds are withdrawn. As in the case of the IRA, there is a penalty for premature withdrawals before age 59½, and withdrawals must start after reaching age 70½.

The determination of the amount an individual may contribute to a Keogh account is somewhat confusing. The individual may contribute up to 25 percent of net earned income, but the calculation of net earned income subtracts the pension contribution as a business expense. The effect is that the individual can contribute 20 percent of income before the contribution. Consider a self-employed individual who earns $100,000 before the pension contribution. If that individual contributes $20,000 (i.e., 20 percent of $100,000), he or she has contributed 25 percent of income after deducting the pension contribution:

Net income after contribution: $100,000 − $20,000 = $80,000.

Contribution as percent of net earned income: $20,000/$80,000 = 25%.

It is probably easier to determine one's maximum possible contribution by taking 20 percent of income before the contribution than by determining 25 percent of net earned income.[2]

---

[2]The formula for determining the maximum contribution is $\dfrac{\text{income} \times 0.25}{1 + 0.25}$.

If the individual's income is $100,000, the maximum contribution is $\dfrac{\$100,000 \times 0.25}{1 + 0.25} = \dfrac{\$25,000}{1.25} = \$20,000.$

⊕ **Point of Interest**

THE USE OF PERSONAL COMPUTERS TO COMPLETE YOUR 1040

For many investors, record keeping, tax planning, and the completion of tax forms required for filing with the IRS can be complicated, time-consuming, and expensive. However, by using a personal computer and a tax preparation package, the investor may significantly reduce the amount of work necessary for the completion of the required tax forms. There are many tax packages to choose among, including *Turbo Tax* from Intuit and *J. K. Lasser's Your Income Tax*. The investor should consider the following when acquiring such a program.

- The investor needs to identify the use of the program. There are many tax packages available, offering a wide range of features. Modest tax packages will complete the most frequently used tax schedules (e.g., form 1040 and schedules A, B, C, D, and E). If, however, the

investor needs to complete other schedules, a more elaborate (and more expensive) program may be necessary.

- Computer programs designed to complete tax papers are "cookbooks." They can do only what the investor tells them to perform. Their primary advantages are the reduction in mathematical errors and the simplification of both tax planning and the completion of the tax forms. For example, the investor may enter into the program charitable deductions, interest expenses, or business deductions throughout the year. Such running entries will simplify year-end tax planning. However, the investor must still know what to enter. The tax preparation package is not a substitute for knowledge of the tax laws.

A self-employed person may open an IRA in addition to a Keogh account. The contribution to the IRA, however, may not be deductible from taxable income if the individual's income exceeds the limits discussed above. If the self-employed person has funds to finance only one account, it is probably more advantageous to have the Keogh account because the amount that may be contributed (and sheltered from current income taxes) is larger.

If a self-employed person does open a Keogh plan, it must also apply to other people employed by this individual. There are some exceptions, such as new and young employees; however, if a self-employed individual establishes a Keogh account for himself or herself, other regular employees cannot be excluded. By establishing the account, the self-employed individual takes on fiduciary responsibilities for the management of Keogh accounts for his or her employees.

This individual can avoid these responsibilities by establishing a *Simplified Employee Pension (SEP)* plan. SEPs were designed by Congress to encourage small employers to establish pension plans for their employees while avoiding the complexities of the pension laws. In a SEP plan, employers make IRA contributions on behalf of employees and thus avoid the administrative costs associated with developing their own pension plans. The limitations on contributions to regular IRA accounts do not apply to SEP plans. In addition to employee contributions, the tax law permits employers to use salary reductions to make contributions to their SEP, so the SEP-IRA can also serve as a 401(k) plan.

Nondeductible IRAs—The Roth IRA

In 1997, enabling legislation created the Roth IRA, named after its sponsor, Senator Roth from Delaware. Like the deductible IRA, the Roth IRA is designed to encourage saving for retirement and is an illustration of a tax shelter. However, unlike the traditional IRA in which the contributions are deducted up front, the Roth IRA's advantage occurs when the funds are withdrawn. While the contributions are not tax deductible, the *withdrawals are not subject to income tax*. As was explained earlier, withdrawals from a deductible IRA are subject to income taxation.

Like the deductible IRA, the Roth IRA is subject to limitations concerning the amount of the contribution. For 2010 the limitation is $5,000 annually for an individual's account. Contributions may be made as long as adjusted gross income is less than $167,000 ($105,000 if single). For adjusted gross income in excess of these levels, the contributions are phased out.

You can have both types of IRAs but cannot contribute $5,000 to each. You could invest $2,500 in each account for a total of $5,000, but that strategy avoids the important question: Which is better; the deductible or the nondeductible IRA? The deductible provides an immediate tax break but you pay taxes later. The nondeductible requires that you pay the tax now and receive the tax break later. Which is better depends on your current tax bracket and your anticipated tax bracket, and as is illustrated in Appendix 4, there may be no difference between the two alternatives.

Tax-Deferred Annuities

tax-deferred annuity
A contract sold by an insurance company in which the company guarantees a series of payments and whose earnings are not taxed until they are distributed.

In addition to tax-deferred pension plans, an individual may acquire a **tax-deferred annuity**, which is a contract for a series of payments in the future whose earnings are not subject to current income taxation. Tax-deferred annuities are sold by life insurance companies, and they work like life insurance in reverse. Instead of periodically paying for the insurance, the individual who owns the annuity receives regular payments from the insurance company. A tax-deferred annuity has two components: a period in which funds accumulate and a period in which payments are made by the insurance company to the owner of the annuity.

The investor buys the annuity by making a payment to the insurance company (e.g., a lump-sum distribution from a pension plan may be used to buy an annuity). The insurance company then invests the funds and contractually agrees to a repayment schedule, which can start immediately or at some other time specified in the contract. While the funds are left with the insurance company, they earn a return for the annuity's owner. The individual's personal income tax obligation on these funds is deferred until the earnings are actually paid out by the insurance company. Since the tax on the earnings is deferred, it is possible that the amount of tax actually paid will be less than would have been the case if the earnings were taxed as accumulated.

Many individuals use annuities to accumulate funds for retirement. If after reaching retirement their income has fallen, their tax bracket may be reduced. In this case, the withdrawals from the annuity will be taxed at a lower rate. Of course, it is possible that if the individual has saved sufficiently through pension plans, IRA accounts, Keogh accounts, and personal savings, the tax bracket could be higher instead of lower when funds are withdrawn from any of the tax-sheltered accounts (including the tax-deferred annuity). But even if a higher tax rate were to apply in the future, the individual still would have had the advantage of tax-free accumulation during the period when the tax obligation was deferred.

THE EFFICIENT MARKET HYPOTHESIS

The first sections of this chapter have provided a basic introduction to financial planning, asset allocation, and taxation that affects investment decisions. Initially you determine your financial goals and analyze your financial position. Then you allocate your resources to construct a portfolio designed to meet your financial objectives. Your understanding of taxation should help you allocate your resources to better manage your tax obligations. All of your investment decisions, however, are made in financial markets that are competitive. You need to be aware of that competitiveness and one of its important implications: Financial markets are very efficient.

Perhaps it is conceit that makes some individuals think they can beat the market. The important consideration from a financial planning perspective, however, is not beating the market but earning a return that is commensurate with the risk you bear. If you bear more risk, you should earn a higher return, but that does not necessarily mean you beat the market on a risk-adjusted basis.

The distinction between "beating the market" and "beating the market on a risk-adjusted basis" is important. The popular press often compares returns to the return on the market and announces that X outperformed (or underperformed) the market. Frequently, comparisons are on an absolute basis and not on a risk-adjusted basis. Of course, if a particular portfolio manager pursues a risky strategy, that individual should earn a higher return (i.e., beat the market on an absolute basis). Conversely, if an individual manages a conservative, low-risk portfolio, that individual should earn a lower return. Failure to consider risk is, in effect, omitting one of the most important considerations in investing and portfolio construction. To beat the market, the portfolio manager or individual investor must do better than the return that would be expected given the amount of risk the investor bears. This implies that the investor could earn a lower return than the market but still outperform the market after adjusting for risk.

efficient market hypothesis (EMH)

A theory that stock prices correctly measure the firm's future earnings and dividends and that investors should not consistently outperform the market on a risk-adjusted basis.

The last section of this chapter is devoted to the **efficient market hypothesis (EMH)**, which suggests that investors cannot expect to outperform the market consistently on a risk-adjusted basis. Notice that the hypothesis does not say an individual will not outperform the market, since obviously some investors may do exceptionally well for a period of time. Being an occasional winner is not what is important.

The efficient market hypothesis is based on several assumptions, including that (1) there are a large number of competing participants in the securities markets, (2) information is readily available and virtually costless to obtain, and (3) transaction costs are small. The first two conditions seem obvious. Brokerage firms, insurance companies, investment and asset management firms, and many individuals spend countless hours analyzing financial statements seeking to determine the value of a company. The amount of information available on investments is nothing short of staggering, and the cost of obtaining much of the information used in security analysis is often trivial.

The third condition may not hold for individual investors, who pay commissions to brokerage firms for executing orders. The condition does apply to financial institutions, such as trust departments and mutual funds. These institutions pay only a few cents per share and this insignificant cost does not affect their investment decisions. Today, as a result of electronic trading, even the individual investor may now be able to buy and sell stock at a cost that is comparable to financial institutions. However, investors who continue to use traditional full-service brokers pay substantial commissions to trade stocks, and these commissions do affect the investment's return.

Because securities markets are highly competitive, information is readily available, and transactions may be executed with minimal transaction costs, the efficient market hypothesis argues that a security's price adjusts rapidly to new information and must reflect all known information concerning the firm. Since securities prices fully incorporate known information and prices change rapidly, day-to-day price changes will follow in a random walk over time. A *random walk* essentially means that *price changes are unpredictable and patterns formed are accidental.* If prices do follow a random walk, trading rules are useless, and various techniques, such as charting moving averages cannot lead to superior security selection. (These techniques are discussed in Chapter 12.)

The conventional choice of the term *random walk* to describe the pattern of changes in securities prices is perhaps unfortunate for two reasons. First, it is reasonable to expect that over a period of time, stock prices will rise. Unless the return is entirely the result of dividends, stock prices must rise to generate a positive return. In addition, stock prices will tend to rise over time as firms and the economy grow.

Second, the phrase *random walk* is often misinterpreted as meaning that securities prices are randomly determined, an interpretation that is completely backwards. It is *changes* in securities prices that are random. Securities prices themselves are rationally and efficiently determined by such fundamental considerations as earnings, interest rates, dividend policy, and the economic environment. Changes in these variables are quickly reflected in a security's price. All known information is embodied in the current price, and only new information will alter that price. New information has to be unpredictable; if it were predictable, the information would be known and stock prices would have already adjusted for that information. Hence, new information *must be random*, and a security's price should change randomly in response to that information. If changes in securities prices were not random and could be predicted, then some investors could consistently outperform the market (i.e., earn a return in excess of the expected return given the amount of risk) and securities markets would not be efficient.

The Speed of Price Adjustments

For securities markets to be efficient, prices must adjust rapidly. The efficient market hypothesis asserts that the market prices adjust extremely rapidly as new information is disseminated. In a world of advanced communication, information is rapidly dispersed in the investment community. The market then adjusts a security's price in accordance with the impact of the news on the firm's future earnings and dividends. By the time that the individual investor has learned the information, the security's price probably will have already changed. Thus, the investor will not be able to profit from acting on the information.

This adjustment process is illustrated in Figure 4.1, which plots the price of Google (GOOG) near the end of January 2006. The stock was trading around $433 when it announced that per-share earnings had *increased* from $0.71 to $1.22. While such a large increase should be bullish, it was *less than analysts' forecasts.* The stock opened the next day at $389, a 10 percent *decline* from the previous day's close. Such price behavior is exactly what the efficient market hypothesis suggests. Prices adjust rapidly to new information. Once the announcement is made, securities dealers immediately alter bid and ask prices to adjust for the new information. By the time a typical investor knows the new information, it is too late to react.

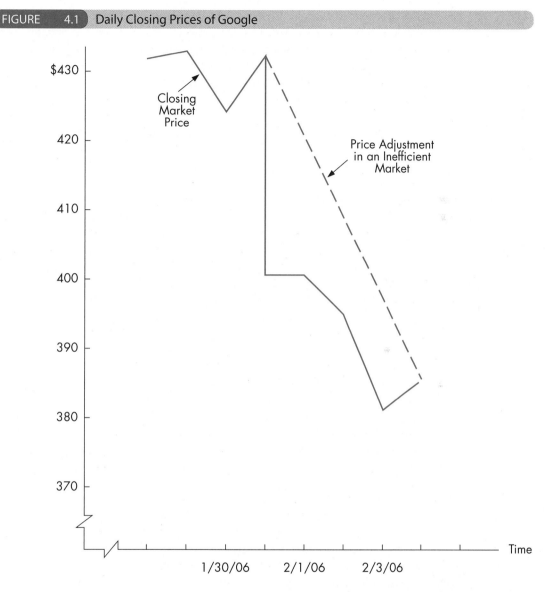

FIGURE 4.1 Daily Closing Prices of Google

If the market were not efficient and prices did not adjust rapidly, some investors would be able to adjust their holdings and take advantage of differences in investors' knowledge. Consider the broken line in Figure 4.1. If some investors knew that the earnings increase would be less than the forecasts but others did not know, the former could sell their holdings to those who were not informed. The price then might fall over a period of time as the knowledgeable sellers accepted progressively lower prices in order to unload their stock. Of course, if a sufficient number of investors had learned quickly, the price decline would be rapid as these investors adjusted their valuations of the stock in accordance with the new information. That is exactly what happened, because a sufficient number of investors were rapidly informed and the efficient market quickly adjusted the stock's price.

If an investor were able to anticipate the earnings before they were announced, that individual could avoid the price decline. Obviously, some investors did sell their shares just before the announcement, but it is also evident that some individuals bought those shares. Certainly one reason for learning the material and performing the various types of analysis throughout this text is to increase one's ability to anticipate events before they occur. However, the investor should realize that evidence supports the efficient market hypothesis and strongly suggests few investors will, over a period of time, outperform the market consistently.

Forms of the Efficient Market Hypothesis

The previous discussion of the efficient market hypothesis suggested that financial markets are efficient. The competition among investors, the rapid dissemination of information, and the swiftness with which securities prices adjust to this information produce efficient financial markets in which an individual cannot expect to consistently outperform the market. Instead, the investor can expect to earn a return that is consistent with the amount of risk he or she bears.

Although you may know that financial markets are efficient, you may not know *how* efficient. The degree of efficiency is important, because it determines the value the individual investor places on various types of analysis to select securities. If financial markets are inefficient, then many techniques may aid in selecting securities, and these techniques will lead to superior results. However, as markets become more efficient and various tools of analysis become well known, their usefulness for security selection is reduced, since they will no longer produce superior results (i.e., beat the market on a risk-adjusted basis).

You may believe that the financial markets are weakly efficient, semistrongly efficient, or strongly efficient. The *weak form* of the efficient market hypothesis suggests that the fundamental analysis discussed in Chapters 8 and 9 may produce superior investment results but that the technical analysis discussed in Chapter 12 will not. Thus, studying past price behavior and other technical indicators of the market will not produce superior investment results. For example, if a stock's price rises, the next change cannot be forecasted by studying previous price behavior. According to the weak form of the efficient market hypothesis, technical indicators do not produce returns on securities that are in excess of the return consistent with the amount of risk borne by the investor.

The *semistrong form* of the efficient market hypothesis asserts that the current price of a stock reflects the public's known information concerning the company. This knowledge includes both the firm's past history and the information learned through studying a firm's financial statements, its industry, and the general economic environment. Analysis of this material cannot be expected to produce superior investment results. Notice that the hypothesis does not state that the analysis cannot produce superior results. It just asserts that superior results should not be expected. However, there is the implication that even if the analysis of information produces superior results in some cases, it will not produce superior results over many investment decisions.

This conclusion should not be surprising to anyone who thinks about the investment process. Many investors and analysts study the same information. Their thought processes and training are similar, and they are in competition with one another. Certainly, if one perceives a fundamental change in a particular firm, this information will be readily transferred to other investors, and the price of the security will change. The competition among the potential buyers and the potential sellers will result in the security's price reflecting the firm's intrinsic worth.

As may be expected, the investment community is not particularly elated with this conclusion. It implies that the fundamental analysis considered in Chapters 8 and 9 will not produce superior investment results. Thus, neither technical nor fundamental analysis will generate consistently superior investment performance. Of course, if the individual analyst is able to perceive fundamental changes before other analysts do, that individual can outperform the market as a whole. However, few, if any, individuals should be able to consistently perceive such changes. Thus, there is little reason to expect investors to achieve *consistently* superior investment results.

There is, however, one major exception to this general conclusion of the semistrong form of the efficient market hypothesis. If the investor has access to *inside information*, that individual may consistently achieve superior results. In effect, this individual has information that is not known by the general investing public. Such privileged information as dividend cuts or increments, new discoveries, or potential takeovers may have a significant impact on the value of the firm and its securities. If the investor has advance knowledge of such events and has the time to act, he or she should be able to achieve superior investment returns.

Of course, most investors do not have access to inside information or at least do not have access to information concerning a number of firms. An individual may have access to privileged information concerning a firm for which he or she works. But as was previously pointed out, the use of such information for personal gain is *illegal*. To achieve continuously superior results, the individual would have to have a continuous supply of correct inside information and use it illegally. Probably few, if any, investors have this continuous supply, which may explain why both fundamentalists and technical analysts watch sales and purchases by insiders as a means to glean a clue as to the true future potential of the firm as seen by its management.

The *strong form* of the efficient market hypothesis asserts that the current price of a stock reflects all known (i.e., public) information and all privileged or inside information concerning the firm. Thus, even access to inside information cannot be expected to result in superior investment performance. Once again, this does not mean that an individual who acts on inside information cannot achieve superior results. It means that these results cannot be expected and that success in one case will tend to be offset by failure in other cases, so over time the investor will not achieve superior results.

This conclusion rests on a very important assumption: Inside information cannot be kept inside! Too many people know about the activities of a firm. This information is discerned by a sufficient number of investors, and the prices of the firm's securities adjust for the informational content of this inside knowledge. Notice that the conclusion that the price of the stock still reflects its intrinsic value does not require that all investors know this additional information. All that is necessary is for a sufficient number to know. Furthermore, the knowledge need not be acquired illegally. It is virtually impossible to keep some information secret, and there is a continual flow of rumors concerning a firm's activities. Denial by the firm is not sufficient to stop this spread of rumors, and when some are later confirmed, it only increases the credibility of future rumors as a possible means to gain inside information.

Although considerable empirical work has been designed to verify the forms of the efficient market hypothesis, these tests generally support only the weak and semistrong forms. The use of privileged information may result in superior investment performance, but the use of publicly known information cannot be expected to produce superior investments. Thus, neither technical nor fundamental analysis may be of help to the individual investor, because the current price of a stock fully incorporates this information.

Empirical Evidence for the Efficient Market Hypothesis: The Anomalies

While it is generally believed that securities markets are efficient, the question as to how efficient markets are remains to be answered. This raises a second question: If the financial markets are not completely efficient, what are the exceptions? This question has led to the identification of exceptions to market efficiency, referred to as *anomalies*. A market anomaly is a situation or strategy that cannot be explained away but would not be expected to happen if the efficient market hypothesis were true. For example, if buying shares in companies that announced a dividend increase led to excess returns, such a strategy would imply that securities markets are not completely efficient.

Most empirical testing of various types of technical indicators supports the weak form of the efficient market hypothesis, and the techniques explained in Chapter 12, do not lead to superior investment results. The evidence suggests that successive price changes are random and that the correlation between stock prices from one period to the next period is virtually nil. Thus, past price behavior provides little useful information for predicting future stock prices.

At the other extreme, the strong form of the efficient market hypothesis asserts that even access to inside information will not lead to excess returns. Initial empirical evidence does not support the strong form and suggests that insiders may be able to trade profitably in their own stocks. More recent evidence confirms these initial results that insider trading anticipates changes in stock prices. Insider purchases rise before an increase in the stock's price and insider sales precede decreases in the stock's price. Such evidence suggests that financial markets are not completely efficient.

By far the most research and the most interest lie with the semistrong form of the efficient market hypothesis. Studies of strategies that use publicly available information, such as the data found in a firm's financial statements, have generally concluded that this information does not produce superior results. Prices change very rapidly once information becomes public, and thus the security's price embodies all known information. If an investor could anticipate the new information and act before the information became public, that individual might be able to outperform the market, but once the information becomes public, it rarely can be used to generate superior investment results.

While the evidence generally supports the semistrong form of the efficient market hypothesis, there are exceptions. Two of the most important anomalies are the *P/E effect* and the *small-firm effect*. The P/E effect suggests that portfolios consisting of stocks with low price/earnings ratios have a higher average return than portfolios with higher P/E ratios. (P/E ratios are covered in more detail in Chapter 9.) The small-firm effect (or *small cap* for small capitalization) suggests that returns diminish as the size of the firm rises. Size is generally measured by the market value of its stock. If all common stocks on the New York Stock Exchange are divided into five groups, the smallest quintile (the smallest 20 percent of the total firms) has tended to earn a return that exceeds the return on investments in the stocks that compose the largest quintile, even after adjusting for risk.

Subsequent studies have found that the small-firm effect occurs primarily in January, especially the first five trading days. This anomaly is referred to as the *January effect*. However, there is no negative mirror-image December effect (i.e., small stocks do not consistently underperform the market in December) that would be consistent with December selling and January buying. The January effect is often explained by the fact that investors buy stocks in January after selling for tax reasons in December. And there is some evidence that within a size class those stocks whose prices declined the most in the preceding year tend to rebound the most during January.

The *neglected-firm* effect suggests that small firms that are neglected by large financial institutions (e.g., mutual funds, insurance companies, trust departments, and pension plans) tend to generate higher returns than those firms covered by financial institutions. By dividing firms into the categories of highly researched stocks, moderately researched stocks, and neglected stocks (based on the number of institutions holding the stock), researchers have found that the last group outperformed the more well-researched firms. This anomaly is probably another variation of the small-firm effect, and both the neglected-firm effect and the small-firm effect suggest that the market gets less efficient as firms get smaller. Because large financial institutions may exclude these firms from consideration, their lack of participation reduces the market's efficiency.

Besides the January effect, there is also a *day-of-the-week effect*. Presumably, there is no reason to anticipate that day-to-day returns should differ except over the weekend, when the return should exceed the return earned from one weekday to the next. However, research has suggested that the weekend generates not a higher return but a *lower* return. If this anomaly is true, it implies that investors anticipating the purchase of stock should not buy on Friday but wait until Monday. Investors anticipating the sale of stock should reverse the procedure. If this anomaly does exist, it should be erased by investors selling short on Friday and covering their positions on Monday (i.e., an act of arbitrage should erase the anomaly). The existence of the anomaly is generally resolved by asserting that the excess return is too small to cover transaction costs.

The *overreaction effect* is the tendency of securities prices to overreact to new information and is also inconsistent with efficient markets. There are many illustrations of securities prices experiencing large changes in response to new information. Evidence does support this anomaly that the market does overreact, but the overreaction appears to be asymmetric. Investors overreact to bad news but not to good news.

There also appears to be evidence that a security's price may drift in a particular direction over a period of time (a *drift* anomaly), especially after a surprise announcement of some magnitude. Bad news is interpreted by the market to be prolonged and stocks continue to decline even if the firm's fundamentals subsequently change. The converse would also be true: The market assumes good news will continue indefinitely. The former situation creates a buying opportunity, while the latter creates a selling opportunity. Presumably, in efficient markets, the change would occur immediately, since the new price embodies the new information. (The overreaction and the drift anomalies appear to be at odds, but that interpretation need not be correct. The subsequent rebound may occur soon following the initial price change after which the price drift resumes.)

While evidence does support the efficient market hypothesis, the preceding discussion indicates that there appear to be exceptions. Perhaps the observed exceptions are the result of flaws in the research methodology. Furthermore, any evidence supporting a particular inefficiency cannot be used to support other possible inefficiencies; it applies only to the specific anomaly under study.

Point of Interest

THE MONEY MASTERS

The efficient market hypothesis suggests that few, if any, investors will outperform the market for an extended period of time. Nine individuals who seem to have achieved that feat are highlighted in a fascinating book, *The Money Masters*, by John Train (Harper and Row, 1980). In this book, Train explores the ideas and strategies of these nine portfolio managers who achieved extraordinary records of capital appreciation for a period of at least ten years.*

The strategies and characteristics of these nine individuals have common threads. They sought undervalued securities and tended to avoid stocks that were currently popular. They avoided new ventures, well-known firms (the so-called *blue chips*), and gimmicks, such as options. They made realistic appraisals and favored stocks that tended to sell below book value. Each of these investors

was patient and willing to wait until the prices of his stocks rose to reflect the securities' true value.

These nine men (there were no women) tended to be loners. While they were obviously very well informed concerning Wall Street, they were geographically dispersed and not necessarily located in New York City. While their success could be interpreted to refute the efficient market hypothesis, the opposite inference is more correct. The paucity of individuals who have achieved such success is strong support for the hypothesis that few individuals will achieve superior returns over an extended period of time.

*In 1987, John Train published *The New Money Masters* (Harper and Row), which added the next generation of portfolio managers (e.g., Peter Lynch) to Train's initial list. He repeated the process in 2003 when he published *Money Masters of Our Time* (Collins Business).

Before you rush out to take advantage of these alleged inefficiencies, you should remember several sobering considerations. First, the empirical results are only consistent with inefficiencies; they do not prove their existence. Second, for you to take advantage of the inefficiency, it must be ongoing. Once an inefficiency is discovered and investors seek to take advantage of it, the inefficiency may disappear. Third, transaction costs are important, and you must pay the transaction costs associated with the strategy. If a substantial amount of trading is required, any excess return may be consumed by transaction costs. Fourth, you still must select individual issues. Even if small firms outperform the market in the first week of January, you cannot purchase all of them. There is no assurance that the selected stocks will be those that outperform the market in that particular year.

Implications of the Efficient Market Hypothesis

Ultimately, you must decide for yourself the market's degree of efficiency and whether the anomalies are grounds for particular strategies. Any investor who has a proclivity toward active investment management may see the anomalies as an opportunity. Those investors who prefer more passive investment management may see them as nothing more than interesting curiosities.[3]

Whether you follow a passive strategy or one that is designed to take advantage of an anomaly, you need to understand the efficient market hypothesis. First, an efficient

---

[3]For an excellent perspective on market efficiency, see Simon M. Keane, "The Efficient Market Hypothesis on Trial," *Financial Analysts Journal* (March/April 1986): 58–63. Keane suggests that the burden of proof of market inefficiency must fall on those individuals advocating an active strategy designed to take advantage of market inefficiencies. Even if inefficiencies were perceived by highly skilled financial specialists, that is insufficient evidence that the market is inefficient for the vast number of participants. For ordinary investors to benefit, any inefficiencies used by the financial specialist must be transmittable to the nonspecialist. Without evidence of such transferability of a market inefficiency, only passive strategies are defensible given the cost to execute an active strategy.

market implies that investors and financial analysts are using known information to value correctly what a security is worth. You may not be able to use public information to achieve superior investment results because the investment community is already using and acting on that information. If the investment community did not use this information and properly apply it to security valuation, the individual could achieve superior investment results. It is the very fact that investors as a whole are competent and are trying to beat each other that helps to produce efficient financial markets.

Second, while securities markets are efficient, such efficiency may not apply to other markets. For example, the investor may buy and sell nonfinancial assets in an inefficient market. This means that the current prices of these assets need not reflect their intrinsic value—that is, the price may not reflect the asset's potential flow of future income or price appreciation. If the markets for assets other than financial assets are dispersed and all transactions are, in effect, over-the-counter, the dissemination of information and prices is limited. This tends to reduce the efficiency of markets and to result in prices that can be too high or too low. While such a situation may offer excellent opportunities for the astute and the knowledgeable, it can also spell disaster for the novice.

The third and perhaps most important implication of the efficient market hypothesis applies to an individual's portfolio. The efficient market hypothesis seems to suggest that the individual investor could randomly select a diversified portfolio of securities and earn a return consistent with the market as a whole. Furthermore, once the portfolio has been selected, there is no need to change it. The strategy, then, is to buy and hold. Such a policy offers the additional advantage of minimizing commissions.

The problem with this naive policy is that it fails to consider the reasons an investor saves and acquires securities and other assets. The goals behind the portfolio are disregarded, and different goals require different portfolio construction strategies. Furthermore, goals and conditions change, which in turn requires changes in an individual's portfolio. Altering the portfolio for the sake of change will result in additional commissions and will not produce superior investment returns. However, when the investor's goals or financial situation change, the portfolio's asset allocation should be altered in a way that is consistent with the new goals and conditions.

The importance to the individual investor of the efficient market hypothesis is not the implication that investment decision making is useless. Instead, it brings to the foreground the environment in which the investor must make decisions. The hypothesis should make the investor realize that investments in securities may not produce superior returns. Rather, the investor should earn a return over a period of time that is consistent with the return earned by the market as a whole and the amount of risk borne by the investor. This means that individual investors should devote more time and effort to the specifications of their investment goals and the selection of securities to meet those goals than to the analysis of individual securities. Since such analysis cannot be expected to produce superior returns, it takes resources and time away from the important questions of why we save and invest.

SUMMARY

Because investments are made in efficient financial markets, it is difficult for an investor to outperform the market consistently. However, this does not imply that financial assets should be acquired randomly. Instead, the investor should develop a financial plan in which financial goals are defined and priorities determined. Next, the individual should analyze his or her financial position by constructing a personal balance sheet and a cash budget. The balance sheet enumerates what the individual owns and owes. The cash budget enumerates receipts and disbursements. These financial statements may be created for the present and may be projected for some time period in the future. Once these steps have been taken, an asset allocation can be determined to meet the goals.

Taxation can have a significant impact on investment decisions. Although tax laws are enacted by all levels of government, the important tax laws affecting investments have primarily been passed by the federal government. These laws include the differentiation between long-term and short-term capital gains. Long-term capital gains are taxed at a lower rate. Pension plans and individual retirement plans also offer tax advantages. In many cases, federal income taxes are deferred until the individual removes funds from the retirement account.

Investments are made in competitive financial markets. This competition as well as the rapid dissemination of information and the rapid changes in securities prices result in efficient securities markets. The efficient market hypothesis suggests that the individual investor cannot expect to outperform the market on a risk-adjusted basis over an extended period of time. Instead, the investor should earn a return that is consistent with the market return and the amount of risk the individual bears.

Empirical evidence tends to support the efficient market hypothesis, at least the weak and semistrong forms. There are, however, anomalies that are inconsistent with the efficient market hypothesis. Financial markets may have pockets of inefficiency that the investor may be able to exploit. Such anomalies imply that financial markets are not completely efficient and that an investor may earn an excess return. Such a return is greater than should be expected given the market return and the risk the investor takes.

Summary of Offsetting Capital Gains and Losses

This summary illustrates six cases of short-term gains and losses: (1) short- and long-term gains, (2) short- and long-term losses, (3) short-term loss less than long-term gain, (4) short-term loss exceeding long-term gain, (5) short-term gain less than long-term loss, and (6) short-term gain exceeding long-term loss.

Case 1 *Short-term and long-term gains*
    short-term gain: $300
    short-term loss: $200
      net short-term gain: $100
    long-term gain: $600
    long-term loss: $400
      net long-term gain: $200
    tax implication:
      $100 taxed as ordinary income
      $200 taxed as long-term capital gain

Case 2 *Short-term and long-term losses*
    short-term gain: $100
    short-term loss: $200
      net short-term loss: ($100)

long-term gain: $300
long-term loss: $400
   net long-term loss: ($100)
tax implication:
   $200 is used to offset taxable income from other sources

Case 3 *Short-term loss is **less than** long-term gain*
   short-term gain: $300
   short-term loss: $400
      net short-term loss: ($100)
   long-term gain: $600
   long-term loss: $400
      net long-term gain: $200
   tax implication:
      $100 short-term loss is used to offset long-term gain; net
      $100 gain is taxed as long-term capital gain

Case 4 *Short-term loss **exceeds** long-term gain*
   short-term gain: $300
   short-term loss: $500
      net short-term loss: ($200)
   long-term gain: $500
   long-term loss: $400
      net long-term gain: $100
   tax implication:
      $200 short-term loss is used to offset $100 long-term gain; net $100 loss is
      used to offset other taxable income

Case 5 *Short-term gain **exceeds** long-term loss*
   short-term gain: $400
   short-term loss: $200
      net short-term gain: $200
   long-term gain: $400
   long-term loss: $500
      net long-term loss: $100
   tax implication:
      $100 long-term loss is used to offset short-term gain; net $100 gain is taxed
      as ordinary income

Case 6 *Short-term gain **less than** long-term loss*
   short-term gain: $300
   short-term loss: $200
      net short-term gain: $100
   long-term gain: $400
   long-term loss: $600
      net long-term loss: $200
   tax implication:
      $200 long-term loss is used to offset short-term gain; net $100 loss is used to
      offset taxable income from other sources

QUESTIONS

1. What are the steps for constructing a financial plan? What role do financial statements play in the construction of financial plans?

2. What is the difference between an individual's forecasted balance sheet and forecasted cash budget? Which of the following should be part of an individual's balance sheet and which should be part of the cash budget?
   a) Mortgage
   b) Principal repayment to be made
   c) Dividend payments
   d) Stock
   e) Social Security payments
   f) Mutual fund shares
   g) Interest owed
   h) Antiques
   i) Credit card balances
   j) 401(k) contributions

3. What is a tax shelter? Does a tax shelter imply that the individual avoids paying taxes?

4. What is a capital gain, and is it subject to taxation? May capital losses be used to offset capital gains and income from other sources?

5. Which of the following illustrates a tax shelter?
   a) Dividend income
   b) Interest earned on a savings account
   c) A stock purchased for $10 that is currently worth $25
   d) An IRA
   e) A Roth account
   f) The sale of a stock purchased in 2005 for a $1,000 capital gain.

6. What are IRA, 401(k), and Keogh plans? What are their primary advantages for investors?

7. What differentiates a deductible IRA from a Roth IRA? What conditions favor the Roth IRA?

8. Taxes affect financial planning. Go to an Internet site such as the IRS website (**http://www.irs.ustreas.gov**) and answer the following questions. Other possible sites include TurboTax (**http://www.turbotax.intuit.com**) or 1040.com (**http://www.1040.com**).
   a) What are the marginal tax brackets for a single individual and for a couple filing a joint return if their taxable incomes are $50,000, $75,000, or $150,000?
   b) What is the maximum amount that taxpayers can contribute to a Roth IRA?
   c) What are the current maximum rates on short-term and long-term capital gains?
   d) Are contributions to your college's alumni fund tax deductible?

9. Does the efficient market hypothesis suggest that an investor cannot outperform the market? What effect does the dissemination of information (as required by the full disclosure laws) have on the efficiency of financial markets? How rapidly do securities prices change in response to new information in an efficient market?

10. What are the three forms of the efficient market hypothesis? What are possible exceptions (anomalies) to the efficient market hypothesis?

PROBLEMS

1. a) An individual in the 28 percent federal income tax bracket and 15 percent long-term capital gains tax bracket bought and sold the following securities during the year:

	Cost Basis of Stock	Proceeds of Sale
ABC	$24,500	$28,600
DEF	35,400	31,000
GHI	31,000	36,000

What are the taxes owed on the short-term capital gains?

   b) An individual in the 35 percent federal income tax bracket and 15 percent long-term capital gains tax bracket bought and sold the following securities during the year:

	Cost Basis of Stock	Proceeds of Sale
ABC	$34,600	$28,600
DEF	29,400	31,000
GHI	21,500	19,000

What are the taxes owed or saved as a result of these sales?

2. An investor is in the 33 percent tax bracket and pays long-term capital gains taxes of 15 percent. What are the taxes owed (or saved in the case of losses) in the current tax year for each of the following situations?
   a) Net short-term capital gains of $3,000; net long-term capital gains of $4,000
   b) Net short-term capital gains of $3,000; net long-term capital losses of $4,000
   c) Net short-term capital losses of $3,000; net long-term capital gains of $4,000
   d) Net short-term capital gains of $3,000; net long-term capital losses of $2,000
   e) Net short-term capital losses of $4,000; net long-term capital gains of $3,000
   f) Net short-term capital losses of $1,000; net long-term capital losses of $1,500
   g) Net short-term capital losses of $3,000; net long-term capital losses of $2,000

3. You are in the 28 percent income tax bracket and pay long-term capital gains taxes of 15 percent. What are the taxes owed or saved in the current year for each of the following sets of transactions?
   a) You buy 100 shares of ZYX for $10 and after seven months sell it on December 31, 200X, for $23. You buy 100 shares of WER for $10 and after 15 months sell it on December 31, 200X, for $7. You buy 100 shares of DFG for $10 and after nine months, on December 31, 200X, it is selling for $15.
   b) You buy 100 shares of ZYX for $60 and after seven months sell it on December 31, 200Y, for $37. You buy 100 shares of WER for $60 and after 15 months sell it on December 31, 200Y, for $67. You buy 100 shares of DFG for $60 and after nine months sell it on December 31, 200Y, for $76.
   c) On January 2, 200X, you buy 100 shares of ZYX for $40 and sell it for $31 after 22 months. On January 2, 200X, you buy 100 shares of WER for $40 and sell it for $27 after 15 months. On January 2, 200X, you buy 100 shares of DFG for $40 and sell it for $16 after 18 months.
   d) On January 2, 200X, you buy 100 shares of ZYX for $60. On October 2, 200X, you sell 100 shares of ZYX for $40. On October 10, 200X, you purchase 100 shares of ZYX for $25.

4. You are in the 25 percent income tax bracket. What are the taxes owed or saved if you
   a) contribute $2,000 to a 401(k) plan
   b) contribute $2,000 to a Roth IRA
   c) withdraw $2,000 from a traditional IRA
   d) withdraw $2,000 from a Keogh account

5. Your traditional IRA account has stock of GFH, which cost $2,000 20 years ago when you were 50 years old. You have been very fortunate, and the stock is now worth $23,000. You are in the 35 percent income tax bracket and pay 15 percent on long-term capital gains.
   a) What was the annual rate of growth in the value of the stock?
   b) What are the taxes owed if you withdraw the funds?

6. You are 60 years old. Currently, you have $10,000 invested in an IRA and have just received a lump-sum distribution of $50,000 from a pension plan, which you roll over into an IRA. You continue to make $2,000 annual payments to the regular IRA and expect to earn 9 percent on these funds until you start withdrawing the money at age 70 (i.e., after ten years). The IRA rollover will earn 9 percent for the same duration.
   a) How much will you have when you start to make withdrawals at age 70?
   b) If your funds continue to earn 9 percent annually and you withdraw $17,000 annually, how long will it take to exhaust your funds?
   c) If your funds continue to earn 9 percent annually and your life expectancy is 18 years, what is the maximum you may withdraw each year?

7. Bob places $1,000 a year in his IRA for ten years and then invests $2,000 a year for the next ten years. Mary places $2,000 a year in her IRA for ten years and then invests $1,000 a year for the next ten years. They both have invested $30,000. If they earn 8 percent annually, how much more will Mary have earned than Bob at the end of 20 years?

8. Bob and Barbara are 55 and 50 years old. Bob annually contributes $1,500 to Barbara's IRA. They plan to make contributions until Bob retires at age 65 and then to leave the funds in as long as possible (i.e., age 70 to ease calculations).

   Mike and Mary are 55 and 50 years old. Mike annually contributes $2,000 to Mike's IRA. They plan to make contributions until Mike retires at age 65 and then leave the funds in as long as possible (i.e., age 70 to ease calculations). Both Barbara's and Mike's IRAs yield 10 percent annually.

   The combined life expectancy of both couples is to age 85 of the wife. What will be each couple's annual withdrawal from the IRA based on life expectancy? (This problem is designed to illustrate an important point in financial planning for retirement. What is the point?)

The Financial Advisor's Investment Case
Retirement Planning and Federal Income Taxation

Your financial planning practice services several sophisticated individuals who have accumulated a substantial amount of assets but who are naive concerning potential strategies to reduce taxes. To increase their awareness, one client suggested that you offer a complimentary seminar to explain fundamental means for reducing taxes. Your immediate reaction was that each individual's tax situation differs, so the seminar would be of little benefit. On further reflection, however, you thought a focused presentation could be beneficial, especially if you limit the discussion to one topic, retirement planning, and cover other tax strategies such as capital gains or estate planning only to the extent that they affect retirement planning.

To illustrate the differences in retirement planning, you selected two very different case studies. Mary Brost is a single parent with one teenage son. She has a well-paying, secure job that offers a 401(k) plan, life insurance, and other benefits. While Ms. Brost has sufficient resources to finance her son's college education, he works in a local CPA office that provides him with sufficient spending money, including the cost of insurance for his car.

Jason Agens has two young children, and his wife has returned to graduate school to complete an advanced degree. He is self-employed in an industry with large cyclical swings in economic activity. Although Agens did not sustain any losses during the prior recession, he has previously experienced losses that have affected his willingness to assume risk. During the good years, he has accumulated a sizable amount of liquid assets that he believes may be needed during any future periods of economic downturn.

You decide that both individuals offer sufficient differences to cover many facets of tax planning for retirement. To ease your presentation, you assume that both are in the 25 percent marginal tax bracket and that retirement will not occur for at least 20 years. Although you would like to illustrate how much each individual could accumulate, you believe that discussion should be deferred until some other time in order to concentrate on the tax implications of possible retirement strategies. To help generate discussion, you decide to start your presentation by answering the following specific questions that you distributed prior to the seminar:

1. Can Mary set up an IRA and deduct the contribution from her income that is subject to federal income taxation? Does the same apply to Jason? Could Mary's or Jason's children have IRA accounts?

2. Can Mary or Jason set up a Keogh account and deduct the contribution from income that is subject to federal income taxation? Could their children establish Keogh accounts?

3. Is there any reason why Mary or Jason should prefer a 401(k) or Keogh retirement account to an IRA?

4. Is the income generated by Mary's 401(k) account subject to current federal income taxation? If Jason created a retirement account, would the income be subject to current federal income taxation?

5. If either Mary or Jason were to withdraw funds from their retirement accounts, would they pay federal income taxes and penalties?

6. If Mary or Jason purchased stock outside of a retirement account, should the purchases emphasize income or capital gains? Would purchasing stock outside a retirement account be a desirable strategy?

7. Would the purchase of an annuity offer tax benefits that are similar to a retirement account?

8. What general strategies would you suggest to an individual seeking to accumulate funds for retirement?

Appendix 4

THE DEDUCTIBLE VERSUS THE NONDEDUCTIBLE IRA

Although it may appear that the deductible IRA is preferred because the contribution is *currently* exempt from taxation, that is not necessarily the correct choice. Instead, the choice depends on the investor's current income tax bracket and anticipated tax bracket in the future when the funds are withdrawn. In general, if the tax bracket is higher when the contributions are made, the deductible IRA should be preferred. The converse would be true if the investor expects to be in a higher tax bracket when the funds are withdrawn. Then the nondeductible IRA should be preferred. If the tax brackets are the same, it may not matter which IRA the individual chooses. (There are other differences between the deductible and the nondeductible plans, such as mandatory withdrawal from a deductible IRA starting at age 70½. The nondeductible IRA does not have mandatory withdrawals. Such differences may favor one plan over the other independently of the individual's tax bracket.)

To verify this, consider the following three cases in which an investor has $40,000 in adjusted gross income and can earn 8 percent annually on invested funds for 20 years. In the first case, the investor is in the 25 percent income tax bracket and expects to be in that bracket when the funds are withdrawn. (For simplicity, assume that the 25 percent tax rate applies to all taxable income instead of part of the income being taxed at a lower rate and some being taxed at the marginal rate as currently required by the federal income tax code.) With the deductible IRA, disposable income after the IRA contribution and taxes is as follows:

Adjusted gross income	$40,000
Deductible IRA contribution	2,000
Taxable income	38,000
Income taxes	9,500
Disposable income	$28,500

If this individual chooses the nondeductible IRA, the following analysis applies:

Adjusted gross income	$40,000
Deductible IRA contribution	0
Income taxes	10,000
Nondeductible IRA contribution	1,500
Disposable income	$28,500

Notice that in both cases disposable income is the same, so the situations are comparable.

The $2,000 annual contribution in the deductible IRA grows to $91,524[a] over 20 years at 8 percent, while the $1,500 in the nondeductible IRA grows to $68,643.[b] If the funds are withdrawn over 20 years and continue to earn 8 percent annually, the deductible IRA will generate $9,322[c] a year. Taxes then are paid on the entire distribution, so the investor gets to keep $6,991 [$9,322 − 0.25($9,322)]. The nondeductible IRA yields $6,991,[d] which the investor may keep; there is no further tax liability. Notice that the net amount received after taxes is the same independently of which IRA the individual selected.

To prefer one IRA over the other requires differences in the assumed tax rates for the amounts invested. Consider the effect of assuming a 25 percent tax rate when the funds are invested but a 20 percent tax rate when the funds are withdrawn. With the deductible IRA, disposable income after the IRA contribution and taxes is as follows:

Adjusted gross income	$40,000
Deductible IRA contribution	2,000
Taxable income	38,000
Income taxes	9,500
Disposable income	$28,500

If this individual chooses the nondeductible IRA, the following analysis applies:

Adjusted gross income	$40,000
Deductible IRA contribution	0
Income taxes	10,000
Nondeductible IRA contribution	1,500
Disposable income	$28,500

Since the initial 25 percent income tax rate is unaltered, the analysis is the same as above. The difference occurs when the funds are withdrawn.

Once again, the $2,000 annual contribution in the deductible IRA grows to $91,524[a] and the $1,500 annual contribution to the nondeductible IRA grows to $68,643.[b] When the funds are withdrawn, the deductible IRA generates $9,322[c] a year, and the investor nets after taxes $7,457.60 [$9,322 − 0.2($9,322)]. The nondeductible IRA yields only $6,991,[d] so the deductible IRA is the better choice because there is more tax saving up front.

The opposite occurs if the tax rates are assumed to be 20 percent when the funds are contributed to the retirement account but 25 percent when they are withdrawn. In that case the IRA contribution and taxes are as follows:

Adjusted gross income	$40,000
Deductible IRA contribution	2,000
Taxable income	38,000
Income taxes	7,600
Disposable income	$30,400

If this individual chooses the nondeductible IRA, the following analysis applies:

Adjusted gross income	$40,000
Deductible IRA contribution	0
Income taxes	8,000
Nondeductible IRA contribution	1,600
Disposable income	$30,400

The initial income tax rate is now 20 percent, so the results are altered. Since disposable income is increased for the deductible IRA, the contribution to the nondeductible IRA is increased to maintain comparability.

Once again, the $2,000 annual contribution in the deductible IRA grows to $91,524[a] but the $1,600 in the nondeductible IRA grows to $73,219.[e] When the funds are withdrawn, the deductible IRA generates $9,322[c] a year, and the investor retains $6,992 [$9,322 − 0.25($9,322)]. The nondeductible IRA yields $7,458,[f] so the nondeductible IRA is the better choice because the tax saving is greater when the funds are withdrawn (i.e., the tax rate is higher during the withdrawal period than during the accumulation period).

The first case illustrates that if disposable income is maintained under each IRA and the tax rates are the same during the accumulation and withdrawal periods, there is no difference between the deductible and the nondeductible IRAs. The subsequent cases show that if the tax rate is higher during the accumulation stage, the deductible IRA is better and that if the tax rate is higher during the withdrawal stage, the nondeductible IRA is better.

The last case considers when the tax rates are the same (25 percent during the accumulation and the withdrawal periods) and the annual contribution is the same ($2,000) for either IRA. To compare equal contributions, the investor must reduce disposable income to cover the taxes paid on the income contributed to the nondeductible IRA.

For the deductible IRA, the analysis is as follows:

Adjusted gross income	$40,000
Deductible IRA contribution	2,000
Taxable income	38,000
Income taxes	9,500
Disposable income	$28,500

For the nondeductible IRA, the analysis is:

Adjusted gross income	$40,000
Deductible IRA contribution	0
Income taxes	10,000
Nondeductible IRA contribution	2,000
Disposable income	$28,000

The difference in disposable income is $500, which is the tax on the income invested in the nondeductible IRA.

The question now is what does the investor who chose the deductible IRA do with the $500? If the money is spent, then there is no question that the nondeductible IRA will produce the higher flow of income during the withdrawal period. The withdrawals will be the same in both cases, but the deductible IRA payments will be subject to income tax while the nondeductible payments will be tax-exempt. If the individual invests the $500, there is an array of possibilities, but unless it is assumed the return exceeds the return on the nondeductible IRA, the analysis will favor the Roth IRA. The following analysis considers two possibilities: (1) the $500 is invested in a tax-exempt security and (2) the $500 is invested in a non-dividend-paying stock, so that any profits will be taxed as long-term capital gains.

Calculator Solution

Function Key	Data Input
(e) PV =	0
FV =	?
PMT =	−1600
N =	20
I =	8
Function Key	Answer
FV =	73,219

Function Key	Data Input
(f) PV =	73219
FV =	0
PMT =	?
N =	20
I =	8
Function Key	Answer
FV =	7,458

Calculator Solution

Function Key	Data Input
(g) PV =	0
FV =	?
PMT =	−500
N =	20
I =	6
Function Key	Answer
FV =	18,393

If the individual annually invests $500 for 20 years in a tax-exempt fund and the fund earns 6 percent, the total grows to $18,393.[g] (In the 25 percent tax bracket, 6 percent after taxes is equivalent to 8 percent before taxes. See the discussion of tax equivalence in the section on municipal bonds in Chapter 15.) If the funds continue to earn 6 percent for 20 years, the saver may withdraw $1,604[h] annually. This $1,604 plus the $6,992 after-tax withdrawal from the deductible IRA generates total cash flow of $8,596, which is inferior to the $9,322 generated by the nondeductible IRA.

If the saver annually invests the $500 in non-dividend-paying growth stocks that grow at 8 percent, the total is $22,881,[i] of which $10,000 is the amount invested and $12,881 is the appreciation that is subject to long-term capital gains taxation. If the long-term capital gains tax rate is 20 percent, the investor nets $10,305 after tax for a total of $20,305. At 8 percent, $20,305 generates $2,068[j] before tax for the next 20 years. Thus, $2,068 plus $6,992 after taxes from the deductible IRA totals $9,060. This amount is also inferior to the $9,322 annual withdrawal from the nondeductible IRA.

In both scenarios, the nondeductible IRA is the better choice. Why is this so? The answer lies in the fact that the extra $500 generates a return that will not be taxed when withdrawn from the nondeductible IRA. However, the $500 investment outside of the IRA will have tax implications, which must be considered when selecting between the two strategies. In the first case, the nontaxable 6 percent return can never exceed the 8 percent return earned in the nondeductible IRA. In the second case, the 8 percent growth is the same as that earned in the Roth IRA but is subject to long-term capital gains taxation. In both cases, the after-tax return is insufficient to cover the tax break from the nondeductible IRA. Unless a higher return is assumed for the additional $500 investment, the nondeductible IRA is always the superior choice, because the return will be insufficient to offset the tax advantage. (Of course, assuming a higher return can justify any strategy.)

In summary, if the individual can forgo current spending (that is, make the $2,000 contribution and *cover the taxes on that income*), the nondeductible IRA will be the better choice. If, however, the individual can only save the $2,000 and not cover the tax, there is no substantive difference between the two IRAs. The cash withdrawals will be the same as long as the tax rates are the same. The choice between the deductible and the nondeductible then depends on the expected income tax rate when the funds are withdrawn. If the expected income tax rate exceeds the current rate, the individual should choose the nondeductible IRA.[1] If the expected income tax rate is less than the current rate, the saver should select the deductible IRA.[2]

[1]Differences in the income limitations on contributions and when funds must be withdrawn also favor the nondeductible Roth IRA over the deductible IRA.
[2]The Roth IRA offers interesting possibilities for students who are currently earning modest amounts and who are in low tax brackets. For example, if a 17-year-old high school student earns $1,000, that income will not be subject to federal income tax. If the $1,000 were invested in a Roth IRA that earned 8 percent and the funds were left to compound until age 67 (50 years), the account would be worth $46,902. This amount could then be withdrawn and not be subject to income tax. This illustration assumes, of course, the student is willing to part with the $1,000 and that Congress does not change the tax laws.

CHAPTER

Risk and Portfolio Management

In February 2004, the Mega Millions jackpot reached $230 million. People drove for miles and stood in long lines to buy a ticket. The odds of their winning were approximately 135 million to 1. The odds were obviously not on any individual's side. Perhaps they should have listened to George Patton, who in *War As I Knew It* wrote, "Take calculated risks; that is quite different from being rash." All investments involve risk because the future is uncertain, but the possible returns on investments are perceptibly more certain than the returns on a state-sponsored lottery.

This chapter is an introduction to the sources and measurements of risk and how these measurements are used in portfolio theory. Risk may be measured by a standard deviation, which measures the dispersion (or variability) around a central tendency, such as an average return. Risk also may be measured by a beta coefficient, which is an index of the volatility of a security's return relative to the return on the market. Much of this chapter is devoted to an exposition of these measures of risk and the reduction of risk through the construction of diversified portfolios.

The chapter ends with a discussion of portfolio theory and explanations of security returns. Portfolio theory is built around the investor seeking to construct an efficient portfolio that offers the highest return for a given level of risk or the least amount of risk for a given level of return. Of all the possible efficient portfolios, the individual investor selects the

LEARNING OBJECTIVES

After completing this chapter you should be able to:

1. Identify the sources of risk.
2. Identify the relationship between securities that is necessary to achieve diversification.
3. Contrast the sources of return and differentiate between expected and realized returns.
4. Explain how standard deviations and beta coefficients measure risk, and interpret the difference between beta coefficients of 1.5, 1.0, and 0.5.
5. Contrast efficient and inefficient portfolios and identify which portfolio the individual will select.
6. Compare the explanation of a stock's return according to the Capital Asset Pricing Model and arbitrage pricing theory.

portfolio that offers the highest level of satisfaction or utility.

Models of security returns are built around the specification of what variables affect an asset's return. In the Capital Asset Pricing Model (CAPM), a security's return primarily depends on interest rates (such as the rate on safe Treasury securities), movements in securities prices in general, and how the individual stock responds to changes in the market. In arbitrage pricing theory, security returns are related to more variables, which may include unexpected changes in inflation or industrial production.

RETURN

Investments are made to earn a return, but to earn the return, you must accept the possibility of loss. Portfolio theory is concerned with risk and return. Its purpose is to determine the combination of risk and return that allows the investor to achieve the highest return for a given level of risk. To do this, means for measuring risk and return must be devised. Initially, this chapter considers various usages for the term *return*, followed by an extensive discussion of the measurement of risk. Risk and return are then combined in the discussion of portfolio theory.

The word *return* is often modified by an adjective, including the *expected return*, the *required return*, and the *realized return*. The **expected return** is the anticipated flow of income and/or price appreciation. An investment may offer a return from either of two sources. The first source is the flow of income that may be generated by the investment. A savings account generates interest income. The second source of return is capital appreciation. If an investor buys stock and its price subsequently increases, the investor receives a capital gain. All investments offer the investor potential income and/or capital appreciation. Some investments, like the savings account, offer only income, whereas other investments, such as an investment in land, may offer only capital appreciation. In fact, some investments may require that expenditures (e.g., property tax on the land) be made by the investor.

This expected return is summarized in Equation 5.1:

5.1
$$E(r) = \frac{E(D)}{P} + E(g).$$

The symbols are

$E(r)$ the expected return (as a percentage)
$E(D)$ the expected dividend (or interest in the case of a debt instrument)
P the price of the asset
$E(g)$ the expected growth in the value of the asset (i.e., the capital gain).

If an investor buys a stock for $10 and expects to earn a dividend of $0.60 and sell the stock for $12 so there is a capital gain of 20 percent [($12 − $10)/$10], the expected return is

$$E(r) = \frac{\$0.60}{\$10} + 0.2 = 0.26 = 26\%.$$

The investor expects to earn a return of 26 percent during the time period. (Since the time period has not been specified, this return should not be confused with an *annual* rate of return. In Chapter 10, returns that do not specify the time period are referred to as *holding period returns*. The calculation of *annual rates of return* is also addressed in Chapter 10.)

It is important to realize that this return is anticipated. The yield that is achieved on the investment is not known until after the investment is sold and converted to cash. It is important to differentiate between the *expected return*, the *required return*, and the *realized return*. The expected return is the incentive for accepting risk, and it must be compared with the investor's **required return**, which is the return necessary to induce the investor to bear the risk associated with a particular investment. The required return includes (1) what the investor may earn on alternative investments,

expected return

The sum of the anticipated dividend yield and capital gains.

required return

The return necessary to induce the investor to purchase an asset.

such as the risk-free return available on Treasury bills, and (2) a premium for bearing risk that includes compensation for the expected rate of inflation and for fluctuations in security prices. Since the required return includes a measure of risk, the discussion of the required return must be postponed until the measurement of risk is covered.

realized return

The sum of income and capital gains earned on an investment.

The **realized return** is the return actually earned on an investment and is essentially the sum of the flow of income generated by the asset and the capital gain. The realized return may, and often does, differ from the expected and required returns.

The realized return is summarized by Equation 5.2:

5.2
$$r = \frac{D}{P} + g.$$

This is essentially the same as the equation for expected return with the expected value sign, E, removed. If an investor buys a stock for $10 and collects $0.60 in dividends, and the stock appreciates by 20 percent, the realized return is

$$r = \frac{\$0.60}{\$10} + 0.2 = 0.26 = 26\%.$$

Expected Return Expressed as a Probability

Probability theory measures or indicates the likelihood of something occurring. If you are certain that something will happen, the probability is 100 percent. (Remember the old joke about death and taxes.) The sum of all the probabilities of the possible outcomes is 100 percent. The expected value (the anticipated outcome) is the sum of each outcome multiplied by the probability of occurrence. For example, an investor is considering purchasing a stock. The possible returns and the investor's estimate of their occurring are as follows:

Return	Probability
3%	10%
10	45
12	40
20	5

The sum of all the probabilities is 100 percent, and the returns encompass all the possible outcomes. The expected value or, in this illustration, the expected return $[E(r)]$ is the probability of the outcome times each individual return. That expected value is

$$E(r) = (0.10).03 + (0.45).10 + (0.40).12 + (0.05).20$$
$$= 0.003 + 0.045 + 0.048 + 0.01 = 0.106 = 10.6\%.$$

Each of the expected returns is weighted by the probability of occurrence. The results are then added to determine the expected return, 10.6 percent.

While it is possible that the return on the stock could be as low as 3 percent or as high as 20 percent, their weights are relatively small. They contribute only modestly to the expected return. The return of 10 percent carries more weight (45 percent) in the determination of the expected return. Notice, however, that the expected return is not 10 percent, nor is it any of the four possible outcomes. The expected return is a weighted average in which each outcome is weighted by the probability of the outcome occurring.

The investor may also use this information to construct cumulative probabilities. Cumulative probability distributions answer questions such as, What is the probability that the return will be at least 10 percent, or What is the probability that the investor will not earn 12 percent? The answer to the former question is 90 percent (45% + 40% + 5%) percent, because that percentage includes all the probabilities that the return will be 10 percent or greater. The answer to the second question is 55 percent, because it includes all the probabilities that the stock's return will be less than 12 percent.

Probability lends itself to studying different situations. By changing the individual probabilities, the outcome (the expected value) is altered. For example, the probabilities in the preceding example could be changed, which would affect the weighted average (i.e., the expected return). If the individual returns remain the same but their probability of occurring are changed as follows:

Return	Probability
3%	20%
10	35
12	40
20	5

the expected return $[E(r)]$ becomes

$$E(r) = (0.20).03 + (0.35).10 + (0.40).12 + (0.05).20$$
$$= 0.006 + 0.035 + 0.048 + 0.01 = 0.099 = 9.9\%.$$

A greater weight is now assigned to the lowest return, which has the effect of reducing the expected return from 10.6 percent to 9.9 percent.

In addition to changing the probabilities and determining the impact of the expected return, it is also possible to change the individual returns to determine how sensitive the expected return is to an individual observation. (This type of analysis cannot be applied to the probabilities. Changing one probability requires changing another since the sum of the probabilities must equal 100 percent.) Suppose the third return (the third observation) were to change by 1 percent from 12 percent to 13 percent. The impact on the expected return is

$$E(r) = (0.20).03 + (0.35).10 + (0.40).13 + (0.05).20$$
$$= 0.006 + 0.035 + 0.052 + 0.01 = 0.103 = 10.3\%.$$

If the fourth observation were changed by 1 percent from 20 percent to 21 percent, the expected return would be

$$E(r) = (0.20).03 + (0.35).10 + (0.40).12 + (0.05).21$$
$$= 0.006 + 0.035 + 0.048 + 0.0105 = 0.0995 = 9.95\%.$$

The expected return is more sensitive to the change in the first case when the individual return rose from 12 to 13 percent. In the second illustration, the expected return is not sensitive to the change.

This type of sensitivity analysis can play an important role in portfolio management. It helps answer questions such as, If stock A's return declines, what impact will the decline have on the portfolio's return? How sensitive is the portfolio return to a specific stock's return? If, for example, a large proportion of an individual's portfolio was invested in Enron when it imploded, the impact was significant. The portfolio return was sensitive to the Enron bankruptcy. If, however, Enron constituted a small proportion of an individual's portfolio, the impact was minor. The portfolio return was not sensitive to the return of an individual stock. (An investor might want to answer the following series of questions: What is the worst case scenario? What is the probability that the worst case will occur? What is the impact if the worst case does occur?)

A Monte Carlo simulation takes this process to an extreme. Named after combining mathematics with gambling casinos, a Monte Carlo approach ties together simulations and probability distributions. A computer randomly selects a value for each variable and computes the expected value and the dispersion around that expected value. (That variability or dispersion around the expected value is measured by the standard deviation, which is discussed later in this chapter.) This process of selecting values for each variable and determining the expected value is repeated numerous times. The results are then combined into one final expected value and measure of dispersion around that value.

SOURCES OF RISK

systematic risk
Associated with fluctuation in security prices; e.g., market risk.

Risk refers to the uncertainty that the actual return the investor realizes will differ from the expected return. As is illustrated in Exhibit 5.1, the sources of this variability in returns are often differentiated into two types of risk: systematic and unsystematic risk. **Systematic risk** refers to those factors that affect the returns on all comparable investments. For example, when the market as a whole rises, the prices of most individual securities also rise. There is a systematic relationship between the return on a specific asset and the return on all other assets in its class (i.e., all other comparable assets). Because this systematic relationship exists, diversifying the portfolio by acquiring comparable assets does not reduce this source of risk; thus, systematic risk is often referred to as *nondiversifiable risk*. While constructing a diversified portfolio has little impact

---

EXHIBIT 5.1 The Sources of Risk

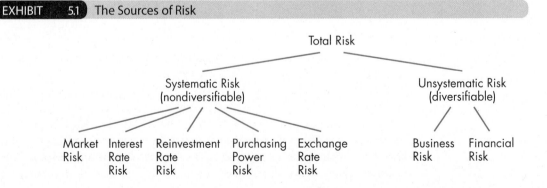

on systematic risk, you should not conclude that this nondiversifiable risk cannot be managed. One of the objectives of this text is to explain a variety of techniques that help manage the various sources of systematic risk.

market risk

Systematic risk; the risk associated with the tendency of a stock's price to fluctuate with the market.

Market risk refers to the tendency of security prices to move together. While it may be frustrating to invest in a firm that appears to be undervalued and then to watch the price of its stock fall as the market as a whole declines, that is the nature of market risk. Security prices do fluctuate, and the investor must either accept the risk associated with those fluctuations or not participate in the market.

While market risk is generally applied to stocks, the concept also applies to other assets, such as precious metals and real estate. The prices of these assets fluctuate. If the value of houses were to rise in general, then the value of a particular house would also tend to increase. But the converse is also true because the prices of houses could decline, causing the value of a specific house to fall. Market risk cannot be avoided if you acquire assets whose prices may fluctuate.

interest rate risk

The uncertainty associated with changes in interest rates; the possibility of loss resulting from increases in interest rates.

Interest rate risk refers to the tendency of security prices, especially fixed-income securities, to move inversely with changes in the rate of interest. As is explained in detail in Chapter 14, the prices of bonds and preferred stock depend in part on the current rate of interest. Rising interest rates decrease the current price of fixed-income securities because current purchasers require a competitive yield. The investor who acquires these securities must face the uncertainty of fluctuating interest rates that, in turn, cause the price of these fixed-income securities to fluctuate.

reinvestment rate risk

The risk associated with reinvesting earnings or principal at a lower rate than was initially earned.

Reinvestment rate risk refers to the risk associated with reinvesting funds generated by an investment. If an individual receives interest or dividends, these funds could be spent on goods and services. For example, many individuals who live on a pension consume a substantial portion, and perhaps all, of the income generated by their assets. Other investors, however, reinvest their investment earnings in order to accumulate wealth.

Consider an individual who wants to accumulate a sum of money and purchases a $1,000 bond that pays $100 a year and matures after ten years. The anticipated annual return based on the annual interest and the amount invested is 10 percent ($100/$1,000). The investor wants to reinvest the annual interest, and the question then becomes what rate will be earned on these reinvested funds: Will the return be more or less than the 10 percent initially earned? The essence of reinvestment rate risk is the uncertainty that the investor will earn less than the anticipated return when payments are received and reinvested.

The investor must also bear the risk associated with inflation. Inflation is the loss of purchasing power through a general rise in prices. If prices of goods and services increase, the real purchasing power of the investor's assets and the income generated by them is reduced. Thus, purchasing power risk is the risk that inflation will erode the buying power of the investor's assets and income. The opposite of inflation is deflation, which is a general decline in prices. During a period of deflation, the real purchasing power of the investor's assets and income is increased.

purchasing power risk

The uncertainty that future inflation will erode the purchasing power of assets and income.

Investors will naturally seek to protect themselves from loss of purchasing power by constructing a portfolio of assets with an anticipated return that is higher than the anticipated rate of inflation. It is important to note the word *anticipated*, because it influences the selection of particular assets. If inflation is expected to be 4 percent, a savings account offering 6 percent will produce a gain and thereby "beat" inflation. However, if the inflation rate were to increase unexpectedly to 7 percent, the savings account would result in a loss of purchasing power. The real rate of return would be negative. If the higher rate of inflation had been expected, the investor would not have chosen the savings account but would have purchased some other asset with a higher expected return.

The last source of systematic risk in Exhibit 5.1 refers to the currency risk associated with foreign investments. The price of one currency in terms of another is the **exchange rate**, and currencies may be expressed in terms of each other:

exchange rate

The price of a foreign currency in terms of another currency.

Country	U.S. $ Equivalent	Currency per U.S. Dollar
Britain (UK)	1.4345	0.6971

The entries indicate that the dollar cost of the British pound is $1.4345, or that $1.00 buys 0.6971 pounds. The 0.6971 is derived by dividing $1 by the price of the pound: $1/$1.4345 = 0.6971 units of the British currency.

revaluation

An increase in the value of one currency relative to other currencies.

Currencies trade daily, so exchange rates change virtually all the time. If the dollar cost of the pound rises to $1.45, that is a **revaluation** (appreciation) of the British currency. It is also a decline or **devaluation** in the value of the dollar, since more dollars are necessary to purchase one pound. If the dollar price of the pound falls to $1.40, that is a devaluation of the pound but a revaluation of the dollar.

devaluation

A decrease in the value of one currency relative to other currencies.

Fluctuating exchange rates mean that the value of any investment denominated in another currency rises and falls with changes in the exchange rate. **Exchange rate risk** is the uncertainty of the future value of a currency, since the foreign investment must be converted back to the domestic currency. Of course, this source of risk applies only if the investor acquires foreign investments denominated in another currency, such as the stock of a Brazilian company. The individual, however, may not be able to avoid exchange rate risk by limiting purchases of stock to domestic companies. Firms such as Coca-Cola (KO) or Tupperware (TUP) generate more than half their sales and earnings from foreign operations, so U.S. investors indirectly bear exchange rate risk when they buy stock in Coca-Cola and Tupperware.

exchange rate risk

The uncertainty associated with changes in the value of foreign currencies.

unsystematic risk

The risk associated with individual events that affect a particular security.

Unsystematic risk, which is also referred to as *diversifiable risk*, depends on factors that are unique to the specific asset. For example, a firm's earnings may decline because of a strike. Other firms in the industry may not experience the same labor problem, and thus their earnings may not be hurt or may even rise as customers divert purchases from the firm whose operations are temporarily halted. In either case, the change in the firm's earnings is independent of factors that affect the industry, the market, or the economy in general. Because this source of risk applies only to the specific firm, it may be reduced through the construction of a diversified portfolio.

business risk

The risk associated with the nature of a business.

The sources of unsystematic risk may be subdivided into two general classifications: business risk and financial risk. **Business risk** is the risk associated with the nature of the enterprise itself. Not all businesses are equally risky. Drilling for new oil deposits is more risky than running a commercial bank. The chances of finding oil may be slim, and only one of many new wells may actually produce oil and earn a positive return. Commercial banks, however, can make loans that are secured by particular assets, such as residences or inventories. While these loans are not risk-free, they may be relatively safe because even if the debtor defaults, the creditor (the bank) can seize the asset to meet its claims. Some businesses are by their very nature riskier than others, and, therefore, investing in them is inherently riskier.

All assets must be financed. Either creditors or owners or both provide the funds to start and to sustain the business. Firms use debt financing for two primary reasons. First, under current tax laws interest is a tax-deductible expense while dividends paid to stockholders from earnings are not. Second, debt financing is a source of financial leverage that may increase the return on equity (i.e., the return to the owners). If the firm earns more on the borrowed funds than it must pay in interest, the return on equity is increased.

For many firms the use of debt financing is a major source of funds. Leveraged buyouts and corporate restructuring often involve the issuing of a substantial amount of debt and have led to the development of high-yield securities often called *junk bonds*. Even conservatively managed firms use debt financing. Virtually every firm has some debt outstanding even if the debt is limited to accrued wages and accounts payable generated by the normal course of business.

financial risk

The risk associated with a firm's sources of financing.

This use of financial leverage is the source of **financial risk**. Borrowing funds to finance a business may increase risk, because creditors require that the borrower meet certain terms to obtain the funds. The most common of these requirements is the paying of interest and the repayment of principal. The creditor can (and usually does) demand additional terms, such as collateral or restrictions on dividend payments, that the borrower must meet. These restrictions mean that the firm that uses debt financing bears more risk

---

⊕ Point of Interest

OTHER TERMS USED TO DESCRIBE SOURCES OF RISK

The body of the text dichotomized the sources of risk into unsystematic/diversifiable risk, which may be reduced through the construction of well-diversified portfolios, and systematic/nondiversifiable risk, which cannot be reduced through diversification. These two general classes of risk were then subdivided into the sources of risk illustrated in Exhibit 5.1. Other terms or words are also used to describe sources of risk. Whether these are different sources or subsets for (or synonymous with) the sources in Exhibit 5.1 is probably open to debate. But if an investor's goal is risk management, such semantic discussions are probably immaterial.

Default risk refers to the probability that borrowers (e.g., a firm or government) will not meet their debt obligations. Such risk is firm-specific and may be considered as part of financial risk, the impact of which is reduced through the construction of a well-diversified portfolio. *Sovereign risk* (also called *political risk*) refers to the risk associated with investing in a specific country. Such risk is obvious for an investment in a country whose government may subsequently nationalize the assets—as occurred when Castro seized

power in Cuba. Sovereign risk may also apply to investments in emerging nations, whose economies and political environments are not stable. Since sovereign risk applies to specific nations, its impact may be reduced through diversification or avoided entirely by not investing in countries with unstable, volatile economies and governments.

Event risk refers to the possibility of loss from a specific event. This source of risk may be firm-specific. For example, A.H. Robbins's Dalkon Shield bankrupted the company. Specific events can also affect the market as a whole. The oil embargo of the 1970s caused a dramatic shift in the price of oil, which, in turn, had an impact on inflation and the level of economic activity. Stock prices and interest rates were also negatively affected. Whether the investor wants to consider as the source of risk the specific "event" or the expected increases in inflation and higher interest rates is probably immaterial. The ultimate effect was a general reduction in stock prices and lower bond prices, the impact of which could not have been reduced through the construction of a well-diversified portfolio.

because it must meet these obligations in addition to its other obligations. When sales and earnings are rising, these constraints may not be burdensome, but during periods of financial stress the failure of the firm to meet these terms may result in financial ruin and bankruptcy. A firm that does not use borrowed funds to acquire its assets does not have these additional responsibilities and does not have the element of financial risk.

TOTAL (PORTFOLIO) RISK

portfolio risk

The total risk associated with owning a portfolio; the sum of systematic and unsystematic risk.

diversification

The process of accumulating different securities to reduce the risk of loss.

The combination of systematic and unsystematic risk is defined as the total risk (or **portfolio risk**) that the investor bears. Unsystematic risk may be significantly reduced through **diversification**, which occurs when the investor purchases the securities of firms in different industries. Buying the stock of five telecommunication companies is not considered diversification, because the events that affect one company tend to affect the others. A diversified portfolio may consist of stocks and bonds issued by a communications company, an electric utility, an insurance firm, a commercial bank, an oil refinery, a retail business, and a manufacturing firm. This is a diversified mixture of industries and types of assets. The impact of particular events on the earnings and growth of one firm need not apply to all the firms; therefore, the risk of loss in owning the portfolio is reduced.

How diversification reduces risk is illustrated in Figure 5.1, which shows the price performance of three stocks and their composite. Stock A's price initially falls, then rises, and starts to fall again. Stock B's price ultimately rises but tends to fluctuate. Stock C's price fluctuates the least of the three but ends up with only a modest gain.

FIGURE	5.1	Prices of Three Stocks

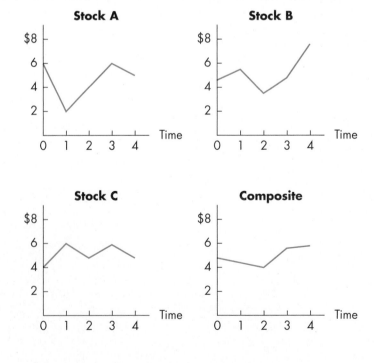

Purchasing stock B and holding it would have produced a substantial profit, while A would have generated a moderate loss.

The last quadrant illustrates what happens if the investor buys an equal dollar amount of each stock (i.e., buys a diversified portfolio).[1] First, the value of the portfolio as a whole may rise even though the value of an individual security may not. Second, and most important, the fluctuation in the value of the portfolio is less than the fluctuations in individual security prices. By diversifying the portfolio, the investor is able to reduce the risk of loss. Of course, the investor also gives up the possibility of a large gain (as was achieved by stock B).

In effect, a diversified portfolio *reduces unsystematic risk*. The risk associated with each individual investment is reduced by accumulating a diversified portfolio of assets. Even if one company fails (or does extremely well), the impact on the portfolio as a whole is reduced through diversification. Distributing investments among different industries, however, does not eliminate market risk and the other types of systematic risk. The value of a group of securities will tend to follow the market values in general. The price movements of securities will be mirrored by the diversified portfolio; hence, the investor cannot eliminate this source of systematic risk.

How many securities are necessary to achieve a diversified portfolio that reduces and almost eliminates unsystematic risk? The answer may be "surprisingly few." Several studies have found that risk has been significantly reduced in portfolios consisting of from 10 to 15 securities.[2]

This reduction in unsystematic risk is illustrated in Figure 5.2. The vertical axis measures units of risk, and the horizontal axis gives the number of securities. Since

FIGURE 5.2 Portfolio Risk: The Sum of Systematic and Unsystematic Risk

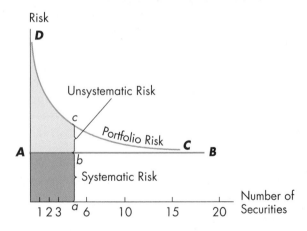

---

[1] Later in this chapter, the statistical condition that must be met to achieve diversification is discussed and illustrated using returns from investments in the common stocks of Mobil and Public Service Enterprise Group.
[2] For further discussion, see the following: Bruce D. Fielitz, "Indirect versus Direct Diversification," *Financial Management* (winter 1974): 54–62; William Sharpe, "Risk, Market Sensitivity and Diversification," *Financial Analysts Journal* (January–February 1972): 74–79, and Meir Statman, "How Many Stocks Make a Diversified Portfolio?" *Journal of Financial and Quantitative Analysis* (September 1987): 353–364. However, George Frankfurter suggests that even well-diversified portfolios have a substantial amount of nonsystematic risk. See his "Efficient Portfolios and Nonsystematic Risk," *The Financial Review* (fall 1981): 1–11.

systematic risk is independent of the number of securities in the portfolio, this element of risk is illustrated by a line, *AB*, that runs parallel to the horizontal axis. Regardless of the number of securities that an individual owns, the amount of nondiversifiable risk remains the same.[3]

Portfolio risk (i.e., the sum of systematic and unsystematic risk) is indicated by line *CD*. The difference between line *AB* and line *CD* is the unsystematic risk associated with the specific securities in the portfolio. The amount of unsystematic risk depends on the number of securities held. As this number increases, unsystematic risk diminishes; this reduction in risk is illustrated in Figure 5.2 where line *CD* approaches line *AB*. For portfolios consisting of ten or more securities, the risk involved is primarily systematic.

Such diversified portfolios, as mentioned previously, do not consist of ten public utilities but of a cross section of stocks. Investing $20,000 in ten stocks (i.e., $2,000 for each) may achieve a reasonably well diversified portfolio. Although such a portfolio costs more in commissions than two $10,000 purchases, the small investor achieves a diversified mixture of securities, which should reduce the risk of loss associated with investment in a specific security. Unfortunately, the investor must still bear the systematic risk associated with movements in the markets, the risk of loss in purchasing power that results from inflation, and the other sources of nondiversifiable risk.

THE MEASUREMENT OF RISK

Portfolio theory determines the combination of risk and return that achieves the highest return for a given level of risk. The previous section addressed the expected and realized return; the measurement of risk is the focus of the next sections of this text.

Risk is concerned with the uncertainty regarding whether the realized return will equal the expected return. The measurement of risk places emphasis either on the extent to which the return varies from the average return or on the volatility of the return relative to the return on the market. The variability of returns is measured by a statistical concept called the *standard deviation*, while volatility is measured by what has been termed a *beta coefficient*. (In terms of Figure 5.2, the standard deviation measures the total risk—that is, the distance *ac*. The beta measures systematic risk—distance *ab*. As may be seen in the figure, total risk approaches systematic risk as the portfolio becomes more diversified, so that in a well-diversified portfolio, the two measures of risk are essentially equal.) This section considers the standard deviation as a measure of risk. Beta coefficients are covered later in the chapter.

A measurement of risk is implied when individuals refer to the annual range in an asset's price. One may encounter such statements as "The stock is trading near its low for the year," or "245 stocks reached new highs while only 41 fell to new lows." Some individuals plan their investment strategy as if a stock trades within a price range. If the stock is near the low for the year, it may be a good time to purchase. Correspondingly, if it is trading

---

[3]The sources of systematic risk may be managed through techniques that are covered throughout this text. For example, the investor bears less market risk by constructing a portfolio that is less responsive to changes in securities prices. (See the discussion of beta coefficients later in this chapter.) Interest rate and reinvestment rate risk may be managed using "duration" or constructing a laddered bond portfolio (covered in Chapter 14). Exchange-rate risk may be reduced through the use of derivatives. (See the discussions of options, futures, and swaps in Chapters 17–19.)

near the high for the year, it may be a good time to sell. The range in the stock's price, then, can be used as a guide to strategy, because the price tends to gravitate to a mean between these two extremes. In other words, there is a *central tendency* for the price of the stock. The range in a stock's price then becomes a measure of risk. Stocks with wider ranges are "riskier" because their prices tend to deviate farther from the average (mean) price.

One problem with using the range as a measure of risk is that two securities with different prices can have the same range. For example, a stock whose price ranges from $10 to $30 has the same range as a stock whose price varies from $50 to $70. The range is $20 in both cases, but an increase from $10 to $30 is a 200 percent increment, whereas the increase from $50 to $70 is only a 40 percent increase. The price of the latter stock appears to be more stable; hence, less risk is associated with this security, even though both stocks involve equal risk according to the range.

Dispersion Around an Investment's Return

The problem inherent in using only two observations (e.g., a stock's high and low prices) to determine risk may be avoided by analyzing **dispersion** around an average value, such as an investment's average return. This technique considers all possible outcomes. If there is not much difference among the individual returns (i.e., they are close together), then the dispersion is small. If most of the returns are near the extremes and differ considerably from the average return, then the dispersion is large. The larger this dispersion, the greater the risk associated with a particular stock.

dispersion
Deviation from the average.

This concept is perhaps best illustrated by a simple example. An investment in either of two stocks yields an average return of 15 percent, but stocks could have the following returns:

Stock A	Stock B
13½%	11%
14	11½
14¼	12
14½	12½
15	15
15½	17½
15¾	18
16	18½
16½	19

Although the average return is the same for both stocks, there is an obvious difference in the individual returns. Stock A's returns are close to the average value, whereas stock B's returns are closer to the high and low values. The returns of stock A cluster around the average return. Because there is less variability in returns, it is the less risky of the two securities.

These differences in risk are illustrated in Figure 5.3, which plots returns on the horizontal axis and the frequency of their occurrence on the vertical axis. (This is basically the same information that was previously given for stocks A and B, except that more observations would be necessary to construct such a graph. While only nine observations are used in the illustration, the figure is drawn as if there were a large number of observations.) Most of stock A's returns are close to the average return, so the

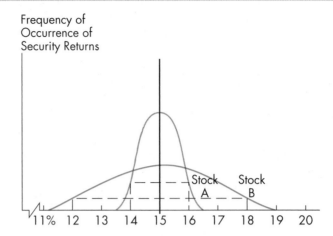

FIGURE   5.3   Distribution of the Returns of Two Stocks

frequency distribution is higher and narrower. The frequency distribution for stock B's return is lower and wider, which indicates a greater dispersion in that stock's returns.

The large dispersion around the average return implies that the stock involves greater risk because the investor can be less certain of the stock's return. The larger the dispersion, the greater is the chance of a large loss from the investment, and, correspondingly, the greater is the chance of a large gain. However, this potential for increased gain is concomitant with bearing more risk. Stock A involves less risk; it has the smaller dispersion. But it also has less potential for a large gain. A reduction in risk also means a reduction in possible return on the investment.

Standard Deviation as a Measure of Risk: One Asset

This dispersion around the mean value (i.e., the average return) is measured by the standard deviation. (The variance, which is the square of the standard deviation, is also used to measure risk.) See the discussion of the variance and semivariance in the appendix to this chapter. Since the standard deviation measures the tendency for the individual returns to cluster around the average return and is a measure of the variability of the return, it may be used as a measure of risk. The larger the dispersion, the greater the standard deviation and the larger the risk associated with the particular security.

The standard deviation of the returns for stock A is 1.01. The actual calculation of the standard deviation is illustrated in the appendix to this chapter. Plus or minus one standard deviation has been shown to encompass approximately 68 percent of all observations (in this case, 68 percent of all the returns). Since the standard deviation for A is 1.01, then approximately 68 percent of the returns fall between 13.99 and 16.01 percent. These returns are simply the average return (15 percent) plus 1.01 and minus 1.01 (i.e., plus or minus the standard deviation).

For stock B the standard deviation is 3.30, so approximately 68 percent of the returns fall between 11.7 and 18.3 percent. Stock B's returns have a wider dispersion from the average return, and this fact is indicated by the greater standard deviation.

These differences in the standard deviations are illustrated in Figure 5.4, which reproduces Figure 5.3 but adds the standard deviations. The average return for both

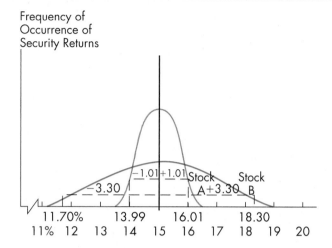

stocks is 15 percent, but the standard deviation is greater for stock B than for stock A (i.e., 3.30 for B versus 1.01 for A). By computing the standard deviation, the analyst quantifies risk. This will help in the selection of individual securities, since the investor will prefer those assets with the least risk for a given expected return.

If this were an illustration of selecting between two securities, the individual would select investment A because it has the lower standard deviation for a given return. If this were an illustration comparing the historical or actual returns between two investments, the individual would conclude that investment A had outperformed investment B because the returns were the same but B's return had been more variable.

Such comparisons are easy when the returns are the same, because the analysis is limited to comparing the standard deviations. The comparisons are also easy when the standard deviations are the same, because then the analysis is limited to comparing the returns. Such simple comparisons are rare, since investment returns and standard deviations often differ. Investment A may offer a return of 10 percent with a standard deviation of 4 percent, while investment B offers a return of 14 percent with a standard deviation of 6 percent. Since neither the returns nor the standard deviations are the same, they may not be compared. Investment A offers the lower return and less risk; therefore, it cannot be concluded that it is the superior investment.

This inability to compare may be overcome by computing the *coefficient of variation*, which divides the standard deviation by the return. This process, which is illustrated in the appendix to this chapter, expresses risk relative to return. Higher coefficients of variation imply more risk, because a higher numerical value means more variability per unit of return.

The Return and Standard Deviation of a Portfolio

Although the preceding discussion was limited to the return on an individual security and the dispersion around that return, the concepts can be applied to an entire portfolio. A portfolio also has an average return and a dispersion around that return. The investor is concerned not only with the return and the risk associated with each investment but also with the return and risk associated with the portfolio as a whole. This aggregate is, of course, the result of the individual investments and of each one's weight in the portfolio (i.e., the value of each asset, expressed in percentages, in proportion to the total value of the portfolio).

Consider a portfolio consisting of the following three stocks:

Stock	Return
1	8.3%
2	10.6
3	12.3

If 25 percent of the total value of the portfolio is invested in stocks 1 and 2 and 50 percent is invested in stock 3, the return is more heavily weighted in favor of stock 3. The return is a weighted average of each return times its proportion in the portfolio.

Return	×	Weight (Percentage Value of Stock in Proportion to Total Value of Portfolio)	=	Weighted Average
8.3%	×	0.25	=	2.075%
10.6	×	0.25	=	2.650
12.3	×	0.50	=	6.150

The return is the sum of these weighted averages.

$$2.075\%$$
$$2.650$$
$$\underline{6.150}$$
$$10.875\%$$

The previous example is generalized in Equation 5.3, which states that the return on a portfolio r_p is a weighted average of the returns of the individual assets $[(r_1) \ldots (r_n)]$, each weighted by its proportion in the portfolio $(w_1 \ldots w_n)$:

5.3
$$r_p = w_1(r_1) + w_2(r_2) + \cdots + w_n(r_n).$$

Thus, if a portfolio has 20 securities, each plays a role in the determination of the portfolio's return. The extent of that role depends on the weight that each asset has in the portfolio. Obviously those securities that compose the largest part of the individual's portfolio have the largest impact on the portfolio's return.[4]

Unfortunately, an aggregate measure of the portfolio's risk (i.e., the portfolio's standard deviation) is more difficult to construct than the weighted average of the returns. This is because securities prices are not independent of each other. However, while securities prices do move together, there can be considerable difference in these price movements. For example, prices of stocks of firms in home building may be more sensitive to recession than stock prices of utilities, whose prices may decline only moderately. These

---

[4]The same general equation may be applied to expected returns, in which case the expected return on a portfolio, $E(r_p)$, is a weighted average of the expected returns of the individual assets $[(E(r_1) \ldots E(r_n)]$, each weighted by its proportion in the portfolio $(w_1 \ldots w_n)$:

$$E(r_p) = w_1E(r_1) + w_2E(r_2) + \cdots + w_nE(r_n).$$

relationships among the assets in the portfolio must be considered in the construction of a measure of risk associated with the entire portfolio. These inner relationships among stocks are called *covariation*. Covariation considers not only the variability of the individual asset but also its relationship with the other assets in the portfolio.

Since the calculation of a portfolio's standard deviation becomes complicated for a portfolio of many assets, the following illustrations will be limited to portfolios of only two assets. Three cases are illustrated in Figure 5.5. In the first case, the two assets' returns move exactly together; in the second, the two assets' returns move exactly opposite; and in the third, the returns are independent of each other. While these examples are simple, they do illustrate how a portfolio's standard deviation is determined and the effect of the relationships among the assets in the portfolio on the risk associated with the portfolio as a whole.

The standard deviation of the returns on a portfolio (S_d) with two assets is given in Equation 5.4:

5.4
$$S_d = \sqrt{w_a^2 S_a^2 + w_b^2 S_b^2 + 2w_a w_b \, \text{cov}_{ab}}.$$

Although this looks formidable, it says that the standard deviation of the portfolio's return is the square root of the sum of (1) the squared standard deviation of the return of the first asset (S_a) times its squared weight in the portfolio (w_a) plus (2) the squared standard deviation of the return on the second asset (S_b) times its squared weight (w_b)

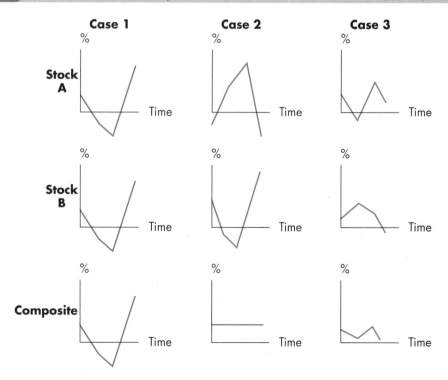

FIGURE   5.5   Stock Returns, Individually and Combined

in the portfolio plus (3) two times the weight of the first asset times the weight of the second asset times the covariance of the two assets.[5]

The calculation of covariation (like the calculation of the standard deviation) is illustrated in the appendix to this chapter. As is also explained in the appendix, the correlation coefficient combines the standard deviations of the two variables and the covariance, so the covariance is computed before the correlation coefficient. However, it is often convenient to express the covariance of returns on assets a and b (cov_{ab}) in terms of the correlation coefficient:

$$\text{cov}_{ab} = S_a \times S_b \times \text{(correlation coefficient of } a \text{ and } b).$$

Although the calculation of the correlation coefficient is illustrated in the appendix to this chapter, for this discussion it is necessary to know only that the numerical values of the correlation coefficient range from $+1.0$ for perfect positive correlation to -1.0 for perfect negative correlation.

To illustrate the determination of the portfolio's standard deviation, consider the returns earned by securities A and B and the returns' standard deviations in the following three cases in which the portfolio is divided equally between the two securities. The three cases are also shown in Figure 5.5, which plots the returns on the assets and on the portfolio composed of equal amounts invested in each (i.e., 50 percent of the portfolio in each asset).

Case 1

Perfect Positive Correlation (Correlation Coefficient = 1.0)

Year	Return on Security A	Return on Security B	Return on Portfolio
1	10%	10%	10%
2	−12	−12	−12
3	−25	−25	−25
4	37	37	37
Average return	2.5%	2.5%	2.5%
Standard deviation of security returns	27.16	27.16	?

---

[5]While Equation 5.4 expresses the standard deviation of a portfolio consisting of two assets, most portfolios consist of more than two assets. The standard deviations of portfolios consisting of more assets are computed in the same manner, but the calculation is considerably more complex. For a three-security portfolio, the calculation requires portfolio weights for securities a, b, and c, and the covariance of ab, ac, and bc. For a six-security portfolio, the calculation requires each security's weight and the covariance of ab, ac, ad, ae, af, bc, bd, be, bf, cd, ce, cf, de, df, and ef for a total of 15 covariances. The number of required covariances is

$$\frac{(n^2 - n)}{2},$$

in which n is the number of securities in the portfolios. For a six-security portfolio that is

$$\frac{(6^2 - 6)}{2} = 15.$$

For a portfolio with 100 securities, the required number of covariances is

$$\frac{(100^2 - 100)}{2} = 4,950.$$

While such calculations can be performed by computers, a two-security portfolio is sufficient to illustrate the computation of the portfolio standard deviation and its implication for diversification.

In this case, the securities move exactly together (i.e., their correlation coefficient is 1.0). The standard deviation of the portfolio is computed as follows:

$$S_d = \sqrt{w_a^2 S_a^2 + w_b^2 S_b^2 + 2 w_a w_b \text{cov}_{ab}}$$

$$= \sqrt{w_a^2 S_a^2 + w_b^2 S_b^2 + 2 w_a w_b S_a S_b \text{ Correlation Coefficient}_{ab}}$$

$$= \sqrt{0.5^2 (27.16)^2 + 0.5^2 (27.16)^2 + 2(0.5)(0.5)(27.16)(27.16)(1)}$$

$$= 27.16.$$

Case 2

Perfect Negative Correlation (Correlation Coefficient $= -1.0$)

Year	Return on Security A	Return on Security B	Return on Portfolio
1	−15%	25%	5%
2	12	−2	5
3	25	−15	5
4	−37	47	5
Average return	−3.75%	13.75%	5%
Standard deviation of security returns	27.73	27.73	?

In this case the returns move exactly opposite (i.e., the correlation coefficient is -1.0), and the standard deviation of the portfolio is

$$S_d = \sqrt{w_a^2 S_a^2 + w_b^2 S_b^2 + 2 w_a w_b \text{cov}_{ab}}$$

$$= \sqrt{0.5^2 (27.73)^2 + 0.5^2 (27.73)^2 + 2(0.5)(0.5)(27.73)(27.73)(-1)}$$

$$= 0.$$

Case 3

Partial Negative Correlation (Correlation Coefficient $= -0.524$)

Year Security A	Return on Security A	Return on Security B	Return on Portfolio
1	10%	2%	6%
2	−8	12	2
3	14	6	10
4	4	−2	1
Average return	5%	4.5%	4.75%
Standard deviation of security returns	9.59	5.97%	?

In this last case the returns do not move together. In the first and third years they both generated positive returns, but in the other two years one generated a loss while the other produced a positive return. In this illustration the correlation coefficient between the returns equals -0.524. Thus, the standard deviation of the portfolio is

$$S_d = \sqrt{w_a^2 S_a^2 + w_b^2 S_b^2 + 2w_a w_b cov_{ab}}$$
$$= \sqrt{0.5^2(9.59)^2 + 0.5^2(5.97)^2 + 2(0.5)(0.5)(9.59)(5.97)(-0.524)}$$
$$= 4.11.$$

Notice how, in the first case, the standard deviation of the portfolio is the same as the standard deviation of the two assets. Combining these assets in the portfolio has no impact on the risk associated with the portfolio. In Case 2, the portfolio's risk is reduced to zero (i.e., the portfolio's standard deviation is zero). This indicates that combining these assets whose returns fluctuate exactly in opposite directions has the effect on the portfolio of completely erasing risk. The fluctuations associated with one asset are exactly offset by the fluctuations in the other asset, so there is no variability in the portfolio's return.

Notice that in the second case the elimination of risk does not eliminate the positive return. Of course, if one asset yielded a return of $+10$ percent while the other asset yielded -10 percent, the net return is 0 percent. That is, however, a special case. If in one period the return on one asset is $+15$ percent while the other is -5 percent, the net is 5 percent.[6] If, in the next period, the first asset yielded -1 percent while the other yielded 11 percent, the net is still 5 percent. The swing in the first asset's return is -16 percent ($+15$ to -1), while the swing in the second asset's return is $+16$ percent (-5 to $+11$). The movements are exactly opposite, so the correlation coefficient would be -1.0, but the return on a portfolio *equally* invested in the two securities would be $+5$ percent for both periods.

In the third case, which is the most realistic of the three illustrations, the standard deviation of the portfolio is less than the standard deviations of the individual assets. The risk associated with the portfolio as a whole is less than the risk associated with either of the individual assets. Even though the assets' returns do fluctuate, the fluctuations partially offset each other, so that by combining these assets in the portfolio, the investor reduces exposure to risk with almost no reduction in the return.

Diversification and the reduction in unsystematic risk require that assets' returns not be highly positively correlated. When there is a high positive correlation (as in Case 1), there is no risk reduction. When the returns are perfectly negatively correlated (as in Case 2), risk is erased (i.e., there is no variability in the combined returns). If one asset's return falls, the decline is exactly offset by the increase in the return earned by the other asset. The effect is to achieve a risk-free return. In the third case, there is neither a perfect positive nor a perfect negative correlation. However, there is risk reduction, because the returns are poorly correlated. The lower the positive correlation or the greater the negative correlation among the returns, the greater will be the risk reduction achieved by combining the various assets in the portfolio.

While the above illustration is extended, it points out a major consideration in the selection of assets to be included in a portfolio. The individual asset's expected return and risk are important, but the asset's impact on the portfolio as a whole is also important. The asset's return and the variability of that return should be considered in a portfolio context. It is quite possible that the inclusion of a volatile asset will reduce the risk exposure of the portfolio as a whole if the return is negatively correlated with the

---

[6]Remember: The return is a weighted average of the individual returns, so in this illustration the return is (0.5) (0.15) + (0.5) (−0.05) = 0.05 = 5%.

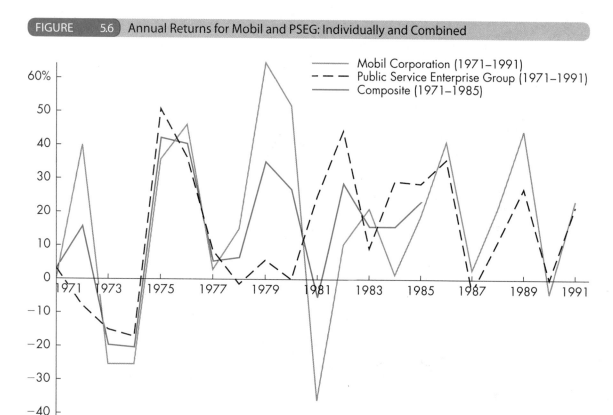

FIGURE 5.6 Annual Returns for Mobil and PSEG: Individually and Combined

—— Mobil Corporation (1971–1991)
– – – Public Service Enterprise Group (1971–1991)
—— Composite (1971–1985)

returns offered by the other assets in the portfolio. Failure to consider the relationships among the assets in the portfolio could be counterproductive if including the asset reduces the portfolio's potential return without reducing the variability of the portfolio's return (i.e., without reducing the element of risk).[7]

RISK REDUCTION THROUGH DIVERSIFICATION: AN ILLUSTRATION

The previous discussion has been abstract, but the concept of diversification through securities whose returns are not positively correlated may be illustrated by considering the returns earned on two specific stocks, Public Service Enterprise Group and Mobil Corporation. Public Service Enterprise Group is primarily an electric and gas utility whose stock price fell with higher interest rates and inflation. Prior to its merger with Exxon, Mobil was a resource company whose stock price rose during inflation in response to higher oil prices but fell during the 1980s as oil prices weakened and inflation receded.

The annual returns (dividends plus price change) on investments in these two stocks are given in Figure 5.6. As may be seen in the graph, there were several periods when the

[7]The correlation between assets is an essential topic in portfolio management and appears frequently in this text, especially when considering diversification through the use of fixed-income securities, real estate, collectibles, or foreign securities.

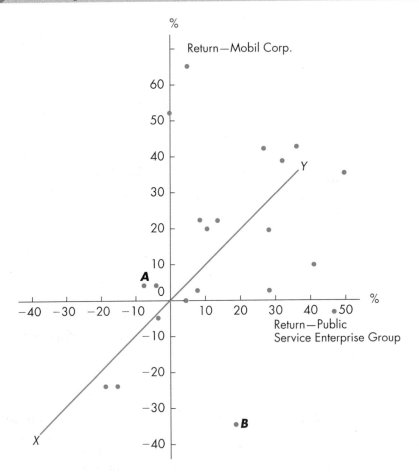

FIGURE   5.7   Scatter Diagram of Returns for Mobil and PSEG

returns on the two stocks moved in opposite directions. For example, during 1971 and 1978, an investment in Public Service Enterprise Group generated a loss while an investment in Mobil produced a gain. However, the converse occurred during 1981 as the trend in Public Service Enterprise Group's stock price started to improve. From 1980 to 1985 the price of Public Service Enterprise Group doubled, but the price of Mobil's stock declined so that most of the return earned on Mobil's stock during the mid-1980s was its dividend.

Figure 5.7 presents a scatter diagram of the returns on these two stocks for 1971–1991. The horizontal axis presents the average annual return on Public Service Enterprise Group, while the vertical axis presents the average annual return on Mobil Corporation. As may be seen in the graph, the individual points lie throughout the plane representing the returns. For example, point A represents a positive return on Mobil but a negative return on Public Service Enterprise Group, and point B represents a positive return on Public Service Enterprise Group but a negative return on Mobil.

Combining these securities in a portfolio reduces the individual's risk exposure, as is also shown in Figures 5.6 and 5.7. The line representing the composite return in Figure 5.6 runs between the lines representing the returns on the individual securities. Over the entire time period, the average annual returns on Mobil and Public Service

⊕ Point of Interest

TANGIBLE ASSETS AND DIVERSIFICATION

Perhaps the strongest rationale for acquiring collectibles and other nonfinancial assets is their possible impact on diversification. The returns on most financial assets tend to be positively correlated. When stock prices rise, the prices of most individual stocks rise in sympathy. The factors that cause stock prices to rise often cause bond prices to rise. Lower interest rates tend to be bullish for both stocks and bonds. Inflation tends to cause the prices of both stocks and bonds to fall as earnings are squeezed and tighter monetary policy raises interest rates.

The returns on some physical assets (e.g., gold and other precious metals, real estate, and art objects) may be negatively correlated with returns on financial assets. The inflation that hurts stocks and bonds may be beneficial for precious metals or real estate. This suggests that these assets can play an important role in the construction of a diversified portfolio. The attractiveness of tangible assets then may not be the returns they offer but the possibility of risk reduction, in which case they are not alternatives to financial assets but complementary to them.

Enterprise Group were 16.6 and 13.0 percent, respectively. The average annual return on the composite was 14.8 percent. The risk reduction (i.e., the reduction in the dispersion of the returns) can be seen by comparing the standard deviations of the returns. For the individual stocks, the standard deviations were 26.5 percent and 19.4 percent, respectively, for Mobil and Public Service Enterprise Group. However, the standard deviation for the composite return was 18.9, so the dispersion of the returns associated with the portfolio is less than the dispersion of the returns on either stock by itself.[8]

In this illustration the correlation coefficient between the two returns is 0.34. This lack of correlation is visible in Figure 5.7. If there were a high positive correlation between the two returns, the points would lie close to the line XY. Instead, the points are scattered throughout the figure. Thus, there is little correlation between the two returns, which is why combining the two securities reduces the individual's risk exposure.

It should be noted that combining these two stocks achieved diversification in the past because their returns were not highly correlated. Such diversification, however, may not be achieved in the future if the returns become highly positively correlated. This higher correlation appears to have occurred since 1985. The annual returns plotted in Figure 5.6 appear to have moved together from 1985 through 1991. This movement suggests that investing in these two stocks had little impact on diversification after 1985. This inference is confirmed because the correlation coefficient for the years 1971 through 1985 is 0.231, but 0.884 for 1986 through 1991. (The correlation remained high after 1991 and was 0.732 for the 15 years 1985–1999. This high correlation suggests that acquiring Mobil and PSEG would have had at best a small impact on the variability of the portfolio's return during that period.)

Diversification and Asset Allocation

One purpose of asset allocation is the diversification of a portfolio. As an investment policy, asset allocation determines what proportion of the portfolio should be invested in different classes or types of assets. A financial planner may recommend that a client construct a portfolio of 10 percent liquid assets such as money market mutual funds to meet financial

---

[8] The calculation is $\sqrt{(0.5)^2(26.5)^2 + (0.5)^2(19.4)^2 + 2(0.5)(0.5)(26.5)(19.4)(0.34)} = 18.9$.

emergencies, 30 percent fixed-income securities (bonds) to generate income, and 60 percent stocks to generate growth. The stock component of the portfolio may be allocated one-third to large companies (i.e., large cap), one-third to smaller companies (i.e., mid and small cap stocks), and one-third to foreign securities. The foreign stocks may be allocated between emerging economies such as China and developed economies such as Japan.

A portfolio of 60 percent stock, 30 percent bonds, and 10 percent cash should help achieve diversification. Of course, for this allocation to diversify a portfolio, the returns on the various assets would have to lack high, positive correlation. To some extent, this lack of correlation is self-evident. The modest return on the liquid assets should not be correlated with the return on the stocks. Combining these assets with stocks should reduce the variability of the portfolio without necessarily reducing the return.

PORTFOLIO THEORY

Harry Markowitz is credited with being the first individual to use the preceding material to develop a theory of portfolio construction employing returns and risk as measured by a portfolio's standard deviation.[9] This contribution was a major advance in finance and led to the development of the Capital Asset Pricing Model (CAPM) and subsequently to the arbitrage pricing model, generally referred to as *arbitrage pricing theory* (APT). Both the CAPM and the APT seek to explain portfolio and security returns as a response to change in identifiable variables.

The Markowitz Model

The Markowitz model is premised on a risk-averse individual constructing a diversified portfolio that maximizes the individual's satisfaction (generally referred to as *utility* by economists) by maximizing portfolio returns for a given level of risk. This process is depicted in Figures 5.8 through 5.10, which illustrate the optimal combinations of risk and return available to investors, the desire of investors to maximize their utility, and the determination of the optimal portfolio that integrates utility maximization within the constraint of the available portfolios.

Figure 5.8 illustrates the determination of the optimal portfolios *available* to investors. The vertical axis measures portfolio expected returns expressed as a percentage. The horizontal axis measures the risk associated with the portfolio, using the portfolio's standard deviation (σ_p). In Figure 5.8, the shaded area represents possible portfolios composed of various combinations of risky securities. This area is generally referred to as the *attainable* or *feasible* set of portfolios. Some of these portfolios are **inefficient** because they offer an inferior return for a given amount of risk. For example, portfolio A is inefficient since portfolio B offers a higher return for the same amount of risk.

All portfolios that offer the highest return for a given amount of risk are referred to as **efficient**. The line that connects all these portfolios (XY in Figure 5.8) defines the *efficient frontier* and is referred to as the *efficient set* of portfolios. Any portfolio that offers the highest return for a given amount of risk must lie on the efficient frontier. Any portfolio that offers a lower return is inefficient and lies below the efficient frontier in

inefficient portfolio
A portfolio whose return is not maximized given the level of risk.

efficient portfolio
The portfolio that offers the highest expected return for a given amount of risk.

[9]Harry M. Markowitz, "Portfolio Selection," *Journal of Finance* (March 1952); and Harry M. Markowitz, *Portfolio Selection: Efficient Diversification of Investments* (New York: Wiley, 1959).

FIGURE	5.8	The Efficient Frontier

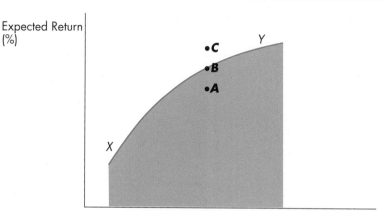

Risk: Portfolio Standard Deviation (σ_p)

the shaded area. Since inefficient portfolios will not be selected, the efficient frontier establishes the best set of portfolios available to investors.

A portfolio such as *C* that lies above the efficient frontier offers a superior yield for the amount of risk. Investors would prefer that portfolio to portfolio *B* on the efficient frontier because *C* offers a higher return for the same level of risk. Unfortunately, combination *C* of risk and return does not exist. It is not a feasible solution. No combination of risk and expected return that lies above the efficient frontier is attainable.

While the efficient frontier gives all the best attainable combinations of risk and return, it does not tell *which* of the possible combinations an investor will select. That selection depends on the individual's willingness to bear risk. The combining of the efficient frontier and the willingness to bear risk determines the investor's optimal portfolio. Figure 5.8 gives only the efficient frontier; it says nothing about the investor's willingness to bear risk.

This willingness to bear risk may be shown by the use of indifference curves, which are often used in economic theory to indicate levels of an individual's utility (i.e., consumer satisfaction) and the impact of trading one good for another. While satisfaction cannot be measured, the analysis permits the *ranking of levels of satisfaction*. A higher level of satisfaction may be reached by obtaining more of one good without losing some of an alternative good. For example, a consumer will prefer a combination of five apples and five oranges to a combination of five apples and four oranges, because the individual has more apples but has not lost any oranges.

While five apples and five oranges is preferred to five apples and four oranges, it cannot be concluded that the individual will prefer six apples and four oranges to five apples and five oranges. To obtain the sixth apple, the consumer gave up one orange. If the consumer prefers the additional apple to the lost orange, then a higher level of satisfaction is achieved. If the consumer does not prefer the additional apple, then the level of satisfaction is reduced. It is also possible that the additional satisfaction gained by the additional apple exactly offsets the satisfaction lost, so the individual is indifferent between five apples and five oranges and six apples and four oranges. Notice that instead of measuring satisfaction, the analysis seeks to determine *levels* of satisfaction—that is, which combination of goods is preferred.

FIGURE 5.9 Indifference Map

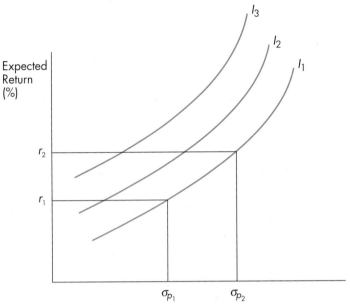

Risk: Portfolio Standard Deviation (σ_p)

When applied to portfolio theory, the economic theory of consumer behavior develops the trade-off between risk and return (instead of the trade-off between two goods such as apples and oranges). This trade-off between risk and return is also shown by indifference curves. A set of these indifference curves is illustrated in Figure 5.9. Each indifference curve represents a level of satisfaction, with higher curves indicating higher levels of satisfaction. Movements along a given curve indicate the same level of satisfaction (the individual is indifferent). For example, on indifference curve I_1, the investor would be willing to accept a modest return, such as r_1 and bear a modest amount of risk (σ_{p_1}). The same investor would also be willing to bear more risk for a higher return (e.g., r_2 and (σ_{p_2}). The additional return is sufficient to induce bearing the additional risk, so the investor is *indifferent between the two alternatives*. Thus, all the points on the same indifference curve represent the same level of satisfaction.

The indifference curves in Figure 5.9 are for a risk-averse investor; hence, additional risk requires more return. However, notice that these curves are concave from above; their slope increases as risk increases. This indicates that investors require ever-increasing amounts of additional return for equal increments of risk to maintain the same level of satisfaction.

Investors would like to earn a higher return without having to bear additional risk. A higher return without additional risk increases total satisfaction. Higher levels of satisfaction are indicated by indifference curves I_2 and I_3, which lie above indifference curve I_1. Once again the investor is *indifferent between any combination of risk and return* on I_2. All combinations of risk and return on indifference curve I_2 are preferred to all combinations on indifference curve I_1. Correspondingly, all points on indifference curve I_3 are preferred to all points on I_2. Since there is an indefinite number of levels of satisfaction, an indefinite number of indifference curves could be constructed for an

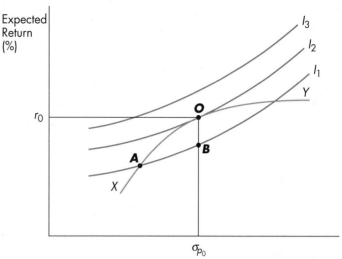

FIGURE   5.10   Determination of the Optimal Portfolio

Risk: Portfolio Standard Deviation (σ_p)

individual. Each would represent a different level of satisfaction, and the higher the curve, the higher the level of satisfaction. (One of the advantages offered by this type of analysis is that indifference curves themselves do not measure satisfaction; they only indicate rankings—that is, I_2 is preferred to I_1.)

The investor seeks to reach the highest level of satisfaction but is, of course, constrained by what is available. The best combinations of risk and return available are given by the efficient frontier. Superimposing the indifference curves on the efficient frontier defines the investor's optimal portfolio. This is shown in Figure 5.10, which combines Figures 5.8 and 5.9. The optimal combination of risk and return represented by point O is the investor's optimal combination of risk and return.

If the investor selects any other portfolio with a different combination of risk and return on the efficient frontier (e.g., A), that portfolio would not be the individual's best choice. While portfolio A is an efficient combination of risk and return, it is not the optimal choice, as may be seen using the following logic. Portfolio B is equal to portfolio A (i.e., the investor is indifferent between A and B), but B is not efficient and is inferior to portfolio O, since O offers a higher level of return for the same amount of risk. Portfolio O must be preferred to B, and because A and B are equal, O must also be preferred to A. By similar reasoning, only one portfolio offers the highest level of satisfaction *and* lies on the efficient frontier. That unique combination of risk and return is represented by portfolio O, which occurs at the *tangency* of the efficient frontier and indifference curve I_2.

If an indifference curve cuts through the efficient frontier (e.g., I_1), it is attainable but inferior, and it can always be shown that the investor can reach a higher level of satisfaction by altering the portfolio. If an indifference curve lies above the efficient frontier (e.g., I_3), such a level of satisfaction is not obtainable. The investor would like to reach that level of satisfaction, but no combination of assets offers such a high expected return for that amount of risk.

Different investors may have varying indifference curves. If the investor is very risk-averse, the curves tend to be steep, indicating a large amount of additional return is necessary to induce this individual to bear additional risk and maintain the same level of satisfaction. If the curves are relatively flat, the individual is less risk-averse. Only a modest amount of additional return is necessary to induce this individual to bear additional risk and still maintain the same level of satisfaction. However, both investors are still averse to bearing risk. The difference is the degree of risk aversion.

THE CAPITAL ASSET PRICING MODEL

Although indifference curves cannot be observed or estimated, combining them with the efficient frontier produced a major step forward for portfolio theory. For the first time, the Markowitz model explained diversified portfolio construction in the utility-maximization framework generally used by economists. This model subsequently led to the development of the Capital Asset Pricing Model (CAPM) by William F. Sharpe, John Lintner, and Jan Mossin.[10] The CAPM is among the most important *theoretical concepts* in finance; it advances the relationship between risk and return in an efficient market context, adds the possibility of earning a risk-free return, and is easier to implement than the Markowitz model. The CAPM is an outgrowth of the Markowitz model and extends the concept of optimal diversified portfolios to the market in general and to the valuation of individual securities. That is, the concept is applied in both a *macro* context that specifies the relationship between risk and the return on a portfolio and a *micro* context that specifies the relationship between risk and the return on a specific asset.

The macro aspect of the CAPM is the development of the *capital market line*. Figure 5.11 begins with all the possible efficient portfolios of risky securities and adds line

---

| FIGURE | 5.11 | Capital Market Line |

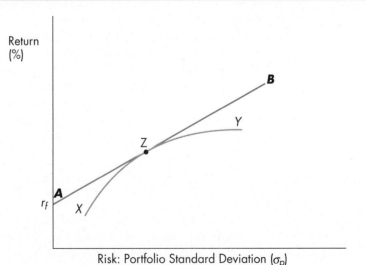

---

[10]For the seminal work on CAPM, see William Sharpe, "Capital Asset Prices: A Theory of Market Equilibrium," *Journal of Finance* (September 1964): 425–442; John Lintner, "The Valuation of Risk Assets and the Selection of Risk Investments in Stock Portfolios and Capital Budgets," *Review of Economics and Statistics* (February 1965): 13–37; and Jan Mossin, "Equilibrium in a Capital Asset Market," *Econometrica* (October 1966): 768–783. The contributions of Markowitz and Sharpe to the analysis of risk and the development of portfolio theory are so important that they, along with Merton Miller, were awarded the Nobel Prize in economics in 1990.

AB, which begins at r_f on the Y-axis and is tangent to the efficient frontier. *AB* is the capital market line specified by the Capital Asset Pricing Model. Each point on the line represents a combination of the risk-free security and a portfolio encompassing risky securities. If investors bear no risk and invest their entire portfolios in risk-free assets, they should earn a return equal to r_f. As investors substitute risky securities for the risk-free assets, both risk and return increase (i.e., there is movement along the capital market line). Point *Z*, the point of tangency, represents a portfolio consisting solely of risky securities. To the right of *Z*, an investor is using margin to increase return further, but the use of margin continues to increase risk. In effect, the capital market line *AZB* becomes the efficient frontier. Combinations of risk and return on this line represent the best attainable portfolios, and these combinations range from portfolios with no risk earning only the risk-free return to portfolios in which securities are bought on margin.

The equation for the capital market line is based on the equation for a straight line:

$$Y = a + bX,$$

in which *Y* is the return on the portfolio (r_p); *a*, the intercept, is the risk-free rate (r_f), *X* measures risk; and *b* is the slope of the line. The equation for the capital market line is

5.5
$$r_p = r_f + \left(\frac{r_m - r_f}{\sigma_m}\right)\sigma_p.$$

This equation states that the return on a portfolio (r_p) is the sum of the return earned on a risk-free asset (risk-free return $= r_f$) such as a Treasury bill and a risk premium that depends on (1) the extent to which the return on the market exceeds the risk-free return (i.e., $r_m - r_f$) and (2) the dispersion of the portfolio (σ_p) relative to the dispersion of the market (σ_m). If the dispersion of the portfolio is equal to the dispersion of the market, these two considerations cancel; the return on such a portfolio depends solely on the risk-free rate and the risk premium associated with investing in securities. If, however, the dispersion of the portfolio is greater than the dispersion of the market, the return will have to exceed the return associated with the market. The risk premium is larger. Thus, the capital market line indicates that to earn larger returns, the investor is required to take greater risks.

The Capital Asset Pricing Model and Beta Coefficients

The second component of the Capital Asset Pricing Model is the specification of the relationship between risk and return for the *individual* asset. At the micro level this relationship is referred to as the *security market line* (SML). Although this relationship is very similar to the capital market line, the difference is important. In the capital market line, risk is measured by the portfolio's standard deviation. In the security market line, the individual asset's risk is measured by a *beta coefficient*. Understanding the security market line requires understanding beta coefficients. Thus, it is necessary to explain this measure of risk before discussing its use in the Capital Asset Pricing Model.

BETA COEFFICIENTS

beta coefficient

An index of risk; a measure of the systematic risk associated with a particular stock.

When an individual constructs a well-diversified portfolio, the unsystematic sources of risk are diversified away. That leaves the systematic sources of risk as the relevant risks. A **beta coefficient** is a measure of systematic risk; it is an index of the volatility of the individual asset relative to the volatility of the market. The beta coefficient for a specific security (βi) is defined as follows:

5.6 $$\beta_i = \frac{\text{Standard deviation of the return on stock } i}{\text{Standard deviation of the return on the market}} \times \text{the return on the stock and the return on the market} \cdot$$

Thus, beta depends on (1) the variability of the individual stock's return, (2) the variability of the market return (both measured by their respective standard deviations), and (3) the correlation between the return on the security and the return on the market. (The computation of beta is illustrated in the section on regression analysis in the appendix to this chapter.)

The ratio of the standard deviations measures how variable the stock is relative to the variability of the market. The more variable a stock's return (i.e., the larger the standard deviation of the stock's return) relative to the variability of the market's return, the greater the risk associated with the individual stock. The correlation coefficient indicates whether this greater variability is important.

The impact of different numerical values for the standard deviation of the stock's return and for the correlation coefficient on the beta coefficient is illustrated in Exhibit 5.2. The exhibit has two parts. In the first, the stock return moves exactly with the market, so the correlation coefficient between the return on the stock and the return on the market is 1.0. Since the correlation coefficient is equal to 1.0, there is a strong, positive relationship between the return on the market and the return on the stock. Whether the stock has more or less market risk depends on the variability of the stock's return relative to the variability of the market return. When the stock's return is less variable than the market return (e.g., when the standard deviation is 2 percent),

EXHIBIT   5.2   Various Values of Beta Coefficients

Part 1	
Standard deviation of the market	10%
Correlation coefficient of the returns on the stock and on the market	1.0
Standard Deviation of the Stock	Beta
2%	(2/10)(1) = 0.2
6	(6/10)(1) = 0.6
10	(10/10)(1) = 1.0
14	(14/10)(1) = 1.4
18	(18/10)(1) = 1.8

Part 2	
Standard deviation of the market	10%
Standard deviation of the stock	10%
Correlation Coefficient	Beta
−1.0	(10/10)(−1.0) = −1.0
−0.5	(10/10)(−0.5) = −0.5
0.0	(10/10)(0.0) = 0.0
0.5	(10/10)(0.5) = 0.5
1.0	(10/10)(1.0) = 1.0

⊕ **Point of Interest**

A PRACTICAL CAPITAL MARKET LINE

The prior discussion indicates that one facet of the Capital Asset Pricing Model is a theory explaining the determination of an individual's optimal portfolio as a combination of a riskless asset and a portfolio of risky securities in which the capital market line specifies the relationship between a portfolio's risk and return. The slope of the line indicates the additional return associated with each additional unit of risk. Illustrations such as Figure 5.12 are sometimes used to indicate how individual classes of assets may fall on the capital market line and how the substitution of one class of assets increases the investor's return and risk exposure.

Although the discussion of each type of security in Figure 5.12 is deferred until its appropriate place in the text, the illustration suggests that there are specific assets, such as short-term U.S. Treasury bills or federally insured savings accounts, that generate a modest return without risk. As you move farther to the right, returns increase as the investor acquires riskier assets. Risk-free assets are followed by money market securities with marginally higher yields. These are succeeded by bonds with intermediate-term maturities of one to ten years. Bonds with longer terms to maturity tend to offer higher returns but expose the investor to greater risk. Stocks of large corporations and small firms offer even more return but require the

individual to bear even greater risk. At the extreme right of the figure, such assets as options, foreign investments, real estate, collectibles, and futures contracts produce the highest returns but carry the greatest amount of risk.

While Figure 5.12 indicates that some assets offer higher returns for additional risk-taking, the Capital Asset Pricing Model suggests that investors combine these various assets in efficient diversified portfolios. If an investor's particular portfolio does not lie on the efficient frontier, that individual alters the combination of assets to obtain an efficient portfolio. Then the investor determines if that efficient portfolio offers the highest level of satisfaction. If it does not, the investor further alters the portfolio until both conditions are met, so that the portfolio is efficient while achieving the highest level of satisfaction.

This process is no different than individuals' allocating their income among various goods and services so that the highest level of consumer satisfaction is achieved with the given amount of income. The amount of income constrains the consumer just as the efficient frontier constrains the investor. Given these constraints, individuals still behave in such a way as to maximize their consumer satisfaction. In portfolio theory, that maximization is indicated by the tangency of the efficient frontier and the individual investor's indifference curves.

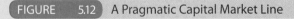

| FIGURE | 5.12 | A Pragmatic Capital Market Line |

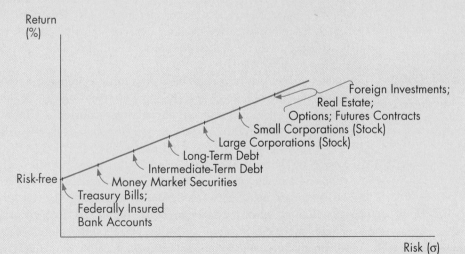

the beta is 0.2. The stock is less volatile than the market, and the stock has only a small amount of market risk. When the standard deviation is 18 percent, the beta is 1.8. The stock is more volatile than the market and has a large amount of market risk.

In the second part of Exhibit 5.2, the standard deviations of the stock and the market are equal, but the value of the correlation coefficient varies. When the returns on the stock and the market move in exactly opposite directions, the correlation coefficient is −1.0 and the beta is −1.0. While the variability of the stock and the market are the same, the volatility of the stock and the market returns are exactly opposite. Conversely, if the correlation coefficient is +1.0, the beta is +1.0. The variability of the stock and market returns are identical, and the volatility of the stock is the same as the market. If there is no relationship between returns on the stock and the market (i.e., the correlation coefficient is 0.0), the beta equals 0.0. The return on the stock does not respond to changes in the market; there is no market risk. The stock's return can vary, but this variability must be explained by other sources of risk.

As long as there is a strong relationship between the return on the stock and the return on the market (i.e., the correlation coefficient is not a small number), the beta coefficient has meaning. Since the numerical values of the correlation coefficients can range from −1.0 to +1.0, they are often squared to obtain the *coefficient of determination*, or (R^2). As is explained in the statistical appendix to this chapter, the coefficient of determination gives the proportion of the variation in one variable explained by the variation in the other variable. Beta coefficients with low coefficients of determination suggest that the beta is of little use in explaining the movements in the stock, because some factor other than the market is causing the variation in the stock's return.

If a stock has a beta of 1.0, the implication is that the stock's return moves exactly with an index of the market. A 10 percent return in the market could be expected to produce a 10 percent return on the specific stock. Correspondingly, a 10 percent decline in the market would result in a 10 percent decline in the return on the stock. A beta coefficient of less than 1.0 implies that the return on the stock would tend to fluctuate less than the market as a whole. A coefficient of 0.7 indicates that the stock's return would rise by only 7 percent as a result of a 10 percent increase in the market but would fall by only 7 percent when the market declined by 10 percent. A coefficient of 1.2 means that the return on the stock could be expected to be 12 percent if the market return was 10 percent, but the return on the stock would decline by 12 percent when the market declined by 10 percent.

The greater the beta coefficient, the more systematic market risk associated with the individual stock. High beta coefficients may indicate higher profits during rising markets, but they also indicate greater losses during declining markets. Stocks with high beta coefficients are referred to as *aggressive*. The converse is true for stocks with low beta coefficients, which should earn lower returns than the market during periods of rising stock prices but earn higher (or less negative) returns than the market during periods of declining prices. Such stocks are referred to as *defensive*.

This relationship between the return on a specific security and the market index as a whole is illustrated in Figures 5.13 and 5.14. In each graph the horizontal axis represents the percentage return on the market index and the vertical axis represents the percentage return on the individual stock. The line *AB*, which represents the market, is the same in both graphs. It is a positive-sloped line that runs through the point of origin and is equidistant from both axes (i.e., it makes a 45-degree angle with each axis).

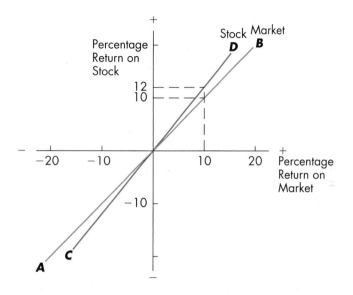

FIGURE   5.13   Stock with a Beta Coefficient of Greater Than 1.0

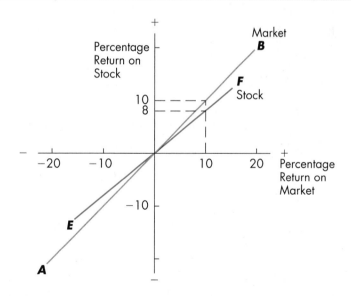

FIGURE   5.14   Stock with a Beta Coefficient of Less Than 1.0

Figure 5.13 illustrates a stock with a beta coefficient of greater than 1.0. Line *CD* represents a stock whose return rose and declined more than the market. In this case the beta coefficient is 1.2, so when the return on the market index is 10 percent, this stock's return is 12 percent.

Figure 5.14 illustrates a stock with a beta coefficient of less than 1.0. Line *EF* represents a stock whose return rose (and declined) more slowly than that of the market. In this case the beta coefficient is 0.8, so when the market's return is 10 percent, this stock's return is 8 percent.

EXHIBIT 5.3	Selected Beta Coefficients as Computed by *Value Line*							
	Beta Coefficient							
Company	1986	1992	1995	1998	2001	2004	2007	2009
AT&T	0.90	0.85	0.85	NMF	1.00	NMF	1.10	0.80
ExxonMobil	0.80	0.75	0.60	0.85	0.80	0.80	0.90	0.80
Altria (Philip Morris Inc.)	0.95	1.05	1.20	1.00	0.70	0.70	0.80	NMF
Johnson & Johnson	0.95	1.05	1.10	1.10	0.85	0.70	0.65	0.55
IBM	1.05	0.95	1.00	1.15	1.00	1.05	1.00	0.90
GE	1.05	1.10	1.10	1.25	1.25	1.30	1.20	0.95
Viacom	1.05	1.00	1.05	0.90	1.20	1.50	NMF	1.00
E. I. Du Pont	1.20	1.10	1.00	1.10	1.00	1.00	1.00	1.00
McDonald's	1.10	0.95	1.05	0.90	0.85	1.00	1.10	0.75
Alcoa	1.15	1.25	1.05	0.95	0.90	1.30	1.40	1.40
Boeing	1.20	1.05	1.00	0.95	0.95	1.00	1.10	0.90

NMF = No meaningful figure.
Source: http://www.valueline.com.

Beta coefficients do vary among firms. This is illustrated in Exhibit 5.3, which presents the beta coefficients for selected firms as computed by *Value Line*. As may be seen in the table, some firms (e.g., ExxonMobil) have relatively low beta coefficients, while the coefficients for other firms (e.g., GE) are higher. Investors who are willing to bear more risk may be attracted to these stocks with higher beta coefficients. Investors who are less inclined to bear risk may prefer the stocks with low beta coefficients. Although these investors forgo some potential return during rising market prices, they should suffer smaller losses during periods of declining stock prices.

Computing beta coefficients is a tedious job. (How betas are estimated is illustrated in the appendix to this chapter.) Fortunately, betas are readily available through the Internet from several sources. A list of possible sources is provided in the Investment Assignment at the end of Chapter 1 on page 16. You should be warned that beta coefficients from different sources often vary for the same stock. Such differences in betas are illustrated in the Point of Interest: Will the Real Beta Please Stand Up?

To be useful, beta coefficients must be reliable predictors of future stock price behavior. For example, a low-risk investor who desires stocks that will be stable will probably purchase stocks with low beta coefficients. An investor selecting a stock with a beta coefficient of 0.6 will certainly be upset if the market prices decline by 10 percent and this stock's price falls by 15 percent, since a beta coefficient of 0.6 indicates that the stock should decline by only 6 percent when the market declines by 10 percent.

Beta coefficients are constructed with historical price data. Although such data may be accumulated and tabulated for many years, this does not mean that coefficients based on historical data will be accurate predictors of future movements in stock prices. Beta coefficients can and do change over time. Empirical studies have shown that beta coefficients for individual securities may be unstable (e.g., the decrease in McDonald's beta in Exhibit 5.3). In general, the evidence suggests that the numerical value of beta coefficients moves toward 1.0 (i.e., riskier securities become less volatile and vice versa). Therefore, the investor should not rely solely on these coefficients for selecting a particular security. However, beta coefficients do give the investor some indication of the market risk associated with specific stocks and thus can play an important role in the selection of a security.

Unlike the beta coefficient for individual securities, the beta coefficient for a diversified portfolio is fairly stable over time. Changes in the different beta coefficients tend to average out; while one stock's beta coefficient is increasing, the beta coefficient of another stock is declining. A portfolio's historical beta coefficients, then, can be used as a tool to forecast its future beta coefficient, and this projection should be more accurate than forecasts of an individual security's beta coefficient. For example, in both 1978 and 2004 the average beta coefficient of the portfolio illustrated in Exhibit 5.3 is approximately 1.0.[11] If an equal dollar amount were invested in each security, the value of the portfolio should follow the market value fairly closely, even though individual beta coefficients are greater or less than 1.0. This tendency of the portfolio to mirror the performance of the market should occur even though selected securities may achieve a return that is superior (or inferior) to that of the market as a whole.

Beta and the Security Market Line

Beta's primary use in finance has been its incorporation into the Capital Asset Pricing Model as the key variable that explains individual security returns. The relationship between risk, as measured by beta, and an asset's return is specified in the security market line (SML). The security market line stipulates the return on a stock (r_s) as

5.7 $$r_s = r_f + (r_m - r_f)\beta.$$

The return on a stock depends on the risk-free rate of interest (r_f) and a risk premium composed of the extent to which the return on the market (r_m) exceeds the risk-free rate and the individual stock's beta coefficient.[12] This relationship (i.e., the security market line) is shown in Figure 5.15.

FIGURE   5.15   Security Market Line

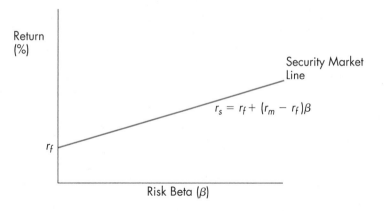

[11]The average for the stocks in Exhibit 5.3 was, 1.031 in 1986, 1.025 in 1992, 1.021 in 1995, 0.995 in 1998, 0.963 in 2001, 1.035 in 2004, 1.025 in 2007, and 0.91 in 2009. This consistency suggests that the beta for a portfolio consisting of these stocks would have changed only marginally over the years even though the individual betas may have changed.
[12]The return on Standard & Poor's 500 stock index is often used as a proxy for the return on the market. Another alternative measure is the return estimated by Ibbotson Associates and reported in the *Stock, Bonds, Bills, and Inflation (SBBI) Annual Yearbook.*

Although these measures of the returns on the market may be appropriate for investments in many securities and diversified portfolios, they may be inappropriate for particular investments—such as the returns on the mutual fund specializing in gold stocks. The return on an index of gold or precious metal stocks may be a more relevant measure of the market return in such cases.

The similarity of the capital market line and the security market line are immediately apparent if Figure 5.15 is compared to Figure 5.11. The Y-axis is the same, and the relationship between risk and return is represented as a straight line (i.e., $Y = a + bX$). The difference between the two figures is the measure of risk on the X-axis. The capital market line uses the portfolio's standard deviation, while the security market line uses the individual security's beta coefficient.

The difference between the two concepts, however, is more than the distinction between the two measures of risk. Both the capital market line (Equation 5.5) and the security market line (Equation 5.7) are part of the Capital Asset Pricing Model, which seeks to explain security returns. The capital market line, or the macro component, suggests that the return on a well-diversified portfolio depends on the yield of a risk-free security and the portfolio's response to an aggregate measure of risk—the portfolio's standard deviation. The security market line, or the micro component, suggests that the return on an individual asset depends on the risk-free rate and the security's response to changes in the market, with that response being measured by an index of the security's market risk—the beta coefficient.

In addition to being a theory of the determination of security returns, the Capital Asset Pricing Model plays an important role in the valuation of securities and the analysis of portfolio performance. For example, in Chapter 9, the security market line component of the CAPM is used to determine the required return for an investment in common stock. This return is then used in the dividend-growth model to determine the value of a common stock. The model is also used in portfolio evaluation in Chapter 6, in which the realized return is compared to the required return specified by using the Capital Asset Pricing Model. Thus, the CAPM not only is an integral part of the theory of portfolio construction and the determination of security returns but also establishes a criterion for assessing portfolio performance.

Portfolio Betas

The security market line relates a particular stock's beta to the security's return. However, beta coefficients may also be computed for an entire portfolio and related to the portfolio's return. If a portfolio is well diversified, its beta is an appropriate index of the portfolio's risk, since diversification virtually eliminates the portfolio's unsystematic risk. The portfolio beta is a weighted average of each security in the portfolio and its beta. Thus, if a portfolio has the following stocks and their betas,

Stock	Amount Invested	Percent of Portfolio	Beta
A	$100	10%	0.9
B	200	20	1.2
C	300	30	1.6
D	400	40	1.7

the portfolio's beta is

$$(0.1)(0.9) + (0.2)(1.2) + (0.3)(1.6) + (0.4)(1.7) = 1.49.$$

This portfolio's beta is greater than 1.0, which indicates that the portfolio is more volatile than the market. Of course, the portfolio beta would have been different if

⊕ Point of Interest

WILL THE REAL BETA PLEASE STAND UP?

Exhibit 5.3 provided the beta coefficient for several stocks as computed by the *Value Line Investment Survey*. The following table reproduces selected beta coefficients and adds the beta coefficients reported by Yahoo! Finance (**http://finance.yahoo.com**).

Although the *Value Line* betas may be obtained through subscribing to its service (**http://www.valueline.com**), the Yahoo! betas are complimentary.

Company	*Value Line* Beta	Yahoo Beta
Alcoa	1.40	2.22
AT&T	0.80	0.86
ExxonMobil	0.80	0.46
GE	0.95	1.21
IBM	0.90	0.91
Johnson & Johnson	0.55	0.58

Immediately it is apparent that the estimated beta coefficients differ, and the differences are not consistent in one direction.

Why are there differences, and do the differences matter? The answer to the first question is easier. Beta coefficients are calculated using regression analysis that estimates the slope of a line that relates an independent variable (the market) to a dependent variable (the stock). Differences in the slope (the beta) may arise because the estimates use a different measure of the market (e.g., the *Value Line* stock index and not the

Standard & Poor's 500 stock index). Another possible source of the difference is the time period covered. For example, one estimate may use weekly returns over five years while another uses weekly returns over three years. Betas will also differ if the calculation considers only price changes in the stock and the market instead of total returns, which include price changes and dividends received.

Whether the differences are important may depend on the usage of the betas. If the purpose is to determine which stocks have more systematic risk (i.e., to determine the relative amount of systematic risk), variations in the betas may not be a problem. Even if the estimates differ, it is unlikely that one estimate will be 2.1 (indicating a large amount of market risk) while another estimate is 0.9, indicating less volatility than the market. Beta coefficients, however, are also used in the valuation of stock (see Chapter 9) and in measuring performance of mutual funds (see Chapter 6). Since lower beta coefficients indicate less risk, that argues for a higher valuation, in which case the investor would be willing to pay more for the stock. Unfortunately, there is no answer as to which estimate is "correct." While an individual could accept one beta as the basis for stock valuation, an alternative strategy would be to use more than one beta and develop a range of stock values before making a final investment decision.

---

the weights were different. If the portfolio had been more heavily weighted in stock A instead of stock D, for example, the numerical value of the beta would have been lower.

In addition to betas for individual stocks, betas may be computed for portfolios or mutual funds. For example, Morningstar provides beta coefficients for the mutual funds in its database, and the American Association of Individual Investors supplies betas for the funds covered by its *Top Mutual Funds Guide*. The interpretation of these betas is essentially the same as that for common stock. A numerical value of beta that is greater than 1.0 suggests an aggressive mutual fund whose return is more volatile than the market. A numerical value less than 1.0 suggests the opposite: that the fund has less market risk. (Morningstar also provides the coefficient of determination, [R^2], which is one measure of the quality of the estimated beta. A small R^2 would suggest that nonmarket factors are the primary contributors to the variability of the fund's return. See the appendix to this chapter for a discussion of the correlation coefficient and the coefficient of determination.)

In addition to indicating market risk, portfolio betas can play an important role in the evaluation of performance, since betas are a means to standardize each fund's return relative to its market risk. The discussion of assessing portfolio performance is deferred until the material on portfolio assessment in Chapter 6 on investment companies.

ARBITRAGE PRICING THEORY

The previous material discussed beta coefficients and their use in the Capital Asset Pricing Model. While the CAPM is a major component in financial theory, it has been criticized as being too limited. The model reduces the explanation of a stock's return to two variables: (1) the market return and (2) the volatility of the stock in response to movements in the market (i.e., the beta). Of course in a well-diversified portfolio, systematic risk is *the* important source of risk. However, unsystematic risk may be important in the determination of an individual stock's return, if the stock's price is responsive to changes in some other variable. For example, an increase in the rate of inflation or a decrease in the euro relative to the dollar could have an important impact on an individual stock's return. Thus, other factors could play an important role in the explanation of security returns.

arbitrage

Simultaneous purchase and sale to take advantage of price differences in different markets.

Arbitrage pricing theory (APT), initially developed by Stephen A. Ross, seeks to add additional variables to the explanation of security returns.[13] It is a multivariable model in which security returns are dependent on several variables in addition to the volatility of the market. APT derives its name from the economic premise that prices cannot differ in two markets. **Arbitrage** is the act of buying a good or security and simultaneously selling it in another market at a higher price. (Individuals who participate in these transactions are called "arbitrageurs." (Arbitrage is discussed further in the chapters on options and futures.) If IBM stock is selling for $50 in New York and $60 in San Francisco, an opportunity for a riskless profit exists. Arbitrageurs would buy the stock in New York and simultaneously sell it in San Francisco, thus earning the $10 profit without bearing any risk. Of course, the act of buying in New York will drive up the stock's price and the act of selling in San Francisco will drive down the price until the prices in the two markets are equal and the opportunity for arbitrage is erased.

Arbitrage also implies that portfolios with the same risk generate the same returns. If portfolio A has the same risk as portfolio B, the two are substitutes for each other. Just as the stock of IBM must trade for the same price in New York and San Francisco, the returns on portfolios A and B must be the same or an opportunity for arbitrage would exist. Once again, the role of arbitrage is to erase differentials. Differences in returns then must be related to differences in how the portfolios respond to the changes in the sources of risk that the investor faces. These sources of risk may be a major determinant of the return the investor earns.

In arbitrage, the security's price movement and return are *not* explained by a relationship between risk and return. The CAPM is built on an assumption concerning investors' willingness to bear risk (i.e., investors must expect to earn a higher return to

---

[13]See Stephen A. Ross, "The Arbitrage Theory of Capital Asset Pricing," *Journal of Economic Theory* (December 1976): 341–360; and "Return, Risk, and Arbitrage," in I. Friend and J. L. Bicksler, eds., *Risk and Return in Finance* (Cambridge, MA: Ballinger, 1977), Section 9.

be induced to bear more risk). While this assumption may be reasonable, APT explains movements in securities prices without making an assumption concerning risk preferences. Security returns are the result of arbitrage as investors seek to take advantage of perceived differences in prices of risk exposure.

Arbitrage pricing theory states that the return on a security (r_s) depends on the expected return (r_e) and on a set of factors $(F_1 \ldots F_n)$. For example, if the number of factors were four, the general model would be

5.8
$$r_s = r_e + b_1F_1 + b_2F_2 + b_3F_3 + b_4F_4 + e.$$

The individual parameters (i.e., the estimated coefficients $b_1 \ldots b_4$) measure the responsiveness or sensitivity of the return on the stock (or portfolio) to changes in the respective factors. The e represents an error term. If the model captures the important factors, the errors tend to cancel out (i.e., a positive error is canceled by a negative error), and the numerical value of the error term should be zero ($e = 0$). If there is a consistent error, the error term will not be equal to zero and the model is misspecified—that is, at least one important factor has been excluded.

The factors that could affect the return on a stock (or a portfolio) are numerous. Empirical work on APT generally classifies these variables into *sector* influences and *systematic* influences. An example of a sector variable is a firm's industry. What affects a bank stock may not affect a retailer or an airline. A systematic influence may be interest rates or the level of economic activity. For example, high-dividend-paying stocks may more readily respond to changes in interest rates, while cyclical stocks may more readily respond to changes in the level of economic activity.

While there could be a large number of possible variables, empirical results suggest that only a few seem to have a lasting or continuous impact on security returns. For example, a change in inflation may have an important impact on security returns. However, it is unanticipated (rather than anticipated) inflation that has the impact. In competitive financial markets, expected inflation is already incorporated into a security's price. If inflation is expected to rise from 4 percent to 8 percent, securities prices would have been previously adjusted downward and yields would be higher. It is the unexpected change that arbitrage pricing theory is seeking to build into the return. The expected return plus the responsiveness to the unexpected change in inflation (and to other factors) determine the realized return.

Unexpected events will always occur, so realized returns usually deviate from expected returns. What the investor does not know is which unexpected events will occur and how the individual stock will respond to the change. In addition, not all securities or portfolios will respond in the same direction or by the same amount. Two portfolios may respond differently to a change in a particular factor; hence, the returns on two (or more) portfolios may also differ.

Consider the following three-variable multifactor model:

$$r_s = 0.12 + b_1F_1 + b_2F_2 + b_3F_3 + e,$$

in which the return on a stock will be 12 percent (the expected return) plus the impact of three risk factors. However, the estimated parameters for two stocks differ. Suppose the estimated equations for stocks A and B are

$$r_{sA} = 0.12 + 0.02F_1 - 0.01F_2 + 0.01F_3$$

and

$$r_{sB} = 0.12 + 0.05F_1 + 0.01F_2 + 0.02F_3.$$

The error terms wash out (i.e., $e = 0$), and the equations for the returns on the two stocks differ. The stocks have different responsiveness to changes in the risk factors, so the returns on each stock must differ. For example, the estimated coefficients for the second factor have different signs (minus versus plus), indicating this factor has an opposite impact on the returns of the two stocks.

Suppose the numerical values of the factors are 0, 1, and 2, respectively. The returns on the stocks will be

$$r_{sA} = 0.12 + 0.02(0) - 0.01(1) + 0.01(2) = 0.13 = 13\%$$

and

$$r_{sB} = 0.12 + 0.05(0) + 0.01(1) + 0.02(2) = 0.17 = 17\%.$$

Since the numerical value of factor 1 is 0 during the time period, the expected value for this factor and the actual value were the same (i.e., $F_1 = 0$), so this factor had no impact on the returns. The actual values of factors 2 and 3 differed from the expected values; thus, these two variables affected each security's return. Factor 2 had a negative impact on stock A and a positive impact on stock B, while factor 3 had a positive influence on both stocks, with a slightly larger effect (0.02 versus 0.01) on stock B.

While there may be many possible factors, research suggests that four are preeminent. These are (1) unexpected inflation, (2) unexpected changes in the level of industrial production, (3) unanticipated shifts in risk premiums, and (4) unanticipated changes in the structure of yields (measured by the slope of the curve illustrating term structure of interest rates).[14]

Again, since expected changes are already incorporated into the expected return, APT stresses the importance of unanticipated change. If the actual values and expected values are equal, the factor washes out. If factor 1 in the preceding model is the difference between the actual rate of inflation and the expected rate of inflation, the equation would be

$$r_s = 0.12 + b_1 \text{ (actual rate of inflation } - \text{ expected rate of inflation)} + b_2F_2 + b_3F_3.$$

If the actual rate of inflation is 4 percent and the expected rate of inflation is also 4 percent, this factor has no impact on the stock's return, that is, $b_1(0.04 - 0.04) = 0$.

The factors will have an impact on the stock's return only when the actual values differ from the expected values. If the actual rate of inflation is 7 percent (an increase from the expected 4 percent), this risk factor becomes relevant and has an impact on the stock's return. The amount of impact and its direction depend on the estimated parameter (i.e., the estimated coefficient and its sign). An increase in the rate of inflation could cause the returns on some stocks (e.g., utilities) to fall and cause the returns to rise on others (e.g., resource companies).

---

[14]The term structure of interest rates is discussed in Chapter 13 in the section on yields and in the chapter's appendix.

How each stock and each portfolio responds to the differences between the realized and the expected variables is crucial to the returns earned. Even though two stocks have the same beta coefficients and have responded in a similar fashion to a change in the market, they may respond differently to changes in other factors. For this reason, a portfolio stressing fixed-income securities may experience a larger response to a change in inflation than a portfolio stressing economic growth. This difference in responsiveness may play a crucial role in security selection or portfolio management. It suggests that buying low beta stocks may not be a defensive strategy if the securities are responsive to another variable that is subject to change.

Unfortunately, one of the largest problems facing the investor or portfolio manager who seeks to apply APT is the measurement of unanticipated changes in the factors. If one of the factors changes (e.g., an unanticipated increase in the rate of inflation) and the financial portfolio manager seeks to analyze how the market (or particular stock) responds to the change, that individual cannot separate the movement in the price caused by changes in expected inflation and the movement caused by unanticipated inflation. The movement in the market or the stock's price would encompass both. This is, of course, a major hurdle in the implementation of the model.

APT is currently in the process of being further developed and may someday supplant the Capital Asset Pricing Model as the primary model relating risk and return. Intuitively, APT is appealing because it is less limiting than the Capital Asset Pricing Model. The CAPM is based on an assumption concerning risk preferences and explains returns solely in terms of movements in the market. In the CAPM, the impact of asset-specific variables is erased through the construction of a diversified portfolio, so the volatility of the stock relative to the volatility of the market is the prime variable that explains an asset's risk and return. APT, however, suggests that differences in returns are driven by an arbitrage process and that two securities or portfolios with the same risk must generate the same return. APT permits the inclusion of more explanatory variables. The inclusion of these other factors, especially economic variables, such as unexpected changes in industrial production, make APT an appealing alternative explanation of an asset's return. Additional econometric research obviously is necessary to make the model more usable by individuals and portfolio managers, but it is reasonable to anticipate that further research will occur and that arbitrage pricing theory will remain at the forefront of security valuation and portfolio management.

SUMMARY

Because the future is uncertain, all investments involve risk. The return the investor anticipates through income and/or capital appreciation may differ considerably from the realized return. This deviation of the realized return from the expected return is the risk associated with investing.

Risk emanates from several sources, which include fluctuations in market prices, fluctuations in interest rates, changes in reinvestment rates, fluctuations in exchange rates, and loss of purchasing power through inflation. These sources of risk are often referred to as *systematic risk* because the returns on assets tend to move together (i.e., there is a systematic relationship between security returns and market returns).

Systematic risk is also referred to as *nondiversifiable risk* because it is not reduced by the construction of a diversified portfolio.

Diversification does, however, reduce *unsystematic risk*, which applies to the specific firm and encompasses the nature of the firm's operation and its financing. Because unsystematic risk applies only to the individual asset, there is no systematic relationship between the source of risk and the market as a whole. A portfolio composed of 10 to 15 unrelated assets—for example, stocks in companies in different industries or different types of assets, such as common stock, bonds, mutual funds, and real estate—virtually eradicates the impact of unsystematic risk on the portfolio as a whole.

Risk may be measured by the standard deviation, which measures the dispersion around a central tendency, such as an asset's or a portfolio's average return. If the individual returns differ considerably from the average returns, the dispersion is larger (i.e., the standard deviation is larger) and the risk associated with the asset is increased.

An alternative measure of risk, the beta coefficient, measures the responsiveness or variability of an asset's return relative to the return on the market as a whole. If the beta coefficient exceeds 1.0, the stock's return is more volatile than the return on the market; but if the beta is less than 1.0, the return on the stock is less volatile. Since the beta coefficient relates the return on the stock to the market's return, it is an index of the systematic risk associated with the stock.

Portfolio theory is built around risk and return. Portfolios that offer the highest return for a given amount of risk are *efficient*; portfolios that do not offer the highest return for a given level of risk are *inefficient*. A major component of portfolio theory is the Capital Asset Pricing Model (CAPM), which has a macro (aggregate) and a micro component. In the macro component, the capital market line gives the return on each efficient portfolio associated with each level of risk, which is measured by the portfolio's standard deviation. The individual investor selects the efficient portfolio that generates the highest level of satisfaction or utility.

In the micro component of the Capital Asset Pricing Model, beta coefficients are used to explain an individual security's return. Riskier securities with higher beta coefficients should have greater returns to justify bearing the additional risk. The security market line gives the return on a specific asset associated with each level of risk as measured by the asset's beta coefficient.

The use of beta as the primary explanatory variable of security returns has been criticized as too limiting. An alternative explanation of security returns is arbitrage pricing theory (APT), which is a multivariable model. In this model, such variables as unexpected inflation or unexpected changes in industrial production may affect security returns in addition to the security's response to changes in the market.

QUESTIONS

1. What is the difference between nondiversifiable (systematic) risk and diversifiable (unsystematic) risk?
2. What is a diversified portfolio? What type of risk is reduced through diversification? How many securities are necessary to achieve this reduction in risk? What characteristics must these securities possess?

3. What are the sources of return on an investment? What are the differences among the expected return, the required return, and the realized return?
4. If the expected returns of two stocks are the same but the standard deviations of the returns differ, which security is to be preferred?
5. If an investor desires diversification, should he or she seek investments that have a high positive correlation?
6. Indifference curves used in portfolio theory relate risk and return. How is the portfolio's risk measured? If one investor's indifference curves are steeper than another investor's, what does that indicate about their respective willingness to bear risk?
7. What is a beta coefficient? What do beta coefficients of 0.5, 1.0, and 1.5 mean?
8. If the correlation coefficient for a stock and the market equals 0, what is the market risk associated with the stock?
9. How are the capital market line and the security market line different? What does each represent?
10. How does arbitrage pricing theory advance our understanding of security returns?

PROBLEMS

1. You are considering three stocks with the following expected dividend yields and capital gains:

	Dividend Yield	Capital Gain
A	14%	0%
B	8	6
C	0	14

    a) What is the expected return on each stock?
    b) How may transactions costs and capital gains taxes affect your choices among the three securities?

2. A portfolio consists of assets with the following expected returns:

	Expected Return	Weight in Portfolio
Real estate	16%	20%
Low-quality bonds	15	10
AT&T stock	12	30
Savings account	5	40

    a) What is the expected return on the portfolio?
    b) What will be the expected return if the individual reduces the holdings of the AT&T stock to 15 percent and puts the funds into real estate investments?

3. You are given the following information concerning two stocks:

	A	B
Expected return	10%	14%
Standard deviation of the expected return	3.0	5.0
Correlation coefficient of the returns		−.1

a) What is the expected return on a portfolio consisting of 40 percent in stock A and 60 percent in stock B?
b) What is the standard deviation of this portfolio?
c) Discuss the risk and return associated with investing (a) all your funds in stock A, (b) all your funds in stock B, and (c) 40 percent in A and 60 percent in B. (This answer *must* use the numerical information in your answers derived above.)

4. You are given the following information:

Expected return on stock A	12%
Expected return on stock B	20%
Standard deviation of returns:	
stock A	1.0
stock B	6.0
Correlation coefficient of the returns on stocks A and B	+.2

a) What are the expected returns and standard deviations of a portfolio consisting of:
    1. 100 percent in stock A?
    2. 100 percent in stock B?
    3. 50 percent in each stock?
    4. 25 percent in stock A and 75 percent in stock B?
    5. 75 percent in stock A and 25 percent in stock B?
b) Compare the above returns and the risk associated with each portfolio.
c) Redo the calculations assuming that the correlation coefficient of the returns on the two stocks is −0.6. What is the impact of this difference in the correlation coefficient?

5. What is the beta of a portfolio consisting of one share of each of the following stocks, given their respective prices and beta coefficients?

Stock	Price	Beta
A	$10	1.4
B	24	0.8
C	41	1.3
D	19	1.8

How would the portfolio beta differ if (a) the investor purchased 200 shares of stocks B and C for every 100 shares of A and D and (b) equal dollar amounts were invested in each stock?

6. What is the return on a stock according to the security market line if the risk-free rate is 6 percent, the return on the market is 10 percent, and the stock's beta is 1.5? If the beta had been 2.0, what would be the return? Is this higher return consistent with the portfolio theory explained in this chapter? Why?

7. You are considering purchasing two stocks with the following possible returns and probabilities of occurrence:

Investment A	Return	Probability of Occurrence
	−10%	20%
	5	40
	15	30
	25	10

Investment B	Return	Probability of Occurrence
	−5%	20%
	5	40
	7	30
	39	10

Compare the expected returns and risk (as measured by the standard deviations) of each investment. Which investment offers the higher expected return? Which investment is riskier? Compare their relative risks by computing the coefficient of variation. For explanations and illustrations of the required calculations, see the appendix to this chapter.

8. Using the material on the standard deviation and the coefficient of variation presented in the appendix to this chapter, rank the following investments with regard to risk.

a)

Investment Returns	
Stock A	Stock B
2.50%	7.50%
2.75	8.25
3.00	9.00
3.25	9.75
3.50	10.50

b)

Investment Returns	
Stock A	Stock B
1.70%	7.40%
1.85	7.70
2.00	8.00
2.15	8.30
2.30	8.60

9. This problem illustrates how beta coefficients are estimated and uses material covered in the appendix to this chapter. It may be answered using any program that performs linear regression analysis such as Excel. The following information is given:

Period	Market	Return on	
		Stock X	Stock Y
1	10%	−2%	13%
2	26	13	41
3	−2	3	3
4	−14	−7	−7
5	7	9	9
6	14	5	19
7	−5	2	−8
8	19	13	13
9	8	−3	17
10	−5	8	−14

Using regression analysis, compute the estimated equations relating the return on stock X to the return on the market and the return on stock Y to the return on the market. According to the equations, what is each stock's beta coefficient? What does each beta coefficient imply about the systematic risk associated with each stock?

What is the difference between the return on each stock given by the estimated equation for period 10 and the actual return? What may account for any differences in the estimated return and the actual return? (To answer this question, use the estimated equation, and compare the results with the actual results.)

What is the R^2 for each equation? Interpret the R^2. What does the R^2 imply about the other sources of risk as they apply to stocks X and Y?

10. Given the returns on a domestic stock and a foreign stock, what are the correlation coefficients relating the returns for the 20 years and for each five-year time period: 1989–1993, 1994–1998, 1999–2003, and 2004–2008? What do the coefficients imply about diversification for the entire period and the five-year subperiods? Did the potential for diversification change during the 20 years? (This problem illustrates how correlation coefficients are computed and their importance to investments. You may perform the calculations manually as illustrated in the appendix to this chapter. You may also calculate the correlation coefficients using a spreadsheet such as Excel. To calculate the correlation coefficients, go to the section "Data Analysis" under "Tools.")

Year	Domestic Stock	Foreign Stock
1989	31.5%	10.6%
1990	−3.2	−23.0
1991	30.6	12.8
1992	7.7	−12.1
1993	10.0	33.1
1994	1.3	8.0
1995	37.4	11.5
1996	23.1	6.3

Year	Domestic Stock	Foreign Stock
1997	33.4	2.0
1998	28.5	20.3
1999	21.0	27.2
2000	−9.0	−13.9
2001	−11.8	−21.2
2002	−22.0	−15.6
2003	28.6	39.1
2004	10.9	20.7
2005	4.9	14.0
2006	15.8	26.9
2007	5.5	11.6
2008	−31.9	−43.1

INVESTMENT ASSIGNMENT (PART 2)

In Chapter 1, you selected ten stocks and invested $10,000 in each. This assignment adds to what you have already done.

a. Obtain the beta coefficient for each stock and calculate the beta for your portfolio.
b. What does your portfolio's beta coefficient tell you about the tendency of the portfolio to move with the market?
c. Find the beta coefficients from another source for each stock. Does the ranking from least risky to most risky for the ten stocks differ? Are the two portfolio beta coefficients different? What does any difference in the portfolio betas imply about the accuracy of the measures of systematic risk associated with your portfolio?
d. How has each stock performed since the assignment began? What is the portfolio currently worth? What is the percentage change in the portfolio?
e. How did an index of the market such as the Standard & Poor's 500 stock index perform? Did your portfolio follow the market?
f. Compare the percentage change in the value of your portfolio with the percentage change in the market. Was your portfolio's performance better or worse after considering the change in the market and the portfolio's beta?
g. If an investor desired to construct a well-diversified portfolio with moderate market risk, do the stocks you have selected achieve that objective?

The Financial Advisor's Investment Case
Inferior Investment Alternatives

Although investing requires the individual to bear risk, the risk can be controlled through the construction of diversified portfolios and by excluding any portfolio that offers an inferior return for a given amount of risk. While this concept seems obvious, one of your clients, Laura Spegele, is considering purchasing a stock that you believe will offer an inferior return for the risk she will bear. To convince her that the acquisition is not desirable, you want to demonstrate the trade-off between risk and return.

While it is impractical to show the trade-off for all possible combinations, you believe that illustrating several combinations of risk and return and applying the same analysis to the specific investment should be persuasive in discouraging the purchase. Currently, U.S. Treasury bills offer 7 percent. Three possible stocks and their betas are as follows:

Security	Expected Return	Beta
Stock A	9%	0.6
Stock B	11	1.3
Stock C	14	1.5

1. What will be the expected return and beta for each of the following portfolios?
   a) Portfolios 1 through 4: All of the funds are invested solely in one asset (the corresponding three stocks or the Treasury bill).
   b) Portfolio 5: One-quarter of the funds are invested in each alternative.
   c) Portfolio 6: One-half of the funds are invested in stock A and one-half in stock C.
   d) Portfolio 7: One-third of the funds are invested in each stock.
2. Are any of the portfolios inefficient?
3. Is there any combination of the Treasury bill and stock C that is superior to portfolio 6 (i.e., half the funds in stock A and half in stock C)?
4. Since your client's suggested stock has an anticipated return of 12 percent and a beta of 1.4, does that information argue for or against the purchase of the stock?
5. Why is it important to consider purchasing an asset as part of a portfolio and not as an independent act?

The Financial Advisor's Investment Case
Foreign Country Funds and Diversification

Floria Scarpia believes that many of her clients could benefit from using international investments to diversify their portfolios, but many are reluctant to invest abroad—especially since they may be unfamiliar with foreign economies and businesses. Previously, all suggestions to diversify internationally have met resistance. At best, clients have been willing to invest in U.S. firms with international operations, such as Coca-Cola or IBM.

To overcome this reluctance, Scarpia has decided to demonstrate the reduction in portfolio risk from foreign investments. For the demonstration, she has selected a single-country fund to illustrate the variability of returns from combining a country fund with an index fund based on the S&P 500 stock index. The S&P 500 has averaged a return of 10 percent with a standard deviation of 10 percent. The country fund specializes in Japanese stocks and has a beta of 1.0 when compared to the returns on the Japanese market. The return has averaged 10 percent with a standard deviation of 14 percent. The fund has no investments in U.S. stocks and historically the correlation coefficients relating the returns on the funds to the S&P 500 stock index have been 0.4. To isolate the impact of selecting the fund for diversification, Scarpia assumes that the return on the fund and on the S&P 500 stock index will continue to be 10 percent, so that the investor can anticipate earning 10 percent regardless of which choice is made. The only consideration will be the reduction in the variability of the returns (i.e., the reduction in risk as measured by the standard deviation). To show the reduction, compute the standard deviation of the return when combining the U.S. index fund with the Japanese fund for each of the following investment proportions:

Proportion Invested in the U.S. Fund	Proportion in the Foreign Fund
100%	0%
90	10
80	20
70	30
60	40
50	50
40	60
30	70
20	80
10	90
0	100

1. What happens to the portfolio standard deviation as the investor substitutes the foreign securities for the U.S. securities? What combination of U.S. and Japanese stocks minimizes risk?
2. Repeat the analysis but assume that the correlation coefficient is −0.2 instead of 0.4.
3. Should a Japanese investor who owns only Japanese stocks acquire U.S. stocks?
4. How would each of the following affect a U.S. investor's willingness to acquire foreign stocks?
   a) The dollar is expected to strengthen.
   b) Globalization of financial markets should accelerate.

Appendix 5

STATISTICAL TOOLS

The old saying that "statistics never lie, but liars use statistics" certainly may apply to investments. Mathematical computations and statistics often play an important role in financial and security analysis and in portfolio construction. You do not have to be a statistician or a securities analyst to have a fundamental knowledge of the statistics provided by such investment services as Value Line or Morningstar. Understanding these basic statistical concepts should increase your comprehension of investment analysis.

This appendix briefly explains and illustrates with financial examples the statistical concepts that appear in the body of the text. These include measures of variability (such as the standard deviation), regression analysis, and the reliability of the estimates.

The Standard Deviation

While averages are often used in investment analysis, they indicate nothing about the variability of the individual observations. Do the observations cluster around the average or is there considerable variation in the individual numbers? Consider two stocks presented in the body of the text that earned the following annual returns:

| | Return | |
Year	Stock A	Stock B
1	13.5%	11.0%
2	14.0	11.5
3	14.25	12.0
4	14.5	12.5
5	15.0	15.0
6	15.5	17.5
7	15.75	18.0
8	16.0	18.5
9	16.5	19.0

The arithmetic average return is 15 percent (135/9) in both cases, but B's returns are obviously more diverse than A's. In B the individual observations cluster around the extreme values, so there is more variation in the annual returns.

This dispersion or variability around the mean is measured by the *standard deviation*. The equation for the computation of the standard deviation (σ) is

5A.1
$$\sigma = \sqrt{\frac{\Sigma(r_n - \bar{r})^2}{n - 1}}.$$

This equation states that the standard deviation is the square root of the sum of the squared differences between the individual observation (r_n) and the average ($\bar{r}$), divided by the number of observations (n) minus 1.[1] The steps necessary to calculate the standard deviation follow:

1. For the range of possible returns, subtract the average return from the individual observations.
2. Square this difference.
3. Add these squared differences.
4. Divide this sum by the number of observations less 1.
5. Take the square root.

For stock A, the standard deviation is determined as follows:

Individual Return	Average Return	Difference	Difference Squared
13.50%	15%	−1.5	2.2500
14	15	−1	1.0000
14.25	15	−0.75	0.5625
14.50	15	−0.5	0.25
15	15	0	0
15.50	15	0.5	0.25
15.75	15	0.75	0.5625
16	15	1	1.000
16.50	15	1.5	2.2500
		The sum of the squared differences:	8.1250

The sum of the squared differences divided by the number of observations less 1:

$$\frac{8.1250}{8} = 1.0156.$$

The square root:

$$\sqrt{1.0156} = \pm 1.01.$$

Thus, the standard deviation is 1.01. (A square root is a positive [+] or negative [−] number. For example, the square root of 9 is +3 *and* −3 since (3)(3) = 9 and (−3)(−3) = 9.

---

[1] The subscript n represents the total observations from 1 through n. The line over the r indicates that the number is the average of all the observations. The $n − 1$ represents the *degrees of freedom*, because there can be only $n − 1$ independent observations. Consider the following analogy. If you know (1) the average of a series of 10 numbers and (2) 9 of the 10 numbers, the remaining number can be determined. It cannot be independent, so there are only 10 − 1 (i.e., $n − 1$) independent numbers.

When computing the standard deviation from sample data, $n − 1$ is generally used in the denominator. However, the difference between n and $n − 1$ is very small for large numbers of observations. For large samples, n and $n − 1$ are virtually the same, and n may be used instead of $n − 1$. When all observations are known (i.e., when computing the standard deviation of a population), n is also used. See, for instance, a text of statistics, such as David R. Anderson, Dennis J. Sweeney, and Thomas A. Williams, *Statistics for Business and Economics*, 8th ed. (Mason, OH: South-Western Publishing, 2002).

Average rates of return (and their standard deviations) are illustrations of samples, because not every possible period is included. Even computations of annual rates of return are samples because the annual returns may be computed for January 1, 20X0 through January 1, 20X1 but exclude rates computed using January 2, 20X0 through January 2, 20X1; January 3, 20X0 through January 3, 20X3; etc. The presumption is that if enough periods are included in the computation, the results are representative of all possible outcomes (representative of the population). The large samples would also mean that the difference between n and $n − 1$ is small and should not affect the estimate of the variability around the mean.

However, in the calculation of the standard deviation, only positive numbers are used—that is, the sum of the squared differences—so the square root must be a positive number.)

The investor must then interpret this result. Plus and minus 1 standard deviation has been shown to encompass approximately 68 percent of all observations (in this case, 68 percent of the returns). The standard deviation for stock A is 1.01, which means that approximately two-thirds of the returns fall between 13.99 and 16.01 percent. These returns are simply the average return (15 percent) plus 1.01 and minus 1.01 percent (i.e., plus and minus the standard deviation).

The standard deviation for B is 3.30, which means that approximately 68 percent of the returns fall between 11.7 percent and 18.3 percent. Stock B's returns have a wider dispersion from the average return, and this fact is indicated by the greater standard deviation.

While the standard deviation measures the dispersion around the mean, it is an absolute number. In the previous illustration, the average return was 15 percent for both A and B, so the larger standard deviation for B indicates more variability. If the average returns for A and B differed, a comparison of their standard deviations may not indicate that B's returns are more diverse.

The standard deviation may also be computed for expected values and their probabilities. The body of this chapter illustrated the computation of an expected return. In that illustration, the returns and their probabilities were as follows:

Return	Probability
3%	10%
10	45
12	40
20	5

The expected value (return) was

$$E(r) = (0.10).03 + (0.45).10 + (0.40).12 + (0.05).20$$

$$= 0.003 + 0.045 + 0.048 + 0.01 = 0.106 = 10.6\%.$$

To calculate the dispersion (the standard deviation) around the expected value, use the following process:

Individual Return	Expected Return	Difference	Difference Squared and Weighted by the Probability
3%	10.6%	−7.6	(57.76)(0.10) = 5.776
10	10.6	−.6	(0.36)(0.45) = 0.162
12	10.6	1.4	(1.96)(0.40) = 0.784
20	10.6	9.4	(88.36)(0.05) = 4.418
			11.14

Subtract the expected value from the individual observation. Square the difference and weight the squared difference by the probability of occurrence. The sum of the weighted squared differences is the variance (11.14). The standard deviation is the square root of the variance ($\sqrt{11.14} = 3.338$). The standard deviation is simply a weighted average of the differences from the expected value.

Although the standard deviation measures the dispersion around the mean (or expected mean), it is an absolute number. In the first illustration of the calculation of the standard deviation, the average return was 15 percent for both A and B, so the larger standard deviation for B indicates more variability.

Suppose that over a period of years, firm A had average earnings of $100 with a standard deviation of $10, while firm B's average earnings were $100,000 with a standard deviation of $100. Since $10 is less than $100, it would appear that firm A's earnings were less variable. Such a conclusion, however, does not make sense, since B's average earnings are so much larger than A's average earnings.

The *coefficient of variation* (CV) is used to adjust for such differences in scale. The coefficient of variation is a relative measure of dispersion and is defined as the ratio of the standard deviation divided by the mean. That is,

5A.2
$$CV = \frac{\text{The standard deviation}}{\text{The average}}.$$

The coefficients of variation for firms A and B are

$$CV_A = \frac{\$10}{\$100} = 0.1 \text{ and } CV_B = \frac{\$100}{\$100,000} = 0.001.$$

From this perspective, B's earnings are less variable than A's, even though B's standard deviation is larger. (The Sharpe index discussed in Chapter 6 for evaluating portfolio performance is, in effect, a coefficient of variation since it is the ratio of the return divided by the standard deviation.)

In some cases, the *variance* is used instead of the standard deviation as a measure of risk. (It is not unusual for the risk/return model to be referred to as the "mean-variance" model.) The variance is the square of the standard deviation (i.e., the variance is the sum of the squared differences). As with the standard deviation, variances can be used to rank the amount of risk, but the variance is harder to interpret. While a mean of 25 percent with a standard deviation of 10 percent suggests that approximately two-thirds of the returns fall between 15 and 35 percent, the variance has no such useful interpretation.

The standard deviation does have a weakness in that it considers both positive and negative performance. Investors are probably not disappointed if the return is higher than the average. It is the negative return that concerns them, but the standard deviation does not differentiate between upside and downside variability. The computation of the standard deviation squares both the returns that exceed the average (the positive differences) and the returns that are less than the average (i.e., the negative differences).

Semivariance

Risk is often measured by the dispersion around a central value such as an investment's average return or the investment's required or target returns. As was illustrated in the previous section, dispersion may be measured by the variance or the standard deviation, which is the square root of the variance. The standard deviation is easier to interpret since approximately two-thirds of all observations lie within 1 standard deviation of the mean. If a mutual fund's average return is 12 percent with a standard deviation of 3, then approximately two-thirds of the time, the fund's return lies between 9 and 15 percent.

The variance and the standard deviation do not differentiate between variability that exceeds the average, which presumably investors want, and variability that is less than the average, which investors do not want. Investors are primarily concerned with downside risk, the possibility of loss and not the possibility of a large gain. When variance is used as a measure of risk, it may be advantageous to analyze only the extent to which the return is less than the average or target (i.e., to consider downside variability).

An alternative to the variance is the *semivariance*, which considers only the returns that fall below the average or target.[2] Since the semivariance isolates only the returns below the average, it is a measure of downside risk. Consider the two following investments and their returns for each time period:

Period	Investment A	Investment B
1	−7%	0%
2	−5	−2
3	6	−7
4	8	11
5	13	13

The average returns, variances, and standard deviations are the same (3.0 percent, 74.5, and 8.6, respectively). In terms of return and risk, the two investments are the same. Investment A, however, has larger losses, which are offset by the larger gains, so the two investment returns are the same.

The semivariance uses the same method of computation as the variance but includes only the observations below the average. The effect of considering only the observations that are less than the average may be seen by computing the sum of the squared differences for both investments but limiting the calculation to only those observations that are below the average return. For investment A that calculation is

Investment A

Individual Return	Average Return	Difference	Difference Squared
−7	3%	−10	100
−5	3	−8	64
The sum of the squared differences:			164

For investment B the calculation is

Investment B

Individual Return	Average Return	Difference	Difference Squared
0	3%	−3	9
−2	3	−5	25
−7	3	−10	100
The sum of the squared differences:			134

[2]Semivariance is primarily used by professional portfolio managers. See, for instance, David Spaulding, *Measuring Investment Performance* (New York: McGraw-Hill, 1997) and Frank J. Fabozzi, *Investment Management,* 2nd ed. (Upper Saddle River, NJ: Prentice Hall, 1999.)

The sum of the squared differences is larger for investment A, which suggests that A is the riskier investment.

Covariation and Correlation

Sometimes it is desirable to know not only how a return varies relative to its average return but also its variability to other returns. This variability is measured by the *covariance* or *correlation coefficient*. To illustrate the calculation of covariance and the correlation coefficient, consider the following annual returns for two mutual funds.

	Return	
Year	Fund A	Fund B
1	10%	17%
2	14	3
3	8	16
4	8	21
5	10	3
Average return	10%	12%

The arithmetic average return is 10 percent for A and 12 percent for B. (The standard deviations of the returns are 2.449 and 8.426, respectively.)

Both funds have positive returns, and the higher return for B is associated with more variability—that is, a higher standard deviation. There is also variability between the returns in a given year. For example, A did well in year 5 when B earned a small return, but B did very well in year 4 when A earned a modest return. Covariance and correlation measure the variability of the returns on funds A and B relative to each other and indicate if the returns move together or inversely.

The covariance is found by considering simultaneously how the individual returns of A differ from its average and how the individual returns of B differ from its average. The differences are multiplied together, summed, and the sum is divided by the number of observations minus 1 $(n - 1)$. For the previous returns, the calculation of the covariance is as follows:

Average Return on A	Individual Return on A	Difference	Average Return on B	Individual Return on B	Difference	Product of the Difference
10%	10	0	12%	17	−5	0
10	14	−4	12	3	9	−36
10	8	2	12	16	−4	−8
10	8	2	12	21	−9	−18
10	10	0	12	3	9	0
				The sum of the product of the differences:		−62

To determine the covariance (cov_{AB}), the sum of the product of the differences is divided by the number of observations minus 1:

$$\text{cov}_{AB} = \frac{-62}{5 - 1} = -15.5.$$

Notice that unlike the computation for the standard deviation, the differences are not squared, so the final answer can have a negative number. The negative number indicates that the variables move in opposite directions, and a positive number indicates they move in the same direction. Large numerical values indicate a strong relationship between the variables, while small numbers indicate a weak relationship between the variables.

Since the covariance is an absolute number, it is often converted into the *correlation coefficient*, which measures the strength of the relationship and is easier to interpret than the covariance. The correlation coefficient (R_{AB}) is defined as

5A.3 $$R_{AB} = \frac{\text{Covariance of AB}}{(\text{Standard deviation of A})(\text{Standard deviation of B})}.$$

(By algebraic manipulation, the covariance is

$$\text{cov}_{AB} = S_A \times S_B \times (\text{correlation coefficient of A and B})$$

and is frequently used in this form in this text.)

The numerical value of the correlation coefficient ranges from $+1$ to -1. If two variables move exactly together (i.e., if there is a perfect positive correlation between the two variables), the numerical value of the correlation coefficient is 1. If the two variables move exactly opposite of each other (i.e., if there is a perfect negative correlation between the two variables), the numerical value of the correlation coefficient is -1. All other possible values lie between the two extremes. Low numerical values, such as -0.12 or 0.19, indicate little relationship between the two variables. In this example, the correlation coefficient of AB is

$$R_{AB} = \frac{-15.5}{(2.499)(8.426)} = -0.7511.$$

A correlation coefficient of -0.7511 indicates a reasonably strong negative relationship between the two variables.

The correlation coefficient is often converted into the coefficient of determination, which is the correlation coefficient squared and is often referred to as R^2. The coefficient of determination gives the proportion of the variation in one variable explained by the other variable. In the preceding illustration, the coefficient of determination is 0.5641 $((-0.7511)(-0.7511))$, which indicates that 56.41 percent of the variation in fund A's return is explained by the variation in fund B's return. (Correspondingly, 56.41 percent of the variation in B's return is explained by A's return. No causality is claimed by the coefficient of determination. It is the job of the analyst to determine if one of the variables is dependent on the other.) Obviously, some other variable(s) must explain the remaining 43.59 percent of the variation.

Since the R^2 gives the proportion of the variation in one variable explained by the other, it is an important statistic in investments. For example, Morningstar reports the volatility of a mutual fund's return relative to the return on the market. This volatility is measured by an index referred to in the chapter as a *beta coefficient*. The beta has little meaning if the relationship between the fund's return and the market return is weak. The strength of the relationship is indicated by the R^2. If the $R^2 = 0.13$, the beta has little meaning, since the variation in the return is caused by something other than the movement in the market (i.e., the stock has little market risk). If the $R^2 = 0.94$, it is reasonable to conclude that the variability of the return is primarily the result of the variability of the market, (i.e., the stock's primary source of risk is movements in the market).

Regression Analysis

Although the correlation coefficient and the coefficient of determination provide information concerning the closeness of the relationship between two variables, they cannot be used for forecasting. Regression analysis, on the order hand, estimates an equation between two variables that may be used in forecasting. Regression analysis is also used to estimate the beta coefficient referred to in the previous paragraph. As was explained in the body of this chapter, betas are very important in investments as an index of the systematic, nondiversifiable risk.[3]

Correlation coefficients do not imply any causality. The correlation coefficient relating X to Y is the same as the correlation coefficient for Y to X. Regression does have an implication of a causal relationship, because variables are specified as *independent* and *dependent*. Consider the following data relating the independent variable, the return on the market (r_m), and the dependent variable, the return on a stock (r_s).

Return on the Market (r_m)	Return on a Stock (r_s)
14%	13%
12	13
10	12
10	9
5	4

Return on the Market (r_m)	Return on a Stock (r_s)
2	−1
−1	2
−5	−7
−7	−8
−12	−10

Each pair of observations represents the return on the market and the return on the stock for period of time, such as a week or a year. The data are plotted in Figure 5A.1, with each point representing one set of observations. For example, point A represents a 4 percent return on the stock in response to a 5 percent increase in the market. Point B represents a −7.0 percent return on the stock and a −5.0 percent return on the market.

The individual points like A and B tell very little about the relationship between the return on the market and the return on the stock, but all the observations, taken as a whole, may. In this illustration, the points suggest a strong positive relationship between the return on the market and the return on the stock, but inferences from visual inspection may be inaccurate.

The problem of accuracy is reduced by regression analysis, in which the individual observations are summarized by a linear equation relating the return on the market (the independent variable) and the return on the stock (the dependent variable). (In this

---

[3]For a more detailed explanation of regression analysis, consult a specialized statistics textbook such as William Mendenhall and Terry Sincich, *A Second Course in Statistics: Regression Analysis,* 6th ed. (Upper Saddle River, NJ: Prentice Hall, 2003).

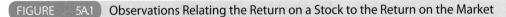

FIGURE   5A.1   Observations Relating the Return on a Stock to the Return on the Market

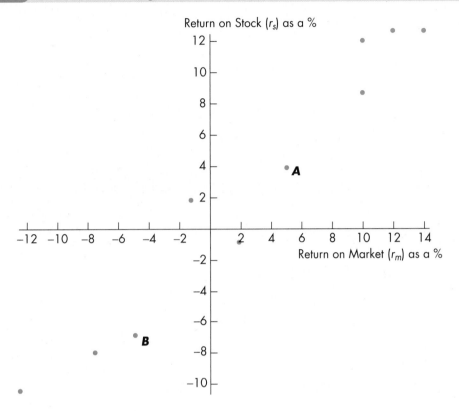

illustration there is only one independent variable. Multiple regression, however, incorporates more than one independent variable.) The general form of the equation is

$$r_s = a + br_m + e,$$

in which r_s and r_m are the return on the stock and the return on the market, respectively, a is the Y-intercept, b is the slope of the line, and e is an error term. (The analysis assumes that the error term is equal to 0, since errors should be both positive and negative and tend to cancel out. If the errors do not cancel out, the equation is misspecified.)

Although the actual computations of the intercept and slope are performed by a computer, a manual demonstration of the process is presented in Exhibit 5A.1, from which the following equation is derived:

$$r_s = -0.000597 + 0.9856 \, r_m.$$

The Y-intercept is −0.000597 and the slope of the line is +0.9856. In the body of this chapter, this slope is referred to as the stock's beta coefficient. This equation is given as line XY in Figure 5A.2, which reproduces Figure 5A.1 but adds the regression line. As may be seen from the graph, line XY runs through the individual points. Some of the observations are above the line, while others fall below it. Some of the individual points are close to the line, while others appear farther away. The closer the points are to the line, the stronger is the relationship between the two variables.

EXHIBIT 5A.1 Manual Calculation of a Simple Linear Regression Equation

$X(r_m)$	$Y(r_s)$	X^2	Y^2	XY
0.14	0.13	0.0196	0.0169	0.0182
0.12	0.13	0.0144	0.0169	0.0156
0.10	0.12	0.0100	0.0144	0.0120
0.10	0.09	0.0100	0.0081	0.0090
0.05	0.04	0.0025	0.0016	0.0020
0.02	−0.01	0.0004	0.0001	−0.0002
−0.01	0.02	0.0001	0.0004	−0.0002
−0.05	−0.07	0.0025	0.0049	0.0035
−0.07	−0.08	0.0049	0.0064	0.0056
−0.12	−0.10	0.0144	0.0100	0.0120
$\Sigma X = 0.28$	$\Sigma Y = 0.27$	$\Sigma X^2 = 0.0788$	$\Sigma Y^2 = 0.0797$	$\Sigma XY = 0.775$

n = the number of observations (10)

$$b = \frac{n\Sigma XY - (\Sigma X)(\Sigma Y)}{n\Sigma X^2 - (\Sigma X)^2}$$

$$= \frac{(10)(0.0775) - (0.28)(0.27)}{(10)(0.0788) - (0.28)(0.28)}$$

$$= \frac{0.7750 - 0.0756}{0.7880 - 0.0784} = 0.9856$$

The a is computed as follows:

$$a = \frac{\Sigma Y}{n} - b = \frac{\Sigma Y}{n}$$

$$= \frac{0.27}{10} - (0.9856)\frac{0.28}{10} = 20.000597$$

The estimated equation is $r_m = -0.000597 + 0.9856r_s$.

FIGURE 5A2 Regression Line Relating the Return on a Stock to the Return on the Market

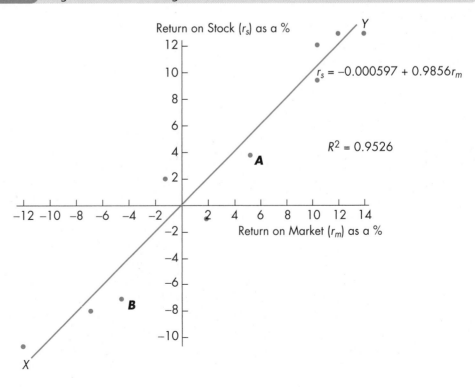

Since the individual observations lie close to the estimated regression line, that suggests a high correlation between the two variables. In this illustration, the actual correlation coefficient is 0.976, which indicates a very strong relationship between the return on the stock and the return on the market. The coefficient of determination, the R^2, is 0.9526, which indicates the over 95 percent of the return on the stock is explained by the return on the market.

A small R^2 (e.g., $R^2 = 0.25$) would suggest that other factors affected the stock's return. The stock would have more unsystematic, diversifiable risk, and the beta coefficient may be a poor predictor of the stock's future performance. That, however, need not imply that the beta is useless. The portfolio beta, which is an aggregate of the individual betas, may be a good predictor of the return the investor can expect from movements in the market. Factors that adversely affect the return on one security may be offset by factors that enhance the return earned on other securities in the portfolio. In effect, the errors cancel.

Manually calculating the regression equation, the correlation coefficient, and the coefficient of determination is tedious and time-consuming. Fortunately, spreadsheet software applications, such as Excel, include a simple linear regression program. Some electronic calculators also perform regression, although the number of observations is limited.

Skewed Distributions

An average is a measure of central tendency and the standard deviation is a measure of dispersion around that average. While averages are frequently used in business and investments, potential problems exist. Consider the following three sets of data:

A	B	C
9	6	3
10	7	12
11	8	12
12	9	13
13	10	14
14	29	15
Average: 11.5	11.5	11.5

The average is the same in all three cases: 11.5. However, the distribution of the individual observations differs. The numbers in set A are symmetrically distributed around the average. For set B, all the numbers except one are less than the average, and that one large number increases the average. For set C, all the numbers are greater than the average except for one observation, and that one small number brings down the average. Distributions B and C are skewed. Case B is skewed to the right or "positively skewed." More of the individual observations are less than the average, which is pulled up by the one large observation. (The number 29 produces a "tail" to the right.) Case C is skewed to the left or "negatively skewed." More of the individual observations exceed the average, which is pulled down by the one small observation. (The number 3 produces a "tail" to the left.) Skewed distributions are often illustrated as in

FIGURE 5A3 Normal and Skewed Distributions

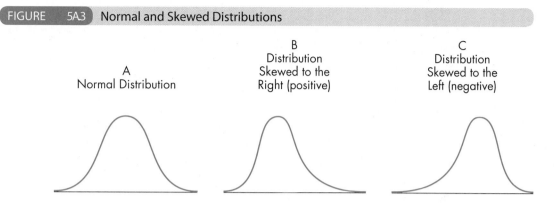

	B	C
	Distribution	Distribution
	Skewed to the	Skewed to the
A	Right (positive)	Left (negative)
Normal Distribution		

Figure 5A.3. Example A is the symmetric distribution, while B and C are skewed to the right (positive) and to the left (negative), respectively. In B, the "tail" in the figure is to the right, so the average exceeds most of the observations. In C, the "tail" is to the left, so the average is less than most of the observations.

Although the mean is 11.5 in all three cases, using these averages may be misleading. The usual purpose for computing an average is to provide a measure of central tendency such as a baseball player's batting average or the average price-to-earnings ratios for a group of stocks. If the distribution is skewed, the average may be a poor measure of central tendency. An alternative measure of central tendency is the median, which splits the distribution into two equal halves. The median is often used when the data are skewed. For example, average family income may be a poor indicator of the typical family's income because a few large incomes will skew the distribution. For this reason, family income is often reported using both the average family income and the median family income.

One means to measure if a distribution is skewed is the *skewness coefficient*. If the distribution is symmetric, the numerical value of this coefficient is 0. If the distribution is skewed to the right, the coefficient is a positive number, and if the distribution is skewed to the left, the coefficient is negative. The larger the absolute value of the coefficient, the larger is the amount of the skewness.

Peaked Distributions

A distribution can be symmetric but have most of the individual observations close to the average. In this case the distribution will have a greater peak around the average. If most of the observations lie away from the average, the distribution will be flatter. That is, the distribution has "broad shoulders." *Kurtosis* measures whether the distribution is peaked or flat relative to a normal distribution. If the distribution is peaked, the numerical value of kurtosis is positive. The further the tails are from the average and the sharper the peak, the larger will be the positive value for kurtosis. The distribution is said to have a peak and fat tails.

If the distribution is flat and has broad shoulders, the numerical value of kurtosis is negative. These differences in kurtosis are illustrated in Figure 5A.4. Part A illustrates a peaked distribution with fat tails. Part B illustrates a distribution with broad shoulders. Both A and B include the normal distribution for comparison.

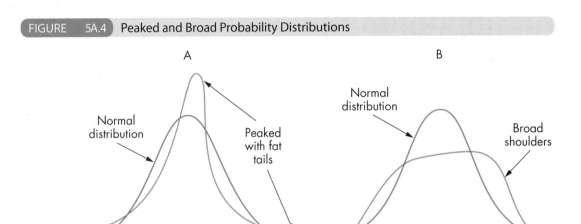

FIGURE **5A.4** Peaked and Broad Probability Distributions

Skewness and kurtosis coefficients are usually provided as part of the output for descriptive statistics. If you use Excel to compute descriptive statistics, the results include the mean, the median, the standard deviation (and the variance, which is the standard deviation squared), and the numerical values for skewness and kurtosis.

Averages are frequently used as a tool in investments. For example, the average P/E ratios may be used to compare and value stocks (Chapter 9) and to analyze financial statements (Chapter 8). In each case the analyst compares financial ratios for a firm with comparable ratios for other firms or with industry averages. In each usage, there is the implication that the distributions are not skewed and that the mean is an appropriate measure of central tendency. Whether the distribution is in fact symmetric is rarely addressed or even mentioned, so you will have to take the averages and the results on faith.

Normal distributions are also used in valuing securities, especially options. The Black-Scholes option valuation model in Chapter 18 assumes that the logarithms of the returns on the underlying stocks are normally distributed. If this assumption does not hold and kurtosis exists, the resulting option values may be incorrect.

PART

Two

Investment Companies

Many individuals find selecting specific securities and managing their own portfolios to be difficult. Instead they pass the decisions to financial planners and the managers of investment companies. These planners and portfolio managers invest the funds on behalf of these individuals. In many cases the portfolios of investment companies are well diversified, holding a wide spectrum of stocks, bonds, or a combination of both. Thus, the investor receives both the benefits of professional management and diversification.

Part 2 is devoted to investment companies. Chapter 6 covers "open-end" investment companies, which are commonly called mutual funds. Chapter 7 deals with "closed-end" investment companies and other alternatives to the mutual fund, especially the exchange-traded fund. Mutual funds are the more popular, but this popularity may have more to do with salesmanship than substance. Brokers and some financial planners have an incentive to push particular mutual funds because they produce generous commissions. While sales of alternative investments will generate commissions, mutual fund sales often are more profitable to the salesperson.

Your interest in investment companies will in part depend on how actively you want to manage your portfolio. If you wish to buy and sell individual stocks and bonds for your account, your interest in mutual funds may be limited to specific niches to fill in your asset allocation. If, however, you do not have the inclination or time to select specific stocks and bonds, then investment companies offer a means to accumulate a portfolio designed to meet your financial goals. Investment companies may be even more important if you believe that you lack the knowledge to manage your portfolio. In that case, the material in the next two chapters should be among the most important that you will read in this text.

CHAPTER 6

Investment Companies: Mutual Funds

LEARNING OBJECTIVES

After completing this chapter you should be able to:

1. Differentiate between closed-end and open-end investment companies.
2. Define net asset value.
3. Identify the costs of investing in mutual funds.
4. Differentiate between loading fees, exit fees, and 12b-1 fees.
5. List the advantages offered by mutual funds.
6. Distinguish among the types of mutual funds based on their portfolios or investment strategies.
7. Differentiate between an actively managed portfolio and a passively managed index fund.
8. Identify factors to consider when selecting a specific mutual fund.
9. Compare performance on the basis of risk and return.

There are two types of investment companies: closed-end and open-end. The open-end investment company is generally referred to as a mutual fund and is by far the more popular. The chapter begins with a discussion of the mechanics of buying and selling the shares of mutual funds, the difference between load and no-load funds, and the investment styles and strategies used to construct a fund's portfolio. The next sections cover factors to consider when selecting a mutual fund, including historical returns, the fees charged, and income taxation.

The chapter ends with means to compare mutual fund performance. Although the absolute return is important, the risk assumed to earn that return is also important. The measures of performance assessment encompass both risk and return. As was discussed in the previous chapter, risk may be measured by the standard deviation of a portfolio's return or by beta coefficients. These measures are used to construct indexes of performance on the basis of risk, realized return, and the required return specified by the Capital Asset Pricing Model.

INVESTMENT COMPANIES: ORIGINS AND TERMINOLOGY

Investment companies are not a recent development but were established in Britain during the 1860s. Initially, these investment companies were referred to as trusts because the securities were held in trust for the firm's stockholders. These firms issued a specified number of shares and used the funds that were obtained through the sale of the stock to acquire shares of other firms. Today, the descendants of these companies are

closed-end investment company
An investment company with a fixed number of shares that are bought and sold in the secondary securities markets.

open-end investment company
A mutual fund; an investment company from which investors buy shares and to which they resell them.

mutual fund
An open-end investment company.

@

referred to as **closed-end investment companies** because the number of shares is fixed (i.e., closed to new investors).

Whereas the first trusts offered a specific number of shares, the most common type of investment company today does not. Instead, the number of shares varies as investors buy more shares from the trust or sell them back to the trust. This **open-end investment company** is commonly called a **mutual fund**. Such funds started in 1924 when Massachusetts Investor Trust offered new shares and redeemed (i.e., bought) existing shares on demand by stockholders.

The rationale for investment companies is simple and appealing. The firms receive the funds from many investors, pool them, and purchase securities. The individual investors receive (1) the advantage of professional management of their money, (2) the benefit of ownership in a diversified portfolio, (3) the potential savings in commissions, as the investment company buys and sells in large blocks, and (4) custodial services (e.g., the collecting and disbursing of funds).

The advantages and services help explain why both the number of mutual funds and the dollar value of their shares have grown dramatically during the last 40 years. According to data available through ICI (the Investment Company Institute at http://www.ici.org), the total number of funds in 1970 was 361. In 1990 the number had risen to 2,362, and by the end of 2008 the number of mutual funds exceeded 8,800. As of 2008, about 2,700 companies traded on the NYSE. The number of funds was more than triple the number of common stocks traded on the NYSE.

Just as the number of funds has grown, so have their total assets. Excluding money market mutual funds, assets grew from $17.9 billion in 1970 to $571 billion in 1990. The growth then exploded to $5.2 trillion in 1999 for a 28 percent annual compound rate of growth for the period 1970–1999. (Closed-end investment companies also grew, but the value of their assets is less than 10 percent of the value of mutual fund assets.) The bear market in 2000–2002 took its toll on mutual funds, but by 2005, total assets had recouped those losses. The 2008 market decline decreased mutual fund assets by $2.7 trillion. (The major U.S. stock market indexes declined by almost 40 percent during 2008.)

Investment companies receive special tax treatment. Their earnings (i.e., dividend and interest income received) and realized capital gains are exempt from taxation. Instead, these earnings are taxed through their stockholders' tax returns. Their dividends, interest income, and realized capital gains (whether they are distributed or not) must be reported by their shareholders, who pay the appropriate income taxes.

For this reason, income that is received by investment companies and capital gains that are realized are distributed. The companies, however, offer their stockholders the option of having the fund reinvest these distributions. While such reinvestments do not erase the stockholders' tax liabilities, they are an easy, convenient means to accumulate shares. The advantages offered by the dividend reinvestment plans of individual firms that will be discussed in Chapter 8 also apply to the dividend reinvestment plans offered by investment companies. Certainly the most important of these advantages is the element of forced savings. Because the stockholder does not receive the money, there is no temptation to spend it. Rather, the funds are immediately channeled back into additional income-earning assets.

One term frequently encountered in a discussion of an investment company is its **net asset value**. The net worth of an investment company is the total value of its stocks,

net asset value (NAV)
The asset value of a share in an investment company; total assets minus total liabilities divided by the number of shares outstanding.

bonds, cash, and other assets minus any liabilities (e.g., accrued fees).[1] The net asset value (NAV) of any share of stock in the investment company is the net worth of the fund divided by the number of shares outstanding. Thus, net asset value may be obtained as follows:

Value of stock owned	$1,000,000
Value of debt owned	+1,500,000
Value of total assets	$2,500,000
Liabilities	−100,000
Net worth	$2,400,000
Number of shares outstanding	1,000,000
Net asset value per share	$2.40

The net asset value is extremely important for the valuation of an investment company, for it gives the value of the shares should the company be liquidated. Changes in the net asset value, then, alter the value of the investment company's shares. Thus, if the value of the fund's assets appreciates, the net asset value will increase, which may also cause the price of the investment company's stock to increase.

MUTUAL FUNDS

load fee

Sales charge levied by mutual funds.

Mutual funds are investment companies whose shares are not traded in the secondary markets like stocks and bonds. Instead, an investor purchases shares directly from the fund at the net asset value plus any applicable sales charge, which is called a **load fee** or load charge or simply "load." After receiving the cash, the mutual fund issues new shares and purchases assets with the newly acquired funds.

If an investor owns shares in the fund and wants to liquidate the position, the shares are sold back to the mutual fund minus any applicable sales charge. (Most funds do not charge an "exit fee" if the investor has held the shares for at least six months.) The shares are redeemed at their net asset value, and the fund pays the investor from its cash holdings. If the fund lacks sufficient cash, it will sell some of the securities it owns to redeem the shares. The fund cannot suspend this redemption feature except in an emergency, and then it may be done only with the permission of the Securities and Exchange Commission.

The buying and redeeming of mutual fund shares at their net asset value (plus or minus the applicable fees) is extremely important. When you place an order to buy, you do not know the cost you will pay. When you place an order to redeem, you do not know the amount you will receive. When you place the order during the day, it is executed at the *net asset value as of the end of the day*. If the NAV rises during the day (perhaps because the market as a whole rises), you will pay more than you anticipated. The reverse also applies to redemptions; you may receive less. Since there is no

---

[1]Some investment companies use debt financing to leverage the returns for their stockholders. For example, the High Yield Income Fund (a closed-end investment company) reported in its August 31, 2008, *Annual Report* that the fund has a $23,500,000 loan outstanding. This loan was 41 percent of the fund's total assets. Although the amount that the investment companies may borrow is modest relative to their assets, such use of margin increases the potential return or loss and increases their stockholders' risk exposure.

secondary market in the shares of mutual funds, there is no price. You cannot specify market orders, limit orders, or stop-loss orders for the purchase and sale of mutual funds. You pay the NAV plus any applicable load fees and receive the NAV minus any applicable exit fees.

no-load mutual fund

A mutual fund that does not charge a commission for buying or selling its shares.

load fund

A mutual fund that charges a commission to purchase or sell its shares.

The loading fee ranges from zero for **no-load mutual funds** to between 3 and 6 percent for **load funds**. If the individual makes a substantial investment, the loading fee is usually reduced. You should be warned that mutual funds state the loading charge as a percentage of the offer price. For example, if the net asset value is \$20 and the loading charge is 5.75 percent, then the offer price is $\$20/(1 - 0.0575) = \$21.22$. Since the loading fee is based on the offer price, then you pay a fee of \$1.22, which is 5.75 percent of the offer price $(0.0575 \times \$21.22 = \$1.22)$. The effect of the fee being a percentage of the offer price and not a percentage of the net asset value is to increase the effective percentage charged. If American Balanced Fund's loading charge is 5.75 percent, the effective loading charge based on the net asset value is 5.75%/$(1 - 0.575) = 5.75/0.9425 = 6.1\%$, which is higher than the stated 5.75 percent loading charge. (The effective rate may also be determined by dividing the load fee by the net asset value. In this example, that is \$1.22/\$20 = 6.1%.)

In addition to loading charges, investors in mutual funds have to pay a variety of other expenses. Each mutual fund is required to disclose in its prospectus these various costs, which are generally referred to as "fees and expenses." The costs associated with researching specific assets, brokerage fees charged when the fund buys and sells securities, and compensation to management are all costs that the investor must bear. These expenses are the cost of owning the shares and are in addition to any sales fees (loading charges) the investor pays when the shares are purchased. The costs of owning the shares are generally expressed as a percentage of the fund's assets. A total expense ratio of 1.6 percent indicates that the fund's expenses are \$1.60 for every \$100 of assets. It should be obvious that the fund must earn at least \$1.60 for each \$100 in assets just to cover these costs, so if a fund earns 11.2 percent on its assets, the investor nets 9.6 percent.

The fees and expenses for three no-load mutual funds (Legg Mason High Yield Portfolio, Legg Mason Total Return Trust, and Schwab International Index Fund) are illustrated in Exhibit 6.1. The first three rows list the fees related to purchasing the shares. Because all three funds are no-load funds, there are no sales costs, but the Schwab International Fund does have a fee for early withdrawals. Such exit fees are designed to discourage frequent redemptions by investors seeking short-term gains. If the investor holds the shares for six months, the charge does not apply.

The management fee compensates the investment advisor for the general management of the fund's affairs. This fee generally runs from 0.5 to 1.0 percent of the fund's assets. Operating expenses cover record keeping, transaction costs, directors' fees, and legal and auditing expenses. The sum of these expenses tends to range from 0.3 to 0.7 percent of the fund's assets; including management and other expenses, the range increases to 0.8 to 1.7 percent of the fund's assets.

While management and other expenses are necessary fees, 12b-1 fees are nonessential costs. As is discussed later in this chapter, these are special charges for marketing and distribution services and may include commissions to brokers who sell the shares. The Schwab fund does not have a 12b-1 fee, but the two Legg Mason funds do. In contrast to the Legg Mason full-service brokerage firm, Schwab's brokers do not work

EXHIBIT 6.1	Cost Disclosures for Selected No-Load Mutual Funds		
	Legg Mason High Yield Portfolio	Legg Mason Total Return Trust	Schwab International Index Fund
Sales load	None	None	None
Early withdrawal fees	None	None	0.75%
Exchange fees	None	None	None
Management fees	0.65%	0.75%	0.45
Operating expenses	0.44	0.19	0.50
12b-1 fees	0.50	1.00	None
Total expenses	1.59	1.94	0.95

Source: Each fund's prospectus.

on commission. The 12b-1 fee then compensates the Legg Mason brokers for selling the shares and covers any other expenses associated with advertising and marketing the fund. (The 12b-1 fee is discussed in the section on fees and expenses.)

Investors in mutual funds earn a return from dividends and capital appreciation. Any income from dividends and interest earned by the fund is distributed as income (after deducting the fund's expenses). If the fund's assets appreciate in value and the fund realizes these gains, they are distributed as capital gains. If the value of the assets appreciates and the gains are not realized, the fund's net asset value also appreciates. The investor then may redeem the shares at the higher net asset value.

THE PORTFOLIOS OF MUTUAL FUNDS

The portfolios of investment companies may be diversified or specialized, such as the money market mutual funds covered later in this chapter. The more traditional funds may be classified by investment type or investment style. Investment type refers to the class or type of securities the fund acquires, such as income-producing bonds. Investment style refers to the fund's investment philosophy or strategy. Possible styles include the size of the firms acquired by the fund or the approach used to select securities.

Income funds stress assets that generate dividend and/or interest income. As its name implies, the Value Line Income Fund's objective is income. Virtually all of its assets are stocks such as utilities that distribute a large proportion of their earnings and periodically increase the dividend as their earnings grow. Growth funds, however, stress appreciation in the value of the assets and give little emphasis to current income. The portfolio of the Value Line Fund consists of common stocks of companies with potential for growth. These growth stocks may include large, well-known companies and smaller companies that may offer superior growth potential.

Even within the class of growth funds, there can be considerable differences. Some funds stress riskier securities in order to achieve faster appreciation and larger returns. For example, Janus Venture seeks capital appreciation by investing in small companies. Other growth funds, however, are more conservative. The Fidelity Fund is a growth fund emphasizing larger companies that are considered to offer capital appreciation but whose earnings are more stable and reliable.

⊕ **Point of Interest**

SERVICES OFFERED BY MUTUAL FUNDS

Custodial services, such as monthly statements and the reinvestment of dividends and capital gains distributions, are obvious services offered by mutual funds. These funds, however, offer the investor other services designed to encourage the investor to acquire shares in that particular fund or family of funds. Some of these services include check writing and credit cards to access money market funds. While subject to a minimum amount, the money market fund may pay a rate of interest higher than that available through an interest-bearing checking account with a commercial bank. A fund may offer an automatic investment or an automatic withdrawal plan in which money is transferred from or to the investor's checking account.

Other possible services include direct deposit of payroll checks, access to automated teller machines,

telephone or on-line exchange of shares from one fund to another within a family of funds, telephone redemption of shares, statements sent to a third party (such as an accountant or financial planner), trading through a personal computer, cross reinvestment (in which the distributions from one fund are used to purchase shares in another fund), and faxed transactions.

Not all funds offer all services, and changes in technology and customer demand will affect which services continue to be offered. The investor, however, should realize that the costs of the services are hidden in the fund's expenses and thus reduce the return the fund earns. Individuals who do not need or want these services are, in effect, subsidizing those who do use them.

Balanced funds own a mixture of securities that sample the attributes of many types of assets. The Fidelity Balanced Fund owns a variety of stocks, some of which offer potential growth while others are primarily income producers. A balanced fund's portfolio may also include short-term debt securities (e.g., Treasury bills), bonds, and preferred stock. Such a portfolio seeks a balance of income from dividends and interest plus some capital appreciation.

Investment style is built around the size of the firms acquired by the fund or the approach (growth or value) used to select stocks for inclusion in the portfolio. Firm size is referred to as large cap, mid cap, or small cap. The word *cap* is short for capitalization, which refers to the market value of the company. The market value is the number of shares outstanding times the market price. Large cap stocks are the largest companies, with market value exceeding $10 billion. A small cap stock is a much smaller firm, perhaps with a total value of less than $1 billion. Mid cap is, of course, between the two extremes ($1 to $10 billion). Some classifications further divide small cap into micro or mini cap for even smaller firms.

Two companies illustrate this difference in capitalization. Louisiana Pacific (LPX) has 103 million shares outstanding. At a price of $4.00 the total value (capitalization) of the stock is $412 million. LPX would be classified as a small cap stock. Coca-Cola (KO) has 2.3 billion shares outstanding. At a price of $42.20, the total value of the stock is approximately $97 billion. KO would be classified as a large cap stock. It is obvious that LPX is small compared to KO and would not be an acceptable investment for a large cap portfolio even if the portfolio manager believed that the stock was undervalued.

An alternative strategy to capitalization-based investing is "style" investing based on value or growth. A "value" manager acquires stock that is undervalued or "cheap." A value approach stresses fundamental analysis based on analytical tools such as

contrarians

Investors who go against the consensus concerning investment strategy.

comparisons of the financial statements covered in Chapter 8 and P/E ratios covered in Chapter 9. Contrarian investors may also use a value approach, since they try to identify strong stocks that are currently out of favor.

A "growth" fund portfolio manager identifies firms offering exceptional growth based on the industry's potential and the firm's position within the industry. Many technology stocks illustrate the difference between the growth and value approaches. Amazon (AMZN) may appeal to growth portfolio managers because the company has potential for growth through its dominant sales position on the Internet and the recently developed Kindle, a system for providing books online instead of through the traditional bound (paper) form. From a value perspective, Amazon has at best meager earnings relative to the stock's price and sells for substantially above its value based on its financial statements. Such a stock would not appeal to value investors.

A fund can have more than one style, such as "small cap–value," which suggests that the portfolio manager acquires shares in small companies that appear to be undervalued. A "small cap–growth" fund would stress small companies that offer exceptional growth potential but are not necessarily operating at a profit and are not perceived as unvalued.

One convenient means to summarize the portfolio strategy of a particular fund is a "style box." The general form covers value/growth and capitalization. For example, the style boxes for a small cap–value fund or a fund with a balanced portfolio of large cap stocks would be as follows:

	Small Cap–Value Fund			Balanced Large Cap Fund		
	Value	Blend	Growth	Value	Blend	Growth
Large					X	
Mid						
Small	X					

While the layouts may differ, such style boxes are often used in the financial press. See, for instance, Morningstar (**http://www.morningstar.com**) or the American Association of Individual Investors (**http://www.aaii.com**).

While various investment styles may seem complementary, a portfolio manager's style can be important, especially when evaluating performance. Presumably, a style portfolio manager offers the investor two things: (1) the style and (2) the investment skill. If a portfolio manager's style stresses small cap growth, that fund's performance should not be compared to the performance of large cap funds. Only through a consistent comparison of funds with similar strategies or styles can the portfolio manager's investment skill be isolated.

Specialized Mutual Funds

Investment trusts initially sought to pool the funds of many savers to create a diversified portfolio of assets. Such diversification spread the risk of investing and reduced the risk of loss to the individual investor. While a particular mutual fund had a specified goal, such as growth or income, the portfolio was still sufficiently diversified so that the element of firm-specific, unsystematic risk was reduced.

Today, however, a variety of funds have developed that have moved away from this concept of diversification and the reduction of risk. Instead of offering investors a cross section of American business, many funds have been created to offer investors specialized investments. For example, a mutual fund may be limited to investments in the securities of a *particular sector* of the economy (e.g., Fidelity Select Multimedia) or a *particular industry*, such as gold (e.g., INVESCO Gold). There are also funds that specialize in a *particular type of security*, such as bonds (e.g., American General Bond Fund).

While these funds have a specialization in a sector, industry, or security, they are usually diversified within their area of concentration. For example, a high-yield bond fund may acquire poor-quality bonds, but the fund would own a variety of these bonds issued by different firms in different industries. Thus, the portfolio is diversified even though the fund is specialized. For example, the Corporate High Yield Fund reported that it held bonds issued by over 100 companies in almost 40 different industries. While its portfolio would certainly react to changes in interest rates and to changes in the market for high-yield securities, the impact of one specific bond on the portfolio as a whole would be marginal. (The various types of high-yield bonds are discussed in Chapter 13.)

There are, however, a few funds that are not well diversified and have a portfolio focused on a few securities. The FPA Paramount Fund, the Sequoia Fund, and the Yacktman Fund each have fewer than 20 stocks in their portfolios. If the fund's management selects well, the fund can achieve high returns. The converse, however, is also true. By focusing on only a few investments, the ability of diversification to reduce the variability of returns is diminished; a focused fund's return may be exceptionally high during one period and exceptionally low during another.

In addition to funds with specialized portfolios, other investment companies offer individuals real alternatives to the traditional, diversified stock mutual fund. The money market fund (discussed in the next section) provides a means to invest in money market securities. Funds that acquire foreign securities permit the individual to have foreign investments without having to acquire foreign stocks. Real estate investment trusts (REITs) are closed-end investment companies that specialize in properties or mortgages. Other examples of specialized funds that help investors manage risk or participate in other markets include the index fund and the municipal bond fund.

index fund

A mutual fund whose portfolio seeks to duplicate an index of stock prices.

An **index fund** duplicates a particular measure (index) of the market. The fund's purpose is almost diametrically opposed to the traditional purpose of a mutual fund. Instead of identifying specific securities for purchase, the managements of these funds seek to duplicate the composition of an index of the market. The Vanguard Index Trust–500 Portfolio is based on the Standard & Poor's 500 stock index. Other funds seek to duplicate different indexes. The Vanguard Index Trust-Extended Market Portfolio seeks to duplicate the Wilshire 5000 stock index, which is even more broadly based than the S&P 500 stock index. Some index funds are less broadly based, such as the Rushmore Over-the-Counter Index Plus. This index, based on the Nasdaq 100 stock index, is limited to the 100 largest over-the-counter stocks. (The composition of stock indexes is covered in Chapter 10.)

Index funds offer investors, especially those with modest funds, a means to participate in the equity markets without having to select individual stocks. Index funds are essentially passive investments, since the fund duplicates the index. Once the portfolio is constructed, changes are infrequent and occur in response to changes in the composition of the index. Such minimal changes reduce the cost of managing the fund, so they are a cost-effective means to buy the market.

After the initial success of the index fund, a variation was created: exchange-traded funds, commonly referred to as ETFs. As the name implies, an exchange-traded fund is an investment company whose shares are traded on an exchange. Essentially, ETFs are a type of closed-end investment company, since their shares are not bought from the fund but are bought and sold like stocks in the secondary markets. ETFs have become extremely popular investment vehicles that offer investors an array of alternatives to traditional financial assets and mutual funds. Since they are a type of closed-end investment company, the discussion of these important investment alternatives is deferred to the next chapter on closed-end investment companies.

MONEY MARKET MUTUAL FUNDS

money market mutual funds

Mutual funds that specialize in short-term securities.

money market instruments

Short-term securities, such as Treasury bills, negotiable certificates of deposit, or commercial paper.

As the name implies, **money market mutual funds** are investment companies that acquire **money market instruments**, which are short-term securities issued by banks, non-bank corporations, and governments. Money market mutual funds specialize solely in short-term assets and provide investors with an alternative to savings and time deposits offered by banks. Money market mutual funds thus compete directly with commercial banks and other depository institutions for the deposits of savers, while regular mutual funds offer an alternative means to own stocks and bonds.

The money funds invest in short-term securities such as the negotiable CDs just discussed. Other money market instruments include the short-term debt of the federal government (Treasury bills), commercial paper issued by corporations, repurchase agreements (commonly referred to as *repos*), bankers' acceptances, and tax anticipation notes. Of course, the individual investor may acquire these securities directly, but the large denominations of some short-term securities (e.g., the minimum

U.S. Treasury bill

Short-term debt of the federal government.

negotiable certificates of deposit (jumbo CDs)

A certificate of deposit in which the rate and the term are individually negotiated by the bank and the lender and which may be bought and sold.

Eurodollar certificates of deposit (Eurodollar CDs)

Time deposit in a foreign bank and denominated in dollars.

commercial paper

Short-term promissory notes issued by the most creditworthy corporations.

repurchase agreement

Sale of a short-term security in which the seller agrees to buy back the security at a specified price.

banker's acceptance

Short-term promissory note guaranteed by a bank.

tax anticipation note

Short-term government security secured by expected tax revenues.

denomination of negotiable CDs and commercial paper is $100,000) exclude most investors.

The safest short-term security is the **U.S. Treasury bill** (commonly referred to as a *T-bill*), which is issued by the federal government. Prior to the political confrontation over the federal budget in 1995, there was no question that the federal government would retire the principal and pay the interest on its obligations. (The pricing of and yields earned on T-bills are covered in Chapter 15.) The short term of the bills also implies that if interest rates were to rise, the increase would have minimum impact on the bills, and the quick maturity means that investors could reinvest the proceeds in the higher-yielding securities.

Negotiable certificates of deposits (CDs or "jumbo" CDs) are issued by commercial banks. As their name implies, the CDs are "negotiable," which means they may be bought and sold. The ability to buy and sell jumbo CDs differentiates them from the certificate of deposit that most savers acquire. Savings CDs cannot be bought and sold; you redeem them at the issuing bank and probably pay a penalty for early redemption. Jumbo CDs are also differentiated from savings CDs because they are issued in units of $100,000, which precludes most individual investors from acquiring negotiable CDs.

Large American banks with foreign operations also issue **Eurodollar certificates of deposit (Eurodollar CDs)**. These CDs are similar to domestic negotiable CDs except they are issued either by the branches of domestic banks located abroad or by foreign banks. Eurodollar CDs are denominated in dollars (instead of a foreign currency) and are actively traded, especially in London, which is the center of the Eurodollar CD market. Because they are issued in a foreign country, these CDs are considered riskier than domestic CDs, so Eurodollar CDs offer higher yields to induce investors to purchase them.

Commercial paper is a *promissory note* (i.e., debt) issued by a corporation as an alternative to borrowing funds from commercial banks. Only firms with excellent credit ratings are able to sell commercial paper; hence, the risk of default is small, and the repayment of principal is virtually assured. Once again, the term is short, so there is little risk from an investment in commercial paper.

A **repurchase agreement** (or "repo") is a sale of a security in which the seller agrees to buy back (repurchase) the security at a specified price at a specified date. Repos are usually executed using federal government securities, and the repurchase price is higher than the initial sale price. The difference between the sale price and the repurchase price is the source of the return to the holder of the security. By entering into the repurchase agreement, the investor (the buyer) knows exactly how much will be made on the investment and when the funds will be returned.

Banker's acceptances are short-term promissory notes guaranteed by a bank. These acceptances arise through international trade. Suppose a firm ships goods abroad and receives a draft drawn on a specific bank that promises payment after two months. If the firm does not want to wait for payment, it can take the draft to a commercial bank for acceptance. Once the bank accepts the draft, the draft may be sold. The buyer purchases the draft for a discount, which becomes the source of the return to the holder. Banker's acceptances are considered to be good short-term investments because they are supported by two parties: the firm on which the draft is drawn and the bank that accepts the draft.

Tax anticipation notes are issued by states or municipalities to finance current operations before tax revenues are received. As the taxes are collected, the proceeds are used to retire the debt. Similar notes are issued in anticipation of revenues from future bond issues and other sources, such as revenue sharing from the federal government. These anticipation notes do not offer the safety of Treasury bills, but the interest is exempt from federal income taxation. (The tax exemption of interest paid on state and local municipal debt is discussed in Chapter 15.) Commercial banks and securities dealers maintain secondary markets in them, so the notes may be liquidated should the noteholder need cash.

Money market mutual funds can invest in any of the money market instruments (negotiable certificates of deposit, Eurodollar CDs, Treasury bills, commercial paper, repurchase agreements, banker's acceptances, and tax anticipation notes). Some of the funds, however, do specialize, such as the Schwab U.S. Treasury Money Fund, which invests solely in U.S. government securities or securities that are collateralized by obligations of the federal government. Other funds invest in a wider spectrum of short-term debt obligations. For example, as of January 2009, the Schwab Money Market Fund had 0 percent of its assets in Treasury obligations, 24.4 percent in negotiable CDs, 42.2 percent in commercial paper, and the remaining percentage in various other short-term assets, such as repurchase agreements.

The yields earned on investments in money market funds closely mirror the yields on short-term securities. Since the Schwab U.S. Treasury Money Fund invests solely in government or government-backed securities, the yield it offers investors mirrors the return on these government securities. This relationship must occur because when the short-term debt held by the fund matures, the proceeds can be reinvested only at the going rate of interest paid by short-term government securities. Hence changes in short-term interest rates paid by these securities are quickly transferred to the individual money market mutual fund.

Prior to 2008, the risk of loss from an investment in a money market mutual fund was considered virtually nonexistent. Money market mutual fund shares were always priced at their $1.00 net asset value. The short-term debt instruments held by the fund could decline and cause the net asset value to fall below the $1.00 (called "breaking the buck"). This had occurred once before when the Mercury Finance Corporation defaulted on its commercial paper, but the Strong family of funds covered the losses sustained by its money market mutual funds and maintained the $1.00 net asset value.

This changed in 2008 with the financial crisis. When Lehman filed for bankruptcy, it defaulted on its commercial paper. The value of several money funds fell below $1.00, which caused investors to rush to withdraw funds. Such withdrawals would have the same effect as the runs on banks during the 1930s. The money funds could not liquidate sufficient assets at their face value and sustain the $1.00 net asset value of mutual fund shares. In order to stop the run on money market mutual funds, the U.S. Treasury offered temporary guarantees for most money market funds and the Federal Reserve guaranteed certain commercial paper issuers. These actions by the U.S. federal government stopped massive withdrawals from the money funds.

The guarantees achieved the same objective as that of the Federal Deposit Insurance Corporation (FDIC). FDIC insures bank deposits up to a specified limit. If a bank were to fail, FDIC would reimburse each depositor up to the limit. As most individuals do not have more than the limit on deposit, these investors know that their principal is safe and will not make a massive run on banks to withdraw deposits.

(You should realize that deposit insurance is *not* automatic but must be purchased from FDIC by the bank. A few banks have chosen not to purchase the insurance. If safety of your principal is a major concern, you should deposit funds only in an account insured by FDIC.)

SELECTING MUTUAL FUNDS

Most mutual funds are created by investment management companies that administer money for institutional investors such as pension plans, foundations, and endowments. These money management firms include commercial banks, insurance companies, and investment counsel/planning firms (e.g., Fidelity Investments). After a mutual fund is created, it has its own portfolio managers who select the assets included in the fund's portfolio. The originating investment management company then becomes an advisor to the fund.

Many investment management firms offer a wide spectrum of mutual funds, often referred to as a "family of funds." Each fund has a separate financial objective and hence a different portfolio. For example, Fidelity Investments offers investors the opportunity to choose among over 125 different funds covering a broad array of alternatives. An investor seeking income may acquire shares in an equity income fund, a government bond fund, or a corporate bond fund. These varied investment alternatives give the individual a diversified portfolio of income-earning assets.

⊕ Point of Interest

SOCIALLY RESPONSIBLE INVESTING

Socially responsible investing refers to buying securities in firms that produce socially desirable goods and services or pursue socially desirable policies. Of course, what is considered socially desirable is determined by each individual. For one investor, manufacturers of military and defense products or electric utilities with nuclear facilities may be examples of firms that do not produce socially desirable products. Another investor, however, may believe that a strong defense is socially responsible or that nuclear power is less polluting than oil and coal-fired generators.

Socially responsible inivesting may be applied to other facets of business enterprise. Does the firm have a good record for promoting women and minorities? Does the firm perform research on live animals? Does the firm sponsor socially desirable programs, such as research on cancer or AIDS?

If socially responsible investing appeals to an individual, he or she must determine which firms meet the social goals or criteria that are deemed important. In one sense, this process is no different from selecting among various stocks and bonds, except that social criteria are added to (or substituted for) financial criteria to identify acceptable investments.

If the investor does not want to select individual socially conscientious firms, a possible alternative is to acquire shares in socially conscientious mutual funds with portfolios that are consistent with the individual's social criteria. A current list of socially responsible funds may be obtained from the Social Investment Forum, a nonprofit organization that promotes the practice of socially responsible investing. The Forum may be reached at its website (http://www.socialinvest.org). General information on social investing and social economics may be found through Green America (http://greenamericatoday.org), the Coalition for Environmentally Responsible Economics (http://www.ceres.org), the Investor Responsibility Research Center (http://www.irrc.org), and Social Funds (http://socialfunds.com).

In addition to offering a variety of funds from which to choose, a family of funds generally permits the individual to shift investments from one fund to another within the family without paying fees. An individual who currently has a growth fund may shift to an income fund upon retiring. Such a shift is achieved by redeeming the shares in the growth fund and buying shares in the income fund. While the redemption is a taxable event (unless the shares are in a tax-deferred account such as an IRA), the investor may make the switch without paying commissions on the transactions.

With so many mutual funds available, you cannot acquire all of the funds but must choose among the alternatives. While mutual funds may relieve investors from selecting particular stocks and bonds, they do not relieve you from having to select among the funds that meet your financial goals and asset allocation objectives.

The next three sections cover factors to consider when selecting mutual funds. These include returns funds have earned, the fees and expenses they charge, and income and capital gains taxation. Obviously, these factors are interrelated because higher expenses reduce returns, and taxes reduce the amount of the return the investor gets to keep. Looking at only one of these considerations, such as a fund's historical returns, may be misleading. As will be explained, reported returns rarely equal realized returns when all the costs and taxes are added into the equation.

Mutual Fund Returns

One of the advantages associated with investing in mutual funds is professional management, but this management cannot guarantee to outperform the market. A particular fund may do well in any given year but perform poorly in subsequent years. Several studies have been undertaken to determine if professional management by portfolio managers results in superior performance for mutual funds.

The first study found that the performance of mutual funds was not significantly different from that of an unmanaged portfolio of similar assets. About half the funds outperformed Standard & Poor's indexes, but the other half underperformed these aggregate measures of the market. In addition, there was no evidence of superior performance by a particular fund over a number of years. These initial results were confirmed by later studies. When loading charges are included in the analysis, the return earned by investors tends to be less than that which would be achieved through a random selection of securities.

Exhibit 6.2 provides annualized returns and their standard deviations for several classes of funds for four overlapping five-year time periods: 1996–2000, 1998–2002, 2001–2005, and 2005–2008. The impact of the 2000–2002 bear market on the returns is readily apparent. During each time period, many of the fund returns were less than the return on the S&P 500 stock index, and their standard deviations were larger. These data support the general conclusion that in the aggregate, funds do not tend to outperform the market and that this inferior return is often accompanied by increased, not decreased, risk.

Consistency of Returns

More recently, the question of the consistency of a fund's performance has been addressed. Even if funds in the aggregate do not outperform the market, some individual funds may have earned higher returns and continue to perform well. That is, the portfolio managers of some funds consistently outperform the market. This argues

EXHIBIT	6.2	Returns on Various Types of Low-Load and No-Load Mutual Funds						
Fund Classification	Return 1996–2000	Standard Deviation of Return	Return 1998–2002	Standard Deviation of Return	Return 2001–2005	Standard Deviation of Return	Return 2004–2008	Standard Deviation of Return
Large cap	17.0%	18.8%	−0.9%	19.1%	0.8%	10.3%	−2.4%	17.2%
Small cap	15.1	31.1	1.2	23.8	8.5	14.9	−2.4	21.0
Growth style	16.1	19.5	−1.5	26.7	−0.8	12.9	−2.8	20.0
Value style	14.4	18.1	2.6	17.4	8.8	11.6	−1.2	17.1
Balanced	11.8	11.0	2.5	10.9	4.7	6.6	0.9	11.0
S&P 500	18.3	17.7	−0.5	18.8	0.6	9.2	−2.2	15.3

Source: *The Individual Investor's Guide to Low-Load Mutual Funds,* 20th ed. (Chicago: American Association of Individual Investors, 2001), 30; *The Individual Investor's Guide to Top Mutual Funds,* 22nd ed. (Chicago: American Association of Individual Investors, 2003), 71; *The Individual Investor's Guide to the Top Mutual Funds,* 25th ed. (Chicago: American Association of Individual Investors, 2006), 69; *The Individual Investor's Guide to the Top Mutual Funds,* 28th ed. (Chicago: American Association of Individual Investors, 2009), 69.

for purchasing shares in funds that have done well on the premise that the best-performing funds will continue to do well. Certainly the large amount of publicity in the popular financial press given to the funds that do well during a particular time period encourages individuals to invest in those funds (i.e., go with the "hot hands"). Money certainly does flow into funds that have a superior track record, and, since fees increase as the funds under management grow, it should not be surprising to learn that mutual funds tout any evidence of superior performance.

Consistency of mutual fund performance is intuitively appealing. Such consistency seems to apply to many areas of life. For example, several baseball teams do well and make the playoffs virtually every year. However, the material on efficient markets suggests the opposite may apply to mutual funds. Essentially the question is: If stock market prices have no memory and past stock performance has no predictive power, why should historical mutual fund performance have predictive power? The answer, of course, may be the superior skills of the fund's managers. If fund managers have superior skills, then the portfolios they manage should consistently outperform the portfolios of less-skilled managers.

Studies have been conducted to determine the consistency of fund returns. Non-academic studies tend to suggest consistency. For example, a study by the Institute for Economic Research indicated that past performance did predict future performance.[2] The results were consistent over different time horizons; for example, 26-week returns forecasted the next 26-week returns and one-year returns predicted the next year returns. Results tended to be best over the longest time horizons. Funds with the highest returns over a period of five years consistently did better during the next two years than the funds with the lowest returns.

The results of academic studies, however, are ambiguous. Although some support consistency, others do not.[3] At least one study explained the observed consistency on

---

[2]"Mutual Fund Hot Hands: Go with the Winners," Institute for Economic Research (April 1998). Information concerning this study may be obtained from the Institute at 2200 S.W. 10th St., Deerfield Beach, FL 33442.

[3]"A sampling of this research includes: Ronald N. Kahn and Andrew Rudd, "Does Historical Performance Predict Future Performance?" *Financial Analysts Journal* (November–December 1995): 43–51. This study found consistency only in fixed-income funds. William N. Goetzmann and Roger G. Ibbotson, "Do Winners Repeat?" *Journal of Portfolio Management* (winter 1994): 9–18. This study found consistency in both raw returns and after adjusting for risk using the Jensen alpha. W. Scott Bauman and Robert E. Miller, "Can Managed Portfolio Performance Be Predicted?" *Journal of Portfolio Management* (summer 1994): 31–39. This study found consistency over long periods of time (i.e., stock cycles).

the basis of the fund's investment objective or style and not on the basis of the port-folio manager's skill.[4] For example, suppose large cap stocks do well while small cap stocks do poorly. Large cap mutual funds should consistently outperform small cap funds. Once the returns are standardized for the investment style, the consistency of the returns disappears. The superior performance of the large cap mutual funds is the result of market movements and not the result of the skill of the portfolio managers. The consistently better-performing large cap stocks give the impression that the large cap mutual funds are the consistently better-performing mutual funds. These findings, of course, support the concept of efficient markets. One set of portfolio managers is not superior to another. Their better performance in one period does not predict superior returns in the next period. Once again, past performance is not indicative of future per-formance. Past prices have no memory and do not predict future prices.

One major problem facing all studies of the consistency of returns is "survival bias." Suppose an investment management firm has two mutual funds, A and B, which earn 20 and 5 percent, respectively. For some reason (possibly skill, possibly luck) the management of fund A did perceptibly better than the management of fund B. Can the investment management firm erase fund B's performance? The answer is yes! One possibility is to merge fund B into fund A. Since fund A survives, the performance data of B are buried. That is the essence of survival bias—poorly performing funds cease to exist and their performance data disappear.[5]

Does this happen? The answer is unequivocally yes, and there are stunning illus-trations. In 1993, the $334 million Putnam Strategic Income Fund was merged into Putnam Equity Income. Prior to the merger, the Putnam Equity Income Fund had only $1 million in assets, so the merger buried the performance of a much larger fund. Dur-ing the mid-1990s Dreyfus merged or liquidated 14 funds. In late 1998, a plan existed to merge and combine several Steadman funds, which were among the industry's worst performing funds. As would be expected, the 2008 market decline generated fund mergers. Pioneer Investments combined 22 funds. For example, Pioneer Select Equity, which lost 32 percent, was merged into Pioneer Global Equity, which buried the perfor-mance of Pioneer Select Equity.

From the investor's perspective, liquidations and mergers are important when inter-preting data concerning the consistency of performance. If funds that did poorly cease to exist while funds that do well continue to operate, the investor may conclude that funds perform better than is the case. Returns from poor funds are ignored. Of course, investors who owned the poorly performing funds will have actual returns that are perceptibly less than the returns reported by the surviving fund.

Fees and Expenses

Fees and expenses obviously affect the return earned by the investor. Management fees, commissions to brokers for executing the fund's trades, and 12b-1 fees (discussed

---

[4]See, for instance, F. Larry Detzel and Robert A. Weigand, "Explaining Persistence in Mutual Fund Performance," *Financial Services Review* 7, no. 1 (1998): 45–55; and Gary E. Porter and Jack W. Trifts, "Performance of Experienced Mutual Fund Managers," *Financial Services Review* 7, no. 1 (1998): 56–68.

[5]For example, Burton Malkiel has suggested that performance consistency is largely explained by survival bias. His study found that mutual funds tend to underperform the market and that consistency, which may have existed in the 1970s, has subsequently disappeared. See Burton G. Malkiel, "Returns from Investing in Equity Mutual Funds, 1971–1991," *Journal of Finance* (June 1995): 549–572.

below) are paid from the fund's income before determining the fund's earnings available to shareholders. These expenses are across all shares and are already accounted for in the return reported by the fund. Presumably, lower expenses contribute to a higher return, and differences in expenses among the funds may be a reason for selecting a particular fund.

Front-end load fees are paid when the shares are purchased, and exit fees are paid when the shares are redeemed. These fees apply only to those individuals who are buying and redeeming shares and do not apply to other shareholders who are neither buying nor redeeming shares. These fees, however, affect the investor's realized return and increase the difficulty of comparing the performance reported by the fund and the return actually realized by the investor.

Consider a front-loaded mutual fund that charges 6.0 percent. If the net asset value of the fund is $10, the investor must remit $0.64 to purchase a share. This cost of the share is determined as follows:

$$\$10/(1 - 0.06) = \$10/0.94 = \$10.64.$$

The loading fee is $0.64, which is 6.0 percent of the amount invested ($10.64 × 0.06 = $0.64). As was discussed earlier in this chapter, loading fees are figured on the amount invested and not on the net asset value.

The mutual fund earns $1 during the year, so the net asset value grows to $11. The fund's management reports a return of 10 percent, but the individual investor has certainly not earned 10 percent. Instead, the actual amount invested ($10.64) has grown to $11, an increase of less than 3 percent. Over a period of years, the loading fee significantly reduces the return. For example, if the fund were to earn 12 percent compounded annually for seven years, its net asset value would grow from $10 to $22.11.[a] However, the investor's return would be only 11 percent as the actual amount invested ($10.64) rises to $22.11.[b]

This comparison problem created by fees is considerably lessened for a no-load mutual fund if (1) the management fees of the no-load fund are no higher than the management fees of the load fund and (2) the no-load fund does not have an exit fee. Some no-load funds assess a sales charge when the investor redeems the shares. Since the fund lacks a traditional front-end load fee, it may refer to itself as a no-load fund.

The impact of a back-end load fee can be considerable even though the charge may be expressed as a modest 2 or 3 percent. Consider the preceding illustration in which the net asset value grew from $10 to $22.11 in seven years for a 12 percent annual increase. If the fund assesses a 3 percent back-end fee, the investor receives $21.44 ($22.11 − [0.03][$22.11]), so the realized return is reduced from 12 percent annually to 11.5 percent.[c]

If the fund has both a front-end and back-end load, the investor's return is reduced even further. To continue the preceding example, the individual spends $10.64 to acquire a share with a net asset value of $10. The net asset value then compounds at 12 percent for seven years to $22.11, and the fund assesses a 3 percent back-end load. The investor receives $21.44, so that individual has in effect invested $10.64 to receive $21.44 over seven years. This is a return of 10.5 percent annually, which is almost two percentage points below the 12 percent that the fund can report as the growth in the net asset value.[d]

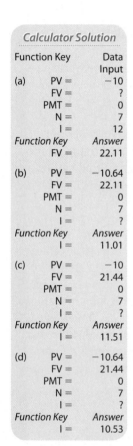

Calculator Solution

Function Key	Data Input
(a) PV =	−10
FV =	?
PMT =	0
N =	7
I =	12
Function Key	Answer
FV =	22.11
(b) PV =	−10.64
FV =	22.11
PMT =	0
N =	7
I =	?
Function Key	Answer
I =	11.01
(c) PV =	−10
FV =	21.44
PMT =	0
N =	7
I =	?
Function Key	Answer
I =	11.51
(d) PV =	−10.64
FV =	21.44
PMT =	0
N =	7
I =	?
Function Key	Answer
I =	10.53

Calculator Solution	
Function Key	Data Input
(e) PV =	−10
FV =	?
PMT =	0
N =	12
I =	12
Function Key	Answer
FV =	38.96
(f) PV =	−10.31
FV =	38.96
PMT =	0
N =	12
I =	?
Function Key	Answer
I =	11.72
(g) PV =	−10.00
FV =	37.79
PMT =	0
N =	12
I =	?
Function Key	Answer
I =	11.72
(h) PV =	−50000
FV =	?
PMT =	0
N =	20
I =	12
Function Key	Answer
FV =	482,315
(i) PV =	−47000
FV =	?
PMT =	0
N =	20
I =	12
Function Key	Answer
FV =	453,376

Actually, the impact on the terminal value of an investment in the fund is the same for a back-end and a front-end loading fee as long as the percentages are the same. For example, fund A charges a 3 percent front-end load fee, while fund B charges a 3 percent exit fee. The initial net asset value of each is $10, which grows annually at 12 percent for 12 years. The investor spends $10.31 ($10/[1 − 0.03]) to acquire a share of fund A and $10 to acquire a share of fund B. The terminal value of both funds is

$$\$10(3.8960) = \$38.96.^{(e)}$$

The investor in fund B, however, receives only $37.79 ($38.96 − [0.03][$38.96]). The return on each investment, however, is 11.72 percent: $10.31 grows to $38.96 at 11.72 percent,[f] and $10.00 grows to $37.79 at 11.72 percent.[g] In both cases the return is the same.

The impact of loading fees is substantial when the rate differences are compounded over many years. Consider a $50,000 investment in a fund that is left to compound at 12 percent for 20 years. The $50,000 grows to $482,315.[h] However, if the fund had charged an initial load fee of 6.0 percent, the investor would have only $47,000 ($47,000/[1 − 0.06] = $50,000) actually invested by the fund. At 12 percent compounded annually for 20 years, the terminal value would be $453,376.[i] This is $28,939 less than would be earned with the no-load fund.

Suppose the investor had purchased shares in a no-load fund with an exit fee of 3 percent. In this case, the investor receives $467,846 ($482,315 − $14,469). If the investor had purchased a load mutual fund with a 6.0 percent front load and a 3 percent back-end load, this individual would have netted only $439,775, or $42,540 less than the no-load fund with no exit fee. Obviously, the loading fees can have a considerable impact on the net return the investor ultimately earns, even though the net asset value increased by the same percentage in each case!

Individuals who sell load funds may disagree, but the preceding illustrations suggest that the investor should not view the load as a one-time fee whose impact is reduced over time as it is spread over an ever-increasing investment. Instead, the opposite is true. The longer the investor holds the shares, the greater the absolute differential will be between the terminal values of the load and no-load funds. The funds not lost to the load fee are being compounded over a longer period of time; thus, the terminal value of the no-load fund becomes even larger.

12b-1 Fees

Although this discussion suggests that investors should purchase no-load mutual funds in preference to those with load fees, the investor still needs to be aware of an expense some no-load funds charge that may prove over a period of time to be more costly than the loading fees. The purpose of the loading fee is to compensate those individuals who sell the fund's shares. No-load funds do not have a salesforce and thus do not have this expense. They may, however, use other marketing devices, such as advertising, that must be paid for.

Some load and no-load funds have adopted an SEC rule that permits management to use the fund's assets to pay for these marketing expenses. These are referred to as **12b-1 fees**, which are often called a 12b-1 plan by the industry. The 12b-1 fees are named after the SEC rule that enables funds to assess the fee that, in

12b-1 fees

Fees that a mutual fund may charge to cover marketing and advertising expenses.

effect, is an ongoing charge that shareholders pay. The fee covers a variety of costs, such as advertising, distribution of fund literature, and even sales commissions to brokers. Unlike a front-load fee, which is charged when the shares are purchased, this 12b-1 fee can be a continuous annual expense. Thus, over a number of years, investors in funds assessing this charge may pay more than they would have paid in loading fees.

Over a period of years, 12b-1 fees can significantly reduce the return the investor earns, because the fee is paid not only in good years but also in years when the fund experiences losses and a decline in its net asset value. You need to be aware of 12b-1 fees when selecting a mutual fund, since the growth in the fund's net asset value will be reduced by the fee. Suppose one fund charges a fee that averages 1.0 percent of total assets and another fund does not assess the fee. Both funds earn 12 percent on assets before the fees, so after the fee is paid the returns are 12 percent for the fund without the fee but 11 percent for the fund with the 12b-1 fee. Obviously, the return is reduced, and over time the impact of this reduction can be surprisingly large. Consider an initial investment of $1,000. After 20 years the $1,000 at 12 percent grows to $9,646 in the fund without the fee but grows to only $8,062 in the fund with the fee. The difference ($1,584) is, of course, the result of the 12b-1 fee.

A, B, and C Shares

Some funds have adopted different classes of shares and the fees for each class differ. Class A shares have front-end load fees but tend to have lower 12b-1 fees and lower annual expenses. Class B shares have no front-end loads but have exit fees and higher 12b-1 fees. Class C shares do not have front- or back-end load fees. They do, however, have higher 12b-1 fees and higher annual expenses. If held for many years, class C shares will be more expensive as the 12b-1 fees offset the benefit associated with no-loads. If the investor anticipates holding the shares for many years, class A shares would be better, but the individual cannot know, when the investment is made, which alternative will prove to be the best. That will be known only after the fact.

⊕ Point of Interest

THE REGULATION OF MUTUAL FUNDS

Mutual funds operate under the Investment Company Act of 1940, which is administered by the Securities and Exchange Commission. The general purpose of this regulation is the same as that which applies to the securities market: the disclosure of information so the individual investor can make an informed decision. Mutual funds must register their shares with the SEC and provide prospective shareholders with a prospectus. The prospectus specifies the fund's investment objectives, the composition of its portfolio, fees and expenses that the investor pays, the composition of the fund's board of directors, and insider transactions.

Regulation does not specify maximum fees nor does it apply to the execution of the fund's objective or its performance. It is assumed that excessive fees or poor performance will lead to the demise of the fund, just as the poor management of a firm will lead to its failure. Regulation cannot ensure that investors will earn profits, nor does it protect them from their own folly or greed.

TAXATION

Investment companies do not pay income and capital gains taxes. Instead, applicable taxes are paid by shareholders. Distributions from mutual funds (and closed-end investment companies) are specified as income or capital gains on the 1099 forms sent to each shareholder so the investor knows the proper classification of the distributions for tax purposes. In addition, sales of fund shares are subject to capital gains taxes. While the fund will include sales on the 1099, the cost basis of the shares, which is necessary to determine capital gains or losses, is each investor's responsibility.

A mutual fund cannot know its stockholders' tax brackets, and it reports returns on a before-tax basis. Even if the fund reports returns on an after-tax basis, the tax rates used may not be applicable for all investors. For this reason, individuals may not be able to compare their realized, after-tax return with the return reported by the fund.

In addition to the noncomparability of a fund's return and an investor's realized return, taxes can have an important impact on the selection of a particular fund. Even if the fund's objectives are consistent with the investor's financial goals, the fund's management may follow an investment strategy that is not in the best interest of the individual's tax strategy. Considerations such as hidden capital gains and losses, the timing of year-end purchases and a fund's year-end distributions, and a fund's tax efficiency affect the decision to acquire one fund in preference to another. The investor also needs to be aware of the tax implications of redeeming fund shares, especially when he or she liquidates part but not all of a position in a fund.

Hidden Capital Gains

The individual mutual fund can have built into its portfolio the potential for a considerable tax liability that may not be obvious to the investor. In some cases this liability may fall on investors who do not experience the gains. This potential tax liability is the result of the fund experiencing paper profits on its portfolio (i.e., profits that have not been realized). As long as the gains are not realized, there will be no taxation, which only occurs once the investment company sells the appreciated assets and thus realizes the capital gain.

This potential tax liability is perhaps best seen by a simple illustration. If a mutual fund is started by selling shares for $10 (excluding costs), the net asset value of a share is $10. The fund invests the money in various securities, which appreciate in value during the year. At the end of the year the net asset value of a share is now $14. Since the fund has not sold any of its holdings, its stockholders have no tax liability.

This fund is a going concern and like all mutual funds offers to redeem its shares and sell additional shares to investors. Suppose an original investor redeems shares at the net asset value of $14. This individual has a capital gain because the value of the shares rose from the initial offer price of $10 to $14. Such a capital gain is independent of whether or not the fund realizes the capital gain on its portfolio, because the investor realizes the gain.

Suppose, however, this individual had not redeemed the shares but continued to hold them. The fund then realizes the $4 per share profit and distributes the capital gain. Once again this investor must pay the appropriate capital gains tax. These two cases are exactly what you should expect. If you redeem the shares and realize the gain or if the fund realizes the gain, you are responsible for the taxes.

It is, however, possible for an investor to be responsible for the taxes without experiencing the capital gain. Suppose you purchase shares at the current net asset value of $14 for a cost basis of $14. On the next day the management of the fund realizes the profits on the portfolio (i.e., sells its securities) and distributes the capital gain. The investors who purchased the initial shares at $10 have earned a profit and must pay any appropriate capital gains tax. The individual who has just purchased the shares for $14 also receives a capital gain distribution and thus is also subject to the capital gains tax. Even though you paid $14 per share, you are the holder of record for the distribution and thus responsible for the tax.

When the capital gain distribution is made, the value of the stock declines. In this illustration the net asset value of the shares declines by $4 (i.e., the amount of the distribution) to $10. You bought the shares for $14 but could offset the $4 distribution by redeeming the shares. Since the shares cost $14 but are now worth only $10, you sustain a $4 loss. Such a sale offsets the distribution, and thus you no longer have any tax obligation.

Could you have anticipated this potential tax liability? The answer is yes when the investor realizes that the source of the tax is the unrealized capital gains embedded in the mutual fund's net asset value. If a fund's portfolio has risen in value, the fund has unrealized capital gains. When the gains are realized, they accrue to the shareholders to whom they are distributed. These shareholders are not necessarily the stockholders who owned shares when the appreciation occurred. If the individual compares the cost basis of the fund's portfolio and the current value of that portfolio, any unrealized capital gains would be apparent. If, for example, the fund has $100,000,000 in assets that cost only $60,000,000, there is $40,000,000 in unrealized gains. If these profits are realized, they will create tax liabilities for current—rather than former—stockholders.

Hidden Capital Losses

Whereas unrealized gains imply the potential for future tax liabilities, unrealized capital losses offer the possibility of tax-free gains. Suppose a mutual fund started with a net asset value of $10 but as the result of a declining market currently has a net asset value of $6. Any individual who originally bought the shares at $10 and now has redeemed them for $6 has sustained a capital loss, and he or she will use that loss to offset other capital gains or income (up to the limit allowed by the current tax code).

If, however, an individual purchases shares at the current net asset value of $6, the value of the portfolio could rise without necessarily creating a tax liability for that investor. Suppose the portfolio's net asset value rises back to $10, at which time the mutual fund sells the securities. Since the cost basis to the fund of the sold securities is $10, the fund has no capital gain. The shareholder has seen the net asset value rise from $6 to $10 without any tax liability being created by the mutual fund.

If the net asset value continues to rise to $12 and the fund sells the securities, it realizes a $2 gain ($12 − $10). The investor who bought the shares at $6 will be subject to capital gains tax only on the $2, because the fund's cost basis is $10. The investor has seen his or her investment rise from $6 to $12 but is subject to tax only on the appreciation from $10 to $12. As long as the investor *does not redeem the shares acquired for $6*, the tax on the $4 appreciation from $6 to $10 is deferred even if the mutual fund sells the securities. Thus, if the fund has unrealized losses, this may offer the individual an opportunity for tax savings just as the unrealized capital gains may create future tax liabilities.

The investor should realize that a fund with unrealized losses is not necessarily an attractive investment. The losses may be the result of inept management, and if such performance continues, the fund will generate larger losses. However, if the investor believes that the fund will be acquired or will turn around and perform well so that its net asset value increases, the unrealized tax losses embedded in the fund's portfolio can magnify the investor's after-tax return.

Year-End Distributions and Income Taxation

Distributions from mutual funds are subject to income or capital gains taxation. Most mutual funds make two distributions. The first is a six-month income distribution. A second and year-end distribution consists of both income and capital gains. The recipient of the distribution is responsible for the tax on the dividend income and the capital gains tax on the capital gain. If you buy the shares at the NAV ($34) just prior to the distribution, you pay the appropriate tax even though the appreciation occurred prior to the purchase. Thus, it may be desirable to defer the purchase until after the dividend payment. (Of course, this tax issue is irrelevant if the shares are held in a tax-deferred retirement account.)

Tax Efficiency

Mutual fund fees obviously affect an investor's return. Load charges, operating expenses, 12b-1 fees, and commissions paid by the fund reduce the return the investor earns. While funds with lower fees may be preferred, there are reasons why some fees are larger and the increased expense is justified. For example, funds that specialize in foreign investments may have larger expenses because foreign operations cost more and obtaining information on which to base security purchases or sales may be more difficult. Obviously, if the investor wants shares in the foreign fund for some purpose (e.g., diversification), the higher fees may be justified.

While fees affect the fund's return, taxes affect the return the investor retains. Mutual fund returns are before tax, but income and capital gains taxes affect the return the investor retains. Consider three funds: The net asset value of each is $20 and each earns a return of 10 percent. The investor buys one share for $20. Fund A consists solely of stocks that are never sold, so at the end of the second year, the fund's net asset value is $22 ($20 × 1.1), and the investor has stock worth $22.

Fund B collects interest of 10 percent on its debt securities. Thus, during the first year, the fund earns $2 and distributes $2. The fund's earnings initially increase its NAV to $22, but after the $2 income distribution, the NAV returns to $20. The individual reinvests the $2 into 0.1 share and has 1.1 shares worth $22.

Fund C invests in stock that appreciates 10 percent, then sells it and distributes the gain. The fund's NAV initially increases to $22, but after the $2 capital gain distribution, the NAV returns to $20. The individual reinvests the $2 into 0.1 share and has 1.1 share worth $22.

All three cases end with the investor having funds worth $22. However, there is a tax difference. Fund A had no security sales, and the investor has no tax obligations. Fund B's $2 distribution is subject to income taxes, and fund C's $2 distribution is subject to capital gains taxation. There is an obvious difference in the investor's tax obligations generated by each fund.

The ability of the fund to generate returns without generating large amounts of tax obligations is the fund's "tax efficiency." Obviously, if the fund never realizes any capital gains and does not receive any income, there will be no distributions and the investor has no tax obligations. This, however, is unlikely. (Even a passively managed index fund may receive dividend income from its portfolio. This income is distributed and the investor becomes liable for taxes on the distribution.) At the other extreme are the funds that frequently turn over their portfolios. Each security sale is a taxable event. Such frequent turnover implies the fund will *not generate long-term capital gains*. The capital gains and the distributions will be short-term and subject to tax at the stockholder's marginal federal income tax rate.

If the fund turns over its portfolio less frequently, the capital gains it realizes and the subsequent distributions may be long-term. Since long-term capital gains are taxed at favorable (lower) rates, the fund's ability to generate long-term instead of short-term capital gains is more favorable to the investor from a tax perspective.

Tax efficiency is an index that converts mutual fund returns to an after-tax basis by expressing the after-tax return as a percentage of the before-tax return, which permits comparisons based on a fund's ability to reduce stockholder tax obligations. The computation of tax efficiency requires assumptions concerning tax rates. In the following example, an income tax rate is assumed to be 35 percent, and the long-term capital gains tax rate is assumed to be 15 percent. Fund A's return consists solely of unrealized capital appreciation. Since there is no tax, the after-tax and before-tax returns are equal so the tax efficiency is 100 percent. Fund B's return is entirely subject to income tax of $0.70 (0.35 × $2 = $0.70). While the before-tax return is 10 percent, the after-tax return is 6.5 percent ($1.30/$2). The tax efficiency index is 65 (6.5%/10%). Fund C's return consists of realized long-term capital gains, which generate $0.30 in taxes (0.15 × $2.00). The after-tax return is 8.5 percent ($1.70/$2), so the tax efficiency index is 85. Since the tax efficiency index for each of the three funds is 100, 65, and 85, on an after-tax basis the performance ranking is A, C, and B.

Under the federal tax law effective in 2009, if fund B's income had been dividends on stock investments and not interest on bond investments, the appropriate tax rate would have been 15 percent. In that case the taxes owed would have been $0.30 and the after-tax return would have been 8.5 percent. The tax efficiency index would be 85, the same as the index for fund C, which had only long-term capital gains. From a tax perspective, the composition of a fund's return is obviously important. Funds that avoid taxes or have returns taxed at favorable rates have higher tax efficiency ratings.

While the tax efficiency index may seem appealing, it has several weaknesses. To construct the tax efficiency index, the investor needs the composition of the returns and the appropriate tax rates in effect when the returns were earned. Tax rates vary with changes in the tax laws, but even without changes in the tax laws, the appropriate income tax rate may differ as the investor moves from one tax bracket to another. The tax efficiency index varies among investors, and published tax efficiency rankings may not be appropriate for an investor whose tax brackets differ from those used to construct the index.

A second weakness is that a high tax efficiency index may be achieved when the fund does not realize capital gains. When these gains are realized, the tax efficiency ratio will decline. In terms of the illustration, fund A's high rating will fall when the gains are realized. Thus, while a high tax efficiency ratio indicates lower taxes in the past, it may also imply higher taxes in the future. For this reason the index needs to be computed over a period of years so that differences in the timing of securities sales from one year to the next are eliminated.

A third weakness is that high efficiency may not alter performance rankings. Funds with similar objectives and styles (e.g., long-term growth through investments in large cap stocks) may generate similar tax obligations. Suppose one fund's return is 20 percent while another fund generates 16 percent. All gains are distributed and are long-term. The tax efficiency for both funds is the same, so the relative ranking is unchanged. Unless the second fund can perceptibly save on taxes, its performance is likely to remain inferior on both a before- and after-tax basis.

Actually, the tax efficiency index may be only another measure of a fund's portfolio turnover. Low turnover suggests that the fund will generate more long-term gains and thus reduce taxes relative to a fund with a high turnover. If management turns over the entire portfolio during the year, all gains will be short-term. If the portfolio turns over every two years, many of the gains may be long-term. Thus, if the investor is concerned with the taxes, a portfolio with low turnover should tend to generate lower taxes than a fund with high turnover.

The Determination of Which Mutual Funds Shares Are Redeemed

While redemption of mutual fund shares is taxed as a capital gain, the process is trickier than just reporting the information supplied by the fund on Form 1099. The general rule is first purchased, first sold. For example, if an investor buys 100 shares in January and 100 shares in February and redeems 100 shares in December, the shares purchased in January are considered to have been sold. If their cost basis is lower, taxes owed will be higher.

To determine the taxes owed, the investor must maintain detailed records of purchases and sales. If the investor makes only a few purchases, the record keeping required for tax purposes is modest. But, if additional shares are acquired through the reinvestment of distributions, accurate record keeping can be a substantial chore. Consider the following series of purchases.

Date	Shares Acquired	How Acquired	Average Price	Cost Basis
1/2/X0	100	Initial purchase	$20	$2,000
12/30/X0	4	$100 distribution	25	100
6/6/X1	50	Second purchase	72	3,600
12/30/X1	6	$360 distribution	60	360
1/31/X2	40	Third purchase	155	6,200

The investor has acquired 200 shares with a total cost basis of $12,260, which includes the purchases and the distributions. Notice that the cost basis of the shares acquired through the reinvestment of a distribution is the amount of the distribution. Each distribution was taxed in the year in which it was received even though the funds were reinvested. If the investor does not add in the amount of the distributions ($460) to the cost basis, he or she may believe that the total cost of the shares is $11,800. If all the shares are sold and the investor uses only $11,800 as the cost basis, any capital gain will be *overstated* and hence the taxes owed will be *higher*.

The investor now sells 40 shares. Under first purchased, first sold, 40 of the initial 100 shares were sold, so the cost basis of the 40 sold shares is $800 ($20 × 40). If the last 40 shares had been sold, the cost basis would have been $6,200. Any capital gains would have been smaller (or capital loss would have been larger). To have the higher cost basis apply, the investor writes the fund or broker and instructs that the shares purchased on 1/31/X2 be sold. The broker or fund will then confirm the shares purchased on 1/31/X2 were redeemed. Such documentation is necessary if the investor wants the 1/31/X2 shares sold for tax purposes in preference to the shares acquired on 1/2/X0.

Now consider what happens if the investor sells 150 shares. Under first bought, first sold, the 100 shares purchased 1/2/X0, the 4 shares purchased on 12/30/X0 with the $100 distribution, and 46 of the 50 shares acquired on 6/6/X1 are sold. The cost basis is $5,412 [$2,000 + 100 + (46/50)$3,600]. If the investor makes frequent purchases (e.g., a monthly purchase plan) and has distributions reinvested, the record keeping can become substantial.

An alternative technique lets the investor determine the average cost of all the shares and use that for the cost basis. In the preceding illustration, the average cost of a share is $61.30 ($12,260/200). If 40 shares are sold, the cost basis is $2,452, and if 150 shares are sold, the cost basis is $9,195. Averaging ends the investor's ability to select which shares to sell. If, for instance, the investor wanted to sell the 40 shares that were purchased last and at the highest cost, such a strategy is precluded once the investor has started averaging the cost basis.

 Point of Interest

RETAINING YOUR MUTUAL FUND STATEMENTS

Although IRS requires that you retain your 1040 for only three years, you must retain information concerning the cost of your investments until it is needed to complete your tax forms. If, for example, you purchased a stock for $1,000 in 1965, you should retain the purchase confirmation because the cost basis of the stock is necessary to complete your 1040 when the stock is sold. (The confirmation statement will also verify the cost in case of an audit.) This retention principle applies to mutual fund statements, especially if you are reinvesting distributions.

Distributions are taxed even though they may be reinvested. If you do not retain these statements indicating the purchases, you will not have the cost basis to complete the required tax forms. You may even forget that the shares were purchased with after-tax funds and pay tax on the entire proceeds of the sale. Failure to retain mutual fund statements only increases the probability that you will be unaware of the cost basis of your shares.

If you take distributions in cash and do not reinvest them, the need to retain statements to determine the cost basis is eliminated. You may find this less burdensome, especially when receiving monthly distributions from a fixed-income fund and making periodic share purchases by check. And, of course, if the shares are held in your tax-deferred retirement account and distributions are reinvested, there are no tax implications until you withdraw the funds—at which time the entire distribution is taxed, and the cost basis of the shares is irrelevant.

REDEEMING MUTUAL FUND SHARES

Most material on mutual funds is concerned with acquiring the shares and covers such topics as the objectives and strategy of various funds, their expenses, and historic returns. Not much is written concerning the redeeming of the positions in the funds. There is, however, no reason to assume that shares once acquired will be held forever; indeed there are many reasons why investors may redeem their shares.

Presumably the individual acquires the shares to meet financial objectives, so the most obvious reason for redeeming the shares is that the objective has been achieved. For example, funds acquired to finance a college education are redeemed to meet that expense. A growth fund acquired while the investor is working may be redeemed when the individual retires and needs a flow of income provided by a bond fund or a balanced fund.

Meeting one's financial objectives is only one of many reasons for redeeming shares. While a particular fund may be bought to meet a specific objective, these objectives are not static. The birth of a child, a death in the family, a change in employment, divorce, or a major illness may alter an investor's financial situation and necessitate a change in the portfolio. A mutual fund that met prior financial objectives may no longer be suitable—in which case, the position is liquidated and the funds used for current needs.

Shares may be redeemed for tax purposes. If an investor has a capital loss from another source, the investor may liquidate a position in a mutual fund to offset the tax loss. Conversely, if an investor has a loss in the fund, the shares may be redeemed to offset capital gains from other sources. If the investor has no offsetting capital gains, the loss may be used to reduce ordinary income (subject to the limitations on capital gain losses offsetting ordinary income as discussed in Chapter 4). The proceeds may be used to invest in an alternative fund with the same or similar goals.

The three previous reasons for liquidating a position (financial goals have been met, financial goals have changed, and tax considerations) apply to the individual investor. There are also reasons for liquidating a position that pertain to the individual fund. A fund's specified objective may change, or the fund's portfolio may not appear to meet its objective. For example, an investor may question the appropriateness of a growth fund's purchasing shares in a regulated telecommunications company such as AT&T. In response, this investor may redeem the shares to place the proceeds in an alternative fund with a more appropriate portfolio.

The fund may change its investment strategies while maintaining its objective. For example, a growth fund may start using derivative securities in an attempt to increase its return. A large proportion of the fund's portfolio may be invested in foreign securities or in securities of firms in emerging economies. While these strategies may be consistent with the fund's objective, they may be inconsistent with the investor's willingness to bear risk, in which case the individual may redeem the shares.

A change in the fund's management may also be cause for liquidating a position. While the management of a corporation may be replaced, it may take years for the firm to be transformed—if it is changed at all. For example, it is doubtful that a new management at Hershey's or Heinz will change the basic products sold by these firms. However, a change in a fund's portfolio manager can have an immediate impact, since the portfolio may be easily altered. A fund with a poor performance record may improve while a fund with an excellent record may deteriorate after a change in its principal portfolio manager. For instance, the investor who supports the theory concerning a fund's consistency of performance would consider a change in a fund's portfolio manager to be exceedingly important and may redeem the shares in response to the change.

Past performance may also induce the investor to redeem shares. If the fund consistently underperforms its peer group, the investor may redeem the shares and invest the proceeds elsewhere. The rationale for such a move again supports the consistency argument: Poor-performing funds will continue to underperform. However, the investor needs to define underperformance and its duration. Does underperformance mean 0.5 percent, 2 percent, or a larger percentage? Is consistency two quarters, two years, or longer?

There are still other possible reasons for redeeming shares: (1) the fund's expenses are high relative to the expenses of comparable funds, (2) the fund becomes too large, or (3) the fund merges with or acquires another fund. Once again, the investor will have to make a judgment as to what constitutes "higher expenses" or "too large" or if the merger is potentially detrimental. If there were obvious answers to these questions, investing would be simple and mechanical. But investing is neither simple nor mechanical, and acquiring shares in mutual funds does not absolve the individual from having to make investment decisions. Although the individual does not determine which specific assets to include in the portfolio, investing in mutual funds requires some active management. A portfolio of mutual funds may require less supervision than a portfolio of individual stocks and bonds, but it should not be considered a passive investment strategy.

MEASURES OF RISK-ADJUSTED PERFORMANCE

Investments are made to earn a return, but making investments requires the individual to bear risk. A higher return by itself does not necessarily indicate superior performance. It may simply be the result of taking more risk. Unfortunately, many investors and the popular press appear to stress return and omit risk.

It should be obvious that returns from funds with different objectives are not comparable. Returns on bond funds are obviously not comparable to returns on growth funds. Even returns on funds with the same objective, such as capital appreciation, may not be comparable if they are not equally risky. From the investor's perspective, a return of 15 percent achieved by a low-risk portfolio is preferred to 15 percent earned on a high-risk portfolio. If you compare absolute returns, you are implicitly assuming that both funds are equally risky. To compare returns, the investor needs to standardize for differences in risk to determine if the fund's management outperformed other funds or the market.

The phrases "outperformed the market" or "beat the market" are often used regarding performance, but the phrases can be misleading. In the popular press, the phrases are essentially comparing the portfolio manager's return to the market return. This implies the goal of the fund is to earn a return that exceeds the market return. In addition, two considerations are omitted: (1) What is the appropriate market or benchmark and (2) what is the risk. In the academic and (usually) the professional literature, the phrases mean a risk-adjusted return in excess of the market return. If the portfolio manager's risk-adjusted return exceeds the market return, then the fund outperformed the market (i.e., beat the market).

Three techniques for the measurement of performance that incorporate both risk and return have been developed. These measures, which are often referred to as "composite performance measures," are (1) the Jensen index, (2) the Treynor index, and (3) the Sharpe index, each named after the individual who first used the technique to measure performance. All three measures address the questions of the index of the appropriate market and the adjustment of the return for risk associated with the portfolio. Thus, all three composite measures provide risk-adjusted measures of performance. They encompass both elements of investment performance: the return and the risk taken to earn that return.

The benchmark frequently used to measure the market is the S&P 500 stock index, since it is a comprehensive, value-weighted index. Because many portfolios, especially mutual funds, trust accounts, and pension plans, are composed of the securities represented in the S&P 500 index, this index is considered to be an appropriate proxy for the market. However, if the portfolios include bonds, real estate, and numerous types of money market securities, the S&P 500 stock index may be an inappropriate benchmark for evaluating portfolio performance.

The differences among the three composite performance measures rest primarily with the adjustment for risk and the construction of the measure of evaluation. The measurement of risk is particularly important because a lower return is not necessarily indicative of inferior performance. Obviously, the return on a money market mutual fund should be less than the return earned by a growth fund during a period of rising securities prices. The more relevant question is this: Was the growth fund manager's performance sufficient to justify the additional risk?

All three composite measures are an outgrowth of the Capital Asset Pricing Model (CAPM), presented in Chapter 5. That model specified that the return on an investment (r) depends on (1) the return the individual earns on a risk-free asset, such as a U.S. Treasury bill, and (2) a risk premium. This risk-adjusted return was expressed as

$$r = r_f + (r_m - r_f)\beta,$$

in which r_f represents the risk-free rate and r_m is the return on the market. The risk premium depends on the extent to which the market return exceeds the risk-free rate (i.e., $r_m = r_f$) adjusted by the systematic risk associated with the asset (i.e., its beta coefficient). This relationship is shown in Figure 6.1, which replicates Figure 5.16,

FIGURE   6.1   CAPM Risk-Adjusted Returns

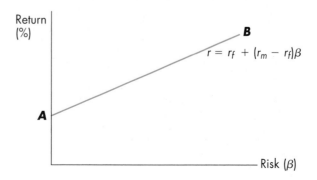

the security market line. The Y-axis represents the return, and the X-axis represents the risk as measured by beta. Line *AB* gives all the combinations of return at each level of risk. If the investor bears no risk, the return on the Y-axis represents the risk-free rate, and higher returns are associated with bearing increased risk.

The Jensen Performance Index

Although the CAPM is used to determine the return that is required to make an investment, it may also be used to evaluate realized performance for a well-diversified portfolio: that is, given the realized return and the risk, did the investment earn a sufficient return? The Jensen performance index determines by how much the realized return differs from the return required by the CAPM. The realized return (r_p) on a portfolio (or on a specific investment if applied to the return on an individual asset) is

6.1 $$r_p = r_f + (r_m - r_f)\beta + e.$$

Equation 6.1 is basically the same as the CAPM equation except that (1) the realized return is substituted for the return and (2) a random error term (e) has been added.[6] In this form, the model is used to evaluate performance and not to determine the required return necessary to make an investment.[7]

If the risk-free return is subtracted from both sides, the equation becomes

6.2 $$r_p - r_f = (r_m - r_f)\beta + e.$$

In this form, Equation 6.2 indicates that the actual risk premium earned on the portfolio equals the market risk premium times the beta plus the error term. Since the errors are assumed to be random, the value of e should be zero.

Figure 6.2 reproduces Figure 6.1 and adds line *CD*, which represents Equation 6.1. The two lines, *AB* and *CD*, are parallel, and since the risk-free rate has been subtracted from both sides of Equation 6.1 to derive Equation 6.2, line *CD* has no positive intercept on the Y-axis. Equation 6.2 indicates that after subtracting the risk-free rate, higher returns are related solely to the additional risk premium associated with the portfolio. Actual performance, however, may differ from the return implied by Equation 6.2. The possibility that the realized return may differ from the expected return is indicated by

6.3 $$r_p - r_f = a + (r_m - r_f)\beta,$$

---

[6]Two methods for computing returns, dollar-weighted and time-weighted rates of return, are discussed in Chapter 10. The dollar-weighted return (the internal rate of return) determines the rate that equates all an investment's cash inflows with its cash outlays. The time-weighted return computes the return for each period and averages these holding period returns. The computation may be an arithmetic or a geometric average, with the latter being preferred because it considers compounding.

Although dollar-weighted or time-weighted rates of return may be used for comparisons, the investor needs to apply the computation consistently. If, for instance, an individual computes time-weighted rates of return as required by the Association for Investment Management and Research, then any comparisions must be made with rates computed using the same method. If the investor or portfolio manager compares his or her performance with rates derived from another source, such as the returns earned by mutual funds reported in Morningstar, that individual needs to be certain that all returns were calculated using the same method of computation.

[7]Application of the Jensen model may require an adjustment in the risk-free rate. Usually, a short-term security, such as a U.S. Treasury bill, is the appropriate proxy for this rate. However, if the time period being covered by the evaluation is greater than a year, it is inappropriate to use a short-term rate, and a different risk-free rate is required for each time interval during the evaluation period. If, for example, the evaluation of the performance of two portfolio managers is being done on an annual basis over five years, a different one-year risk-free rate would have to be used for each of the five years during the evaluation period.

Jensen Performance Index—Risk-Adjusted Returns Including and Excluding the Risk-Free Rate

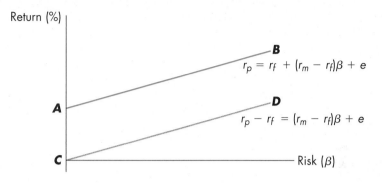

in which a (often referred to as *alpha*) represents the extent to which the realized return differs from the required return or the return that would be anticipated for a given amount of risk.

After algebraic manipulation, Equation 6.3 is often presented in the following form:

6.4
$$a = r_p - [r_f + (r_m - r_f)\beta],$$

Jensen performance index (alpha)

A measure of performance that compares the realized return with the return that should have been earned for the amount of risk borne by the investor.

which is referred to as the **Jensen performance index**. Because alpha is the difference between the realized return and the risk-adjusted return that should have been earned, the numerical value of a indicates superior or inferior performance.

If the portfolio manager consistently does better than the capital asset model projects, the alpha takes on a positive value. If the performance is consistently inferior, the alpha takes on a negative value. For example, if portfolio manager X achieved a return of 15.0 percent with a beta of 1.1 when the market return was 14.6 percent and the risk-free rate was 7 percent, the alpha is

$$a = 0.15 - [0.07 + (0.146 - 0.07)1.1] = -0.0036,$$

which indicates inferior performance. If portfolio manager Y achieved a 13.5 percent return with a beta of 0.8, the alpha is

$$a = 0.135 - [0.07 + (0.146 - 0.07)0.8] = 0.0042,$$

which indicates superior performance. Even though portfolio manager Y had the lower realized return, the performance is superior on a risk-adjusted basis.

The Jensen performance index permits the comparison of portfolio managers' performance relative to one another or to the market. The numerical values of alpha permit the ranking of performance, with the higher scores indicating the best performance. The sign of the alpha indicates whether the portfolio manager outperformed the market after adjusting for risk. A positive alpha indicates superior performance relative to the market, and a negative alpha indicates inferior performance. Thus, in the previous example, portfolio manager Y's performance was superior not only to portfolio manager X's performance but also to the market. In other words, portfolio manager Y outperformed the market on a risk-adjusted basis.

The Jensen performance index measures risk premiums in terms of beta, so the index assumes that the portfolio is well diversified. Since a well-diversified portfolio's total risk is primarily its systematic risk, beta is the appropriate index of that risk. Thus, the Jensen performance index would be an appropriate measure for large cap growth mutual funds whose portfolios are well diversified. If the portfolio were not sufficiently diversified, portfolio risk would include both unsystematic and systematic risk, and the standard deviation of the portfolio's returns would be a more appropriate measure of risk.

The Treynor Performance Index

Treynor index

A risk-adjusted measure of performance that standardizes the return in excess of the risk-free rate by the portfolio's systematic risk.

The Treynor and Sharpe indexes are alternative measures of portfolio evaluation. The Treynor index (T_i) for a given time period is

6.5
$$T_i = \frac{r_p - r_f}{\beta},$$

in which r_p is the realized return on the portfolio and r_f is the risk-free rate. The extent to which the realized return exceeds the risk-free rate (i.e., the risk premium that is realized) is divided by the portfolio beta (i.e., the measure of systematic risk). Thus, if portfolio manager X achieved a return of 15 percent when the risk-free rate was 7 percent and the portfolio's beta was 1.1, the Treynor index is

$$T_x = \frac{0.15 - 0.07}{1.1} = 0.0727.$$

If portfolio manager Y achieved a return of 13.5 percent with a beta of 0.8, the Treynor index is

$$T_y = \frac{0.135 - 0.07}{0.8} = 0.08125.$$

This indicates that portfolio manager Y outperformed portfolio manager X on a risk-adjusted basis, which is the same conclusion regarding the relative performance of the two portfolio managers derived by the Jensen index of performance. However, it cannot be concluded from the Treynor index that either portfolio manager outperformed or underperformed the market, because there is no source for comparison. The Treynor performance index must be computed for the market to determine whether the portfolio manager outperformed the market. If, during the time period, the market return was 14.6 percent, then the Treynor index for the market is

$$T_M = \frac{0.146 - 0.07}{1.0} = 0.076.$$

(Notice that the numerical value of the beta for the market is 1.0.) Since the Treynor index for the market is 0.076, portfolio manager X underperformed while portfolio manager Y outperformed the market on a risk-adjusted basis.

This conclusion is illustrated in Figure 6.3. Line *AB* represents the returns (r_p) that would be anticipated using the Capital Asset Pricing Model for a given risk-free rate, a given return on the market, and different levels of beta. The Y-intercept measures the risk-free return, which in the preceding illustration is 7 percent. The return on the market is 14.6 percent, and the X-axis gives different levels of beta. Thus, the equation for line *AB* is

$$r_p = r_f + (r_m - r_f)\beta = 0.07 + (0.146 - 0.07)\beta.$$

| FIGURE | 6.3 | Realized Returns Compared to the Market Return |

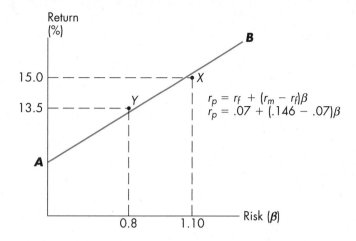

If the portfolio manager outperforms the market on a risk-adjusted basis, the realized combination of risk and return will lie above line *AB*. Conversely, if the performance is inferior to the market, the realized combination of risk and return will lie below line *AB*.

The beta of portfolio X is 1.1, so the anticipated return is

$$r_x = 0.07 + (0.146 - 0.07)1.1 = 15.36\%.$$

The *realized return* is 15.0 percent, which is less than the expected return of 15.36 percent, and the portfolio underperformed the market after adjusting for risk. This realized return is represented by point X in Figure 6.3, and the point does lie below line *AB*.

The beta of portfolio Y is 0.8, so the anticipated return is

$$r_y = 0.07 + (0.146 - 0.07)0.8 = 13.08\%.$$

The realized return is 13.5 percent, which exceeds the expected return of 13.08 percent; thus, the portfolio outperformed the market after adjusting for risk. The realized return is represented by point Y in Figure 6.3, and the point does lie above line *AB*.

The Jensen and Treynor performance measures are similar. They include the same information: the return on the portfolio, the risk-free and the market returns earned during the time period, and the portfolio's beta. The Treynor measure computes a relative value, the return in excess of the risk-free rate divided by the measure of risk. While the Treynor index may be used to determine whether a portfolio's performance was superior or inferior to the market on a risk-adjusted basis, the numerical value of the index may be difficult to interpret. For example, in the preceding illustration, the Treynor indexes for portfolios X and Y were 0.0727 and 0.08125, respectively. When these values were compared to the Treynor index for the market (0.076), the comparisons indicated inferior and superior results, but the results do not indicate by how much each portfolio under- or outperformed the market.

The Jensen measure computes an absolute value, the alpha, which may be easier to interpret and does indicate the degree to which the portfolio over- or underperformed the market. In the example, the alphas of portfolios X and Y were −0.0036 and 0.0042, respectively. Portfolio X performed 0.36 percent less than the market, while portfolio

Y performed 0.42 percent better than the market. The Jensen measure also offers an additional advantage. By using regression analysis it may be possible to determine if the alpha is statistically significant. For example, portfolio Y's alpha was 0.42 percent—but that difference could be the result of chance. If the alpha is statistically significant, then the difference is not the result of chance and confirms that the portfolio manager out-performed the market on a risk-adjusted basis.

The Sharpe Performance Index

Sharpe performance index

A risk-adjusted measure of performance that standardizes the return in excess of the risk-free rate by the standard deviation of the portfolio's return.

The third measure of performance, the **Sharpe performance index** (S_i), is

6.6
$$S_i = \frac{r_p - r_f}{\sigma_p}.$$

The only new symbol in the index is σ_p, which represents the standard deviation of the portfolio. If the previous examples are continued and portfolio manager X's returns had a standard deviation of 30 percent (0.3), while portfolio manager Y's returns had a standard deviation of 25 percent, their respective indexes are

$$S_x = \frac{0.15 - 0.07}{0.3} = 0.267$$

and

$$S_y = \frac{0.135 - 0.07}{0.25} = 0.260.$$

Because portfolio manager X has the higher score, the performance is superior to that of portfolio manager Y. The additional return (i.e., 15 versus 13.5) more than compensates for the additional risk (i.e., the higher standard deviation).

The Sharpe ranking of X over Y is opposite to the ranking determined using the Treynor and Jensen indexes of performance. In those measurements, portfolio manager Y had the higher score, which indicated better performance. The reason for the difference in the rankings is the measure of risk. The Sharpe performance index uses the standard deviation of the returns as the measure of risk. Since the index uses the standard deviation, it does not assume the portfolio is well diversified. In effect, the index standardizes the return in excess of the risk-free rate by the variability of the return. The Treynor index uses the portfolio's beta and does assume the portfolio is well diversified. In effect, it standardizes the return in excess of the risk-free rate by the volatility of the return.

It is important to realize that variability and volatility do not mean the same thing. (This is so at least in an academic usage; words may be interchanged in the popular press.) Variability compares one period's return with the portfolio's average return. That is, how much did the return vary from period to period? A variable return implies that over time there will be large differences in the annual returns. Volatility compares the return relative to something else. That is, how volatile was the stock's return compared to the market return? A volatile return implies that the return on the portfolio fluctuates more than some base (i.e., the return on the portfolio is more volatile than the return on the market). A portfolio could have a low beta; its return relative to the market would not be volatile (i.e., the return on the market would fluctuate more). However, from year to year there could be a large variation in the portfolio's return, so the returns are variable even though the portfolio is less volatile than the market.

Because the measures of risk used in the Sharpe and Treynor indexes differ, it is possible for the two indexes to rank performance differently. Suppose the average return on a utility fund is 8 percent with a standard deviation of 9 percent. This indicates that during 68 percent of the time, the return ranges from −1 to 17 percent. Returns ranging from −1 to 17 percent may indicate large variability in the return for that type of fund and indicate considerable risk unique to that fund (i.e., a large amount of diversifiable risk). The fund, however, may have a beta of only 0.6, indicating that its returns are less volatile than the market returns. The fund has only a modest amount of nondiversifiable, systematic risk. The large standard deviation may generate an inferior risk-adjusted performance using the Sharpe index because the fund has excessive diversifiable risk. The low beta may generate a superior risk-adjusted return when the Treynor index is used because that index considers only the fund's nondiversifiable risk.

As with the Treynor index, the Sharpe measure of performance does not indicate whether the portfolio manager outperformed the market. No statement can be made concerning performance relative to the market unless the Sharpe performance index also is computed for the market. If the standard deviation of the market return is 20 percent (0.2), the Sharpe index for the market is

$$S_M = \frac{0.146 - 0.07}{0.2} = 0.38.$$

Since this value exceeds the numerical values computed for portfolio managers X and Y (i.e., 0.267 and 0.26), the inference is that both underperformed the market on a risk-adjusted basis.

Preference for one performance measure may depend on the portfolios being evaluated and whether the evaluation should be based on total risk or diversifiable risk. If the specific portfolio constitutes all of an individual's assets, total risk is the appropriate measure. This argues for the Sharpe performance index because it uses the standard deviation of the returns, which measures total risk. If, for instance, an individual had most of his or her funds invested in a growth equity fund in a 401(k) plan, then the Sharpe index would indicate how that plan performed based on the total risk borne by the individual.

If the portfolio manager being evaluated represents only one of many portfolios the individual holds, then the Treynor or Jensen indexes may be preferred. If the individual has acquired the shares of several diverse funds, then that individual has achieved diversification—each fund does not represent the investor's total risk. Instead, the investor is concerned with the nondiversifiable risk associated with each fund, in which case beta is the appropriate measure of risk. In effect, the investor is evaluating the ability of the portfolio manager to generate a return for the systematic risk the investor bears. (The individual could then determine the aggregate return and standard deviation of all the various funds to evaluate the fund selection process.)

The Benchmark Problem

The Jensen, Treynor, and Sharpe indexes of performance use an index such as the S&P 500 stock index to measure the market. However, this index may not be appropriate. Certainly, a stock index is an inappropriate benchmark for an income fund with a portfolio devoted to bonds. A stock index may even be inappropriate for a portfolio devoted to stock if that portfolio is not similar in composition to the benchmark.

⊕ **Point of Interest**

NEGATIVE SHARPE RATIOS

The Sharpe ratio compares portfolio performance by standardizing the return in excess of the risk-free rate by the portfolio's standard deviation. Greater numerical values, which are obtained by either higher returns or smaller standard deviations (lower risk), imply better performance. For example, consider the following investments:

Investment	Return	Standard Deviation	Sharpe Ratio
A	10%	5%	0.2
B	5%	5%	0.1

Both have the same risk but A earned a higher return. The numerical value of the Sharpe ratio is greater, indicating better performance.

Although the ratio correctly ranks risk-adjusted returns during risking markets, the converse is not necessarily true during declining markets when the numerical value of the ratio is negative. Consider the following three illustrations.

Case 1: the returns differ but the risk is the same.

Investment	Return	Standard Deviation	Sharpe Ratio
A	−10%	5%	−0.2
B	−5%	5%	−0.1

Both investments have the same risk but Investment A has the larger loss. Its Sharpe ratio is a larger, negative number. Since −0.1 is a smaller negative number than −0.2, the Sharpe ratio indicates that B is superior to A. (A smaller negative number is the larger of the two numbers; −0.1 is greater than −0.2 in a scale that moves from negative to positive numbers.) This result is intuitively correct, since a greater loss for the same amount of risk would indicate inferior performance.

Case 2: the returns are equal but the risk differs.

Investment	Return	Standard Deviation	Sharpe Ratio
A	−10%	5%	−0.2
B	−10%	10%	−0.1

Both investments have the same return, but Investment A has less risk. Once again the numerical value of its Sharpe ratio is a larger, negative number. Since −0.1 is a smaller negative number than −0.2, the Sharpe ratio again indicates that B was superior to A. Both investments generated the same return, but since B should have lost more but did not, its performance was better than A. From an investor's perspective, this result makes no sense. Since investors do not want to sustain a loss, lower risk would be preferred to more risk for an equal loss. Perhaps Case 2 is only a mathematical anomaly.

Case 3: both the returns and risk differ.

Investment	Return	Standard Deviation	Sharpe Ratio
A	−8%	2%	−0.4
B	−10%	10%	−0.1

Investment A loses less and has less risk than Investment B; however, its Sharpe ratio is a larger, negative number. Once again, the Sharpe ratios indicate that B's risk-adjusted performance is superior to A's. This conclusion has to be incorrect. A has less risk and a smaller loss. Its performance has to be superior, but the Sharpe ratio for A is the larger, negative number and indicates inferior performance. The reason for the larger, negative number is that as risk decreases, the denominator decreases. The lower denominator increases the ratio.

For rising markets and positive returns, the Sharpe ratio accurately ranks performance. However, in declining markets, negative Sharpe ratios need to be interpreted carefully since they may imply that lower risk and smaller losses indicate inferior performance. (For a possible adjustment in the Sharpe ratio, see "Sharpening the Sharpe Ratio," *Financial Planning* (January 2003), available through **http://www.financialplanning.com**).

This problem is referred to as the *benchmark problem*. The essence of the problem is that performance of many portfolios should not be compared to a limited aggregate measure of the U.S. stock market. If, for example, a fund invested in European stocks did outperform the S&P 500, it may not have outperformed an aggregate measure of European stocks. The comparison of the fund to the S&P 500 is not meaningful.

These problems raise the question: Does the investor have to compute the performance indexes? The answer is both yes and no. If the investor wants to do the calculations, a good starting point is *The Individual Investor's Guide to the Top Mutual Funds* (published annually by the American Association of Individual Investors, http://www.aaii.com). This publication includes (1) a fund's returns for three, five, and ten years, (2) the standard deviation of the returns, and (3) the fund's beta. Unfortunately, this publication does not include all funds and does not report all the data necessary to calculate the three comparative measures of performance. If the investor does not want to calculate the performance measures, subscription services such as Morningstar (http://www.morningstar.com) provide the alphas and the Sharpe index, and they should be sufficient for an investor to compare funds' performance.

SUMMARY

Instead of directly investing in securities, individuals may buy shares in investment companies. These firms, in turn, invest the funds in various assets, such as stocks and bonds.

There are two types of investment companies. A closed-end investment company has a specified number of shares that are bought and sold in the same manner as the stock of firms such as AT&T. An open-end investment company (i.e., a mutual fund) has a variable number of shares sold directly to investors. Investors who desire to liquidate their holdings sell them back to the company.

Mutual funds offer several advantages, including professional management, diversification, and custodial services. Dividends and the interest earned on the firm's assets are distributed to stockholders. In addition, if the value of the fund's assets rises, the shareholders profit as capital gains are realized and distributed.

Mutual funds may be classified by the types of assets they own. Some stress income-producing assets, such as bonds, preferred stock, and common stock of firms that distribute a large proportion of their income. Other mutual funds stress growth in their net asset values through investments in firms with the potential to grow and generate capital gains. There are also investment companies that specialize in special situations or particular sectors of the economy, and some mutual funds seek to duplicate an index of the stock market.

Although investment companies are professionally managed, the returns that mutual funds have earned over a period of years have not consistently outperformed the market, especially after considering expenses and load fees.

Performance may be judged using the Jensen index by comparing the realized return with the risk-adjusted return that should have been earned. If the realized return exceeds this risk-adjusted return, then there was truly an excess return, and the investor beat the market during that time period. Alternative approaches for portfolio evaluation standardize the realized return by a measure of risk, such as the portfolio's standard deviation (the Sharpe index) or its beta (the Treynor index). The resulting index of performance may be compared with similar standardized indexes of performance by mutual funds or the market to determine if the particular portfolio did exceptionally well during the time period.

QUESTIONS

1. Are mutual funds subject to federal income taxation? Are distributions from mutual funds taxable?
2. What is a loading charge? Do all investment companies charge this fee?
3. What is a specialized mutual fund? What differentiates large and small cap funds? Value and growth funds?
4. What advantage do "families" of funds offer?
5. What differentiates a traditional savings accounts at a commercial bank from a money market mutual fund? Are investments in money market funds as safe as savings accounts and certificates of deposit with a commercial bank?
6. What assets do money market mutual funds acquire? Could an individual investor with $12,345 to invest in a safe, short-term security acquire these assets?
7. Should an investor expect a mutual fund to outperform the market? If not, why should the investor buy the shares?
8. What are the differences among loading fees, exit fees, and 12b-1 fees?
9. Why may the annual growth in a fund's net asset value not be comparable to the return earned by an individual investor?
10. How may beta coefficients be used to standardize returns for risk to permit comparisons of mutual fund performance?
11. If a portfolio manager earned 15 percent when the market rose by 12 percent, does this prove that the manager outperformed the market?
12. How may realized returns be adjusted for risk so that investment performance may be judged on a risk-adjusted basis?

PROBLEMS

1. What is the net asset value of an investment company with $10,000,000 in assets, $790,000 in current liabilities, and 1,200,000 shares outstanding?
2. If a mutual fund's net asset value is $23.40 and the fund sells its shares for $25, what is the load fee as a percentage of the net asset value?
3. If an investor buys shares in a no-load mutual fund for $31.40 and the shares appreciate to $44.60 in a year, what would be the percentage return on the investment? If the fund charges an exit fee of 1 percent, what would be the return on the investment?
4. An investor buys shares in a mutual fund for $20 per share. At the end of the year the fund distributes a dividend of $0.58, and after the distribution the net asset value of a share is $23.41. What would be the investor's percentage return on the investment?
5. Consider the following four investments.
   a) You invest $3,000 annually in a mutual fund that earns 10 percent annually, and you reinvest all distributions. How much will you have in the account at the end of 20 years?
   b) You invest $3,000 annually in a mutual fund with a 5 percent load fee so that only $2,850 is actually invested in the fund. The fund earns 10 percent annually, and you reinvest all distributions. How much will you have in

the account at the end of 20 years? (Assume that all distributions are not subject to the load fee.)

c) You invest $3,000 annually in a no-load mutual fund that charges 12b-1 fees of 1 percent. The fund earns 10 percent annually before fees, and you reinvest all distributions. How much will you have in the account at the end of 20 years?

d) You invest $3,000 annually in no-load mutual fund that has a 5 percent exit fee. The fund earns 10 percent annually before fees, and you reinvest all distributions. How much will you have in the account at the end of 20 years?

In each case you invest the same amount ($3,000) every year; the fund earns the same return each year (10 percent), and you make each investment for the same time period (20 years). At the end of the 20 years, you withdraw the funds. Why is the final amount in each mutual fund different?

6. You are given the following information concerning several mutual funds:

Fund	Return in Excess of the Treasury Bill Rate	Beta
A	12.4%	1.14
B	13.2	1.22
C	11.4	0.90
D	9.8	0.76
E	12.6	0.95

During the time period, the Standard & Poor's stock index exceeded the Treasury bill rate by 10.5 percent (i.e., $r_m - r_f = 10.5\%$).

a) Rank the performance of each fund without adjusting for risk and adjusting for risk using the Treynor index. Which, if any, outperformed the market? (Remember, the beta of the market is 1.0.)

b) The analysis in part (a) assumes each fund is sufficiently diversified so that the appropriate measure of risk is the beta coefficient. Suppose, however, this assumption does not hold and the standard deviation of each fund's return was as follows:

Fund	Standard Deviation of Return
A	0.045 (= 4.5%)
B	0.031
C	0.010
D	0.014
E	0.035

Thus, fund A earned a return of 12.4 percent, but approximately 68 percent of the time this return has ranged from 7.9 percent to 16.9 percent. The standard deviation of the market return is 0.01 (i.e., 1 percent), so 68 percent of the time, the return on the market has ranged from 9.5 to 11.5 percent. Rank the funds using this alternative measure of risk. Which, if any, outperformed the market on a risk-adjusted basis?

The Financial Advisor's Investment Case
Retirement Plans and Investment Choices

Ken Saffaf's 22-year-old daughter Bozena has just accepted a job with Doctor Medical Systems (DMS), a firm specializing in computer services for doctors. DMS offers employees a 401(k) plan to which employees may contribute 5 percent of their salary. DMS will match $0.50 for every dollar contributed. Bozena's starting salary is $32,000, so she could contribute up to $1,600 and DMS would contribute an additional $800. If she did decide to contribute to the plan, she has the following choices of funds, all managed by Superior Investments. She may select any combination of the funds and change the selection quarterly.

a. U.S. Value Fund—a fund invested solely in stocks of U.S. firms that management believes to be undervalued
b. Research & Technology Fund—a fund specializing in stocks of companies or firms primarily emphasizing computer services and programming
c. Global Equities—a fund invested solely in stocks of firms with international operations, such as Sony
d. Government Bond Fund—a fund devoted to debt issued or guaranteed by the federal government
e. High-Yield Debt—a fund devoted to bonds with non–investment grade ratings
f. Money Fund—a fund investing solely in short-term money market instruments

The historic returns of each fund, the standard deviation of the returns, the fund's beta (computed relative to the S&P 500 stock index), and the R^2 of beta are as follows:

	Return	Standard Deviation of Return	Beta	R^2
a. USVF	13%	20%	0.7	0.3
b. RTF	12	10	1.1	0.9
c. GE	15	40	1.5	0.6
d. GBF	7	8	0.3	0.2
e. HYD	10	12	0.4	0.3
f. MF	4	1	0.0	0.0

Ken's employer offers a defined benefit pension plan in which his retirement income depends on the average of his salary for the last five years in which he works. Since the employer guarantees and funds the plan, Ken does not understand Bozena's choices. He believes that she should participate but does not know the advantages and risks associated with each choice. Since Ken is your cousin, he has asked you to answer the following questions to convince Bozena to participate in the 401(k) plan and to help her choose among the six alternative funds.

1. If Bozena participates and the 401(k) earns 10 percent annually, how much will she have accumulated in 45 years (to age 67) even if her salary does not change?
2. If she does not participate and annually saves $1,600 on her own, how much will she have accumulated if she earns 10 percent (before tax) and is in the 20 percent federal income tax bracket?
3. If she retires at age 67, given the amounts in (1) and (2), how much can Bozena withdraw and spend each year for 20 years from each alternative? Assume she continues to earn 10 percent (before tax) and remains in the 20 percent federal income tax bracket.
4. If her salary grows, what impact will the increase have on the 40l(k) plan? To illustrate the effect on her accumulated funds, assume a $5,000 increment every five years so that she is earning $72,000 in years 41–45 (ages 63–67).
5. What are the risks and potential returns associated with each of the six alternative funds?
6. Who bears the risk associated with Bozena's retirement income?
7. Why does Ken not have to make these investment decisions? What are the risks associated with his retirement plan?
8. At this point in Bozena's life, which alternative(s) do you suggest she select?

CHAPTER 7

Closed-end Investment Companies, Real Estate Investment Trusts (REITs), and Exchange-Traded Funds (ETFs)

LEARNING OBJECTIVES

After completing this chapter you should be able to:

1. Compare and contrast closed-end and open-end investment companies.
2. Describe the difference between shares selling for a discount and shares selling for a premium from their net asset values.
3. Differentiate among the types of real estate investment trusts (REITs).
4. Describe the features and advantages associated with exchange-traded funds (ETFs).
5. Explain why an ETF trades for virtually no discount or premium (i.e., at its net asset value).
6. Explain why the operating expenses incurred by an ETF may be less than the operating expenses incurred by many mutual funds.
7. Differentiate hedge funds and private equity funds from other investment companies.
8. Use investment companies and especially ETFs to take positions in foreign financial markets.
9. Explain the necessary condition for foreign investments to diversify a domestic portfolio.

The previous chapter covered the shares of mutual funds, which are bought and sold directly from the fund. This chapter adds closed-end investment companies, real estate investment trusts, and exchange-traded funds. The shares of these investment companies are traded on the secondary markets such as the NYSE or Nasdaq. This ease of trading has significantly increased investor interest in these investment companies, especially exchange-traded funds.

Closed-end investment companies have many of the essential features and advantages of open-end mutual funds, such as diversification and professional management. However, the fact that closed-end investment company shares trade in the securities markets clearly differentiates them from mutual funds. Many closed-end investment companies are specialized; some invest solely in the securities of a specific region such as Asia or specific country such as Korea. Others specialize in debt instruments such as municipal bonds issued in a state such as Virginia or New Jersey.

Real estate investment trusts, commonly referred to as REITs (pronounced REETs), are closed-end investment companies that specialize in real estate interests such as mortgages, apartments, or shopping malls. REITs permit investors to have a position in real estate without actually owning and operating the buildings themselves.

Exchange-traded funds (common referred to as ETFs) are a relatively new investment vehicle. Initially ETFs were created as a type of index fund whose shares trade in the secondary securities markets. These ETFs tracked an index such as the Standard & Poor's 500 stock index or an index of foreign securities. Today, however, the number of ETFs has exploded, so that ETFs cover virtually every possible investment alternative including sectors, countries, debt obligations, currencies, and commodities. There are even ETFs stressing specific investment strategies such taking short positions instead of long positions.

The last sections of this chapter briefly cover investment companies with foreign investments, hedge funds, and private equity firms. This variety of investment companies offers individuals a means to diversify and manage their portfolios. The existence of investment companies permits an individual to construct a well-diversified portfolio and to alter its composition among various types of securities, various sectors within the economy, different countries, or even different investment strategies without ever having to select individual securities. Thus, these investment companies can play an extremely important role in the individual's portfolio construction and asset allocation.

CLOSED-END INVESTMENT COMPANIES

Mutual fund shares are bought from the fund and sold back to the fund. Shares in closed-end investment companies are bought and sold through the securities markets. The shares are originally sold to the general public through an initial public offering (IPO) and subsequently trade on an exchange or through the over-the-counter markets. No new shares are created when an investor buys stock because the shares are purchased from another individual and not from the investment company.

A closed-end investment company has a fixed capital structure that may be composed of all stock or a combination of stock and debt. The number of shares and the dollar amount of debt that the company may issue are specified. (In a mutual fund the number of shares varies as investors purchase and redeem them.) Since a closed-end investment company has a specified number of shares, an individual who wants to invest in a particular company must buy the shares from existing stockholders. Conversely, any investor who owns shares and wishes to liquidate the position must sell the shares to another investor. Individuals may obtain the current price of the shares by entering the ticker symbol in the same way that they would obtain the price of IBM stock.

Discounts and Premiums

discount (from net asset value)

The extent to which the price of a closed-end investment company's stock is below its net asset value.

premium (over net asset value)

The extent to which the price of a closed-end investment company's stock exceeds the share's net asset value.

While shares in mutual funds are bought and redeemed at the fund's net asset value (plus or minus any applicable load fees), the price of a share in a closed-end investment company need not equal its net asset value. The price may be above or below the NAV depending on the demand and the supply of the stock. If the market price is less than the net asset value of the shares, the shares are selling for a **discount**. If the market price is above the net asset value, the shares are selling for a **premium**.

These differences between the investment company's net asset value per share and the stock price are illustrated in Exhibit 7.1, which gives the price, the net asset value, and the discount or the premium for several closed-end investment companies. Three sold for a discount (i.e., below their net asset values). The cause of this discount is not really known, but it is believed to be the result of taxation. The potential impact of capital gains taxation on the price of the shares is illustrated in the following example.

A closed-end investment company initially sells stock for $10 per share and uses the proceeds to buy the stock of other companies. If transaction costs are ignored, the net asset

| EXHIBIT 7.1 | Net Asset Values and Market Prices of Selected Closed-end Investment Companies as of June 12, 2009 |

Company	Price	Net Asset Value	(Discount) or Premium as a Percentage of Net Asset Value
Adams Express	$8.67	$10.35	(16.5)%
Gabelli Trust	5.01	4.20	19.3
General American Investors	19.47	23.59	(17.5)
Royce Focus Trust	8.87	10.34	(14.2)

Source: *Wall Street Journal,* June 15, 2009, C5.

value of a share is $10, and the shares may trade in the secondary market for $10. The value of the firm's portfolio subsequently rises to $16 (i.e., the net asset value is $16). The firm has a potential capital gain of $6 per share. If it is realized and these profits are distributed, the net asset value will return to $10 and each stockholder will receive $6 in capital gains, for which he or she will pay the appropriate capital gains tax.

Suppose, however, that the capital gains are not realized (i.e., the net asset value remains at $16). What will the market price of the stock be? This is difficult to determine, but it will probably be below $16. Why? Suppose an investor bought a share for $16 and the firm then realized and distributed the $6 capital gain. After the distribution of the $6, the investor would be responsible for any capital gains tax, but the net asset value of the share would decrease to $10.

Obviously this is not advantageous to the buyer. Individuals may be willing to purchase the shares only at a discount that reduces the potential impact of realized capital gains and the subsequent capital gains taxes. Suppose the share had cost $14 (i.e., it sold for a discount of $2 from the net asset value) and the fund realized and distributed the gain. The buyer who paid $14 now owns a share with a net asset value of $10 and receives a capital gain of $6. Although this investor will have to pay the appropriate capital gains tax, the impact is reduced because the investor paid only $14 to purchase the share whose total value is $16 (the $10 net asset value plus the $6 capital gain).

Although many closed-end investment companies sell for a discount, some do sell for a premium. In Exhibit 7.1, Gabelli Trust sold for $5.01 when its net asset value was $4.20, a premium of 19.3 percent above the net asset value. Often, closed-end investment companies that sell for a premium have a specialized portfolio that appeals to some investors. For example, as of June 2009, the India Fund commanded a premium of 17.5 percent. This fund invests primarily in a country that places restrictions on foreign investments. If individuals want to acquire shares in firms in such countries (perhaps for potential growth or for diversification purposes), a closed-end investment company is a viable means to make the investments. The effect may be to bid up the price of the shares so that the closed-end investment company sells for a premium over its net asset value.

Since the shares may sell for a discount or a premium relative to their net asset value, it is possible for the market price of a closed-end investment company to fluctuate more or less than the net asset value. For example, during 2003, the net asset value of Salomon Brothers Fund rose from $10.75 to $14.04 (a 30.6 percent increase), but the stock increased 31.9 percent ($9.12 to $12.03) as the discount fell from 16.2 to

⊕ Point of Interest

INITIAL PUBLIC OFFERINGS OF CLOSED-END INVESTMENT COMPANIES

As was explained in Chapter 2, the shares of companies are originally sold to the public through investment bankers in an initial public offering (or IPO). The shares of closed-end investment companies are originated through the same process. These shares are initially sold to the public for a premium over their net asset value. If the price to the public is $15 and the investment banking fee is $0.85, then the net asset value is reduced from $15.00 to $14.15. In effect, the shares are sold for a premium of 6 percent over their net asset value.

While some initial public offerings do well in the secondary markets, many do not. The prices of these closed-end investment company shares decline until the premium disappears, and the shares may even sell for a discount. The SEC has reported that the shares of bond and stock closed-end investment funds declined 6 and 23 percent, respectively, within the first four months of trading. These results suggest that it is not prudent to purchase initial offerings of closed-end investment companies. While no satisfactory explanation has been given as to why individuals pay the initial premium, the usual explanation involves the persuasive power of the brokers who sell the securities for the investment bankers.

14.3 percent. Since the market price can change relative to the net asset value, an investor is subject to an additional source of risk. The value of the investment may decline not only because the net asset value may decrease but also because the shares may sell for a larger discount from their net asset value.

Some investors view the market price relative to the net asset value as a guide to buying and selling the shares of a closed-end investment company. If the shares are selling for a sufficient discount, they are considered for purchase. If the shares are selling for a small discount or at a premium, they are sold. Of course, determining the premium that will justify the sale or the discount that will justify the purchase is not simple (and may even be arbitrary).

Sources of Return from Investing in Closed-end Investment Companies

Investing in closed-end investment companies involves several costs. First, since the shares are purchased in the secondary markets, the individual must pay the brokerage commission for the purchase and for any subsequent sale. Second, the investment company charges a fee to manage the portfolio. This fee is subtracted from any income that the firm's assets earn. These management fees generally range from 0.5 to 2 percent of the net asset value. Third, when the investment company purchases or sells securities, it also has to pay brokerage fees, which are passed on to the investor.

Investors in closed-end investment companies earn returns in a variety of ways. First, if the investment company collects dividends and interest on its portfolio, this income is distributed to the stockholders. Second, if the value of the firm's assets increases, the company may sell the assets and realize the gains. These profits are then distributed as capital gains. Such distributions usually occur in a single payment near the end of the calendar year and, for most individuals, the tax year. Third, the net asset value of the portfolio may increase, which will cause the market price of the

| EXHIBIT | 7.2 | Annual Returns on an Investment in Salomon Brothers Fund, a Closed-end Investment Company |

Distributions and Price Changes	2003	2002	2001	2000	1999	1998	1997	1996
Per-share income distributions	$ 0.13	0.11	0.11	0.14	0.18	0.27	$0.27	0.33
Per-share capital gains distributions	—	$0.07	0.33	2.41	3.63	3.19	$2.63	2.09
Year-end net asset value	$14.04	10.75	14.07	16.27	19.24	18.76	$18.51	17.26
Year-end market price	$12.03	9.12	12.42	16.25	20.375	18.19	$17.625	16.00
Annual return based on prior year's market price								
a. Dividend yield	1.4%	0.8	0.7	0.7	1.0	1.5	1.7%	2.5
b. Capital gains yield	—	0.5	1.8	11.8	20.2	18.1	16.4%	15.6
c. Change in price	31.9%	−35.2	−13.4	−20.2	12.0	3.2	10.2%	19.6
Total return	33.3%	−33.9	−10.9	−7.7	33.2	22.8	28.3%	37.7

Source: Salomon Brothers Fund (SBF) annual reports.

company's stock to rise. In this case, the investor may sell the shares in the secondary market and realize a capital gain. Fourth, the market price of the shares may rise relative to the net asset value (i.e., the premium may increase or the discount may decrease); the investor may then earn a profit through the sale of the shares.

These sources of return are illustrated in Exhibit 7.2, which presents the distributions and price changes over several years for Salomon Brothers Fund from December 31, 1996, through December 31, 2003. As may be seen in the exhibit, the investment company distributed cash dividends of $0.27 and capital gains of $2.63 in 1997. The net asset value rose from $17.26 to $18.51, and the price of the stock likewise rose (from $16 to $17.625). An investor who bought the shares on December 31, 1996, earned a total annual return of 28.3 percent (before commissions) on the investment.[1]

The potential for loss is also illustrated in Exhibit 7.2. If the investor bought the shares on December 31, 2000, he or she suffered a loss during 2001. While the fund distributed $0.11 in income and $0.33 in capital gains, the net asset value and the price of the stock declined sufficiently to more than offset the income and capital gains distributions.

Notice in Exhibit 7.2 that Salomon Brothers Fund consistently sold for a discount. Except for 1999, the year-end market price (line 4) was less than the net asset value (line 3). The persistency of the discount led some shareholders to demand that the fund be converted from a closed-end to an open-end investment company. Since open-end mutual funds are bought and redeemed at the fund's net asset value, the switch would end the shares selling for a discount. In 2005, the fund's board adopted a plan for conversion, and Salomon Brothers Funds did convert to a mutual fund whose shares are bought and redeemed at their net asset value plus any adjustments required by applicable load fees.

---

[1] The calculation of the annual return is

$$\frac{\$17.625 + \$0.27 + \$2.63 - \$16}{\$16} = 28.3\%.$$

Unit Trusts

unit trust

A passive investment company with a fixed portfolio of assets that are self-liquidating.

A variation on the closed-end investment company is the fixed-unit investment trust, commonly referred to as a **unit trust** or unit investment trust (UIT). These trusts, which are formed by brokerage firms and sold to investors, hold a fixed portfolio of securities. The portfolio is designed to meet a specified investment objective, such as the generation of interest income, in which case the portfolio would include federal government or corporate bonds, municipal bonds, or mortgage loans.

A unit trust is a passive investment, as its assets are not traded but are frozen. No new securities are purchased, and securities originally purchased are rarely sold. The trust collects income (e.g., interest on its portfolio) and, eventually, the repayment of principal. The trust is self-liquidating because as the funds are received, they are not reinvested but are distributed to stockholders. Such trusts are primarily attractive to retirees who seek a steady, periodic flow of payments. If the investor needs the funds earlier, the shares may be sold back to the trust at their current net asset value, which may be lower than the initial cost.

Unit trusts are also of interest to investors whose financial goals are matched by the objectives of the trust. Such individuals acquire shares in a diversified portfolio of assets that are sold in affordable units. Unlike other investment companies, the fixed portfolio means that operating expenses, which would reduce the current flow of income to the owners of the trust, are minimal.

As with any investment, however, unit trusts do have disadvantages. The investor pays an initial up-front fee of 3 to 5 percent when the trust is formed, and even though there are minimal management fees, the trustees do have custodial expenses that are paid from the earnings of the trust. Although the trust may acquire high-quality securities, there is no certainty that the bonds will not default. There is the risk that the realized return may be less than anticipated.

The concept of a unit trust has been extended to a broader spectrum of securities. For example, Merrill Lynch developed a trust consisting solely of emerging growth stocks. After a specified period of time, the stocks will be sold and the funds distributed to unit holders. Once again, the trust is a passive investment that holds a portfolio for a specified time period and is liquidated. Such a trust may appeal to an investor seeking capital appreciation through a diversified portfolio but who needs the funds at a specific time in the future (e.g., at retirement). Because the liquidation date is specified, that individual knows when the funds will be received.

Although the investor knows when the funds will be received, he or she does not know the amount. The prices of the stocks held by the trust could rise or fall. If the value of the stocks were to rise, the investor would earn a profit. However, if the prices of the securities were to decline, the trust's management cannot wait beyond the liquidation date for the stocks to recoup their lost value.

real estate investment trust (REIT)

Closed-end investment company that specializes in real estate or mortgage investments.

REAL ESTATE INVESTMENT TRUSTS (REITs)

Real estate investment trusts (REITs) are closed-end investment companies that specialize in real estate assets, primarily properties or mortgages. REITs provide investors with a means to have positions in real estate *without having to acquire and operate the*

EXHIBIT 7.3	Selected REITs and Their Dividend Yields		
REIT	Price as of June 18, 2009	Annual Dividend	Dividend Yield
Analy Capital Management (NLY)	$14.76	$2.00	13.55%
National Retail Properties (NNN)	17.04	1.50	8.80
Senior Housing Properties Trust (SNH)	16.73	1.40	8.97
UDR Inc (UDR)	10.44	0.72	6.90
Washington Real Estate Investment Trust (WRE)	20.98	1.68	8.01

Source: http://finance.yahoo.com, June 18, 2009.

properties. Since REITs are a type of closed-end investment company, they receive the same tax treatment as other investment companies such as mutual funds. As long as a REIT derives 75 percent of its income from real estate (e.g., interest on mortgage loans and rents) and distributes at least 90 percent of the income as cash dividends, the trust is exempt from federal income tax. Thus, REITs, like mutual funds and other closed-end investment companies, are conduits through which earnings pass to the shareholders.

Shares of REITs are bought and sold like the stocks of other companies.[2] Some of the shares are traded on the New York Stock Exchange (e.g., National Retail Properties), while others are traded on the American Stock Exchange and Nasdaq. The existence of these markets means that the shares of REITs may be readily sold. This liquidity certainly differentiates shares of REITs from other types of real estate investments.

Since a REIT distributes virtually all its earned income to maintain its tax status, the result is greater dividend yields than may be available through most stock investments. Selected dividend yields offered by REITs are provided in Exhibit 7.3, and yields in excess of 8 percent are common from investments in REITs, especially REITs that invest in mortgage loans such as Analy Capital Management.

Dividends paid by REITs are not the same as dividends paid by corporations such as AT&T. Corporate dividends are paid from after-tax income and as of 2010 are taxed at a maximum federal rate of 15 percent. REIT dividends are *not* paid from after-tax income and do *not* receive the favorable 15 percent federal tax rate. Instead, the dividends are taxed at the investor's marginal tax rate. Actually, the payments from a REIT are not "dividends" but "distributions." Distributions are often related to the trust's cash flow from operations, and the payments may include income, capital gains from sale of properties, and the return of the investor's capital. (For a more detailed discussion of the taxation of REIT distributions, see the accompanying Point of Interest.)

Classification of REITs

REITs may be grouped according to either the types of assets they acquire or their capital structure. **Equity trusts** own property and rent it to other firms (i.e., they lease their property to others). **Mortgage trusts** make loans to develop property and finance

equity trust

A real estate investment trust that specializes in acquiring real estate for subsequent rental income.

mortgage trust

A real estate investment trust that specializes in loans secured by real estate.

[2] Information concerning a REIT may be obtained from the trust. Use its name or ticker symbol to locate the trust's Web address. Information may also be obtained through the SEC EDGAR database (**http://www.sec.gov**), Edgar Online (**http://www.edgar-online.com**), or specialized sources such as the National Association of Real Estate Investment Trusts (**http://www.reit.com**), REITNet (**http://www.reitnet.com**), and Realty Stocks and Funds (**http://www.realtystocks.com**).

⊕ Point of Interest

REIT DISTRIBUTIONS AND FEDERAL TAXES

Many companies make cash distributions to stockholders. These are often called *dividends*, but the use of that term is not necessarily correct when applied to distributions by REITs. In common usage, a cash dividend implies a distribution of earnings. But a REIT's cash distribution could be from earnings, capital gains, or a return of capital.

Consider the following REIT with per-share earnings from operations of $1.00, a per-share gain from the sale of property of $0.60, and per-share funds from operations of $2.10. Since a REIT's expenses include noncash depreciation charges, the firm can generate more funds than earnings. Noncash expenses explain why operating income can be $1.00 while funds from operations is $2.10. (They also explain why financial analysts may use funds from operations instead of earnings when valuing a REIT.)

The REIT now distributes $1.90 per share to its stockholders. What are the tax implications of this distribution? One dollar of the distribution is income and is taxed as income. That is, the $1.00 in dividends from earnings is taxed at the individual's marginal tax rate (i.e., tax bracket). Another $0.60 of the distribution is classified as a capital gain. Since property is generally held for more than a year, the $0.60 will be a long-term capital gain and taxed at a lower rate than the tax on the dividend from earnings.

One dollar in income plus $0.60 in capital gains account for only $1.60 of the $1.90 distribution. What is the tax on the remaining $0.30? The answer is nothing. Thirty cents is a return of the investor's capital and is not taxed. Instead, the investor's cost basis for the stock is reduced by $0.30. If the investor paid $13.45 per share for the stock, the adjusted cost basis becomes $13.15. This adjustment becomes important when the investor sells the stock and must pay capital gains tax on any profits. As the cost basis is reduced by the return of capital, potential capital gains taxes increase. Of course, as long as the stockholder retains the stock, there is no capital gains tax.

Distributions from REITs are occasionally touted as being partially nontaxable. To some extent this is true, since any return of capital is nontaxable. But, the statement is also misleading because the cost basis is reduced by the amount of distribution, which may result in future capital gains taxes. The informed investor realizes that REIT dividends are not necessarily dividends in the traditional sense of the term and that nontaxable distribution can produce capital gains taxes in the future. If an investor wants to know if previous distributions made by a REIT were nontaxable, that information is available through the National Association of Real Estate Investment Trusts (NAREIT) website (**http://www.nareit.com**).

buildings. There is a considerable difference between these two approaches to investing in real estate. Loans to help finance real estate, especially developmental loans, can earn high interest rates, but some of these loans can be very risky. Contractors may be unable to sell or lease the completed buildings, which may consequently cause them to default on their loans. In addition, any appreciation in the value of the property cannot be enjoyed by the lender, who owns a fixed obligation.

In an equity trust, the REIT owns the property and rents space. This also is risky because the properties may remain vacant. Unleased property, of course, does not generate revenue, but the owner still has expenses, such as insurance, maintenance, and depreciation. These fixed expenses can generate large fluctuations in earnings of an equity trust. However, should there be an increase in property values, the trust may experience capital appreciation.

The second method for differentiating REITs is according to their capital structures or the extent to which they use debt financing. Some trusts use modest amounts of debt financing, while others use a large amount of leverage. The latter can be very risky investments. If mortgage loans turn sour and the borrowers default, or if the properties

EXHIBIT 7.4	Selected REITs by Type of Assets and Capital Structure	
REIT	Real Estate as a Percentage of Total Assets	Ratio of Debt to Total Assets
Analy Capital Management (NLY)	0%	87.5%
Washington Real Estate Investment Trust (WRE)	90.9	70.3
UDR INC (UDR)	92.3	69.4
National Retail Properties (NNN)	94.0	41.8
Senior Housing Properties Trust (SNH)	97.1	30.7

Source: 2008 annual reports.

become vacant, the trust may have difficulty meeting its own obligations. Thus, while the use of debt financing magnifies fluctuations in a REIT's cash flow and earnings, low use of financial leverage suggests a REIT is better positioned to survive a period of recession and declining economic growth. This certainly proved to be the case in 2008 when homeowners did default on mortgages. Mortgage trusts such as New Century Financial, which primarily invested in high risk "subprime" mortgages, filed for bankruptcy and inflicted large losses on its stockholders and creditors.

These differences among REITs are illustrated in Exhibit 7.4, which presents real estate as a percentage of the trust's assets and its use of debt financing as measured by the ratio of debt to total assets. The entries are listed in descending order according to their debt ratios. Analy Capital Corporation is a mortgage trust that owns no properties. United Dominion REIT (UDR) is an equity trust (primarily apartments) with over 60 percent of its assets debt financed. National Retail Properties (NNN) is also an equity trust but finances its assets with less debt. While NNN's use of less debt financing suggests that it is the less risky of the two trusts, its commercial properties may be subject to increased vacancy rates. It has more business risk than United Dominion.

REITs and Securitization

REITs are an illustration of securitization, the process of converting illiquid assets into a liquid, marketable asset. Even if they had the resources, few investors would be willing to own an apartment complex or office building. And even fewer would be able to own a mall. Contractors and developers are able to package together these types of properties and spin them off as REITs. By this process they convert an asset that is not easily sold (e.g., apartment buildings) into an asset for which a ready market exists (i.e., the shares of the REIT). For example, Cornerstone Realty Income Trust was formed when real estate operations were converted into a trust. Individual ownership of the shares then facilitated the trust's acquiring additional properties through issuing publicly traded stock in exchange for the properties. Individual ownership also meant that the trust could raise additional funds by selling additional shares to the general public.

A company may use the formation of a REIT as a means to divest an operation without actually selling the assets and thereby avoid paying income taxes on any gains from the sale. Other companies may form a REIT to remove assets (and liabilities) that no longer meet their strategic plans. Getty Petroleum split into two operations. One piece received service stations (and any debt such as mortgages associated with the stations). The operation was renamed Getty Realty (GTY) and reorganized as a real estate investment trust. Virtually all of Getty Realty's assets are service stations under long-term leases to Getty. Owners of the trust will receive cash flow from the leases, and Getty divested itself of the service stations and their associated liabilities. In effect, the company has converted an illiquid asset, the service stations, into a marketable asset, shares in the trust.

EXCHANGE-TRADED FUNDS (ETFs)

The inability of many mutual funds to outperform the market (or outperform an appropriate benchmark) led to increased interest in index funds, which mirror the market (or a subsection of the market). Their appeal is obvious. The advantages include (1) portfolio diversification, (2) a passive portfolio with minimal turnover resulting in lower operating expenses, and (3) lower taxes since the index fund has few realized capital gains. By 2000, about 50 index funds tracked the S&P 500 and other indexes, such as the Dreyfus S&P MidCap Index Fund, which specializes in moderate-sized stocks that match the S&P MidCap 400 index. The Vanguard Balanced Index Fund mimics a combination of stocks and bonds, and the Schwab International Index Fund tracks the 350 largest non–U.S. firms.

Financial markets are not static; new products evolve. The creation of the index fund led to the creation of the exchange-traded fund (ETF). Index funds permit investors to take a position in the market as a whole without having to select individual securities. Purchases and redemptions, however, occur only at the end of the day when the fund's net asset value is determined. Standard & Poor's Depository Receipts or SPDRs (pronounced "spiders") overcame this limitation. The shares may be bought and sold on an exchange during operating hours. In effect, SPDRs are index funds that trade like stocks and bonds, hence the name "exchange-traded fund" or "ETF." (The phrase "exchange-traded portfolio" is also used.)

The first SPDR comprised all the stocks in the S&P 500 stock index. The second SPDR was based on the S&P MidCap stock index and was followed by nine "Select Sector SPDRs" based on subsections of the S&P 500 stock index. These sectors include basic industry, consumer products, utilities, health care, financial, technology, and energy stocks. If you believe that large cap energy companies will do well, you do not have to select specific companies. You can buy the energy SPDRs. Since each SPDR includes *all* the stocks in the appropriate subsection, there is no selection process for the SPDR. Operating expenses should be minimal, and the performance of the SPDR should mirror the return earned by the subsection (e.g., energy).

Since SPDRs and ETFs trade like the shares of any closed-end investment company, can their shares sell for a discount or premium over net asset value? The answer is no. ETFs permit large institutions to exchange shares in the companies for ETF shares and vice versa. Suppose an ETF were to sell for a discount from NAV. The financial institutions could buy the ETF shares and exchange them for shares in the underlying companies. Simultaneously, the financial institution would sell the exchanged shares in the secondary markets and make the difference between the cost of the ETF and the proceeds from the sale of the underlying stock. The process would be reversed if the ETF shares

SOURCES OF INFORMATION ON ETFs

As you might anticipate, a large number of Internet sites provide information on exchange-traded funds. As a starting point you may use Index Funds, Inc. **http://www.indexfunds.com**, which provides information on index and exchange-traded funds.

Information sources on specific ETFs include the following: **http://www.sectorspdr.com** for the nine sector SPDRs based on the S&P 500 index

http://www.ishares.com for iShares

http://www.holdrs.com for HOLDRs. Bank of New York, which acts as the trustee and transfer agent for the securities, also provides a website devoted to depository receipts

http://www.adrbnymellon.com. Information includes current pricing and a link that provides the composition of each HOLDR portfolio.

http://www.streettracks.net for streetTracks

http://www.vanguard.com for ETFs created by the Vanguard Group, Inc.

were selling for a premium. The financial institution would buy the underlying shares, exchange them for shares in the ETF, and simultaneously sell the ETF shares. Once again, the financial institution would make the difference between the cost of the underlying stock and the proceeds from the sale of the ETF shares. These actions by the financial institutions would assure that the price of an ETF approximates its net asset value. Any remaining difference would be small, perhaps trivial. For example, PowerShares Dynamic Insurance (PIC), which tracks an index of insurance companies, sold for $13.72 when its NAV was $13.74, for a discount of only 0.15 percent.

The simultaneous buying and selling of ETF shares and the underlying securities is an illustration of arbitrage. Arbitrage was defined in Chapter 5 as the simultaneous selling and buying of the same security or commodity to take advantage of differences in prices. If the price of the securities and an ETF NAV differ, *arbitrage assures that the price differences are erased*. Arbitrage is an important concept in finance and economics; because of it price differentials for the same asset cannot exist. Arbitrage appears many times in this text. The first reference was in the section on arbitrage pricing theory. It reappears in Chapter 16 on convertible bonds, where it determines the minimum price of a convertible bond. In Chapters 17–19 on options and futures, arbitrage assures that a derivative security must sell for at least its value as the underlying asset.

Although the potential for arbitrage assures that an ETF will sell for approximately its net asset value, the net asset value may not track the index. Consider an ETF designed to track an index of foreign stocks such as the EAFE (Europe, Australasia, and Far East).[3] Suppose the index rises by 10 percent; will the ETF also increase by 10 percent? Notice that the question did not ask: "Will the return be 10 percent?" One reason why the return may be less would be the expenses associated with the ETF. The return might be 9.6 percent after operating expenses are subtracted. Of course, all investment companies have operating expenses, so this discrepancy between the investor's return and the change in the benchmark index should be expected. (One means for choosing

---

[3] Australasia is a region in Oceania that encompasses Australia, New Zeland, New Guinea, and neighboring islands.

among investment companies is to select funds with lower expenses, such as the 12b-1 fees covered in the previous chapter.)

There is, however, an important reason why the change in the ETF's value may not be equal to the change in its benchmark. Suppose an ETF mimicked an index that encompassed 100 stocks. To achieve the same percentage change as the benchmark, the ETF would have to *own all 100 stocks in the same proportion as the index*. ETFs rarely do this; instead they own a set of stocks that are highly correlated with the index. For example, iShares US Medical Devices (IHI) tracks the Dow Jones U.S. Medical Equipment index. The fund usually invests 90 percent of its assets in the stocks in the index. The fund, however, does not invest in all the stocks in the index, and over 50 percent of its assets are in just ten stocks. The fund may also invest in other assets that management believes will track the index. For this reason the change in an ETF's price can deviate from the change in the index. The difference is referred to as the "tracking error." If you acquire an ETF with a large tracking error, you may not earn the return generated by the underlying index.

In addition to the tracking error, an ETF may not duplicate the return on the underlying index because the ETF does not seek to mimic the index. As is explained in Chapter 10 on stock indexes, the S&P 500 stock index is a value-weighted index that gives more emphasis to large companies such as Microsoft and ExxonMobil. You might expect that an ETF based on the S&P 500 would also give more weight to large companies, but that need not be the case. The RevenueShares Large Cap ETF (RWL) ranks the stocks in the index based on *sales* and not on capitalization. Companies such as Wal-Mart Stores are given more weight in this ETF's portfolio. The Rydex S&P Equal Weight ETF (RSP) treats each stock equally so that smaller companies have more impact on that ETF's performance than would be the case of an ETF that mimics the S&P 500's stock weightings.

Specialized ETFs

After the initial success of index funds and SPDRs, the next logical step was to extend the concept to other areas. Barclays Global Investors created "iShares," which extended the concept to foreign stock indexes. Investors could buy iShares based on a broad overview of international stock markets such as the iShares MSCI EAFE Index Fund (ticker symbol: EFA) or specific countries such as the iShares Germany Index Fund (EWG). (MSCI stands for Morgan Stanley Capital International and the EAFE index encompasses Europe, Australasia and the Far East.) ETFs were created for geographical regions such as the iShares S&P Europe 350 Index Fund (IEV) and for emerging markets such as the iShares Brazil Index Fund (EWZ).

Merrill Lynch created "HOLDRs" (Holding Company Depository Receipts), each of which owns a fixed portfolio of approximately 20 stocks in a sector such as biotech, pharmaceuticals, or regional banks. (The pharmaceutical portfolio includes Abbott Laboratories, Allergan, Johnson & Johnson, and Merck.) Once the portfolio is acquired, it is maintained indefinitely, so there is no active management of the portfolio, which reduces annual expenses.

HOLDRs added a different twist on the ETF. Investors who purchase a HOLDR are considered to own the stock in the portfolio. An investor may take delivery of the individual securities. If a HOLDR were to sell for a discount from its net asset value, investors could short the stocks, buy the HOLDR at the discounted price, have the individual stocks delivered, and use them to cover the short sales. This arbitrage process guarantees a profit, and the act of buying the HOLDR drives up its price to the value of the underlying securities. While other ETFs offer this opportunity for arbitrage to large financial institutions, they do not, in effect, make the same offer to the individual investor: The minimum size of the necessary transaction is too large for individual investors to execute, so they are excluded. A HOLDR extends the opportunity for arbitrage to all of its stockholders.

In addition to SPDRs, iShares, and HOLDRs, other ETFs include streetTracks, which track specialized indexes such as the Dow Jones small cap growth stocks or the Wilshire index of real estate investment trusts. These various ETFs have become popular vehicles for investors. ETFs based on the S&P 500 and the Nasdaq 100 (commonly referred to by its symbol QQQQ or the "QQQs") are among the most actively traded securities on the various securities markets.

Although exchange-traded funds are not riskless (the B2B HOLDR declined from a high of $60 in August 2000 to less than $5 in August 2001), they do offer advantages not available through index funds. Operating expenses of both index funds and ETFs are modest and both facilitate asset allocation strategies, so investors may readily trade ETFs. Investors can easily move from one ETF to another just as they can buy and sell the stock of individual companies. Purchases and sales of index mutual funds occur only once at the end of the day. In addition, an investor who believes one area or sector is overpriced may sell the exchange-traded shares short. Such short sales are not possible with mutual funds and would require substantial commissions if a large number of stocks were sold short.

In a sense, exchange-traded funds let passive investors actively manage their positions. Instead of having to select individual securities (as active portfolio management requires), the investor may move between sectors and types of securities. Even if the investor wants to acquire individual assets in a specific sector, exchange-traded funds offer flexibility. The investor may initially acquire an ETF and then research individual stocks. Once the desired companies have been identified, the investor unwinds (i.e., sells) the position in the ETF and substitutes the desired stocks. This process may be spread over a period of time during which the investor maintains exposure to the sector through the exchange-traded fund. As more individual stocks are added to the portfolio, the position in the ETF is liquidated.

Leveraged ETFs

One type of ETF that has gained in popularity is the leveraged ETF, which seeks to duplicate a multiple of the daily change in an index. For example, Proshares Ultra Dow (DDM) generates a return that is twice the daily performance of the Dow Jones Industrial Average. If the average rises 3 percent, DDM should generate a return of 6 percent. Suppose the Dow is 10,000 and the ETF is 100. If the Dow rises by 3 percent to 10,300, the ETF should increase by 6 percent to 106. Of course, leverage works both ways, so if the average were to decline by 2 percent, the Proshares Ultra Dow would decline by 4 percent. That is, if the Dow declines by 2 percent from 10,000 to 9,800, the ETF should decline from 100 to 96.

You might think that a 2 percent decline in the average would be offset by a 2 percent increase. However, a 2 percent increase and a 2 percent decrease do not

ETFs AND REITs

If you do not want to select individual REITs, an alternative strategy is to acquire shares in an exchange-traded fund that tracks an index of REITs. Several REIT ETFs are available. The oldest is the iShares Dow Jones (IYR), which uses the Dow Jones U.S. Real Estate Index. While this index is primarily composed of REITs, it also includes stocks of real estate operating companies. The streetTracks Wilshire REIT Fund (RWR) tracks the Wilshire REIT Index, which is an index of publicly traded REITs. The iShares Cohen & Steers Realty Majors Fund (ICF) tracks the Cohen & Steers Realty Majors Index, which emphasizes large, actively traded REITs. The MSCI US REIT index encompasses over 100 REITs, and

the Vanguard REIT ETF (VNQ) is based on this index. Notice that each ETF tracks a different index, so its performance may differ. All four, however, offer you the advantage of not having to select individual REITs or select portfolio managers who, in turn, select individual REITs. Like all exchange-traded funds, the REITs ETFs let you take a long position in real estate with the advantage of modest operating expenses. (If you prefer to invest in the builders instead of the owners of properties, you may consider ETFs that track homebuilders and construction companies. These funds include SPDR Homebuilders (XHB) and iShares Dow Jones US Home Construction (ITB).)

produce the same absolute price change. Suppose the Dow were to increase by 2 percent from 10,000 to 10,200 (1.02 × 10,200) and subsequently decline by 2 percent to 9,996 (0.98 × 10,200). The ETF would initially rise by 4 percent from 100 to 104 and subsequently decline by 4 percent to 99.84 (0.96 × 104). (For an explanation of averaging percentage changes, see Chapter 10 on indexes and the computation of returns.)

One implication of this mathematical reality is that these securities are only appropriate for short-term traders. In a stagnating market in which prices fluctuate but do not trend in a particular direction, a leveraged ETF will generate losses for investors with long positions in the security. Over time the price of the ETF will actually tend to decline as the index stagnates. This process is referred to as "decaying." To see the impact, work through Problem 5, in which the index price starts at 100, fluctuates, and ends the period at 100. The price of the leveraged ETF, however, declines!

Several brokerage firms have acknowledged that leveraged ETFs are not appropriate for many of their clients. In July 2009, UBS Wealth Management suspended purchase of leveraged ETFs, asserting that their short-term emphasis was not consistent with its clients' long-term investment objectives. Previously, LPL Investment Holdings had prohibited the sale of leveraged products, and Ameriprise Financial told its financial advisors to stop soliciting orders for leveraged ETFs.

HEDGE FUNDS AND PRIVATE EQUITY FIRMS

The word *hedge* generally implies a course of action designed to reduce risk, and the phrase "hedge fund" might imply a type of mutual fund that pursues low-risk strategies, but neither inference is correct. Hedge funds (and private equity firms) are pools of money that are used to acquire a variety of assets with the intent to earn higher returns. The strategies necessary to generate these higher returns often require taking substantial risks.

Hedge funds are generally organized as limited partnerships, with the fund's managers serving as general partners while the investors are limited partners. Hedge funds are "private" organizations that generally limit the number of investors to less than 100. Each individual (or financial institution such as an endowment fund or pension plan) has to meet specified criteria in order to participate. These criteria often specify a minimum net worth such as $1,000,000 and minimum annual income. The required investment is also substantial, with minimums of $1,000,000 being common.

Because hedge funds are private, they are not subject to many of the disclosure requirements and other regulations associated with public investment companies. However, the financial crisis experienced during 2008 has led to new proposals for the regulation of financial markets and financial institutions including hedge funds. Although increased regulation is a virtual certainty, how it will affect hedge funds is unknown. It is also possible that the funds will change their locations to countries with fewer and less costly regulations.

You might think that not having to meet financial regulations and disclosure requirements would imply that the costs to investors in hedge funds would be low. Once again that inference would be incorrect. Hedge fund portfolio managers are exceedingly well compensated through salary and performance bonuses. Typical fees are 2 percent of the value of the assets under management and 20 percent of the fund's performance. This large compensation paid to the portfolio managers and the companies that organize the funds helps explain why so many investment firms are willing to create hedge funds.

If the fund does not generate a positive return, the investors still pay the management fee. If the fund loses 10 percent, the managers continue to collect the 2 percent of the net asset value. (A $1 billion portfolio generates a fee of $20,000,000!) In many cases, the performance bonus may not be restored until the fund recoups the lost 10 percent. But fund managers may get around this inconvenience by closing and liquidating the fund and then starting a new hedge fund. This process wipes out the poor performance and ends the need to recoup the losses before performance bonuses are resumed.

Since a hedge fund is private, no secondary market exists for its shares. Once the individual invests in a hedge fund, that person cannot sell the shares. The fund generally has a "withdrawal" policy by which the investor may liquidate a position. There are, however, significant limitations on the withdrawals. For example, the hedge fund may refuse to repurchase shares until a period of time has elapsed. (A one-year "lock-up" is common.) The fund may also limit repurchases to some percentage of the outstanding shares. These exit policies should be clearly detailed in the fund's general offering statement, and a potential investor should obviously read that statement carefully prior to acquiring the shares.

Traditional mutual funds are precluded from using risky strategies such as selling short or buying stocks and bonds of firms in bankruptcy, but hedge funds may follow such strategies. A common hedge fund practice is to buy a particular stock and simultaneously short another. If the fund's analysts thought that Home Depot was undervalued relative to Lowe's, the fund would buy Home Depot and short Lowe's. (The proceeds of the short sale would be used to cover the cost of the long position.) Of course, identical movements in the two stocks would offset each other. A $1 increase in Home Depot would be offset by a $1 increase in Lowe's if the same number of shares were bought and sold short. But that is not the point. The expectation is that Home Depot will increase relative to Lowe's or that Lowe's will decline relative to Home Depot. If the analysis is correct and Home Depot proves to be undervalued relative to Lowe's, the gains more than offset the losses. The price of Home Depot rises more than the price of Lowe's, and the two positions generate a net profit.

While such a combination of a long and a short may appear to be a hedge position, it is not. The strategy may produce large losses and is certainly not comparable to the hedge positions that are explained in Chapter 19 on futures contracts. The hedges using futures are designed to erase the impact of a price change. For example, the farmer with a crop in the ground (a long position) sells a futures contract (a short position) to lock in the price. The above positions using Home Depot do not lock in a price but are designed to take advantage of an anticipated price change in one stock relative to the other. If the anticipated price changes were to occur, the strategy would generate a profit. If, however, the price of Lowe's rises relative to Home Depot, the loss on the short in Lowe's would exceed the gain on the long in Home Depot, and there would be a net loss on the strategy.

Since hedge fund portfolio managers have virtually complete discretion as to how to run the fund, their strategies have led to some large hedge fund losses. In 2006, Amaranth lost $6 billion in a matter of days. The fund took large positions in natural gas that were heavily leveraged (i.e., financed with debt). When natural gas prices declined, the value of Amaranth's assets declined from over $9 billion to $3.5 billion.

Perhaps the most important hedge fund failure occurred in 1998. Long-Term Capital Management (LTCM) had an equity base of $4.5 billion but was able to borrow more than $200 billion. While this huge amount of leverage initially produced spectacular results for the investors, the collapse of the Russian financial system led to widespread selling of poorer-quality debt. LTCM was unable to liquidate its positions and sustained large losses. Without additional financing, LTCM would have had to declare bankruptcy and would have been forced into liquidation. Bankruptcy would mean that the holders of the $200 billion in LTCM debt would not be repaid. In the end, the Federal Reserve stepped in and essentially forced large banks to put in additional funds. The fear that such a large failure could lead to a panic in the financial market (such as was experienced during the 1930s) forced banks to concede to the Federal Reserve's demand for additional funds for LTCM.

Private equity firms are also large pools of cash, but they are not comparable to hedge funds. While hedge funds use a variety of strategies to increase returns, private equity firms' primary objective is to make large focused investments. For example, an equity firm may use its cash to acquire a company and take it private. The intent is to make the acquired firm exceedingly profitable (often through aggressively cutting costs) and then sell the firm to another company or to resell the firm to public stockholders through an initial public offering. If the acquired firm does prosper and the company is sold, the private equity firm may reap a large return on its investment. In a variation on this strategy, a firm with a minority of public stockholders may be taken private. The majority stockholders (often a family or the firm's management) use the help of a private equity firm. After the minority stockholders are bought out, the company becomes private. Once the firm is private, SEC and Sarbanes-Oxley disclosure requirements no longer apply. Management may then direct the firm without the oversight and regulations imposed on publicly held firms.

The amount of money raised by private equity firms is often substantial. In fall 2006, Blackstone Group sought to raise $20 billion. Such large amounts are necessary if the firm wants to acquire large companies. During 2006, the private equity arm of Merrill Lynch commenced the purchase of HCA Inc. (a hospital chain) for a total cost in excess of $21 billion.

Hedge funds and private equity firms are obviously not appropriate for and not available to the vast majority of investors. They do, however, appeal to a select group of investors, and the dollar amount invested in hedge and private equity firms has grown dramatically. Their alleged advantages include higher returns and the potential for diversification of a traditional portfolio. The word *alleged* applies because returns cannot be verified. Hedge funds self-report their returns. While funds with high returns have an incentive to announce superior results, funds with inferior returns need not report their performance. All mutual funds must report returns, so an average fund return encompasses the best and the worst performers. An average of hedge fund returns, however, will have an upward bias if inferior-performing funds are excluded from the calculation.

To verify that hedge funds diversify an investor's portfolio requires knowing the correlation between returns. Failure to report returns or the selective reporting of returns increases the difficulty of estimating meaningful correlation coefficients. As with the assertion of higher returns, the individual will have to take on faith that hedge funds do reduce an investor's risk exposure by contributing to the diversification of the portfolio.

One means to overcome or at least reduce these disadvantages is to acquire shares in a fund that invests in different hedge funds. This "fund of funds" offers the potential for diversification since it owns positions in several hedge funds. Presumably the management of a fund of funds has better access to information and may be able to make more informed investment decisions. However, from the individual's perspective these funds are expensive, since the investor *pays two sets of management fees*, one to the managers of the fund of funds and a second to the managers of the hedge funds acquired by the fund of funds.

INVESTMENT COMPANIES AND FOREIGN INVESTMENTS

Mutual funds, closed-end investments, and ETFs offer American investors a simple, convenient means to acquire securities issued in foreign countries. Although investors continue to bear the risks associated with foreign investments (e.g., fluctuations in the value of foreign currencies and the political risks associated with each country), they do not have to do the analysis to select individual stocks and bonds. Instead, that task is performed by the management of the investment company.

global funds

Mutual funds whose portfolios include securities of firms with international operations that are located throughout the world.

international funds

American mutual funds whose portfolios are limited to non–American firms.

regional funds

Mutual funds that specialize in a particular geographical area.

emerging market fund

Investment company that specializes in securities from less-developed countries.

There are four types of mutual funds with international investments. **Global funds** invest in foreign and U.S. securities. Many U.S. mutual funds are global, as they maintain some part of their portfolios in foreign investments. Although these funds do not specialize in foreign securities, they do offer the individual investor the advantages associated with foreign investments: returns through global economic growth, diversification from assets whose returns are not positively correlated, and possible excess returns from inefficient foreign financial markets.

In addition to global funds, there are **international funds**, which invest solely in foreign securities and hold no U.S. securities, and **regional funds**, which specialize in a particular geographical area, such as Asia. The regional funds obviously specialize, and the international funds may also specialize during particular time periods. Thus it is not unusual for a fund to invest a quarter or more of its assets in the shares of firms in a particular country.

The last type of mutual fund with international investments is the **emerging market fund**, which specializes in securities of firms located in less-developed nations. In many cases, emerging market funds specialize in specific countries, such as the Indonesia Fund or the Turkish Investment Fund. Such funds give the U.S. investor the opportunity to invest in specific markets without specialized knowledge of local firms or laws concerning security transactions in that country. In addition, the governments of some countries with emerging securities markets forbid foreign ownership of securities (perhaps to avoid foreign control or influence). Such governments, however, may grant a specific investment company the right to own securities issued in that country. In such cases, the only means by which the U.S. investor may participate in that specific market is through the ownership of shares in the emerging market fund.

Many of the regional and emerging market funds are closed-end investment companies. A sampling is provided in Exhibit 7.5. Ticker symbols are given to facilitate obtaining information on a particular fund. The prices of these closed-end investment companies can be volatile, since the price depends on both the fund's net asset value and speculative interest in the shares. For example, in November 1989, the price of the Germany Fund was $10.63. The fund's net asset value was $9.46, so the shares sold for a 12 percent premium. Within ten weeks, the price of the fund rose to $23.50 and sold for an 85 percent premium over its net asset value of $12.69. The explanation for the large premium was a major shift in the German political climate (the fall of the Berlin Wall). While the political change dramatically increased speculative interest in German securities, the large premium was not sustained. In less than a year, the shares were trading for $11, which approximated their net asset value of $11.03.

Such a large premium has not been limited to the Germany Fund. At various times, the shares of many closed-end funds that specialize in a single county have sold for substantial premiums above their net asset value. Buying these shares for a large premium over their net asset value may seem illogical. However, these funds may be the only means by which the individual investor may participate in a country's stock markets, since local laws may ban or severely limit foreign ownership of the securities.

ETFs offer an alternative to investing in mutual funds and closed-end investment companies that specialize in foreign securities. The initial foreign ETFs were "iShares."

EXHIBIT 7.5 Selected Specialized Country Closed-end Investment Companies and ETFs

Fund	Ticker Symbol
Developed Nations	
Japan Equity Fund	JEQ
Spain Fund	SNF
Swiss Helvetia Fund	SWZ
Emerging Markets	
Chile Fund	CH
China Fund	CHN
India Growth Fund	IFN
Indonesia Fund	IF
Korea Fund	KF
Malaysia Fund	MF
Singapore Fund	SGF
Taiwan Fund	TWN
Thai Fund	TTF
Turkish Investment Fund	TKF
iShares Traded on the American Stock Exchange	
Australia Index Series	EWA
Austria Index Series	EWO
Belgium Index Series	EWK
Canada Index Series	EWC
France Index Series	EWQ
Germany Index Series	EWG
Hong Kong Index Series	EWH
Italy Index Series	EWI
Japan Index Series	EWJ
Malaysia (Free) Index Series	EWM
Mexico (Free) Index Series	EWW
Netherlands Index Series	EWN
Singapore (Free) Index Series	EWS
Spain Index Series	EWP
Sweden Index Series	EWD
Switzerland Index Series	EWI
U.K. Index Series	EWU

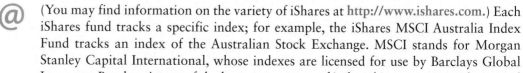

(You may find information on the variety of iShares at http://www.ishares.com.) Each iShares fund tracks a specific index; for example, the iShares MSCI Australia Index Fund tracks an index of the Australian Stock Exchange. MSCI stands for Morgan Stanley Capital International, whose indexes are licensed for use by Barclays Global Investors. Barclays is one of the largest managers of indexed investment products, and it created the MSCI iShares that are actively traded on the American Stock Exchange.

⊕ Point of Interest

GLOBAL INVESTING AND THE WORLD WIDE WEB

Finding information on foreign firms is not as easy as on American firms, especially since most foreign firms do not have their shares registered with the SEC for trading in the United States. Global Investor (http://www .global-investor.com) may be used to determine which foreign securities have American Depositary Receipts and where the securities are traded. The Bank of New York (http://www.bnymellon.com) provides similar service and offers company profiles and website links. Global Financial Data, Inc. (http://www.globalfinancialdata.com) furnishes historical databases that cover stock markets, interest rates, and exchange rates for over 50 countries. Although Global Financial Data offers information through subscription, it does provide some complimentary data such as annual data for many stock indexes, including markets in developed countries and the emerging markets.

As you would expect, foreign stock markets have websites, usually with information in English. For example, the Mexican stock market (Bolsa Mexicana de Valores) may be found at http://www.bmv.com.mx. Other sites, such as ADR.com (J.P. Morgan) (http://adr.com) provide links to foreign markets. One especially convenient Web source is the *Financial Times,* which reproduces surveys at its website (http://www.ft.com/reports). Coverage includes financial markets, emerging markets, global industries, and individual countries. If, for example, you wanted information on Singapore, this website is a good place to start. Topics include an overview, financial services, the country's foreign policy, and even social issues such as individual freedoms.

Although the value of iShares fluctuates with changes in the underlying index, the fund need not duplicate the index. Instead, the sponsors construct a portfolio that is highly correlated with the index. These exchange-traded funds are usually fully invested and there is minimal turnover of their portfolios. This lack of turnover also reduces the cost of managing the fund and generates fewer capital gains that the stockholders must report for income tax purposes.

A sampling of iShares is provided in Exhibit 7.5. Since these ETFs trade in the United States, their prices are expressed in dollars. The securities they own, however, are denominated in the local currency, so an American investor's return is affected by changes in the exchange rate as well as changes in the value of the index and any distributions by stocks in the portfolio. Dividends received by the ETFs are, in turn, distributed to their stockholders after covering the fund's expenses. If the value of the dollar were to rise, the value in dollars of an iShares portfolio would decline. Thus, the investor could sustain a loss even though the stock market in that particular country rose.

This exchange rate risk, of course, applies to all foreign investments, but the management of an iShares fund cannot take actions that might offset this risk. Since an iShares portfolio is fully invested, its management cannot sell the securities and convert to dollars in anticipation that the dollar will rise. If that were to happen, the fund would no longer track the index. The managers of a specialized country mutual fund or closed-end fund, however, can actively manage the portfolio. If they anticipate that the dollar will rise, they can liquidate securities and move the funds into dollars. These managers may also take positions in derivatives such as puts and calls (Chapters 17 and 18) and futures contracts on currencies (Chapter 19) to hedge the risk of loss from fluctuations in exchange rates.

SUMMARY

Stock in closed-end investment companies is initially sold to the general public through an initial public offering. The shares subsequently trade in the secondary securities markets. Although the shares may sell for a premium above their net asset value, they often sell for a discount from net asset value. Returns from an investment in a closed-end fund are earned from distributions, increases in the fund's market price, and changes in the discount or premium relative to the fund's net asset value.

Unit trusts are passive investments with a fixed portfolio that is often self-liquidating. Real estate investment trusts (REITs) are closed-end investment companies that specialize in real estate. REITS make loans to develop properties, originate and acquire mortgage loans, or purchase properties such as apartments and shopping malls and lease the buildings to tenants such as Wal-Mart Stores. REITs offer individuals a means to invest in real estate without owning and operating the properties. The current tax code permits REITs to avoid income taxes provided that at least 75 percent of their income is generated by real estate and they distribute 90 percent of their income to stockholders.

Exchange-traded funds (ETFs) combine features of mutual funds and closed-end investment companies. Their shares trade through the secondary securities markets, so they may be readily bought and sold by investors. As the result of an arbitrage process, the price of an ETF tends to equal its net asset value. The first ETFs tracked an aggregate market index such as the S&P 500 stock index. Subsequently, ETFs were created to track sectors of the S&P 500 and to track other indexes or to replicate investment strategies.

Hedge funds and private equity firms offer a small number of investors another alternative to traditional assets. The word *hedge* implies investment strategies that reduce risk. That need not be the case, as individual hedge funds may employ risky strategies to increase returns. Participation in a hedge fund is limited to individuals and institutions such as endowment funds or pension plans with substantial cash to invest. Hedge funds and private equity firms are not publicly traded and in past have not been subject to many of the regulations associated with publicly traded securities. These alternative investments are appropriate only for investors who understand and can accept the risk associated with these funds.

Investment companies are an excellent means to take positions in foreign securities. Instead of selecting individual foreign stocks and bonds, the investor acquires shares in investment companies with foreign securities. Some funds specialize in stocks of a specific country or region. Other investment companies take a more global view. The investor may also acquire shares in an ETF that tracks an index of foreign securities, such the Europe, Australasia, and Far East (EAFE) index. The returns on the foreign ETFs should mirror the underlying index and not depend on the portfolio manager's ability to select individual foreign securities.

QUESTIONS

1. What are the differences between a closed-end investment company and a mutual fund? What are the sources of return from an investment in a closed-end investment company?

2. Why can a closed-end investment company sell for a discount from net asset value but a mutual fund cannot sell for a discount?

3. What differentiates a real estate investment trust (REIT) from a firm involved in building, developing, and owning properties? What differentiates a mortgage trust from an equity trust? What advantages do REITs offer investors over direct investments in real estate properties?

4. Using the information in the Point of Interest on the taxation of REIT distributions, what was the tax status of recent annual distributions made by Plum Creek Timber (PCU), UDR INC. (UDR), and Washington Real Estate Investment Trust (WRE)?

5. How do exchange-traded funds (ETFs) differ from mutual funds? Why may they be considered alternatives to index mutual funds?

6. Why does arbitrage virtually assure that an ETF will sell for its net asset value?

7. How may mutual funds, closed-end investment companies, and ETFs be used to take positions in foreign securities?

8. Why are hedge funds and private equity funds of little interest to most investors?

9. Why may investing in an ETF such as the various iShares be preferable to acquiring shares in a mutual fund that makes foreign investments?

10. Exhibit 7.5 lists several closed-end investment companies and iShares that invest in the same country. Select at least one pair such as the Japan Equity Fund (JEQ) and the iShares Japan Index Series (EWJ). Compare their monthly percentage changes (i.e., monthly returns) for three years and compute the correlation coefficient between the two sets of returns. Repeat the process using an index of U.S. stocks such as the S&P 500 stock index. How may this information be used to help you diversify your portfolio? What additional information may be desirable? You may obtain historical prices and dividends from a source such as Yahoo! Finance (**http://finance.yahoo.com**).

PROBLEMS

1. a) A closed-end investment company is currently selling for $10 and its net asset value is $10.63. You decide to purchase 100 shares. During the year, the company distributes $0.75 in dividends. At end of the year, you sell the shares for $12.03. At the time of the sale, net asset value is $13.52. What percentage return do you earn on the investment? What role does the net asset value play in determining the percentage return?

   b) A closed-end investment company is currently selling for $10 and you purchase 100 shares. During the year, the company distributes $0.75 in dividends. At end of the year, you sell the shares for $12.03. The commission on each transaction is $50. What percentage return do you earn on the investment?

   c) You buy 100 shares in a mutual fund at its net asset value of $10. The fund charges a load fee of 5.5 percent. During the year, the mutual fund distributes $0.75 in dividends. You redeem the shares for their net asset value of $12.03, and the fund does not charge an exit fee. What percentage return do you earn on the investment?

d) You buy 100 shares in a no-load mutual fund at its net asset value of $10. During the year, the mutual fund distributes $0.75 in dividends. You redeem the shares for their net asset value of $12.03, but the fund charges a 5.5 percent exit fee. What percentage return do you earn on the investment?

e) You buy 100 shares in a no-load mutual fund at its net asset value of $10. During the year, the mutual fund distributes $0.75 in dividends. You redeem the shares for their net asset value of $12.03, and the fund does not charge an exit fee. What percentage return do you earn on the investment?

f) Compare your answers to parts (a) through (e). What are the implications of the comparisons? How would each of the following affect the percentage returns?

- You buy and sell stocks through an online broker instead of a full-service broker.
- You are in the 25 percent federal income tax bracket.
- The distributions are classified as long-term instead of short-term term.
- The purchases and sales occur in your retirement account (e.g., IRA).

2. You purchase a REIT for $50. It distributes $3 consisting of $1 in income, $0.50 in long-term capital gains, $0.30 in short-term capital gains, and $1.20 in return of capital. After a year, you sell the stock for $56. If you are in the 30 percent income tax bracket and 15 percent long-term capital gains bracket, what are your taxes owed? (Review the Point of Interest "REIT Distributions and Federal Taxes," if necessary.)

3. REITs pay dividends in order to retain their favorable tax status. As the next chapter on stock explains, corporate dividends are made from earnings. REIT dividends often are not made from earnings but the distributions are made from funds from operations (FFO). REIT accounting earnings are adjusted for noncash expenses such as depreciation to determine funds from operations. In addition, a REIT may sell a property and distribute the proceeds. For these reasons, financial analysts often use FFO instead of earnings to analyze a REIT. Distributions are often more highly correlated to per-share funds from operation than they are with earnings per share (EPS). Consider the following FFO and EPS for Washington Real Estate Trust:

Year	Distributions	FFO	EPS
1999	$1.16	$1.57	$1.24
2000	1.23	1.79	1.26
2001	1.31	1.96	1.38
2002	1.39	1.97	1.32
2003	1.47	2.04	1.13
2004	1.55	2.05	1.09
2005	1.60	2.07	1.84
2006	1.64	2.12	0.88
2007	1.68	2.31	1.34
2008	1.72	2.12	0.67

To verify that the dividend distribution is more strongly correlated to FFO than to EPS, compute the correlation coefficients relating the distributions to FFO and to EPS.

4. The portfolio manager of a hedge fund believes that stock A is undervalued and stock B is overvalued. Currently their prices are $30 and $30, respectively. The portfolio manager of the fund buys 100 shares of A and sells 100 shares of B short.

    a) Why does the portfolio manager establish these two positions?
    b) What is the initial cash outflow from the two positions?
    c) What are the net profits and losses on the positions if, after a period of time, the prices of each stock are

Price of A	Price of B
$25	$25
27.50	27.50
30	30
32.50	32.50
35	35

    d) What are the net profits and losses if, after a period of time, the prices are

Price of A	Price of B
$30	$30
32.50	27.50
35	25
37.50	22.50
40	20

    e) What are the net profits and losses if, after a period of time, the prices are

Price of A	Price of B
$30	$30
27.50	32.50
25	35
22.50	37.50
20	40

    f) What are the net profits and losses on the positions if, after a period of time, the prices of each stock are

Price of A	Price of B
$25	$20
27.50	25
30	30
32.50	35
35	40

g) What are the net profits and losses on the positions if, after a period of time, the prices of each stock are

Price of A	Price of B
$25	$27.50
27.50	28.25
30	30
32.50	31.25
35	32.50

h) What are the net profits and losses on the positions if, after a period of time, the prices of each stock are

Price of A	Price of B
$25	$35
27.50	32.50
30	30
32.50	27.50
35	25

i) For the portfolio manager's expectation to be fulfilled, the prices of the stocks have to follow which of the above six patterns? What are the implications if the other patterns of stock prices occur?

5. Currently a stock index stands at 100 and the leveraged ETF is selling for $100. The ETF should generate a return that is twice the daily return on the index. Over the next 21 days the value of the index and its daily percentage change are as follows:

Day	Value of the Index	Daily Percentage Change
1	100	—
2	110	10.0%
3	100	−9.1
4	90	−10.0
5	80	−11.1
6	70	−12.5
7	90	28.6
8	110	22.2
9	130	18.2
10	100	−23.1
11	105	5.0
12	101	−3.8
13	99	−2.0
14	105	6.1
15	98	−6.7
16	105	7.1
17	98	−6.7
18	106	8.2
19	109	2.8
20	126	15.6
21	100	−20.6

150

What is the value of the ETF at the end of each day? Notice that at the end of 21 days, the index is back to its starting value of 100. What is the value of the ETF at the end of 21 days? Suppose that on day 22, the index rises 50 percent from 100 to 150; what is the percentage change in the ETF from day 1 through day 22? If you bought the ETF on day 1 and held it through day 22, did you earn the leveraged return that you expected?

6. In October 2009, Ares Capital Corporation (ARCC) announced that it was acquiring Allied Capital (ALD). The terms of the acquisition specified that one share of ALD would become 0.325 share of ARCC. Prior to the announcement, the closing daily prices of the two stocks were the following:

Days Prior to Announcement	ALD	ARCC
4	$2.85	$10.81
3	2.82	10.60
2	2.85	10.89
1	2.73	10.69

After the announcement, the closing daily prices of the two stocks were the following:

Days After Announcement	ALD	ARCC
1	$3.61	$11.99
2	3.52	11.73
3	3.20	10.61
4	3.38	11.19

a) What is the value of ALD stock in terms of ARCC stock prior to the announcement?

b) What is the value of ALD stock in terms of the closing prices of ARCC after the announcement? Is there a difference between the actual price of ALD and its value in terms of ARCC?

c) A hedge fund manager believes the difference in pricing offers an opportunity for arbitrage. On the day of the announcement, this portfolio manager establishes two positions by purchasing 1,000 shares of ALD and selling 325 shares of ARCC short. What is the cash inflow and cash outflow from the two positions?

d) If the acquisition is completed, what are the profits or losses on the two positions for the following prices of ARCC: $8, 9, 10, 11, and 12?

e) What is the potential profit or loss if the acquisition is canceled and the stocks return to their prices prior to the announcement?

The Financial Advisor's Investment Case

Investment Companies and Asset Allocation

Your clients, Eva and Walther Sachs, operate a successful catering business specializing in Germanic and eastern European foods. It is a family business with part-time workers during peak periods. Most of the part-time employees have regular full-time jobs and work part time for their love of the specialty foods. The business has been profitable for years and consumes a large amount of Eva's and Walther's time. They have accumulated over $250,000, which has been invested solely in a large cap growth mutual fund. They have no retirement accounts and have not thought about an exit strategy in which they would sell or liquidate the business.

You realize that the Sachses love their business and that it is essentially their life, so it would not be wise to discuss an exit strategy at this time. However, you do believe that their asset allocation needs serious adjustment and want to propose that they make fundamental changes in their portfolio. By focusing all of their funds in a large cap growth fund, the Sachses are not diversified and could sustain a substantial loss if the market for large cap stocks were to decline and they needed to liquidate the shares. In addition, since they have no retirement accounts, they are missing an opportunity to reduce current federal income taxes. Exhibit 1 provides a correlation matrix for several ETFs and historical returns on the indexes they track.

Based on the information in Exhibit 1 you must develop a simple illustration of asset allocation that uses a variety of investment companies and encompasses the following questions and considerations:

1. What differentiates an exchange-traded fund from other investment companies? How easily are ETF shares bought and sold? Do they sell for a premium or discount from their net asset values?

2. What are the tax implications if the Sachses sell the stock they currently hold to obtain funds to invest in other alternatives?

3. Should Eva and Walther open a retirement account? Which of the various ETFs may be the most appropriate to acquire in a retirement account?

4. Develop an illustrative allocation. (Express the allocation in both dollars and percentages.) What is the purpose of each component of your allocation?

5. What is the importance of the correlation coefficients between the returns?

6. Assume that the cost basis of the current large cap mutual fund is $250,000. If the returns in Exhibit 1 are maintained, how much will the portfolio be worth after ten years? Has the asset allocation changed and, if so, what steps may be taken?

7. Based on your answers to the above questions, what course(s) of action do you suggest that Eva and Walther Sachs take?

EXHIBIT 1	Correlation Coefficients Relating Returns for Selected ETFs					
	Large Cap	Small Cap	Corporate Bonds	Money Market	Real Estate	Foreign Stocks	Returns on Indexes
Large cap	1.00						10.0%
Small cap	0.78	1.00					12.0%
Corporate bonds	0.23	0.12	1.00				6.0%
Money market securities	0.10	0.05	0.65	1.00			4.0%
Real estate	0.26	0.35	0.14	0.03	1.00		14.0%
Foreign stocks	0.35	0.26	0.17	0.14	0.28	1.00	12.0%

PART
Three

Investing in Common Stock

For many individuals the word *investing* is synonymous with buying and selling common stock. Although alternatives are certainly available, common stocks are a primary instrument of investing, perhaps because of the considerable exposure individuals have to them. Newspapers report stock transactions, market averages are quoted on the nightly news, brokerage firms advertise the attractiveness of such investments, and information concerning stocks is readily available through the Internet.

Unlike bonds, which pay a fixed amount of interest, common stocks may pay a dividend and offer the potential to grow. As the economy prospers and corporate earnings rise, the dividends and the value of common stocks may also increase. For this reason, common stocks are a good investment for individuals who have less need for current income but desire capital appreciation.

This section discusses investing in common stocks. Various techniques are used to analyze a firm and its financial statements with the purpose of identifying the stocks that have the greatest potential or are the most undervalued. This section also considers how measures of the market are constructed and the returns that investors in the aggregate have earned over a period of years.

CHAPTER 8

Stock

LEARNING OBJECTIVES

After completing this chapter you should be able to:

1. Describe and contrast the features of common and preferred stock.
2. Explain why dividend payments generally follow changes in earnings.
3. List the important dates for dividend payments and enumerate the advantages offered by dividend reinvestment plans.
4. Determine the impact of cash dividends, stock dividends, and stock splits on the firm's earning capacity and the price of its stock.
5. Differentiate between (a) the current ratio and the quick ratio, (b) accounts receivable turnover and the average collection period, (c) the gross profit margin, the operating profit margin, and the net profit margin, (d) the return on assets and the return on equity.
6. Apply ratios to analyze the financial condition of a firm and locate Internet sources that provide an analysis of a firm's financial statements.
7. Analyze the sources and uses of a firm's funds and the change in its cash position.

Investment companies permit you to own and manage a portfolio without having to select individual stocks and bonds. The selection process is delegated to the investment company's portfolio managers. For many individuals, this strategy makes sense; they may lack the time, knowledge, or inclination to actively select securities for their portfolios. They can use the various investment companies to construct a well-diversified portfolio designed to meet their financial objectives.

Other investors, however, want to take a more active role in the management of their financial assets. Presumably these individuals believe they can do better or at least not worse than the managers of the investment companies. Financial theory suggests these individuals are not wrong, since investments are made on a level playing field in efficient markets. Over time, their returns should tend to track market returns adjusted for the risk they bear. In addition, if you manage your own financial assets, you avoid paying fees and have the excitement associated with investing.

In either case you need to know the basics concerning securities analysis and selection, which are the subjects of the remainder of this text. For many individuals, investing implies buying and selling stock, but bonds (Part 4) and derivatives (Part 5) may be part of your investment strategy. This chapter begins with a description of the features of common stock. The second section covers dividends. Many firms do not distribute cash dividends; instead they retain their earnings to finance growth. Most large firms such as Coca-Cola and IBM have a policy of distributing part of their earnings and have annually increased their dividends for years.

The third section is devoted to preferred stock. While the term "stock" often implies common stock, some firms have issued preferred stock. As the name implies, its position is superior to common stock for the payment of dividends and distribution of assets if the firm is liquidated.

A large portion of this chapter covers the analysis of financial statements using ratios. There are many ratios that the financial analyst may compute, but each may be classified into one of five groups. Liquidity ratios seek to determine if the firm can meet its financial obligations as they come due. Activity ratios tell how rapidly assets flow through the firm; profitability ratios measure performance. Leverage ratios measure the extent to which the firm uses debt financing, and coverage ratios measure the firm's ability to make ("cover") a specific payment.

THE CORPORATE FORM OF BUSINESS AND THE RIGHTS OF COMMON STOCKHOLDERS

stock

A security representing ownership in a corporation.

certificate of incorporation

A document creating a corporation.

charter

A document specifying the relationship between a firm and the state in which it is incorporated.

bylaws

A document specifying the relationship between a corporation and its stockholders.

voting rights

The rights of stockholders to vote their shares.

director

A person who is elected by stockholders to determine the goals and policies of the firm.

A corporation is an artificial legal economic unit established (i.e., chartered) by a state. Stock, both common and preferred, represents ownership, or equity, in a corporation. Under state laws, the firm is issued a certificate of incorporation that indicates the name of the corporation, the location of its principal office, its purpose, and the number of shares of stock that are authorized (i.e., the number of shares that the firm may issue). In addition to a certificate of incorporation, the firm receives a charter that specifies the relationship between the corporation and the state. At the initial meeting of stockholders, bylaws are established that set the rules by which the firm is governed, including such issues as the voting rights of the stockholders.

Firms may issue both preferred and common stock. As the name implies, preferred stock holds a position superior to common stock. For example, preferred stock receives dividend payments before common stock and, in the case of liquidation, preferred stockholders are compensated before common stockholders. Although preferred stock is legally equity and hence represents ownership, its features are more similar to the characteristics of debt than of common stock.

In the eyes of the law, a corporation is a legal entity that is separate from its owners. It may enter into contracts and is legally responsible for its obligations. Creditors may sue the corporation for payment if it defaults on its obligations, but the creditors cannot sue the stockholders. Therefore, an investor knows that if he or she purchases stock in a publicly held corporation such as General Electric, the maximum that can be lost is the amount of the investment.[1] If a large corporation (e.g., Enron or WorldCom) does go bankrupt, limited liability means its stockholders are safe from the firm's creditors.

Because stock represents ownership in a corporation, investors have all the rights of ownership. These rights include the option to vote the shares. The stockholders elect a board of directors that selects the firm's management. Management is then responsible to the board of directors, which in turn is responsible to the firm's stockholders. If the stockholders do not think that the board is doing a competent job, they may elect another board to represent them.

For publicly held corporations, such democracy rarely works. Stockholders are usually widely dispersed, while the firm's management and board of directors generally

---

[1]Stockholders in privately held corporations who pledge their personal assets to secure loans do not have limited liability. If the corporation defaults, the creditors may seize the assets that the stockholders have pledged. In this event, the liability of the shareholders is not limited to their investment in the firm.

form a cohesive unit. Rarely does the individual investor's vote mean much.[2] However, there is always the possibility that if the firm does poorly, another firm may offer to buy the outstanding stock held by the public. Once such purchases are made, the stock's new owners may remove the board of directors and establish new management. To some extent this encourages a corporation's board of directors and management to pursue the goal of increasing the value of the firm's stock.

A stockholder generally has one vote for each share owned, but there are two ways to distribute this vote. With the traditional method of voting, each share gives the stockholder the right to vote for one individual for *each* seat on the board of directors. Under this system, if a majority group voted as a block, a minority group could never elect a representative. The alternative system, **cumulative voting**, gives minority stockholders a means to obtain representation on the firm's board.

How cumulative voting works is best explained by a brief example. Suppose a firm has a board of directors composed of five members. With traditional voting, a stockholder with 100 shares may vote 100 votes for a candidate for each seat. The total 500 votes are split among the seats. Under cumulative voting, the individual may cast the entire 500 votes for a candidate for one seat. Of course, then the stockholder cannot vote for anyone running for the remaining four seats.

A minority group of stockholders can use the cumulative method of voting to elect a representative to the firm's board of directors. By banding together and casting all their votes for a specific candidate, the minority may be able to win a seat. Although this technique cannot be used to win a majority, it does offer the opportunity for representation that is not possible through the traditional method of distributing votes (i.e., one vote for each elected position). As would be expected, management rarely supports the cumulative voting system.

Since stockholders are owners, they are entitled to the firm's earnings. These earnings may be distributed in the form of cash dividends, or they may be retained by the corporation. If they are retained, the individual's investment in the firm is increased (i.e., the stockholder's equity increases). However, for every class of stock, the individual investor's relative position is not altered. Some owners of common stock cannot receive cash dividends, whereas others have their earnings reinvested. The distribution or retention of earnings applies equally to all stockholders.[3]

Although limited liability is one of the advantages of investing in publicly held corporations, stock ownership does involve risk. As long as the firm prospers, it may be able to pay dividends and grow. However, if earnings fluctuate, dividends and growth may also fluctuate. It is the owners—the stockholders—who bear the business risk associated with these fluctuations. If the firm should default on its debt, it can be taken to court by its creditors to enforce its obligations. If the firm should fail or become bankrupt, the stockholders have the last claim on its assets. Only after all the creditors have been paid will the stockholders receive any funds. In many cases of bankruptcy, this amounts to nothing. Even if the corporation survives bankruptcy proceedings, the amount received by the stockholders is uncertain.

cumulative voting

A voting scheme that encourages minority representation by permitting each stockholder to cast all of his or her votes for one candidate for the firm's board of directors.

---

[2]There are exceptions. One of the biggest occurred when Penn Central stockholders voted down a merger with Colt Industries. Management supported the merger but lost the vote: 10,245,440 shares against versus 10,104,220 shares in favor.
[3]Some corporations have different classes of stock. For example, Food Lion, Inc., has two classes of common stock, both of which are publicly traded. The class A stock does not have voting power while the class B does. However, if management chooses to pay dividends to the class B stock, it must pay a larger dividend to the class A stock.

⊕ Point of Interest

STANDARD & POOR'S *CORPORATION RECORDS* AND MERGENT'S MANUALS

Two of the most important sources of factual information concerning firms and their securities are the *Corporation Records* published by Standard & Poor's and the various manuals published by Mergent. S&P's *Corporation Records* contains descriptions of companies listed on the major exchanges and many over-the-counter stocks. (Firms that are included pay a fee for the service. For small firms this fee is an inexpensive means for them to meet disclosure requirements, especially state "blue-sky" laws.) These corporate records are updated quarterly and include the most recent fiscal year's financial statements. For larger firms, S&P's *Corporation Records* includes descriptions of the firm's various securities, its earnings, dividends, and the annual range of security prices for the previous decade.

Previously, Mergent manuals were called Moody's manuals and were published by Financial Information Services (FIS). That name has been changed to Mergent FIS and the manuals now bear the Mergent name.

Mergent's manuals compile information similar to S&P's *Corporation Records*, but Mergent publishes this material in specialized volumes. The titles include *Mergent Industrial Manual, Mergent Bank and Finance Manual, Mergent Public Utility Manual, Mergent Municipal & Government Manual, Mergent Transportation Manual, Mergent International Manual*, and *Mergent OTC Industrial Manual*. In addition to these annually published manuals, Mergent also publishes *News Reports*, which continually updates the material in the manuals.

Like S&P's *Corporation Records*, Mergent manuals require that the firm or government pay an annual fee for inclusion. Material in these manuals includes descriptions of the firm, its securities, and recent financial statements. The manuals are an excellent reference for descriptions of the important features of a firm's securities, especially its bonds.

S&P's *Corporation Records* and the Mergent manuals include essentially the same information. However, occasionally a firm is listed in one and not the other. This is particularly true for small firms whose securities are traded over-the-counter. Corporations whose securities are traded on the major exchanges generally choose to be included in both S&P's *Corporation Records* and Mergent's manuals.

Preemptive Rights

preemptive rights
The right of current stockholders to maintain their proportionate ownership in the firm.

Some stockholders have **preemptive rights**, which is their prerogative to maintain their proportionate ownership in the firm. If the firm wants to sell additional shares to the general public, these new shares must be offered initially to the existing stockholders in a sale called a **rights offering**. If the stockholders wish to maintain their proportionate ownership in the firm, they can exercise their rights by purchasing the new shares. However, if they do not want to take advantage of this offering, they may sell their privilege to whoever wants to purchase the new shares.

rights offering
Sale of new securities to existing stockholders.

Preemptive rights may be illustrated by a simple example. If a firm has 1,000 shares outstanding and an individual has 100 shares, that individual owns 10 percent of the firm's stock. If the firm wants to sell 400 new shares and the stockholders have preemptive rights, these new shares must be offered to the existing stockholders before they are sold to the general public. The individual who owns 100 shares would have the right to purchase 40, or 10 percent, of the new shares. If the purchase is made, then that stockholder's relative position is maintained, for the stockholder owns 10 percent of the firm both before and after the sale of the new stock.

Although preemptive rights are required in some states for incorporation, their importance has diminished and the number of rights offerings has declined. Some firms have changed their bylaws in order to eliminate preemptive rights. For example, AT&T asked its stockholders to relinquish these rights. The rationale for this request was that issuing new shares through rights offerings was more expensive than selling the shares to the general public through an underwriting. Investors who desired to maintain their relative position could still purchase the new shares, and all stockholders would benefit through the cost savings and the flexibility given to the firm's management. Most stockholders accepted management's request and voted to relinquish their preemptive rights. Now AT&T does not have to offer any new shares to its current stockholders before it offers them publicly.

CASH DIVIDENDS

dividend

A payment to stockholders that is usually in cash but may be in stock or property.

Corporations may pay their stockholders dividends, which can be in the form of cash or additional shares. A **dividend** is a distribution from earnings. Companies that pay cash dividends often have a dividend policy that is known to the investment community. Even if the policy is not explicitly stated by management, the continuation of such practices as paying quarterly dividends implies a specific policy.

regular dividends

Steady dividend payments that are distributed at regular intervals.

While most American companies that distribute cash dividends pay a **regular dividend** on a quarterly basis, there are other types of dividend policies. For example, some companies pay a quarterly dividend plus an additional or **extra dividend**. In 2004, Limited Brands declared its regular quarterly dividend of $0.12 per share plus an extra dividend of $1.23 per share because the company had strong cash flows. Such a policy is appropriate for a firm with fluctuating cash flows. Management may not want to increase the dividend and then have difficulty maintaining the higher dividend. By having a set cash payment that is supplemented with extras in good years, management is able to maintain a fixed payment that is relatively assured and to supplement the cash dividend when the extra is warranted by earnings and cash flow.

extra dividend

A sum paid in addition to the firm's regular dividend.

Occasionally a firm distributes property as a supplement to or instead of cash dividends. For example, Freeport-McMoran distributed shares in two of its subsidiaries, Freeport-McMoran Energy Partners, Ltd. and Freeport-McMoran Copper and Gold Company. These property distributions supplemented the firm's usual quarterly cash dividend. Distributing property (i.e., stock in the subsidiaries) permits the stockholders to benefit directly from the market value of the subsidiaries, both of which became publicly traded, and from any of the subsidiaries' cash dividends.

irregular dividends

Dividend payments that either do not occur in regular intervals or vary in amount.

Other firms pay cash dividends that are **irregular**: There is no set dividend payment. For example, real estate investment trusts (frequently referred to as REITs and discussed in Chapter 7) are required by law to distribute their earnings to maintain their favorable tax status. Since the earnings of such trusts can fluctuate, the cash dividends may also fluctuate. The special tax laws pertaining to REITs cause them to have irregular dividend payments.

Dividends are paid from earnings. The payment reduces the firm's cash and retained earnings. These funds could be used to acquire more assets or to retire debt. If these assets generate additional earnings, the firm will grow and be able to pay additional dividends in the future. Cash dividends and the retention of earnings are mutually exclusive. If the firm retains the earnings, its capacity to grow increases. If the firm distributes the earnings, it will have to obtain funds elsewhere in order to grow.

⊕ **Point of Interest**

THE LONGEVITY OF CASH DIVIDENDS

The dividend-growth model presented in Chapter 9 assumes that firms pay cash dividends indefinitely. Do firms in fact continue to pay cash dividends year after year? For many corporations the answer is yes! Several have paid a cash dividend every year for more than 100 years.

Many of these firms are banks because banking was one of the first important industries to develop. The Bank of New York started paying dividends in the eighteenth century (1785).

America's industrial giants developed after the banks, and while their dividend longevity records may not be as impressive as those of the banks, the accompanying list illustrates the extended period over which some industrial firms have maintained cash dividends.

Do dividend payments ever end? Unfortunately, the answer is also yes. The financial difficulty Unisys experienced caused the firm to cease paying cash dividends. Previously the firm had paid a cash dividend every year since 1895.

Firm	Year Annual Cash Dividends Began
Cincinnati Gas and Electric (CINergy)	1853
Stanley Works	1877
AT&T	1881
ExxonMobil	1882
Consolidated Edison	1885
Eli Lilly	1885
UGI	1885
Procter & Gamble	1891
Coca-Cola	1893
Colgate-Palmolive	1895
General Mills	1898
General Electric	1899
PPG Industries	1899

The distribution of earnings should depend on who has the better use for the funds, the stockholders or the corporation. If management can earn a higher return on the funds, then retaining and reinvesting the earnings is the logical choice. Management, however, does not know the stockholders' alternative uses for the funds. Instead management pursues a policy believed to be in the best interests of the stockholders and the company. Stockholders who do not like the dividend policy may sell their shares. If sellers exceed buyers, the stock price will fall, and management will become aware of investors' attitude toward the dividend policy.

Some managements view dividends as a residual. The rationale is simple and pragmatic. If management does not know the stockholders' preference and the firm has attractive investment opportunities, these may be financed through the retention of earnings. After all attractive investments have been made, any residual is left for distribution to stockholders. Such a policy places emphasis on growth and, if the firm does have excellent investment alternatives, may lead to higher stock prices over a period of time.

payout ratio

The ratio of dividends to earnings.

retention ratio

The ratio of earnings not distributed to earnings.

Management may also view dividend policy as the distribution of a certain proportion of the firm's earnings. This policy may be expressed in terms of a **payout ratio**, which is the proportion of the earnings that the firm distributes. Conversely, the **retention ratio** is the proportion of the earnings that are not paid out and are retained. For example, Hershey Foods earned $4.68 in 2006 and paid cash dividends of $2.06. The payout ratio is 44.0 percent ($2.06/$4.68), and the retention ratio is $2.62/$4.68 = 56.0 percent. (The retention ratio is also equal to 1 − payout ratio, which is 100 − 44.0 = 56.0 percent for Hershey Foods.)

For some firms, the payout ratio has remained relatively stable over time. Such consistency suggests that management views the dividend policy in terms of distributing a certain proportion of the firm's earnings to stockholders. For example, SCANA's management stated that the "goal is to increase the common stock dividend at a rate that reflects the growth in our principal businesses, while maintaining a payout ratio of 50–55 percent of earnings." The obvious implication is that higher earnings will lead to higher dividends as management seeks to maintain the payout ratio.

Management, however, rarely increases the cash dividend immediately when earnings increase because it wants to be certain that the higher level of earnings will be maintained. The managements of many publicly held corporations are reluctant to reduce the dividend because the decrease may be interpreted as a sign of financial weakness. In addition, a decrease in earnings may not imply that the firm's capacity to pay the dividend has diminished. For example, an increase in noncash expenses, such as depreciation, reduces earnings but not cash, and the same applies to a write-down of the book value of an asset. In both cases, the firm's capacity to pay the dividend is not affected, because the expense does not affect cash. Management then maintains the dividend payment to signal that the firm's financial condition has not deteriorated.

This pattern is illustrated in Figure 8.1, which presents the quarterly per-share earnings (after extraordinary gains and losses) and the cash dividend for Hershey Foods

FIGURE 8.1   Dividends and Earnings per Share (Before Extraordinary Items and a 2 for 1 stock split) of Hershey Foods (1998–2008)

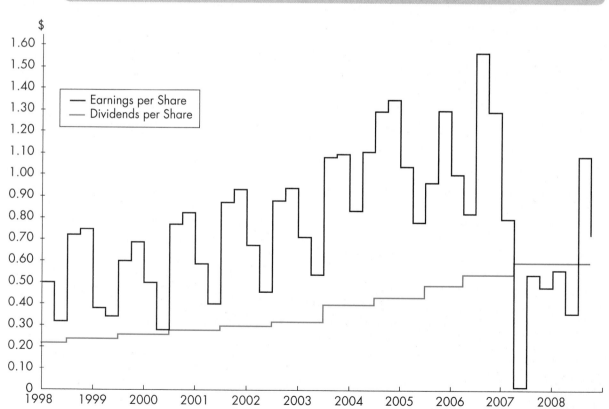

for 1998–2008. As may be seen in the figure, earnings fluctuate more than the cash dividend. The declines in earnings experienced during the first two quarters of each year do not lead to dividend cuts. The increases in earnings during the last two quarters do not lead to dividend increments. Instead, the pattern of rising earnings during the 11 years is associated with the steady annual increments in the cash dividend.

Notice in Figure 8.1 that Hershey's annual dividend increments ceased in 2008. Earnings during 2007 and 2008 were perceptibly below the earnings in the previous years. Even with the lower earnings, management maintained the cash dividend. Such action is consistent with management's reluctance to reduce dividends. In general, however, the stigma associated with dividend cuts completely changed during 2008–2009. The economic recession and the large decline in corporate earnings led several managements to reduce and in some cases eliminate cash dividends. The large losses sustained by banks such as Wells Fargo and Bank of America resulted in their cutting dividends. Major manufacturing firms such as GE and pharmaceutical firms such as Pfizer also reduced dividend payments. Previously such dividend cuts would have been considered drastic actions and would have produced a backlash causing the value of the stocks to fall. However, in 2009, managements' reduction or suspension of the dividend to conserve cash had the opposite effect. The prices of many of these stocks rose!

While U.S. firms tend to follow a policy of quarterly dividend distributions, firms in other countries may not. Many foreign firms often make only two payments. The first payment may be called a "preliminary" dividend and the second (made at the end of the firm's fiscal year) may be called a "final" dividend. For example, Canon paid $0.412 in June 2007 and then distributed $0.447 in December 2007.

Even if the cash payments from foreign firms occur at regular intervals, the dollar amount tends to vary. This variation is the result of fluctuation in the dollar value of each currency. For example, if the value of the dollar falls relative to the euro, any dividends that are distributed in euros translate into more dollars when the euros are converted. The converse is also true. If the dollar value of the euro should fall, the dividend buys fewer dollars when the currency is converted. Americans who want predictable flows of dividends are usually advised to purchase American stocks and avoid foreign securities.

The Distribution of Dividends

date of record

The day on which an investor must own shares in order to receive the dividend payment.

The process by which dividends are distributed occurs over time. First, the firm's directors meet. When they declare a dividend, two important dates are established. The first date determines who is to receive the dividend. On the **date of record**, the ownership books of the corporation are closed, and everyone who owns stock in the company at the end of that day receives the dividend.

ex-dividend

Stock that trades exclusive of any dividend payment.

If the stock is purchased after the date of record, the purchaser does not receive the dividend. The stock is traded **ex-dividend**, for the price of the stock does not include the dividend payment. This **ex-dividend date** is two trading days prior to the date of record, because the settlement date for a stock purchase is three working days after the transaction.

This process is illustrated by the following time line:

ex-dividend date

The day on which a stock trades exclusive of any dividends.

Declaration date (January 2)	Ex-div date (January 30)	Date of record (February 1)	Distribution date (March 1)

On January 2, the board of directors declares a dividend to be paid March 1 to all stockholders of record February 1. To receive the dividend, the individual must own the stock at the close of trading on February 1. To own the stock on February 1, the stock must have been purchased on or before January 29. If the stock is bought January 29, settlement will occur after three days on February 1 (assuming three workdays), so the investor owns the stock on February 1. If the investor buys the stock on January 30, that individual does not own the stock on February 1 (the seller owns the stock) and cannot be the owner of record on February 1. On January 30, the stock trades exclusive of the dividend (ex-dividend or "ex-div"), and the buyer does not receive the dividend.

In the financial press, transactions in the stock on the ex-dividend date are indicated by an x for "ex-div." The following entry indicates the stock of Reynolds and Reynolds traded exclusive of the dividend.

	DIV	DIV %	LAST	NET CHG
Reyn&Reyn REY x	.44	2.0	22.50	+0.31

The $0.11 (i.e., $0.44 ÷ 4) quarterly dividend will be paid to whoever bought the stock on the previous day and will not be paid to investors who purchased the stock on the ex-dividend date.

The investor should realize that buying or selling stock on the ex-dividend date may not result in a windfall gain or a substantial loss. If a stock that pays a $1.00 dividend is worth $100 on the day before it goes ex-dividend, it cannot be worth $100 on the ex-dividend date. If it were worth $100 on both days, investors would purchase the stock for $100 the day before the ex-dividend date, sell it for $100 on the ex-dividend date, and collect the $1 dividend. If investors could do this, the price would be bid up and exceed $100 on the day preceding the ex-dividend date and would be less than $100 on the ex-dividend date as a result of the sales. In effect, this price pattern does occur because this stock would sell for $100 and then be worth $100 minus $1 on the ex-dividend date.

This price change is illustrated in the previous example. There was an increase in the price of Reynolds and Reynolds stock for the ex-dividend date. This indicates that the closing price on the previous day was $22.30 and not $22.19 (22.50 − 0.31), as might be expected. Since the current buyers will not receive the dividend, the net change in the price of the stock is reduced for the dividend. The net change is figured from the adjusted price (i.e., $22.30 minus the $0.11 dividend). If the stock had closed at 23.00, the net change would have been +0.81, and if it had closed at 22.00, the net change would have been −0.19.

distribution date

The date on which a dividend is paid to stockholders.

The second important date established when a dividend is declared is the day on which the dividend is paid, or the **distribution date**. The distribution date may be several weeks after the date of record, as the company must determine who the owners were as of the date of record and process the dividend checks. The company may not perform this task itself; instead, it may use the services of its commercial bank, for which the bank charges a fee. The day that the dividend is received by the stockholder is thus likely to be many weeks after the board of directors announces the dividend payment. For example, the distribution date for a Black & Decker dividend that was declared on July 17 was September 25, which was almost two weeks after the date of record, September 14.

Many firms try to maintain consistency in their dividend payment dates. Textron makes payments on the first business days of January, April, July, and October. Public Service Enterprise Group pays its dividends on the last days of March, June, September, and December. Such consistency in payments is beneficial to investors and the firm, as both can plan for this receipt and disbursement.

Dividend Reinvestment Plans

dividend reinvestment plan (DRIP)

A plan that permits stockholders to have cash dividends reinvested in stock instead of received in cash.

Many corporations that pay cash dividends also have **dividend reinvestment plans (DRIPs)** in which the cash dividends are used to purchase additional shares of stock. Dividend reinvestment programs started in the 1960s, but the expansion of the programs occurred in the early 1970s, so that currently more than 2,000 companies offer some version of the dividend reinvestment plan.[4]

There are two general types of dividend reinvestment programs. In most plans a bank acts on behalf of the corporation and its stockholders. The bank collects the cash dividends for the stockholders and in some plans offers the stockholders the option of making additional cash contributions. The bank pools all the funds and purchases the stock on the open market (i.e., in the secondary market). The bank does charge a fee for its service, but this fee is usually modest, and in some cases is paid by the firm.

In the second type of reinvestment plan, the company issues new shares of stock for the cash dividend, and the money is directly rechanneled to the company. The investor may also have the option of making additional cash contributions. This type of plan offers the investor an additional advantage in that the brokerage fees are completely circumvented. The entire amount of the cash dividend is used to purchase shares, with the cost of issuing the new shares being paid by the company.

Some brokerage firms also offer dividend reinvestment plans. For example, Charles Schwab will reinvest dividends for stock registered in street name. Under its *Stock-Builder Plan*, Schwab purchases the shares for the investor. Schwab benefits by any profits on the spread between the bid and ask prices on securities bought and sold and by inducing individuals to invest through Schwab instead of competing brokerage firms.

Dividend reinvestment plans offer advantages to both firms and investors. For stockholders, the advantages include the purchase of shares at a substantial reduction in commissions. Even reinvestment plans in which the fees are paid by the stockholder offer this savings. Both types of plans are particularly attractive to the small investor, for few brokerage firms are willing to buy $100 worth of stock, and substantial commissions are charged on such small transactions.

Perhaps the most important advantage to investors is the fact that the plans are automatic. The investor does not receive the dividends, for the proceeds are automatically reinvested. For any investor who lacks the discipline to save, such forced saving may be a means to systematically accumulate shares. For the firm, the primary advantages

[4]Mergent's annual *Dividend Record* lists firms that offer dividend reinvestment plans. The American Association of Individual Investors annually publishes similar information and includes phone numbers, minimum-maximum optional cash purchases, fees, and discounts (if available). There is even an investment advisory service, the DRIP Investor (**http://www.dripinvestor.com**), which provides timely information on the plans. Information concerning dividend reinvestment plans is readily available on the Internet from DRIP Central (**http://www.dripcentral.com**) and Netstock Direct (**http://www.sharebuilder.com**). Netstock Direct not only provides detailed plan summaries but its software also allows companies to publish their plans. Links to the firms provide investors with immediate access to each firm's dividend reinvestment or direct purchase stock plan.

are the goodwill that is achieved by providing another service for its stockholders. The plans that involve the issue of new shares also raise new equity capital. This automatic flow of new equity reduces the need for the sale of shares through underwriters.

The Internal Revenue Service considers dividends that are reinvested to be no different from cash dividends that are received. Such dividends are subject to federal income taxation. The exclusion from federal income taxation of dividend income that is reinvested has been considered as one possible change in the tax code, but as of 2009 reinvested dividends continued to be subject to federal income tax.

STOCK DIVIDENDS

stock dividend

A dividend paid in stock.

recapitalization

An alteration in a firm's sources of finance, such as the substitution of long-term debt for equity.

Some firms make a practice of paying stock dividends in addition to or in lieu of cash dividends. **Stock dividends** are a form of **recapitalization** and do *not* affect the assets or liabilities of the firm. Since the assets and their management produce income for the firm, a stock dividend does not by itself increase the potential earning power of the company. Some investors, however, may believe that stock dividends will enhance the earning capacity of the firm and consequently the value of the stock.

The following balance sheet demonstrates the transactions that occur when a firm issues a stock dividend:

Assets		Liabilities and Equity	
Total assets	$10,000,000	Total liabilities	$2,500,000
		Equity: $2 par common stock (2,000,000 shares authorized; 1,000,000 outstanding)	2,000,000
		Additional paid-in capital	500,000
		Retained earnings	5,000,000

Since a stock dividend is only a recapitalization, the assets and the liabilities are not affected by the declaration and payment of the stock dividend. However, the entries in the equity section of the balance sheet are affected. The stock dividend transfers amounts from retained earnings to common stock and additional paid-in capital. The amount transferred depends on (1) the number of new shares issued through the stock dividend and (2) the market price of the stock.

If the company in the preceding example issued a 10 percent stock dividend when the price of the common stock was $20 per share, 100,000 shares would be issued with a market value of $2,000,000. This amount is subtracted from retained earnings and transferred to common stock and additional paid-in capital. The amount transferred to common stock will be 100,000 times the par value of the stock ($2 × 100,000 = $200,000). The remaining amount ($1,800,000) is transferred to additional paid-in capital. The balance sheet then becomes:

Assets		Liabilities and Equity	
Total assets	$10,000,000	Total liabilities	$2,500,000
		Equity: $2 par common stock	2,200,000
		(2,000,000 shares authorized;	
		1,100,000 outstanding)	
		Additional paid-in capital	2,300,000
		Retained earnings	3,000,000

Note that no funds (i.e., money) have been transferred. While there has been an increase in the number of shares outstanding, there has been no increase in cash and no increase in assets that may be used to earn profits. All that has happened is a recapitalization: The equity entries have been altered.

The major misconception concerning the stock dividend is that it increases the ability of the firm to grow. If the stock dividend is a substitute for a cash dividend, then this belief may be partially true, because the firm retains the cash that would have been paid to stockholders if a cash dividend had been declared. However, the firm will still have the cash even if it does not pay the stock dividend. Hence, the decision to pay the stock dividend does not increase the amount of cash; it is the decision *not to pay* the cash dividend that conserves the money. When a stock dividend is paid in lieu of cash, it may even be interpreted as a screen: The stock dividend is hiding management's reluctance to pay cash dividends.

Although the stock dividend does not increase the wealth of the stockholder, it does increase the number of shares owned. In the previous example, a stockholder who owned 100 shares before the stock dividend had $2,000 worth of stock. After the stock dividend is distributed, this stockholder owns 110 shares that are also worth $2,000, for the price of the stock falls from $20 to $18.18. The price of the stock declines because there are 10 percent more shares outstanding, but there has been no increase in the firm's assets and earning power. The old shares have been diluted, and hence the price of the stock must decline to indicate this **dilution**.[5]

dilution

A reduction in earnings per share due to the issuing of new securities.

If the price of the stock did not fall to adjust for the stock dividend, all companies could make their stockholders wealthier by declaring stock dividends. However,

---

[5]A stock dividend must reduce the price of the stock because the firm does not receive funds and earnings per share must decline. However, when new shares are issued, dilution may not occur. Presumably, management will use the funds for profitable investments or to retire debt, so earnings per share may not decline. One study, however, found that management is concerned with the dilution of existing stockholders' positions and this concern affects their decision to issue *new* stock to raise funds. See John Graham and Campbell Harvey, "The Theory and Practice of Corporate Finance: Evidence from the Field," *Journal of Financial Economics* 60 (May/June 2001): 187–243.

because the stock dividend does not increase the assets or earning power of the firm, investors are not willing to pay the former price for a larger number of shares; hence, the market price must fall to adjust for the dilution of the old shares.

There are some significant disadvantages associated with stock dividends. The primary disadvantage is the expense. The costs associated with these dividends include the expense of issuing new certificates, payments for any fractional shares, any taxes or listing fees on the new shares, and the revision of the firm's record of stockholders. These costs are indirectly borne by the stockholders. There are also costs that fall directly on the stockholders, including increased transfer fees and commissions (if the new securities are sold).

Perhaps the primary advantage of the stock dividend is that it brings to the current stockholders' attention the fact that the firm is retaining its cash in order to grow. The stockholders may subsequently be rewarded through the firm's retention of assets and its increased earning capacity. By retaining its assets, the firm may be able to earn more than the stockholders could if the funds were distributed. This should increase the price of the stock in the future. However, this same result may be achieved without the expenses associated with the stock dividend.

THE STOCK SPLIT

stock split

Recapitalization that affects the number of shares outstanding, their par value, the earnings per share, and the price of the stock.

After the price of a stock has risen substantially, management may decide to split the stock. The rationale for the **stock split** is that it lowers the price of the stock and makes it more accessible to investors. For example, when Finova split its stock 2 for 1, management stated in the *Annual Report* that "the split would help broaden our investor base." The management of MindSpring went even further in a press release announcing a 2-for-1 split: "This action will help widen the distribution and enhance the marketability of MindSpring's common stock, and bring the price per share . . . into a range which should generate increased interest from current and new shareholders." Implicit in this reasoning are the beliefs that investors prefer lower-priced shares and that reducing the price of the stock benefits the current stockholders by widening the market for their stock.

Like the stock dividend, the stock split is a recapitalization. It does not affect the assets or liabilities of the firm, nor does it increase its earning power. The wealth of the stockholder is increased only if investors prefer lower-priced stocks, which will increase the demand for this stock.

The balance sheet used previously for illustrating the stock dividend may also be used to illustrate a 2-for-1 stock split. In a 2-for-1 stock split, one old share becomes two new shares, and the par value of the old stock is halved. There are no changes in the additional paid-in capital or retained earnings. The new balance sheet becomes:

Assets		Liabilities and Equity	
Total assets	$10,000,000	Total liabilities	$2,500,000
		Equity: $1 par common stock	2,000,000
		(2,000,000 shares authorized;	
		2,000,000 outstanding)	
		Additional paid-in capital	500,000
		Retained earnings	5,000,000

There are now twice as many shares outstanding, and each new share is worth half as much as one old share. If the stock had sold for $80 before the split, each share becomes worth $40. The stockholder with 100 old shares worth $8,000 now owns 200 shares worth $8,000 (i.e., $40 × 200).

An easy way to find the price of the stock after the split is to multiply the stock's price before the split by the reciprocal of the terms of the split. For example, if a stock is selling for $54 per share and is split 3 for 2, then the price of the stock after the split will be $54 × ⅔ = $36. Such price adjustments must occur because the old shares are diluted and the earning capacity of the firm is not increased.

Stock splits may use any combination of terms. The most common is 2 for 1, but splits such as 3 for 2 or 3 for 1 are not unusual. There is no obvious explanation for a particular set of terms other than that management wanted to reduce the stock's price to a particular level and selected the terms that would achieve the desired price.

There are also reverse splits such as the 1-for-20 split executed by Friedman, Billings, Ramsey Group in June 2009. A reverse split reduces the number of shares and raises the price of the stock. The purpose of such a split is to add respectability to the stock (i.e., to raise the price above the level of the "cats and dogs"). Since many financial institutions, pension plans, and endowments cannot invest in stocks with low prices, the reverse split raises the price sufficiently to be considered for purchase by these potential buyers. A cynic might also suggest that the reverse split is designed to hide poor performance. After the 1-for-20 reverse split, Friedman, Billings, Ramsey Group also changed its name to Arlington Asset Management Group. As would be expected, reverse splits were common during 2009 after the severe price declines experienced during 2008–2009.

Stock splits, like stock dividends, do not increase the assets or earning capacity of the firm. The split does decrease the price of the stock and thereby may increase its marketability. Thus, the split stock may be more widely distributed, which increases investor interest in the company. This wider distribution may increase the wealth of the current stockholders over time.

Academic studies, however, are inconclusive as to whether stock splits or stock dividends increase the value of stock.[6] These studies generally show that other factors, such as increased earnings, increased cash dividends, or a rise in the general market, result in higher prices for individual stocks. In fact, stock splits generally occur *after* the price of the stock has risen. Instead of being a harbinger of good news, they mirror an increase in the firm's earnings and growth.

From the investor's point of view, there is little difference between a stock split and a stock dividend. In both cases the stockholders receive additional shares, but their proportionate ownership in the firm is unaltered. In addition, the price of the stock adjusts for the dilution of per-share earnings caused by the new shares.

Accountants, however, do differentiate between stock splits and stock dividends. Stock dividends are generally less than 20 to 25 percent. A stock dividend of 50 percent would be treated as a 3-for-2 stock split. Only the par value and the number of

---

[6]Evidence that stock splits may increase investors' wealth is provided in David L. Ikenberry, Graeme Rankine, and Earl K. Stice, "What Do Stock Splits Really Signal," *Journal of Financial and Quantitative Analysis* (September 1996): 357–375. For an extensive review of the literature on stock splits and stock dividends, refer to H. Kent Baker, Aaron L. Philips, and Gary E. Powell, "The Stock Distribution Puzzle: A Synthesis of the Literature on Stock Splits and Stock Dividends," *Financial Practice and Education* (spring/summer 1995): 24–37.

shares that the firm has outstanding would be affected. There would be no change in the firm's retained earnings. A stock split of 11 for 10 would be treated as a 10 percent stock dividend. In this case, retained earnings would be reduced, and the amount would be transferred to the other accounts (i.e., common stock and paid-in capital accounts). Total equity, however, would not be affected.

Federal Income Taxes and Stock Dividends and Stock Splits

The federal government taxes cash dividends. Does it also tax shares received in stock dividends and stock splits? The answer is no. There is no taxation of stock dividends and stock splits unless the investor sells the shares.

If you bought 100 shares for $5,000 ($50 a share) and the firm pays a 10 percent stock dividend, your 100 shares become 110 shares. The total cost remains $5,000 and the cost basis per share is $45.45 ($5,000/110). As long as you do not sell the shares, there is no taxable transaction. If you sell the entire 110 shares, the cost basis is $5,000. If, however, you sell only part of the 110 shares, your cost basis is figured using the adjusted $45.45 cost per share. If you sell 50 shares, the cost basis is $2,272.50.

If the firm splits the stock, the investor's cost basis is also adjusted for the split. If you own 100 shares that cost $5,000 ($50 a share) and the stock is split 2 for 1, you now have 200 shares that cost $5,000. The cost basis is adjusted to $25 a share. If you sell 100 shares for $40 a share, your capital gain is $1,500 ($4,000 − 2,500) and taxed at the appropriate capital gains tax rate. If you sell 50 shares for $10 share, your capital loss is $750 ($500 − 1,250). That loss may then be used to offset capital gains from other transactions.

STOCK REPURCHASES AND LIQUIDATIONS

A corporation with excess cash may choose to repurchase some of its outstanding stock. Such repurchases are often perceived as an alternative to paying cash dividends. Instead of distributing the money as cash dividends, the company offers to repurchase shares from its stockholders. If the stockholders do not want to sell the shares and pay any applicable capital gains taxes, they may retain their shares. If the stockholders prefer the money, they may sell the shares. The decision to sell rests with the stockholder while the decision to distribute cash dividends is made by the firm's management.

One argument that is often made for repurchasing in preference to distributing cash dividends is the decrease in the number of shares outstanding. The decrease in the number of shares increases earnings per share because the earnings are spread over fewer shares. The higher per-share earnings could, in turn, result in a higher stock price, especially if the P/E ratio remains the same.

Whether stock repurchases do produce higher stock prices is indeterminate. Teledyne repurchased 8.7 million shares at $200 for an outlay in excess of $1.7 billion. At the time of the offer, the stock was selling for $156, so the repurchase price represented a 28 percent premium over the market price. The repurchase raised earnings per share by more than $7. After the repurchase the price of the stock did not decline back to $156 but continued to increase, reaching $240 a share within a few weeks. In 2004, Limited Brands repurchased over 125 million shares at an average price of $24.92 for a total outlay in excess of $3.1 billion. The stock, however, was trading for approximately the same price a year later, so in this illustration the repurchase did not increase the value of the remaining shares.

Repurchased shares are generally held in the firm's "treasury" for future use. (See, for instance, the stockholders' equity section of Hershey Foods Corporation's balance sheet in Exhibit 8.2.) While the cost of the repurchased shares reduces the firm's equity, the shares are not retired but held by the company. If the shares were retired and management subsequently wanted to issue the stock to employees or the general public, the shares would have to be reregistered with the SEC in order to be publicly traded.

Issuing shares to employees or selling the shares back to the public offsets the impact on earnings from the repurchases. Many companies use the repurchases to obtain shares to issue when employees exercise stock options. In this case, current stockholders may be worse off, since the proceeds the company receives when the options are exercised are less than the company paid to repurchase the shares.

There are other reasons for management to buy back shares that may explain why the stock's price does not rise. Management can repurchase shares in an effort to prop up the price of the stock. Such actions often result in the company paying an artificially higher price for the stock. Management can repurchase shares to reduce the chance of an unwanted takeover. If the firm has a large amount of cash, it may become the prey of another firm. The firm executing the takeover borrows the required cash from another source (such as a group of commercial banks), acquires the firm, and then uses the cash obtained through the takeover to retire the loan. If management believes it is threatened with a hostile takeover, then repurchasing the shares serves two purposes. The reduction in the cash reduces the possibility of the takeover, and the reduction in the number of outstanding shares increases management's proportionate ownership and strengthens its control over the firm. Either of these reasons favors management at the stockholders' expense and may explain why the share buyback did not produce a higher stock price even though earnings per share increased.

Occasionally a firm is liquidated. The final distribution of the firm's assets is sometimes called a *liquidating dividend*. This is a bit misleading, because the distribution is not really a dividend. It is treated for tax purposes as a distribution of capital and is taxed at the appropriate capital gains tax rate. Thus, liquidating dividends are treated in the same manner as realized sales for federal income tax purposes.

A simple example illustrates how such a dividend works. A firm decides to liquidate and sells all its assets for cash. The stockholders then receive the cash. If the sales raise $25 in cash per share, a stockholder surrenders the stock certificate and receives $25 in cash. The capital gain is then determined by subtracting the stockholder's cost basis of the share from the $25. If the stockholder paid $10 for the share, the capital gain would be $15. The stockholder then pays the appropriate capital gains tax. If the cost basis were $40, the investor would suffer a capital loss of $15, which may be used for tax purposes to offset other capital gains or income. In either case, this is no different than if the stockholder had sold the shares. However, with a repurchase the stockholder does have the option to refuse to sell and thus may postpone any capital gains tax. In a liquidation the stockholder must realize the gain or loss. Once the firm has adopted a plan of liquidation, it must execute the plan or face penalties. When a firm liquidates, the stockholder cannot postpone the capital gains tax.

In the preceding example, the liquidating dividend was cash. However, the dividend need not be cash but may be property. For example, a real estate holding company could distribute the property it owns. Or a company that has accumulated stock in other companies could distribute the stock instead of selling it. Such distributions may be desirable if the stockholders want the particular assets being distributed. However, if the stockholders want or need cash (perhaps to pay the capital gains tax), then the burden of liquidating the assets is passed on to them.

An example of a firm that did liquidate is Tishman Realty. The stockholders adopted a plan of liquidation; the firm then sold most of its assets to Equitable Life Assurance for $200 million. The company paid an initial $11 per share liquidating dividend. After additional cash distributions were made, a partnership was established to hold the remaining assets, which consisted primarily of mortgages on properties sold. These partnership shares were then distributed to stockholders to complete the liquidation.

PREFERRED STOCK

preferred stock

A class of equity whose claim is prior to that of common stock on the corporation's earnings, and on its assets in case of liquidation or reorganization.

Preferred stock is an equity instrument that usually pays a fixed dividend that is not guaranteed but receives preference over common stock. Preferred stock also has a prior claim on the firm's assets if the firm ceases to exist and is liquidated or if the firm is reorganized. Since preferred stock is a form of equity, the holders of the stock may have voting rights. For example, the owners of the CenturyTel preferred stock have the right to vote their shares just as the owners of the common stock have the right to vote the shares.

While most firms have only one issue of common stock, they may have several issues of preferred stock. (Some corporations have also issued a *preference* stock, which is subordinated to preferred stock but has preference over common stock with regard to the payment of dividends. Such stock is another level of preferred stock, and in this text no distinction is made between the two.) As may be seen in Exhibit 8.1, Virginia Electric and Power has eight issues of preferred stock. In seven cases the dividend is fixed. Thus, for the series $5.00 preferred, the annual dividend is $5.00, which is

---

EXHIBIT   8.1   The Preferred Stocks of Virginia Electric and Power

Preferred Stock Not Subject to Mandatory Retirement	
Annual Dividend per Share	Outstanding Shares
$4.04	12,926
4.20	14,797
4.12	32,534
4.80	73,206
5.00	106,677
7.05	500,000
6.98	600,000
Money market preferred (variable rate)	1,250,000

Source: 2008 Dominion Resources Form 10-K.

distributed at the rate of $1.25 per quarter. For the money market preferred stock, the dividend is reset every 49 days with changes in money market rates.

The dividend is expressed either as a dollar amount or as a percentage based on the preferred stock's par value. The par value is the stated value of the shares and is also the price at which the shares were initially sold. In the case of the Virginia Electric $5.00 preferred, the par value is $100, so the dividend rate is 5.0 percent based on the par value.

Preferred stock dividends are paid from the firm's earnings. If the firm does not have the earnings, it may not declare and pay the preferred stock dividends. If the firm should omit the preferred stock's dividend, the dividend is said to be *in arrears*. The firm does not have to remove this **arrearage**. In most cases, however, any omitted dividends have to be paid in the future before dividends may be paid to the holders of the common stock. Such cases in which the preferred stock's dividends accumulate are called **cumulative preferred**. Most preferred stock is cumulative, but there are examples of **noncumulative preferred stocks** whose dividends do not have to be made up if not paid. For example, Bank of America, issued a perpetual noncumulative preferred stock in 2008. The annual dividend is 8.20 percent, but payment is not a legal obligation of the company and Bank of America is not required to make up any missed payments.

For investors holding preferred stock in firms having financial difficulty, the difference between cumulative and noncumulative preferred may be immaterial. Forcing the firm to pay dividends to erase the arrearage may further weaken the company and hurt the owner of the preferred stock more than forgoing the dividends. Once the firm has regained its profitability, erasing the arrearage may become important to both the holders of the stock and the company, especially if the firm needs to raise external funds. For example, Unisys paid the arrearages on its preferred stock when the company regained profitability.

Preferred stock may be perpetual or it may have a finite life, in which case the corporation must retire the preferred stock. Both offer advantages and disadvantages. If the stock is perpetual, the corporation does have to raise the funds to retire it. However, if management wants to retire perpetual stock to erase the dividend payment, it may have to offer a premium price to induce investors to sell the shares back to the company. With a finite life preferred stock, the corporation must generate sufficient funds to retire the stock.

Since preferred stock pays a fixed dividend, it is purchased primarily by investors who want a fixed flow of income. Although preferred is an equity instrument, its features are more similar to debt (bonds) than to common stock. As is explained in Chapter 14, the value of a fixed income security is the present value of the future flow of income discounted back to the present. For this reason, the analysis and valuation of preferred stock is deferred until after discussion of debt instruments in Part 4.

ANALYSIS OF FINANCIAL STATEMENTS

Ratios may be the most frequently used tool to analyze a company. They are readily understood and can be computed with ease. In addition, the information used in ratio analysis is easy to obtain, for financial ratios employ data available in a firm's annual and quarterly reports. Ratios are used not only by investors and financial analysts but also by a firm's

arrearage

Cumulative preferred dividends that have not been paid.

cumulative preferred stock

A preferred stock whose dividends accumulate if they are not paid.

noncumulative preferred stock

Preferred stock whose dividends do not accumulate if the firm misses a dividend payment.

management and its creditors. Management may use ratio analysis to plan, to control, and to identify weaknesses within the firm. Creditors use the analysis to establish the ability of the borrower to pay interest and retire debt. Stockholders are primarily concerned with performance and employ ratio analysis to measure profitability.[7]

Although a variety of people use ratio analysis, they should select those ratios that are best suited to their specific purposes. A creditor is concerned primarily with the firm's ability to pay interest and repay principal and is less concerned with the rate at which the firm's equipment is used. While the rate at which fixed assets turn over may affect the ability of the company to pay the interest and principal, the typical creditor is more concerned with the firm's capacity to generate cash.

The investor may find that a specific industry requires additional ratios or more sophisticated versions of a particular ratio. For example, the ratios used to analyze public utilities are different from those used to analyze railroads. Although both are highly regulated and have similarities, such as large investments in plant and equipment, the natures of the industries are different, including factors such as the labor requirements, competition, and demand for each service. Emphasis, then, is placed on different factors, such as miles traveled per ton of freight for railroads versus the peak load requirements relative to the average demand for electricity for an electric utility.

time-series analysis

An analysis of a firm over a period of time.

cross-sectional analysis

An analysis of several firms in the same industry at a point in time.

Ratios may be computed and interpreted from two perspectives. They may be compiled for a number of years to perceive trends, which is called **time-series analysis**, or they may be compared at a given time for several firms within the same industry, known as **cross-sectional analysis**. Time-series and cross-sectional analyses may be used together, as the analyst compares the firm to its industry over a period of years.

One ratio by itself means little, but several ratios together may give a clear picture of a firm's strengths and weaknesses. Rarely will all the ratios indicate the same general tendency. However, when they are taken as a group, the ratios often give an indication of the direction in which the firm is moving and its financial position in comparison to other firms in its industry.

The subsequent sections of this chapter cover a variety of ratios. The illustrations of these ratios employ data taken from the balance sheet and income statements of Hershey Foods Corporation (HSY—the NYSE trading symbol). Hershey's balance sheet and income statement for 2006 through 2008 are given in Exhibits 8.2 and 8.3. The 2008 data are used to illustrate the ratios.

Before proceeding, you need to be forewarned that several ratios have more than one definition. The definition used by one analyst may differ from that used by others. These differences can arise from averaging the data. (See, for instance, the two approaches to inventory turnover discussed below.) Another source of differences can be what is included or excluded. (See, for instance, the various definitions of the debt ratios.) As is illustrated later in this chapter, you cannot assume that the analysis obtained from one source is comparable to that provided by an alternative source. This problem may be particularly acute with analyses of financial statements that may be found on the Internet. Of course, you can avoid this problem by performing the analysis yourself!

---

[7]Benjamin Graham is considered to be the father of modern financial analysis that employs ratio analysis of financial statements. His text is a classic and employs many of the ratios described in this chapter. See Benjamin Graham, David L. Dodd, Sidney Cottle, and Charles Tatham, *Security Analysis: Principles and Techniques,* 5th ed. (New York: McGraw-Hill, 1988). See especially part 4, "The Valuation of Common Stock," for the conservative financial approach to the analysis of common stock.

EXHIBIT 8.2 Hershey Foods Corporation Consolidated Balance Sheet
As of December 31 (in millions)

	2008	2007	2006
ASSETS			
Current assets			
Cash and cash equivalents	$ 37.1	$ 130.0	$ 97.1
Accounts receivable	445.2	487.3	522.7
Inventories	592.5	600.2	648.8
Other	270.2	209.1	103.0
Total current assets	1345.0	1426.6	1417.8
Property, plant, and equipment	1458.9	1539.7	1651.3
Other assets	830.8	1280.8	1088.5
Total assets	$3,634.7	$4,247.1	$4,157.6
LIABILITIES AND STOCKHOLDERS' EQUITY			
Current liabilities			
Accounts payable	249.5	223.0	155.5
Accrued liabilities	504.1	539.0	454.0
Short-term debt	483.1	850.3	655.2
Other	33.5	6.5	188.8
Total current liabilities	1270.2	1618.8	1453.5
Long-term debt	1506.0	1280.0	1248.1
Other long-term liabilities	505.0	544.0	486.5
Deferred income taxes	3.6	180.8	286.0
Total liabilities	3284.8	3623.6	3474.1
Stockholders' equity			
Common stock	359.8	359.9	359.9
Additional paid-in capital	352.4	335.3	298.2
Retained earnings	3975.8	3927.3	3965.4
Treasury stock repurchased at cost	−4010.0	−4001.6	−3801.9
Other adjustments	−359.9	28.0	−138.2
Total stockholders' equity	318.1	592.9	683.4
Total liabilities and stockholders' equity	$3,634.7	$4,247.1	$4,157.6

Source: Adapted from Hershey Foods Corporation Proxy Statement and 2008 and 2006 10-K Reports.

EXHIBIT 8.3 Hershey Foods Corporation Statement of Income for the years ended
December 31 (in millions except per-share data)

	2008	2007	2006
Net sales	$5,132.8	$4,946.7	$4,944.2
Costs and expenses			
Cost of good sold	3375.1	3315.1	3076.7
Selling, marketing, administrative	1073.0	895.9	860.4
Other	94.8	276.8	14.6
Earnings before interest and taxes (EBIT)	$ 589.9	$ 458.9	$ 992.5
Interest expense	97.9	118.6	116.1
Provision for income taxes	180.7	126.1	317.4
Net income	$ 311.3	$ 214.2	$ 559.0
Net income per share	$ 1.27	$ 0.87	$ 2.19
Cash dividends per share	$ 1.19	$ 1.135	$ 1.03

Source: Adapted from Hershey Foods Corporation Proxy Statement and 2008 and 2006 10-K Reports.

LIQUIDITY RATIOS

Liquidity is the ease with which assets may be quickly converted into cash without the firm's incurring a loss. If a firm has a high degree of liquidity, it will be able to meet its debt obligations as they become due. Therefore, liquidity ratios are a useful tool for the firm's creditors, who are concerned with being paid. Liquidity ratios are so called because they indicate the degree of liquidity or "moneyness" of the company's assets.

The Current Ratio

current ratio

Current assets divided by current liabilities; a measure of liquidity.

The **current ratio** is the ratio of current assets to current liabilities.

$$\text{Current ratio} = \frac{\text{Current assets}}{\text{Current liabilities}}.$$

It indicates the extent to which the current liabilities, which must be paid within a year, are "covered" by current assets. For HSY, the current ratio as of December 31, 2008, was

$$\frac{\$1,345.0}{\$1,270.2} = 1.06,$$

which indicates that for every $1 that the firm had to pay within the year, there was $1.06 in the form of either cash or an asset that was to be converted into cash within the year.

For most industries, it is desirable to have more current assets than current liabilities. It is sometimes asserted that a firm should have at least $2 in current assets for every $1 in current liabilities, or a current ratio of at least 2:1. If the current ratio is 2:1, then the firm's current assets could deteriorate in value by 50 percent and the firm would still be able to meet its short-term liabilities.

Although such rules of thumb are convenient, they need not apply to all industries. For example, electric utilities usually have current liabilities that exceed their current assets (i.e., a current ratio of less than 1:1). Does this worry short-term creditors? No, because the short-term assets are primarily accounts receivable from electricity users and are of high quality. Should a customer fail to pay an electricity bill, the company threatens to cut off service, and this threat is usually sufficient to induce payment. The higher the quality of the current assets (i.e., the greater the probability that these assets can be converted to cash at their stated value), the less vital it is for the current ratio to exceed 1:1. The reason, then, for selecting a rule of thumb such as a current ratio of at least 2:1 is for the protection of the creditors, who are aware that not all current assets will, in fact, be converted into cash.

Both creditors and equity investors want to know if the firm has sufficient liquid assets to meet its bills. Obviously, a low current ratio is undesirable because it indicates financial weakness, but a high current ratio may also be undesirable. A high current ratio may imply that the firm is not using its funds to best advantage. For example, the company may have issued long-term debt and used it to finance an excessive amount of inventory or accounts receivable. The high current ratio may also indicate that the firm is not taking advantage of available short-term financing or is mismanaging its current assets, which reduces its profitability. A high or low numerical value for the current ratio may be a signal to creditors and stockholders that the management of short-term assets and liabilities should be revised.

⊕ **Point of Interest**

GENERALLY ACCEPTED ACCOUNTING PRINCIPLES (GAAP)

Accounting statements provide financial information concerning an enterprise. Although the emphasis in this text is the statements' applications to firms, financial statements may be constructed for governments (e.g., the local municipality), nonprofit organizations (such as the Metropolitan Opera), or individuals. In all cases, these statements show the financial condition of the entity and its assets and how they were financed. This information can then be used to aid financial decision making.

To be useful in decision making, financial statements must be reliable, understandable, and comparable. Reliability requires the statements to be objective and unbiased. The data included on the statements should be verifiable by independent experts. This does not mean that two accountants working with the same information will construct identical financial statements. Individual opinions and judgments may lead to different financial statements. An example that involves the accountant's judgment is the allowance for doubtful accounts receivable. Two accountants may establish differing amounts that will affect the firm's financial statements. However, it should not be concluded that two accountants will construct widely different statements. While the financial statements may differ, the amount of differentiation should be modest.

Accountants' second goal is that financial statements be understandable. The statement should be presented in an orderly manner and be readable by informed laypersons as well as professionals. Investors and other individuals who use financial statements need not know all the principles used to construct a financial statement. However, an intelligent individual should be able to read a firm's profitability, its assets and liabilities, and its cash flow.

Comparability requires that one set of financial statements can be compared to the same financial statements constructed over different accounting periods. The principles used to construct one year's statements should be used for subsequent years. If the principles being applied are changed, the previous years' statements should be restated. If the firm's operations change, the financial statements should also reflect these changes. If, for example, the firm discontinues part of its operations, its sales, expenses, and profits for previous years should be restated. If this adjustment is not made, the users of the financial statements will be unable to compare the firm's financial condition and performance over a period of time for its continuing operations.

To increase the objectivity of financial statements, a general framework for accounting and financial reports has been established by the Financial Accounting Standards Board (FASB). Accounting principles that are "generally accepted" also receive the support of the American Institute of Certified Public Accountants and the Securities and Exchange Commission (SEC). Although these bodies establish the principles under which financial statements are constructed, it should not be concluded that the principles are static. Their conceptual framework changes over time with changes in the business environment and the needs of the statements' users. For example, increases in foreign investments and fluctuations in the value of foreign currencies have generated a need for better methods of accounting for these foreign investments. This problem, plus others such as inflation, pension liabilities, and stock options, have resulted in changes in accounting principles as the profession seeks to improve the informational content of financial statements.

The Quick Ratio

The current ratio gives an indication of the company's ability to meet its current liabilities as they become due, but it has a major weakness. It is an aggregate measure of liquidity that does not differentiate between the degrees of liquidity of the various types of current assets, which may be in the form of cash, accounts receivable, or inventory. Cash is a liquid asset, but it may take many months before inventory is sold and turned into cash. This failure of the current ratio to distinguish between the degrees of liquidity has led to the development of the quick ratio, which omits inventory from the calculation.

quick ratio (acid test)

Current assets excluding inventory divided by current liabilities; a measure of liquidity.

The **quick ratio** or *acid test* (both names are used) is determined as follows:

$$\text{Quick ratio} = \frac{\text{Current assets} - \text{Inventory}}{\text{Current liabilities}}.$$

For HSY, the quick ratio is

$$\frac{\$1,345.0 - \$592.5}{\$1,270.2} = 0.59,$$

which is lower than the current ratio of 1.06. The difference lies, of course, in the inventory that the company is carrying, which is excluded from the acid test.[8]

A low quick ratio implies that the firm may have difficulty meeting its current liabilities as they become due if it must rely on converting inventory into cash. However, a low quick ratio does not indicate that the firm will fail to pay its bills. The ability to meet liabilities is influenced by such factors as (1) the rate at which cash flows into the firm, (2) the time at which bills become due, (3) the relationship between the company and its creditors and their willingness to roll over debt, and (4) the firm's ability to raise additional capital. The acid test merely indicates how well the current liabilities are covered by cash and by highly liquid assets that may be converted into cash relatively quickly. Because this ratio takes into account that not all current assets are equally liquid, it is a more precise measure of liquidity than is the current ratio.

ACTIVITY RATIOS

Activity ratios indicate at what rate the firm is turning its inventory and accounts receivable into cash. The more rapidly the firm turns over its inventory and receivables, the more quickly it acquires cash. High turnover indicates that the firm is rapidly receiving cash and is in a better position to pay its liabilities as they become due. Such high turnover, however, need not imply that the firm is maximizing profits. For example, high inventory turnover may indicate that the firm is selling items for too low a price in order to induce quicker sales. A high receivables turnover may be an indication that the firm is offering large discounts for rapid payment, which could result in lower profits.

Inventory Turnover

inventory turnover

The speed with which inventory is sold.

Inventory turnover is defined as annual sales divided by average inventory. That is,

$$\text{Inventory turnover} = \frac{\text{Sales}}{\text{Average inventory}}.$$

This ratio uses average inventory throughout the year. Such an average reduces the impact of fluctuations in the level of inventory. If only year-end inventory was used and it

---

[8]The quick ratio may also be defined as

$$\frac{\text{Cash} + \text{Cash equivalents} + \text{Accounts receivable}}{\text{Current liabilities}}.$$

It might appear the two definitions are the same, but they are not if the firm has current assets other than cash, cash equivalents, accounts receivable, and inventory. This second definition excludes other current assets such as prepaid expenses, while the definition in the text does not. If this second definition is used for Hershey, the quick ratio is ($37.1 + $445.2)/$1,270.2 = 0.38, which is lower and suggests the firm is less liquid.

was abnormally high at the end of the fiscal year, the turnover would appear to be slower. Conversely, if inventory was lower than normal at the year's end, the turnover would appear faster than in fact it was. Averaging the inventory reduces the impact of these fluctuations. Management may use any number of observations (e.g., monthly or weekly) to determine the average inventory. The information available to investors, however, may be limited to the level of inventory given in the firm's quarterly and annual reports.

For HSY, inventory was $592.5 in 2008 and $600.2 in 2007. The average for the two years was

$$\frac{\$592.5 + \$600.2}{2} = \$596.1.$$

Thus, for HSY, inventory turnover was

$$\frac{\text{Sales}}{\text{Average inventory}} = \frac{\$5,132.8}{\$596.1} = 8.6.$$

This indicates that annual sales are about 8 times the level of inventory. Inventory thus turns over 8.6 times a year, or about once every 6 weeks.

Inventory turnover may also be defined as the cost of goods sold divided by the inventory. That is,

$$\text{Inventory turnover} = \frac{\text{Cost of good sold}}{\text{Average inventory}}.$$

If this definition is used, HSY's inventory turnover is

$$\frac{\$3,375.1}{\$596.1} = 5.7.$$

This definition places more emphasis on recouping the cost of the goods. However, creditors may prefer to use sales, since sales produce the funds to service the debt. Dun and Bradstreet uses sales in its industry averages, and any creditors who use Dun and Bradstreet data as a source of comparison must remember to use sales instead of cost of goods sold to be consistent.

Average Collection Period (Days Sales Outstanding)

average collection period (days sales outstanding)
The number of days required to collect accounts receivable.

The **average collection period**, which is also referred to as *days sales outstanding*, measures how long it takes a firm to collect its accounts receivable. The faster the company collects its receivables, the more rapidly it receives cash and hence can pay its obligations, such as its interest expense. The average collection period (ACP) is determined as follows:

$$\text{ACP} = \frac{\text{Receivables}}{\text{Sales per day}}.$$

Sales per day are total sales divided by 360 (or 365) days. For HSY the average collection period is

$$\frac{\$445.2}{\$5,132.8 \div 360} = 31.2.$$

This indicates that the firm takes 31 days to convert its receivables into money.

receivables turnover
The speed with which a firm collects its accounts receivable.

Receivables turnover, which is another way of viewing the average collection period, may be defined as annual credit sales divided by receivables. Some analysts may prefer to average the accounts receivable in the same way that inventory was averaged for the inventory turnover ratio. By this definition,

$$\text{Receivables turnover} = \frac{\text{Annual credit sales}}{\text{Accounts receivable}}.$$

An alternative definition of receivables turnover substitutes annual sales for annual credit sales. That is,

$$\text{Receivables turnover} = \frac{\text{Annual sales}}{\text{Accounts receivable}}.$$

Either definition is acceptable as long as it is applied consistently. Although management has access to the information used in both formulas, investors may be limited to the data provided by the firm. If annual credit sales are not reported by the firm, the investor will have no choice but to use annual sales.

Since the HSY income statement does not give annual credit sales, the first definition cannot be used; hence, for HSY,

$$\text{Receivable turnover} = \frac{\$5,132.8}{\$445.2} = 11.5.$$

This indicates that annual sales are 11.5 times the amount of receivables. The larger the ratio, the more rapidly the firm turns its credit sales into cash. A turnover of 11.5 times per year indicates that receivables are paid off on the average of every month. This is the same information that was derived by computing the average collection period, since 31.2 days is approximately one month.

While days sales outstanding and receivables turnover may on the surface appear to have little interest for stockholders, that conclusion is incorrect. An increase in days sales outstanding (reduction in turnover) indicates that receivables are increasing relative to sales. The firm may be offering more generous credit terms to generate sales or being lax in collection policies. Even though these credit sales may be profitable, they do not generate cash until the receivables are collected. Thus, an increase in days sales outstanding may be a subtle flag that stockholders (and creditors) may interpret as problems that lie ahead!

Fixed Asset Turnover

Inventory and accounts receivable turnover stress the speed with which current assets flow up the balance sheet. Rapid inventory turnover means inventory is quickly sold and converted into either cash or an account receivable. The average collection period tells how long it takes the firm to collect the account (i.e., how long it takes to receive cash from a credit sale).

fixed asset turnover
Ratio of sales to fixed assets; tells how many fixed assets are needed to generate sales.

Turnover ratios may also be constructed for long-term assets. Such a ratio is the **fixed asset turnover**.

$$\text{Fixed asset turnover} = \frac{\text{Annual sales}}{\text{Fixed assets}}.$$

Fixed assets are the firm's plant and equipment, and this ratio indicates the amount of plant and equipment that were used to generate the firm's sales. For HSY, the fixed asset turnover was

$$\text{Fixed asset turnover} = \frac{\$5{,}132.8}{\$1{,}458.9} = 3.52.$$

This indicates that HSY generated $3.52 in sales for every $1 invested in plant and equipment (i.e., fixed assets).

Many firms such as utilities must have substantial investment in plant and equipment to produce the output they sell. Other firms, especially those providing services, need only modest amounts of fixed assets. Thus, the ratio is obviously sensitive to the firm's industry. Fixed asset turnover is also hard to interpret. It is a measure of management's ability to efficiently use long-term assets, but a low numerical value is not necessarily bad, and, conversely, a high value is not necessarily good. With the passage of time, plant and equipment are depreciated. Their book value diminishes, which would increase the numerical value of the ratio. New investments in plant and equipment would decrease fixed asset turnover. A low fixed asset turnover may be indicative of increased investment in plant and equipment and not necessarily inefficient use of fixed assets. Thus, the analyst should consider changes in fixed asset turnover over time and not the absolute value of the ratio.

Total Asset Turnover

total asset turnover
Ratio of sales to total assets; tells how many total assets are used to generate sales.

Total asset turnover considers the firm's sales relative to all of the assets:

$$\text{Total asset turnover} = \frac{\text{Annual sales}}{\text{Total assets}}.$$

For HSY, the total asset turnover is

$$\text{Total asset turnover} = \frac{\$5{,}132.8}{\$3{,}634.7} = 1.4.$$

Like the other turnover ratios, total asset turnover tells the analyst how many assets were required to generate the firm's sales. However, since it aggregates the firm's total assets, it does not differentiate between current and long-term ratios. Since it aggregates the assets, it cannot indicate the source of any problem that may be identified by receivables, inventory, or fixed asset turnover.

All of the turnover ratios need to be interpreted with caution. These ratios are static, for they use information derived at a given time (i.e., the year-end figures on the balance sheet). The ratios, however, are dealing with dynamic events; they are concerned with the length of time it takes for an event to occur. Because of this problem with time, these turnover ratios, which are based on year-end figures, may be misleading if the firm has (1) seasonal sales, (2) sporadic sales during the fiscal year, or (3) any growth in inventory and sales during the fiscal year. Creditors and bondholders need to be aware of these potential problems since they can lead to incorrect conclusions concerning the firm's capacity to service its debt.

PROFITABILITY RATIOS

The amount that a firm earns is particularly important to investors. Earnings accrue to stockholders and either are distributed to them as dividends or are retained. Retained earnings represent an additional investment in the corporation by stockholders. Obviously, a firm's performance is a crucial element in fundamental analysis.

gross profit margin

Percentage earned on sales after deducting the cost of goods sold.

Profitability ratios are measures of performance that indicate the amount the firm is earning relative to some base, such as sales, assets, or equity. The **gross profit margin** is

$$\text{Gross profit margin} = \frac{\text{Sales} - \text{Cost of goods sold}}{\text{Sales}}.$$

For HSY, the gross profit margin for 2008 was

$$\text{Gross profit margin} = \frac{\$5{,}132.8 - \$3{,}375.1}{\$5{,}132.8} = 34.2\%,$$

which indicates the firm earned $0.342 on every dollar of sales before considering administrative expenses, depreciation, and financing costs.

operating profit margin

Percentage earned on sales before adjusting for nonrecurring items, interest, and taxes.

The **operating profit margin** is operating income divided by sales.

$$\text{Operating profit margin} = \frac{\text{Operating earnings}}{\text{Sales}}.$$

Operating income is often defined as earnings before interest and taxes, and in most cases that is sufficient unless the firm has extraordinary or nonrecurring items included in earnings before interest and taxes. While management will report these items as a separate entry, they may be included in income before interest and taxes. If operating income does include extraordinary items, it is not indicative of operating income. (In 1999, HSY had a large gain of $243.7 million from the sale of a business. The inclusion of the gain increased operating income from $558.4 million to $802.4 million. The larger number would overstate operating income and net income so the operating profit margin and net profit margin would be misleading.)

For 2008, HSY had operating income of $589.9, so its operating profit margin is

$$\text{Operating profit margin} = \frac{\$589.9}{\$5{,}132.8} = 11.5\%.$$

This indicates that HSY earned about $0.115 on every dollar of sales before considering interest expense and income taxes.

net profit margin

The ratio of earnings after interest and taxes to sales.

The **net profit margin** is the ratio of profits after taxes to sales. That is,

$$\text{Net profit margin} = \frac{\text{Earnings after taxes}}{\text{Sales}}.$$

For HSY, the net profit margin was

$$\text{Net profit margin} = \frac{\$311.3}{\$5{,}132.8} = 6.1\%.$$

The net profit margin indicates that HSY earned $0.061 on every $1 of sales.

Although the computation of all three profit margin ratios may seem unnecessary, they tell the analyst different things about profitability. The gross profit margin is sensitive only to changes in the cost of goods sold. The operating profit margin is affected by all operating expenses. Changes in advertising or depreciation affect the operating but not the gross profit margin. By computing both ratios, the financial analyst can determine whether changes in the cost of goods sold or changes in other operating expenses are affecting operating income.[9]

The net profit margin adds the impact of financing expenses and taxes on profitability. A change in income tax rates affects net profits but not operating profits. This impact may be important for stockholders who are concerned with the bottom line (net income) but not for bondholders whose interest is paid before income tax. Bondholders may be concerned with expenses that affect operating income but not those that affect net income.

return on assets

The ratio of earnings to total assets.

Other profitability ratios measure the **return on assets** and the return on equity. The return on assets is net earnings divided by assets. That is,

$$\text{Return on assets} = \frac{\text{Earnings after taxes}}{\text{Total assets}}.$$

For HSY, the return on assets was

$$\frac{\$311.3}{\$3,634.7} = 8.6\%.$$

Thus, HSY earned $.086 on every $1 of assets. This ratio measures the return on the firm's resources (i.e., its assets). It is an all-encompassing measure of performance that indicates the total that management is able to achieve on all the firm's assets. This return on assets takes into account the profit margin and the rate at which the assets are turned over (e.g., the rate at which the firm sells its inventory and collects its accounts receivable) as well as taxes and extraordinary items.

Although return on assets gives an aggregate measure of the firm's performance, it does not tell how well management is performing for the stockholders. This performance is indicated by the **return on equity**. The return on equity uses earnings after taxes, which are the earnings available to the firm's stockholders. For HSY, the return on equity is

return on equity

The ratio of earnings to equity.

$$\text{Return on equity} = \frac{\text{Earnings after taxes}}{\text{Equity}} = \frac{\$311.3}{\$318.1} = 97.9\%.$$

Equity is the sum of stock, additional paid-in capital (if any), and retained earnings (if any). The return on equity measures the amount that the firm is earning on the stockholders' investment. A return on equity of 97.9% is exceptionally high. For this reason, it is desirable to compute the ratio over a period of time to establish a more accurate indication of the continuing return that management is able to earn for stockholders.

Many stockholders may be concerned not with the return on the firm's total equity but with the return earned on the equity attributable to the common stock. To

---

[9]Some financial analysts also determine profit margins using earnings before interest, taxes, and depreciation and amortization (EBITDA). Depreciation is the allocation of the cost of a tangible asset (i.e., plant and equipment) over a period of time. Amortization is the allocation of an intangible asset such as goodwill over a period of time. Both depreciation and amortization are noncash expenses. As is explained later in this chapter in the section on the statement of cash flows, noncash expenses are added back to earnings to determine the cash generated by operations.

By using EBITDA instead of operating income (EBIT), the financial analyst is subtracting only cash expenses (e.g., cost of goods sold) from revenue. If two firms have identical EBIT but one has larger depreciation expenses, its cash expenses are lower. Lower cash expenses means that EBITDA is larger; the firm has lower cash outflows. By using earnings before interest, taxes, and depreciation and amortization expenses (EBITDA) as well as operating earnings (EBIT) and net earnings, the financial analyst is better able to determine the firm's ability to generate cash. Such cash then may be used to retire debt, distributed to stockholders, or invested in potentially profitable assets.

determine this return on common stock, adjustments must be made for any preferred stock the firm has outstanding. First, the dividends that are paid to preferred stockholders must be subtracted from earnings to obtain earnings available to common stockholders. Second, the contribution of the preferred stock to the firm's equity must be subtracted to obtain the investment in the firm by the common stockholders. Thus, the return to common stockholders is

$$\text{Return on common equity} = \frac{\text{Earnings after taxes} - \text{Preferred stock dividends}}{\text{Equity} - \text{Preferred stock}}.$$

Of course, if the firm has no preferred stock, the return on equity and the return on the common equity are identical.

For HSY, the return on common equity for 2008 was

$$\text{Return on common equity} = \frac{\$311.3 - 0}{\$318.1 - 0} = 97.9\%.$$

The ratio indicates that HSY earned a return of $0.979 for every $1 invested by common stockholders. Thus, while HSY achieved only 8.6 percent on its total assets, it was able to earn 97.9 percent on the stockholders' investment.

LEVERAGE (CAPITALIZATION) RATIOS

financial leverage
The use of borrowed funds to acquire an asset.

debt ratio
The ratio of debt to total assets; a measure of the use of debt financing.

How can a firm magnify the return on its stockholders' investment? One method is the use of **financial leverage**. By successfully using debt financing, management can increase the return to the owners, the common stockholders. The use of financial leverage may be measured by capitalization ratios, which indicate the extent to which the firm finances its assets by debt. These ratios are also referred to as **debt ratios**.

Because debt financing can have such impact on the firm, each of these ratios is extremely valuable in analyzing the financial position of the firm. The most commonly used capitalization ratios are (1) the debt-to-equity ratio and (2) the debt-to-total assets ratio. These ratios are

$$\frac{\text{Debt}}{\text{Equity}} \text{ and } \frac{\text{Debt}}{\text{Total assets}}.$$

For HSY, the values for these ratios for 2008 were as follows:

$$\frac{\text{Debt}}{\text{Equity}} = \frac{\$3,284.8}{\$318.1} = 10.3,$$

$$\frac{\text{Debt}}{\text{Total assets}} = \frac{\$3,284.8}{\$3,634.7} = 90.4\%.$$

For HSY, the debt-to-equity ratio indicates that there was $10.30 in debt for every $1 of stock. The ratio of debt to total assets indicates that debt was used to finance 90.4 percent of the firm's assets.

Since these ratios measure the same thing (i.e., the use of debt financing), you may wonder which is preferred. Actually, either is acceptable. The debt-to-equity ratio expresses debt in terms of equity, while the debt-to-total assets ratio gives the proportion of the firm's total assets that are financed by debt. Financial analysts or investors should choose the one they feel most comfortable working with.

These capitalization ratios are aggregate measures. They both use total debt and hence do not differentiate between short-term and long-term debt. The debt-to-equity ratio uses total equity and does not differentiate between the financing provided by preferred and common stock. The debt-to-total assets ratio uses total assets and hence does not differentiate between current and long-term assets.

Some definitions of debt ratio use only long-term debt (i.e., long-term debt/total assets). The argument is that short-term debt has to be quickly retired and is not part of the firm's permanent capital structure. There are three possible arguments against this reasoning. First, a firm may always have some current liabilities (e.g., trade accounts payable), and such liabilities are part of its permanent capital structure. Second, during periods of higher interest rates, management may issue short-term debt as a temporary source of funds prior to refinancing once interest rates have declined. Third, there are periods when short-term debt may be used prior to issuing long-term debt. For example, when a plant is being constructed, it may be financed with short-term debt prior to more permanent financing once the plant is completed and put into operation. In this text, the term *debt ratio* will always include both short- and long-term debt.

There is also the question of whether to include the deferred income taxes as part of the debt structure and hence include them in the calculation of the debt ratio. Since deferred taxes finance less than 1 percent of HSY's assets ($3.6/$3,634.7), they have little impact on the firm's sources of funds. The argument for exclusion of deferred taxes is that they may be deferred indefinitely. Inclusion ultimately depends on when the financial analyst believes the taxes will be paid. Changes in tax laws or in the firm's operations can accelerate or retard paying these deferred obligations. An acceleration, of course, argues for their inclusion in the calculation.

In spite of the variety of definitions of the debt ratio, all the ratios measure the extent to which assets are financed by creditors. The smaller the proportion of total assets financed by creditors, the larger the decline in the value of assets that may occur without threatening the creditors' position. Capitalization ratios thus give an indication of risk. Firms that have a small amount of equity capital are considered to involve greater risk because there is less cushion to protect creditors if the value of the assets deteriorates. For example, the ratio of debt to total assets for HSY was 90.4 percent. This indicates that the value of the assets may decline by 9.6 percent (100% − 90.4%) before only enough assets remain to pay off the debt. If the debt ratio had been 60 percent, a decline of 40 percent in the value of the assets would endanger the creditors' position.

Capitalization ratios indicate risk as much to investors as they do to creditors, because firms with a high degree of financial leverage are riskier investments. If the value of the assets declines or if the firm experiences declining sales and losses, the equity deteriorates more quickly for firms that use financial leverage than for those that do not use debt financing. Hence, the debt ratios are an important measure of risk for both investors and creditors.

That capitalization ratios differ among firms is illustrated in Exhibit 8.4, which presents the debt ratios for four industrial and manufacturing firms. This exhibit is arranged in descending order from the firm that uses the greatest amount of debt financing (Ford Motor, whose liabilities *exceed* its assets) to the firm that uses the least (VF Corp.). The debt ratios calculated for Exhibit 8.4 use total debt. The ratios may be considerably different if only long-term debt is used. The Coca-Cola Company debt ratio declines to only 6.9 percent if current liabilities are excluded from the calculation.

| EXHIBIT 8.4 | Ratio of Total Debt to Total Assets for Selected Firms as of December 2008 |

Firm	Debt Ratio
Ford Motor Company	107.8
Hershey Foods	90.4
Coca-Cola Company	49.4
VF Corp. (Vanity Fair)	44.7

Source: 2008 annual reports.

undercapitalized

Having insufficient
equity financing.

Financial theory suggests that there is an optimal combination of debt and equity financing that maximizes the value of a firm. The optimal use of financial leverage benefits common stockholders by increasing the per-share earnings of the company and by permitting faster growth and larger dividends. If, however, the firm uses too much financial leverage or is **undercapitalized**, creditors will require a higher interest rate to compensate them for the increased risk. Investors will invest their funds in a corporation with a large amount of financial leverage only if the anticipated return is higher. Thus, the debt ratio, which measures the extent to which a firm uses financial leverage, is one of the most important ratios that managers, creditors, and stockholders may calculate.

COVERAGE RATIOS

times-interest-earned

Ratio of earnings before interest and taxes divided by interest expense; a coverage ratio that measures the safety of debt.

Although leverage ratios measure the firm's use of debt financing, coverage ratios measure the ability of the firm to service its debt and preferred stock. For debt, the ratios indicate to creditors and bondholders how much the firm is earning from its operations relative to what is owed. The coverage for interest payments is called **times-interest-earned**. Times-interest-earned is the ratio of earnings that are available to pay the interest (i.e., operating income) divided by the amount of interest. That is,

$$\text{Times-interest-earned} = \frac{\text{Earnings before interest and taxes}}{\text{Annual interest expense}}.$$

A ratio of 2 indicates that the firm has $2 after meeting other expenses to pay $1 of interest charges. The larger the times-interest-earned ratio, the more likely it is that the firm will be able to meet its interest payments.

For HSY, times-interest-earned is

$$\frac{\$589.9}{\$97.9} = 6.03,$$

which indicates the firm has operating income of $6.03 for every $1 of interest expense.

The ability to cover the interest expense is important, for failure to meet interest payments as they become due may throw the firm into bankruptcy. A decline in the times-interest-earned ratio indicates declining income relative to debt, or stable income but increased use of debt. It serves as an early warning to creditors and investors, as well as to management, of a deteriorating financial position and the increased probability of default on interest payments.

For preferred stock, coverage ratios indicate the ability of the firm to pay the dividend. The preferred dividend depends on *net* earnings. (Times-interest-earned uses *operating* income since interest is paid before taxes.) The coverage ratio for preferred stock, **times-dividend-earned**, is

times-dividend-earned ratio

Earnings divided by preferred dividend requirements.

$$\text{Times-dividend-earned} = \frac{\text{Earnings after taxes}}{\text{Dividends on preferred stock}}.$$

The larger this ratio, the safer the preferred stock's dividend should be. Notice that the numerator consists of *total* earnings. Although the preferred stock dividends are subtracted from the total earnings to derive the earnings available to the common stockholders, all the firm's earnings are available to pay the preferred stock dividend.

A variation on this ratio is **earnings per preferred share**. This ratio is

earnings per preferred share

The total earnings divided by the number of preferred shares outstanding.

$$\text{Earnings per preferred share} = \frac{\text{Earnings after taxes}}{\text{Number of preferred shares outstanding}}.$$

The larger the earnings per preferred share, the safer the dividend payment. However, neither of these ratios indicates whether the firm has sufficient cash to pay the dividends. They can indicate only the extent to which earnings cover the dividend requirements of the preferred stock.

Since HSY does not have preferred stock, the coverage ratios do not apply. However, how each ratio is computed can be illustrated by the following simple example. A firm in the 40 percent tax bracket has earnings of $6 million before income taxes. It has 100,000 shares of preferred stock outstanding, and each share pays a dividend of $5. The times-dividend-earned ratio is

$$\frac{\$6,000,000 - \$2,400,000}{\$500,000} = 7.2,$$

and the earnings per preferred share are

$$\frac{\$6,000,000 - \$2,400,000}{100,000} = \$36.$$

Both ratios, in effect, show the same thing. In the first, the preferred dividend is covered by a multiple of 7.2 to 1. The second ratio shows an earnings per preferred share of $36, which is 7.2 times the $5 dividend paid for each share.

As with times-interest-earned, high numerical values imply the dividend is safe. Greater earnings and more liquidity imply that the dividend payment will be made. Even if the coverage is low or negative or if the firm is experiencing a loss, management may continue to pay preferred dividends if the firm has sufficient cash. The preferred dividends might be paid despite any losses to indicate that the loss is expected to be temporary and that the firm is financially sound.

ANALYSIS OF FINANCIAL STATEMENTS, SECURITIES SELECTION, AND THE INTERNET

If you do not want to calculate the ratios used to analyze a firm's financial statements, you may find much of the analysis at various Internet sites such as Yahoo!. Financial firms, especially electronic brokerage firms such as Schwab or Scottrade,

EXHIBIT 8.5 Ratios from Different Internet Sources for Hershey Foods

Ratio	MSN Money	Reuters	Yahoo!	Scottrade
Current Ratio	1.1	1.1	1.1	1.1
Operating Profit Margin	—	11.9%	15.2	11.9
Net Profit Margin	6.2%	6.2	6.2	6.2
Return on Assets	8.6%	8.6	13.0	8.6
Return on Equity	68.9%	68.9	68.9	68.9

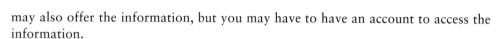

Addresses for each site:
MSN Money: **http://moneycentral.msn.com**
Reuters: **http://www.reuters.com**
Yahoo!: **http://finance.yahoo.com**
Scottrade: **http://scottrade.com**

may also offer the information, but you may have to have an account to access the information.

Exhibit 8.5 provides selected financial ratios for Hershey Foods that are readily available on the Web. Not all the ratios may be given, and the values can differ for different sites. Such differences may be the result of the time periods used, such as the last 12 months, referred to as "trailing twelve months" or TTM, versus the firm's last fiscal year. Different data may be used in the calculation. For example, one source may use earnings without adjusting for nonoperating and other gains and losses while another source may use adjusted earnings. Varying definitions of a particular ratio may also explain differences.

These differences pose a problem for the investor who wants to make comparisons. One obvious solution is for the individual to compute the ratios, in which case the definitions and time periods can be applied consistently. A more pragmatic solution may be to use one source exclusively. The choice could then depend on which source provides the desired data. For example, one source may provide both the company's ratios and the ratios for the industry.

Once you have determined the appropriate source for the data, ratios can be used to screen companies to isolate firms that meet specific criteria. For example, you can specify a return on equity of at least 20 percent, and a dividend yield of 2.5 percent. The computer then searches the database to identify all firms that meet these specified criteria. If the number is large, the criteria may be made more rigorous or additional criteria may be added to the screening process.

Unfortunately, a data search does not answer the fundamental question: Is the stock under- or overvalued? The search only isolates all stocks that meet the specified criteria. If you want to identify all stocks with a dividend yield of 2.5 percent and a return on equity of 20 percent, the resulting list will be based on the current dividend. There is no assurance that the current dividend will be maintained. The return on equity will be based on the firm's income statement and balance sheet, both of which are historical. The next year's earnings could be lower, so the desired return on equity might not be maintained. While screening limits the number of stocks to those that meet the criteria, these filter techniques are at best starting points in the analysis of securities for possible inclusion in a portfolio.

ANALYSIS OF CASH FLOW

The previous sections have been devoted to the analysis of a firm's income statement and balance sheet with emphasis placed on profitability and *net* earnings available to the common stockholder. However, increased interest has developed among financial analysts in a firm's *operating* earnings and cash flow. Net earnings may be affected by numerous factors that have little meaning from the perspective of a firm's operations. For example, the use of straight-line depreciation instead of accelerated depreciation will increase earnings (and taxes) but does not affect the firm's operations. Other items, such as the sale of an appreciated asset, an increase in reserves to cover losses on accounts receivable, or changes in inventory valuation, can have an impact on the firm's net income, but these events need not affect current or future operations.

The previous examples suggest that earnings could be affected without affecting operations. Because these examples may be nonrecurring (e.g., the sale of an asset occurs only once), net income from different accounting periods may not be comparable. In addition, the firm could have recurring earnings and still not be generating cash. For example, if firm A owns stock of firm B, this investment can affect earnings but not operations. Firm A may report as part of its earnings the earnings of firm B (i.e., firm A picks up its proportional share of firm B's earnings), but that does not necessarily mean that firm A receives cash. If firm B retains the earnings, firm A obviously does not receive any cash for the earnings it is reporting. For a firm like Berkshire Hathaway, which has substantial equity investments in other firms, a large proportion of its earnings are independent of its own operations and do not represent the receipt of cash.

Because net earnings may be affected by nonrecurring items or need not represent cash, many financial analysts place more emphasis on cash flow. The argument is that the cash flow generated by a firm's operations is a better indication of its profitability and value. Instead of isolating income, these analysts determine the capacity of the firm to generate cash and use this information for their valuation of the firm.

Statement of Cash Flows

statement of cash flows

An accounting statement that enumerates a firm's cash inflows and cash outflows.

The increased emphasis on the generation of cash has led to the creation of the **statement of cash flows**. This statement determines changes in the firm's holding of cash and cash equivalents (i.e., short-term liquid assets, such as Treasury bills). The emphasis is not on income or the firm's assets and liabilities but on the inflows and outflows of cash from the firm's operations, investments, and financing decisions.

The statement of cash flows for Hershey Foods Corporation is presented in Exhibit 8.6. The statement is divided into three sections: (1) operating activities, (2) investment activities, and (3) financing activities. Each section enumerates the inflow and outflow of cash. The cash inflows are the following:

1. A decrease in an asset
2. An increase in a liability
3. An increase in equity

| EXHIBIT | 8.6 | Hershey Foods Corporation Consolidated Statement of Cash Flows for the Years Ended December 31 (in millions) |

	2008	2007	2006
Operating activities			
Net income	311.4	214.2	559.0
Adjustments to reconcile net income to net cash (used in) provided by operating activities			
Depreciation and amortization	249.5	310.9	199.9
Deferred income taxes	−17.1	−124.3	4.2
(Gains) losses on sales of business net of tax	0.0	0.0	0.0
Other	108.7	261.3	0.4
Changes in operating assets and liabilities, net of acquisitions and dispositions			
Accounts receivable	31.6	40.5	−14.9
Inventories	7.7	45.3	−12.5
Accounts payable and accrued expenses	26.4	62.2	−13.2
Other assets and liabilities	−198.6	−31.3	0.3
Net cash provided by (used in) operating activities	519.6	778.8	723.2
Investing activities			
Purchases of property, plant, and equipment	−262.6	−189.7	−183.5
Proceeds from (purchases of) sale of businesses	82.8	0.0	0.0
Other	−18.4	−9.5	−32.0
Net cash provided by (used in) investing activities	−198.2	−304.4	−215.5
Financing activities			
Net borrowing (payments) on credit lines	−371.4	195.1	−163.8
Payments on long-term debt	−5.0	−188.9	0.0
Proceeds from issuance of long-term debt	247.8	0.0	496.7
Proceeds from issuances of common stock	37.0	50.5	37.1
Repurchase of stock	−60.4	−256.3	−621.6
Dividends paid	−262.9	−252.3	−235.1
Other	−1.5	−9.0	−9.5
Net cash provided by (used in) financing activities	−413.4	−442.4	−477.7
Increase (decrease) in cash equivalents	−92.1	32.1	30.0
Cash and cash equivalents at beginning of year	129.2	97.1	67.2
Cash and cash equivalents at end of year	37.1	129.2	97.2

Source: Adapted from Hershey Foods Corporation Proxy Statement and 2008 and 2006 10-K Reports.

The cash outflows are the following:

1. An increase in an asset
2. A decrease in a liability
3. A decrease in equity

The statement of cash flows starts with a firm's earnings and works through various entries to determine the change in the firm's cash and cash equivalents. As is illustrated in Exhibit 8.6, Hershey Foods starts with earnings of $311.4 million. Since earnings are not synonymous with cash, adjustments must be made to put earnings on a cash basis. The first adjustment is to add back all noncash expenses and deduct noncash revenues. The most important of these adjustments is usually depreciation, the noncash expense that allocates the cost of plant and equipment over a period of time. Other noncash expenses may include depletion of raw materials and amortization of intangible assets such as goodwill. In this illustration, Hershey has depreciation expense of $249.5 million, which is added to the firm's earnings.

Next, deferred taxes are added to earnings plus noncash expenses. Earnings are determined after subtracting taxes owed for the time period but not necessarily paid. A firm may be able to defer paying some taxes until the future, so these deferred taxes do not result in an outflow of cash during the current accounting period. Although taxes actually paid are a cash outflow, deferred taxes recognized during the time period are not a cash outflow and are added back to earnings to determine the cash generated by operations.

In 2008, Hershey experienced a decrease in deferred taxes of $17.1 million. Since the taxes were paid, there was a cash outflow, and the amount of the deferred tax is subtracted to determine cash from operations. An increase in deferred taxes would indicate that deferred taxes were not paid and were a cash inflow. In that case, the change in deferred taxes would be added, as occurred during 2006.

Gains from the sale of plant and equipment are also subtracted. Since these gains are included in the sale of the plant and equipment in the section on investment activities, failure to subtract the gain (or add any loss) would double count the profit as generating cash from the sale and from the earnings from the sale. For Hershey no gains or losses occurred in 2008. The last line in the section on operating activities is miscellaneous cash flows ("other"). For Hershey these cash outflows were primarily cash contributions to pension plans made during 2008.

The next set of entries refers to changes in the firm's current assets and liabilities resulting from operations. Some of these generate cash while others consume it. If accounts receivable increase, that means the firm experienced a net increase in credit sales. These credit sales do not generate cash until the receivables are collected. If the receivables had declined, the firm would have experienced an increase in collections, which would be a cash inflow. In 2008, Hershey's receivables declined by $31.6, which is inflow.

An increase in inventory, like an increase in accounts receivable, is a cash outflow. More inventory is purchased than is sold, so there is a cash outflow. If the firm's inventory declines, it experiences a cash inflow. A reduction in inventory indicates that less inventory was purchased than was sold. This cash inflow would be added to determine cash generated by operations. During 2008, Hershey's inventory decreased by $7.7, and this cash inflow is added to determine cash generated by operations.

These effects on cash by changes in accounts receivable and inventory also apply to other current assets. An increase in a current asset, other than cash or cash equivalents, is a cash outflow, while a decrease is a cash inflow. For example, if the firm prepays an insurance policy or makes a lease or rent payment at the beginning of the month, these payments are cash outflows. However, they are also increases in the asset prepaid expense; thus, the increase in the asset represents a cash outflow.

In addition to changes in current assets, normal day-to-day operations will alter the firm's current liabilities. Wages will accrue and other trade accounts may rise. An increase in the firm's payables is a cash inflow, because the cash has not yet been paid. A decrease in payables results when the accounts are paid, thus becoming a cash outflow. Hershey experienced an increase of $26.4 million in accounts payable and other accrued expenses.

The sum of all the adjustments to income and the changes in operating current assets and current liabilities is the net cash provided by operating activities. Hershey experienced a net cash inflow from operations of $519.6 million during 2008. This operating cash flow exceeded the firm's reported income of $311.4 million.

After the adjustments to income and the changes in current assets and current liabilities from operations, the statement of cash flows considers cash generated by investment activities. The acquisition of plant and equipment requires a cash outflow, whereas the sale of plant and equipment generates cash (an inflow). Expanding firms often need additional investments in plant and equipment, which consume cash. A stagnating firm with excess capacity may sell plant and equipment, which generates cash. Hershey purchased plant and equipment ($262.6 million), which is a cash outflow. The firm also bought a business (a cash outflow of $82.8 million). The remaining entry is a cash outflow of $18.4 million. The net effect of its investment decisions was a cash outflow of $198.2 million.

The third part of the statement of cash flows covers the firm's financing decisions. Financing activities can be for either the long or the short term. Issuing new debt produces a cash inflow, so an increase in short-term liabilities (such as a bank loan) or long-term liabilities (such as a bond) is a source of cash. (Notice that a change in the current liability "net borrowings on credit lines" is treated in the section on financing activities and is not included with the changes in other current liabilities under operating activities.) A reduction in bank loans or outstanding bonds requires a cash outflow. Issuing new stock (an increase in equity) generates a cash inflow, while redeeming stock or paying cash dividends are cash outflows.

The cash inflows and outflows from Hershey Foods Corporation's financing decisions include net reduction in short-term borrowing ($371.4 million) and a net increase in long-term debt of $242.8 million ($-5.0 + 242.8$). Hershey repurchased stock (an outflow of $60.4 million) and paid $262.9 million in dividends. Other cash outflows were $1.5 million and included the exercising of options by employees.

The bottom line in the statement of cash flows indicates the firm's cash position at the end of the accounting period. If the sum of the cash inflows from operations, investments, and financing is positive, the firm experienced a cash inflow. If the sum is negative, the result is a cash outflow. For Hershey Foods, outflows exceeded inflows by $92.1, which decreased the cash and cash equivalents from $129.2 million to $37.1 million.

What does the statement of cash flows add to the financial analyst's knowledge? By placing emphasis on inflows and outflows, the statement highlights where the firm generated cash and how the funds were used. Hershey experienced an increase in cash from operations, which was used to buy plant and equipment, and pay cash dividends. These outflows, however, exceeded the cash inflows from operations, so the net effect was to reduce the firm's cash position.

SUMMARY

A corporation is an economic unit created (i.e., chartered) by a state. Ownership in a corporation is represented by stock, which may be readily transferred from one individual to another. In addition, investors in publicly held corporations have limited liability.

After a corporation generates earnings, it may distribute them as dividends or retain them to finance future growth or retire debt. As earnings grow, dividends may also increase, but there is usually a lag between an increase in earnings and an increase in the cash dividend.

In addition to cash dividends, some firms distribute stock dividends. These dividends and stock splits do not increase the earning capacity of the firm. Instead they are recapitalizations that alter the number of shares the firm has outstanding. Since stock dividends and stock splits do not alter the firm's earning capacity, the price of the stock adjusts for the change in the number of shares.

Ratio analysis is frequently used to analyze a firm's financial statements. These ratios are easy to compute and employ data that are readily available on a firm's financial statements. Ratios facilitate comparisons. A firm's current financial position may be compared to those of previous years or to other firms within its industry. A summary of the ratios presented in this chapter is provided below.

Financial analysis also places emphasis on the firm's ability to generate cash. The statement of cash flows enumerates the firm's cash inflows and outflows. Increases in liabilities or equity and decreases in assets are inflows. Decreases in liabilities or equity and increases in assets are outflows. By specifying cash inflows and outflows, the statement of cash flows indicates where funds come from and how they are used. It determines if the firm's cash position has improved or deteriorated.

Although ratios are often used to analyze a firm's financial position, they do not answer this question: Should the stock be bought or sold? Ratios by themselves cannot answer that question. A high return on equity, a low debt ratio, or sufficient liquidity to meet current obligations are all positive factors, but they do not put a value on the stock. That valuation is the subject of the next chapter.

Summary of Ratio Definitions

1. Liquidity ratios:
Current ratio:

$$\frac{\text{Current assets}}{\text{Current liabilities}}$$

Quick ratio:

$$\frac{\text{Current assets} - \text{inventory}}{\text{Current liabilities}}$$

2. Activity ratios
Inventory turnover:

$$\frac{\text{Sales}}{\text{Average inventory}}$$

or

$$\frac{\text{Cost of goods sold}}{\text{Average inventory}}$$

(The denominator may be defined as year-end inventory instead of average inventory.)
Average collection period:

$$\frac{\text{Receivables}}{\text{Sales per day}}$$

Receivables turnover:

$$\frac{\text{Annual credit sales}}{\text{Accounts receivable}}$$

or

$$\frac{\text{Annual sales}}{\text{Accounts receivable}}$$

(If credit sales are not given, the first definition of receivables turnover cannot be computed.)

Fixed asset turnover:

$$\frac{\text{Annual sales}}{\text{Fixed assets}}$$

Total asset turnover:

$$\frac{\text{Annual sales}}{\text{Total assets}}$$

3. Profitability ratios

Gross profit margin:

$$\frac{\text{Sales} - \text{Cost of goods sold}}{\text{Sales}}$$

Operating profit margin:

$$\frac{\text{Operating earnings}}{\text{Sales}}$$

Net profit margin:

$$\frac{\text{Earnings after taxes}}{\text{Sales}}$$

Return on assets:

$$\frac{\text{Earnings after taxes}}{\text{Total assets}}$$

Return on equity:

$$\frac{\text{Earnings after taxes}}{\text{Equity}}$$

Return on common equity:

$$\frac{\text{Earnings after taxes} - \text{Preferred dividends}}{\text{Equity} - \text{Preferred stock}}$$

4. Leverage ratios

Debt/net worth:

$$\frac{\text{Debt}}{\text{Equity}}$$

Debt ratio:

$$\frac{\text{Debt}}{\text{Total assets}}$$

5. Coverage ratios
Times-interest-earned:

$$\frac{\text{Earnings before interest and taxes}}{\text{Annual interest expense}}$$

Times-dividend-earned:

$$\frac{\text{Earnings after taxes}}{\text{Dividend on preferred stock}}$$

Earnings per preferred share:

$$\frac{\text{Earnings after taxes}}{\text{Number of preferred shares outstanding}}$$

QUESTIONS

1. What does it mean for investors who purchase IBM stock to have limited liability?
2. What is the purpose of each of the following?
   a) Preemptive rights
   b) Cumulative voting
   c) The board of directors
3. Why may a dividend increment lag after an increase in earnings? Why may a firm distribute dividends even though earnings decline?
4. What are the differences among the *ex-dividend date*, the *date of record*, and the *distribution date*?
5. What are the advantages associated with dividend reinvestment plans?
6. How do stock dividends differ from cash dividends? How do stock dividends differ from stock splits?
7. What are the tax implications of the following?
   a) Dividend reinvestment plans
   b) Stock dividends
   c) Stock splits
   d) Corporate stock repurchases?
8. How does preferred stock differ from common stock?
9. If a preferred stock is in arrearage, what does that imply about the dividend payment?
10. What is the difference between the following?
    a) Cross-sectional and time-series analysis
    b) The current ratio and the quick ratio
    c) Receivables turnover, inventory turnover, and fixed asset turnover
    d) The gross profit margin, the operating profit margin, and the net profit margin
    e) The return on assets and the return on equity
    f) Debt to total assets and debt to equity
    g) Times-interest-earned and times-dividend-earned
11. What does the statement of cash flows add to the analyst's knowledge of the firm?

12. Obtain Hershey's financial statements for the subsequent years and update the ratios presented in this chapter. Has the firm's financial position deteriorated, improved, or essentially stayed the same? You may find the financial statements at Hershey's home page http://www.hersheys.com. Financial statements are also available through Mergent Online (http://mergentonline.com). Compare your results with ratios found on the Internet at sites such as Yahoo! (http://finance .yahoo.com) or Reuters (http://www.reuters.com). Are there major differences between your results and the ratios you located through the Internet?

13. Select three firms in an industry such as pharmaceuticals or homebuilding and compare the following ratios for the three firms: current ratio, debt ratio, return on assets, return on equity, and net profit margin. Are there similarities among the firms in each industry group? You may use the sites provided in the previous question to obtain the ratios.

PROBLEMS

1. An investor buys 100 shares of a $40 stock that pays an annual cash dividend of $2 a share (a 5 percent dividend yield) and signs up for the dividend reinvestment plan.

   a) If neither the dividend nor the price changes, how many shares will the investor have at the end of ten years? How much will the position in the stock be worth?

   b) If the price of the stock rises by 6 percent annually but the dividend remains at $2 a share, how many shares are purchased each year for the next ten years? How much is the total position worth at the end of ten years?

   c) If the price of the stock rises by 6 percent annually but the dividend rises by only 3 percent annually, how many shares are purchased each year for the next ten years? How much is the total position worth at the end of ten years? Since dividend plans credit fractional shares, use three decimal places in parts (b) and (c).

2. A firm has the following items on its balance sheet:

Cash	$ 20,000,000
Inventory	134,000,000
Notes payable to bank	31,500,000
Common stock ($10 par; 1,000,000 shares outstanding)	10,000,000
Retained earnings	98,500,000

Describe how each of these accounts would appear after the following:

   a) A cash dividend of $1 per share

   b) A 10 percent stock dividend (fair market value of stock is $13 per share)

   c) A 3-for-1 stock split

   d) A 1-for-2 reverse stock split

3. A company whose stock is selling for $60 has the following balance sheet:

Assets	$30,000,000	Liabilities	$14,000,000
		Preferred stock	1,000,000
		Common stock ($12 par;	
		100,000 shares outstanding)	1,200,000
		Paid-in capital	1,800,000
		Retained earnings	12,000,000

   a) Construct a new balance sheet showing the effects of a 3-for-1 stock split. What is the new price of the stock?
   b) Construct a new balance sheet showing the effects of a 10 percent stock dividend. What will be the approximate new price of the stock?

4. Using the income statement and balance sheet presented here, compute the following ratios. Compare your results with the industry averages. What strengths and weaknesses are apparent?

Ratio	Industry Average
Current ratio	2:1
Acid test (quick ratio)	1:1
Inventory turnover	
a. Annual sales	4.0×
b. Cost of goods sold	2.3×
Receivables turnover	
a. Annual credit sales	5.0×
b. Annual sales	6.0×
c. Average collection period	2.5 months
Operating profit margin	26%
Net profit margin	19%
Return on assets	10%
Return on equity	15%
Debt ratio	
a. Debt/equity	33%
b. Debt/total assets	25%
Times-interest-earned	7.1×

Income Statement for XYZ
for the period ending December 31, 20X1

Sales	$100,000
Cost of goods sold	60,000
Gross profit	40,000
Selling and administrative expense	15,000
Operating profit	25,000
Interest expense	5,000
Earnings before taxes	20,000
Taxes	3,200
Earnings available to stockholders	$ 16,800
Number of shares outstanding	10,000
Earnings per share	$1.68

(To compute the inventory turnover, assume that the prior year's inventory was $40,000.)

Firm XYZ
Balance Sheet as of December 31, 20X1 Assets

Current assets		
Cash and marketable securities		$ 10,000
Accounts receivable	$ 32,000	
Less allowance for doubtful accounts	2,000	30,000
Inventory		
Finished goods	30,000	
Work in progress	5,000	
Raw materials	7,000	42,000
Total current assets		$ 82,000
Investments		$ 10,000
Long-term assets		
Plant and equipment	100,000	
Less accumulated depreciation	30,000	70,000
Land		10,000
Total long-term assets		$ 80,000
Total assets		$172,000

Liabilities & Stockholders' Equity

Current liabilities	
Accounts payable	$ 10,000
Accrued wages	11,000
Bank notes	15,000
Accrued interest payable	4,000
Accrued taxes	1,000
Total current liabilities	$ 41,000
Long-term debt	$ 15,000
Total liabilities	$ 56,000
Stockholders' equity	
Common stock ($1 par value; 20,000 shares authorized; 10,000 shares outstanding)	$ 10,000
Additional paid-in capital	20,000
Retained earnings	86,000
Total stockholders' equity	$116,000
Total liabilities and equity	$172,000

5. You have taken the following information from a firm's financial statements. As an investor in the firm's debt instruments, you are concerned with its liquidity

position and its use of financial leverage. What conclusions can you draw from this information?

	2010	2009	2008
Sales	$1,700,000	$1,500,000	$1,000,000
Cash	18,000	7,000	5,000
Accounts receivable	152,000	130,000	125,000
Inventory	200,000	190,000	200,000
Current liabilities	225,000	210,000	175,000
Operating income	170,000	145,000	90,000
Interest expense	27,000	23,000	20,000
Taxes	53,000	45,000	25,000
Net income	90,000	77,000	45,000
Debt	260,000	250,000	200,000
Equity	330,000	300,000	200,000

6. What is the debt/equity ratio and the debt ratio for a firm with total debt of $700,000 and equity of $300,000?

7. A firm with sales of $500,000 has average inventory of $200,000. The industry average for inventory turnover is four times a year. What would be the reduction in inventory if this firm were to achieve a turnover comparable to the industry average?

8. If a firm has sales of $42,791,000 a year, and the average collection period for the industry is 40 days, what should be this firm's accounts receivable if the firm is comparable to the industry?

9. Two firms have sales of $1 million each. Other financial information is as follows:

	Firm A	Firm B
EBIT	$150,000	$150,000
Interest expense	20,000	75,000
Income tax	50,000	30,000
Equity	300,000	100,000

What are the operating profit margins and the net profit margins for these two firms? What is their return on equity? Why are they different? If total assets are the same for each firm, what can you conclude about their respective uses of debt financing?

10. Determine the times-dividend-earned ratio given the following information:

   30% corporate income tax rate
   $10,000 earnings before interest and taxes
   $2,000 interest owed
   $2,000 preferred stock dividends

11. A firm with earnings before interest and taxes of $500,000 needs $1 million of additional funds. If it issues debt, the bonds will mature after 20 years and pay interest of 8 percent. The firm could issue preferred stock with a dividend rate of 8 percent. The firm has 100,000 shares of common stock outstanding and is in the 30 percent income tax bracket. What are the (1) earnings per common share under the two alternatives, (2) the times-interest-earned if the firm uses debt financing, and (3) the times-dividend-earned if the firm uses preferred stock financing?

INVESTMENT ASSIGNMENT (PART 3)

In Part 1 you invested $10,000 in each of ten stocks and set up a watch account at a site such as Yahoo! Finance. Some of the sites provide the ratios illustrated in this chapter. This assignment asks you to determine if any of the stocks you selected meet any of the following ratio requirements:

Current ratio	at least 1:1
Profit margin	minimum of 8%
Return on assets	minimum of 10%
Return on equity	minimum of 15%
Long-term debt to total assets	not to exceed 40%

(Most sources use long-term debt and not total liabilities. If you wish to use total liabilities to compute the debt ratio, you may find that information on the firm's balance sheet.)

Although these ratios do not indicate whether the stock is over- or undervalued (that is addressed in the next chapter), they can be a good place to start. For example, if the return on assets and the return on equity are negative, you might want to ask if you desire to own a stock that is operating at a loss.

The Financial Advisor's Investment Case
Strategies to Increase Equity

Christina Molitoris is preparing for a meeting of the board of directors of Chesapeake Bay Corporation, a developer of moderate-priced homes and vacation homes in the Chesapeake Bay area. The combination of the location near major metropolitan areas with the recreational facilities associated with the Chesapeake Bay has made the firm one of the most successful homebuilders in the nation. During the last five years, the firm's cash dividend has risen from $2.10 to $3.74, and the price of its stock has risen from $36 to $75. Since the firm has 1,200,000 shares outstanding, the market value of the stock is $90,000,000. Given the volatile nature of its industry, the increases in the price of the stock and in the dividend were substantial achievements.

Management, however, is considering entering into nonbuilding areas in an effort to diversify the firm. These new investments will require more financing. Although additional debt financing is a possibility, management believes that it is unwise to issue only new debt and not increase the firm's equity base. New equity could be obtained by issuing additional stock or reducing the dividend and thus retaining a larger proportion of the firm's earnings. Two major points had previously been raised against these strategies: Issuing additional shares may dilute the existing stockholders' position, and reducing the dividend could cause the value of the stock to decline.

Even though it is possible that no change will be made and that the firm will continue its present course, the board believes that a thorough discussion of all possibilities is desirable. Ms. Molitoris has been instructed to develop alternatives to the two strategies for the next meeting of the board in two weeks.

The short period for preparation means that a thorough analysis may be impossible, especially of the possible impact of a dividend cut on the value of the stock, but Ms. Molitoris presumes that some additional alternatives do exist. One of her assistants suggested that the firm institute a dividend reinvestment plan, in which additional shares would be sold to stockholders to raise additional equity capital. Her other assistant suggested that the company substitute a 5 percent stock dividend for the cash dividend. Before making either (or both) suggestions to the board, Ms. Molitoris decided to seek your help in answering several questions:

1. Would implementing the suggestions dilute the existing stockholders' position?
2. How much new equity would be raised by each action?
3. What may happen to the price of the stock?
4. What are the costs associated with each strategy?
5. Would a stock split combined with either strategy help raise additional equity financing?
6. Would an increase in the cash dividend coupled with the dividend reinvestment plan help raise additional equity financing?
7. Is there any reason to prefer or exclude any one of the four strategies (that is, issuing new shares, reducing the dividend, instituting a dividend reinvestment plan, or substituting a stock dividend for the cash dividend)?

CHAPTER 9

The Valuation of Common Stock

LEARNING OBJECTIVES

After completing this chapter you should be able to:

1. Identify the components of an investor's required rate of return.
2. Distinguish between required and expected returns.
3. Examine the determinants of a stock's price.
4. Calculate the value of a stock using a simple present value model.
5. Explain how to use P/E ratios, price-to-sales ratios, price-to-book ratios, and PEG ratios to select stocks.
6. Identify the weaknesses associated with ratios such as P/E, P/S, and P/B.
7. Discern the implication of the Fama-French study of investment returns.

You are considering purchasing IBM's stock and want information to facilitate your decision. From a source such as MSN Money (**http://moneycentral.msn.com**) or Yahoo! Finance (**http://finance.yahoo.com**) you type in the IBM ticker symbol, which leads you to price quotes and various links such as company profile, analyst ratings, and financials. Financials sounds dull and you believe that you already know IBM's profile. You click on analyst ratings and find 20 ratings ranging from "strong buy" to "strong sell." You also find earnings estimates for the next year which range from $4.84 to $5.55. You click on an additional link for evaluation. The evaluation tells you the stock's price is in a "buy zone" and the buy zone ranges from $66 to $111. If you do buy the stock at its current price of $100, the stock could decline 34 percent and still be in the buy zone.

You are facing one of the most elusive and perplexing questions for every investor. What is the stock worth? What is its current value? Without some estimate of the current value, the decision to buy will be based on hunches, intuition, or tips. What do you do? A financial psychologist (or cynic) might suggest that you latch on to the specific information that confirms a preconceived desire to buy IBM. But in any event, you must have some notion as to the value of the stock in order to justify the purchase of IBM.

Conceptually, the valuation of a stock is the same as the valuation of a bond or any asset. In each case, future cash flows are discounted back to their present value. For debt instruments this process is relatively easy because debt instruments pay a fixed amount of interest and mature at a specified date. Common stock, however, does not pay a fixed dividend, nor does it mature. These two facts considerably increase the difficulty of valuing common stock.

Initially this chapter considers the expected return, which is the sum of dividends and capital gains. This expected or required return is used in a discounted cash flow model for the valuation of common stock. After this initial presentation, the investor's required return is adjusted for the systematic risk associated with the stock.

The dividend-discounted flow model cannot be applied to non-dividend-paying stocks. Alternative methods for valuation include multiplier techniques such as the price-to-earnings (P/E) ratio, the price-to-book (P/B) ratio, the price-to-sales (P/S) ratio, and the PEG ratio. The chapter ends with a discussion of stock valuation and the efficient market hypothesis. Some evidence does exist to suggest that markets are not completely efficient and that the use of fundamental analysis of a firm's financial statements may lead to higher risk-adjusted returns.

THE INVESTOR'S EXPECTED RETURN

Investors purchase stock with the anticipation of a total return consisting of a dividend yield and a capital gain. The dividend yield is the flow of dividend income paid by the stock. The capital gain is the increase in the value of the stock that is related to the growth in earnings. If the firm is able to achieve growth in earnings, then dividends can be increased, and over time the shares should grow in value.

The expected return on an investment, which was discussed in Chapter 5 and expressed algebraically in Equation 5.1, is reproduced here:

$$E(r) = \frac{E(D)}{P} + E(g).$$

The expected return, $E(r)$, is the sum of the dividend yield, which is the expected dividend $E(D)$ divided by the price of the stock (P) plus the expected growth rate $E(g)$. If a firm's $0.93 dividend is expected to grow at 7 percent to $1.00 and the price of the stock is $25, the anticipated annual return on an investment in the stock is

$$E(r) = \frac{\$1}{\$25} + 0.07 = 0.11 = 11\%.$$

For an investment to be attractive, the expected return must be equal to or exceed the investor's required return. (Specification of the required return will be discussed later in this chapter.) If an individual requires an 11 percent return on investments in

---

⊕ Point of Interest

REAL RETURNS

As used in this text, the word *returns* implies nominal returns; no adjustment is made for the rate of inflation. If such an adjustment were made, the resulting returns would be expressed in *real* terms. Real returns measure the increase in purchasing power earned by the investor. If the nominal return was 15 percent when the rate of inflation was 10 percent, the investor is worse off than the investor who earns a nominal return of 10 percent during a period when prices increase by only 3 percent. In the latter case, the investor earns a higher real return.

The real return (i.e., the inflation-adjusted return) that the investor earns may be determined by the following equation:

$$\left(\frac{1 + \text{nominal return}}{1 + \text{rate of inflation}} - 1\right) \times 100\%.$$

Thus, if the rate of nominal return is 15 percent when the rate of inflation is 10 percent, the real return is

$$\left(\frac{1 + 0.15}{1 + 0.10} - 1\right) \times 100\% = 4.545\%.$$

This rate is less than the real return when the nominal return is 10 percent and the rate of inflation is 3 percent. Under that circumstance the real return is

$$\left(\frac{1 + 0.10}{1 + 0.03} - 1\right) \times 100\% = 6.796\%.$$

There is no doubt that inflation has eroded the purchasing power of the dollar. Research on returns and inflation indicates that, over an extended period, the return on common stocks has exceeded the rate of inflation by about 6 percent.* This suggests that individuals who invested for the long haul earned a real return on their positions in common stock.

*See *Stocks, Bonds, Bills, and Inflation Yearbook* (Chicago: Ibbotson Associates, published annually). The Web address is **http://corporate.morningstar.com**.

common stock of comparable risk, then this stock meets the investor's requirement. If, however, the investor's required rate of return is in excess of 11 percent, the anticipated yield on this stock is inferior, and the investor will not purchase the shares. Conversely, if the required rate of return on comparable investments in common stock is 10 percent, this particular stock is an excellent purchase because the anticipated return exceeds the required rate of return.

In a world of no commission fees and in which the tax on dividends is the same as on capital gains, investors would be indifferent to the composition of their return. An investor seeking an 11 percent return should be willing to accept a dividend yield of zero if the capital gain is 11 percent. Conversely, a capital growth rate of zero should be acceptable if the dividend yield is 11 percent. Of course, any combination of growth rate and dividend yield with an 11 percent return should be acceptable.

However, because of commissions and taxes, the investor may be concerned with the composition of the return. To realize the growth in the value of the shares, the investor must sell the security and pay commissions. This cost suggests a preference for dividend yield. In addition, capital gains occur in the future and may be less certain than the flow of current dividends. The uncertainty of future capital gains versus the likelihood of current dividends also favors dividends over capital appreciation.

Prior to the changes in the federal tax laws in 2003, dividends were taxed at a higher rate than long-term capital gains. As of 2010, the highest rate on both is 15 percent. (The rate on short-term capital gains is the individual's marginal tax rate. This difference in the taxation of short-term and long-term capital gains is an obvious incentive to hold the stock for at least a year and a day.) The 15 percent tax rate on dividends and long-term capital gains certainly levels the playing field. However, there remains a tax argument favoring long-term capital gains. The tax may be deferred until the gains are realized; the tax on dividends cannot be deferred. (The frequent changes in the federal income tax laws points out the need to keep abreast of tax regulations and to reconsider their impact on the composition of your portfolio.)

VALUATION AS THE PRESENT VALUE OF DIVIDENDS AND THE GROWTH OF DIVIDENDS

Value investing primarily focuses on what an asset is worth—its intrinsic value. As with the valuation of any asset, the valuation of stock involves bringing future cash inflows (e.g., dividends) back to the present at the appropriate discount factor. For the individual investor, that discount factor is the required return, which is the return the investor demands to justify purchasing the stock. This return includes what the investor may earn on a risk-free security (e.g., a Treasury bill) plus a premium for bearing the risk associated with investments in common stock.

The process of valuation and security selection is similar to comparing expected and required returns, except the emphasis is placed on determining what the investor believes the security is worth. Future cash inflows are discounted back to the present at the required rate of return. The resulting valuation is then compared with the stock's current price to determine if the stock is under- or overvalued. Thus, valuation compares dollar amounts. The dollar value of the stock is compared with its price. Returns compare percentages. The expected percentage return is compared to the required return. In either case, the decision will be the same. If the valuation exceeds the price, the expected return will exceed the required return.

The process of valuation and security selection is readily illustrated by the simple case in which the stock pays a fixed dividend of $1 that is not expected to change. That is, the anticipated cash inflow is

Year	1	2	3	4	. . .
Dividend	$1	$1	$1	$1	. . .

The current value of this indefinite flow of payments (i.e., the dividend) depends on the discount rate (i.e., the investor's required rate of return). If this rate is 12 percent, the stock's value (V) is

$$V = \frac{\$1}{(1 + 0.12)^1} + \frac{1}{(1 + 0.12)^2} + \frac{1}{(1 + 0.12)^3} + \frac{1}{(1 + 0.12)^4} + \cdots,$$

$$V = \$8.33.$$

This process is expressed in the following equation in which the new variables are the dividend (D) and the required rate of return (k):

9.1
$$V = \frac{D}{(1 + k)^1} + \frac{D}{(1 + k)^2} + \cdots + \frac{D}{(1 + k)^\infty},$$

which simplifies to

9.2
$$V = \frac{D}{k}.$$

If a stock pays a dividend of $1 and the investor's required rate of return is 12 percent, then the valuation is

$$\frac{\$1}{0.12} = \$8.33.$$

Any price greater than $8.33 will result in a yield that is less than 12 percent. Therefore, for this investor to achieve the required rate of return of 12 percent, the price of the stock must not exceed $8.33.

There is, however, no reason to anticipate that common stock dividends will be fixed indefinitely into the future. Common stocks offer the potential for growth, both in value and in dividends. For example, if the investor expects the current $1 dividend to grow annually at 6 percent, the anticipated flow of dividend payments is

Year	1	2	3	. . .
Dividend	$1.06	$1.124	$1.191	. . .

The current value of this indefinite flow of growing payments (i.e., the growing dividend) also depends on the discount rate (i.e., the investor's required rate of return). If this rate is 12 percent, the stock's value is

$$V = \frac{1.06}{(1 + 0.12)^1} + \frac{1.124}{(1 + 0.12)^2} + \frac{1.191}{(1 + 0.12)^3} + \cdots,$$

$$V = \$17.67.$$

dividend-growth valuation model

A valuation model that uses dividends and their growth properly discounted back to the present.

Equation 9.1 may be modified for the growth in dividends. This is expressed in Equations 9.3 and 9.4. The only new variable is the rate of growth in the dividend (*g*). If it is assumed that this growth rate *is fixed and will continue indefinitely* into the future, the **dividend-growth valuation model** is

9.3
$$V = \frac{D(1 + g)^1}{(1 + k)^1} + \frac{D(1 + g)^2}{(1 + k)^2} + \frac{D(1 + g)^3}{(1 + k)^3} + \cdots + \frac{D(1 + g)^\infty}{(1 + k)^\infty},$$

which simplifies to

9.4
$$V = \frac{D_0(1 + g)}{k - g}.$$

The stock's intrinsic value depends on (1) the current dividend, (2) the growth in earnings and dividends, and (3) the required rate of return. Notice the current dividend is D_0, with the subscript 0 representing the present. The application of this dividend-growth model may be illustrated by a simple example. If the required rate of return is 12 percent and the stock is currently paying a $1 per share dividend growing at 6 percent annually, the stock's value is

$$V = \frac{\$1(1 + 0.06)}{0.12 - 0.06} = \$17.67.$$

Any price greater than $17.67 will result in a total return of less than 12 percent. Conversely, a price of less than $17.67 will produce an expected return in excess of 12 percent. For example, if the price is $20, the expected return is

$$E(r) = \frac{\$1(1 + 0.06)}{\$20} + 0.06$$

$$= 11.3\%.$$

(Notice the expected dividend is $1.06, which is the $1 current dividend plus the anticipated $0.06 (6 percent) increment in the dividend.) Because this return is less than the 12 percent required by the investor, this investor would not buy the stock and would sell it if he or she owned it.

If the price is $15, the expected return is

$$E(r) = \frac{\$1(1 + 0.06)}{\$15} + 0.06$$

$$= 13.1\%.$$

This return is greater than the 12 percent required by the investor. Since the security offers a superior return, it is undervalued. This investor then would try to buy the security.

Only at a price of $17.67 does the stock offer a return of 12 percent. At that price it equals the return available on alternative investments of the same risk. The investment will yield 12 percent because the dividend yield during the year is 6 percent and the earnings and dividends are growing annually at the rate of 6 percent. These relationships are illustrated in Figure 9.1, which shows the growth in dividends and prices of the stock that will produce a constant yield of 12 percent. After 12 years, the dividend will have grown to $2.02 and the price of the stock will be $35.55. The total return on

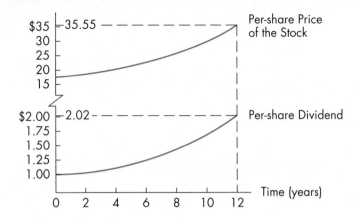

FIGURE   9.1   Earnings, Dividends, and Price of Stock over Time Yielding
                 12 Percent Annually

this investment remains 12 percent. During that year, the dividend will grow to $2.14, giving a 6 percent dividend yield, and the price will continue to appreciate annually at the 6 percent growth rate in earnings and dividends.

If the growth rate had been different (and the other variables remained constant), the valuation would have differed. The following illustration presents the value of the stock for various growth rates:

Growth Rate	Value of the Stock
0%	$ 8.83
3%	$ 11.78
9%	$ 35.33
11%	$106.00
12%	undefined (denominator = 0)

As the growth rate increases, so does the valuation, until the value becomes undefined (an exceedingly large number) when the growth rate equals the required return. This positive relationship indicates that when a stock offers more potential for capital gains, its valuation increases (if the dividend and the required return are *not affected* by the growth).

The dividend-growth valuation model assumes that the required return exceeds the rate of growth (i.e., $k > g$). While this may appear to be a restrictive assumption, it is logical. The purpose of the dividend-growth model is to *determine what the stock is worth and then to compare this value to the actual price in order to determine whether the stock should be purchased.* If a stock offers 14 percent when the investor requires 12 percent, the valuation is immaterial. It does not matter what the stock costs. Whether the price is $1 or $100,000 is irrelevant because you anticipate earning 14 percent on the amount invested when only 12 percent is required. Valuation can be material only if the growth rate (i.e., the potential capital gain) is less than the required return.

Although the previous model assumes that the firm's earnings will grow indefinitely and that the dividend policy will be maintained, such need not be the case. The dividend-growth model may be modified to encompass a period of increasing or declining growth or one of stable dividends. Many possible variations in growth patterns can be built into the model. Although these variations change the equation and make it appear far more complex, the fundamentals of valuation remain unaltered. Valuation is still the process of discounting future cash flows back to the present at the appropriate discount rate.

To illustrate such a variation, consider the following pattern of expected earnings and dividends.

Year	Earnings	Yearly Dividends	Percentage Change in Dividends from Previous Year
1	$1.00	$0.40	...
2	1.60	0.64	60.0%
3	1.94	0.77	20.3
4	2.20	0.87	13.0
5	2.29	0.905	4.0
6	2.38	0.941	4.0
7	2.48	0.979	4.0

After the initial period of rapid growth, the firm matures and is expected to grow annually at the rate of 4 percent. Each year the firm pays dividends, which contribute to its current value. However, the simple model summarized in Equation 9.4 cannot be used, because the earnings and dividends are not growing at a constant rate. Equation 9.3 can be used, and when these values, along with a required rate of return of 12 percent, are inserted into the equation, the stock's value is

$$V = \frac{\$0.40}{(1 + 0.12)^1} + \frac{\$0.64}{(1 + 0.12)^2} + \frac{\$0.77}{(1 + 0.12)^3} + \frac{\$0.87}{(1 + 0.12)^4}$$

$$+ \frac{\$0.905}{(1 + 0.12)^5} + \frac{\$0.941}{(1 + 0.12)^6} + \frac{\$0.979}{(1 + 0.12)^7} + \cdots$$

$$= \$9.16.$$

This answer is derived by dividing the flow of dividends into two periods: a period of super growth (years 1 through 4) and a period of normal growth (from year 5 on). The present value of the dividends in the first four years is

$$V_{1-4} = \frac{\$0.40}{(1 + 0.12)^1} + \frac{\$0.64}{(1 + 0.12)^2} + \frac{\$0.77}{(1 + 0.12)^3} + \frac{\$0.87}{(1 + 0.12)^4}$$

$$= \$0.36 + \$0.51 + \$0.55 + \$0.55$$

$$= \$1.97.$$

The dividend-growth model is applied to the dividends from year 5 on, so the value of the dividends during normal growth is

$$V_{5-\infty} = \frac{\$0.87(1 + 0.04)}{0.12 - 0.04} = \$11.31.$$

This $11.31 is the value at the end of year 4, so it must be discounted back to the present to determine the current value of this stream of dividend payments. That is,

$$\frac{\$11.31}{(1 + 0.12)^4} = \$11.31(0.636) = \$7.19.$$

The value of the stock, then, is the sum of the two parts.[1]

$$V = V_{1-4} + V_{5-\infty}$$
$$= \$1.97 + 7.19 = \$9.16.$$

As this example illustrates, modifications can be made in this valuation model to account for the different periods of growth and dividends. Adjustments can also be made for differences in risk. You should realize that the model does not by itself adjust for different degrees of risk. If a securities analyst applies the model to several firms to determine which stocks are underpriced, there is the implication that investing in all the firms involves equal risk. If the analyst uses the same required rate of return for each firm, then no risk adjustment has been made. The element of risk is assumed to be the same for each company.

THE INVESTOR'S REQUIRED RETURN AND STOCK VALUATION

One means to adjust for risk is to incorporate into the valuation model the security market line presented earlier in Chapter 5. In that chapter, beta coefficients, which are an index of the market risk associated with the security, were used as part of the Capital Asset Pricing Model to explain returns. In this context, beta coefficients and the Capital Asset Pricing Model are used to specify the risk-adjusted required return on an investment.

The required return has two components: the risk-free rate (r_f) that the investor can earn on a risk-free security such as a U.S. Treasury bill, and a risk premium. The risk premium is also composed of two components: (1) the additional return that investing in securities offers above the risk-free rate, and (2) the volatility of the particular security relative to the market as a whole (i.e., the beta). The additional return is the extent to which the return on the market (r_m) exceeds the risk-free rate $(r_m - r_f)$. Thus, the required return (k) is

9.5
$$k = r_f + (r_m - r_f)\beta.$$

---

[1]This valuation procedure may be summarized by the following general equation:

$$V = V_s + V_n.$$

V_s is the present value of the dividends during the period of super growth; that is,

$$V_s = \sum \frac{D_0(1 + g_s)^t}{(1 + k)^t}$$

V_n is the present value of the dividends during the period of normal growth; that is,

$$V_n = \left[\frac{D_n(1 + g)}{k - g}\right]\left(\frac{1}{(1 + k)^n}\right).$$

The value of the stock is the sum of the individual present values; that is,

$$V_s = \sum \frac{D_0(1 + g_s)^t}{(1 + k)^t} + \left[\frac{D_n(1 + g)}{k - g}\right]\left(\frac{1}{(1 + k)^n}\right).$$

Equation 9.5 is the same equation as the security market line in Chapter 5, which was used to explain a stock's return. In that context, the Capital Asset Pricing Model states that the realized return depends on the risk-free rate, the risk premium associated with investing in stock, and the market risk associated with the particular stock. In this context, the same variables are used to determine the return the investor requires to make the investment. This return encompasses the expected yield on a risk-free asset, the expected risk premium associated with investing in stock, and the expected market risk associated with the specific stock. The differences between the two uses concerns time and historical versus anticipated values. In one case the expected values are being used to determine if a specific stock should be purchased now. In the other application, historical values are employed to explain the realized return on an investment that was previously made.

The following examples illustrate how to use the equation for the required return. The risk-free rate is 3.5 percent and the investor expects that the market will rise by 10 percent. (Historical returns suggest that over a period of years stocks have yielded a return of 6 to 7 percent in excess of the return on U.S. Treasury bills. Thus, if the bills are currently yielding 3.5 percent, an expected return on the market of 10 percent is reasonable. Treasury bills are covered in more detail in Chapter 15 on government securities.) Stock A is relatively risky and has a beta coefficient of 1.8 while stock B is less volatile and has a beta of 0.8. What return is necessary to justify purchasing either stock? Certainly it would not be correct to require a return of 10 percent for either, since that is the expected return on the market. Since stock A is more volatile than the market, the required return should exceed 10 percent. However, the required return for B should be less than 10 percent; it is less volatile (less risky) than the market as a whole.

Given this information concerning the risk-free rate and the anticipated return on the market, the required returns for stocks A and B are

$$k_{A} = 3.5\% + (10\% - 3.5\%)1.8 = 3.5\% + 11.7\% = 15.2\%$$

and

$$k_{B} = 3.5\% + (10\% - 3.5\%)0.8 = 3.5\% + 5.2\% = 8.7\%.$$

Thus the required return for stocks A and B are 15.2 percent and 8.7 percent, respectively. These required returns differ from each other and from the expected return on the market because the analysis now explicitly takes into consideration risk (i.e., the volatility of the individual stock relative to the market). Stock A's required rate of return is greater than the expected return on the market (15.2 percent versus 10 percent) because stock A is more volatile than the market. Stock B's required rate of return is less than the return expected for the market (8.7 percent versus 10 percent) because stock B is less volatile than the market as a whole.

The relationship between the required rate of return and risk expressed in Equation 9.5 is illustrated in Figure 9.2. The horizontal axis represents risk as measured by the beta coefficient, and the vertical axis measures the required rate of return. Line *AB* represents the required rates of return associated with each level of risk. Line *AB* uses the information given in the preceding example: The Y-intercept is the risk-free return (3.5 percent), and the slope of the line is the difference between the market return and the risk-free return (10 percent minus 3.5 percent). If the beta coefficient were 1.80, the figure indicates that the required return would be 15.2 percent; if the beta coefficient were 0.8, the required return would be 8.7 percent.

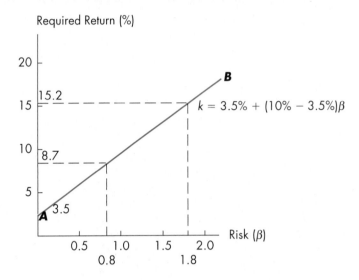

FIGURE   9.2   Relationship Between Risk and Required Return

How the risk-adjusted required return may be applied to the valuation of a specific stock using the dividend-growth model is illustrated in the following example. A firm's current dividend is $2.20, which is expected to grow annually at 5 percent. The risk-free rate is 3.5 percent, and the market is expected to rise by 10 percent. If the beta is 0.8, the required return is 8.7 percent. What is the maximum an investor should be willing to pay for this stock? If the dividend-growth model is used, the answer is

$$V = \frac{D_0(1 + g)}{k - g}$$

$$= \frac{\$2.20(1 + 0.05)}{0.087 - 0.05}$$

$$= \frac{\$2.31}{0.037}$$

$$= \$62.43.$$

At a price of $62.43 (and only at $62.43), the expected and required returns are equated. If the market price is below $62.43, the stock would be considered undervalued and a good purchase. Correspondingly, if the price exceeds $62.43, the stock is overvalued and should be not purchased. The investor should sell it short.

ALTERNATIVE VALUATION TECHNIQUES: MULTIPLIER MODELS

The dividend-growth model is theoretically sound: It *discounts future cash flows back to the present at the required return*, and the required return incorporates differences in market risk. The discounting of dividends is used by professional securities analysts. For example, one securities analyst at JMP Securities stated in an investment report,

"Using a dividend discount model, we calculate the fair value of . . ." This analyst was obviously using some form of a dividend discount model to determine if the stock was under- or overvalued.

Making the dividend-growth model operational, however, can be difficult. A problem immediately arises if the stock does not pay a dividend, and many corporations do not pay dividends. Without a dividend payment, the numerator is $0.00, which makes the value equal $0.00.

While this problem is obvious, there are additional problems associated with each of the variables in the model. One problem is the choice of the beta coefficient. As was discussed in Chapter 5, there can be differences in estimated betas for the same stock, which raises a question as to which beta to use. The same question applies to the risk-free rate. Although a short-term rate on federal government securities may be used, investments in stock often have a longer time horizon. The question becomes which to use, a short-term or long-term rate? (A corollary question is this: Is it appropriate to use a short-term rate for valuing a long-term investment?) Even if the analyst does use a short-term rate, there is still the question of which short-term rate: a three-month, a six-month, or any other risk-free short-term rate?

Similar problems exist with the return on the market and the future growth rate. One possible solution is to use historical data to forecast returns and growth rates. The results, however, may depend on the period selected, and on the method used for the calculation. In addition, using historical data assumes that the past is applicable to the future.

The problems with making the dividend-growth model applicable, however, are not a sufficient basis for discarding it or any other valuation model. Valuation models are built on discounting future cash flows. The analyst is forced to identify real economic forces (e.g., earnings and growth rates) and the returns on alternative investments (e.g., the risk-free rate and the return on the market). Without such analysis, the

---

⊕ Point of Interest

INFLATION AND THE INVESTOR'S REQUIRED RETURN

Although inflation is not explicitly part of the equation for the required rate of return, it is implicitly included. Anticipation of inflation will increase the rate on Treasury bills and the required return on the market. Higher rates of inflation will increase the T-bill rate as (1) the Federal Reserve takes steps to reduce inflation and (2) individuals seek to protect themselves by investing only if yields are sufficiently high to compensate them for the anticipated inflation.

A higher T-bill rate will result in an increase in the required return on the market. Investors certainly will not buy risky securities in general if their return declines relative to the T-bill rate. Increases in the T-bill rate must lead to corresponding increases in the required return on the market. The net effect will be to increase the required rate of return on an investment in common stock. For example, suppose the expected rate of inflation rises by 2 percent from 4 to 6 percent, which, in turn, causes the T-bill rate to rise from 6 to 8 percent and the required return on the market to increase from 12 to 14 percent. If a stock has a beta of 1.2, the required return rises from

$$k = 0.06 + (0.12 - 0.06)1.2 = 13.2\%$$

to

$$k = 0.08 + (0.14 - 0.08)1.2 = 15.2\%.$$

investor may have to rely on hunches, intuition, and just plain guessing to select assets. Such an approach has no conceptual or theoretical basis.

P/E Ratios

Value investing is concerned with the components of the dividend-growth model even if the analyst does not apply the actual model. The financial analyst or portfolio manager may employ alternative approaches to identify stocks for possible purchase. One of these approaches is the use of the ratio of the stock's price to earnings per share, or the P/E ratio.

The process by which price/earnings ratios may be used to value a stock is summarized by the following simple equation:

9.6 $$P = (m)(EPS),$$

which states that the value of the stock is the product of the earnings per share (*EPS*) and some multiple. This multiple is the appropriate price/earnings ratio. Once the expected earnings and the appropriate multiple are estimated, the intrinsic value of the stock is easily determined. For example, if the financial analyst determines that the appropriate P/E ratio is 10 and the firm's earnings are $4.50 per share, the value of the stock is

$$(10)(\$4.50) = \$45.$$

The implication is that if the stock is currently selling for $35, it is undervalued and should be purchased. If it is selling for $55, it is overvalued and should be sold.

Financial analysts often express the P/E ratio in terms of *future* earnings. For example, suppose the price of the stock is $36 when the estimated earnings are $4.50. The P/E using the estimated earnings is $36/\$4.50 = 8.0$. If the appropriate P/E is 10, a P/E of 8 suggests that the stock is undervalued and that the price of the stock will rise over time as the forecasted earnings are realized. The difference between these two approaches is the starting point. In the first case, current earnings and the appropriate P/E ratio are used to determine a value, which is compared to the current price. In the second case, the current price is divided by the estimated earnings to determine a P/E ratio, which is compared to the appropriate P/E ratio. In either case, the crux of the analysis is (1) the appropriate P/E ratio and (2) earnings.

The use of a P/E approach to valuation and security selection is often found in the financial press (if not the academic press). For example, a financial analyst may recommend purchase of IBM by stating that the "shares trade at 12.7 times our EPS projection of $4.90." A similar statement may be: "The shares appear undervalued at 13 times our earnings estimate of $4.90." Such material is typical of brokerage firms' purchase recommendations for common stocks.

The previous discussion considered a unique P/E ratio, but stocks may be treated as if they trade within a range of P/E ratios. Consider the P/E ratios over a five-year period for Bristol-Myers Squibb in Exhibit 9.1. On the average, the P/E ratio has ranged from a high of 29.3 to a low of 21.8. If the current ratio moves outside this range, the investor may want to look further at Bristol-Myers Squibb. For example, during 2009, the P/E was perceptibly lower than the average P/E. Unless something fundamental had changed, such as the Food and Drug Administration (FDA) not approving a new

EXHIBIT 9.1	Price/Earnings Ratio for Bristol-Myers Squibb

Year	High	Low
2008	17.2	10.0
2007	36.8	29.2
2006	42.6	32.4
2005	14.7	15.4
2004	30.5	21.8
Average	29.3	21.8

blockbuster drug developed by Bristol-Myers Squibb, the P/E was suggesting that the stock was undervalued.

Weaknesses in the Use of P/E Ratios

The first major problem concerning the use of P/E ratios is the appropriate ratio. The preceding illustration used a P/E of 10, but no explanation is given as to why 10 is appropriate. The Bristol-Myers Squibb illustration makes the point that the average ratio ranged from 29.3 to 21.8 but does not explain why either of these numbers would be appropriate or why the P/E ratio should stay within the range.

One possible solution is to use the industry average P/E ratio. This is a common solution to the problem of determining an appropriate ratio. This approach, however,

⊕ Point of Interest

VALUATION TECHNIQUES AND UNIQUE VALUES

The goal of valuation is to determine a unique value that can be compared to the stock's price. Unfortunately, the various techniques can lead to different values, and instead of determining a unique price, the analysis may generate a range of values. Both of these points are illustrated in the valuation provided to the management of Life Technologies by the investment banking firm Goldman Sachs. Life Technologies requested the valuation after Dexter Corporation offered to purchase the company for $37 a share. The board of Life Technologies employed Goldman Sachs as a financial advisor to determine if the $37 offer was reasonable and fair to Life Technologies' stockholders.

Goldman Sachs used several of the techniques developed in this text to determine the value of Life Technologies stock, including discounted cash flows and a comparable analysis of selected companies. The discounted cash flow models brought back to the present estimates of future cash flows. The comparability analysis compared the firm with similar firms using price/earnings ratios, forecasted earnings, and estimates of growth. Using these techniques, Goldman Sachs determined values ranging from $7.74 to $64.85.

The implication of this illustration is obvious. The techniques used to value stock often produce different amounts, and in the final analysis the values are often expressed in terms of a range and not a unique number (although the range is usually smaller than in this illustration). Valuation is not an exact science. If it were, investment decisions would be obvious, and incorrectly priced stocks could not exist.

implicitly assumes that a particular firm is comparable to the firms used to determine the average P/E. Although many firms in an industry are similar, each is unique in some way. Wal-Mart Stores, Target, Sears, Federated Department Stores, and Limited Brands are all retailers, but each tries very hard to differentiate itself from the other retailers. Are industry average P/E ratios for retailers appropriate to analyze each of these companies?

An additional problem using P/E ratios concerns earnings. The essential problems revolve around which earnings should be used. Companies report total and per-share earning, but these "bottom line" numbers may include extraordinary items that are nonrecurring. Should the earnings be adjusted for these isolated events?

Obviously, the P/E ratio will be affected by the choice of earnings. Extraordinary gains produce higher earnings and lower the P/E ratio and perhaps suggest that the stock is undervalued. If the gain is excluded and EPS are lower, the P/E ratio will be higher, which may indicate that the stock is not undervalued. The converse applies to extraordinary charges to income. Lower EPS cause the P/E ratio to be higher, so the stock may appear to be overvalued.

One possible solution is to adjust EPS for extraordinary items and use that figure to calculate the P/E. This is a reasonable approach if the items are unique, nonrecurring events. A firm, however, may have extraordinary items on a recurring basis. In one year, bad investments may be written off. In the next year, management may sell a subsidiary for a loss. In the third year, a loss of foreign exchange transactions may decrease earnings. Recurring extraordinary losses may imply poor management, so the use of the actual, *unadjusted* earnings may be appropriate.

Even if the analyst can determine which reported earnings to use, there remains the question of the appropriateness of using historical data to select an investment whose return will be earned in the future. The analyst may replace historical earnings with forecasted earnings, but that approach requires estimates of future earnings. Forecasted earnings may be available through the Internet, and some sites report P/E ratios based on both historical and estimated earnings. See, for instance, Money Central (http://moneycentral.msn.com) and Yahoo! Finance (http://finance.yahoo.com).

Similarities Between the Use of P/E Ratios and the Dividend-Growth Valuation Model

Even though P/E ratios have serious weaknesses from the perspective of valuing common stocks, they are useful for comparing firms with different earnings and stock prices. Current earnings and the price of the stock are combined in a P/E ratio, and this standardization facilitates comparisons. If a firm's P/E ratio differs from the industry average, the investor may want to ask why and analyze the firm further before making an investment decision.

The previous discussion suggested how P/E ratios may be used to compare firms and help select individual stocks. The approach appears to be different from the dividend-growth model presented earlier in this chapter. They are, however, essentially similar. The dividend-growth model was

$$V = \frac{D_0(1 + g)}{k - g}.$$

The firm's current dividend (D_0) is related to its current earnings (E_0) and the proportion of the earnings that are distributed (d). That is, the dividend is the product of the earnings and the proportion distributed:

$$D_0 = dE_0.$$

When this is substituted back into the dividend-growth model, the model becomes

$$V = \frac{dE_0(1 + g)}{k - g}.$$

If both sides of the equation are divided by earnings (E_0), the stock's valuation is expressed as a P/E ratio:

$$\frac{V}{E_0} = \frac{d(1 + g)}{k - g}.$$

From this perspective, a P/E ratio depends on the same fundamental financial variables as the dividend-growth model: the dividend (which depends on earnings), the firm's ability to grow, and the required return.

The use of P/E ratios instead of the dividend-growth model offers one major advantage and one major disadvantage. The advantage is that P/E ratios may be applied to common stocks that are not currently paying cash dividends. The major weakness of the use of P/E ratios is that these ratios do not tell the analyst if the stock is under- or overvalued. The ratio may indicate whether the firm's stock is selling near its historic high or low P/E ratio and then the investor draws an inference from this information. The dividend-growth model establishes a value based on the investor's required rate of return, the firm's dividends, and the future growth in those dividends. This valuation is then compared to the actual price to answer the question of whether the stock is under- or overvalued.

Price/Cash Flow

An alternative to using earnings in security valuation is cash flow and the ability of the firm to generate cash. (The statement of cash flows, which emphasizes the change in a firm's cash position, was covered in Chapter 8.) For growing firms, the ability to generate cash may be initially as important as earnings, since generating cash implies the firm is able to grow without requiring external financing. After the initial period of operating at a loss but producing positive cash flow, the firm may grow into a prosperous, profitable operation.

The valuation process using cash flow is essentially the same as is used with P/E ratios, except cash flow is substituted for earnings and emphasis is placed on the growth in cash flow rather than the growth of earnings. For example, in its August issue of *Private Client Monthly* a Scott & Stringfellow analyst recommended purchasing XTO Energy stock. Besides the company's successful exploration for and production of natural gas, the analyst pointed out that XTO was trading "below 5 times discretionary cash flow." In this illustration, 5 times cash flow was being used instead of 5 times earnings to justify purchasing the stock.

The estimation of future cash flow and the determination of the appropriate multiplier are, of course, at the discretion of the investor or analyst. For firms with substantial

⊕ Point of Interest

JOHN BOGLE'S BATTLE FOR THE SOUL OF CAPITALISM

The issues of investor capitalism and corporate board oversight are addressed in John Bogle's *The Battle for the Soul of Capitalism* (New Haven: Yale University Press, 2005). Bogle, founder of Vanguard and developer of the first index mutual fund, believes that corporate boards of directors do not exercise proper oversight and that corporate managers often maximize their compensation at the expense of stockholders. Accountants, who manage a firm's earnings, and investment bankers, who profit from underwriting and consulting fees, compound the problems.

According to Bogle, greedy corporate managers, accountants, and investment bankers are not the only source of the current problems with corporate America. Stock traders with short-term investment horizons, who emphasize rapid turnover of securities, also contribute to an environment that places emphasis on quarterly earnings and immediate returns.

Bogle would like to see a return to long-term investing, that is, an "own-a-stock" instead of a "rent-a-stock" mentality. He suggests that valuation should be based on *cash flow* and a *firm's capacity to pay dividends* and create wealth for investors. He even recommends increasing taxation of short-term gains to discourage the quick sale of securities. Bogle's discussion of the need for corporate managers to operate in stockholders' best interests is must reading for anyone interested in corporate governance and the reformation of financial markets.

Adapted from *Choice*, June 2006.

---

investments in plant or natural resources, noncash depreciation (and depletion expense) help recapture the cost of these investments and contribute to the firm's cash flow. The same applies to real estate investments, and funds from operations are often used instead of earnings when valuing properties and real estate investment trusts. Such valuations are the essence of value investing practiced by individuals such as Warren Buffett. Whether a value approach is superior to a growth approach will be addressed in the section on efficient markets.

Price/Book Ratio

While the P/E ratio may receive the most coverage in the financial press, financial analysts often use it in conjunction with other ratios such the ratio of the stock price to the per-share book value. (Book value is the sum of stock, additional paid-in capital, and retained earnings on a firm's balance sheet.) Essentially the application is the same as with the P/E ratio. The securities analyst compares the price of the stock with its per-share book value. For example, according to Louisiana Pacific's 2008 Annual Report, LPX's book value was $11.47. As of June 2009, the price of the stock was less than $4.20, so the stock was selling for less than book value. A low ratio may suggest that the stock is undervalued while a high ratio suggests the opposite. Determining what constitutes a "low" or a "high" ratio is left to the discretion of the analyst. Often, if a stock is selling for less than its book value (i.e., less than 1), it is considered undervalued. However, just because LPX is selling for less than book value and Coca-Cola with a price/book ratio of 5.5 is selling for more does not necessarily mean that LPX is undervalued while Coke is overvalued.

P/E ratios and the ratio of market to book are convenient means to compare stocks and are important to the value approach for security selection. Value investing emphasizes stocks that are anticipated to grow more slowly than average but may be selling for low prices (i.e., are undervalued). These stocks often have low P/E and market-to-book ratios, and the firms often operate in basic or low-tech industries. The essence of this approach is that the market has overlooked these stocks. A value strategy is obviously opposite to a growth strategy, which emphasizes the selection of stocks with greater-than-average growth potential.

Price/Sales (P/S) Ratio

A third valuation ratio is the ratio of the price of the stock to per-share sales. For example, LPX reported 2008 sales per share of $11.35. Since the price of the stock was $4.20, the price-to-sales ratio was 0.37($4.20/$11.35). (Coca-Cola's price-to-sales ratio was 3.6.) The price-to-sales ratio offers one particular advantage over the P/E ratio. If a firm has no earnings, the P/E ratio has no meaning, and the ratio breaks down as a tool for valuation and comparisons. The P/S ratio, however, can be computed even if the firm is operating at a loss, thus permitting comparisons of all firms, including those that are not profitable.

Even if the firm has earnings and thus has a positive P/E ratio, the price/sales ratio remains a useful analytical tool. Earnings are ultimately related to sales. A low P/S ratio indicates a low valuation; the stock market is not placing a large value on the firm's sales. Even if the firm is operating at a loss, a low P/S ratio may indicate an undervalued investment. A small increase in profitability may translate these sales into a large increase in the stock's price. When the firm returns to profitability, the market may respond to the earnings, and both the P/E and P/S ratios increase. Thus, a current low price/sales ratio may suggest that there is considerable potential for the stock's price to increase. Such potential would not exist if the stock were selling for a high price/sales ratio.

While the ratio of price/sales is used as a tool for security selection, the weaknesses that apply to P/E ratios (and to price/book ratios) also apply to price/sales. Essentially, there is no appropriate or correct ratio to use for the valuation of a stock. While some financial analysts believe that a low P/E ratio is indicative of financial weakness, other securities analysts draw the opposite conclusion. The same applies to price/sales ratios. Some financial analysts isolate firms with low ratios and then suggest that these firms are undervalued. Other analysts, however, would argue the opposite. Low price/sales ratios are characteristic of firms that are performing poorly and not worth a higher price. The low ratio then does not indicate undervaluation but is a mirror of financial weakness.

How the price/sales ratio may be used in combination with the price/book and price/earnings ratios is illustrated in Exhibit 9.2, which gives the price/sales, price/book, and price/earnings for three telephone service providers. As may be seen in the exhibit, Sprint Nextel has the lowest P/S ratio and the lowest P/B ratio. But those lowest values are not a sufficient reason to prefer Sprint Nextel to the other companies. For example, AT&T has operated profitably and may be preferred to Sprint Nextel. However, AT&T's P/S ratio is the highest of the three firms. As is often the case, the ratios rarely suggest that one firm is the best investment. If that were the case, investors would buy the stock, drive up its price, and all ratios with the price in the numerator would rise.

EXHIBIT 9.2	Price/Sales, Price/Book, and Price/Earnings Ratios			
		Price/Sales	Price/Book	Price/Earnings
AT&T	(T)	1.19	1.52	11.6
Sprint Nextel	(S)	0.44	0.79	NE
Verizon Communications	(VZ)	0.85	2.03	13.1

NE   no earnings; firm operated at a loss.
Source: Yahoo! Finance (**http://finance.yahoo.com**), June 15, 2009.

Ratios that Combine Two Ratios

The P/E, P/B, and P/S ratios value a stock relative to its earnings, book value, and sales. Additional techniques that combine tools of analysis, such as the "PEG" ratio, have been developed. This section describes several of these methods, but as with the P/E, P/B, and P/S these valuation techniques cannot identify which stocks to buy or sell. They can, however, reduce the number of stocks you may choose to analyze further.

The PEG Ratio

PEG ratio

The price/earnings ratio divided by the growth rate of earnings.

The **PEG ratio** came into prominence during the late 1990s and is defined as

$$\frac{\text{Price/earnings ratio}}{\text{Earnings growth rate}}.$$

If the stock's P/E ratio is 20 and the per-share earnings growth rate is 10 percent, the value of the ratio is

$$\frac{20}{10} = 2.$$

The PEG ratio standardizes P/E ratios for growth. It gives a relative measure of value and facilitates comparing firms with different growth rates.

If the growth rate exceeds the P/E ratio, the numerical value is less than 1.0 and suggests that the stock is undervalued. If the P/E ratio exceeds the growth rate, the PEG ratio is greater than 1.0. The higher the numerical value, the higher the valuation and the less attractive is the stock. A PEG of 1.0 to 2.0 may suggest the stock is reasonably valued, and a ratio greater than 2.0 may suggest the stock is overvalued. (What numerical value determines under- and overvaluation depends on the financial analyst or investor.)

As with the price/earnings, price/sales, and price/equity ratios, the PEG ratio can have significant problems. Certainly all the questions concerning the use of price/earnings ratios apply to the PEG ratio, since the P/E ratio is the numerator in the PEG ratio. Should earnings include nonrecurring items or be adjusted for nonrecurring items? Should the analyst use historical or projected earnings (i.e., should the P/E ratio be based on past earnings or future earnings)? Should the growth rate be the historical or the expected rate of growth in earnings? Analysts often use a *five-year expected growth rate* when calculating the PEG ratio, but that raises questions concerning how the future growth rate is estimated.

EXHIBIT 9.3	Selected PEG and P/E Ratios	
	PEG Ratio	P/E Ratio
Archer Daniels Midland	0.4	8.9
Coca-Cola	2.1	19.9
Corning	1.2	5.8
Dominion Resources	1.8	13.5
EMC	NA	20.7
ExxonMobil	1.7	9.5
Ford Motor Company	NE	NE
Honeywell	1.2	9.9
Illinois Tool Works	6.3	16.1

NA not given.
NE no earnings; firm operated at a loss.
Source: Yahoo! Finance (**http://finance.yahoo.com**), June 15, 2009.

Because the PEG ratio standardizes for growth, it offers one major advantage over P/E ratios. The PEG ratio facilitates comparisons of firms in different industries that are experiencing different rates of growth. Rapidly growing companies may now be compared to companies experiencing a lower rate of growth. This comparison is illustrated in Exhibit 9.3, which gives the PEG and P/E ratios for several firms. Several of the firms (e.g., EMC) have high P/E ratios and may be considered overvalued based solely on that ratio. However, some firms (e.g., Illinois Tool Works) are expected to grow more rapidly, so when the P/E ratio is standardized for growth, these stocks appear less overvalued. Other firms such as Coca-Cola have relatively high PEG and P/E ratios, which would suggest they are overvalued. And at the other extreme, Archer Daniels Midland has a low P/E and a low PEG, which suggests the stock is undervalued. Of course, the investor may want to ask why both ratios are so low for Archer Daniels Midland. The low PEG and the low P/E ratios may be a good starting point but are probably not sufficient to conclude that stock is a good purchase.

In addition, there may be inconsistencies in the data. Computing a P/E ratio requires earnings. Computing a PEG ratio requires both a P/E and a growth rate. So you might ask, how can there be a PEG ratio and *not a P/E ratio*? The most likely explanation is that the P/E was based on reported earnings. If the firm operated at a loss during the previous year, there could be no positive P/E value based on the historical earnings. The PEG ratio, however, may have been based on forecasted earnings, in which case the source could provide a numerical value for the ratio.

The Adjusted PEG

The PEG ratio presented in the previous section divided the P/E by the growth rate. Returns, however, encompass both growth and dividends, so an alternative definition of the PEG ratio encompasses a stock's dividend yield. That is

$$\frac{\text{Price/earnings ratio}}{\text{Growth rate + dividend yield}}.$$

In the example in the previous section, a stock's P/E was 20 and the earnings growth rate was 10 percent, so the PEG ratio was 2.0. If the dividend yield is 2 percent, the adjusted PEG is

$$\frac{20}{10 + 2} = 1.7.$$

Lower values of the adjusted PEG are better than higher numerical values because they indicate the investor is paying less for earnings, growth, and dividends. The fundamental question, however, remains: What is a desirable numerical value for the adjusted PEG ratio? When is the numerical value sufficiently low to justify buying the stock?

Return on Equity to Price/Book

The return on equity is earnings divided by a firm's equity and is a measure of performance. While higher earnings increase the return on equity, the return earned by stockholders on their investment is affected by the price of the stock. Since the stock may sell for more than the book value (i.e., the P/B ratio may exceed 1.0), the return on equity may not be a good measure of performance from a stockholder's perspective.

To overcome this problem, financial analysts and portfolio managers may compute an adjusted return on equity:

$$\frac{\textbf{Return on equity}}{\textbf{Price/book ratio}}.$$

For example, if a firm's return on equity is 10 percent and the price-to-book ratio is 2.0, the adjusted return on equity is

$$\frac{10\%}{2.0} = 5\%.$$

The effect of this ratio is to reduce the return on equity based on the price of the stock. If the stock is selling for less than book value (e.g., P/B = 0.8), the adjusted return on equity is

$$\frac{10\%}{0.8} = 12.5\%.$$

The return on the equity based on the price of the stock is increased. While a high return on equity may be important, it is also important to adjust for the price the investor pays to buy the stock. Rarely does a firm's stock sell for its book value. Adjusting the return on the book value by the actual price of the stock gives investors a better indicator of the performance management is actually achieving for its stockholders based on the current market price of the stock.

Profit Margin to Price/Sales

A firm's profit margin is the ratio of earnings to sales. The ratio tells the investor what the firm earns on every $1 of sales and is a measure of profitability. While high profit margins on sales are important, the profit margin (the return) earned by stockholders is affected by the price of the stock. High profit margins may not increase an investor's return if the stock sells for more than the per-share sales. For this reason, the profit margin may not be a good measure of profitability from a stockholder's perspective.

To overcome this problem, financial analysts and portfolio managers may compute an adjusted profit margin:

$$\frac{\textbf{Profit margin}}{\textbf{Price/sales ratio}}.$$

For example, if a firm's profit margin on sales is 10 percent and the price-to-sales ratio is 2.0, the adjusted profit margin is

$$\frac{10\%}{2.0} = 5\%.$$

The effect is to reduce the profit margin from the investor's perspective. If the stock is selling for less than per-share sales (e.g., P/S = 0.8), the adjusted profit margin is

$$\frac{10\%}{0.8} = 12.5\%.$$

The profit margin based on the sales and the price of the stock is increased. Although a high profit margin may be important, it is also important to adjust for the price the investor pays to buy the stock. Since a firm's stock usually sells for more or less than per-share sales, adjusting the profit margin gives investors a better indicator of the profitability management is actually achieving for its stockholders.

Exhibit 9.4 illustrates the application of these ratios. Part (a) presents the return on equity relative to the price-to-book ratio. The high returns on equity generated by Coca-Cola and Corning are perceptibly less impressive when they are adjusted by the ratio of the price-to-book value. For both companies, the market price of the stock exceeds the book value. Although the firm is earning a high return on the book value, you are paying more than the book value, so the return on the market price is less.

Part (b) presents the net profit margin relative to the price-to-sales ratio. Once again Coca-Cola and Corning have large profit margins on sales that are less impressive when you realize that the price of the stock exceeds per-share sales. Archer Daniels Midland's low profit margin does not look so bad when you realize that you are paying less for the stock since the price-to-sales ratio is less than 1.0.

VALUATION AND THE EFFICIENT MARKET HYPOTHESIS

The valuation methods and ratios described in the previous sections may give the impression that stock selection is mechanical. Nothing could be further from the truth. Stock valuation is often subjective, and analytical techniques may be manipulated to achieve any preconceived results. If you want to buy a stock, increasing the valuation makes it easier to rationalize the purchase. Increased growth rates, lower beta

---

EXHIBIT 9.4 Modified Return on Equity and Profit Margins for Selected Firms

(a) Return on Equity and Adjusted Return on Equity

	Return on Equity	Return on Equity Price to Book
Archer Daniels Midland	15.2%	10.9
Coca-Cola	25.9	4.7
Corning	36.3	19.1
Dominion Resources	13.9	7.3
EMC	9.9	5.0
ExxonMobil	33.8	9.9
Honeywell	30.0	8.3
Illinois Tool Works	14.3	5.7

(b) Profit Margin and Adjusted Profit Margin Selected Firms

	Profit Margin	Profit Margin Price to Sales
Archer Daniels Midland	2.7%	10.8
Coca-Cola	17.8	5.0
Corning	79.7	17.2
Dominion Resources	8.4	7.2
EMC	8.9	4.8
ExxonMobil	9.5	10.8
Honeywell	7.3	9.7
Illinois Tool Works	7.9	6.2

 Source: Yahoo! Finance (**http://finance.yahoo.com**), June 15, 2009.

coefficients, higher estimates of earnings, and lower PEG ratios make a stock look better and may justify its purchase. The converse would be true if you want to sell.

Stock valuation and the selection of securities are not mechanical. Neither are they scientific. Personal judgment and expectations can play a large role in the process, and personal bias often affects decisions. Even if an individual can overcome these biases and apply the analysis methodically, few (if any) investors and financial analysts will be consistently correct. That, of course, is the basic idea of the efficient market hypothesis. Securities markets are exceedingly competitive. Prices tend to mirror current information and current expectations, and changes in information and expectations affect securities prices rapidly. The result is that few investors and securities analysts consistently outperform the market on a risk-adjusted basis.

There is, however, some evidence that using fundamental financial analysis may lead to superior risk-adjusted returns. For example, Fama and French considered the relationship between stock returns and the ratio of book value to market value. Book value to market value is the reciprocal of the ratio of market value to book value. While the two ratios essentially measure the same things from different perspectives, each appears in the financial literature. Price-to-book primarily appears in the professional literature and the popular press. Book-to-price appears in the academic literature pertaining to investments.

⊕ Point of Interest

JUST BY THE NUMBERS AND INVESTOR BEHAVIOR

Financial analysts, investors, and portfolio managers use the various techniques covered in this chapter and in Chapter 8 to identify superior stocks for possible purchase. After identifying stocks by using the numbers, do these individuals violate the numbers and use other or additional criteria for stock selection? The answer is yes; human nature being what it is, you may find the perfect stock but not buy it for some reason. And, what may be worse, you may buy a stock that has not met your established mathematical criteria.

How can personal bias be avoided? How can you acquire only stocks that meet predetermined mathematical criteria? Although the individual investor may never be able to overcome personal bias, there are mutual funds that invest *solely* on the quantitative analysis performed by computers. Instead of the active human management of a portfolio, "quant funds" select stocks on the

basis of fundamental analysis of a firm's financial statements and the stock's price. Computers do not sample the firm's products, visit corporate headquarters, and interview management. Instead the computers are used for data mining populations of companies to look for stocks with superior potential.

Returns earned by quant funds have done well. While they underperformed during the late 1990s and the Internet bubble, these funds have tended to outperform other funds during the subsequent period. Part of this better performance may be explained by avoiding investor error and by the lower expenses associated with computer-generated stock selection. If you are interested in pursuing this avenue of investing, possible quant funds include Janus Intech Risk-Managed Stock (JRMXS, a large cap fund), Vanguard Strategic Equity (VSEQX, a mid cap fund), and Bridgeway Small-Cap Growth (BRSGX, a small cap fund).

Fama and French's results indicated that stocks with low book-to-market ratios generated lower returns.[2] The immediate implication is that investors who use the ratio of book value to market value to select securities (i.e., individuals who follow a "value" instead of a "growth" strategy) earn a higher return without bearing additional risk. Such a result is inconsistent with the efficient market hypothesis, which asserts that higher returns are available only when the investor bears more risk. The Fama and French study is also important for its implications concerning a value strategy versus a growth strategy. Companies classified as growth stocks often have high price-to-book ratios, and these are precisely the stocks the Fama-French results show generate lower returns and higher risks. Instead the results argue for a value strategy, since these stocks generally have lower price-to-book ratios.

Before concluding that value always beats growth, you should ask yourself whether these results are consistent over time. Just because a strategy appears to have generated higher returns in the past does not mean that it will generate higher returns in the future. In addition, one type of analysis may work under one set of conditions while

---

[2] Eugene F. Fama and Kenneth R. French, "The Cross-Section of Expected Returns," *Journal of Finance* (June 1992): 427–465. The French-Fama study also reported that returns were not related to the beta used in the Capital Asset Pricing Model. Low-beta stocks generated higher returns, which is inconsistent with the Capital Asset Pricing Model. Further support for these results may be found in Josef Lakonishok, "Contrarian Investment, Extrapolation, and Risk," *Journal of Finance* (December 1994): 1541–1578. This study found that value strategies (investments in firms whose stock price is low relative to earnings and other fundamentals, such as the book value of the equity) did better than growth strategies. For a basic discussion of the value approach, see Robert A. Haugen, The *New Finance: The Case Against Efficient Markets,* 3d ed. (Upper Saddle River, NJ: Prentice Hall, 2002).

an alternative strategy may work under a different set of circumstances. However, the Fama-French results do suggest that the fundamental analysis and stock valuation covered in this chapter may generate higher returns. Certainly securities analysts, portfolio managers, and individual investors need to know the basic tools of fundamental analysis and stock valuation.

SUMMARY

Investors in common stock anticipate a return from dividends and capital (price) appreciation. Capital gains tax laws favor price appreciation over cash dividends. Cash dividends are taxed as received while capital gains taxes are deferred until the stock is sold.

In finance, valuation is the process of determining the present value of future cash flows. One model, the dividend-growth model, determines the present value of common stock by discounting future dividends and the future growth in earnings back to the present at the investor's required rate of return. The required return encompasses the return on a risk-free investment, the anticipated return on the market, and the firm's systematic risk as measured by its beta coefficient.

Alternative and simpler methods for valuation and stock selection use ratios such as the price of the stock relative to earnings (P/E), price-to-book value (P/B), price-to-per-share sales (P/S), and the P/E relative to earnings growth (PEG). These ratios facilitate comparisons of firms but do not indicate if a stock is over- or undervalued. The conclusion requires judgment by the analyst or investor. Evidence exists that the application of valuation techniques may lead to superior returns. Such evidence is inconsistent with the efficient market hypothesis, which asserts that investors cannot expect to consistently earn superior risk-adjusted returns.

Exhibit 8.5 in the previous chapter provided several Internet sources for much of the data necessary to perform the valuation techniques covered in this chapter. Unless you do the calculations yourself, the Internet sources are a pragmatic place to start your valuation of possible stocks to buy or to sell.

Summary of Equations

Valuation of common stock (constant dividend):

9.2
$$V = \frac{D}{k}$$

Valuation of common stock (constant rate of growth):

9.4
$$V = \frac{D_0(1 + g)}{k - g}$$

Required return:

9.5
$$k = r_f + (r_m - r_f)\beta$$

Valuation using a multiple (e.g., a P/E ratio):

9.6
$$P = (m)(EPS)$$

QUESTIONS

1. What is the difference between the expected return and the required return? When should the two returns be equal?

2. What is the difference between the value of a stock and its price? When should they be equal?

3. What variables affect the value of a stock according to the dividend-growth model? What role do earnings play in this model?

4. How do interest rates and risk affect a stock's price in the Capital Asset Pricing Model?

5. The efficient market hypothesis suggests that it is difficult to outperform the market on a consistent basis. Are there possible exceptions to the hypothesis that concern the valuation of common stock?

6. The price of a stock is often expressed relative to a base such as earnings. The resulting ratio is then used to value the stock. Go to a website that provides information such as the price-to-earnings ratio, price-to-sales ratio, price-to-book ratio, the PEG ratio, dividends, estimated growth rate, profit margin, and return on equity. Compare several firms within the same industry, such as telecommunications (e.g., AT&T and Verizon Communications), food products (e.g., Del Monte, Heinz, and Kellogg), or retailers (Best Buy, Limited Brands, Target, and Wal-Mart). Compare the firms' valuation and performance ratios. Which stock appears to be the best buy in each group? (Remember that a particular website may not provide all of the needed information, so you may have to consult more than one.)

7. Apply the dividend-growth model to value the firms in the previous question. (You will have to locate each firm's growth rate, dividend, and beta coefficient. If any of the firms has ceased to pay a dividend, exclude that stock from your analysis.) To obtain the required return, use the Capital Asset Pricing Model. To obtain the risk-free rate, use the 12-month U.S. Treasury bill rate, which you may find from numerous sites such as the Federal Reserve (http://federalreserve .gov) or the federal government's public debt site (http://publicdebt.treas.gov). After obtaining the risk-free rate, add 6 percent as a means to obtain the return on the market, since the return on the market has over time tended to average about 6 percent more than the U.S. Treasury bill rate. Compare your valuations to the stock's current price. Are any of the stocks undervalued? If you use the dividend-growth model to rank stocks, do you get the same rankings as in the previous question?

PROBLEMS

1. Given the following data, what should the price of the stock be?

Required return	10%
Present dividend	$1
Growth rate	5%

a) If the growth rate increases to 6 percent and the dividend remains $1, what should the stock's price be?

b) If the required return declines to 9 percent and the dividend remains $1, what should the price of the stock be? If the stock is selling for $20, what does that imply?

2. An investor requires a return of 12 percent. A stock sells for $25, it pays a dividend of $1, and the dividends compound annually at 7 percent. Will this investor find the stock attractive? What is the maximum amount that this investor should pay for the stock?

3. A firm's stock earns $2 per share, and the firm distributes 40 percent of its earnings as cash dividends. Its dividends grow annually at 7 percent.

a) What is the stock's price if the required return is 10 percent?

b) The firm borrows funds and, as a result, its per-share earnings and dividends increase by 20 percent. What happens to the stock's price if the growth rate and the required return are unaffected? What will the stock's price be if after using financial leverage and increasing the dividend to $1, the required return rises to 12 percent? What may cause this required return to rise?

4. The annual risk-free rate of return is 9 percent and the investor believes that the market will rise annually at 15 percent. If a stock has a beta coefficient of 1.5 and its current dividend is $1, what should be the value of the stock if its earnings and dividends are growing annually at 6 percent?

5. You are considering two stocks. Both pay a dividend of $1, but the beta coefficient of A is 1.5 while the beta coefficient of B is 0.7. Your required return is

$$k = 8\% + (15\% - 8\%)\beta.$$

a) What is the required return for each stock?

b) If A is selling for $10 a share, is it a good buy if you expect earnings and dividends to grow at 5 percent?

c) The earnings and dividends of B are expected to grow annually at 10 percent. Would you buy the stock for $30?

d) If the earnings and dividends of A were expected to grow annually at 10 percent, would it be a good buy at $30?

6. You are offered two stocks. The beta of A is 1.4 while the beta of B is 0.8. The growth rates of earnings and dividends are 10 percent and 5 percent, respectively. The dividend yields are 5 percent and 7 percent, respectively.

a) Since A offers higher potential growth, should it be purchased?

b) Since B offers a higher dividend yield, should it be purchased?

c) If the risk-free rate of return were 7 percent and the return on the market is expected to be 14 percent, which of these stocks should be bought?

7. Your broker suggests that the stock of QED is a good purchase at $25. You do an analysis of the firm, determining that the $1.40 dividend and earnings should continue to grow indefinitely at 8 percent annually. The firm's beta coefficient is 1.34, and the yield on Treasury bills is 7.4 percent. If you expect the market to earn a return of 12 percent, should you follow your broker's suggestion?

8. The required return on an investment is 12 percent. You estimate that firm X's dividends will grow as follows:

Year	Dividend
1	$1.20
2	2.00
3	3.00
4	4.50

For the subsequent years you expect the dividend to grow but at the more modest rate of 7 percent annually. What is the maximum price that you should pay for this stock?

9. Management has recently announced that expected dividends for the next three years will be as follows:

Year	Dividend
1	$2.50
2	3.25
3	4.00

For the subsequent years, management expects the dividend to grow at 5 percent annually. If the risk-free rate is 4.3 percent, the return on the market is 10.3 percent, and the firm's beta is 1.4, what is the maximum price that you should pay for this stock?

10. Management has recently announced that expected dividends for the next three years will be as follows:

Year	Dividend
1	$3.00
2	2.25
3	1.50

The firm's assets will then be liquidated and the proceeds invested in the preferred stock of other firms so that the company will be able to pay an annual dividend of $1.25 indefinitely. If your required return on investments in common stock is 10 percent, what is the maximum you should pay for this stock?

INVESTMENT ASSIGNMENT (PART 4)

Part 3 in the previous chapter requested that you obtain ratios such as the return on equity and the profit margin. A high profit margin and a high return on equity are desirable, but those data are derived from the firm's balance sheet and do not consider the actual *price that you have to pay for the stock*. The following ratios add the stock's price to help determine whether you should buy or sell the stock.

1. Fill in the following table for each of your companies.

Stock	P/E	P/B	P/S	PEG	Profit margin divided by P/S	Return on equity divided by P/B

2. Rank the stocks from best to worst (e.g., lowest P/E to highest P/E, lowest P/B to highest P/B, and so on for each ratio).

Stock	P/E	P/B	P/S	PEG	Profit margin divided by P/S	Return on equity divided by P/B

3. Are the rankings consistent? Based on the valuation ratios, which stocks appear to be the best and the worst? Are you having trouble drawing a conclusion?

4. Add the beta coefficients to the initial table.

Stock	P/E	P/B	P/S	PEG	beta

Is there a relationship between the betas and each ratio? A low beta and a low valuation ratio may suggest that the stock is undervalued.

5. The next table concerns dividends and earnings.

Stock	Dividend	Dividend Yield	Estimated growth rate	Historical growth rate

You may have trouble finding growth rates, especially if the firm is operating at a loss. High dividend yields and high growth rates increase the stock's attractiveness.

6. Based on the information that you derived, would you sell any of the ten stocks that you selected?

The Financial Advisor's Investment Case
Blue Jeans and Stock Selection

H.B. Babalola often observed that the clothes worn by his daughters and their friends were made of denim. No matter what the style, blue jeans and other clothes made of denim were popular. While certain styles would remain popular for only brief periods, the use of denim continued year after year. Babalola reasoned that the manufacturers of denim may be potentially attractive investments, as there appeared to him to be little fluctuation in the demand for denim.

Babalola discovered that the primary manufacturer and importer of denim was Dentex. Dentex specializes in denim and produces only a modest amount of other types of cloth. Its sales of denim account for one-third of the total denim market, both domestic and abroad. Dentex's balance sheets and income statements for the last two years are presented in Exhibit 1. Dentex's per-share earnings and dividends are given in Exhibit 2. With the exception of the most recent year, 2010, and 2007, per-share earnings have steadily increased, and dividends have risen every year for the last ten years. This pattern of earnings and dividend growth impressed Babalola, who tended to think of textiles as a dull industry with little growth potential.

Babalola realized that for the firm to be a good investment, it should have strong fundamentals and be financially sound. So he decided to use ratios to analyze the firm's financial statements. From other sources, he found the industry averages given in Exhibit 3.

Currently Dentex's stock sells for $50. Babalola could invest in U.S. Treasury bills that yield 3.5 percent, but he believes that the stock market may offer a return over a period of years of 9.5 percent. Should he buy the stock of Dentex? To help Babalola with his decision, answer the following questions:

1. What conclusion(s) are indicated by the ratio analysis?
2. What is the firm's current payout ratio compared to its historical payout ratio?
3. What are the annual growth rates in the earnings per share and the dividend?
4. Is there any reason to believe that the firm has changed its dividend policy?
5. Risk is affected by many factors. How may each of the following affect the firm-specific (unsystematic) risk associated with Dentex?
   a) Its product line
   b) Its use of debt financing
   c) Foreign competition
6. Does Dentex's P/E ratio suggest the firm is undervalued?
7. Why is the growth rate in the dividend *not* sustainable?
8. If a dividend growth rate of 4 percent can be sustained, is the stock a good purchase if the required return is 9.5 percent?
9. If the beta coefficient were 0.8 and the sustainable growth is assumed to be 4 percent, should the stock be purchased if the risk-free rate is 3.5 percent and the anticipated return on the market is 9.5 percent?

EXHIBIT 1 Financial Statements of Dentex

Consolidated Statement of Income (for the years ending)

	2010	2009
Sales (in thousands)	$668,000	$730,000
Cost of goods sold	531,000	571,000
Selling and administrative expense	54,000	52,000
Depreciation	24,000	22,000
Interest expense (net)	3,000	3,000
	612,000	648,000
Income before taxes	56,000	82,000
Income taxes	24,000	35,000
Net income	$ 32,000	$ 47,000
Earnings per share	$5.87	$8.82
Dividends per share	2.20	2.00

Consolidated Balance Sheet (as of December 31)

	2010	2009
Assets (in thousands)		
Current assets		
Cash and short-term investments	$ 23,000	$ 5,000
Accounts receivable	80,000	114,000
Inventory	120,000	118,000
Total current assets	223,000	237,000
Property, plant, and equipment		
Land	3,000	3,000
Buildings and equipment	177,000	156,000
Other	20,000	17,000
	200,000	176,000
Total assets	$423,000	$413,000

	2010	2009
Liabilities (in thousands)		
Current liabilities		
Long-term debt due within a year	$ 6,000	$ 4,000
Accounts payable	22,000	22,000
Accrued expenses	30,000	35,000
Income taxes owed	3,000	10,000
Total current liabilities	61,000	71,000
Long-term debt	20,000	22,000
Stockholders' equity		
Common stock	57,000	57,000
Paid-in capital	5,000	5,000
Retained earnings	280,000	258,000
Total stockholders' equity	342,000	320,000
Total liabilities and stockholders' equity	$423,000	$413,000

EXHIBIT	2	Earnings per Share and Dividends of Dentex

	Earnings per share	Dividends
2010	$5.87	$2.20
2009	8.82	2.00
2008	7.49	1.80
2007	6.21	1.60
2006	6.75	1.35
2005	4.90	0.95
2004	3.97	0.75
2003	2.51	0.70
2002	1.58	0.55
2001	1.33	0.51
2000	1.00	0.50

EXHIBIT	3	Industry Averages for Selected Ratios

Current ratio	3.2:1
Quick ratio	1.6:1
Average collection period	55 days
Inventory turnover (sales/average inventory)	3.7 a year
Fixed asset turnover	4.5 a year
Debt ratio (debt/total assets)	33%
Times-interest-earned	10 ×
Net profit margin	3.3%
Return on assets	4.5%
Return on equity	7.0%

The Financial Advisor's Investment Case

Determining the Value of a Business

Amanda Monaco has just inherited her father's company. Prior to his death, Mr. Monaco was the sole stockholder, and he left the entire company to his only daughter. Although Amanda has worked for the firm for many years as a commercial artist, she does not feel qualified to manage the operation. She has considered selling the firm while it is still a viable operation and before her father's absence causes the value of the firm to deteriorate. Amanda realizes that selling the firm will result in losing control, but her father granted her a long-term contract that guarantees employment or a generous severance package. Furthermore, if Amanda were to sell for cash, she should receive a substantial amount of money, so her financial position would be secure.

Even though Amanda would like to sell out, she has enough business sense to realize that she does not know how to place an asking price (a value) on the firm. The IRS had established a value on her father's stock of $100 a share, and since he owned 100,000 shares, the value of the company for estate tax purposes was $10,000,000. Amanda thought that was a reasonable amount but decided to consult with Sophie Ryer, the CPA who completed the estate tax return.

Ryer suggested that the firm could be valued using a discounted cash flow method in which the current and future dividends are discounted back to the present to determine the value of the firm. She explained to Amanda that this technique, the dividend-growth model, is an important theoretical model used for the valuation of companies. In addition, she suggested that the price/earnings ratio of similar firms may be used as a guide to the value of the firm. Amanda asked Ryer to prepare a valuation of the stock based on P/E ratios and the dividend-growth model. While Amanda realized that she could get only one price, she requested a range of values from an optimistic price to a minimum, rock-bottom value.

To aid in the valuation process, Ryer assembled the following information. The firm earned $8.50 a share and distributed 60 percent in cash dividends during its last fiscal year. This payout ratio had been maintained for several years, with 40 percent of the earnings being retained to finance future growth. The per-share earnings for the past five years were as follows:

Year	Earnings per share
2006	$6.70
2007	7.40
2008	7.85
2009	8.20
2010	8.50

Publicly held firms in the industry have an average P/E ratio of 12, with the highest being 17 and the lowest 9. The betas of these firms tend to be less than 1.0, with 0.85 being typical. While the firm is not publicly held, it is similar in structure to other firms in the industry. It is, however, perceptibly smaller than the publicly held firms. The Treasury bill rate is currently 5.2 percent, and most financial analysts anticipate that the market as a whole will average a return of 6 to 6.5 percent greater than the Treasury bill rate.

Amanda has come to you to help devise a financial plan after the company is sold. Such a plan would encompass the construction of a well-diversified portfolio with sufficient resources to meet temporary needs for cash. You do not want to blindly accept the IRS estate value of $10,000,000. Obviously, if the firm could be sold for more, that would be beneficial to your client. In addition, you want an indication of the value Ryer may place on the firm, so you resolve to answer the following questions.

1. Based on the background information, what are the highest and lowest values of the stock based on P/E ratios?

2. What has been the firm's earnings growth rate (i.e., the rate of growth from $6.70 to $8.50) for the prior five years?
3. What are the highest and lowest values of the stock based on the dividend-growth model?
4. What assumptions must be made to determine these values using these two techniques?
5. Explain the impact each of the following would have on the valuation of the stock:

a) The anticipated return on the market rises.
b) The rate of growth declines.
c) The average P/E is 15 instead of 12.

6. If the estate tax rate is 55%, what is the implication of a valuation if less than $100 per share?

Appendix 9

TESTING THE EFFICIENT MARKET HYPOTHESIS: THE EVENT STUDY

One method employed to test the efficient market hypothesis is to study how a stock responds to the change in a variable, such as an unexpected increase in earnings or a decrease in the dividend. This technique is called an *event study*. If the market anticipated the event, the price should have already adjusted (i.e., the information is fully discounted), and the announcement of the event should have no impact. If the market did not anticipate the event, the price should immediately adjust for the new information so that few, if any, individuals are able to profit by acting on the announcement of the event. If the market is not completely efficient, prior to the announcement the price should move in the direction implied by the event but not fully discount the event.

These three scenarios are illustrated in Figure 9A.1. Panel (a) illustrates the case in which the information is fully discounted and the price has already adjusted before the event, which occurs at t_1. Even though some individuals may acquire the stock before the announcement, the time lapse between the price increase from A to B in panel (a) is sufficient that the time value of money consumes any possible excess return. For example, if individuals buy a stock in anticipation of a $1 dividend increment and bid up the stock's price, any excess return implied by the dividend increment is consumed by the cost of carrying the security until the announcement is made. This pattern is consistent with market efficiency.

Panel (b) illustrates the case in which there is no price change prior to the event, at which time the price quickly adjusts for the new information. Since the price change [i.e., the vertical distance AB in panel (b)] is rapid and by an amount equal to the valuation of the event, there is no opportunity for an excess gain once the information is public. This price pattern also is consistent with efficient markets.

Panel (c) illustrates the case in which the market is not efficient; some price change [i.e., the movement from A to B in panel (c)] occurs prior to the event, but either the amount of the increment or its timing is insufficient to discount fully the impact of the announcement. Thus, investors who buy the stock prior to the announcement earn an excess return. If this pattern exists for several events (e.g., for all dividend increments), then the individual investor who perceives the pattern may earn consistent excess returns. For such inefficiency to exist, it is not necessary that every, or even many, investors perceive the pattern. If some investors, whether they are skilled or have some particular knowledge of the event, are able to outperform the market consistently, the market is not completely efficient.

Testing for the patterns illustrated in Figure 9A.1 would appear to be easy, but two important observations need to be made. First, at any moment in time many factors (e.g., a movement in the market, a change in interest rates, a change in expected inflation, or a political event) may be affecting a stock's price, so the impact of one event must be isolated to determine if it has an impact on the stock's price and hence on the return. Second, returns must be adjusted for risk. One individual may acquire a very

FIGURE   9A.1   Stock Price Changes in Response to an Event

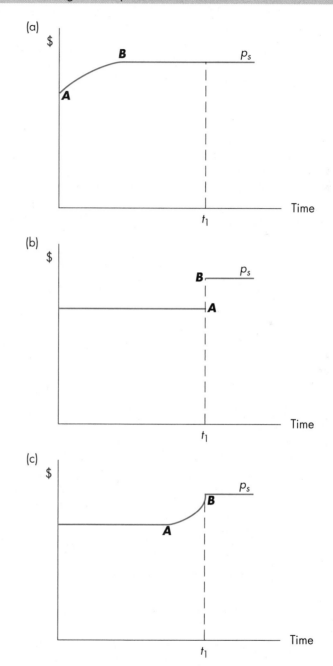

risky portfolio and achieve a higher return than the market. Another individual may acquire a portfolio consisting of certificates of deposit and achieve a lower return. The different returns earned by these individuals are not sufficient evidence that the former outperformed the market while the latter underperformed the market. A higher (or lower) return may be the result of a different amount of risk. Thus, returns must be adjusted for risk. To demonstrate market inefficiency, the individual must consistently achieve a higher (or lower) return on a *risk-adjusted basis*. Thus, it is possible for a return to be less than the market return but still be considered superior after adjusting for risk, in which case the return indicates an inefficient market.

Testing of the efficient market hypothesis using event studies assumes that the stock's return (r_s) is a function of the return the security would earn in response to the return on the market ($a + br_m$) and the impact of a firm-specific event represented by the e in the following equation:

$$r_s = a + br_m + e.$$

The a measures the return the stock would earn if the market return equals zero. The r_m measures the market return during the period, while the b gives the response of the individual stock's return to the market return (i.e., it is the stock's beta). The e, or error term, picks up the impact of a firm-specific event, such as a reduction in the dividend.

Rearranging the equation to solve for e gives an estimate of the firm-specific component of the return:

$$e = r_s - (a + br_m).$$

This equation states that if the return associated with changes in the market (i.e., $a + br_m$) is subtracted from the actual return (i.e., r_s), the residual is the firm-specific component of the return. The impact of this residual, of course, plays an important role in the rationale for the diversification of a portfolio. Because diversification erases the impact of firm-specific events, the value of e approaches zero as the number of securities increases, and the impact of firm-specific events is eliminated.

In an event study, however, the e is used to test for the impact of a firm-specific event, such as a dividend cut. The value of e will not equal zero if the event has an impact on the stock's return. If, for example, a dividend cut has a negative impact on a stock's return, e will be negative after subtracting the return generated by the movements in the market. It is possible that e could be positive if the market approves of the dividend cut and causes the stock's return to exceed the return associated with movements in the market as a whole. If the firm-specific event has no impact, the value of e is zero, and the stock's return is completely explained by the movement in the market.

Even though an investor can earn an excess return or sustain an excess loss in a single event, that is not sufficient evidence to verify an inefficiency. To overcome this, researchers measure superior performance by computing the "cumulative excess return" the investor earns. If the individual consistently outperforms the market, these excess returns will grow over time. The three possible patterns (i.e., consistently superior excess returns, consistently inferior returns, and no excess returns) are illustrated in Figure 9A.2. The efficient market hypothesis suggests that the pattern of cumulative excess returns should look like panel (c), in which returns fluctuate around zero. If the investor consistently outperforms the market, the cumulative excess returns will rise [i.e., panel (a)]. Conversely, if the performance is consistently inferior, the cumulative excess returns will be negative and falling [i.e., panel (b)].

How cumulative excess returns may be used to test for an inefficiency can be illustrated by employing one of the so-called technical indicators, such as the 200-day moving average. (Technical analysis is covered in Chapter 12.) The 200-day moving

FIGURE 9A.2 Cumulative Returns

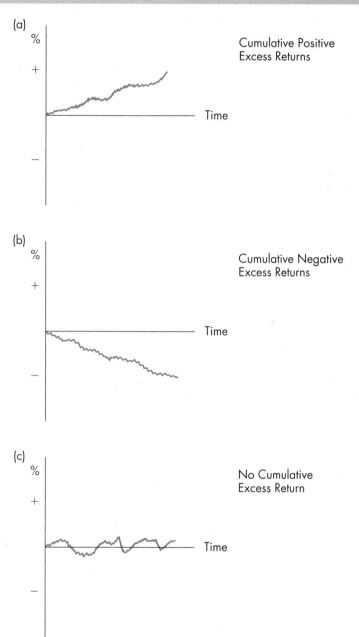

(a) Cumulative Positive Excess Returns

(b) Cumulative Negative Excess Returns

(c) No Cumulative Excess Return

average suggests buying or selling a stock when the price of the stock goes through the 200-day moving average. For example, if the moving average has been declining, the daily price of the stock will have been less than the moving average. If the price of the stock rises sufficiently so that it is equal to the moving average and then moves above the average, the movement is interpreted to be a buy signal. Conversely, if the moving average has been rising, the daily price of the stock will have been greater than the moving average. If the price of the stock declines sufficiently to equal the moving average and subsequently moves below the average, that is interpreted as a sell signal.

Such buy and sell signals beg to be tested. The stock returns generated by strategies such as this should be compared to the returns generated by the market during each time period. That is, the residuals (i.e., the excess returns) are isolated and summed. If the strategy outperformed the market, then the cumulative excess return would rise over time. Such a pattern would indicate superior performance and suggest the market is not efficient, at least with regard to the particular buy-sell strategy being tested.

CHAPTER 10

Investment Returns and Aggregate Measures of Stock Markets

LEARNING OBJECTIVES

After completing this chapter you should be able to:

1. Differentiate between a simple price-weighted average, a value-weighted average, and a geometric average.
2. Contrast the composition and method of calculation of aggregate measures of the stock market.
3. Explain the differences among the holding period return, an average rate of return, and the true annual rate of return.
4. Compute the rate of return on an investment.
5. Compare the results of various studies concerning the rates of return earned on investments in common stock.
6. Differentiate between dollar-weighted and time-weighted returns.
7. Identify the advantages associated with dollar cost averaging and averaging down.

From 1996 through 1999, the Standard & Poor's 500 stock index rose 26.435 percent annually. Is it reasonable to expect that stock prices will continue to increase at 26.435 percent? At that rate, $1,000 will grow to $108,980 in 20 years. If you could invest $1,000 each year for 20 years, you would accumulate $408,473.

It was proven during 2007–2008 that such returns do not continue indefinitely into the future. What return is it reasonable to assume will occur? What return has the stock market achieved over an extended period of time, such as 20 years? As will be covered later in this chapter, the large companies that compose the S&P 500 stock index have averaged about 10 percent annually. Even at that rate, $1,000 grows to $6,727 in 20 years, and $1,000 invested every year for 20 years grows to $57,275. Even if combined state and federal taxes consume 20 percent of the total, the investor still nets $5,381 and $45,820, respectively.

Historical returns are important because they give you perspective. Current high or low returns should not be sustained; returns should revert to historical levels. For this reason, historical returns are useful to forecast future returns, at least over an extended period, and may be used in valuation models such as the dividend-growth model presented in the previous chapter.

Aggregate measures of the market and the historical returns earned by investments in stocks are the primary focus of this chapter. The first section discusses the construction of aggregate measures of the securities markets. These include the Dow Jones averages, the Standard & Poor's 500 stock index, the New York Stock Exchange index, the Wilshire 5000 Total Market stock index, and selected specialized indexes that have recently been developed.

The second section is devoted to historical returns earned on investments in securities. The coverage includes various methods employed to compute and show returns and academic studies of returns actually realized. The chapter concludes with a discussion of buying stock systematically to smooth out fluctuations in prices and returns experienced from year to year.

MEASURES OF STOCK PERFORMANCE: AVERAGES AND INDEXES

Constructing an aggregate measure of stock prices may appear to be easy, but there are several important considerations. The first concerns which securities to include. Unless the measure encompasses all stocks, choices must be made as to which to include in the index. The second important consideration concerns the weight given to each security. For example, consider two stocks. Company A has 1 million shares outstanding and the stock sells for $10. Company B has 10 million shares outstanding, and its stock sells for $20. The total market value (or capitalization) of A is $10 million while the total market value of B is $200 million. How should these two securities be weighted? There are several choices: (1) treat each stock's price equally, (2) adjust for B's larger number of shares, or (3) use an equal dollar amount invested in each stock.

Price-Weighted Arithmetic Average

The first choice is the arithmetic average of both stocks whereby the two prices are treated equally and the average price is

$$\frac{(\$10 + \$20)}{2} = \$15.$$

If the prices of the stocks rise to $18 and $22, respectively, the new average price is

$$\frac{(\$18 + \$22)}{2} = \$20.$$

In both calculations, the simple average gives equal weight to each stock price and does not recognize the difference in the number of shares outstanding.

Value-Weighted Average

An alternative means used to measure stock performance is to construct an average that allows for differences in the number of shares each company has outstanding. If the preceding numbers are used, the total value of A and B is

$$\text{Price} \times \text{Number of shares} = \text{Total value}$$
$$\$10 \times 1,000,000 = \$10,000,000$$
$$+$$
$$\underline{\$20 \times 10,000,000 = 200,000,000}$$
$$\$210,000,000.$$

The value-weighted average price of a share of stock is

$$\text{Average price} = \text{Total value of all shares} \div \text{Total number of shares},$$

$$\text{Average price} = \frac{\$210,000,000}{(10,000,000 + 1,000,000)}$$
$$= \$19.09.$$

If the prices of the stocks rise to $18 and $22, respectively, the new total value of all shares is

$$\begin{array}{l} \$18 \times 1,000,000 = \$18,000,000 \\ + \\ \underline{\$22 \times 10,000,000 = 220,000,000} \\ \hspace{3cm} \$238,000,000 \end{array}.$$

The average value of a share of stock becomes

$$\text{Average price} = \frac{\$238,000,000}{(10,000,000 + 1,000,000)}$$

$$= \$21.64.$$

The value-weighted average gives more weight to companies with more shares outstanding, and that affects the average.

Geometric Average

A third alternative means to calculate an aggregate measure of securities prices is to construct a geometric average. Instead of adding the prices of the various stocks and dividing by the number of entries, a geometric average multiplies the various prices and then takes the nth root with n equal to the number of stocks. For example, if the prices of two stocks are $10 and $20, the geometric average is

$$\text{Average price} = \sqrt{(\$10)(\$20)} = \$14.14.$$

If the prices of the stocks rise to $18 and $22, the new geometric average price is

$$\text{Average price} = \sqrt{(\$18)(\$22)} = \$19.90.$$

Notice that in each calculation the averages and the changes in the averages differ. The simple average rose from $15 to $20 (a 33.3 percent increase), but the value-weighted average rose from $19.09 to $21.64 (a 13.3 percent increase). The geometric average rose from $14.14 to $19.90 for a 40.7 percent increase. All of these averages may be used to construct an aggregate measure of the stock market. For example, the Dow Jones Industrial Average is a simple arithmetic average; the Standard & Poor's 500 stock index uses a value-weighted average, and the Value Line stock index is constructed using a geometric average.

While aggregate measures of the market may use any of the averages, the difference between arithmetic and geometric averages is crucial for the calculation of returns. Consider the following stock prices and the percentage change in each. Over the time period the stock rose from $20 to $30.

Year	Price of Stock	Percentage Change
1	$20	—
2	34	70.0%
3	25	−26.5
4	30	20.0

The percentage changes indicate what the investor earned each year and may be used to compute a return. The average return for the three years is 21.17 percent:

$$\frac{(70.0 - 26.5 + 20.00)}{3}.$$

You would think that if an investor earned 21.17 percent each year, the total gain would be

$$\$20 \times 3 \times .2117 = \$12.70$$

and the $20 would now be worth $32.70 instead of $30. Something is obviously wrong, and the error would be even larger if the calculation had used compounding:

$$\$20(1 + 0.2117)^3 = \$35.58.$$

The error is the result of averaging plus and minus percentage changes. A price movement from $20 to $25 is a 25 percent gain. A price change from $25 to $20 is a 20 percent decline. Averaging the two percentage changes produces an average of 2.5 percent, but a change from $20 to $25 to $20 indicates no change and no return. In both cases the stock moves $5, but the percentage changes differ because the base or starting price differs—thus biasing the return upward.

This problem is avoided if a geometric average return is computed. The computation is as follows:

$$\sqrt[3]{(1 + 0.70)(1 + [-0.265])(1 + 0.2)} = \sqrt[3]{1.4994} = 1.1446.$$

The geometric average return is

$$1.1446 - 1 = 14.46\%.$$

Notice that the calculation is not

$$\sqrt[3]{(70)(-26.5)(20)} = \sqrt[3]{-37100},$$

which *fails to consider the decimal* (i.e., 70 percent does not equal 70) and produces a negative number. The correct calculation requires adding the percentage, expressed as a decimal, to 1. Positive percentage changes generate numbers greater than 1. Negative percentage changes result in numbers less than 1, but all numbers must be positive. After the appropriate root is determined, the 1 is subtracted to obtain the geometric average return, which in the illustration is an annual return of 14.46 percent.

Does the 14.46 percent seem reasonable? The answer is yes. Suppose a $20 investment earned 14.46 percent each year; the gain would be

$$\$20 \times 3 \times 0.1446 = \$8.676$$

and the $20 would now be worth $28.676. Something still remains wrong, but once compounding is considered, the correct return is verified:

$$\$20(1 + 0.1446)^3 = \$29.99 \approx \$30.$$

Since the use of the geometric average has generated the true return, its use is crucial to investments.

THE DOW JONES INDUSTRIAL AVERAGE

One of the first measures of stock prices was the average developed by Charles Dow.[1] Initially, the average consisted of the stock from only 11 companies, but it was later expanded to include more firms. Today, this average is called the Dow Jones Industrial Average (ticker symbol: ^DJI) and it is probably the best known and most widely quoted average of stock prices.

The Dow Jones Industrial Average is a simple price-weighted average. Initially, it was computed by summing the price of the stocks of 30 companies and then dividing by 30. Over time, the divisor has been changed so that substitutions of one firm for another (e.g., replacing GM and Citigroup with Travelers and Cisco Systems in 2009) or a stock split has no impact on the average. If the computation were simply the sum of the current prices of 30 divided by 30, the substitution of one stock for another or a stock split would affect the average.

To see the possible impact of substituting one stock for another, consider an average that is computed using three stocks (A, B, and C) whose prices are $12, $35, and $67, respectively. The average price is $38. For some reason, the composition of the average is changed. Stock B is dropped and replaced by stock D, whose price is $80. The average price is now $53 [($12 + 35 + 80)/30]. The substitution of D for B has caused the average to increase even though there has been no change in stock prices. To avoid this problem, the divisor is changed from 3 to the number that does not change the average. To find the divisor, set up the following equation:

$$\frac{(\$12 + 67 + 80)}{X} = \$38.$$

Solving for X gives a divisor of 4.1842. When the prices of stocks A, C, and D are summed and divided by 4.1842, the average price is

$$\frac{(\$12 + 67 + 80)}{4.1842} = \$38,$$

so the average price has not been altered by the substitution of stock D for B.

A similar situation occurs when one of the stocks is split. (Stock splits and their impact on the price of a share were covered in Chapter 8.) Suppose stock D is split 2 for 1 so its price becomes $40 instead of $80 (two new shares at $40 = one old share at $80). The investor's wealth has not changed; the individual continues to hold stock worth a total of $159 ($12 + 67 + 40 + 40). The price average, however, becomes ($12 + 67 + 40)/4.1842 = $28.44 instead of $38. According to the average, the stock is worth less. The average has been affected by something other than a price movement—in this case, the stock split. Once again, this problem is solved by changing the divisor so that the average price remains $38. To find the divisor, set up the following equation:

$$\frac{(\$12 + 67 + 40)}{X} = \$38.$$

---

[1]In 1882 Edward Jones joined Charles Dow to form a partnership that grew into Dow, Jones and Company. Information on the Dow Jones averages may be found at **http://www.djindexes.com**.

Solving for X gives a divisor of 3.1316. When the individual prices of stocks A, C, and D are summed and divided by 3.1316, the average price is

$$\frac{(\$12 + 67 + 40)}{3.1316} = \$38,$$

so the average price has not been altered by the stock split.

While the Dow Jones Industrial Average is adjusted for stock splits, stock dividends in excess of 10 percent, and the substitution of one firm for another, no adjustment is made for the distribution of cash dividends. Hence, the average declines when stocks like ExxonMobil go ex-div (pay a dividend) and their prices decline. (The reason for a stock's price to decline when the firm pays a dividend was explained in Chapter 8.)

The failure to include dividend payments means that the annual percentage change in the Dow Jones Industrial Average understates the true return. This failure to include the dividend can have an amazing impact when compounding is considered. Suppose the average rises 8 percent annually when dividends are excluded but the return is 10 percent when dividends are included and reinvested. (The dividend yield on the Dow Jones Industrial Average was 3.80% as of February 2009.) Over 20 years, $1,000 grows to $4,661 at 8 percent but to $6,728 at 10 percent. If the time period is extended to 50 years, these values become $46,902 and $117,391, respectively.[2]

This understatement of the true annual return is, of course, true for all stock indexes that do not add back the dividend payment. The bias is greater for those indexes that cover the largest companies, since they tend to pay dividends. Although some small cap stocks do distribute dividends, they tend to pay out a smaller proportion of their earnings, and the dividend constitutes a small, perhaps even trivial, part of the total return.

The Dow Jones Industrial Average for the period from 1950 through 2009 is presented in Figure 10.1, which plots the high and low values of the average for each year. During the 1970s, the Dow Jones Industrial Average (and the stock market) certainly did not experience steady growth. (In 1970 and in 1974 the Dow Jones Industrial Average even fell below the high achieved in 1959.) The period from 1985 through 1999, however, showed a different pattern, as stock prices soared and the Dow Jones Industrial Average rose to 11,497 at the end of 1999. This continual growth came to a crashing end in 2000, when the average declined 6.2 percent and continued to decline through 2002. Even in 2005, the Dow Jones Industrial Average traded 15 percent below the 1999 closing.

The Dow's performance in 2008 was even worse! After reaching a high in excess of 14,200 in 2007, the Dow collapsed in 2008. The low for 2008 barely exceeded the low for 2002 and was less than the high achieved in 1997. This performance by the Dow stocks suggests that many investors were worse off in 2008 than they were in 1997. If an investor purchased the components of the Dow during 1997, the value of the stocks would be less in 2008 than their cost in 1997!

During 2009, the Dow continued to decline and fell to 6,440 in March, for an additional decline of 26 percent in less than three months. From this nadir, the Dow

---

[2]One study found that from its inception through December 31, 1998, the Dow Jones Industrial Average grew from 40.94 to 9,181.43, for a 5.42 percent annual growth rate. However, if dividends had been reinvested, the Dow Jones would have been 652,230.87, for an annual growth rate of 9.89 percent. See Roger G. Clarke and Meir Statman, "The DJIA Crossed 652,230," *Journal of Portfolio Management* (winter 2000): 89–93.

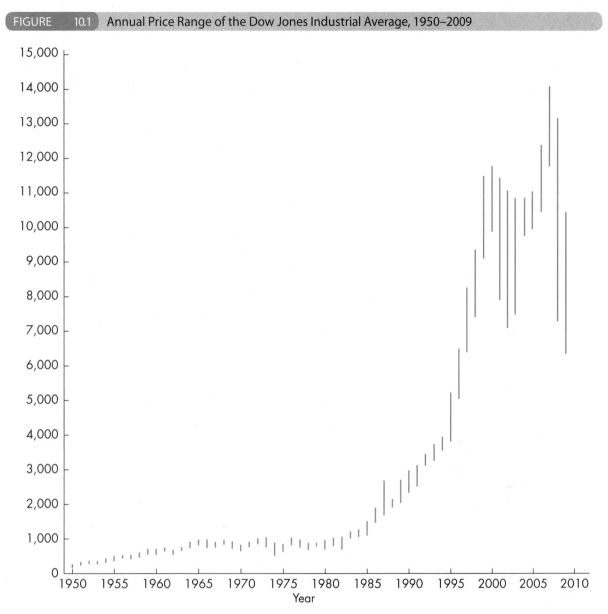

FIGURE 10.1 Annual Price Range of the Dow Jones Industrial Average, 1950–2009

Source: First issue of the *Wall Street Journal* for each year.

rebounded, reached a high of 10,606, and ended the year at 10,494. While the Dow recouped the losses experienced during late 2008 through March 2009, it remained well below the 14,200 high achieved during 2007. To regain that level, the Dow would have had to rebound over 100 percent. (Once again, comparing negative and positive percentage changes is misleading. A decline from 14,200 to 6,440 is a 55 percent loss but would require a gain of 120 percent to recoup the loss.)

There may be an interesting parallel between the recent performance of the stock market and its performance during the 1970s. In 1972 the Dow Jones Industrial Average broke 1,000, and it reached 1,052 in 1973. Then it fell to 578 in 1974 for a 45 percent decline and did not pass its previous high until 1982. In 2007, the Dow rose to 14,280 and then fell, bottoming out in March 2009 at 6,440, a decline in excess of 55 percent. If history repeats itself, the Dow will not pass its previous high until 2017!

Graphical Illustrations

While a picture may be worth 1,000 words, pictures can be misleading. So, before proceeding to the discussion of other indexes of stock prices, it is desirable to consider the composition of graphs (i.e., the pictures) used to illustrate indexes of stock prices. The choice of the scale affects the graph. This choice can influence the reader's perception of the index and, hence, the performance of the stock market.

This impact may be illustrated by the following monthly range of stock prices and percentage increases:

Month	Price of Stock	Percentage Change in Monthly Highs
January	$5–10	—
February	10–15	50
March	15–20	33
April	20–25	25

Even though the monthly price increases are equal ($5), the percentage increments decline. The investor who bought the stock at $10 and sold it for $15 made $5 and earned a return of 50 percent. The investor who bought it at $20 and sold for $25 also made $5, but the return was only 25 percent.

These monthly prices may be plotted on graph paper that uses absolute dollar units for the vertical axis. This is done on the left-hand side of Figure 10.2. Such a graph gives the appearance that equal price movements yield equal percentage changes. However, this is not so, as the preceding illustration demonstrates.

FIGURE 10.2 The Use of Different Scales to illustrate Stock Price Movements

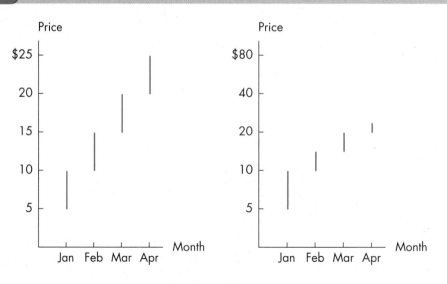

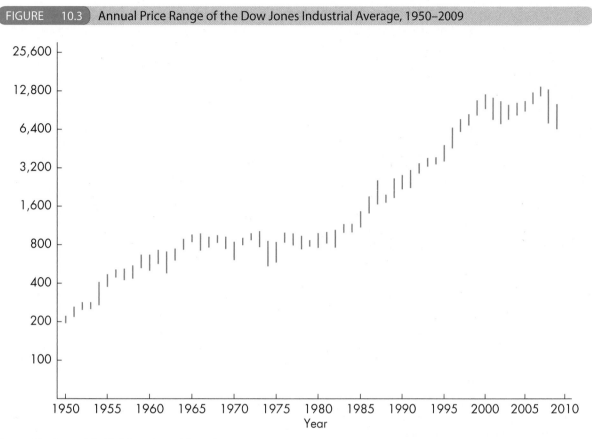

FIGURE 10.3 Annual Price Range of the Dow Jones Industrial Average, 1950–2009

Source: First issue of the *Wall Street Journal* for each year.

To avoid this problem, a different scale can be used, as illustrated in the right-hand side of Figure 10.2. Here, equal units on the vertical axis represent percentage change. Thus, a price movement from $10 to $15 appears to be greater than one from $20 to $25, because in percentage terms it is greater.

The impact of using the percentage scale may be seen by comparing Figures 10.1 and 10.3. Both present the annual price range of the Dow Jones Industrial Average, but Figure 10.1 uses an absolute scale while Figure 10.3 expresses prices in relative terms. The general shape is the same in both cases, but the large absolute increase in the Dow Jones Industrial Average during the late 1990s is considerably less impressive in Figure 10.3. Because absolute price changes are reduced to relative price changes, graphs like Figure 10.3 are better indicators of securities price movements and the returns investors earn.

OTHER INDEXES OF AGGREGATE STOCK PRICES

Unlike the Dow Jones Industrial Average, the Standard & Poor's 500 stock index (^GSPC, commonly referred to as the S&P 500) is a value-weighted index. The index was 10 in the base year, 1943. Thus, if the index is currently 100, the value of these stocks is ten times their value in 1943. Standard & Poor's also computes an index of 400 industrial stocks and indexes of 20 transportation, 40 utility, and 40 financial companies.

Since the S&P 500 is a value-weighted index, large capitalization stocks such as Microsoft and ExxonMobil, whose market values were $274 billion and $328 billion as of January 2010, have more impact on the index than Alcoa, whose market value was $15.2 billion. Although the number of stocks in the S&P 500 remains constant, the composition of the index changes over time. Mergers and acquisitions are one cause of changes in the index as a firm is acquired and is replaced in the index by another stock. A financially weak firm whose stock has experienced a major decline in value may be dropped in favor of a company in better financial condition. Also, if the market value of a company declines, it may be dropped from the index and replaced by a stock with a larger capitalization. For example, McDermott International was dropped and MedcoHealth Solutions was added. The reason given for the switch was the decline in McDermott's market capitalization.

The impact of price of the stock that is added is usually positive. Any increase, however, is not the result of the company receiving favorable recognition but of buying by the index funds, which must now include the stock in their portfolios. Conversely, if a firm is dropped from the index, the index funds will sell their positions, which may cause the price of the stock to decline.

The S&P 500 is essentially an index of large cap stocks. Standard & Poor's also has an index of 400 moderate-sized firms (the S&P 400 MidCap index, ^MID) and an index of 600 small firms (the S&P 600 SmallCap index, ^SML). There is also an index (the S&P 1500, ^SPSUPX), which combines all the stocks in the S&P 500, the S&P MidCap, and the S&P SmallCap indexes. (For information on the S&P indexes, go to http://www.standardandpoors.com.)

The New York Stock Exchange Composite Index (^NYA) includes all common stocks listed on the NYSE. Like the S&P 500, the NYSE Composite Index is a value-weighted index. In 2002, the NYSE reconstituted the index to include all common stocks, American Depository Receipts (ADRs) of foreign stock traded on the NYSE, and real estate investment trusts (REITs), and to exclude preferred stocks, closed-end and exchange-traded funds, and derivatives. (Each of these types of securities is covered in various places in this text.) The index's base was changed from 50 to 5,000 starting as of December 31, 2002. Returns on the index are reported for both price changes and for price changes plus dividends. (For information on the NYSE Composite Index, go to the NYSE webpage: http://www.nyse.com.)

The Value Line Geometric index (^VLIC) of approximately 1,700 stocks differs from the Dow Jones, S&P, and NYSE indexes in two important ways. It includes the stocks covered by the Value Line survey. This coverage encompasses stocks that are traded on the NYSE and on Nasdaq but are not necessarily in the Dow Jones Industrial Average and the NYSE Composite Index. Since some of the stocks covered by Value Line are not large cap stocks, they are excluded from the S&P 500 even though they may be in the S&P 400 and the S&P 600. The second important difference is the method of calculation. Value Line uses a geometric average that gives equal weight to each stock included in the average. The Dow Jones Industrial Average and S&P indexes are arithmetic and value-weighted averages. (Value Line also publishes an arithmetic average, ^VAY.)

Other aggregate measures include the Russell indexes, the Amex index, and the Nasdaq index. The Russell 1000 (^RUI) uses the 1,000 largest firms traded on the NYSE and on Nasdaq. The Russell 2000 (^RUT) consists of the next 2,000 largest firms, and the Russell 3000 (^RUA) combines the stocks in the Russell 1000 and the Russell 2000. The American Stock Exchange Composite Index (^AMEX) is a value-weighted index that encompasses all the common stock traded on that exchange. The Nasdaq Composite Index (^IXIC) of over-the-counter stocks covers more than 3,000 issues. Perhaps the broadest-based aggregate measure of stock prices is the Dow Jones Wilshire 5000 (^DWC), which is constructed using all the stocks traded on the NYSE and the Amex plus actively traded Nasdaq stocks (i.e., virtually every publicly traded U.S. company). While the name implies a total of 5,000 stocks, the actual number exceeds 7,000.

Specialized Indexes

The previous section considered aggregate measures of the market or measures based on the size or capitalization of the company. The S&P 500 and the NYSE Composite Index are obviously aggregate measures that emphasize large cap stocks, and the Dow Jones Wilshire 5000 is a very broad-based measure of stocks. In addition to these aggregate measures, there are many averages and indexes based on specific subsections of the market. Initially, Dow Jones computed not only its industrial average consisting of 30 stocks but also averages for 20 transportation stocks (^DJT), 15 utility stocks (^DJU), and an aggregate average of all 65 stocks (^DJA). In recent years, Dow Jones has developed specialty measures for industries such as Composite Internet (^DJINET), individual countries (e.g., the Dow Jones Japan Titans 100 Trust, ^XLJNTR), or world markets (e.g., Dow Jones Asia/Pacific Large Cap, ^P1LRG).

Specialized market measures are not a monopoly of Dow Jones. Standard & Poor's has indexes based on economic sectors. Each stock in the S&P 500 is classified into one of ten sectors based on the firm's largest source of revenue. (See the Point of Interest for the ten sectors.) In reality there are a large number of indexes that cover the subsets of the securities markets. A sampling of these indexes is given in Exhibit 10.1, which provides the ticker symbol for each index. This large number of specialized measures means that the individual investor, financial analyst, or portfolio manager can monitor market movements in virtually any desired area. Information on a particular index is readily available through Internet sources such as Yahoo! Finance. Use the ticker symbol to access a particular index.

While it may seem unnecessary to have so many indexes (and obviously an individual cannot follow all of them), each index can serve an important purpose. In Chapter 6 on mutual funds, assessing a portfolio manager's performance requires a benchmark for comparison. While a large cap growth fund may be compared to the S&P 500, such a comparison would not be appropriate for the manager of a fund that specialized in energy stocks or small cap stocks. This question of comparability applies to any specialized investment portfolio. If assessment is to be based on market comparison, then appropriate measures of the relevant market's performance are necessary. Certainly the large number of indexes serves this purpose.

The individual investor, however, should be aware of a potential weakness. With so many aggregate measures available, a portfolio manager may be able to find an index that puts that manager's performance in a favorable light. If, for example, the S&P 500

EXHIBIT 10.1	Selected Specialized Indexes and Ticker Symbols

Index	Ticker Symbol
American Markets	
AMEX Internet	^IIX
AMEX Networking	^NWX
Pacific Exchange Technology	^PSE
Philadelphia Semiconductor	^SOXX
PHLX TheStreet.Com Internet	^DOT
Nasdaq Industrials	^IXID
Nasdaq Banks	^IXBX
Nasdaq Biotech	^NBI
Nasdaq Computer	^IXK
Nasdaq Insurance	^IXIS
Nasdaq Telecommunications	^IXUT
Nasdaq Transportation	^IXTR
Foreign Markets	
World Leaders	^NIN
Nikkei 225 (Tokyo)	^N225
FTSE-100 (London)	^FTSE
Hang Seng Index (Hong Kong)	^HIS
Shanghai Composite (China)	^SSEC
Seoul Composite (Korea)	^KSII

indicates inferior performance but the Dow Jones Wilshire 5000 indicates superior performance, an obvious incentive exists for the portfolio manager to use the Wilshire 5000 when reporting performance comparisons. Switching from one index to another may be a red flag and certainly should raise a question concerning the validity of the comparison. Of course, if the portfolio manager is consistent and uses the same index for several consecutive years, there may be periods of underperformance. The efficient market hypothesis suggests that such performance may be expected, since consistent superior performance is hard to achieve.

Aggregate Measures of Stock Prices and Correlation

As may be expected, the correlation between aggregate measures of the American stock markets is high. This is illustrated in Figure 10.4 (on page 354), which plots the Dow Jones Industrial Average, the S&P 500, and the NYSE Composite Index for 1980–2000. (The Dow Jones values have been divided by 10 to put them on a common basis with the other two indexes.)

By visual inspection, the correlation between the aggregate measures appears to be high. The correlation of the monthly price changes for the data used in Figure 10.4 for the S&P 500 and the NYSE Composite Index is 0.99. Merrill Lynch Quantitative Analysis estimated the correlation coefficient relating the S&P 500 and the Dow Jones Industrial Average to be 0.95, and the correlation coefficient between the S&P 500

⊕ **Point of Interest**

THE VARIETY OF SECTORS

The composition of the various sectors of the stock market depends on which source you are using. The following lists the sectors used by Dow Jones, Standard & Poor's, and Morningstar. The listing starts with the Dow Jones in alphabetical order and then provides the comparable sector for Standard & Poor's and Morningstar. In some cases, there appears to be no comparable sector (e.g., the omission of transportation by Morningstar). Since the sectors differ, the firms included in each will also differ. And although the returns on the various sectors are correlated, the degree of correlation does differ (i.e., the correlation coefficients between two sectors such as the Dow Jones consumer goods and the S&P consumer stables need not equal 1.0).

Dow Jones	S&P	Morningstar
Basic materials	Basic materials	Industrial materials
—	Communication services	Telecommunications
—	—	Media
Consumer goods	Consumer stables	Consumer goods
Consumer services	Consumer cyclicals	Consumer services
Financials	Financials	Financial services
Health care	Health care	Health care
Industrials	—	—
Oil & gas	Energy	Energy
Technology	Technology	Software
Transportation	Transportation	—
Utilities	Utilities	Utilities
—	—	Hardware

and the NYSE composite approximated 1.0. The NYSE reported that the correlation between its index and the S&P 500 was 0.968.

Bond Averages and Indexes

In addition to stock indexes, there are also aggregate measures of the bond markets. These averages and indexes differ from stock indexes in several ways. The first is the units. Bond averages may be expressed in terms of yields instead of prices. This is illustrated in Figure 10.5, which presents the Dow Jones 200 bond composite and the yields on Moody's Aaa-rated bonds for 1978–2000. The average is expressed in dollars and the yields are in percentages. The figure vividly illustrates an inverse relationship between bond prices and yields. For example, the bond average declined from 85.4 to 55.4 between January 1979 and September 1981 when yields rose from 9.3 percent to over 15 percent. Then yields started to decline and bond prices rose. This pattern continued into the early 2000s when bond yields were at lows not seen in decades. (This negative relationship between interest rates and bond prices is explained in Chapter 14 on the valuation of fixed-income securities.)

Measures of the bond markets that are expressed in terms of yields are obviously not comparable to stock indexes such as the S&P 500, which are based on prices. Even

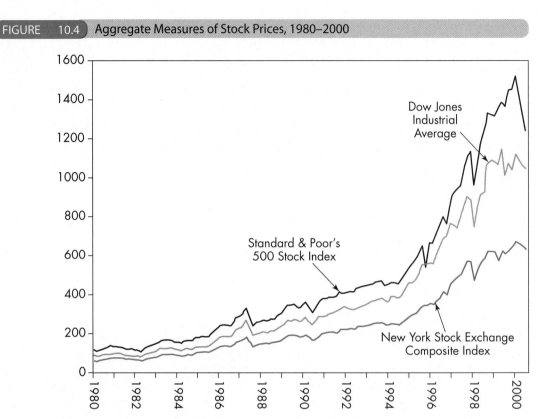

FIGURE   10.4   Aggregate Measures of Stock Prices, 1980–2000

Source: *Federal Reserve Bulletin,* various issues.

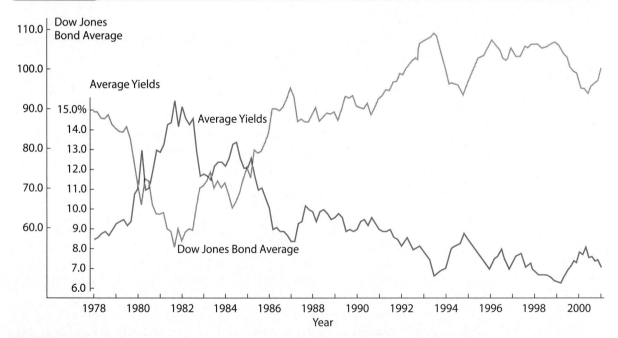

FIGURE   10.5   Dow Jones Bond Average and Yields on Mergent's (Moody's) Aaa-Rated Bonds, 1978–2000

Source: *Moody's Bond Record,* various issues, 1978–1999; *Mergent's Bond Record,* various issues, 2000; *The Wall Street Journal Index* (Ann Arbor, MI: UMI Company), 1978–2000.

measures of the bond markets that are expressed in terms of price may not be comparable to measures of stocks. Instead of experiencing the price appreciation associated with stocks, bond investors collect interest payments. Their return primarily consists of the flow of interest income, while the primary source of return to stockholders is price appreciation.

One means to overcome this problem of comparability is to select a starting point such as January 200X and then use the price plus the interest that is earned and *reinvested*. Over time, the value of the bond average should increase as the interest compounds. The Dow Jones corporate bond index has been reconstituted to include the reinvestment of interest payments, so the bond average is more comparable to the Dow Jones stock averages.

As with stock indexes, there are aggregate measures of the bond market in addition to the Dow Jones bond average. A sampling of these measures for U.S. Treasury debt and their ticker symbols is as follows:

30-year Treasury Bond	^TYX
10-year Treasury Bond	^TNX
5-year Treasury Bond	^FVX
13-Week Treasury Bill	^IRX

You may easily access these indexes by using an Internet source that provides stock prices and entering the ticker symbol. Bond indexes for corporate debt include Barclays aggregate bonds (AGG), Barclays high-yield bonds (JNK), and Barclays Asia bonds (AGZ). You may readily buy and sell exchange-traded funds that track these indexes. Use the ticker symbols provided after the index.

The Volatility Index (VIX)

One index that has received considerable publicity during the recent financial crises is the Volatility Index, which is commonly referred to by its ticker symbol: VIX. (Use ^VIX to obtain values of the index.). The VIX is a measure of investors' expectations or "sentiment" about near-term stock market volatility. Since the VIX is a gauge of investor expectations, it also measures market psychology and is often referred to as the "fear" index.

The actual calculation of the VIX is based on the S&P 500 index options and is expressed in percentages. (Options are explained in Chapters 17 and 18.) For example, a numerical value of 20 suggests that market participants expect the S&P 500 to swing by 20 percent over the next 12 months. Low values such as 10 suggest little volatility; market participants are not pessimistic or are even complacent. As they become more pessimistic and the stock market becomes more volatile and less certain, the value of the index rises. A value of 50 suggests an expectation of large swings in the S&P 500.

During 2005–2006, the value of the VIX fluctuated between 10 and 18 and remained in that range through July 2007. As financial problems started to emerge and people became more aware of them, the VIX rose. By January 2008, the index had risen to over 38 and continued to increase through the year. During October, the VIX rose from 39 to a historic 89 in a matter of days and ended the month at 55. As the financial crises started to recede, the VIX also declined and by 2010 stood at 20.

RATES OF RETURN ON INVESTMENTS IN COMMON STOCK

What returns have you earned on investments in securities? To answer this question, you should consider the purchase price of the security, the sale price, the flow of income (such as dividends or interest), and how long you owned the asset. The easiest (and perhaps the most misleading) return is the **holding period return (HPR)**. It is derived by dividing the gain (or loss) plus any income by the price paid for the asset. That is,

holding period return (HPR)

Income plus price appreciation during a specified time period divided by the cost of the investment.

10.1
$$\text{HPR} = \frac{P_1 + D - P_0}{P_0},$$

in which P_1 is the sale price, D is the income, and P_0 is the purchase price. If an investor buys a stock for \$40, collects dividends of \$2, and sells the stock for \$50, the holding period return is

$$\text{HPR} = \frac{\$50 + \$2 - \$40}{\$40} = 30\%.$$

The holding period return has a major weakness because it *fails to consider how long it took to earn the return*. This problem is immediately apparent if the information in the previous example had been a stock that cost \$40, paid annual dividends of \$1, and was sold at the end of the *second* year for \$50. Given this information, what is the return? Although the holding period return remains the same, 30 percent is obviously higher than the true annual return. If the time period is greater than a year, the holding period return overstates the true annual return. (Conversely, for a period that is less than a year, the holding period return understates the true annual return.)

Because the holding period return is easy to compute, it is frequently used, producing misleading results. Consider the following example. You buy a stock for \$10 per share and sell it after ten years for \$20. What is the holding period return on the investment? This simple question can produce several misleading answers. You may respond by answering, "I doubled my money!" or "I made 100 percent!" That certainly sounds impressive, but it completely disregards the *length of time* needed to double your money. You may compute the arithmetic average and assert that you made 10 percent annually (100% ÷ 10 years). This figure is less impressive than the claim that the return is 100 percent, but it is also misleading because it fails to consider compounding. Some of the return earned during the first year in turn earned a return in subsequent years, which was not taken into consideration when you averaged the return over the ten years.

rate of return (internal rate of return or IRR)

The discount rate that equates the cost of an investment (cash outflows) with the cash inflows generated by the investment.

The correct way to determine the **rate of return** or **internal rate of return (IRR)** that was earned is to phrase the question as follows: "At what rate does \$10 grow to \$20 after ten years?" You should recognize this as another example of the time value of money. The equation used to answer this question is

$$P_0(1 + r)^n = P_n,$$

in which P_0 is the cost of the security, r is the rate of return per period, n is the number of periods (e.g., years), and P_n is the price at which the security is sold. When the values are substituted in the equation, the answer is

$$\$10(1 + r)^{10} = \$20,$$
$$(1 + r)^{10} = 2,$$
$$r = \sqrt{2} - 1 = 1.0718 - 1 = 7.18\%,$$

Calculator Solution

Function Key	Data Input
PV =	−10
FV =	20
PMT =	0
N =	10
I =	?
Function Key	Answer
I =	7.18

so the annual rate of return is 7.18 percent. The correct rate of return on the investment (excluding any dividend income) is considerably less impressive than "I doubled my money!" or "I averaged 10 percent each year."

The inclusion of income makes the calculation of a rate of return more difficult. Consider the example in which you bought a stock for $40, collected $2 in dividends, and then sold the stock for $50 after two years. What is the rate of return? The holding period return is overstated because it fails to consider the time value of money. If you compute the rate of growth and consider only the original cost and the terminal value, the rate of return is understated because the dividend payments are excluded.

These problems are avoided by computing an investment's internal rate of return that equates the present value of all an investment's future cash inflows with the present cost of the investment. The general equation for the internal rate of return (r) for a stock is

10.2
$$P_0 = \frac{D_1}{(1 + r)} + \cdots + \frac{D_n}{(1 + r)^n} + \frac{P_n}{(1 + r)^n},$$

in which D is the annual dividend received in n years, and P_n is the price received for the stock in the nth year. The same equation is used to determine the yield to maturity in Chapter 14. The yield to maturity is the internal rate of return on an investment in a bond that is purchased today and redeemed at maturity.

If the internal rate of return were computed for the previous illustration of a stock that cost $40, paid an annual dividend of $1, and was sold at the end of the second year for $50, the equation to be solved is

$$\$40 = \frac{\$1}{(1 + r)} + \frac{\$1}{(1 + r)^2} + \frac{\$50}{(1 + r)^2}.$$

Notice that there are three cash inflows: the dividend received each year and the sale price. The internal rate of return equates *all* cash inflows with the cost of the investment. These cash inflows include periodic payments as well as the sale price. (The calculation for the holding period return combined the dividend plus the capital gain on the investment and treated them as occurring at the end as a single cash inflow.)

Solving this equation is tedious, especially if there is a large number of years. Select a rate (e.g., 12 percent) and substitute it into the equation. If the results equate both sides of the equation, the internal rate of return has been determined. If the sides are not equal, select another rate and repeat the process. For example, if 12 percent is selected, then

$40 = $1 × (interest factor for the present value of an annuity at 12 percent for two years) + $50 × (interest factor for the present value of $1 at 12 percent for two years)

= $1(1.690) + $50(0.797) = $41.54.

Since the two sides are not equal, 12 percent is not the internal rate of return. Since $41.54 exceeds $40, the rate is too small, so a greater rate would be selected and the process repeated.

This tedious process is made considerably easier with the use of a financial calculator or software. When the data are entered into the calculator, the internal rate of return on the investment, 14.17 percent, is readily determined. This 14.17 percent is the true, annualized rate of return on the investment. (The use of a financial calculator facilitates the computation of the internal rate of return, but calculators do have weaknesses. In this illustration, the yearly payments are equal and are entered into the calculator as an annuity. If the yearly payments were unequal, each payment would have to be individually entered. Because calculators limit the number of individual entries, they may not be used to determine the internal rate of return for problems with large numbers of cash inflows.)

The internal rate of return has two potential problems. The first concerns the reinvestment of cash inflows received by the investor. The internal rate of return assumes that cash inflows are *reinvested at the investment's internal rate*. In the preceding illustration that means the $1 received in the first year is reinvested at 14.17 percent. If the dividend payment is reinvested at a lower rate or not reinvested (e.g., it is spent), the true annualized return on the investment will be less than the rate determined by the equation. Conversely, if the investor earns more than 14.17 percent when the $1 is reinvested, the true return on the investment will exceed the internal rate of return determined by the equation.

The second problem occurs when you make more than one purchase of the security. Although the problem is not insurmountable, it makes the calculation more difficult. Suppose you buy one share for $40 at the beginning of the first year, buy a second share for $42 at the end of the first year, and sell both shares at the end of the second year for $50 each. The firm pays an annual dividend of $1, so $1 is collected at the end of year 1 and $2 at the end of year 2. What is the return on the investment?

To answer this question using the internal rate of return, you must equate the present value of the cash inflows and the cash outflows. The cash flows are as follows:

Time	Year 0	End of Year 1	End of Year 2
Cash outflow	$40	$42	—
Cash inflow	—	$ 1	$2 + $100

There are two cash outflows (the purchases of $40 and $42) that occur in the present (year 0) and at the end of year 1. There are two cash inflows, the $1 dividend received at the end of year 1 and the $2 dividend at the end of year 2 plus cash from the sale of the shares ($100) at the end of year 2. The equation for the internal rate of return is

$$\$40 + \frac{42}{(1 + r)} = \frac{\$1}{(1 + r)} + \frac{2 + 100}{(1 + r)^2}$$

and the internal rate of return is 16.46 percent.

In this example, you own one share during the first year and two shares during the second year. The return in the second year has more impact on the overall return than

Calculator Solution

Function Key	Data Input
PV =	−40
FV =	50
PMT =	1
N =	2
I =	?
Function Key	Answer
I =	14.17

dollar-weighted rate of return

The rate that equates the present value of cash inflows and cash outflows; the internal rate of return.

time-weighted rate of return

Geometric average of individual holding period returns.

the rate earned during the first year when you owned only one share. Since the number of shares and hence the amount invested differ each year, this approach to determining rates of return is sometimes referred to as a dollar-weighted rate of return.

An alternative to the dollar-weighted or internal rate of return is the time-weighted return, which ignores the amount of funds invested during each time period. This technique computes the return for each period and averages the results. In effect, it computes the holding period return for each period and averages them. In the illustration, the initial price was $40; the investor collected $1 in dividends and had stock worth $42 at the end of the year. The return for the first year was

$$(\$42 + 1 - 40) \div 40 = 7.5.$$

During the second year, a share rose from $42 to $50 and paid a $1 dividend. The return was

$$(\$50 + 1 - 42) \div 42 = 21.43\%.$$

The simple average return is

$$(7.5\% + 21.43) \div 2 = 14.47\%,$$

and the geometric average return is

$$\sqrt{(1.075)(1.2143)} - 1 = \sqrt{1.3054} - 1 = 1.1425 - 1 = 14.25\%.$$

As discussed earlier, the geometric average is the true compound rate, while the simple average tends to overstate the true annual rate of return.

In this illustration, the dollar-weighted return (i.e., the internal rate of return) is greater than the time-weighted return. This is the result of the stock performing better in the second year when the investor owned more shares. The results would have been reversed if the stock had performed better the first year than during the second year (i.e., 21.4 percent in year 1 and 7.5 percent in year 2). In that case, the larger amount invested would have earned the smaller return, so the dollar-weighted return would have been less than the time-weighted return.

Which of the two methods, the dollar-weighted return or the time-weighted return, is preferred? There is no absolute right answer. Because the investor is concerned with the return earned on *all* the dollars invested, the dollar-weighted return would appear to be superior. However, there is an argument for the use of a time-weighted return to evaluate the performance of a portfolio manager. For example, a firm may make periodic contributions to its employee pension plan. Because the timing and amount of the cash inflows are beyond the pension plan manager's control, the use of a dollar-weighted return is inappropriate. Thus, money managers often use a time-weighted return instead of a dollar-weighted return to evaluate portfolio performance.[3]

[3]The CFA Institute (**http://www.cfainstitute.org**) requires its members to calculate time-weighted returns at least quarterly using a geometric average. The purpose of the calculation is to inform clients of the portfolio manager's performance. The portfolio managers must also present measures of risk, such as the standard deviations of the returns.

⊕ Point of Interest

WHEN A 75 PERCENT RETURN PRODUCES A LOSS

You invest $100 in a mutual fund that earns 25 percent annually for three years. Unfortunately, it loses 75 percent during the fourth year but then comes back and earns 25 percent for the next three years. That's a total return of 75 percent. Because seven years were required to earn the 75 percent, the average return is 10.7 percent.

Unfortunately, the calculation (6) (25) – 75 does give 75, but that is not the rate of return. What actually happened to the investment is as follows:

Year	Value of Investment
0	$100.00
1	125.00
2	156.25
3	195.31
4	48.83
5	61.04
6	76.29
7	95.37

You lost money; the true rate of return is negative! This example points out two things. First, adding percentage changes is misleading. This problem is avoided by the following calculation:

$$(1.25)(1.25)(1.25)(0.25)(1.25)(1.25)(1.25)$$
$$= 0.9537.$$

On an annualized basis, the rate of return is

$$\$100(1 + r)^7 = \$95.37$$
$$r = 0.9537^{0.14286} - 1 = -0.7\%.$$

Second, one bad year can wipe out the gains of several good years. The 75 percent loss in the fourth year requires a 300 percent increase to offset it. If your stock declines from $195.31 to $48.83 (a 75 percent decrease), the stock must rise by a factor of 4 to go from $48.83 to $195.31, which is a 300 percent increase.

You may not experience such a large decline in the value of your stock. If, however, such a decline occurs when you need to sell the securities, the large loss will obviously have an impact on your wealth. The possibility of a worst-case scenario (i.e., a large loss when funds are needed) should be a consideration if you are anticipating selling the securities for a specific purpose. If, for example, your aim is to finance your daughter's college education, taking profits early may be desirable to avoid the possibility of a large loss occurring when the tuition bill comes due!

STUDIES OF INVESTMENT RETURNS

Several studies have estimated the annualized returns earned by investments in common stock. The initial studies found an annual return approximating 9 percent, but there were periods when the annual return rose to 15 percent.

Ibbotson and Sinquefield extended the results of the prior studies to include the returns on corporate bonds, federal government bonds, short-term Treasury bills, and the rate of inflation. The results are updated annually by Ibbotson Associates in *The Stocks, Bonds, Bills, and Inflation (SBBI) Yearbook*.

For 1926 through 2007, the annual return for common stock as measured by the S&P 500 stock index was 10.4 percent, but there was considerable variation from the annualized return. The standard deviation of returns was 20.2, which indicates that 68 percent of the returns fell between −10.2 percent and 30.6 percent. (Two standard deviations would indicate years in which the annual returns exceeded 50 percent and were less than −30 percent. For example, stocks rose by 52.6 percent in 1954 and declined by 26.5 percent during 1974.) The returns and their variability were less for corporate and Treasury bonds but the returns on small stocks were more volatile. For example, during 1967, small stocks rose 83.6 percent but lost 30.9 percent in 1973. (The definition of small stocks is *not* cheap, inexpensive stocks traded through Nasdaq. Small stocks are the firms with the smallest capitalization in the S&P 500.)

As the time period increases, the range in the returns diminishes. The impact of years with high returns is offset by years with low returns so that the average over a span of years approaches the average for the entire period. In addition, as the number of years increases, negative returns diminish and even vanish. Prior to 2009, if you consider ten-year time horizons, not one period sustained a loss. The worse case was 1965 through 1974, during which the annual return was only 1.4 percent. However, that conclusion changed during 2000–2009, when the S&P 500 declined by 9.1 percent, making it the worst decade ever for that index. (The decline during the 1930s was only −0.3 percent.)

Although historical results indicate positive returns over extended periods of time, the investor may want to ask questions such as "Do securities traded in a particular market such as the Nasdaq stock market generate higher returns than stocks traded on another market such as the New York Stock Exchange?" An even more important question is "Will past returns forecast future returns?"

The time period selected is important. (The SBBI returns for 1926 through 2007 do not include the impact of the large decline experienced during 2008–2009. The returns, however, do include the impact of the 1930s.) Consider Figure 10.6, which plots the Nasdaq market index against the S&P 500. While a few stocks (e.g., Microsoft) are in both indexes, the essential composition of each index differs. Figure 10.6 has two parts, and each index has been adjusted to establish a common starting value: 100 for 1980–1994 and 100 for 1995–2000. Part (a) covers 1980–1994 and indicates that the Nasdaq rose slightly more than the S&P 500, about 11 percent annually versus 10 percent annually over the period. The figure also indicates the high correlation between the two indexes, which essentially moved together. The return earned by the Nasdaq may have been higher because that market consisted of riskier securities.

Part (b) suggests a similar result from the *beginning* of 1995 to the *ending* value at the beginning of 2004. But those returns do not hold if a different time period is selected as the starting point or ending point for comparing the returns. Figure 10.6 clearly illustrates the large increase experienced by the Nasdaq stock market starting in 1998 and continuing into 2000, and the subsequent large decline that started in 2000 and continued through 2002. If an individual purchased Nasdaq stocks during 1999 and held them until the end of 2003, that investor sustained a loss, and several years later, the Nasdaq index remained below its closing value of December 2000.

Whether historical returns can be used to forecast is certainly an important question. In part (b) of Figure 10.6, after the large increase the Nasdaq reverted to its prior pattern. (This is sometimes referred to as "reverting to the mean.") This pattern suggests that historical returns have predictive power. An obvious implication would be that the large market declines experienced during 2007–2009 are another illustration of the pattern in part (b) of Figure 10.6, except inverted. The essential question would be "Will the markets revert to their historical patterns and resume annualized returns approximating 10 percent?"

FIGURE 10.6 S&P 500 Stock Index and Nasdaq Stock Index, 1980–2003

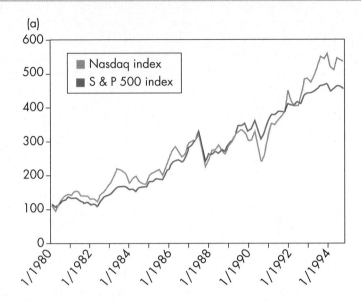

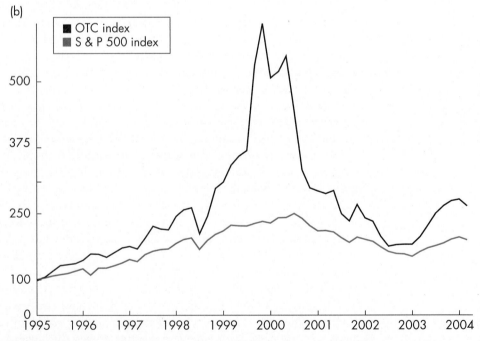

Source: Data from Commodity Systems, Inc. (CSI) available through Yahoo! at **http://finance.yahoo.com** under the section "Historical Prices."

The Reinvestment Assumption

Before jumping to conclusions as to what an investor in the stock market will earn, you should realize that studies of investment return are aggregates. Your portfolio may not mirror the market return. In addition, historical returns may not be indicators of future returns. Studies of historical returns make a crucial assumption that investors may not be able to fulfill. The studies compute internal rates of return that assume that *cash inflows (i.e., dividend and interest income) are reinvested at the internal rate*. For most individuals, that assumption does not apply. While it obviously does not apply if you spend the payments, the assumption still would not apply even if the income were reinvested. Because income taxes would have to be paid on the dividend and interest income, the funds available to reinvest would be reduced. If all the funds were reinvested, you would have to pay the tax from other sources. In either case, the comparability of the historical returns with the return the investor earns is diminished. (This is, of course, the same problem covered in Chapter 6. In that discussion, a mutual fund's return was stated before tax but the individual had to pay the income tax on the distributions, so the realized returns were after tax.)

At best, historical returns may be taken as starting points in the valuation of stock. They may be used in the Capital Asset Pricing Model to help determine the required return, which in turn is used as the discount factor in the dividend-growth model. Thus, historical returns are important to the determination of whether a stock is overvalued or undervalued.

Time Diversification

Historical returns can also lead to an incorrect conclusion concerning risk. As the time period increases, the variability of returns appears to decrease, implying a decrease in risk. This misperception is sometimes referred to as "time diversification," and it suggests that as the time horizon is increased, risk is reduced. This conclusion concerning risk reduction is counterintuitive. A longer time horizon should imply greater uncertainty and greater risk. Certainly the next six months are more certain than the next twelve months, and the next year is more certain than ten years into the future. This uncertainty should increase as the time horizon increases.

Actually, the concept of time diversification is the result of the mathematical calculation of the standard deviation. Consider the following prices of a stock and the annualized returns:

	One-Year Returns	Two-Year Returns	Four-Year Returns	Five-Year Returns
$100	—			
$120	20.0%	—		
$130	8.3	14.0%		
$160	23.1	15.5	—	
$140	−12.5	3.8	8.8%	—
$170	21.4	3.1	9.1	11.2%
Geometric average return	11.2%	9.0%	9.0%	11.2%
Standard deviation of the return	14.9	6.6	0.2	0.0

In this illustration, the standard deviation of the returns declines as the number of years increases. In fact, there is no variability in the return for the five-year time period.

The standard deviation is 0.0, indicating no variability and no risk. This lack of variability is, of course, the result of only one observation, the five-year return.

The conclusion that there is no risk is false. Certainly the individual making the investment now does not know the value of the portfolio at the end of the time period. Risk is the uncertainty of the future value, when the asset is sold. This future price cannot be known with certainty, and the future price should become less certain as the time period increases. The standard deviation does measure the variability of returns and is an important tool for comparing performance (as in the Sharpe Index for ranking risk-adjusted performance of portfolio managers, presented in Chapter 6). Its use, however, to justify a longer investment time horizon on the basis of risk reduction is a misuse of an important mathematical tool.

The importance of time rests not with risk reduction but with the realization that time works in the investor's favor. Most individuals have limited resources; the accumulation of wealth through investments requires the passage of time. The Ibbotson studies suggest that over time, equity investors earn the highest returns when compared to other financial assets. Compounding has a greater impact the longer the time period. These considerations obviously argue for the investor to adopt a long time horizon.

While long time horizons are important, any investor who had to liquidate in late October 1987 or during the last half of 2002 into 2003 or 2008 into 2009 learned that investments still involve risk even if the assets were accumulated over an extended period of time. "Time diversification" and its implication that increased time reduces risk is unfortunate, since risk management and diversification are among the most important concepts in investments. The construction of a diversified portfolio reduces the risk associated with specific securities. Once the investor has developed an appropriate asset allocation and constructed a well-diversified portfolio, the risk exposure essentially depends on movements in the market and the portfolio's response to those movements. That risk is not reduced if the investor has a long time horizon.

REDUCING THE IMPACT OF PRICE FLUCTUATIONS: AVERAGING

One strategy for accumulating shares and reducing the impact of price fluctuations is to "average" the position. By buying shares at different times, the investor accumulates the shares at different prices. Such a policy may be achieved through the dividend reinvestment plans offered by mutual funds and many companies. An alternative is to systematically purchase shares of stock. There are two basic methods for achieving this averaging: the periodic purchase of shares and the purchase of additional shares if the stock's price falls.

Periodic Purchases

dollar cost averaging
The purchase of securities at different intervals to reduce the impact of price fluctuations.

Under the periodic purchase plan, the investor buys additional shares of a stock at regular intervals. For example, you may elect to buy $2,000 worth of a stock every quarter or every month. This purchase is made at the appropriate interval, no matter what the price of the stock is. Since the dollar amount is the same, this technique is referred to as **dollar cost averaging**.

EXHIBIT 10.2 Average Position When $2,000 in EMEC Stock Is Purchased Each Quarter

Date	Price of Stock	Number of Shares Purchased	Cumulative Number of Shares Owned	Average Cost of Share
1/1/X0	$25	80	80	$25.00
4/1/X0	28	71	151	26.50
7/1/X0	33	60	211	28.44
10/1/X0	27	74	285	28.07
1/1/X1	21	95	380	26.32
4/1/X1	18	111	491	24.44
7/1/X1	20	100	591	23.69
10/1/X1	25	80	671	23.85

The effect of such a program is illustrated in Exhibit 10.2, which shows the number of shares of EMEC stock purchased at various prices when $2,000 is invested each quarter. The first column gives the dates of purchase, and the second column presents the various prices of the stock; the third and fourth columns list the number of shares purchased and the total number of shares held in the position. The last column presents the average price of the stock held in the position. You should notice that when the price of the stock declines, $2,000 buys more shares. For example, at $33 per share, $2,000 buys only 60 shares, but at $18 per share you receive 111 shares. Because more shares are acquired when the price of the stock falls, this has the effect of pulling down the average cost of a share. In this example, after two years the average cost of the stock had fallen to $23.85 and you have accumulated 671 shares. If the price of the stock subsequently rises, you will earn more profits on the lower-priced shares and thus will increase the return on the entire position.

Averaging Down

Some investors find it difficult to purchase stock periodically, especially if the price of the stock has increased. Instead, they prefer to purchase additional shares of the stock only if the price declines. Such investors are following a policy of "averaging down." Averaging down is a means by which the investor reduces the average cost basis of an investment in a particular security by buying more shares as the price declines so that the average cost of a share is reduced. This may be particularly rewarding if the price subsequently rises, because you have accumulated shares at lower prices and earn a gain when the price increases. You may dollar cost average, which means that you spend the same dollar amount on shares each time a purchase is made. Or you may average down by purchasing the same number of shares (i.e., share averaging) every time a purchase is made.

share averaging

A system for the accumulation of shares in which the investor periodically buys the same number of shares.

Exhibit 10.3 illustrates these averaging down strategies. The price of the stock is given in column 1. Column 2 uses the dollar cost averaging method; the investor purchases $1,000 worth of stock every time the price declines by $5. As is readily seen in column 2, the number of shares in each successive purchase is larger. The last entries in the column give the total amount that the investor has spent ($5,000), the total number of shares that have been purchased (289), and the average cost of the shares ($17.30). The average cost of the total position has declined perceptibly below the $30 price of

EXHIBIT	10.3	Averaging Down Strategies

Price of the Stock	Number of Shares Purchased ($1,000 Each Purchase)	Cost of 100 Shares
$30	33	$ 3,000
25	40	2,500
20	50	2,000
15	66	1,500
10	100	1,000
	289 shares (for a cost of $5,000 and an average cost of $17.30 per share)	$10,000 (500 shares, for a cost of $10,000 and an average cost of $20 per share)

the initial commitment. However, if the price of the stock were to increase to $30, the entire position would be worth $8,670. You would have made a profit of $3,670 and earned a gain of 73 percent on the entire position.

Column 3 in Exhibit 10.3 illustrates the share averaging method, which means that the same number of shares are bought every time you make a purchase. When the price declines by $5, the investor buys 100 shares. If the price of the stock were to fall to $10, you would have accumulated 500 shares under share averaging, for a total cost of $10,000. If the price of the stock were to return to $30, the entire position would be worth $15,000, and the profit would be $5,000, for a gain of 50 percent.

There is a greater reduction in the average cost of the entire position with dollar cost averaging than with share averaging. When the investor dollar cost averages, the amount spent is held constant and the number of shares purchased varies. When the investor share averages, the number of shares purchased is held constant and the dollar amount varies. Because the investor purchases a fixed number of shares with share averaging regardless of how low the price falls, the average cost of a share in the position is not reduced to the extent that it is with dollar cost averaging.

The preceding discussion and examples explain the essentials of averaging. You may choose any number of variations on this basic concept. For example, you may choose to average down on declines of any dollar amount in the price of the stock or may select any dollar amount to invest for periodic purchases or for averaging down. The effect is the same—that is, to reduce the average cost basis of the position in that particular security.

Averaging down obviously requires that you have the funds to acquire the additional shares once the price has declined. Such purchases may not be cost-efficient when considering commissions. Dividend reinvestment plans that permit additional contributions may alleviate the problem of commission costs, but the purchases then cannot be made at a particular desired price. Instead, you must accept the price on the day the funds are invested.

If you follow a policy of averaging down, you should not assume that such a strategy will lead to a positive return. The stock's price may continue to decline, or many years may pass before the price rises to its previous level. You should view the funds spent on the initial investment as a fixed or sunk cost that should not influence the

⊕ Point of Interest

DOLLAR COST AVERAGING AND MUTUAL FUNDS

One of the advantages offered by mutual funds is dollar cost averaging. You may make equal, periodic investments. With such a strategy, you acquire fewer shares when prices rise but more shares when prices fall. The larger purchases reduce the average cost of a share, and, if the value of the stock subsequently rises, the low-cost stock generates more capital gains.

While you may follow such a strategy by purchasing stock through brokers, transaction fees reduce the attractiveness of dollar cost averaging, especially if you are investing a modest amount (e.g., less than $500).

Transaction costs may be eliminated or at least reduced through the use of mutual funds. Avoidance of fees is obvious in the case of no-load funds, but reduction in costs may also apply to load funds. Suppose you seek to invest $300 a month; many brokers may not execute such a small order. If they do buy $300 worth of stock, brokerage firms (including discount brokerage firms) will charge the minimum commission. Thus even with loading fees, mutual funds can still offer investors with modest sums a cheaper means to achieve the advantage associated with dollar cost averaging.

decision to buy additional shares. This type of reasoning is difficult to put into practice. Many individuals will not readily admit that they have made a poor investment. Unfortunately, they then follow a program of averaging down in the belief that it will vindicate their initial investment decision.

You should not automatically follow a policy of averaging down. Before additional purchases are made, the stock should be reanalyzed. If the potential of the company has deteriorated (which may be why the price of the stock has fallen), it would be wiser to discontinue averaging down, to sell the stock, and to take a tax loss. If the stock lacks potential, it makes no sense to throw good money (the money used to buy the additional shares) after bad (the money previously invested in the stock). Some questions that should be asked are "Does the firm still have potential?" or "Is there a substantive reason for maintaining the current position in the stock?" If the answer is yes, then averaging down and periodic purchases are two means of accumulating shares while reducing their average cost basis. Such strategies reduce the impact of price fluctuations, but it cannot be assumed the strategies produce superior returns, since excess returns are inconsistent with the efficient market hypothesis. Averaging strategies do, however, offer a means to save and systematically accumulate securities.

SUMMARY

Securities prices fluctuate daily. Many averages and indexes have been developed to track these price movements. Aggregate measures of the market include the Dow Jones averages, Standard & Poor's stock indexes, the NYSE index, the Russell stock indexes, and the Value Line stock index. There are also measures of segments of the market (e.g., large cap stocks) or sectors (e.g., tech stocks).

The composition and method of calculation of each measure differ. The composition ranges from the Dow Jones Industrial Average of 30 companies to the Dow Jones Wilshire 5000, which encompasses over 7,000 companies. The method of calculation is based on averages, which include price-weighted averages (e.g., the Dow Jones industrials), value-weighted averages (e.g., the S&P 500), and geometric averages (e.g., the Value Line index).

An index may be used to compute stock returns. Just as there are several ways to calculate an average, there are several ways to compute a return. The holding period return is the percentage change in the price of the investment over the entire time period. The holding period return may also include any income generated by the investment. Since the holding period return does not consider time, it does not include the impact of compounding and often overstates the true, compounded return. Dollar-weighted returns and time-weighted returns do include the impact of time. The dollar-weighted return (or internal rate of return) equates the percentage value of an investment's cash inflows with the investment's cash outflows. The time-weighted return is a geometric average of each period's return.

Although studies of common stock return have found that investors have earned an annual return in excess of 10 percent, there has been considerable variation from year to year. The late 1990s produced exceptional returns in excess of 25 percent annually, but 2007–2009 produced one of the strongest reversals ever experienced by investors, and by the end of 2009, market indexes were considerably below their historic highs.

Averaging is one strategy designed to reduce the impact of security price fluctuations. You may make periodic purchases (dollar cost averaging) or buy additional shares after the price has declined (averaging down). Such strategies may reduce the average cost of the stock in the position and generate larger returns. But to earn the higher returns, the price of the stock must rise, and such price increases are not assured.

QUESTIONS

1. What is a value-weighted average? Why does such an average place more emphasis on such firms as Microsoft and ExxonMobil than on other companies?
2. How does the computation of the Dow Jones Industrial Average differ from Standard & Poor's 500 stock index and the Value Line index?
3. Why may averaging percentage changes produce an inaccurate measure of the true rate of return?
4. Historically, what rates of return have investors earned on investments in common stocks?
5. What is the advantage of using a relative rather than an absolute scale to construct graphs of security prices?
6. What is dollar cost averaging? What is averaging down? Why may averaging down result in poor investment decisions?
7. The 1999 year-end values of several measures of the market were as follows:

Dow Jones Industrial Average	(^DJI)	11,497
S&P 500 stock index	(^SPX)	1,469
Nasdaq stock index	(^IXIC)	4,069

What were the percentage changes for these measures of the stock market in subsequent years?

8. You purchased $1,000 of IBM stock at the end of each quarter from 2000 through 2006. Excluding commissions, how many shares have you accumulated? As of January 2010, IBM was selling for $130. What was the position worth in January 2010? (For questions 7 and 8 you may obtain historical price data from Yahoo! Finance.)

9. The following correlation matrix gives the correlation coefficients for several sectors within the S&P 500. What can you conclude concerning investing in the sectors to diversify a portfolio?

	Consumer Staples	Financials	Health Care	Utilities
Consumer Staples	1.00			
Financials	0.72	1.00		
Health Care	0.69	0.59	1.00	
Utilities	0.31	0.36	0.23	1.00

PROBLEMS

1. You buy a stock for $20. After a year the price rises to $25 but falls back to $20 at the end of the second year. What was the average percentage return and what was the true annualized return?

2. The S&P 500 declined 38.49 percent during 2008, its third-worse performance in history. (The largest declines were 47.07 percent and 38.59 percent and occurred during 1931 and 1937, respectively.) What percentage increase is necessary to recoup the 38.49 percent loss?

3. You make an investment and the annual returns are as follows:

Year	Return
1	25%
2	3
3	−18
4	−10
5	15

The average annual return is 3 percent. What is the true annualized return?

4. Given the following information concerning four stocks,

	Price	Number of Shares
Stock A	$10	100,000
Stock B	17	50,000
Stock C	13	150,000
Stock D	20	200,000

a) Construct a simple price-weighted average, a value-weighted average, and a geometric average.

b) What is the percentage increase in each average if the stocks' prices become:
   i. A: $10, B: $17, C: $13, D: $40
   ii. A: $10, B: $34, C: $13, D: $20?
c) Why were the percentage changes different in (i) and (ii)?

5. You are given the following information concerning four stocks: ◾

Stock		A	B	C	D
Shares outstanding		1,000	300	2,000	400
Price	20X0	$50	30	20	60
	20X1	50	30	40	60
	20X2	50	60	20	60

Using 20X0 as the base year, construct three aggregate measures of the market that simulate the Dow Jones Industrial Average, the S&P 500 stock index, and the Value Line stock index (i.e., a simple average, a value-weighted average, and a geometric average).

a) What is the percentage change in each aggregate market measure from 20X0 to 20X1, and 20X0 to 20X2? Why are the results different even though only one stock's price changed and in each case the price that changed doubled?

b) If you were managing funds and wanted a source to compare your results, which market measure would you prefer to use in 20X2?

6. An investor buys a stock for $35 and sells it for $56.38 after five years.
   a) What is the holding period return?
   b) What is the true annual rate of return?

7. You sold a security for $980 that you purchased five years before for $795. What was the holding period return? Prove that this return overstates the annualized, compound return.

8. You invest $1,000 in a large company stock and $1,000 in a corporate bond. If you earn 10.0 percent on the stock and 6.0 percent on the bond and hold each security for 10 years, what are the terminal values for each investment? If you continue to hold each security and earn the same returns for 20 years, how much more will the stock generate than the bond over the entire time period? (When you invest for retirement or to finance a child's college education, you should think about the answer to this problem.)

9. In 2000, the Dow Jones Industrial Average's range was 11,723–9,796. If the historical returns on stock were 10.4 percent, what should have been the range in the Dow Jones Industrial Average for 2009 if that return had continued to be achieved for 2000 through 2009? Compare your estimated range with the actual range. What inference(s) can you draw? During 1973, the range of the Dow Jones Industrial Average was 1,052–788 and during 1982, the range was 1,074–766. Do you see any similarities between the two time periods (1973–1982 and 2000–2009)? What do these time periods suggest about using a buy and hold strategy or an index strategy?

10. Determine the value of the Dow Jones Industrial Average as of your date of birth and as of your most recent birthday. What was the annualized return on the average between the two dates? Since this return does not include dividend income, it understates the return. Assume that you collected dividends of 2 percent and compare the return on the Dow (including the dividends) with the historical return of 10.4 percent. Information on the Dow Jones averages and indexes may be found at http://www.djindexes.com.

11. A stock costs $80 and pays a $4 dividend each year for three years.
    a) If an investor buys the stock for $80 and expects to sell it for $100 after three years, what is the anticipated annual rate of return?
    b) What would be the rate of return if the purchase price were $60?
    c) What would be the rate of return if the dividend were $1 annually and the purchase price were $80 and the sale price were $100?

12. You purchase a stock for $100 that pays an annual dividend of $5.50. At the beginning of the second year, you purchase an additional share for $130. At the end of the second year, you sell both shares for $140. Determine the dollar-weighted return and the time-weighted compounded (i.e., geometric) return on this investment. Repeat the process but assume that the second share was purchased for $110 instead of $130. Why do the rates of return differ?

13. You purchase a stock for $40 and sell it for $50 after holding it for five years. During this period you collected an annual dividend of $2. Did you earn more than 12 percent on your investment? What was the annual dollar-weighted rate of return?

14. You purchase shares in an investment company such as a mutual fund for $35 a share. The fund makes the following cash payments ("distributions"):

Year	Distribution
1	$1.00
2	3.15
3	2.09
4	1.71

At the end of the fourth year, you sell the shares for $41. What was the dollar-weighted rate of return on your investment?

15. You invest $100 in a mutual fund that grows 10 percent annually for four years. Then the fund experiences an exceptionally bad year and declines by 60 percent. After the bad year, the fund resumes its 10 percent annual return for the next four years.
    a) What is the average percentage change for the nine years?
    b) If you liquidate the fund after nine years, how much do you receive?
    c) What is the annualized return on this investment using a dollar-weighted calculation and using a time-weighted calculation?

16. You sold a stock short for $50 and maintained the position for two years during which the stock paid an annual dividend of $2. At the end of two years, you closed your position when the stock was selling for $35. The margin requirement for short sales was 100 percent, so you could not borrow any funds. Excluding the impact of commissions, what was the annual rate of return on this investment?

17. You read that stock A is trading for $50 and is down 50 percent for the year. Stock B is also trading for $50 but has risen 100 percent for the year. If the investor had purchased one share of each stock at the beginning of the year, what can you conclude has happened to the value of the portfolio?

18. You believe that QED stock may be a good investment and decide to buy 100 shares at $40. You subsequently buy an additional $4,000 worth of the stock every time the stock's price declines by an additional $5. If the stock's price declines to $28 and rebounds to $44, at which time you sell your holdings, what is your profit? (Assume that no fractional shares may be purchased.)

19. On January 31, 2001, you bought 100 shares of AVAYA (AV) for $17.50 a share. Subsequent prices of AV were

January 1, 2002	$8.60
January 1, 2003	2.50
January 1, 2004	17.50

You owned the stock for three years (2001 to January 2004). What were your (1) holding period return, (2) average percentage return, and (3) true return on this investment?

The Financial Advisor's Investment Case
The Calculation of Returns

As a portfolio manager, you are required to provide clients with a measure of your performance, a comparison with the market, and a measure of risk. Initially, your portfolio was worth $10 a share. During the last five years, the ending values of the portfolio, the cash distributions, and the annual return on the market were as follows:

Year	Ending Value of Your Portfolio	Cash Distributed	Market Return
1	$10.50	$0.30	12%
2	12.00	1.00	17
3	11.25	0.50	2
4	12.50	1.00	−3
5	14.00	1.25	14

1. Over the entire five years, what was the time-weighted compound annual rate of return and the comparable rate of return on the market?

2. Was your return more or less volatile than the market? Did your investors bear more or less systematic risk than the market?

3. Were your returns more or less variable than the market returns?

4. Do your answers to Questions 2 and 3 indicate that your portfolio was more or less risky than the market?

5. Over the entire five years, what was the dollar-weighted compound annual rate of return?

6. If an individual bought 100 shares (i.e., $1,000) at the beginning of year 1, how much did the investor have in the account at the end of year 5, assuming that all cash distributions were reinvested in your fund at the year-end values? Based on these beginning and ending values, what was the annual rate of return?

7. Why do the rates calculated in Questions 1, 5, and 6 differ?

8. If an individual invested $1,000 at the beginning of each year, how much did the investor have in the account at the end of year 5 if cash distributions were also reinvested? (Assume that the year-end values are the beginning values of the subsequent year.) Using this strategy, the dollar-weighted internal rate of return is almost 20 percent. Why is the annual rate so much higher than those in which the investor made only the initial investment? Which of these rates best indicates your performance even when the individual invests $1,000 each year?

CHAPTER 11

The Macroeconomic Environment for Investment Decisions

Many events affect investment decisions. Some may cause securities markets to react, but the reaction is varied and difficult to anticipate. On April 18, 2001, the Federal Reserve unexpectedly lowered interest rates and the Dow Jones Industrial Average rose 372 points. Subsequently, on May 15 and on July 26, the Federal Reserve again lowered interest rates and the stock market yawned; the market did not react. During 2007, the economy continued to grow but its rate of growth declined. Whether the economy had entered a recession was a big point of debate during the first part of 2008. That debate occurred after the fact! The economy entered into a recession in December 2007, ending a period of economic growth that began in 2001.

Do these events matter from the investor's perspective? The positive response to the April 18 decline in interest rates affected investors who owned stocks. But the May 15 decrease in interest rates had no immediate impact. The recession that started in 2007 certainly did affect investors. The stock market had its third-worst year on record during 2008 and in 2009 traded more than 50 percent below the high achieved in 2007. The market recovery experienced in 2009 only partially recouped the losses generated during 2008.

This chapter considers the aggregate economic environment in which investment decisions are made.

LEARNING OBJECTIVES

After completing this chapter, you should be able to:

1. Define gross domestic product and specify its components.
2. Identify the factors that affect a specific rate of interest.
3. Differentiate the discount rate, the federal funds rate, and the target federal funds rate.
4. Describe the tools of monetary policy and the mechanics of open market operations.
5. Contrast the different measures of the money supply.
6. Explain how monetary and fiscal policy and a federal government deficit may affect securities prices.
7. Determine which investments may be desirable in an inflationary environment.

Emphasis is placed on the Federal Reserve's monetary policy, especially the impact on interest rates and the supply of money. Since the risk-free rate is part of the required return in the Capital Asset Pricing Model, anything that affects interest rates should affect securities prices. The chapter ends by raising two questions: Will the stimulatory fiscal and monetary policy started during 2009 have inflationary consequences? If inflation does occur, what investments should you make now to offset the impact of an anticipated inflationary environment?

THE LOGICAL PROGRESSION OF SECURITIES ANALYSIS

Financial planning has a logical process from the general to the specific. It starts with the specification of goals and prioritization of investment objectives followed by an analysis of the individual's resources and available funds. Then the funds are allocated among various assets to construct a diversified portfolio designed to meet the individual's financial objectives.

Fundamental securities analysis also follows a logical process from the general to the specific. Initially the analyst considers macroeconomic issues. Such concerns as economic growth and employment, inflation and commodity prices, currency flows and the balance of foreign trade, and the geopolitical environment can affect both the securities markets and the value of individual assets.

The analyst then proceeds to the various sectors of the economy such as energy, health, or technology. Questions the analyst needs to address include regulatory issues and the impact of government intervention. Certainly the election of President Obama raised questions concerning the regulation of health care. The incursion of government, of course, is not limited to regulation, since subsidies and tax policy are often designed to stimulate demand for specific products such as more fuel-efficient cars. Public policy often shifts the demand and supply for specific products and services. It may affect product pricing and the amount of funds that firms divert for investments in specific products.

Sectors are broad divisions within the economy and may be broken down into specific industries. For example, the sector "health" includes pharmaceuticals, health providers such as hospitals, and producers of medical devices. "Energy" encompasses oil and natural gas drillers, refiners, distributors, and retailers. Within each industry the analyst needs to be aware of the degree of competition, cost structures, pricing environments, and anticipated growth for each industry. Such background is necessary prior to analyzing the individual firm.

After taking into account the macroeconomy, the sector, and the industry, the securities analyst moves on to consider the specific firm. The product mix, management, sources of funds, measures of performance such as the return on assets and equity, and capacity to generate cash are all part of the process to value the company. Ultimately the purpose of the analysis is to determine if the firm's securities (i.e., its stocks and bonds) are undervalued and should be purchased for inclusion in an individual's portfolio.

Although the above process applies to all firms, the impact varies. What applies to the economy or industry may not apply to a specific firm. Some firms do poorly even when the economy prospers, and the converse also applies. During the 1990s, US Airways Group operated at a loss even though many airlines were profitable. During the 2000s, Southwest Airlines operated profitably when several airlines were generating losses and going through bankruptcy restructurings.

THE ECONOMIC ENVIRONMENT

All investment decisions are made within the economic environment. This environment varies as the economy goes through stages of economic prosperity and growth. This process used to be called the "business cycle," which was an unfortunate choice of words since the word *cycle* implies a regularly repeated sequence of events, such as the seasons of the year. The economy does not follow a regularly repeated sequence of events. Instead there are periods of growth and periods of stagnation, even contraction.

Each of these periods differs with regard to length and severity, and circumstances that affect the economy during one period may cease to exist or have marginal impact during subsequent periods. The oil embargo and the resulting sudden and large increase in the price of oil severely affected the economy during the 1970s. This was followed by a period of stable oil prices, but the economy continued to go through periods of growth and stagnation. As of January 1999, oil was $19 a barrel, but by late 2004 its price reached $53 a barrel. In July 2006, the price rose to $77; a year later it exceeded $90. In July 2008, the price reached $147 a barrel. That large increase was a contributing factor to the economic downturn that started in late 2007 and continued into 2009.

During the 1930s, the failures of many commercial banks had an enormous impact on the economy and contributed to the Great Depression. During the late 1980s, the failure of many savings and loan associations and commercial banks created a financial crisis, but unlike those of the 1930s, the financial crises had little impact on the aggregate economy. Such was not the case with the credit and banking crisis of 2008, which—like the large increase in the price of oil—contributed to the severe decline in the economy.

In many cases there is a strong relationship between stock prices and the aggregate economy. This was certainly illustrated during 2007–2009 when the aggregate economy experienced a sharp decline, and the decline in stock prices was one of the most severe in history. However, the large plunge in stock prices during October 1987 appears in retrospect to have been a nonevent. At that time, there were predictions that the large decline was forecasting another depression. Such a depression did not occur. Instead, the economy continued to prosper and the stock market rebounded to new highs. Of course, some investors did sustain major losses during October 1987, but other individuals who purchased stocks after the decline did well. Such transfers among investors, however, do not have the same impact on the country that is associated with a decline in the general level of economic activity.

Each of these events is important. The dramatic increase in the price of oil, the collapse of segments of the banking and financial system, and the severe decline in stock prices did inflict losses on investors during 2007 through 2009. It is, however, possible that none of these events will be repeated or repeated simultaneously; the next economic crisis may be perceptibly different from prior crises. If such repetitions were to occur, individuals would soon recognize the patterns and adjust accordingly. Such adjustments, of course, would ensure that the future would not be a replay of the past.

MEASURES OF ECONOMIC ACTIVITY

gross domestic product (GDP)

Total value of all final goods and services newly produced within a country by domestic factors of production.

Economic activity is measured by aggregate indicators such as the level of production and national output. Perhaps the most commonly quoted measure is **gross domestic product (GDP)**, which is the total dollar value of all *final* goods and services newly produced within the country's boundaries with *domestic* factors of production. Cars made in the United States by Toyota are included in GDP, while IBM computers produced in Europe are not. Gross domestic product has replaced gross national product

(GNP) as the primary measure of a nation's aggregate national output. (GNP is the total value of all final goods and services newly produced by an economy and includes income generated abroad—that is, income earned abroad by U.S. firms is added and income earned in the United States by foreign firms is subtracted.) The change from GNP to GDP emphasizes the country's output of goods and services within its geographical boundaries. Alternative measures of economic activity stress prices and employment. Emphasis is often placed on unemployment, especially the rate of unemployment, which measures output lost.

GDP may be computed by adding the expenditures of the sectors of an economy or by adding all sources of income. From the individual investor's perspective, the former is more useful since corporate earnings are related to expenditures by the various sectors of the economy. These expenditures are personal consumption (C), gross private domestic investment (I), government spending (G), and net exports (E). The sum, GDP, is often indicated by the following equation:

11.1 $$GDP = C + I + G + E.$$

Equation 11.1 points out the importance to economic activity of personal spending, investment in plant, equipment, and inventory by firms, government spending, and the exporting of goods. Government taxation, of course, reduces the ability of individuals and firms to spend, but the tax revenues are spent—they contribute to the nation's GDP. Correspondingly, the importing of goods increases the GDP of other nations, while foreign spending here increases gross domestic product. (In a sense the Mercantilists of the fifteenth through the seventeenth centuries had it right: Export goods and receive gold. Perhaps they placed the emphasis incorrectly on the accumulation of wealth and national power. They should have said, "Export goods and increase the domestic economy by increasing output and employment.")

Since the GDP is the sum of spending by each sector, if one sector of the economy were to decline, then GDP would also decline if another sector did not increase. For example, a reduction in federal government spending puts pressure on business to expand jobs and invest in plant and equipment. Without such expansion in the business sector to offset the decline in government spending, consumer income and spending may not rise and the economy may stagnate.

Equation 11.1 also points out the importance of fiscal and monetary policies on the nation's economy. Excluding the direct impact of government spending, the thrust of a specific policy is its effect on the firms' and consumers' ability to, or incentive to, spend. For example, lower interest rates encourage additional spending by firms on plant, equipment, and inventory and by individuals on durable goods such as cars and homes. Higher interest rates have the opposite effect. These changes in business and consumer spending have an immediate impact on the aggregate level of output; that is, they affect the level of GDP.

Over time, GDP grows but the rate of growth varies. As the economy expands, employment also tends to increase. There are, however, periods when the economy contracts and unemployment increases. If the contraction lasts for more than two quarters, it is referred to as a **recession**. From 1964 through 1990, the economy experienced four periods of recession as determined by the National Bureau of Economic Research (NBER): December 1969–November 1970, November 1973–March 1975, January 1980–July 1980, and July 1981–November 1982. The length of these recessions varied

recession

A period of rising unemployment and declining national output.

from a few months in 1980 to almost a year and a half from 1981 to 1982. The periods of economic growth also varied from a short period of growth in late 1980 to mid-1981 to the long period of growth that started at the end of 1982 and lasted to July 1990. That recession ended in March 1991, and economic growth continued to the spring of 2001.

The recession of 2001 ended in November; it was very short and mild, and economic growth resumed. During the 2000s, housing prices, fueled by excessive and easy credit, rose dramatically. The situation completely changed in late 2007. Housing prices, which had never declined after World War II, started to fall. Many homeowners failed to make payments on their mortgages and lenders foreclosed on the properties. Bank failures in the United States and worldwide led to the reduction and availability of credit, which precipitated a liquidity and solvency crisis. Major firms were forced into bankruptcy, and others received funds from the government in order to survive. The price of a barrel of oil spiked to new highs and unemployment rose dramatically.

During this period stock prices experienced one of the sharpest declines in history. From a high exceeding 14,200 in 2007, the Dow Jones Industrial Average sank to below 6,500 in 2009, a decline is excess of 50 percent in less than two years. Since there is a relationship between stock prices and economic activity, securities analysts and portfolio managers follow various indicators of economic activity to help formulate possible investment strategies. These individuals need to know the direction of economic change *before* it occurs. Hence the emphasis is placed on *leading* indicators of economic activity. The National Bureau of Economic Research (http://www.nber.org) tabulates a series of economic indicators. Eleven are leading indicators, four are coincident indicators, and seven are lagging indicators. The data are reported individually for each series, and the NBER groups these indicators into three composite indexes.

The Conference Board also publishes composite economic indicators. As with the NBER indicators, some are leading while others are coincident and lagging indicators. The ten leading indicators are the following:

1. Average weekly hours of manufacturing production workers
2. Average weekly initial claims for unemployment insurance
3. Manufacturers' new orders (consumer goods and materials)
4. Time for deliveries
5. Manufacturers' new orders of nondefense capital goods
6. Building permits, new private housing units
7. Stock prices (S&P 500 stock index)
8. Money supply (M-2)
9. Interest rate spread (difference between ten-year Treasury bond yields and short-term rates)
10. Index of consumer expectations

Information concerning these indicators may be found at the Conference Board's home page, http://www.conference-board.org. However, there are two important caveats to consider. First, the time lapse between the initial decline in the index and the subsequent start of the recession differs. The 1973 recession started nine months after the decrease in the index, but the index declined for over a year and a half before the 1990 recession. Second, the index may give false signals. The index decreased in both 1984 and 1987 without a similar decline in the economy.

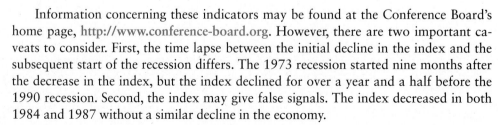

Measures of Consumer Confidence

One leading economic indicator that receives special attention is a measure of consumer sentiment or confidence. Consumer confidence affects spending, which has an impact on corporate profits and levels of employment. Two such measures include the Consumer Confidence Index (CCI) and the Consumer Sentiment Index (CSI). The CCI is published monthly by the Consumer Research Center of the Conference Board (http://www.conference-board.org) in the *Consumer Confidence Survey* and in the *Statistical Bulletin*; the CSI is published monthly by the Survey Research Center of the University of Michigan (http://www.sca.isr.umich.edu). The CSI is used by the Department of Commerce as one of its leading indicators. Both the CCI and the CSI provide indicators of consumer attitudes by focusing on (1) consumer perceptions of business conditions, (2) consumer perceptions of their financial condition, and (3) consumer willingness to purchase durables, such as automobiles, homes, and other large dollar-cost items. An increase in confidence forecasts that consumers will increase spending, which leads to economic growth.

The absolute level of either index is not as important as changes in the index. That is, changes in the indexes suggest changes in consumer optimism or pessimism. A decline in consumer confidence forecasts a reduction in the level of economic activity. Individuals who are worried about losing their jobs or who anticipate a decline in income will demand fewer goods and services and will not borrow to finance durable purchases. An increase in the indexes has, of course, the opposite implication. To some extent, a reduction in consumer confidence and a resulting decline in the demand for goods and services may be a self-fulfilling prophecy. If consumers do cut back and purchase fewer goods and services, firms will have to contract, laying off workers and cutting payrolls.

From an investor's perspective, the change in the economy resulting from a change in consumer confidence could lead to a shift in the individual's portfolio. A reduction in confidence that leads to economic contraction argues for movement out of growth companies into defensive stocks such as utilities or large firms (IBM or Merck) and debt instruments. The reduction in the level of economic activity should hurt firms' earnings and reduce their capacity to pay dividends or reinvest funds. However, the lower level of economic activity may induce the Federal Reserve to pursue a stimulatory monetary policy. At least initially, an easy-money policy will reduce interest rates, as the Federal Reserve puts money into the economy. Investors with long-term debt instruments in their portfolios should experience capital gains as bond prices rise in response to lower interest rates.

While investors may follow leading indicators to help formulate investment strategies, the usefulness of the index of leading indicators for trading in stocks is limited, because *stock prices are one of the leading indicators*. By the time the index of indicators has given a signal, stock prices have (probably) already changed. It is still possible, however, that one of the specific leading indicators leads the stock market. For example, if changes in the stock market precede changes in economic activity by four months and changes in the money supply precede the change in economic activity by seven months, then changes in the money supply might predict changes in the stock market three months before the event. Unfortunately, there is variation in the individual components of the leading indicators. While a specific indicator may lead one recession by three months, it may lead another recession by nine months. One indicator by itself is not an accurate forecaster. (If it were, there would be no need for an *index* of leading indicators.)

In addition, it is virtually impossible to tell when an indicator has changed. Peaks and valleys (i.e., changes in the indicators) are generally determined after the fact. It is impossible to tell when a recession has started (or ended) until the change has occurred, and the same principle would apply to a specific indicator's forecasting changes in stock prices.

This inability to forecast changes in stock prices is consistent with the efficient market hypothesis. If one variable or an index of several variables could be used to forecast the direction of stock prices, individuals using the technique would consistently outperform the market. Such performance is unlikely using publicly known information, so the inability to use economic data to forecast stock prices is further support for the semistrong form of the efficient market hypothesis.

THE CONSUMER PRICE INDEX

In addition to aggregate measures of economic activity and leading indicators, measures of inflation can have an important impact on investor behavior. Inflation is a general rise in prices and was previously discussed as an important source of risk. While prices are expressed in units of a currency (e.g., dollars), inflation is generally measured by an index. Two commonly used indexes are the Consumer Price Index (CPI) and the Producer Price Index (PPI). The CPI is calculated by the Bureau of Labor Statistics and measures the cost of a basket of goods and services over time. The PPI is calculated by the U.S. Department of Labor and measures the wholesale cost of goods over a period of time. Since goods are manufactured prior to their sale to consumers, changes in the Producer Price Index often forecast changes in the Consumer Price Index. Information concerning federal government statistics such as the Consumer Price Index may be found through the Bureau of Labor Statistics home site: http://stats.bls.gov.

 An alternative measure of inflation to the CPI is the index of Personal Consumption Expenditures (PCE) computed by the Bureau of Economic Analysis (BEA at http://www.bea.gov). Notice the difference in wording. The Consumer Price Index measures inflation by the change in the prices of a basket of goods and services. The Personal Consumption Expenditures index measures consumer spending. The PCE seeks to take into consideration consumers' response to changes in price. By measuring the response, the PCE measures expenditures and the impact of changes in prices on consumer behavior.

While aggregate prices are measured by an index, the rate of inflation is measured by changes in the index. If the CPI rises from 100 to 105.6 during the year, the annual rate of inflation is 5.6 percent. Over time, there has been considerable variation in the rate of inflation. During 1930, the inflation rate was −6.0 percent (i.e., prices in the aggregate fell). During 1980, the rate was 12.4 percent. For 1926 through 2005 the annual rate of inflation was 3 percent, with a standard deviation of 4.3. This result indicates that for 68 percent of the years, the rate of inflation ranged from a low of −1.3 percent to a high of 7.3 percent. For the 1955–2008 period, there were no years in which consumer prices fell.

The impact of inflation on individuals varies with their consumption of goods and services. Since inflation is a general rise in prices and the Consumer Price Index measures the price of a basket of goods and services, the impact on individuals depends on the extent to which they consume the particular goods whose prices are inflating. For example, higher housing costs do not affect individuals equally. Homeowners seeking to sell may benefit from the higher prices at the expense of those seeking to acquire housing. Prices also do not rise evenly over geographic areas. Heating costs may rise more in the north than in the south, and correspondingly the cost of air-conditioning may rise more in the south than the north. These differences and other problems—such as how the index is calculated and the inability to adjust the index for technological change in the goods consumed—have led some analysts to argue that the CPI overstates the true rate of inflation. (The Bureau of Labor surveys buying patterns about every ten years and reconstructs the basket of goods and services consumed by the average household.)

During deflation, which is a general decline in prices, the real purchasing power of assets and income rises as the prices of goods and services decline. Since World War II, inflation has been a common occurrence, but deflation is rare. While prices of specific goods and services may decline in response to lower demand or to lower costs of production, prices in general tend to be "sticky"—they do not decline. This stickiness is apparent in the labor market, in which an aggregate reduction in the demand for labor does not result in lower wages. Instead, workers are laid off and individuals looking for jobs are unable to find them, so the level of unemployment rises.

Even though deflation had not happened since the 1950s, the possibility of its occurring during 2008–2009 was a frequent concern facing policy makers and participants in financial markets. The CPI rose approximately 4 percent during 2007 but was virtually unchanged during 2008, and it rose 2.7 percent from January 2008 through December 2009. In addition there were 12-month periods during which the CPI actually declined. For example, from July 2008 through July 2009, the index declined 2 percent. Some of these changes in the CPI could be explained by the swings in energy and food prices, which are more volatile than prices in general. (For example, food prices are sensitive to changes in the weather.) The reality, however, was that consumer prices in general were very stable and had the potential to decline. That possibility of deflation raised the fear that economic activity and employment would decline.

THE FEDERAL RESERVE

Federal Reserve
The central bank of the United States.

In addition to forecasts of aggregate economic activity, investors are concerned with the monetary policy of the **Federal Reserve** (the "Fed"). The Federal Reserve is the country's central bank (http://www.federalreserve.gov). Although in many countries the central bank is part of the federal government, in the United States they are separate. However, both the federal government and the Federal Reserve share the same general goals of full employment, stable prices, and economic growth.

The Federal Reserve pursues these economic goals through its impact on the supply of money and the cost of credit. Monetary policy refers to changes in the supply of money and credit. When the Federal Reserve wants to increase the supply of money and credit to help expand the level of income and employment, it follows an *easy* monetary policy. When it desires to contract the supply of money and credit to help fight inflation, it pursues a *tight* monetary policy.

Determination of Interest Rates

The impact of the Federal Reserve's monetary policy is felt through its effect on the rate of interest—that is, the impact on the cost of borrowing funds. The rate of interest is determined by the demand for and supply of loanable funds. As interest rates decline, the quantity demanded of loanable funds increases. Lower rates increase the profitability of investments in assets such as plant, equipment, and inventory; reduce the cost of carrying a home mortgage; and increase the quantity demanded of borrowed funds. As interest rates rise, the converse applies. Higher returns encourage firms and individuals to spend less and save more.

The actual rate an individual borrower pays (and the investor earns) depends on several variables, such as the term of the loan or the riskiness of the borrower. The types and features of bonds and the impact of fluctuations in interest rates on bond prices is covered in Part 4 of this text. A specific interest rate may be expressed as a simple equation:

11.2 $$i = i_r + p_i + p_d + p_l + p_t.$$

The current nominal interest rate (i) is the sum of the real risk-free rate (i_r) plus a series of premiums: the premium for expected inflation (p_i), the premium for default risk (p_d), the premium for liquidity (p_l), and the premium for the term to maturity (p_t). Thus, the observed current rate of interest is the result of the interplay of several complex variables, each of which is simultaneously affecting the rate.

The *real risk-free rate* is the return investors earn without bearing any risk in a noninflationary environment. While no exact measure of the real risk-free rate exists, analysts generally believe it ranges from 2 to 4 percent. The real risk-free rate varies with the general level of economic activity, rising during periods of economic expansion and contracting during periods of economic stagnation. During a period of rapid economic growth, the real risk-free rate may rise to 4 percent, but the actual observed interest rate will be higher as a result of the other contributing factors.

The *inflation premium* depends on expectations of future inflation. A greater anticipated rate argues for a higher rate of interest. Since inflation may vary from year to year, the expectation also varies. If the expected inflationary rate is 4 percent for one year and 6 percent for the second year, the premiums will differ. In this case, the one-year rate of interest would be less than the two-year rate. The investor would have to earn only 4 percent for a one-year loan to cover the expected rate of inflation but would require a higher interest rate on a two-year loan to be compensated for the higher anticipated rate of inflation in the second year. This relationship would be reversed if the expected rate of inflation were 6 percent for the next year and 4 percent for the second year. In that case, the rate on a two-year debt instrument could be lower than the rate on a one-year security. (The inflation premium on the one-year security would have to be 6 percent to compensate for that year's rate of inflation, while the premium on the two-year security could be 5 percent annually to compensate the investor for the expected 10 percent inflation over the two-year time period.)

The *default premium* depends on investors' expectations or the probability that the lender will not pay the interest and retire the principal. The higher the probability of default, the greater will be the interest required to induce investors to purchase the securities. Rating systems give some indication of default risk, and the difference in yields and prices between bonds with different ratings is illustrated in Figure 14.1 in Chapter 14.

The *liquidity/marketability premium* is related to the ease with which the asset may be converted into cash near its original cost. Although there is an active secondary market in debt securities, there are differences in the depth of these markets. The bonds of a well-known company such as AT&T may be readily sold, but the secondary market for the bonds of a small company may be inactive. The size of an issue of bonds also affects its marketability. A large $500 million bond issue will have an active secondary market. A small issue, however, may not have an active secondary market.

The *term premium* is associated with the time (or term to maturity) when the bond will be redeemed. Investors prefer short-term to long-term bonds. As is explained in Chapter 14, when interest rates rise, bond prices fall, and the amount of the price decline is greater the longer the term of the bond. To compensate for the possibility of higher interest rates inflicting capital losses on bondholders, investors demand a higher interest rate as the term of the bond increases.

As this discussion indicates, the interest rate is affected by many factors. The actual observed current nominal rate of interest is the result of the simultaneous interplay of all these factors. Thus, anomalies in bond yields are possible. For example, the interest rate on a poor-quality bond that matures in one year may be less than the rate on a high-quality bond that matures in ten years, if the premium for the longer term exceeds the default premium. Another possible explanation for the difference in the yields could be that the poor-quality bond is actively traded, while the higher-quality bond is a small issue with an inactive secondary market. Or investors could anticipate an increase in the rate of inflation. This expectation would lead to higher rates for the ten-year bond but have little impact on the rate paid by the bond that matures within a year.

The Impact of the Federal Reserve on Interest Rates

The determination of interest rates is complicated by the actions of the Federal Reserve. The Federal Reserve seeks to affect the level of economic activity by changing interest rates. Through its impact on the cost of credit, the Federal Reserve seeks to control inflation or to stimulate employment and economic growth. The Federal Reserve affects interest rates through its power to change the money supply by using the tools of monetary policy: the reserve requirements of banks, the discount rate, and open market operations.

The Federal Reserve influences the money supply and interest rates through the lending capacity of the fractional reserve banking system. Depository institutions (commercial banks and savings institutions, such as savings and loan associations) must hold reserves against their deposit liabilities. These reserves are divided into *required reserves* and *excess reserves*. This division depends on the **reserve requirement**, which is the percentage set by the Federal Reserve that depository institutions must hold against deposit liabilities. (Deposit liabilities are primarily checking and savings accounts, but the Federal Reserve may set reserve requirements against other accounts, such as time

reserve requirement

The percentage of cash that banks must hold against their deposit liabilities.

deposits.) If the reserve requirement is 10 percent and $100 cash is deposited, $10 must be held against the deposit (the required reserve) and $90 is available for lending (the excess reserves). Only a fraction of the new cash (10 percent) must be held against the deposit liability.

When the commercial banking system lends the excess reserves, the supply of money and credit is expanded. The converse occurs when the reserve requirement is increased and banks are forced to contract their lending. The supply of money and credit declines as excess reserves are removed from the system. By altering the reserve requirement, the Federal Reserve affects the capacity of banks to lend and thus affects the supply and cost of credit.

discount rate

The rate of interest that the Federal Reserve charges banks for borrowing reserves.

The **discount rate** is the interest rate the Federal Reserve charges depository institutions for borrowing reserves. When banks borrow from the Federal Reserve, they receive excess reserves. When these reserves are loaned, they expand the supply of money and credit. Depository institutions may also borrow from the Federal Reserve when they determine that they have insufficient reserves to meet their reserve requirements. In that case, borrowing the required reserves would not expand the supply of money and credit, because the expansion had already occurred at the time the loans were made. By borrowing the necessary reserves, banks will not have to liquidate assets in order to obtain the funds to meet their reserve requirements. Such liquidations would cause the system to contract, so in this case, borrowing the reserves from the Federal Reserve maintains the supply of money and credit.

Although the Federal Reserve does change the discount rate, such changes may be more symbolic than substantive. There are other, more effective (and subtler) means to alter the supply of money and credit. Instead of relying on the discount rate and the reserve requirement, the Federal Reserve uses the **federal funds rate** (or *Fed funds rate*) and open market operations. While the term *federal funds rate* includes "federal" and "rate," this rate should not be confused with the discount rate or the rate on federal government debt. The federal funds rate is the interest charged by banks when they lend reserves to each other. Banks with excess reserves can put those funds to work by lending them to other banks in the federal funds market, and the bank in need of reserves acquires them without having to borrow from the Federal Reserve.

federal funds rate

The rate of interest a bank charges another bank for borrowing reserves.

Unlike the discount rate, the federal funds rate is not set by the Federal Reserve. Instead, it is established by the interaction of the demand and supply of funds available in the federal funds market. The Federal Reserve, however, can affect the supply of funds and thereby affect the federal funds rate. During the 1990s and 2000s, the Federal Reserve set a target federal funds rate and changed that target as a primary indicator of monetary policy.

Fluctuations in the federal funds rate are illustrated in Figure 11.1, which presents the target rate from 1998 through 2009. While the federal funds rate reached 6.5 percent during January 2000, the Fed responded to subsequent sluggish economic behavior by lowering the rate. After economic growth increased during 2003, the Fed began to raise the target rate in 0.25 percent increments so that by mid-2006, the rate reached 5.25 percent. The pattern was reversed in 2007, and the target rate was rapidly reduced during 2007–2008 so that by year's end it was virtually 0 percent (0.00 to 0.25). Such a rate was an unprecedented response to the financial crisis and subsequent increases in unemployment, defaults, home foreclosures, and bankruptcies.

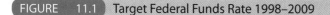

FIGURE 11.1 Target Federal Funds Rate 1998–2009

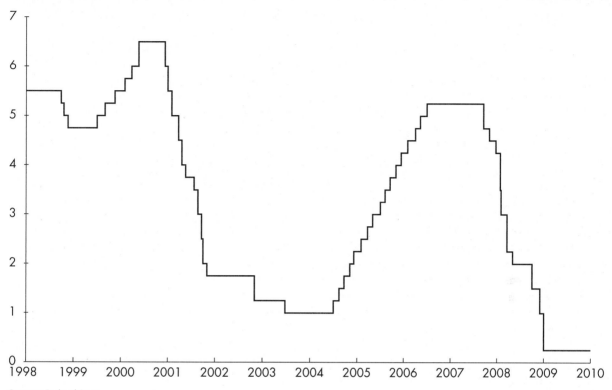

Source: Federal Reserve.

open market operations

The buying or selling of Treasury securities by the Federal Reserve.

The Fed achieves the desired effect on the federal funds rate through its most important tool of monetary policy, open market operations. **Open market operations** are the buying and selling of securities (primarily short-term Treasury bills) by the Federal Reserve. The Fed may buy or sell these securities in any quantity at any time. When the Federal Reserve follows an expansionary policy, it purchases securities. When the Federal Reserve pays for the securities, the funds are deposited into commercial banks, putting reserves into the banking system. Because only a percentage of the reserves will be required against the deposit liabilities, the remainder become excess reserves. When these newly created excess reserves are loaned by the banking system, the supply of money and credit is increased.

A tight (contractionary) monetary policy is designed to drain reserves from the banking system. The Federal Reserve sells securities, which are then purchased by the general public or banks. When the securities are paid for, funds flow from deposits to the Federal Reserve. The effect is to reduce the reserves of depository institutions. The reduction in reserves decreases the banks' capacity to lend and contracts the supply of money and credit.

Open market operations have a direct and immediate impact on interest rates. Purchasing securities increases prices and simultaneously drives down yields. The opposite occurs when the Federal Reserve sells securities, which reduces their price and

⊕ Point of Interest

THE RATE OF INTEREST PAID BY THE FED ON BANK RESERVES

In October 2008, the Federal Reserve announced that it would start paying interest on banks' reserves. Initially, the rate on required reserves was set at the average targeted federal funds rate minus 0.10 percent. The rate on excess reserves was set at the targeted federal funds rate minus 0.75 percent.

Since the federal funds rate is the result of the interaction of supply and demand for overnight loans by banks, the Fed can only affect but not control that rate. The rate paid on reserves, however, is set by the Federal Reserve. By paying interest on reserves, the Fed establishes a lower bound on the federal funds rate and provides both liquidity and stability to the financial system.

Without this lower bound, interest rates could be less than the Fed's targeted federal funds rate. Bank A, however, will not lend to Bank B at a rate that is less than the Fed's rate on reserves. Instead Bank A will leave reserves with the Fed and earn that risk-free rate. The rate on reserves thus establishes a floor on interest rates.

The lower bound should be particularly important when the Fed seeks to tighten credit. If the Fed wants to tighten credit, it raises the rate paid on reserves. Banks then have an incentive to leave the reserves with the Federal Reserves and not to lend them elsewhere, which reduces liquidity within the system. Any increase by the Fed in the rate paid on reserves would drive up all other rates in the financial system.

In 2010, discussion revolved around replacing the targeted federal funds rate with the rate on excess reserves as the benchmark for the Fed's interest rate policy. The essence of the argument was that using the rate on reserves as the benchmark short-term rate should give the Federal Reserve more power over interest rates. More control should increase financial stability and help achieve the Fed's objectives of maximum employment with price stability. Whether this new benchmark will be adopted, however, was only conjecture when this text went to press.

increases yields. The change in yields is transferred to other interest rates. As was explained earlier, interest rates are the result of several factors including the risk-free rate, the default premium, the liquidity/marketability premium, and the term premium. Since short-term U.S. Treasury bills are the safest of all debt instruments, their yield is often used as the risk-free rate. Changes in that risk-free rate must have an impact on interest rates in general.

Changes in monetary policy should also affect stock prices. This impact may be the result of a change in the required return used to discount future cash flows. For example, in the Capital Asset Pricing Model, a higher risk-free rate would lead to a higher required return and lower stock valuations. Monetary policy may also affect stock prices through its effect on a firm's earning capacity. An easy monetary policy that reduces the cost of credit may increase earnings, resulting in higher dividends and more growth through the retention of earnings. A tight monetary policy should have the opposite impact. Higher interest rates should reduce earnings, which reduces the firm's ability to expand and pay dividends.

Determining the Direction of Monetary Policy

To take advantage of changes in interest rates, the investor needs to know the direction that the Federal Reserve is following. It should come as no surprise then that Fed watching is a major activity among securities analysts and portfolio managers. Major changes in monetary policy occur after the Federal Reserve's Board of Governors' meetings and may be signaled by changes in the target federal funds rate. Analysts also track changes in the nation's money supply and bank reserves in an effort to determine current monetary policy.

Unfortunately, monetary statistics, which are released weekly, do not clearly indicate the Federal Reserve's monetary policy. Although the Fed's purpose is to control the money supply to stimulate economic growth and to maintain stable prices and full employment, there is disagreement as to the composition of the money supply. The simplest definition of the supply of money (commonly referred to as **M-1**) is the sum of currency, coins, and checking accounts (including interest-bearing checking accounts) in the hands of the public. A broader definition (**M-2**) adds savings accounts to this definition. Thus, if individuals shift funds from savings accounts to checking accounts, the money supply is increased under the narrow definition (M-1) but is unaffected under the broader definition (M-2).

The growth rate in the money supply will depend on the definition used by the analyst. Figure 11.2 plots M-1 and M-2 for 1986 through 2000. Over the entire period, both M-1 and M-2 rose, but there were periods in which the rates of growth differed. For example, during 1994 through 2000, M-2 grew by over 32 percent while M-1 was virtually unchanged. An opposite pattern occurred during 1991. There were even periods (such as 1996) when M-1 declined while M-2 rose.

An alternative measure to determine the direction of change in monetary policy is the "monetary base" or "high-powered money." The monetary base is the sum of coins, paper money (currency), and bank reserves kept within a bank or at the Federal Reserve. Since banks' capacity to lend is ultimately related to banks' reserves, changes in the monetary base should mirror current monetary policy.

The measures of the money supply may present conflicting signals, but the consensus is that the Federal Reserve systematically expands the money supply over time to maintain economic growth. (Over the 15-year period in Figure 11.2, M-1 and M-2 grew annually at 3.85 percent and 4.75 percent, respectively.) From the individual investor's perspective, the growth in the money supply is related to economic growth and economic growth is related to stock prices. If the money supply rises too slowly, economic growth will be constrained, which should reduce stock prices. If the money supply rises too rapidly, inflation will result, which is associated with higher rates of interest and lower stock prices. The goal is to determine what rate of growth in the money supply will over time sustain economic growth without creating stagnation or inflation.

Although the monetary policy of the Federal Reserve can have an important impact on bond and stock investments, developing a successful investment strategy based on monetary policy is exceedingly difficult, if not impossible. In addition, the stock market is a leading indicator of economic activity. The market anticipates change in monetary policy and often does not react to the policy change unless the change is unanticipated. Hence, to use changes in monetary policy as a guide for an investment strategy, it is necessary to differentiate between expected changes—the effects of which are already embodied in stocks' prices—and unanticipated changes, which can have an impact on stock prices. This means that the investor must correctly anticipate and act before the unexpected change. In efficient financial markets, the investor must have superior insight or luck to use changes in monetary policy to consistently generate superior stock market returns.

M-1

Sum of demand deposits, coins, and currency.

M-2

Sum of demand deposits, coins, currency, and savings accounts at banks.

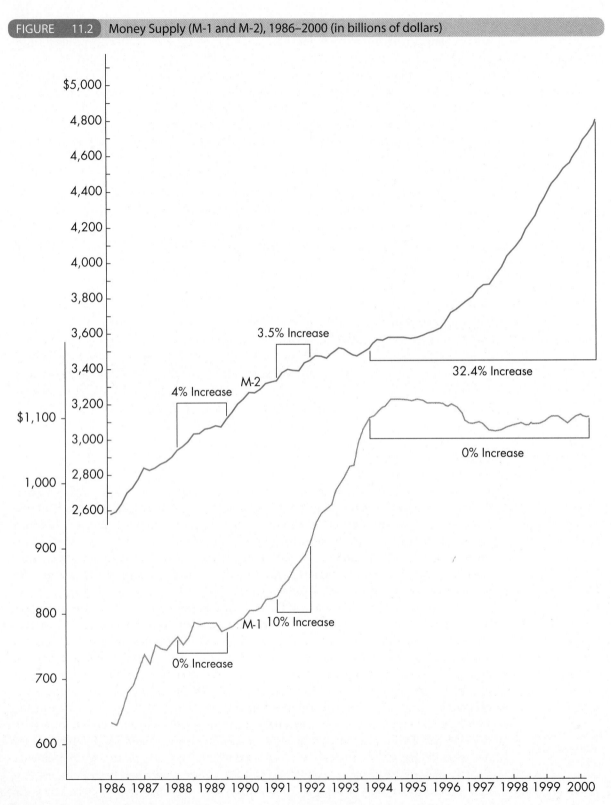

FIGURE   11.2   Money Supply (M-1 and M-2), 1986–2000 (in billions of dollars)

Source: *Federal Reserve Bulletin,* various issues.

⊕ **Point of Interest**

FED WATCHING

Because changes in interest rates can have a major impact on securities prices, it is not surprising that investors watch the Fed with the hope of determining the next change in monetary policy. This watching primarily revolves around meetings of the Federal Open Market Committee and the statements of the chairman of the Board of Governors of the Federal Reserve.

The Federal Open Market Committee is individually the most powerful component of the Fed because it has control over open market operations. The committee consists of 12 members, 7 of whom are the members of the Board of Governors of the Federal Reserve. The remaining 5 members are presidents of some of the 12 Federal Reserve district banks. Membership on the Open Market Committee rotates among 11 of the district bank presidents. The president of the New York district bank is a permanent member.

The most important individual member of the Fed is the chair of the Board of Governors. During the 1990s to 2006, Alan Greenspan served as chair, followed by Ben Bernanke. As chair of the Board of Governors, Bernanke is the chief spokesperson for the Fed. The chair's frequent testimony to Congress (and the announcements and minutes of Board meetings) are scrutinized for clues to future Fed actions. The market does react to the chair's statements. In December 1996, Chairman Greenspan remarked that recent increases in stock prices exhibited "irrational exuberance." The next day, the Dow Jones Industrial Average declined 145 points. In June 2006, the announcement of an increase in the target federal funds rate was accompanied by a statement suggesting that further rate increases might not be necessary. The Dow promptly rose more than 200 points.

These illustrations indicate that the remarks of the chair and announcements from the Fed can have an immediate impact on securities prices. The impact, however, may be short-lived. The Dow rose more than 1,000 points within six months after the "irrational exuberance" statement. Thus, it should be evident that the Fed should not be the sole or perhaps even the primary basis for investment decisions.

FISCAL POLICY

fiscal policy

Taxation, expenditures, and debt management of the federal government.

In addition to the monetary policy of the Federal Reserve, the fiscal policy of the federal government can have an important impact on the securities markets. **Fiscal policy** is taxation, expenditures, and debt management by the federal government. The Council of Economic Advisors annually publishes the *Economic Report of the President*, which details the fiscal policy (i.e., taxation and expenditures) of the federal government and is available at **http://www.access.gpo.gov/eop/**. Like monetary policy, fiscal policy may be used to pursue the economic goals of price stability, full employment, and economic growth.

Obviously, taxation can have an impact on stock prices. Corporate income taxes reduce earnings and hence reduce firms' capacity to pay dividends and to retain earnings for growth. Personal income taxes reduce disposable income. This reduces demand for goods and services as well as savings that would be invested in some asset. Federal taxes also affect the demand for specific securities, such as tax-exempt bonds discussed in Chapter 15. Thus the tax policies may affect not only the level of securities prices but also relative prices, as certain types of assets receive favorable tax treatment.

deficit spending

Government expenditures exceeding government revenues.

The potential impact of the federal government's fiscal policy is not limited to taxation. Expenditures can also affect securities prices. This should be obvious with regard to the specific products bought by the government. Such purchases may increase a particular firm's earnings and enhance its stock's price. However, expenditures in general, especially **deficit spending**, in which expenditures exceed revenues, can affect the financial markets and securities prices.

⊕ Point of Interest

FINDING GOVERNMENT PUBLICATIONS ON THE WEB

The federal government and its agencies publish a substantial amount of material, some of which may interest the individual investor. This material includes historical data, forecasts, and regulations, such as the tax laws. Although the information is available in print form, the investor may find it easier to access the documents directly through the Internet.

The following is a list of Web addresses that should facilitate obtaining government material:

Federal Government
Economic Report of the President
http://www.access.gpo.gov/eop/
Bureau of Labor Statistics
http://stats.bls.gov
Bureau of Economic Analysis
http://www.bea.gov
Federal Deposit Insurance Corporation
http://www.fdic.gov

U.S. Treasury
http://www.ustreas.gov

Federal Reserve
Federal Reserve Board of Governors
http://www.federalreserve.gov
Federal Reserve Bank of New York
http://www.ny.frb.org

From this list, you may obtain the *Economic Report of the President,* information on interest rates (from the Federal Reserve or the Federal Reserve Bank of New York), employment statistics and consumer prices (Bureau of Labor Statistics), foreign exchange rates (Federal Reserve), and copies of tax laws and tax forms (IRS). There is also a Global Information Locator service (http://www.gils.net/index.html) to facilitate locating specific information and data published by the federal government.

When the federal government's expenditures exceed revenues, the federal government may obtain funds to finance this deficit from three sources: (1) the general public, (2) banks, and (3) the Federal Reserve. When the federal government sells securities to the general public to finance the deficit, these securities compete directly with all other securities for the funds of savers. This increased supply of federal government securities will tend to decrease securities prices and increase their yields.

A similar conclusion applies to sales of Treasury securities to banks. If the banks lend money to the federal government, they cannot lend these funds to individuals and businesses. The effect will be to raise the cost of loans as the banks ration their supply of loanable funds. Higher borrowing costs should tend to reduce securities prices for several reasons. First, higher costs should reduce corporate earnings, which will have an impact on dividends and growth rates. Second, higher borrowing costs should reduce the attractiveness of buying securities on credit (i.e., margin) and thus reduce the demand for securities. Third, the higher costs of borrowing will encourage banks to raise the rates they pay depositors. Since all short-term rates are highly correlated, increases in one rate will be transferred to other rates. Once again, the higher interest rates in general produce lower securities prices.

If the Federal Reserve were to finance the federal government's deficit, the impact would be the same as if the Fed had purchased securities through open market operations. In either case, the money supply would be increased. In effect, when the Fed buys the securities issued to finance the federal government's deficit, the Fed is monetizing the debt because new money is created.

surplus

Receipts exceeding disbursements.

The opposite of deficit spending is a **surplus**, in which government revenues (receipts) exceed government expenditures (disbursements). Prior to the late 1990s, the federal government had not had a budgetary surplus since the Nixon administration. The period of federal government surpluses, however, did not last long and the federal government was once again operating with expenditures exceeding revenues.

THE 2009 ECONOMIC ENVIRONMENT

Fiscal policy and deficit spending took on a whole new meaning in reaction to the events of 2007–2008. The financial crisis, the decline in home values, and the large increase in unemployment resulted in the federal government taking unprecedented steps designed to stimulate economic activity. The "stimulus" package proposed by the newly elected President Obama and subsequently passed in 2009 by Congress created a federal deficit in excess of a trillion dollars ($1,000,000,000,000).

Simultaneously the Federal Reserve pursued a highly expansionary monetary policy by driving interest rates to historic lows. As of 2009, the discount rate was 0.5 percent and the federal funds rate was virtually 0 percent. Previously, open market operations focused on the buying and selling of Treasury securities; now, however, the Fed extended its purchases to include a variety of debt instruments. Such purchases had the effect of increasing the money supply. This increase is illustrated in Figure 11.3, which plots the money supply from 2000 through May 2009, and Figure 11.4, which plots the six-month percentage changes in M-1 and M-2. The large increases in M-1 and M-2 are readily apparent. From January 2000 through 2007, M-1 rose 22.9 percent or 2.9 percent annually. From January 2008 through May 2009, M-1 rose 15.8 percent or approximately 1 percent a month.

The obvious intent of this expansionary fiscal and monetary policy was to end the country's worst economic crisis since the depression experienced during the 1930s. While the ultimate outcome is unknown, the impact of these policies on the economy and the investment environment will be experienced for years. One potential impact is the return of inflation, not the modest 2–4 percent annual rate experienced during the previous 20 years but the possibility of inflation exceeding the rate experienced from 1978 through 1981. During that period, the CPI rose at an annual rate in excess of 13 percent.

FIGURE   11.3   M-1 and M-2, January 2000–May 2009 (in billions of dollars)

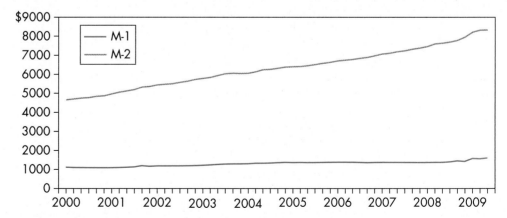

Source: Data available through the Federal Reserve.

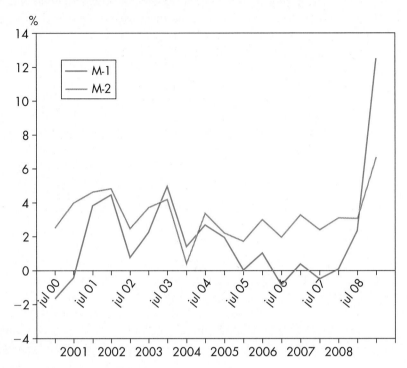

FIGURE   11.4   Six-Month Percentage Change in M-1 and M-2 (2000–2008)

Source: Data available through the Federal Reserve.

The Expectation of Inflation and Investment Strategy

The expectation of inflation changes investor psychology and strategies. During 2009 some investment advisors were recommending individuals alter their portfolios toward assets that may perform well in an inflationary environment. Recommendations stressed the importance of precious metals, commodities, currencies, and debt instruments whose payments are tied to the rate of inflation.

The most frequently recommended precious metal is gold, but other metals such as silver and copper should appreciate during an inflationary period. The same would apply to commodities such as oil and natural gas. The argument for currencies revolves around a deteriorating dollar relative to other currencies. Higher inflation should result in the selling of dollars as investors seek to move into currencies with more stable prices. The essence of the argument for variable-rate debt securities is the reality that inflation will lead to higher interest rates. Since these debt securities pay a variable rate, the interest payments will increase in response to the higher rates and offset the impact of inflation.

How to make such investments is perceptibly easier today than in the past. Exchange-traded funds (ETFs) permit investors to establish positions in precious metals, commodities, and currencies without having to select specific assets. The investor no longer has to buy gold bars to have a position in the precious metal. The investor does not have to select individual oil and copper companies to have a position in commodities. And the same applies to currencies. American investors do not have to buy euros to have a position in the currency. Instead, investors may establish positions in an ETF that tracks a commodity or a currency index or that holds positions in commodities or currencies. Possible ETFs for gold include iShares COMEX Gold Trust (IAU), streetTRACKS Gold Shares (GOLD), and SPDR Gold Shares (GLD). These ETFs hold either cash or gold, so the net asset value tracks the price of gold; all three ETFs are a pure play on the price of gold and avoid the disadvantages (e.g., storage and insurance) associated with actually owning the metal.

PowerShares DB Gold (DGL), Ultra Gold ProShares (UGL), and UltraShort Gold ProShares (GLL) are ETFs based on gold futures contracts. (Futures are explained in Chapter 19.) The UltraShort Gold ProShares is the opposite of the other two ETFs, because it is premised on a *decline* in the price of gold. Buying shares in UltraShort Gold ProShares is taking a short position in gold. Market Vectors Gold Miners (GDX) is based on gold mining companies such as Barrick Gold (ABX) and Newmont Mining (NEM), and it mimics the NYSE Arca Gold Miners Index.

Possible ETFs for currencies include the following:

- Euro Currency Trust (FXE)
- British pound (FXB)
- Canadian dollar (FCX)
- Mexican peso (FXM)
- Swedish krona (FXC)
- Australian dollar (FXA)
- Swiss franc (FXF)

Each ETF tracks the specific currency; their returns are based solely on the dollar cost of the currency. You buy these ETFs in anticipation that the foreign currency will rise against the dollar. If the dollar were to rise, then prices of the currency ETFs would fall, and you would sustain a loss.

A possible ETF for variable interest rates is the iShares Barclays TIPS Bond (ticker symbol: TIP). TIPS stands for Treasury Inflation Protected Security. These variable-rate bonds are discussed in Chapter 15 on government securities.

SUMMARY

Portfolio planning, securities analysis, and investment decisions are made in a logical progression from the general to the specific. The starting point should be the macroeconomy; it affects an individual's employment, income, and wealth and affects a firm's cost of funds and earnings. Measures of economic output and national income include the gross domestic product (GDP). Other economic measures include the Consumer Confidence Index (CCI), the Consumer Sentiment Index (CSI), and Consumer Price Index (CPI).

The Federal Reserve (the "Fed") is the nation's central bank. Its goals are full employment, economic growth, and stable prices. The Fed seeks to achieve these economic goals through its impact on the rate of interest or the supply of money. The specific interest rate that a borrower pays depends on the risk-free rate plus a series of premiums related to the expectation of inflation, the borrower's risk of default, and the liquidity of the debt. As the Fed affects interest rates, it affects the supply of credit and the cost of funds.

The Fed executes monetary policy through its impact on the reserves of the banking system and the supply of money. The discount rate is the rate the Fed charges banks when they borrow reserves. Although the discount rate is one tool of monetary policy, the Fed emphasizes the federal funds rate, which is the rate banks charge each other for borrowing reserves. The Fed affects the federal funds rate through open market operations—the buying and selling of securities by the Fed. Buying securities puts liquidity (money) into the economy while selling securities has the opposite impact as it takes liquidity out of the economy.

Fiscal policy is federal government spending, taxation, and debt management. When the federal government spends more than it receives in revenues, it runs a deficit. When the federal government spends less than its revenues, it runs a surplus. Deficit spending by the federal government may be used to stimulate the economy and is often financed by selling securities to the Federal Reserve. The Fed's financing of the federal government's deficit will increase the money supply, which may increase the fear of future inflation. To protect themselves from the anticipated inflation, investors often acquire assets such as commodities and precious metals (gold) whose prices tend to rise in an inflationary environment.

QUESTIONS

1. What is the impact on GDP if consumer spending increases? Would the answer be different if the consumer spending was directed toward foreign goods?
2. What differentiates inflation and deflation? If both GDP and unemployment were simultaneously rising, would this period be classified as a recession?
3. What factors, besides the expected rate of inflation, may affect the rate of interest a borrower pays?
4. What is the Federal Reserve? What are its economic goals?
5. How does the Fed pursue its economic goals? How may the tools of monetary policy affect securities prices?
6. What is the difference between the discount rate and the targeted federal funds rate?
7. What are M-1 and M-2? How does the Fed alter M-1 or M-2?
8. Do the fundamental economic goals of fiscal policy differ from those of monetary policy? If the Federal Reserve finances the federal government's deficit, what will happen to the supply of money?
9. The seasonally adjusted data (in billions) for M-1 for the two-month periods from January 2008 through May 2009 are as follows:

January	$1368
March	1373
May	1374
July	1400
September	1452
November	1524
January	1576
March	1562
May	1596

 During the period September 2008 through May 2009, M-1 experienced a large percentage increase. Go to the Federal Reserve website (http://www.federalreserve .gov) and continue the above data. What subsequently happened to the rate of change in M-1? What is the inflationary implication of the change in M-1? Have consumer prices reacted as you would have anticipated?

CHAPTER 12

Behavioral Finance and Technical Analysis

LEARNING OBJECTIVES

After completing this chapter you should be able to:

1. Explain how behavior affects investment decisions.
2. State the purpose of technical analysis.
3. Differentiate among the various technical indicators.
4. Calculate and use a moving average.
5. Interpret resistance and support lines.
6. Construct a portfolio based on the Dogs of the Dow.
7. Explain the implications of research concerning technical analysis.

Alan Greenspan's comment that financial markets were experiencing "irrational exuberance" captures the reality that human behavior affects financial markets. While the stock and bond markets are driven by rational individuals making investment decisions designed to maximize returns for the risk taken, human emotions such as hope, fear, and greed affect investing. Behavioral finance applies psychological principles to finance and studies how human behavior affects financial decisions. Once the individual is aware that emotions may lead to poor investment decisions, it may be possible to overcome these emotions or at least reduce their impact.

One method to remove emotion from the investment process is to use *technical analysis*. Since these techniques accumulate and summarize data in a variety of figures and charts, it gives the impression of being "technical," hence the name. Investors who use these techniques are often referred to as *chartists*. Technical analysis focuses on the trend in a stock's price or a particular price pattern to determine if the pattern has changed. Once a technical indicator generates a buy or sell signal, the investor executes the appropriate trade. Emotion is removed from the decision to buy or to sell.

This chapter is a brief introduction to behavioral finance and technical analysis. It begins by describing behavioral traits and how they affect investment decisions. This is followed by several methods used in technical analysis. These techniques, such as moving averages, may be applied to aggregate financial markets or to individual stocks. The chapter also includes empirical evidence that suggests that technical analysis need not lead to superior investment results.

BEHAVIORAL FINANCE

Many financial models such as the Capital Asset Pricing Model in Chapter 5 and the Black-Scholes option valuation model in Chapter 18 have their basis in economics. These models assume that investors are rational, that they make unbiased forecasts, and that financial markets are competitive. Although these assumptions are often sufficiently correct in the aggregate to create efficient markets, they need not apply to individual investors, securities analysts, or portfolio managers. And there are periods during which investors appear to behave irrationally. During these bubbles, investors appear to be willing to throw caution to the wind and bid up securities prices to levels that make little or no sense from a fundamental valuation perspective.

Behavioral finance is a new and growing academic discipline that merges finance and psychology and studies investor behavior. Investors are human, make mistakes, and may behave irrationally. These realities affect the decision-making process, which, in turn, reduces returns. By studying behavior and identifying mistakes, behavioral finance can contribute to improving returns or reducing investors' risk.

The terminology used by behavioral finance is based on psychology and not finance. It includes such phrases as "cognitive dissonance" and "familiarity bias." If you read material on behavioral finance, terms like *growth stock* or *P/E ratio* are encountered only intermittently. The emphasis is not on stock valuation or portfolio construction but on behavior that may be detrimental to the returns investors earn. This brief discussion covers several important contributions that behavioral finance has made to investments, and you may recognize several that apply to your decision-making process.

Overconfidence

Making investment decisions requires confidence, but overconfidence leads investors to overestimate their knowledge and abilities. If you ask investors if their stocks will outperform the market or outperform the stocks they decided not to buy, the answer is often yes. This answer is obvious. If investors expected the other stocks to do better, why would they have bought the stocks they did acquire?

Overconfident investors often believe they know more than other investors. A vast amount of information is available through the Internet, so individuals can become knowledgeable about a specific company, trading technique, or valuation process. These individuals become overconfident in their ability to select securities or apply investment tools. If they experience success, these investors attribute their success to their ability to analyze the markets and select superior stocks and strategies. They become even more confident. If they make poor decisions, they may attribute the losses to "bad luck" and not to lack of ability.

As confidence increases, it often leads investors to take larger risks. These individuals often focus their investments and do not sufficiently diversify their portfolios. They also trade securities more frequently, which increases commission costs and produces short-term gains. These gains are taxed at their marginal tax rate instead of the lower rates that apply to long-term gains. The result is to reduce after-tax returns, so the overconfident investors realize lower returns while taking more risk.

Disposition Effect

One Wall Street adage is to "cut your losses and let your profits run." Investors, however, often do the exact opposite; they take small gains but let losses increase. Psychology suggests that investors feel *pride* in their successes so they want to realize their gains. Losses, however, cause feelings of *regret*. Investors want to postpone those feelings so they continue to hold stocks in which they have losses. Even the possibility of a tax loss and resulting reduction in taxes owed (up to the legal limit) may not induce an investor to sell.

The tendency to retain a losing position is particularly strong if the investor buys a stock and it subsequently falls during a rising market. The investor regrets the purchase and does not want to admit the mistake. If the investor buys the stock and the market declines, the disposition effect is weaker. The investor may rationalize that the purchase was sound and it was the market that caused the stock to decline. Since the market is the cause and not the investor's decision, the disposition effect is smaller. The investor may say, "If the stock returns to its original price, I'll sell it." Unfortunately, that price increase may not occur or may occur after the passage of many years.

The Ostrich Effect

The ostrich effect is a variation on the disposition effect in which investors are reluctant to cut their losses. During rising markets, investors readily watch securities prices and track the value of their portfolios. The experience is pleasurable. In declining markets, investors stop watching. They do not want to know or acknowledge that something bad has happened. If you do not know that the value of your portfolio has declined, it is easier to deny that you have sustained a loss. You avoid the pain. Such action is analogous to the ostrich with its head in the sand. You pretend that the losses do not exist, but acknowledging those losses is the first step toward taking corrective action.

The House Money Effect

Gamblers who lose may double their bets in an attempt to recoup the loss. If they lose $1, they place a bet for $2. If they lose again, the next bet is $4, and the process continues until they win and "break even." Notice that with each additional bet, the gamblers increase their risk exposure.

If they win, gamblers may also increase their bets. They do not consider the winnings their own but the "house's money"; if they lose the gains, they rationalize that they are no worse off than when they started. Gamblers increase the bets to change small winnings into large ones. Consider betting on horse racing. You bet $1 on a horse whose odds are 3 to 1, and you win. Your $1 generated $3, two of which are "house money." On the next race you may bet $2 on a horse with odds of 15 to 1. If you win, you convert $2 into $30. If you lose, you still have your initial $1. Notice that winning induces you to bet more and increase your risk.

Investors may follow similar strategies. If they buy a stock and lose, they buy riskier stocks in an effort to recoup the initial losses and break even. If they buy a stock and win, they may buy a riskier stock to magnify returns. Also notice that the initial win increases investors' confidence. They obviously know how to select a stock, so this overconfidence induces them to acquire riskier securities.

Familiarity

Familiarity with how to perform a task or solve a problem builds confidence and a feeling of control. Investors often buy stocks in companies they are familiar with. Many national firms have visible products, such as Ford, Coca-Cola, or Verizon Communications. Local stocks may also be visible; local newspapers run stories about them. Friends and neighbors work for the firms or shop in their stores. This visibility increases individuals' comfort with the companies and induces them to buy the firms' securities.

Taken to an extreme, the company with which many people are most familiar is the one they work for. It is not unusual for employees to own the stock of their employers. While this may be obvious for managers who are granted options to buy the stock, it also applies to many employees who own company stock through pension plans. Often 401(k) retirement plans offer company stock to employees as one of the possible alternatives, and a surprising number invest their funds in the company's stock.

Such investments certainly increase risk exposure. Instead of diversifying the portfolio, these investments increase the portfolio's focus and increase risk. As many employees learned through the Enron debacle, investing in your company's stock is a risky proposition. The possibility exists that the individual will lose both employment and the funds invested. Common sense should indicate that the strategy is not wise, but familiarity with the company increases the investors' comfort level, perhaps to their detriment.

Mental Budgeting

In its simplest form, a budget is a list of receipts and disbursements. Various types of receipts and disbursements are put into categories. An individual's budget may include disbursements such as food, mortgage payments, insurance payments, entertainment, clothing, and charitable gifts. Notice that each item is treated individually; there is a blank to be filled for each type of disbursement. While the sum of receipts and disbursements provides a bottom line (change in cash or need to borrow), any interaction between the items may be lost because each is treated individually.

Individuals often put different investments in separate mental accounts. They may have funds to meet emergencies in a local bank's savings account or money market mutual fund. Their 401(k) plans may have a variety of mutual funds; money in a college savings plan may also be invested in similar mutual funds. The tendency is to see each investment separately from the others and not as part of a portfolio. The mental budgeting reduces the individual's ability to perceive opportunities for diversification and tax savings. If the funds in both the 401(k) plan and the college savings plan are invested in large cap growth stocks, an opportunity for diversification is lost. One of the accounts could hold one type of security and the other account a different type. The mental separation of the accounts increases the difficulty of seeing each investment as part of the whole portfolio.

There may also be negative tax implications. Funds taken from a 401(k) plan will be taxed at the individual's tax rate. Long-term capital gains receive favorable tax treatment. If the large cap growth stock appreciates, the potential for long-term capital gains is lost. From a tax perspective it would be better for the individual to keep fixed-income, interest-paying investments in the tax-deferred account. The interest will not be taxed until it is removed from the account and then will be taxed at the individual's tax rate. There is no potential for long-term capital gains, and the tax advantages associated with lower long-term rates are irrelevant. The growth fund could be held outside the tax-deferred accounts, and realized long-term gains would receive the favorable taxation associated with long-term gains.

Cognitive Dissonance

Cognitive dissonance refers to memory, specifically the tendency to selectively remember. You will tend to remember good investments; they make you look informed and smart. Bad investments produce the opposite effect, hence the dissonance. The mind remembers the successful investment decisions but represses the bad ones. An implication of this cognitive dissonance is that an investor's memory of returns earned tends to exceed the returns that were actually realized.

One of the great adages concerning history is that if you do not remember the lessons of history, you are doomed to repeat them. If you do not remember your investment mistakes and what caused you to make those decisions, you probably will repeat them. Your mind's repressing unpleasant information only increases the probability that you will continue to repeat the same investment errors.

Herding

The previous traits are associated with individuals, but individuals can act in concert and create a herding effect. A consensus forms and many investors act in the same way. Speculative bubbles are the result of such herding. During the late 1990s, the Internet and dot-com stocks rose dramatically as individual investors clamored to acquire these stocks. The dramatic price increases reinforced the herd effect. Eventually the bubble burst and many investors sustained substantial losses. Stocks such as Ask Jeeves and Ariba (examples of initial public offerings in Chapter 2) collapsed as investors sought to sell when there were few buyers.

The herd effect magnifies individual investors' biases. If the individual buys a stock that just seems to continue to rise, there is less chance of experiencing regret, especially since many other investors are also acquiring the stock. "Feeling" replaces analysis; the old methods for selecting stocks are considered passé. Phrases such as "new paradigm" or "new economy" replace traditional tools of securities analysis such as P/E ratio, price-to-book ratio, estimated earnings, and discounted cash flows.

During such periods, old valuation techniques are even more important. They often indicate that current prices violate logical sense. How can a company with sales of $10 million and no earnings be worth $1 billion? If you invested $1 billion in a savings account that paid only 2 percent, you would earn $20 million, which exceeds the firm's sales! Traditional analysis would point out the irrationality of current prices, but during a bubble, such contrary views are hard for individuals to have. It requires that they be pessimistic during a period of extreme optimism and sell securities instead of buying them.

It may be even harder to go against the herd during a period of extreme pessimism (i.e., to buy stocks when prices are falling). However, a contrarian might say, "When everyone is racing for the door and selling their securities, hold the door for them but don't follow." Certainly the large decline experienced during early 2009 occurred because many investors were selling their positions. Contrarian buyers, however, did very well when prices subsequently rebounded and closed over 60 percent above the lows for the year.

Overcoming Personal Biases

Human behavior obviously affects investment decisions, and this impact may be detrimental to investment results. Individuals often act irrationally and make investments that do not maximize their returns for a given level of risk. This reality is inconsistent with the portfolio theory presented in Chapter 5. That theory suggests investors determine which combination of assets maximizes utility and generates the highest return for the risk taken. The obvious question is, how does the individual remove emotion from investment decisions?

⊕ **Point of Interest**

THE ADAPTIVE MARKET HYPOTHESIS

The adaptive market hypothesis combines elements of financial theory such as the efficient market hypothesis and behavioral finance with evolutionary biology. The adaptive market hypothesis becomes a means to reconcile behavioral finance with the efficient market hypothesis. Behavioral finance stresses human behavior that appears to be irrational and inconsistent with the foundations of efficient market theory. This behavior leads to poor investment decisions, which do not maximize returns for a given level of risk. The efficient market hypothesis, of course, assumes that investors make rational decisions that produce maximum returns for a given level of risk.

The adaptive market hypothesis suggests that investors use trial and error methods and discard those that do not work. Through this process investors learn and adjust their behavior to changing market conditions. Securities markets, financial analysis and valuation methods, and investment products evolve. Failure to adapt forces market participants to fail and drop out of the market, so the remaining participants are those who are able to learn and adapt. Behavior and human biases are no longer viewed as a deviation from rationality. Instead they are part of the process by which investors evolve and the market maintains efficiency.

As you might expect, there is no shortage of material on behavioral finance. The following is a sampling covering different facets of behavioral finance and investing.

Woody Dorsey, *Behavior Trading*. (Thomson, 2004).

Explores methods for measuring investor sentiment.

Mark Fenton-O'Creevy et al., *Traders: Risk, Decisions, and Management in Financial Markets*. (Oxford University Press, 2005).

Discusses biases in professional traders and market makers, which are essentially the same found in individual investors.

John R. Nofsinger, *Investment Blunders of the Rich and Famous*. (Pearson Education, 2002).

Chronicles major losses sustained by rich individuals, professional financial analysts, and portfolio managers.

John R. Nofsinger, *The Psychology of Investing*, 4th ed. (Prentice Hall, 2010).

An easy-to-read, concise primer on behavioral finance.

Harlan D. Platt, *Counterintuitive Investing*. (Thomson, 2005).

Tests how to profit from investors' tendency to overreact.

Hersh Shefrin, *Beyond Greed and Fear*. (Oxford University Press, 2002).

Perhaps the most thorough book on behavioral finance, with extensive references to empirical work that verify behavioral finance concepts.

It certainly would be easy to conclude that the applications of the valuation models in Chapter 9 are one means to avoid bias. That, however, may not be the case, since data used in the models may be manipulated to achieve a desired result. Increased estimates of growth may make a stock appear to be currently undervalued and help rationalize its purchase. The possibility that earnings may rebound and cause the price of the stock to rise may help justify maintaining a position in which the investor has a loss. The applications of valuation models may give investors confidence in their abilities that is not warranted, especially if the data are skewed to obtain a predetermined outcome.

The remainder of this chapter considers technical analysis, which is another method to remove emotion from investment decision making. Strict application of these methods should be devoid of emotion, since decisions depend on the buy and sell signals given by the various technical indicators. Few investors, however, are able to use only one method for stock selection, and the decision of which methods to use and when can once again bias the results. Buy and sell signals may also be difficult to follow, especially if a sell signal indicates the investor has made a mistake and now must feel the pain of regret.

TECHNICAL ANALYSIS

In Bizet's *Carmen*, three gypsies use cards to foretell their future. One foresees a young lover who sweeps her off her feet to experience never-ending love. Another foresees a rich, old gentleman who marries her. She will have diamonds and gold and soon become a widow. Carmen foresees death.

Wouldn't investing be easier if we could read the cards and foresee the future? Or if we could find a trading rule that told us when to buy or sell? Then you would not have to perform the analysis described in the previous chapters and could avoid your emotions that color your investment decisions. The technical approach to securities selection purports to do just that. By analyzing how the market (or a specific stock) has performed, the investor may forecast how the market or the stock will perform in the future. The study of historical price and volume data substitutes for analysis of the economy, the industry, financial statements, and estimates of growth in earnings and dividends.

Technical analysts often assert that technical analysis measures (or at least mirrors) that which cannot be measured: supply and demand. Ultimately securities prices depend on the demand for and supply of the specific stock or bond. Increased demand will lead to higher prices while increased supply will depress prices. Unfortunately, supply and demand cannot be measured, but stock patterns and trends mirror their impact, so that technical analysts often say they are measuring supply and demand. In addition, it is often stated that technical analysis measures human psychology. The analysis assumes that human psychology is constant so that, like weather forecasting, past behavior predicts future behavior. Investor sentiment and fear do not change. If markets (or a specific stock's price) are rising, they will continue to rise. Momentum is driving prices higher and, unless it is broken, the current price direction will continue. Technical analysis also acknowledges that securities prices may oscillate, so until the pattern is broken, prices will continue to trade within an identifiable range.

There are many approaches to technical analysis; the remainder of this chapter can cover only a few. These are classified into two groups. The first techniques are designed to indicate the general direction of the market. Since securities prices move together, the direction of the market is an important, perhaps overriding, factor in the decision to buy or to sell securities. The second set of technical approaches is designed to discern the movement of the market and of specific securities. Much of this material is readily available through the Internet, so the individual investor need not make the numerous calculations or draw the various charts that are the backbone of technical analysis.

Before reading further, you should be forewarned that the presentation of the various approaches makes their application appear to be easy. In actual practice the signals may be less obvious. A technical indicator is drawn with data as they become available. Often, you can look back and see a pattern has developed (e.g., a sell signal). If you had sold, you would have made the correct decision. Hindsight, however, is 20/20. Seeing the pattern after the fact is not the same as perceiving the pattern as it is unfolding. Of course, you must perceive the indicator as it develops to act on it.

MARKET INDICATORS

Dow Theory

A technical approach based on the Dow Jones averages.

The **Dow Theory** is one of the oldest technical methods for analyzing securities prices. It is an aggregate measure of securities prices and hence does not predict the direction of change in individual stock prices. What it purports to show is the direction that the market will take. Thus, it is a method that identifies the top of a bull market and the bottom of a bear market.

The Dow Theory developed from the work of Charles Dow, who founded Dow Jones and Company and was the first editor of the *Wall Street Journal*. Dow identified three movements in securities prices: primary, secondary, and tertiary. Primary price movements are related to the security's intrinsic value. Such values depend on the earning capacity of the firm and the distribution of dividends. Secondary price movements, or "swings," are governed by current events that temporarily affect value and by the manipulation of stock prices. These price swings may persist for several weeks and even months. Tertiary price movements are daily price fluctuations to which Dow attributed no significance.

Although Charles Dow believed in fundamental analysis, the Dow Theory evolved into a technical approach to the stock market. It asserts that stock prices demonstrate patterns over four to five years and that these patterns are mirrored by indexes of stock prices. The Dow Theory employs two of the Dow Jones averages, the industrial average and the transportation average. The utility average is generally ignored.

The Dow Theory is built on the assertion that measures of stock prices tend to move together. If the Dow Jones Industrial Average is rising, then the transportation average should also be rising. Such simultaneous price movements suggest a strong bull market. Conversely, a decline in both the industrial and transportation averages suggests a strong bear market. However, if the averages are moving in opposite directions, the market is uncertain as to the direction of future stock prices.

If one of the averages starts to decline after a period of rising stock prices, the two are at odds. For example, the industrial average may be rising while the transportation average is falling. This suggests that the industrials may not continue to rise but may soon start to fall. Hence, the smart investor will use this signal to sell securities and convert to cash.

The converse occurs when, after a period of falling securities prices, one of the averages starts to rise while the other continues to fall. According to the Dow Theory, this divergence suggests that the bear market is over and that securities prices in general will soon start to rise. The investor will then purchase securities in anticipation of the price increase.

Barron's Confidence Index

Barron's confidence index

An index designed to identify investors' confidence in the level and direction of security prices.

Barron's confidence index is based on the belief that the differential between the returns on quality bonds and bonds of lesser quality will forecast future price movements. During periods of optimism, investors will be more willing to bear risk and thus will move from investments in higher-quality debt to more speculative but higher-yielding, lower-quality debt. This selling of higher-quality debt will depress its price and raise its yield. Simultaneously, the purchase of poor-quality debt should drive up its price and lower the yield. Thus, the difference between the two yields will diminish. The opposite occurs when sentiment turns bearish. Investors will sell poor-quality debt and purchase higher-quality debt. This will have the effect of increasing the spread between the yields, as the price of poor-quality debt falls relative to that of the higher-quality debt.

Barron's confidence index is constructed by using Barron's index of yields on higher- and lower-quality bonds. When the yield differential is small (i.e., when the yields on high-quality debt approach those that can be earned on poor-quality debt), the ratio rises. This is interpreted as showing investor confidence. Such confidence means that securities prices will tend to rise. Conversely, when the index declines, that is an indication that securities prices will fall.

Like the Dow Theory, Barron's confidence index may indicate a tendency; however, it may not give conclusive signals. Since the signals of the Barron's confidence index are often ambiguous or there is a considerable time lag between the signal and the change forecasted, the index can be of only modest use for investors. Like many technical indicators, it may point to the direction that securities prices will follow, but it is not a totally reliable predictor of future stock prices.

Investment Advisory Opinions

The advisory opinion theory suggests that financial analysts are often wrong. This approach is often referred to as a *contrarian* view, since it takes the opposite side of most financial analysts. The theory suggests that when most financial analysts become bearish and forecast declining securities prices, that is the time to purchase securities. When the majority become bullish and forecast rising securities prices, the wise investor liquidates (i.e., sells securities). This technical indicator seems perverse, as it suggests that those most likely to know are unable to forecast the direction of securities prices accurately.

Advances/Declines

The advance-decline cumulative series is an indicator based on the cumulative net difference between the number of stocks that rose in price relative to the number that declined. Consider the following summaries of daily trading on the New York Stock Exchange:

Day	1	2	3	4
Issues advancing	1,200	820	480	210
Issues declining	400	760	950	1,190
Issues unchanged	200	220	370	400
Net advances (declines)	800	60	(470)	(980)
Cumulative net advances (declines)	800	860	390	(590)

During the first day, 800 more stocks rose than declined. While this pattern continued during the second day, the number of stocks rising was less than during the previous day, so the cumulative total registered only a small increment. During the third day, the market weakened, and the prices of more stocks fell than rose. However, the cumulative total remained positive. During the fourth day, the number of stocks that declined rose farther, so that the cumulative total now became negative.

According to technical analysis, the cumulative total of net advances gives an indication of the general direction of the market. If the market is rising, the net cumulative total will be positive and expanding; however, when the market changes direction, the cumulative total will start to diminish and will become negative as prices continue to decline. Of course, the converse applies at market bottoms. When the market declines, the net advances fall (i.e., the negative cumulative total increases). Once the bottom in the market has been reached and securities prices start to rise, the number of advances will start to exceed the number of declines, which will cause the net advances to increase. Changes in the direction of advances/declines becomes a barometer of the trend in the market. (This technique is similar to moving averages, which are discussed later in this chapter and which are used to measure the direction of prices both in individual stocks and in the market as a whole.)

SPECIFIC STOCK INDICATORS

The preceding section discussed several technical approaches to the market as a whole. This section considers several techniques that may be applied to either the market or individual securities. When applied to the market, their purpose is to identify the general trend. When applied to individual securities, these techniques attempt to time when to buy, when to sell, or when to maintain current positions in a specific security.

Point-and-Figure Charts (X-O Charts)

point-and-figure chart (X-O chart)

A chart composed of Xs and Os that is used in technical analysis to summarize price movements.

Most technical analysis has an underlying basis in economics. In effect, these analytical techniques seek to measure supply and demand. Because an increase in demand will lead to higher prices and an increase in supply will lead to lower prices, an analysis that captures shifts in supply and demand will be able to forecast future price movements. **Point-and-figure charts**, also called **X-O charts**, attempt to identify changes in supply and demand by charting changes in securities prices.

If a stock's price rises, that movement is caused by demand exceeding supply. If a stock's price falls, then supply exceeds demand. If a stock's price is stable and trades within a narrow range, the supply of the stock coming onto the market just offsets the current demand. However, when the stock's price breaks this stable pattern of price movements, there has been a fundamental shift in demand and/or supply. Thus, a movement upward suggests a change in demand relative to supply, while a movement downward suggests the opposite.

Point-and-figure charts identify these fundamental changes through the construction of graphs employing Xs and Os. Such an X-O chart is constructed by placing an X on the chart when the price of the stock rises by some amount, such as $1 or $2, and an O on the chart when it declines by that amount. (Some presentations use only Xs.) Notice that an entry is made on the chart only if the price changes by the specified amount. This process avoids small changes in the price and facilitates identifying shifts in supply and demand.

Buy and sell signals are illustrated in Figure 12.1. After a period of stable prices, a deviation signals a fundamental change. The left-hand side (A) illustrates an increase in demand. After a period of trading between $52 and $58, the price of the stock rises to a new high of $60; the trading range is broken. This suggests that a new upward price trend is being established, which is a buy signal. The right-hand side (B) illustrates the

FIGURE	12.1	Buy and Sell Signals

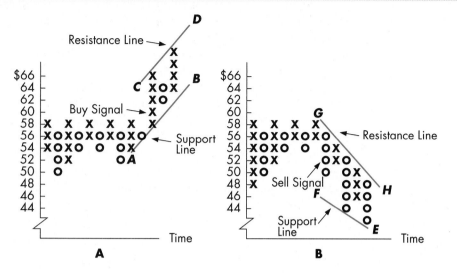

opposite case. The price declines below $52, which suggests a new downward price trend is being established. If the investor owns the stock, the shares should be sold.

In both the cases illustrated in Figure 12.1, the purchases and sales appear to be made at the wrong time. In the case of the purchase, it is made after the stock already increased in price. Conversely, the sale is made after the stock has declined in price. Thus, purchases are not made at the lows, and sales are not made at the highs. Instead, the purchases appear to be made when the stock is reaching new highs, and the sales are made when the stock is reaching new lows. The rationale for this behavior rests primarily on the belief that the charts indicate new trends. There has been a *fundamental change in the demand and supply of the stock*. Despite the fact that the investor missed the high prices for the sale and the low prices for the purchase, if the price change that is being forecasted proves accurate, then the investor will have made the correct investment decision even though the purchases and sales were not made at the exact turning points.

Besides indicating the buy or sell signals when trends are being established, these charts suggest possible trading strategies during the trends, which are also illustrated in Figure 12.1. While the left-hand side shows a price that is obviously rising, the price is still fluctuating. The right-hand side illustrates a downward trend, but the price is also fluctuating. During the upward trend, each high is higher than the preceding high price, and each low is higher than the preceding low price. Obviously, if an investor buys this stock and holds it, the return will be positive over this period. However, the return may be increased by judiciously buying at each low, selling at each high, and repeating the process when the cycle within the trend is repeated.

In order to isolate these opportunities, a set of lines has been drawn in Figure 12.1 connecting the high and the low prices that the stock is achieving. These lines are believed to have special significance because they indicate when to make the buy and sell decisions. The bottom lines (*AB* and *EF*), which connect the lowest prices, suggest a price level that generates "support" for the stock. Technical analysis asserts that when the price of the stock approaches a support line, the number of purchases will increase, which will stop further price declines. Hence, the approach of a stock's price toward a support line suggests that a buying opportunity is developing. Should the price reach the line and then start to climb, the investor should buy the stock.

The opposite occurs at the top lines (*CD* and *GH*), which represents "resistance." Since the price of the stock has risen to that level, more investors will want to sell their stock, which will thwart further price advances. Accordingly, the investor should sell the stock when the price reaches a line of resistance. After the stock has been sold, the investor then waits for the price to decline to the level of price support.

The buy and sell signals indicated by stocks bouncing off lines *AB* or *EF* and *CD* or *GH* should not be confused with the buy and sell signals that occur when the resistance and support lines are broken. The former is a trading signal; you buy and sell within the trading range. Breaking the resistance or support lines indicates a shift in supply or demand. Instead of selling the stock when the resistance line is broken, the penetration is a strong buy signal. Once the purchases are made, this long position will be maintained until a new price pattern emerges. The opposite occurs when the support line is broken. Any long positions are sold.

Bar Graphs

bar graph
A graph indicating the high, low, and closing prices of a security.

Bar graphs are similar to point-and-figure charts. Like the X-O charts, they require a day-to-day compilation of data and use essentially the same information. Preference for one over the other is a matter of choice.

A bar graph is constructed by using three price observations—the high, the low, and the closing price for the day. If the prices were

Price	Monday	Tuesday	Wednesday	Thursday	Friday
High	$10	$9.50	$9.88	$10.50	$12
Low	9	9	9.25	9.88	10.13
Close	9	9.37	9.87	10	11.50

the bar graphs for each day would be

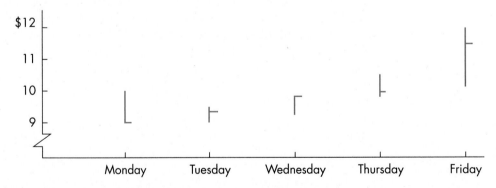

The vertical lines represent the range of the stock's price (i.e., the high and the low prices), and the horizontal lines represent the closing price.

As with the X-O chart, the bar graph is supposed to indicate future price movements in the stock by the pattern that emerges. There are several possible patterns, each with a descriptive name, such as head and shoulder, rounded tops, and descending triangles.

| FIGURE | 12.2 | Head-and-Shoulder Pattern |

Space limits this discussion to only one pattern: the head and shoulder. If you are interested in the variety of patterns you should consult a source that explains the different patterns and how they are used to predict future stock prices.[1]

head-and-shoulder pattern

A tool of technical analysis; a pattern of security prices that resembles a head and shoulders.

A **head-and-shoulder pattern** does just what its name implies: The graph forms a pattern that resembles a head and shoulders. Such a pattern is illustrated in Figure 12.2. Initially, the price of the stock rises. Then it levels off before rising to a new high, after which the price declines, levels off, and then starts to fall. To illustrate the head-and-shoulder pattern, several lines have been imposed on the graph. These lines are similar to the lines of resistance and support found on the X-O charts, and these charts also develop head-and-shoulder patterns. Line *AB* shows the left shoulder and also represents a line of resistance. However, once it is penetrated, the price of the stock rises to a new high, where it meets new resistance (line *CD*).

When the stock is unable to penetrate this new resistance, the price starts to decline and forms the head. However, after this initial decline in price the stock reaches a new level of support, which forms the right shoulder (line *EF*). When the price falls below line *EF*, the head-and-shoulder pattern is completed. This is interpreted to mean that the stock's price will continue to fall and is taken as a bearish sign by followers of this type of analysis.

While the head-and-shoulder pattern in Figure 12.2 indicates that the price of the stock will subsequently fall, the same pattern upside down implies the exact opposite. In this case, penetration of the right shoulder indicates that the price of the stock will rise and is taken as a bullish sign by those who use bar graphs.

Candlesticks

Sometimes the bar graphs are drawn as "candlesticks." Candlestick graphs require four prices: the open, the close, the high, and the low. A thin line (the "shadow") connects the high and low prices. The body of the candlestick connects the opening and closing

---

[1]See, for instance, Jake Bernstein, *The Compleat Guide to Day Trading Stocks* (New York: McGraw-Hill, 2000); Robert D. Edwards, John Magee, and W. H. C. Bassetti, *Technical Analysis of Stock Trends,* 9th ed. (New York: AMACOM, 2007); Michael N. Kahn, *Technical Analysis Plain and Simple,* 2nd ed. (Upper Saddle River, NJ: Pearson Education, 2006); Richard Lehman, *Far from Random* (New York: Bloomberg Press, 2009); John J. Murphy, *Technical Analysis of the Financial Markets* (New York: New York Institute of Finance, 1999); Martin Pring, *Technical Analysis Explained: The Successful Investor's Guide to Spotting Investment Trends and Turning Points,* 4th ed. (New York: McGraw-Hill, 2002).

prices. If the opening price exceeds the closing price, indicating that the price fell, the body of the candlestick is filled in (i.e., is black). If the opening price is less than the closing price (the price rose), the body is left open (i.e., is white). For example, suppose a stock had the following prices during the week:

	Monday	Tuesday	Wednesday	Thursday	Friday
High	$10.00	$9.50	$10.00	$10.00	$10.00
Open	9.50	9.50	9.50	9.25	9.50
Close	9.25	9.25	9.75	9.50	9.50
Low	9.00	9.00	9.50	9.00	9.00

the candlestick graphs for each day would be

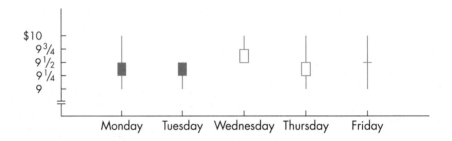

As perhaps would be expected, dark candlesticks (especially long sticks, which indicate a large decline from the opening to the closing price) are bearish indicators, while light candlesticks are bullish. Candlesticks may also be used to construct head-and-shoulder patterns and other configurations that technical analysts use to forecast the direction of stock prices.

Moving Averages

moving average

An average in which the most recent observation is added and the most distant observation is deleted before the average is computed.

A **moving average** is an average computed over time. For example, suppose the closing monthly values for the Dow Jones Industrial Average were as follows:

January	9,287	April	9,258	July	9,347	October	9,374
February	9,284	May	9,315	August	9,334	November	9,472
March	9,267	June	9,335	September	9,328	December	9,547

A six-month moving average of the Dow Jones industrials would be computed as follows. The average for the first six months is computed first.

$$\frac{9{,}287 + 9{,}284 + 9{,}267 + 9{,}258 + 9{,}315 + 9{,}335}{6} = \frac{55{,}746}{6} = 9{,}291.$$

Then the average is computed again, but the entry for July (9,347) is added in and the entry for January (9,287) is deleted:

$$\frac{9{,}284 + 9{,}267 + 9{,}258 + 9{,}315 + 9{,}335 + 9{,}347}{6} = \frac{55{,}806}{6} = 9{,}301.$$

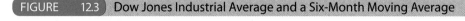

FIGURE 12.3 Dow Jones Industrial Average and a Six-Month Moving Average

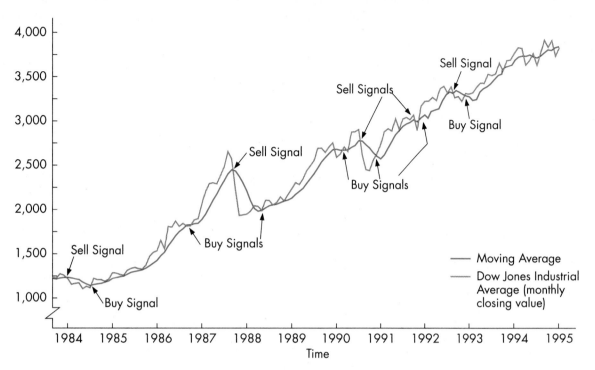

The average is now 9,301, which is greater than the average for the preceding six months (9,291).

To obtain the next entry, the average is computed again, with August being added and February being dropped. The average in this case becomes 9,309. By continuing this method of adding the most recent entry and dropping the oldest entry, the averages move through time.

Figure 12.3 presents both the Dow Jones Industrial Average and the six-month moving average. As may be seen from the figure, the moving average follows the Dow Jones industrials. However, when the Dow Jones industrials are declining, the moving average is greater than the industrial average. The converse is true when the Dow Jones Industrial Average is rising: The moving average is less than the industrial average. At several points the two lines cross. For example, the Dow Jones Industrial Average crossed the six-month moving average in early 1988. Technicians place emphasis on such a crossover, for they believe that it is indicative of a change in the direction of the market. (It may also indicate a change in a specific security's price when the moving average is computed for a particular stock.) In this illustration, there appears to be some validity to the claim of the predictive power of the moving average, as the market rose after the buy signals and fell after the sell signals.

Averages that are often used include the 50-day, 100-day, and 200-day moving averages. These averages may be used together. For example, if the 50-day moving average rises above the daily price, that may be interpreted as a buy signal. The investor, however, may wait for the 100-day moving average to rise above the daily price to confirm the initial buy signal. If the 200-day also crosses the daily price, the signal may be considered an even stronger buy signal.

Other possibilities are a 30-day or 5-day moving average, and any of the averages may be combined with other technical indicators such as point-and-figure charts.[2] Since the creation of the Internet, investors have ready access to these averages and do not have to make their own calculations. There is, however, little evidence that using moving averages of different durations produces inferior or superior results. If one average were superior to the others, only that average would be tracked. The existence of so many moving averages might cause the individual to ask "Why so many?"

Volume

The preceding techniques emphasized price movements as measured by point-and-figure charts, bar graphs, and moving averages. Technical analysts also place emphasis on the volume of transactions and deviations from the normal volume of trading in a specific stock. A large deviation from normal volume is interpreted to mean a change in the demand for or supply of the stock.

Since a price change can occur on small volume or on large volume, the price change itself says nothing concerning the breadth of the change in demand or supply. A price increase on small volume is not as bullish as one accompanied by heavy trading. Conversely, a price decline on small volume is not as bearish as a decline accompanied by a large increase in the number of shares traded. When a price decline occurs on small volume, that indicates that only a modest increase in the supply of the stock was offered for sale relative to the demand. However, if the price decline were to occur on a large increase in volume, that would indicate many investors were seeking to sell the stock, which would be considered bearish.

Moving Average Convergence Divergence (MACD)

Point-and-figure charts, bar graphs, and moving averages are relatively simple to construct. There are, however, a variety of additional technical indicators such as the moving average convergence divergence (MACD) that are more complicated. Fortunately, sources such as Yahoo! Finance provide these indicators for the individual investor who may want to use them. Type in the stock's ticker symbol such as AA for Alcoa and then click on the link for "basic tech. analysis." Immediately a variety of technical indicators such the MACD are available. (The site also presents a variety of moving averages, bar charts, and candlesticks.)

MACD is an "oscillator" and is premised on a stock price's tendency to fluctuate back and forth around some value. This oscillation is used to identify short-term price reversals. MACD is constructed using two exponential moving averages, one average for a period such as 12 days and another for a period such as 26 days. While an arithmetic moving average equally weights each day's price, the exponential moving average gives more weight to the recent prices. A moving average convergence divergence indicator places less emphasis on older stock prices and more emphasis on recent stock prices. After determining the two moving averages, MACD uses the difference between

---

[2]See, for instance, Kenneth Tower, "Applying Moving Averages to Point and Figure Charts," in Rick Bensignor, ed., *New Thinking in Technical Analysis* (Princeton, NJ: Bloomberg Press, 2000).

the moving averages. When the difference is positive and increasing, that is a bullish indicator. Short-term demand for the stock exceeds short-term supply. If the MACD is positive but decreasing, the averages are converging. That suggests that short-term supply exceeds short-term demand, which is a bearish indicator. The converse applies to a difference that is negative. An increase in a negative divergence implies that prices are falling, but if the difference is diminishing, that suggests demand exceeds supply and prices should rise.

There are several variations on this type of technical indicator. Just as changing the number of days used in a moving average from 50 to 200 may change the implied investment strategy, so too changing the number of days in the MACD will affect the results and may alter the implied investment strategy. Individuals who are interested in pursuing different types of oscillators and other technical indicators should consult several of the books enumerated in footnote 1.

TECHNICAL ANALYSIS IN AN EFFICIENT MARKET CONTEXT

At first glance, technical analysis seems so appealing. You need only obtain a set of charts and follow the signal given by the analysis. You, however, must realize that the efficient market hypothesis suggests that technical analysis will not lead to superior investment results. In addition, technical analysis may require frequent buying and selling, which generates commissions. The returns must obviously more than cover these costs for you to outperform the market on a risk-adjusted basis.

Many studies have sought to test the validity of technical analysis.[3] The majority of this research has failed to verify the various technical approaches to investing. This large body of empirical evidence has resulted in a general rejection of technical analysis by many academically trained teachers of finance. In addition, many investors have also concluded that technical analysis does not lead to superior investment performance. An investor would do just as well to buy a randomly selected portfolio and hold it indefinitely.

Although technical analysis has found little support in the financial academic community, some studies have supported technical analysis.[4] These results suggested that a simple set of trading rules using moving averages and support and resistance levels did improve returns over a buy-and-hold strategy. Another study, however, concluded that when transaction costs are factored into the analysis, returns are not improved over buy-and-hold.[5] This result is, of course, consistent with efficient markets. (With the advent of electronic trading and its minimal transaction costs, it may become possible to use trading rules, pay the commissions, and beat a buy-and-hold strategy. Stay tuned.)

---

[3]A summary of empirical evidence is provided in Burton G. Malkiel, *A Random Walk Down Wall Street,* 9th ed. (New York: W. W. Norton, 2008).

[4]William Brock, Josef Lakonishok, and Blake LeBaron, "Simple Technical Trading Rules and the Stochastic Properties of Stock Returns," *Journal of Finance 47* (December 1992): 1731–1764; and Andrew Lo, Harry Mamaysky, and Jiang Wang, "Foundation of Technical Analysis," *Journal of Finance 55* (August 2000): 1705–1765. However, another study did not replicate these results. See Mark J. Ready, "Profits from Technical Trading Rules," *Financial Management* (autumn 2002): 43–61.

[5]Hendrick Bessembinder and Kolok Chan, "Market Efficiency and the Returns to Technical Analysis," *Financial Management* (summer 1998): 5–17.

⊕ Point of Interest

THE MARKET TECHNICIANS ASSOCIATION

The Market Technicians Association is an organization for individuals whose "professional efforts are spent practicing financial technical analysis that is either made available to the investing public or becomes a primary input into an active portfolio management process and for whom technical analysis is the basis of the decision making process." Affiliate memberships are open to individuals who are interested in technical analysis but do not meet the above requirements. The association publishes the *Market Technicians Association Journal* to "promote the investigation and analysis of price and volume activities of the world's financial markets." Information concerning the association is available at http://www.mta.org.

One major reason why technical approaches may not lead to superior investment results is the speed with which securities prices change. Information is readily disseminated among the investors, and prices adjust accordingly. Thus, if an investor were to develop an approach that outperformed the market, it would only be a matter of time before the technique would be learned by others. The method would no longer achieve the initial results as additional investors applied it. A system that works (if one can be found) can succeed only if it is not known by many investors. Thus, it is naive for an investor to believe that he or she can use a known technical approach to beat the market. A new and unknown system is needed. However, when you realize that many investors are looking for and testing various approaches, it is hard to believe that the individual investor will find a technical approach that can beat the market.

Even though empirical results do not favor the use of technical analysis, some investors and portfolio managers continue to use this type of analysis. This usage has the potential to affect securities prices. For example, breaking a trend line may suggest a buying (or selling) opportunity. Heavy buying (or selling) could occur even though the firm's fundamentals have not changed. By knowing technical trading rules, an investor may avoid buying when the technicians are buying and perhaps artificially raising the stock's price.

Even if investors and portfolio managers do not employ technical analysis as the sole criterion for investment decisions, they may apply the analysis to confirm decisions based on fundamental analysis. One possible explanation for the continued use is the accuracy of the empirical tests. These tests must specify a confidence level, such as 95 percent. Consider a technical approach that generates a return of 12.2 percent when the average return is 12 percent. Can the investor assert with a 95 percent level of confidence that the 0.2 percent difference is the result of the approach's ability to outperform or is the difference the result of chance?[6] Even if the returns had been 15 percent versus 12 percent and

---

[6]An analogy with batting averages may help clarify the point. A player with a batting average of .256 has a .298 season. Since baseball is a game of streaks, is the higher average the result of improved skills or chance (i.e., a lucky streak during the season)? The answer is obviously important since management may pay for improved skills but trade the player if the improved average is the result of chance.

⊕ Point of Interest

SERIAL CORRELATION AND STOCK RETURNS

Correlation coefficients measure the extent to which two series are related. For example, if the returns on assets A and B were

Period	A	B
1	15%	12%
2	10	10
3	6	8
4	−4	−9
5	−8	−6

an obvious positive correlation exists between the two series. In this illustration, the numerical value of the correlation coefficient is 0.960. Such correlation coefficients appear frequently in this text to illustrate the potential for diversification. If the returns on assets lack strong positive correlation, combining the assets in a portfolio reduces risk, because the lack of correlation reduces the variability of the portfolio's return.

Serial correlation measures the correlation between the data for one of the variables. The individual returns for A appear to be serially correlated, since the return in each subsequent period is smaller than the return in the previous period. This serial correlation suggests that the return in one period forecasts the return in the next period.

Serial correlation may be used to test technical analysis, especially the assertion that stock prices move in trends or have momentum in a particular direction. The *Stocks, Bonds, Bills, and Inflation Yearbook* reported that serial correlation between stocks' returns was virtually nil. Such a result is consistent with the weak form of the efficient market hypothesis. Other studies tend to support the lack of serial correlation between returns. However, while the returns for large company stocks may lack serial correlation, it may exist for small company stocks. If this is true and the returns on small company stocks are serially correlated, that result is not consistent with the efficient market hypothesis and suggests that the investor may be able to earn excess returns through a trading strategy.

the probability of the difference being statistically significant were higher, the 3 percent difference could still be the result of chance.

Empirical tests often use 95 percent as the level of confidence, with 90 percent being the lowest acceptable level. If it cannot be shown with at least a 90 percent level of confidence that the results are attributable to the technical indicator, the empirical test concludes that the difference is the result of chance. Supporters of technical analysis may argue that 95 percent or even the less rigorous 90 percent is too high a level of confidence. If a technique works only 70 percent of the time, it still generates a higher return. If this return is 0.2 percent greater than the average return, then over a period of years the difference will generate a higher terminal value (i.e., in 20 years, $100,000 grows to $999,671 at 12.2 percent but only $964,629 at 12 percent). Even if the additional return is the result of chance, it is doubtful the investor would say, "I don't want the additional $35,000. It was not earned but was the result of luck!"

The debate concerning the efficacy of technical analysis will continue, and the Internet will increase access to technical analysis by the individual investor. Data are readily available that permit you to track stocks and apply technical analysis. Even if you do not use the analysis, its jargon permeates the popular, if not the academic, press on investments. Thus, you need to be aware of technical analysis even if you never use it as part of an investment strategy.

THE DOGS OF THE DOW

One investment strategy that has come into prominence is the Dogs of the Dow.[7] (Weak stocks or low-priced stocks are sometimes referred to as "dogs.") This simple strategy is neither a technical approach nor a fundamental approach to the selection of securities. Since it requires no analysis of past stock prices, volume of trading, or any other method of technical analysis, it is not readily classifiable as a technical approach. The Dogs of the Dow, however, also avoids the fundamental analysis of financial statements, the valuation of cash flows, and the estimation of future growth rates. Since the Dow dog strategy is mechanical, it is more comparable to technical approaches than to valuation methods for selecting stocks and is included in this chapter.

The Dogs of the Dow strategy requires the investor to rank all 30 stocks in the Dow Jones Industrial Average from highest to lowest based on their dividend yields (dividend divided by the price of the stock). The investor then buys an equal dollar amount of the ten stocks with the highest dividend yields. (An alternative strategy is to buy the five lowest-priced "small dogs" of the ten highest-yielding dividend stocks.) After one year, the process is repeated. The Dow stocks are once again ranked, and, if a stock continues to be among the ten highest dividend yields, it is retained. If the stock is no longer among the ten, it is sold and replaced by a new Dow dog that is one of the ten stocks with the highest dividend yields.

This strategy has obvious appeal. First, since it is rebalanced only once a year, commission costs are modest. Second, by waiting one additional day so the portfolio adjustments occur after a year, all capital gains are long-term. (The dividend payments are also taxed.) Third, by buying the Dow stocks with the highest dividend yields, this yield may offer some downside protection from further price declines. Fourth, buying the Dow dogs is acquiring the stocks in the Dow that are currently out of favor and is consistent with a contrarian strategy.

Does the system work? There is evidence that the Dow dividend strategy produces higher returns than the Dow itself.[8] The evidence, however, also shows that the standard deviations of the returns on the Dow dogs exceeded the standard deviations of the returns on the Dow Jones Industrial Average and the S&P 500 stock index. (A Dow dog portfolio is less diversified, so the expectation would be for greater variability in the returns.) This result is, of course, consistent with efficient markets: More risk-taking generates higher returns. The empirical results also suggest that over long periods, such as a decade, a strategy of buying and holding all the Dow stocks was a better alternative after considering risk, taxes, and transaction costs.

[7]The Dow dividend strategy was popularized in Michael O'Higgins, *Beating the Dow* (New York: Harper Perennial, 1992). Information concerning the Dow dogs, such as which stocks would currently compose a Dow dog portfolio, may be found at **http://www.dogsofthedow.com**.
[8]Evidence that the strategy generates larger returns but the returns are more variable may be found in George Wunder and Herbert Mayo, "Study Supports Efficient Market Hypothesis," *Journal of Financial Planning* (July 1995): 128–135; and Grant McQueen, Kay Shields, and Steven R. Thorley, "Does the Dow-10 Investment Strategy Beat the Dow Statistically and Economically?" *Financial Analysts Journal* (July–August 1997): 66–72.

SUMMARY

Behavioral finance combines psychology and finance and identifies human traits that affect investment decisions. These emotions include being overconfident, feeling regret when investment decisions generate losses, and perceiving gains as the "house's" money. Individuals tend to acquire assets with which they are familiar; they isolate (mentally budget) individual investment decisions and selectively remember investment results. Investors also follow a herd mentality. These are some of the personal traits that often lead to poor investment decisions.

Technical analysis seeks to identify potential investments by examining the past performance of the market or individual securities. Technical analysts or "chartists" stress the past as a means to predict the future. Technical analysis removes emotion and is diametrically opposed to the fundamental analysis that stresses future earnings and dividends (i.e., cash flows) appropriately discounted back to the present.

Several technical approaches such as the Dow Theory and Barron's confidence index attempt to identify changes in the direction of the market. Because individual securities prices move together, the determination of a change in the market's direction should identify future movements in individual stock prices. Other technical indicators such as point-and-figure charts, bar graphs, and moving averages may be applied to the market and to individual securities. By constructing various charts, the technical analyst determines when specific securities should be bought or sold.

Whether technical approaches to market timing and stock selection lead to superior returns is an empirical question. With some exceptions, academic research has produced little support for technical analysis. These results suggest that investors may achieve similar or even superior results by purchasing and holding a well-diversified portfolio of securities.

QUESTIONS

1. What are several human traits that tend to affect investment decisions?
2. Why do the supporters of behavioral finance suggest that emotions lead to inferior investment decisions?
3. What is the purpose of technical analysis, and why are those who use technical analysis referred to as *chartists*?
4. What changes produce a sell signal in the Dow Theory and Barron's confidence index?
5. What is a moving average? What is the significance when a stock's price crosses a moving average of the stock's price?
6. What is the problem with time lags in technical analysis and why may the analysis lead to self-fulfilling predictions?
7. What is the difference between "support" and "resistance" in technical analysis?
8. Why does technical analysis receive little support from academically oriented students of investments?
9. Which Dow Jones Industrial Average stocks would be considered "dogs"? Determine the Dow dogs as of January 1; invest $1,000 in each dog. At the end of a time period such as the semester or year, compare the dogs' performance with the

performance of the Dow. Be certain to remember to include the dividends in your calculation.

10. Locate graphs of moving averages for International Business Machines (IBM) and Cisco. Based on the moving averages, should you be long or short in each of these stocks? After answering this question, continue to follow the stocks' prices for a period of time. Did your position prove to be profitable? Various moving averages are available at many of the Internet sites given throughout this text.

INVESTMENT ASSIGNMENT (PART 5)

Return to Investment Assignment Part 4, in which you identified the stocks you thought were the best and the worst. Presumably you would be purchasing the former and selling the latter. Technical analysis may help you time those purchases and sales. Locate the 50-day, 100-day, and 200-day moving average of each stock's price at a site such as http://finance.yahoo.com. Based solely on each average, should you be a buyer or a seller? Do all three averages confirm the implied direction of change in the price of each stock?

PART

Four

Investing in Fixed-Income Securities

Part 4 considers investments in securities that pay a fixed annual income: bonds and preferred stock. While preferred stock does pay a fixed dividend, the emphasis in Part 4 is on debt securities that pay a fixed annual rate of interest. The next four chapters are concerned with these bonds and cover (1) the characteristics common to all debt instruments, (2) the risks associated with investing in debt, (3) the mechanics of purchasing bonds, (4) the retirement of debt, and (5) bond pricing. Like stock, bonds may be purchased initially through a private placement or through a public offering. Once the securities are issued, secondary markets develop. While many stocks trade through organized stock markets, the secondary market for bonds is primarily an over-the-counter market. This fact does not limit the individual's ability to invest in bonds. Investors may readily buy or sell the bonds issued by many corporations and governments just as they may buy and sell shares of stock.

Some investors may believe that bonds are not exciting investments, and other investors may believe that bonds are inappropriate for their portfolios. These investors may be wrong on both counts. The variety of debt instruments with a wide range of features and the possibility to earn large returns through investing in particular debt instruments suggest these securities can be exciting investments. The wide price fluctuations in bond prices experienced during the 2000s when many firms defaulted and the increases in bond prices experienced when interest rates fell during the early 2000s suggest that bonds can generate large losses and gains. Bonds can be exciting investments, but many individual issues cannot be considered safe investments that are appropriate for conservative investors seeking income and preservation of capital.

Bonds can also play an important role in diversifying a portfolio. In some cases, such as acquiring bonds in a tax-deferred retirement account, bonds may be more appropriate than acquiring stock that offers potential long-term capital gains. The income tax on the interest is deferred until the funds are withdrawn, and the favorable long-term capital gains tax rate is lost if the gains come through a tax-deferred retirement account. Thus, bonds are often a viable alternative that all investors should consider when constructing their portfolios.

CHAPTER 13

The Bond Market

LEARNING OBJECTIVES

After completing this chapter you should be able to:

1. Describe the features common to all bonds.
2. Explain the purpose of the indenture and the role of the trustee.
3. Identify the sources of risk to the bondholder.
4. Describe the procedure for buying a bond and the paying or receiving of accrued interest.
5. Differentiate among the types of corporate bonds.
6. Differentiate the variety of high-yield bonds, their sources of risk, and realized returns.
7. Distinguish among the ways bonds are retired.

In *The Merchant of Venice*, Antonio secured his debt with Shylock with a "pound of flesh." And you thought your credit card interest rate was bad! Perhaps that is why Polonius advised Laertes in *Hamlet* "neither a borrower nor a lender be." The terms of a loan can be onerous, but corporations and governments do borrow, often under burdensome terms, to finance investments in plant, equipment, or inventory or for the construction of roads and schools. Internally generated funds are often insufficient to finance such investments on a pay-as-you-go basis. Bonds, which mature at the end of a term longer than one year, permit firms and governments to acquire assets now and pay for them over a period of years. This long-term debt is then retired for corporations by the cash flow that is generated by plant and equipment and for governments by the fees or tax revenues that are collected.

This chapter is concerned with bonds. Initially it considers (1) the characteristics common to all debt instruments, (2) the risks associated with investing in bonds, and (3) the mechanics of investing in debt. Next follows a description of the various bonds issued by corporations, and the chapter ends with a discussion of retiring debt. Chapter 14 covers the valuation of fixed-income securities. The emphasis in that chapter is on corporate bonds. Federal, state, and municipal government securities are covered in detail in Chapter 15.

Like stock, bonds may initially be purchased by financial institutions in a private placement or by investors through a public offering. Once the bonds have been sold to the general public, these debt securities may subsequently be bought and sold through organized exchanges or in the over-the-counter markets. There is an active secondary market for many debt securities, so the investor may readily increase or liquidate positions in bonds.

GENERAL FEATURES OF BONDS

Interest and Maturity

bond

A long-term liability with a specified amount of interest and specified maturity date.

principal

The amount owed; the face value of a debt.

maturity date

The time at which a debt issue becomes due and the principal must be repaid.

interest

Payment for the use of money.

coupon rate

The specified interest rate or amount of interest paid by a bond.

current yield

Annual income divided by the current price of the security.

yield to maturity

The yield earned on a bond from the time it is acquired until the maturity date.

yield curve

The relationship between time to maturity and yields for debt in a given risk class.

All **bonds** (i.e., long-term debt instruments) have similar characteristics. They represent the indebtedness (liability) of their issuers in return for a specified sum, which is called the **principal**. Virtually all debt has a **maturity date**, which is the particular date by which it must be paid off. When debt is issued, the length of time to maturity is set, and it may range from one day to 20 or 30 years or more. (Disney has an outstanding bond that matures in 2093.) If the maturity date falls within a year of the date of issuance, the debt is referred to as short-term debt. Long-term debt matures more than a year after it has been issued. (Debt that matures in from one to ten years is sometimes referred to as *intermediate debt*.) The owners of debt instruments receive a flow of payments, which is called **interest**, in return for the use of their money. Interest should not be confused with other forms of income, such as the cash dividends that are paid by common and preferred stock. *Dividends are distributions from earnings*, whereas *interest is an expense* of borrowing.

When a debt instrument such as a bond is issued, the rate of interest to be paid by the borrower is established. This rate is frequently referred to as the bond's **coupon rate** (e.g., the 8.375 percent for the IBM bond in Exhibit 13.2). The amount of interest is usually fixed over the lifetime of the bond. (There are exceptions; for example, see the section on variable interest rate bonds later in this chapter.) The return earned by the investor, however, need not be equal to the specified rate of interest because bond prices change. They may be purchased at a discount (a price below the face amount or principal) or at a premium (a price above the face amount of the bond). The return actually earned depends on the interest received, the purchase price, and what the investor receives upon selling or redeeming the bond.

The potential return offered by a bond is referred to as the *yield*. Yield is frequently expressed in two ways: the **current yield** and the **yield to maturity**. Current yield refers only to the annual flow of interest or income. The yield to maturity refers to the yield that the investor will earn if the debt instrument is held from the moment of purchase until it is redeemed at par (face value) at maturity. The difference between the current yield and the yield to maturity is discussed in the section on the pricing of bonds in Chapter 14.

There is a relationship between yield and the length of time to maturity for debt instruments of the same level of risk. Generally, the longer the time to maturity, the higher the rate of interest. This relationship is illustrated in Figure 13.1, which plots the yield on various U.S. government securities as of April 2004. This figure, which is frequently referred to as a **yield curve**, shows that the bonds with the longest time to maturity have the highest interest rates. For example, short-term securities (three months to maturity) had yields of 0.92 percent; one-year bonds paid yields of 1.19 percent, and bonds that matured after 20 years paid almost 4.8 percent.

One would expect such a relationship because the longer the time to maturity, the longer the investor will tie up his or her funds. To induce investors to lend their money for lengthier periods, it is usually necessary to pay them more interest. Also, there is more risk involved in purchasing a bond with a longer period to maturity, since the future financial condition of the issuer is more difficult to estimate for the longer term.

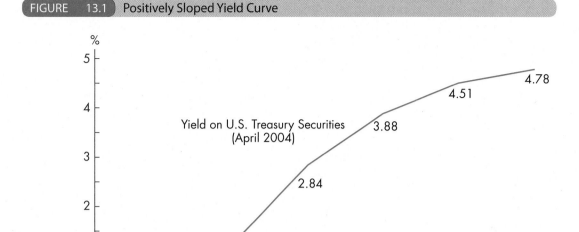

FIGURE   13.1   Positively Sloped Yield Curve

Source: Data derived from the *Wall Street Journal.*

This means that investors will ordinarily require additional compensation to bear the risk associated with long-term debt.

Although such a relationship between time and yield does usually exist, there have been periods when the opposite has occurred (i.e., when short-term interest rates exceeded long-term interest rates). This happened from 1978 to 1979, and again in 1981, when short-term interest rates were higher than long-term rates. The yields on Treasury securities (securities issued by the Treasury Department) in June 1981 are illustrated in Figure 13.2. In this case the yield curve has a negative slope, which indicates that as the length of time to maturity increased, the interest rates declined. Thus, securities maturing in less than a year had a yield of greater than 14 percent, while the long-term debt that matured after ten years yielded 13 percent.

Such a yield curve can be explained by inflation, which exceeded 10 percent in 1981 to 1982. The Board of Governors of the Federal Reserve was pursuing a tight monetary policy in order to fight inflation. It sold short-term government securities (i.e., Treasury bills) in an effort to reduce the capacity of commercial banks to lend. These sales depressed the prices of all fixed-income securities, which resulted in higher yields. (As is explained in Chapter 14, yields on debt instruments rise as their prices fall.) The yields on short-term securities rose more than those on long-term securities, and this, coupled with other events in the money and capital markets, resulted in the negatively sloped yield curve. When the rate of inflation abated during the mid-1980s, the yield curve returned to the positive slope that it maintains during most periods.

There have been periods when the yield curve was flat. This is illustrated in Figure 13.2 by the yield curve for October 2006. The yield on short-term debt with three

> **FIGURE   13.2**   Yield Curves (Yields on Federal Government Securities)

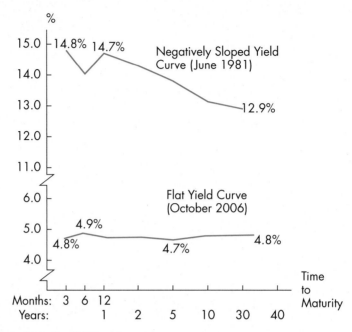

Source: Data derived from the *Wall Street Journal*.

to six months to maturity was approximately 4.8 percent, and the yield for the bonds with 20 to 30 years to maturity was approximately 4.8 percent. While there was some slight differences in yields, for all practical purposes, the yield curve was flat.

Figures 13.1 and 13.2 also illustrate that interest rates do change. (You should remember that the interest rate is the *current* rate paid for credit. That rate should not be confused with the coupon rate, which is *fixed when the debt is issued*.) Although all interest rates fluctuate, short-term rates fluctuate more than long-term rates. These differences in fluctuations are illustrated in Figure 13.3, which plots the yields on a six-month Treasury bill and on a 30-year Treasury bond. As may be seen in the figure, the fluctuations for the short-term debt are greater than for the 30-year bond. For example, the yields on the six-month Treasury bill decreased from 7 percent in late 1990 to below 4 percent in early 1992 while the yield on the bond declined from 8.5 to 7.9 percent during the same period. Figure 13.3 also illustrates how quickly rates can change. Short-term rates rose from 10.1 to 15 percent in only three months during 1980 in response to change in the demand and supply of short-term credit.

Figure 13.4 presents the yields on the six-month Treasury bill and the 30-year bond for 2006 through 2008. The stunning decline in the yield on the six-month bill during 2008 is obvious in the figure. During 2006, the yield on the bill fluctuated between 4.3 and 5.0 percent while the yield on the 30-year bond fluctuated between 4.7 and 5.2 percent. There was little difference between the two yields. During 2008, the yield on the 30-year bond declined from 4.7 percent to 2.9 percent at the end of the year. The rate on the bill, however, plummeted from 2.7 percent to virtually nothing (0.26 percent).

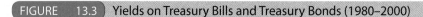
FIGURE 13.3 Yields on Treasury Bills and Treasury Bonds (1980–2000)

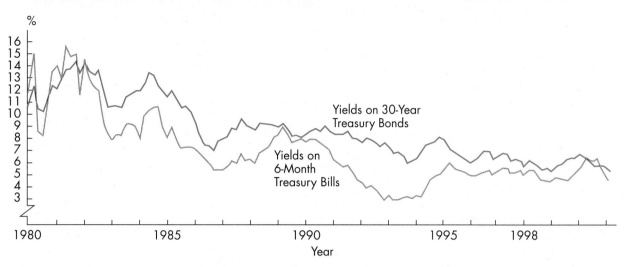

Source: *Federal Reserve Bulletin*, various issues.

FIGURE 13.4 Yields on Treasury Bills and Treasury Bonds (2006–2008)

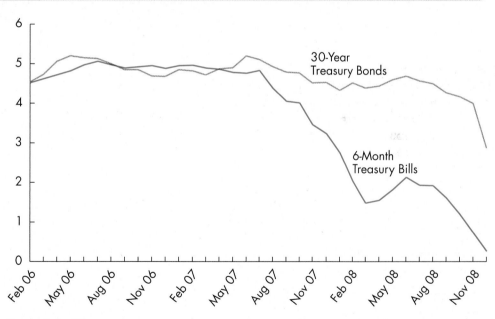

Source: Federal Reserve.

The Indenture

indenture

The document that specifies the terms of a bond issue.

Each debt agreement has terms that the debtor must meet. These are stated in a legal document called the **indenture**. (For publicly held corporate bond issues, the indenture is filed with the Securities and Exchange Commission.) These terms include the coupon rate, the date of maturity, and any other conditions required of the debtor. One of the more frequent of these requirements is the pledging of collateral, which is property that the borrower must offer to secure the loan. For example, the collateral for a mortgage loan is the building. Any other assets owned by the borrower, such as securities or inventory, may also be pledged to secure a loan. If the borrower defaults on the debt, the creditor may seize the collateral and sell it to recoup the principal. **Default** occurs when the borrower fails to meet not only the payment of interest but *any* of the terms of the indenture. The other conditions of the indenture are just as important as meeting the interest payments on time, and often they may be more difficult for the debtor to satisfy.

default

The failure of a debtor to meet any term of a debt's indenture.

Examples of common loan restrictions include (1) limits on paying dividends, (2) limits on issuing additional debt, and (3) restrictions on merging or significantly changing the nature of the business without the prior consent of the creditors. In addition, loan agreements usually specify that if the firm defaults on any other outstanding debt issues, this debt issue is also in default, in which case the creditors may seek immediate repayment. Default on one issue, then, usually puts all outstanding debt in default.

These examples do not exhaust all the possible conditions of a given loan. Since each loan is separately negotiated, there is ample opportunity for differences among loan agreements. During periods of scarce credit, the terms of a loan agreement will be stricter, whereas during periods of lower interest rates and more readily available credit, the restrictions will tend to be more lenient. The important point, however, is that if any part of the loan agreement is violated, the creditor may declare that the debt is in default and may seek a court order to enforce the terms of the indenture.

The Role of the Trustee

trustee

An appointee, usually a commercial bank, responsible for upholding the terms of a bond's indenture.

Many debt instruments are purchased by individual investors who may be unaware of the terms of the indenture. To protect their interests, a **trustee** is appointed for each publicly held bond issue. It is the trustee's job to see that the terms of the indenture are upheld and to take remedial action if the company defaults on the terms of the loan. For performing these services, the trustee receives compensation from the issuer of the debt.

Trustees are usually commercial banks that serve both the debtor and the bondholders. They act as transfer agents for the bonds when ownership is changed through sales in the secondary markets. These banks receive from the debtor the funds to pay the interest, and this money is then distributed to the individual bondholders. It is also the job of the trustee to inform the bondholders if the firm is no longer meeting the terms of the indenture. In case of default, the trustee may take the debtor to court to enforce the terms of the contract. If there is a subsequent reorganization or liquidation of the company, the trustee continues to act on behalf of the individual bondholders to protect their principal.

registered bond

A bond whose ownership is registered with the commercial bank that distributes interest payments and principal repayments.

bearer bond

A bond with coupons attached or a bond whose possession denotes ownership.

Forms of Debt

Debt instruments are issued in one of two forms: (1) **registered bonds** or (2) **bearer bonds** to which coupons are attached (therefore, they are also called **coupon bonds**). Registered bonds are similar to stock certificates; the bonds are registered in the owner's name. Delivery of the bonds is made to the registered owner, who also receives the interest payments from the trustee bank. When the bond is sold, it is registered in the name of the new owner by the transfer agent.

coupon bond

A bond with coupons attached that are removed and presented for payment of interest when due.

While many bonds may be registered in the name of the owner, most registered bonds are issued in *book form*. No actual bonds are printed; instead, a computer record of owners is maintained by the issuer or the issuer's agent, such as a bank. If a bond is sold only in book form, the investor cannot take delivery, and the bond must be registered in the street name of the investor's brokerage firm or whoever is holding the bond for the investor. Such a system is obviously more efficient than physically issuing the bond.

Bearer bonds are entirely different. Ownership is evidenced by mere possession and is transferred simply by passing the bond from the seller to the buyer. No new certificates are issued. Securities in this form are easy to transfer. They are like currency if lost, so the possibility of theft has to be a real concern. If the bonds are stolen, they may not be traceable. For this reason, many brokerage firms will not accept bearer bonds for sale or to put on an account unless the individual has proof of purchase.

Since the issuer of bearer bonds does not know the names of the owners of the securities, coupons are attached to the bond. The owner detaches the coupon and sends it in for payment to collect the interest. In the past, most bonds were issued in this form. Investors who relied on fixed-income payments for their livelihood were frequently called "coupon clippers," and the term "coupon" continues to mean the interest payment made by a bond.

Under current federal law, all newly issued corporate and municipal bonds must be registered in the name of the owner or whoever holds the bond for the owner (e.g., a brokerage firm). The primary reason for this ban on issuing bearer bonds with coupons attached is that they are an easy means to evade taxes. When the coupons are cashed, there may be no record of the interest payment, so income taxes may not be paid. Since possession is indication of ownership, the bonds may also be used to evade estate taxes. When the owner dies, the bonds may pass to an heir without being included in the estate. Since the transfer of ownership through the estate is avoided, the value of the bonds may not be reported for purposes of estate taxation. Given the ease with which these bonds facilitate tax evasion, it should hardly be surprising that the federal government outlawed bearer bonds.

Even though new bearer bonds may not be issued in the United States, the investor should not conclude they do not exist. While the supply is diminishing as they mature and are retired, some coupon bonds remain. In addition, bearer bonds may be issued in other countries. Laws in other countries differ from U.S. laws and may permit the issuance of bearer bonds. However, in the United States it is only a matter of time before all corporate and municipal bonds will be in registered form.

RISK

An important characteristic of all debt is risk: risk that the interest will not be paid (i.e., risk of default); risk that the principal will not be repaid; risk that the price of the debt instrument may decline; risk that inflation will continue, thereby reducing the purchasing power of the interest payments and of the principal when it is repaid; risk that the bond will be retired (i.e., called) prior to maturity, thereby denying the investor the interest payments for the term of the bond; and risk that interest rates will fall, resulting in lower interest income when the proceeds are reinvested. These risks vary with different types of debt. For example, there is no risk of default on the interest payments and principal repayments of the debt of the federal government. The reason for this absolute safety is that the federal government has the power to tax and to create money. The government can always issue the money that is necessary to pay the interest and repay the principal.[1]

The procedure is more subtle than just printing new money. The federal government issues new debt and sells it to the Federal Reserve Board. With the proceeds of these sales, the federal government retires the old debt. The money supply increases because newly created money is used to pay for the debt. The effect of selling debt to the Federal Reserve Board and then using the proceeds to retire existing debt (or to finance a current deficit) is no different from printing and spending new money. The money supply expands in either case. Thus, the federal government can always pay its interest expense and retire its debt when it becomes due.

Even though the federal government can refund its debt and hence is free of the risk of default, the prices of the federal government's bonds can and do fluctuate. In addition, the purchasing power of the dollar may decline as a result of inflation, and, therefore, the purchasing power of funds invested in debt also may decline. Thus, investing in federal government securities is not free of risk, since the investor may suffer losses from price fluctuations of the debt or from inflation.

The debt of firms, individuals, and state and local governments involves even greater risk, for all these debtors may default on their obligations. To aid buyers of debt instruments, several companies have developed **credit rating systems**. The most important of these services are Moody, Dun and Bradstreet, and Standard & Poor's. Although these firms do not rate all debt instruments, they do rate the degree of risk of a significant number.

credit rating systems
Classification schemes designed to indicate the risk associated with a particular security.

Exhibit 13.1 gives the risk classifications presented by Moody and Standard & Poor's. The rating systems are quite similar, for each classification of debt involving little risk (high-quality debt) receives a rating of triple A, while debt involving greater risk (poorer-quality debt) receives progressively lower ratings. Bonds rated triple B or better are considered investment grade, while bonds with lower ratings are often referred to as *junk bonds* or *high-yield securities*. The growth in this poor-quality debt was one of the phenomena within the financial markets during the 1980s. (The variety of features found in junk bonds is covered later in this chapter.)

Even within a given rating, both Moody and Standard & Poor's fine-shade their rankings. Moody adds the numbers 1 through 3 to indicate degrees of quality within a ranking, with 1 representing the highest rank and 3 the lowest. Thus a bond rated A1 has a higher rating than a bond rated A3. Standard & Poor's uses + and − to indicate shades of quality. Thus a bond rated A + has a higher rating than an A bond, which, in turn, has a better rating than an A− bond.

Since the rating services analyze similar data, their ratings of specific debt issues should be reasonably consistent. This consistency is illustrated in Exhibit 13.2, which gives the ratings for several different bond issues. Generally, both Moody and Standard & Poor's assigned comparable ratings, such as the A+ and A1 for the IBM bond. When the ratings are different, the discrepancies are small. Moody ranked the NY Telephone bond A, which is higher than the Standard & Poor's Baa3 rating.

---

[1]The decline in the value of the dollar in foreign countries may reduce the attractiveness of federal obligations. Fluctuations in the value of the dollar impose an additional risk for foreigners who invest in these securities.

EXHIBIT	13.1	Bond Ratings

Moody's Bond Ratings*

Aaa	Bonds of highest quality		B	Bonds that lack characteristics of a desirable investment
Aa	Bonds of high quality			
A	Bonds whose security of principal and interest is considered adequate but may be impaired in the future		Caa	Bonds in poor standing that may be defaulted
			Ca	Speculative bonds that are often in default
			C	Bonds with poor prospects of any investment value (lowest rating)
Baa	Bonds of medium grade that are neither highly protected nor poorly secured			
Ba	Bonds of speculative quality whose future cannot be considered well assured			

For ratings Aa through B, 1 indicates the high, 2 indicates the middle, and 3 indicates the low end of the rating class.

Standard & Poor's Bond Ratings†

AAA	Bonds of highest quality		BB	Bonds of lower-medium grade with few desirable investment characteristics
AA	High-quality debt obligations			
A	Bonds that have a strong capacity to pay interest and principal but may be susceptible to adverse effects		B	Primarily speculative bonds with great uncertainties and major risk if exposed to adverse conditions
BBB	Bonds that have an adequate capacity to pay interest and principal but are more vulnerable to adverse economic conditions or changing circumstances		CCC	
			C	Income bonds on which no interest is being paid
			D	Bonds in default

Plus (+) and minus (−) are used to show relative strength and weakness within a rating category.

*__Source:__ Adapted from *Mergent's Bond Record*, January 2006.
†__Source:__ Adapted from *Standard & Poor's Bond Guide*, January 2006.

EXHIBIT	13.2	Ratings for Selected Bonds as of June 2009

Issuer	Coupon Rate of Interest	Year of Maturity	Moody's Rating	Standard & Poor's Rating
IBM	8.375	2019	A+	A1
Bank of NY	5.700	2020	A+	Aa3
GE Capital	5.250	2021	AA+	Aa2
Coca-Cola Enterprise	8.500	2022	A	A3
NY Telephone	6.700	2023	A	Baa3

__Sources:__ *Mergent's Bond Record* and *Standard & Poor's Bond Guide*.

These ratings play an important role in the marketing of debt obligations. Since the possibility of default may be substantial for poor-quality debt, some financial institutions and investors will not purchase debt with a low credit rating. Many financial institutions, especially commercial banks, are prohibited by law from purchasing bonds with a rating below Baa. Thus, if the rating of a bond issued by a firm or a municipality is low or declines from the original rating, the issuer may have difficulty selling its debt. Corporations and municipal governments try to maintain good credit ratings, because high ratings reduce the cost of borrowing and increase the marketability of the debt.

Although the majority of corporate and municipal bonds are rated, there are exceptions. If a firm or municipality believes it will be able to market the securities without a rating, it may choose not to incur the costs necessary to have the securities rated. Unrated securities tend to be small issues and, because they lack the approval implied by a rating, probably should be viewed as possessing considerable risk.

Besides the risk of default, creditors are also subject to the risk of price fluctuations. Once debt has been issued, the market price of the debt will rise or fall depending on market conditions. If interest rates rise, the price of existing debt must fall so that its fixed interest payments relative to its price become competitive with the higher rates. In the event that interest rates decline, the opposite is true. The higher fixed-interest payments of the bond make the debt more attractive than comparable newly issued bonds, and buyers will be willing to pay more for the debt issue. Why these fluctuations in the price of debt instruments occur is explained in more detail in Chapter 14, which discusses the valuation of debt instruments.

There is, however, one feature of debt that partially compensates for the risk of price fluctuations. The holder knows that the debt ultimately matures: The principal must be repaid. If the price of the bond decreases and the debt instrument sells for a discount (i.e., less than the face value), the value of the debt must appreciate as it approaches maturity, because on the day of maturity, the full amount of the principal must be repaid.

Since interest rates fluctuate, bondholders may also bear reinvestment rate risk. Of course, this risk does not apply if the investor is spending payments as they are received, but that is often not the case. Instead, the payments are reinvested, and lower interest rates imply the individual will earn less and accumulate a lower terminal value. The converse would also apply if interest rates were higher. The reinvested payments would earn more and the investor would accumulate a larger terminal value.

Bondholders and creditors also endure the risk associated with inflation, which reduces the purchasing power of money. During periods of inflation the debtor repays the loan in money that purchases less. Creditors must receive a rate of interest that is at least equal to the rate of inflation to maintain their purchasing power. If lenders anticipate inflation, they will demand a higher rate of interest to help protect their purchasing power. For example, if the rate of inflation is 3 percent, the creditors may demand 6 percent. Although inflation still causes the real value of the capital to decline, the higher interest rate partially offsets the effects of inflation.

If creditors do not anticipate inflation, the rate of interest may be insufficient to compensate for the loss in purchasing power. Inflation, then, hurts the creditors and helps the debtors, who are repaying the loans with money that purchases less.

The supposed inability of creditors to anticipate inflation has led to a belief that during inflation it is better to be a debtor. However, creditors invariably make an effort to protect their position by demanding higher interest rates. There is a transfer of purchasing power from creditors to debtors only if the creditors do not fully anticipate the inflation and do not demand sufficiently high interest rates. A transfer of purchasing power from debtors to creditors will occur in the opposite situation. If inflation is anticipated but does not occur, many debtors may pay artificially high interest rates, which transfers purchasing power from them to their creditors. Debtors may seek to protect themselves from the anticipated inflation *not* occurring by having the bond be callable. The call feature is discussed later in this chapter. Hence, the transfer of purchasing power can go either way if one group inaccurately anticipates the future rate of inflation.

If the investor acquires bonds denominated in a foreign currency, there is the additional risk that the value of the currency will decline relative to the dollar. Payments received in yen, euros, or pounds have to be converted into dollars before they may be spent in the United States, so fluctuations in the value of the currency affect the number of dollars the investor will receive. Of course, the value of the foreign currency could rise, which means the investor receives more dollars, but the value could also fall.

All the sources of risk to bondholders (default, fluctuations in bond prices from fluctuations in interest rates, reinvestment rate risk, loss of purchasing power from inflation, and foreign exchange rate risk) are essentially the same as the sources of risk to investors in stock. While a diversified bond portfolio reduces the risk identified with a specific asset (i.e., the risk of default), the risks associated with bond investments in general are not reduced by diversification. Even diversified bond investors must still bear the risks of fluctuations in interest and reinvestment rates, loss of purchasing power from inflation, and declining exchange rates.

THE MECHANICS OF PURCHASING BONDS

Bonds may be purchased in much the same way as stocks. The investor can buy them through a brokerage firm, and some bonds (e.g., federal government securities) can be purchased through commercial banks. The various purchase orders that may be used to buy stock (e.g., the market order or the limit order with a specified price) also apply to the purchase of bonds. Bonds may be bought with cash or through the use of margin.

The bonds of many companies are listed on the New York and American stock exchanges. In addition, there is a large volume of trading in bonds in the over-the-counter markets. After the debt has been purchased, the broker sends a confirmation statement. Exhibit 13.3 presents simplified confirmation statements for the purchase and subsequent sale of $10,000 in face value worth of Tesoro Petroleum bonds. In addition to a description of the securities, the confirmation statements include the price, the commission, accrued interest, and net amount due.

accrued interest

Interest that has been earned but not received.

Bonds earn interest every day, but the firm distributes the interest payments only twice a year. Thus, when a bond is purchased, the buyer owes the previous owner accrued interest for the days that the owner held the bond. In the case of the first transaction, the purchase was made after the last interest payment, so the accrued interest amounted to $54.00. This interest is added to the purchase price that the buyer must pay. When the bond is sold, the seller receives the accrued interest. The second transaction occurred soon after the interest payment, and in this case the accrued interest was only $12.00, which was added to the proceeds of the sale.

Interest on bonds accrues daily. At 5.25 percent, the interest on $10,000 is $525, or approximately $1.44 a day. If the purchase of the bond occurs 37 days after the payment date, the accrued interest owed is $53.28. If the sale occurs 8 days after the

EXHIBIT 13.3 Simplified Confirmation Statements for the Purchase and Sale of a Bond

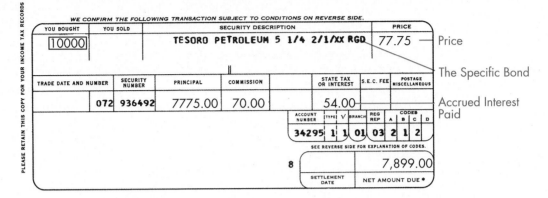

Source: Adapted from Scott & Stringfellow, Inc.

interest payment, the accrued interest received is $12.52. Accrued interest amounts in Exhibit 13.3 are rounded to facilitate the calculation of gains (or losses) in Exhibit 13.4.

The profit or loss from the investment cannot be figured as the difference between the proceeds of the sale and the amount that is due after the purchase (i.e., $8,667.00 minus $7,899.00). Instead, an adjustment must be made for the accrued interest. This procedure is illustrated in Exhibit 13.4. First, the accrued interest must be subtracted from the amount due to obtain the cost of the bond. Thus, $7,899.00 minus $54.00 is the cost ($7,845.00) of this purchase. Second, the accrued interest must also be subtracted from the proceeds of the sale. Thus, $8,667.00 minus $12.00 yields the revenues from the sale. To determine the profit or loss, the cost basis is subtracted from the sale value. In this particular instance, that is $8,655.00 (the sale value) minus $7,845.00 (the cost basis), which represents a gain of $810.00.

A few bonds trade without accrued interest. These bonds are currently in default and are not paying interest. Such bonds are said to trade **flat**, and an *F* is placed next to them in the transactions reported by the financial press. These bonds are of little interest except to speculators. The risk in buying them is substantial, but some do resume interest payments that can result in substantial returns.

flat

A description of a bond that trades without accrued interest.

| EXHIBIT 13.4 | Determination of Profit or Loss on the Sale of a Bond |

Cost basis of the bond:	
Amount due	$7,899.00
Less accrued interest	−54.00
	$7,845.00
Revenue from the sale:	
Proceeds of the sale	$8,667.00
Less accrued interest	−12.00
	$8,655.00
Profit (or loss) on the investment:	
Return from the sale of the bond	$8,655.00
Cost basis of the bond	7,845.00
Profit (or loss) on the investment	$810.00

VARIETY OF CORPORATE BONDS

Corporations issue many types of bonds: mortgage bonds, equipment trust certificates, debenture bonds and subordinated debentures, income bonds, convertible bonds, variable interest rate bonds, and zero coupon bonds. These corporate debt instruments are either secured or unsecured. If a debt instrument is secured, the debtor pledges a specific asset as collateral. In case of default, the creditor may seize this collateral (through a court proceeding). Bonds that are not collateralized by specific assets are unsecured. If the debtor were to default, there would be no specific assets the creditors could seize to satisfy their claims on the borrower. Such unsecured debt instruments are supported by the general capacity of the firm to service its debt (i.e., pay the interest and repay the principal). Thus, the capacity of the borrower to generate operating income (i.e., earnings before interest and taxes) is crucial to the safety of unsecured debt obligations.

Mortgage Bonds

mortgage bond
A bond that is secured by property, especially real estate.

Mortgage bonds are issued to purchase specific fixed assets, which are then pledged to secure the debt. This type of bond is frequently issued by utility companies. The proceeds that are raised by selling the debt are used to build power plants, and these plants secure the debt. As the plants generate revenues, the firm earns the cash flow that is necessary to service (pay interest on) and retire the debt. If the firm defaults on the interest or principal repayment, the creditors may take title to the pledged property. They may then choose to hold the asset and earn income from it (to operate the fixed asset) or to sell it. These options should give investors cause for thought: How many creditors could operate a power plant? If the investors choose to sell it, who would buy it?

These two questions illustrate an important point concerning investing in corporate debt. Although property that is pledged to secure the debt may decrease the lender's risk of loss, the creditor is not interested in taking possession of and operating the property. Lenders earn income through interest payments and not through the operation of the fixed assets. Such creditors are rarely qualified to operate the assets should they take possession of them. If they are forced to seize and sell the assets, they may find few buyers and may have to sell at distress prices. Despite the fact that pledging assets to secure debt increases the safety of the principal, the lenders prefer the prompt payment of interest and principal.

Equipment Trust Certificates

equipment trust certificate

A serial bond secured by specific equipment.

Not all collateral has questionable resale potential. Unlike the mortgage bonds that are issued by utility companies, **equipment trust certificates** are secured by assets with substantial resale value. These certificates are issued to finance specific equipment, which is pledged as collateral. Equipment trust certificates are primarily issued by railroads and airlines to finance rolling stock (railroad cars) and airplanes. As the equipment is used to generate cash flow, the certificates are retired. The collateral supporting these certificates is generally considered to be of excellent quality, for, unlike some fixed assets (e.g., the aforementioned utility plants), this equipment may be readily *moved* and sold to other railroads and airlines in the event that the firm defaults on the certificates.

Investors, however, should realize that while equipment may be more readily sold than power plants, these investors could still suffer losses. For example, when Eastern, Pan Am, and several small airlines went bankrupt, they dumped a large number of aircraft on the market, so prices for used aircraft declined. This, of course, meant that even the secured creditors did not receive their principal from the proceeds of the sales of the planes.

Other Asset-Backed Securities and Securitization

securitization

The process of converting an illiquid asset into a marketable security.

While equipment trust certificates are secured by equipment such as railroad cars and mortgages are secured by real estate, other assets may also be used as collateral for a debt issue. For example, a firm may issue and sell debt securities backed by its accounts receivable. (The firm may also sell the receivables outright to a financial institution or factor, who, in turn, issues debt instruments secured by the assets.) As the accounts are collected, the funds are used to retire the securities and pay the interest. The advantage to the issuing firm is simple. It obtains the funds immediately and does not have to wait for the collection of the receivables. The advantage to the investors, especially large pension plans, is that they receive an interest-paying security that is relatively safe since it is secured by the underlying assets.

The process of converting illiquid assets such as accounts receivable into liquid assets is called **securitization**. Textron, a manufacturer of Bell helicopters, Cessna aircraft, automotive products, and fastening systems, sells a variety of products, which generates accounts receivable. In its 2005 annual report, Textron reported that it securitized over $400 million in assets. The proceeds of the sales were then used to retire debt previously issued by Textron.

Debentures

debenture

An unsecured bond.

Debentures are unsecured promissory notes that are supported by the general creditworthiness of the firm. This type of debt involves more risk than bonds that are supported by collateral. In the case of default or bankruptcy, the unsecured debt is redeemed only after all secured debt has been paid off. Some debentures are subordinated, and these involve even more risk, for they are redeemed after the other general debt of the firm has been redeemed. Even unsecured debt has a position superior to the subordinated debenture. These bonds are among the riskiest debt instruments issued by firms and usually have higher interest rates or other attractive features, such as convertibility into the stock of the company, to compensate the lenders for assuming the increased risk.

Financial institutions, such as commercial banks or insurance companies, prefer a firm to sell debentures to the general public. Since the debentures are general obligations of the company, they do not tie up its specific assets. Then, if the firm needs additional funds from a commercial bank, it can use specific assets as collateral, in which case the bank will be more willing to lend the funds. If the assets had been previously pledged, the firm would lack this flexibility in financing.

Although the use of debentures may not decrease the ability of the firm to issue additional debt, default on the debentures usually means that all senior debt is in default as well. A common indenture clause states that if any of the firm's debt is in default, all debt issues are also in default, and in this case the creditors may declare that all outstanding debt is due. For this reason, a firm should not overextend itself through excessive amounts of unsecured debt.

Income Bonds

income bond
A bond whose interest is paid only if it is earned by the firm.

Income bonds are the riskiest bonds issued by corporations. Interest is paid only if the firm earns it. If the company is unable to cover its other expenses, it is not legally obligated to pay the interest on these bonds. Owing to the great risk associated with them, income bonds are rarely issued by corporations. One notable exception is an issue of Disney bonds that could pay as much as 13.5 percent annually if a package of 20 Disney movies grosses over $800 million. If, however, the gross is less, the bonds could yield as little as 3 percent.

Although income bonds are rarely issued by firms, a similar type of security is often issued by state and municipal governments. These are *revenue bonds*, which are used to finance a particular capital improvement that is expected to generate revenues (e.g., a toll road or a municipal hospital). If the revenues are insufficient, the interest is not paid.

There is, however, one significant difference between income bonds and revenue bonds. Failure to pay interest does not result in default for an income bond, but it does mean that a revenue bond is in default. Most projects financed by revenue bonds have generated sufficient funds to service the debt, but there have been notable exceptions. Perhaps the most famous default was the multibillion-dollar default by the Washington Public Power Supply System. As of 2006, the defaulted bonds were virtually worthless.

Convertible Bonds

convertible bond
A bond that may be exchanged for (i.e., converted into) common stock.

Convertible bonds are a hybrid-type security. Technically they are debt: The bonds pay interest, which is a fixed obligation of the firm, and have a maturity date. But these bonds have a special feature: The investor has the option to convert the bond into a specified number of shares of common stock. For example, the Continental

---

⊕ **Point of Interest**

BONDS AND THE INTERNET

While obtaining information on bonds using the Internet is not as easy as for stocks, a variety of sites do exist. Yahoo! Finance Bonds Center (**http://finance.yahoo .com/bonds**) provides yields and news, and lets you screen for specific types of bonds. Since Yahoo! is a major free site for information on stocks, it may be a good place to start your search for information on bonds. Investing in Bonds (**http://www.investinginbonds.com**) is sponsored by the Securities Industry and Financial Markets Association, which is the bond market's trade association.

In addition to data, it provides information on current issues concerning bonds.

Other possibilities include:

BondsOnline (**http://www.bondsonline.com**)
Briefing.com (**http://www.briefing.com**)
Morningstar (**http://www.morningstar.com**)
Morgan Stanley (**http://www.morganstanley.com**)

While the composition of each site varies, they all provide information, tutorials, commentary, and data.

Airlines ¼ percent of the year 2023 bond may be converted into 50 shares of Continental Airlines common stock. The market price of convertible bonds depends on both the value of the stock and the interest that the bonds pay. If the price of the common stock rises, then the value of the bond must rise. The investor thus has the opportunity for capital gain should the price of the common stock rise. If, however, the price of the common stock does not appreciate, the investor still owns a debt obligation of the company and therefore has the security of an investment in a debt instrument.

Convertible bonds have been popular with some investors, and thus firms have issued these bonds as a means to raise funds. However, since convertible bonds are a hybrid-type security, they are difficult to analyze. For this reason, a detailed discussion is deferred until Chapter 16, which follows the discussion of nonconvertible debt and precedes the discussion of options.

Variable Interest Rate Bonds

variable interest rate bond

A long-term bond with a coupon rate that varies with changes in short-term rates.

Generally, the interest that a bond pays is fixed at the date of issuance; however, some corporations issue **variable interest rate bonds**. Citicorp was the first major American firm to offer bonds with variable interest rates to the general public. Two features of the Citicorp bond were unique at the time it was issued: (1) a variable interest rate that was tied to the interest rate on Treasury bills and (2) the right of the holder to redeem the bond at its face value.

The interest rate to be paid by the Citicorp bond was set at 1 percent above the average Treasury bill rate during a specified period. This variability of the interest rate means that if short-term interest rates rise, the interest rate paid by the bond must increase. The bond's owner participates in any increase in short-term interest rates. Of course, if the short-term interest rates decline, the bond earns a lower rate of interest.

The second unique feature of the Citicorp bond was that two years after it was issued, the holder had the option to redeem the bond for its face value or principal. This option recurred every six months. If the owner needed the money more quickly, the bond could have been sold in the secondary market, for it was traded on the New York Stock Exchange. An important implication of the variable coupon is that the market price of the bond fluctuates less than the price of a fixed coupon bond. As is explained in the next chapter, the price of a fixed coupon bond fluctuates inversely with interest rates. Such price changes will not occur with a variable rate bond because the interest paid fluctuates with interest rates in general. Hence these bonds avoid one of the major sources of risk associated with investing in bonds: higher interest rates driving down the bond's market value.

Zero Coupon Bonds

zero coupon bond

A bond on which interest accrues and is paid at maturity, and is initially sold at a discount.

In 1981 a new type of bond was sold to the general public. These bonds pay no interest and are sold at large discounts. The pathbreaking issue was the J.C. Penney **zero coupon bond**. This bond was initially sold for a discount ($330) but paid $1,000 at maturity in 1989. The investor's funds grew from $330 to $1,000 after eight years. The annual rate of growth (i.e., the yield on the bond) was 14.86 percent.[2]

After the initial success of this issue, other firms, including IBM Credit Corporation (the financing arm of IBM) and ITT Financial, issued similar bonds. In each case the firm pays no periodic interest. The bond sells for a large discount, and the investor's return accrues from the appreciation of the bond's value as it approaches maturity.

Because the return on an investment in a zero coupon bond depends solely on the firm's capacity to retire the debt, the quality of the firm is exceedingly important. Zero coupon bonds issued by such firms as Sears or IBM Credit Corporation are of excellent quality and should be retired at maturity. In these cases the investor will earn the expected return that accrues when the bond approaches maturity. If, however, the investor purchases low-quality zero coupon bonds, these bonds may never be redeemed. If the firm were to go bankrupt, the investor might receive nothing. Thus, it is possible for the individual who buys zero coupon bonds to lose the entire investment and never receive a single interest payment.

Eurobonds

Many U.S. firms also issue bonds in foreign countries to raise funds for foreign investments (e.g., plant and equipment).[3] These bonds fall into two basic types, depending on

Calculator Solution

Function Key	Data Input
PV =	−330
N =	8
PMT =	0
FV =	1000
I =	?
Function Key	*Answer*
I =	14.86

[2]The yield or interest rate on a zero coupon is calculated using the time value equation

$$P_0(1+i)^n = P_n,$$

which is solved for *i*. In this example,

$$\$330(1+i)^8 = \$1,000$$
$$(1+i)^8 = \$1,000/\$330 = 3.030$$
$$i = \sqrt[8]{3.030} - 1$$
$$i = 0.1486 = 14.86\%.$$

If you do not have access to a calculator with a y^x key or a financial calculator, then the future value table can be used, but you will derive an approximate answer of 15 percent.

[3]Bonds are also issued in the United States by foreign firms and these are sometimes referred to as "Yankee" bonds. Other colorful names are also applied to foreign bonds issued in other domestic markets: the "Bulldog" market for foreign bonds issued in the United Kingdom and the "Samurai" market for foreign bonds issued in Japan.

the currency in which they are denominated. U.S. firms can sell bonds denominated in the local currency (e.g., British pounds or European euros). For example, ExxonMobil reported in its 2000 10-K report that $650 million of its $7.28 billion of long-term debt (8.9 percent) was denominated in foreign currencies. The firm can also sell abroad bonds denominated in U.S. dollars called **Eurobonds**. This term applies even though the bonds may be issued in Asia instead of Europe.

Eurobond
A bond denominated in U.S. dollars but issued abroad.

When a firm issues a Eurobond, the U.S. firm promises to make payments in dollars. This means that the U.S. investor does not have to convert the payments from the local currency (e.g., British pounds) into dollars. As is explained in Chapter 5, fluctuation in the value of one currency relative to another is a major source of risk that every individual who acquires foreign securities must bear. By acquiring Eurobonds, the U.S. investor avoids this currency risk. However, foreign investors do bear this risk. They have to convert the dollars into their currency, so the yields on Eurobonds tend to be higher than on comparable domestic securities. The higher yield is a major reason some investors find Eurobonds attractive.

LIBOR

LIBOR is an acronym for the London InterBank Offer Rate, which is established daily by the British Bankers' Association. LIBOR is the interest rate at which large international banks are willing to lend to each other for periods ranging from one day (referred to as "overnight") to one year. Generally LIBOR is about half a percentage point above the rate on U.S. federal government securities with the same maturities. This differential increases during periods of financial strife such as the last quarter of 2008.

LIBOR is important for two fundamental reasons. First, LIBOR is calculated in ten currencies and has become the global benchmark for global lending and interest rates. Second, although LIBOR is not the rate paid on a particular type of debt instrument, it plays an important role in the determination of borrowing costs and hence yields. Many debt instruments have variable rates of interest that are tied to LIBOR. Thus, increases in LIBOR are transferred throughout the world to all debt instruments tied to that rate. These instruments include the corporate high-yield bonds covered in the next section, small business loans, student loans, and adjustable-rate mortgages. (See Point of Interest: The Variety of Mortgage Terms in Chapter 15.) The rates on these loans are often several percentage points above the LIBOR rate, which means that if LIBOR rises from 2 to 3 percent, an adjustable mortgage set 5 percentage points above LIBOR will rise from 7 to 8 percent.

HIGH-YIELD SECURITIES

high-yield securities
Non-investment-grade securities offering a high return.

High-yield securities (sometimes referred to as *junk bonds*) are not a particular type of bond but refer to any debt of low quality (i.e., bonds rated below triple B). These bonds have the same general features associated with investment-grade debt. In addition to the interest payment (the coupon) and the maturity date, junk bonds often have call features and sinking funds. Although junk bonds are usually debentures and may be subordinated to the firm's other debt obligations, some do have collateral (i.e., they are mortgage bonds). As is subsequently discussed, some high-yield securities have variations on the basic features associated with all bonds.

The poor quality of junk bonds requires that they offer high yields, at least relative to investment-grade debt. Generally, triple B or better is considered investment grade, and many financial institutions, such as trust departments of commercial banks, are allowed to purchase only investment-grade bonds. Anything with a lower credit rating is not an acceptable risk.

Junk bonds (and high-yield preferred stock) are often issued to finance takeovers and mergers or to finance start-up firms with little credit history. The bonds are purchased by financial institutions and individuals who are accustomed to investing in poor-quality debt and who are willing and able to accept the larger risk in order to earn the higher yields. These investors may treat the bonds as if they are equity instruments that will generate their potential return if the firm generates cash flow and survives. In many cases, the additional return may be 3 or 4 percentage points greater than the yield on investment-grade debt.

High-yield securities may be divided into two classes. First are the bonds that were initially investment grade but whose credit ratings were lowered as the issuing firms developed financial problems. This type of high-yield bond is often referred to as a **fallen angel**. When RJR Nabisco was purchased and taken private, the surviving firm issued substantial new debt that resulted in the downgrading of outstanding RJR Nabisco bonds. The prices of what were previously high-quality debt declined dramatically, and the issues became high-yield securities. Of course, the high yields were to be earned by new buyers and not by the original investors who suffered losses when the prices of the previously issued bonds declined.

Some fallen angels ultimately go bankrupt. Manville, Public Service of New Hampshire, and Texaco all went bankrupt and defaulted on their debts. However, bonds in default continue to trade, and there is always the possibility that the firm will recover and the price of the bonds will rise. This did occur in the case of Texaco. One of the attractions of the high-yield security market is the possibility that the financial condition of the issuing firm will improve. A higher credit rating should be beneficial to the holders of the firm's debt, because the bonds' prices should increase as the firm's financial condition improves.

The second class of high-yield securities is composed of bonds and preferred stock issued by firms with less than investment-grade credit ratings. The maturities of these securities can range from short-term (i.e., high-yield commercial paper) to long-term (i.e., bonds and preferred stock).

fallen angel
Investment-grade security whose quality has deteriorated.

Split Coupon Bonds

split coupon bond
Bond with a zero or low initial coupon followed by a period with a high coupon.

A **split coupon bond** combines the features of zero coupon and high coupon bonds. During the first three to five years, the bond pays initially no (or a small amount of) interest. The interest accrues like a zero coupon bond. After this initial period, the bond pays a high coupon. For example, Dr Pepper issued a split coupon bond that pays no interest for the first four years and then must pay a coupon of 11.5 percent for the next six years, until the bond matures.

⊕ **Point of Interest**

MEZZANINE FINANCING

Although there are secondary markets for high-yield securities, junk bonds tend to lack liquidity. The spreads between the bid and ask prices are often large, and there may be little or no market for small issues. This lack of liquidity for small issues has led to "mezzanine financing." In a theater, the mezzanine is between the orchestra seats and the balcony seats. That analogy describes mezzanine financing, which tends to be a modest-sized debt issue ranging from $50 million to $200 million.

Modest-sized issues are often too small to attract buyers of high-yield securities (e.g., pension plans or mutual funds specializing in low-quality debt) but too large for most commercial banks. To place such issues, investment bankers have formed specialized groups to arrange offerings of mezzanine debt. The securities are privately placed with one or more buyers who intend to hold the securities until maturity. Since there will be no secondary market for the securities, the yields tend to be higher, which compensates the buyers for the lack of liquidity.

These bonds, which are also referred to as *deferred interest bonds*, initially sell at a discounted price that is calculated using the coupon rate in effect when the bond starts to pay cash. For the Dr Pepper bond, the flow of payments per $1,000 bond is

Interest:	
Years 1–4	$0
Years 5–10	$115
Principal repayment at end of year 10:	$1,000

The advantage to the firm issuing split coupon bonds is that debt service is eliminated during the initial period. Split coupon bonds conserve cash, but the accrual of interest is tax deductible to the issuing firm. Split coupon bonds are often issued in leveraged buyouts and other recapitalizations that result in the firm issuing substantial amounts of debt.

Split coupon bonds tend to be very costly to the firm issuing them. The high yield to investors means a high cost of funds to the issuers. There is an incentive for the firm to retire the securities as soon as possible. Thus most split coupon bonds have call features that permit the firm to retire the securities before their maturity. For example, Safeway Stores called half of its issue of junior subordinated debentures only 11 months after the bonds were originally issued.

Reset Securities and Increasing Rate Bonds

reset bond

Bond whose coupon is periodically reset.

Although the coupons are fixed when most high-yield securities are issued, there are exceptions. With a **reset bond**, the coupon is adjusted at periodic intervals, such as six months or every year. The coupon is usually tagged to a specified rate, such as the six-month Treasury bill rate plus 5 percent, and there is often a minimum and a maximum coupon. For example, American Shared Hospital Service issued a reset note whose coupon can range from 14 to 16.5 percent.

Since the coupon is permitted to change, price fluctuations associated with changes in interest rates are reduced. The minimum coupon, however, means that if interest rates fall on comparably risky securities, the price of the bond will rise since the coupon becomes fixed at the lower bound. And the same applies when interest rates rise. If the coupon reaches the upper limit, further increases in comparable yields will decrease the bond's price. However, within the specified range the changing coupon should stabilize the price of the bond. Of course, if the firm's financial condition changes, the price of the bond will change independently of changes in interest rates.

increasing rate bond
Bond whose coupon rises over time.

An **increasing rate bond** is a debt security whose coupon increases over time. For example, RJR Holdings issued $5 billion of increasing rate notes. One issue had an initial coupon of 14.5625 percent, but future coupons will be the higher of 13.4375 percent or 4 percent plus the three-month London Interbank Offer (LIBOR) rate. Subsequent coupons increase by 0.5 percent quarterly for two years and 0.25 percent quarterly for years three and four. Unless yields decline dramatically so that 13.4375 percent becomes the coupon, the yield on this bond will rise over time. Obviously, increasing rate securities are an expensive means for any firm to raise funds, so the investor can anticipate that the issuer will seek to retire the debt as rapidly as possible, which is precisely what occurred as RJR Holdings refinanced after interest rates fell and its financial position improved.

Extendible Securities

In the previous discussion, the high-yield securities had differing coupons but fixed maturity dates. Split coupon bonds have periods during which interest accrues but is not paid. Reset and increasing rate notes and bonds have coupons that vary. Each of the types of high-yield securities has a fixed maturity date. However, a firm may issue

extendible security
Bond whose maturity date may be extended into the future.

an **extendible security** in which the term to maturity may be lengthened by the issuer. For example, Mattel issued a bond with an initial maturity date in 1990, but the company could extend the bond for one-, two-, or three-year periods with a final maturity in 1999. Thus the investor who acquired this bond did not know if the bond would be outstanding for one year or six years or longer. Only the final maturity in 1999 was known.

The ability to extend the maturity date is, of course, beneficial to the issuer. If the firm does not have the capacity to retire the debt at the initial maturity date, the date may be extended. This buys time for the firm to find the funds or to refinance the debt. Failure to retire the debt at the final maturity, of course, throws the bond into default.

Spreads and Returns

The coupons on high-yield securities are promised or anticipated yields. In many cases the promised return will be realized as the firm makes timely payments and retires the securities on schedule. However, securities markets and firms are dynamic entities. Change is always occurring, so the returns actually earned by investors often differ from the expected yields. The actual returns could be higher, especially if interest rates decline or the firm's financial condition improves. In either case, the price of the high-yield security should rise, so that the investor earns a higher return.

While earning higher returns is possible, the greater concern is usually that something will go wrong and that the investor will earn a lower return. Firms that issue high-yield securities are obviously not financially strong and some will not survive. If the investor is unfortunate enough to select those firms, he or she could lose a substantial amount of money—perhaps all the funds invested. Avoiding such an outcome is obviously desirable and is the purpose of analyzing the issuer's financial condition and determining the quality of its debt.

Analysis of investment-grade debt revolves around the firm's current and future capacity to service the debt. This analysis may start with such ratios as the debt ratio or times-interest-earned. For high-yield securities the emphasis is often placed on cash flow (operating income plus noncash expenses such as depreciation), since interest is paid with funds from operations and not with earnings. Even if the firm is operating at an accounting loss, it may still generate sufficient cash to service its debt.

The spread in yields (i.e., the difference) between high-yield and investment-grade debt can be substantial. This difference is usually expressed in terms of basis points. A **basis point** is 0.01 percent, so that a difference of 50 basis points is 0.5 percent. If the yield on AAA-rated bonds is 4.6 percent and the yield on a B-rated bond is 5.2 percent, the difference is 60 basis points. If the yields were 4.6 percent and 7.2 percent, the difference is 260 basis points.

During December 2008, the spread between high-yield junk bonds and AAA-rated bonds reached over 2,100 basis points. In other words, if high-quality debt yielded 4 percent, junk bonds were yielding over 25 percent. Eighteen months earlier the spread was about 200 basis points. Even as the financial crises appeared to abate, the spread still exceeded 1,000 basis points in June 2009.

Investors may use the spread as a guide for an investment strategy. When the spread increases, the investor sells the quality debt and purchases the lower-quality debt. The process would be reversed when the spread diminished. Essentially, the spread must be sufficient to compensate for the additional risk. Even if only 5 percent of the bonds were to default, the total loss on each bond may offset a substantial proportion of the yield advantage.

Studies have concluded that returns on portfolios of high-yield debt generate higher returns than investment-grade bonds. Even after adjusting for defaults, the returns were higher. Of course, this would be expected, since the investor bears more risk. If the returns were consistently lower, no one would buy poor-quality debt. The surprise, however, was that high-yield bonds were less volatile. During periods of changing interest rates, their prices did not fluctuate as much.

This lower volatility seems inconsistent with the concept of risky, high-yield bonds. However, as is discussed in the next chapter, the prices of bonds with higher coupons tend to fluctuate less than the prices of bonds with lower coupons. Higher-yield bonds have higher coupons than investment-grade bonds, so their prices are less sensitive to change in interest rates. It is the firm-specific risk (i.e., the unsystematic risk) and not the market or interest rate that is the primary source of risk. The firm-specific source of risk is reduced, if not eliminated, by the construction of a well-diversified portfolio of high-yield securities.

Even though studies concluded that high-yield bonds have done well and exhibit less price volatility, you should realize that historical returns are not future returns. Even if there have been periods when high-yield securities produced greater returns than investment-grade debt, you should not conclude these bonds will continue to do well. Many firms that issue junk bonds ultimately default. Some will be reorganized and

basis point
0.01 percent.

survive, but many will not and their bonds will become worthless. During 2007–2009, many firms did default and filed for bankruptcy. Their bonds sold for mere pennies on the dollar. Such valuations suggest that the market did not anticipate the companies and their bonds would survive.

ACCRUED INTEREST, ZERO COUPON BONDS, ORIGINAL-ISSUE DISCOUNT BONDS, AND INCOME TAXATION

Bonds accrue interest every day, and that reality affects income taxation. Taxation, of course, affects financial planning and portfolio management. As was illustrated in the section on the mechanics of purchasing a bond, you pay the prior owner accrued interest. In Exhibit 13.3, the accrued interest paid was $54.00. When you receive the six-month $262.50 interest payment (($10,000 × .0525)/2 = $262.50), only $208.50 is subject to income taxation. When you sell the bond, the accrued interest that you receive ($12.00 in Exhibit 13.3) is subject to income taxation.

Zero coupon bonds are initially sold for less than their face value and do not annually pay interest. Instead the interest accrues daily and is received when the bond matures. Tax on the accrued interest, however, occurs every year as if the interest were received. Consider a four-year $1,000 zero coupon bond that sells for $683 if the interest rate is 10 percent and the interest is paid annually. (FV = 1000, N = 4, I = 10, PMT = 0, and PV = ?. See the next chapter for the explanation of bond pricing.) After one year the price of the bond is $751 if interest rates do not change. The appreciation from $683 to $751 ($68) is the accrual of interest, and that $68 is subject to income taxation. At the end of the second, third, and fourth years, the bond's values are $826, $909, and $1,000. The accrued interest earned in each year is $75, $83, and $91.

Notice that the interest earned each year is *not* an average of the discount: ($1,000 − $683)/4 = $79.25. Each year the accrued interest is determined on the principal and added to the prior year's principal. Thus, the $68 earned in year one is added to $683, which becomes the principal owed ($751) at the end of the first year. This process is repeated until the bond is redeemed at maturity for $1,000. The accrued interest, however, continues to be taxed each year.

The prices in the previous example were determined assuming that interest rates do not change and that the value of the bond increases with the accrual of interest. After the first year, the bond could sell for more or less than $751. If the bond is sold for $773 instead of $751, there is a gain of $90 ($773 − $683). The appreciation, however, is not a capital gain since $68 is the result of the accrued interest. The $68 is taxed as income and the $22 is taxed at the appropriate capital gains tax rate if the bond were sold.

If the price of the bond is $723 and the investor sells the bond, the appreciation is only $723 − $683 = $40. The accrued interest, however, remains $68, so the investor experiences a capital loss of $40 − $68 = ($28). This loss is applied against other capital gains and ordinary income. (The use of capital losses to offset capital gains and ordinary income was discussed in Chapter 4.)

Original-issue discount bonds combine the features of a zero coupon and a coupon bond. When they are issued, the coupon is less than the yield on comparable debt, so the bond sells for a discount. Since the bond does pay some interest, the amount of the discount is less than the discount associated with a zero coupon bond. Over time the discount disappears as the interest accrues and the bond is redeemed for its face value at maturity. The taxation of the accrual for an original-discount bond is the same as the taxation of a zero coupon bond.

The taxation of the accrued interest that is earned but not received until maturity suggests investors may have little reason to purchase zero coupon bonds. There is, however, one major exception: tax-deferred pension plans. The tax on the accrued interest is deferred until the funds are withdrawn from the account. So the primary reason for acquiring zero coupon bonds is to use them as part of a tax-deferred retirement account.

RETIRING DEBT

Debt issues must ultimately be retired, and this retirement must occur on or before the maturity date of the debt. When the bond is issued, a method for periodic retirement is usually specified, for very few debt issues are retired in one lump payment at the maturity date. Instead, part of the issue is systematically retired each year. This systematic retirement may be achieved by issuing the bond in a series or by having a sinking fund.

Serial Bonds

serial bond

A bond issue in which specified bonds mature each year.

In an issue of **serial bonds**, some bonds mature each year. (Preferred stock may also be issued in series.) This type of bond is usually issued by corporations to finance specific equipment, such as railroad cars, which is pledged as collateral. As the equipment depreciates, the cash flow that is generated by profits and depreciation expense is used to retire the bonds in a series as they mature.

The advertisement presented in Exhibit 13.5 is for equipment trust certificates issued by Union Pacific Railroad Company. These equipment trust certificates were sold in 1985 and were designed so that one-fifteenth of the securities matured each year. Thus, the firm retired $2,337,000 of the certificates annually as each series within the issue matured. At the end of 2001, the entire issue of certificates had been retired.

Few corporations, however, issue serial bonds. They are primarily issued by state and local governments to finance capital improvements, such as new school buildings, or by ad hoc government bodies, such as the Port Authority of New York, to finance new facilities or other capital improvements. The bonds are then retired over a period of years by tax receipts or by revenues generated by the investment (e.g., toll roads).

Sinking Funds

sinking fund

A series of periodic payments to retire a bond issue.

Sinking funds are generally employed to ease the retirement of long-term corporate debt. A **sinking fund** is a periodic payment to retire part of the debt issue. One type of sinking fund requires the firm to make payments to a trustee, who invests the money to earn interest. The periodic payments plus the accumulated interest retire the debt when it matures.

Another type of sinking fund requires the firm to set aside a stated sum of money and to randomly select the bonds that are to be retired. The selected bonds are called and

EXHIBIT 13.5 Example of a Serial Bond Issue (Equipment Trust Certificate)

This announcement is under no circumstances to be construed as an offer to sell or as a solicitation of an offer to buy any of these securities. The offering is made only by the Offering Circular Supplement and the Offering Circular to which it relates.

NEW ISSUE   July 17, 1985

$35,055,000

Union Pacific Railroad Company

Equipment Trust No. 1 of 1985

Serial Equipment Trust Certificates
(Non-callable)

Price 100%
(Plus accrued dividends, if any, from the date of original issuance.)

MATURITIES AND DIVIDEND RATES.

(To mature in 15 equal annual installments
of $2,337,000, commencing July 15, 1987.)

1987	6.500%	1992	7.500%	1997	7.800%
1988	7.000	1993	7.600	1998	7.800
1989	7.125	1994	7.700	1999	7.875
1990	7.300	1995	7.700	2000	7.875
1991	7.375	1996	7.750	2001	7.875

These Certificates are offered subject to prior sale, when, as and if issued and received by us, subject to approval of the Interstate Commerce Commission.

Merrill Lynch Capital Markets

Thomson McKinnon Securities Inc.

Source: Reprinted with permission of the Union Pacific Railroad Company.

redeemed, and the holder surrenders the bond because it ceases to earn interest once it has been called. This type of sinking fund is illustrated in Exhibit 13.6 by an advertisement taken from the *Wall Street Journal*. The specific bonds being retired are selected by a lottery. Once they are chosen, these bonds are called. The owners must surrender the bonds to obtain their principal. If the bonds are not presented for redemption, they

EXHIBIT   13.6   Example of a Sinking Fund Retiring Debt

NOTICE OF REDEMPTION
To the Holders of

Issuing Authority ──────────────→ **New York State Urban Development Corporation**

Bond Issue ────────────────→ **Project Revenue Bonds (Center for Industrial Innovation)**

Coupon ────────────────────→ **Series 1982 Bonds 11⅛% Due January 1, 2013**

Maturity Date ────────────────── **(CUSIP NO. 650033BD4)***

NOTICE IS HEREBY GIVEN THAT, pursuant to the provisions of a resolution adopted by the New York State Urban Development Corporation (the "Corporation"), on November 18, 1982, as amended and restated on December 10, 1982, and entitled "Project Revenue Bond (Center for Industrial Innovation) General Resolution" (the "General Resolution"), as supplemented by a resolution of the Corporation entitled "Series 1982 Project Revenue Bonds (Center for Industrial Innovation) Series Resolution" (the "Series Resolution") authorizing the issuance of the above described Bonds, the Corporation will redeem

Sinking Fund Provision ──────── and the Trustee under the General Resolution has drawn by lot for redemption on January 1, 1993 (the "Sinking Fund Redemption Date"), through the operation of the sinking fund created under the Series Resolution, $465,000 aggregate principal amount of the above described Bonds as set forth below.

Amount to Be Redeemed ────────

Coupon Bonds called for redemption each bearing the
Prefix A and each in the Denomination of $5,000, are as follows:

Specific Bonds ─────── 386   424   854   3472   3987   4417   5417   5438   5513   6024   6304   6746   6920

Being Retired

Registered Bonds called for redemption, in whole or in part, each bearing the
Prefix AR, are as follows:

Bond Number	Denomination	Amount Called	Bond Number	Denomination	Amount Called
26...	$ 500,000 ...	$15,000	87...	$2,435,000 ...	$30,000
39...	50,000 ...	5,000	88...	2,460,000 ...	30,000
51...	5,000 ...	5,000	89...	2,435,000 ...	35,000
81...	490,000 ...	10,000	90...	2,465,000 ...	20,000
82...	95,000 ...	5,000	91...	2,405,000 ...	40,000
84...	2,430,000 ...	40,000	92...	2,450,000 ...	35,000
85...	2,420,000 ...	35,000	93...	1,945,000 ...	30,000
86...	2,480,000 ...	20,000	94...	2,415,000 ...	45,000

On the Sinking Fund Redemption Date, there shall become due and payable on each of the above mentioned Bonds to be redeemed, the sinking fund redemption price, namely 100% of the principal amount thereof. Interest accrued on such Bonds to said Sinking Fund Redemption Date will be paid in the usual

Interest Will Cease to Accrue ──── manner. From and after the Sinking Fund Redemption Date, interest on the Bonds described above shall cease to accrue.

IN ADDITION THE CORPORATION HAS ELECTED TO REDEEM ON JANUARY 1, 1993 (THE "REDEMPTION DATE") ALL REMAINING OUTSTANDING BONDS NOT HERETOFORE CALLED FOR SINKING FUND REDEMPTION AT A REDEMPTION PRICE EQUAL TO 103% OF THE PRINCIPAL AMOUNT THEREOF. INTEREST ACCRUED ON SUCH BONDS TO THE REDEMPTION DATE WILL BE PAID IN THE USUAL MANNER. FROM AND AFTER THE REDEMPTION DATE, INTEREST ON THE BONDS SHALL CEASE TO ACCRUE.

The Bonds specified herein to be redeemed shall be redeemed on or after both the Sinking Fund Redemption Date and the Redemption Date upon presentation and surrender thereof, together, in the case of coupon Bonds, with all appurtenant coupons attached, if any, maturing after January 1, 1993, to Bankers Trust Company, as Trustee and Paying Agent, in person or by registered mail (postage prepaid) at the following addresses:

IN PERSON:

Bankers Trust Company
Corporate Trust and Agency Group
First Floor
123 Washington Street
New York, New York

BY MAIL:

Bankers Trust Company
Corporate Trust and Agency Group
P.O. Box 2579
Church Street Station
New York, NY 10008
Attn: Bond Redemption

If any of the Bonds designated for redemption are in registered form, they should be accompanied by duly executed instruments of assignment in blank if payment is to be made to other than the registered holder thereof.

Coupons maturing January 1, 1993 appertaining to the coupon Bonds designated for redemption should be detached and presented for payment in the usual manner. Interest due January 1, 1993 on registered Bonds designated for redemption will be paid to the registered holders of such registered Bonds in the usual manner.

 NEW YORK STATE URBAN DEVELOPMENT CORPORATION
By: BANKERS TRUST COMPANY, *as Trustee*

Source: Empire State Development Corporation.

EXHIBIT 13.7		Selected Examples of Sinking Funds for GT&E Bonds
GTE (A Telephone Subsidiary of Verizon) Bonds		**Sinking Fund Feature**
9⅛%	2016	$12,500,000 face amount retired each year to retire 95% of the issue prior to maturity.
7.9%	2027	No sinking fund.

are still outstanding and are obligations of the company, but the debtor's obligation is limited to refunding the principal, since interest payments cease at the call date.

Since each debt issue is different, there can be wide variations in sinking funds. A strong sinking fund retires a substantial proportion of the debt before the date of maturity. For example, if a bond issue is for $10 million and it matures in ten years, a strong sinking fund may require the firm to retire $1 million, or 10 percent, of the issue each year. Thus, at maturity only $1 million is still outstanding. With a weak sinking fund, a substantial proportion of the debt is retired at maturity. For example, a sinking fund for a debt issue of $10 million that matures in ten years may require annual payments of $1 million commencing after five years. In this example, only $5 million is retired before maturity. The debtor must then make a lump sum payment to retire the remaining $5 million. Such a large final payment is called a **balloon payment**.

balloon payment

The large final payment necessary to retire a debt issue.

Different sinking funds are illustrated in Exhibit 13.7, which presents the sinking fund requirements for two GT&E bonds. (GT&E subsequently merged with Bell Atlantic to form Verizon.) One of the sinking funds is quite strong. The 9⅛ percent bond has a sinking fund that retires 95 percent of the issue prior to maturity. However, there is no sinking fund for the 7.9 percent bond that matures in 2027. Unless GT&E calls the bond and retires it prior to maturity, the entire issue may be outstanding until it matures in 2027.

The strength of a sinking fund affects the element of risk. A strong sinking fund requirement means that a substantial amount of the debt issue is retired during its lifetime, which makes the entire debt issue safer. The sinking fund feature of a debt issue, then, is an important factor in determining the amount of risk associated with investing in a particular debt instrument.

Repurchasing Debt

If bond prices decline and the debt is selling for less than face value (i.e., at a discount), the firm may try to retire the debt by purchasing it on the open market. The purchases may be made from time to time, in which case the sellers of the bonds need not know that the company is purchasing and retiring the debt. The company may also offer to purchase a specified amount of the debt at a certain price within a particular period. Bondholders may then tender their bonds at the offer price; however, they are not required to sell their bonds and may continue to hold the debt. If more bonds are tendered than the company offered to buy, the firm prorates the amount of money that it had allocated for the purchase among the number of bonds being offered.

The advantage of repurchasing debt that is selling at a discount is the savings to the firm. If a firm issued $10 million in face value of debt and the bonds are currently selling for $0.60 on the $1, the firm may reduce its debt by $1,000 with a cash outlay of only $600, resulting in a $400 savings for each $1,000 bond that is purchased. This savings is translated into income, and is reported under the heading "other gains and losses." For example, General Cinema reported a gain of $419.6 million from the purchase of Harcourt Brace Jovanovich's debt at a discount as part of the acquisition of the publisher. The low interest rates of the late 1990s and early 2000s caused bond prices to rise. (See the next chapter for the explanation of changes in interest rates and their impact on bond prices.) The increase in bond prices meant the opportunity to repurchase bonds at a discount had disappeared.

On the surface, a firm's retiring debt at a discount may appear desirable. However, using money to repurchase debt is an investment decision, just like buying plant and equipment. If the company repurchases debt, it cannot use the funds for other purposes. Management must decide which is the better use of the money: purchasing other income-earning assets or retiring the debt and saving the interest payments. Unlike a sinking fund requirement (which management must meet), purchasing and retiring debt at a discount is a voluntary act. The lower the price of the debt, the greater the potential benefit from the purchase, but management must still determine if it is the best use of the firm's scarce resource, cash.

Call Feature

call feature

The right of an issuer to retire a debt issue prior to maturity.

Some bonds may have a **call feature** that allows for redemption prior to maturity. (Bonds that lack a call feature may be referred to as "bullets.") In most cases after the bond has been outstanding for a period of time (e.g., five years), the issuer has the right to call and retire the bond. The bond is called for redemption as of a specific date. After that date, interest ceases to accrue, which forces the creditor to relinquish the debt instrument.

Such premature retiring of debt through a call feature tends to occur after a period of high interest rates. If a bond has been issued during such a period and interest rates subsequently decline, it may be advantageous for the company to issue new bonds at the lower interest rate. The proceeds can then be used to retire the older bonds with the higher coupon rates. Such **refunding** reduces the firm's interest expense.

refunding

The act of issuing new debt and using the proceeds to retire existing debt.

Of course, premature retirement of debt hurts the bondholders who lose the higher-yield bonds. To protect these creditors, a call feature usually has a **call penalty**, such as the payment of one year's interest. If the initial issue had a 9 percent interest rate, the company would have to pay $1,090 to retire $1,000 worth of debt. This call penalty usually declines over the lifetime of the debt. Exhibit 13.8 illustrates the call penalty associated with the AT&T 8⅛ of 2020. In 2005 the penalty was $33.09 per $1,000, but it declines to nothing in 2015. Such a call penalty does protect bondholders, and the debtor has the right to call the bond and to refinance debt if interest rates fall sufficiently to justify paying the call penalty.

call penalty

A premium paid for exercising a call feature.

Several such refinancings occurred during the 1990s and 2000s when interest rates fell to lows that had not been seen in 20 to 40 years. In particular, utility companies that had issued debt when interest rates were higher sold new bonds with lower yields, called the old debt, and paid the call penalty. Bell Atlantic retired $125 million of bonds with 7.5 percent coupons. The company paid 101.5 per bond (i.e., $1,015 per

EXHIBIT 13.8	Schedule for the Call Penalty of the AT&T 8⅛ Debenture Maturing in 2020		
Year	Percentage of Face Value	Amount Required to Retire $1,000 of Debt	Amount of Call Penalty
2005	103.309	$1,033.09	$33.09
2006	102.978	$1,029.78	$29.78
2007	102.647	$1,026.47	$26.47
.	.	.	.
.	.	.	.
.	.	.	.
2010	101.655	$1,016.55	$16.55
.	.	.	.
.	.	.	.
.	.	.	.
2015	100.000	$1,000.00	0.00

$1,000) for a penalty of $15 per bond. Nonutility companies also retired debt whose coupons exceeded the current rate of interest. Texas Instruments retired $200 million of its 12.7 percent bonds. It paid $1,047 to retire $1,000 in face value of debt (i.e., a premium of $47 per bond). These refinancings sufficiently reduced the companies' interest expense to justify paying the call premium.

Escrowed to Maturity

As is explained in the previous section, many firms and state and local governments that had previously issued debt when interest rates were higher will refund the bonds after interest rates decline. Such a refunding is essentially issuing new debt to retire old debt. The option to refund is, of course, one reason to have the call feature, but calling the debt is not necessarily a refunding. The firm can have funds from other sources such as earnings or a new issue of stock and may use those funds to retire the debt. (Some bond indentures permit the firm to call and retire the bond prior to maturity but do not permit a refunding in which new bonds are issued to retire an existing issue.)

While refunding may be profitable when interest rates decline, there is the possibility that interest rates will decline before the bond is callable. Suppose, for example, a company issued a bond in 1999 that matures in 2019 and is callable in 2009. Interest rates declined perceptibly during 2000–2003, so management wanted to refund the initial bond. Since the bonds cannot be called until 2009, there is the risk that interest rates will subsequently increase and the opportunity to save on interest expense will vanish.

Management may avoid this risk by issuing new bonds at the current and lower rate of interest and using the proceeds from the sale to purchase U.S government securities with the same maturity date as the call date. In the above example, management would invest the proceeds in Treasury bonds that mature in 2009. When the Treasury bonds mature, the proceeds will then be used to call the old bonds. This original issue will now be referred to as having been "escrowed to maturity," since funds have been separated and earmarked for the bonds' retirement. The interest earned on the U.S. securities may offset all or at least part of the interest expense on the old bonds, so that there may be a net interest savings to the firm.

Does this strategy increase the perception that the firm is using more financial leverage? It now has two debt issues: the original bonds and the new bonds. The answer to that question is no. Since the old bonds are escrowed to maturity, they are considered to have been retired and are removed from the issuer's balance sheet. Even though the actual retirement will occur in the future, from an accounting perspective, the bonds are retired and any appearance that the firm is more financially leveraged is avoided.

SUMMARY

This chapter discussed the general features of long-term debt. The terms of a debt issue include the coupon rate of interest and the maturity date. A trustee is appointed for each bond issue to protect the rights of the individual investors. The risks associated with investing in debt are attributable to price fluctuations and inflation as well as to the possibility of default on interest and principal repayment. To help investors, several firms have developed rating services that classify debt issues according to risk.

The mechanics of purchasing debt are very similar to those of buying stocks. However, while stocks are purchased through brokerage firms, some debt instruments (e.g., federal government securities) may be purchased through banks.

Debt may be retired in several ways. Some bonds are issued in a series, with a specified amount of debt maturing each year. Other debt issues have sinking funds that retire part of the bond issue prior to maturity. For some debt issues, the firm has the right to call the bonds prior to maturity. The debtor can also offer to buy the debt back from investors before it matures. Since creditors are as concerned with the return of their principal as they are with the payment of interest, the ability of the firm or government to retire its liabilities is one of the foremost factors in determining the risks associated with investing in debt.

QUESTIONS

1. What is the difference between the following?
    a) The indenture and the trustee
    b) The coupon rate and the current rate of interest
    c) Debentures and secured bonds
    d) A sinking fund and a call feature
    e) Mortgage bonds and equipment trust certificates
    f) Serial bonds and term bonds
    g) Zero coupon and coupon bonds
    h) High-yield and investment-grade bonds
2. What is the relationship between interest rates and the length of time to maturity? Figures 13.1 through 13.3 give various yield curves for U.S. Treasury securities. What is the current yield curve for U.S. Treasury securities? Possible sources for the answer to this question are Bloomberg (http://www.bloomberg.com under Market Data: Rates & Bonds) or the TreasuryDirect (http://www.treasurydirect.gov under the section on access data).

3. Even though bonds are debt obligations, investing in them involves risk. What are the sources of risk? What role do rating services play in managing risk?
4. How do you purchase a publicly traded bond?
5. When you purchase a bond, why do you have to pay accrued interest?
6. A call penalty protects whom from what? Why may firms choose to retire debt prior to maturity? Would you expect a callable bond to have a higher or lower coupon rate of interest than a noncallable bond?

PROBLEMS

1. Bell Corp. issues a bond with the following features:

Principal	$1,000
Coupon	0%
Maturity	5 years

   The current interest rate on comparable debt is 7 percent, so the bond initially sells for $713. What is the accrued interest on the bond for each of the next five years?

2. You purchase a 6 percent $10,000 bond for $9,180 plus $156 in accrued interest for a total outlay of $9,336. Subsequently you receive a $300 interest payment. You are in the 20 percent income tax bracket. How much tax do you owe on the interest payment?

3. You sell a 6 percent $10,000 bond for $9,180 plus $156 in accrued interest for a total of $9,336. Soon thereafter the company makes a $300 interest payment. You are in the 20 percent income tax bracket.

   a) How much tax do you owe on the interest?

   b) Compare your answers for Problems 2 and 3. Why do they differ?

4. Molly Matters Inc. issues a split-coupon $1,000 bond that matures in seven years. Interest payments are $80 a year (8 percent) and start after three years have lapsed. The bond initially sells for a discounted price of $794.

   a) You are in the 30 percent income tax bracket and purchase the bond. What are the annual taxes owed on the interest?

   b) You are in the 30 percent income tax bracket and purchase the bond in your IRA. What are the annual taxes owed on the interest?

The Financial Advisor's Investment Case
Corporate Bonds as a Viable Investment Vehicle

The Sourland Mountain in New Jersey investment club has recently asked you to give a presentation on investing in corporate bonds. Club members have previously invested solely in corporate stocks, but several members have expressed an interest in diversifying the portfolio through investing in bonds. Although you do not often give presentations, you believe that this one exception may introduce your financial planning services to potential clients.

Since you don't know the background of the club members or what they expect in the presentation, you suggested that they send you several questions as a means to start the general discussion. You received the following questions:

1. What are the primary differences between investments in corporate stock versus corporate bonds?
2. Since bonds pay interest, does that imply the individual's risk exposure is less for investing in bonds rather than stock?
3. What are the mechanics of purchasing bonds? May the investor leave the bonds with his or her broker?
4. Since a bond has a maturity date, does that imply the investor holds the bond to maturity?
5. Can the investor expect to earn higher returns on a firm's bonds than on its stock?
6. Are high-yield securities an acceptable investment for an investment club or its members?

The questions obviously cover many facets to consider when investing in bonds. You believe that the presentation will be improved if you also illustrate bond investments as part of a tax-deferred retirement account or a means to achieve diversification, so you pose these additional questions:

7. From a tax perspective, which should an investor acquire for a retirement account: a firm's stock or its bonds?
8. If an individual owns stock and acquires bonds issued by the same company, does the purchase diversify the investor's portfolio?
9. How does an individual construct a diversified bond portfolio? How can an investor use bonds to help diversify the total portfolio?

THE TERM STRUCTURE OF INTEREST RATES

The relationship between the rate of interest and the length of time to maturity is often referred to as the *term structure of interest rates*. During most periods of hisory, the longer the term to maturity, the higher the rate of interest (for example, see the yields in Figure 13.1). One possible explanation for this relationship is that investors have a preference for liquidity. To induce these individuals to commit their funds for a longer term, the interest rate has to be higher to compensate them for the loss of liquidity.

This explanation is very plausible, but there have been periods when short-term interest rates have been higher than long-term rates. This has led to the development of an alternative explanation of the structure of yields based on investor expectations concerning future interest rates. This expectations theory suggests that the long-term rate is an average of the current short-term rate and the expected future short-term rate.

Consider an investor faced with the two following investment alternatives:

One-year bond	6%
Two-year bond	8%

If the investor purchases the two-year bond, the yield is locked in for two years. However, if the one-year bond is purchased, the investor will have to reinvest the proceeds when the bond matures. He or she will seek to earn the same return on either alternative: (1) the one-year bond in combination with a second one-year bond or (2) the two-year bond. Thus, the choice between the two alternatives depends on what the expected future rate on the one-year bond will be.

For the yields on the two alternatives to produce the same return over two years, the funds reinvested when the one-year bond matures must earn 10 percent during the second year. The average yield is 8 percent in both cases. The yield on the two-year bond equals the yield on the combination of the 6 percent and 10 percent one-year bonds.

However, suppose the investor anticipates that the one-year rate in the future will be 12 percent. If the current one-year bond is purchased, the individual can reinvest the funds when it matures and earn 12 percent for one year. The average return over the two years is 9 percent and beats the 8 percent annual yield on the two-year bond. Obviously, the two one-year securities will be preferred. However, if the investor anticipates that the future one-year rate will be 9 percent, the average yield over the two years is 7.5 percent annually, which is inferior to the 8 percent earned annually on the two-year bond.

Although an individual may move between the one- and two-year bonds, this is not true in the aggregate. Investors as a whole cannot alter their portfolios by selling one security and purchasing another. Such attempts to alter portfolios change the securities' prices and yields. If all investors expected the future one-year rate to be 12 percent, they would seek to sell the two-year bond. The effect would be to drive up its yield. One possible set of one-year and two-year yields that could emerge is:

One-year bond	8%
Two-year bond	10%

In this case, the average yield on the two one-year bonds is 10 percent (8 percent for one year and 12 percent for the other year). The average yield on the two-year bond is 10 percent. Since the average yield on either investment alternative is the same (for a given risk class), an expectation of higher future interest rates requires a positively sloped yield curve. If investors anticipate that the one-year rate next year will be 12 percent and that two-year bonds are paying 10 percent, the one-year rate today *must be 8 percent*. At 8 percent the average yield on the two alternatives is 10 percent for both. If the current rate on the one-year bond is 8 percent, the term structure is positive. The one-year bond is paying 8 percent and the two-year bond is paying 12 percent, which is a positive relationship between yields and time to maturity.

If, however, investors expect the future one-year rate to be 7 percent while the two-year bond pays 10 percent annually, the current one-year rate must be 13 percent. Only if the current rate is 13 percent will a combination of it and the expected future one-year rate of 7 percent equal the average annual yield offered by the two-year bond. If the current one-year rate is 13 percent, then the current term structure of yields is negative. The one-year bond offers 13 percent and the two-year bond offers 10 percent, which is a negative relationship between yields and time to maturity. Thus, the expectation of lower rates in the future requires a negatively sloped yield curve in the present.

In addition to the liquidity preference and expectations theories of the term structure of yields, a third alternative explanation has been suggested. It is referred to as the *segmentation theory*, and it suggests that yields depend on the demand for and supply of credit in various segments of the financial markets. For example, suppose funds were to flow from savings and loan associations and other savings institutions to money market mutual funds. Since the S&Ls make mortgage loans but money market mutual funds make only short-term loans and no mortgage loans, there has been a change in the supply of credit in the two markets. The supply of mortgage money has decreased, and the rate charged on these loans should rise. Simultaneously, the supply of short-term credit has increased, which should tend to reduce short-term interest rates. The structure of yields thus depends on the supply and demand for credit from the various segments of the economy. A flow from one segment to another alters the supply of this credit, causing yields (i.e., the term structure of interest rates) to change. A flow of funds from financial institutions that grant short-term loans to those making long-term loans will then result in a negatively sloped yield curve.

There is no consensus as to which of the three theories is correct. Each has appealing elements, but there is insufficient empirical evidence to suggest that the structure of yields is solely explained by only one of the three theories. It is probably safe to assume that all three play some role in the determination of the term structure of interest rates.[1]

---

[1]The illustration of the expectation theory in this appendix is limited to two years. It may be generalized to more years so that the current structure of yields reflects expected short-term rates three, four, five, or more years in the future. For a comprehensive explanation of the expectations theory, see a financial institutions or money and banking book such as David S. Kidwell, David W. Blackwell, David A. Whidbee, and Richard L. Peterson, *Financial Institutions, Markets, and Money*, 10th ed. (New York: Wiley, 2008).

CHAPTER 14

The Valuation of Fixed-Income Securities

In June 2009, a 10-year $1,000 federal government bond was selling for $1,332. A 15-year bond was selling for $1,389. A $1,000 bond issued by IBM was selling for $1,286. Why would anyone pay these high prices for a $1,000 bond? These investors will receive only $1,000 when the bonds mature. They could have bought a different $1,000 federal government bond for $1,000.

As you learned in the previous chapter, corporations issue a variety of debt instruments that are sold to the general public. An active secondary market exists for these bonds. Since the bonds trade daily, what establishes their prices? Why do some bonds trade for $1,300 while others trade for much less? Which bonds' prices tend to be more volatile? These are some of the essential questions concerning investing in fixed-income securities, especially bonds.

Although a variety of debt instruments exists, each with its specific name and characteristics, for the purpose of this chapter the term *bond* will be used to represent all types of debt instruments. As will be explained in detail, comparable bonds are priced so their yields are the same. What is important is how much you earn and not how much you pay. The price of any bond (for a given risk class) is primarily related to (1) the interest paid by the bond, (2) the interest rate that investors may earn on comparable, competitive bonds, and (3) the maturity date. Bond pricing is followed by a discussion of the various uses of the word *yield*, including the current yield, the yield to maturity, and the yield to call.

The valuation of preferred stock follows the coverage of bond pricing and yields. Preferred stock pays a fixed dividend, which is analogous to the fixed interest payment made by a bond. For this reason, the pricing of preferred stock is essentially the same as the pricing of a bond.

The remainder of the chapter is devoted to the risks associated with investing in bonds. This begins with a discussion of risk and its impact on yields. Next follows the impact of reinvestment rate risk. The calculation of a bond's yield to maturity assumes that the interest payments are reinvested at the bond's yield to maturity. This assumption rarely holds, and a bond's duration is one means to manage this source of risk. The chapter ends with additional methods including the laddered and matching strategies designed to reduce the interest rate risk associated with bond portfolios.

PERPETUAL SECURITIES

Some securities have an indefinite life. A corporation and its common stock may exist for centuries. Many issues of preferred stock have no maturity dates and are perpetual. There are even a few debt issues that are perpetual. The issuer never has to retire the principal; it only has to meet the interest payment and the other terms of the indenture. The British government issued perpetual bonds called *consols* to refinance (i.e., consolidate) the debt issued to support the Napoleonic Wars. These bonds will never mature, but they do pay interest, and there is an active secondary market in them.

Although there are few perpetual bonds, they facilitate illustrating the process of the valuation of debt instruments. Bond valuation is essentially the same as common stock valuation: future cash inflows are discounted back to the present. The discount rate is the return that the investor can earn on comparable securities. (That is, the perpetual interest payments are brought back to the present at the current rate paid by bonds with the same degree of risk.) For example, a perpetual bond pays the following interest payment annually:

Year 1	Year 2	...	Year 20	...	Year 100	...	Year 1000	...
$80	$80		$80		$80		$80	

How much are these interest payments currently worth? To answer the question, the investor must know the rate of interest that may be earned on alternative investments. If the investor can earn 10 percent elsewhere, the present value or price (P) is

$$P = \frac{\$80}{(1 + 0.10)^1} + \frac{\$80}{(1 + 0.10)^2} + \cdots + \frac{\$80}{(1 + 0.10)^{20}}$$

$$+ \cdots + \frac{\$80}{(1 + 0.10)^{100}} + \cdots + \frac{\$80}{(1 + 0.10)^{1000}}$$

$$= \$80(0.909) + \$80(0.826) + \cdots + \$80(0.149)$$

$$+ \cdots + \$80(0.000) + \cdots + \$80(0.000)$$

$$= 72.72 + \$66.08 + \cdots + \$11.92 + \cdots + 0$$

$$= \$800.$$

The $80 interest payments received in the near future contribute most to the present value of the bond. Dollars received in the distant future have little value today. The sum of all of these present values is $800, which means that if alternative investments yield 10 percent, an investor would be willing to pay $800 for a promise to receive $80 annually for the indefinite future.

The preceding may be stated in more formal terms. If *PMT* is the annual interest payment and *i* is the rate of return that is being earned on comparable investments, then the present value is

$$P = \frac{PMT}{(1 + i)^1} + \frac{PMT}{(1 + i)^2} + \frac{PMT}{(1 + i)^3} + \cdots.$$

This is a geometric series, and its sum may be expressed as

14.1
$$P = \frac{PMT}{i}.$$

Equation 14.1 gives the current value of an infinite stream of equal interest payments. If this equation is applied to the previous example in which the annual interest payment is $80 and alternative investments can earn 10 percent, then the present value of the bond is

$$P = \frac{\$80}{0.10} = \$800.$$

If market interest rates of alternative investments were to increase to 20 percent, the value of this perpetual stream of interest payments would decline; if market interest rates were to fall to 8 percent, the value of the bond would rise. These changes occur because the bond pays a *fixed flow of income*; that is, the dollar amount of interest paid by the bond is constant. Lower interest rates mean that more money is needed to purchase this fixed stream of interest payments, and with higher interest rates, less money is needed to buy this fixed flow of income.

The inverse relationship between interest rates and bond prices is illustrated in Exhibit 14.1, which presents the value of the preceding perpetual bond at different interest rates. As may be seen from the exhibit, as current market interest rates rise, the present value of the bond declines. Thus, if the present value is $1,000 when interest rates are 8 percent, the value of this bond declines to $400 when interest rates rise to 20 percent.

A simple example may show why this *inverse relationship between bond prices and interest rates* exists. Suppose two investors offered to sell two different bond issues. The first is the perpetual bond that pays $100 per year in interest. The second is also a perpetual bond, but it pays $120 per year in interest. If the offer price in each case is $1,000, which bond would be preferred? If they are equal in every way except in the amount of interest, a buyer would prefer the second bond that pays $120. What could the seller of the first bond do to make the bond more attractive to a buyer? The obvious answer is to lower the asking price so that the yield the buyer receives is identical for both bonds. Thus, if the seller were to ask only $833 for the bond that pays $100 annually, the buyer should be indifferent as to which to purchase. Both bonds would

EXHIBIT   14.1   Relationship Between Interest Rates and the Price of a Perpetual Bond

Current Interest Rate (i)	Annual Interest Paid by the Bond (PMT)	Present Price of the Bond $\left(P = \frac{PMT}{i}\right)$
4%	$80	$2,000
6	80	1,333
8	80	1,000
10	80	800
15	80	533
20	80	400

then offer a yield of 12 percent (i.e., $100 ÷ $833 for the first bond and $120 ÷ $1,000 for the second bond).

BONDS WITH MATURITY DATES

The majority of bonds are not perpetual but have a finite life. They mature, and this fact must affect their valuation. A bond's price is related not only to the interest that it pays but also to its face amount (i.e., the principal). The current price of a bond equals the present value of the interest payments plus the present value of the principal to be received at maturity. Although most bonds pay interest semiannually, this initial discussion uses annual compounding to facilitate the explanation. Semiannual compounding is illustrated in the next section. A few bonds pay interest quarterly, and there are examples of bonds that pay monthly.

The value of a bond with a finite life is the present value of its cash flows (interest and principal repayment). This value is expressed algebraically in Equation 14.2 in terms of the present value formulas discussed in Chapter 3. A bond's value is

14.2
$$P_B = \frac{PMT}{(1 + i)^1} + \frac{PMT}{(1 + i)^2} + \cdots + \frac{PMT}{(1 + i)^n} + \frac{FV}{(1 + i)^n},$$

in which P_B indicates the current price of the bond; PMT, the interest payment; n, the number of years to maturity; FV, the future value, or the principal repayment; and i, the current interest rate.

The calculation of a bond's price using Equation 14.2 may be illustrated by a simple example. A firm has a $1,000 bond outstanding that matures in three years with a 10 percent coupon rate ($100 annually). All that is needed to determine the price of the bond is the current interest rate, which is the rate being paid by newly issued, competitive bonds with the same length of time to maturity and the same degree of risk. If the competitive bonds yield 10 percent, the price of this bond will be par, or $1,000, for

$$P_B = \frac{\$100}{(1 + 0.10)^1} + \frac{\$100}{(1 + 0.10)^2} + \frac{\$100}{(1 + 0.10)^3} + \frac{\$1,000}{(1 + 0.10)^3}$$

$$= \$100(0.909) + 100(0.826) + 100(0.751) + 1,000(0.751)$$

$$= \$999.60 \approx \$1,000.$$

If competitive bonds are selling to yield 12 percent, this bond will be unattractive to investors. They will not be willing to pay $1,000 for a bond yielding 10 percent when they could buy competing bonds at the same price that yield 12 percent. For this bond to compete with the others, its price must decline sufficiently to yield 12 percent. In terms of Equation 14.2, the price must be

$$P_B = \frac{\$100}{(1 + 0.12)^1} + \frac{\$100}{(1 + 0.12)^2} + \frac{\$100}{(1 + 0.12)^3} + \frac{\$1,000}{(1 + 0.12)^3}$$

$$= \$100(0.893) + 100(0.797) + 100(0.712) + 1,000(0.712)$$

$$= \$952.20.$$

discount (of a bond)

The extent to which a bond's price is less than its face amount, or principal.

The price of the bond must decline to approximately $952; that is, it must sell for a **discount** (a price less than the stated principal) in order to be competitive with comparable bonds. At that price investors will earn $100 per year in interest and approximately $50 in capital gains over the three years, for a total annual return of 12 percent on their investment. The capital gain occurs because the bond is purchased for $952.20, but when it matures, the holder will receive $1,000.

If comparable debt were to yield 8 percent, the price of the bond in the previous example would have to rise. In this case, the price of the bond would be

$$P_B = \frac{\$100}{(1 + 0.08)^1} + \frac{\$100}{(1 + 0.08)^2} + \frac{\$100}{(1 + 0.08)^3} + \frac{\$1,000}{(1 + 0.08)^3}$$

$$= \$100(0.926) + 100(0.857) + 100(0.794) + 1,000(0.794)$$

$$= \$1,051.70.$$

premium (of a bond)

The extent to which a bond's price exceeds the face amount of the debt.

The bond, therefore, must sell at a **premium** (a price greater than the stated principal). Although it may seem implausible for the bond to sell at a premium, this must occur if the market interest rate falls below the coupon rate of interest stated on the bond.

(The answers in the text differ slightly from the answers in the margin that were derived using a financial calculator. The differences are the result of rounding. For example, the numerical values for $1/(1 + 0.08)^1$ and $1/(1 + 0.12)^1$ in the interest tables are carried only to three decimals (0.893 and 0.926, respectively), while the financial calculator carries the numbers to more decimals.)

These price calculations are lengthy, but the number of computations can be reduced when one realizes that the valuation of a bond has two components: a flow of interest payments and a final repayment of principal. Since interest payments are fixed and are paid every year, they may be treated as an annuity. The principal repayment may be treated as a simple lump-sum payment. If a $1,000 bond pays $100 per year in interest and matures after three years, its current value is the present value of the $100 annuity for three years and the present value of the $1,000 that will be received after three years. If the interest rate is 12 percent, the current value of the bond is

$$P_B = \$100(2.402) + \$1,000(0.712) = \$952.20,$$

in which 2.402 is the interest factor for the present value of a $1 annuity at 12 percent for three years and 0.712 is the interest factor for the present value of $1 at 12 percent after three years. This is the same answer that was derived earlier (except for the rounding error), but the amount of arithmetic has been reduced.

These examples illustrate the same general conclusion that was reached earlier concerning bond prices and changes in interest rates. They are inversely related. When the current rate of interest rises, the prices of existing bonds decline. When the market rate of interest falls, bond prices rise. This relationship is illustrated in Exhibit 14.2, which gives the prices of the $1,000 bond with a 10 percent coupon that matures after three years for various interest rates. As may be seen in the exhibit, higher interest rates depress the bond's current value. Thus, the bond's price declines from $1,000 to $951.96 when interest rates rise from 10 to 12 percent; the price rises to $1,051.54 when interest rates decline to 8 percent. (Factors that affect the amount of the price change are covered later in this chapter.)

The inverse relationship between the price of a bond and the interest rate suggests a means to make profits in the bond market. All that investors need to know is the direction of *future* changes in the interest rate. If investors anticipate that interest

EXHIBIT 14.2   Relationship Between Interest Rates and a $1,000 10 Percent Coupon Bond Maturing after Three Years

Current Interest Rate	Present Price of the Bond
4%	$1,166.51
6	1,106.92
8	1,051.54
10	1,000.00
12	951.96
14	907.13
18	826.06
20	789.35

Source: Prices determined using a financial calculator.

rates will decline, then they are expecting the price to rise for previously issued bonds with a given number of years to maturity and of a certain risk. This price increase must occur in order for previously issued bonds to have the same yield as currently issued bonds. The reverse is also true, for if investors anticipate that interest rates will rise, they are also anticipating that the price of currently available bonds will decline. This decline must occur for previously issued bonds to offer the same yield as currently issued bonds. Therefore, if investors can anticipate the direction of change in interest rates, they can also anticipate the direction of change in the price of bonds.

Investors, however, may anticipate incorrectly and thus suffer losses in the bond market. If they buy bonds and interest rates rise, then the market value of their bonds must decline, and the investors suffer capital losses. These individuals, however, have something in their favor: The bonds must ultimately be retired. Since the principal must be redeemed, an investment error in the bond market may be corrected when the bond's price rises as the bond approaches maturity. The capital losses will eventually be erased. The correction of the error, however, may take years, during which time the investors have lost the higher yields that were available on bonds issued after their initial investments.

Semiannual Compounding

The valuation of a bond with a finite life presented in Equation 14.2 is a bit misleading, because most bonds pay interest twice a year (i.e., semiannually), and the equation assumes that the interest payments are made only annually. However, Equation 14.2 may be readily modified to take into consideration semiannual (or even quarterly or weekly) compounding. This is done by adjusting the amount of each payment and the total number of these payments. To adjust the previous example, each interest payment will be $50 if payments are semiannual, and instead of three annual payments, the bond will make a total of six $50 semiannual payments. Hence, the flow of payments that will be made by this bond is

Year 1		Year 2		Year 3		
$50	$50	$50	$50	$50	$50	$1,000

This flow of payments would then be discounted back to the present to determine the bond's current value. The question then becomes, what is the appropriate discount factor?

If comparable debt yields 12 percent, the appropriate discount factor is not 12 percent; it is 6 percent per period. Six percent interest paid twice a year yields 12 percent interest compounded semiannually. Thus, to determine the present value of this bond, the comparable interest rate is divided in half (just as the annual interest payment is divided in half). However, the number of interest payments to which this 6 percent is applied is doubled (just as the number of payments is doubled). Hence, the current value of this bond, which pays interest twice a year (is compounded semiannually), is

$$P_B = \frac{\$50}{(1 + 0.06)^1} + \frac{\$50}{(1 + 0.06)^2} + \frac{\$50}{(1 + 0.06)^3} + \frac{\$50}{(1 + 0.06)^4}$$

$$+ \frac{\$50}{(1 + 0.06)^5} + \frac{\$50}{(1 + 0.06)^6} + \frac{\$1,000}{(1 + 0.06)^6}$$

$$= \$50(0.943) + 50(0.890) + 50(0.840)$$

$$+ 50(0.792) + 50(0.747) + 50(0.705) + 1,000(0.705)$$

$$= \$47.15 + 44.50 + 42.00 + 39.60 + 37.35 + 35.25 + 705$$

$$= \$950.85.$$

With semiannual compounding, the current value of the bond is slightly lower (i.e., $950.85 versus $952.20). This is because the bond's price must decline more to compensate for the more frequent compounding. An investor would prefer a bond that pays $50 twice per year to one that pays $100 once per year, because the investor would have use of some of the funds more quickly. Thus, if interest rates rise, causing bond prices to fall, the decline will be greater if the interest on bonds is paid semiannually than if it is paid annually.

Equation 14.2 may be altered to include semiannual compounding. This is done in Equation 14.3. Only one new variable, c, is added, which represents the frequency of compounding (i.e., the number of times each year that interest payments are made).

14.3
$$P_B = \frac{\frac{PMT}{c}}{\left(1 + \frac{i}{c}\right)^1} + \frac{\frac{PMT}{c}}{\left(1 + \frac{i}{c}\right)^2} + \cdots + \frac{\frac{PMT}{c}}{\left(1 + \frac{i}{c}\right)^{n \times c}} + \frac{FV}{\left(1 + \frac{i}{c}\right)^{n \times c}}.$$

When Equation 14.3 is applied to the earlier example, the price of the bond is

$$P_B = \frac{\frac{\$100}{2}}{\left(1 + \frac{0.12}{2}\right)^1} + \frac{\frac{\$100}{2}}{\left(1 + \frac{0.12}{2}\right)^2} + \cdots + \frac{\frac{\$100}{2}}{\left(1 + \frac{0.12}{2}\right)^{3 \times 2}} + \frac{\$1,000}{\left(1 + \frac{0.12}{2}\right)^{3 \times 2}}$$

$$= \$50(0.943) + 50(0.890) + \cdots + 50(0.705) + 1,000(0.705)$$

$$= \$950.85,$$

which is the same answer derived in the immediately preceding example.

FLUCTUATIONS IN BOND PRICES

As the preceding examples illustrate, a bond's price depends on the interest paid, the maturity date of the bond, and the yield currently earned on comparable securities. The illustrations also demonstrated that when interest rates rise, bond prices fall, and when interest rates fall, bond prices rise.

The amount of price fluctuation depends on (1) the amount of interest paid by the bond, (2) the length of time to maturity, and (3) risk. The smaller the amount of interest, the larger the relative price fluctuations will tend to be. The longer the term, or time to maturity, the greater the price fluctuations will be. Riskier bonds may also experience greater fluctuations in price.

This section is concerned with the first two factors that affect price fluctuations, the amount of interest and the term to maturity. The impact of risk is covered in a subsequent section. The effect of the amount of interest and term to maturity may be seen by the following illustrations. In the first case, consider two bonds with equal lives (i.e., ten years to maturity) but unequal coupons. Bond A pays $80 a year (an 8 percent coupon), and bond B pays $140 annually (a 14 percent coupon). Exhibit 14.3 gives the prices of each bond at various rates of interest. For example, if interest rates rise from 10 percent to 14 percent, the price of bond A declines from $877 to $687. Bond B's price falls from $1,246 to $1,000. These are 22 and 20 percent declines, respectively. If interest rates continue to rise, the bonds' prices decline further. At 20 percent, the values of the bonds are $497 and $748. The percentage declines in the bond with the lower coupon are greater. (The extreme case would be a zero coupon bond whose price depends solely on the repayment of the principal.)

The length of time to maturity also affects the fluctuation in a bond's price. Consider the two bonds in the second part of Exhibit 14.3. Both bonds pay $100 interest annually (a 10 percent coupon), but bond A matures after one year and bond B matures after ten years. If interest rates are 10 percent, each bond sells for its principal value ($1,000). If interest rates rise to 12 percent, the prices of the bonds decline to $982 and $887. The short maturity of bond A, however, cushions the impact of the change in interest rates. At the extreme case of 20 percent, the price of bond A declines only to $917 while the price of bond B declines to $581.

If interest rates fall, the prices of both bonds will rise, but the price of the bond with the longer term will rise more. For this reason, individuals who are speculating on a decline in interest rates will favor bonds with a longer term to maturity, but investors who are concerned with both interest income and safety of principal will prefer short-term debt. These investors will accept less interest income for safety and liquidity. Of course, the extreme form of such investments is the money market mutual fund, which invests solely in short-term investments (e.g., commercial paper and Treasury bills), for such investments offer liquidity that cannot be obtained through investments in longer-term debt.

Bond Valuation Applications to Nontraditional Bonds

In the previous examples of valuation, all the bonds paid interest annually and were retired at maturity. In the previous chapter, bond features were not limited to a fixed payment and maturity date. For example, zero coupon bonds accrue interest but do not

EXHIBIT 14.3 Fluctuations in Bond Prices

Case 1 Differences in Coupons and Equal Maturity Dates

	Prices:	
Current Rate of Interest	Bond A 8 Percent Coupon 10 Years to Maturity	Bond B 14 Percent Coupon 10 Years to Maturity
4%	$1,324	$1,811
6	1,147	1,589
8	1,000	1,403
10	877	1,246
12	774	1,113
14	687	1,000
16	613	903
18	551	820
20	497	748

Case 2 Differences in Maturity Dates and Equal Coupons

	Prices:	
Current Rate of Interest	Bond A 10 Percent Coupon 1 Year to Maturity	Bond B 10 Percent Coupon 10 Years to Maturity
4%	$1,058	$1,487
6	1,038	1,294
8	1,018	1,134
10	1,000	1,000
12	982	887
14	965	791
16	948	710
18	932	640
20	917	581

Calculator Solution

Function Key	Data Input
PV =	?
FV =	1000
PMT =	0
N =	10
I =	7
Function Key	*Answer*
PV =	−508.35

distribute it. Several high-yield securities (e.g., the split coupon bond, the reset bond, or the extendable bond) have features that differ from the traditional bond.

Although bonds can have these varying features, their valuations remain the same: the present value of future cash flows. For example, what would an investor pay for a $1,000 zero coupon bond that matures after ten years? The answer has to be the present value of the $1,000—that is, the present value of the future cash flow. If the investor requires a return of 7 percent, then the value is

$$P_B = \frac{\$1,000}{(1 + 0.07)^{10}} = \$1,000(0.508) = \$508.$$

If the required return had been 10 percent, the value of the bond would be $1,000(0.386) = $386.

The valuation of split coupon and reset bonds is essentially the same. Consider the Dr Pepper bond in the previous chapter that illustrated a split coupon bond. That bond

Calculator Solution

Function Key	Data Input
PV =	?
FV =	1000
PMT$_1$ =	0
PMT$_2$ =	0
PMT$_3$ =	0
PMT$_4$ =	0
PMT$_5$ =	115
PMT$_6$ =	115
PMT$_7$ =	115
PMT$_8$ =	115
PMT$_9$ =	115
PMT$_{10}$ =	115
N =	10
I =	15
Function Key	Answer
PV =	−496

(This solution requires a financial calculator that accepts uneven cash payments.)

paid $0 in interest during the first four years, $115 annually for the next six years, and matured after ten years. How much would an investor pay if the required return were 15 percent? The answer is

$115 × the present value of an annuity for six years at 15 percent

× the present value of one dollar for four years at 15 percent

+ 1,000 × the present value of one dollar at 15 percent for ten years

= $115(3.785)(0.572) + $1,000(0.247)

= $496.

If interest rates declined (or the firm's financial condition improved) so the comparable rate is 12 percent, the bond's price would rise to

$$\$115(4.111)(0.636) + \$1,000(0.322) = \$623$$

for a 25.6 percent increase. Of course, the converse is also true; higher yields would cause the price of the split coupon bond to decline.

The valuations of zero coupon and split coupon bonds are essentially no different from the valuation of a regular coupon bond since the payments (their amounts and timing) are known. With a reset bond or an extendable bond, the payments and their timing are not known. The interest payments or the maturity date or both are permitted to vary. While the valuation process remains the present value of future cash inflows, the investor must make assumptions concerning these inflows. For example, in the case of an extendable bond, the investor must assume a particular repayment date. If the investor expects the bond's maturity date to be extended, then the longer term is used to value the bond. Using a shorter term may result in the bond receiving a higher valuation, in which case the investor would pay too much and realize a smaller return if the maturity is extended.

THE VALUATION OF PREFERRED STOCK

The process of valuing preferred stock is essentially the same as that used to price bonds because preferred is a fixed-income security. The future payments are brought back to the present at the appropriate discount rate. If the preferred stock does not have a required sinking fund or call feature, it may be viewed as a perpetual debt instrument. The fixed dividend (D) will continue indefinitely. These dividends must be discounted by the yield being earned on newly issued preferred stock (k). This process for determining the present value of the preferred stock (P) is:

$$P = \frac{D}{(1 + k)^1} + \frac{D}{(1 + k)^2} + \frac{D}{(1 + k)^3} + \cdots.$$

As in the case of the perpetual bond, this equation is reduced to

$$P = \frac{D}{k}.$$

which is the same as Equation 14.1 used to value a perpetual bond. If a preferred stock pays an annual dividend of $4 and the appropriate discount rate is 8 percent, the present value of the preferred stock is

$$P = \frac{\$4}{(1 + 0.08)^1} + \frac{\$4}{(1 + 0.08)^2} + \frac{\$4}{(1 + 0.08)^3} + \cdots$$

$$= \frac{\$4}{0.08} = \$50.00.$$

If an investor buys this preferred stock for $50.00, he or she can expect to earn 8 percent ($50.00 × 0.08 = $4) on the investment. Of course, the realized rate of return on the investment will not be known until the investor sells the stock and adjusts this 8 percent return for any capital gain or loss. However, at the current price, the preferred stock is selling for an 8 percent dividend yield.

　　If the preferred stock has a finite life, this must be considered in determining the stock's value. As with the valuation of long-term debt, the amount that is repaid when the preferred stock is retired must be discounted back to the present value. Thus, when preferred stock has a finite life, the valuation equation becomes

$$P = \frac{D}{(1 + k)^1} + \frac{D}{(1 + k)^2} + \cdots + \frac{D}{(1 + k)^n} + \frac{S}{(1 + k)^n},$$

where S represents the amount that is returned to the stockholder when the preferred stock is retired after n number of years.

　　This is the same as Equation 14.2, which is used to value a bond with a finite life. If the preferred stock in the previous example is retired after 20 years for $100 per share, its current value would be

$$P = \frac{\$4}{(1 + 0.08)^1} + \cdots + \frac{\$4}{(1 + 0.08)^{20}} + \frac{\$100}{(1 + 0.08)^{20}}$$

$$= \$4(9.818) + \$100(0.215)$$

$$= \$60.77,$$

Calculator Solution	
Function Key	Data Input
PV =	?
FV =	100
PMT =	4
N =	20
I =	8
Function Key	Answer
PV =	−60.73

in which 9.818 is the interest factor for the present value of an annuity of $1 for 20 years at 8 percent and 0.215 is the present value of $1 to be received after 20 years when yields are 8 percent. Instead of selling the stock for $50.00, the nonperpetual preferred stock would sell for $60.77. At a price of $60.77, the yield is still 8 percent, but the return in this case consists of a current dividend yield of 6.58 percent ($4 ÷ $60.77) and a capital gain as the price of the stock rises from $60.77 to $100 when it is retired 20 years hence.

YIELDS

The word *yield* is frequently used with regard to investing in bonds. There are three important types of yields with which the investor must be familiar: the current yield, the yield to maturity, and the yield to call. This section will differentiate among these three yields.

The Current Yield

The current yield is the percentage that the investor earns annually. It is simply

14.4 $$\frac{\text{Annual interest payment}}{\text{Price of the bond}}.$$

The discounted bond discussed previously has a coupon rate of 10 percent. Thus, when the price of the bond is $952, the current yield is

$$\frac{\$100}{\$952} = 10.5\%.$$

The current yield is important because it gives the investor an indication of the current return that will be earned on the investment. Investors who seek high current income prefer bonds that offer a high current yield.

However, the current yield can be misleading, for it fails to consider any change in the price of the bond that may occur if the bond is held to maturity. Obviously, if a bond is bought at a discount, its value must rise as it approaches maturity. The opposite occurs if the bond is purchased for a premium, because its price will decline as maturity approaches. For this reason it is desirable to know the bond's yield to maturity.

The Yield to Maturity

The yield to maturity considers the current income generated by the bond as well as any change in its value when it is held to maturity. If the bond referred to earlier is purchased for $952 and is held to maturity, after three years the investor will receive a return of 12 percent. This is the yield to maturity, because this return considers not only the current interest return of 10.5 percent but also the price appreciation of the bond from $952 at the time of purchase to $1,000 at maturity. Since the yield to maturity considers both the flow of interest income and the price change, it is a more accurate measure of the return offered to investors by a particular bond issue.

The yield to maturity may be determined by using Equation 14.2. That equation is

$$P_B = \frac{PMT}{(1 + i)^1} + \frac{PMT}{(1 + i)^2} + \cdots + \frac{PMT}{(1 + i)^n} + \frac{FV}{(1 + i)^n}.$$

The yield to maturity is a specific application of the internal rate of return discussed in Chapter 10. Equation 14.2 is simply a restatement of Equation 10.2 for the determination of an investment's internal rate of return. The i is the current rate of interest paid by newly issued bonds with the same term to maturity and the same degree of risk. If the investor buys a bond and holds it to maturity, the yield that is being paid by newly issued bonds (i) will also be the yield to maturity.

Determining the yield to maturity when the coupon rate of interest, the bond's price, and the maturity date are known is not easy, except with the use of a financial calculator. For example, if the bond were selling for $952 and the investor wanted to know the yield to maturity, the calculation would be

$$\$952 = \frac{\$100}{(1 + i)^1} + \frac{\$100}{(1 + i)^2} + \frac{\$100}{(1 + i)^3} + \frac{\$1,000}{(1 + i)^3}.$$

Solving this equation can be a formidable task because there is no simple arithmetical computation to determine the value of i. Instead, the investor selects a value for i and plugs it into the equation. If this value equates the left-hand and right-hand sides of the equation, then that value of i is the yield to maturity.

If the value does not equate the two sides of the equation, another value must be selected. This process is repeated until a value for i is found that equates both sides of the equation. Obviously, that can be a long process. For example, suppose the investor selects 14 percent and substitutes it into the right-hand side of the equation. The result is

$$P_B = \frac{\$100}{(1 + 0.14)^1} + \frac{\$100}{(1 + 0.14)^2} + \frac{\$100}{(1 + 0.14)^3} + \frac{\$1,000}{(1 + 0.14)^3}$$

$$= \$100(2.321) + 1,000(0.675)$$

$$= \$232.10 + 675$$

$$= \$907.10.$$

Unfortunately, $907.10 does not equal $952. That means the selected yield to maturity was too high, so the investor selects another, lower rate. If the investor had selected 12 percent, then

$$P_B = \$100(2.402) + \$1,000(0.712)$$

$$= \$240.20 + 712$$

$$= \$952.20,$$

and thus 12 percent is the yield to maturity (compounded annually). If you obtain a price greater than the correct price, the yield to maturity is too low, and you should select a higher rate.

The yield to maturity may be readily computed using a financial calculator. To determine the yield to maturity, enter the amount of each interest payment (PMT = 100), the principal repayment in the future (FV = 1,000), the term to maturity (N = 3), and the current price of the bond (PV = −963.66), and instruct the calculator to determine the interest (I). (Enter the present value as a negative number, since the calculator is programmed to view the price as a cash outflow and the interest and principal repayment as cash inflows.) When these figures are entered, the calculator determines the interest rate—or the yield to maturity—to be 11.50 percent. This procedure is considerably easier than the process described using interest tables.

If the bond pays interest semiannually, enter each six-month interest payment (PMT = 50), the principal repayment (FV = 1,000), the term on the bond (N = 6), and the current price of the bond (PV = −963.66). Instruct the calculator to determine the interest (I). The calculator determines the yield to maturity to be 5.73 percent per period or 11.46 percent compounded semiannually. Notice that the yield to maturity is marginally lower because the timing of the interest payments is slightly faster ($50 after six months followed by the next $50 after 12 months instead of the entire $100 after 12 months.) To equalize the yields, the bond with the semiannual interest payments would sell for a slightly lower price ($963 instead of $963.66). Since the interest is paid semiannually, you do not have to invest as much to earn a specified return (i.e., 11.5 percent), so the price would be lower. If the prices of the two bonds were the same ($963.66), you would have overpaid for the bond with the semiannual interest payments and your return would have been lower (11.46 percent versus 11.5 percent).

EXHIBIT 14.4	Current Yields and Yields to Maturity for a Ten-Year Bond with an 8 Percent Annual Coupon

Price of Bond	Current Yield	Yield to Maturity
$1,100	7.27%	6.60%
1,050	7.62	7.28
1,000	8.00	8.00
950	8.42	8.77
900	8.89	9.60
850	9.41	10.49
800	10.00	11.46
750	10.67	12.52

A Comparison of the Current Yield and the Yield to Maturity

The current yield and the yield to maturity are equal only if the bond sells for its principal amount, or par. If the bond sells at a discount, the yield to maturity exceeds the current yield. This may be illustrated by the bond in the previous example. When it sells at a discount (e.g., $952), the current yield is only 10.5 percent. However, the yield to maturity is 12 percent. Thus, the yield to maturity exceeds the current yield.

If the bond sells at a premium, the current yield exceeds the yield to maturity. For example, if the bond sells for $1,052, the current yield is 9.5 percent ($100 ÷ $1,052) and the yield to maturity is 8 percent. The yield to maturity is less in this case because the loss that the investor must suffer when the price of the bond declines from $1,052 to $1,000 at maturity has been included in the calculation.

Exhibit 14.4 presents the current yield and the yield to maturity at different prices for a bond with an 8 percent annual coupon that matures in ten years. As may be seen in the table, the larger the discount (or the smaller the premium), the greater are both the current yield and the yield to maturity. For example, when the bond sells for $850, the yield to maturity is 10.49 percent, but it rises to 12.52 percent when the price declines to $750.

Discounted bonds offer investors attractive opportunities for financial planning. For example, a person who is currently 60 years old may purchase discounted bonds that mature after five years to help finance retirement. This investor may purchase several bonds that mature five, six, seven years, and so on, into the future. This portfolio will generate a continuous flow of funds during retirement as the bonds mature.

Discounted bonds generally result from an increase in interest rates. If interest rates fall, bonds would sell for a premium, so the previous strategy cannot be executed. An alternative but similar strategy uses zero coupon bonds, which always sell for a discount. This strategy is illustrated in Exhibit 14.5, in which the individual needs funds for the years 2013 through 2017 and buys a series of U.S. Treasury zero coupon bonds. For a total outlay of $4,271, the investor will receive $1,000 for each of the five years.

Although the two strategies illustrated are similar, there are differences. First, as was previously explained, bonds with higher coupons experience less price fluctuation with changes in interest rates, so the zero coupon bond strategy subjects the investor to more price volatility. Such price fluctuations are relevant only if interest rates rise and the investor needs to sell the bonds before their maturity dates. Second, the discounted

		Price (per $1,000	
Coupon Rate	Maturity Year	Face Value)	Yield to Maturity
0%	2013	$944	1.56%
0	2014	907	2.09
0	2015	836	2.80
0	2016	821	2.95
0	2017	763	3.43

EXHIBIT 14.5 Selected U.S. Treasury Zero Coupon Bonds (as of June 2009)

Source: Yahoo! Finance, June 10, 2009.

bonds pay some interest each year, while the zero coupon bonds pay nothing. If the investor wants cash flow each year prior to the bonds' maturity dates, the discounted bonds may be the better choice.

The Yield to Call

Some bonds will never reach maturity but are retired before they become due. In some cases the issuer may call the bonds before maturity and redeem them. In other cases, the sinking fund will randomly call selected bonds from the issue and retire them. For these reasons the **yield to call** may be a more accurate estimate of the return actually earned on an investment in a bond that is held until redemption.

yield to call

The yield earned on a bond from the time it is acquired until the time it is called and retired by the firm.

The yield to call is calculated in the same way as the yield to maturity except that (1) the expected call date is substituted for the maturity date and (2) the principal plus the call penalty (if any) is substituted for the principal. Note that the anticipated call date is used. Unlike the maturity date, which is known, the date of a call can only be anticipated.

The following example illustrates how the yield to call is calculated. A bond that matures after ten years and pays 8 percent interest annually is currently selling for $935.00. The yield to maturity is 9 percent. However, if the investor believes that the company or government will call the bond after five years and will pay a penalty of $50 per $1,000 bond to retire the debt permanently, the yield to call (i_c) is

$$\$935 = \frac{\$80}{(1 + i_c)^1} + \cdots + \frac{\$80}{(1 + i_c)^5} + \frac{\$1,050}{(1 + i_c)^5}$$

$$i_c = 10.55\%.$$

Calculator Solution

Function Key	Data Input
PV =	−935
FV =	1050
PMT =	80
N =	5
I =	?
Function Key	Answer
I =	10.55

In this example, the yield to call is higher than the yield to maturity because (1) the investor receives the call penalty and (2) the principal is redeemed early and hence the discount is erased sooner. Thus, in the case of a discounted bond, the actual return the investor earns exceeds the yield to maturity if the bond is called and retired before maturity.

However, if this bond were selling for a premium such as $1,147 with a yield to maturity of 6 percent and the firm were to call the bond after five years, the yield to call would become

$$\$1,147 = \frac{\$80}{(1 + i_c)^1} + \cdots + \frac{\$80}{(1 + i_c)^5} + \frac{\$1,050}{(1 + i_c)^5}$$

$$i_c = 5.46\%.$$

Calculator Solution

Function Key	Data Input
PV =	−1147
FV =	1050
PMT =	80
N =	5
I =	?
Function Key	Answer
I =	5.46

This return is less than the anticipated yield to maturity of 6 percent. The early redemption produces a lower return for the investor because the premium is spread out over fewer years, reducing the yield on the investment. If an investor expected the bond to be called for $1,050 after five years and wanted to earn 6 percent, the price would have to be $1,122.

Which case is more likely to occur? If a firm wanted to retire debt that was selling at a discount before maturity, it would probably be to its advantage to purchase the bonds instead of calling them. (See the section on repurchasing debt in the previous chapter.) By doing so, the firm would avoid the call penalty and might even be able to buy the bonds for less than par. If the firm wanted to retire debt that was selling at a premium, it would probably be advantageous to call the bonds and pay the penalty. If the bonds were selling for more than face value plus the call penalty, this would obviously be the chosen course of action.

An investor should not expect a firm to prematurely call a bond issue that is selling at a discount. However, if interest rates fall and bond prices rise, the firm may refinance the debt. It will then issue new debt at the lower (current) interest rate and use the proceeds to retire the old and more costly debt. In this case the yield to the anticipated call is probably a better indication of the potential return offered by the bonds than is the yield to maturity.

The preceding example also illustrates the importance of the call penalty. If an investor bought the bond in anticipation that it would yield 6 percent at maturity (i.e., the investor paid $1,147) and the bond is redeemed after five years for the principal amount ($1,000), the return on the investment is only 4.6 percent. Although the $50 call penalty does not restore the return to 6 percent, the investor does receive a yield of 5.46 percent, which is considerably better than 4.6 percent.

RISK AND FLUCTUATIONS IN YIELDS

Stock investors will bear risk only if they anticipate a sufficient return to compensate for the risk, and a higher anticipated return is necessary to induce them to bear additional risk. This principle also applies to investors who purchase bonds. Bonds involving greater risk must offer higher yields to attract investors. Therefore, the lowest yields are paid by bonds with the highest credit ratings, and low credit ratings are associated with high yields.

This relationship is illustrated by Exhibit 14.6, which presents Standard & Poor's ratings and the anticipated yields to maturity for three bonds that will mature in the year 2023. As may be seen in the exhibit, the bonds with the highest credit ratings have

EXHIBIT   14.6   Credit Ratings and Yields to Maturity for Selected Bonds Maturing in the Year 2023

Bond Issue	Standard & Poor's Bond Rating	Yield to Maturity
GE Capital 5.5 23	AA+	6.0%
NY Telephone 6.7 23	A	6.9
USX 8.5 23	BBB+	7.6

Source: *Standard & Poor's Bond Guide.*

the lowest anticipated yield to maturity. A GE Capital bond with an AA+ rating was selling to yield less than the BBB+-rated bond of USX. The difference, or *spread*, in the yields is partially due to the difference in risk between the two bonds. While the GE Capital bond is considered to be relatively safe (as judged by its rating), the USX bond is viewed as involving more risk.

Because interest rates change over time, the anticipated yields on all debts vary. However, the yields on debt involving greater risk tend to fluctuate more. This is illustrated in Figure 14.1, which plots the yields on Moody's Baa-rated bonds in the top line and the yields on its Aaa-rated bonds in the bottom line. In this particular period there was considerable change in the yields to maturity. During periods of higher interest rates, the poorer-quality debt offered a higher yield and the spread between the yields was also greater. For example, during 1982 the yields rose to 14.8 and 14.9 percent, and the spread between the bonds also rose to 2.1 percent.

| FIGURE 14.1 | Fluctuations in Yield to Maturity for Moody's Aaa- and Baa-Rated Industrial Bonds (1980 through 2008) |

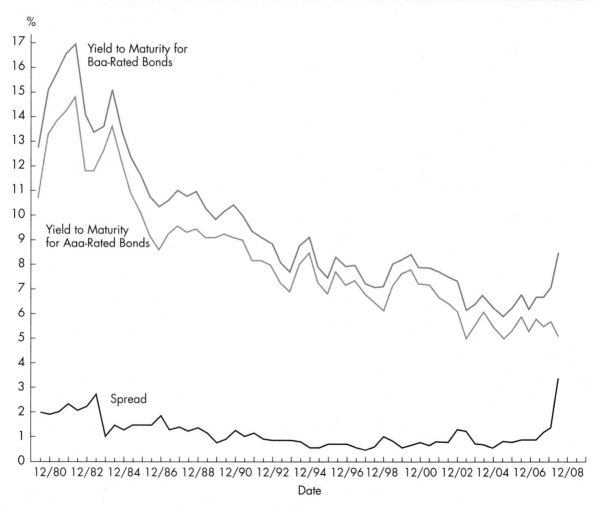

Source: *Moody's Bond Record*, various issues, 1980–2008, *Mergent's Bond Record*, various issues.

After 1982, yields and spreads fell. During the 1990s, the spread between Aaa and Baa industrial bonds averaged less than 1.0 percent (less than 100 basis points). In the early 2000s, interest rates declined, but the spread actually increased, and by the end of 2008, the spread exceeded 3 percent (over 300 basis points). During the 2008 financial crisis, investors moved from poorer-quality debt into higher-quality debt. (The data in Figure 14.1 use averages yields. There were numerous examples of bonds with Baa ratings that sold for much higher yields. For example, an AMBAC debenture with an Aa2 rating sold for less than $0.50 on the $1.00 with a yield to maturity in excess of 17.1 percent. Obviously investors did not trust its rating.)

Changes in Risk

Previous sections demonstrated that when interest rates change, bond prices fluctuate in the opposite direction. If interest rates rise after a bond is issued, it will sell for a discount as the price adjusts so that the yield to maturity will be comparable with bonds being currently issued. If interest rates fall after the bond is issued, it will sell for a premium so that once again the yield to maturity is comparable to current interest rates.

The amount of price change depends on the coupon, the term of the bond, and the risk. The smaller the coupon, the greater the price fluctuation for a given maturity and level of risk. The longer the term of the bond, the greater the price fluctuation for a given coupon and level of risk. For given coupons and maturity dates, the prices of riskier bonds tend to fluctuate more.

The coupons and maturity dates of a bond are set when the bond is issued. However, the risk of default on a bond may vary over time as the financial condition of the issuer varies. Firms that were financially sound when their bonds were issued may fall on hard times. Their credit ratings deteriorate. Other firms' financial positions may improve. These changes in risk will, of course, affect the value of outstanding bonds. Consider Moody's ratings for the bonds of Jersey Central Power and Light, part owner of the Three Mile Island nuclear power plant. The 1979 accident at that power plant changed the risk exposure of JCP&L's bonds. The ratings dropped from Baa, the lowest investment-grade rating, to Ba. The price of the bonds declined dramatically, and they sold at a substantial discount. However, the subsequent improvement in the firm's financial condition resulted in improved credit ratings, so that by 1990, the rating was higher than before the Three Mile Island accident.

REALIZED RETURNS AND THE REINVESTMENT ASSUMPTION

The yield to maturity makes an important assumption that answers the following questions: What happens to the interest received in year one, year two, and so on (i.e., does the recipient pocket the money or reinvest the funds)? If the funds are reinvested, what rate do they earn? The yield to maturity calculation assumes that *all interest payments are reinvested at the yield to maturity*. This is an exceedingly important assumption because if the payments are not reinvested at that rate, the yield to maturity will not be realized. This also means that when an investor purchases a bond, the yield to maturity is an expected yield that will not necessarily be the realized yield, even if the bond is held to maturity.[1] The debtor could make all the interest payments and redeem the bond at maturity, but the yield over the lifetime of the bond could be different from the yield to maturity the investor anticipated when the bond was purchased.

The reinvestment rate assumption is the essential difference between compounding and not compounding. If an investor buys a $1,000 bond with an 8 percent coupon at par and spends the interest as received, the investor is earning a simple, noncompounded rate of 8 percent. The yield to maturity, however, assumes that the interest received will be reinvested at 8 percent (i.e., compounded at 8 percent). If the funds are not being reinvested, the compounded yield will be less than the simple 8 percent rate.

The reinvestment rate that the investor does achieve could be greater or less than the anticipated yield to maturity. If interest rates rise (and the price of this bond declines), the individual can reinvest the interest payments at the now higher rate. The yield earned over the lifetime of the bond will exceed the anticipated yield to maturity. If interest rates fall (and the price of this bond rises), the individual can only reinvest the interest payments at the lower rate. The yield earned over the lifetime of the bond will be less than the anticipated yield to maturity.

Perhaps the best way to see the importance of the reinvestment rate assumption is through several illustrations. In each of the following cases, the investor purchases an 8 percent, $1,000 coupon bond that matures after ten years. The investor wants the funds to accumulate and is curious as to how much will be available at the end of the tenth year. Essentially, this question may be restated in the following way: If I invest $80 each year at some rate for ten years and receive $1,000 at the end of the tenth year, how much will I have accumulated? The final amount will depend on the rate earned each year. This is the reinvestment rate.

Case 1: All Interest Payments Are Reinvested at 8 Percent

In this case, the terminal value will be $80 times the interest factor for the future sum of an annuity of $1 at 8 percent for ten years. The future value of this annuity is

$$\$80(14.487) = \$1,158.96.$$

This amount is added to the $1,000 principal received at maturity so the investor has a total of $2,158.96 at the end of ten years.

What is the return on this investment that initially cost $1,000 and has grown into $2,158.96? This is a future value of $1 problem:

$$\$1,000(\text{interest factor for 10 years at } i \text{ percent}) = \$2,158.96$$

$$\$1,000IF = \$2,158.96$$

$$IF = 2.159.$$

An interest factor (*IF*) for the future value of $1 of 2.159 indicates that $1,000 grows to $2,159 in ten years at 8 percent. The yield on this investment over its lifetime (i.e., the yield to maturity) is the anticipated 8 percent.

Calculator Solution

Function Key	Data Input
PV =	0
FV =	?
PMT =	80
N =	10
I =	8
Function Key	*Answer*
FV =	−1158.92

Calculator Solution

Function Key	Data Input
PV =	−1,000
FV =	2158.96
PMT =	0
N =	10
I =	?
Function Key	*Answer*
I =	8

[1]The reinvestment assumption also applies to the yield to call, which assumes that cash inflows are reinvested at the yield to call. All time-value calculations assume that inflows are reinvested at the discount rate, or interest rate. If this reinvestment rate is not achieved, then the present value, or future value, or rate of return, or number of years being determined by the calculation to solve a specific problem are inaccurate.

Case 2: All Interest Payments Are Reinvested at 12 Percent

Suppose immediately after buying the bond, interest rates rise to 12 percent. Of course, the bond would now sell for a discount and the investor has sustained a loss. But the bond was purchased to receive a flow of interest payments that the individual intended to reinvest at the current rate. So the loss of value is only a paper loss. The bond is not sold, and the loss is not realized. Instead, the bond is held and the interest payments are now reinvested at the higher rate. What will be the return on this investment? Will this return be equal to the 8 percent yield to maturity that was anticipated when the bond was purchased?

In this case, the terminal value of the interest payments will be $80 times the interest factor for the future sum of an annuity of $1 at 12 percent for ten years. The future value of this annuity is

$$\$80(17.549) = \$1,403.92.$$

This amount is added to the $1,000 principal received at maturity so the investor has a total of $2,403.92 at the end of ten years.

What is the return on this investment that initially cost $1,000 and has grown into $2,403.92? Once again this is a future value of $1 problem:

$$\$1,000(\text{interest factor for 10 years at } i \text{ percent}) = \$2,403.92$$

$$\$1,000IF = \$2,403.92$$

$$IF = 2.404.$$

The interest table reveals that an interest factor of 2.404 means that in ten years $1,000 grows to $2,404 at between 9 and 10 percent (9.17 percent to be more precise). The actual yield on this investment over its lifetime (i.e., the realized yield to maturity) exceeds the anticipated 8 percent. Thus, the investor who purchased the bond anticipating a yield to maturity of 8 percent actually earns more. Even though interest rates rose, which caused the market value of the bond to fall, the return over the lifetime of the bond exceeds the expected yield to maturity.

Case 3: All Interest Payments Are Reinvested at 5 Percent

In this case, the terminal value of the interest payments will be $80 times the interest factor for the future value of an annuity of $1 at 5 percent for ten years. The future value of this annuity is

$$\$80(12.578) = \$1,006.24.$$

The sum of this amount and the $1,000 principal received at maturity is $2,006.24.

What is the return on this investment that initially cost $1,000 and has grown into $2,006.24? The answer is

$$\$1,000(\text{interest factor for 10 years at } i \text{ percent}) = \$2,006.24$$

$$\$1,000IF = \$2,006.24$$

$$IF = 2.006.$$

An interest factor of 2.006 indicates that $1,000 grows to $2,006 in ten years at less than 8 percent (7.21 to be more precise). Even though interest rates fell and the price of the bond initially rose, the yield on the investment in this bond is only 7.21 percent.

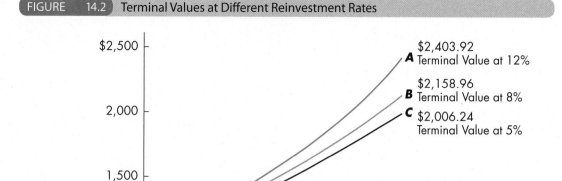

FIGURE   14.2   Terminal Values at Different Reinvestment Rates

The actual return is less than the expected yield to maturity (i.e., the anticipated 8 percent).

These three illustrations are compared in Figure 14.2, which shows the initial $1,000 and the terminal values achieved through the investment of the interest at the different reinvestment rates. Lines *OA*, *OB*, and *OC* represent the growth in each investment at 12 percent, 8 percent, and 5 percent, respectively. The terminal values, $2,403.92, $2,158.96, and $2,006.24, generated through the reinvestment of interest income, are shown on the right-hand side of the figure. Of course, the highest terminal value and consequently the highest realized return occur at the highest reinvestment rate.

Actually, there is little reason to expect the investor will earn the anticipated yield to maturity. To obtain that yield, interest rates must remain unchanged and the bond must be held to maturity. The probability of these conditions being met is very small. Interest rates change virtually every day, and few bonds remain outstanding to maturity. Most bonds are retired through sinking funds or are called. In either case, only a few bonds of the initial issue may remain outstanding at maturity.

Since many bonds are retired prior to maturity, the investor may want to purchase only those bonds that are noncallable. Some bonds have this feature written into their indentures. They cannot be retired prior to maturity, in which case there is no uncertainty concerning when these bonds will be redeemed. Since this uncertainty has been erased, such bonds tend to sell for lower yields. Thus, the investor purchases the certainty of when the bond will be retired by forgoing some interest income.

Even if the investor acquires noncallable bonds, there is still the uncertainty associated with changes in interest rates. Thus, the realized yield over the lifetime of these noncallable bonds may not equal the yield to maturity that was anticipated when the bonds were purchased. A noncallable feature may reduce one source of risk but cannot erase all the possible sources of risk associated with investing in bonds.

There is only one type of bond that erases both the uncertainty of when the bond will be retired and the reinvestment rate. That bond is the noncallable, zero coupon bond. The entire yield occurs at maturity, and the discounted price considers the compounding of the implicit interest. These bonds offer actual yields to maturity that are equal to the expected yields. As long as the issuer does not default (i.e., repays the principal on the maturity date), the yield to maturity will be the realized return.

DURATION

The price volatility of bonds with equal coupons and different terms may be compared on the basis of time. For a given risk class, the price of the bond with the longer term to maturity should be more volatile. Bonds with equal maturities but different coupons may be compared on the basis of the interest payments. For a given risk class, the price of the bond with the smaller coupon will tend to be more volatile. Bonds, however, may have different coupons and different maturity dates. Computing the yield to maturity is one method for comparing bonds.[2] However, the yields to maturity on bonds with different maturities and different coupons may not be comparable, and the yield to maturity does not indicate which bonds' prices tend to be more volatile.

The previous discussion also indicated that the actual return the investor earns over a bond's lifetime will not equal the yield to maturity if the reinvestment rate differs from the yield to maturity. An alternative calculation that may be used to compare bonds with different coupons and different terms to maturity has been developed. This technique is called the bond's **duration** and seeks to compare bonds with different coupons and different maturity dates by determining each bond's price sensitivity to changes in interest rates.

duration

The average time it takes to collect a bond's interest and principal repayment.

Duration is defined as the average time it takes the bondholder to receive the interest and the principal. It is a weighted average that encompasses the total amount of the bond's payments and their timing, then standardizes for the bond's price. To illustrate how duration is determined, consider a $1,000 bond with three years to maturity and a 9 percent coupon. The annual payments are as follows:

Year	Payment
1	$ 90
2	90
3	1,090

Currently, the rate of interest on comparable bonds is 12 percent, so this bond's price is $927.95. The bond's duration is the sum of the present value of each payment weighted by the time period in which the payment is received, with the resulting quantity divided by the price of the bond. Thus, for this bond, the duration is determined as follows:

Number of Each Payment		Amount of Payment		Present Value Interest Factor at 12 Percent		
1	×	$ 90	×	0.893	=	$80.37
2	×	90	×	0.797	=	143.46
3	×	1,090	×	0.712	=	2,328.24
						$2,552.07

$$\text{Duration} = \frac{\$2,552.07}{\$927.95} = 2.75 \text{ years.}$$

[2] As is explained in the second appendix to this chapter, bonds in the same risk class and with the same maturity but with different coupons may have different yields to maturity. Thus, it cannot be assumed that all bonds with the same maturity date and same risk offer the same returns.

A duration of 2.75 years means that the bondholder collects, on the average, all the payments in 2.75 years. Obviously, all the payments are not made exactly at 2.75 years into the future. Ninety dollars is received at the end of year one; $90 is received at the end of year two; and $1,090 is received at the end of year three. The weighted average of all these payments is 2.75 years. Duration may be computed when payments are semiannual, in which case the annual payment and interest rate on comparable debt are divided by 2 and the number of payments is multiplied by 2. If this example had used semiannual compounding, the bond's price would be $926.24, and the computation of duration is

Number of Each Payment		Amount of Payment		Present Value Interest Factor at 6 Percent		
1	×	$ 45	×	0.943	=	$42.44
2	×	45	×	0.890	=	80.04
3	×	45	×	0.840	=	113.40
4	×	45	×	0.792	=	142.56
5	×	45	×	0.747	=	168.08
6	×	1,045	×	0.705	=	4,420.35
						$4,966.87

$$\text{Duration} = \frac{\$4,966.87/2}{\$926.24} = 5.3624/2 = 2.68 \text{ years.}$$

The duration is marginally smaller because the cash inflows are received slightly faster as the result of semiannual compounding.

The calculation of duration (D) may be formally expressed as:

14.5
$$D = \frac{\sum_{t=1}^{m} PVCF_t \times t}{P_B}.$$

The numerator states that the cash flow in each year (CF_t) is stated in present value terms (PV) and weighted by the number of the period (t) in which the payment is received. The individual present values are summed from $t = 1$ to $t = m$ (maturity), and the resulting amount is divided by the current price of the bond (P_B).

Notice that duration is not the sum of the present value of each payment. (That sum is the price of the bond.) Duration takes the present value of each payment and weights it according to when the payment is received. Payments that are to be received farther into the future have more weight in the calculation. If two bonds pay the same coupon but the term of one bond is 10 years while the term of the other is 20 years, the weights given to the payments in years 11 through 20 result in a larger weighted average. The duration, or the weighted average of when all the payments will be received, is longer for the second bond.

The preceding calculation of duration can be tedious. An alternative method simplifies the problem.

14.6
$$D = \frac{1 + y}{y} - \frac{(1 + y) + n(c - y)}{c[(1 + y)^n - 1] + y}.$$

Although this equation looks formidable, its application is relatively easy. The variables represent the following:

$$c = \text{the annual coupon (as a percentage)}$$

$$n = \text{the number of years to maturity}$$

$$y = \text{the yield to maturity (reinvestment rate)}$$

Applying the numbers from the preceding illustration yields

$$\text{Duration} = \frac{1 + 0.12}{0.12} - \frac{(1 + 0.12) + 3(0.09 - 0.12)}{0.09[(1 + 0.12)^3 - 1] + 0.12}$$

$$= 2.75,$$

which is the same answer (2.75) derived earlier.

By making this calculation for bonds with different coupons and different maturities, the investor standardizes for price fluctuations. Bonds with the same duration will experience similar price fluctuations, while the prices of bonds with a longer duration will fluctuate more. For example, consider the following two bonds. Bond A has a 10 percent coupon, matures in 20 years, and currently sells for $1,000. Bond B has a 7 percent coupon and matures after 10 years with a current price of $815.66. (In this illustration it is assumed that the bonds sell for the same yield to maturity. While generally the long-term bond should offer a higher yield, this assumption facilitates comparisons for a given change in interest rates.) If interest rates rise, the price of both bonds will fall, but which bond's price will fall more? Since the bonds differ with regard to maturity date and coupon, the investor does not know which bond's price will be more volatile.

In general, the longer the term to maturity, the more volatile the bond's price. By that reasoning, bond A will be more volatile. However, lower coupons are also associated with greater price volatility, and by that reasoning bond B's price should be more volatile. Thus, the investor cannot tell on the basis of term and coupon which of these two bonds' prices will be more volatile. However, once their durations have been determined (9.36 and 7.22, respectively), the investor knows that the price of bond A will decline more in response to an increase in interest rates. For example, if interest rates rise to 12 percent, the prices of the two bonds become $850.61 and $717.49, respectively. Bond A's price declined by 15 percent while bond B's price fell by 12 percent, so bond A's price was more volatile.

Duration may also be used to determine the amount by which a bond's price will fluctuate for small changes in interest rates. The percentage change in a bond's price for a change in the yield to maturity is

$$\frac{\Delta P_B}{P_B} = -D \times \frac{\text{Change in the yield to maturity}}{1 + y}$$

$$\frac{\Delta P_B}{P_B} = -D \times \frac{\Delta y}{1 + y},$$

in which P_B is the current price of the bond, D is the bond's duration, and y is the yield to maturity. By rearranging terms, the change in the price of a bond is

14.7
$$\Delta P_B = -D \times \frac{\Delta y}{1 + y} \times P_B.$$

The equation may be illustrated by using bond A above, which sold for $1,000 when the yield to maturity was 10 percent, and whose duration was 9.36. If interest rates rise to 10.2 percent, the change in the price of bond A is

$$\Delta P_B = \frac{(-9.36)(0.002)}{1.1} \times \$1,000 = \$-17.$$

The increase in interest rates from 10 to 10.2 percent causes the price of the bond to decline from $1,000 to $983. If interest rates were to fall from 10 to 9.8 percent (-0.002), the price of the bond would rise to $1,017.[3]

Since bonds with larger durations are more volatile, investors reduce the risk associated with changes in interest rates by acquiring bonds with shorter durations. This, however, is not synonymous with buying bonds with shorter maturities.[4] If two bonds have the same term to maturity, the bond with the smaller coupon will have the longer duration, since a larger proportion of the bond's total payment is repayment of principal. If two bonds have the same coupon, the one with the longer maturity will have the longer duration, as the payments are spread over a longer period of time. However, if one bond has a smaller coupon and a shorter term, its duration could be either greater or smaller than the duration of a bond with a higher coupon and longer term to maturity. Thus, it is possible to buy a bond with a longer term to maturity that has a shorter duration. In such a case, the longer-term bond will experience smaller price fluctuations than the bond with the shorter maturity but longer duration.

Duration and Portfolio Immunization

Pension plan managers and some portfolio managers (e.g., managers of a life insurance company's bond portfolio) use duration as a tool of risk management. These professional investors know reasonably well the time and the amount of funds needed for distributions. They then match the duration of their portfolios with the timing of the need for funds. This strategy is often referred to as "immunization," because it reduces the risk associated with interest rate fluctuations and the reinvestment of interest payments.

Consider a portfolio manager who needs $2,200 at the end of seven years and purchases at par a high-yield 12 percent coupon bond that matures at the end of seven years. If interest rates remain at 12 percent, the investor will have $2,211 because the coupons are reinvested at 12 percent. The terminal value is

$$\$1,000 + \$120(10.089) = \$2,211.$$

(The $1,000 is the repayment of the principal and the $120[10.089] is the future value of all the interest payments compounded annually at 12 percent.)

If interest rates rise and the portfolio manager reinvests at 14 percent, the terminal value is

$$\$1,000 + \$120(10.730) = \$2,288,$$

---

[3]The usefulness of duration to forecast a bond's price change due to a given change in interest rates diminishes as the change in interest rates increases. For example, if interest rates had increased from 10 to 12 percent, Equation 14.7 indicates that bond A's price would have declined by $170, whereas the bond valuation equation indicates that the price should be $851, a decline of $149. (See the next section on bond convexity.)

[4]The only time duration equals the term to maturity occurs when the bond makes no interest payments (i.e., it is a zero coupon bond). All the payments then occur at maturity.

and the portfolio manager is even better off. A problem arises when interest rates fall and the coupons are reinvested at a lower rate. For example, if interest rates decline to 8 percent, the terminal value is

$$\$1,000 + \$120(8.923) = \$2,071,$$

and the portfolio manager does not have the required $2,200. The lower reinvestment of the interest payments resulted in an insufficient terminal value.

The portfolio manager could have avoided the shortage by acquiring a bond whose duration (and not its term) is equal to seven years. For example, if the portfolio manager purchases a bond with a 12 percent coupon that matures in 12 instead of 7 years, that bond has a duration of 6.9 years that almost matches when the $2,200 is needed. (The 12 percent 7-year bond has a duration of 5.1 years.) As will be subsequently illustrated, the purchase of the 12-year bond instead of the 7-year bond eliminates the reinvestment risk.

Since the 12-year bond will have to be sold at the end of seven years, the obvious question is: At what price? The price could rise (if interest rates fall) or decline (if interest rates rise). Should the portfolio manager be concerned with interest rate risk (i.e., the fluctuation in the bond's price), which would not apply if the bond matured at the end of seven years? The answer is no. The bond's price of course will change, but the impact of the price fluctuation is offset by the change in the reinvestment of the interest payments. The effect, then, of *both reinvestment rate risk and interest rate risk is eliminated.*

Suppose interest rates immediately rise to 14 percent after the portfolio manager buys the bond. The portfolio manager holds the bond for seven years and reinvests the interest payments at 14 percent. How much will this investor have at the end of seven years? The answer is the sum of the interest payments reinvested at 14 percent for seven years [$120(10.730) = $1,288] plus the sale price of the bond. Since the bond has five years to maturity, its price is

$$\$120(3.433) + \$1,000(0.519) = \$931.$$

Thus, the portfolio manager has $1,288 + $931 = $2,219, which meets the desired amount ($2,200). The loss on the sale of the bond is offset by the increased interest earned when the annual interest payments are reinvested at the higher rate.

Suppose interest rates immediately decline to 8 percent after the bond is purchased. The portfolio manager holds the bond for seven years and reinvests the interest payments at 8 percent. How much will the investor have at the end of seven years? The answer in this case is the sum of the interest payments reinvested at 8 percent for seven years [$120(8.923) = $1,071] plus the sale price of the bond. Since the bond has five years to maturity, its price is

$$\$120(3.993) + \$1,000(0.681) = \$1,160.$$

Thus, the portfolio manager has $1,071 + $1,160 = $2,231, which once again meets the desired amount ($2,200). The gain on the sale of the bond offsets the reduction in interest earned when the interest payments are reinvested at the lower rate.

Notice that in both cases the individual achieves the investment goal of $2,200 at the end of seven years. Lower reinvestment income from a decline in interest rates is offset by the increase in the price of the bond, while higher reinvestment income from an increase in interest rates is offset by the decline in the price of the bond. Thus, the impact of reinvestment rate risk and interest rate risk is eliminated. Of course, the portfolio manager has lost the opportunity to earn a higher return, but the purpose of the strategy is to ensure a particular amount in the future.

As this discussion indicates, the concept of duration is exceedingly important for any investor who knows when funds will be needed and in what amount. Pension managers know both when payments must be made and their amount. Mortality tables help establish the same information for life insurance companies. Portfolio managers immunize their risk exposure and ensure that the desired funds are available when needed. (These portfolio managers, of course, still have the risk of default or incorrect forecasts, such as changes in a mortality table.)

Individual investors will probably find duration less useful. For example, even if parents know when their children will attend college, they do not necessarily know the cost—hence the future value is unknown. In addition, the duration of each bond is not readily available and, as is explained in the next section, the value changes with each change in the bond's price. Thus, individual investors who want to apply this concept will have to perform the calculation themselves and frequently adjust their portfolios as the duration of each bond in the portfolio fluctuates.

BOND PRICE CONVEXITY AND DURATION

Duration may be used to rank bonds with regard to their price volatility and to determine their price change for a given change in interest rates. The accuracy of the price change, however, varies with the amount of the fluctuation in interest rates. Consider an 8 percent, 10-year bond that is currently selling for par ($1,000). The first three columns in Exhibit 14.7 list various interest rates, the price of the bond based on the

EXHIBIT 14.7 Forecasted Bond Prices Using Duration and Actual Prices

Interest Rate	Price of the Bond	Change in Bond's Price	Duration	Forecasted Change in Price	Difference
20.0%	$497	$−503	6.000	$−805	$302
15.0	649	−397	6.524	−470	119
12.0	774	−226	6.837	−268	42
11.0	823	−176	6.941	−201	25
10.0	877	−123	7.044	−134	11
9.0	936	−64	7.146	−67	3
8.8	948	−52	7.166	−53	1
8.4	974	−26	7.207	−27	1
8.2	987	−13	7.227	−13	—
8.0	1,000	—	7.247	—	—
7.8	1,014	14	7.267	13	1
7.6	1,027	26	7.287	27	1
7.2	1,056	56	7.327	53	3
7.0	1,070	70	7.347	67	3
6.0	1,147	147	7.445	134	13
4.0	1,324	324	7.637	268	56
2.0	1,539	539	7.823	403	136
1.0	1,663	663	7.912	470	193

rates, and resulting change in price from the initial par value. As expected, the price of the bond rises in response to lower rates, and the price of the bond declines in response to higher rates.

The fourth column gives the bond's duration at the various prices. This value may be used in Equation 14.7 to forecast the price change in the bond for a given change in interest rates. The fifth column presents the forecasted price change using Equation 14.7 and starting with the bond selling for par with a duration of 7.247. The last column presents the absolute difference in the forecasted price change and the actual change in column 3. As may be seen in the sixth column, the forecasted error is small for a small change in interest rates. For example, a change in interest rates from 8 percent to 9 percent or from 8 percent to 7 percent produces an error of $3. However, the difference between the actual change and the forecasted change increases with larger changes in interest rates. If interest rates were to rise or fall by 4 percentage points to 12 percent or 4 percent, the errors are $42 and $56, respectively. These differences between the actual and forecasted price changes reduce the usefulness of the duration.

The source of the error may be seen in Figure 14.3. Line *BB* plots the various prices of the bond against the different interest rates. (In effect, line *BB* replicates the second column in Exhibit 14.7.) Line *AA* gives the bond prices forecasted using duration, with the difference between *AA* and *BB* being the error. Notice that as interest rates move further above or below the initial 8 percent, the error increases.

The source of the error is that duration predicts the same price change for each 1 percent movement in the interest rate, but the actual price change varies. As may be seen in the figure, *AA* is a straight line while *BB* is a curve and is convex to the origin.

FIGURE   14.3   Bond Prices Forecasted by Duration and Actual Prices

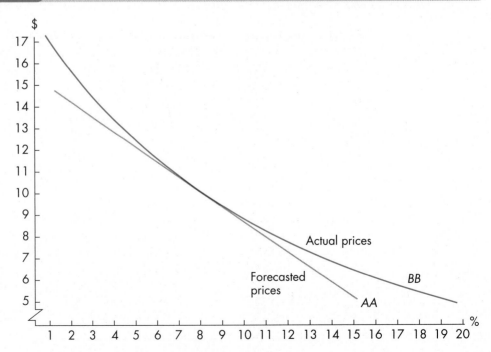

The price of the bond moves along the curve. For a given change in interest rates (e.g., 8 percent to 9 percent or 9 percent to 10 percent), the amount of price change varies. The forecasted price moves along the straight line. For a given change in interest rates (e.g., 8 percent to 9 percent or 9 percent to 10 percent), the amount of price change is the same, so the forecasted error increases.

This "convexity" of line *BB* decreases the practicality of using a unique value of duration (e.g., the 7.247 used to construct Exhibit 14.7 and Figure 14.3) to forecast price changes. Equation 14.5, which determines the numerical value of duration, uses the price of the bond in the denominator. As the price of the bond changes, so must its duration. This change in the bond's duration is also illustrated in Exhibit 14.7 in the fourth column. While the initial duration is 7.247 when the bond sells for $1,000, the value rises to 7.445 when interest rates decline to 6 percent and falls to 6.524 when interest rates rise to 15 percent.

To use duration as a tool for managing a bond portfolio, the investor must adjust for changes in the value of a bond's duration. An immediate implication of the change in duration is the need to alter the composition of a bond portfolio when a specific numerical value for duration is desired. Such changes in the portfolio suggest that an actively managed bond portfolio requires constant supervision and that such a portfolio cannot be a passive investment in which the portfolio manager accumulates a collection of bonds and then idly sits and collects the interest. Although a bond portfolio may be passively managed, a bond portfolio designed to generate a specified amount of funds at a specified date cannot be passively managed if the portfolio duration is to be matched with the specified time when the funds are needed.

MANAGEMENT OF BOND PORTFOLIOS

Since bonds pay a fixed income and mature at a specified date, they are conducive to passive management. The investor may acquire a portfolio of bonds and simply hold them to maturity (i.e., a buy-and-hold strategy). Each year the interest is received and at maturity the principal is repaid. During the interim, the value of the portfolio could rise (i.e., interest rates fall), or the value of the portfolio could fall (i.e., interest rates rise). Such fluctuations in the value of the portfolio may have little meaning to the investor who is passively holding the portfolio and collecting the interest until the bonds mature. Of course, if the individual had to sell the bonds for any reason, their prices would become crucial since the investor would receive only what the bonds were currently worth.

Not all bondholders, however, are passive investors. As was explained in the previous section, using duration for the management of reinvestment rate risk requires frequent trading of bonds. A strategy designed to take advantage of an expected change in rates paid by one type of bond relative to a different type requires the swapping of one bond for another. A strategy designed to reduce interest rate risk may require the construction of a portfolio with many bonds with different maturity dates. A strategy designed to match the timing of a bond portfolio's cash flows with when the funds are needed may require frequent trading of bonds. None of these constitutes passive management of a bond portfolio.

Management of Interest Rate Risk

Since interest rates change daily, the value of a bond portfolio fluctuates daily. Of course, the investor could avoid these fluctuations by acquiring only short-term debt obligations. This strategy generates less income since shorter maturities generally have lower yields than bonds with longer maturities. The opposite strategy of purchasing only very long-term bonds will increase income but also increases the risk associated with changes in interest rates.

The investor could construct a portfolio of bonds with maturities distributed over a period of time. Such a strategy is sometimes referred to as a *laddered* approach. For example, a $1,000,000 portfolio could acquire $100,000 worth of bonds that mature for each of the next ten years. If interest rates change, the prices of the bonds with the shorter terms (i.e., the bonds with one to five years to maturity) will fluctuate less than the prices of the bonds with the longer terms (i.e., years six through ten). Hence, such a portfolio reduces the impact of changes in interest rates.

In addition to reducing the impact on the value of the portfolio from fluctuating interest rates, a laddered portfolio offers two important advantages. First, since the structure of yields is generally positive, the interest earned on the bonds will tend to be greater than would be earned on a portfolio of short-term debt instruments. (Correspondingly, it would be smaller than the interest earned on a portfolio consisting solely of bonds with long terms to maturity.) Second, some of the bonds mature each year. If the individual needs the funds, they are available; if the individual does not need the funds, they may be reinvested. If the funds are reinvested each year in bonds with a ten-year maturity, the original structure of the portfolio is retained.

The previous example illustrates a straight ladder. The width of each step is the same and the distance between each step is the same. But both the width and the distance may vary. For example, suppose the investor anticipates needing more funds further into the future. The top of the ladder could be expanded and the base could be narrowed. The ten-year $1,000,000 ladder could be constructed so that $50,000 matures in the first year and that amount increases each year ($75,000 in year two, $100,000 in year three, $125,000 in year four, and so on). This strategy will increase annual income if the yield curve is positively sloping, but it also exposes the investor to more interest rate risk. If interest rates do rise, the value of the bonds with the longest maturity will decline more. Investing a larger proportion in the longer-term bonds may produce a larger loss if the interest rates rise and the investor must sell the ladder.

The possibility of an increase in interest rates suggests the opposite strategy: widen the ladder at the base. The investor may allocate the $1,000,000 ladder so that $200,000 matures in the first year, $175,000 in the second year, $150,000 in the third year, and so on. If interest rates do rise, the funds received when the shorter-term bonds mature can be reinvested at the higher rates. Of course, if interest rates do not rise, this strategy generates less income than the ladder with more invested further into the future. Certainly the investor's need for funds or expectation of an increase in interest rates affects the construction of the shape of the ladder.

One disadvantage associated with a ladder strategy is that if the investor wants to (or needs to) alter the portfolio, virtually all the bonds have to be liquidated. If the investor anticipates lower interest rates, then a portfolio consisting of only long maturities is desirable. All the bonds with short to intermediate terms would have to be sold and reinvested in bonds with long maturities. The opposite would occur if the individual anticipates higher rates. In that case, the individual wants only short-term securities, so all the bonds with intermediate to long terms would have to be sold.

This lack of flexibility and the need to change a large proportion of the portfolio if the investor seeks to take advantage of anticipated changes in interest rates has led to an entirely different strategy for management of a bond portfolio. In this strategy, which is sometimes referred to as a *barbell*, the investor acquires a portfolio consisting of very long- and very short-term maturities. If the individual has $1,000,000 to invest, $500,000 may be used to purchase bonds with short maturities (e.g., six months to a year) and $500,000 to purchase 20-year bonds. If the investor then anticipates a change in interest rates, only half of the portfolio needs to be changed. Expectation of lower rates would imply selling the short-term bonds and investing the proceeds in the long-terms. If the investor anticipates higher interest rates, he or she would do the opposite: sell the long-terms and move into the short-term bonds.

A barbell strategy will reduce the impact of fluctuating interest rates if the investor anticipates correctly. It will magnify the impact if the investor is incorrect. A movement into long-term bonds just prior to an increase in interest rates could inflict a substantial loss on the value of the portfolio. The strategy also has a second major disadvantage: With the passage of time, the short-term bonds will mature, and the maturities of the long-term bonds will diminish. Thus, this bond strategy requires active management, as the proceeds of the maturing bonds will have to be reinvested and some of the longer bonds may have to be sold and the proceeds invested in bonds with even longer maturities. Failure to take these steps means that the investor's cash position will increase and the term of the remaining bonds will decrease.

Matching Strategies

The "barbell strategy" is designed to facilitate swapping bonds of different terms to benefit from anticipated changes in interest rates. The "immunized portfolio" discussed earlier matches the duration of the bond portfolio with the investor's cash needs. This particular strategy requires the investor to monitor the portfolio and adjust it should the duration differ from the time when the funds will be needed.

An alternative to the immunized portfolio is the "dedicated bond portfolio," which matches the receipt of cash flows with the need for the funds. The interest payments and principal repayments are matched with when the investor anticipates needing these cash inflows to make payments. For example, a parent may construct a portfolio of zero coupon bonds, each of which matures when the child's tuition is due. While this is perhaps an exceptionally obvious example, the strategy would also apply to the trustees of a pension plan. In that case, the timing and amount of the payments to the retirees are known. The trustees then acquire bonds such that the interest payments and principal repayments match the required payments.

An individual could follow a similar strategy with funds in an IRA. While the investor will not know exactly when the funds will be needed, he or she can estimate cash requirements. For example, suppose a retiree owns a house with no mortgage, a new car, and supplementary medical insurance. That individual may not know how much each payment will be in the future, but he or she knows when property taxes and insurance payments are due. The retiree may also have an estimate of annual maintenance requirements for the house and the car and when the car would be replaced. Acquiring bonds that pay interest or mature at the same time these payments fall due should facilitate making the payments.

Interest rate risk is irrelevant for both immunized and dedicated bond portfolios. By matching the duration of the portfolio with the duration of the investor's liabilities or by timing the cash received with cash needs, the impact of fluctuations in interest rates is minimized. Such strategies are better than a simple buy-and-hold strategy because they seek to match the portfolio with the need for funds. Since a simple buy-and-hold does not consider when the funds will be needed, the investor will be subject to interest rate risk. The funds may possibly be needed during a period of higher interest rates, in which case the investor will not realize the value of the initial investment.

Interest Rate Swaps

Interest rate swaps have emerged as one of the major recent innovations in finance and are discussed in Chapter 19. Few individual investors are concerned with the market for interest rate swaps. Instead, these swaps are a means by which financial institutions, such as commercial banks or savings and loan institutions, manage risk.

Many financial institutions have mismatched assets and liabilities. For example, a savings and loan's primary assets may be long-term mortgages, while its primary liabilities are short to intermediate term (i.e., deposits and certificates of deposit). When interest rates rise, a savings and loan institution loses on two counts: The higher interest rate reduces the value of its assets and increases the interest it must pay to attract depositors. To reduce this risk, the savings and loan needs a flow of payments that will vary with changes in interest, so the savings and loan swaps the flow of fixed-interest payments it will receive on the mortgages for a series of variable payments.

The swap is made with a corporation that has the need to make fixed payments. For example, suppose a utility has a large number of fixed-coupon bonds outstanding. The utility agrees to make variable payments to the savings and loan in exchange for the fixed-interest payments. Now the utility will have the funds coming in to make the interest payments. In effect, the utility is substituting variable-interest payments to the savings and loan for the fixed-interest payments that it would have to make to its bondholders, while the savings and loan substitutes the receipt of variable-interest payments for fixed-interest payments from the mortgages. The swap helps both firms better match their receipts and disbursements and manage their assets and liabilities.

SUMMARY

The price of a bond depends on the interest paid, the maturity date, and the return offered by comparable bonds. If interest rates rise, the price of existing bonds falls. The opposite is also true—if interest rates fall, the price of existing bonds rises.

The current yield considers only the flow of interest income relative to the price of the bond. The yield to maturity considers the flow of interest income as well as any price change that may occur if the bond is held to maturity. The yield to call is similar to the yield to maturity, but it substitutes the call date and the call price for the maturity date and the principal.

Discounted bonds may be attractive to investors seeking current income, some capital appreciation, and the return of the principal at a specified date. Since many such bonds are redeemed at maturity, the investor knows when the principal is to be received.

All bond prices fluctuate in response to changes in interest rates and changes in risk, but the prices of bonds with smaller coupons, longer maturities, or poorer credit ratings tend to fluctuate more. These bonds may sell for larger discounts or higher premiums than bonds with shorter maturities or better credit ratings. Such bonds may be attractive investments for individuals who want higher returns and who are willing to bear additional risk.

Investors may determine bonds' duration to ascertain which bonds' prices will fluctuate more. Duration is a weighted average of all of a bond's interest and principal payments standardized by the bond's price. Bonds with smaller durations tend to have smaller price fluctuations in response to changes in interest rates. Duration may also be used to manage reinvestment rate risk by timing a bond's duration with when the funds will be needed.

The individual may passively or actively manage a bond portfolio. Passive strategies range from buy and hold to a laddered portfolio consisting of bonds with different maturity dates. Active strategies include swapping among different bonds to take advantage of mispricings, expected changes in interest rates, and tax losses and to match the need for funds and the receipt of interest payments and principal repayments.

Preferred stock is legally equity, but because it pays a fixed dividend, it is similar to debt. Preferred stock's value fluctuates with changes in interest rates. When interest rates rise, the price of preferred stock falls; when interest rates decline, the price of preferred stock rises. Because its price behavior is the same as the price behavior of bonds, preferred stock is valued and analyzed as an alternative to long-term debt.

The prime advantage to the firm issuing preferred stock is that it is less risky than debt because preferred stock does not represent an unconditional obligation to pay dividends. The major disadvantage to the issuing firm is that the dividends are not a tax-deductible expense.

The primary purpose for purchasing a preferred stock is the flow of dividend income. However, since preferred stock is riskier than debt (from the viewpoint of the individual investor), preferred stock is not a popular investment with individuals. The majority of preferred stock is purchased by corporations, especially insurance companies, which receive favorable tax treatment on the preferred stock dividends they receive.

Summary of Equations

Perpetual Bond (i.e., perpetual fixed income security)

14.1
$$P = \frac{PMT}{i}$$

Bond with Finite Maturity—Annual Interest Payments

14.2
$$P_B = \frac{PMT}{(1 + i)^1} + \frac{PMT}{(1 + i)^2} + \cdots + \frac{PMT}{(1 + i)^n} + \frac{FV}{(1 + i)^n}$$

Bond with Finite Maturity (Semiannual Compounding: $c = 2$)

14.3
$$P_B = \frac{\frac{PMT}{c}}{\left(1 + \frac{i}{c}\right)^1} + \frac{\frac{PMT}{c}}{\left(1 + \frac{i}{c}\right)^2} + \cdots + \frac{\frac{PMT}{c}}{\left(1 + \frac{i}{c}\right)^{n \times c}} + \frac{FV}{\left(1 + \frac{i}{c}\right)^{n \times c}}.$$

Current Yield

14.4
$$\text{Current yield} = \frac{\text{Annual interest payment}}{\text{Price of the bond}}$$

Duration

14.5
$$D = \frac{\sum\limits_{t=1}^{m} PVCF_t \times t}{P_B}$$

14.6
$$D = \frac{1 + y}{y} - \frac{(1 + y) + n(c - y)}{c[(1 + y)^n - 1] + y}$$

Change in the Price of a Bond

14.7
$$\Delta P_B = -D \times \frac{\Delta y}{1 + y} \times P_B$$

QUESTIONS

1. What causes bond prices to fluctuate?
2. Define the current yield and the yield to maturity. How are they different?
3. What advantages do discounted bonds offer to investors? Why may a bond be called if it is selling at a premium?
4. Although all bond prices fluctuate, which bond prices tend to fluctuate more?
5. What is the yield to call? How does it differ from the yield to maturity?
6. What differentiates the term of a bond and its duration? If bond A has a 10 percent coupon while bond B has a 5 percent coupon and they both mature after ten years, which bond has the shorter duration?
7. Why is a barbell strategy more flexible than a laddered strategy if an investor anticipates a decline in interest rates?
8. If interest rates rise, bond prices will fall. Given the following pairs of bonds, indicate which bond's price will experience the greater price decline.
   a) Bond A   Coupon: 10%
                Maturity: 5 years
      Bond B   Coupon: 6%
                Maturity: 5 years
   b) Bond A   Coupon: 10%
                Maturity: 7 years
      Bond B   Coupon: 10%
                Maturity: 15 years
   c) Bond A   Coupon: 10%
                Maturity: 5 years

Bond B   Coupon: 6%
          Maturity: 8 years
d) Bond A   Coupon: 10%
          Maturity: 1 year
Bond B   Coupon: zero percent
          Maturity: 10 years

PROBLEMS

Before doing these problems, here are two notes. First, the majority of bonds pay interest semiannually, but the points illustrated by these problems apply to annual payments as well as semiannual interest payments. Ask your instructor which you should use, annual or semiannual payments, to solve the problems. Appendix B provides answers to selected problems using both annual and semiannual calculations. Second, several of the problems include questions that are not explicitly covered in this chapter, such as sinking funds and call features or the computation of returns. If necessary, review the material in the previous chapter that describes bond features or the material in Chapter 10 on the computation of returns.

1. A $1,000 bond has a coupon rate of 8 percent and matures after ten years.
   a) What is the current price of the bond if the comparable rate of interest is 8 percent?
   b) What is the current price of the bond if the comparable rate of interest is 10 percent?
   c) What are the current yields given the prices determined in parts (a) and (b)?
   d) Why are the prices in (a) and (b) and the current yields in (c) different?
2. A $1,000 bond has a coupon rate of 10 percent and matures after eight years. Interest rates are currently 7 percent.
   a) What will the price of this bond be if the interest is paid annually?
   b) What will the price be if investors expect that the bond will be called with no call penalty after two years?
   c) What will the price be if investors expect that the bond will be called after two years and there will be a call penalty of one year's interest?
   d) Why are your answers different for questions (a), (b), and (c)?
3. A company has two bonds outstanding. The first matures after five years and has a coupon rate of 8.25 percent. The second matures after ten years and has a coupon rate of 8.25 percent. Interest rates are currently 10 percent. What is the present price of each $1,000 bond? Why are these prices different?
4. If a $1,000 bond with a 9 percent coupon (paid annually) and a maturity date of ten years is selling for $939, what is the current yield and the yield to maturity?
5. A $1,000 zero coupon bond sells for $519 and matures after five years. What is the current yield and the yield to maturity?
6. What are the holding period and the annualized compounded returns if you buy a zero coupon bond for $519 and it is redeemed after five years for $1,000? Compare the answer to the answer for Problem 5.

7. Given the following information:
    XY Inc. 5% bond
    AB Inc. 14% bond
   Both bonds are for $1,000, mature in 20 years, and are rated AAA.
   a) What should be the current market price of each bond if the interest rate on triple-A bonds is 10 percent?
   b) Which bond has a current yield that exceeds its yield to maturity?
   c) Which bond would you expect to be called if interest rates are 10 percent?
   d) If CD Inc. had a bond outstanding with a 5 percent coupon and a maturity date of 20 years but it was rated BBB, what would you expect its price to be relative to the XY Inc. bond?

8. a) A stock costs $900 and pays an annual $40 cash dividend. If you expect to sell the stock for $1,000 after five years, what is your anticipated return on the investment?
   b) A $1,000 bond has a 4 percent coupon and currently sells for $900. The bond matures after five years. What is the bond's anticipated return? Compare this return with the answer to part (a).

9. a) If a preferred stock pays an annual dividend of $6 and investors can earn 10 percent on alternative and comparable investments, what is the maximum price that should be paid for this stock?
   b) If the preferred stock in part (a) had a call feature and investors expected the stock to be called for $100 after ten years, what is the maximum price that investors should pay for the stock?
   c) If investors can earn 12 percent on comparable investments, what should be the price of the preferred stock in part (a)? What would be the price if comparable yields are 8 percent? What generalization do these answers imply?

10. What should be the prices of the following preferred stocks if comparable securities yield 6 percent, 8 percent, and 10 percent?
    a) MN Inc., $4 preferred ($100 par).
    b) CH Inc., $4 preferred ($100 par with the additional requirement that the firm must retire the preferred after 20 years).
    Why should the prices of these securities be different?

11. Company X has the following bonds outstanding:

Bond A		Bond B	
Coupon	8%	Coupon	Variable—changes annually to be comparable
Maturity	10 years		to the current rate
		Maturity	10 years

Initially, both bonds sold at $1,000 with yields to maturity of 8 percent.
    a) After two years, the interest rate on comparable debt is 10 percent. What should be the price of each bond?
    b) After two additional years (i.e., four years after issue date), the interest rate on comparable debt is 7 percent. What should be the price of each bond?
    c) What generalization may be drawn from the prices in questions (a) and (b)?

12. A high-yield bond has the following features:

Principal amount	$1,000
Interest rate (the coupon)	11.50%
Maturity	10 years
Sinking fund	None
Call feature	After two years
Call penalty	One year's interest

   a) If comparable yields are 12 percent, what should be the price of this bond?
   b) Would you expect the firm to call the bond if yields are 12 percent?
   c) If comparable yields are 8 percent, what should be the price of the bond?
   d) Would you expect the firm to call the bond today if yields are 8 percent?
   e) If you expected the bond to be called after three years, what is the maximum price you would pay for the bond if the current interest rate is 8 percent?

13. What is the price of the following split coupon bond if comparable yields are 12 percent?

Principal	$1,000
Maturity	12 years
Annual coupon	0% ($0) for years 1–3
	10% ($100) for years 4–12

   If comparable yields decline to 10 percent, what is the appreciation in the price of the bond?

14. A bond has the following terms:

Principal amount	$1,000
Annual interest payment	$140 starting after five years have passed (i.e., in year 6)
Maturity	12 years
Callable at $1,140 (i.e., face value + one year's interest)	

   a) Why do you believe that the terms were constructed as specified?
   b) What is the bond's price if comparable debt yields 12 percent?
   c) What is the bond's current yield?
   d) Even though interest rates have fallen, why may you not expect the bond to be called?

15. Tinker Spy Corp. has a high-yield junk bond with the following features:

Principal	$1,000
Coupon	0% for years 1 through 5 and 10% for years 6 through 10
Maturity	10 years

   The *current* interest rate on comparable debt is 10 percent. If you expect that the interest rate will be 8 percent five years from now, what is your potential gain or loss if your expectation is correct and interest rates are 8 percent after five years?

16. An extendable bond has the following features:

Principal	$1,000
Coupon	9.5% ($95 annually)
Maturity	8 years but the issuer may extend the maturity for 5 years

    a) If comparable yields are 12 percent, what will be the price of the bond if investors anticipate that it will be retired after eight years?
    b) What impact will the expectation that the bond will be retired after 13 years have on its current price if comparable yields are 12 percent?
    c) If comparable yields remain 12 percent, would you expect the firm to retire the bond after eight years?

17. Stella's Dog Biscuits Inc. has outstanding a high-yield bond with the following features:

Principal	$1,000
Coupon	10%
Maturity	5 years
Special features:	Company may extend the life of the bond to 10 years

    The current interest rate on comparable debt is 8 percent.
    a) If you expect that interest rates will be 8 percent five years from now, how much would you currently pay for this bond?
    b) What is your potential gain or loss if you buy the bond based on that expectation but interest rates are 12 percent five years from now?

18. You purchase a 7 percent $1,000 bond with a term of ten years and reinvest all interest payments. If interest rates rise to 10 percent after you purchase the bond, what is the return on your investment in the bond?

19. The prices of longer-term bonds are more volatile than the prices of shorter-term bonds with the same coupon. The prices of bonds with smaller coupons are more volatile than bonds with larger coupons for the same term to maturity. However, you cannot compare the relative price changes on bonds with different coupons and maturities unless you consider their durations. Consider the following bonds:

Bond	Coupon	Term
A	8%	8 years
B	14%	10 years

    The price of which bond will fall more if interest rates rise from the current yield to maturity of 8 percent? To answer the question, calculate the duration of both bonds.

20. Compute the duration for bond C, and rank the bonds on the basis of their price volatility. The current rate of interest is 8 percent, so the prices of bonds A and B are $1,000 and $1,268, respectively.

Bond	Coupon	Term	Duration
A	8%	10 years	7.25
B	12%	10 years	6.74
C	8%	5 years	?

Confirm your ranking by calculating the percentage change in the price of each bond when interest rates rise from 8 to 12 percent. (Bond A's and B's prices become $774 and $1,000, respectively.)

21. a) What is the price of each of the following bonds ($1,000 principal) if the current interest rate is 9 percent?

Firm A	Coupon	6%
	Maturity	5 years
Firm B	Coupon	6%
	Maturity	20 years
Firm C	Coupon	15%
	Maturity	5 years
Firm D	Coupon	15%
	Maturity	20 years
Firm E	Coupon	0% (zero coupon bond)
	Maturity	5 years
Firm F	Coupon	0% (zero coupon bond)
	Maturity	20 years

   b) What is the duration of each bond?
   c) Rank the bonds in terms of price fluctuations with the least volatile bond first and the most volatile bond last as judged by each bond's duration.
   d) Confirm your volatility rankings by determining the percentage change in the price of each bond if interest rates rise to 12 percent.
   e) What generalizations about duration can be made from the above exercise concerning (a) low- versus high-coupon bonds, (b) intermediate- versus long-term bonds, and (c) zero coupon bonds?

22. A ten-year bond with a 9 percent coupon will sell for $1,000 when interest rates are 9 percent. What is the duration of this bond? Using duration to forecast the change in the price of the bond, calculate the difference between the forecasted and the actual price change according to the bond valuation model for the following interest rates: 9.2, 9.4, 9.6, 9.8, 10, 10.5, 11, and 12 percent.

23. You own the following $1,000 bonds:

Bond A	4 percent coupon due in three years
Bond B	5 percent coupon due in five years
Bond C	7 percent coupon due in ten years.

Currently the structure of yields is positive so that each bond sells for its par value. However, you expect that inflation will increase and cause interest rates to rise so that the structure of yields becomes inverted (i.e., a negatively sloped yield curve). You anticipate that interest rates will be 10, 9, and 8 percent for three-, five-, and ten-year bonds, respectively.

   a) Given the current $1,000 price of each bond, what is each bond's duration?
   b) Given each bond's duration, what is the forecasted change in the value of the bond?

c) If interest rates do change as you expected, what is the new price of each bond?

d) What is the forecasting error based on duration and the actual change in each bond's price?

24. Portfolio A consists entirely of $1,000 zero coupon bonds that mature in 8, 9, and 10 years. Portfolio B consists of $1,000, 8 percent coupons that mature in 10, 15, and 20 years.

a) Based on this information, which portfolio appears to be riskier? Why?

b) If the rate of interest on comparable bonds is 8 percent, what are the price and duration of each bond?

c) What is the average duration of each portfolio based on each bond's duration? Does this information change your answer to (a)?

d) What is the percentage loss for each portfolio if the comparable interest rate rises to 10 percent?

e) What does the previous answer imply about the importance of duration to the management of risk?

25. In the section on the yield to call, a bond pays annual interest of $80 and matures after ten years. The bond is valued at $1,147 if the comparable rate is 6 percent and the bond is held to maturity. If, however, an investor expects the bond to be called for $1,050 after five years, the value of the bond would be $1,122. Investor A expects the bond to be called and investor B expects the bond not to be called. Investor A sells the bond to B for $1,122. What is the annual return earned by B if the bond is not called? Why is this yield greater than the 6 percent earned on comparable securities?

26. (This problem uses the material in Appendix 14B concerning bond valuation.) Two bonds have the following features:

Bond A		Bond B	
Principal	$1,000	Principal	$1,000
Coupon	6%	Coupon	12%
Maturity	5 years	Maturity	5 years

The structure of yields is

Term	Interest Rate
1 year	6%
2 years	7%
3 years	8%
4 years	9%
5 years	10%

a) What is the valuation of each security based on the yield to maturity for a five-year bond?

b) What is the valuation based on the structure of yields?

c) Given the valuations in (b), what is each bond's yield to maturity?

d) Do the yields to maturity in (c) differ from each other and from the assumed yield to maturity in (a)?

e) Given the price of bond A in (a), what would you do? Why?

The Financial Advisor's Investment Case

Bonds, Bonds, and More Bonds

Kavita De Falla is an individual with low risk tolerance who has just inherited $100,000. She has no immediate needs for the funds but would like to supplement her current income. Thus, De Falla is considering investing these funds in debt instruments, since the interest and repayment of principal are legal obligations of the issuer. While she realizes that the borrower could default on the payments, she believes this is unlikely, especially if she limits her choices to triple- or double-A-rated bonds. De Falla does realize that she could earn more interest by purchasing lower-rated bonds but is not certain that she is capable of bearing the risk.

Besides risk and expected return, De Falla decides that tax considerations must also play a role in this investment decision. She is currently in the 28 percent federal income tax bracket and pays state income tax of 5 percent. She believes that her job is relatively secure and that her salary will increase over time but does not expect it to rise sufficiently so that her income tax brackets will be significantly increased.

De Falla quickly learned that there are many bonds among which to choose. For example, the PHONE Company has four double-A bonds outstanding. Their annual interest payments (or coupon rate), term to maturity, price, and yield to maturity are

Bond	Interest per $1,000 Bond	Coupon
A	$ 50	5%
B	100	10
C	100	10
D	80	8

Bond	Term	Price	Yield to Maturity
A	1 year	$ 981	7.0%
B	5 years	1,035	9.1
C	10 years	1,000	10.0
D	20 years	742	11.3

Currently the interest rate of long-term debt ranges from 9 to 11.5 percent, but De Falla expects that this rate will fall, as inflation is declining. In addition, the level of unemployment is increasing, so De Falla anticipates that the Federal Reserve will take actions to stimulate the economy through reductions in the rate of interest. She believes that interest rates could fall to 8 percent within a year. Of course, she also realizes that this decline may not occur—or even if it does, that interest rates could rise again after the initial decline. De Falla decided to analyze the four PHONE Company bonds to determine which may be the best investment under various assumptions concerning future interest rate behavior. To do this she sought your help in answering the following questions:

1. a) What would be the expected price of each bond one year from now if interest rates were 8 percent?
    b) What would be the expected price two years from now if interest rates initially fall but subsequently rise to 12 percent at the end of the second year?
2. If interest rates were expected to fall and not rise back to 12 percent, which alternative is best?
3. If interest rates were expected to decline initially and then rise, which alternative should be selected?
4. If bond A were selected, what would happen after a year elapses? What decision must then be made?

The answers to these questions emphasize to De Falla the importance of expected future interest rates on the selection of a bond. Since she firmly believes that interest rates will fall and remain below current levels for several years, she has decided to select bond D, the longest-term bond that would lock in the current high yields. However, she has also decided to consider other bonds to determine what additional returns she could earn for bearing more risk, along with the tax implications of her selections. She has noticed that the following ten-year bonds are available:

Bond	Interest per $1,000	Price	Yield to Maturity	Rating
U.S. Treasury	$ 0	$ 463	8%	—
U.S. Treasury	80	1,000	8	—
WEAK Inc.	140	1,000	14	B
WEAK Inc.	120	896	14	B

At this point De Falla is sufficiently frustrated and asks your advice. As her financial advisor, which bond(s) do you recommend? In your advice, specifically explain the tax implications (both in terms of income and capital gains) of each bond. Also consider her willingness to bear risk and the anticipated flow of income both from the bonds and her job. Then construct a portfolio that you believe meets her needs and willingness to bear risk. Assume that the bonds are sold in units of $1,000 with a minimum purchase of $10,000. Exclude the impact of commissions and accrued interest.

The Financial Advisor's Investment Case
High-Yield Securities and Relative Risk

Stephanie Waldron is an aggressive individual whose career as a self-employed management consultant has blossomed. Waldron is both willing and able to bear substantial risk in order to earn a higher return. She is also very independent, preferring to make her own investment decisions after considering various alternatives. She has a Keogh account that she manages herself. Although she could select various types of mutual funds as investment vehicles for the account, she prefers to select specific assets. The account's value exceeds $200,000, and Waldron recently liquidated several securities whose prices had risen sufficiently so that she believed further price increases to be unlikely.

As her financial planner, you believe that high-yield debt instruments would be an attractive alternative to stocks, whose prices have risen recently. High-yield securities offer larger returns but may involve substantial risk. The combination of high risk and high return are consistent with Waldron's investment philosophy, so she has asked you to suggest several alternative high-yield bonds. The terms of several B-rated bonds are as follows:

Company	Coupon	Maturity Date (Years)	Price	Yield to Maturity
A	10%	10	$ 900	11.75%
B	15	15	1,200	12.055
C	0	7	487	10.825
D	7	10	772	10.847

Waldron is interested in each of the bonds but has several questions concerning their risk. Since each bond has the same rating, it seems reasonable to conclude that the probability of default is about the same for each bond. However, there may be considerable difference in their price volatility. Waldron has asked you to rank each bond from the least to the most price volatile. She also wants you to compare the bonds' price volatility with the triple-A-rated bonds with the same terms to maturity. To do this, you have found four triple-A-rated bonds with the following terms:

Company	Coupon	Maturity Date (Years)	Price	Yield to Maturity
E	6.50%	10	$ 900	7.99%
F	10.5	15	1,200	8.143
G	0	7	587	7.908
H	4.5	10	772	7.879

If interest rates rise by 3 percent across the board, what will be the new price of each of the eight bonds? What do these new prices suggest about the price volatility of high-yield versus high-quality bonds? To answer this last question, compare bond A to bond E, B to F, C to G, and D to H. Which bonds' prices were more volatile? If two bonds with the same term to maturity sell for the same price, which bond may subject the investor to more interest rate risk? Does acquiring bonds with higher credit ratings and less default risk also imply the investor has less interest rate risk?

The Financial Advisor's Investment Case
Risk Reduction through the Active Management of a Bond Portfolio

Fiona Corcoran is responsible for meeting distributions for EEM Health and Life Insurance Company. An actuary, Robert Bjornsund, has forecasted that a specific policy will require $210,000 after ten years. Current interest rates are 8 percent, and RPM Restoration equipment trust certificates (i.e., collateralized bonds) are available for possible investment. Their terms are

Bond A: zero percent coupon with maturity in 10 years,
Bond B: 8 percent coupon with maturity in 10 years,
Bond C: 8 percent coupon with maturity in 18 years.

Bjornsund, who has not been trained in investments, is dubious that the three alternatives will meet the required cash in a timely fashion and asks several questions.

1. What does an equipment trust certificate imply?
2. What is the cost of each bond if it is priced to yield 8 percent?
3. How much will have to be invested in the zero coupon bond to meet the objective?
4. Assuming that the amount determined in (3) is invested in each bond and that yields do not change, will each bond meet the objective? Can the answer be verified?

Corcoran's answers do not satisfy Bjornsund's concerns and he asks the following questions.

5. Can the prices of the bond change?
6. If interest rates rise to 10 percent and remain there for ten years, will each bond meet the objective?
7. If interest rates decline to 5 percent and remain there for ten years, will each bond meet the objective?

Corcoran points out that bond management is not limited to the pricing of bonds and tells Bjornsund that it is also important to know a bond's duration. Duration is important because it reduces interest rate and reinvestment rate risk and facilitates selecting bonds to meet a financial objective.

8. Given the current prices of each bond, what is the duration of each bond?
9. Given the durations, which bonds, if any, will meet the investment objective? Can the answer to this question be verified?
10. What generalization can be drawn from the answers to (8) and (9)?

If you were Corcoran, how would you answer the questions?

Appendix 14A

BOND DISCOUNTS/PREMIUMS AND DURATION COMPARED

The discussion in the body of the chapter explained how increases in interest rates cause the prices of existing bonds to fall. Declining interest rates have the opposite effect; bond prices rise. For bonds with the same coupon, the amount of the price change varies with the term of the bond. The longer the term, the greater is the price fluctuation. The discussion also indicated that longer duration is associated with greater price fluctuations. Since both discussions were concerned with price fluctuations, both were also concerned with risk.

The two concepts, however, are different. Consider the two bonds in Exhibit 14A.1 and illustrated in Figure 14A.1. Both bonds have an 8 percent coupon rate of interest; the difference between the bonds is the term, 10 years and 20 years. The exhibit and figure give the premium or discount and the duration for each bond at different interest rates. At a current rate of 3 percent, both bonds sell for a premium, but the 20-year bond sells for a larger premium. As the current interest rate rises, the prices of both bonds fall. They sell for their face value when the coupon and the current rate of interest are equal at 8 percent. As the market rate of interest continues to rise, both bonds sell for a discount. Both the discount and the premium are larger for the bond with the

EXHIBIT 14A.1 Premiums or (Discounts) and the Durations for 8 Percent Bonds with Terms to Maturity of 10 and 20 Years at Different Rates of Interest

Interest Rate	10-Year Bond		20-Year Bond	
	Premium/(Discount)	Duration	Premium/(Discount)	Duration
3%	$429	7.60	$748	12.65
4	327	7.50	547	12.18
5	234	7.39	377	11.71
6	149	7.29	231	11.23
7	71	7.18	107	10.76
8	0	7.07	0	10.29
9	(65)	6.95	(92)	9.83
10	(125)	6.84	(172)	9.39
11	(179)	6.73	(241)	8.95
12	(229)	6.61	(301)	8.53
13	(275)	6.49	(354)	8.13
14	(318)	6.37	(400)	7.75
.	.	.	.	.
.	.	.	.	.
.	.	.	.	.
20	(511)	5.65	(587)	5.85

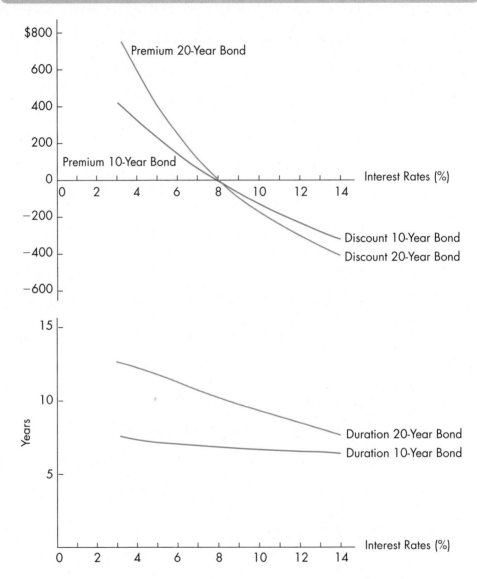

FIGURE   14A.1   Premiums, Discounts, and Durations for 8 Percent Coupon, 10-Year and 20-Year Bonds at Different Rates of Interest

longer term, but the difference between the discounts diminishes as the interest rate continues to rise. Since the maximum possible discount is the face amount of the bond ($1,000), the discount for the bond with the shorter term approaches the discount for the bond with the longer term.

Duration also declines for both bonds as the market interest rate rises. Although the duration for the 10-year bond does decline, the change is small (e.g., from 7.6 to 6.37 years as interest rates rise from 3 to 14 percent). The decline in the duration of the 20-year bond is much larger (e.g., from 12.65 to 7.75 years as interest rates rise from 3 to 14 percent). The duration of the 20-year bond approaches the duration of the bond with the smaller term. At 21.5 percent the durations are equal, and for higher interest rates, the duration of the 20-year bond is actually less than the duration of the 10-year bond.

Exhibit 14A.2 and Figure 14A.2 present the premiums and discounts and the durations for bonds with *different coupons* and 10- and 20-year terms to maturity when the current rate of interest is 8 percent. Exhibit 14A.1 held constant the bond's coupon and varied the rate of interest; Exhibit 14A.2 holds constant the rate of interest and varies the coupon. The bonds with the lower coupons sell for a larger discount, and the longer the term, the greater is the discount. The zero coupon 20-year bond's price is $208 (a discount of $792), while the 10-year bond would sell for $446 and a $554 discount. As the coupon increases, the discount decreases. When the coupon exceeds the current rate of interest, the bond sells for a premium, and the longer the term of the bond, the larger is the premium. For example, the 10- and 20-year bonds with the 12 percent coupons sell for premiums of $272 and $396, respectively.

The coupon also affects each bond's duration. Higher coupons imply that cash is received faster, so the duration declines as the coupon increases. This relationship is also verified in Exhibit 14A.2. While the durations are equal to the term of the bond for the zero coupon bonds, the durations diminish as the coupons increase. As is also indicated in the exhibit, the numerical value of the 20-year bonds' duration declines more rapidly than the duration of the 10-year bonds.

EXHIBIT 14A.2 Premiums or (Discounts) and the Durations When Interest Rates Are 8 Percent for Bonds with Terms to Maturity of 10 and 20 Years at Different Coupons

Interest Rate	10-Year Bond Premium/(Discount)	10-Year Bond Duration	20-Year Bond Premium/(Discount)	20-Year Bond Duration
0%	($554)	10.00	($792)	20.00
2	(407)	8.76	(594)	14.03
3	(340)	8.33	(495)	12.79
4	(272)	7.99	(396)	12.00
5	(204)	7.70	(297)	11.38
6	(136)	7.45	(198)	10.92
7	(68)	7.25	(99)	10.57
8	0	7.07	0	10.29
9	68	6.91	99	10.06
10	136	6.78	198	9.87
11	204	6.65	297	9.71
12	272	6.61	396	9.57
13	340	6.44	495	9.45
14	407	6.35	594	9.34
.	.	.	.	.
.	.	.	.	.
20	815	5.96	1188	8.91

FIGURE 14A.2 Discounts, Premiums, and Durations for 10- and 20-Year Bonds with Different Coupons (Interest Rate = 8 Percent)

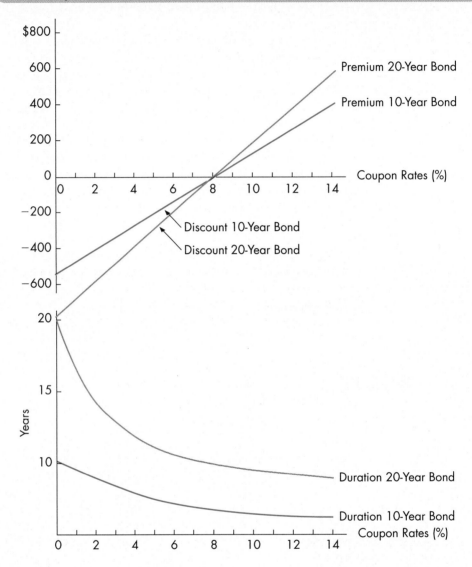

Notice that in both exhibits as the numerical value of the left-hand column increases, that is, the interest rate or the coupon increases, the duration diminishes. Higher interest rates (i.e., lower bond prices and larger discounts) and higher coupons produce smaller durations. The investor is receiving more cash flow earlier, so the duration is smaller. This relation is different than the relationship between the values in the left-hand column and the premium/discount column. Higher interest rates and *lower* coupons produce larger discounts, while smaller interest rates and larger coupons generate *larger* premiums.

Appendix 14B

USING THE STRUCTURE OF YIELDS
TO PRICE A BOND

In the body of this chapter, once the price of a bond is known, the yield to maturity can be determined. That yield is the discount rate that equates the cash inflows (the interest payments and principal repayment at maturity) from the bond and its price (the initial cash outflow). The discussion also illustrated how the price of a bond may be determined. The price of a bond is the present value of all the cash flows discounted back at the appropriate discount factor (i.e., rate of interest).

The use of the yield to maturity to determine that value, however, may misprice the bond. The source of this mispricing is the assumption that the yield to maturity is the appropriate rate to discount all the future payments. For this assumption to apply, the yield curve (the structure of yields) must be flat so that all payments should be discounted at that unique rate, the yield to maturity. (The same assumption was made in the illustrations of the impact of changes in the reinvestment rate on the terminal value. Since all interest payments were reinvested at the same rate, the assumption has to be that the yield curve is flat. That is, the yield is the same for all terms to maturity.)

If the yield curve is positively sloping, then using the yield to maturity to price a bond undervalues the security. Consider a five-year bond with an 8 percent coupon. The structure of yields is as follows:

Term	Interest Rate
1 year	6%
2 years	7
3 years	8
4 years	9
5 years	10

If 10 percent (the yield on a five-year bond) is used to determine the value, the bond is worth $924.18. (PMT = $80; FV = $1,000; N = 5, and I = 10; PV = −$924.18.) Is this valuation accurate? Since the value of a bond is the present value of the cash flows, the value of the first $80 should be discounted at 6 percent. The second, third, and fourth interest payments should be discounted at 7, 8, and 9 percent, respectively. The $1,080 to be received at the end of the fifth year is discounted at 10 percent. What is the present value of these cash inflows, each of which is discounted at a different rate? The answer is $936.13 [$80(0.943) + 80(0.873) + 80(0.794) + 80(0.708) + 1,080(0.621)].

Given the structure of yields, the bond should sell for $936.12 and not the $924.18 determined when 10 percent was used to discount all the cash inflows. If the investor does buy the bond for $936.13, the yield to maturity is 9.67 percent. (PMT = $80, FV = $1,000, N = 5, and PV = −$936.13; I = 9.67.) The actual yield to maturity is less than 10 percent. The use of 10 percent underprices the bond, which overstates its yield.

If the bond did sell for $924.18, an opportunity for an arbitrage profit would exist.[1] The investor buys the bond and strips the coupons (removes the interest payments from the principal). Each of the coupons and the principal are then sold separately as if they were a zero coupon bond. That is, the $80 coupon paid after one year is sold as a one-year zero coupon bond priced to yield 6 percent ($75.47). The second coupon is sold as a two-year zero coupon bond priced to yield 7 percent ($69.88). The third-, fourth-, and fifth-year coupons are sold as three-, four-, and five-year zero coupon bonds. The principal is also sold as a five-year zero coupon bond at 10 percent. What is the value of all these zero coupon bonds? The answer is $936.13, the price of the bond when the structure of yields is used to value the bond. Thus, if an investor could purchase the bond for $924.18 (the value using the yield to maturity based on the bond's term), separate the individual cash payments, and sell each payment as a zero coupon bond, that individual would be assured of a profit. The source of the profit is, of course, the undervaluation of the bond that results from using the yield to maturity to price the bond.

When the yield to maturity is used to determine the value of a bond, all bonds with the same term and risk class (i.e., same credit rating) must have that same yield. This would be true even if the bonds have different coupons. When valuation is based on the structure of yields, bonds with different coupons may have different yields to maturity. Consider two five-year bonds, one of which has a 4 percent coupon and the other a 10 percent coupon. The current structure of yields is as follows:

Term	Interest Rate
1 year	5%
2 years	6
3 years	7
4 years	8
5 years	9

Their valuations based on the structure of yields are $811.72 and $1,054.30, respectively. Given these prices, the yield to maturity for the 4 percent coupon bond is 8.82 percent. (PV = $ −811.72, PMT = $40, FV = $1,000, N = 5; I = 8.82.) The yield to maturity for the 10 percent coupon bond is 8.62 percent. (PV = $ −1,054.3, PMT = $100, FV = $1,000, N = 5; I = 8.62.) The differences in the coupons and the use of the structure of yields to value the bonds result in their having different yields to maturity even though their terms to maturity are the same.

---

[1]Arbitrage is the act of buying in one market and simultaneously selling in another to take advantage of differences in prices between the two markets. It is explained in more detail in the sections on the intrinsic value of an option, put-call parity, and programmed trading and index arbitrage.

CHAPTER 15

Government Securities

During the 2000s, one of the big political issues in Washington was the size of the federal government's deficit. During the later 1990s, the issue was the opposite: what to do with the federal government's surplus. Government deficits occur when disbursements (expenditures) exceed receipts (revenues). Whenever a deficit occurs, someone must finance it. In order to raise funds to cover its deficit, the federal government issues a variety of debt instruments. This variety helps tap different sources of funds that are available in the money and capital markets.

Chapter 13 discussed a variety of corporate debt securities. This chapter extends the discussion to debt securities issued by the federal government, its agencies, and state and municipal governments. Many of the features associated with corporate debt (e.g., interest payments, maturity dates, and call features) apply to government securities. This specific material is not repeated; instead the emphasis is on the features that differentiate government securities from corporate bonds.

The chapter begins with a discussion of the various types of debt securities issued by the federal government. These debt instruments range from EE bonds issued in small denominations to short-term Treasury bills and long-term bonds. The federal government also has created agencies such as the Government National Mortgage Association. These agencies also issue debt securities, whose interest rates generally exceed the rate paid by the bonds of the federal government. The chapter ends with coverage of the debt issued by state and local governments. These bonds, often referred to as "municipal bonds," offer a real alternative to corporation and federal government bonds because they pay interest that is exempt from federal income taxation.

THE VARIETY OF FEDERAL GOVERNMENT DEBT

According to the Economic Report of the President, the federal government made interest payments of $312.6 billion in 2007 on its debt. This sum was substantial and amounted to about 11 percent of the total expenditures made by the federal government in that year. The debt was financed by a variety of investors, including individuals, corporations, and financial institutions. To induce this diverse group of investors to purchase its debt, the federal government has issued different types of debt instruments that appeal to the various potential buyers. (Information concerning the public debt is available through the Treasury's public debt website, http://www.treasurydirect.gov, and includes yields on savings bonds and Treasury bills [as of the auction date], and how the investor may buy these Treasury obligations directly from the federal government.)

For investors, the unique advantage offered by the federal government's debt is its safety. These debt instruments are the safest of all possible investments, for there is no question that the U.S. Treasury is able to pay the interest and repay the principal. The source of this safety is the federal government's constitutional right to tax and to print money. Because there is no specified limitation on the federal government's capacity to create money, only Congress can enact legislation (e.g., the debt ceiling) that restricts the federal government's ability to retire or refinance its debt.

The various types of federal government debt and the amount outstanding of each are illustrated in Exhibit 15.1. As may be seen in the exhibit, there has been an emphasis on the use of short- and intermediate-term (five years or less) financing by the Treasury. This emphasis is partially explained by interest costs. Interest rates on short-term debt are usually lower than those on long-term debt. Hence, the use of short-term financing reduces the Treasury's interest expense. Furthermore, Congress restricts the interest rate that the Treasury may pay on long-term debt, but it does not restrict the interest rate on short-term securities. Thus, during periods of high interest rates, the Treasury may not be permitted to sell long-term securities even if it desires to do so.

Series EE bonds

Savings bonds issued in small denominations by the federal government.

Nonmarketable Federal Government Debt

Perhaps the most widely held federal government debt is the Series EE bonds. Originally Series E bonds were issued in 1941 to help finance World War II. They were sold at a

---

EXHIBIT   15.1   The Variety and Amount of Federal Government Debt as of January 1, 2009

	Length of Time To Maturity	Value (in Billions of Dollars)	Percentage of Total Debt
Treasury bills	Up to 1 year	$ 1,867	17.4%
Intermediate-term bonds	1 to 10 years	2,792	25.9
Long-term bonds	10 or more years	594	5.5
Inflation-protected bonds	various maturities	530	4.9
Savings bonds	various maturities	194	1.8
Other*	various maturities	4,784	44.5
		$10,761	100.0%

*Primarily debt held by U.S. government agencies, trust funds, and state and local governments
Source: Bureau of Public Debt.

discount in small denominations such as $25, $50, and $100, so virtually every person could save and contribute to the war effort.

 On January 2, 1980, the Treasury started to issue Series EE bonds to replace the Series E bonds. In November 1982, the Treasury changed the method for computing interest on EE bonds from a fixed rate to a variable rate, which is changed every six months. (You may find the current rate by dialing 1-800-US BONDS. Additional information concerning E and EE bonds may be obtained from SavingsBonds.com (http://www.savingsbonds.com), which offers a service that provides interest earned, cash-in values, and final maturity dates of all issues of E and EE bonds. The service also tells you which bonds have ceased earning interest.) The variable rate permits the small investor to participate in higher yields when interest rates rise, but you will earn less when interest rates fall.

EE bonds mature after 17 years. If the bonds are not redeemed at maturity, they will continue to earn interest for an additional 13 years, for a total of 30 years. The interest rate is announced every May 1 and November 1 and applies for the following six months. The new rate is 90 percent of an average of the rate paid by five-year Treasury securities for the preceding three months. Interest is added to the value of the bonds every six months after they are purchased.

An important difference between Series EE bonds and other bonds is the lack of a secondary market. If the investor needs immediate cash, the bonds cannot be sold. Instead, they are redeemed at a financial institution such as a commercial bank. Nor can the bonds be transferred as a gift, although they can be transferred through an estate. The Treasury also forbids using EE bonds to secure a loan. Although corporate bonds can be used as collateral, EE bonds cannot.

In addition to EE bonds, the Treasury issued HH bonds. Unlike EE bonds, whose interest accrues and is paid when the bond is redeemed, HH bonds were sold at par and paid interest twice a year. In 1998, the U.S. Treasury started selling a new security, Series I bonds. Over time the new bonds replaced HH bonds, and the Treasury stopped issuing HH bonds in 2004.

Series I bonds are sold in denominations ranging from $50 to $10,000, and the interest rate is set by the Treasury every May and November for the next six months. The interest payment combines a fixed rate and an additional amount based on the Consumer Price Index. Thus, I bonds offer a guaranteed minimum rate plus an adjustment for inflation. (HH bonds paid a fixed rate with no adjustment for inflation.) The maturity date is 20 years after date of issue but may be extended for an additional 10 years, after which interest payments cease. Interest is exempt from state income taxation and may be excluded from federal income tax if the interest is used to pay qualified higher education expenses.

Treasury Bills

Treasury bills

Short-term federal government securities.

Short-term federal government debt is issued in the form of **Treasury bills**. These bills are sold in denominations of $10,000 to $1,000,000 and mature in 3 to 12 months. Like Series EE bonds, they are sold at a discount; however, unlike Series EE bonds, the discounted price is not set. Instead, the Treasury continually auctions off the bills, which go to the highest bidders. For example, if an investor bids $9,700 and obtains the bill, he or she will receive $10,000 when the bill matures, which is a yield of 3.1 percent ($300 ÷ $9,700) for the holding period. If the bid price had been higher, the interest cost to the Treasury (and the yield to the buyer) would have been lower.

Once Treasury bills have been auctioned, they may be bought and sold in the secondary market. They are issued in book-entry form and are easily marketed. There is an active secondary market in these bills, and they are quoted daily in the financial press and many city newspapers. For Treasury bills the quotes are given in the following form:

Maturity	Days to Maturity	Bid	Asked	Ask Yield
12/06/0X	126	3.49	3.47	3.56

These quotes indicate that for a Treasury bill maturing on December 6, 200X, buyers were willing to bid a discounted price that produced a discount yield of 3.49 percent. Sellers, however, were willing to sell (offer) the bills at a smaller discount (higher price) that returned a discount yield of 3.47 percent. The annualized yield on the bill based on the asked price is 3.56 percent.

The reason for the difference between the discount yield and the annualized yield is that Treasury bills are sold at a discount and are quoted in terms of the discount yield. The discount yield is not the same as (nor is it comparable to) the annualized yield on the bill or the yield to maturity on a bond. The discount yield is calculated on the basis of the face amount of the bill and uses a 360-day year. The annualized yield, which is sometimes referred to as the "bond-equivalent yield," depends on the price of the bill and uses a 365-day year.

The difference between the two calculations may be seen in the following example. Suppose a three-month $10,000 Treasury bill sells for $9,800. The *discount yield* (i_d) is

15.1
$$i_d = \frac{\text{Par value} - \text{Price}}{\text{Par value}} \times \frac{360}{\text{Number of days to maturity}}$$

$$\frac{\$10,000 - \$9,800}{\$10,000} \times \frac{360}{90} = 8\%.$$

The *annualized yield* (i_a) is

15.2
$$i_a = \frac{\text{Par value} - \text{Price}}{\text{Price}} \times \frac{365}{\text{Number of days to maturity}}$$

$$\frac{\$10,000 - \$9,800}{\$9,800} \times \frac{365}{90} = 8.277\%.$$

Since the discount yield uses the face amount and a 360-day year, it understates the yield the investor is earning. The discount yield may be converted to the annualized yield by the following equation:

$$i_a = \frac{365 \times i_d}{360 - (i_d \times \text{Days to maturity})}.$$

Thus, if the discount rate on a three-month Treasury bill is 8 percent, the annualized yield is

$$i_a = \frac{365 \times 0.08}{360 - (0.08 \times 90)} = 8.277\%,$$

which is the same answer derived using the annual yield equation.[1]

Treasury bills may be purchased through brokerage firms, commercial banks, and any Federal Reserve bank. These purchases may be new issues or bills that are being traded in the secondary market. Bills with one year to maturity are auctioned once a month. Shorter-term bills are auctioned weekly. If the buyer purchases the bills directly through the Federal Reserve bank, there are no commission fees. Brokers and commercial banks do charge commissions, but the fees are modest compared with those charged for other investment transactions, such as the purchase of stock.

Treasury bills are among the best short-term debt instruments available to investors who desire safety and some interest income. The bills mature quickly, and there are many issues from which the investor may choose. Thus, the investor may purchase a bill that matures when the principal is needed. For example, an individual who has ready cash today but who must make a payment after three months may purchase a bill that matures at the appropriate time. In doing so, the investor puts the cash to work for three months.

Perhaps the one feature that differentiates Treasury bills from all other investments is risk. These bills are considered the safest of all possible investments. There is no question concerning the safety of principal when investors acquire Treasury bills. The federal government always has the capacity to refund or retire Treasury bills because it has the power to tax and the power to create money.

The primary buyers of Treasury bills are corporations with excess short-term cash, commercial banks with unused lending capacity, money market mutual funds, and foreign investors seeking a safe haven for their funds. Individual investors may also purchase them. However, the minimum denomination of $10,000 excludes many savers. Individual investors who desire such safe short-term investments may purchase shares in money market mutual funds that specialize in buying short-term securities, including Treasury bills.

Treasury notes

The intermediate-term debt of the federal government.

Treasury Notes and Bonds

Intermediate-term federal government debt is in the form of **Treasury notes**. These notes are issued in denominations of $1,000 to more than $100,000 and mature in

Calculator Solution

Function Key	Data Input
PV =	−9800
FV =	10000
PMT =	0
N =	.24657
I =	?
Function Key	*Answer*
I =	8.54

---

[1] The annualized yield is a simple (i.e., noncompounded) rate. The determination of the compound rate (i_c) is

$$\$9,800(1 + i_c)^n = \$10,000,$$

in which $n = 90/365$. The solution is

$$\$9,800(1 + i_c)^{90/365} = \$10,000$$

$$(1 + i_c)^{0.2466} = \frac{\$10,000}{\$9,800} = 1.0204.$$

$$i_c = (1.0204)^{4.0556} - 1 = 0.0854 = 8.54\%.$$

Treasury bonds

The long-term debt of the federal government.

one to ten years. **Treasury bonds**, the government's debt instrument for long-term debt, are issued in denominations of $1,000 to $1,000,000, and these bonds mature in more than ten years from the date of issue. Notes and bonds are issued in book-entry and registered forms. These issues are the safest intermediate- and long-term investments available and are purchased by pension funds, financial institutions, or savers who are primarily concerned with moderate income and safety. Since these debt instruments are so safe, their yields are generally lower than that which may be obtained with high-quality corporate debt, such as IBM bonds. For example, in 2009, ExxonMobil bonds that were rated triple A yielded 5.1 percent, while Treasury bonds with approximately the same time to maturity yielded 4.4 percent.

Like Treasury bills, new issues of Treasury bonds may be purchased through commercial banks and brokerage firms. These firms will charge commissions, but the individual may avoid such fees by purchasing the securities from any of the Federal Reserve banks or their branches. Payment, however, must precede purchase, except when the individual pays cash. Unless the individual investor submits a competitive bid, the purchase price is the average price charged institutions that buy the bonds through competitive bidding. By accepting this noncompetitive bid, the individual ensures matching the average yield earned by financial institutions, which try to buy the securities at the lowest price (highest yield) possible.

Once the bonds are purchased, they may be readily resold, as there is an active secondary market in U.S. Treasury bonds. Price quotes, however, are different from the quotes for stock, since Treasury bonds are quoted in 32nds. If a bond were quoted 107:13–107:15, that means the bid price is 107 13/32 and the ask price is 107 15/32. These amounts are $10,740.63 and $10,746.88 per $10,000 face amount of debt.

Treasury bonds are among the safest investments available to investors. As with Treasury bills, there is no question that the federal government can pay the interest and refund its debt, but there are ways in which the holder of Treasury notes and bonds can suffer losses. These debt instruments pay a fixed amount of interest, which is determined when the notes and bonds are issued. The fixed interest means the bonds are subject to interest rate risk. If interest rates subsequently rise, existing issues will not be as attractive, and their market prices will decline. If an investor must sell the debt instrument before it matures, the price will be lower than the principal amount and the investor will suffer a capital loss.

Interest rates paid by Treasury debt have varied over time. The extent of this variation was illustrated by Figure 13.3 in Chapter 13, which showed the yields on Treasury bills and Treasury bonds. Yields also can fluctuate rapidly. For example, yields on three-month Treasury bills changed from a high of 15 percent in March 1980 to 8.7 percent *only two months* later. These fluctuations in yields are due to variations in the supply of and demand for credit in the money and bond markets. As the demand and supply vary, so will the market prices and the yields on all debt instruments, including the debt of the federal government. When demand for bonds becomes strong and exceeds supply at the old prices, bond prices will rise and yields will decline. The reverse occurs when supply exceeds demand: Bond prices decline and yields rise.

An investor may also lose through investments in Treasury debt when the rate of inflation exceeds the interest rate earned on the bonds. For example, during 1974 the yields on government bonds rose to 7.3 percent, but the rate of inflation for consumer goods exceeded 10 percent. The investor then suffered a loss in purchasing power, for interest payments were insufficient to compensate for the inflation.

These two factors, fluctuating yields and inflation, illustrate that investing in federal government debt, like all types of investing, subjects the investor to interest rate risk and purchasing power risk. Therefore, although federal government debt is among the safest of all investments with regard to the certainty of payment of interest and principal, some element of risk still exists.

Foreign investors have the additional risk associated with exchange rates when they purchase U.S. federal government securities. If the value of their currency rises relative to the dollar, then the interest and principal repayment is reduced when the dollars are converted into their currency. However, the value of the dollar could rise, in which case the return on the investment is enhanced. During periods of economic uncertainty in other countries, foreign investors will buy dollars both as a safe haven and for the enhanced return that will occur if their currency declines and the value of the dollar rises.

The Variability of Federal Government Bond Returns

One argument for investing in federal government securities is their safety: the probability of default on interest and principal repayment is nil. However, as was previously discussed, there always exists the possibility of loss from inflation and higher interest rates driving down the price of federal government bonds.

During the 1980s, the returns on federal government bonds became more variable. This increased variability is illustrated in Figure 15.1, which plots the annualized standard deviations of monthly returns for stocks and long-term government bonds for three ten-year time periods: 1950–1959, 1979–1988, and 1993–2002. For the period 1950–1959, the standard deviations of the long bond averaged 4.2 percent and were consistently below the standard deviations of the stock returns. Starting in the late 1970s, the return on the government bonds became much more variable, and the standard deviations of the returns exceeded 20 percent during several years. (The average was 15.3 percent.) The standard deviation of the bond returns even exceeded the standard deviation of the stock returns in 1981, when interest rates rose dramatically and drove down the prices of the bonds.

During the late 1980s, this variability declined. While the standard deviations of the returns did not revert to the levels experienced during the 1950s, they are perceptibly below the levels experienced during 1979–1988. Although 1979–1988 was an aberration, the data suggest that federal government bonds have become riskier as their returns have become more variable.

Zero Coupon Treasury Securities

With the advent of Individual Retirement Accounts (IRAs), corporations started issuing zero coupon bonds. Because the Treasury did not issue such bonds at that time, selected brokerage firms created their own zero coupon Treasury securities. For example, Merrill Lynch created the Treasury Investment Growth Receipt (TIGR, generally

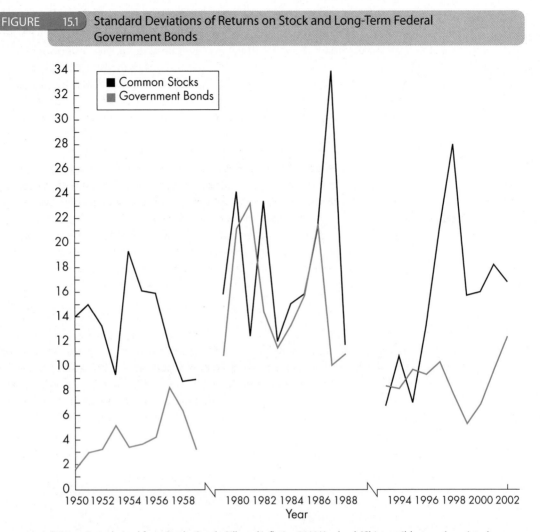

FIGURE   15.1   Standard Deviations of Returns on Stock and Long-Term Federal Government Bonds

Source: Data derived from *Stocks, Bonds, Bills and Inflation 2003 Yearbook* (Chicago: Ibbotson Associates).

referred to as *Tigers*). Merrill Lynch bought a block of Treasury bonds, removed all the coupons, and offered investors either the interest to be received in a specific year or the principal at the bonds' maturity. Since payment was limited to the single payment at the specified time in the future, these Tigers were sold at a discount. In effect, they were zero coupon bonds backed by Treasury securities originally purchased by Merrill Lynch and held by a trustee.

Other brokerage firms created similar securities by removing coupons from existing Treasury bonds. Some of these zero coupon Treasury securities were given clever acronyms, such as Salomon Brothers' CATS (Certificates of Accrual on Treasury Securities). In other cases they were just called Treasury Receipts (T.R.s). In each case, however, the brokerage firm owns the underlying Treasury securities. The actual security purchased by the investor is an obligation of the brokerage firm and not of the federal government.

STRIPS

In 1985, the Treasury introduced its own zero coupon bonds, called STRIPS, for Separate Trading of Registered Interest and Principal Securities. Investors who purchase such STRIPS acquire a direct obligation of the federal government. Since these securities are direct obligations, they tend to have slightly lower yields than Tigers, CATS, and the other zero coupon securities created by brokerage firms.

In any case, the primary appeal of these securities is their use in retirement accounts. The interest earned on a zero coupon bond is taxed as it accrues, even though the holder does not receive annual cash interest payments. Thus, there is little reason to acquire these securities in accounts that are not tax sheltered. They are, however, excellent vehicles for retirement accounts, since all the funds (i.e., principal and accrued interest) are paid in one lump sum at maturity. Because any tax on a retirement account is paid when the funds are withdrawn, the tax disadvantage of zero coupon bonds is circumvented. The investor can purchase issues that mature at a desired date to meet retirement needs. For example, a 40-year-old investor could purchase zero coupon government securities that mature when he or she reaches the age of 65, 66, and so on. Such a laddered bond strategy would ensure that the funds were received after retirement, at which time they would replace the individual's earned income that ceases at retirement.

If the investor does acquire zero coupon bonds, that individual should be aware that these securities have the most price volatility of all federal government bonds. As was discussed in Chapter 14, changing interest rates generate fluctuations in bond prices. The longer the term or the smaller the coupon, the greater is the price fluctuation. Zero coupon bonds make no periodic interest payments; thus, for a given term to maturity, their prices are more volatile than coupon bonds with the same maturity. For example, if interest rates were 8 percent compounded annually, a ten-year zero coupon bond would sell for $463.19, while a ten-year 8 percent coupon bond would sell for $1,000. If interest rates rose to 10 percent, the price of the zero coupon bond would fall to $385.50 for a decline of approximately 17 percent. The price of the 8 percent coupon bond would fall to $877.11 for a decline of approximately 13 percent. If the terms of these bonds had been 20 years, the respective prices at 8 percent would be $214.55 and $1,000 and would fall to $148.64 and $829.73 at 10 percent. Such price declines are approximately 30 and 17 percent.

The reason for a zero coupon bond's increased price volatility in response to changes in interest rates is that the entire return falls on the single payment at maturity. Since the current price of any bond is the present value of the interest and principal payments, the price of a zero coupon bond is solely the result of the present value of the single payment received at maturity. No interest payments will be received during the early years of the bond's life that reduce the responsiveness of the bond's price to changes in interest rates.

This price volatility suggests that zero coupon bonds may well serve a laddered bond strategy and may be excellent candidates for purchase in anticipation of lower interest rates. In the laddered strategy, there is no intention to sell the bond prior to maturity. Instead, the investor expects to collect the payment at the bond's maturity, so price volatility is unimportant. Bond purchases made in anticipation of lower interest rates are made to take advantage of the price increase that would accompany lower rates.

Inflation-Indexed Treasury Securities

inflation-indexed securities

Securities whose principal and interest payments are adjusted for changes in the Consumer Price Index.

In addition to traditional marketable debt instruments, the federal government also issues **inflation-indexed securities**, sometimes referred to as TIPS (Treasury Inflation-Protection Securities). There are two basic types of marketable federal government inflation-indexed debt. The first is notes, which are issued annually on January 15 and July 15 and mature after ten years. The second is the inflation-indexed bond, which is a 30-year security issued every October 15.

Inflation-indexed notes and bonds pay a modest rate of interest plus make an adjustment for changes in the Consumer Price Index (i.e., the rate of inflation). The interest rate is the "real yield" earned by the investor. The adjustment occurs by altering the amount of principal owed by the federal government; *no* adjustment is made in the semiannual interest *rate*. The amount of the change in the principal depends on the current CPI relative to the CPI when the securities were issued. For example, the ten-year notes issued in January 1999 have a real interest rate of 3⅞ percent. The base CPI to be used for determining subsequent changes in the principal is 164. Two years later, in January 2001, the CPI was 174, and the principal was increased by a factor of 1.06098 (174/164). A $1,000 note was increased to $1,060.98. The investor would then receive interest of $41.075 ($1,060.98 × .03875) instead of the $38.75, which was the amount initially earned when the note was issued.[2] Since the principal and the amount of interest received are increased with the rate of inflation, the investor's purchasing power is maintained.

Inflation-indexed bonds appeal to individuals who are primarily concerned that the rate of inflation will increase so that an investment in a traditional, fixed-rate bond will result in a loss of purchasing power. If, for example, the rate of inflation is 2 percent and an investor purchases a 5 percent, ten-year bond and the rate of inflation rises to 6 percent, the interest is insufficient to cover the higher rate of inflation. The purchasing power of the investor's principal is also eroded. If that investor had acquired an inflation-indexed security, the principal owed and the interest earned would rise sufficiently to cover the increased inflation and provide a modest return.

While federal government inflation-indexed notes and bonds are a means to manage purchasing power risk, there are risks associated with an inflation-indexed bond. The fixed, real rate paid by the bonds is less than the nominal rate that could be earned by an investment in a traditional bond. For example, the rate of interest on 20-year bonds in 2004 was 4.8 percent, which was more than the real rate on the inflation-indexed 20-year bond. Of course, if the rate of inflation were to increase, the real return on the traditional note would diminish while the inflation-indexed note would continue to earn its 2 percent real rate. If, however, inflation does not increase, the inflation-indexed security produces an inferior return.

Inflation-indexed federal government notes and bonds are, of course, illustrative of an important trade-off investors must accept. To obtain protection and reduce the risk from inflation, investors may acquire the indexed bonds. If, however, the rate of inflation does not increase, this strategy earns a lower rate of interest. Investors can earn a

[2]This illustration assumes annual interest payments, while the notes (and the bonds) distribute interest semiannually. The index factors for adjusting the principal may be found at **http://www.treasurydirect.gov** under the subhead of inflation-indexed notes and bonds.

higher rate by not acquiring the indexed bonds, but then they bear the risk associated with inflation. Although the traditional bond may generate more current interest income, the investors who acquire them in preference to the indexed bond bear the risk associated with the loss of purchasing power from inflation.

The possibility also exists that the CPI may decline. If deflation were to occur, the inflation-indexed principal would be *reduced*, which decreases the periodic interest payments. If the inflation-adjusted principal were less than the original par value at maturity of the security, the federal government would repay the initial par value. The buyer is assured of receiving the initial amount invested in inflation-indexed securities (when they are issued) if they are held to maturity. Only the periodic interest payments would be reduced.

In addition to these risks, there is a tax disadvantage associated with the federal government's inflation-indexed debt securities. The addition to the principal is considered taxable income even though it is not received until the instrument matures (or is sold). In the preceding example, the principal amount rose from $1,000 to $1,060.89. The $60.89 is taxable income during the two years in which the accretion occurred even though the investor received only interest of 3⅞ percent of the principal value. This tax treatment of the accretion in the principal value may reduce the attractiveness of inflation-indexed notes and bonds except for usage in tax-deferred retirement accounts.

FEDERAL AGENCIES' DEBT

In addition to the debt issued by the federal government, certain agencies of the federal government and federally sponsored corporations issue debt. These debt instruments encompass the entire spectrum of maturities, ranging from short-term securities to long-term bonds. Like many U.S. Treasury debt issues, there is an active secondary market in some of the debt issues of these agencies, and price quotations for many of the bonds are given daily in the financial press.

Several federal agencies have been created to fulfill specific financial needs. For example, the Banks for Cooperatives were organized under the Farm Credit Act. These banks provide farm business services and make loans to farm cooperatives to help purchase supplies. The Federal Home Loan Mortgage Corporation was established to strengthen the secondary market in residential mortgages insured by the Federal Housing Administration. This federal corporation buys and sells home mortgages to give them marketability and thus increase their attractiveness to private investors. The Student Loan Marketing Association was created to provide liquidity to the insured student loans made under the Guaranteed Student Loan Program by commercial banks, savings and loan associations, and schools that participate in the program. This liquidity should expand the funds available to students from private sources.

federal agency bonds
Debt issued by an agency of the federal government.

moral backing
Nonobligatory support for a debt issue.

Federal agency bonds are not issued by the federal government and are not the debt of the federal government. Hence, they tend to offer higher yields than those available on U.S. Treasury debt. However, the bonds are extremely safe because they have government backing. In some cases, this is only **moral backing**, which means that in case of default the federal government does not have to support the debt (i.e., to pay the interest and meet the terms of the indenture). Some of the debt issues, however, are *guaranteed* by the U.S. Treasury. Should these issues go into default, the federal government is legally required to assume the obligations of the debt's indenture.

The matter of whether the bonds have the legal or the moral backing of the federal government is probably academic. All these debt issues are excellent credit risks, because it is doubtful that the federal government would let the debt of one of its agencies go into default. Since these bonds offer slightly higher yields than those available on U.S. Treasury debt, the bonds of federal agencies have become attractive investments for conservative investors seeking higher yields. This applies not only to individual investors who wish to protect their capital but also to financial institutions, such as commercial banks, insurance companies, or credit unions, which must be particularly concerned with the safety of the principal in making investment decisions.

Federal agency debt can be purchased by individuals, but few individual investors do own these bonds, except indirectly through pension plans, mutual funds, and other institutions that own the debt. Many individual investors are probably not even aware of the existence of this debt and the potential advantages it offers. Any investor who wants to construct a portfolio with an emphasis on income and the relative safety of the principal should consider these debt instruments.

Ginnie Mae Securities

Ginnie Mae

Mortgage pass-through bond issued by the Government National Mortgage Association.

One of the most important and popular debt securities issued by a government agency and supported by the federal government is the **Ginnie Mae**, a debt security issued by the Government National Mortgage Association (GNMA or Ginnie Mae), a division of the Department of Housing and Urban Development (HUD). The funds raised through the sale of Ginnie Mae securities are used to acquire a pool of FHA/VA guaranteed mortgages. (FHA and VA are the Federal Housing Administration and Department of Veterans Affairs, respectively.) The mortgages are originated by private lenders, such as savings and loan associations and other savings institutions, and packaged into securities that are sold to the general public and guaranteed by GNMA. The minimum size of the individual Ginnie Mae securities sold to the public is $25,000.[3]

To understand how a Ginnie Mae (or any mortgage-backed security) works, it is necessary to understand the payments generated by a mortgage. This process is illustrated in Exhibit 15.2. The individual buys a house with a down payment and finances the balance of the cost of the house through a mortgage. The homeowner makes periodic equal payments that cover the interest and retire the principal. The amount of the payment is fixed when the mortgage is granted. In Exhibit 15.2 the mortgage loan is $150,000; the interest rate is 8 percent; and the term of the mortgage is 25 years (300 months). Each monthly payment is $1,157.72, which consists of an interest payment and a principal repayment. The first column of the table gives the number of payment. These range from 1 to 300 because the loan requires 12 monthly payments for 25 years for a total of 300 payments. The second column presents the interest payment, and the third column gives the amount of principal repayment. The balance of the loan

---

[3]Individuals with less to invest may acquire shares in a mutual fund that invests in mortgage-backed securities. Since Ginnie Maes convert an illiquid asset (a mortgage loan) into a marketable security, they are an illustration of securitization. Few investors are willing to hold a mortgage, because mortgage notes are difficult to sell. A Ginnie Mae, however, may be readily sold. The effect, then, is to convert an illiquid asset into a marketable asset. See the discussion of securitization in Chapter 13.

EXHIBIT 15.2	Selected Payments from a Repayment Schedule for a $150,000 Mortgage Loan at 8 Percent for 25 years (Monthly Payment: $1,157.72)

Number of Payment	Interest Payment	Principal Repayment	Balance of Loan
1	$1,000.00	$157.72	$149,842.28
2	998.95	158.78	149,683.50
3	997.89	159.83	149,523.67
—	—	—	—
—	—	—	—
—	—	—	—
148	738.84	418.89	110,407.01
149	736.05	421.68	109,985.33
150	733.24	424.49	109,560.84
—	—	—	—
—	—	—	—
—	—	—	—
298	22.85	1,134.88	2,292.50
289	15.28	1,142.44	1,150.06
300	7.67	1,150.06	0.00

is given in the last column. Since the amount of interest is determined on the balance owed, the amount of interest remitted with each payment declines, and the amount of the payment used to retire the principal rises. For example, the amount of interest in the third payment is $997.89, but in payment number 148, interest is $738.84. Since the amount of interest declines, the principal repayment increases from $159.83 in payment number 3 to $418.89 in payment number 148. Payments during the early years of the mortgage loan primarily cover the interest owed, but payments near the end of the life of the loan primarily reduce the balance of the loan.

The periodic payment required to cover the interest and retire the loan is determined through the use of present value calculations presented in Chapter 3. The following simple example illustrates this calculation. An individual borrows $10,000 for ten years and agrees to make annual payments that retire the loan and pay 12 percent interest on the declining balance owed.[4] What is the annual payment? The answer is

$$\$10,000 = \frac{PMT}{(1 + 0.12)^1} + \cdots + \frac{PMT}{(1 + 0.12)^{10}}.$$

Calculator Solution

Function Key	Data Input
PV =	10000
FV =	0
PMT =	?
N =	10
I =	12
Function Key	Answer
PMT =	−1,769.84

Since the periodic payments will be equal, this equation may be solved by the use of the present value of an annuity table. The problem collapses to

$$\$10,000 = PMT \text{ times the interest factor for the present value}$$
$$\text{of an annuity of \$1 at 12\% for 10 years,}$$

$$\$10,000 = PMT(5.650),$$

$$PMT = \frac{\$10,000}{5,650} = \$1,769.91.$$

---

[4]Mortgage rates are currently considerably less than the 12 percent in the example. The 12 percent, however, facilitates the illustration in footnote 5, which illustrates using interest tables to construct a monthly mortgage payment.

Annual payments of $1,769.91 for ten years will retire the loan and pay 12 percent on the declining balance owed.[5]

Ginnie Mae securities serve as a conduit through which the interest and principal repayments are received from the homeowners and distributed to investors. The investor acquires part of the Ginnie Mae pool. As interest and principal repayments are made to the pool, the funds are channeled to the Ginnie Mae's owners. The investor receives a monthly payment that is his or her share of the principal and interest payments received by the pool. Since payments to the pool vary from month to month, the amount received by the investors also varies monthly. Thus, a Ginnie Mae is one example of a long-term debt instrument whose periodic payments are not fixed. (See the mortgage problems at the end of this chapter.)

Ginnie Mae securities have become popular with investors financing retirement or accumulating funds in retirement accounts. The reason for their popularity is safety, since the federal government insures the payment of principal and interest. Thus, if a mortgage payer were to default, the federal government would make the required payments. This guarantee virtually assures the timely payment of interest and principal to the holder of the Ginnie Mae.

In addition to safety, Ginnie Maes offer higher yields than federal government securities. Since the yields are ultimately related to the mortgages acquired by the pool, they depend on mortgage rates rather than on the yields of federal government bills and bonds. This yield differential can be as great as 2 percentage points (usually referred to as 200 basis points) over the return offered by long-term federal government bonds.

Ginnie Mae securities are also useful to investors seeking a regular flow of payments, since interest and principal repayments are distributed monthly. The mortgage repayment schedules define the minimum amount of the anticipated payments. However, if the homeowners speed up payments or pay off their loans before the full term of the mortgage, the additional funds are passed on to the holder of the Ginnie Mae securities.

These securities are supported by the full faith and credit of the federal government, but there are risks associated with Ginnie Maes. One is the loss of purchasing power through inflation. Of course, investors will not purchase Ginnie Maes if the anticipated yield is less than the anticipated rate of inflation.

Even if the anticipated return is sufficient to justify the purchase, investors could still lose if interest rates rise. All the mortgages in a particular pool have the same

---

[5]This illustration is an oversimplification because interest payments (at least on a mortgage) are generally made monthly and not annually. Adjustments may be made to determine monthly payments. Divide the interest rate by 12 months and multiply the number of periods by 12. In this case, that is

$$\$10,000 = \frac{PMT}{\left(1 + \frac{0.12}{12}\right)} + \cdots + \frac{PMT}{\left(1 + \frac{0.12}{12}\right)^{10\times12}}$$

$10,000 = x$ times the interest factor for the present value of an annuity of $1 at 1 percent for 120 time periods

$10,000 = x(69.698)$

$x = \$143.48$.

The monthly payment is $143.48 and is not $1,769.91 divided by 12 months ($147.49). Since the loan is being retired more rapidly (i.e., every month the principal is reduced), the effect is to reduce the total amount of interest paid and thus decrease the total monthly payment to $143.48 instead of $147.49.

This example also illustrates the limitation of using interest tables, which have a limited number of percentages and time periods. Financial calculators permit the use of any interest rate and time period. For example, the payment on a $10,000 loan at 7.35 percent for 11.5 years is $1,318.06 annually, or $107.56 monthly.

Calculator Solution

Function Key	Data Input
PV =	10000
FV =	0
PMT =	?
N =	120
I =	1
Function Key	Answer
PMT =	−143.47

Point of Interest

THE VARIETY OF MORTGAGE TERMS

As is illustrated in Exhibit 15.2, the conventional mortgage consists of monthly payments that cover the interest and reduce the principal. There are, however, many variations on that basic pattern of payments. An "adjustable-rate mortgage" or "ARM" substitutes a variable rate for a fixed rate. As interest rates change, the rate on the mortgage changes. For example, the rate may change 0.5 percent each year with a limit of 2.5 percent over the lifetime of the loan. If the borrower obtains a loan at 6 percent, the rate could rise as high as 8.5 percent. Another variation is the "graduated payment" mortgage. Under this type of mortgage, the amount of the payment is not fixed (although the rate of interest may be fixed) but it rises over the lifetime of the loan. This type of loan can be disastrous if the borrower's income does not rise sufficiently to cover the increased cost of the mortgage.

A "two-step mortgage" combines the conventional and the adjustable-rate mortgage. During the initial period, the rate is fixed, but after a period of time such as five years, the interest rate is changed. Another version is the "renegotiable mortgage" in which the terms are renegotiated at specific intervals. Although the term of the mortgage may be 25 years, the lender may renegotiate the interest rate. If interest rates rise, the borrower is forced to pay the higher, current rate of interest. There are even mortgages in which the borrower pays only the interest for a period of time before principal payments must be made.

Such variations certainly increase the risk associated with the loans, since economic conditions may change and reduce the borrower's capacity to service the loan, especially those mortgages whose payments increase over time. (This problem is compounded when the borrower does not understand the implications of the various terms.) The variety of terms also makes valuing a mortgage difficult. As is often discussed in this text, valuation is the process of discounting future cash inflows back to the present. Even without default by the borrowers, the various mortgage terms makes estimating future cash inflows difficult. For this reason, two investors may determine perceptibly different values for the same mortgage.

interest rate, and since Ginnie Maes are fixed-income debt securities, their prices fluctuate with interest rates. Higher interest rates will drive down their prices. Thus, if an investor were to seek to sell the security in the secondary market (and there is an active secondary market in Ginnie Maes), he or she could sustain a capital loss resulting from the rise in interest rates. Of course, the investor could experience a capital gain if interest rates were to decline, thus causing the security's value to rise.

The last source of risk concerns the reinvestment rate, which reduces the certainty of the monthly payments. Homeowners can (and do) repay their mortgage loans prematurely. This occurs when individuals move and sell their homes and when interest rates fall. Lower rates encourage homeowners to refinance their mortgages (i.e., obtain new mortgages at the current, lower rate and pay off the old, higher-rate mortgages). Since the old loans are retired, the owners of the Ginnie Mae receive larger principal repayments but can relend the funds only at the current, lower rate of interest. The opposite would occur if interest rates rise. Homeowners will not refinance and prepayments will decline, so the holder of the Ginnie Mae receives lower principal repayments.

This uncertainty of the timing of payments affects the valuation of Ginnie Mae securities. Pricing Ginnie Maes is essentially the same as any other bond: The interest and principal repayments are discounted back to the present at the current rate of interest. Because of reinvestment rate risk, the amount of each principal payment is not certain. If a large number of homeowners rapidly pay off their mortgages, the payments will quickly retire the Ginnie Maes. (This disadvantage associated with Ginnie Maes may be reduced by acquiring collateralized mortgage obligations [CMOs], which are discussed later.)

This uncertainty of future payments can lead to differences in the estimated yields. Consider a Ginnie Mae that has an expected life of 12 years[6] and that is currently selling for a discount (which could result if interest rates rose after this Ginnie Mae pool had been assembled and sold). In such a case, the price of the Ginnie Mae would decline so that the anticipated yield is comparable with securities currently being issued. For the Ginnie Mae selling at a discount, the yield would depend on the flow of interest payments and how *rapidly the mortgage loans are paid off.*

If the mortgages are paid off more rapidly than expected (i.e., if the life of the pool is less than the expected 12 years), the realized return will be higher because the discount will be erased more rapidly. However, if the mortgages are retired more slowly, the realized return will be less than the expected return. Thus it is possible that the actual yield may differ from the yield assumed when the security was purchased. This makes it possible for two dealers to assert different yields for the same Ginnie Mae sold at the same discounted price. If one dealer assumes that the mortgage loans will be retired more quickly, a higher yield is anticipated. However, another dealer may make a more conservative assumption as to the rate at which the mortgages will be retired.

The speed with which the mortgages are paid off depends in part on the interest rates being paid on mortgage loans. If the Ginnie Mae mortgage loans have relatively high rates, homeowners will seek to refinance these loans when rates decline, so the original mortgages are retired rapidly. The opposite holds when the rates on the Ginnie Maes' mortgage loans are lower than current interest rates. In this case, there is little incentive for early retirement, which will tend to extend the life of the mortgage pool. Thus, a Ginnie Mae that sells for a discount because the mortgage loans have lower interest rates will tend to have a longer life than a Ginnie Mae selling at a premium because its mortgage loans have a higher rate of interest.

The investor who purchases a Ginnie Mae security should be aware that the payment received represents both earned interest income and return of invested funds. If the investor spends all the payment, that individual is depleting his or her principal. Thus the investor should be fully aware that the individual payments received are composed of both interest and principal repayment and that the latter should be spent only if there is reason for the investor to consume the principal.

Collateralized Mortgage Obligations (CMOs)

While Ginnie Maes are supported by the federal government so the investor knows that the interest and principal will be paid, the amount of each monthly payment is unknown. Because principal repayments vary as homeowners refinance their homes, the amount of principal repayment received by the investor changes every month. This variation in the monthly cash flow may be a disadvantage to any individual (e.g., a retiree) seeking a reasonably certain flow of monthly cash payments.

---

[6] Although the maturity of a Ginnie Mae may be 25 to 30 years, the average life (according to the Government National Mortgage Association) is 12 years.

⊕ Point of Interest

POINT

"Heads I win; tails you lose." That saying may appropriately describe *points,* which many financing institutions charge to grant a mortgage loan. These points are in addition to other costs associated with buying a home, such as a mortgage application fee, lawyers' fees to transfer title, surveying, and title insurance.

Points are expressed as a percentage of the mortgage loan. Two points means that 2 percent is added to the amount being borrowed. If the home owner requests a loan for $100,000, the cost of the loan is increased by $2,000. This money is paid to the lending institution up front. If the home owner does not have the $2,000, he or she will have to borrow an additional $2,000 to cover the points. This effectively increases the cost of the loan, since the individual does not have the use of the entire $102,000 that has been borrowed.

Points charged by lending institutions vary. One lender may offer the loan for 8 percent plus one point while a competing lender may offer the loan for 7.5 percent plus two points. The differences in the interest rates and the points increase the difficulty in comparing the loans. Points may also be tax deductible (if the individual itemizes), which further complicates the analysis.

If the individual anticipates living in the home for a short period (e.g., less than five years) before selling, accepting the loan with the higher interest rate and lower points is usually preferable. The anticipation of lower interest rates and the possibility of refinancing also argues for accepting the higher interest and lower points alternative. If, however, the individual expects to be paying the mortgage over many years (i.e., not moving or refinancing), then accepting the lower interest rate and paying the higher points is a better option. Over the extended number of years, the lower interest costs will tend to more than offset the higher points.

---

collateralized mortgage obligation (CMO)

Debt obligation supported by mortgages and sold in series.

tranche

Subdivision of a bond issue.

A **collateralized mortgage obligation (CMO)** reduces, but does not erase, this uncertainty. Collateralized mortgage obligations are backed by a trust that holds Ginnie Mae and other federal government-supported mortgages. When a CMO is created, it is subdivided into classes (called **tranches**). For example, a $100 million CMO may be divided into four tranches of $25 million each. The principal repayments received by the CMO are initially paid to the first class until that tranche has been entirely retired. Once the first tranche has been paid off, mortgage principal repayments are directed to the holders of the CMOs in the second tranche. This process is repeated until all the tranches have been repaid.

Within a tranche, principal repayments may be made on a pro rata basis or by lottery. Whether a pro rata or a lottery system is used to determine repayment is specified in the CMO's indenture; thus, investors know which system applies to a particular CMO. In either case, no principal repayments are made to the next tranche until all the funds owed the first tranche are paid.

This pattern of payment is illustrated by the following CMO with four tranches. Each tranche consists of a $200,000 loan ($800,000 total outstanding), $100,000 of which is retired each year. Interest is paid annually on the amount of the loan outstanding in each tranche. The rate of interest varies with the expected life of each tranche. The interest rates start at 7 percent for tranche A and rise to 10 percent for tranche D. For accepting later repayment of principal, the investor can expect to earn a higher interest rate. The tranche with the shortest expected life earns the lowest interest rate, while the one with the longest expected life earns the highest rate.

The annual payments to each tranche are as follows if the anticipated payment schedules are made:

| | Tranche Payment | | | | | | | |
| | A | | B | | C | | D | |
Year	Interest	Principal	Interest	Principal	Interest	Principal	Interest	Principal
1	$14,000	$100,000	$16,000	$0	$18,000	$0	$20,000	$0
2	7,000	100,000	16,000	0	18,000	0	20,000	0
3	0	0	16,000	100,000	18,000	0	20,000	0
4	0	0	8,000	100,000	18,000	0	20,000	0
5	0	0	0	0	18,000	100,000	20,000	0
6	0	0	0	0	9,000	100,000	20,000	0
7	0	0	0	0	0	0	20,000	100,000
8	0	0	0	0	0	0	10,000	100,000

This schedule indicates that tranche D is a loan for $200,000 at 10 percent, so the annual interest payment is $20,000 for the first 7 years and $10,000 in year 8. Repayment of principal does not occur until all the preceding tranches are retired. Under the anticipated schedule, the principal repayments of $100,000 occur in years 7 and 8, which is why the interest payment is $10,000 instead of $20,000 in year 8.

Over the eight years, the borrower pays a total of $326,000 in interest for the use of the funds and retires the $800,000 loan. While the owners of the different tranches receive different interest rates, the borrower pays the same rate on the entire loan. The trustee structures the tranches to coincide with the loan payments. In this illustration, the borrower's repayment schedule is as follows:

Year	Principal Owed at the End of the Year	Interest Payment	Principal Repayment
0	$800,000		
1	700,000	$ 72,448	$100,000
2	600,000	63,392	100,000
3	500,000	54,336	100,000
4	400,000	45,280	100,000
5	300,000	36,224	100,000
6	200,000	27,168	100,000
7	100,000	18,112	100,000
8	0	9,056	100,000
		$326,016	

The rate of interest on the loan is 9.056 percent on the declining balance. (The 9.056 percent is a forced number. Generally, the terms of the loan are established and the trustee constructs the tranches to match the borrower's payments. Since the purpose of this example is to illustrate the payments to the tranches, the loan is being forced to approximate the payments to the investors.)

The total interest paid by the borrower is $326,016, and the interest payments approximate those received by the tranches. Notice that the borrower's interest rate of

9.056 percent applies to the entire $800,000 loan, while each tranche receives a different rate of interest. In effect, the early tranches subsidize the later tranches. Investors in the early tranches accept a lower rate for a more rapid repayment of principal, while the investors who acquire the longer tranches accept later payments in order to earn a higher rate of interest. The borrower's payments, however, do not make this distinction. The trustee who makes the loan to the borrower establishes the tranches and converts the borrower's debt obligation into a series of securities that different investors with different financial needs find acceptable.

When an investor purchases a CMO, an estimated *principal repayment window* is known. As in the preceding illustration, the schedule gauges when the investor can expect to receive principal repayments and when a particular tranche will be entirely redeemed. As with Ginnie Mae payments, the CMO payment schedule is based on historical repayment data, but the actual timing of the repayments cannot be known with certainty. Lower interest rates will tend to speed up payments as homeowners refinance, while higher interest rates will tend to retard principal repayments.

Since the actual timing of principal repayment is not known, CMOs reduce but do not erase this source of risk. However, less timing risk exists with CMOs than with a Ginnie Mae. When the investor acquires a Ginnie Mae, the repayments are spread over the life of the entire issue. With a CMO, the repayments are spread over each tranche. The investor who acquires a CMO can better match the anticipated need for cash. For example, a 65-year-old retiree may have less immediate need for cash than an 80-year-old. The latter may acquire the first tranche, while the former acquires the third tranche within a CMO. The 65-year-old would receive the current interest component but the principal repayment would be deferred until the first and second tranches were entirely retired.

STATE AND LOCAL GOVERNMENT DEBT

State and local governments also issue debt to finance capital expenditures, such as schools or roads. The government then retires the debt as the facilities are used. The funds used to retire the debt may be raised through taxes (e.g., property taxes) or through revenues generated by the facilities themselves.

Unlike the federal government, state and local governments do not have the power to create money. These governments must raise the funds necessary to pay the interest and retire the debt, but the ability to do so varies with the financial status of each government. Municipalities with wealthy residents or valuable property within their boundaries are able to issue debt more readily and at lower interest rates because the debt is safer. The tax base in these communities is larger and can support the debt.

municipal (tax-exempt) bond

A bond issued by a state or one of its political subdivisions whose interest is not taxed by the federal government.

The Tax Exemption

The primary factor that differentiates state and local government debt from other forms of debt is the tax advantage that it offers to investors. The interest earned on state and municipal government debt is exempt from federal income taxation. Hence, these bonds are frequently referred to as **tax-exempt** or **municipal bonds**. Although state and local governments may tax the interest, the federal government may not. The rationale for this tax exemption is legal and not financial. The Supreme Court ruled that the federal government does not have the power to tax the interest paid by the debt of state and municipal governments. Since the interest paid by all other debt, including corporate bonds, is subject to federal income taxation, this exemption is advantageous to state and local governments, for they are able to issue debt with substantially lower interest rates.

Investors are willing to accept a lower return on state and local government debt because the after-tax return is equivalent to higher yields on corporate debt. For example, if an investor is in the 28 percent federal income tax bracket, the return after taxes is the same for a corporate bond that pays 10 percent as for a state or municipal government bond that pays 7.2 percent: The after-tax return is 7.2 percent in either case.

The willingness of investors to purchase state and local government debt instead of corporate and U.S. Treasury debt is related to their income tax bracket. If an investor's federal income tax rate is 28 percent, a 4.5 percent nontaxable municipal bond gives the investor the same yield after taxes as a 6.25 percent corporate bond, the interest of which is subject to federal income taxation. The individual investor may determine the equivalent yields on tax-exempt bonds and nonexempt bonds by using the following equation:

15.3
$$i_c(1 - t) = i_m,$$

in which i_c is the interest rate paid on corporate debt, i_m is the interest rate paid on municipal debt, and t is the individual's tax bracket (i.e., the marginal tax rate). This equation is used as follows. If an investor's tax bracket is 28 percent and tax-exempt bonds offer 4.5 percent, then the equivalent corporate yield is

$$i_c(1 - 0.28) = 0.045$$

$$i_c = \frac{0.045}{0.72} = 6.25\%.$$

If the investor lives in a state that taxes income, Equation 15.3 may be modified to include the impact of the local tax. Equation 15.4 includes the impact of the federal income tax rate (t_f) and the state and/or local income tax rate (t_s):

15.4
$$i_c(1 - t_f - t_s) = i_m.$$

If the investor's federal income tax bracket is 25 percent and the state income tax bracket is 6 percent, then a high-yield, low-quality bond offering 10 percent has an inferior after-tax yield to a local municipal bond offering more than 6.9 percent $(10\% [1 - 0.25 - 0.06] = 6.9\%)$.

Exempting the interest on these bonds from federal income taxation has been criticized because it is an apparent means for the "rich" to avoid federal income taxation. Since the minimum denomination for municipal bonds is $5,000 and dealers may require larger purchases (e.g., $25,000), individuals with modest amounts to invest are excluded from this market except through investing in mutual funds that invest in tax-exempt bonds. The exemption does, however, reduce the interest cost for the state and municipal governments that issue debt, which in effect subsidizes those governments. From an economic point of view, the important question is whether the exemption is the best means to aid state and local governments. Other means, such as federal revenue sharing, could be used for this purpose. Thus, the interest exemption is primarily a political question. Changes in the legal structure may alter the tax exemption in the future.

Until that time, however, the interest on state and municipal debt remains exempt from federal income taxation, with the effects being that (1) state and local governments can issue debt with interest rates that are lower than those individuals and corporations must pay, and (2) these bonds offer the wealthier members of our society a means to obtain tax-sheltered income.

Although state and local government debt interest is tax-exempt at the federal level, it may be taxed at the state level. States do exempt the interest paid by their own local governments but tax the interest paid by other states and their local governments. Interest earned on New York City obligations is not taxed in New York, but it is taxed in New Jersey. While New Jersey taxes the interest earned on New York City obligations, it exempts interest earned on New Jersey municipal bonds.

It should also be noted that state and local governments cannot tax the interest paid by the federal government. While interest earned on series EE bonds and Treasury bills, notes, and bonds is taxed by the federal government, this interest cannot be taxed by state and local governments. In states with modest or no income taxes, this exemption is meaningless. However, in states with high income taxes, such as Massachusetts or New York, this tax exemption may be a major reason for acquiring U.S. Treasury securities. For example, the yield on a Treasury bill on an after-tax basis may exceed the yield on a federally insured certificate of deposit or the yield offered by a money market mutual fund. In such cases, the tax laws will certainly encourage the investor to acquire the federal security, because that investor has both a higher after-tax yield and less risk (i.e., the full faith and credit of the federal government).

Yields on Municipal Bonds

Like the yields on other debt securities, the yields on tax-exempt bonds have varied over time. Figure 15.2 shows the average yields on municipal bonds rated Aaa and Baa by Moody's for the period 1990 to January 2009. From 1990 to 2007, the yields on Aaa bonds ranged from over 7 percent to less than 4 percent. These yields, however, are considerably less than the 12 percent on Aaa bonds and the 14 percent on Baa bonds experienced during 1982. In addition to showing the fluctuation in yields, the figure shows the difference or spread in yields. As would be expected, the yields on the Baa-rated bonds exceeded those on the Aaa-rated bonds. Although this spread does vary, it was relatively stable until the 2008 financial crisis. During 2008, the spread rose from less than 1 percent (100 basis points) to over 2 percent (200 basis points) at the beginning of 2009.

A similar pattern applies to the yields on Aaa-rated municipal bonds and U.S. Treasury long-term bonds. Generally, the yields on taxable federal government bonds exceed the yields on nontaxable municipal bonds. Over time this differential has diminished as lower federal income tax rates reduced the attractiveness of municipal bonds relative to federal government bonds. There have been periods when the nontaxable municipal bonds offered higher yields. Recent proposals to raise federal income tax rates may, however, increase the attractiveness of these bonds, which should increase their prices and lower their yields.

Any change in the attractiveness of one type of bond relative to another type points out that the yields and prices on bonds ultimately depend on the demand for and supply of the various types of bonds. If many state and local governments seek credit and issue

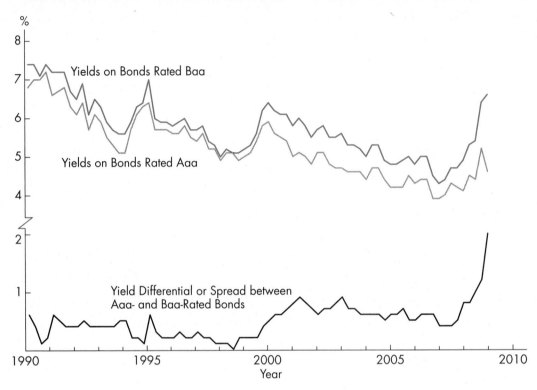

FIGURE 15.2 Average Yields and the Spread between Aaa- and Baa-Rated Municipal Bonds (January 1990–2009)

Source: *Mergent's Bond Record*, various issues.

bonds, the yields on tax-exempt bonds will rise. In addition, changes in the conditions in the financial markets and changes in income tax rates will also affect demand and hence change bond prices and yields.

Of course, an increase in demand means the prices of existing bonds must rise and their yields must fall. Conversely, a decrease in demand implies higher prices and lower yields. The equations used to determine the price of a bond and its yield also apply to the valuation of municipal and state bonds. Like corporate debt, these bonds can sell at a discount or for a premium, depending on the direction of change in interest rates. Hence, investors in tax-exempt bonds bear the same risk associated with fluctuations in interest rates.

general obligation bond

A bond whose interest does not depend on the revenue of a specific project; government bonds supported by the full faith and credit of the issuer (i.e., authority to tax).

Types of Tax-Exempt Securities

State and local governments issue a variety of debt instruments; these can be classified either according to the means by which the security is supported or according to the length of time to maturity (i.e., short- or long-term). State and municipal debt is supported by either the taxing power of the issuing government or the revenues generated by the facilities that are financed by the debt. If the bonds are secured by the taxing power, the debt is a **general obligation** of the government.

⊕ Point of Interest

COPs

In addition to general obligation and revenue bonds and notes issued in anticipation of taxes and other revenues, some municipalities have sold *certificates of participation* (COPs). COPs are issued to finance specific projects (e.g., equipment such as police vehicles, correction facilities, or administrative buildings) that are subsequently leased to the municipality. The rental payments cover the debt-service payments to the holders of the certificates. The municipal government is not responsible for payments to the investors who purchase the COPs; the municipality only makes the lease or rental payments.

COPs are often issued by governments seeking to circumvent limits on their ability to issue debt or to avoid having to obtain voter approval to sell debt. Since the government makes lease payments and not interest and principal repayments, the debt is not considered an obligation of the government. This exclusion of the debt from the municipality's balance sheet understates its obligations.*

The removal also increases the investor's risk. Unlike the required interest and principal repayment of general obligation bonds, there is no assurance the government will allocate the funds to make the lease payments. Legislative

bodies in Brevard County, Florida, and Florence, South Carolina, have threatened to withhold the lease payments. Without such appropriations, payments to the investors would not be made and the COPs would go into default. While such a default has not occurred, any default on a specific certificate could affect all COPs and lead to their downgrading by the rating services. This increased risk associated with COPs results in their offering higher yields (from 0.1 to 0.5 percentage points) than are available through traditional municipal bonds of the same credit rating.

*An analogous situation applies to firms that lease plant and equipment. However, corporate accounting may require that the firm *capitalize* the lease. That is, the corporation must determine the present value of the lease obligation and put that amount on its balance sheet as a long-term obligation. In effect, the lease obligation is acknowledged as an alternative to a bond. Both require periodic payments, and both increase the financial risk associated with the firm.

Managements that do not want the lease obligation to appear on the firm's balance sheet must be certain that the terms of the lease do not meet the accounting requirements that cause the lease to be capitalized. Even if the lease obligation does not have to be capitalized, it must be disclosed in a footnote to the firm's accounting statements.

revenue bond

A bond whose interest is paid only if the debtor earns sufficient revenue.

A bond supported by the revenue generated by the project being financed with the debt is called a **revenue bond**. Revenue bonds are issued to finance particular capital improvements, such as a toll road that generates its own funds. As these revenues are collected, they are used to pay the interest and retire the principal.

General obligation bonds are safer than revenue bonds, since the government is required to use its taxing authority to pay the interest and repay the principal. General obligation bonds may have to be approved by popular referendum, and public approval of the bonds may be difficult to obtain. These characteristics associated with issuing the debt reduce the risk of investing in general obligation bonds. Revenue bonds are supported only by funds generated by the project financed by the sale of the bonds. If the project does not generate sufficient revenues, the interest cannot be paid and the bonds go into default. For example, the Chesapeake Bay Bridge and Tunnel did not produce sufficient toll revenues, so its publicly held bonds went into default. The default, of course, caused the price of the bonds to fall. Since the bondholders could not foreclose on the bridge, their only course of action was to wait for a resumption of interest payments. After several years elapsed, toll revenues rose sufficiently, such that interest payments to the bondholders were resumed.

Tax-exempt bond are issued in minimum denominations of $5,000 face value. Although a secondary market exists for this debt, small denominations tend to lack marketability. That does not mean you cannot sell one $5,000 bond issued by a small municipality, but the market is exceedingly thin. The spread between the bid and ask prices may be substantial. (One municipal bond salesperson referred to the $5,000 muni bond as a "roach motel." Once you are in, you can't get out. The unit is just too small for bond dealers to buy it. If you do acquire municipal securities in small units, you had best plan to hold the bond until it is retired.)

Although most corporate bonds are issued with a maturity date and a sinking fund requirement, many tax-exempt bonds are issued in a series. With a serial issue, a specific amount of the debt falls due each year. Such an issue is illustrated in Exhibit 15.3, which reproduces a tombstone advertisement for bonds sold by the North Carolina Eastern Municipal Power Agency. (These advertisements are placed by the underwriting syndicate to describe a public offering. They are frequently referred to as *tombstones* because of their resemblance to an epitaph on a tombstone.) About half of the $113 million issue is in serial bonds. A portion of the issue matures each year. For example, $2,895,000 worth of the bonds matured on January 1, 2003, and another $5,185,000 matures on January 1, 2013. Serial bonds offer advantages to both the issuer and the buyer. In contrast to corporate debt, in which a random selection of the bonds may be retired each year through the sinking fund, the buyer knows when each bond will mature. The investor can then purchase bonds that mature at the desired time, which helps in portfolio planning. Because a portion of the issue is retired periodically with serial bonds, the issuing government does not have to make a large, lump-sum payment. Since these bonds are scheduled to be retired, there is no call penalty. If the government wants to retire additional debt, it can call some of the remaining bonds. For example, if the agency wanted to retire some of these bonds prematurely, it would call the term A bonds that are due in 2021 or the term B bonds due in 2026. (Most issues like the bonds shown in Exhibit 15.3 require that any debt retired before maturity be called in reverse order. Thus, the term bonds with the longest time to maturity are called and redeemed first.)

Although most of the debt sold to the general public by state and local governments is long-term, there are two exceptions: tax or revenue anticipation notes. A tax or revenue **anticipation note** is issued by a government anticipating certain receipts in the future—it issues a debt instrument against these receipts. When the taxes or other revenues are received, the notes are retired. The maturity date is set to coincide with the timing of the anticipated receipts so that the notes may be easily retired.

anticipation note
A short-term liability that is to be retired by specific expected revenues (e.g., expected tax receipts).

Tax-Exempt Securities and Risk

Although the sources of risk associated with investing in tax-exempt bonds were alluded to in the preceding discussion, it is helpful to summarize them. First, there is the market risk associated with changes in interest rates. Higher interest rates will drive down the prices of existing bonds. The investor may reduce this source of risk by purchasing bonds of shorter maturity, because the prices of bonds with longer terms to maturity fluctuate more. If the investor is concerned with price fluctuations and the preservation of capital, then shorter-term tax-exempt bonds should be preferred to long-term bonds. The investor, however, should realize that shorter-term bonds generally pay less interest.

The second source of risk is the possibility that the government might default on the interest and principal repayment. Unfortunately, finding information on particular bond

EXHIBIT 15.3 Tombstone for an Issue of Serial and Term Bonds

Issuing Authority →

Tax Exemption →

Serial Bonds →

Term Bonds →

Lead Underwriters →

All of these securities have been sold. This announcement appears as a matter of record only.

New Issue

$1,614,620,000

North Carolina Eastern Municipal Power Agency

$113,000,000 Power System Revenue Bonds, Series 1993 A
$1,501,620,000 Power System Revenue Bonds, Refunding Series 1993 B

The Bonds are dated January 1, 1993 for Fixed Rate Bonds and the Date of Delivery for Structured Yield Curve Notes, are due January 1, as shown below and are subject to redemption prior to maturity as described in the Official Statement.

In the opinion of Bond Counsel, under existing statutes and court decisions, interest on the 1993 Bonds is excluded from gross income for federal income tax purposes and is not an item of tax preference for purposes of the federal alternative minimum tax imposed on corporations and taxpayers other than corporations. See "Tax Exemption" in the Official Statement for a description of certain other provisions of law which may affect the federal tax treatment of interest on the 1993 Bonds. In the opinion of Bond Counsel, under existing laws of the State of North Carolina, the 1993 Bonds, their transfer and the income therefrom (including any profit made on the sale thereof) are free from taxation by the State of North Carolina or any political subdivision or any agency of either thereof, excepting inheritance or gift taxes.

$113,000,000 1993 A Bonds

Amount	Due	Interest Rate	Price or Yield		Amount	Due	Interest Rate	Yield or Price		Amount	Due	Interest Rate	Yield
$2,145,000	1997	4.60%	100%		$2,895,000	2003	5⅝%	5.80%		$3,855,000	2008	6⅛%	6.30 %
2,245,000	1998	4.85	100		3,055,000	2004	5¾	5.90		4,090,000	2009	6	6.138†
2,350,000	1999	5.10	100		3,230,000	2005	6	100		4,335,000	2010	6⅛	6.184†
2,470,000	2000	5¼	5.30		3,425,000	2006	6	6.15		4,600,000	2011	6⅛	6.227†
2,600,000	2001	5⅜	5.50		3,630,000	2007	6⅛	6.25		4,880,000	2012	6.20	6.279†
2,740,000	2002	5½	5.65							5,185,000	2013	6.20	6.279†

$55,270,000 6.40% Term Bonds due January 1, 2021 — Yield 6.50%
(Accrued interest to be added)

$1,501,620,000 1993 B Bonds

Amount	Due	Interest Rate	Price		Amount	Due	Interest Rate	Yield		Amount	Due	Interest Rate	Price or Yield
$3,580,000	1995	3.85%	100%		$4,470,000	2000	5¼%	5.30%		$ 39,910,000	2005	6 %	100%
3,715,000	1996	4.35	100		4,705,000	2001	5⅜	5.50		42,600,000	2006	6	6.10
3,880,000	1997	4.60·	100		4,960,000	2002	5½	5.65		44,760,000	2007	7¼	6.20
4,055,000	1998	4.85	100		5,230,000	2003	5⅝	5.80		123,355,000	2008	7	6.25
4,255,000	1999	5.10	100		5,525,000	2004	5¾	5.90		127,060,000	2009	6⅛	6.30

$248,055,000 6¼% Term Bonds due January 1, 2012 — Yield 6.457%
$ 40,345,000 6 % Term Bonds due January 1, 2013 — Yield 6.437%
$146,625,000 5½% Term Bonds due January 1, 2017 — Yield 6.27 %†
$ 97,790,000 6 % Term Bonds due January 1, 2018 — Yield 6.30 %††
$194,510,000 5½% Term Bonds due January 1, 2021 — Yield 6.45 %
$157,740,000 6 % Term Bonds due January 1, 2022 — Yield 6.41 %
$ 60,180,000 6¼% Term Bonds due January 1, 2023 — Yield 6.33 %†
$ 45,030,000 6¼% Term Bonds due January 1, 2023 — Yield 6.415%
$ 16,875,000 6 % Term Bonds due January 1, 2025 — Yield 6.42 %
$ 16,610,000 6 % Term Bonds due January 1, 2026 — Yield 6.42 %
(Accrued interest to be added)

$55,800,000 6%* ("Bond Rate") Structured Yield Curve Notes due January 1, 2014 — NRO**

---

†Payment of principal and interest when due will be insured by Financial Guaranty Insurance Company.
††Payment of principal and interest when due will be insured by AMBAC Indemnity Corporation.
*Subject to change as described in the Official Statement.
**Not reoffered.

The 1993 Bonds are offered subject to the approval of legality by Hawkins, Delafield & Wood, New York, New York, Bond Counsel. Certain legal matters in connection with the 1993 Bonds are subject to the approval of Poyner & Spruill, Rocky Mount, North Carolina, North Carolina counsel to Power Agency, and Brown & Wood, New York, New York, counsel to the Underwriters.

Smith Barney, Harris Upham & Co.
Incorporated

Morgan Stanley & Co.
Incorporated

Goldman, Sachs & Co.

J. P. Morgan Securities Inc.

Alex. Brown & Sons
Incorporated

First Charlotte Company
Division of J.C. Bradford & Co.

Interstate/Johnson Lane

J. Lee Peeler & Company, Inc.

Legg Mason Wood Walker
Incorporated

Wheat, First Securities, Inc.

Source: Reprinted with permission of North Carolina Eastern Municipal Power Agency.

issues can be difficult for the individual investor. Municipal bonds are not registered with the Securities and Exchange Commission (SEC) prior to their sale to the general public, and state and local governments do not publish annual reports and send them to bondholders. Fortunately for investors, several firms rate a considerable number of the tax-exempt bonds that are sold to the general public. These ratings are based on a substantial amount of data, for the rating services require the municipal and state governments to provide them with financial and economic information. Since failure of the bond issue to receive a favorable rating will dissuade many potential buyers, the state and local governments supply the rating services with the required information.

The investor can take several steps to reduce the risk associated with default. The first is to purchase a diversified portfolio of tax-exempt bonds, which spreads the risk associated with any particular government. Second, the investor may limit purchases to debt with high credit ratings. If the investor purchases only bonds with AAA or AA credit ratings, there is little risk (perhaps no real risk) of loss from default.

A third means by which the investor may limit the risk of default is to purchase municipal bonds that are insured. Several insurance companies guarantee the payment of interest and principal of the municipal bonds they insure. For example, Edison Township, New Jersey, bonds are insured by Financial Security Assurance and have a AAA rating by Standard & Poor's. Other municipal bond insurers include MBIA (Municipal Bond Insurance Association), which is traded on the NYSE (MBI), and FGIC (Financial Guaranty Insurance Co.), which is part of GE Capital.

The existence of these risks does not imply that an investor should avoid tax-exempt bonds. The return offered by these bonds is consistent with the amount of risk the investor must bear. If a particular bond were to offer an exceptionally high return, it would be readily purchased and its price driven up so that the return was in line with comparably risky securities. Tax-exempt bonds should be purchased by investors with moderate-to-high incomes who are seeking tax-free income and who do not need liquidity. Like any investment, tax-exempt bonds may fit into an individual investor's portfolio and offer a return (after tax) commensurate with the risk the investor must endure.

AUTHORITY BONDS AND BUILD AMERICA BONDS

In addition to general obligation and revenue bonds, some local and state governments have created industrial authorities that issued bonds, built facilities, and leased them to firms. Local governments sold these industrial revenue bonds to stimulate economic growth or obtain a desired facility, such as a hospital. Since the local government authority and not the user issued the debt, the interest is tax-exempt. (An "authority" is a government body created for a single purpose such as the building of an industrial complex. The authority then leases the facility to a corporation. Authorities are also created to build and operate toll roads, bridges, tunnels, ports, and airports. Examples include the New York Port Authority and the New Jersey Turnpike Authority.) The interest payments are the responsibility of the industrial authority and not the local or state government that created the authority (i.e., the bonds are revenue bonds of the authority and not general obligations of the state or its municipalities). If the firm using the facilities fails to make the required payments, the industrial authority would be unable to make the interest payments to the bondholders. Although this suggests

⊕ Point of Interest

DEFAULT: WPPSS/WHOOPS AND CALIFORNIA

Tax-exempt bonds have generally been free from default. This has been especially true for general obligation bonds that are supported by the taxing authority of the issuing government.

Such safety need not apply to tax-exempt bonds that are not general obligations. The most spectacular demonstration of risk through default is the Washington Public Power Supply System (WPPSS and cynically referred to as WHOOPS), which sold $2.25 billion of debt to build two nuclear power plants. The plants, however, were not completed, so the utilities that initially agreed to buy the power refused to make construction payments. In addition, the power authority was not allowed by the courts to raise its rates for electricity generated in the authority's other facilities. Because the plants were not completed and the authority could not recover its costs, the bonds went into default.

The bleak financial environment that started in 2008 may now cause even general obligations to have risk of default. In December 2008, California's finance director announced that the state "will begin delaying payments or paying in registered warrants." These warrants would be issued to the state's suppliers and contractors and are a promise of future payment plus interest. In January 2009, the state's controller announced that California would start to delay $3.7 billion in tax refunds for 30 days because the state "is running out of money." Payments for social services and mental health programs were also to be delayed. While the controller said that debt payments would continue, investors in California's tax-exempt, general obligation bonds have to consider the possibility that the state would default, an event that had not occurred since the Great Depression.

industrial revenue bonds can be risky investments, many are among the safest municipal securities because the payments are supported by major corporations. For example, the Waynesboro, Virginia, Industrial Authority bonds are supported by DuPont.

The American Recovery and Reinvestment Act of 2009 authorized the creation of a new taxable bond issued by state and local governments during 2009 and 2010. The funds raised by the sale of the "Build America Bonds" must be used to finance infrastructure projects such as road and building repairs. Since the interest on Build America Bonds is higher than the interest on nontaxable municipal securities, 35 percent of the borrowing costs are subsidized by the federal government.

Because the expected life of the financed projects extends over many years, Build America Bonds are long-term debt instruments. They are primarily attractive to financial institutions such as insurance companies and pension plans whose obligations extend over many years. Even if the Build America Bonds are of marginal interest to individual investors, their existence will have at least one important implication for individuals who purchase the traditional tax-exempt bond: The supply of tax-exempt municipal bonds will decrease, and that decrease should increase their prices and lower their yields.

In addition to taxable municipal bonds, the interest on some nontaxable bonds may be subject to the alternative minimum tax that some individuals must pay. This alternative tax is designed to ensure that individuals who may not be subject to federal income tax under the regular tax laws will be required to make some federal income tax payments. Hence, tax-exempt interest may be subject to the alternative taxation.

An example of tax-exempt debt subject to the alternative minimum tax was the issue of bonds sold by the Richmond, Virginia, Redevelopment and Housing Authority. The funds raised by the issue were used to develop condominiums, apartments, and

⊕ Point of Interest

PREREFUNDED MUNICIPAL BONDS

Municipal bonds are initially issued with terms of 15, 20, or 25 years. Bonds may even have maturity dates that are farther in the future. Some are noncallable, and the call date for others is often many years after the date of issue. For example, the University of Virginia Hospital Authority issued nontaxable revenue bonds in 1985 with coupons in excess of 8 percent and maturities extending beyond the year 2000. The bonds could not be called until 1995, ten years after being issued. After 1985, interest rates declined, so it would have been advantageous to refinance. Issuing new bonds with lower coupons and retiring the more expensive debt would reduce interest expense, but the inability to call the bonds meant such an action was not feasible.

Although the bonds could not be called, an alternative strategy was used to reduce interest expense. A second series of bonds was issued, and the proceeds were used to acquire U.S. Treasury bonds that matured when the original issue was callable. The interest earned on the Treasury bonds was then used to pay the interest on the original bonds. In effect, the municipal authority paid interest only on the new bonds: When the original bonds became callable, only the proceeds from the maturing Treasury securities retired the original debt issue.

Once a municipal government (or authority in the case of the UVA hospital bonds) issues the new bonds, segregates the proceeds, and acquires the Treasury securities, the original issue of bonds is referred to as *prerefunded*. The bonds will be retired on the call date, and the maturity date is no longer relevant. From the investor's perspective, the uncertainty as to when the bonds will be retired is eliminated. In addition, since the proceeds of the Treasury securities are earmarked to pay the interest and retire the debt, default risk is eliminated. Although prerefunded municipal bonds still have some interest rate and reinvestment rate risk, these tax-free bonds are as safe as Treasury securities.

retail space. Part of the financing, which included both private and public participation, was a $100 million issue of authority bonds. Although the interest was exempt from regular federal income taxation, it was subject to the alternative minimum tax.

FOREIGN GOVERNMENT DEBT SECURITIES

American investors are not limited to the securities issued by the federal government, its agencies, the states, and their political subdivisions. Investors can also purchase the debt of foreign governments. These foreign securities may offer a higher yield because they have additional risk, such as the risks associated with changes in exchange rates and with default.

Investments in foreign government securities have exchange rate risk—that is, the currency in which the debt is denominated. Unless the debt is denominated in dollars, the American investor bears the risk associated with fluctuations in exchange rates. Since the value of the dollar relative to other currencies changes daily, higher promised yields in the local currency may translate into modest or even negative returns once the local currency is converted into dollars.

The second source of risk is the risk of default. The failure to pay the interest and redeem the bonds is highly unlikely by the governments of world financial powers, such as the United Kingdom. The risk of default, however, is perceptibly greater for the governments of such countries as Russia and China. Such default could be based on political as well as economic events. For example, when Castro came to power, Cuba nationalized assets held by U.S. firms and repudiated debts the government owed. (Cuban bonds continued to trade in the United States even after their maturity dates had passed and interest had not been paid for years.) More recent defaults led to the development of Brady bonds.

Brady Bonds

The economies of many developing nations have experienced periods of rapid growth. These nations, especially those with such natural resources as oil reserves, issued debt that was readily bought by Western commercial banks. The countries were eager to issue this debt to avoid constraints imposed by accepting grants from Western nations or borrowing from Western government-sponsored banks (e.g., the World Bank). The commercial banks readily granted the loans to the developing nations to earn higher rates of interest. Increasing commodity prices suggested that these countries could easily service the debt.

Commodity prices, however, did not increase indefinitely, and many of these governments either defaulted or had to borrow additional funds to pay the interest on their bonds. Such borrowing, of course, only further increased the amount they owed. Many of the bonds sold in the secondary markets for substantial discounts. In effect, these bonds became another illustration of high-yield, junk securities. The defaults led to a period of restructuring, and it was during this period that Brady bonds were developed.

Brady bonds, named for Nicholas Brady, who was responsible for their development, advanced a plan to reduce the amount of foreign debt through an exchange of old bonds for new bonds. For the debt restructuring to occur, the debtor nation had to undergo economic reforms. After economic progress had been made, the old bonds were exchanged for new bonds—the Brady bonds. The face value or principal amount of the new bonds was less than the original amount of the debt (i.e., some of the debt was forgiven). Initial interest payments were less than current interest rates but would rise over time.

Lower interest payments and principal forgiveness are common features in restructuring. What differentiated Brady bonds was that the principal was guaranteed by U.S.

⊕ Point of Interest

EXCHANGE-TRADED FUNDS (ETFs) AND BONDS

A large number of exchange-traded funds exist for stocks, so you should expect exchange-traded funds for bonds. Several iShares for debt securities have been created by Barclays Global Investors. The iShares Lehman Aggregate Bond Fund (AGG) tracks the performance of the highest-quality American investment-grade bonds. About 40 percent of the index is devoted to U.S. government and agency bonds and another 40 percent to corporate bonds rated AAA. The iShares iBoxx $ Investment Grade Corporate Bond Fund (LQD) encompasses a broader range of the investment grade bonds with emphasis on debt rated AA or A.

Four iShare ETFs are composed of federal government bonds. Three of these funds emphasize a specified term to maturity: the iShares Lehman 1–3 Year Treasury Bond Fund (SHY), the iShares Lehman 7–10 Year Treasury Bond Fund (IEF), and the iShares Lehman 20+ Year Treasury Bond Fund (TLT). The fourth government ETF is the iShares Lehman U.S. Treasury Inflation Protected Securities Bond Fund (TIP), which tracks the yields on inflation-protected securities (commonly called TIPs) issued by the federal government. All four ETFs offer the advantages of participating in their defined markets, but since exchange-traded funds are passive investments, the operating expenses are less than the investor would have to pay for an actively managed bond mutual fund. Information concerning all six bond ETFs may be obtained from iShares at **http://www.ishares.com**.

federal government securities. U.S. zero coupons with maturity dates that coincided with the maturity dates of the exchanged bonds were used as collateral for the new bonds issued by the emerging nation's government. This guarantee was exceedingly important because it removed default risk (at least for the principal). It also removed exchange rate risk because the principal amount is collateralized in dollars.

It is important to realize that Brady bonds are not obligations of the federal government and that the federal government is not making the loans. Instead, the Brady bonds were created through an exchange of old bonds for new bonds, and are not new loans. Once issued, Brady bonds may be bought and sold in the secondary market like any other debt security. Investing in Brady bonds still involves risk. Interest payments may not be made, and a bond's price will vary with changes in interest rates, so yields are higher than those available on investment-grade debt. In effect, Brady bonds are a type of government high-yield security whose principal repayment is guaranteed by U.S. federal government obligations. (Information concerning Brady bonds, such as prices and ratings, may be found at BradyNet Incorporated's Web address: http://www.bradynet.com).

GOVERNMENT SECURITIES AND INVESTMENT COMPANIES

Closed-end investment companies and mutual funds are tailor-made for investing in government securities. Although investment companies are available for equities, some individuals prefer to manage their own portfolios. There is no denying the potential excitement or satisfaction of acquiring a stock and then having its price rise. (The converse would be true if the individuals sold the stock short and its price subsequently declined.) Even if the investor does not outperform the market over a period of time (and efficient markets suggest that the individual will not outperform the market on a risk-adjusted basis), there is satisfaction from the process of security selection and personal management of the portfolio.

Even these individuals, however, may prefer to use mutual funds for the acquisition of government securities. Several reasons have been alluded to throughout this chapter, two of which are the lack of marketability of some government securities and the lack of readily available information on which to base an investment decision. A third reason is the size of the unit of trading, and a fourth is diversification.

While federal government securities have active secondary markets, that is not true for many tax-exempt securities. Even if the investor is able to acquire the bonds, the spread between the bid and ask prices can be substantial, especially for small issues or if the individual acquires small denominations, such as a $5,000 face amount.

The inability of the investor to obtain financial information concerning the issuing government authority is also related to the size of the issue. Municipal bonds are not registered with the SEC. Information on many issues is not readily available. Prices are not quoted, and though bond values may be provided by brokers on the investor's monthly statements, the values are at best approximations and are not indicative of actual trades or available bid prices.

A third disadvantage is the size of the unit of trading, and that minimum size has implications for diversification. For example, Ginnie Mae bonds are sold in units of $25,000, and municipal bonds are sold in units of $5,000. (Some brokers require larger minimum purchases. For example, the minimum unit from Schwab is $10,000.) The large unit for trading in buying Ginnie Maes suggests that investors may prefer to buy shares in a mutual fund that specializes in these mortgage-backed bonds. Certainly the unit of trading is small, but the funds offer an additional advantage. The fund's portfolio would encompass many issues, which increases diversification. Since Ginnie Maes are supported by the federal government, the need to diversify the risk of default is minimal. What a diversified portfolio of Ginnie Maes accomplishes is an increase in the certainty of monthly payments. Since these payments are a combination of interest and principal repayment, prepayments and refinancings imply that monthly cash flows are uncertain. The more different issues of Ginnie Maes that the investor owns, the more certain the monthly payments will be. Repayments and refinancing cannot be the same for each issue; hence, a portfolio of Ginnie Mae bonds should have a more certain flow of monthly cash payments than the monthly payments from a single issue of Ginnie Mae bonds.

Diversifying a municipal government bond portfolio also requires purchasing a variety of issues. However, diversifying may not be important if the investor limits the bonds to those with investment-grade ratings, since bonds with these ratings should not default. (Of course, the investor still must bear the risk associated with changes in interest rates since all bond prices will change with an increase or a decrease in the rate of interest.) Diversifying a bond portfolio will require a variety of issues, whose features would differ in order for their returns not to be perfectly correlated. Diversification would obviously be important if the investor constructed a portfolio of less-than-investment-grade municipal bonds or a portfolio of foreign government debt issues. Such a diversified portfolio will require a substantial investment, since the minimum unit of trading increases the total cost of diversifying the portfolio.

These disadvantages associated with managing an individual government bond portfolio are avoided by acquiring shares in investment companies. The shares are easily bought and redeemed (in the case of mutual funds) or bought and sold (in the case of closed-end investment companies). Information is, of course, readily available on the investment company, such as its size, past performance, management, and fees. Information on the specific securities held by the investment company may be irrelevant to the individual investor. Instead, the information is relevant to the fund's professional managers.

The size of the unit is also not a problem for the investor. Presumably the fund has the resources to buy and sell the individual debt security using a cost-efficient unit of trading. The investor then buys the shares of the closed-end investment company on the open market or buys the shares directly from the open-end mutual fund. The amount of the purchase can be as small as the investor wishes, subject to minimum size of purchase from the fund (e.g., $1,000) or the minimum amount to be cost-effective to acquire the publicly traded shares of the closed-end investment company.

Last, diversification is one of the advantages offered by investment companies. Unless the individual acquires shares solely in specialized investment companies, the individual has a piece of a diversified portfolio. Even if the investor acquires a position in a specialized fund, that portfolio is diversified within the specialization.

Specialized Government Investment Companies

Many investment companies have portfolios that specialize in particular debt instruments. Although many money market mutual funds hold a cross section of short-term debt instruments, some hold only Treasury bills and other short-term securities guaranteed by the U.S. government. These funds pay the lowest rates available from money market funds, but they are also the absolute safest of all the money market funds.

Other mutual funds specialize in intermediate-term federal government bonds, while others hold long-term bonds. The latter funds may move into intermediate-term bonds if the portfolio manager anticipates higher interest rates. Such a movement would protect investors if long-term rates did rise. This portfolio manager would follow an opposite strategy in anticipation of lower rates, since the prices of the longest-term bonds would increase the most in response to lower rates. Other portfolio managers may follow a more passive strategy, which emphasizes the collection of interest and the repayment of principal and not the timing of interest rate changes.

Among the most important government securities funds are those specializing in municipal bonds. These include (1) money market mutual funds that acquire short-term municipal debt, (2) general bond funds that hold a cross section of municipal bonds, and (3) state municipal bond funds with portfolios devoted entirely to the government bonds issued in a particular state. The short-term municipal bond funds are always open-end mutual investment companies, but the general bond funds and the specialized state funds can be either open-end or closed-end investment companies whose shares are traded on the secondary markets.

The appeal of the general municipal bond funds is primarily directed to investors seeking income that is exempt from federal income taxation. For example, Dreyfus Muni Bond Fund holds 100 percent of its assets in municipal bonds issued in various states. In 2005, this fund earned (and distributed) $0.51 a share on a net asset value of $11.88 for a yield of 4.29 percent. All the income was exempt from federal income taxation. The distributions, however, were subject to state income taxes, but if the individual lived in a state with no income tax, then the distribution was not taxed at the state level.

Individuals who live in states with high state income taxes may prefer the specialized municipal bond funds. These specialized funds are obviously designed to attract the funds of investors who live in the particular state. For example, Nuveen New Jersey Premium Income Municipal Fund (NNJ) is a closed-end investment company that owns investment-grade municipal bonds issued by the state of New Jersey and its political subdivisions. NNJ's shares are traded on the New York Stock Exchange, and, although any investor may acquire the stock, its primary appeal is to residents of New Jersey, who pay both federal and state income tax. For residents in the top bracket, the total tax rate is 43.97 percent (35 percent federal plus 8.97 percent state). If the investor in the top bracket acquires the shares of NNJ and earns 4.50 percent, that is the equivalent of 8.03 percent on a taxable investment.

SUMMARY

In order to tap funds from many sources, the federal government issues a variety of debt instruments. These range from Series EE and I bonds, which are sold in small denominations, to short-term Treasury bills and long-term bonds, which are sold in large denominations.

Because there is no possibility of default, federal government debt is the safest of all possible investments. However, the investor still bears the risk of loss through fluctuations in interest rates and (except for indexed bonds) inflation. If interest rates rise, the prices of federal government bonds decline. If the rate of inflation exceeds the yield on debt instruments, the investor experiences a loss of purchasing power.

In addition to the debt issued by the federal government itself, bonds are issued by its agencies. These bonds tend to offer slightly higher yields, but they are virtually as safe as the direct debt of the federal government. In some cases, the agency's debt is even secured by the full faith and credit of the U.S. Treasury.

Among the most popular securities issued by a federal government agency are the mortgage pass-through bonds issued by the Government National Mortgage Association, or *Ginnie Mae*. These bonds serve as a conduit through which interest and principal repayments are made from homeowners to the bondholders. Payments are made monthly, so Ginnie Mae bonds are popular with individuals desiring a flow of cash receipts. These bonds expose investors to risk of loss from fluctuating interest rates or from inflation, but the interest payments and principal repayments are guaranteed by an agency of the federal government.

Alternatives to Ginnie Maes are collateralized mortgage obligations (CMOs), which are issued by a trust that holds mortgages guaranteed by the federal government. CMOs are sold in series, or tranches, with the obligations in the shortest tranche being retired before any of the CMOs in the next series are retired.

State and local governments issue long-term debt instruments to finance capital improvements, such as schools and roads. The debt is retired over a period of time by tax receipts or revenues. Some of these bonds are supported by the taxing authority of the issuing government, but many are supported only by the revenues generated by the facilities financed through the bond issues.

State and municipal debt differs from other investments because the interest is exempt from federal income taxation. These bonds pay lower rates of interest than taxable securities (e.g., corporate bonds), but their after-tax yields may be equal to or even greater than the yields on taxable bonds. The nontaxable bonds are particularly attractive to investors in high income tax brackets, because the bonds provide a means to shelter income from taxation.

Tax-exempt bonds can be risky investments, since the capacity of state and local governments to service the debt varies. Moody's and Standard & Poor's rating services analyze this debt based on the government's ability to pay the interest and retire the principal. Such ratings indicate the risk associated with investing in a particular debt issue. In addition, investors must bear the risks associated with fluctuations in securities prices and the lack of liquidity associated with tax-exempt bonds.

QUESTIONS

1. Why is the debt of the federal government considered to be the safest of all possible investments?
2. What distinguishes EE bonds from Treasury bills?
3. When interest rates rise, what happens to the price of federal government bonds? What happens to the price of state and local government bonds?

4. What is the difference between the following?
    a) A bond secured by a moral obligation and a bond secured by full faith and credit
    b) A revenue bond and a general obligation bond

   Are there any similarities between a bond secured by a moral obligation and a revenue bond?

5. What are the sources of risk from investing in the following?
    a) Federal government debt
    b) Municipal debt

6. How do Treasury inflation-indexed securities help the investor manage risk?

7. What is the difference between a term bond issue and a serial bond issue? Why are many capital improvements made by state and local governments financed through serial bonds?

8. What is a mortgage pass-through bond? What risks are associated with investing in Ginnie Mae bonds? What is the composition of the payment received from a mortgage pass-through bond?

9. If interest rates increase, what should happen to the following?
    a) The price of a Ginnie Mae bond and the price of a municipal bond
    b) The payments received from a Ginnie Mae bond and the payments received from a municipal bond

   Contrast your answers to parts (a) and (b).

10. Identify which government securities may be appropriate for the following investors:
    a) A retired couple seeking income
    b) An individual in the highest tax bracket seeking a liquid investment
    c) An individual seeking a government bond for inclusion in an individual retirement account (IRA)
    d) A child with no income and a modest amount to invest
    e) A corporation with $100,000,000 to invest for less than three months
    f) A church seeking to invest a modest endowment fund

11. Selected interest rates may be found in Federal Reserve Economic Data (FRED), which may be accessed through the Federal Reserve Bank of St. Louis's home page: http://www.stlouisfed.org. Based on this information, what is the current difference between the yield on a six-month Treasury bill and the 20-year Treasury bond? What is the difference in the yields on corporate bonds rated Aaa and Baa by Moody's?

12. What is the yield currently being offered by Series EE bonds? (Information concerning EE bonds may be found through the U.S. Treasury: http://www.treasurydirect .gov.)

PROBLEMS

1. If a six-month Treasury bill is purchased for $0.9675 on a dollar (i.e., $96,750 for a $100,000 bill), what is the discount yield and the annual rate of interest? What will these yields be if the discount price falls to $0.94 on a dollar (i.e., $94,000 for a $100,000 bill)?

2. An investor is in the 28 percent income tax bracket and can earn 6.3 percent on a nontaxable bond. What is the comparable yield on a taxable bond? If this same investor can earn 8.9 percent on a taxable bond, what must be the yield on a non-taxable bond so that the after-tax yields are equal?

3. An investor in the 35 percent tax bracket may purchase a corporate bond that is rated double A and is traded on the New York Stock Exchange (the bond division). This bond yields 9.0 percent. The investor may also buy a double-A-rated municipal bond with a 5.85 percent yield. Why may the corporate bond be preferred? (Assume that the terms of the bonds are the same.)

4. What is the price of the following zero coupon bonds if interest rates are (a) 4 percent, (b) 7 percent, and (c) 10 percent?
   - Bond A: zero coupon; maturity 5 years
   - Bond B: zero coupon; maturity 10 years
   - Bond C: zero coupon; maturity 20 years

   What generalization can be made concerning the term of a zero coupon bond and its price in relation to changes in the level of interest rates?

5. You are in the 28 percent federal income tax bracket. A corporate bond offers you 6.8 percent while a tax-exempt bond with the same credit rating and term to maturity offers 4.1 percent. On the basis of taxation, which bond should be preferred? Explain.

6. A six-month $10,000 Treasury bill is selling for $9,844. What is the annual yield according to the discount method? Does this yield understate or overstate the true annual yield? Explain.

7. What is the current taxable equivalent yield for an individual in the 35 percent federal income tax bracket for intermediate bonds (10 or fewer years to maturity) and long-term bonds (30 years to maturity)? Estimates of prevailing yields on municipal bonds may be found through Bloomberg's information on U.S. financial markets: **http://www.bloomberg.com/markets**.

8. The federal government issues two four-year notes. The first is a traditional type of debt instrument that pays 6 percent annually ($60 per $1,000 note). The second pays a real yield of 3 percent with the amount of interest being adjusted with changes in the CPI. The CPI was 100 when the notes were initially issued.

   a) What is the annual amount of interest paid each year on each security if the CPI is as follows?

Year	CPI
1	102
2	96
3	103
4	110

   b) What is the amount of principal repaid at maturity by each note?
   c) Using the dollar-weighted return explained in Chapter 10, what is the nominal, annual rate of return on each security?
   d) Based on the answer to part (c), which alternative produced the higher return and why?

9. (This problem illustrates "riding the yield curve," which is covered in the appendix to this chapter.) The U.S. Treasury issues a ten-year, zero coupon bond.

a) What will be the original issue price if comparable yields are 6 percent? (Assume annual compounding.)

b) What will be the price of this zero coupon bond after three, six, and nine years have passed if the comparable yield remains 6 percent? What are the annualized returns the investor earns if the bond is sold after three, six, or nine years?

c) When the bond was issued, the structure of yields was as follows:

Years to Maturity	Yield
1	3
4	4
7	5
10	6

What will be the price of the bond after three, six, and nine years have passed if this structure of yields does not change? What is the annualized return the investor earns if the bond is sold after three, six, or nine years?

d) Assume the structure of yields does change to the following:

Years to Maturity	Yield
1	2
4	3
7	4
10	5

What will be the price of the bond after three, six, and nine years have passed? What is the annualized return the investor earns if the bond is sold after three, six, or nine years?

e) Assume the structure of yields changes to the following:

Years to Maturity	Yield
1	4
4	5
7	6
10	7

What will be the price of the bond after three, six, and nine years have passed? What is the annualized return the investor earns if the bond is sold after three, six, or nine years?

f) Why are the annualized returns different in parts (b)–(e)?

10. (This problem illustrates the impact of a call feature. Review the material in the previous chapter, if necessary.) In 2005, a brokerage firm offered a tax-exempt 4.5 percent Ocean City, New Jersey, bond that was due in 11 years for a price of $105.30 with a yield to maturity of 3.89 percent. The bond was callable as follows:

4 years at $101.00
5 years at $100.50
6 and all subsequent years at $100.00.

The call feature is exercisable at the end of each year.

As of the day of offer, the structure of yields on comparable debt was as follows:

Years to Maturity	Yield
4	2.35%
5	2.65%
6	3.07%
7	3.18%

Does the callable bond produce a higher or lower return than the comparable bonds? To answer the question, determine the potential return (yield) on the callable bond for each of the call dates. What is an important implication of your results?

Problems 11 through 14 illustrate factors that may affect Ginnie Maes. The first (problem 11) covers the determination of the mortgage schedule, that is, the payments received by a Ginnie Mae. The next three problems illustrate how the life of a Ginnie Mae may be affected by refinancing and the possible impact on the bond's valuation. Problem 12 considers refinancing, which reduces the number of years a mortgage is outstanding. Problem 13 illustrates valuation based on different assumptions concerning the expected life of the pool. Problem 14 illustrates the potential interest savings to the homeowner by periodically retiring the mortgage faster.

11. Determine the annual repayment schedule for the first two years (i.e., interest, principal repayment, and balance owed) for each of the following. (Assume that only one payment is made annually.) Compare the payments required by each mortgage. What conclusions can you draw?
    a) A $60,000 conventional mortgage for 25 years at 10 percent
    b) A $60,000 conventional mortgage for 20 years at 10 percent
    c) A $60,000 conventional mortgage for 25 years at 8 percent

12. As a result of lower interest rates, you are considering refinancing your mortgage. The existing mortgage has a 12 percent interest rate. The balance owed is $50,000, and the remaining term is 18 years, and your annual payment (i.e., interest plus principal) is $6,897. A bank is willing to lend you the money at 10 percent to retire the old loan. The term of the new loan will be 18 years, so you are not increasing the number of years required to pay off the mortgage. (There is no reason why the number of years should be the same. If there is a reduction in your mortgage payment, you could restore the original payment and retire the loan quicker. Or you may increase the amount of the loan and use the additional funds to improve the property.) Unfortunately, the bank will charge you an application fee of $500 and an additional fee (*points*) equal to 2 percent of the amount of the mortgage. There will also be additional costs (e.g., court recording costs of the new mortgage) that are estimated to be $500. To help determine if it is profitable to refinance, answer the following questions.
    a) What are the total expenses to obtain the new loan?
    b) How much will you have to borrow to retire the loan when the refinancing expenses are included, and what will be the annual payment required by the new loan?
    c) What is the difference between the annual payments under the new and the old mortgages? What is the implied course of action?

13. You acquire a debt security that is a claim on a mortgage pool (e.g., a Ginnie Mae pass-through security). The mortgages pay 9 percent and have an expected life of 20 years. Currently, interest rates are 9 percent, so the cost of the investment is its par value of $100,000.

    a) What are the expected annual payments from the investment?
    b) If interest rates decline to 7 percent, what is the current value of the mortgage pool based on the assumption that the loans will be retired over 20 years?
    c) If interest rates decline to 7 percent and you expect homeowners to refinance after four years by repaying the loan, what is the current value of the mortgages? (To answer this question, you must determine the amount owed at the end of four years.)
    d) Why do your valuations differ?
    e) You acquire the security for the price determined in part (c) but homeowners do not refinance, so the payments occur over 20 years. What is the annual return on your investment? Did you earn your expected return?

14. (This problem is designed to illustrate the potential savings from paying a mortgage off faster. It may be viewed as an illustration of an assured, risk-free return, except that the return is the interest you save instead of interest you earn.)

    You have a 20-year $100,000 mortgage with a 9 percent interest rate. (To reduce the size of this problem, assume that payments are made annually and not monthly as would be the normal case with a mortgage.)

    a) Determine the repayment schedule.
    b) How much is owed after ten years?
    c) How much will be the total payments made over the 20 years?
    d) How much interest is paid over the 20 years?
    e) If you increase your first-year payment to include the *next year's principal payment*, how much interest will you pay at the end of the second year?
    f) If each year your payment includes the current required payment and the subsequent year's principal repayment, what will be the life of the mortgage?
    g) If you follow the process in (f), what are the total payments and the interest payments made over the life of the mortgage?
    h) What are the advantages and disadvantages associated with this early payment strategy?
    i) If interest rates decline to 7 percent, what is the current value of the mortgage based on the assumption that the loan will be outstanding for 20 years? (That is, if you were buying this mortgage as an investment for a mortgage pool, how much would you be willing to pay?)
    j) If interest rates decline to 7 percent and you follow the strategy in (f), what is the current value of the mortgage?
    k) If interest rates decline to 7 percent and you expect to refinance after four years (i.e., repay the loan with no prepayment penalty), what is the current value of the mortgage?
    l) Why do your valuations in (i) through (k) differ?

The Financial Advisor's Investment Case
Building a Bond Portfolio

Kris Trejo, who recently retired, has come to you for financial help. At the initial consultation, you realized that he is an investor with a very low risk tolerance who wants to increase current income. Trejo has $300,000 invested in certificates of deposit with maturities of one to three years earning rates of 3 percent. While you believe that such a large amount invested in one type of asset at one financial institution is a decidedly inferior strategy, you also realize that Trejo would not be willing to alter the portfolio in any way that would largely impact on risk.

Since he is primarily concerned with income and safety of principal, you believe that initially the best strategy would be to alter the portfolio by substituting quality bonds for a substantial proportion of the certificates of deposit. Thus, you suggest that $250,000 be invested in a laddered bond portfolio. Of the $250,000, $25,000 would be invested in triple-A- or double-A-rated bonds with one year to maturity, $25,000 with two years to maturity, and so on until the last $25,000 is invested in bonds with ten years to maturity. Thus, none of the bonds would have a maturity exceeding ten years, none of the bonds would have a rating of less than double A, and each year $25,000 of the bonds' face amounts would mature.

Trejo agreed to the basic strategy but required that all the bonds be federal government obligations. Currently the structure of interest rates is as follows:

Term to Maturity	Coupon Rate of Interest
1	4.0%
2	4.0
3	4.0
4	5.0
5	5.0
6	5.0
7	6.0
8	6.0
9	7.0
10	7.0

All the bonds are currently selling at par ($1,000 per $1,000 face amount). Trejo still has doubts concerning the risk of loss of principal, but he likes the fact that additional income can be generated by the bonds with the higher coupons. To help convince him this is an acceptable strategy, answer the following questions:

1. If the interest on the CDs was $9,000, what is the increase in income generated by this laddered strategy?
2. What is the advantage of investing $25,000 in bonds maturing each year instead of investing the entire $250,000 in the ten-year bonds?
3. How much could Trejo lose of the $250,000 if he follows this strategy and, *after one year*, interest rates rise across the board by 1 percent (100 basis points)?
4. Would the additional earned interest offset the loss from the rise in interest rates?
5. How much additional loss would be incurred compared to the loss in Question 3 if Trejo invests the entire $250,000 in the ten-year bonds and one year later the interest rates rise to 10 percent?
6. What should Trejo do with the $25,000 from the bond that matures after one year if he finds that he does not need the principal?

Appendix 15

USING YIELD CURVES

Yield curves relate the term, or time to maturity, and yields to maturity (not coupon or nominal rates) for bonds of a given risk class. These curves were illustrated in Figures 13.1 and 13.2, which plotted yields and time to maturity for U.S. Treasury securities during three different time periods. Figure 13.1 presented a positive yield curve, indicating that longer-term bonds offered higher yields. Figure 13.2 presented (1) a negatively sloped yield curve, which indicated that as the term of the bond increases, the yield to maturity declines; and (2) a flat yield curve, in which yields are essentially the same no matter how long the bond is outstanding.

YIELD CURVES AND ACTIVE BOND STRATEGIES

Generally, yield curves are positively sloping, but curves do shift and change their shape. These fluctuations may offer investors an opportunity to increase returns or decrease risk by adjusting their portfolios of debt securities. For example, in Figure 15A.1, the original, negatively sloped yield curve (YC_1) shifts to a positively sloped

FIGURE 15A.1 Shifting Yield Curves

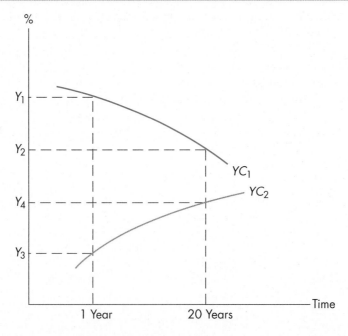

yield curve (YC_2). While all yields decrease, the shape of the yield curve changes. Short-term rates decline more than the decline in long-term rates, and the yield becomes upward sloping, indicating that long-term yields now exceed short-term yields. (A shift from YC_2 to YC_1 would indicate the opposite: that short-term rates now exceed long-term rates.)

The individual may infer that a negatively sloped yield curve argues for investing in short-term and avoiding long-term bonds in order to earn the higher rates (i.e., shift funds from long-term to short-term). The investor may execute this strategy if he or she expects rates to remain unchanged or to increase.

The shift from long-term to short-term, however, will not benefit from a decline in interest rates. If the yield curve returns to its normal, positive slope (i.e., YC_1 shifts to YC_2), acquiring short-term securities precludes the opportunity to lock in currently high long-term rates. For example, if the investor acquires one-year securities offering yield Y_1, that individual will experience a large decline in yields if the curve shifts from YC_1 to YC_2. If this investor had purchased the 20-year security with a yield of Y_2, that individual would have locked in the higher rate. If the investor had initially acquired higher-yielding short-term securities, that individual will earn only Y_3 if the short-term securities are retained and Y_4 if the funds are invested for 20 years.[1]

Acquiring the long-term debt does run the risk that the bonds will be called after interest rates fall and the yield curve returns to its normal shape. Even if the bonds are called, the investor can roll over the funds, and any call penalty offsets (at least partially) lost interest. (Financial managers of corporations realize that they may save interest expense if they borrow for the short-term at the higher rate on YC_1 and refinance at the subsequent lower rate on YC_2. One reason why the short-term rate is higher on YC_1 than the long-term rate is that financial managers expect rates to fall and are reluctant to borrow for the long-term. Instead, they increase the demand for short-term funds, which increases the short-term rate of interest.)

Another possible shift in yield curves is illustrated in Figure 15A.2, in which the yield curve shifts upward from YC_1 to YC_2. While the positive slope of both curves indicates that the longest-term bonds continue to offer the highest yields, higher yields are now available with shorter maturities. The investor can earn Y_1 but will have to commit the funds for only 10 years instead of 20 years. By shortening the maturity of the portfolio, the investor may be able to reduce risk from fluctuations in interest rates, the reinvestment rate, having the bond called prior to maturity, and the loss of purchasing power. The risk reduction may be achieved without having to forgo interest income.

Of course, if the investor had purchased the 20-year bond prior to the shift in the yield curves from YC_1 to YC_2, that individual will experience a capital loss. In this case, the better strategy would be to acquire short-term debt and forgo some interest income. Unfortunately, few investors can predict the direction of change in interest rates and must bear the risk associated with their fluctuations.

---

[1] These fluctuations in yield curves also illustrate reinvestment rate risk. If the investor acquires long-term debt (e.g., the 20-year bond yielding Y_2 in Figure 15A.1), the actual return will be less if the yield curve shifts from YC_1 to YC_2 because the interest payments cannot be reinvested at Y_2.

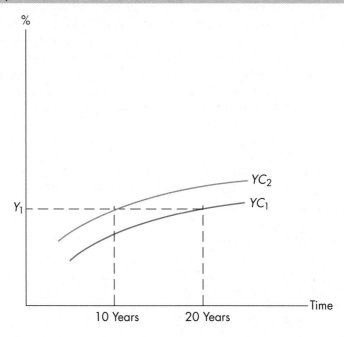

FIGURE 15A.2 An Upward Shift in Yield Curves

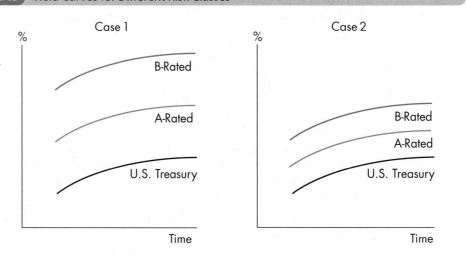

FIGURE 15A.3 Yield Curves for Different Risk Classes

The prior discussion was limited to yield curves for bonds with the same default risk (i.e., bonds with comparable ratings such as U.S. Treasury securities). Figure 15A.3 illustrates two cases for yield curves of bonds with different credit ratings. In both cases, the yield curves are positively sloped, and lower ratings are associated with higher yields. The difference between case 1 and case 2 is the distance or spread between the yield curves. Figure 14.1 illustrated fluctuations in the yields of triple-A- and triple-B-rated corporate bonds. The same information for Aaa- and Baa-rated municipal bonds was presented in Figure 15.2. The yields on the lower-quality bonds always exceeded the yields on the higher-quality debt, but the difference between the yields (i.e., the spread between the yield curves) fluctuated over time.

When the spreads increase (i.e., when the yield curves are farther apart as in case 1), the investor may sell the safer bonds and purchase the riskier bonds. This strategy will earn the higher return. If increased default risk is excluded, this bond swap may also decrease the investor's risk exposure. First, if the term remains the same (e.g., ten years), the investor earns the higher return without increasing purchasing power risk. Second, interest rate risk is related to the decline in the price of the bonds when interest rates increase. If rates do increase, there may be less of a decline in the market value of the riskier bonds because they pay higher coupons. The smaller price fluctuation from the higher coupon bonds suggests that swapping the safer, lower-coupon bond for the higher-coupon bond may reduce rather than increase interest rate risk. (The higher coupon weights the cash flows toward the earlier years of the bond's life. The duration of these bonds is smaller, which indicates that their price volatility is less than those bonds with the smaller coupons.) Third, reinvestment rate risk is related to the rate earned when the interest payments are reinvested and applies if interest rates decline. After the swap the additional interest offsets (at least partially) any interest lost from reinvesting the coupons at lower rates.

This suggests that the investor can use yield curves to actively manage a bond portfolio. Shifts in the curves may encourage alterations in the composition of a bond portfolio to increase returns or reduce risk. Such a plan opposes the laddered strategy discussed in the section on managing interest rate risk in Chapter 14. By staggering maturities in a laddered strategy, the investor adopts a passive strategy and is not concerned with the shape of or shifts in the yield curve.

RIDING THE YIELD CURVE TO ENHANCE SHORT-TERM YIELDS

In addition to active bond strategies, the investor may use a positive yield curve as a means to magnify the return on a short-term investment. Consider an individual with $10,000 to invest in Treasury bills. Four investment possibilities follow:

Term	Price	Annual Yield
3 months	$9,800	8.42%
6 months	9,500	10.80
9 months	9,100	13.40
12 months	8,800	13.64

Notice that in this example the yield curve in Figure 15A.4 is positively sloped because as the term of the bill increases, the yields become higher. The three-month bill yields 8.42 percent and the 12-month bill yields 13.64 percent. The exaggerated

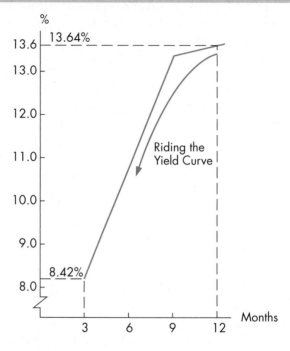

FIGURE 15A.4 Riding the Yield Curve

Calculator Solution

Function Key	Data Input
PV =	−9800
FV =	10000
PMT =	0
N =	.25
I =	?
Function Key	*Answer*
PV =	8.42

difference in the yields is designed to illustrate this concept—it is not typical of the actual differences in yields. The determination of the annualized (compound) yield is

$$\$9,800(1 + i)^n = \$10,000,$$

in which $n = 0.25$. The solution is

$$\$9,800(1 + i)^{0.25} = \$10,000$$

$$(1 + i)^{0.25} = \frac{\$10,000}{9,800} = 1.0204$$

$$i = (1.0204)^4 - 1 = 0.0842 = 8.42\%.$$

The investor may purchase any of the four T-bills. For example, if the individual wants to invest the funds for one year, he or she can buy the 12-month bill or buy the 3-month bill and reinvest the funds for an additional 9 months when the 3-month bill matures. Even if the individual wants the investment for only 6 months, any of the T-bills may be purchased, because the 3-month bill can be rolled over into another bill and the 9-month or 12-month bills can be sold after 6 months. Since there are active secondary markets in T-bills, the investor could buy the 12-month bill, hold it for 6 months, and then sell it.

Whether the individual wants to invest for 3 months, 6 months, or a year, it may be possible to increase the yield by purchasing the 12-month bill and selling it after a period of time. This strategy is referred to as *riding the yield curve*. To see how the yield may be increased, consider the investor who buys the 12-month bill with the intention of selling it after 6 months. What will be the price of the bill when it is sold? There are three general possibilities: (1) the structure of yields will remain the same, (2) yields will rise, and (3) yields will fall.

If after 6 months the structure of yields has not changed, the 12-month bill becomes a 6-month bill with a price of $9,500 and an annual yield of 10.80 percent. (Remember: T-bills are sold at a discount that declines as the bill approaches maturity.) The bill has moved up two steps in the preceding table of prices and yields and has moved down the yield curve in Figure 15A.4. That means the investor may sell the bill for a profit of $700 ($9,500 − $8,800), for a 6-month holding period return of 7.95 percent ($700/$8,800). The annualized yield is 16.54 percent.[2] This gain is greater than the $500 earned by purchasing the 6-month bill for $9,500 and redeeming it for $10,000 at maturity, thus realizing an annualized return of 10.80 percent.

If interest rates have risen, the prices of the bills will not rise as much. For example, suppose after 6 months the structure of yields is

Term	Price	Annual Yield
3 months	$9,750	10.66%
6 months	9,410	12.93
9 months	9,000	15.08
12 months	8,600	16.28

The original 12-month bill can now be sold for $9,410, which generates an annual return of 14.3 percent. The investor did not fare as well in this case (14.3 percent versus 16.8 percent) because the bill's price did not rise as much. However, unless interest rates rise precipitously and rapidly, as did occur during 1980 (see Figure 13.3), the investor will earn a return that exceeds the yield available through purchasing the 6-month bill and holding it to maturity.

If interest rates have fallen, the strategy of buying the 12-month bill produces an even higher return. Suppose after 6 months the structure of yields is

Term	Price	Annual Yield
3 months	$9,850	6.23%
6 months	9,600	8.51
9 months	9,400	8.60
12 months	9,120	9.65

---

[2]The determination of the annualized (compound) rate (i) is

$8,800(1 + i)^n = $9,500,$

in which $n = 0.5$. The solution is

$8,800(1 + i)^n = $9,500$

$$(1 + i)^{0.5} = \frac{\$9,500}{\$8,800} = 1.07955$$

$$i = (1.07955)^2 - 1 = 0.1654 = 16.54\%.$$

Since interest rates have fallen, the price of the 12-month bill has risen even more than it would have had there been no change in the yield structure. In this case, the investor may now sell the bill for $9,600, generating a profit of $800 and an annual return of 19.0 percent. This is obviously the best scenario, since the investor benefits from both riding the yield curve and the declining interest rates.

The opportunity to increase returns by riding the yield curve suggests that a positively sloped yield curve may be unstable. If many investors try to ride the yield curve, they will sell the shorter-term bills in order to purchase the longer-term bills. The sales will depress the price of the shorter-term bills and increase their yields while simultaneously increasing the price of the longer-term bills and decreasing their yields. These forces will tend to flatten the yield curve.

The actual shape of the yield curve at a point in time depends on the interplay of many factors. These include the Federal Reserve's interest rate policy, investors' preference for liquidity and their expectations of future interest rates, and borrowers' need for short- or long-term funds. These factors as well as the impact of individuals and portfolio managers seeking higher returns by riding the yield curve ultimately determine the structure of yields. (You may obtain the current structure of yields daily in the *Wall Street Journal*, which publishes a figure [usually on page 2 of section C] that shows the current structure and the prior structures for one month and one year.)

CHAPTER 16

Convertible Bonds and Convertible Preferred Stock

LEARNING OBJECTIVES

After completing this chapter you should be able to:

1. Describe the features common to all convertible bonds.
2. Determine the *floor*, or minimum price, of a convertible bond.
3. List the factors that affect the price of a convertible bond.
4. Identify the two premiums paid for a convertible bond.
5. Explain why the two premiums are inversely related.
6. Compare convertible bonds with convertible preferred stock.
7. Explain the advantage offered by a put bond.

The previous chapters discussed the variety of bonds and preferred stock and the valuation of these securities. This chapter considers bonds and preferred stock with a special feature: The owner may convert the security into the issuing firm's common stock. Generally, convertible securities offer more income (higher interest or higher dividends) than may be earned through an investment in the firm's common stock. In addition, convertible securities have some potential for capital gains if the price of the underlying stock rises. Convertibles are issued by a variety of firms, generating a range of securities from high-quality to extremely risky convertibles.

This chapter discusses investing in convertible bonds and convertible preferred stocks. Initially, the features and terms of convertible bonds are described, followed by a discussion of their pricing. This includes the premiums paid for convertible bonds, and the relationship between their price and the price of the stock into which they may be converted. The third section is devoted to convertible preferred stock. These shares are similar to convertible bonds but lack the safety implied by the debt element of convertible bonds. Next follows the brief histories of three convertible bonds that illustrate the potential returns and risk associated with investing in them. The chapter ends with a description of a bond that permits the holder to sell the security back to the issuer prior to maturity for the bond's face value.

FEATURES OF CONVERTIBLE BONDS

convertible bond

A bond that may be exchanged for (i.e., converted into) stock.

Convertible bonds are debentures (i.e., unsecured debt instruments) that may be converted at the holder's option into the stock of the issuing company. Since the firm has granted the holder the right to convert the bonds, these bonds are usually subordinate to the firm's other debt. They also tend to offer a lower interest rate (i.e., coupon rate)

549

than is available on nonconvertible debt. Thus, the conversion feature means that the firm can issue lower-quality debt at a lower interest cost. Investors are willing to accept this reduced quality and interest income because the market value of the bond will appreciate if the price of the stock rises. These investors are thus trading quality and interest for possible capital gains.

Since convertible bonds are long-term debt instruments, they have features that are common to all bonds. They are usually issued in $1,000 denominations, pay interest semiannually, and have a fixed maturity date. If the bonds are converted into stock, the maturity date is irrelevant because the bonds are retired when they are converted. Convertible bonds frequently have a sinking fund requirement, which, like the maturity date, is meaningless once the bonds are converted.

Convertible bonds are *always callable*. The firm uses the call to force the holders to convert the bonds. Once the bond is called, the owner must convert, or any appreciation in price that has resulted from an increase in the stock's value will be lost. Such forced conversion is extremely important to the issuing firm, because it no longer has to pay the interest and retire the debt.

Convertible bonds are attractive to some investors because they offer the safety features of debt. The firm must meet the terms of the indenture, and the bonds must be retired if they are not converted. The flow of interest income usually exceeds the dividend yield that may be earned on the firm's stock. In addition, since the bonds may be converted into stock, the holder will share in the growth of the company. If the price of the stock rises in response to the firm's growth, the value of the convertible bond must also rise. It is this combination of the safety of debt and the potential for capital gain that makes convertible bonds an attractive investment, particularly to investors who desire income and some capital appreciation.

Like all investments, convertible bonds subject the holder to risk. If the company fails, the holder of a bond stands to lose the funds invested in the debt. This is particularly true with regard to convertible bonds, because they are usually subordinate to the firm's other debt. Thus, convertible bonds are riskier than senior debt or debt that is secured by specific collateral. In case of a default or bankruptcy, holders of convertible bonds may at best realize only a fraction of the principal amount invested. However, their position is still superior to that of the stockholders.

In addition to the risk of default, prices of convertible bonds fluctuate. As the next section explains, their price is partially related to the value of the stock into which they may be converted. Fluctuations in the price of the stock produce fluctuation in the price of the bond. These fluctuations are in addition to price movement caused by changes in interest rates. During periods of rising rates, convertibles are doubly cursed. Their lower coupons cause their prices to decline more than those of nonconvertible debt with higher coupons. This, coupled with a decline in the value of the underlying stock, results in considerable price declines for convertible bonds.

There are three possible outcomes for a convertible bond. If the price of the stock rises, the value of the bond rises and the bond is converted. If the firm defaults, the bond is reissued as part of a reorganization or the bond becomes worthless. If the value of the stock does not rise, the bond remains outstanding until the issuing company retires the debt.

THE VALUATION OF CONVERTIBLE BONDS

The valuation of a convertible bond depends on (1) the price of the stock into which the bond may be converted and (2) the value of the bond as a debt instrument. Although each of these factors affects the market price of the bond, the importance of each element varies with changing conditions in the securities markets. In the final analysis, the valuation of a convertible bond is difficult, because it is a hybrid security that combines debt and equity.

This section has three subdivisions. The first considers the value of the bond solely as stock. The second covers the bond's value only as a debt instrument, and the last section combines these values to show the hybrid nature of convertible bonds. To differentiate the value of the bond as stock from its value as debt, subscripts are added to the symbols used. *S* will represent stock, and *D* will represent debt. Although this may make the equations appear more complex, it will clearly distinguish the value of the bond as stock from the value as debt.

The Convertible Bond as Stock—The Conversion Value

conversion value as stock

Value of the bond in terms of the stock into which the bond may be converted.

The value of a convertible bond in terms of the stock, its **conversion value** (C_s), depends on (1) the face value or principal amount of the bond (FV), (2) the conversion (or exercise) price of the bond (P_e), and (3) the market price of the common stock (P_s). The face value divided by the *conversion price* of the bond gives the number of shares into which the bond may be converted. For example, if a $1,000 bond may be converted at $20 per share, then the bond may be converted into 50 shares ($1,000 ÷ $20). The number of shares times the market price of a share gives the value of the bond in terms of stock. If the bond is convertible into 50 shares and the stock sells for $15 per share, then the bond is worth $750 in terms of stock ($15 × 50).

The conversion value of the bond as stock may be expressed in equation form. The number of shares into which the bond may be converted is called the *conversion ratio*, or

$$\text{Conversion ratio} = \frac{FV}{P_e}.$$

The conversion value of the bond is the product of the conversion ratio and the price of the stock.[1] The conversion value of the bond as stock is expressed in Equation 16.1:

16.1
$$C_s = \frac{FV}{P_e} \times P_s$$

and is illustrated in Exhibit 16.1. In this example a $1,000 bond is convertible into 50 shares (i.e., a conversion price of $20 per share). The first column gives various prices of the stock. The second column presents the number of shares into which the bond is convertible (i.e., 50 shares). The third column gives the value of the bond in terms of

---

[1]The conversion price (the face value divided by the number of shares into which the bond may be converted) may be expressed using the conversion ratio. That is,

$$\text{Conversion price} = \frac{FV}{\text{Conversion ratio}}.$$

EXHIBIT   16.1   The Relationship Between the Price of a Stock and the Value of a Convertible Bond as Stock

Price of the Stock	Shares into Which the Bond Is Convertible	Value of the Bond in Terms of Stock
$ 0	50	$ 0
5	50	250
10	50	500
15	50	750
20	50	1,000
25	50	1,250
30	50	1,500

stock (i.e., the product of the values in the first two columns). As may be seen in the exhibit, the value of the bond in terms of stock rises as the price of the stock increases.

This relationship between the price of the stock and the conversion value of the bond is illustrated in Figure 16.1. The price of the stock (P_s) is given on the horizontal axis, and the conversion value of the bond (C_s) is shown on the vertical axis. As the price of the stock rises, the conversion value of the bond increases. This is shown in the graph by line C_s, which represents the intrinsic value of the bond in terms of stock. Line C_s is a straight line running through the origin. If the stock has no value, the value of the bond in terms of stock is also worthless. If the exercise price of the bond and the market price of the stock are equal (i.e., $P_s = P_e$, which in this case is $20), the bond's value as stock is equal to the principal amount (i.e., the bond's face value). As the price of the stock rises above the exercise price of the bond, the bond's value in terms of stock increases to more than the principal amount of the debt.

The market price of a convertible bond cannot be less than the bond's conversion value. If the price of the bond were less than its value as stock, an opportunity for arbitrage would exist. Arbitrageurs would sell the stock short, purchase the convertible bond, exercise the conversion feature, and use the shares acquired through the conversion to cover the short sale. They would then make a profit equal to the difference between the price of the convertible bond and the conversion value of the bond. For

FIGURE   16.1   The Relationship Between the Price of the Stock and the Conversion Value of the Bond

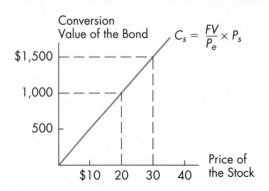

example, if in the preceding example the bond were selling for $800 when the stock sold for $20 per share, arbitrageurs would enter the market. At $20 per share, the bond is worth $1,000 in terms of the stock (i.e., $20 × 50). Arbitrageurs would sell 50 shares short for $1,000. At the same time they would buy the bond for $800 and exercise the option (i.e., convert the bond). After the shares had been acquired through the conversion of the bond, the arbitrageurs would cover the short position and earn $200 (before commissions).

As arbitrageurs purchase the bonds, they will drive up their price. The price increase will continue until there is no opportunity for profit. This occurs when the price is equal to or greater than the bond's value as stock. Thus, the conversion value of the bond as stock sets the minimum price of the bond. Because of arbitrage, the market price of a convertible bond will be at least equal to its conversion value.

However, the market price of the convertible bond is rarely equal to the conversion value of the bond. The bond frequently sells for a premium over its conversion value because the convertible bond may also have value as a debt instrument. As a pure (i.e., nonconvertible) bond, it competes with other nonconvertible debt. Like the conversion feature, this element of debt may affect the bond's price. Its impact is important, for it also has the effect of putting a minimum price on the convertible bond. It is this price floor that gives investors in convertible bonds an element of safety that stock lacks.

The Convertible Bond as Debt—The Investment Value

investment value as debt

The value of a convertible as if it were nonconvertible debt.

The **investment value** of a convertible bond (C_D) is related to (1) the annual interest that the bond pays (PMT), (2) the current interest rate that is paid on comparable nonconvertible debt (i), and (3) the requirement that the principal (FV) be retired at maturity (after n number of years) if the bond is not converted. In terms of present value calculations, the value of a convertible bond as nonconvertible debt is given in Equation 16.2:

16.2
$$C_D = \frac{PMT}{(1 + i)^1} + \frac{PMT}{(1 + i)^2} + \cdots + \frac{PMT}{(1 + i)^n} + \frac{FV}{(1 + i)^n}.$$

(Equation 16.2 is simply the current price of any bond and was discussed in Chapter 14.)

Equation 16.2 may be illustrated by the following example. Assume that the convertible bond in Exhibit 16.1 matures in ten years and pays 5 percent annually. Nonconvertible debt of the same risk class currently yields 8 percent. When these values are inserted into Equation 16.2, the investment value of the bond as nonconvertible debt is $798.50:

$$C_D = \frac{\$50}{(1 + 0.08)^1} + \frac{\$50}{(1 + 0.08)^2} + \cdots + \frac{\$50}{(1 + 0.08)^9}$$
$$+ \frac{\$50}{(1 + 0.08)^{10}} + \frac{\$1,000}{(1 + 0.08)^{10}}$$
$$C_D = \$50(6.710) + \$1,000(0.463) = \$798.50.$$

This equation may be solved by the use of present value tables or a financial calculator. The 6.710 is the interest factor for the present value of an annuity of $1 for ten years at 8 percent, and 0.463 is the interest factor for the present value of $1 to be

Calculator Solution	
Function Key	Data Input
PV =	?
FV =	1000
PMT =	50
N =	10
I =	8
Function Key	Answer
PV =	−798.70

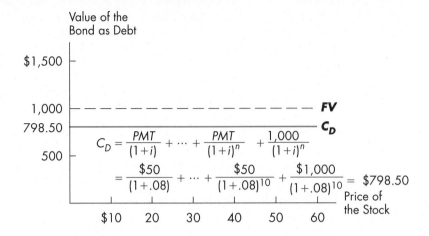

FIGURE   16.2   The Relationship Between the Price of Common Stock and the Value of the Bond as Nonconvertible Debt

received ten years in the future when it is discounted at 8 percent. To be competitive with nonconvertible debt, this bond would have to sell for $798.50.

The relationship between the price of the common stock and the value of this bond as nonconvertible debt is illustrated in Figure 16.2. This figure consists of a horizontal line (C_D) that shows what the price ($798.50) of the bond would be if it were not convertible into stock, in which case the price is independent of the value of the stock. The principal amount of the bond is also shown in Figure 16.2 by the broken line FV, which is above line C_D. The principal amount exceeds the value of the bond as pure debt because this bond must sell at a discount to be competitive with nonconvertible debt.

The investment value of the convertible bond as debt varies with market interest rates. Since the interest paid by the bond is fixed, the value of the bond as debt varies inversely with interest rates. An increase in interest rates causes this value to fall; a decline in interest rates causes the value to rise.

The relationship between the value of the preceding convertible bond as debt and various interest rates is presented in Exhibit 16.2. The first column gives various interest

EXHIBIT   16.2   The Relationship Between Interest Rates and the Investment Value of a Bond

Interest Rate	Coupon Rate	Investment Value of a Ten-Year Bond (Interest Paid Annually)
3%	5%	$1,170.60
4	5	1,081.11
5	5	1,000.00
6	5	926.40
7	5	859.53
8	5	798.70
10	5	692.77
12	5	604.48

FIGURE   16.3   The Actual Minimum Price of a Convertible Bond

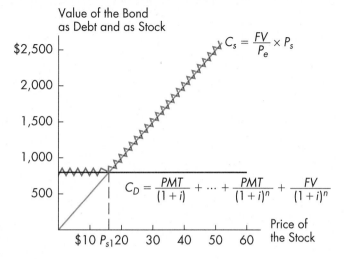

rates; the second column gives the nominal (i.e., coupon) rate of interest; and the last column gives the value of the bond as nonconvertible debt. The inverse relationship is readily apparent, for as the interest rate rises from 3 to 12 percent, the value of the bond declines from $1,170.60 to $604.48.

The value of the bond as nonconvertible debt is important because it sets another minimum value that the bond will command in the market. At that price the convertible bond is competitive with nonconvertible debt of the same maturity and degree of risk. If the bond were to sell below this price, it would offer a more attractive (i.e., higher) yield than nonconvertible debt. Investors would seek to buy the bond to attain this higher yield. They would bid up the bond's price until its yield was comparable to that of nonconvertible debt. Thus, the bond's value as nonconvertible debt becomes a floor on the price of the convertible bond. Even if the value of the stock into which the bond may be converted were to fall, this floor would halt the decline in the price of the convertible bond.

The actual minimum price of a convertible bond combines its value as stock and its value as debt. This is illustrated in Figure 16.3, which combines the preceding figures for the value of the bond in terms of both stock and nonconvertible debt. The bond's price is always greater than or equal to the higher of the two valuations. If the price of the convertible bond were below its value as common stock, arbitrageurs would bid up its price. If the bond sold for a price below its value as debt, investors in debt instruments would bid up the price.

The minimum price of the convertible bond is either its value in terms of stock or its value as nonconvertible debt, but the importance of these determinants varies. For low stock prices (i.e., stock prices less than P_{s1} in Figure 16.3), the minimum price is set by the bond's value as debt. However, for stock prices greater than P_{s1}, it is the bond's value as stock that determines the minimum price.

FIGURE   16.4   Market Price of a Convertible Bond

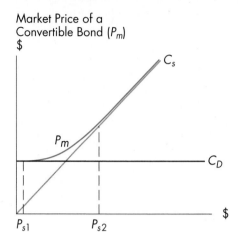

The Bond's Value as a Hybrid Security

The market price (P_m) of the convertible bond combines both the conversion value of the bond and its investment value as nonconvertible debt. If the price of the stock were to decline significantly below the exercise price of the bond, the market price of the convertible bond would be influenced primarily by the bond's value as nonconvertible debt. In effect, the bond would be priced as if it were a pure debt instrument. As the price of the stock rises, the conversion value of the bond rises and plays an increasingly important role in the determination of the market price of the convertible bond. At sufficiently high stock prices, the market price of the bond is identical with its conversion value.

These relationships are illustrated in Figure 16.4, which reproduces Figure 16.3 and adds the market price of the convertible bond (P_m). For prices of the common stock below P_{s1}, the market price is identical to the bond's value as nonconvertible debt. For prices of the common stock above P_{s2}, the price of the bond is identical to its value as common stock. At these extreme stock prices, the bond may be analyzed as if it were either pure debt or stock. For all prices between these two extremes, the market price of the convertible bond is influenced by the bond's value both as nonconvertible debt and as stock. This dual influence makes the analysis of convertible bonds difficult, since the investor pays a premium over the bond's value as stock and as debt.

PREMIUMS PAID FOR CONVERTIBLE DEBT

One way to analyze a convertible bond is to measure the premium over the bond's value as debt or as stock. For example, if a particular convertible bond is commanding a higher premium than is paid for similar convertible securities, perhaps this bond should be sold. Conversely, if the premium is relatively low, the bond may be a good investment.

The premiums paid for a convertible bond are illustrated in Exhibit 16.3, which reproduces Exhibit 16.1 and adds the value of the bond as nonconvertible debt (column 4)

EXHIBIT	16.3	Premiums Paid for Convertible Debt				
Price of the Stock	Shares into Which the Bond May Be Converted	Conversion Value of the Bond in Terms of Stock	Investment Value of the Bond as Non-convertible Debt	Hypothetical Market Price of the Convertible Bond	Premium in Terms of Stock*	Premium in Terms of Non-convertible Debt[†]
$ 0	50	$ 0	$798.50	$ 798.50	$798.50	$ 0.00
5	50	250	798.50	798.50	548.50	0.00
10	50	500	798.50	798.50	298.50	0.00
15	50	750	798.50	900.00	150.00	101.50
20	50	1,000	798.50	1,100.00	100.00	301.50
25	50	1,250	798.50	1,300.00	50.00	501.50
30	50	1,500	798.50	1,500.00	0.00	701.50

*The premium in terms of stock is equal to the hypothetical price of the convertible bond minus the value of the bond in terms of stock.
[†]The premium in terms of nonconvertible debt is equal to the hypothetical price of the convertible bond minus the value of the bond as nonconvertible debt.

along with hypothetical market prices for the bond (column 5). The premium that an investor pays for a convertible bond may be viewed in either of two ways: the premium over the bond's value as stock or the premium over the bond's value as debt. Column 6 gives the premium in terms of stock. This is the difference between the bond's market price and its conversion value as stock (i.e., the value in column 5 minus the value in column 3). This premium declines as the price of the stock rises and plays a more important role in the determination of the bond's price. Column 7 gives the premium in terms of nonconvertible debt. This is the difference between the bond's market price and its investment value as debt (i.e., the value in column 5 minus the value in column 4). This premium rises as the price of the stock rises, because the debt element of the bond is less important.

The inverse relationship between the two premiums is also illustrated in Figure 16.5. The premiums are shown by the difference between the line representing the market

FIGURE	16.5	Premium Paid for a Convertible Bond

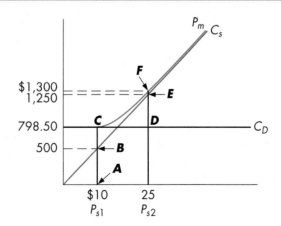

price (P_m) and the lines representing the value of the bond in terms of stock (C_s) and the value of the bond as nonconvertible debt (C_D).

When the price of the stock is low and the bond is selling close to its value as debt, the premium above the bond's intrinsic value as stock is substantial, but the premium above the bond's value as debt is small. For example, at P_{s1} the price of the stock is $10, the bond's value in terms of stock is $500 (line *AB* in Figure 16.5), and the premium is $298.50 (line *BC*). However, the bond is selling for its value as nonconvertible debt ($798.50), and there is no premium over its value as debt. When the price of the stock is $25 and the bond is selling for $1,300, the premium in terms of stock is only $50 (line *EF*). However, the bond's premium over its value as nonconvertible debt is $501.50 (line *DF*).

As these examples illustrate, the premium paid for the bond over its value as stock declines as the price of the stock rises. This decline in the premium is the result of the increasing impact of the conversion value on the bond's market price and the decreasing impact of the debt element on the bond's price.

As the price of the stock rises, the safety feature of the debt diminishes. If the price of the common stock ceased to rise and started to fall, the price of the convertible bond could decline considerably before it reached the floor price set by the nonconvertible debt. For example, if the price of the stock declined from $30 to $15 (a 50 percent decline), the price of the convertible bond could fall from $1,500 to $798.50 (a 46.8 percent decline). Such a price decline would indicate that the floor value of $798.50 had little impact on the decline in the price of the bond.

In addition, as the price of the stock (and hence the price of the convertible bond) rises, the probability that the bond will be called rises. When the bond is called, it can be worth only its value as stock. The call forces the holder to convert the bond into stock. For example, when the price of the stock is $30, the bond is worth $1,500 in terms of stock. Should the company call the bond and offer to retire it for its face value ($1,000), no one would accept the offer. Instead, they would convert the bond into $1,500 worth of stock. If the investor paid a premium over this conversion value (such as $1,600) and the bond were called, the investor would then suffer a loss. Thus, as the probability of a call increases, the willingness to pay a premium over the bond's value as stock declines, and the price of the convertible bond ultimately converges with its value as stock.

This decline in the premium also means that the price of the stock will rise more rapidly than the price of the bond. As may be seen in both Exhibit 16.3 and Figure 16.5, the market price of the convertible bond rises and falls with the price of the stock, because the conversion value of the bond rises and falls. However, the market price of the convertible bond does not rise as rapidly as the conversion value of the bond. For example, when the stock's price increased from $20 to $25 (a 25 percent increase), the convertible bond's price rose from $1,100 to $1,300 (an 18.2 percent increase). The reason for this difference in the rate of increase is the declining premium paid for the convertible bond. Since the premium declines as the price of the stock rises, the rate of increase in the price of the stock must exceed the rate of increase in the price of the bond.

Some investors may have the misconception that convertible bonds offer the best of both worlds: high return plus the safety of debt. In many cases, a convertible bond may prove to be an inferior investment. For example, if the price of the

⊕ Point of Interest

THE CONVERSION PARITY

In the body of the text, the analysis is based upon the value of the bond as stock (the conversion value) and the value of the bond as a debt instrument (the investment value). The analysis may be reversed to express the value of the stock in terms of the price of the bond, which is referred to as the *conversion parity*. This indicates what the stock is worth given the price of the bond. That is,

$$\text{Conversion parity} = \frac{\text{Price of the bond}}{\text{Conversion ratio}}.$$

If the price of the bond is $900 and the bond is convertible into 20 shares (i.e., convertible at $50 a share), the conversion parity is

$$\frac{\$900}{\$1,000/\$50} = \frac{\$900}{20} = \$45.$$

The conversion parity indicates that a share of stock is worth $45 in terms of the bond. If the price of the stock is $35, the bond is selling for a premium of $10 a share (i.e., a total premium of $200 based on the number of shares into which the bond may be converted).

The conversion parity offers another means to determine the premium paid for a convertible. In Exhibit 16.3, the bond's premium over its value as stock is the price of the bond minus the conversion value of the bond ($900 − $700 = $200 in this illustration). The conversion parity reverses the process. If the price of the bond is $900, the stock is worth $45 a share. Since the stock sells for $35 ($10 less than $45), the bond commands a premium of $200 ($10 × 20 shares) over its value as stock. The premium is $200 in either case.

stock rises rapidly, the stock is a superior investment because it will *produce a larger capital gain*. The stock outperforms the bond because the investor paid a premium for the convertible bond. In the opposite case when the price of the stock does not rise, a nonconvertible bond will outperform the convertible bond because it *pays more interest*. Thus, the very sources of a convertible bond's attractiveness (i.e., the potential capital growth plus the safety of debt) are also the reasons for its lack of appeal (i.e., the inferior growth relative to the stock and the inferior interest income relative to nonconvertible debt).

There is also potential for loss if the convertible bond is purchased for a substantial premium over its value as debt (i.e., over its investment value). For example, when the price of the stock was $30 in Exhibit 16.3, the bond sold for $1,500 (its conversion value). At that price the investor paid a premium of $701.50 over the bond's value as debt. If the price of the stock were to decline to $10, the value of the bond could fall to $798.50, inflicting a capital loss of $701.50 on the investor. While the decline in the bond's value is less than the decline in the value of the stock (47 versus 67 percent), the significant decrease certainly suggests that investors in convertible bonds could sustain a substantial loss even when interest rates remain the same and the company does not default.

These risks suggest that investors should approach convertible bonds cautiously. However, convertible bonds do offer some combination of potential capital gains, interest income, and the safety associated with debt. If the price of the stock rises, the price of the bond must also rise, and the investor receives interest income. If the stock's price does not rise, the convertible bond must eventually be retired because it is a debt obligation of the firm. Hence the bond does offer an element of safety that is not available through an investment in stock, as well as some growth potential that is not available through an investment in nonconvertible debt.

CONVERTIBLE PREFERRED STOCK

convertible preferred stock

Preferred stock that may be exchanged for (i.e., converted into) common stock.

In addition to convertible bonds, many firms have issued **convertible preferred stock**. As its name implies, this stock may be converted into the common stock of the issuing corporation. For example, the Rouse Company 6 percent preferred is convertible into 1.311 shares of the company's common stock.

Several of these issues of convertible preferred stock are the result of mergers. The tax laws permit firms to combine through an exchange of stock, which is not taxable (i.e., it is a tax-free exchange). If one firm purchases another firm for cash, the stockholders who sell their shares have an obvious realized sale. Profits and losses from the sale are then subject to capital gains taxation. However, the Internal Revenue Service has ruled that an exchange of *like securities* is not a realized sale and thus is not subject to capital gains taxation until the investor sells the new shares.

This tax ruling has encouraged mergers through the exchange of stock. In many cases, the firm that is taking over (the surviving firm) offers to the stockholders of the firm that is being taken over an opportunity to trade their shares for a new convertible preferred stock. Since the stock is convertible into the common stock of the surviving firm, it is a "like" security. Thus, the transaction is not subject to capital gains taxation. To encourage the stockholders to tender their shares, the surviving firm may offer a generous dividend yield on the convertible preferred stock. For this reason many convertible preferred stocks have more generous dividend yields than that which is available through investing in the firm's common stock.

Convertible preferred stock is similar to convertible debt, but there are some important differences. The differences are primarily the same as those between nonconvertible preferred stock and nonconvertible debt. Preferred stock is treated as an equity instrument. Thus, the firm is not under any legal obligation to pay dividends. In addition, the preferred stock may be a perpetual security, and unlike debt, may not have to be retired. However, many convertible preferred stocks do have a required sinking fund, and all convertible preferred stocks are callable, so the firm can force stockholders to convert.

The value of convertible preferred stock (like convertible bonds) is related to the price of the stock into which it may be converted and to the value of competitive nonconvertible preferred stock. As with convertible bonds, these values set floors on the price of the convertible preferred stock. It cannot sell for any significant length of time below its value as common stock. If it did, investors would enter the market and buy the preferred stock, which would increase its price. Thus, the minimum value of the convertible preferred stock (like the minimum value of the convertible bond) must be equal to the conversion value of the stock (P_c). In equation form that is

16.3
$$P_c = P_s \times N,$$

where P_s is the market price of the stock into which the convertible preferred stock may be converted, and N is the number of shares an investor obtains through conversion.

Equation 16.3 is similar to Equation 16.1, which gave the intrinsic value of the convertible bond as stock.

The convertible preferred stock's value as nonconvertible, perpetual preferred stock (P_{pfd}) is related to the dividend it pays (D_{pfd}) and to the appropriate discount factor (k_{pfd}), which is the yield earned on competitive nonconvertible preferred stock. In equation form that is

16.4
$$P_{pfd} = \frac{D_{pfdr}}{k_{pfd}},$$

which is essentially the same as the convertible bond's value as debt except that the preferred stock has no definite maturity date. However, this value does set a floor on the price of a convertible preferred stock because at that price it is competitive with nonconvertible preferred stock.

As with convertible bonds, the convertible preferred stock is a hybrid security whose value combines its worth both as common stock and as nonconvertible preferred stock. Convertible preferred stock tends to sell for a premium over its value as common stock and its value as straight preferred stock. Figures 16.4 and 16.5, which illustrated the value of the convertible bond at various prices of the stock into which it may be converted, also apply to convertible preferred stock. The only difference is the premium that the preferred stock commands over the value as common stock, which tends to be smaller. The reason for this reduced premium is that the preferred stock does not have the element of debt. Its features are more similar to common stock than are the features of the convertible bond. Thus, its price usually commands less of a premium over its value as common stock.

Convertible-Exchangeable Preferred Stock

Convertible-exchangeable preferred stock is a security that includes two options. The holder may convert the shares into the firm's common stock, or the company may force the holder to exchange the shares for the firm's bonds.[2] For example, the Federal Paper Board $2.3125 convertible-exchangeable preferred stock could be converted at the holder's option into 2.51 shares of common stock. However, the firm had the option to exchange each share for $25 worth of the firm's 9¼ percent convertible debentures.

The exchange option gives the firm more control over the preferred stock, as it is a means to force retirement of the shares without an outlay of cash if the value of the common stock rises *or* falls. If the value of the common stock rises, the investor may voluntarily convert the preferred stock. However, the firm may exercise its option to exchange the bonds for the preferred stock, thus forcing the stockholder to convert or

---

[2] A variation on the convertible-exchangeable preferred stock is the Premium Income Equity Securities or PIES. (Lehman Brothers Inc. has the rights to the terms "Premium Income Equity Securities" and "PIES.") These securities consist of a stock purchase contract that the holder must fulfill and a debt obligation that the issuer must meet. For example, Dominion Resources issued PIES with a 9.5 percent coupon that must be converted into common stock at $61.20. If the price of the stock rises above $61.20, the value of the PIES will rise. But the converse is also true. If the price of the stock declines below $61.20, the holder is obligated to exchange the PIES for the stock. If an investor purchases a convertible bond and the price of the underlying stock falls, the investor may hold the bond and receive the principal at maturity. With a Premium Income Equity Security, the investor must exchange the security for the underlying stock.

lose the appreciation in the preferred stock's value. In this case the exchange option operates as a call feature—it forces conversion.

If the value of the common stock were to decline, no one would exercise the option to convert the stock. Without the exchange option, there is nothing the firm could do to retire the stock and rid itself of the required dividend payments except repurchase the shares. However, the exchange option allows the firm to force the preferred stockholder to exchange the shares for debt. The firm will now have to make interest payments, but these are tax-deductible expenses, while preferred dividends are paid from earnings and are not tax deductible.

Preferred Equity Redemption Cumulative Stock (PERCS)

Preferred equity redemption cumulative stock (PERCS) is a preferred stock that will be exchanged in the future for the issuing firm's common stock. Like convertible preferred stock it combines elements of preferred stock with some potential for growth. The cash dividend paid by a PERCS is established when the security is issued and is generally about twice the amount of the dividend being paid by the common stock. Since the stock pays a fixed dividend, the security is similar to preferred stock.

The potential for growth occurs through the redemption feature. This preferred stock may not be converted at the holder's option and will not be called by the firm. Instead, the preferred stock is redeemed (i.e., exchanged) at a specified future date into the firm's common stock (usually three years after date of issue). For example, the PERCS issued on February 21, 1992, by Sears would be exchanged for Sears common stock on February 21, 1995. The PERCS paid an annual dividend of $3.75 while the common paid a dividend of $2.00. At the end of three years, the stock would be exchanged for one share of common as long as the price of the common was $59.00 or less. If the price of the common exceeded $59, the number of common shares exchanged would be adjusted so that the holder of the PERCS received common stock worth $59.00. Thus, if Sears were selling for $75, the holder of the PERCS would receive 0.7867 ($59/$75) shares. On February 21, 1995, Sears stock did not sell for more than $59, so each share of preferred was exchanged for a share of common stock.

What advantages do PERCS shares offer investors? The primary advantage is the higher dividend yield. Suppose the price of Sears stagnates; at the end of the three years, the investor receives one share of common stock whose value has not changed, but the investor has received more dividends during the three years than would have been paid to holders of the common stock. If the value of the common stock declines, the additional dividends offset some of the price decline. Thus, if the price of the stock remains stable or declines, the investor ends up better off with the PERCS compared to holding the underlying common stock.

If the price of the common stock rises, the value of the preferred equity cumulative redemption stock also rises up to the specified maximum price, which sets a ceiling on the price increase. If the price of the common continues to rise, the price of the PERCS cannot rise since further price increases are offset by the decline in the number of shares into which the PERCS will be exchanged. Thus, PERCS is of interest to investors who seek additional dividend income and who do not believe that the price of the underlying stock will rise dramatically during the time period. Of course, the best outcome for the investor in the PERCS would be for the price of the stock to rise to the maximum

ADDITIONAL HYBRID SECURITIES

Hybrid cars have motors that combine the use of gasoline and an alternative source of power such as electricity from batteries. Debt-equity hybrid securities combine elements of debt and equity. They are similar to convertible bonds, but they are not convertible into the firm's underlying stock at the investor's option. Instead these hybrids have features that blur the distinctions between debt and equity.

"Trust Preferred Securities" ("TruPS") are preferred stock but are considered debt even though the name uses the word *preferred*. These securities make regular payments like traditional bonds, and tax lawyers (with the IRS's blessing) claim the payments are tax-deductible for the firm. Trust-preferred shares have long maturities (often 50 or more years from date of issue), which makes them more like equity than a debt instrument, which has

a more finite life. Credit agencies consider a proportion of trust-preferred stock as debt and a part as equity when rating the creditworthiness of the firm. This prorating of the security makes the firm appear to be using less financial leverage.

In 2006, Wachovia Capital Trust III issued Income Trust Securities (called "WITS"). These securities originate as a subordinated bond that pays a fixed rate of interest. After five years, the bond transforms into a perpetual preferred stock that pays a variable rate. Other variations on this theme include bonds whose payments increase when the securities transform from debt to equity. Notice that the company does not call and the investor does not convert the bond. The transformation occurs automatically if the company does not redeem the issue.

exchange price. Then the investor would receive the higher dividend and realize the highest possible capital gain. The only loss would be an opportunity loss from the price of the common stock rising above the exchange price.

SELECTING CONVERTIBLES

Because convertible bonds are a hybrid security, they are more difficult to analyze than nonconvertible bonds. These securities are debt instruments and pay a fixed flow of interest income, so they appeal to conservative, income-oriented investors. However, since the bonds sell for a premium over their investment value as debt, investors forgo some of the interest income and safety associated with nonconvertible bonds.

A convertible bond also offers the potential for capital gains if the value of the stock into which the bond may be converted were to rise. Possible capital gains increase the bond's attractiveness to investors seeking capital appreciation. Since the investor pays a premium over the bond's value as stock, the potential price appreciation is less than is available through an investment in the firm's common stock. However, the investor who purchases the bond does collect the interest, which usually exceeds the dividends paid on an equivalent number of shares into which the bond may be converted.

The interest advantage may be seen by considering the 8 percent convertible bond issued by Petrie Stores. Each bond may be converted into 45.2 shares of common stock. The stock paid dividends of $0.20 a share (i.e., the equivalent of $9.04 on 45.2 shares), but the bond paid interest of $80. The bondholder collected $70.96 more in interest income than the stockholder collected on an equivalent number of shares.

⊕ **Point of Interest**

FEDERAL INCOME TAXES AND CONVERTIBLE BONDS

The federal government taxes interest paid by convertible bonds as income, and it taxes any capital gains that occur if the bond is sold for a profit. Does it also levy taxes when the investor converts the bonds into stock? The answer is no. The cost basis of the bond is transferred to the stock.

You buy a convertible bond for $1,000 and it is convertible into 40 shares. The cost basis for the bond is $1,000, and that is used when the bond is sold to determine any capital gains or losses. If you convert the bond, the cost of the 40 shares of stock is also $1,000 ($25 a share). As long as you hold the shares, there has been no taxable transaction. If you sell the 40 shares for $1,600 ($40 a share), your capital gain is $600 ($1,600 − 1,000). If you sell the 40 shares for $10 a share, your capital loss is $600 ($400 − 1,000). Whether these capital gains or losses are short-term or long-term depends on the total time you held the securities. Thus, the determination of long-term or short-term includes both the periods when you held the bond and when you owned the stock.

This additional flow of income offers one way to analyze the premium paid for a convertible bond. If the bond is held for a sufficient amount of time, the additional income will offset the premium. This time period is sometimes referred to as *years to payback* or the *break-even time*. The following example illustrates how this break-even time period may be computed. Consider a $1,000 convertible bond with a 7 percent coupon that is convertible into 50 shares of stock. The stock currently sells for $16 a share and pays a dividend of $0.40 a share. In terms of stock the bond is worth $800 (50 × $16). If the bond's price is $1,000, the premium over the bond's value as stock is $200 ($1,000 − $800). The bondholder receives $70 a year in interest but would receive only $20 ($0.40 × 50) on the stock. Thus purchasing the bond instead of an equivalent number of shares generates $50 in additional income, which offsets the premium over the bond's value as stock in four years ($200/$50 = 4).

This series of calculations may be summarized as follows:

Market value of the bond	$1,000
Minus bond's conversion value	800
Premium over the conversion value	$ 200
Bond's annual income	$ 70
Minus annual income from stock	20
Annual income advantage to bond	$ 50

$$\text{Payback period} = \frac{\text{Premium over the conversion value}}{\text{Annual income advantage}}$$

$$= \frac{\$200}{\$50} = 4 \text{ years.}$$

If the additional income offsets the premium paid over the bond's value as stock in a moderate period of time (e.g., three to four years), the convertible bond may be an attractive alternative to the stock. (This, of course, assumes that the stock is also sufficiently attractive and offers the potential for growth.) If the time period necessary to overcome the premium is many years (e.g., ten years), then the bond should not be purchased as an alternative to the stock but should be viewed solely as a debt instrument and analyzed as such.

The individual should realize that this technique is relatively simple and does not consider (1) differences in commission costs to buy bonds instead of stock, (2) possible growth in the cash dividend, which will increase the time period necessary to recapture the premium, and (3) the time value of money. The premium is paid in the present (i.e., when the bond is purchased), but the flow of interest income occurs in the future. However, the technique does permit comparisons of various convertible bonds. If the individual computes the time period necessary to recapture the premium for several bonds, he or she may identify specific convertible bonds that are more attractive potential investments.

THE HISTORY OF SELECTED CONVERTIBLE BONDS

Perhaps the best way to understand investing in convertible bonds is to examine the history of several convertible bonds. The first is a success story, in that the price of the common stock rose and therefore the value of the bond also rose. The second is a not-so-successful story, for the price of the stock declined and so did the value of the bond. However, the story of this bond is not a tragedy, for the bond was still a debt obligation of the company and was retired at maturity even though it was not converted into stock. The third bond illustrates a more typical case in which the bond's price rises but the increase occurs over an extended period of time.

The American Quasar Convertible Bond

American Quasar was a firm devoted to exploring and drilling for oil and gas. The discovery of oil wells (called *wildcats*) can prove to be highly lucrative; however, the majority of drilling leads only to dry holes (i.e., no oil or natural gas is found). Because of the nature of its operations, American Quasar was a speculative firm at best. Speculative firms, however, need funds to operate, so the firm issued $17,500,000 in face value of convertible bonds. The coupon rate was set at 7¼ percent and the exercise price of the bond was $21 (i.e., it was convertible into 47.6 shares), which was a premium of 17 percent over the approximate price of the stock ($18) at the date of issue.

After the bond was issued, American Quasar's stock did particularly well and the price rose to $32. The value of the convertible bond also increased with the price of the stock. The prices of the bond and the stock moved closely together, and less than two years after being issued the bond was called, which forced conversion of the bond into the stock.

What was the return earned by investors in these securities? Obviously, an investment in either the stock or the bond was quite profitable, since the price of the stock rose so rapidly. The bond's price rose from an initial sale price of $1,000 to approximately $1,500 during the time it was outstanding. The bond paid $72.50 in interest. The holding period return earned over the 15 months on an investment in the bond was

$$\frac{\text{Price appreciation + Interest earned}}{\text{Cost}} = \frac{\$1,500 - \$1,000 + \$72.50}{\$1,000}$$

$$= \frac{\$572.50}{\$1,000} = 57.25\%.$$

For the stock the holding period return was

$$\frac{\text{Price appreciation + Dividends}}{\text{Cost}} = \frac{\$32 - \$18 + \$0}{\$18} = \frac{\$14}{\$18} = 77.7\%.$$

(The bond paid only one year's interest since it was converted prior to the next interest payment, and the stock did not pay any cash dividends while the bond was outstanding.) As may be seen by these calculations, the returns are both positive. The stock did better because the bond was initially sold for a premium over its value as stock. However, an investor who purchased this convertible bond certainly would have little cause for complaint.

The Pan American World Airways Convertible Bonds

Although the previous example illustrated how the price of convertible bonds may rise as the price of the stock rises, the Pan American World Airways convertible bonds demonstrate the opposite. The 4½ percent convertible bond was issued when Pan Am was riding the crest of popularity. For investors purchasing either the stock or the bond, Pam Am's popularity vanished, and through years of continued deficits, the price of the stock declined drastically. Both the stock and the bond fell to "bargain basement" prices, as the market expected the firm to default. At that time the bond reached a low of $130 for a $1,000 bond!

Pan Am, however, did not default, and the bond remained an obligation that had to be retired. Thus, when Pan Am did redeem the bond, investors who purchased it initially for $1,000 received their principal. Holders of the Pan Am convertible bonds due in 2010 and the nonconvertible debt due in 2003 and 2004 were not so lucky, because the firm eventually failed and ceased operations. These bonds thus illustrate that investors who acquire both convertible and nonconvertible bonds of financially weak firms can lose their entire investments if the firm fails.

The Seagate Technology Convertible Bond

The American Quasar bond was in existence only briefly because the underlying stock price rose and the bond was converted soon after it was issued. The Pan Am convertible bond lasted the entire term and was retired at par. Between the two extremes is the Seagate Technology convertible bond. Issued in 1993, this 6¾ percent bond continued to trade, with its price moving with the price of the underlying stock. The Seagate convertible illustrates the importance of holding the bond for many years if the bondholder expects to earn a higher return on the bond than on the stock. For example, an investor could have bought the bond in 1993 for $860, while the stock sold for $16. Since the bond was convertible into 23.529 shares, its value as stock was $376 (23.529 × $16). At those prices the bond sold for a premium of $484 ($860 − $376) over the value of the underlying stock. Since the bond paid annual interest of $67.50, it would take over seven years ($484/$67.50) for the interest to offset the premium.

In 1996, the stock had risen to over $60, and Seagate called bonds for $1,013.50 plus accrued interest. At $60, the bonds were worth $1,411.74, so it was obviously advantageous to convert. The call occurred three years after the bonds were issued, so the interest could not cover the premium. The investor who purchased the stock for $16 and sold it for $60 earned an annualized return in excess of 55 percent. The investor who purchased the bond for $860, collected the interest, and sold the bond for $1,412 earned an annualized return of 24.7 percent.

CALLING CONVERTIBLES

Two of the previous illustrations (the American Quasar and Seagate Technology bonds) resulted in the bond's being called. Why do companies call their convertible bonds, and when? The answer to the first question is almost self-evident. Calling the bond and forcing it to be converted into stock results in saving the interest payments. Once the bond is converted, interest payments cease. The forced conversion also improves the firm's balance sheet. There is less debt outstanding and additional equity. The debt ratio declines and indicates that the firm is less financially leveraged. This reduction in debt is achieved without a cash outflow to repay the principal.

The mechanics of calling has two considerations. First, the price of the stock must exceed the exercise price of the bond. If the exercise price of a $1,000 convertible bond is $50 and the price of the stock is $40, no one will convert. The bond is convertible into 20 shares ($1,000/$50) and those shares are worth only $800. No investor will convert the bond but instead will accept the call price. If the price of the stock is $80, virtually all investors will convert. The 20 shares are worth $1,600. Few, if any, will accept the call price and not convert the bond.

Once the bond is called, there is the chance that the price of the stock may decline. The call is not instantaneous; it occurs over a period of time such as four weeks. If the price of the above stock is $53, the value of the bond as stock is only $1,060. If the firm calls the bond and the price of the stock declines to $49, investors will not convert. This defeats the purpose of the call to force conversion. Management will wait until the price of the stock has risen sufficiently to make it a virtual certainty that the price of the stock will not decline to the point that bondholders accept the call price instead of converting.

The second consideration is the actual timing of the call. The call virtually always occurs prior to an interest payment. If the bond pays interest every June 1 and December 1, calling the bond on December 10 occurs after the interest payment is made. It would be better to call the bond prior to December 1. Even calling the bond on November 15 would not avoid the interest payment. The four-week period during which the bondholders may convert would result in their holding the bond until the interest payment is made and then converting the bond. Thus, calls tend to occur more than one month prior to the interest payment (e.g., October 15 in the previous example) but rarely after the interest payment.

CONTINGENT CONVERTIBLE BONDS

A variation on the convertible bond is the "contingent convertible" or CoCo bond. Unlike a straight convertible bond, which has the convertible feature when issued, a CoCo bond becomes convertible *if* the price of the firm's stock rises a specified amount, such as 30 percent, from the date when the bond is issued.

While this distraction may seem like splitting hairs, the difference is important from an accounting perspective. When a convertible bond is exchanged for stock, the number of outstanding shares is increased, which reduces earnings per share (EPS). Companies must report EPS on a fully diluted basis, so a straight convertible bond reduces EPS even though the bond has not been, and may not be, converted. CoCo bonds, however, are not convertible when issued. They become convertible only if the contingency is met, so CoCo bonds do not dilute current earnings.

Since CoCo bonds avoid the dilution associated with straight convertible bonds, they have become a popular means to raise funds. This accounting advantage, however, may cease to exist. The Financial Accounting Standards Board (FASB) is considering changing the rules and requiring that earnings be adjusted for the potential dilution caused by contingency convertible bonds from date of issue. While the accounting change will not affect interest paid or a firm's cash flow, it will affect reported earnings and may decrease the attractiveness of the bonds to issuers.

The Textron 4.5 Convertible Senior Note due 2013 illustrates the contingency bond. The conversion price of the bond is $13.125 (76.19 shares of TXT stock). Once the stock trades for 30 consecutive days above $17.06 (a 30 percent premium over the conversion price), the bond could be converted into the common stock. This occurred in December 2009, so the bond became convertible in January 2010. With the stock trading for approximately $19, the bond was worth $1,448 as stock.

What should the bondholder do? The option to convert lasts for 90 days, after which the bond would no longer be convertible until the stock once again trades for 30 days at a price that exceeds 30 percent of the conversion price. If the investor does convert into TXT stock, the value of the stock may decline. The investor could decide not to convert, continue to hold the bond, and collect the interest. Now, however, the investor could lose the appreciation in the value of the bond (unless the stock continues to trade for the 30 percent premium over the conversion price). Of course, the investor could choose to sell the bond or sell the shares after converting the bond. The sale, however, is a taxable event. As with so many investment alternatives, no single choice may be preferred until the individual analyzes the choices in the context of his or her investment goals and strategies.

PUT BONDS

put bond

A bond that the holder may redeem (i.e., sell back to the issuer) at a specified price and a specified time.

Most of this chapter has been devoted to convertible bonds, which are debt instruments that investors may, at their option, exchange for stock. If the price of the stock rises, the investor profits because the conversion value of the bond rises.

During the 1980s, another type of bond was created with a different type of option. This **put bond** permits the holder to sell the instrument back to the issuer. In effect, the firm must redeem the bond at a specified date for its principal amount. Since the owner of these bonds has the option to sell the bond back to the firm, this option is analogous to a put option—hence the name, *put bond*. (Put options to sell stock are explained in the next chapter.) A typical illustration of a put bond is a Dominion Resource bond, which the investor could redeem five years after being issued for the principal amount. Put bonds also have a call feature, which gives the company the right to redeem the bonds. Thus, both the issuer and the buyer have options to redeem the bonds at par as of a specified date.

Fear that interest rates would increase and thereby inflict losses on bondholders led to the development of put bonds. Firms and governments need long-term financing, but some investors do not want to commit their funds for extended periods of time, especially if they fear rising interest rates. Put bonds permit firms and governments to sell long-term debt to investors who are reluctant to buy bonds with maturity dates 20 to 30 years into the future.

If, after these put bonds were issued, interest rates were to rise and thereby drive down the price of the bonds, the investor would exercise the put option at the specified redemption date. He or she would receive the principal and could immediately invest it at the current (and higher) rate of interest. Of course, if interest rates were to fall, the individual would not exercise the option. There would be no reason for the investor to seek the early redemption of the principal if interest rates have fallen. Instead, the investor may sell the bond on the market for more than the principal amount (i.e., for a premium).

Firms and governments are willing to offer investors this put option for much the same reason that they were willing to offer convertibility: lower interest costs. If an investor acquires an option, he or she must pay a price. For regular puts and calls that price (or *premium* as it is called in the jargon of options) is the amount paid to purchase the option. With a convertible bond or a put bond, the option's price is more subtle. Its price is the reduction in interest the investor must accept to acquire the option. (This price may be expressed in present value terms—it is the difference between the value of the bond with and the value of the bond without the option. See Problem 4.) Without the option the put bond's coupon would have had to be higher to induce investors to purchase the long-term bond.

The put option's potential impact on the value of a bond as interest rates fluctuate may be seen by the following illustration. A firm issues a bond due in 20 years with a 10 percent coupon. It grants the investor the option to redeem the bond at par at the end of 5 years. If the option is not exercised, the bond will remain outstanding for an additional 15 years. (This is a simple illustration with only one future date at which the investor may exercise the put option. Some bonds may grant the bondholder the option to redeem the bond more frequently, such as every 5 years.)

If the current interest rate is 8 percent, the value of the bond is

$$\$100(9.818) + \$1,000(0.215) = \$1,196.80.$$

The interest factors are 9.818 and 0.215 for the present value of an annuity and the present value of $1 at 8 percent for 20 years. Twenty years is the appropriate number of years because, since interest rates have fallen, the investor will not redeem the bond. The option thus has no impact on the increase in the price of the bond.

If the current interest rate is 12 percent, the value of the bond is

$$\$100(3.605) + \$1,000(0.567) = \$927.50.$$

Calculator Solution

Function Key	Data Input
PV =	?
FV =	1000
PMT =	100
N =	20
I =	8
Function Key	*Answer*
PV =	−1196.36

Calculator Solution

Function Key	Data Input
PV =	?
FV =	1000
PMT =	100
N =	5
I =	12
Function Key	*Answer*
PV =	−927.90

Calculator Solution

Function Key	Data Input
PV =	?
FV =	1000
PMT =	100
N =	20
I =	12
Function Key	*Answer*
PV =	−850.61

The interest factors are 3.605 and 0.567 for the present value of an annuity and the present value of $1 at 12 percent for *five* years. Five years is the appropriate number of years because if the current rate of interest exceeds 10 percent, the investor will exercise the option and redeem the bond.

The impact of the put option on the value of the bond can be seen by comparing the value above and the bond's value *without* the put option. In that case, if the current interest rate were 12 percent, the value of the bond would be

$$\$100(7.469) + \$1,000(0.104) = \$850.90.$$

The interest factors are 7.469 and 0.104 for the present value of an annuity and the present value of $1 at 12 percent for 20 years. Twenty years is the appropriate number of years because the bond lacks the put option. In this illustration, the put option increases the value of the bond by $76.60 ($927.50 − $850.90). Thus the put option affects the value of the bond if interest rates increase. Its impact is to reduce the amount by which the bond's price will decline, because the expected life is the redemption date rather than the maturity date.

Since bonds with put options are relatively new securities, one can only speculate as to their future popularity. However, granting the option does alter the interest paid, so one of the participants (i.e., the issuer or the investor) profits from the option. If interest rates remain below the coupon rate, the issuer profits, because the firm (or government) was able to sell a debt instrument with a lower rate than would have been required to sell the bonds without the put option. However, if interest rates rise, investors profit, because they are no longer locked into a debt instrument with an inferior yield. The issuer then will have to pay the higher rates in order to reborrow the funds. Obviously, if the investor (1) anticipates rising interest rates or (2) is particularly uncertain as to the direction of future interest rates and wants to hedge against rates increasing, bonds with put options may be attractive alternatives to other types of long-term debt instruments.

BONDS WITH PUT AND CALL FEATURES COMPARED

Put bonds and callable bonds are both illustrations of bonds with built-in options. In the case of the put bond, the option rests with the investor who has the right to sell the bond back to the issuer after a period of time for the bond's principal. This feature protects the bondholder from higher interest rates. Higher interest rates mean that the market price of the bond would decline, which hurts the bondholder. The put feature thus protects the investor from an increase in interest rates.

A callable bond gives the issuer the right to retire the bond (usually at face value plus a penalty). The feature protects the issuer from lower interest rates. Lower interest rates mean that the issuer is paying more on the existing debt than it would pay if it currently issued debt. The ability to call the debt suggests that the issuer may refund existing debt that requires a higher interest payment and substitute lower interest payments.

In either case, the option comes at the expense of one of the parties. That is, the option has a cost. The put feature favors the investor, so the interest rate on a put bond

⊕ **Point of Interest**

CONVERTIBLE, CALLABLE, AND PUTABLE BONDS

The features of convertible and put bonds are explained in the body of this chapter. May a bond have a conversion and a put feature? May the investor have the option to convert the bond? May the firm have the option to call the bond and force the bondholders to convert? May the investor have the option to sell the bond back to the issuer? The answer to all questions is yes.

In September 2006, New Plan Excel Trust issued a bond with all three features. The bonds pay a 3.7 percent coupon and are due in 2026. A $1,000 bond may be converted into 30.553 shares of stock, a conversion price of $1,000/30.553 = $32.73. (The conversion price was 22 percent higher than the $26.83 price of the stock when the terms were finalized.) If the price of the stock rises, the bondholders may convert the bonds into stock. If the dividend paid by the stock is higher than the interest earned on the bonds, such conversion makes sense.

After five years New Plan Excel Trust may redeem the bonds. By calling and redeeming the bonds, the company will force conversion if the price of the stock has risen. The bondholders may require New Plan Excel Trust to repurchase the bonds in September 2011, 2016, and 2021. Forcing redemption makes sense if the price of the stock has not risen and the interest return is inferior to other alternatives. So this issue of New Plan Excel Trust bonds has all three features: bondholders may voluntarily convert, bondholders may be forced to convert, and bondholders may force the company to repurchase the bonds. Hence this issue is convertible, callable, and putable.

should be lower. The cost of the option is the lost interest. The call feature favors the issuer, so the interest rate on the callable bond should be higher. The cost of the option is the higher interest payment. In either case one party gives up something and receives something in return. In the case of the put bond, the investors give up interest for the right to sell the bond back. In the case of the callable bond, the issuer pays higher interest for the right to retire the debt before maturity. In each case, one of the parties has to be wrong. If interest rates do not rise, then the interest cost of the put bond to the issuer is lower. The issuer benefits at the investors' expense. With the callable bond, the issuer loses if interest rates do not decline. The investors receive the higher interest payments.

The benefits and costs of options are not limited to debt instruments. They are a major component of all derivative securities. The market for derivative securities is large and plays an important role in both speculation and risk management. The benefits and costs of options to buy and sell stock are developed in more detail in the next three chapters, which are concerned with the features, valuation, and strategies that employ options and futures to buy and sell securities and other assets.

INVESTMENT COMPANIES AND CONVERTIBLE SECURITIES

Although an investor may acquire convertible securities, they are not as actively traded as the underlying stock, and the spreads between the bid and ask prices tend to be larger for the convertible bonds than for the stock. Only a handful of convertible prices are reported daily in the financial press. In addition, the large increases in securities prices experienced during the late 1990s and mid-2000s resulted in many convertibles being called, so the existing supply of convertible bonds and preferred stocks diminished.

These factors suggest that investors wanting to buy convertible securities may prefer to acquire shares in investment companies that hold convertibles. Both mutual funds and closed-end investment companies exist that specialize in convertible bonds and convertible preferred stock.

Fidelity Convertible Securities (FCSX) illustrates a no-load mutual fund that specializes in convertibles. At least 80 percent of its portfolio consists of convertible securities. Advent Claymore Convertible Securities and Income Fund (AVK) and Calamos Convertible and High Income Fund (CHY) illustrate closed-end investment companies that also specialize in convertibles. However, unlike a mutual fund, the shares of a closed-end investment may sell for a premium or discount from net asset value. As of June 2009, the Advent Claymore funds sold for a discount while the Calamos fund sold for a premium.

SUMMARY

A convertible bond is a debt instrument that may be converted into stock. The value of this bond depends on the value of the stock into which the bond may be converted and on the value of the bond as a debt instrument.

As the value of the stock rises, so does the conversion value of the convertible bond. If the price of the stock declines, the conversion value of the bond will also fall. However, the stock's price will decline faster, because the convertible bond's investment value as debt will halt the fall in the bond's price.

Since a convertible bond's price rises with the price of the stock, the bond offers the investor an opportunity for appreciation as the value of the firm increases. In addition, the bond's value as a debt sets a floor on the bond's price, which reduces the risk of loss to the investor. Should the stock decline in value, the debt element reduces the risk of loss to the bondholder.

Convertible bonds may sell for a premium. For these bonds, the premium may be viewed relative to the bond's value as stock or its value as debt. These two premiums are inversely related. When the price of the stock rises, the premium that the bond commands over its value as stock diminishes, but the premium over its value as debt rises. When the price of the stock falls, the premium over the bond's value as stock rises, but the premium relative to the bond's value as debt declines.

Convertible preferred stock is similar to convertible debt, except that it lacks the safety implied by a debt instrument. Its price is related to its conversion value, the flow of dividend income, and the rate that investors may earn on nonconvertible preferred stock.

A recent innovation in the debt instrument market is the put bond, which permits the holder to redeem the bond for its principal amount at some specified time in the future. If interest rates increase, the bondholder may exercise the put option. He or she redeems the bond, receives the principal, and thus is able to reinvest the funds at the higher current rate of interest. However, if interest rates fall, the bondholder will not exercise the option, as there is no reason to redeem the bond prior to maturity. Hence, the advantage put bonds offer investors is protection against being locked into an inferior rate of interest if the rates were to increase in the future.

Summary of Convertible Bond Equations

$$\text{Conversion ratio} = \frac{FV}{P_e}$$

$$\text{Conversion price} = \frac{FV}{\text{Conversion ratio}}$$

Conversion value (value of the bond as stock):

16.1
$$C_s = \frac{FV}{P_e} \times P_s$$

$$\text{Conversion premium (in dollars)} = \text{Price of the bond} - \text{Conversion value}$$

$$\text{Conversion premium (percentage)} = \frac{(\text{Price of the bond} - \text{Conversion value})}{\text{Conversion value}}$$

$$\text{Conversion parity (value of the stock based on the price of the bond)} = \frac{\text{Price of the bond}}{\text{Conversion ratio}}$$

Investment value (value of the bond as debt):

16.2
$$C_D = \frac{PMT}{(1+i)} + \cdots + \frac{PMT}{(1+i)^n} + \frac{FV}{(1+i)^n}$$

$$\text{Investment premium (in dollars)} = \text{Price of the bond} - \text{Investment value}$$

$$\text{Investment premium (percentage)} = \frac{(\text{Price of the bond} - \text{Investment value})}{\text{Investment value}}$$

$$\text{Payback period (breakeven time)} = \frac{\text{Conversion premium}}{(\text{Bond income} - \text{Stock income})}$$

QUESTIONS

1. What differentiates convertible bonds from other bonds?
2. How is the value of a convertible bond in terms of stock determined? What effect does this conversion value have on the price of the bond?
3. How is the value of a convertible bond in terms of debt determined? What effect does this investment value have on the price of the bond?
4. Why may convertible bonds be called by the firm? When are these bonds most likely to be called?
5. Why are convertible bonds less risky than stock but usually more risky than non-convertible bonds?
6. Why does the premium over the bond's conversion value decline as the value of the stock rises?

7. How are convertible preferred stocks different from convertible bonds?
8. What advantages do convertible securities offer investors? What are the risks associated with these investments?
9. Why may an investor prefer a debenture with a put feature in preference to a bond with a call feature?
10. If you expected a common stock's price to appreciate over a period of time, would you prefer to invest in a put bond, a callable convertible bond, or a convertible-exchangeable preferred stock issued by the firm?

PROBLEMS

1. Given the following information concerning a convertible bond:

Principal	$1,000
Coupon	5%
Maturity	15 years
Call price	$1,050
Conversion price	$37 (i.e., 27 shares)
Market price of the common stock	$32
Market price of the bond	$1,040

a) What is the current yield of this bond?
b) What is the value of the bond based on the market price of the common stock?
c) What is the value of the common stock based on the market price of the bond?
d) What is the premium in terms of stock that the investor pays when he or she purchases the convertible bond instead of the stock?
e) Nonconvertible bonds are selling with a yield to maturity of 7 percent. If this bond lacked the conversion feature, what would the approximate price of the bond be?
f) What is the premium in terms of debt that the investor pays when he or she purchases the convertible bond instead of a nonconvertible bond?
g) If the price of the common stock should double, would the price of the convertible bond double? Briefly explain your answer.
h) If the price of the common stock should decline by 50 percent, would the price of the convertible bond decline by the same percentage? Briefly explain your answer.
i) What is the probability that the corporation will call this bond?
j) Why are investors willing to pay the premiums mentioned in parts (d) and (f)?

2. The following information concerns a convertible bond:

Coupon	6% ($60 per $1,000 bond)
Exercise price	$25
Maturity	20 years
Call price	$1,040
Price of the common stock	$30

a) If this bond were nonconvertible, what would be its approximate value if comparable interest rates were 12 percent?
b) Into how many shares can the bond be converted?
c) What is the value of the bond in terms of stock?
d) What is the current minimum price that the bond will command?
e) If the current market price of the bond is $976, what should you do?
f) Is there any reason to anticipate that the firm will call the bond?
g) What do investors receive if they do not convert the bond when it is called?
h) If the bond were called, would it be advantageous to convert?
i) If interest rates rise, would that affect the bond's current yield?
j) If the stock price were $10, would your answer to part (i) be different?

3. Given the following information concerning a $2.00 convertible preferred stock:

One share of preferred is convertible into 0.50 shares of common stock	
Price of common stock:	$34
Price of convertible preferred stock:	$25

a) What is the value of the preferred stock in terms of common stock?
b) What is the premium over the preferred stock's value as common stock?
c) If the preferred stock is perpetual and comparable preferred stock offers a dividend yield of 10 percent, what would be the minimum price of this stock if it were not convertible?
d) If the price of the common stock rose to $60, what would be the minimum increase in the value of the preferred stock that you would expect?

4. Two bonds have the following terms:

Bond A	
Principal	$1,000
Coupon	8%
Maturity	10 years

Bond B	
Principal	$1,000
Coupon	7.6%
Maturity	10 years

Bond B has an additional feature: It may be redeemed at par after five years (i.e., it has a put feature). Both bonds were initially sold for their face amounts (i.e., $1,000).

a) If interest rates fall to 7 percent, what will be the price of each bond?
b) If interest rates rise to 9 percent, what will be the decline in the price of each bond from its initial price?
c) Given your answers to questions (a) and (b), what is the trade-off implied by the put option in bond B?
d) Bond B requires the investor to forgo $4 a year (i.e., $40 if the bond is in existence for ten years). If interest rates are 8 percent, what is the present value of this forgone interest? If the bond had lacked the put feature but had a coupon of 7.6 percent and a term to maturity of ten years, it would sell for $973.16 when interest rates were 8 percent. What, then, is the implied cost of the put option?

5. Two firms have common stock and convertible bonds outstanding. Information concerning these securities is as follows:

	Firm A	Firm B
Common stock		
Price of common stock	$46	$30
Cash dividend	none	$1
Convertible bond		
Principal	$1,000	$1,000
Conversion price	$50	$33¹/₃
	(20 shares)	(30 shares)
Maturity	10 years	10 years
Coupon	7.5%	7.5%
Market price	$1,100	$1,100

a) What is the value of each bond in terms of stock?
b) What is the premium paid over each bond's value as stock?
c) What is each bond's income advantage over the stock into which the bond may be converted?
d) How long will it take for the income advantage to offset the premium determined in part (b)?
e) If after four years firm A's stock sells for $65 and the firm calls the bond, what is the holding period return and the annual rate of return earned on an investment in the stock or in the bond? (You may wish to review the material on calculating rates of return presented in Chapter 10.)

6. Corporation RTY has the following convertible bond outstanding:

Coupon	7%
Principal	$1,000
Maturity	10 years
Conversion price	$64.516
Call price	$1,000 + one year's interest

The bond's credit rating is A. Other bonds issued by the company have a AA rating. Comparable AA-rated bonds yield 9 percent, and A-rated bonds yield 10 percent. The firm's stock is selling for $60 and pays a dividend of $2 a share. The convertible bond is selling for par ($1,000).

a) What is the value of the bond in terms of stock?
b) What is the premium paid over the bond's value as stock?
c) What is the bond's income advantage?
d) Given the bond's income advantage, how long must the investor hold the bond to overcome the premium over the bond's value as stock?
e) What is the probability that the firm will currently call the bond?
f) If after three years the price of the stock has risen annually by 10 percent to $80, what must have happened to the price of the bond?

    g) If the price of the bond rises to $1,240 at the end of three years, what is the *total* percentage return (i.e., the holding period return) the investor earns on the stock and on the bond?

    h) Why is the holding period return misleading?

    i) If the price of the bond rises to $1,240 at the end of three years, what is the annualized return the investor earns? Does this return exceed the return earned on the stock?

    j) If the stock is split 2 for 1, what impact will that have on the price of a convertible bond?

    k) If the convertible bond is held to maturity, what does the investor receive? What is the annualized return?

    l) If the price of the stock rises to $90 a share while interest rates on A-rated bonds rise to 12 percent, what impact does the increase in interest rates have on this convertible bond?

7. Dash Incorporated has the following convertible bond outstanding:

Coupon	5%
Principal	$1,000
Maturity	12 years
Conversion price	$33.34
Conversion ratio	30 shares
Call price	$1,000 + one year's interest

The bond's credit rating is BB, and comparable BB-rated bonds yield 9 percent. The firm's stock is selling for $25 and pays a dividend of $0.50 a share. The convertible bond is selling for $1,000.

    a) What is the premium paid over the bond's value as debt? What justifies this premium?

    b) Given the bond's income advantage, how long must the investor hold the bond to overcome the premium over the bond's value as stock?

    c) If the price of the stock were to decline by 50 percent, what is the worst performance that the bond should experience and why?

    d) If after four years the price of the stock has risen to $40, what is the minimum percentage increase in the bond's price?

    e) If the company pays a 20 percent stock dividend (i.e., not a cash dividend), what impact will that payment have on the price of the convertible bond?

    f) If the bond is not converted, what does the investor receive when the bond matures? What is the annual return on the investment?

    g) Is there any reason to expect that the firm will currently call the bond?

    h) If the price doubles and if the bond is called and investors do not convert, what do they receive?

8. A company issued a $100 preferred equity redemption cumulative stock with an annual dividend of $8. The preferred may be exchanged for two shares of common stock as long as the price of the stock is $60 or less. If the price of the stock exceeds $60, the number of shares is adjusted so the investor receives stock worth $60 a share. If the price of the stock is less than $40, the number of shares is adjusted so the investor receives stock worth $30 a share. The preferred

stock currently sells for $95. The common stock sells for $40 and does not pay a dividend.

a) What is the value of the exchangeable preferred stock based on the current value of the common stock?

b) Is the preferred stock selling for a premium over its value as common stock?

c) What may explain the existence of the premium?

d) What is the preferred stock's current yield?

e) What will be the value of the preferred stock as stock if the common stock sells for $10, $20, $40, $50, $60, $70, and $80?

f) If at the end of four years the common stock sells for $75 a share, which alternative generated the higher annualized return?

g) If at the end of four years the common stock sells for $45 a share, which alternative generated the higher annualized return?

h) If the price of the common stock declines to $25, what is the maximum possible loss experienced by the preferred stock excluding the dividend? If the dividend is included, what is the total loss or gain from the preferred stock?

The Financial Advisor's Investment Case
The Pros and Cons of Investing in a Convertible Bond

Many of your clients own small to medium-sized private businesses. One of your clients, Maurice Roussel, is planning to finance the education of his two children, ages 10 and 12. Currently, neither child has any assets, so Roussel is considering investing a modest amount in convertible bonds in their names with his wife, Lili, as custodian. Lili Roussel has doubts because she does not believe that it is wise to risk their hard-earned money on risky investments. Mr. Roussel believes that the money to be transferred is small enough to risk. Besides, he is fascinated with the convertible bonds issued by UT&T, a large company with a good, if not superior, credit rating.

Currently, the UT&T bonds trade for par ($1,000), have a coupon of 8 percent, mature in ten years, and are convertible into the stock at $10 a share (100 shares per $1,000 bond). Other bonds issued by the company pay 10 percent interest; its stock sells for $8.50 and pays no cash dividends. While Mr. Roussel believes that the bonds are a fine investment, Mrs. Roussel has doubts and raises several questions for you to answer.

1. If the bonds were not convertible, what would they be worth?
2. Since the bonds are convertible, what is their stock value?
3. If the value of the stock rose to $15, what would happen to the value of the bonds?
4. If the price of the stock declined to $5, what would happen to the value of the bonds?
5. If the money were invested in the nonconvertible bonds and the price of the stock changed, what would happen to the value of the bonds?
6. If the price of the stock rose, would the Roussels have to exchange the bonds for the stock?
7. If Mrs. Roussel changed her mind, could she get the principal back?
8. If the company were to fail, what would happen to the bonds?
9. Would buying the bonds be preferable to putting the money in the firm's stock?
10. Would buying the bonds be preferable to putting the money in a certificate of deposit in a federally insured commercial bank?
11. What are the federal income tax implications of owning convertible bonds? Would putting the bonds in the children's names result in any tax savings?

Given the nature of Mrs. Roussel's questions, do you believe that the money should be invested in convertible bonds?

Comprehensive Financial Advisor's Investment Case for Chapters 13–16

The Variety of Bonds and Their Impact on Investment Decision Making

Nikolas Sporer is a financial analyst with an investment company that specializes in fixed-income securities. The firm's portfolio managers have shown an interest in the bonds issued by PetSupport, a rapidly growing firm that specializes in catering to the pets of baby boomers. PetSupport has several bonds outstanding. Each bond matures in 20 years and is sold in units of $1,000. The current price of each bond is $1,000, and the price of the stock is $8.50. The specific features associated with each bond are as follows:

A   4% convertible debenture
      conversion price $10
        (bond may be converted at any time)
      call price $1,000 + one year's interest
      sinking fund retires 10 percent of the
        bond each year starting after ten years
        have elapsed.

B   8% subordinated debenture
      call price $1,000 + one year's interest
      no sinking fund

C   6% mortgage bond
      call price $1,000 + one year's interest
      sinking fund retires 5 percent of the
        issue each year

D   7% callable debenture
      callable after ten years at par
      sinking fund retires 5 percent of the
        issue each year

E   6% put bond
      put may be exercised after ten years
      sinking fund retires 10 percent of the
        bond each year starting after ten years
        have elapsed.

Currently the company is earning $0.85 per share but does not pay a cash dividend. Times-interest-earned is 5.4, and Sporer expects the stock to grow at least 10 percent annually, which should match the comparable stock indexes.

Previous meetings with portfolio managers have raised several questions concerning the risk associated with the company's bonds, especially their price volatility and potential for default. To be well prepared Sporer needs answers to several questions including the following:

1. Which bonds should Sporer expect to have the highest and the lowest credit ratings? What does the times-interest-earned number indicate about the probability of any of the bonds defaulting in the immediate future? Does the times-interest-earned of 5.4 apply to each bond or all of them?

2. Each bond has 20 years to maturity and is selling for its par value. What explains the differences in yields? Are these yields current yields or anticipated yields?

3. Since duration is one measure of price volatility, what is the duration of each bond? What assumptions must be made to answer this question? Why may duration have little applicability to some of the bonds, and which ones?

4. If, after one year, interest rates are essentially unchanged and the price of the stock remains in the doldrums at $8.50, what should be the price of each bond?

5. If, after five years have elapsed and interest rates have risen 2 percentage points (200 basis points) across the board, what should be the price of each bond? What assumptions must be made to answer this question?

6. If, after ten years have elapsed, interest rates have declined by 2 percentage points and the stock indexes have risen 9 percent annually, what should be the price of each bond? What assumptions must be made to answer this question?

7. Given prices in Question 6, what are the annualized returns on each bond? If Sporer believes that the situation in Question 6 is the most likely scenario, what course of action should he recommend today?

PART
Five

Derivatives

Part 5 is devoted to derivative securities. As their name implies, derivatives are based on another asset, and a derivative's value is dependent on the value of that underlying asset. Initially, Part 5 concerns options. An option is a contract that gives the holder the right to buy or sell a security at a specified price within a specified time period.

Options can be very speculative investments, and only those individuals who are willing and able to bear the risk should consider buying and selling them to take advantage of anticipated price movements. Options, however, may also be used in conjunction with other securities to manage risk. Thus, options are both a means to speculate on price movements in stocks and a means to reduce risk. Chapter 17 covers the basic features and positions using options. Chapter 18 presents the Black-Scholes option valuation model and a variety of strategies using options. Because options offer the possibility of a large return, those investors who are willing to bear the risk may find this material to be the most fascinating in the text.

Chapter 19 considers an alternative speculative investment: the futures contract. This contract is for the delivery of a commodity, such as wheat, or a financial asset, such as U.S. Treasury bills. Like options, the value of a futures contract is derived from the value of the underlying commodity. Futures contracts can produce large and sudden profits or losses, and they require that the individual actively participate in the day-to-day management of the investments. Although futures contracts are considered very speculative, they may be combined with other assets to hedge positions and reduce risk. Thus, futures contracts, like options, may be used as a means to speculate or to manage risk.

CHAPTER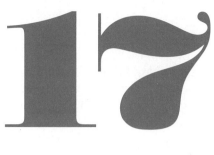

An Introduction to Options

LEARNING OBJECTIVES

After completing this chapter you should be able to:

1. Define the word *option* as it applies to securities and differentiate between an option's market value and its intrinsic value.
2. Identify the risks associated with purchasing an option and the factors affecting an option's time premium.
3. Differentiate the profit and loss from writing a covered call option versus a naked call option.
4. Explain the relationship between the price of a stock and a put option.
5. Compare buying a put with selling short.
6. Identify the advantages offered by stock index options.
7. Differentiate warrants from call options.

In October 2005, you could have bought an option to buy Google stock at $320 for $170. The next day, the option was selling for $1,990 (more than ten times the price the previous day). If you had bought an option to sell the stock at $320 instead of to buy, the option would have cost $1,830. The next day it was worth $5. Why did the prices of these options change so dramatically and in opposite directions? This chapter will help you answer those questions.

An option is often defined as the right to choose. In the securities markets, an option is the right to buy or sell stock at a specified price within a specified time period. The value of an option is derived from (that is, depends on) the underlying security for which the option is a right to buy or sell. Hence, options are often referred to as *derivative* securities. Options take various forms, including calls, puts, and warrants. Some

securities, such as the convertible bonds discussed in the previous chapter, have options built into them.

Investors in options do not receive the benefits of owning the underlying stock. These investors purchase the option because they expect the price of the option to rise (and fall) more rapidly than the underlying stock. Since options offer this potential leverage, they are also riskier investments; an individual could easily lose the entire amount invested in an option.

This chapter is a general introduction to investing in options. Initially, the features common to all options (their intrinsic value, the leverage they offer, and the time premiums they command) are covered. Next follows a discussion of particular options: the call and the put. With the formation of the Chicago Board Options Exchange (CBOE), a secondary market was created for the purchase and sale of call and put options. These options permit investors to take long and short positions and to construct hedge positions to reduce risk. The CBOE transformed securities markets by creating an opportunity for individuals to readily buy and sell options.

The initial success of the CBOE led to the trading of options on other exchanges and to the creation of new types of options, such as the stock index option, which is not based on a specific company's securities but on an index of the market as a whole. These index options permit investors to take long or short positions on the market without having to trade individual securities. The chapter ends with a discussion of warrants to buy stock issued by firms. Although warrants are similar to call options, they are infrequently used by firms as a means to raise funds.

This chapter uses material from Herbert B. Mayo, *Using the Leverage in Warrants and Calls to Build a Successful Investment Program* (New Rochelle, NY: Investors Intelligence, 1974). Permission to use this material has been graciously given by the publisher.

CALL OPTIONS

option

The right to buy or sell something at a specified price within a specified time period.

expiration date

The date by which an option must be exercised.

call option

An option sold by an individual that entitles the buyer to purchase stock at a specified price within a specified time period.

put option

An option to sell stock at a specified price within a specified time period.

intrinsic value

What an option is worth as stock.

exercise (strike) price

The price at which the investor may buy or sell stock through an option.

premium

The market price of an option.

An **option** is the right to buy or to sell stock at a specified price within a specified time period. At the end of the time period, the option expires on its **expiration date**. A **call option** is the right to buy (*call forth*) a specified number of shares (usually 100).[1] The opposite option, which is called a **put**, grants the right to sell a specified number of shares (usually 100) at a specified price within a specified time period. A put option, then, is the right to *place or put* the shares with someone else. (Puts are discussed later in this chapter.)

Notice the phrase "within a specified time period." American put and call options may be exercised at any time prior to expiration. European options may be exercised only at expiration. This difference means that an investor can exercise a call option prior to a dividend payment and receive the dividend. Such is not the case with a European option. Although few American options are exercised prior to expiration, this increased flexibility makes American options more valuable than European options.

The minimum price that a call option will command is its **intrinsic value** as an option. For an option to buy stock, this intrinsic value is the difference between the price of the stock and the per-share **exercise (strike) price** of the option. The market price of an option is frequently referred to as the **premium**. If an option is the right to buy stock at $30 a share and the stock is selling for $40, then the intrinsic value is $10 ($40 − $30 = $10).

If the stock is selling for a price greater than the per-share exercise price, the call has positive intrinsic value. This may be referred to as the option's being *in the money*. If the common stock is selling for a price that equals the strike price, the option is *at the money*. And if the price of the stock is less than the strike price, the call option has no intrinsic value. The option is *out of the money*. No one would purchase and exercise an option to buy stock when the stock could be purchased for a price that is less than the strike price. However, as is explained subsequently, such options may still trade.

The relationships among the price of a stock, the strike price (i.e., the exercise price of an option), and the option's intrinsic value are illustrated in Exhibit 17.1 and Figure 17.1. (Although put and call options generally trade in units of 100 shares, all of the text illustrations are on a per-share basis. The reporting of option prices in the financial press is also on a per-share basis.) In this example, the call is the right to buy the stock at $50 per share. The first column of the exhibit (the horizontal axis on the graph) gives various prices of the stock. The second column presents the strike price of the option ($50), and the last column gives the call's intrinsic value (i.e., the difference between the values in the first and second columns). The values in this third column are illustrated in the figure by line *ABC*, which shows the relationship between the price of the stock and the option's intrinsic value. It is evident from both the exhibit and the figure that as the price of the stock rises, the intrinsic value of the option also rises. However, for all stock prices below $50, the intrinsic value is zero, since securities prices are never negative. Only after the stock's price has risen above $50 does the call's intrinsic value become positive.

---

[1]Actually, call options are not new. They have existed since the 1630s, when options on tulip bulbs played a role in the speculative tulip bulb craze that swept Holland. For a fascinating portrait of such speculative periods, see Burton G. Malkiel, *A Random Walk Down Wall Street*, 9th ed. (New York: W. W. Norton & Company, 2007).

EXHIBIT 17.1	The Price of a Stock and the Intrinsic Value of a Call to Buy the Stock at $50 per Share

Price of the Stock	minus	Per-Share Strike Price of the Option	equals	Intrinsic Value of the Option
$ 0		$50		$ 0
10		50		0
20		50		0
30		50		0
40		50		0
50		50		0
60		50		10
70		50		20
80		50		30
90		50		40

FIGURE 17.1	The Relationship Between the Price of a Stock and the Intrinsic Value of a Call to Buy the Stock at $50 per Share

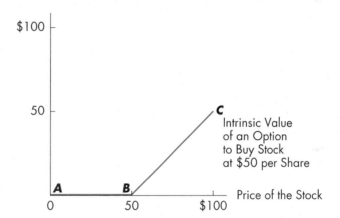

The market price of a call must approach its intrinsic value as the option approaches its expiration date. On the day that the option is to expire, the market price can be only what the option is worth as stock. It can be worth only the difference between the market price of the stock and the exercise price of the option. This fact means that the investor may use the intrinsic value of a call as an indication of the option's future price, for the investor knows that the market price of the option must approach its intrinsic value as the option approaches expiration.

Because of arbitrage, the intrinsic value sets the minimum price that the security will command. As was explained in Chapter 6, arbitrage is the act of simultaneously buying and selling a commodity or security in two different markets to make a profit from the different prices offered by the markets. In the case of an option, the two markets are the market for the stock and the market for the option. The essence of the

EXHIBIT   17.2   The Steps Required for Arbitrage

Givens		
Price of the stock		$60
Per-share strike price of the option		50
Price of the option		6
Step 1		
Buy the call for $6		
Sell the stock short for $60		
Step 2		
Exercise the option, thereby acquiring the stock for $50		
Step 3		
After acquiring the stock, cover the short position		
Determination of Profit or Loss		
Proceeds from the sale of the stock		$60
Cost of the stock		
Cost of the call	$ 6	
Cost to exercise the option	50	
Total cost		56
Net profit		$ 4

arbitrage position is a short sale in the stock and a long position (i.e., a purchase) in the option. After these transactions are effected, the arbitrageur will exercise the option. Then the shares acquired by exercising the call will be used to cover the short position in the stock.

This act of arbitrage may be clarified by using the simple example presented in Exhibit 17.2. If the price of the stock is $60 and the strike price of the option is $50, the option's intrinsic value is $10. If the current market price of the option is $6, an investor can buy the option and exercise it to acquire the stock. By doing so the investor saves $4, for the total cost of the stock is $56 (i.e., $6 for the option and $50 to exercise the option). The investor then owns stock that has a market value of $60.

If the investor continues to hold the stock, the $4 saving can evaporate if the stock's price falls. However, if the investor simultaneously buys the call and sells the stock short, the $4 profit is guaranteed. In other words, the investor uses arbitrage, the required steps for which are presented in Exhibit 17.2. The investor sells the stock short at $60 and purchases the call for $6 (step 1). The stock is borrowed from the broker and delivered to the buyer. Then the investor exercises the option (step 2) and covers the short position with the stock acquired by exercising the option (step 3). This set of transactions locks in the $4 profit, because the investor sells the stock short at $60 per share and simultaneously purchases and exercises the option for a combined cost of $56 per share. By selling the stock short and purchasing the call at the same time, the investor ensures that he or she will gain the difference between the intrinsic value of the option and its price. Through arbitrage the investor guarantees the profit.

Of course, the act of buying the option and selling the stock short will drive up the option's price and put pressure on the price of the stock to fall. Thus, the opportunity to arbitrage will disappear, because arbitrageurs will bid up the price of the option to at least its intrinsic value. Once the price of the call has risen to its intrinsic value, the opportunity for a profitable arbitrage disappears. However, if the price of the call were to fall again below its intrinsic value, the opportunity for arbitrage would reappear, and the process would be repeated. Thus, the intrinsic value of an option becomes the minimum price that the option must command, for arbitrageurs will enter the market as soon as the price of an option falls below its intrinsic value as an option.

If the price of the option were to exceed its intrinsic value, arbitrage would offer no profit, nor would an investor exercise the option. If the call to buy the stock in the previous examples were to sell for $5 when the price of the common stock was $50, no one would exercise the option. The cost of the stock acquired by exercising the call would be $55 (i.e., $50 + $5). The investor would be better off buying the stock outright than purchasing the call and exercising it.

Actually, the opportunity for the typical investor to execute a profitable arbitrage is exceedingly rare. Market makers are cognizant of the possible gains from arbitrage and are in the best possible position to take advantage of any profitable opportunities that may emerge. Hence, if the opportunity to purchase the call for a price less than its intrinsic value existed, the purchases would be made by the market makers, and the opportunity to arbitrage would not become available to the general public. For the general investor, the importance of arbitrage is not the opportunity for profit that it offers but the fact that it sets a floor on the price of an option, and that *floor* is the minimum or intrinsic value.[2]

LEVERAGE

leverage

Magnification of the potential return on an investment.

Options offer investors the advantage of **leverage**. The potential return on an investment in a call may exceed the potential return on an investment in the underlying stock (i.e., the stock that the option represents the right to purchase). Like the use of margin, this magnification of the potential gain is an example of leverage.

Exhibit 17.3, which illustrates the relationship between the price of a stock and a call's intrinsic value, also demonstrates the potential leverage that call options offer. For example, if the price of the stock rose from $60 to $70, the intrinsic value of the option would rise from $10 to $20. The percentage increase in the price of the stock is 16.67 percent ([$70 − $60] ÷ $60), whereas the percentage increase in the intrinsic value of the option is 100 percent ([$20 − $10] ÷ $10). The percentage increase in the intrinsic value of the call exceeds the percentage increase in the price of the stock. If the investor purchased the option for its intrinsic value and the price of the stock then rose, the return on the investment in the call would exceed the return on an investment in the stock.

Leverage, however, works in both directions. Although it may increase the investor's potential return, it may also increase the potential loss if the price of the stock declines. For example, if the price of the stock in Exhibit 17.3 fell from $70 to $60 for a 14.2 percent decline, the intrinsic value of the call would fall from $20 to $10 for a 50 percent decline. As with any investment, the investor must decide if the increase in the potential return offered by leverage is worth the increased risk.

---

[2]As is explained in the next chapter on the Black-Scholes option valuation model, prior to the expiration date the minimum price *must exceed* the option's intrinsic value.

EXHIBIT 17.3	The Relationship Between the Price of a Stock, the Value of a Call, and the Hypothetical Market Price of the Option

	Option		
Price of the Common Stock	Per-Share Strike Price	Intrinsic Value	Hypothetical Market Price
$ 10	$50	$ 0	$ 0
20	50	0	0.02
30	50	0	0.25
40	50	0	1
50	50	0	6
60	50	10	15
70	50	20	23
80	50	30	32
90	50	40	41
100	50	50	50

The Time Premium Paid for a Call

If an option offers a greater potential return than does the stock, investors may prefer to buy the option. In an effort to purchase the option, investors will bid up its price, so the market price will exceed the option's intrinsic value. Since the market price of an option is frequently referred to as the *premium*, the extent to which this price exceeds the option's intrinsic value is referred to as the **time premium** or time value. Investors are willing to pay this time premium for the potential leverage the option offers. This time premium, however, reduces the potential return and increases the potential loss.

time premium

The amount by which an option's price exceeds the option's intrinsic value.

The time premium for a call is illustrated in Exhibit 17.3, which adds to Exhibit 17.1 a hypothetical set of prices in column 4. The hypothetical market prices are greater than the intrinsic values of the call because investors have bid up the prices. To purchase the call, an investor must pay the market price and not the intrinsic value. Thus, in this example when the market price of the stock is $60 and the intrinsic value of the option is $10, the market price of the call is $15. The investor must pay $15 to purchase the call, which is $5 more than the option's intrinsic value.

The relationships in Exhibit 17.3 between the price of the stock and the call's intrinsic value and hypothetical price are illustrated in Figure 17.2. The time premium is easily seen in the graph, for it is the shaded area indicating the difference between the line representing the market price of the call (line *DE*) and the line representing its intrinsic value (line *ABC*). Thus, when the price of the stock and call are $60 and $15, respectively, the time premium is $5 (the price of the option, $15, minus its intrinsic value, $10).

As may be seen in the figure, the amount of the time value varies at the different price levels of the stock. However, the amount of the time premium declines as the price of the stock rises above the option's strike price. Once the price of the stock has risen considerably, the call may command virtually no time premium over its intrinsic value. At $100 per share, the option is selling at approximately its intrinsic value of $50. The primary reason for this decline in the time premium is that as the price of the stock and the intrinsic value of the option rise, the potential leverage is reduced. In addition, at higher prices the potential price decline in the call is greater if the price of the stock falls.

FIGURE 17.2 **The Relationships Among the Price of the Stock and a Call's Intrinsic Value and Hypothetical Price**

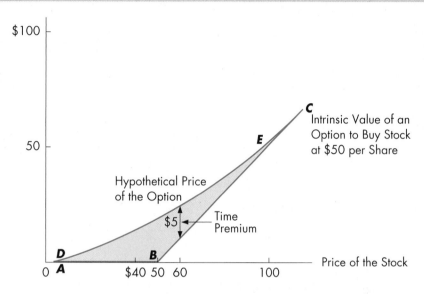

For these reasons investors become less willing to bid up the price of the call as the price of the stock rises, and hence the amount of the time premium diminishes.

The time premium decreases the potential leverage and return from investing in options. If, for example, this stock's price rose from $60 to $70 for a 16.7 percent gain, the call's price would rise from $15 to $23 for a 53.3 percent gain. The percentage increase in the price of the option still exceeds the percentage increase in the price of the stock; however, the difference between the two percentage increases is smaller, since the call sells for more than its intrinsic value. The time premium has substantially reduced the potential leverage that the call offers investors.

Investors who are considering purchasing calls should ask themselves what price increase they can expect in the option if the price of the underlying stock should rise. For the call to be attractive, its anticipated percentage increase in price must exceed the anticipated percentage increase in the price of the stock. The call must offer the investor leverage to justify the additional risk. Obviously an investor should not purchase the call if the stock's price is expected to appreciate in value more rapidly than the option's price. The previous example illustrates that the time premium paid for an option may substantially decrease the potential leverage. Thus, recognition of the time premium that an option commands over its intrinsic value is one of the most important considerations in the selection of an option for investment.

The valuation of a call determines the amount of the time premium (i.e., valuation determines where line *DE* in Figure 17.2 lies in the plane relating the price of the stock and the option's value). Several factors affect an option's value; since these factors differ among companies, time premiums commanded by options on their stocks also differ. While a detailed discussion of option valuation (and hence the time premium) is deferred until the next chapter, the following gives an overview of the determinants of an option's time premium.

⊕ Point of Interest

EUROPEAN OPTIONS

Put and call options are not unique to American financial markets but are also available in some foreign securities markets. However, these put and call options can differ significantly from American options. Specific differences vary from country to country but revolve around the duration of the option and existence of secondary markets. For example, the duration of the traditional British option is three months. Six-month and nine-month options are not available.

Some secondary markets do exist, but not for all foreign puts and calls. For example, there is no secondary market for the traditional three-month British option. Once purchased, the option cannot be sold. The investor must either exercise the option at a specified time or let it expire. Thus the most important difference between an American option and a so-called European option is the requirement that the investor must exercise the European option to realize any gain achieved through appreciation in the option's value.

As an option approaches expiration, its market price must approach the option's intrinsic value. On the expiration date, a call cannot command a price greater than its intrinsic value based on the underlying stock. Thus, as an option nears expiration, it will sell for a smaller time premium, and that premium disappears at the option's expiration.

Other determinants of an option's time premium include the payment of cash dividends, the volatility of the underlying stock, and interest rates. Options of companies that pay cash dividends tend to sell for smaller time premiums. There may be two possible explanations for this relationship. First, companies that retain (do not distribute) earnings will have more funds available for investments. By retaining and reinvesting earnings, a company may grow more rapidly, and this growth may be reflected in the price of its stock. Hence, the potential gain in the price of the call may be greater if the firm retains its earnings and does not pay a cash dividend. Second, if a company pays a dividend, the owner of the option does not receive the cash payment. The call will be less attractive relative to the common stock, for the owner of the option must forgo the dividend. Therefore, investors will not be willing to pay as much for the call and it will sell for a smaller time premium.

Another factor that affects the time premium paid for an option is the price volatility of the common stock. (In the next chapter this volatility will be measured by the variability of the stock's return as measured by the standard deviation of the return.) If the stock's price fluctuates substantially, the option may be more attractive and command a higher time premium. Since the price of the call follows the price of the underlying stock, fluctuations in the price of the stock will be reflected in the option's price. The more volatile the price of the stock, the more opportunity the option offers for a price increase. Thus, options on volatile stocks tend to be more attractive (at least to speculators) and command a higher time premium than options on stocks whose prices are more stable and less volatile.

Interest rates affect options by their impact on the present value of the funds necessary to exercise the option. Since options are exercised in the future, higher interest rates imply that the investor must set aside a lower amount of money to exercise the call. Since a call's intrinsic value is the price of the stock minus the strike price, a lower

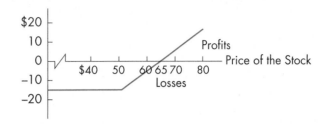

FIGURE 17.3 Profits and Losses at Expiration for the Buyer of a Call

strike price must increase the value of the option. In effect, higher interest rates reduce the present value of the strike price, which makes the call option more valuable.

Purchasing Calls

Calls may be purchased by investors who want to leverage their position in a stock. Should the price of the stock rise, the price of the call will also rise. Since the cost of the call is less than the cost of the stock, the percentage increase in the call may exceed that of the stock, so the investor earns a greater percentage return on the call option than on the underlying stock. If the price of the stock declines, the value of the call also falls, so the investor sustains a larger percentage loss on the option than on the stock. However, since the cost of the call is less than the stock, the absolute loss on the investment in the call may be less than the absolute loss on the stock.

The potential profits and losses at expiration on the purchase of a call for $15 when the stock sells for $60 are illustrated in Figure 17.3. As long as the price of the stock is $50 or less, the entire investment in the call ($15) is lost. As the price of the stock rises above $50, the loss is reduced. The investor breaks even at $65, because the intrinsic value of the call is $15—the cost of the option. The investor earns a profit as the price of the stock continues to rise above $65. (Remember that in this illustration the starting price of the stock was $60. The price has to rise only by more than $5 to assure the investor of a profit on the position in the call.)

Figure 17.4 replicates Figure 17.3 and adds the profits and losses from buying the stock at $60. Both involve purchases and therefore are long positions in the securities. If the price of the stock rises above or declines below $60, the investor earns a profit or sustains a loss. The important difference between the lines indicating the profit and losses on the long positions in the two securities is the possible large dollar loss from buying the stock compared to the limited dollar loss on the call. In the worst-case scenario, the investor could lose $60 on the stock but only $15 on the call.

WRITING CALLS

The preceding section considered purchasing call options to obtain leverage; this section will cover the opposite: selling call options. In the jargon of options, the act of issuing and selling a call is referred to as *writing* the option. While a long position in a call gives the investor an opportunity to profit from the leverage the option offers, the short position (i.e., writing and selling calls) produces revenues from their sale.

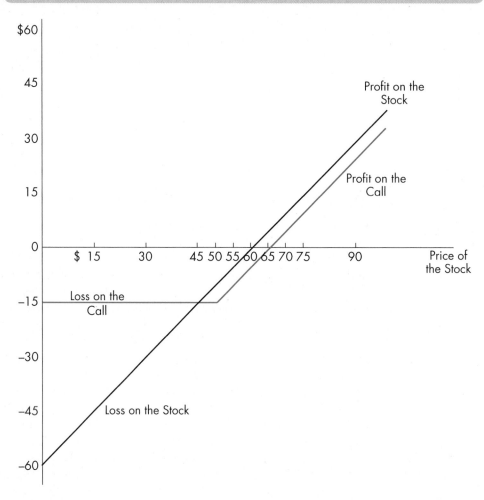

FIGURE   17.4   Profits and Losses of a Long Position in the Stock Compared to a Long Position in the Call

covered option writing

Selling an option for which the seller owns the securities.

naked option writing

The selling (i.e., writing) of an option without owning the underlying security.

There are two ways to write options. The first is the less risky strategy, which is called **covered option writing.** The investor buys (or already owns) the underlying stock and then sells the option to buy that stock. If the option is exercised, the investor supplies the stock that was previously purchased (i.e., *covers* the option with the stock). The second method entails selling the call without owning the stock. This is referred to as **naked option writing,** for the investor is exposed to considerable risk. If the price of the stock rises and the call is exercised, the option writer must buy the stock at the higher market price in order to supply it to the buyer. With naked option writing the potential for loss is considerably greater than with covered option writing.

The reason for writing options is the income to be gained from their sale. The potential profit from writing a covered option may be seen in Exhibit 17.4, which continues the illustration used in the discussion of buying a call. In this example the investor purchases the common stock at the current market price of $60 per share and simultaneously sells for $15 a call to buy the shares at the strike price of $50. Possible future

EXHIBIT 17.4 Profit on a Covered Call (at Expiration) Consisting of the Purchase of Shares of Stock and the Sale of One Call to Buy Shares at $50 a Share

Price of Stock at Expiration of the Call	Net Profit on the Stock	Value of the Call at Expiration	Net Profit on the Sale of the Call	Net Profit on the Position
$35	$−25	$0	$15	$−10
40	−20	0	15	−5
45	−15	0	15	0
50	−10	0	15	5
55	−5	5	10	5
60	0	10	5	5
65	5	15	0	5
70	10	20	−5	5

prices for the stock at the expiration of the call are given in column 1. Column 2 presents the net profit to the investor from the purchase of the stock. Column 3 gives the value of the call at expiration, and column 4 presents the profit to the investor from the sale of the call. As may be seen in column 4, the sale of the call is profitable to the investor as long as the price of the common stock remains below $65 per share. The last column gives the net profit on the entire position. As long as the price of the common stock stays above $45 per share, the entire position will yield a profit before commission fees. The maximum amount of this profit, however, is limited to $5. Thus, by selling the call the investor forgoes the possibility of large gains. For example, if the price of the stock were to rise to $70 per share, the holder of the call would exercise it and purchase the 100 shares from the seller at $50 per share. The seller would then net $5 ($50 from the stock + $15 from the sale of the call − $60 cost of the stock).

If the price of the stock were to fall below $45, the entire position would result in a loss to the seller. For example, if the price of the common stock fell to $40, the investor would lose $20 on the purchase of the stock. However, $15 was received from the sale of the call. Thus, the net loss is only $5. The investor still owns the stock and may now write another call on that stock. As long as the investor owns the stock, the same shares may be used over and over to cover the writing of options. Thus, even if the price of the stock does fall, the investor may continue to use it to write more options. The more options that can be written, the more profitable the shares become. For individuals who write options, the best possible situation would be for the stock's price to remain stable. In that case the investors would receive the income from writing the options and never suffer a capital loss from a decline in the price of the stock on which the option is being written.

The relationship between the price of the stock and the profit or loss on writing a covered call is illustrated in Figure 17.5, which plots the first and fifth columns of Exhibit 17.4. As may be seen from the figure, the sale of the covered option produces a profit (before commissions) for all prices of the stock above $45. However, the maximum profit (before commissions) is only $5.

Option writers do not have to own the common stock on which they write calls. Although such naked or uncovered option writing exposes the investor to a large amount of risk, the returns may be considerable. If the writer of the preceding option

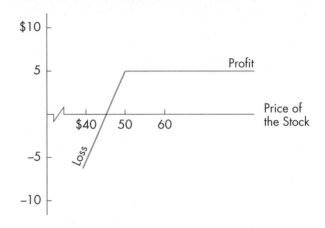

FIGURE **17.5** Profit or Loss on Selling a Covered Call (at Expiration of the Call)

had not owned the stock and had sold the option for $15, the position would have been profitable as long as the price of the common stock remained below $65 per share at the expiration of the call.

The potential loss, however, is theoretically infinite, for the naked option loses $100 for every $1 increase in the price of the stock above the call's exercise price. For example, if the price of the stock were to rise to $90 per share, the call would be worth $4,000 ($40 per share × 100 shares). The owner of the call would exercise it and purchase the 100 shares for $5,000. The writer of the call would then have to purchase the shares on the open market for $9,000. Since the writer received only $1,500 when the call was sold and $5,000 when the call was exercised, the loss would be $2,500. Therefore, uncovered option writing exposes the writer to considerable risk if the price of the stock rises. (This risk may be reduced by an order to purchase the stock at $65. If the price of the stock rises, the order is executed so that the option writer buys the stock and the position in the call is no longer naked.)

The relationship between the price of the stock and the profit or loss on writing a naked call option is illustrated in Figure 17.6. In this case the option writer earns a

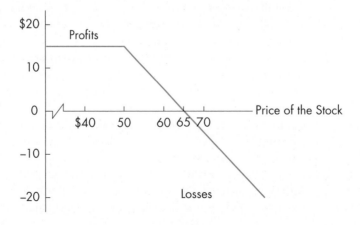

FIGURE **17.6** Profits and Losses at Expiration for a Naked Call Writer

⊕ Point of Interest

BIG PROFITS; BIG LOSSES

Profits and losses can be sustained very rapidly in option trading. Combine options with corporate takeovers and the possible price movements are magnified. Consider the attempted takeover of Cities Service by Gulf Oil. On Wednesday, June 16, 1982, the following options on Cities Service were traded when the stock sold for $37¾.

June Option Exercise Price	Option's Closing Price (6/16/82)
$20	$17⅛
25	12
30	7⅜
35	2
40	⁷⁄₁₆
45	⅛
50	¹⁄₁₆
55	¹⁄₁₆

On Thursday, June 17, 1982, there was no trading in Cities Service stock pending an announcement. The announcement turned out to be that Gulf Oil would buy Cities Service for $63 a share. When trading resumed on Friday, June 18, 1982, Cities Service stock rose to $53⅛. The options' price increases (and the percentage increases from the previous closing prices) were as follows:

June Option Exercise Price	Option's Closing Price (6/18/82)	Percentage Increase in Price
$20	$33¼	94.2%
25	28½	137.5
30	22⅞	210.2
35	18	800.0
40	13⅛	2,900.0
45	9½	7,500.0
50	3½	5,500.0
55	¹⁄₁₆	—

The irony of this incident is that the options were to expire on June 18, 1982. Thus the individual who bought the 40s at ⁷⁄₁₆ ($43.75) with only *two days to expiration* would normally have lost this money. But as a result of the attempted takeover, this speculator earned 2,900 percent in two days!

While few investors earned such a return, the *New York Times* (June 19, 1982, p. 33) reported that several traders who had sold these options without owning the stock (i.e., had sold the options naked) had sustained heavy losses. If a trader had sold 100 contracts at 40 for ⁷⁄₁₆ ($43.75) per contract on Wednesday, those options were worth $4,375 (100 contracts times $43.75 per contract = $4,375). On Friday those calls were worth $131,250 (100 × $1,312.50 = $131,250). The loss to the naked call writer would be $126,875 ($4,375 − $131,250). Thus naked call writers of Cities Service stock suffered large losses as the unexpected happened and gave value to options that normally would have been worthless at expiration.

profit (before commissions) as long as the price of the stock does not exceed $65 at the expiration of the call. Notice that the investor earns the entire $15 if the stock's price falls below $50. However, the potential for loss is considerable if the price of the stock increases.

Investors should write naked call options only if they anticipate a decline (or at least no increase in) the price of the stock. These investors may write covered call options if they believe the price of the stock may rise but are not certain of the price increase. And they may purchase the stock (or the option) and not write calls if they believe there is substantial potential for a price increase.

When Figures 17.3 and 17.6 are combined in Figure 17.7, it becomes apparent that the potential profits and losses from selling a naked call present a mirror image of the losses and profits from purchasing the call. The short position (the sale of the call)

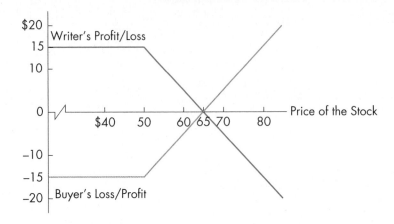

FIGURE 17.7 Profit or Loss on the Purchase of a Call and on the Sale of a Naked Call

exactly mirrors the long position (the purchase). Excluding the impact of commissions, the profits earned by one participant come at the expense of the investor with the opposite position. The buyer is anticipating that the price of the stock will rise and seeks to take advantage of the call's potential leverage. The writer is anticipating that the price of the stock will not rise. Both cannot be right, so the source of profits to one of the participants has to be the source of the loss to the other.

If, however, the writer had sold the call covered, the profits and losses are not directly opposite. The covered writer has a type of hedged position that reduces the risk associated with fluctuations in the price of the stock. The covered writer seeks to take advantage of the option's time premium and accepts a smaller profit. In the previous illustration, that maximum profit was $5—the option's time premium. The naked writer, however, could earn $15 if the price of the stock declined and would earn the $5 time premium even if the price of the stock did not rise (i.e., remained stable). The potential profits and risks assumed by the naked and covered writers are obviously different. Theoretically, the naked writer has no limit to the possible loss whereas the covered writer's worst-case scenario occurs in the unlikely event that the price of the stock declines to $0.

PUTS

A put is an option to *sell* stock (usually 100 shares) at a specified price within a specified time period. As with a call, the time period is short: three, six, or nine months. Like all options, a put has an intrinsic value, which is the difference between the strike price of the put and the price of the stock. Notice that the intrinsic value of a put is the reverse of the intrinsic value of an option to buy (e.g., a call). Compare Exhibits 17.1 and 17.5.

The relationship between the price of a stock and the intrinsic value of a put is illustrated in Exhibit 17.5. This put is an option to sell 100 shares at $30 per share. The first column gives the strike price of the put, the second column presents the hypothetical prices of the stock, and the third column gives the intrinsic value of the put (i.e., the strike price minus the price of the stock).

| EXHIBIT 17.5 | The Relationship Between the Price of a Stock and the Intrinsic Value of a Put |

Strike Price	minus	Price of the Stock	equals	Intrinsic Value of the Put
$30		$15		$15
30		20		10
30		25		5
30		30		0
30		35		0
30		40		0

If the price of the stock is less than the strike price, the put has a positive intrinsic value and is said to be *in the money*. If the price of the stock is greater than the strike price, the put has no intrinsic value and is said to be *out of the money*. If the price of the stock equals the strike price, the put is *at the money*. As with call options, the market price of a put is called *the premium*.

As may be seen in Exhibit 17.5, when the price of the stock declines, the intrinsic value of the put rises. Since the owner of the put may sell the stock at the price specified in the option agreement, the value of the option rises as the price of the stock falls. Thus, if the price of the stock is $15 and the exercise price of the put is $30, the put's intrinsic value as an option must be $1,500 (for 100 shares). The investor can purchase the 100 shares of stock for $1,500 on the stock market and sell them for $3,000 to the person who issued the put. The put, then, must be worth the $1,500 difference between the purchase and sale prices.

Buying Puts

Why should an investor purchase a put? The reason is the same for puts as it is for other speculative options: The put offers potential leverage to the investor. Such leverage may be seen in the example presented in Exhibit 17.5. When the price of the stock declines from $25 to $20 (a 20 percent decrease), the intrinsic value of the put rises from $5 to $10 (a 100 percent increase). In this example a 20 percent decline in the price of the stock produces a larger percentage increase in the intrinsic value of the put. It is this potential leverage that makes put options attractive to investors.

As with call options, investors are willing to pay a price that is greater than the put's intrinsic value: The put commands a time premium above its intrinsic value as an option. As with calls, the amount of this time premium depends on such factors as the volatility of the stock's price, the time to the expiration of the put, and the potential for *decline* in the price of the stock.

The relationships among the price of the stock, the strike price of the put, and the hypothetical prices for the put are illustrated in Exhibit 17.6. The first three columns are identical to those in Exhibit 17.5. The first column gives the strike price of the put, the second column gives the price of the stock, and the third column gives the put's intrinsic value as an option. The fourth column presents hypothetical prices for the put. As may be seen in Exhibit 17.6, the hypothetical price of the put exceeds the intrinsic value, for the put commands a time premium over its intrinsic value as an option.

EXHIBIT   17.6   Relationships Among the Price of the Stock, the Strike Price of the Put, and the Hypothetical Price of the Put

Strike Price of the Put	Price of the Stock	Intrinsic Value of the Put	Hypothetical Price of the Put
$30	$15	$15	$15.25
30	20	10	12
30	25	5	8
30	30	0	6
30	35	0	3.50
30	40	0	1
30	50	0	—

FIGURE   17.8   The Relationships Among the Price of the Stock, the Intrinsic Value of a Put Option, and the Hypothetical Price of the Option

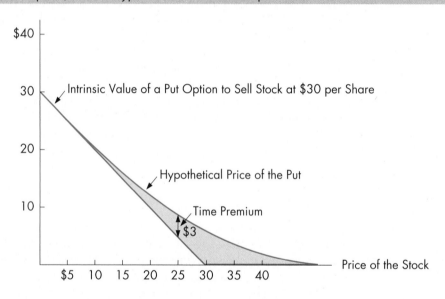

Figure 17.8 illustrates these relationships among the price of the common stock, the intrinsic value of the put, and the hypothetical market value of the put. This figure shows the inverse relationship between the price of the stock and the put's intrinsic value. As the price of the stock declines, the intrinsic value of the put increases (e.g., from $5 to $10 when the stock's price declines from $25 to $20). The figure also readily shows the time premium paid for the option, which is the difference between the price of the put and the option's intrinsic value. If the price of the put is $8 and the intrinsic value is $5, the time premium is $3.

As may be seen in both Exhibit 17.6 and Figure 17.8, the hypothetical market price of the put converges with the put's intrinsic value as the price of the stock declines. If the price of the stock is sufficiently high (e.g., $50 in Exhibit 17.6), the put will not have any market value because the price of the stock must decline substantially for the put to have any intrinsic value. At the other extreme, when the price of the stock is low

EXHIBIT 17.7	Profits and Losses at Expiration from Purchasing a Put	
Price of the Stock	Intrinsic Value of the Put	Net Profit (Loss) on the Purchase
$15	$15	$ 7
20	10	2
25	5	−3
30	0	−8
35	0	−8
40	0	−8

FIGURE 17.9 Profits and Losses at Expiration from Purchasing a Put

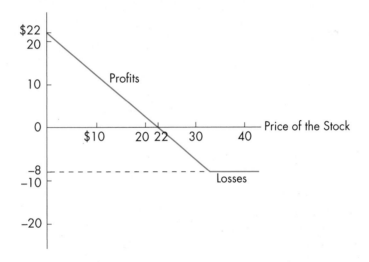

(e.g., $15), the price of the put is equal to the put's intrinsic value as an option. There are two reasons for this convergence. First, if the price of the stock rises, the investor may lose the funds invested in the put. As the price of the stock declines below the strike price of the put, the potential risk to the investor if the price of the stock should start to rise becomes greater. Thus, put buyers are less willing to pay a time premium above the put's intrinsic value. Second, as the intrinsic value of a put rises when the price of the stock declines, the investor must spend more to buy the put; therefore, the potential return on the investment is less. As the potential return declines, the willingness to pay a time premium diminishes.

The potential profit and loss from purchasing a put is illustrated in Exhibit 17.7 and Figure 17.9. If the price of the stock is $25 and the strike price of the put is $30, the intrinsic value is $5 (i.e., the put is in the money). Suppose the price of the put is $8, so it commands a time premium of $3. As may be seen in both Exhibit 17.7 and Figure 17.9, the purchase of the put is profitable as long as the price of the stock is less than $22, and the profit rises as the price of the stock declines. In the unlikely case that the price of the stock were to fall to $0, the maximum possible profit is $22 (the strike price minus the cost of the put).

If the price of the stock rises, the position sustains a loss. As long as the price of the stock is $30 or greater, the put has no intrinsic value (the put is out of the money). No one would exercise an option to sell at $30 if the stock could be sold for a higher price elsewhere. The option would have no value and expire. In this case the investor loses the entire cost of the option ($8). This is, of course, the worst-case scenario, but it emphasizes that the most the investor can lose is the cost of the option. As is explained when comparing purchasing a put to selling a stock short, the latter strategy can generate greater losses.

Writing Puts

Whereas the previous section discussed buying a put, this section will consider its opposite—selling a put. As with call options, investors may either buy or sell a put (i.e., they may *write* a put). The investor buys a put in anticipation of a fall in the price of the stock. The investor who writes a put, on the other hand, believes that the price of the stock will *not* fall. The price of the stock could rise, which is certainly acceptable from the writer's perspective, but the emphasis is on the stock's price *not falling*.

The writer may be either naked or covered. If the investor only sells the put, the position is naked. If the writer simultaneously shorts the stock, the writer is covered. If the put is exercised and the writer buys the stock, the writer could then use the stock to cover the short position. However, since covered put writing is rare, the following discussion is limited to naked put writing.

The possible profits and losses from writing a put may be seen by continuing the example in Exhibit 17.7 and Figure 17.9. In that illustration, the investor purchased the put for $8 to sell stock at $30 when the stock was selling for $25. In the opposite case, the investor writes the put to sell the stock at $30, and receives the $8 proceeds. The writer's possible profits and losses are shown in Exhibit 17.8 and Figure 17.10. As long as the price of the stock exceeds $22, the position generates a profit. The profit rises along with the price of the stock and reaches a maximum of $8 when the price of the stock is $30. The position sustains a loss if the price of the stock is less than $22, and the loss increases as the price of the stock declines. The maximum possible loss is $22 if the price of the stock were to fall to $0.

Figure 17.11 combines the two previous graphs to illustrate the profits and losses to both the buyer and the writer of the put. Like the purchase and sale of a call in Figure 17.7, it should be immediately apparent that the writer's profits and losses mirror

EXHIBIT 17.8 Profits and Losses at Expiration from Selling (Writing) a Put

Price of the Stock	Intrinsic Value of the Put	Net Profit (Loss) on the Sale
$15	$15	$−7
20	10	−2
25	5	3
30	0	8
35	0	8
40	0	8

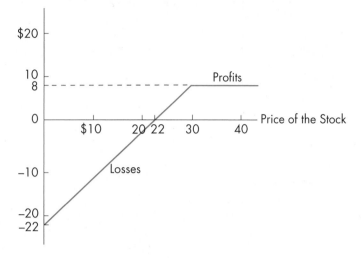

FIGURE 17.10 Profits and Losses from Selling (Writing) a Put

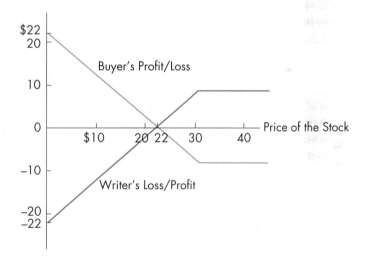

FIGURE 17.11 Profits and Losses to the Buyer and Seller of a Put

the buyer's losses and profits. If the stock sells for $22 at the expiration of the put, the option's intrinsic value is $8—which is exactly what the buyer paid and the writer received. Neither buyer nor seller earns a profit or sustains a loss (before commissions on the trades). If the price of the stock is less than $22, the buyer earns a profit at the writer's expense. If the price of the stock exceeds $22, the writer earns a profit at the buyer's expense. If the price of the stock is $30 or greater, the maximum possible profit to the writer is $8, which is also the buyer's maximum possible loss. If the price of the stock declines to $0, the maximum possible profit to the buyer is $22, which is also the writer's maximum possible loss. Excluding the impact of brokerage commissions on the transactions, the gains and losses offset each other.

Puts Compared with Short Sales

Investors purchase put options when they believe that the price of the stock is going to decline. Purchasing puts, however, is not the only method investors can use to profit from falling securities prices. As was explained in Chapter 2, an investor who believes that the price of a stock is going to fall may profit from the decline by selling short. Buying a put is another form of a short position. However, the put option offers the investor two major advantages over selling short. First, the amount of potential loss is less; second, puts may offer a greater return on the investor's capital because of their leverage.

In order to execute a short position, the investor must sell the stock, deliver the borrowed stock, and later purchase the stock to cover the position. The profit or loss is the difference between the price at which the borrowed stock was sold and the price at which the stock is purchased to repay the loan. If the price of the stock declines, the investor reaps a profit, but if the price of the stock rises, the investor suffers a loss. This loss may be substantial if the stock's price rises significantly. For example, if 100 shares are sold short at $30 and later purchased at $50, the investor loses $2,000 plus commissions on the investment. The higher the price of the stock rises, the greater is the loss that the short position inflicts on the investor. (Notice that once again the investor may limit this potential loss by establishing an order to purchase the stock should the price rise to some predetermined level.)

Purchasing a put option does not subject the investor to a large potential capital loss. If the investor purchases for $300 a put that is the option to sell 100 shares at $30, the maximum amount that the investor can lose is $300. If the price of the common stock rises from $30 to $50, the maximum that can be lost with the put is still only $300. However, the loss on the short position is $2,000 when the price of the stock rises from $30 to $50. Puts reduce the absolute amount that the investor may lose.

Besides subjecting the investor to potentially large losses, the short sale ties up a substantial amount of capital. When the investor sells short, the broker will require that he or she put up funds as collateral. The minimum amount that the investor must remit is the margin requirement set by the Federal Reserve, and individual brokers may require that the investor supply more collateral than this minimum. Selling short thus requires the investor to tie up capital, and the larger the amount that the investor must remit, the smaller the potential return on the short position.

Less capital is required to invest in a put. Although the amount of margin varies at different time periods, it certainly will not be as low as the price of the put. Thus, purchasing the put instead of establishing the short position ties up a smaller amount of the investor's funds. The potential return is greater if the price of the stock declines sufficiently to cover the cost of the put, because the amount invested is smaller. Puts thus offer the investor more leverage than does the short position.

Short sales, however, offer one important advantage over puts. Puts expire, but a short position can be maintained indefinitely. If an investor anticipates a price decline, it must occur during the put's short life for the investment to be profitable. With a short sale, the investor does not have this time constraint and may maintain the position indefinitely.

Protective Puts

Purchasing put options may be viewed as a speculative investment strategy. The buyer profits as the value of the underlying stock declines, which causes the value of the put to rise. Since the long-term trend in stock prices is to increase as the economy expands, purchasing a put seems to be betting against the natural trend in a stock's price.

Although purchases of puts by themselves may be speculative, they may, when used in conjunction with the purchase of stock, reduce the individual's risk exposure. Such a strategy—the simultaneous purchase of the stock and a put—is called a *protective put* because it conserves the investor's initial investment while permitting the investor to maintain a long position in a stock so the profit can grow.

Suppose an individual buys a stock for $40 but does not want to bear the risk associated with a decline in the price of the stock. This investor could purchase a put, whose value would rise if the price of the stock were to decline. Suppose there is a six-month put with a strike price of $40 that is currently selling for $2.50. Exhibit 17.9 presents the benefit of buying the put in combination with the stock. The first two columns give the price of the stock and the profit (loss) on the position in the stock. The third and fourth columns give the intrinsic value of the put at its expiration and the profit (loss) on the position in the put. The last column gives the net profit (loss), which is the sum of the profits (losses) on the positions in the stock and the put.

As shown in the last column of the exhibit, the worst-case scenario is a loss of $2.50. No matter how low the price of the stock falls, the maximum loss to the investor is $2.50. If the price of the stock rises, the maximum possible profit is unlimited. The only effect, then, is that the potential profit is reduced by $2.50, the price of the put. (This reduction in potential profit may be seen by comparing columns 2 and 5.) What the investor has achieved by purchasing the put in conjunction with the purchase of the stock is the assurance of a maximum loss of $2.50.

This protective put strategy may be viewed as an alternative to placing a stop-loss order to sell the stock at $37.50. The advantage of the protective put is that the investor is protected from the price of the stock falling, the stock being sold, and the price subsequently rising. Day-to-day fluctuations in the price of the stock have no impact on the protective put strategy. The disadvantage is that the put ultimately expires, whereas the limit order may be maintained indefinitely. Once the put expires, the investor no

EXHIBIT 17.9	Profit and Loss Resulting from a Protective Put			
Price of the Stock	Profit on the Stock	Intrinsic Value of the Put	Profit on the Put	Total Profit
$20	($20)	$20	$17.50	$−2.50
25	(15)	15	12.50	−2.50
30	(10)	10	7.50	−2.50
35	(5)	5	2.50	−2.50
40	0	0	(2.50)	−2.50
45	5	0	(2.50)	2.50
50	10	0	(2.50)	7.50
55	15	0	(2.50)	12.50
60	20	0	(2.50)	17.50

longer has the protection and would once again be at risk from a decline in the price of the stock. To maintain the protection, the investor could buy another put. In the previous example, the cost of the put was $2.50. If the put were in existence for six months, expired, and the investor bought another put for the same price, the annual cost of the protection is $5. The protective put is similar to buying car or home insurance. The individual must renew the policy in order to maintain the coverage. The limit order, however, has no costs—although the investor may periodically have to instruct the broker to reinstate the limit order.

There is not a clear answer as to whether the limit order or the protective put is the better strategy. The limit order involves no cost but does subject the investor to being sold out on a dip in the price of the stock. The protective put avoids the risk of being sold out by a temporary price decline but requires the investor to pay the cost of the option, which reduces the potential profit from the position in the stock.

PRICE PERFORMANCE OF PUTS AND CALLS

The prices of puts and calls depend on what happens to the price of the underlying stock. This is illustrated in Figures 17.12 and 17.13 for puts and calls on USX (United States Steel) and Teledyne. Figure 17.12 clearly illustrates the impact of the decline in USX's stock price. The stock continuously declined during the time period, causing the

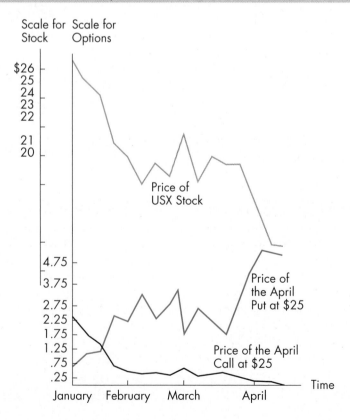

FIGURE 17.12 Price of USX Stock and April Put and Call at $25

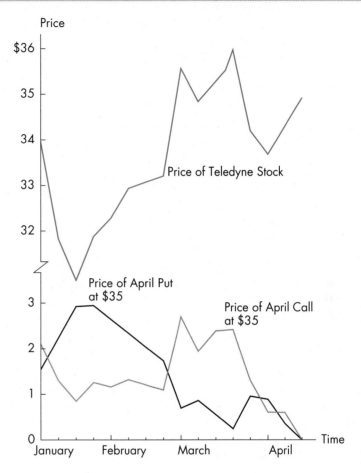

FIGURE 17.13 Prices of Teledyne Stock and the April Put and Call at $35

price of the call to fall while the price of the put rose. The call, which initially traded for $2.50, was worthless at expiration, but during the same time period the price of the put rose from less than $1 to $5.

Figure 17.13 illustrates what happens when the price of the stock does not change. Initially, Teledyne's stock was $34. During the next three and a half months it fell to below $31, then rose to $36, and at the option's expiration was trading for $35, which was the option's strike price. As may be seen in the figure, the price of the put rose rapidly at first (i.e., its price doubled in January); however, the price fell almost as rapidly in February, and the option was worthless at expiration. The price of the call initially fell and then rose in late February in response to the increase in the stock's price. However, in late March the price of the call fell and at expiration the call was worthless.

Perhaps what is most striking about Figure 17.13 is the fact that the ending price of Teledyne's stock was only $1 above the starting price. This small percentage increase of less than 3 percent from January to mid-April caused the value of the put to fall from $1.62 to $0, for a 100 percent decline, and caused the value of the call to fall from $2.12 to $0, also for a 100 percent decline. Even though the price of the stock did rise from $34 to $35, the increase was insufficient to offset the time premium the call initially commanded, so the price of the call fell.

It should be obvious from these illustrations that there can be large variations in the returns from investments in options. Since there are many options for a given stock, the investor has a mind-boggling array of possible strategies. No particular strategy can be expected to yield consistently superior results. If such a strategy existed, many investors would seek to use it, which would reduce the strategy's potential for profit. As with investments in other securities (such as stocks and bonds), profits from investments in options should not tend to exceed the return consistent with the risk borne by the investor.

THE CHICAGO BOARD OPTIONS EXCHANGE

 Prior to the formation of the Chicago Board Options Exchange (CBOE) (http://www .cboe.com), calls were purchased only in the over-the-counter market. If an investor wanted to buy a call option, it was obtained from an options dealer. Each option sold was different, because the exercise price and the expiration date were negotiated with each sale. Once the option was purchased, the investor who desired to sell it had difficulty, because there was no secondary market in options.

With the advent of the CBOE, an organized market in put and call options was created. For the first time, investors could buy and sell call and put options through an organized exchange. An investor purchasing a call on the CBOE knew that there would be a secondary market for that option. This ability to sell options that had been purchased gave a degree of marketability to options that previously did not exist.

The creation of a secondary market in options led to a large increase in option trading. This initial success of the CBOE exceeded expectations, and soon after its formation, other exchanges started to list options. Currently, put and call options are traded not only on the CBOE but also on other exchanges including the New York, American, Pacific, and Philadelphia stock exchanges.

⊕ Point of Interest

THE PUT/CALL RATIO

The ratio of outstanding put and call options may be used as a gauge of investor sentiment. The number of options in existence (the "open interest") is not static; it initially rises and then falls as the options approach expiration. While this pattern applies to all options, the number of puts or calls also changes. If investors become increasingly bullish, they may buy more calls. If they become increasingly bearish, they may buy more puts.

If the number of puts and calls were exactly equal, the ratio would equal 1.0. A ratio greater than 1.0 indicates the existence of more puts than calls. A ratio of less than 1.0 indicates the opposite. As investors become more bearish, the numerical value of the ratio rises, and the open interest in puts exceeds the open interest in calls. Since investors are often optimistic, a put/call ratio exceeding 1.0 occurs less often. A ratio such as 1.6 or 2.1 may be interpreted as a bearish sign. Investors are anticipating that the price of a specific stock will decline (if the options apply to a single stock) or that the market as a whole will decline (if the options are based on a stock index).

EXHIBIT 17.10	The Reporting of Option Trading					
			Call		Put	
Option	Strike	Expiration	Volume	Last	Volume	Last
XXX	60	Aug	1000	3.60	148	0.55
63	60	Sept	500	4.50	20	1.50
63	65	Aug	600	0.60	350	2.60
63	70	Feb	1200	2.90	—	—
63	75	Feb	1400	1.60	—	—

Today transactions are continuously reported, and investors can easily obtain price quotes for puts and calls. Daily summaries of selected transactions appear in leading newspapers. While the formats differ, Exhibit 17.10 illustrates the type of information that is reported. First there is the company name, which is usually abbreviated. Below the company name is the closing price of the stock (63). Next come the strike prices and the expiration dates, which are the third Friday in each of the given months (e.g., the options with a strike price of 65 expire on the third Friday in August). The last entries are the volume of trades and the closing prices for the calls and puts. For the August call at 65, 600 calls traded, with the last one selling for 0.60 ($60). For the August put, 350 options traded with the last trade at 2.60 ($260). There are no entries for the February puts, which means either there were no trades or the option did not exit. The number of trades should not be confused with the number of contracts in existence, which is called the **open interest**.

open interest

Number of contracts with a specified strike price and expiration date on a particular stock.

Exhibit 17.10 also shows price relationships between options. For example, if you compare options with the same strike price but different expiration dates, the option with the longer life commands the higher price. Both the September call and the September put with the 60 strike price traded for a higher price than the call and the put with the August expiration date. This is intuitively obvious, since there is more time for the price of the stock to move and cause the value of the option to change. If you compare options with the same expiration date but different strike prices, there is also a relationship between the option prices. For calls, the option with the lower strike price is more valuable (e.g., $3.60 versus $0.60 for the August calls at 60 and 65). For puts, the pricing relationship is the opposite. The August put at 65 sold for $2.60 while the put at 60 sold for $0.55. These relationships hold because as the price of the stock rises, call options with lower strike prices become more valuable but put options with lower strike prices become less valuable. (Option valuation is covered in more detail in the next chapter on the Black-Scholes option valuation model.)

STOCK INDEX OPTIONS

stock index options

Rights to buy and sell based on an aggregate measure of stock prices.

Although put and call options were initially created for individual stocks, **stock index options** have developed. (As is explained in Chapter 19, there are also stock index futures.) These stock index options are similar to options based on individual stocks, but the index option is based on an aggregate measure of the market, such as the Standard & Poor's 500 stock index. In addition to puts and calls based on the aggregate market, there are options based on subsets of the market, such as computer technology stocks or pharmaceutical stocks. Stock index options have proved to be particularly popular and account for a substantial proportion of the daily transactions in options.

These options are popular because they permit the investor to take a position in the market or a sector without having to select specific companies. For example, suppose an investor anticipates that the stock market will rise. What does this individual do? He or she cannot buy every stock but must select individual stocks. (The investor could buy an index mutual fund, since such funds construct portfolios that mirror aggregate measures of the stock market.) Remember from the discussion of risk in Chapter 5 that there are two sources of risk associated with the individual stock: nondiversifiable systematic risk and diversifiable unsystematic risk. One source of systematic risk is the tendency of a stock's price to move with the market. Unsystematic risk results from price movements generated by the security that are independent of the market (e.g., a takeover announcement, dividend cut, or large increase in earnings).

If the investor buys a particular stock on the expectation of a rising market, it does not necessarily follow that the individual stock's price will increase when the market rises. Investors construct diversified portfolios to reduce the unsystematic risk associated with the individual asset. As the portfolio becomes more diversified, unsystematic risk is reduced further and the return on the portfolio mirrors the return on the market. (Whether the return on the portfolio exceeds the market depends on the portfolio's beta. If the individual selects stocks with high betas, the diversified portfolio should tend to earn higher returns than the market as a whole in rising markets but sustain larger losses than the market in declining markets.)

Index options offer the investor an alternative to creating diversified portfolios as a means to earn the return associated with movements in the market. For example, if the investor anticipates that the market will rise in the near future, he or she may purchase a call option based on an index of the market as a whole (such as the Standard & Poor's 500 stock index). If the market does rise, the value of the call option also increases. The investor has avoided the unsystematic risk associated with the individual stock. In addition, the investor has avoided the commission costs necessary to construct a diversified portfolio.

If the investor anticipates the market will decline, he or she will purchase a stock index put. If the investor is correct and the market does fall, the value of the stock index put rises. Of course, if the market does not decline but rises instead, the investor loses the amount invested in the put option, but *the maximum that the investor can lose is the cost of the option.* An investor who sells stocks short instead of purchasing stock index put options may be exposed to a large loss if stock prices rise.

Stock index options also give investors a means to manage existing portfolios. This is particularly important for portfolio managers with large holdings or individuals who want to improve the tax and risk management of these holdings. Consider a substantial stock portfolio that has appreciated in value. If the investor anticipates declining stock prices and sells the shares, this is a taxable transaction. Instead of selling the stocks, the investor may sell stock index calls or purchase stock index puts (i.e., construct a protective put using stock index puts). Then if the market declines, profits in these positions will help offset the losses on the individual stocks.

If the investor were to sell stock index call options, the value of these options would decline as the market decreased. The gain on the sale would then offset the loss in

⊕ Point of Interest

LEAPS

Initial trading in puts and calls was limited to options of three, six, and nine months. However, in 1990 puts and calls with terms up to two years commenced trading on the CBOE and the AMEX. These options, called LEAPS (Long-Term Equity AnticiPation Securities), work essentially the same as traditional puts and calls, but because the term is longer, LEAPS command a larger time premium. For example, a 5-month call to buy Cisco at $25 sold for $3 and the 19-month call sold for $7.10, while the price of the underlying stock was $23.48. The same price relationship holds for puts. The 5-month and 19-month puts sold for $4.10 and $7.10, respectively.

Investors who anticipate that the price of Cisco will rise may prefer to acquire the LEAPS instead of the short-term option because LEAPS offer additional time for the price of the stock to rise. Conversely, the writer may prefer to sell the longer-term call because the premium is larger. Of course, for the LEAPS option to be profitable for the buyer, the price of Cisco must rise sufficiently to cover the cost of the option. And if that price increase does occur, the writer of the option will sustain a loss.

individual stocks. If the investor were to purchase stock index put options, the value of the options would increase if the market declined. The loss on the portfolio would be offset by the gain on the put option. (The amount offset would depend on how many put options the investor purchased. The number of options necessary to hedge a portfolio is discussed in the next chapter in the section addressing the hedge ratio.) As these two cases illustrate, stock index options offer the investor a means to hedge existing portfolios against a decline in the market without having to liquidate the positions and thus incur the capital gains tax liability. By buying or selling the appropriate stock index option, the investor achieves protection of capital without selling the appreciated securities.

There is one major difference between stock index options and put and call options on specific stocks. With a call option to buy shares of IBM, the owner may exercise the option and buy the stock. With a put option to sell shares of IBM, the owner may exercise the option by delivering shares of IBM stock. Such purchases or deliveries are not possible with a stock index option. The owner of the call cannot exercise it and receive the index. Instead, stock index options are settled in cash. For example, suppose the owner of a call based on the Standard & Poor's 500 index does not sell the option prior to expiration (i.e., does not close the position). At expiration the intrinsic value of the option is determined and that amount is paid by the seller of the option to the owner. Of course, if the option has no intrinsic value at expiration, it is worthless and expires. The seller of the option then has no further obligation to the option's owner. In that case the premium paid for the option (i.e., its price) becomes profit for the seller.

CURRENCY AND INTEREST RATE OPTIONS

While most investors may think of options as the right to buy and sell stock, puts and calls are not limited to equities. There are also options to buy and sell currencies, which trade on the Philadelphia Exchange, and debt securities (interest rate options), which trade on the CBOE. The principles that apply to the options to buy and sell stock also apply to currency and interest rate options.

Individuals may buy or sell these options in anticipation of price movements or to generate income from the sales. Suppose an investor expects the price of the British pound to rise. That investor purchases a call option to buy pounds at a specified price within a specified time period. If the price of the pound did rise, the value of the option would also increase. If the investor expects the price of the British pound to fall, he or she purchases a put option to sell pounds at a specified price within a specified time period. If the price of the pound did fall, the value of the option would increase. In both cases the price of the option is its intrinsic value plus the time premium.

In order for the investor to purchase a currency option, someone has to be selling the put or call. As in the case of options to buy stock, the seller can be naked or covered. The naked seller of the call option is anticipating that the price of the currency will not rise, and the naked seller of the put options is anticipating that that value of currency will not decline. Obviously, both the buyer and the seller of the option cannot be correct. If the price of the currency does rise, the buyer of the call profits at the expense of the seller while the seller of the put option profits at the expense of the buyer.

Currency options, however, are not just used to speculate on an anticipated change in the price of a currency. They are also used to help manage risk. If an investor has a position in a currency, that individual may take the opposite position in a currency option. Suppose an investor owns several British stocks (e.g., has a long position in the stocks) and wants to reduce the risk from a decline in the value of the pound. If that investor purchases a put option on the pound, then the value of the option rises when the currency declines, which helps offset any loss the investor might experience from the value of the currency declining.

Interest rate options work essentially the same way, except the investor has to think of them in reverse. If an investor expects interest rates to *fall*, that individual buys a *call* option. This may seem backwards because the investor is buying the call option in anticipation of interest rates declining. However, since lower interest rates will increase the price of the underlying bond, buying a call option is the correct strategy. If an investor expects interest rates to rise and bond prices to fall, the investor would buy a put. If this individual is right and interest rates do fall, the value of the option increases, since the investor has an option to sell the bond at the price specified in the option.

Individuals who own bonds may use these options to reduce interest rate risk. If the investor were to purchase a put option and interest rates were to rise, the increase in the value of the put would offset some (perhaps all) of the decline in the bonds' value. The investor would continue to collect the interest paid by the bonds, and, in the event the bonds had to be sold, the loss on the bonds would be offset by the gain on the option. This offsetting of loss means that the investor has reduced the risk associated with changes in interest rates.

warrant

An option issued by a company to buy its stock at a specified price within a specified time period.

WARRANTS

The preceding material covered calls and puts. The remainder of this chapter is devoted to warrants and rights offerings. A **warrant** is an option issued by a company to buy its stock at a specified price within a specified time period. This definition includes the essential elements of all warrants, but there can be subtle differences. For example, the specified exercise price may rise at predetermined intervals (e.g., every five years) or the firm may have the right to extend the expiration date or to call the warrant.

Most warrants are an option, or right, to buy one share of common stock. Some warrants, however, are the option to buy more or less than one share. Such terms may be the result of stock dividends, stock splits, or a merger. For example, a warrant that is the option to buy 0.4 share may have evolved through a merger. The warrant initially represented the option to purchase one share of the company. However, when the company subsequently merged into another firm, the terms of the merger were 0.4 share of the acquiring firm (i.e., the surviving company) for each share of the company being acquired. The warrant then became an option to buy one share that had been converted into 0.4 share of the surviving company.

If a warrant is an option to buy more or less than one share, the strike price and the market price of the warrant can be readily converted to a per-share basis. Such conversion is desirable to facilitate comparisons among warrants. Consider, for example, an option that gives the right to buy 0.4 share at $10 and is currently selling for $4. The warrant's strike price and market price are divided by the number of shares that the warrant is an option to buy. Thus, the per-share strike price is $25 ($10 ÷ 0.4), and the per-share market price is $10 ($4 ÷ 0.4). Stated differently, 2.5 warrants are necessary to buy one share for $25.

Warrants are usually issued by firms in conjunction with other financing. They are attached to other securities, such as debentures or preferred stock, and are a sweetener to induce investors to purchase the securities. For example, AT&T and Chrysler Corporation issued bonds and preferred stock with warrants attached. The warrants were an added inducement to purchase the securities.[3]

When a warrant is exercised, the firm issues new stock and receives the proceeds. For this reason, most warrants usually have a finite life. The expiration date ultimately forces the holder to exercise the option if the strike price is less than the current market price of the stock. However, if the strike price exceeds the stock's price at expiration (i.e., if the warrant has no intrinsic value), the warrant will not be exercised and will expire. After the expiration date, the warrant is worthless. This was the case with the Berkshire Realty warrant, which was the option to buy the stock at $11.79. The stock sold for $9.625 on the expiration date. No one would exercise a warrant to buy stock at $11.79 that could be bought for $9.625, so the warrant expired.

Warrants are very similar to calls; their definitions are essentially identical. They offer speculators potential leverage because the price of a warrant moves with the price of the underlying stock. Since the warrant sells for a lower price than the underlying stock, the percentage increase in the price of the warrant tends to exceed the percentage increase in the price of the stock. The converse is also true: The percentage decline in the price of the warrant will exceed the percentage decline in the price of the stock. Again, leverage works both ways.

---

[3]Warrants are often used in private placements of new securities. RCN Corp. sold $50 million worth of stock with warrants. The sale price of the stock was $6.53, which approximated the current market price of the stock at the time of the sale. The exercise price of the warrant was $12.93 with an expiration date of 4½ years. If the price of RCN rises to above $12.93, the buyer can exercise the warrant and subsequently sell shares for a profit. The effect is to increase the potential return on the initial sale without the investor's making an additional current cash outlay. (RCN subsequently went bankrupt, so the warrant was not exercised.)

Although warrants are similar to calls, they have several distinguishing features. First, warrants are issued by companies, whereas call options are issued by individuals or financial institutions like pension plans. Second, the term of a warrant tends to be longer than the term of a call. The expiration date of a warrant may be several years into the future. Calls are of relatively short duration: three, six, or nine months. (There are some longer-term calls; see the Point of Interest box on LEAPS.) Third, when a warrant is exercised, the firm issues new stock and receives the proceeds. The seller of a call, however, cannot issue new stock when the call is exercised but must either purchase the stock on the open market or surrender the stock from personal holdings. When the stock is supplied for the exercised call option, the option writer and not the firm receives the proceeds.

SUMMARY

In the securities markets, an option gives the holder the right to buy or sell a stock (or index of stocks) at a specified price within a specified time period. The value of an option depends in part on the value of the underlying security, so options are often referred to as *derivative* securities. A call is an option written by an individual to buy stock. A put is an option to sell stock. A call writer may either own the underlying stock and write *covered* call options or not own the stock and write *naked* call options. If the call writer does not own the stock, that individual is exposed to a large potential loss should the price of the stock rise dramatically.

Options permit investors to buy and take long positions without acquiring the stock. Options also permit investors to sell and take short positions without selling the stock. Investors purchase options in anticipation of price changes. Options are a means for buyers to leverage the potential profits and limit the potential losses. Writers seek to take advantage of the time premiums that buyers are willing to pay for the options. Options may be used to hedge against a price change. For example, the owner of a stock may acquire a put to protect against a decline in the stock's price.

The intrinsic value of an option to buy is the difference between the price of the stock and the strike (exercise) price of the option. As the price of the stock rises, the value of the call rises. The intrinsic value of a put is the reverse: the difference between the strike price and the price of the stock. As the price of the stock declines, the value of the put rises.

Options tend to sell for more than their intrinsic values—that is, they command a *time premium*. This time premium works against the holder of the option, because it reduces the option's potential leverage. This premium declines with the passage of time, because on the expiration date the option must sell for its intrinsic value. Unless the price of the underlying stock changes sufficiently, the disappearance of the time premium inflicts a loss on the investor who purchased the option.

Since the creation of the Chicago Board Options Exchange (CBOE), put and call options have been traded on organized exchanges. These secondary markets have increased the popularity of options because investors know there are markets in which they may liquidate their positions. The initial success of option trading has led to the creation of varied types of puts and calls, such as stock index options. These index options are puts and calls based on an aggregate measure of the stock market instead of a specific security. Stock index options offer investors a means to manage their exposure to systematic risk by permitting them to take positions in the market as a whole.

In addition to call options, warrants are options issued by a firm to buy a stock at a specified price within a specified time period. While warrants are similar to calls, the firm issues new shares and receives the proceeds when the option is exercised.

The following table summarizes the maximum possible gains and losses for the basic positions using options:

Bullish

Buy the stock	Maximum possible gain: unlimited
	Maximum possible loss: cost of the stock
Buy the call	Maximum possible gain: unlimited
	Maximum possible loss: cost of the call
Sell the put	Maximum possible gain: price of the put
	Maximum possible loss: strike price of the put minus the cost of the put

Bearish

Short the stock	Maximum possible gain: price of the stock
	Maximum possible loss: unlimited
Buy the put	Maximum possible gain: strike price of the put minus the cost of the put
	Maximum possible loss: cost of the put
Sell the call	Maximum possible gain: price of the call
	Maximum possible loss: unlimited

Neutral

| Covered call | Maximum possible gain: time premium of the call |
| | Maximum possible loss: price of the stock minus the price of the call |

QUESTIONS

1. What is an option? How is an option's minimum (or intrinsic value) determined? How does arbitrage ensure that the price of an option will not be less than the option's intrinsic value? If you saw that the price of a share of stock was $20, the exercise price of an option to buy the stock was $10, and the price of the option was $5, what would you do?

2. What is the source of leverage in a call option? Why may an option be considered a speculative investment?

3. What is the CBOE, and why are secondary markets crucial to the popularity of options?

4. What is the difference between covered and naked call writing? Why do some individuals buy call options while others write calls?

5. If an individual buys a call option and the price of the underlying stock declines, what should happen to the option? What is the maximum amount the investor can lose?

6. In what ways are calls similar to warrants? How do they differ?

7. Why does the intrinsic value of a call rise with the price of the stock, whereas the intrinsic value of a put declines as the stock's price rises?

8. What should happen to an option's time premium as the option approaches expiration? What happens to an out-of-the-money option at expiration?

9. If an individual sells a call or a put option, how may that investor close the position?

10. What advantage does purchasing a stock index option offer over buying options on individual securities?

11. Why does a protective put reduce the potential loss from a long position in a stock?

12. You may track option prices through a variety of Internet sources. Go to the CBOE home page (http://www.cboe.com) and select an index option based on the S&P 500 and the Russell 1000. Select a call and a put option with the same expiration dates and a strike price close to the current value of each index. Track the prices of the options and each index for a period of two to four weeks. What were the percentage changes in the indexes and in the put and call options?

PROBLEMS

1. A particular call is the option to buy stock at $25. It expires in six months and currently sells for $4 when the price of the stock is $26.

   a) What is the intrinsic value of the call? What is the time premium paid for the call?

   b) What will the value of this call be after six months if the price of the stock is $20? $25? $30? $40?

   c) If the price of the stock rises to $40 at the expiration date of the call, what is the percentage increase in the value of the call? Does this example illustrate favorable leverage?

   d) If an individual buys the stock and sells this call, what is the cash outflow (i.e., net cost) and what will the profit on the position be after six months if the price of the stock is $10? $15? $20? $25? $26? $30? $40?

   e) If an individual sells this call naked, what will the profit or loss be on the position after six months if the price of the stock is $20? $26? $40?

2. What are the intrinsic values and time premiums paid for the following options?

Option	Price of the Option	Price of the Stock
Calls: XYZ, Inc., 30	$7.00	$34
XYZ, Inc., 35	2.50	34
Puts: XYZ, Inc., 30	1.25	34
XYZ, Inc., 35	4.25	34

If the stock sells for $31 at the expiration date of the preceding options, what are the profits or losses for the writers and the buyers of these options?

3. The price of a stock is $51. You can buy a six-month call at $50 for $5 or a six-month put at $50 for $2.

   a) What is the intrinsic value of the call?

   b) What is the intrinsic value of the put?

   c) What is the time premium paid for the call?

   d) What is the time premium paid for the put?

   e) If the price of the stock falls, what happens to the value of the put?

    f) What is the maximum you could lose by selling the call covered?

    g) What is the maximum possible profit if you sell the stock short?

After six months, the price of the stock is $58.

    h) What is the value of the call?

    i) What is the profit or loss from buying the put?

    j) If you had sold the stock short six months earlier, what would your profit or loss be?

    k) If you had sold the call covered, what would your profit or loss be?

4. Given the following information,

price of a stock	$101
strike price of a six-month call	$100
market price of the call	$5
strike price of a six-month put	$100
market price of the put	$4

answer the following sentences.

    a) Which option is "in" the money?

    b) What is the time premium paid for the put?

    c) If an investor establishes a naked call position, what amount is received?

    d) What is the most the buyer of the call can lose?

    e) What is the maximum amount a short seller (of the stock) can lose?

At the expiration of the options (i.e., after six months have elapsed), the price of the stock is $93.

    f) What is the profit (loss) from buying the stock?

    g) What is the profit (loss) from buying the call?

    h) What is the profit (loss) from writing the call covered?

    i) What is the profit (loss) from selling the put?

    j) At expiration, what time premium is paid for the call?

5. A particular put is the option to sell stock at $40. It expires after three months and currently sells for $2 when the price of the stock is $42.

    a) If an investor buys this put, what will the profit be after three months if the price of the stock is $45? $40? $35?

    b) What will the profit from selling this put be after three months if the price of the stock is $45? $40? $35?

    c) Compare the answers to (a) and (b). What is the implication of the comparison?

6. A LEAPS call with an expiration date of two years is an option to buy stock at $24. The current market price of the stock is $35, and the market price of the LEAPS is $15.

    a) What is the option's intrinsic value?

    b) What is the time premium paid for the LEAPS?

    c) If after two years the stock is selling for $50, what will be the price of the LEAPS? What is the percentage increase in the value of the stock and in the value of the option?

    d) Why does the time premium disappear?

    e) If after two years the stock is selling for $22, what will be the price of the LEAPS? What is the percentage decrease in the value of the stock and in the value of the option?

7. A stock that is currently selling for $47 has the following six-month options outstanding:

	Strike Price	Market Price
Call option	$45	$4
Call option	50	1

   a) Which option(s) is (are) in the money?
   b) What is the time premium paid for each option?
   c) What is the profit (loss) at expiration given different prices of the stock—$30, $35, $40, $45, $50, $55, and $60—if the investor buys the call with the $45 strike price?
   d) What is the profit (loss) at expiration given different prices of the stock—$30, $35, $40, $45, $50, $55, and $60—if the investor buys the call with the $50 strike price? Compare your answers to (c) and (d).
   e) What is the range of stock prices that will generate a profit if the investor buys the stock and sells the call with the $50 strike price?
   f) What is the range of stock prices that will generate a profit if the investor buys the stock and sells the call with the $45 strike price? Compare your answers to (e) and (f).

8. An investor buys a stock for $36. At the same time a six-month put option to sell the stock for $35 is selling for $2.
   a) What is the profit or loss from purchasing the stock if the price of the stock is $30, $35, or $40?
   b) If the investor also purchases the put (i.e., constructs a protective put), what is the combined cash outflow?
   c) If the investor constructs the protective put, what is the profit or loss if the price of the stock is $30, $35, or $40 at the put's expiration? At what price of the stock does the investor break even?
   d) What is the maximum potential loss and maximum potential profit from this protective put?
   e) If, after six months, the price of the stock is $37, what is the investor's maximum possible loss?

9. Options may also be used with other securities to devise various investment strategies. For example, an investor has the following alternative investments and their prices:

Common stock	$ 100
Six-month call to buy 100 shares at $100	$ 400
Six-month $10,000 U.S. Treasury bill	$9,600

   The investor has $10,000 and thus could buy (a) 100 shares of the stock or (b) one call plus the Treasury bill. After six months how much profit or loss will the investor have earned on each alternative (excluding commissions) if the price of the stock is $110, $105, $100, $95, or $90? Which alternative is less risky?

10. If you anticipate that the price of a stock will rise, you could (1) buy the stock, (2) buy a call, (3) sell a covered call, or (4) sell a put. All four positions may

generate profits if the price of the stock rises, but the cash inflows or outflows, the amount of any gains, and the potential losses differ for each position. Currently, the price of a stock is $86; four-month calls and puts with a strike price of $85 are trading for $10.50 and $8.25, respectively.

    a) What are the cash inflows or outflows associated with each of the four positions?

    b) Construct a profit/loss profile for each position at the following prices of the stock.

	Profit/Loss			
Price of the Stock	Bought the Stock	Covered Call	Bought the Call	Sold the Put
$110				
100				
95.50				
90				
86				
80				
76.75				
75.50				
70				
65				

As this profile illustrates, each strategy produces a gain but the amounts and potential losses differ.

    c) What are the prices of the stock that generate breakeven for each position?

    d) Compare the cash inflows/outflows, profits, and potential loss from the covered call and sale of the put. Which is better if you are able to invest any cash inflows and earn $1.25?

    e) Which strategy has the smallest potential dollar loss?

    f) What price of the stock produces a loss on all four positions?

    g) Which position generates the highest possible gain in dollar and in percentage terms?

    h) Suppose the price of the stock declines, and the put is exercised (i.e., you have to buy the stock). Since the option is exercised, what is your cost basis of the stock? Compare this cost basis to your initially buying the stock instead of selling the put.

INVESTMENT ASSIGNMENT (PART 6)

Options are a means to leverage your position and increase the potential returns, but they also magnify the potential for loss. Select two of your ten stocks and locate prices for the stocks and for call options on those stocks. (Many Internet sites have option prices and well as stock prices.) Select three call options on each stock:

a.   A call whose strike price exceeds the price of the stock (an "out-of-the-money" call)

b.   A call whose strike price approximates the price of the stock (an "at-the-money" call)

c.   A call whose strike price is less than the price of the stock (an "in-the-money" call)

Select options that will expire within three to six weeks, and answer the following questions:

1. What the intrinsic value of each option?
2. What is the time premium paid for each option?
3. What is the maximum you could lose if you bought each option?
4. What is the maximum you could lose if you bought the underlying stock? What is the probability of that occurring within three to six weeks?

Track the prices of the stock and the three options until the options expire and answer the following questions.

5. What are the changes in the price of the stock and the changes in the price of each option over the time period?
6. What are the percentage returns for the stock and each option?
7. Suppose you had bought the stock and sold one of the options (i.e., constructed a covered call). What would have been your return?
8. Why do all of the returns differ?
9. In retrospect, which position performed worst and which performed best?

The Financial Advisor's Investment Case
A Speculator's Choices

Cosima Wagner is an optimist who likes to speculate. She enjoys watching prices change rapidly and believes that she could make large profits by judiciously taking advantage of price swings. Thus it is easy to see why she is attracted to options whose prices may change rapidly from day to day. She especially likes the securities associated with Fasolt and Fafner (F&F) Construction Corporation, a large building and engineering firm that also has considerable holdings of coal and oil reserves.

Currently the economy is in a recession. F&F is doubly cursed: The recession has resulted in a significant decline in construction, and commodity prices, including oil and gas, are declining. These two factors have reduced profit margins so that per-share earnings have plummeted from $5.50 to $1.00 during the latest fiscal year. The stock, which at one time had been an outstanding performer, has declined from a high of more than $80 to its current price of $15.

Wagner believes that the stock market has overreacted to the decline in earnings. Furthermore, there are signs that the recession is ending. Retail sales have risen and interest rates are falling. A more robust economy should certainly help F&F's sales and earnings, which Wagner believes would result in a higher stock price. F&F's fundamentals are sound, as its profit margins have historically been among the highest in the industry. However, the firm has a considerable amount of long-term debt outstanding. Even though the company pays no cash dividends, it has had to issue long-term bonds because retained earnings were insufficient to finance expansion and acquisitions.

Wagner firmly believes that the company offers an excellent opportunity for profit, but she is very uncertain as to the correct strategy to follow. In addition to the stock, the firm has outstanding a ten-year, high-yield debenture with a 7.2 percent coupon. The bond is currently selling for $780 per $1,000 face amount for a yield to maturity of 10.92 percent. It is rated double B by one rating service but only single B by another service.

Options on the stock are also actively traded. Currently the following options and their prices are available:

Exercise Price	Three-Month		Six-Month		Nine-Month	
	Call	Put	Call	Put	Call	Put
$15	$2.00	$1.50	$3.50	$2.25	$5	$3
20	0.75	5.50	1.50	6	2	6.25

To help determine the potential returns from the various alternatives, Wagner decided that answers to the following questions may be useful.

1. What is the current yield offered by the stock, the bond, and the calls and puts?
2. What is the value of the bond in terms of the stock?
3. What is the intrinsic value of each option?
4. What are the time premiums paid for each option?
5. What will be the price of each security if after six months the fundamental economic picture is not changed and the price of the stock remains at $15?
6. Although Wagner considers a further decline in F&F's situation to be unlikely, the possibility does exist that after six months the stock would fall to $10. What impact would that have on the prices of the various securities?
7. Wagner believes that the price of the stock will rise to $25 a share within six months. What impact would such a price increase have on the prices of the various securities?

As an outside financial advisor to Cosima Wagner, what course of action would you suggest with regard to Fasolt and Fafner's securities? In formulating your answer, consider the pros and cons of each of the alternatives and which conditions favor each security.

CHAPTER 18

Option Valuation and Strategies

The previous chapter presented the basics concerning options. It described their features, the reasons why investors may purchase or sell them, and how they are used as speculative investments or as a means to reduce risk. The chapter also explained how an option sells for a time premium that disappears with the passage of time, so that the option sells for its intrinsic value on the day it expires.

This chapter develops the material on options by (1) discussing the Black-Scholes option valuation model, (2) explaining how stock, bond, and option markets are interrelated so that changes in one are transmitted to the other markets, and (3) illustrating several strategies using options. Options are a very involved topic that can be approached from a sophisticated mathematical perspective. The approach used in this chapter seeks to reduce the abstractions while liberally illustrating the concepts, so that the individual investor can understand the fundamentals and importance of option valuation even if he or she never intends to apply them.

LEARNING OBJECTIVES

After completing this chapter you should be able to:

1. Determine the relationship between the value of an option and the variables specified in the Black-Scholes option valuation model.
2. Calculate the value of a call option using the Black-Scholes option valuation model.
3. Illustrate how arbitrage ensures that a change in the market for stock is transferred to the market for options and vice versa.
4. Explain how the hedge ratio is used to reduce the risk associated with a position in a stock.
5. Determine the potential profits and losses from option strategies.
6. Differentiate speculative from risk management strategies using options.
7. Explain how incentive-based stock options may affect a firm's earnings.

BLACK–SCHOLES OPTION VALUATION

Valuation is a major theme in finance and investments. The valuation of bonds, preferred stock, and common stock composes a substantial proportion of the chapters devoted to these securities. The valuation of options is also important but is more difficult than most of the material covered in this text. This section will briefly cover the model initially developed by Fischer Black and Myron Scholes for the valuation of warrants and subsequently applied to call options.[1] This valuation model, commonly referred to as Black-Scholes, permeates the literature on put and call options. It has also been applied to other areas of finance in which there are options. For example, if a firm has the right to retire a bond issue prior to maturity, the bond has a built-in option. By valuing the option and separating that value from the amount of the debt, the financial analyst determines the cost of the debt.

The following discussion explains and illustrates the Black-Scholes option valuation model. (The derivation of the model is not given, so you will have to take the model on faith.) The question of valuation of an option is illustrated in Figure 18.1, which essentially reproduces Figure 17.2. Lines AB and BC represent the option's intrinsic value, and line DE represents all the values of the option to buy for the various prices of the stock. The questions are: "Why is line DE located where it is? Why isn't line DE higher or lower in the plane? What variables cause the line to shift up or down?" The Black-Scholes model determines the value of the option for each price of the stock and thus locates DE in the plane.

In Black-Scholes, the value of a call option (V_o) depends on all of the following:

P_s, the current price of the stock
P_e, the option's strike price
T, the time in years to the option's expiration date (i.e., if expiration is 3 months, $T = 0.25$)
σ, the standard deviation of the stock's annual rate of return
r, the annual risk-free rate of interest on an asset (e.g., Treasury bill) with a term equal to the time to the option's expiration

FIGURE 18.1 Profits and Losses at Expiration for the Buyer of a Call

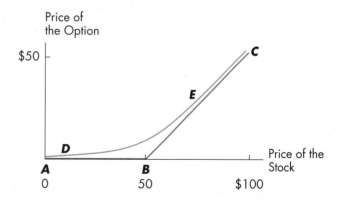

[1]The initial model was published in Fischer Black and Myron Scholes, "The Pricing of Options and Corporate Liabilities," *Journal of Political Economy* (May/June 1973): 637–654.

The relationships between the value of a call (the dependent variable) and each of these independent variables (assuming the remaining variables are held constant) are as follows:

- An increase in the price of the stock (an increase in P_s) increases the value of a call option (V_o). This is true since the intrinsic value of the option rises as the price of the stock rises.
- An increase in the strike price (an increase in P_e) decreases the value of a call option. Higher strike prices reduce the option's intrinsic value for a given price of the stock.
- An increase in the time to expiration (an increase in T) increases the value of a call option. As time diminishes and the option approaches expiration, its value declines.
- An increase in the variability of the stock (an increase in σ) increases the value of a call option. A speculator will find an option on a volatile stock more attractive than an option on a stock whose price tends to be stable. Decreased variability decreases the value of an option.
- An increase in interest rates (an increase in r) increases the value of a call option. Higher interest rates are associated with higher call option valuations.

Most of the relationships between the independent variables and an option's value seem reasonable with the exception of a change in the interest rate. Throughout this text, an increase in interest rates decreases the value of the asset. Higher interest rates reduce the present value of a bond's interest payments and principal repayment, thus reducing the value of the bond. Higher interest rates increase the required return for a common stock, thus decreasing the valuation of the common stock. This negative relationship between changes in interest rates and a security's value does not hold for call options. Higher interest rates increase the value of an option to buy stock.

Although the positive relationship between interest rates and the value of a call option seems perverse, the relationship makes sense. Remember that the intrinsic value of a call option is the difference between the price of the stock and the strike price. The investor, however, does not have to exercise the call option immediately but may wait until its expiration. The funds necessary to exercise the option may be invested elsewhere. Higher interest rates mean these funds earn more. You need to invest less at the higher rate to have the funds to exercise the option at expiration. Thus the present value of the strike price (i.e., the funds necessary to exercise the call option) declines as interest rates rise. This reduction in the present value of the strike price increases the value of the option.

It should be noted that dividends are excluded from the Black-Scholes model. In its initial formulation, the valuation model was applied to options on stocks that did not pay a dividend. Hence the dividend played no role in the determination of the option's value. The model has been extended to dividend-paying stocks. Since the extension does not significantly change the basic model, this discussion will be limited to the original presentation.

Black-Scholes puts the variables together in the following equation for the value of a call option (V_o):

18.1
$$V_o = P_s \times F(d_1) - \frac{P_e}{e^{rT}} \times F(d_2).$$

The value of a call depends on two pieces: the price of the stock times a function, $F(d_1)$; and the strike price, expressed in present value terms, times a function, $F(d_2)$. While the price of the stock (P_s) presents no problem, the strike price (P_e) expressed as a present value (P_e/e^{rT}) needs explanation. The strike price is divided by the number $e = 2.71828$ raised to rT, the product of the risk-free interest rate and the option's time to expiration. The use of $e = 2.71828$ expresses compounding on a continuous basis instead of discrete (e.g., quarterly or monthly) time periods.

The definitions of the functions $F(d_1)$ and $F(d_2)$ are

18.2
$$d_1 = \frac{\ln\left(\frac{P_s}{P_e}\right) + \left(r + \frac{\sigma^2}{2}\right)T}{\sigma\sqrt{T}}$$

and

18.3
$$d_2 = d_1 - \sigma\sqrt{T}.$$

The ratio of the price of the stock and the strike price (P_s/P_e) is expressed as a natural logarithm (ln). The numerical values of d_1 and d_2 represent the area under the normal probability distribution. Applying Black-Scholes requires a table of the values for the cumulative normal probability distribution. Such a table is readily available in statistics textbooks, and one is provided in Exhibit 18.1 for convenience. Once d_1 and d_2 have been determined and the values from the cumulative probability distribution located, it is these values that are used in the Black-Scholes model (i.e., substituted for $F(d_1)$ and $F(d_2)$ in Equation 18.1).

How the model is applied may be seen by the following example. The values of the variables are

Stock price (P_s)	$52
Strike price (P_e)	$50
Time to expiration (T)	0.25 (three months)
Standard deviation (σ)	0.20
Interest rate (r)	0.10 (10% annually)

Thus the values of d_1 and d_2 are

$$d_1 = \frac{\ln\left(\frac{52}{50}\right) + \left(0.1 + \frac{0.2^2}{2}\right) \times 0.25}{0.2\sqrt{0.25}}$$

$$= \frac{0.0392 + (0.1 + 0.02)0.25}{0.1} = 0.692$$

and

$$d_2 = 0.692 - 0.2\sqrt{0.25} = 0.692 - 0.1 = 0.592.$$

The values from the normal distribution are[2]

$$F(0.692) \approx 0.755$$

$$F(0.592) \approx 0.722.$$

---

[2]$F(0.69) = 0.7549$ and $F(0.59) = 0.7224$, which approximates the values given in the text.

EXHIBIT 18.1 Cumulative Normal Distribution

d	F(d)	d	F(d)	d	F(d)	d	F(d)	d	F(d)	d	F(d)	d	F(d)	d	F(d)	d	F(d)	d	F(d)	d	F(d)
-3.09	0.001	-2.51	0.0060	-1.93	0.0268	-1.35	0.0885	-0.77	0.2207	-0.19	0.4247	0.39	0.6517	0.94	0.8264	1.49	0.9319	2.04	0.9793	2.59	0.9952
-3.08	0.001	-2.50	0.0062	-1.92	0.0274	-1.34	0.0901	-0.76	0.2236	-0.18	0.4286	0.40	0.6554	0.95	0.8289	1.5	0.9332	2.05	0.9798	2.6	0.9953
-3.07	0.0011	-2.49	0.0064	-1.91	0.0281	-1.33	0.0918	-0.75	0.2266	-0.17	0.4325	0.41	0.6591	0.96	0.8315	1.51	0.9345	2.06	0.9803	2.61	0.9955
-3.06	0.0011	-2.48	0.0066	-1.90	0.0287	-1.32	0.0934	-0.74	0.2297	-0.16	0.4364	0.42	0.6628	0.97	0.834	1.52	0.9357	2.07	0.9808	2.62	0.9956
-3.05	0.0011	-2.47	0.0068	-1.89	0.0294	-1.31	0.0951	-0.73	0.2327	-0.15	0.4404	0.43	0.6664	0.98	0.8365	1.53	0.937	2.08	0.9812	2.63	0.9957
-3.04	0.0012	-2.46	0.0069	-1.88	0.0301	-1.30	0.0968	-0.72	0.2358	-0.14	0.4443	0.44	0.67	0.99	0.8389	1.54	0.9382	2.09	0.9817	2.64	0.9959
-3.03	0.0012	-2.45	0.0071	-1.87	0.0307	-1.29	0.0985	-0.71	0.2389	-0.13	0.4483	0.45	0.6736	1.00	0.8413	1.55	0.9394	2.1	0.9821	2.65	0.996
-3.02	0.0013	-2.44	0.0073	-1.86	0.0314	-1.28	0.1003	-0.70	0.242	-0.12	0.4522	0.46	0.6772	1.01	0.8438	1.56	0.9406	2.11	0.9826	2.66	0.9961
-3.01	0.0013	-2.43	0.0075	-1.85	0.0322	-1.27	0.102	-0.69	0.2451	-0.11	0.4562	0.47	0.6808	1.02	0.8461	1.57	0.9418	2.12	0.983	2.67	0.9962
-3.00	0.0013	-2.42	0.0078	-1.84	0.0329	-1.26	0.1038	-0.68	0.2483	-0.10	0.4602	0.48	0.6844	1.03	0.8485	1.58	0.9429	2.13	0.9834	2.68	0.9963
-2.99	0.0014	-2.41	0.0080	-1.83	0.0336	-1.25	0.1057	-0.67	0.2514	-0.09	0.4641	0.49	0.6879	1.04	0.8508	1.59	0.9441	2.14	0.9838	2.69	0.9964
-2.98	0.0014	-2.40	0.0082	-1.82	0.0344	-1.24	0.1075	-0.66	0.2546	-0.08	0.4681	0.50	0.6915	1.05	0.8531	1.6	0.9452	2.15	0.9842	2.7	0.9965
-2.97	0.0015	-2.39	0.0084	-1.81	0.0351	-1.23	0.1093	-0.65	0.2578	-0.07	0.4721	0.51	0.695	1.06	0.8554	1.61	0.9463	2.16	0.9846	2.71	0.9966
-2.96	0.0015	-2.38	0.0087	-1.80	0.0359	-1.22	0.1112	-0.64	0.2611	-0.06	0.4761	0.52	0.6985	1.07	0.8577	1.62	0.9474	2.17	0.985	2.72	0.9967
-2.95	0.0016	-2.37	0.0089	-1.79	0.0367	-1.21	0.1131	-0.63	0.2643	-0.05	0.4801	0.53	0.7019	1.08	0.8599	1.63	0.9484	2.18	0.9854	2.73	0.9968
-2.94	0.0016	-2.36	0.0091	-1.78	0.0375	-1.20	0.1151	-0.62	0.2676	-0.04	0.484	0.54	0.7054	1.09	0.8621	1.64	0.9495	2.19	0.9857	2.74	0.9969
-2.93	0.0017	-2.35	0.0094	-1.77	0.0384	-1.19	0.117	-0.61	0.2709	-0.03	0.488	0.55	0.7088	1.10	0.8643	1.65	0.9505	2.2	0.9861	2.75	0.997
-2.92	0.0018	-2.34	0.0096	-1.76	0.0392	-1.18	0.119	-0.60	0.2743	-0.02	0.492	0.56	0.7123	1.11	0.8665	1.66	0.9515	2.21	0.9864	2.76	0.9971
-2.91	0.0018	-2.33	0.0099	-1.75	0.0401	-1.17	0.121	-0.59	0.2776	-0.01	0.496	0.57	0.7157	1.12	0.8686	1.67	0.9525	2.22	0.9868	2.77	0.9972
-2.90	0.0019	-2.32	0.0102	-1.74	0.0409	-1.16	0.123	-0.58	0.281	0.00	0.5	0.58	0.719	1.13	0.8708	1.68	0.9535	2.23	0.9871	2.78	0.9973
-2.89	0.0019	-2.31	0.0104	-1.73	0.0418	-1.15	0.1251	-0.57	0.2843	0.01	0.504	$d_2 \rightarrow$ 0.59	0.7224	1.14	0.8729	1.69	0.9545	2.24	0.9875	2.79	0.9974
-2.88	0.002	-2.30	0.0107	-1.72	0.0427	-1.14	0.1271	-0.56	0.2877	0.02	0.508	0.60	0.7257	1.15	0.8749	1.7	0.9554	2.25	0.9878	2.8	0.9974
-2.87	0.0021	-2.29	0.0110	-1.71	0.0436	-1.13	0.1292	-0.55	0.2912	0.03	0.512	0.61	0.7291	1.16	0.877	1.71	0.9564	2.26	0.9881	2.81	0.9975
-2.86	0.0021	-2.28	0.0113	-1.70	0.0446	-1.12	0.1314	-0.54	0.2946	0.04	0.516	0.62	0.7324	1.17	0.879	1.72	0.9573	2.27	0.9884	2.82	0.9976
-2.85	0.0022	-2.27	0.0116	-1.69	0.0455	-1.11	0.1335	-0.53	0.2981	0.05	0.5199	0.63	0.7357	1.18	0.881	1.73	0.9582	2.28	0.9887	2.83	0.9977
-2.84	0.0023	-2.26	0.0119	-1.68	0.0465	-1.10	0.1357	-0.52	0.3015	0.06	0.5239	0.64	0.7389	1.19	0.883	1.74	0.9591	2.29	0.989	2.84	0.9977
-2.83	0.0023	-2.25	0.0122	-1.67	0.0475	-1.09	0.1379	-0.51	0.305	0.07	0.5279	0.65	0.7422	1.20	0.8849	1.75	0.9599	2.3	0.9893	2.85	0.9978
-2.82	0.0024	-2.24	0.0125	-1.66	0.0485	-1.08	0.1401	-0.50	0.3085	0.08	0.5319	0.66	0.7454	1.21	0.8869	1.76	0.9608	2.31	0.9896	2.86	0.9979
-2.81	0.0025	-2.23	0.0129	-1.65	0.0495	-1.07	0.1423	-0.49	0.3121	0.09	0.5359	0.67	0.7486	1.22	0.8888	1.77	0.9616	2.32	0.9898	2.87	0.9979
-2.80	0.0026	-2.22	0.0132	-1.64	0.0505	-1.06	0.1446	-0.48	0.3156	0.1	0.5398	0.68	0.7517	1.23	0.8907	1.78	0.9625	2.33	0.9901	2.88	0.998
-2.79	0.0026	-2.21	0.0136	-1.63	0.0516	-1.05	0.1469	-0.47	0.3192	0.11	0.5438	$d_2 \rightarrow$ 0.69	0.7549	1.24	0.8925	1.79	0.9633	2.34	0.9904	2.89	0.9981
-2.78	0.0027	-2.20	0.0139	-1.62	0.0526	-1.04	0.1492	-0.46	0.3228	0.12	0.5478	0.7	0.758	1.25	0.8943	1.8	0.9641	2.35	0.9906	2.9	0.9981

d	F(d)	d	F(d)	d	F(d)	d	F(d)	d	F(d)	d	F(d)	d	F(d)	d	F(d)	d	F(d)	d	F(d)	d	F(d)
-2.77	0.0028	-2.19	0.0143	-1.61	0.0537	-1.03	0.1515	-0.45	0.3264	0.13	0.5517	0.71	0.7611	1.26	0.8962	1.81	0.9649	2.36	0.9909	2.91	0.9982
-2.76	0.0029	-2.18	0.0146	-1.60	0.0548	-1.02	0.1539	-0.44	0.33	0.14	0.5557	0.72	0.7642	1.27	0.898	1.82	0.9656	2.37	0.9911	2.92	0.9982
-2.75	0.003	-2.17	0.0150	-1.59	0.0559	-1.01	0.1562	-0.43	0.3336	0.15	0.5596	0.73	0.7673	1.28	0.8997	1.83	0.9664	2.38	0.9913	2.93	0.9983
-2.74	0.0031	-2.16	0.0154	-1.58	0.0571	-1.00	0.1587	-0.42	0.3372	0.16	0.5636	0.74	0.7703	1.29	0.9015	1.84	0.9671	2.39	0.9916	2.94	0.9984
-2.73	0.0032	-2.15	0.0158	-1.57	0.0582	-0.99	0.1611	-0.41	0.3409	0.17	0.5675	0.75	0.7734	1.30	0.9032	1.85	0.9678	2.4	0.9918	2.95	0.9984
-2.72	0.0033	-2.14	0.0162	-1.56	0.0594	-0.98	0.1635	-0.40	0.3446	0.18	0.5714	0.76	0.7764	1.31	0.9049	1.86	0.9686	2.41	0.992	2.96	0.9985
-2.71	0.0034	-2.13	0.0166	-1.55	0.0606	-0.97	0.166	-0.39	0.3483	0.19	0.5753	0.77	0.7793	1.32	0.9066	1.87	0.9693	2.42	0.9922	2.97	0.9985
-2.7	0.0035	-2.12	0.0170	-1.54	0.0618	-0.96	0.1685	-0.38	0.352	0.2	0.5793	0.78	0.7823	1.33	0.9082	1.88	0.9699	2.43	0.9925	2.98	0.9986
-2.69	0.0036	-2.11	0.0174	-1.53	0.063	-0.95	0.1711	-0.37	0.3557	0.21	0.5832	0.79	0.7852	1.34	0.9099	1.89	0.9706	2.44	0.9927	2.99	0.9986
-2.68	0.0037	-2.10	0.0179	-1.52	0.0643	-0.94	0.1736	-0.36	0.3594	0.22	0.5871	0.80	0.7881	1.35	0.9115	1.9	0.9713	2.45	0.9929	3	0.9987
-2.67	0.0038	-2.09	0.0183	-1.51	0.0655	-0.93	0.1762	-0.35	0.3632	0.23	0.591	0.81	0.791	1.36	0.9131	1.91	0.9719	2.46	0.9931	3.01	0.9987
-2.66	0.0039	-2.08	0.0188	-1.50	0.0668	-0.92	0.1788	-0.34	0.3669	0.24.	0.5948	0.82	0.7939	1.37	0.9147	1.92	0.9726	2.47	0.9932	3.02	0.9987
-2.65	0.004	-2.07	0.0192	-1.49	0.0681	-0.91	0.1814	-0.33	0.3707	0.25	0.5987	0.83	0.7967	1.38	0.9162	1.93	0.9732	2.48	0.9934	3.03	0.9988
-2.64	0.0041	-2.06	0.0197	-1.48	0.0694	-0.90	0.1841	-0.32	0.3745	0.26	0.6026	0.84	0.7995	1.39	0.9177	1.94	0.9738	2.49	0.9936	3.04	0.9988
-2.63	0.0043	-2.05	0.0202	-1.47	0.0708	-0.89	0.1867	-0.31	0.3783	0.27	0.6064	0.85	0.8023	1.40	0.9192	1.95	0.9744	2.5	0.9938	3.05	0.9989
-2.62	0.0044	-2.04	0.0207	-1.46	0.0721	-0.88	0.1894	-0.30	0.3821	0.28	0.6103	0.86	0.8051	1.41	0.9207	1.96	0.975	2.51	0.994	3.06	0.9989
-2.61	0.0045	-2.03	0.0212	-1.45	0.0735	-0.87	0.1922	-0.29	0.3859	0.29	0.6141	0.87	0.8078	1.42	0.9222	1.97	0.9756	2.52	0.9941	3.07	0.9989
-2.60	0.0047	-2.02	0.0217	-1.44	0.0749	-0.86	0.1949	-0.28	0.3897	0.3	0.6179	0.88	0.8106	1.43	0.9236	1.98	0.9761	2.53	0.9943	3.08	0.999
-2.59	0.0048	-2.01	0.0222	-1.43	0.0764	-0.85	0.1977	-0.27	0.3936	0.31	0.6217	0.89	0.8133	1.44	0.9251	1.99	0.9767	2.54	0.9945	3.09	0.999
-2.58	0.0049	-2.00	0.0228	-1.42	0.0778	-0.84	0.2005	-0.26	0.3974	0.32	0.6255	0.90	0.8159	1.45	0.9265	2	0.9772	2.55	0.9946		
-2.57	0.0051	-1.99	0.0233	-1.41	0.0793	-0.83	0.2033	-0.25	0.4013	0.33	0.6293	0.91	0.8186	1.46	0.9279	2.01	0.9778	2.56	0.9948		
-2.56	0.0052	-1.98	0.0239	-1.40	0.0808	-0.82	0.2061	-0.24	0.4052	0.34	0.6331	0.92	0.8212	1.47	0.9292	2.02	0.9783	2.57	0.9949		
-2.55	0.0054	-1.97	0.0244	-1.39	0.0823	-0.81	0.209	-0.23	0.409	0.35	0.6368	0.93	0.8238	1.48	0.9306	2.03	0.9788	2.58	0.9951		
-2.54	0.0055	-1.96	0.0250	-1.38	0.0838	-0.80	0.2119	-0.22	0.4129	0.36	0.6406										
-2.53	0.0057	-1.95	0.0256	-1.37	0.0853	-0.79	0.2148	-0.21	0.4168	0.37	0.6443										
-2.52	0.0059	-1.94	0.0262	-1.36	0.0869	-0.78	0.2177	-0.20	0.4207	0.38	0.648										

Critical Values of z for

Significance Level	Two Tails	Lower Tail	Upper Tail
0.10	±1.65	-1.28	+1.28
0.05	±1.96	-1.65	+1.65
0.01	±2.58	-2.33	+2.33

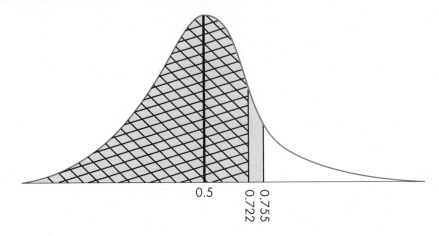

FIGURE 18.2 A Normal Curve with the Areas for d_1 and d_2

These values are represented by d_1 and d_2 in Figure 18.2, which shows the areas under the normal probability distribution for both d_1 and d_2. (The total shaded area represents d_1, while the checkerboard area represents d_2.)

The probability distribution seeks to measure the probability of the option being exercised. If there is a large probability that the option will have positive intrinsic value at expiration, the numerical values of Fd_1 and Fd_2 approach 1, and the option's value will approach the price of the stock minus the present value of the strike price:

$$V_o = (P_s)(1) - \frac{P_e}{e^{rT}}(1) = (P_s) - \frac{P_e}{e^{rT}}.$$

If there is little probability that the option will have positive intrinsic value at expiration, the numerical values of d_1 and d_2 will approach 0, and the option will have little value:

$$V_o = (P_s)(0) - \frac{(P_e)}{e^{rT}}(0) = 0.$$

Given the values for $F(d_1)$ and $F(d_2)$ determined from the normal distribution, the value of the call option is

$$V_o = (\$52)(0.755) - \frac{50}{2.71828^{(0.1)(0.25)}}(0.722) = \$4.00.$$

If the call is selling for more than $4.00, it is overvalued. If it is selling for less, it is undervalued.

If the price of the stock had been $60, the Black-Scholes model determines the value of the option to be $11.25. If the price of the stock were $40, the value of the option is $0.04. By altering the price of the stock, the various values of the option are determined. As shown in Figure 18.3, the different prices of the stock generate the general pattern of option values illustrated by line DE in Figure 18.1.

If one of the other variables (i.e., T, σ, P_e, and r) were to change while holding the price of the stock constant, the curve representing the value of the option would shift.

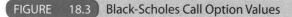

FIGURE   18.3   Black-Scholes Call Option Values

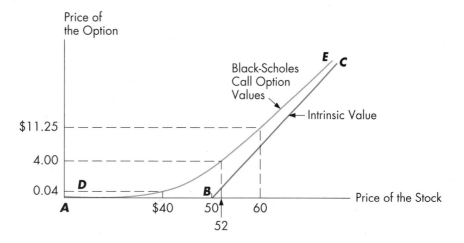

If the life of the option had been nine months instead of three months, the curve would shift up. Increased price volatility, a lower strike price, or higher interest rates would also shift the Black-Scholes option valuation curve upwards. A shorter time to expiration, a lower interest rate, a higher strike price, or smaller volatility would shift the curve downward.

These relationships are illustrated in Exhibit 18.2, which shows the impact of each variable on a call's value using Black-Scholes. This illustration uses the previous example and is divided into five cases. In each case one of the variables is changed while all the others are held constant. The value derived in the initial illustration is underlined in each case. In case 1, the price of the stock varies from $40 to $70, and as the price of the stock rises, so does the valuation of the option. When the option is way out of the money (i.e., when the stock is selling for $40), the valuation is a minimal $0.04. The value rises to $11.25 when the stock sells for $60. At a stock price of $70, the option is way in the money with an intrinsic value of $20, and the Black-Scholes valuation is $21.22.

In case 2, the strike price varies from $40 to $70. As would be expected, the value of the option declines with higher strike prices. Although the option is worth $12.98 when the strike price is $40, the option is virtually worthless at a strike price of $70.

Case 3 illustrates the decline in the value of the option as it approaches expiration. A year prior to expiration, the option at $50 is worth $8.08 when the stock sells for $52. This value declines to $4.00 when three months remain. With two weeks to expiration, the option is worth $2.36, and at expiration, the option is worth only its $2.00 intrinsic value.

In case 4, the variability of the underlying stock's return is altered. Greater variability usually decreases the attractiveness of a security, but the opposite occurs with call options. Increased variability means there is a greater chance the underlying stock's price will rise and increase the intrinsic value of the option. Thus, increased variability

EXHIBIT 18.2 Black-Scholes Option Valuations

Initial values:

Price of the stock	$52.00
Strike price	$50.00
Time to expiration	0.25 (three months, or 90 days)
Standard deviation	0.20
Risk-free interest rate	0.10 (10 percent annually)
Black-Scholes valuation	$4.00

Case 1: Price of the Stock Is Altered

Stock Price	Black-Scholes Option Value
$40	$ 0.04
45	0.55
50	2.62
52	4.00
55	6.50
60	11.25
65	16.22
70	21.22

Case 2: Strike Price Is Altered

Strike Price	Black-Scholes Option Value
$40	$12.98
45	8.18
50	4.00
55	1.37
60	0.31
65	0.03
70	0.01

Case 3: Time to Expiration Is Altered

Days	Black-Scholes Option Value
360	$8.08
270	6.86
180	5.53
90	4.00
60	3.41
30	2.74
15	2.36
7	2.14
1	2.01

Case 4: Standard Deviation Is Altered

Standard Deviation	Black-Scholes Option Value
1.0	$11.56
0.6	7.71
0.3	4.87
0.2	4.00
0.15	3.62
0.1	3.34
0.05	3.22
0.001	3.21

Case 5: Interest Rate Is Altered

Interest Rate	Black-Scholes Option Value
0.20	$4.91
0.15	4.45
0.12	4.18
0.10	4.00
0.08	3.83
0.06	3.66
0.04	3.50
0.02	3.33
0.001	3.18

is associated with higher option valuations, and lower variability is associated with lower option valuations. This relationship is seen in case 4. As the standard deviation of the stock's return declines, so does the value of the option.

In the last case, the interest rate is changed. As was explained earlier, a higher interest rate decreases the present value of the strike price and increases the value of the call option. This relationship is seen in case 5. At an annual interest rate of 20 percent, the option is worth $4.91, but this value decreases as the interest rate declines.

Although Black-Scholes may appear formidable, it is easily applied because computer programs have been developed to perform the calculations. All the variables but one are readily observable. Unfortunately, the standard deviation of the stock's return is not observable, so the individual will have to develop a means to obtain that data to apply the model.

One method to overcome that problem is to reverse the equation and solve for the standard deviation. If the individual knows the price of the stock, the strike price, the price of the option, the term of the option, and the interest rate, Black-Scholes may be used to solve for the standard deviation of the returns. Historical data are then used in Black-Scholes to determine the *implied* historical variability of the underlying stock's returns. If it can be assumed that the variability has not changed, then that value for the standard deviation is assumed to be the correct measure of the stock's current variability and is used to determine the present value of an option.

EXPENSING EMPLOYEE STOCK OPTIONS AND OPTION VALUATION

Many firms grant stock options to select employees as a type of deferred compensation or "incentive-based compensation." For example, Pactiv reported that management and the board of directors receive 25 to 55 percent of their compensation in stock and options. The strike price is set equal to or greater than the market price of the stock. Since there is no positive intrinsic value, the recipient has no immediate tax obligation. (If the strike price were less than the market price of the stock, the option would have positive intrinsic value, which would be taxable.) If the company does well and the price of its stock rises, the value of these incentive options also increases, and the employee will have been compensated for contributing to the firm's success. (The gain on the option may be taxed at the long-term capital gains tax rate, which will be lower than the employee's marginal tax rate.)

Since many firms grant top management incentive-based stock options, a question arises: Does this practice have a cost to the firm? That is, are these options expenses? The initial answer may seem to be no. The option has no intrinsic value and the firm has no cash outflow when the options are issued.

Even if the options have no positive intrinsic value and even if the firm has no cash outflow, that is not the same as stating that out-of-the-money options have no value. The Black-Scholes option valuation model indicates that the value of an option depends not only on the price of the stock and the strike price but also on the risk-free rate, the time to expiration, and the volatility of the underlying stock. Out-of-the-money options have value because of the difference between the price of the stock and the present value of the strike price. Since incentive options often have five to ten years to expiration, the present value of the strike price is often considerably lower than the current stock price. Since the recipient receives this value, the option has a cost to the issuing firm. (Another approach to concluding that incentive-based options are an expense is to use the following reasoning: Instead of granting the option, the firm sells the option and uses the proceeds to compensate the employee. The firm now has a cash outflow, which is an obvious expense.)

Why is the conclusion that incentive stock options have value and should be expensed by the issuing firm important? The answer is the potential impact on the firm's earnings. If the present value of the option were expensed, the firm's earnings would be decreased. *Expensing the options lowers the firm's reported earnings.* Since incentive-based options are a form of compensation, they are a cost that should be currently recognized and deducted from current earnings. The accounting profession has acknowledged that incentive-based compensation involves a cost. Under current reporting requirements, a firm must estimate the cost of incentive-based compensation and provide the impact on earnings on its income statement.

Since the options must be expensed, the question becomes how to determine the value of the options. Currently Black-Scholes is the model most accepted by U.S. firms for valuing options. However, the model does have its weaknesses. For example, applying the model requires an assumption concerning the stock's future price volatility. Also, the recipient may exercise an incentive-based option prior to expiration. The Black-Scholes model requires using a specific date. (The expiration date is generally used because it is known, while the actual date the option will be exercised cannot be known.) These problem areas decrease the model's attractiveness for valuing employee stock options. (An alternative model, the binomial option pricing model, is discussed in the appendix to this chapter.)

PUT–CALL PARITY

Once the value of a call has been determined, so has the value of a put with the same strike price and term to expiration, because the price of the stock, put, and call are interrelated.[3] A change in the value of one must produce a change in the value of the others. If such a change did not occur, an opportunity for a riskless arbitrage would exist. As investors sought to take advantage of the opportunity, prices would change until the arbitrage opportunity ceased to exist.

The relationship between the prices of a put and a call, the price of the underlying stock, and the option's strike price is referred to as put–call parity. In effect, put–call parity says a pie may be cut into pieces of different sizes, but the total pie cannot be affected. According to put–call parity, the price of a stock is equal to the price of the call plus the present value of the strike price minus the price of the put:

18.4
$$P_s = P_c + \frac{P_e}{(1 + i)^n} - P_p.$$

[3]Put–call parity ensures that if the value of a call is determined, the value of the put must also be determined. Since the Black-Scholes model calculates the value of a call, the value of a put with the same strike price and expiration date is also determined. For this reason, software that applies the Black-Scholes model includes the value of a put with the same strike price and expiration date.

In the previous example, the price of the stock was $52, the strike price of the call was $50, and the value of the call was $4 when the annual rate of interest was 10 percent and the option expired in three months. The values imply that the price of a three-month put to sell the stock at $50 must be

$$\$52 = \$4.00 + \frac{\$50}{(1 + 0.1)^{0.25}} - P_p$$

$$P_p = -\$52 + \$4.00 + \$48.82 = \$0.82.$$

Rearranged, the equation says that the price of the stock plus the price of the put minus the price of the call and the present value of the strike price must equal 0. That is,

$$0 = P_s + P_p - P_c - \frac{P_e}{(1 + i)^n}.$$

If the equation does not hold, an opportunity for arbitrage exists. Consider the following example. A stock sells for $105; the strike price of both the put and call is $100. The price of the put is $5, the price of the call is $20, and both options are for one year. The rate of interest is 11.1 percent (11.1 percent is used because the present value of $100 at 11.1 percent is $100/1.111 = $90, which is easier to work with in this illustration). Given these numbers, the equation holds:

$$0 = \$105 + 5 - 20 - 90.$$

If the call sold for $25, then an opportunity for arbitrage would exist. The investor (or the computer) perceives the disequilibrium and executes the following trades:

1. Buy the stock	Cash outflow	$105
2. Buy the put	Cash outflow	5
3. Sell the call	Cash inflow	25
4. Borrow $90 at 11.1%	Cash inflow	90

(Notice there is an important assumption that the investor can either lend funds and earn 11.1 percent or *borrow* funds at that rate.) There is a net cash inflow of $5($25 + 90 - 105 - 5), so the investor has committed no cash and has actually received funds.

An alternative way to see the process of executing the arbitrage is to set up the equation as follows:

$$P_s + P_p = P_c + P_b.$$

In this form, the equation says that the price of the stock plus the price of the put must equal the price of the call plus the price of the bond. If the two sides are not equal, you short the higher side and buy the lower side. Thus if the equation is

$$\$105 + \$5 < \$25 + \$90,$$

you buy the stock and the put and short the call and the bond (i.e., sell the call and borrow the funds). The cash inflows more than cover the cash outflows, and in this illustration the investor receives a net cash inflow of $5.

What are the potential profits from this position a year from now when the options expire and the investor closes the positions if the prices of the stock are $110, $105, and $90? The question is answered as follows:

Price of the Stock	Profit on the Stock Purchased	Profit on the Call Sold	Profit on the Put Purchased	Interest Paid	Net Profit
$110	$ 5	$15	$−5	$−10	$5
105	0	20	−5	−10	5
90	−15	25	5	−10	5

At the highest price ($110), the investor makes $5 on the stock that was purchased for $105. Since the call's intrinsic value is $10, $15 is made on the sale of the call. Since the put's intrinsic value is $0, $5 is lost on the purchase of the put. Interest paid was $10($90 × 0.111), so the net profit on all the positions is $5. At the lowest price ($90), the investor loses $15 on the stock. Since the call's intrinsic value is $0, $25 is made on the sale of the call. Since the put's intrinsic value is $10, $5 is made on the put. Ten dollars was paid in interest, so the net profit is $5. By similar reasoning, if the price of the stock remains at $105, the net profit on the position is $5. No matter what happens to the price of the stock, the investor nets $5. There is no cash outlay and no risk; the $5 is assured.

In the previous illustration the call was overpriced, which led to an arbitrage opportunity. Suppose the put were overpriced and sold for $10. Once again an opportunity for arbitrage would exist. The following trades are executed:

1. Sell the stock (short)	Cash inflow	$105
2. Sell the put	Cash inflow	10
3. Buy the call	Cash outflow	20
4. Lend $90 at 11.1%	Cash outflow	90

There is a net cash inflow of $5($105 + 10 − 20 − 90), so the investor has once again committed no funds but has actually received cash.

What are the potential profits from this position? The answer may be illustrated as follows:

Price of the Stock	Profit on the Stock (Short)	Profit on the Call Purchased	Profit on the Put Sold	Interest Received	Net Profit
$110	$−5	$−10	$10	$10	$5
105	0	−15	10	10	5
90	15	−20	0	10	5

At the $110 price of the stock, the investor loses $5 on the stock. Since the call's intrinsic value is $10, $10 is lost on the purchase of the call. Since the put's intrinsic value is $0, $10 is made on the sale of the put. Ten dollars was collected in interest, so the net profit is $5. At $90, the investor earns $15 on the stock, but loses $20 on the call. Since the put's intrinsic value is $10, there is no gain or loss on the put, and $10 was collected in interest. Once again the net profit is $5. No matter what happens to the price of the stock, the investor nets an assured $5.

Both examples illustrated an opportunity for a riskless arbitrage. In either case, the act of executing the positions would cause the prices of the securities to change until the opportunity ceased to exist and the condition that

$$0 = P_s + P_p - P_c - \frac{P_e}{(1 + i)^n}$$

is fulfilled. In the first example, the call was overpriced, and in the second example, the put was overpriced. In actuality, if any of the securities was mispriced, there would be an opportunity for arbitrage.

Put–call parity may also be used to show interrelationships among financial markets and why a change in one must be transferred to another. Suppose the Federal Reserve uses open-market operations to lower interest rates. The Fed buys short-term securities, which drives up their prices and reduces interest rates. This means the equilibrium prices in the preceding example will no longer hold. The lower interest increases the present value of the strike price. At the existing prices, investors would borrow funds at the new lower rate, buy the stock, sell the call, and buy the put. Executing these transactions generates a net cash inflow and ensures the individual of a profitable riskless arbitrage. Of course, the act of simultaneously trying to buy the stock and the put and to sell the call alters their respective prices until the arbitrage opportunity is negated. The effect of the Federal Reserve's action in one market will then have been transferred to the other financial markets.

THE HEDGE RATIO

In addition to option valuation and the development of put–call parity, the Black-Scholes model provides useful information to investors seeking to hedge positions. Hedged positions occur when the investor takes one position in the stock and the opposite in the option (e.g., a long in the stock and a short in the option). Unfortunately, the price movement in an option and the underlying stock are not equal. This was illustrated in Exhibit 17.3 in which the price of the call option increased from $15 to $23 when the price of the stock rose from $60 to $70. The percentage increase in the call exceeded the percentage increase in the price of the stock, and the absolute price changes were not equal. Since absolute price changes are not equal, the investor cannot use one call option to exactly offset price changes in the stock. Thus a hedge position of one call option cannot exactly offset the price movement in 100 shares of the stock.

To exactly offset a stock's price change, the investor must know the *hedge ratio* of the option. This is the ratio of the change in the price of the call option to the change in the price of the stock (i.e., the slope of the line *DE* relating the price of an option to the price of the stock in Figures 18.1 and 18.3). The hedge ratio is also referred to as an option's *delta*. For a call option, the delta must be a positive number. (For a put the delta is a negative number.) If the delta is 0.5, this means that the per-share price of the option will rise $0.50 for every $1.00 increase in the price of the stock. Thus, if the investor owns 100 shares of the stock and has written two calls, a $1.00 increase in the stock should generate a $1.00 per-share loss in the options (i.e., a $50 increase in the value of each option, which produces a total loss of $100 for the individual who has written two options). The $100 gain in one position (e.g., the long position in the stock) is exactly offset by the $100 loss in the other position (e.g., the short position in the option). The entire position is completely hedged.

If an investor or a portfolio manager wants to exactly offset price changes by using options, the hedge ratio is crucial information. The reciprocal of the hedge ratio, which is

18.5   **Number of call options to hedge 100 shares** $= \dfrac{1}{\text{Hedge ratio}}$,

defines the number of call options that should be sold for each 100 shares purchased. (For short positions in the stock, the ratio indicates the number of calls the individual must buy for every 100 shares sold short.) Thus, in the previous example, the number of call options sold to construct a complete hedge is

$$\frac{1}{0.5} = 2.$$

The portfolio manager must sell two call options for every 100 shares purchased to have a perfectly hedged position.

The hedge ratio may also be viewed as the number of shares of stock that must be purchased for each option sold. In the preceding example, the hedge ratio of 0.5 implies that 50 shares purchased for every call option sold is a completely hedged position. Both views of the hedge ratio are essentially the same. One view determines the number of shares to buy per call option, while the other determines the number of call options to sell per 100 shares of stock.

Fortunately, the hedge ratio is easy to obtain. The numerical value of $F(d_1)$ in the Black-Scholes option valuation model is the hedge ratio. In the preceding illustration of the valuation model, $F(d_1)$ was determined to equal 0.755. Thus at a price of the stock of $52, the number of call options necessary to completely hedge a position in the stock is $1/0.755 = 1.325$ options. Since the investor cannot buy or sell 1.325 call options, the hedge could be expressed as follows: For every call option, the investor takes the opposite position in shares of the stock. Thus one call option hedges 76 shares of the stock.

While the hedge gives the number of call options that must be bought (or sold) for every 100 shares of stock, the numerical value of the ratio frequently changes. This may be seen by observing the curved line *DE* in Figure 18.1, which represents the value of the option at various prices of the stock. The slope of the line changes from being relatively flat for low prices of the stock to being parallel with the line representing the option's intrinsic value. Since the slope of the line increases with a rise in the stock's price, the numerical value of the hedge ratio also increases. This implies that fewer call options must be sold to construct a perfectly hedged portfolio. To maintain a perfectly hedged position, the individual must frequently adjust the positions in the call options or in the underlying securities.

The prior discussion focused on the use of call options and the hedge ratio to reduce the risk associated with a position in a particular stock. Investors, however, may wish to reduce the risk associated with their entire portfolios and may use stock index options to hedge their portfolios. To hedge a portfolio using stock index options, the investor must consider (1) the value of the portfolio, (2) the volatility of the portfolio, (3) the implied value of the option, and (4) the option's hedge ratio.

The value of the portfolio is the sum of the value of all the securities in the portfolio. The volatility of the portfolio is measured by the portfolio's beta. (Failure to include the beta assumes that the portfolio moves exactly with the market [i.e., that the beta = 1.0].) The implied value of the option is the product of the option's strike price and $100. (If an S&P 500 index option's strike price is 560, the implied value of the option is $560 \times \$100 = \$56,000$.) The hedge ratio is derived from the Black-Scholes option valuation model.

The number of index options necessary to hedge a portfolio is given in Equation 18.6.

$$\text{Number of index options} = \frac{\text{Value of the portfolio}}{\text{Implied value of the option}}$$

18.6
$$\times \text{ Portfolio's beta} \times \frac{1}{\text{Hedge ratio}}.$$

Exhibit 18.3 illustrates how an investor may hedge a $200,000 portfolio by writing index call options. The S&P 500 stock index stands at 550, and an out-of-the-money index stock call with a strike price of 560 sells for $800. (The price would be reported as $8 in the financial press, but the cost to the buyer and the proceeds to the seller are 8×100.) The stock index call option's hedge ratio is 0.4.

Equation 18.6 indicates that the investor should write 6.7 calls. Since fractional sales are not possible, the investor sells six calls for $800 each and receives $4,800 before

---

EXHIBIT 18.3 Using Stock Index Call Options to Hedge a $200,000 Portfolio

Givens

Value of portfolio: $200,000
Beta: 0.75
Value of S&P 500 stock index call: 550
Strike price of S&P 500 stock index call: 560
Implied value of S&P 500 stock index option: $100 \times 560 = \$56,000$
Price of the stock index option: $8($800)
Hedge ratio: 0.4
Number of calls necessary to hedge: ($200,000/$56,000)(0.75)(1/0.4) = 6.7
Number of call index options sold: 6
Proceeds from the sale of one option: $800
Total received: $6 \times \$800 = \$4,800$

Market declines by 2 percent to 539

Price of one option: $350
Cost of the repurchase of options: $350 \times 6 = \$2,100$
Gain on call options sold: $4,800 − $2,100 = $2,700
Loss on portfolio: $200,000(1 − 0.02) − $200,000(0.75) = −$3,000
Net loss: $2,700 − $3,000 = −$300

Market rises by 2 percent to 561

Price of one option: $1,100
Cost of the repurchase of options: $1,100 \times 6 = \$6,600$
Loss on call options sold: $4,800 − $6,600 = −$1,800
Gain on portfolio: $200,000(1 + 0.02) − $200,000(0.75) = $3,000
Net gain: $3,000 − $1,800 = $1,200

⊕ Point of Interest

THE DELTA AND OTHER GREEKS

An option's delta is the first derivative (the slope of the line) relating changes in the value of an option to changes in the price of the underlying stock. All the other variables in the Black-Scholes option valuation model are held constant. But these variables can change, and their first derivatives may also be important. Like delta, these slopes may be referred to by letters of the Greek alphabet. You may never use these Greeks, but knowing them should increase your ability to comprehend material that you may encounter in the literature on investments and portfolio management.

"Vega" refers the change in the value of the option with respect to change in volatility. That is, an increase in the standard deviation of the stock's returns causes what change in the value of the option? "Theta" refers to the rate of change in the value of the option with respect to changes in time. As the option approaches expiration, how rapidly does the value of the option decline? "Rho" refers to the rate of change in the option's value with respect to a change in the interest rate. As the interest rate increases, what is the increase in the value of a call option?

Delta, vega, theta, and rho are first derivatives. You may encounter "gamma," which is the second derivative relating the change in the price of an option to the change in the price of the stock. The line representing the value of a call option with respect to the price of the stock (*DE* in Figure 18.3) is a curve. Its slope changes as the price of the stock changes. Gamma measures the rate of change in that slope.

The hedge ratio is derived from the slope relating the price of the option to the price of the stock. This change in the slope means that an investor who uses the delta to hedge a position will have to readjust the number of options as the price of the stock changes. Since gamma measures the rate of change in the delta, sophisticated investors may use it to adjust the number of options. Such adjustments should facilitate their risk management strategies.

commissions. In case 1, the market declines by 2 percent (the S&P 500 declines from 550 to 539). The decline in the market causes the price of the index option to fall from $8 to $3.50. The investor repurchases the six options for $2,100 and earns a profit of $2,700, which almost offsets the $3,000 loss on the portfolio. In case 2, the S&P 500 rises by 2 percent from 550 to 561, and the price of the call rises from $8 to $11. The investor loses $1,800 on the sale of the index options and earns a net profit of $1,200.

As these examples illustrate, using stock index options in hedged positions can reduce the risk of loss, but hedging also reduces and may erase the potential gain from the portfolio. Unlike covered call writing, which seeks to take advantage of the time premium disappearing as the option approaches expiration, the purpose of hedging is to reduce the impact of price fluctuations. This example illustrates the reduction in loss if the market were to decline, but the hedge reduces any gain when the market rises because the option is not at expiration and still commands a time premium. (The call's intrinsic value is $56,100 - 56,000 = 100$, but it costs $1,100 to repurchase the option. The profit would be even smaller if the option commanded a larger time premium and the option price had been higher. At a cost if $1,400, the position would have generated a $200 loss even though the market rose.)

Constructing this hedge requires active portfolio supervision. The data necessary to construct a hedge include the portfolio's beta, which changes with the composition of the portfolio, and the option's hedge ratio. As was discussed earlier, the hedge ratio changes as the price of the option responds to changes in the underlying stock.

Maintaining a well-hedged portfolio requires continuous supervision and frequent re-balancing of the number of index options in the hedge. For the individual investor, using stock index options to hedge a portfolio can be both time-consuming and costly (when commissions are considered) and simply may be impractical. However, using stock index options in hedge positions could be a viable means to reduce the risk of loss for short periods of time when the investor is no longer bullish and does not want to liquidate the portfolio. (Another possibility for hedging a stock or a portfolio is the "collar" strategy considered in the next section on additional option strategies. For the individual investor, a collar may be more practical, since it avoids rebalancing and is a passive strategy.)

ADDITIONAL OPTION STRATEGIES

Even if arbitrage drives option markets toward an equilibrium so that the investor cannot take advantage of mispricings, fairly priced options may still be used in a variety of strategies. For example, in the previous chapter the protective put was illustrated as a means to reduce potential loss. The investor bought a put when buying a stock, so if the value of the stock were to fall, the value of the put would rise and at least partially offset the loss on the stock.

This section covers several other strategies involving options. These include the covered put and the protective call, which mirror the covered call and protective put presented in the previous chapter. Next follow the *straddle*, which combines buying (or selling) both a put and a call, and the *spreads*, which involve the simultaneous purchase and sale of options with different strike prices on the same stock. The last strategy, the *collar*, which involves the stock and both a put and a call, is a means to limit the impact of a decline in the price of the stock. Although these additional strategies do not exhaust all the possible strategies using options, they do give an indication of the variety of possible alternatives available that employ puts and calls.

The Covered Put

The *covered put* is the opposite of the covered call. To construct a covered put, the investor sells the stock short and sells the put. If the put is exercised (forcing the investor to buy the stock), that individual may use the shares to cover the short in the stock. This is, of course, the opposite of the covered call, in which the writer supplies the previously purchased stock if the call option is exercised.

As with the covered call, the covered put limits the potential profit, but it also reduces risk. An investor constructs this position in anticipation of a stable stock price. If the investor anticipates a large change in the price of the stock, an alternative strategy is superior to the covered put. For example, if the investor anticipates a large price decline, selling the stock short or buying the put offers more potential gain if the stock's price were to fall. To see the potential profit and loss from the covered put, consider the following example:

Price of the stock (P_s)	$52
Strike price of the put (P_e)	$55
Price of the put	$ 5.50

The put is in the money, since it has a positive intrinsic value ($P_e - P_s = \$55 - \$52 = \$3$). It is also selling for a time premium ($\$5.50 - \$3 = \$2.50$). Because the investor expects the price of the stock to remain stable or decline modestly, a covered put is constructed by selling the stock short at $52 and selling the put for $5.50. The potential profit and loss at the expiration of the put from this position at various prices of the stock are as follows:

Price of the Stock	Profit (Loss) on the Short	Intrinsic Value of the Put	Profit (Loss) on the Put	Net Profit (Loss)
$40	$12	$15	$(9.50)	$2.50
45	7	10	(4.50)	2.50
50	2	5	.50	2.50
52	0	3	2.50	2.50
55	(3)	0	5.50	2.50
57.50	(5.50)	0	5.50	0
60	(8)	0	5.50	(2.50)
65	(13)	0	5.50	(7.50)

As long as the price of the stock remains below $57.50, the position generates a profit, but the maximum possible net profit is $2.50 (the time premium of the put).

The profit/loss profile is illustrated in Figure 18.4. The horizontal axis presents the price of the stock, and the vertical axis gives the profit and loss on the position. As may be seen in the figure, the maximum possible profit is $2.50 (whenever the price of the stock is equal to or less than $55, the option's strike price). There is no limit to the possible loss if the price of the stock rises. The break-even price of the stock is $57.50.

FIGURE   18.4   Profit or Loss from a Covered Put

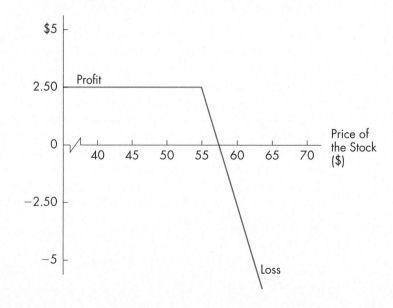

The Protective Call

Obviously, if the investor anticipates a large decline in the price of the stock, the previous strategy is inappropriate because it limits the potential profit from a price decline. Instead, the investor would short the stock (or buy a put). However, there is no limit to the possible loss from a short position if the price of the stock were to rise. The investor could limit the loss by entering a limit order to buy the stock and cover the short if the price of the stock were to rise. A limit order, however, could result in the investor's position being closed by a brief run-up in the price of the stock. An alternative strategy would be for the investor to buy a call. Combining a short in the stock with a call is the *protective call* strategy. The protective call is the opposite of the protective put strategy in which the investor buys the stock and a put. In that case, losses on the stock are partially offset by profits on the put. To see how the protective call strategy works, consider the following extension of the previous illustration.

Price of the stock	$52
Strike price of the call	$55
Price of the call	$ 1.50

In this illustration, the call is out of the money since the strike price exceeds the price of the stock. The option sells for a time premium of $1.50.

To construct a protective call, the investor shorts the stock at $52 and purchases the call for $1.50. The possible profits and losses from the position are as follows:

Price of the Stock	Profit (Loss) on the Short	Intrinsic Value of the Call	Profit (Loss) on the Call	Net Profit (Loss)
$40	$12	$0	$(1.50)	$10.50
45	7	0	(1.50)	5.50
50	2	0	(1.50)	.50
52	0	0	(1.50)	(1.50)
55	(3)	0	(1.50)	(4.50)
60	(8)	5	3.50	(4.50)
65	(13)	10	8.50	(4.50)

In this illustration, the worst case occurs when the price of the stock rises; however, the maximum possible loss is $4.50. Since theoretically there is no limit to the possible loss from a short position, the protective call limits the possible loss from an increase in the price of the stock. To achieve this increased safety, the investor forgoes some possible profit on the short in the stock.

The possible profits and losses at the various prices of the stock are illustrated in Figure 18.5. If the price of the stock rises, the maximum possible loss is limited to $4.50. As long as the price of the stock is less than $50.50, the position is profitable. This figure also includes the possible profits and losses from a short in the stock. Although the potential profit is larger if the price of the stock declines, there is no limit on the possible loss from selling the stock short. There is, however, limited loss from the protective call.

FIGURE 18.5 Profit or Loss from a Protective Call

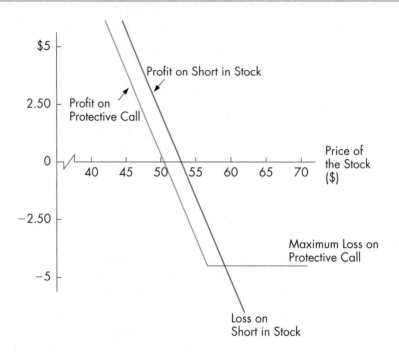

The Straddle

A *straddle* consists of a purchase (or sale) of a put and a call with the same exercise price and the same expiration date. If the investor buys both options, it is possible to earn a profit if the price of the stock rises or falls. The price increase may generate a profit on the call, and the price decline may generate a profit on the put.

Investors construct straddles if they expect the stock's price to move but are uncertain as to the direction. Consider a stock that is trading for $50 as the result of takeover rumors. If the takeover does occur, the price of the stock should rise. That argues for a long position in the stock. If the anticipated takeover does not occur and the rumors abate, the price of the stock will probably decline. That argues for a short position.

A long or a short position by itself may inflict losses if the investor selects the wrong position. To avoid this, the investor purchases both a put and a call. A price movement in either direction generates a profit (if the price movement covers the two premiums), and the maximum possible loss is the cost of the two options.

To see these potential profits and losses, consider the stock and the two options used in the previous illustrations:

Price of the stock	$52
Price of a call at $55	$ 1.50
Price of a put at $55	$ 5.50

Instead of purchasing or shorting the stock, the investor buys both options. The possible profits and losses at the expiration of the options for various prices of the stock are as follows:

Price of the Stock	Intrinsic Value of the Call	Profit (Loss) on the Call	Intrinsic Value of the Put	Profit (Loss) on the Put	Net Profit (Loss)
$40	$0	$(1.50)	$15	$9.50	$8
45	0	(1.50)	10	4.50	3
48	0	(1.50)	7	1.50	0
50	0	(1.50)	5	(.50)	(2)
52	0	(1.50)	3	(2.50)	(4)
55	0	(1.50)	0	(5.50)	(7)
60	5	3.50	0	(5.50)	(2)
62	7	5.50	0	(5.50)	0
65	10	8.50	0	(5.50)	3
70	15	13.50	0	(5.50)	8

The position generates a profit as long as the stock price exceeds $62 or is less than $48 (i.e., the range of stock prices that generates a loss is $48 < P_s < $62). If the price of the stock moves either above $62 or below $48, the investor is assured of a profit. The maximum possible loss is $7, which occurs when the price of the stock equals the options' strike price at their expiration. At that price, neither option has any intrinsic value and both expire, so the investor loses the entire amount invested in both options.

The profits and losses from purchasing a straddle are illustrated in Figure 18.6(a). As may be seen in the figure, the position sustains a loss if the price of the stock is greater than $48 or less than $62, with a maximum possible loss of $7. There is no limit

FIGURE 18.6(a) Profit or Loss from Purchasing a Straddle

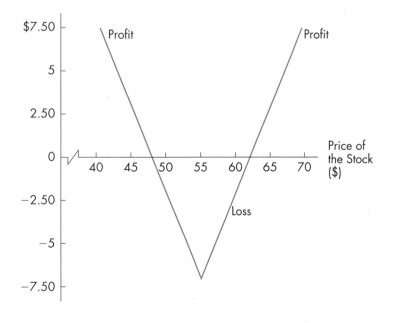

to the potential profit if the price of the stock rises, and the position could generate a profit of $48 in the unlikely case that the price of the stock declines to $0.

Why would the investor construct a straddle in which it is possible to sustain a loss, even if the price fluctuates but does not fluctuate sufficiently to cover the cost of the two options? The answer is that the investor anticipates a large movement in the price of the stock but is uncertain as to the direction. This position offers potential profit if such a price change occurs and limits the loss if the anticipated change does not materialize.

If the investor expects the price of the stock to be stable, that individual writes a straddle. The investor sells a put and a call. This strategy is, of course, the opposite of buying a straddle and its profit/loss profile is the exact opposite:

Price of the Stock	Intrinsic Value of the Call	Profit (Loss) on the Call	Intrinsic Value of the Put	Profit (Loss) on the Put	Net Profit (Loss)
$40	$0	$ 1.50	$15	$(9.50)	$(8)
45	0	1.50	10	(4.50)	(3)
48	0	1.50	7	(1.50)	0
50	0	1.50	5	.50	2
52	0	1.50	3	2.50	4
55	0	1.50	0	5.50	7
60	5	(3.50)	0	5.50	2
62	7	(5.50)	0	5.50	0
65	10	(8.50)	0	5.50	(3)
70	15	(13.50)	0	5.50	(8)

The writer of the straddle profits as long as the price of the stock exceeds $48 but is less than $62. The maximum possible profit is $7, which occurs when the price of the stock is $55 and both options expire worthless. Of course, the writer could sustain a large loss if the price of the stock makes a large movement in either direction.

The profile of profit and loss to the writer of the straddle is illustrated in Figure 18.6(b). Notice that this figure is the exact opposite of Figure 18.6(a). The writer accepts a modest possible profit, but there is no limit to the possible loss if the price of the stock were to rise, and there is also the potential for a large loss if the price of the stock falls below $48.

The Bull Spread

The covered put, the protective call, and the straddle do not exhaust all the possible strategies using puts and calls. The investor can also construct *spreads*, using options with different strike prices and/or expiration dates. In this case, the investor takes a long position in one option and a short position in the other. Consider the following:

Price of the stock	$52
Price of a call at $50	$ 5
Price of a call at $55	$ 1.50

The investor may construct a *bull spread* by purchasing the call with the lower strike price and selling the call with the higher strike price. In this illustration, the investor buys the $50s for $5 and sells (writes) the $55s for $1.50. The net cash outlay is

| FIGURE 18.6(b) | Profit or Loss from Selling a Straddle |

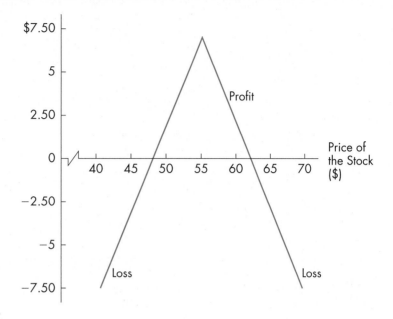

$3.50 (the $5 cost of the call at $50 minus the $1.50 received from the sale of the call at $55). The profile of the possible profit and loss at the options' expiration for various prices of the stock are as follows:

Price of the Stock	Intrinsic Value of the Call at $50	Profit (Loss) on the Call at $50	Intrinsic Value of the Call at $55	Profit (Loss) on the Call at $55	Net Profit (Loss)
$40	$ 0	$(5)	$0	$1.50	$(3.50)
45	0	(5)	0	1.50	(3.50)
50	0	(5)	0	1.50	(3.50)
53.50	3.50	(1.50)	0	1.50	0
55	5	0	0	1.50	1.50
60	10	5	5	(3.50)	1.50
65	15	10	10	(8.50)	1.50

The position generates a profit as long as the price of the stock exceeds $53.50, with a maximum possible profit of $1.50. The maximum possible loss is $3.50 (the net cash outlay). The amount of the profit may seem trivial, but since only $3.50 was at risk, the percentage return (before commissions) is 42.8 percent ($1.50/$3.50).

The Bear Spread

The investor could also reverse the preceding position and construct a *bear spread*. The investor buys the option with the higher strike price and sells the option with the lower strike price. In this illustration, the investor buys the option at $55 for $1.50 and sells the option at $50 for $5. This produces a net cash inflow; however, margin requirements will not permit the individual to remove the entire net proceeds. The possible profits and losses at the options' expiration for various prices of the stock are as follows:

Price of the Stock	Intrinsic Value of the Call at $50	Profit (Loss) on the Call at $50	Intrinsic Value of the Call at $55	Profit (Loss) on the Call at $55	Net Profit (Loss)
$40	$0	$5	$0	$(1.50)	$3.50
45	0	5	0	(1.50)	3.50
50	0	5	0	(1.50)	3.50
53.50	3.50	1.50	0	(1.50)	0
55	5	0	0	(1.50)	(1.50)
60	10	(5)	5	3.50	(1.50)
65	15	(10)	10	8.50	(1.50)

As long as the price of the stock is below $50, the investor earns the maximum profit of $3.50, while the maximum possible loss is $1.50 if the price of the stock is $55 or higher.

Figure 18.7 presents the potential profits and losses at various prices of the stock for the bull and bear spreads. Since they are opposite, the graphs mirror each other. The maximum possible loss is $3.50 in the bull spread if the price of the stock declines, while $3.50 is the maximum possible gain in the bear spread. Conversely, the maximum possible profit in the bull spread is $1.50, and $1.50 is the maximum possible loss in the bear spread.

Both of these spreads are types of hedge positions because they combine a long position and a short position. The effect in both cases is to limit the possible loss, which has the corresponding effect of limiting the potential profit. Neither may be appropriate if the investor anticipates a large movement in the price of the stock in a particular direction. Instead, these spreads are appropriate when the investor anticipates modest price movements in a particular direction. If this expected price change is downward,

FIGURE 18.7 Profit or Loss from Bull and Bear Spreads Using Call Options

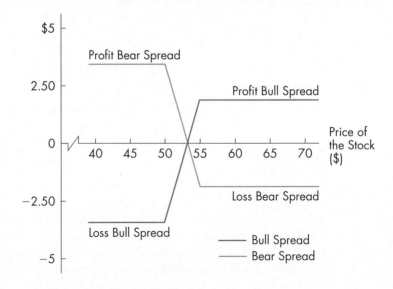

the investor should sell the option with the lower strike price and buy the option with the higher strike price (i.e., construct the bear spread). Conversely, if a modest price increase is anticipated, the investor buys the option with the lower strike price and sells the option with the higher strike price (i.e., constructs the bull spread). In either case, if the price of the stock moves in the anticipated direction, the investor earns a modest profit on a small outlay. If the price of the stock moves against the investor, the spread protects the investor from a large loss.

Collars

If you look at a shirt, there is an opening for the head and the cloth covers the shoulders. Both shoulders are protected but there is room for the individual's head. A collar in investments is similar. The individual is protected on both sides from price movements.

A collar is constructed when an investor owns a stock and for some reason (possible reasons are considered later) wants to hedge against a movement in the stock's price. The investor constructs a collar by selling a call at one strike price and buying a put at a lower strike price. Since this strategy involves both a purchase and a sale, the cash flows offset each other, resulting in either a small cash inflow or, at worst, a modest cash outflow. Consider the following options and their prices:

Strike Price	Price of a Call	Price of a Put
$45	NA	$2
50	$3	NA

The stock is currently selling for $48, and the investor owns 100 shares. The collar requires the investor to sell the call at $50, a $3 cash inflow, and purchase the put at $45, a $2 cash outflow. The result is a net cash inflow of $1. (This small inflow may cover the commissions, in which case the investor has no net cash outflow. No net cash outflow is one of the considerations when selecting options to establish the collar.) The investor now has three positions: (1) a long position in the stock, (2) a short position in the call, and (3) a long position in the put.

The profit/loss profile of these positions at the expiration of the options for various prices of the stock is as follows:

Price of the Stock	Profit on the			Net Profit
	Stock	Call	Put	
$60	$12	($7)	($2)	$3
55	7	(2)	(2)	3
50	2	3	(2)	3
48	0	3	(2)	1
45	(3)	3	(2)	(2)
40	(8)	3	3	(2)
35	(13)	3	8	(2)

In this illustration, if the price of the stock rises, there is a modest gain. If the price of the stock declines, there is a modest loss. The investor's aim to avoid a possible large loss has been achieved.

The profit/loss profile for the collar is similar to the profit/loss profile for a bull spread. The positions, however, are different and serve different purposes. With a collar, the investor *owns* the stock and is attempting to avoid the impact of a price decline. Movements in the price of the stock in either direction have little or no effect. In a bull spread the investor buys the call with the lower strike price and sells the call with the higher strike price. The investor *does not own the stock*. In a bull spread, the investor anticipates an increase in the price of the stock and wants to make a large percentage return on the modest amount invested. The purpose of the spread is to magnify the price increase while limiting the potential loss if the price of the stock declines.

Why would an investor construct a collar? There are several reasons, which revolve around the timing of sales and limits on the investor's ability to sell. Consider the situation of an investor who bought the preceding stock at $20 and would like to sell at $48. The sale, however, produces a capital gain, which the investor would prefer to defer to the next taxable year. Constructing the collar locks in the price and the profit on the stock because if the price does change, the profits/losses on the various components cancel each other. The original appreciation in the stock from $20 to $48 is retained and the taxes are deferred until the positions are unwound, which could occur in the next taxable year.

Another, and more likely, reason for constructing the collar is to protect a gain when the investor is forbidden to sell the stock. Prior to an initial public offering, a firm may issue employees stock as compensation or grant employees options to buy the stock. For instance, a firm expects to go public and sell stock at $50 and grants current employees shares based on the following formula. Each employee is to receive stock based on 40 percent of that individual's prior year's compensation. That dollar value then will be divided by $50, the initial anticipated price of the IPO, to determine the number of shares that will be granted prior to the initial public offering. If an employee earned $80,000, the number of shares to be received is 640 shares (0.4[$80,000/$50]). The employee, however, cannot immediately sell the shares. Shares are restricted units, one third of which may be sold on the anniversary dates of the initial public offering for the next three years. The employee can sell only 213 shares a year for the next three years. (The purpose of such restrictions is to avoid the dumping of stock right after an initial public offering, especially if the price of the stock rises. See the discussion of lock-ups in Chapter 2.)

Suppose that six months after the initial public offering the price of the stock is $72. The employees would like to sell and realize the $22 profit, but the stock cannot be sold. Of course, further price increases would be welcome, but a price decline could inflict a loss or at least reduce existing gains. By constructing a collar, these employees are able to freeze the price of the stock until they are able to sell it. Although they forgo the possibility of further gains, they lock in existing profits. Since the investment objective is to hedge against a price decline, the collar protects these employees against the possibility of a price decline.

A third reason for constructing a collar is essentially a variation on the previous case. Many top executives receive additional compensation in the form of stock options instead of cash. (See the section on expensing options.) These stock options are similar to calls and give the executives the right to buy the stock at specified prices for specified time periods. Although the calls traded on the CBOE and other exchanges are of relatively short duration, options granted executives often may be exercised after many years.

Once again, the use of collars protects the investors from a price decline. If an executive exercises a profitable stock option, there may be legal or tax reasons why the stock may not be immediately sold. By constructing the collar, the executive freezes the current price of the stock and protects the gain.

Collars are also used in merger agreements to lock in a specified price or range of stock prices. When Georgia Pacific (GP) offered to buy Fort James, the terms established a maximum price of $40. GP offered $29.60 plus 0.2644 shares of Georgia Pacific for every share of Fort James. If GP sold above $40, the number of shares would be decreased. The effect is to set a maximum cost and a minimum cost to Georgia Pacific. If GP sold for more than $40, the reduction in the number of shares limits the upside cost to $40. Thus, if GP were to sell for $50, the stockholders of Fort James would receive $29.60 plus 0.208 shares. The 0.208 shares would be worth $10.40, which plus the $29.60 is a total of $40. At the other extreme, in the unlikely case that the price of Georgia Pacific stock collapsed, the stockholders of Fort James would receive $29.60. The effect is to guarantee Fort James stockholders $29.60 to $40 and to limit the cost to Georgia Pacific of the acquisition from $29.60 to $40. Such merger agreements, which guarantee a minimum but limit the upside price, are common when the acquiring firm offers to swap its stock for the other firm's stock.

The VIX and Option Strategies

As was explained in Chapter 10 on indexes and returns, the VIX stands for the CBOE volatility index and is a measure of expected market volatility. Since volatility is associated with market uncertainty, the VIX is also a measure of investor sentiment and is often referred to as an indication or gauge of investor fear.

The index is based on *implied volatility* of various in- and out-of-the-money put and call options based on the S&P 500 stock index. The VIX is built upon normal probability distributions (the so-called bell curve). For example, picture highly peaked, not very wide bell curves. Under these conditions, the numerical value of the VIX is small (e.g., 10–15) and indicates less volatility. Flatter and wider bell curves produce larger numerical values (e.g., 40–50) in the VIX and indicate more volatility. As you would expect, the historical values of the VIX have been relatively small during periods of relative market complacency. For example, during the mid-1990s, the VIX ranged between 10 and 20. The opposite occurred during 2008 when the VIX rose almost to 90, but by January 2010 the numerical value had retreated to approximately 20.

You cannot buy and sell the index, but you may purchase put and call options on the VIX. This offers you the potential to speculate or develop option strategies based on investor expectations. If you expected volatility to increase, you could purchase calls or sell puts. If you anticipated volatility to decrease, you could sell calls or purchase puts based on the VIX. Of course, if you are incorrect, you will sustain losses on your positions.

Options on the VIX may also be used as tools of risk management. For example, you could construct a variation on the protective put. If you anticipated that increased volatility would lead to lower stock prices, you might purchase a call based on the index. If you were correct and the market as a whole declined as volatility increased, then the gain on the call would offset at least some of the losses on the stocks.

Such a strategy assumes that increased volatility is negatively correlated with stock prices. That was true during 2008 when the VIX increased dramatically and stock prices fell just as dramatically. However, it may be dangerous to assume that the relationship always exists. During a period of relative stability, the negative relationship might not exist. From December 2004 through 2007, the VIX was virtually unchanged while the S&P 500 rose approximately 8.7 percent. The CBOE, however, has reported on its website (http://www.cboe.com) that the VIX and S&P 500 move in opposite directions 88 percent of the time. On the average, the VIX rose 16.8 percent when the S&P 500 fell 3 percent, and the correlation coefficient relating the return on the two indexes is −0.67.

BUYING THE CALL AND A TREASURY BILL VERSUS BUYING THE STOCK—AN ALTERNATIVE TO THE PROTECTIVE PUT

An alternative to the protective put is purchasing a call and a Treasury bill in preference to purchasing the stock and the put. (This strategy is not to be confused with purchasing a stock and a put versus purchasing a call and a bond. If the financial markets are in equilibrium, put–call parity implies that these two positions produce the same results. See Problem 6.) Suppose a stock is selling for $100 and the call to buy the stock after one year is $6. A one-year Treasury bill is selling for $96 for a 4.19 percent yield. The investor could purchase the stock or purchase both the call and the bill. Notice that the costs of the two positions differ: $100 for the stock versus $102 for the call plus the bill. (You may infer that the price of a one-year put option to sell the stock at $100 is $2, because put–call parity requires that the sum of the cost of the stock and the put equal the sum of the cost of the call and the bill.)

What are the potential profits and losses on the two positions at various prices of the stock? The answer to this question is given in the following profit/loss profile.

Price of the Stock	Profit (Loss) on the Stock	Profit (Loss) on the Call	Profit (Loss) on the Bill	Net on the Call + Bill
$110	$10	$4	$4	$8
105	5	(1)	4	3
100	0	(6)	4	(2)
95	(5)	(6)	4	(2)
90	(10)	(6)	4	(2)

As may be seen in the profit/loss profile, the combination of the call and the bill is similar to the stock on the upside but limits the loss on the downside. If the price of the stock rises, the bill-call strategy generates almost the same profit. The $2 difference is the result of the difference in the initial cash outflows.

If the above profit/loss profile is compared to Exhibit 17.9 in the previous chapter, the profit/loss pattern is the same. Hence, this strategy is essentially another version of the protective put. Both limit the downside loss but do not limit the upside potential. If the price of the stock does not rise or declines, the worst-case scenario for the call-bill combination is a loss of $2, the initial cash outflow. The worst-case scenario

Point of Interest

ETFs AND THE USE OF OPTIONS

Do exchange-traded funds (ETFs) use options to magnify returns? Since the portfolios of ETFs are designed to mimic an index such as the S&P 500 or the Nasdaq 100 index, the general answer is no. They acquire the stocks in the index or a portfolio that is highly correlated with the index so the return on the ETF mimics the return on the index.

But there are exceptions. ProShares has designed ETFs to magnify the return offered by the index. By using options to leverage the position, the portfolio managers hope to magnify the return on the underlying index. For example, if the S&P 500 index increases by 10 percent, the return on the Ultra S&P500 ProShares may rise by 20 percent. Of course, increased return implies increased risk; leverage works both ways. If the S&P 500 falls by 10 percent, the value of the leveraged ETF may decline by 20 percent.

Leveraged ETFs violate two important advantages offered by exchange-traded funds. Since ETFs are passive investments, they have low operating expenses. Low portfolio turnover means that ETFs generate few capital gains tax obligations for stockholders. The buying and selling of options increases a leveraged ETF's operating expenses and the commissions on the transactions. If the ETF's management is successful and increases the return, the profitable option transactions produce short-term gains, which will generate tax obligations for the ETF's stockholders.

Obviously leveraged ETFs are not appropriate for many investors. But if you want to try market timing or leverage your positions in index funds, these ETFs offer advantages. You do not have to select individual stocks, and you do not have the risk associated with buying and selling index call or put obligations. If leveraged ETFs interest you, possible choices include Ultra QQQ ProShares (QLD), Ultra MidCap400 ProShares (MVV), and Ultra Dow30 ProShares (DDM) in addition to the Ultra S&P500 ProShares (SSO).

for the stock is that the investor could lose the entire $100. This reduction in potential loss suggests that the strategy reduces the investor's risk but the reduction in risk only marginally limits the potential gain.

SUMMARY

While the previous chapter presented the basics concerning options, this chapter expanded that material by covering the Black-Scholes option valuation model; by explaining how the stock, bond, and option markets are interrelated so that changes in one are transmitted to the others; and by illustrating several strategies using options.

The Black-Scholes option valuation model specifies that the value of a call option is positively related to the price and to the volatility of the underlying stock. As the price of the stock rises, the value of the option rises. The same relationship holds for variability of returns, as options on volatile stocks command higher valuations. Call option values are also positively related to the life of the option. As the term of the option diminishes and the option approaches expiration, the option's value declines.

Although an increase in interest rates generally depresses the value of a financial asset, this negative relationship does not apply to options to buy stock. An increase in interest rates increases the value of the option, because higher rates reduce the present value of a call's strike price. The lower strike price then increases the value of the option to buy the stock.

In addition to being used to value publicly traded puts and calls, the Black-Scholes model may be applied to options issued by firms to selected employees, especially senior management. These options are part of incentive-based compensation packages. If the firm is successful and the value of its stock rises, the value of the options also increases. Since incentive options are part of the employee's compensation, an accounting question arises: Should the cost of the options be expensed? Expensing requires a valuation, and the Black-Scholes model is often used to value incentive options in order to determine their cost.

The Black-Scholes option valuation model also calculates the hedge ratio, which determines the number of options necessary to completely hedge a stock portfolio. A completely hedged portfolio means that any loss generated on one side (e.g., a long position in stocks) is offset by the gain on the opposite side (e.g., a short position in the options). Such a hedging strategy is executed by portfolio managers to reduce risk. Such risk reduction may not be available to individual investors, since the portfolio has to be frequently rebalanced as the hedge ratio changes.

Put–call parity explains the interrelationships among financial markets. In equilibrium, the price of the underlying stock, the price of the puts and calls on the stock, and the present value of the strike price (as affected by the rate of interest) must balance or an opportunity for a risk-free arbitrage would exist. As investors seek to execute the arbitrage, the prices of the various securities are affected. An implication of put–call parity is that any change in one of the markets (e.g., an increased demand for stocks) must be transmitted to the other markets.

Strategies using options include the covered put and the protective call, which are the reverse of the covered call and the protective put. Other possible option strategies are straddles; bull and bear spreads; and collars. Straddles and spreads involve buying or selling more than one option on the same stock. Straddles and spreads permit investors to take long, short, or hedged positions in stocks without actually owning or selling the stocks. Collars permit investors who own stock but cannot sell it to lock in the current price. All these strategies using options alter the individual's potential returns and risk exposure from investing in financial assets. Options, thus, are both a means to speculate on anticipated price movements in the underlying stocks and to manage the risk from actual price movements in the underlying stocks.

QUESTIONS

1. What, according to the Black-Scholes option valuation model, is the relationship between the value of a call option and each of the following?
   a) Risk as measured by the variability of the underlying stock's return
   b) Interest rates
   c) The term of the option (i.e., the length of time to expiration)
2. According to Black-Scholes option valuation and put–call parity, what will happen to the value of a put option if interest rates decline?
3. How may the Black-Scholes option valuation model be used to determine the risk associated with the underlying stock?
4. An investor sells a stock short in July and its price declines in November—the position has generated a profit. However, the individual does not want to close the

position and realize the profit during this tax year. Instead, the investor wants to maintain the position until January so the gain will be taxed next year. How can the hedge ratio be used to reduce the risk associated with the price of the stock rising while still transferring the gain to the next tax year?

5. An investor expects the price of a stock to remain stable and writes a straddle. What is this individual's risk exposure? How may the investor close the position?

6. You expect the price of a stock to decline but do not want to sell the stock short and run the risk that the price of the stock may rise dramatically. How could you use a bear spread strategy to take advantage of your expectation of a lower stock price?

7. You sell a stock short. How can you use an option to reduce your risk of loss should the price of the stock rise?

8. How do collars, the hedge ratio, the protective call, and the protective put help investors manage risk?

9. If you thought a stock was fairly valued and its price would not change, how could you use a straddle to take advantage of your valuation? If you follow this strategy and the stock's price does not remain stable, have you increased your risk exposure?

10. The Black-Scholes valuation model shows that higher interest rates result in higher call option valuations. Do these higher interest rates and call valuations imply that put values will also rise?

PROBLEMS

Apply the Black-Scholes option valuation model to solve the following problems.

1. A stock sells for $30. What is the value of a one-year call option to buy the stock at $25, if debt currently yields 10 percent? (Assume $F(d_1)$ and $F(d_2) = 1$.)

2. A call option is the right to buy stock at $50 a share. Currently the option has six months to expiration, the volatility of the stock (standard deviation) is 0.30, and the rate of interest is 10 percent (0.1 in Exhibit 18.2).
   a) What is the value of the option according to the Black-Scholes model if the price of the stock is $45, $50, or $55?
   b) What is the value of the option when the price of the stock is $50 and the option expires in six months, three months, or one month?
   c) What is the value of the option when the price of the stock is $50 and the interest rate is 5 percent, 10 percent, or 15 percent?
   d) What is the value of the option when the price of the stock is $50 and the volatility of the stock is 0.40, 0.30, or 0.10?
   e) What generalizations can be derived from the solutions to these problems?

3. One useful piece of information derived from the Black-Scholes model for the valuation of a call option is the hedge ratio, which gives the slope of the line relating the change in the price of an option to the change in the price of the stock.
   a) If the delta is 0.6 and the investor owns 600 shares of stock, how may the investor use call options to hedge the position?
   b) If the investor buys a call option on 100 shares, what position in the stock and how many shares will offset movement in the price of the option?

4. Problems 4–11 illustrate arbitrage. Problems 5–8 use put–call parity while 9–11 are based on Black-Scholes.

    Put–call parity in effect states that long positions in a call and a risk-free bond plus a short position in a put must be the same value as the underlying stock. If not, at least one market is in disequilibrium. The resulting arbitrage alters the securities' prices until the value of the three securities equals the value of the stock. Currently, the price of a stock is $50, while the price of a call option at $50 is $3, the price of the put option is $1.50, and the rate of interest is 10 percent—so that the investor may purchase a $50 discounted note for $45.50.

    Given these prices, an arbitrage opportunity exists. Verify this by setting up a riskless arbitrage. Show the possible profit if the price of the stock is $45, $50, or $55 at the expiration of the options.

5. In the body of this chapter, disequilibrium of the following equation indicated an opportunity for a riskless arbitrage:

$$0 = P_s + P_p - P_c - \frac{P_e}{(1 + i)^n}$$

or

$$P_s + P_p = P_c + \frac{P_e}{(1 + i)^n}.$$

The equation was illustrated as follows. A stock sells for $105; the strike price of both the put and call is $100. The price of the put is $5, the price of the call is $20, and both options are for one year. The rate of interest is 11.1 percent, so the present value of the $100 strike price is equal to $90. Given these values, the equation holds:

$$0 = \$105 + 5 - 20 - 90$$

or

$$\$105 + 5 = \$20 + 90.$$

The opportunity for the riskless arbitrage was then illustrated by two cases, one in which the call was overpriced ($25) and one in which the put was overpriced ($10). For each of the following sets of values, verify that a riskless arbitrage opportunity exists by determining the profit if the price of the stock rises to $110, falls to $90, or remains unchanged at $105.

	Price of the Stock	Price of the Call	Price of the Put	Interest Rate
a.	$105	$10	$5	11.1%
b.	105	20	3	11.1
c.	105	20	5	5.263
d.	105	20	5	19
e.	112	20	5	11.1
f.	101	20	5	11.1

When will the opportunity for arbitrage cease, and what are the implications for the prices of each security?

6. Put–call parity asserts that if the markets are in equilibrium, a *long position* in a stock and a put produces the same return (or profit/loss) as a *long position* in a discounted bond and call with the same strike price as the put. You are given the following information:

Price of the stock	$50
Interest rate	5%
Price of a $50 bond discounted at the current interest rate	$47.62
Price of a call to buy the stock at $50	$ 5.38
Price of a put to sell the stock at $50	$ 3.00

Use the following prices of the stock ($60, $50, and $40) to verify the above statement.

7. Put–call parity basically says that combination of a stock and a put produces the same return as the comparable position in a call and a risk-free bond. If not, at least one market is in disequilibrium. The resulting arbitrage alters the securities' prices until the value of the stock plus the put equals the prices of the call and the bond. Put–call parity also demonstrates that a short position in the stock is mimicked by short positions in the call and the bond and a long position in the put. Currently, the price of a stock is $100 while the price of a call option at $100 is $9; the price of the put option at $100 is $3, and the price of a discounted bond is $94. Verify that a short position in the stock produces the same performance as a short position in the call and the bond plus a long position in the put.

8. Put–call parity asserts that the sum of the prices of the stock and put must equal the prices of the call and the bond. If they do not, an arbitrage opportunity exists and you can generate a risk-free return. Given the following information,

Price of the stock	$50.00
Interest rate	5%
Price of a $50 bond discounted at the current interest rate	$47.62
Price of a call to buy the stock at $50	$4.38
Price of a put to sell the stock at $50	$4.00

an arbitrage opportunity exists. Unfortunately, you construct the wrong positions (do everything backwards). Verify that you always lose at the following prices of the stock: $40, $45, $50, $55, and $60.

9. You are given the following:

Price of the stock	$26
Price of a six-month call at $25	2
Price of a six-month call at $30	4

An investor buys the $25 call and sells the $30 call. What are the profits if the stock's price at expiration is $20, $25, $30, or $35? Arbitrage implies what about the price of the call with the higher strike price?

10. Currently a stock that sells for $57 has a put option at $55 and another at $60. The prices of the options are $6 and $3, respectively. What would you do? Illustrate and explain your actions.

11. Black-Scholes demonstrates that the value of a put option increases the longer the time to expiration. Currently the price of a stock is $100 and there are two put options to sell the stock at $100. The three-month option sells for $7.00 and the six-month option sells for $4.50.
    a) What would you do and why?
    b) How much do you earn or lose after three months at the following prices of the underlying stock ($85, $90, $95, $100, $105, and $110)? Assume the worst-case scenario.
    c) Is there any reason to anticipate earning a higher return than your answers in (b)?

Various option strategies (e.g., the straddle) were explained in this chapter. The following problems apply these strategies.

12. A put and a call have the following terms:

Call:	strike price	$30
	term	three months
	price	$3
Put:	strike price	$30
	term	three months
	price	$4

The price of the stock is currently $29. You sell the stock short. Illustrate how to use the call or the put to reduce your risk exposure.
    a) What is the maximum possible profit on the position?
    b) What is the maximum possible loss on the position?
    c) What range of stock prices generates a profit?
    d) What advantage does this position offer?

13. You are given the following:

Price of the stock	$18
Price of a three-month call at $20	2
Price of a three-month call at $15	5

    a) What is the profit (loss) at the expiration date of the options if the price of the stock is $14, $20, or $25 and if the investor buys the option with the $20 strike price and sells the other option?
    b) Compare the profit (loss) from this strategy with shorting the stock at $18.
    c) What is the profit (loss) at the expiration date of the options if the price of the stock is $14, $20, or $25 and if the investor buys the option with the $15 strike price and sells the other option?
    d) Compare the profit (loss) from this strategy with buying the stock at $18.

14. A straddle occurs when an investor purchases both a call option and a put option. Such a strategy makes sense when the individual expects a major price movement but is uncertain as to the direction. For example, a firm may be a rumored

takeover candidate. If the rumor is wrong, the stock's price could decline and make the put profitable. If the rumor is correct and a takeover bid does occur, the price of the stock may rise and the call becomes profitable. There is also the possibility (probably small, at best) that the price of the stock could rise and subsequently fall, so the investor earns a profit on both the call and the put. The following problem works through a straddle.

Given the following,

Price of the stock	$50
Price of a six-month call at $50	5
Price of a six-month put at $50	3.50

the individual establishes a straddle (i.e., buys one of each option).

a) What is the profit (loss) on the position if, at the expiration date of the options, the price of the stock is $60?

b) What is the profit (loss) on the position if, at the expiration date of the options, the price of the stock is $40?

c) What is the profit (loss) on the position if, at the expiration date of the options, the price of the stock is $50?

15. An insider purchased a stock prior to the IPO for $10 a share. Once public, the stock runs up to $55 a share but the insider cannot sell the stock for a year. Since put and call options exist, the individual decides to construct a collar for protection from a possible decline in the price of the stock. Information concerning the options is as follows:

	Strike price	Market price
Put	$55	$3.00
Call	$55	$3.00

a) Describe the position you establish.

b) Verify that the position achieves its objective by determining the profit/loss profile on the collar if the price of the stock rises to $60, remains at $55, or declines to $40.

c) Why does the position work (i.e., why does it achieve its objective)?

16. As an executive, you received stock options that you recently exercised. However, you cannot legally sell the stock for the next six months. Currently the stock is selling for $38.25. A call to buy the stock at $40 is selling for $3.38 and a put to sell the stock at $35 is selling for $1.94. How could you use a collar to reduce your risk of loss from a decline in the price of the stock? Verify that the collar does achieve its objective.

Option strategies are not limited to covered puts and calls, protective puts and calls, straddles, bull and bear spreads, and collars. Other strategies include the "strip," the "strap," and the "butterfly spread." The following problems illustrate these strategies. (You could also construct strips, straps, and butterflies using puts.)

17. Strips and straps are variations on the straddle. The investor buys a straddle (i.e., buys a put and a call with the same strike price and expiration date) when he or

she expects the price to move but is uncertain of the direction of change. A *strip* involves buying one call and two puts with the same strike price and expiration date. The strip places more emphasis on the price of the stock declining. A *strap* consists of buying two calls and one put. It places more emphasis on the price of the stock rising. (Another variation is a *strangle* in which the investor buys a put and a call with the same expiration dates but different strike prices.) Suppose a stock is selling for $41 and there are three-month options at $40. The call is selling for $3, and the put is selling for $1.

    a) What would be the gains or losses at the options' expiration if you construct a straddle, a strip, or a strap when the following are the prices of the stock: $30, $35, $38, $40, $42, $45, and $50?

    b) What is the maximum possible loss under each strategy?

    c) What is the range of stock prices that produces a loss under each strategy?

18. *Butterfly* spreads combine the bull and bear spreads and require involve three options with different strike prices and the same expiration date. If the investor expects the price of the stock to be stable (the butterfly will "not flap its wings"), the individual buys the options with the highest and lowest strike prices and *sells two options* with the strike price in the middle. If the investor expects the price of the stock to fluctuate (i.e., the butterfly will "flap its wings"), the process is reversed. The investor sells the outer options and buys two of the calls with the strike price in the middle.

    For example, suppose a stock is selling for $61 and there are three-month call options at $57, $60, and $64. The prices of the options are $6, $3, and $1, respectively.

    a) The investor expects the price of the stock to be stable. What would the investor gain or lose at the options' expiration from constructing an appropriate butterfly spread at the following prices of the stock: $50, $55, $57, $60, $63, $65, and $60?

    b) What is the maximum possible loss?

    c) What is the maximum possible gain?

    d) What is the range of stock prices that produces a gain from constructing this butterfly?

    e) Did the butterfly achieve its objective based on the expectation that the price of the stock would be stable?

The Financial Advisor's Investment Case
Profits and Losses from Straddles

Julian Herrara, a sophisticated investor who is both willing and able to take risk, has just noticed that Go-West Airlines has become the target of a hostile takeover. Prior to the announcement of the offer to purchase the stock for $72 a share, the stock had been selling for $59. Immediately after the offer, the stock rose to $75, a premium over the offer price. Such premiums are often indicative that investors expect a higher price to be forthcoming. Such a higher price could occur if a bidding war erupts for the company or if management leads an employee or management buyout of the firm. Of course, if neither of these scenarios occurs, the price of the stock could fall back to the $72 offer price. In addition, if the offer were to be withdrawn or defeated by management, the price of the stock could fall below the original stock price.

Herrara has no reason to anticipate that any of these possibilities will be the final outcome, but he realizes that the price of the stock will not remain at $75. If a bidding war erupts, the price could easily exceed $100. Conversely, if the takeover fails, he expects the price to decline below $55 a share, since he previously believed that the price of the stock was overvalued at $59. With such uncertainty, Herrara does not want to own the stock but is intrigued with the possibility of earning a profit from a price movement that he is certain must occur.

Currently there are several three-month put and call options traded on the stock. Their strike and market prices are as follows:

Strike Price	Market Price of Call	Market Price of Put
$50	$26.00	$0.125
55	21.50	.50
60	17.00	1.00
65	13.25	1.75
70	8.00	3.50
75	4.25	6.00
80	1.00	9.75

Herrara decides the best strategy is to purchase both a put and a call option (to establish a straddle). Deciding on a strategy is one thing; determining the best way to execute it is quite another. For example, he could buy the options with the extreme strike prices (i.e., the call at $80 and the put at $50). Or he could buy the options with the strike price closest to the original $72 offer price (i.e., buy the put and the call at $70).

To help determine the potential profits and losses from various positions, Herrara developed profit profiles at various stock prices by filling in the following chart for each position:

Price of the Stock	Intrinsic Value of the Call	Profit on the Call	Intrinsic Value of the Put	Profit on the Put	Net Profit
$50					
55					
60					
65					
70					
75					
80					
85					

To limit the number of calculations, he decided to make three comparisons: (1) the purchase of two inexpensive options—buy the call with the $80 strike price and the put with the $60 strike price, (2) the purchase of the options with the $70 strike price, and (3) the purchase of the options with the price closest to the original stock price (i.e., the options with the $60 strike price).

Construct Herrara's profit profiles and answer the following questions.

1. Which strategy works best if a bidding war erupts?
2. Which strategy works best if the hostile takeover is defeated?
3. Which strategy works best if the original offer price becomes the final price?
4. Which of the three positions produces the worst result and under what condition does it occur?
5. If you were Herrara's financial advisor, which strategy would you advise he establish? Or would you argue that he not speculate on this takeover?

Appendix 18

BINOMIAL OPTION PRICING

The Black-Scholes model determines the value of a European option, and put–call parity demonstrates through arbitrage the linkage among the prices of put and call options, the underlying stock, and the rate of interest earned by lending or paid from borrowing. This appendix adds the binomial option pricing model. The model is referred to as "binomial," because it is initially built on an assumption that there are only two possible outcomes. The binomial model is less restrictive than Black-Scholes since it assumes an option may be exercised prior to expiration.

Illustrating this process of valuation requires an extended example. Consider an option to buy stock at $50 at the end of a time period such as a year. To ease the analysis, assume that the option can be exercised *only* at expiration (i.e., it is a European option). Currently, the price of the stock is $50, so the option is at the money. The price of the stock could rise to $65 or decline to $40. These prices are the only two possible outcomes, one of which involves a rising stock price and the other of which involves a declining stock price. The investor can purchase or sell the stock or the investor can purchase or sell the call. Since sales produce cash inflows, the funds may be invested at the going rate of interest (i.e., the investor can purchase a one-year bond). Since purchases require cash outflows, the funds may be borrowed at the going rate of interest. Assume the borrowing and lending rates of interest are both 10 percent and that the principal amount is $50, the current price of the stock. Given this information, what should be the value of the call? To answer that question, consider the two possible outcomes:

Current price of the stock	$50	
Future price of the stock	$65	$40
Future value of the option at expiration	$15	$ 0

If the price of the stock rises to $65, the value of the call must be $15 at expiration. If the price of the stock declines to $40, the call must be worth $0. The binomial option pricing model asks the following question: What combination of the stock and the bond produces the same result?

To answer that question, set up two equations for the possible outcomes:

$$65S + 55B = 15$$

$$40S + 55B = 0$$

The 65 and 40 are the two future prices of the stock, and the 55 is the value of the bond plus the 10 percent interest ($50 + $5). Since there are two equations with two unknowns, they may be solved. First, subtract the second equation from the first and solve for S:

$$65S + 55B = 15$$

$$\underline{-40S + 55B = 0}$$

$$65S - 40S = 15$$

$$(65 - 40)S = 15$$

$$S = 15/25 = 0.60.$$

Next, substitute this value in equation 2 and solve for B:

$$40(0.6) + 55B = 0$$

$$B = -40(0.6)/55 = -0.436.$$

The next question is, what are the interpretations of the values 0.6 and −0.436? This information tells us that 0.6 unit of the stock and −0.436 unit of the bond produce the same outcome as buying the call. That is, if an investor is long 0.6 share of the stock and short 0.436 in the bond (the investor borrows 0.436 unit), this combination generates the same results that would be obtained if the investor bought the call.

To verify this statement, consider the cash inflows and outflows. That is, what would be the cash flows if an investor bought 0.6 share of stock and borrowed 0.436 unit of the bond? The answers are

$$\text{Stock: } (0.6)(\$50) = \$30$$

$$\text{Bond: } (0.436)(\$50) = \$21.80.$$

The stock purchase is a cash outflow and borrowing is a cash inflow, so there is a net cash outflow of $8.20($30 − $21.80). As will be shown, that $8.20 must be the value of the call to buy a share of stock at $50. However, before verifying that the price of the call must be $8.20, it is necessary to confirm that the outcome from buying the stock plus borrowing is the same as buying the call.

Consider the outcome if the price of the stock is $65. The stock is worth $65(0.6) = $39, but the borrowed funds must be repaid plus interest. That cash outflow is ($50)(0.436) + (0.1)($50)(0.436) = $23.98 ≅ $24. The cash balance is $15($39 − 24), which is the same result obtained by purchasing the call. If the price of the stock is $65, the call is worth $15 at expiration, so the ending cash is $15 in either case.

If the price of the stock is $40, the investor has stock worth $40(0.6) = $24. When the borrowed funds plus interest [($50)(0.436) + (0.1)($50)(0.436) = $23.98 ≅ $24] are repaid, the balance is $0. This is the same result obtained by purchasing the call. If the price of the stock is $40, the call is worthless at expiration. In either case, the balance is $0.

The preceding illustration stated that the initial cash outflow was $8.20 and that the value of the call must also be $8.20. To see that the value of the call must be $8.20, consider what would happen if the price of the call were not $8.20. For instance, if the option were $10 (i.e., it is overvalued), the investor would sell the call (a cash inflow of $10), buy 0.6 share of stock (cash outflow of $30), and borrow $21.80. The sum of the cash inflows and outflows is an inflow of $1.80($10 − $30 + $21.80 = $1.80). What is the profit or loss on this position if at the expiration of the call, the price of the stock is \$65 or \$40, the two possible outcomes? The answer is

| | Profit (Loss) on | | | |
Price of the Stock	The Call	The Stock	Interest on the Bond	Net Profit
\$65	(\$5)	0.6(\$15) = \$9	−\$2.20	\$1.80
40	10	0.6(−\$10) = −6	−2.20	1.80

Either of the two final outcomes, a higher or a lower stock price, produces the \$1.80 profit.

   If the option were \$5 (i.e., it is undervalued), the investor would reverse the process. The investor buys the call (a cash outflow of \$5), sells 0.6 share of stock (cash inflow of \$30), and lends \$21.80. The sum of the cash inflows and outflows is an inflow of \$3.20 (−\$5 + \$30 − \$21.80 = \$3.20). What is the profit or loss on this position if the price of the stock is \$65 or \$40? The answer is

| | Profit (Loss) on | | | |
Price of the Stock	The Call	The Stock	Interest on the Bond	Net Profit
\$65	\$10	0.6(−\$15) = −\$9	\$2.20	\$3.20
40	(5)	0.6(\$10) = 6	2.20	3.20

Either of the two final possible outcomes produces the \$3.20 profit.

   It is this process of taking both long and short positions that assures the price of the option must be \$8.20. Once again, the opportunity for an arbitrage profit drives prices to eradicate the opportunity. Given the assumptions of the example, the option value must be \$8.20. In addition, the investor can replicate the call by using the stock and the bond. That is, the investor can construct a position in the stock and the bond (borrowing) that produces the same outcome as the call. The investor can buy the call for \$8.20 or achieve the same final outcome by buying 0.6 share of stock and borrowing \$21.80.

   In the preceding illustration, the number of shares that had to be purchased (0.6) and the number of bonds (0.436) were determined by solving the two equations. The values could have been found by doing the following calculations. The 0.6, which is the hedge ratio discussed in the body of the chapter, indicates the amount by which the call rises for every \$1 increase in the stock. This value may be determined by dividing the difference between the call's two possible outcomes by the difference between the ending prices of the stock. That is, the hedge ratio is

$$\frac{\$15 - 0}{\$65 - 40} = 0.6.$$

The amount to be borrowed is equal to the present value of the difference between the lower value of the stock (\$40) and the profit associated with that outcome (\$0 in this illustration). That value is

$$\frac{(0.6)(\$40) - 0}{1 + 0.1} = \$21.82$$

and is 0.436 times the current price of the stock. Thus, if an investor knows the two possible outcomes (e.g., $65 and $40), the rate of the interest (e.g., 10 percent), the price of the stock (e.g., $50), and the strike price (e.g., $50), that individual can determine the value of the call. If the price of the call is not equal to that value, the investor can arbitrage away the price differential. If the individual knows the price of the stock, the interest rate, price of the call, and the strike price, the investor can replicate the call by buying the stock and borrowing the appropriate amount such that either outcome is the same.

The preceding discussion was premised on only two possible outcomes and the time period was a year. What happens if there are more than two outcomes and the time period is not a year? Consider what may happen if the time period is two six-month time periods instead of one twelve-month time period. The following decision tree starts with the same current price of the stock and the original ending prices but adds two possible prices at the end of six months and an additional price at the end of the twelve months.

The price of the stock could go from $50 to $56 or $47 after six months and then proceed to $65, $50, or $40 after a year. Given this information, could the value of the call option be determined? The answer is yes, by following the process previously described for each time period. If the logic holds for the option pricing using two possible outcomes, it can be expanded to encompass three possible outcomes. A current value for the option will be determined, and arbitrage assures that the price is the one and only price.

The preceding illustration could be expanded to encompass a large number of possible outcomes and time periods. As the time periods become smaller, the number of outcomes approaches an infinite number. Computer applications can process a large number of possible time periods and outcomes, but that becomes unnecessary. As the number of outcomes increases, the binomial option pricing model approaches the Black-Scholes option valuation model. The Black-Scholes model reduces option valuation to a single equation that is easily applied.

The importance of the binomial option pricing model is not its applicability but its underlying explanation of option valuation. Through the process of arbitrage and the replication of options using long and short positions in the underlying stock and the bond, the value of an option is determined. The model also identifies the factors that are crucial to option valuation. These include the current price of the stock, the option's strike price, the time to expiration, the rate of interest, possible future prices of the stock, and the risk. This risk is measured by the extreme possible outcome prices. If the range in the extreme possible outcomes were smaller, the stock is less volatile and the outcome is less risky. Notice that the bionomial option pricing model (and the Black-Scholes model) does not include investors' expected future stock prices and investors' aversion to risk. This means that option pricing is independent of investors' expectations and willingness to bear risk. Both are based on the simple premise that two identical positions (the call or the stock and the bond) must have the same price.

CHAPTER 19

Commodity and Financial Futures

LEARNING OBJECTIVES

After completing this chapter you should be able to:

1. Define a futures contract and differentiate between the long and short positions in a commodity futures contract.
2. Contrast the role of margin in the stock market with its role in the commodity futures markets.
3. Distinguish speculators from hedgers and describe the role played by each in the futures markets.
4. Identify the forces that determine the price of a commodity futures contract.
5. Demonstrate how speculators may earn profits or suffer losses in financial and currency futures.
6. Explain how programmed trading links the futures and stock markets.
7. Demonstrate how futures and swaps help manage risk.

Do you want excitement and rapid action? Would you prefer to speculate in pork bellies (i.e., bacon) instead of investing in the stock of Swift or Armour? Then investing in commodity futures may satisfy this speculative desire. These futures contracts are among the riskiest investments available, as prices can change rapidly and produce sudden losses or profits.

There are two participants in the futures markets: the speculators who establish positions in anticipation of price changes and the hedgers who employ futures contracts to reduce risk. The hedgers are growers, producers, and other users of commodities. They seek to protect themselves from price fluctuations, and by hedging they pass the risk of loss to the speculators. The price of a futures contract ultimately depends on the demand for and supply of these contracts by the hedgers and speculators.

This chapter is an elementary introduction to investing in contracts for the future delivery of commodities. The chapter describes the mechanics of buying and selling the contracts, the role of margin, the speculators' long and short positions, and how the hedgers use the contracts to reduce risk. Next follows a discussion of financial futures, since commodity contracts are not limited to physical assets. There are also futures contracts for the purchase and sale of financial assets and foreign currencies. There are even futures based on the Standard & Poor's 500 stock index or the New York Stock Exchange Composite Index. The chapter continues with a discussion of programmed trading and stock index futures and how changes in the futures markets are transferred to the stock market and vice versa. The chapter ends with a brief discussion of swaps, in which participants agree to trade (swap) payments.

Although futures contracts are not appropriate assets for the vast majority of investors, many individuals indirectly participate in these markets. Some corporate financial managers use futures contracts to reduce risk from commodity price fluctuations, changes in interest rates, and changes in currency prices. Portfolio managers also employ futures contracts to reduce risk from fluctuations in securities prices. This usage is often disclosed in the financial statements investors receive from corporations and mutual funds. So, while individual investors may never personally participate in futures markets, they will have a better understanding of financial statements if they have a basic knowledge of these contracts and how the contracts are used for speculating and for hedging.

THE MECHANICS OF INVESTING IN FUTURES

futures contract

An agreement for the future delivery of a commodity at a specified date.

A commodity such as corn may be purchased for current delivery or for future delivery. Investing in futures refers to a contract to buy or to sell (deliver) a commodity in the future. For this reason these contracts are often referred to as *futures*. A **futures contract** is a formal agreement between a buyer or seller and a commodity exchange. In the case of a purchase contract, the buyer agrees to accept a specific commodity that meets a specified quality in a specified month. In the case of a sale, the seller agrees to deliver the specified commodity during the designated month.

Investing in commodity futures is considered to be very speculative. For that reason investors should participate in this market only after their financial obligations and primary financial goals have been met. There is a large probability that the investor will suffer a loss on any particular purchase or sale of a commodity contract. Individuals who buy and sell commodity contracts without wanting to deal in the actual commodities are generally referred to as *speculators*, which differentiates them from the growers, processors, warehousers, and other dealers who also buy and sell commodity futures but really wish to buy or sell the actual commodity.

The primary appeal of commodity contracts to speculators is the potential for a large return on the investment resulting from the leverage inherent in commodity trading. This leverage exists because (1) a futures contract controls a substantial amount of the commodity and (2) the investor must make only a small payment to buy or sell a contract (i.e., there is a small margin requirement). These two points are discussed in detail later in this chapter.

Like stocks and bonds, commodity futures are traded in several markets. One of the most important is the Chicago Mercantile Exchange (CME or "the MERC"), which acquired the Chicago Board of Trade (CBOT) in 2008 (http://www.cme.com) and formed the CME Group Inc. CME Group subsequently acquired the New York Mercantile Exchange (NYMEX). The CME Group trades a variety of commodity futures such as corn and soybeans and futures for currencies and for debt and equity instruments. Other commodities such as sugar, cotton, and coffee trade on the New York Board of Trade (NYBOT at http://www.NYBOT.com or http://www.theice.com).

Individuals acquire commodity contracts through brokers. The broker (or a member of a brokerage firm) owns a seat on the commodity exchange. Membership on each exchange is limited, and only members are allowed to buy and sell the commodity contracts. If the investor's broker lacks a seat, then that broker must have a correspondent relationship with another broker who does own a seat.

The broker acts on behalf of the investor by purchasing and selling contracts through the exchange. The investor opens an account by signing an agreement that requires the contracts to be guaranteed. Since trading commodity contracts is considered to be speculative, some brokers will open accounts only after the investor has proved the capacity both to finance the account and to withstand the losses.

Once the account has been opened, the individual may trade commodity contracts. These are bought and sold in much the same way as stocks and bonds; however, the use of the words *buy* and *sell* is misleading. The individual does not buy or sell a contract, but enters a contract to buy or sell. A buy contract specifies that the individual will *accept* delivery and hence "buy" the commodity. A sell contract specifies that the individual will *make* delivery and hence "sell" the commodity.

⊕ **Point of Interest**

COMMON CHARACTERISTICS THAT ASSETS MUST HAVE TO DEVELOP FUTURES MARKETS

There are markets for many goods and services in which you may be a buyer or a seller. You may buy or sell a house or car; any number of restaurants will sell you a hamburger or slice of pizza. You can hire a pet sitter or sell a used textbook. Markets exist for all of these products and services, but these are not futures markets. Futures markets have developed for specific commodities such as corn or wheat and financial assets such as U.S. Treasury bonds, and each of the assets has several common characteristics.

These common characteristics include the following: (1) There is sufficient demand and supply so no supplier or buyer can develop a monopoly. (2) The goods are easily stored so that a supply of the commodity can come continuously to the market. Disruptions from a lack of supply

are rare, if not nonexistent. (3) The assets are "fungible" so that you cannot tell one from another. One share of AT&T is no different than another share, and one bushel of a particular type of wheat is essentially the same as another bushel. It does not matter which share or which bushel you buy or sell; they are all the same.

As you study this chapter, notice that all the assets traded in futures markets have these characteristics. When differences appear to exist, such as winter and spring wheat or U.S. Treasury bills and bonds, different futures markets exist for each variety of the assets. There can be no confusion as to which asset is being traded, and there must be sufficient supply and demand to create continuous trading and to avoid price-fixing.

A commodity order specifies whether the contract is a buy or a sell, the type of commodity and the number of units, and the delivery date (i.e., the month in which the contract is to be executed and the commodity is bought or sold). The investor can request a market order and have the contract executed at the current market price, or he or she may place orders at specified prices. Such orders may be for a day or until the investor cancels them (i.e., the order is good till canceled). Once the order is executed, the broker provides a confirmation statement for the sale or purchase and charges a commission for executing the order. This fee covers both the purchase and the sale of the contract.

Although a futures contract appears to involve a buyer and a seller, the actual contract is made between the individual and the exchange. If an individual buys a contract, the exchange guarantees the delivery (the sale). If an individual sells a contract, the exchange guarantees to take delivery (the purchase). When a contract is created, the exchange simultaneously makes an opposite contract with another investor. While the exchange has offsetting buy and sell contracts, the effect is to guarantee the integrity of the contracts. If one of the parties were to default (for example, the buyer), the seller's contract is upheld by the exchange.

Commodity Positions

The investor may purchase a contract for future delivery. This is the long position, in which the investor will profit if the price of the commodity and hence the value of the contract rise. The investor may also sell a contract for future delivery. This is the short position, in which the seller agrees to make good the contract (i.e., to deliver the goods) sometime in the future. This investor will profit if the price of the commodity and hence the value of the contract decline. These long and short positions are analogous to the long and short positions that the investor takes in the securities market. Long positions generate profits when the value of the security rises, whereas short positions result in profits when the value of the security declines.

The way in which each position generates a profit can be seen in a simple example. Assume that the **futures price** of wheat is $3.50 per bushel. If a contract is purchased for delivery in six months at $3.50 per bushel, the buyer will profit from this long position if the price of wheat *rises*. If the price increases to $4.00 per bushel, the buyer can exercise the contract by taking delivery and paying $3.50 per bushel. The speculator then sells the wheat for $4 per bushel, which produces a profit of $0.50 per bushel.

The opposite occurs when the price of wheat declines. If the price of wheat falls to $3.00 per bushel, the individual who bought the contract for delivery at $3.50 suffers a loss. But the speculator who sold the contract for the delivery of wheat (i.e., who took the short position) earns a profit from the price decline. The speculator can then buy wheat at the market price (which is referred to as the **spot price**) of $3.00, deliver it for the contract price of $3.50, and earn a $0.50 profit per bushel.

If the price rises, the short position will produce a loss. If the price increases from $3.50 to $4.00 per bushel, the speculator who sold a contract for delivery suffers a loss of $0.50 per bushel, because he or she must pay $4.00 to obtain the wheat that will be delivered for $3.50 per bushel.

Actually, the preceding losses and profits are generated without the goods being delivered. Of course, when a speculator buys a contract for future delivery, there is always the possibility that this individual will receive the goods. Conversely, if the speculator sells a contract for future delivery, there is the possibility that the goods will have to be supplied. However, such deliveries occur infrequently, because the speculator can offset the contract before the delivery date. This is achieved by buying back a contract that was previously sold or selling a contract that is owned.

This process of *offsetting existing contracts* is illustrated in the following example. Suppose a speculator has a contract to buy wheat in January. If the individual wants to close the position, he or she can sell a contract for the delivery of wheat in January. The two contracts cancel (i.e., offset) each other, as one is a purchase and the other is a sale. (This process is analogous to the writer of an option buying back the option. In both cases the investor's position is closed.) If the speculator actually received the wheat by executing the purchase agreement, he or she could pass on the wheat by executing the sell agreement. However, since the two contracts offset each other, the actual delivery and subsequent sale are not necessary. Instead, the speculator's position in wheat is closed, and the actual physical transfers do not occur.

Correspondingly, if the speculator has a contract for the sale of wheat in January, it can be canceled by buying a contract for the purchase of wheat in January. If the speculator were called upon to deliver wheat as the result of the contract to sell, the individual would exercise the contract to purchase wheat. The buy and sell contracts would then cancel each other, and no physical transfers of wheat would occur. Once again the speculator has closed the initial position by taking the opposite position (i.e., the sales contract is offset by a purchase contract).

Because these contracts are canceled and actual deliveries do not take place, it should not be assumed that profits or losses do not occur. The two contracts need not be executed at the same price. For example, the speculator may enter a contract for the future purchase of wheat at $3.50 per bushel. Any contract for the future delivery of

---

futures price

The price in a contract for the future delivery of a commodity.

spot price

The current price of a commodity.

comparable wheat can cancel the contract for the purchase. But the cost of the wheat for future delivery could be $3.60 or $3.40 (or any conceivable price). If the price of wheat rises (e.g., from $3.50 to $3.60 per bushel), the speculator with a long position earns a profit. However, if the speculator has a short position (i.e., a contract to sell wheat), this individual sustains a loss. If the price declines (e.g., from $3.50 to $3.40 per bushel), the short seller earns a profit, but the long position sustains a loss.

The Units of Commodity Contracts

To facilitate trading, contracts must be uniform. For a particular commodity the contracts must be identical. Besides specifying the delivery month, the contract must specify the grade and type of the commodity (e.g., a particular type of wheat) and the units of the commodity (e.g., 5,000 bushels). Thus, when an individual buys or sells a contract, there can be no doubt as to the nature of the obligation. For example, if the investor buys wheat for January delivery, there can be no confusion with a contract for the purchase of wheat for February delivery. These are two different commodities in the same way that AT&T common stock, AT&T preferred stock, and AT&T bonds are all different securities. Without such standardization of contracts there would be chaos in the commodity (or any) markets.

The units of trading vary with each commodity. For example, if the investor buys a contract for corn, the unit of trading is 5,000 bushels. If the investor buys a contract for lumber, the unit of trading is 110,000 board feet. Although the novice investor may not remember the units for a contract, the experienced investor is certainly aware of them. As will be explained later, because of the large units of many commodity contracts, a small change in the price of the commodity produces a considerable change in the value of the contract and in the investor's profits or losses.

Reporting of Futures Trading

Commodity futures prices and the number of contracts in existence are reported in the financial press. Typical reporting is as follows:

	Open	High	Low	Settle	Change	LIFETIME High	Low	Open Interest
Corn (CBT) 5,000 bu; cents per bushel								
Jan	233.0	233.5	230.5	230.50	−3.00	243	210.75	36,790
Mar	240.0	241.5	236.5	237.25	...	270	205.0	10,900
May	244.5	244.5	241.0	241.75	+0.25	286	221.0	5,444

The above illustrates reporting for corn traded on the Chicago Board of Trade (CBT). The unit of trading is 5,000 bushels (bu), and prices are quoted in cents. The opening price for January delivery was 233.0 ($2.330) per bushel. The high, low, and closing (settle) prices were 233.5¢, 230.5¢, and 230.5¢, respectively. This closing price was 3 cents below the closing price on the previous day. The high and low (prior to the reported day of trading) for the lifetime of the contract were 243¢ and 210.75¢, respectively. The **open interest**, which is the number of contracts in existence, was 36,790.

open interest
The number of futures contracts in existence for a particular commodity.

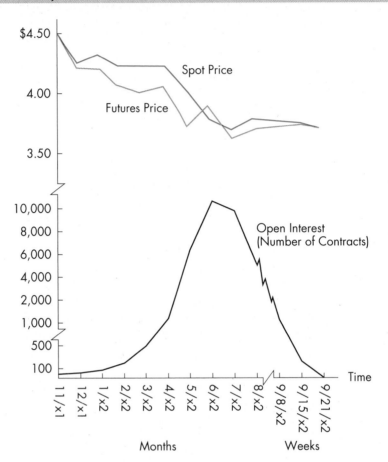

FIGURE 19.1 Spot and Futures Prices and Open Interest for a September Contract for Kansas City Wheat

This open interest varies over the life of the contract. Initially, the open interest rises as buyers and sellers establish positions. It then declines as the delivery date approaches and the positions are closed. This changing number of contracts is illustrated in Figure 19.1, which plots the spot and futures prices and the open interest for a September contract to buy Kansas City wheat. When the contracts were initially traded in November, there were only a few contracts in existence. By June the open interest had risen to over 10,000 contracts. Then, as the remaining life of the contracts declined, the number of contracts fell as the various participants closed their positions. By late September only a few contracts were still outstanding.

As is explained in the section on pricing, futures prices tend to exceed spot prices. If speculators anticipate higher prices, they will buy contracts for future delivery. This anticipation of inflation and the cost of storing commodities usually drives up futures prices relative to the spot price, so the futures price exceeds the current price.

Figure 19.1, however, illustrates that this relationship does not always hold. The figure gives the futures price and the spot price of Kansas City wheat, and, except for a brief period, the spot price exceeds the futures price. This inversion of the relationship occurs if speculators believe the price of the commodity will decline. These speculators sell contracts now to lock in the higher prices so they may buy back the contracts at a lower price. This selling of the futures contracts drives their price down below the spot price.

The futures price must converge with the spot price as the expiration date of the contract approaches. As with options such as puts and calls, the value of the futures contract can be worth only the value of the underlying commodity at the expiration date. This pattern of price behavior is also illustrated in Figure 19.1. In March, April, and May there was a considerable differential between the two prices. However, in late September the futures and spot prices converged and erased the differential.

The Regulation of Commodity Markets

The commodity exchanges, like stock exchanges, are subject to regulation. Until 1974, federal laws pertaining to commodity exchanges and commodity transaction laws were enforced by the Commodity Exchange Authority, a division of the Department of Agriculture. In 1974, Congress created the Commodity Futures Trading Commission (http://www.cftc.gov) to control entry into and operation of the futures markets. As with the regulation of securities transactions, the regulations do not protect investors or speculators from their own folly. Instead, the regulations establish uniform standards for each commodity. The regulatory authority also has control over trading procedures, the hours of trading, and the maximum allowable daily price movements.

LEVERAGE

Commodities are paid for on delivery. Thus, a contract for future delivery means that the goods do not have to be paid for when the individual enters the contract. Instead, the investor (either a buyer or a seller) provides an amount of money, which is called **margin**, to protect the exchange and the broker and to guarantee the contract. This margin should not be confused with the margin that is used in the purchase of stocks and bonds. In the trading of stocks and bonds, margin represents the investor's equity in the position, whereas margin for a commodity contract is a deposit to show the investor's good faith and to protect the broker against an adverse change in the price of the commodity.

In the stock market, the amount of margin required varies with the price of the security, but in the commodity markets, the amount of margin does not vary with the dollar value of the transaction. Instead, each contract has a fixed minimum margin requirement. These margin requirements are established by the commodity exchanges but cannot be below the minimums established by the Commodity Futures Trading Commission. Individual brokers may require more, especially for small accounts.

The margin requirements are only a small percentage of the value of the contract. For example, the $1,400 margin requirement for cocoa gives the owner of the contract a claim on 10 metric tons of cocoa. If cocoa is selling for $1,400 a metric ton, the total value of the contract is $14,000. The margin requirement as a percentage of the value of the contract is only 10 percent ($1,400/$14,000). This small amount of margin is one reason why a commodity contract offers so much potential leverage.

margin

Good faith deposit made when purchasing or selling a futures contract.

The potential leverage from speculating in commodity futures may be illustrated in a simple example. Consider a contract to buy wheat at $3.50 per bushel. Such a contract controls 5,000 bushels of wheat worth a total of $17,500(5,000 × $3.50). If the investor buys this contract and the margin requirement is $1,000, he or she must remit $1,000. An increase of only $0.20 per bushel in the price of the commodity produces an increase of $1,000 in the value of the contract. This $1,000 is simply the product of the price change ($0.20) and the number of units in the contract (5,000). The profit on the contract if sold is $1,000.

What is the percentage return on the investment? With a margin of $1,000 the return is 100 percent, because the investor put up $1,000 and then earned an additional $1,000. An increase of less than 6 percent in the price of wheat produced a return on the speculator's money of 100 percent. Such a return is the result of leverage that comes from the small margin requirement and the large amount of the commodity controlled by the contract.

Leverage, of course, works both ways. In the previous example, if the price of the wheat declines by $0.10, the contract will be worth $17,000. A decline of only 2.9 percent in the price reduces the investor's margin from $1,000 to $500. To maintain the position, the investor must deposit additional margin with the broker. The request for additional funds is referred to as a **margin call**. Failure to meet the margin call will result in the broker closing the position. Since the contract is supported only by the initial margin, further price declines will mean that there is less collateral to support the contract. Should the investor (i.e., the buyer or the seller) default on the contract, the exchange becomes responsible for its execution. The margin call thus protects the exchange.

Actually, there are two margin requirements. The first is the minimum initial deposit, and the second is the maintenance margin. The **maintenance margin** specifies when the investor must deposit additional funds with the broker to cover a decline in the value of a commodity contract. For example, the margin requirement for wheat is $1,000 and the maintenance margin is $750. If the investor owns a contract for the purchase of wheat and the value of the contract declines by $250 to the level of the maintenance margin ($750), the broker makes a margin call. This requires the investor to deposit an additional $250 into the account, which restores the initial $1,000 margin.

Maintenance margin applies to both buyers and sellers. If, in the previous example, the price of wheat were to rise by $250, the speculators who had sold short would see their margin decline from the initial deposit of $1,000 to $750. The broker would then make a margin call, which would require the short sellers to restore the $1,000 margin. Once again this protects the exchange, since the value of the contract has risen and the short seller has sustained the loss.

These margin adjustments occur daily. After the market closes, the value of each account is totaled. In the jargon of futures trading, each account is *marked to the market*. If a position has gained in value, funds are transferred into the account. If a position has lost value, funds are transferred out of the account. The effect is to transfer the funds from the accounts that have sustained losses to those accounts that have experienced gains. If, as a result of the transfer of funds, the account does not meet the maintenance margin requirement, the broker issues a margin call that the individual must meet or the broker will close the position.

margin call

A request by a broker for an investor to place additional funds or securities in an account as collateral against borrowed funds or as a good faith deposit.

maintenance margin

The minimum level of funds in a margin account that triggers a margin call.

The process of marking to the market and daily cash flows may be seen in the following example for a futures contract for 5,000 bushels of a commodity (e.g., wheat or corn). The futures price is $3.00, the margin requirement is $1,500, and the maintenance margin requirement is $800. There are two speculators, one of whom expects the price to rise and buys the contract (i.e., is long) and the other who is short and sells the contract. Both make the initial $1,500 margin payment, so at the end of the first day their respective positions are

Day 1   Futures price: $3.00

	Value of the contract:	$15,000	
	Margin positions:		

Speculator Long	Speculator Short
$1,500	$1,500

During the second day, the futures price rises to $3.05 and the margin accounts are as follows:

Day 2   Futures price: $3.05

Value of the contract: $15,250
Margin positions:

	Speculator Long	Speculator Short
Beginning balance	$1,500	$1,500
Change in balance	+250	−250
Required deposits	—	—
Voluntary withdrawals	250	—
Ending balance	$1,500	$1,250

Notice that Speculator Long has gained $250 while Speculator Short has lost $250 and the appropriate adjustments are made at the end of the day as each account is marked to the market. Since both accounts have more than $800, both meet the maintenance margin requirement, so no deposits of additional funds are needed. Speculator Long, however, may remove $250, since the account exceeds the initial margin requirement. These funds may be invested (e.g., in a money market account) to earn interest.

During the third day, the futures price continues to rise to $3.20 a bushel, so the value of the contract is $16,000. The positions for each account are now

Day 3   Futures price: $3.20

Value of the contract: $16,000
Margin positions:

	Speculator Long	Speculator Short
Beginning balance	$1,500	$1,250
Change in balance	+750	−750
Ending balance	$2,250	$500

Speculator Long may remove an additional $750 since the account again exceeds the margin requirement. Speculator Short's position is now less than the maintenance margin requirement. He or she will have to restore the account to the initial margin ($1,500), which will require an additional $1,000. After these changes the accounts will be

	Speculator Long	Speculator Short
Beginning balance	$1,500	$1,250
Change in balance	+750	−750
Balance	2,250	500
Required deposits	—	1,000
Voluntary withdrawals	−750	—
Closing balance	$1,500	$1,500

Notice that Speculator Long's $1,000 gain equals Speculator Short's $1,000 loss. If the futures price had declined from $3.00 to $2.80, the cash flows would have been reversed. Speculator Short would have $2,500 in the account and could remove $1,000, while Speculator Long would have only $500. Speculator Long would receive a margin call for $1,000 to restore the account to $1,500.

Whether the speculator chooses to meet the margin call is, of course, that person's decision, but a primary purpose of daily marking all positions to the market is to let the process of transferring funds occur. If a participant fails to meet a margin call, the broker closes the position, so that losses will not continue to increase (and put the brokerage firm at risk). Since speculators are highly aware of their risk exposure and often rapidly close positions, the probability they will receive a margin call is small. Such speculators rapidly close losing positions in order to limit their losses.

daily limit

The maximum daily change permitted in a commodity future's price.

Although commodity prices can and do fluctuate, limits are imposed by the markets on the amount of price change permitted each day. The **daily limit** establishes the maximum permissible price increase or decrease from the previous day. The purpose of these limits is to help maintain orderly markets and to reduce the potentially disruptive effects from large daily swings in the price of the futures contract. (The daily limit applies to many futures prices but not all, especially financial futures based on federal government debt and stock index futures.)

Once the price of the futures contract rises by the permissible daily limit, further price increases are not allowed. This does not necessarily mean that trading ceases, because transactions can still occur at the maximum price or below should the price of the commodity weaken. The same applies to declining prices. Once the daily limit has been reached, the price cannot continue to fall, but transactions can still occur at the lowest price or above should the price strengthen. For example, when the 1992 Florida orange crop came in at the higher end of expectations, orange juice futures prices quickly fell. Contracts for January, February, and March delivery declined by the 5¢ daily limit. Although trading could have continued at the lowest price, trading ceased because no one was willing to buy at that level and speculators anticipated further price declines. The same result occurred during the 2003 mad cow disease scare. Even though the Chicago Mercantile Exchange *increased* the daily limit, the futures price of beef declined to the new daily limit and trading ceased. The same principle applies to price increases. In 1995, Hurricane Erin threatened lumber supplies, the price of September lumber rose by the $10 daily limit, and trading ceased.

HEDGING

hedging

Taking opposite positions to reduce risk.

One major reason for the development of commodity futures markets was the desire of producers to reduce the risk of loss through price fluctuations. The procedure for this reduction in risk is called **hedging** and consists of taking opposite positions at the same time. In effect, a hedger simultaneously takes the long and the short position in a particular commodity.

Hedging is best explained by illustrations. In the first example, a wheat farmer expects to harvest a crop at a specified time. Since the costs of production are determined, the farmer knows the price that is necessary to earn a profit. Although the price that will be paid for wheat at harvest time is unknown, the current price of a contract for the future delivery of wheat is known. The farmer can then sell a contract for future delivery. Such a contract is a hedged position, because the farmer takes a long position (the wheat in the ground) and a short position (the contract for future delivery).

Such a position reduces the farmer's risk of loss from a price decline. Suppose the cost to produce the wheat is $2.50 per bushel and September wheat is selling in June for $2.75. If the farmer *sells* wheat for September delivery, a $0.25 per bushel profit is assured, because the buyer of the contract agrees to pay $2.75 per bushel on delivery in September. If the price of wheat declines to $2.50, the farmer is still assured of $2.75. However, if the price of wheat rises to $3.10 in September, the farmer still gets only $2.75. The additional $0.35 gain goes to the owner of the contract who bought the wheat for $2.75 but can now sell it for $3.10.

Is this transaction unfair? Remember that the farmer wanted protection against a decline in the price of wheat. If the price had declined to $2.40 and the farmer had not hedged, the farmer would have suffered a loss of $0.10 (the $2.40 price minus the $2.50 cost) per bushel. To obtain protection from this risk of loss, the farmer accepted the modest profit of $0.25 per bushel and relinquished the possibility of a larger profit. The speculator who bought the contract bore the risk of loss from a price decline and received the reward from a price increase.

Users of wheat hedge in the opposite direction. A flour producer desires to know the future cost of wheat in order to plan production levels and the prices that will be charged to distributors. However, the spot price of wheat need not hold into the future, so this producer *buys* a contract for future delivery and thereby hedges the position. This is hedging because the producer has a long position (the contract for the future delivery of wheat) and a short position (the future production of flour, which requires the future delivery of wheat).

If the producer buys a contract in June for the delivery of wheat in September at $2.75 per bushel, the future cost of the grain becomes known. The producer cannot be hurt by an increase in the price of wheat from $2.75 to $3.10, because the contract is for delivery at $2.75. However, the producer has forgone the chance of profit from a decline in the price of wheat from $2.75 to $2.40 per bushel.

⊕ Point of Interest

FORWARD CONTRACTS

In addition to futures contracts, there are also "forward contracts." These are essentially the same as futures contracts with different features. A futures contract is a standardized contract between two parties that specifies the amount of the commodity and the delivery date. Since the contract is standardized, futures may be bought and sold through organized futures markets. A forward contract is a contract between two parties but is tailor-made for each transaction. The uniqueness of each forward contract makes it adaptable to the specific needs of the respective parties.

Forward contracts are common in the normal course of business. Any contract for the future delivery of a commodity or service is a forward contract. For example, a magazine subscription or an airline ticket illustrate a forward contract. In each case one party contracts to deliver a commodity (the magazine) or service (the plane ride) at specified future dates and for a specified amount of money. The money may be paid when the contract is executed or upon delivery.

Many businesses could not exist without forward contracts in which one party agrees to provide something in the future for a specified price and the other party agrees to take delivery and pay the specified price. Firms, governments, and households enter such contracts, and each contract creates legal obligations on both parties.

Although a forward contract specifies the amount and delivery date, the uniqueness of its features reduces the marketability of the contract. When the contract is written, the intention is to maintain the contract until delivery, so there are no organized forward markets. In effect, forward contracts are illiquid futures contracts. There is, however, some trading of forward contracts over-the-counter among financial institutions. In addition, if a firm has a forward contract to buy a commodity, it may enter into another contract to deliver the commodity. In effect, the two forward contracts cancel each other.

In addition to the lack of liquidity, the other important difference between forward and futures contracts is daily settlement, which applies to futures contracts but not to forward contracts. Forward contracts are not marked to the market daily, and funds are not transferred between the two parties. Final settlement thus occurs when the commodity is delivered and paid for as specified in the contract.

Instead, the possibility of profit from a decline in the price of wheat rests with the speculator who sold the contract. If the price of wheat were to decline, the speculator could buy the wheat in September at the lower price, deliver it, and collect the $2.75 that is specified in the contract. However, this speculator would suffer a loss if the price of September wheat rose over $2.75. The cost would then exceed the delivery price specified in the contract.

These two examples illustrate why growers and producers hedge. They often take the opposite side of hedge positions. If all growers and producers agree on prices for future delivery, there would be no need for speculators; but this is not the case. Speculators buy or sell contracts when there is an excess or an insufficient supply. If the farmer in the preceding example could not find a producer to buy the contract for the future delivery of wheat, a speculator would buy the contract and accept the risk of a price decline. If the producer could not find a farmer to supply a contract for the future delivery of wheat, the speculator would sell the contract and accept the risk of a price increase.

Of course, farmers, producers, and speculators are simultaneously buying and selling contracts. No one knows who buys and who sells at a specific moment. However, if there is an excess or a shortage of one type of contract, the futures price of the commodity changes, which induces a certain behavior. For example, if September wheat is quoted at $2.75 per bushel, but no one is willing to buy at that price, the price declines.

This induces some potential sellers to withdraw from the market and some potential buyers to enter the market. By this process, an imbalance of supply and demand for contracts for a particular delivery date is erased. It is the interaction of the hedgers and the speculators that establishes the price of each contract.

THE SELECTION OF COMMODITY FUTURES CONTRACTS

As with the selection of securities, there are two basic methods for the selection of commodity futures contracts: the technical approach and the fundamental approach. The technical approach uses the same methods that are applied to the selection of securities. Various averages, point-and-figure charts, and bar graphs and their patterns are constructed for various commodities and are used to identify current price movements and to predict future price movements. Since this material was covered in Chapter 12, it is not repeated here.

The fundamental approach is primarily concerned with those factors that affect the demand for and the supply of the various commodities. Although the approach is similar to the selection of securities in that it uses economic data, the specifics are different. The price of a commodity depends on the supply of that commodity relative to the demand. Since the commodities are produced (e.g., wheat) or mined (e.g., silver), there are identifiable sources of supply. Correspondingly, there are identifiable sources of demand. However, there is also a variety of exogenous factors that may affect the supply of or the demand for a particular commodity, and these factors can have a powerful impact on the price of a specific commodity.

To illustrate these points, consider a basic commodity such as wheat. It takes several months for wheat to be produced. It has to be planted, grown, and harvested. The amount of wheat that is planted is known because statistics are kept by the U.S. Department of Agriculture. Such statistics are necessary for government forecasts of the economy, and this information is certainly available to those firms and individuals concerned with the size of the wheat crop.

The size of the crop that is planted and the size that is harvested, however, may be considerably different. The actual harvest depends on other factors. Particularly important is the weather, which can increase or decrease the yield. Good weather at the appropriate time can result in a bountiful harvest. A larger than anticipated supply of wheat should depress its price. On the other hand, bad weather, be it drought or excess rain, will significantly reduce the anticipated supply. A reduction in supply should increase the price of wheat.

Demand, like supply, depends on both predictable and unpredictable forces. The demand for wheat depends on the needs of the firms that use the grain in their products. The producers of flour and cereals are obvious potential customers for wheat. However, the total demand also includes exports. If a foreign government enters the market and buys a substantial amount of wheat, this may cause a significant increase in its price.

Such government intervention in the market is not limited to foreign governments. The U.S. government also buys and sells commodities. Sometimes it buys to absorb excess supplies of a commodity and thus supports the commodity's price. In other cases

TAXATION OF GAINS AND LOSSES FROM TRADING IN FUTURES

Realized profits from trading in futures are taxed as capital gains. In addition, all positions in futures are considered to have been closed at the end of the tax year. Open positions then must be marked to the market on the last day of the tax year and any paper profits taxed as if they were realized capital gains. Any paper losses are treated as realized capital losses.

The profits are arbitrarily apportioned as 60 percent long-term capital gains and 40 percent short-term capital gains. A $1,000 profit would be separated into a $600 long-term capital gain and a $400 short-term capital gain and taxed according to the applicable rates. Losses are treated as capital losses and are used to offset capital gains from trading in futures, capital gains from other securities transactions, and income from other sources, subject to the limitations discussed in Chapter 4.

the federal government may sell from its surplus stocks of a given commodity. This, of course, has the opposite impact on the price of the commodity. The increased supply tends to decrease the price or at least to reduce a tendency for the price to rise. These exogenous forces in the commodity markets are just another source of risk with which the speculator must contend.

Obviously the speculator needs to identify shifts in demand or supply before they occur in order to take the appropriate position. Anticipation of a price increase indicates the purchase of a futures contract, whereas an anticipated price decline indicates the sale of a futures contract. Unfortunately, the ability to consistently predict changes in demand and supply is very rare. This should be obvious! If an individual could predict the future, he or she would certainly make a fortune not just in the commodity futures markets but in any market. Mortals, however, lack such clairvoyance, which leaves them with fundamental and technical analysis as means to select commodity futures for purchase.

Whether an investor uses technical or fundamental analysis, there is an important strategy for trading futures. The speculator should limit losses and permit profits to run. Successful commodity futures trading requires the speculator's ability to recognize bad positions and to close them before they generate large losses. Behavioral finance suggests that many speculators, especially novices, do the exact opposite by taking small profits as they occur but maintaining positions that sustain losses. Then, when price changes produce margin calls, the speculator is forced either to close the position at a loss or to put up additional funds. If the speculator meets the margin call by committing additional funds, that individual is violating the strategy. Instead of taking the small loss, this investor is risking additional funds in the hope that the price will recover.

THE PRICING OF FUTURES

Several factors may affect a futures contract's price. For example, expectations have frequently been discussed as motivating speculators. The expectation of higher prices leads speculators to take long positions, and the expectation of lower prices results in their establishing short positions. Thus, the futures price mirrors what speculators anticipate prices will be in the future. In addition, the futures price and the spot price are not independent of each other. Such factors as the cost of carrying the commodity link the spot and futures prices. The pricing of futures contracts is an involved topic. The following material covers only the basics so an investor can have an understanding of the pricing of a futures contract. More detailed discussions may be found in texts devoted solely to derivatives.[1]

The following discussion is based on a commodity whose spot price is $100; the futures contract is for delivery after one year. Suppose individuals expect the price of the commodity to be $110 after one year. What should be the current price of a one-year futures contract? The answer is $110. Consider how individuals would react if the price were $108. They would buy the futures contract and, after one year, when the price of the commodity was $110, they would exercise the contract to buy the good for $108 and promptly sell it for $110, making a $2 profit. If the futures price exceeded $110 (e.g., $113), they would reverse the procedure and sell the futures contract. After one year, they would buy the commodity for $110, deliver it for the contract price of $113, and clear $3. For any futures price other than $110, speculators would take positions in the futures contracts. Only if the futures price equals the expected price in the future will the market be in equilibrium, and speculators will take no action.

For this reason, futures prices are often considered to be measures of what investors, speculators, and other market participants currently expect the price of the commodity to be in the future. That is, the current futures prices are an indication of what the future holds. (This concept previously appeared in the appendix to Chapter 13, in which the expectations theory of interest rates suggested that the current long-term interest rate is an average of the current short-term rate and expected future short-term rates.) The process of using futures prices as a forecasting tool is sometimes referred to as "price disclosure." The current futures price discloses what market participants believe the future price will be.

If expectations concerning future prices were to change, then the futures price must also change. A major failure of the coffee crop would be expected to increase the future price of coffee, so the expectation of high prices would drive up the current futures price. Of course, if the price of coffee did not rise, those speculators who bought in anticipation of the price increase would lose, while those who sold in anticipation that the price increase would not occur would win.

An additional factor that affects futures prices is the cost of carrying the commodity. In the previous examples, the speculator took only one side, that is, he or she bought or sold the futures in anticipation of a price change and the futures price mirrored the speculator's expected price change. Suppose the individual could buy the commodity now for $100 *and* sell the futures contract at $110. If the price rises to $110, the investor wins because the commodity that cost $100 can be delivered for $110. If the price exceeds $110, this individual still gets $110 and earns the $10. If the price is less than $110, the profit remains $10 because the price is set in the contract at $110. What is the catch?

The problem is the cost of carrying the commodity. If the individual buys the commodity for $100, those funds will not be earning interest (if the investor uses his or

[1]For a more detailed discussion of futures pricing, see Don M. Chance and Robert Brooks, *An Introduction to Derivatives and Risk Management,* 7th ed. (Mason, OH: South-Western Publishing, 2006) or Robert W. Kolb and James A. Overdahl, *Futures, Options, and Swaps,* 4th ed. (Malden, MA: Wiley-Blackwell, 2007).

INVESTING IN COMMODITIES THROUGH EXCHANGE-TRADED FUNDS AND EXCHANGE-TRADED NOTES

Although investing in futures contracts is obviously risky and requires active portfolio management, it offers a means to participate in specialized markets and perhaps contribute to the diversification of a portfolio. Can an individual participate in the market for commodities but avoid the risk associated with margin calls and reduce the need for active management? The answer is yes, by acquiring shares in investment companies that specialize in commodities, especially an exchange-traded fund whose shares are readily bought and sold.

ETFs are associated with tracking an index, so it is easy to assume that no ETFs apply to commodities. That conclusion, however, would be incorrect. The DB Commodity Index Tracking Fund (DBC) tracks six commodities that include agricultural products (corn) and energy (oil). The value of the shares fluctuates with changes in the prices of the underlying commodities in the index.

In 2006, Barclays created a new version of the ETF called *exchange-traded notes* (ETNs). Notice the word *notes* has been substituted for *fund*. These ETNs are *debt obligations of Barclays* that mature after 30 years. Investors

in these ETNs bear two sources of risk: the risk associated with changes in the value of the underlying assets and the credit risk associated with the default of Barclays on its obligation to retire the notes.

The notes also have a redemption feature. Large financial institutions may periodically redeem the ETNs. If the notes were to sell for a discount, an opportunity for arbitrage would exist. The institutions would buy the notes at the discounted price and redeem them for the value of the underlying assets. Presumably this act of arbitrage assures that the notes will sell for the approximate value of the underlying assets.

Barclays initially created two ETNs. The iPath GSCA Total Return Index (GSP) tracks the Goldman Sachs Commodity Index, which is composed of 24 commodities with emphasis on the energy sector. The iPath Dow Jones AIG Commodity Index Total Return (DJP) tracks an index of 19 commodities with less emphasis on energy. Choosing between these two ETNs depends on an investor's desire to have a larger or smaller exposure to swings in energy prices. If these two initial ETNs are successful and generate fees, presumably Barclays will create more.

her own money) or will be requiring interest payments if the funds were borrowed. Suppose the interest rate is 8 percent. Now the individual can borrow $100, buy the commodity for $100, enter into a contract to deliver the commodity after a year for $110, and clear a $2 profit. Thus, *if the futures price exceeds the spot price plus the cost of carry*, then an opportunity for a risk-free arbitrage exists. The arbitrageurs will buy the commodity and sell the futures; they would long the commodity and short the futures. The act of executing these positions will drive up the spot price of the commodity and drive down the futures price. Speculators who anticipate a price of $110 in the future will gladly buy the futures contract for less than $110, since they anticipate earning the difference between $110 and whatever amount they buy the contract for.

If the interest rate were 12 percent, the arbitrageurs would reverse the procedure. They would sell the commodity at the current spot price (receiving the $100) and buy a contract for future delivery at $110. That is, the arbitrageurs would short the commodity and long the futures. Next they would invest (lend) the money received from the sale at 12 percent. At the end of the year, the arbitrageurs would receive the commodity that previously had been sold and make $2 on the transaction. Although the cost of the commodity was $110 and the arbitrageurs received only $100 from the sale, they earned $12 on the sale proceeds and netted $2 on the set of transactions.

Once again the act of executing these positions affects the prices of the commodity. Selling the commodity in the spot market will decrease its price, and buying the futures contract will increase its price. As the futures price increases, the speculators, who anticipate the price will be $110, gladly supply (i.e., sell) the contracts as the futures price rises above $110.

In the previous illustration, the cost of carry was limited to the rate of interest. Although that limitation may apply to a financial contract, it does not apply to a contract for a commodity. For commodities, the cost of carry includes interest expense and warehouse expenses, insurance, and shipping.

Consider the preceding case in which the spot price was $100, the futures price was $110, and the interest rate was 8 percent; the arbitrageurs bought the commodity with borrowed funds and sold the futures contract. Now, however, add a $9 cost of warehousing and shipping the commodity. These additional expenses alter the potential for an arbitrage profit. The futures price must exceed $117 for the arbitrageurs to earn a profit. If they sell the futures contract for $120, they can buy the commodity today for $100 with borrowed funds, pay the $8 interest, cover the $9 in other expenses, and earn a $3 profit without bearing any risk. However, now the futures price must greatly exceed the spot price for the arbitrage opportunity to exist.

FINANCIAL FUTURES AND CURRENCY FUTURES

financial futures
Contract for the future delivery of a financial asset.

currency futures
Contract for the future delivery of foreign exchange.

In the previous discussion, commodity contracts meant futures contracts for physical goods. However, there are also financial and currency futures. **Financial futures** are contracts for the future delivery of securities such as stocks, Treasury bills, and bonds. **Currency futures** are contracts for the future delivery of currency such as the British pound or the European euro. The markets for these contracts, like the market for commodity futures, have two participants: the speculators and the hedgers. It is the interaction of these two parties (i.e., the demand and supply of each contract) that determines the futures price.

The next sections present an introduction to financial futures and currency futures. Initially stock index futures are covered, which includes a discussion of stock index arbitrage and programmed trading. Stock index arbitrage is important because it links the futures markets and the equity markets. If the futures price for stocks rises, arbitrage assures that the prices of stocks also rise. The process also works in reverse. If the futures price for equities declines, arbitrage assures that the decline is transferred to the stock market. A description of futures for debt instruments follows index arbitrage. The last section on futures covers currency futures.

Stock Market Futures

stock index futures
A contract based on an index of security prices.

Stock index futures are futures contracts based on an index of the stock market (e.g., the Standard & Poor's 500 stock index or the New York Stock Exchange Composite Index). These contracts offer speculators and hedgers opportunities for profit or risk reduction that are not possible through the purchase of individual securities. For example, the S&P 500 stock index futures contracts have a value that is 250 times the value of the index. Thus, if the S&P 500 stock index is 1,000, the contract is worth $250,000.

By purchasing this contract (i.e., by establishing a long position), the holder profits if the market rises. If the index were to rise to 1,100, the value of the contract would increase to $275,000. The investor would then earn a profit of $25,000. Of course, if the S&P 500 Index should decline, the buyer would experience a loss. ("Mini" contracts that are worth 50 times the S&P 500 stock index are also available.)

The sellers of these contracts also participate in the fluctuations of the market. However, their positions are the opposite of the buyers' (i.e., they are short). If the value of the S&P 500 stock index were to fall from 1,000 to 900, the value of the contract would decline from $250,000 to $225,000, and the short seller would earn a $25,000 profit. Of course, if the market were to rise, the short seller would suffer a loss. Obviously, if the individual anticipates a rising market, that investor should buy the futures contract. Conversely, if the investor expects the market to fall, that individual should sell the contract.

S&P 500 stock index futures contracts are similar to other futures contracts. The buyers and sellers must make good faith deposits (i.e., margin payments). As with other futures contracts, the amount of this margin (approximately 7 percent of the value of the contract) is modest relative to the value of the contract. Thus, these contracts offer considerable leverage. If stock prices move against the investor and his or her equity in the position declines, the individual will have to place additional funds in the account to support the contract. Since there is an active market in the contracts, the investor may close a position at any time by taking the opposite position. Thus, if the investor had purchased a contract, that long position would be closed by selling a contract. If the investor had sold a contract, that short position would be closed by buying a futures contract.

There is one important difference between stock market index futures and commodity futures contracts. Settlement at the expiration or maturity of the contract occurs in cash. There is no physical delivery of securities as could occur with a futures contract to buy or sell wheat or corn. Instead, gains and losses are totaled and are added to or subtracted from the participants' accounts. The long and short positions are then closed.

One reason for the development of commodity futures markets was the need by producers and users of commodities to hedge their positions against price fluctuations. Stock index futures (and other financial and currency futures) developed in part for the same reason. Portfolio managers buy and sell stock index futures in order to hedge against adverse price movements. For example, suppose a portfolio manager has a well-diversified portfolio of stocks. If the market rises, the value of this portfolio rises. However, there is risk of loss if the market were to decline. The portfolio manager can reduce the risk of loss by selling an NYSE Composite Index futures contract. If the market declines, the losses experienced by the portfolio will be at least partially offset by the appreciation in the value of the short position in the futures contract.

To execute such a hedge, the portfolio manager uses a futures contract that matches the composition of the portfolio. The NYSE Composite Index contract is suitable for a well-diversified stock portfolio but would not be appropriate for a specialized portfolio. Instead, the portfolio manager who is responsible for a portfolio of smaller companies would more likely use futures on the S&P Midcap index, which gives more weight to smaller companies.

To hedge using stock index futures, the portfolio manager divides the value of the portfolio by the value of the contract to determine the number of contracts to sell. For example, if the value of the portfolio is $1,000,000 and the futures contracts are worth $85,000, the individual would sell 11 to 12 contracts ($1,000,000/ $85,000 = 11.76). It may not be possible to exactly hedge the portfolio, since the futures contracts may be unavailable in the desired units. In this example, the portfolio manager would not be able to sell 11.76 futures contracts, but would have to sell either 11 or 12 contracts. This question of units is less of a problem for managers of large portfolios. If the portfolio's value had been $100,000,000, the number of contracts would be 1,176 ($100,000,000/$85,000 = 1,176.47), and the difference between 1,176 and 1,177 is immaterial. The problem facing this portfolio manager will be the market's ability to absorb such a large number of contracts. Is there sufficient demand at current prices to absorb $100,000,000 worth of futures contracts? If the answer is no, then prices will change (which changes the required number of contracts) or the portfolio manager will not be able to completely hedge the long position in the stocks.

In addition to the number of contracts, the portfolio manager must consider the volatility of the portfolio relative to the market. The preceding illustration implicitly assumes that the value of the portfolio exactly follows the index on which the futures contract is based. In effect, the example assumes that the portfolio's beta equals 1.0. If the beta is greater than 1.0, more contracts must be sold to hedge against a price decline, since the value of the contracts sold short will decline less than the value of the portfolio. If the portfolio's beta is less than 1.0, fewer contracts must be sold, since the value of the market will decline more than the value of the portfolio.

The entire process of hedging is illustrated in Exhibit 19.1, in which two portfolio managers want to hedge $2,000,000 portfolios against a price decline. Portfolio A has a beta of 1.25, while portfolio B has a beta of 0.75. Since the portfolio betas differ, portfolio A requires that nine contracts be sold, while portfolio B requires the selling of only five. The market subsequently declines by 10 percent from 1,100 to 990. Each portfolio sustains a loss, but the short positions in the futures contracts generate profits that offset the losses. Except for the problem of units, each investor has successfully hedged against the price decline but has also forgone the opportunity for a gain. If the market had risen, the increase in the value of the contracts would offset the gain in the stocks. Hedging

EXHIBIT 19.1	Using Stock Index Futures to Hedge $2,000,000 Portfolios	
	Portfolio A	Portfolio B
Value of portfolio:	$2,000,000	$2,000,000
Beta:	1.25	0.75
Value of S&P 500 stock index contract:	$250 × 1,100 = $275,000	$250 × 1,100 = $275,000
Number of contracts necessary to hedge:	($2,000,000/$275,000)(1.25) = 9.09	($2,000,000/$275,000)(0.75) = 5.45
Number of contracts sold:	9	5
Gain on futures contracts sold short after market declines by 10 percent to 990:	$275,000 × 9 − 990($250)9 = $247,500	$275,000 × 5 − 990($250)5 = $137,500
Loss on portfolio:	[$2,000,000(1 − 0.1) − $2,000,000] (1.25) = −$250,000	[$2,000,000(1 − 0.1) − $2,000,000](0.75) = −$150,000
Net gain (loss)	$247,500 − $250,000 = ($2,500)	$137,500 − ($150,00) = ($12,500)

⊕ Point of Interest

SINGLE-STOCK FUTURES

There are futures contracts on individual commodities (e.g., wheat); there are contracts on individual stock indexes (e.g., the S&P 500) and broad baskets of stocks; contracts exist on individual currencies (e.g., the pound); and there are even contracts on individual federal government securities (Treasury bills). Beginning in 2001, the Chicago Board Options Exchange, the Chicago Mercantile Exchange, and the Chicago Board of Trade formed a joint venture for trading in single-stock futures.

Single-stock futures essentially work the same as any other futures contract. The participant enters into a contract to buy or to sell the specified stock at the current futures price. If the futures price of the stock rises, the long position wins and the short position loses. The appeal of such contracts is the small margin requirement, so the participant is able to obtain substantial amounts of leverage. However, unlike options, which also may be used to obtain leverage, single-stock futures are marked to the market daily, so gains and losses are settled daily. The cost of an option also varies daily, but the margin requirement for single-stock futures is set and does not change with the futures price. This means that if the price of the stock rose so that the futures price of the stock also rose, the cost of buying or selling the single-stock futures remains the set margin requirement.

with stock index futures works in both directions but is the most appropriate strategy when the portfolio manager expects a price decline and is unwilling to sell the portfolio. For example, the portfolio manager may wish to hedge during a period of greater uncertainty but does not want to sell the securities and generate taxable capital gains.

Besides selling the index futures contract (establishing a short position in futures), the portfolio manager could have hedged by writing an index call option (establishing a covered call position) or by purchasing an index put option (establishing a protective put position). Each of these strategies is designed to protect against a decline in the market as a whole. Each offers potential advantages and has disadvantages, so there is no clear argument to use one exclusively. Selling a futures contract is an easy position to establish and tends to have low transaction costs. If, however, the market were to rise, the loss on the futures contract will offset the gain on the market. Selling the futures eradicates the upside potential.

Selling the call generates income from the sale but the downside protection is limited. If the market were to decline sufficiently to offset the proceeds of the sale of the call, the portfolio will sustain a loss. In addition, if the market rises, the value of the call will increase, which offsets the gain in the portfolio. The protective put does not limit the upside potential. If the market were to rise, the increase in the value of the portfolio is not offset by an equal decrease in the value of the put. But buying the put requires a cash outlay, and the process must be repeated (and cash outlays increased) if the portfolio manager wants to retain the protection from a market decline.

Programmed Trading and Index Arbitrage

Programmed trading arose after the creation of stock index futures and has become a major link between the stock market and the futures market. Through programmed trading and index arbitrage, price changes in one market are transferred to the other and vice versa as the participants move funds between the markets to take advantage of price differentials.

programmed trading
Coordinated buying or selling of portfolios triggered by computers.

The term **programmed trading** refers to the coordinated purchases or sales of an entire portfolio of securities. The managers of mutual funds or financial institutions cannot physically place individual orders to buy and sell large quantities of stocks. Instead, large orders are placed through computers that are programmed (hence the name *programmed trading*) to enter the trades if certain specifications are met.

As explained earlier in this text, arbitrage refers to the simultaneous establishment of long and short positions to take advantage of price differentials between two markets. If, for example, the price of the British pound were $2.46 in Paris and $2.50 in Bonn, the arbitrageur would buy pounds in Paris and simultaneously sell them in Bonn. The pounds bought in Paris could be delivered in Bonn; hence, the individual is assured of a $0.04 profit on the transaction. This riskless arbitrage position ensures that the price of the pound will be approximately the same in Paris and Bonn with minute differentials being explained by transactions costs.

Conceptually, index arbitrage is no different, except the arbitrageur is buying or selling index futures and securities instead of pounds. The principle is the same. If prices deviate in different markets, an opportunity for arbitrage is created. Arbitrageurs will seek to take advantage of the price differentials, and through their actions the differentials are erased. This type of arbitrage is frequently done by mutual funds with large holdings of securities that duplicate the various indexes of stock prices. These funds shuffle money between stocks and futures to take advantage of price differentials.

Programmed trading index arbitrage combines the two concepts: Computers are programmed to enter orders to sell or buy blocks of securities designed to take advantage of arbitrage opportunities that exist in the securities and futures markets. If stock index futures prices rise, the arbitrageurs will short the futures and buy the stocks in the index. If futures prices decline, the arbitrageurs do the opposite. They go long in the futures contracts and short the stocks in the index.

Three potential problems arise: (1) There are some transactions costs that must be covered, so the difference between the value of the futures contracts and the underlying securities must be sufficient to cover this cost. (2) There is an obvious problem with buying or shorting all the securities in a broad-based index. Since the Standard & Poor's 500 stock index uses 500 different stocks, positions would have to be taken in all 500. To get around this problem, the arbitrageurs have developed smaller portfolios called *baskets* that mirror the larger index. The price performance of these stock baskets then mimics the price movements in the index. (3) For arbitrage to be riskless, both positions must be made simultaneously. If they were not, there would be a period when the investor is either long or short (i.e., has only one position) and thus would be at risk. This need for simultaneous executions led to the use of computers that are programmed to coordinate the purchases or sales of the baskets. It is the use of the computers that permits the arbitrageur to enter simultaneous orders to buy or sell large quantities of many individual stocks.

In Chapter 17 it was explained why an option's intrinsic value sets a floor on the option's price. If the price were to decline below the intrinsic value, an opportunity for arbitrage would exist. The same concept applies to stock index futures, except in this case the option is replaced by the index futures and the individual stock by the stock basket.

The idea may be explained by a simple example. Suppose the S&P stock index stands at 300 and the futures contract is trading for 301.5. Assume that the contract has a value of 500 times the index, so the value of each contract is $150,750.

The arbitrageur shorts the futures and buys the $150,000 worth of the stocks in the index (or the shares in the basket). In effect, the arbitrageur has paid $150,000 for $150,750 worth of stock, because the arbitrageur has already entered into a contract for the sale of the stock at $150,750 through the short position in the futures.

If, after executing the position, the futures price declines or the prices of the stocks in the index rise, the arbitrageur will close both positions (referred to as *unwinding*) and make a profit. For example, suppose the prices of the stocks rise sufficiently that the index is 301.50 and the futures contract has only risen to 302. The arbitrageur may now sell the stocks and repurchase the futures contract. The loss on the futures is $250(301.5 × $500 − 302 × $500), while the gain on the stocks is $750(301.5 × $500 − 300 × $500). Since all the transactions can occur in a matter of minutes, the cost of carrying the positions is negligible. The arbitrageur need only cover the transaction cost associated with the trades.

If the differential between the values of the futures and index is not rapidly erased, the arbitrageur can maintain the positions until the expiration date of the futures contracts. As the expiration date approaches, the futures price must converge with the current (i.e., spot) price. Options can be worth only their intrinsic value at expiration, and futures prices must equal the spot prices when the contracts expire. Thus the arbitrageur knows that the differential between the value of the futures contract and the index must disappear and thus assure the profit. The only difference between this and the previous situation is the cost of carrying the stocks, which may be partially offset by income generated by the securities.

If the prices had been reversed (e.g., the futures were trading at 298.5 when the index was 300), so would the procedure. The arbitrageur goes long in the futures and short in the stocks. The simultaneous long and short positions lock in the differential and assure the arbitrageur of the profit. If the price differential rapidly disappears, the positions are unwound and the profit realized. Even if the differential persists, the arbitrageur knows that at expiration the differential must be erased.

This process of index arbitrage is illustrated in Figure 19.2, which presents the differential between the value of the futures contract and the underlying stocks in the index during a trading day. The line at zero represents no differential, and the lines at +0.1 and −0.1 represent the transaction costs of executing index arbitrage. Once the differential between the futures and the index exceeds +0.1 or −0.1, the opportunity for a profitable arbitrage exists.

The computers are then programmed to enter the appropriate buy and sell orders when the differential is sufficient to cover the costs associated with the transactions. For example, at 10:15 A.M., the differential is sufficient on the plus side that the arbitrageur would short the futures and buy the stocks. By 11:45 the differential has vanished, so the positions are closed and the profits are realized. At 2:00 P.M. the differential has once again sufficiently increased (on the negative side) that the arbitrageur goes long in the futures and shorts the stocks. By 3:30, the differential is again erased, and the arbitrageur unwinds the positions.

Of course, as the differentials are erased, the impact is felt in the various markets. Increased demand for futures contracts relative to the underlying stocks generates demand by the arbitrageurs for the stocks and hence their prices rise. In a similar way, an increase in stock prices would be transferred to the futures markets. The converse would also be true. A decline in stock prices would tend to drive down the futures prices.

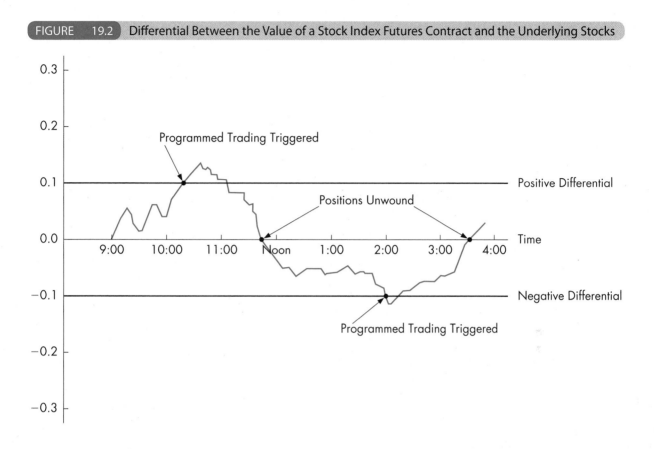

FIGURE 19.2 Differential Between the Value of a Stock Index Futures Contract and the Underlying Stocks

It is important to realize that index arbitrage-programmed trading does *not* depend on the level of stock prices or the level of futures prices. Instead, it depends on (1) spot prices relative to futures prices and (2) synchronized trading. Index arbitrage-programmed trading does not depend on technical analysis, fundamental analysis of a firm's financial statements, changes in information such as an increase in earnings or dividends, or forecasts of the economy.

Programmed trading can distort a stock's price. An individual stock can be fairly valued based on fundamental analysis but experience a large swing in its price if it becomes caught up in programmed trading. As arbitrageurs seek to establish long positions in stocks, the prices of individual securities included in the index or basket can rise rapidly and dramatically. Of course, the converse would be true if arbitrageurs seek to unwind long positions in the stocks or establish short positions. Thus it is possible for the prices of individual securities to be whipsawed during a trading day in response to the establishing or unwinding of arbitrageurs' positions. Such price volatility can create buying (or shorting) opportunities in individual stocks if their prices deviate from their values as indicated by fundamental analysis.

This price volatility may be particularly noticeable near the expiration dates and especially on the four days during the year that are referred to as the *triple witching hour*. On these days the Standard & Poor's 500 stock index futures contract, the Standard & Poor's 100 stock index option contract, and individual option contracts expire.

This convergence of expirations can lead to large volatility in the prices and the volume of the securities traded.

On the triple witching day, the time period is so short that even small differentials can create arbitrage opportunities. The various participants in the markets (i.e., the owners and writers of option contracts and the speculators and hedgers with futures contracts) seek to close their positions, so price differentials can develop, and computers can spot them. If, for example, the futures price becomes marginally higher than the value of the underlying stocks, the arbitrageurs immediately short the futures and buy the stocks knowing that the differential must disappear in a matter of hours. Conversely, if the values of the stocks rise, the arbitrageurs sell the stocks and buy the futures because any difference between the futures contracts and the underlying stocks must disappear at the expiration of the contracts and the options. The possibility of such arbitrage profits, of course, has the effect of increasing the volume of transactions and driving prices so that any disparity is erased.

The large swings in stock prices may create buying (or shorting) opportunities in individual stocks if they become under- or overvalued. Evidence exists that large price changes in individual stocks on the triple witching day are quickly erased during trading on the day after the expiration date. This is, of course, consistent with efficient markets. If, for some reason, an individual stock were to be mispriced, investors would buy or sell the security so that its price would be indicative of what the market believed the security was worth. The unwinding of stock index arbitrage positions can create, albeit briefly, such opportunities.

The volatility of securities prices has raised the question of the desirability of programmed trading. The answer partially revolves around whether programmed trading and index arbitrage are viewed as a cause or as a reaction to other events that are occurring in the securities and futures markets. Consider the case in which speculators believe that the Federal Reserve will ease credit and interest rates will fall. These speculators seek to take long positions and purchase stock index call options and futures contracts. The prices of these contracts rise above the value of the underlying stocks, which triggers programmed selling of futures contracts and large purchases of securities. Stock prices rise dramatically.

The converse applies if speculators expect securities prices to fall. They sell futures contracts that will be transferred to the securities markets. The decline in the futures price would result in programmed trading taking long positions in the futures and short positions in the stocks (i.e., selling stocks). These illustrations, of course, suggest that it is not programmed trading and index arbitrage that are the cause of the changes in stock prices. Instead, it is the speculators who initiated the changes; the programmed trading was only in response to the initial cause.

The existence of index arbitrage is one reason why index futures are followed prior to the opening of the stock market. If index futures are trading higher, that means the stock market will open higher. If the futures are lower, the stock market will open lower. Unfortunately, just because you know that futures are trading higher does not mean that you will be able to take advantage of the information. The market makers will adjust the stocks' prices as trading starts in response to the increased demand resulting from the increase in the futures price. The existence of index arbitrage assures that you will not be able to profit by the price differentials and is another illustration of why financial markets are considered so efficient.

FUTURES FOR DEBT INSTRUMENTS

The previous section covered stock index futures. Futures also exist for debt instruments such as Treasury bills and long-term bonds. Changes in interest rates affect the cost of borrowing and the yields from lending. To reduce the loss from fluctuations in interest rates, borrowers and lenders establish a hedge position to lock in a particular interest rate. Speculators, of course, are not seeking to reduce the risk but to reap large returns from taking risks. The speculators are bearing the risk that the hedgers are seeking to avoid. These speculators try to anticipate the direction of change in interest rates and take a position that will yield profits. The return they earn (if successful) is magnified by the leverage resulting from the small margin requirement necessary to establish the positions.

How financial futures may produce profits for speculators may be illustrated with an example using an interest rate futures contract for the delivery of U.S. Treasury bonds. Suppose a speculator expects interest rates to fall and bond prices to rise. This individual would *buy* a contract for the delivery of Treasury bonds in the future. The individual establishes a *long* position. (Do not confuse yourself; it is easy to get the positions backwards because you anticipate a *decline in interest rates* and the word "decline" implies taking a short position.) If interest rates do fall and bond prices rise, the value of this contract increases because the speculator has the contract for the delivery of bonds at a lower price (i.e., higher yield). If, however, interest rates rise, bond prices fall and the value of this contract declines. The decline in the value of the contract inflicts a loss on the speculator who bought the contract when yields were lower.

If the speculator expects interest rates to rise, that individual *sells* a contract for the future delivery of Treasury bonds (i.e., establishes a *short* position). If interest rates do rise and the value of the bonds declines, the value of this contract must decline, but the speculator earns a profit. This short seller can buy the bonds at a lower price and deliver them at the price specified in the contract. Or the speculator may simply buy a contract at the lower value, thereby closing out the position at a profit. Of course, if this speculator is wrong and interest rates fall, the value of the bonds increases, inflicting a loss on the speculator, who must now pay more to buy the bonds to cover the contract.

CURRENCY FUTURES

Currency futures are contracts for the sale and delivery of a foreign currency such as the British pound. Speculators take positions in anticipation of change in the price of one currency relative to another. Hedgers use the contracts to reduce the risk of loss from the price change. Essentially, currency contracts perform the same role as the contracts for commodities, stock indexes, and debt instruments.

Suppose the dollar price of the British pound is $2. A speculator who anticipates that the price of the pound will rise establishes a long position in the pound. This individual buys a contract for the future delivery of pounds. The futures price may be $2.02 or $1.96. It need not necessarily equal the current, or spot, price. (If many speculators expect the price of the pound to rise, they will bid up the futures price so that it exceeds the current price. If speculators expect the price of the pound to fall, they will then drive down the futures price.) If this speculator buys the futures contract for $2.02 and is correct (i.e., the price of the pound rises), that individual makes a profit. If, for example, the price of the pound were to rise to $2.20, the value of the contract may rise by $0.18 per pound, that is, $2.20 − $2.02. (At expiration the futures and spot prices must be equal. Thus, if the pound is $2.20 on the expiration date, the value of the contract must be $2.20 per pound.) Of course, if the speculator is wrong and the price of the pound declines to $1.80, the value of the contract also declines, and the speculator suffers a loss.

A speculator who anticipated a decline in the value of the pound would establish a short position and sell contracts for the future delivery of pounds. If the speculator is right and the value of the pound declines, he or she may close the position for a profit. Since pounds are now worth less, the speculator may buy the cheaper pounds and deliver them at the higher price specified in the contract. (Actually the speculator would close the short position by buying an offsetting contract for the future delivery of pounds.) If the speculator had been wrong and the price of the pound had risen, that individual would have suffered a loss, as it would have cost more to buy the pounds to make the future delivery required by the contract.

Currency Futures and Risk Reduction through Hedging with Currency Futures

Currency futures offer individuals a means to speculate on price changes, but their use as a means to hedge exchange rate fluctuations is probably more important. American investors who acquire foreign securities and American firms that invest abroad have to bear the risk associated with fluctuations in exchange rates. Currency futures offer a means to manage that risk.

If the prices of currencies were stable, there would be little risk associated with investing in another country. Such is not the case, as is illustrated in Figure 19.3, which

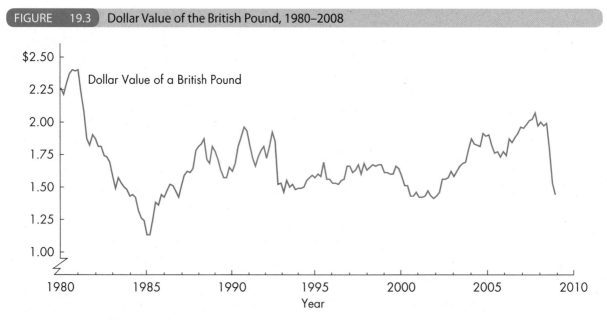

FIGURE   19.3   Dollar Value of the British Pound, 1980–2008

Source: Federal Reserve (**http://www.federalreserve.gov**).

plots the price of the British pound from 1980 through 2008. Consider the price decline experienced in 2008. The pound fell from $2.00 to less than $1.50, a decline in excess of 25 percent. A decline of that magnitude would easily wipe out most positive returns earned on assets denominated in British pounds. If the investors or firms that held the assets established hedged positions, the gains on the hedges would offset (or at least partially offset) the losses from the decline in the dollar value of the pound.

To see how such a hedge works, consider the following example. You purchase 100 shares of stock for £50 a share (£5,000). The pound is currently worth $2.00, so the dollar value of the stock is $10,000. Since you are long in the stock (and hence long in the pound), you need to be short in the futures if you want to hedge against a decline in the pound (i.e., you short pounds). The futures price of the pound is $2.02, that is, $1.00 = £0.4951. (In this example, the futures price exceeds the current or spot price. The converse, in which the futures price is less than the spot price, is also possible.) To establish the short position, you enter into a contract to deliver £5,000 at $2.02. The value of this contract is 5,000 × $2.02 = $10,100, which is almost the same as the value of stock.

Suppose the price of the stock does not change, but the price of the pound declines to $1.90. You have lost nothing on the stock; its price remains £50, but £5,000 are now worth $9,500(5,000 × $1.90). If you were to sell the stock and convert the pounds back to dollars, you would lose $500. The value of the futures contract, however, must have also declined. If the price of the pound is $1.90, the contract is worth $9,500. You could purchase £5,000 for $9,500, deliver them for $2.02 a pound ($10,100), and make $600 on the transaction. The gain on the short in the futures more than offsets the loss from the decline in the dollar value of the pound.

Suppose the price of the stock does not change, but the price of the pound rises to $2.20. You have lost nothing on the stock; its price remains £50, but £5,000 are worth $11,000(5,000 × $2.20). If you were to sell the stock and convert the pounds back to dollars, you would gain $1,000. The value of the futures contract, however, would have also risen. If the price of the pound is now $2.20, the contract is worth $11,000. You would have to pay $11,000 to purchase £5,000, but receive only $10,100($2.02 × 5,000). You would lose $900 on the future contract. The loss on the short in the futures consumes most of the gain from the appreciation in the value of the pound.

A British investor who acquires American stock would follow the opposite strategy. Suppose this investor buys 200 shares of a $50 stock ($10,000). If the price of the dollar is £0.50, the cost of the stock is £5,000($10,000/0.5). He or she will sustain a loss if the value of the pound rises (dollar declines). For example, suppose the price of the stock remains $50, but the pound rises from $2.00 to $2.20. The value of the dollar declines from £0.50(1/$2) to £0.4545(1/$2.20). The 200 shares are now worth £4,545[(200 shares × $50)/2.20]. The British investor sustains a loss of £455(£4,545 − £5,000) when the dollars are converted back to pounds.

To hedge against this loss, the investor enters into a futures contract. This individual has a long position in U.S. securities and enters into a short position in dollars (a long position in pounds). That is, the investor enters into a contract to purchase pounds (deliver dollars). Such a contract rises if the value of the dollar declines. If the investor enters into a contract to sell $10,000 when the future price is £1.00 = $2.02, the value of the contract is £4,950($10,000/2.02). If the value of the dollar declines to £1.00 = $2.20, the stock is worth £4,545 [(200 shares × $50)/2.20]. The British investor, however, may buy $10,000 for £4,545($10,000/2.2) and deliver them for £4,950. The £405 gain almost offsets the £455 loss from the decline in the value of the dollar.

You should notice that in these examples, the investors did not completely hedge their positions. In the first example, the investor had a net gain, and in the second there was a net loss. This inability to hedge completely may result from (1) the difference between the spot price and the futures price or (2) the difference between the size of the contract and the amount invested in the foreign security. Even if investors are unable to hedge completely and to offset exactly the potential loss, the hedge reduces the potential loss from the change in the exchange rate. Many portfolio managers with foreign exchange exposure and corporate financial managers whose firms have foreign operations often use hedging to reduce a substantial amount of the risk associated with fluctuations in exchange rates.

SWAPS

swap

An agreement to exchange payments.

In addition to options and futures, another derivative is the swap. A **swap** is an agreement between two parties who contract to exchange (i.e., swap) payments. A swap is as if I agree to pay your electric bill if you will agree to pay my phone bill. We agree to trade payments. Individuals rarely, if ever, swap payments, but firms and financial institutions often participate in the swap market. Firms make their profits through operations and not from speculating on anticipated price changes. To reduce the risk of loss from price changes, management may enter into a swap agreement. Since accounting disclosure requires swaps to be discussed in annual reports, the investor needs to understand swaps and how corporations use these derivatives to manage the firm's risk exposure.

Currency and Interest Rate Swaps

There are a variety of swap agreements between firms. For example, two firms may swap payments in different currencies (a currency swap). In another case, one firm swaps a series of fixed payments for a series of variable payments. The opposing firm (called the *counterparty*) swaps the variable payments and receives the fixed payments.

The large increase in foreign investments and foreign operations by global firms has greatly increased the use of swap agreements to manage exchange rate risk. Consider a U.S. firm with operations in the United Kingdom that is required to make payments in British pounds. The dollar value of the payments will rise if the pound increases (dollar declines), but the dollar value declines if the pound decreases (dollar increases). The converse is true for a British firm with American operations that must make payments in dollars. Earnings, however, can be increased or *decreased* by fluctuations in the value of the foreign currencies.

One means to reduce the risk of loss is to hedge using the currency futures discussed earlier in this chapter. Swapping payments is another means to reduce the foreign exchange risk. The British firm agrees to make the American firm's required payments in pounds, and the American firm agrees to make the British firm's dollar payments. Since both firms are now making the payments in their native currency, neither has the risk associated with changes in the exchange rate. If the dollar rises (pound falls), the effect on both firms is immaterial.

Swaps involving funds borrowed abroad may also reduce interest expense. Suppose an American firm can borrow in the United States under favorable terms but needs the funds in England where the cost of the loan will be greater. A British firm can borrow in England at a lower rate but needs the funds in the United States. In both cases the firm saves interest expense if it borrows in the domestic market. However, since the funds are needed abroad, they will have to be converted into the local currency. Once converted, the firm now faces exchange rate risk when the funds are exchanged back to retire the loans.

If the American firm could borrow in the United States and the British firm could borrow in England and then agree to swap the liabilities, each firm would have a loan denominated in its currency. To accomplish this swap, the firms use a swap dealer (usually a large financial institution, such as a major commercial bank) who charges a fee for the service. The American firm issues dollar-denominated debt and passes the funds to the dealer. The dealer, in turn, passes the funds to the British firm. Simultaneously, the British firm issues debt denominated in pounds and passes the funds to the dealer, who passes the funds to the American firm.

The British firm now pays interest in pounds, and the American firm pays interest in dollars. The net effect is that the American firm has a dollar-denominated debt on its balance sheet but is able to use pounds. Since the debt is denominated in dollars by the swap agreement, there is no exchange rate risk. In addition, the interest expense may actually be lower if the firm is able to issue debt domestically at a lower interest rate. The converse is true for the British firm, which has borrowed in pounds but can use dollars.

For this swap to occur, both parties must perceive a benefit and the amounts must be comparable. The potential benefits are (1) potential savings in interest expense, (2) reduction in exchange rate risk, or (3) a combination of both. By acting as an intermediary, the swap dealer facilitates the creation of the swap. For this service, the dealer receives a fee.

The potential benefits may be seen by the following simple example in which an American firm needs £625,000 and a British firm needs $1,000,000. A pound costs $1.60. (Conversely, $1.00 buys £0.625.) Given this exchange rate, $1,000,000 equals £625,000. The American firm can borrow $1,000,000 from a domestic bank at 6 percent but must pay 7 percent if it borrows £625,000 from a British bank. The interest payment will be £43,750, and the loan will be denominated in pounds. The British firm can borrow £625,000 for 6 percent in the United Kingdom but must pay 8 percent for $1,000,000 in the United States. The interest cost will be $80,000, and the loan will be denominated in dollars.

In this case, there is an interest savings if the two firms swap obligations. A swap dealer arranges the swap in which each firm borrows the funds in the domestic market and exchanges the obligations. The American firm has the use of £625,000 with an interest cost of £37,500. The interest savings is £6,250, which is $10,000 at the current exchange rate. The British firm has the use of $1,000,000 with an interest cost of $60,000. The interest savings is $20,000, which is £12,500 at the current exchange rate. There is a net interest savings to both firms from the swap.

The previous example illustrates the potential interest savings if each party can borrow at a lower interest cost in a particular market. The next example illustrates the reduction of exchange rate risk. Assume the amounts borrowed and the exchange rate are the same as in the previous example, and the interest rate is 6 percent for both parties in both markets. (Equal interest rates remove the savings from interest payments, so the impact of changing exchange rates is highlighted.) Under these assumptions the American firm borrows $1,000,000 at 6 percent ($60,000 interest payment) and the British firm borrows £625,000 at 6 percent (£37,500 interest payment). The firms swap the funds so both firms get the use of the money in the foreign currency.

Suppose after a year when the loan is repaid, the exchange rate is $1.00 = £0.50 (£1.00 = $2.00). The American firm pays $1,060,000 to retire the loan. If the firm had borrowed £625,000, it would owe £625,000 + £3,750 = £628,750. The cost in dollars of the pounds would be $1,257,500. The savings from the swap is $197,500. The British firm pays £628,750 to retire the loan. If the firm had borrowed $1,000,000, it would owe $1,060,000, which would have cost £530,000. The British firm has lost an opportunity to gain £98,750 ($197,500) from the increased value of the pound. However, the British firm has also avoided any loss that would have occurred if the dollar had risen in value. (The American firm has also lost the opportunity to gain from an increase in the value of the dollar.)

Since firms are generally in business to generate profits from operations and not from exchange rate fluctuations, many firms with international operations participate in swap agreements. For example, in its *2000 Annual Report*, Coca-Cola stated that it had currency swap agreements at the end of 2000 totaling $580,000,000 and that all derivative activities using interest rate swaps, currency swaps, and commodity futures contracts were to manage risk. Without the existence of these derivatives (options, futures, swaps), a firm's exposure to fluctuations in foreign exchange, interest rates, and commodity prices would be increased.

Equity Swaps

In addition to interest rate swaps and currency swaps, there are also equity swaps in which investors swap payments based on a stock index. Consider Investor A with a substantial portfolio of stocks who expects their prices to decline and who would like to move into debt securities. The sale of the stocks may generate taxable gains and will involve transaction costs (commissions). Investor B has substantial holdings of debt securities and anticipates that stock prices will rise. Investor B would like to sell the bonds and purchase stocks. However, the bonds may be illiquid (especially if they are nontaxable municipal bonds) and the sales will involve transaction costs. These two investors could execute a swap agreement that meets each investor's needs.

To see how this equity swap works, assume an amount such as $1,000,000 (the notational principal). If the interest rate is 10 percent, the $1,000,000 earns $100,000 annually. Investor A, who wants the bonds, agrees to pay Investor B the return on the S&P 500 stock index. If the index rises by 5 percent, A pays $50,000($1,000,000 × 0.05). Investor B, who wants the stocks, agrees to pay Investor A $100,000 annually. For each year during which the swap agreement is in effect, Investor A receives $100,000 from Investor B and pays B an amount based on the S&P return. If the S&P 500 rises by 10 percent, A pays B $100,000 and B pays A $100,000, so the amounts cancel. The following table sets out other possible cash flows between the two investors based on the return on the stock index.

Cash Flows Investor A

S&P 500 Return	Payment to B	Payment from B	Net
15%	$150,000	$100,000	($50,000)
4	40,000	100,000	60,000
−3	−30,000	100,000	130,000

Cash Flows Investor B

S&P 500 Return	Payment to A	Payment from A	Net
15%	$100,000	$150,000	$50,000
4	100,000	40,000	(60,000)
−3	100,000	−30,000	(130,000)

If the S&P return is 15 percent, A receives $100,000 but must pay $150,000, so there is a net cash outflow of $50,000 to B. If the S&P return is 4 percent, A receives $100,000 but has to pay only $40,000, so A nets $60,000. In the case when the S&P return is −3 percent, A receives $100,000 from B plus an additional $30,000 because the index return is negative.

Investor B's cash flows are, of course, the mirror image of A's. When the return on the S&P index exceeds 10 percent, Investor A's payments to B exceed the $100,000 B has agreed to make. B then receives a net cash inflow. If the S&P return is less than 10 percent, B's payments to A exceed the cash received, and B experiences a net cash outflow. Actually, only the net cash flow payments are made. If the return on the market is 15 percent, there is no need for A to pay B $150,000 and for B to pay A $100,000. Only the net cash flow payment is made, which in this case would be the $50,000 payment from A to B.

What advantage does this swap offer each investor? The answer is that the swap approximates what would have happened if the parties had made their portfolio changes. Suppose A had sold $1,000,000 worth of stock to buy the 10 percent bonds and the market rose 15 percent. The investor would earn $100,000 in interest but had an opportunity loss of $150,000 in capital appreciation. By entering the swap, the investor experiences a cash outflow of $50,000, so the end result is essentially the same, except the investor avoided all the transaction costs associated with securities sales and subsequent purchases and avoided all the tax consequences of the sales.

From B's perspective, selling the bonds would have resulted in forgoing $100,000 in interest but the stock purchases would have generated $150,000 in appreciation. The net difference is the $50,000, which is essentially the same as the $50,000 cash inflow from the swap. By executing the swap, Investor B avoided the transaction costs and any marketability or liquidity problems associated with selling the debt instruments.

In this illustration, the swap occurred when two investors wanted to alter their portfolios from equity to debt (and vice versa). Other possible equity swaps may occur if investors want to move from one sector to another or to alter their exposure to foreign securities. For example, one investor wants to reduce holdings of large cap stocks in favor of small cap stocks, while another investor wants fewer small cap stocks in favor of large cap stocks. In this case, a swap is based on indexes of large and small

⊕ **Point of Interest**

CREDIT DEFAULT SWAPS

A credit default swap is a contract in which one party, the buyer, makes a series of payments to the seller for protection against a lender defaulting. These swaps were at the center stage of the financial crises of 2008–2009. While not precluded, individual investors rarely, if ever, participate in the market for credit default swaps. However, their impact on the financial markets during the crises had a major affect on individuals' investments and returns.

Credit default swaps are relatively easy to understand. Suppose an investor, such as endowment fund or pension plan, buys debt obligations, such as bonds issued by Company X. The purpose of the investment is to generate interest income but the investor (the lender) is at risk if Company X were to default. The investor then enters into an agreement with a third party (Bank A or Insurance Company Y) to bear the risk. The investor makes payments to the third party, who accepts the risk. If the creditor (Company A) were to default, the third party (e.g., Insurance Company Y) compensates the original investor for the losses.

The purchase of the credit default swap is often used as a hedging strategy. While the purpose is to hedge the risk of loss, the strategy also reduces the return. The investor who purchases the credit default swap nets a lower return since the payments reduce the cash flow generated by the investment. The price paid for the swap is one measure of the perceived risk. As the risk increases, the amount of the payment also increases, as the seller has to be compensated for bearing the additional risk.

While investors may acquire credit default swaps as a hedging tool, they may also buy or sell them as a speculative tool. If an investor anticipates default, that individual or financial institution will purchase the swap. The buyer does not have to own the underlying security on which the swap it based, so the position is not a hedge. It is a speculation on the default. If the borrower were to default, the buyer of the swap profits from receiving the payment from the seller. Of course, if an investor were to anticipate that the borrower will *not* default, that individual would *sell* the swap and collect the payments from the buyer. Both parties to the swap cannot be right; one of the parties to the agreement has to sustain a loss.

Once created, a secondary market can develop in the swap agreements. If one investor buys the swap, that party can sell it to another individual or financial institution. The second buyer now assumes the payments and receives the compensation if the borrower were to default. The seller of the swap may also sell the agreement, in which case the seller no longer receives the payments but is no longer at risk. The prices of these secondary sales should mirror the perceived risks at the time of the sale and that price may not be the price that existed when the credit default swap was initially created.

cap stocks. The investor who wants the large cap stocks would receive payments based on the large cap index and make payments based on the performance of the small cap index. The investor wanting greater exposure to small cap stocks would make and receive the opposite payments (i.e., receive payments based on the small cap index and make payments based on the large cap index).

The same basic principle applies to equity swaps involving foreign securities. Consider an American investor who wants to diversify by including foreign securities. Simultaneously, a foreign investor wants to diversify by owning American securities. Instead of each investor acquiring foreign securities, a swap is arranged. The American investor would receive payment based on an index of foreign securities and make payments based on an index of American securities. The foreign investor would make payments based on his or her domestic index and receive payments based on the performance of the index of American securities. The American investor will receive a net cash inflow if the foreign index generates the higher return but will have to make payments if the foreign index has the lower return. That is essentially the same result that would have occurred if American stocks had been sold to buy foreign stocks. Higher returns abroad would have resulted in an increased return to the American investor, while lower returns abroad would have produced lower returns. The swap agreement achieves a similar result without having to buy and sell individual stocks.

SUMMARY

Investing in futures involves entering contracts for future delivery. The speculator may take a long position, which is the purchase of a contract for future delivery, or a short position, which is the sale of a contract for future delivery. The long position generates profits if the price rises, while the short position results in a gain if the price falls.

Commodity and financial futures contracts are purchased through brokers who own seats on commodity exchanges. The contracts are supported by deposits, which are called *margin*, that signify the investor's good faith. The margin requirement is only a small fraction of the value of the contract, and this produces considerable potential for leverage. A small change in the price of the commodity produces a large profit or loss relative to the small amount of margin. For this reason, commodity contracts are considered very speculative.

Hedging plays an important role in commodity futures markets. Growers, miners, and users of commodities often wish to reduce their risk of loss from price fluctuations and thus hedge their positions. Growers sell contracts for future delivery, and users buy contracts for future delivery. Frequently, it is the speculators who are buying and offering the contracts sought by the hedgers. In this way the risks that the hedgers seek to reduce are passed on to the speculators.

Besides commodity futures there are financial futures, currency futures, and stock index futures. Financial futures are contracts for the delivery of financial assets, such as U.S. Treasury bills and bonds. Currency futures are contracts for the future delivery of foreign moneys, such as Japanese yen or British pounds. Stock index futures are based on a broad measure of the market (e.g., the New York Stock Exchange Composite Index). Speculators who anticipate movements in interest rates, foreign currencies, or the stock market can speculate on these anticipated price changes by taking appropriate positions in futures contracts. As with all commodity contracts, the potential return may be quite large, but the risk of loss is also large. Speculating in commodity futures is probably best left to those few investors who understand these potential risks and can afford to take them.

The creation of stock index futures and the rise of programmed trading have resulted in stock index arbitrage. When the value of a stock index futures contract deviates from the value of the underlying stocks in the index, an opportunity for arbitrage is created. If the value of the contract exceeds the value of the shares, arbitrageurs will short the contracts and buy the shares. The converse occurs when the value of the contract is less than the value of the shares, in which case the arbitrageurs buy the futures and sell the shares. These transactions are done simultaneously through the use of computers that are preprogrammed to enter the buy and sell orders when a divergence between the stock index futures and the stock index develops.

The combining of stock index futures and programmed trading links the securities and futures markets. Changes in one are quickly transferred to the other. This linkage has resulted in significant swings in the prices of individual stocks when the arbitrageurs enter large numbers of buy or sell orders.

A swap is an agreement in which two parties agree to exchange payments. Swap agreements are not a method to increase profits but a means to manage risk, especially exchange rate or interest rate risk. A firm with operations in a foreign country may swap payments with a firm in that country to avoid having to convert one currency to another. A firm that is required to make fixed payments but would prefer to make variable payments may swap the fixed payments with a firm that is obligated to make variable payments. As a result of the swap both firms may be better able to match their cash inflows with required payments.

QUESTIONS

1. What is a futures contract? What are the spot price and the futures price of a commodity? When must the two prices be equal?
2. What is the difference between a long and a short position in a commodity future?
3. What is margin and why is it a source of leverage? What is a margin call? How does margin for futures differ from margin for stocks?
4. Why do farmers and other users of commodity futures hedge their positions?
5. If an investor anticipates a decline in a commodity's price, which futures position should he or she take?
6. How may government intervention affect commodity prices? Are commodity futures markets subject to government regulation?
7. What is a financial futures contract? If you expect interest rates to rise, should you buy or sell a financial futures contract?
8. If you anticipated that the price of the British pound would rise and wanted to speculate on that increase, should you sell or buy a contract for the delivery of pounds?
9. What is the difference between the long and the short positions in a contract for the future delivery of the S&P 500 stock index? If you expect stock prices to fall, do you buy or sell stock index futures?
10. How do changes in the futures market for stock indexes affect the stock market? Why may stock index futures and programmed trading result in dramatic price changes in individual stocks?
11. How does the swapping of payments reduce a firm's risk exposure? When would an individual find it desirable to enter a swap agreement?
12. a) Wheat is traded on which exchange(s), and what is the size of the unit of trading? What is the margin requirement (or "performance bond")? What are the spot price and the futures prices of contacts for one month, three months, and six months?
    b) After a week has elapsed repeat Question (a). What are the price changes in the underlying commodity and the contracts? If you had taken a long position in each contract, what are the percentage changes in the spot price, the contracts, and the return on your margin?

c) Stock index options based on the S&P 500 are traded on which exchange? What are the spot and futures prices for one month, three months, and six months? Based on the unit of trading, what are the values of the contracts?

d) After one week has elapsed, what are the spot and futures prices of the contracts in Question (c)? Was the percentage change in the prices greater for the spot price or the contracts?

To help you answer these questions, consult the following sites:

Kansas City Board of Trade http://www.kcbt.com
Chicago Mercantile Exchange http://www.cme.com

PROBLEMS

1. The futures price of corn is $2.00. The contracts are for 10,000 bushels, so a contract is worth $20,000. The margin requirement is $2,000 a contract, and the maintenance margin requirement is $1,200. A speculator expects the price of the corn to fall and enters into a contract to sell corn.
   a) How much must the speculator initially remit?
   b) If the futures price rises to $2.13, what must the speculator do?
   c) If the futures price continues to rise to $2.14, how much does the speculator have in the account?

2. The futures price of gold is $1,050. Futures contracts are for 100 ounces of gold, and the margin requirement is $5,000 a contract. The maintenance margin requirement is $1,500. You expect the price of gold to rise and enter into a contract to buy gold.
   a) How much must you initially remit?
   b) If the futures price of gold rises to $1,055, what is the profit and percentage return on your position?
   c) If the futures price of gold declines to $1,048, what is the loss and percentage return on the position?
   d) If the futures price falls to $1,038, what must you do?
   e) If the futures price continues to decline to $1,010, how much do you have in your account?
   f) How do you close your position?

3. The futures price of British pounds is $2.00. Futures contracts are for £10,000, so a contract is worth $20,000. The margin requirement is $2,000 a contract, and the maintenance market requirement is $1,200. A speculator expects the price of the pound to fall and enters into a contract to sell pounds.
   a) How much must the speculator initially remit?
   b) If the futures price rises to $2.13, what must the speculator do?
   c) If the futures price continues to rise to $2.14, how much does the speculator have in the account?

4. You expect to receive a payment of £1,000,000 in British pounds after six months. The pound is currently worth $1.60 (i.e., £1 = $1.60), but the six-month futures price is $1.56 (i.e., £1 = $1.56). You expect the price of the pound to decline (i.e., the value of the dollar to rise). If this expectation is fulfilled, you will suffer a loss

when the pounds are converted into dollars when you receive them six months in the future.

    a) Given the current price, what is the expected payment in dollars?

    b) Given the futures price, how much would you receive in dollars?

    c) If, after six months, the pound is worth $1.35, what is your loss from the decline in the value of the pound?

    d) To avoid this potential loss, you decide to hedge and sell a contract for the future delivery of pounds at the going futures price of $1.56. What is the cost to you of this protection from the possible decline in the value of the pound?

    e) If, after hedging, the price of the pound falls to $1.35, what is the maximum amount that you lose? Why is your answer different from your answer to part (c)?

    f) If, after hedging, the price of the pound rises to $1.80, how much do you gain from your position?

    g) How would your answer to part (f) be different if you had not hedged and the price of the pound had risen to $1.80?

5. A portfolio manager owns a bond worth £2,000,000 that will mature in one year. The pound is currently worth $1.65, and the one-year future price is $1.61. If the value of the pound were to fall, the portfolio manager would sustain a loss. If the value of the pound were to rise, the portfolio manager would experience a profit.

    a) What is the expected payment based on the current exchange rate?

    b) What is the expected payment based on the futures exchange rate?

    c) If, after a year, the pound is worth $1.53, what is the loss from the decline in the value of the pound?

    d) If, after a year, the pound is worth $1.72, what is the gain from the increase in the value of the pound?

    e) To avoid the potential loss in part (c) the portfolio manager hedges by selling futures contracts for the delivery of pounds at $1.61. What is the cost of the protection from a decline in the value of the pound?

    f) If, after hedging, the price of the pound falls to $1.53, what is the maximum amount the portfolio manager can lose? Why is this answer different from the answer to part (c) above?

    g) If, after hedging, the price of the pound rises to $1.72, what is the maximum amount the portfolio manager can gain? Why is this answer different from the answer to part (d) above?

6. You expect the stock market to decline, but instead of selling stocks short, you decide to sell a stock index futures contract based on an index of New York Stock Exchange common stocks. The index is currently 600 and the contract has a value that is $250 times the amount of the index. The margin requirement is $2,000 and the maintenance margin requirement is $1,000.

    a) When you sell the contract, how much must you put up?

    b) What is the value of the contract based on the index?

    c) If after one week of trading the index stands at 601, what has happened to your position? How much have you lost or profited?

    d) If the index rose to 607, what would you be required to do?

    e) If the index declined to 594 (1 percent from the starting value), what is your percentage profit or loss on your position?

    f) If you had purchased the contract instead of selling it, how much would you have invested?

    g) If you had purchased the contract and the index subsequently rose from 600 to 607, what would be your required investment?

    h) Contrast your answers to parts (d) and (g).

7. One use for futures markets is "price discovery," that is, the futures price mirrors the current consensus of the future price of the commodity. The current price of gold is $950 but you expect the price to rise to $1,000. If the futures price were $990, what would you do? If your expectation is fulfilled, what is your profit? If the futures price were $1,018, what would you do? What futures price will cause you to take no action? Why?

8. The current price of wheat is $3.70 and the expenses for carrying wheat (combined cost of storage, insurance, shipping) are 20 percent of the price. Based on this information, what should be the price of wheat after a year? What would you do if the futures price were $4.55?

9. Two institutional investors execute a swap agreement for $10,000,000 in which one party agrees to remit to the counterparty the return on the EAFE, an index of European, Australasian, and Far Eastern stocks. The counterparty agrees to remit payments based on the return on the S&P 500. During the next four time periods, the returns on the two indexes are as follows:

Period	S&P 500	EAFE
1	5%	12%
2	−5	8
3	15	0
4	−2	−7

What are the cash flows between the two parties for each time period?

The Financial Advisor's Investment Case
Futures to Defer Taxes

One of your most sophisticated investors, Joseph DeLuca, believes that the stock market will decline and hence reduce the value of his substantial portfolio. However, he does not want to sell the stocks, because the sales would generate a substantial federal capital gains tax liability in the current tax year. He recently read that futures may be used to reduce the risk of loss from price changes as well as vehicles designed to speculate on price changes. You have been his personal financial planner for many years, and he has asked you to develop a strategy using futures to achieve his goal of protecting his gains without selling the securities in the current year.

Since DeLuca has a long position in stocks, you realize that he needs a short position in futures to reduce the risk of loss. Since his portfolio is both substantial and well diversified, you decide to limit your choices to index futures. The portfolio is worth several million dollars, but you decide to use $1,000,000 as the basis for all comparisons since any other amount could be expressed as a multiple of $1,000,000. You notice that an index of the market is 100 and there exists a futures contract with a value that is 500 times the index. The margin requirement is $2,000 per contract. You decide that the best means to explain the strategy using futures is to answer a series of questions that illustrate how the futures may be used to meet DeLuca's goal of deferring the tax obligation until the next year while protecting his gains. These questions are as follows:

1. What is the value of the contract in terms of the index?

2. How many contracts would DeLuca have to sell to hedge $1,000,000? Why should DeLuca sell rather than purchase the contracts?

3. How much cash will DeLuca have to put up to meet the margin requirement? If the annual interest rate on money market securities is 6 percent, what is the interest lost from the margin requirement if the position must be maintained for two months?

4. If the market declined by 5 percent, what will happen to the value of the contracts? Could DeLuca take funds out of the position to reduce the interest lost?

5. If the beta of his portfolio is 1.0 and the market declines by 5 percent, how much would he lose on a $1,000,000 portfolio?

6. If the beta of the portfolio were less than 1.0, could DeLuca hedge his position by selling fewer contracts? If the beta were 0.75, how many contracts would be necessary to hedge the portfolio?

7. Suppose the beta of the portfolio is 0.75 and DeLuca sells 15 contracts. The market then rises by 10 percent; what are the profits and losses on the portfolio and on the contracts? What is the net profit or loss?

8. When the contracts expire, will DeLuca have to deliver the securities he owns to cover the contracts?

9. Does the strategy of using futures contracts achieve its objective?

PART
Six

An Overview

This textbook began by specifying the importance of financial planning, the establishment of financial goals, and the construction of a well-diversified portfolio to meet those goals. Over time that portfolio should generate a positive return, but it also requires the investor to bear risk. While risk may be managed, it cannot be eliminated.

The return depends on the individual assets in the portfolio and the allocation of various assets classes within the portfolio. This last chapter reviews these concepts. There is nothing new in this chapter. Instead, it serves to tie the pieces together.

CHAPTER 20

Investing and Portfolio Management in an Efficient Market Context

Benjamin Britten, in his *Young Person's Guide to the Orchestra*, individually illustrates the instruments of the symphony orchestra. Then Britten reconstructs the orchestra one instrument at a time and ends the work with a glorious fugue that combines all the instruments. In a manner similar to Britten's fugue, the investor combines individual assets to construct a portfolio. Although the individual may acquire one asset at a time, they are all blended together into a portfolio designed to meet the investor's financial goals.

PORTFOLIO CONSTRUCTION AND FINANCIAL PLANNING

As was introduced in the first chapter, portfolio construction is a process in which the individual specifies financial goals, identifies financial resources and obligations, and allocates the assets into a diversified portfolio. Of course, this process is affected by external considerations such as the expectation of inflation and taxation. In addition, changes in the individual's economic or family environment can have an important impact on financial goals. These changes affect the individual's financial plan and the allocation of assets in the portfolio.

Investing can be exciting, especially when you are young and have few obligations. As a graduate student I would randomly buy stocks trading for $2 or less on the American Stock Exchange and sell them after they rose 50 cents. I made money, but no one pointed out how the market rose during that time period and that the prices of junk stocks also tend to increase with the market. I then started to select stocks on the basis on my "knowledge" and lost what I had previously gained. But these gains and loses were of little importance since I did not have a family to support, and retirement was eons into the future.

Of course, my situation changed. Within a few years, I had a family with small children, a house, a mortgage, and so forth, and my perception of investing changed. In effect, I was forced to start making a financial plan and specifying financial goals.

My portfolio became more diversified and my financial assets were allocated over various classes of securities that included both stocks for growth and bonds in my retirement account.

If you manage your own assets or the portfolios of others, several processes simultaneously occur, and they are certainly more sophisticated than my randomly selecting low priced stock. The first is the specification of financial goals and the determination of the asset allocation to achieve those goals. That is, you allocate your resources among the alternatives and construct a portfolio designed to meet your objectives. This requires that you determine which specific assets to include in the portfolio. Of course, an individual's financial resources and willingness to bear risk affect the asset allocation and the selection of which assets to include in the portfolio.

All assets require that you bear risk in order to earn a return. While risk emanates from a variety of sources, there are only two sources of return: income and capital gains. Both sources of return are subject to taxation, and the portfolio's performance should be assessed. Such assessment is necessary to identify possible changes that may improve the investor's ability to meet the specified financial objectives. A summary of this portfolio process is provided in the following flowchart:

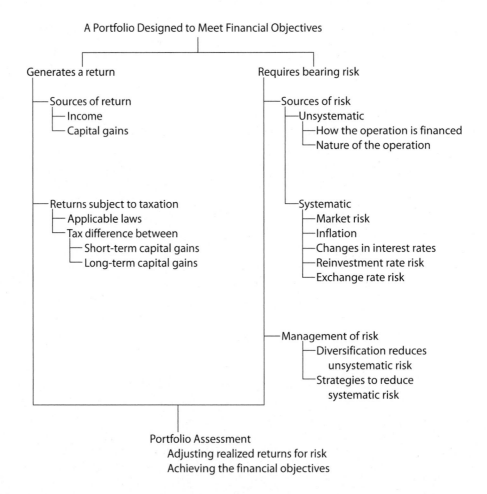

By systematically constructing a portfolio and assessing its performance, the individual investor should be able to achieve the specified financial objectives.

THE IMPORTANCE OF RISK

The number of available assets is so large that no one could possible know them all. In addition, the individual may follow a variety of investment strategies or techniques to select individual assets. Just as you could not possibly know all the specific assets, you could not follow all the strategies. Investing requires making choices. For example, if you are relatively young, you may choose a small cap strategy that involves more risk but offers a higher potential return. But you would then have to make another decision: which individual small cap stocks to purchase. Or you might decide not to buy individual stocks but to acquire shares in a mutual fund with a small cap portfolio or an exchange-traded fund based on an index of small cap stocks.

The allocation of your assets and the investment strategies you employ affect the returns you earn and the risk you bear. Each strategy involves risk. As there is risk associated with each individual asset, there is also the risk associated with each strategy used to select stocks and bonds. To continue the previous example, if you buy small cap stocks, you still must bear the risk associated with that strategy. Even if you diversify away the risk associated with individual small cap stocks, the risk associated with a small cap strategy continues to exist.

Risk also applies to your methods for selecting individual stocks. If you believe that insider trading forecasted movements in stock prices, you could purchase and sell stocks on the basis of insider trading. This method requires the identification of companies whose shares are being bought or sold by insiders. You have to bear the risk associated with using insider trading to select individual stocks. If the method is correct, you should do well. But if it does not work or you apply it incorrectly, the opposite may occur. The same principal applies to the use of a technical indicator such as the tendency of a stock's price to follow a trend within support and resistance lines. If markets are inefficient and you apply the indicator correctly, you may earn a higher return.

Asset-specific risk is reduced and perhaps erased through the construction of a well-diversified portfolio. The risks that remain are the nondiversifiable risks such as movements in the market or inflation or exchange rates. This principle of risk reduction also applies to investment strategies and methods used to select individual assets. Techniques such as insider trading rules and support and resistance lines require that you bear risk. Unless you are willing to accept the risk associated with a particular technique, constructing a portfolio based on several investment strategies reduces the risk associated with each technique.

THE IMPORTANCE OF MARKET EFFICIENCY

As you add more strategies, investment styles, asset classes, or methods for selecting securities, the impact of each on the portfolio declines. You, in effect, diversify away the potential each offers. The portfolio become more like an index portfolio, and the return should mirror the market return. Such mirroring of the market is what the efficient market hypothesis suggests will happen as you construct a well-diversified portfolio. Your return primarily depends on the portfolio's asset allocation and not on your methods for selecting individual assets.

As is discussed in several places in this text, some individuals believe that financial markets are not efficient. For example, it has been suggested that the recent occurrence of "bubbles" is proof that the markets are not efficient. The dot.com craze of the 2000s and its subsequent collapse and the large increase in housing values during the mid 2000s followed by declining home values, mortgage defaults, and foreclosures are often given as illustrations of bubbles. Some analysts suggest that the existence of these bubbles and the large swings in securities prices are indication that financial markets are not efficient.

The essence of the argument that bubbles invalidate the efficient market hypothesis rests on the following points: The efficient market hypothesis is built on the concepts that investors are rational and that prices are the result of investors correctly processing current information and discounting future cash flows. The assertion that the existence of price bubbles proves market are inefficient is based on the premise that participants are acting irrationally and prices could not be the result of discounting cash flows.

There is no denying that there have been periods of extreme changes in security prices. Individuals can act irrationally. A "herd" instinct certainly influences individuals who fear they will be left behind and appear to act irrationally. In some cases they bid up prices. (See, for instance, the extreme run up in the prices of Boston Chicken, Ariba, and Ask Jeeves in the section on IPOs in Chapter 2.) Prices have also dramatically fallen. For example, the Dow Jones Industrial Average declined from 14280 in 2007 to 6440 in March 2009, a decline in excess of 50 percent. That suggests the typical stock portfolio lost about half its value. While proponents of inefficiency offer these periods as evidence of market inefficiency, supporters of efficiency reply that such volatility is what would occur in an efficient market when there is much uncertainty.

Even if financial markets are not always efficient, an important implication of the efficient market hypothesis remains. Investors cannot expect to outperform the market on a risk-adjusted basis consistently. Here is a fundamental question: Who is responsible for verifying the assertion that financial markets are not efficient? Do you think that proponents of efficiency need to prove that it exists or do you think that the proponents of inefficiency should verify that financial markets are not efficient and that is possible to outperform the market on a consistent basis?

Even believers in inefficient markets admit that it is difficult to beat the market. For instance, Robert A. Haugen emphatically believes that a value strategy produces superior results but admits that "it's hard to beat the market because there is a gale of unpredictable price-driven volatility . . ." (See Robert A. Haugen, *The Inefficient Stock Market*, 2nd ed., Upper Saddle River, NJ: Prentice Hall, 2002, p. 134.) Andrew W. Lo and Jasmina Hasanhodzic interviewed several successful investors who use technical analysis in *The Heretics of Finance* (New York: Bloomberg Press, 2009). Most of the individuals "agreed their practice of technical analysis is based on intuition 10 to 50 percent of the time" (p. xix) and "The most successful . . . are those, who through experience, have gained perceptive insight into how the economy and the markets function" (p. xx). Based on these quotes, you might ask yourself: Do I have that "intuition," "experience," or "perceptive insight"? Do I have the time, motivation, and perseverance to develop them?

If the answer is no, then perhaps you should consider learning about more yourself and steps you may take to increase the probability of making fewer investment errors. Two possible places to start are John Nofsinger's, *The Psychology of Investing*, 3rd ed. (Upper Saddle River, NJ: Prentice Hall, 2008) or Richard Lehman's *Far From Random*, (New York: Bloomberg Press, 2009). It is naive to believe that your investment decisions will be independent of your personal biases and tendencies. Understanding yourself may help you avoid mistakes and make better investment decisions in either an efficient *or* inefficient financial market.

The question of market efficiency will in all likelihood not be answered, but your belief in the degree of market efficiency affects your approach to investing. The stronger the belief in inefficiency, the stronger is the argument for active portfolio management. The existence of anomalies offers hope; the ego of some investors and the excitement associated with investing suggest that some individuals will follow an active trading strategy.

For other investors, however, exceptions to market efficiency may be a diversion. If anomalies are of little use, a passive strategy built around well-diversified mutual funds or exchange-traded funds may be more appropriate. Minimal turnover reduces commission costs, and the fewer realized gains reduce the investor's capital gains tax obligations. For the investor who is convinced that financial markets are *sufficiently* efficient, such a strategy may be the best means to achieve his or her financial goals.

Why, then, is there so much emphasis on those investors who do appear to beat the market? Part of the answer rests with the distribution of returns (consider Figure 20.1). The distribution illustrates portfolio returns for a time horizon, such as a year. The mean (15 percent) represents the return on the market. Individual returns are both above and below the market. The figure indicates that some investors and portfolio

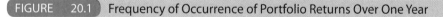

FIGURE 20.1 Frequency of Occurrence of Portfolio Returns Over One Year

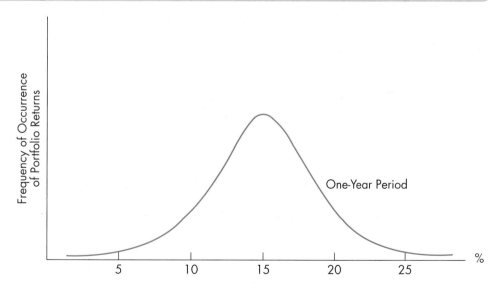

managers did beat the market. There were, of course, some investors and portfolio managers who underperformed the market.

The positive tail clearly suggests that some investors *must outperform the market during a specified time period*. If a portfolio manager does outperform the market, that information is disseminated. Money flows into funds that do well, and a portfolio manager's compensation is often tied both to performance and to the amount of assets under management. Obviously, it is beneficial for portfolio managers and money management firms to capitalize on their success.

The answer is also related to the financial press. Portfolio managers who do exceptionally well often receive publicity and are touted in the popular press. Articles appear in *Money* or *Forbes*. The fund managers may be interviewed on talk shows, and the funds they manage receive "five stars." In a few cases, the portfolio managers develop superstar status. Underperforming portfolio managers, of course, do not receive this kind of publicity.

Although Figure 20.1 presents a distribution for one period, Figure 20.2 adds a distribution for a longer time horizon. During a short period, several investors and portfolio managers do exceptionally well as is illustrated by the flatter distribution, but over longer periods of time, their numbers diminish. The distribution becomes narrower and taller and indicates that more investors earn returns that mirror the markets in which they invested and fewer earn exceptional returns. The positive tail, however, remains. A few, exceptional investors earn higher returns. Perhaps their existence gives false hope to the vast investing public, but these investors and portfolio managers may have exceptional skills that are not transferable to the ordinary investor.

The typical investor, however, should take the concept of efficient financial markets seriously. Instead of trying to emulate the few who have done exceptionally well, most individuals should devote time to developing their financial objectives and constructing

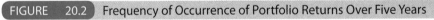

FIGURE 20.2 Frequency of Occurrence of Portfolio Returns Over Five Years

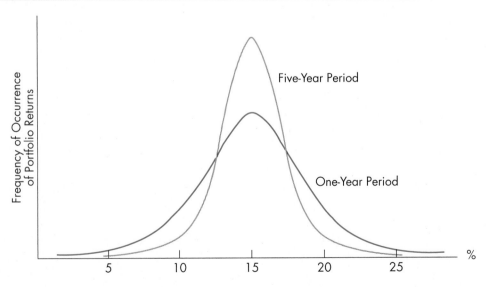

well-diversified portfolios that meet those objectives. Correspondingly, they should spend less time trying to beat the financial markets and not follow the day's investment fad or hot mutual fund.

A large proportion of the material covered in this text can aid in this process of financial planning and investment management even if the information cannot produce superior investment results. This text has described the features of alternative investments, explained factors that affect securities prices, and illustrated many of the analytical tools portfolio managers use to select securities. The text has also argued for the construction of diversified portfolios to reduce the unsystematic risk associated with a specific asset. It is through this construction of well-diversified portfolios and patiently waiting for compounding to work its magic that individuals achieve their financial goals.

The Financial Advisor's Investment Case
Goals and Portfolio Selection

Vanessa Avoletta is a very successful self-employed freelance writer of romantic novels. She has a reputation for writing rapidly and is able to complete at least four books a year, which net after expenses $25,000 to $50,000 per book per year. With this much income, Avoletta is concerned with both sheltering income from taxes and planning for retirement. Currently she is 40 years old, is divorced, and has a child who is entering high school. Avoletta anticipates sending the child to a quality college to pursue a degree in computer sciences.

While Avoletta is intelligent and well informed, she knows very little about finance and investments other than general background material she has used in her novels. Since she does not plan to write prolifically into the indefinite future, she has decided to obtain your help in financial planning.

At your first meeting, you suggested that Avoletta establish a tax-sheltered retirement plan and consider making a gift to her child, perhaps in the form of future royalties from a book in progress. Both of these ideas intrigued Avoletta, who thought that funds were saved, invested to accumulate over time, and then transferred to heirs after death. While Avoletta wanted to pursue both ideas, she thought approaching one at a time made more sense and decided to work on the retirement plan first. She asked you for several alternative courses of action, and you offered the following possibilities.

1. An IRA with a bank with the funds deposited in a variable-rate account.

2. A self-directed Keogh account with a major brokerage firm.
3. A Keogh account with a major mutual fund.
4. An account with a brokerage firm to accumulate common stocks with substantial growth potential but little current income.

Avoletta could not immediately grasp the implications of these alternatives and asked you to clarify several points:

1. What assets would be owned under each alternative?
2. What are the current and future tax obligations associated with each choice?
3. What amount of control would she have over the assets in the accounts?
4. How much personal supervision would be required?

How would you reply to each question? Which course(s) of action would you suggest that she pursue?

Finally, how would each of the following alter your advice?

1. Avoletta has a record of poor health.
2. Avoletta would like to write less and perhaps teach creative writing at a local college.
3. Avoletta has expensive tastes and finds saving to be difficult.

The Financial Advisor's Investment Case
Goals and Asset Allocation

You have new clients, Erik and Senta Bruckner. They are in their mid-30s and have two children, Stella and Chloe, ages 6 and 8. The Bruckners' primary financial objective is to provide for their children's college education. Their secondary objective is to plan for retirement. They own a home with a mortgage and have total family income of $100,000. Senta's employer provides medical insurance and life insurance. She participates in her employer's 401(k) retirement plan and currently has $40,000 in the plan. The funds are invested in her company's stock. Erik is self-employed and works from their home. He has not established a retirement plan. After deducting the amount of the mortgage, the family has total assets of $200,000 available for investing in addition to the $40,000 in the retirement account.

The Bruckners want sufficient liquid assets to cover six months' income as a precaution (0.5 × $100,000 = $50,000). At least 20 percent of the $50,000 should be in exceedingly liquid assets, but the remaining 80 percent may be invested elsewhere provided that the assets meet the objective to provide sufficient liquidity.

The remaining assets ($150,000) are available for other investments. These funds could be allocated in numerous ways. Since the couple is generating income, you expect the Bruckners to conclude that income-producing bonds are not a necessary component of their portfolio. That conclusion, however, is not necessarily correct. Bonds do offer potential diversification and may be included as part of any tax-deferred retirement account. The interest income will not be taxed until the proceeds are removed from the retirement account and the flow of interest income will compound over time. If Senta's employer offers a bond fund as part of the retirement plan, selecting the bond fund instead of the company's stock makes sense from an overall asset allocation perspective.

You decide to develop a sample asset allocation illustration. Once the Bruckners have grasped the concept, you can further subdivide the allocation. The starting amount is $240,000: the $40,000 in the retirement account, the $50,000 needed for liquid assets, and the $150,000 balance. You decide that the retirement account should be invested in bonds and the liquid assets should be in a money market mutual fund that stresses federal government Treasury bills. The balance should be divided equally between large cap and smaller cap stocks. To illustrate the allocation and its possible results over time, prepare answers to the following questions.

1. How much is allocated to each class of assts?
2. The expected returns for each asset class are as follows:

Large company stocks	10%
Small company stocks	12%
Corporate bonds	6%
Treasury bills	3%

How much will be in each account when the girls approach college age ten years from now?
3. Given the terminal values in the previous question, what is the portfolio's asset allocation? What steps should be taken?
4. The expected returns in Question 2 are based on historical returns, but the period 2008–2009 has proven that returns can be much lower than those in Question 2. Suppose the returns on large cap and small cap stocks were only 1.4 and 3.2 percent, respectively. How much would be in the account after ten years? (Assume the yields on corporate bonds and Treasury bills remain 6 percent and 3 percent, respectively.)
5. If the Bruckners do not need the funds to finance their daughters' college educations, how much will be in each account when they approach retirement in their mid-60s under the original allocation? (Use the expected returns in Question 2.)
6. If the rate of inflation is 3 percent, goods and services cost that $100 will cost how much at

their retirement? How much annual income is necessary to maintain the purchasing power of their $100,000 current income?

7. If their combined life expectancy is 15 years at their retirement, can the Bruckners maintain their standard of living if they have the amount determined above and their funds earn 7 percent after they retire? What is the future rate of inflation assumed in your answer? Is that assumption reasonable?

8. Based on the above answers, what are some suggested courses of action the Bruckners should consider taking?

Appendix A

MATHEMATICAL TABLES

The Future Value of $1

The Present Value of $1

The Future Value of an Annuity of $1

The Present Value of an Annuity of $1

The Future Value of $1

Period	1%	2%	3%	4%	5%	6%	7%
1	1.010	1.020	1.030	1.040	1.050	1.060	1.070
2	1.020	1.040	1.061	1.082	1.102	1.124	1.145
3	1.030	1.061	1.093	1.125	1.158	1.191	1.225
4	1.041	1.082	1.126	1.170	1.216	1.262	1.311
5	1.051	1.104	1.159	1.217	1.276	1.338	1.403
6	1.062	1.126	1.194	1.265	1.340	1.419	1.501
7	1.072	1.149	1.230	1.316	1.407	1.504	1.606
8	1.083	1.172	1.267	1.369	1.477	1.594	1.718
9	1.094	1.195	1.305	1.423	1.551	1.689	1.838
10	1.105	1.219	1.344	1.480	1.629	1.791	1.967
11	1.116	1.243	1.384	1.539	1.710	1.898	2.105
12	1.127	1.268	1.426	1.601	1.7496	2.012	2.252
13	1.138	1.294	1.469	1.665	1.886	2.133	2.410
14	1.149	1.319	1.513	1.732	1.980	2.261	2.579
15	1.161	1.346	1.558	1.801	2.079	2.397	2.759
16	1.173	1.373	1.605	1.873	2.183	2.540	2.952
17	1.184	1.400	1.653	1.948	2.292	2.693	3.159
18	1.196	1.428	1.702	2.026	2.407	2.854	3.380
19	1.208	1.457	1.754	2.107	2.527	3.026	3.617
20	1.220	1.486	1.806	2.191	2.653	3.207	3.870
25	1.282	1.641	2.094	2.666	3.386	4.292	5.427
30	1.348	1.811	2.427	3.243	4.322	5.743	7.612

Period	8%	9%	10%	12%	14%	15%	16%
1	1.080	1.090	1.100	1.120	1.140	1.150	1.160
2	1.166	1.188	1.210	1.254	1.300	1.322	1.346
3	1.260	1.295	1.331	1.405	1.482	1.521	1.561
4	1.360	1.412	1.464	1.574	1.689	1.749	1.811
5	1.469	1.539	1.611	1.762	1.925	2.011	2.100
6	1.587	1.677	1.772	1.974	2.195	2.313	2.436
7	1.714	1.828	1.949	2.211	2.502	2.660	2.826
8	1.851	1.993	2.144	2.476	2.853	3.059	3.278
9	1.999	2.172	2.358	2.773	3.252	3.518	3.803
10	2.159	2.367	2.594	3.106	3.707	4.046	4.411
11	2.332	2.580	2.853	3.479	4.226	4.652	5.117
12	2.518	2.813	3.138	3.896	4.818	5.350	5.936
13	2.720	3.066	3.452	4.363	5.492	6.153	6.886
14	2.937	3.342	3.797	4.887	6.261	7.076	7.988
15	3.172	3.642	4.177	5.474	7.138	8.137	9.266
16	3.426	3.970	4.595	6.130	8.137	9.358	10.748
17	3.700	4.328	5.054	6.866	9.276	10.761	12.468
18	3.996	4.717	5.560	7.690	10.575	12.375	14.463
19	4.316	5.142	6.116	8.613	12.056	14.232	16.777
20	4.661	5.604	6.728	9.646	13.743	16.367	19.461
25	6.848	8.623	10.835	17.000	26.462	32.919	40.874
30	10.063	13.268	17.449	29.960	50.950	66.212	85.850

$P_a(1 + i)^n = P_n$ Interest factor $= (1 + i)^n$

The Present Value of $1

Period	1%	2%	3%	4%	5%	6%	7%	8%	9%	10%	12%	14%	15%
1	0.990	0.980	0.971	0.962	0.952	0.943	0.935	0.926	0.917	0.909	0.893	0.877	0.870
2	0.980	0.961	0.943	0.925	0.907	0.890	0.873	0.857	0.842	0.826	0.797	0.769	0.756
3	0.971	0.942	0.915	0.889	0.864	0.840	0.816	0.794	0.772	0.751	0.712	0.675	0.658
4	0.961	0.924	0.889	0.855	0.823	0.792	0.763	0.735	0.708	0.683	0.636	0.592	0.572
5	0.951	0.906	0.863	0.822	0.784	0.747	0.713	0.681	0.650	0.621	0.567	0.519	0.497
6	0.942	0.888	0.838	0.790	0.746	0.705	0.666	0.630	0.596	0.564	0.507	0.456	0.432
7	0.933	0.871	0.813	0.760	0.711	0.665	0.623	0.583	0.547	0.513	0.452	0.400	0.376
8	0.923	0.853	0.789	0.731	0.677	0.627	0.582	0.540	0.502	0.467	0.404	0.351	0.327
9	0.914	0.837	0.766	0.703	0.645	0.592	0.544	0.500	0.460	0.424	0.361	0.308	0.284
10	0.905	0.820	0.744	0.676	0.614	0.558	0.508	0.463	0.422	0.386	0.322	0.270	0.247
11	0.896	0.804	0.722	0.650	0.585	0.527	0.475	0.429	0.388	0.350	0.287	0.237	0.215
12	0.887	0.788	0.701	0.625	0.557	0.497	0.444	0.397	0.356	0.319	0.257	0.208	0.187
13	0.879	0.773	0.681	0.601	0.530	0.469	0.415	0.368	0.326	0.290	0.229	0.182	0.163
14	0.870	0.758	0.661	0.577	0.505	0.442	0.388	0.340	0.299	0.263	0.205	0.160	0.141
15	0.861	0.743	0.642	0.555	0.481	0.417	0.362	0.315	0.275	0.239	0.183	0.140	0.123
16	0.853	0.728	0.623	0.534	0.458	0.394	0.339	0.292	0.252	0.218	0.163	0.123	0.107
17	0.844	0.714	0.605	0.513	0.436	0.371	0.317	0.270	0.231	0.198	0.146	0.108	0.093
18	0.836	0.700	0.587	0.494	0.416	0.350	0.296	0.250	0.212	0.180	0.130	0.095	0.081
19	0.828	0.686	0.570	0.475	0.396	0.331	0.276	0.232	0.194	0.164	0.116	0.083	0.070
20	0.820	0.673	0.554	0.456	0.377	0.312	0.258	0.215	0.178	0.149	0.104	0.073	0.061
25	0.780	0.610	0.478	0.375	0.295	0.233	0.184	0.146	0.116	0.092	0.059	0.038	0.030
30	0.742	0.552	0.412	0.308	0.231	0.174	0.131	0.099	0.075	0.057	0.033	0.020	0.015

Period	16%	18%	20%	24%	28%	32%	36%	40%	50%	60%	70%	80%	90%
1	0.862	0.847	0.833	0.806	0.781	0.758	0.735	0.714	0.667	0.625	0.588	0.556	0.526
2	0.743	0.718	0.694	0.650	0.610	0.574	0.541	0.510	0.444	0.391	0.346	0.309	0.277
3	0.641	0.609	0.579	0.524	0.477	0.435	0.398	0.364	0.296	0.244	0.204	0.171	0.146
4	0.552	0.516	0.482	0.423	0.373	0.329	0.292	0.260	0.198	0.153	0.120	0.095	0.077
5	0.476	0.437	0.402	0.341	0.291	0.250	0.215	0.186	0.132	0.095	0.070	0.053	0.040
6	0.410	0.370	0.335	0.275	0.227	0.189	0.158	0.133	0.088	0.060	0.041	0.029	0.021
7	0.354	0.314	0.279	0.222	0.178	0.143	0.116	0.095	0.059	0.037	0.024	0.016	0.011
8	0.305	0.266	0.233	0.179	0.139	0.108	0.085	0.068	0.039	0.023	0.014	0.009	0.006
9	0.263	0.226	0.194	0.144	0.108	0.082	0.063	0.048	0.026	0.015	0.008	0.005	0.003
10	0.227	0.191	0.162	0.116	0.085	0.062	0.046	0.035	0.017	0.009	0.005	0.003	0.002
11	0.195	0.162	0.135	0.094	0.066	0.047	0.034	0.025	0.012	0.006	0.003	0.002	0.001
12	0.168	0.137	0.112	0.076	0.052	0.036	0.025	0.018	0.008	0.004	0.002	0.001	0.001
13	0.145	0.116	0.093	0.061	0.040	0.027	0.018	0.013	0.005	0.002	0.001	0.001	0.000
14	0.125	0.099	0.078	0.049	0.032	0.021	0.014	0.009	0.003	0.001	0.001	0.000	0.000
15	0.108	0.084	0.065	0.040	0.025	0.016	0.010	0.006	0.002	0.001	0.000	0.000	0.000
16	0.093	0.071	0.054	0.032	0.019	0.012	0.007	0.005	0.002	0.001	0.000	0.000	
17	0.080	0.060	0.045	0.026	0.015	0.009	0.005	0.003	0.001	0.000	0.000		
18	0.069	0.051	0.038	0.021	0.012	0.007	0.004	0.002	0.001	0.000	0.000		
19	0.060	0.043	0.031	0.017	0.009	0.005	0.003	0.002	0.000	0.000			
20	0.051	0.037	0.026	0.014	0.007	0.004	0.002	0.001	0.000	0.000			
25	0.024	0.016	0.010	0.005	0.002	0.001	0.000	0.000					
30	0.012	0.007	0.004	0.002	0.001	0.000	0.000						

$$P_a = \frac{P_n}{(1 + i)^n} \quad \text{Interest factor} = \frac{1}{(1 + i)^n}$$

The Future Value of an Annuity of $1

Period	1%	2%	3%	4%	5%	6%
1	1.000	1.000	1.000	1.000	1.000	1.000
2	2.010	2.020	2.030	2.040	2.050	2.060
3	3.030	3.060	3.091	3.122	3.152	3.184
4	4.060	4.122	4.184	4.246	4.310	4.375
5	5.101	5.204	5.309	5.416	5.526	5.637
6	6.152	6.308	6.468	6.633	6.802	6.975
7	7.214	7.434	7.662	7.898	8.142	8.394
8	8.286	8.583	8.892	9.214	9.549	9.897
9	9.369	9.755	10.159	10.583	11.027	11.491
10	10.462	10.950	11.464	12.006	12.578	13.181
11	11.567	12.169	12.808	13.486	14.207	14.972
12	12.683	13.412	14.192	15.026	15.917	16.870
13	13.809	14.680	15.618	16.627	17.713	18.882
14	14.947	15.974	17.086	18.292	19.599	21.051
15	16.097	17.293	18.599	20.024	21.579	23.276
16	17.258	18.639	20.157	21.825	23.657	25.673
17	18.430	20.012	21.762	23.698	25.840	28.213
18	19.615	21.412	23.414	25.645	28.132	30.906
19	20.811	22.841	25.117	27.671	30.539	33.760
20	22.109	24.297	26.870	29.778	33.066	36.786
25	28.243	32.030	36.459	41.646	47.727	54.865
30	34.785	40.568	47.575	56.085	66.439	79.058

Period	7%	8%	9%	10%	11%	12%
1	1.000	1.000	1.000	1.000	1.000	1.000
2	2.070	2.080	2.090	2.100	2.120	2.140
3	3.215	3.246	3.278	3.310	3.374	3.440
4	4.440	4.508	4.573	4.641	4.770	4.921
5	5.751	5.867	5.985	6.105	6.353	6.610
6	7.153	7.336	7.523	7.716	8.115	8.536
7	8.654	8.923	9.200	9.487	10.089	10.730
8	10.260	10.637	11.028	11.436	12.300	13.233
9	11.978	12.488	13.021	13.579	14.776	16.085
10	13.816	14.487	15.193	15.937	17.549	19.337
11	15.784	16.645	17.560	18.531	20.655	23.044
12	17.888	18.977	20.141	21.384	24.138	27.271
13	20.141	21.495	22.953	24.523	28.029	32.089
14	22.550	24.215	26.019	27.975	32.393	37.581
15	25.129	27.152	29.361	31.772	37.280	43.842
16	27.888	30.324	33.003	35.950	42.753	50.980
17	30.840	33.750	36.974	40.545	48.884	59.118
18	33.999	37.450	41.301	45.599	55.750	68.394
19	37.379	41.446	46.018	51.159	63.440	78.969
20	40.995	45.762	51.160	57.275	72.052	91.025
25	63.249	73.106	84.701	98.347	133.334	181.871
30	94.461	113.283	136.308	164.494	241.333	356.787

$$CS = l(1 + i)^0 + l(1 + i)^1 + \cdots + l(1 + i)^{n-1} \quad \text{Interest factor} = \frac{(1 + i)^n - 1}{i}$$

The Present Value of an Annuity of $1

Period	1%	2%	3%	4%	5%	6%	7%	8%	9%	10%
1	0.990	0.980	0.971	0.962	0.952	0.943	0.935	0.926	0.917	0.909
2	1.970	1.942	1.913	1.886	1.859	1.833	1.808	1.783	1.759	1.736
3	2.941	2.884	2.829	2.775	2.723	2.673	2.624	2.577	2.531	2.487
4	3.902	3.808	3.717	3.630	3.546	3.465	3.387	3.312	3.240	3.170
5	4.853	4.713	4.580	4.452	4.329	4.212	4.100	3.993	3.890	3.791
6	5.795	5.601	5.417	5.242	5.076	4.917	4.766	4.623	4.486	4.355
7	6.728	6.472	6.230	6.002	5.786	5.582	5.389	5.206	5.033	4.868
8	7.652	7.325	7.020	6.733	6.463	6.210	5.971	5.747	5.535	5.335
9	8.566	8.162	7.786	7.435	7.108	6.802	6.515	6.247	5.985	5.759
10	9.471	8.983	8.530	8.111	7.722	7.360	7.024	6.710	6.418	6.145
11	10.368	9.787	9.253	8.760	8.306	7.887	7.499	7.139	6.805	6.495
12	11.255	10.575	9.954	9.385	8.863	8.384	7.943	7.536	7.161	6.814
13	12.134	11.348	10.635	9.986	9.394	8.853	8.358	7.904	7.487	7.103
14	13.004	12.106	11.296	10.563	9.899	9.295	8.745	8.244	7.786	7.367
15	13.865	12.849	11.938	11.118	10.380	9.712	9.108	8.559	8.060	7.606
16	14.718	13.578	12.561	11.652	10.838	10.106	9.447	8.851	8.312	7.824
17	15.562	14.292	13.166	12.166	11.274	10.477	9.763	9.122	8.544	8.022
18	16.398	14.992	13.754	12.659	11.690	10.828	10.059	9.372	8.756	8.201
19	17.226	15.678	14.324	13.134	12.085	11.158	10.336	9.604	8.950	8.365
20	18.046	16.351	14.877	13.590	12.462	11.470	10.594	9.818	9.128	8.514
25	22.023	19.523	17.413	15.622	14.094	12.783	11.654	10.675	9.823	9.077
30	25.808	22.397	19.600	17.292	15.373	13.765	12.409	11.258	10.274	9.427

Period	12%	14%	16%	18%	20%	24%	28%	32%	36%
1	0.893	0.877	0.862	0.847	0.833	0.806	0.781	0.758	0.735
2	1.690	1.647	1.605	1.566	1.528	1.457	1.392	1.332	1.276
3	2.402	2.322	2.246	2.174	2.106	1.981	1.868	1.766	1.674
4	3.037	2.914	2.798	2.690	2.589	2.404	2.241	2.096	1.966
5	3.605	3.433	3.274	3.127	2.991	2.745	2.532	2.345	2.181
6	4.111	3.889	3.685	3.498	3.326	3.020	2.759	2.534	2.339
7	4.564	4.288	4.039	3.812	3.605	3.242	2.937	2.678	2.455
8	4.968	4.639	4.344	4.078	3.837	3.421	3.076	2.786	2.540
9	5.328	4.946	4.607	4.303	4.031	3.566	3.184	2.868	2.603
10	5.650	5.216	4.833	4.494	4.193	3.682	3.269	2.930	2.650
11	5.988	5.453	5.029	4.656	4.327	3.776	3.335	2.978	2.683
12	6.194	5.660	5.197	4.793	4.439	3.851	3.387	3.013	2.708
13	6.424	5.842	5.342	4.910	4.533	3.912	3.427	3.040	2.727
14	6.628	6.002	5.468	5.008	4.611	3.962	3.459	3.061	2.740
15	6.811	6.142	5.575	5.092	4.675	4.001	3.483	3.076	2.750
16	6.974	6.265	5.669	5.162	4.730	4.033	3.503	3.088	2.758
17	7.120	6.373	5.749	5.222	4.775	4.059	3.518	3.097	2.763
18	7.250	6.467	5.818	5.273	4.812	4.080	3.529	3.104	2.767
19	7.366	6.550	5.877	5.316	4.844	4.097	3.539	3.109	2.770
20	7.469	6.623	5.929	5.353	4.870	4.110	3.546	3.113	2.772
25	7.843	6.873	6.097	5.467	4.948	4.147	3.564	3.122	2.776
30	8.055	7.003	6.177	5.517	4.979	4.160	3.569	3.124	2.778

$$PV = \sum_{t-1}^{n} \frac{l}{(1 + i)^l} \quad \text{Interest factor} = \frac{1 - \dfrac{1}{(1 + i)^n}}{l}$$

Appendix B

ANSWERS TO SELECTED PROBLEMS

Chapter 2

1. a) 25% margin: 300%
    c) 75% margin: 100%
2. b) 50% margin: −50%
3. a) 12%
    b) (25%)
    c) (100%)
4. b) $112
5. At price of stock = $40 and margin requirement of 60%:
    Cash account: −21.2%
    Margin account: −42%
    At price of the stock = $70 and margin requirement of 40%:
    Cash account: 31.2%
    Margin account: 63%
6. b) (150%)
7. At price of the stock of $36: 27.8%

Chapter 3

Your answers may vary from the following depending on rounding off, especially when using interest tables. The use of a financial calculator or the accompanying software may lead to different answers than derived when using the interest tables. If the answer obtained from a calculator is 6.1% but only approximately 6% from the interest table, both are "correct."

1. a) $1,191 total interest
    b) $40 annually; $800 total
2. a) $85,913
    c) $147,521; $61,608 in additional funds
3. a) Ordinary annuity: $6,903
       Annuity due: $6,391
    b) Ordinary annuity: $7,950
       Annuity due: $7,572
4. Value: $98,181, which is less than $120,000; don't buy.
5. At 2%: $66,868
    At 4%: $98,601
    $100,000 is sufficient.
6. $19,714
7. a) $87,729
    b) $38,276
    c) $12,619

8. At 6%, select the $900.
   At 14%, select the $150 each year.
   (The higher rate stresses receiving the money faster so it may be invested at the higher rate.)

9. a) Annual compounding: $112
      Semiannual compounding: $112.40
      Monthly compounding: $112.70
   b) Annual compounding: $89.30
      Semiannual compounding: $89.00
      Monthly compounding: $88.70

10. Tom: $102,320
    Joan: $111,529

11. 12 years (12.18)

12. The present value of the annuity payments is $62,868. If the annuity costs $75,000, it is overpriced.

13. At 9%, the present value of the cash flows is $849, which is more than $800. The yield has to be higher than 9% (10.125%) to bring down the present value of the cash flows to $800.

14. $73,212

15. $60,795

16. Budget in year 10: $4,805,550
               15: $8,607,060
               20: $15,400,665

17. Payment for the 9% mortgage: $30,542

18. Between 4 and 5 years (4.5 years)

19. He can withdraw $16,021 annually. To withdraw the desired amount, he must earn 11%.

20. Annual payment starting at the end of the year: $5,393
    Annual payment starting at the beginning of the year: $5,041

21. a) $30,650
    b) $16,250

22. Invest $3,167 annually

23. The $18,000 loan payment = $5,678

24. a) $1,795
    b) Interest ordinary annuity: $1,828
       Interest annuity due: $2,503
    c) Present value ordinary annuity: $65,848
       Present value annuity due: $71,392
    d) 18.638%
    e) Payment at the end of the year: $8,660
       Payment at the beginning of the year: $8,078

Chapter 4

1. a) Capital gains: $4,700
      Tax: $1,316
   b) Tax savings in current year: $1,050

2. b) Net long-term loss after net short-term capital gain: $1,000
      Tax savings: $330
   g) Current year tax savings: $990
3. a) $280
   d) Loss disallowed
4. a) $500 saved
   b) $0
5. b) $8,050
6. a) $10,000 grows to $23,670; the total in all accounts: $172,406 ($172,428 using a financial calculator).
   b) over 25 years (28.3 years)
   c) $19,690
7. Bob: $60,247
   Mary: $77,037
   Difference: $16,790
8. Bob contributes $1,500 for ten years and accumulates $23,906. This amount grows for ten years into $62,012. The final sum is drawn over fifteen years at the rate of $8,153 annually. Mike contributes a larger amount ($2,000) for ten years and accumulates $31,874; however, he must start to withdraw the funds after five years, so the final amount grows to $51,349. This final sum is drawn down over twenty years at the rate of $6,031 annually. Even though Mike contributed more than Bob, the fact that he must start withdrawing the funds earlier means that the amount received each year is less. This problem points out the desirability of leaving funds in a tax-deferred account as long as possible in order to take advantage of the growth in tax-deferred interest.

Chapter 5

1. 14% in all three cases
2. a) 10.3%
3. a) 12.4%
      standard deviation = 3.12
4. a) 50% A/50% B: return = 16%; standard deviation = 3.14
   c) 25% A/75% B: return = 18%; standard deviation = 4.56
6. 12% when beta = 1.5
8. a) coefficient of variation stock B: 0.132
9. a) Beta stock x: 0.352
   c) Stock y: R^2 = 0.82
10. 1989 through 1993: 0.53

Chapter 6

1. $7.68
2. 6.8%
3. percentage (holding period) return: 40.6%
4. 19.96 (20%)
5. a) $171, 825
   c) $153, 480
6. a) The risk-adjusted ranking: E, D, C, A, B
   b) The risk-adjusted ranking: C, D, B, E, A

Chapter 7

1. a) 27.8%
    b) Purchase price: $1,050
       Sale proceeds: $1,153
       16.9%
    d) 21.2%
2. Taxes owed: $1.545 ($1.54.50 on 100 shares)
4. c) $0
    h) ($10), ($5), $0, $5, $10

Chapter 8

1. a) 5.000 shares purchased in year 1
       5.250 shares purchased in year 2
       6.078 shares purchased in year 5
       62.889 total shares purchased
    b) 4.717 shares purchased in year 1
       4.592 shares in year 3
       3.898 shares in year 10
       Value of position: $10,280
    c) 4.858 shares purchased in year 1
       total shares owned: 145.042
2. a) Cash and retained earnings decline by $1,000,000 to $19,000,000 and
       $97,500,000.
    b) 100,000 shares issued
       Common stock: 1,100,000 shares, $10 par; $11,000,000
       Paid-in capital (new entry): $300,000
       Retained earnings: $97,200,000
3. a) Paid-in capital: $1,800,000
       New price of the stock: $20
    b) Paid-in capital: $2,280,000
       New price of the stock: $54.55
4. Current ratio: 2:1
    Quick ratio: 0.98:1
    Inventory turnover: 1.5 (using cost of goods sold)
    Average collection period: 108 days
    Operating profit margin: 25%
    Net profit margin: 16.8%
    Return on assets: 9.8%
    Return on equity: 14.5%
    Debt/Net worth: 48.3%
    Debt/Total assets: 32.6%
    Times-interest-earned: 5
5. Quick ratio 2007: 0.8
    Times-interest-earned 2005: 4.5
6. Debt ratio: 70%
7. Reduction in inventory: $75,000
8. $4,754,556

9. Operating profit margin A: 15%
   Net profit margin B: 4.5%
   Return on equity A: 26.7%
10. Times-dividend earned: 2.8
11. EPS with debt financing: $2.80
    EPS with preferred stock financing: $2.50

Chapter 9

1. $21
2. $21.40, which is less than $25. (Don't buy!)
3. a) $28.53
4. Required return: 18%
5. b) Stock A: $7.78
   d) $12.94
6. Required return for B: 12.6%
8. Present value of dividend payments: $7.66
   Value of stock: $68.86 (using financial calculator)
   $68.91 (using interest tables)
10. $15.45

Chapter 10

1. 2.5%
2. 62.58%
3. 1.8%
4. Simple average: $15
   Value-weighted average: $15.60
   Geometric average: $14.50
6. a) Holding period return: 61%
   b) Annualized return: 10%
11. a) 12% (12.38%)
    c) 9% (8.88%)
12. Dollar-weighted return: 19%
    Time-weighted return: 23.1%
13. At 12%, the present value = $35.56, which is less than $40, so the return is less than 12%. (Return = 9.16%.)
14. 9.4%
15. b) $85.74
    c) −1.7%
18. Average cost per share: $34.55
19. Average percentage return: 159.3%

Chapter 13

1. Year 1: $49.91
   Year 3: $57.14
2. Tax owed: $28.80
4. Interest in year 2: $68.60

Chapter 14

1. a) $1,000
    b) $875
    c) Current yield in b.: 9.1%
2. a) $1,179 (semiannual compounding: $1,181)
    b) $1,054 (semiannual compounding: $1,055)
    c) $1,142 (semiannual compounding: $1,142)
4. Current yield: 9.6%
    Yield to maturity: 10% (semiannual compounding: 10.04%)
5. Yield to maturity: 14%
7. a) 5% coupon bond: $575 (semiannual compounding: $571)
8. 6.4%
9. a) $60
    b) $75.48
11. a) Bond A: $894 (semiannual compounding: $892)
    Bond B: $1,000
13. $636
16. a) $876
    b) $839
19. Bond B: 6.6 years
21. a) Bond A: 4.4 years
    Bond E: 5 years
    c) C, A, E, D, B
23. b) Bond A: ($167)
26. a) Bond A: $848
    b) Bond A: $857

Chapter 15

1. Discount yield: 6.5%; annualized compound yield: 6.83%
2. Taxable yield: 8.75%
4. Bond B: $676, $508, and $386
6. 3.12% discount yield
    3.19% annualized yield
8. b) Indexed bond: $1,100
10. Yield of call after four years: 3.30%
11. a) Interest payment: $6,000
    Principal repayment: $610.11
    Balance owed: $59,289.89
13. a) $10,955
    c) Balance owed after four years: $91,061
14. c) Total payments: $219,093

Chapter 16

1. a) 4.8%
    b) $864
    c) $38.52
    d) $176

e) $817

f) $223

g) At least $1,728

h) At least $817

i) Virtually nil

2. a) $552

b) 40 shares

c) $1,200

d) $1,200 (value as stock)

g) $1,040

3. a) $17

4. a) Bond A: $1,070

b) Bond B: $946

d) $4(6.710) = $26.84

5. c) A: $75

d) A: 2.4 years

e) Stock: 9% annual return

Bond: 10.7% annual return

6. c) $39

f) $1,240

i) Bond: 14%

k) $1,000

8. b) $15

d) 8.4%

Chapter 17

1. a) Intrinsic value: $1; time premium: $3

b)
Price of the stock	Value of the call
$20	$0
30	5
40	15

c) 275%

d) Cash outflow: $22

Price of the stock	Profit
$15	($7)
25	3
26	3
40	3

e) $4, $3, and ($11)

2. XYZ calls: $4 and 0

XYZ puts: 0 and $1

If the price of the stock is $31, the losses to the buyers of the calls are ($6) and ($2.50).

If the price of the stock is $31, the profits to the writers of the puts are $1.25 and $0.25.

3. a) $1

b) $0

    c) $4
    d) $2
    e) rises
    f) $46
    g) $51
    h) $8
    i) ($2)
    j) ($7)
    k) $4
4. b) $4
    d) ($5)
    f) ($8)
    h) ($3)
    i) ($3)
5. a) ($2), ($2), and $3
    b) $2, $2, and ($3)
6. a) $11
    b) $4
    c) $26 (73.3% increase in the LEAPS)
    e) $0 (100% decrease in the LEAPS)
7. c) Loss at the stock price of $35: ($1)
       Loss at the stock price of $50: ($1)
       Gain at the stock price of $60: $11
    d) Profit at the stock price of $35: $7
       Loss at the stock price of $50: ($3)
    e) Loss at the stock price of $35: ($11)
       Profit at the stock price of $50: $4
8. b) Net cash outflow: $38
    d) ($3)
9. If the price of the stock is $110, make $1,000 on the stock versus $1,000 on the call and the Treasury bill. If the price of the stock is $90, lose $1,000 on the stock versus no loss on the call and the Treasury bill.
10. c) Buying the stock: $86.00
      Buying the call: $95.50
      The covered call: $75.50
      Selling the put: $76.75

Chapter 18

1. $30 − $25/(1 + 0.1) = $7.27
2. a) If the price of the stock is $50, value of the call: $5.45
    b) If the expiration is six months, value of the call: $5.45
    c) If the interest rate is 5%, value of the call: $4.82
    d) If the standard deviation is 40% (0.40), value of the call: $6.79
3. a) 10 calls
    b) 60 shares
4. $3

5. a) Profit if
        Price of the stock is $110: $10
        Price of the stock is $105: $10
        Price of the stock is $90: $10
6. Net cash outflow: $0
9. Gain when price of the stock is $20: $2
    Gain when price of the stock is $35: $7
10. Profit when price of the stock is $60: $3
12. a) $26
    b) ($4)
13. Maximum loss: ($2)
14. b) $1.50
15. Gain or loss when the price of the stock is $40: $0.00
16. Maximum loss: ($1.81)

Chapter 19

1. a) $2,000
    b) Value of the contract: $21,300
    c) $1,900
2. b) 10 percent gain
    c) 4 percent loss
4. a) $1,600,000
    b) $1,560,000
    c) ($250,000)
    d) $40,000
    e) $40,000
    f) $0
    g) $200,000
5. a) $3,300,000
    b) $3,220,000
    c) ($240,000)
    e) $80,000
6. a) $2,000
    c) ($250)
    e) $1,500 gain
8. $4.44
9. First transaction: counter-party receives $700,000

Glossary

A

accelerated depreciation: The allocation of the cost of plant and equipment in unequal annual amounts such that most of the cost is recovered in the early years of an asset's life.

accrued interest: Interest that has been earned but not received.

American Depository Receipts (ADRs): Receipts issued for foreign securities held by a trustee.

annuity: A series of equal annual payments.

annuity due: A series of equal annual payments with the payments made at the beginning of the year.

anticipation note: A short-term liability that is to be retired by specific expected revenues (e.g., expected tax receipts).

arbitrage: Simultaneous purchase and sale to take advantage of price differences in different markets.

arrearage: Cumulative preferred dividends that have not been paid.

average collection period (days sales outstanding): The number of days required to collect accounts receivable.

B

balloon payment: The large final payment necessary to retire a debt issue.

banker's acceptance: Short-term promissory note guaranteed by a bank.

bar graph: A graph indicating the high, low, and closing prices of a security.

Barron's confidence index: An index designed to identify investors' confidence in the level and direction of security prices.

basis point: 0.01 percent.

bearer bond: A bond with coupons attached or a bond whose possession denotes ownership.

bearish: Expecting that prices will decline.

best-efforts agreement: Agreement with an investment banker who does not guarantee the sale of a security but who agrees to make the best effort to sell it.

beta coefficient: An index of risk; a measure of the systematic risk associated with a particular stock.

bid and ask: Prices at which a securities dealer offers to buy and sell stock.

bond: A long-term liability with a specified amount of interest and specified maturity date.

book-to-price ratio: The accounting value of a stock divided by the market price of the stock.

broker: An agent who handles buy and sell orders for an investor.

bullish: Expecting that prices will rise.

business risk: The risk associated with the nature of a business.

bylaws: A document specifying the relationship between a corporation and its stockholders.

C

call feature: The right of an issuer to retire a debt issue prior to maturity.

call option: An option sold by an individual that entitles the buyer to purchase stock at a specified price within a specified time period.

call penalty: A premium paid for exercising a call feature.

capital gain: The increase in the value of an asset, such as a stock or a bond.

capital loss: A decrease in the value of an asset such as a stock or a bond.

cash budget: A financial statement enumerating cash receipts and cash disbursements.

certificate of deposit (CD): A time deposit with a specified maturity date.

certificate of incorporation: A document creating a corporation.

charter: A document specifying the relationship between a firm and the state in which it is incorporated.

Chicago Board Options Exchange (CBOE): The first organized secondary market in put and call options.

closed-end investment company: An investment company with a fixed number of shares that are bought and sold in the secondary securities markets.

collateralized mortgage obligation (CMO): Debt obligation supported by mortgages and sold in series.

commercial paper: Short-term promissory notes issued by the most creditworthy corporations.

commissions: Fees charged by brokers for executing orders.

compounding: The process by which interest is paid on interest that has been previously earned.

confirmation statement: A statement received from a brokerage firm detailing the sale or purchase of a security and specifying a settlement date.

contrarians: Investors who go against the consensus concerning investment strategy.

conversion value as stock: Value of the bond in terms of the stock into which the bond may be converted.

convertible bond: A bond that may be exchanged for (i.e., converted into) stock.

convertible preferred stock: Preferred stock that may be exchanged for (i.e., converted into) common stock.

coupon bond: A bond with coupons attached that are removed and presented for payment of interest when due.

coupon rate: The specified interest rate or amount of interest paid by a bond.

covered option writing: Selling an option for which the seller owns the securities.

covering the short sale: The purchase of securities to close a short position.

credit rating systems: Classification schemes designed to indicate the risk associated with a particular security.

cross-sectional analysis: An analysis of several firms in the same industry at a point in time.

cumulative preferred stock: A preferred stock whose dividends accumulate if they are not paid.

cumulative voting: A voting scheme that encourages minority representation by permitting each stockholder to cast all of his or her votes for one candidate for the firm's board of directors.

currency futures: Contract for the future delivery of foreign exchange.

current ratio: Current assets divided by current liabilities; a measure of liquidity.

current yield: Annual income divided by the current price of the security.

D

daily limit: The maximum daily change permitted in a commodity future's price.

date of record: The day on which an investor must own shares in order to receive the dividend payment.

day order: An order placed with a broker that is canceled at the end of the day if it is not executed.

dealers: Market makers who buy and sell securities for their own accounts.

debenture: An unsecured bond.

debt ratio: The ratio of debt to total assets; a measure of the use of debt financing.

default: The failure of a debtor to meet any term of a debt's indenture.

deficit spending: Government expenditures exceeding government revenues.

devaluation: A decrease in the value of one currency relative to other currencies.

dilution: A reduction in earnings per share due to the issuing of new securities.

director: A person who is elected by stockholders to determine the goals and policies of the firm.

discount: The sale of anything below its stated value.

discount (from net asset value): The extent to which the price of a closed-end investment company's stock is below its net asset value.

discount (of a bond): The extent to which a bond's price is less than its face amount, or principal.

discount broker: A broker who charges lower commissions on securities purchases and sales.

discount rate: The rate of interest that the Federal Reserve charges banks for borrowing reserves.

discounting: The process of determining present value.

dispersion: Deviation from the average.

distribution date: The date on which a dividend is paid to stockholders.

diversification: The process of accumulating different securities to reduce the risk of loss.

dividend: A payment to stockholders that is usually in cash but may be in stock or property.

dividend-growth valuation model: A valuation model that uses dividends and their growth properly discounted back to the present.

dividend reinvestment plan (DRIP): A plan that permits stockholders to have cash dividends reinvested in stock instead of received in cash.

dollar cost averaging: The purchase of securities at different intervals to reduce the impact of price fluctuations.

dollar-weighted rate of return: The rate that equates the present value of cash inflows and cash outflows; the internal rate of return.

Dow Jones Industrial Average: An average of the stock prices of 30 large firms.

Dow Theory: A technical approach based on the Dow Jones averages.

duration: The average time it takes to collect a bond's interest and principal repayment.

E

earnings per preferred share: The total earnings divided by the number of preferred shares outstanding.

efficient market hypothesis (EMH): A theory that stock prices correctly measure the firm's future earnings and dividends and that investors should not consistently outperform the market on a risk-adjusted basis.

efficient portfolio: The portfolio that offers the highest expected return for a given amount of risk.

8-K report: A document filed with the SEC that describes a change in a firm that may affect the value of its securities.

emerging market fund: Investment company that specializes in securities from less-developed countries.

equilibrium price: A price that equates supply and demand.

equipment trust certificate: A serial bond secured by specific equipment.

equity trust: A real estate investment trust that specializes in acquiring real estate for subsequent rental income.

Eurobond: A bond denominated in U.S. dollars but issued abroad.

Eurodollar CD: Time deposit in a foreign bank and denominated in dollars.

Eurodollars: Dollar-denominated deposits in a foreign bank.

exchange rate: The price of a foreign currency in terms of another currency.

exchange rate risk: The uncertainty associated with changes in the value of foreign currencies.

exchange-traded fund (ETF): A type of mutual fund whose shares are traded in the secondary markets.

ex-dividend: Stock that trades exclusive of any dividend payment.

ex-dividend date: The day on which a stock trades exclusive of any dividends.

exercise (strike) price: The price at which the investor may buy or sell stock through an option.

expected return: The sum of the anticipated dividend yield and capital gains.

expiration date: The date by which an option must be exercised.

extendible security: Bond whose maturity date may be extended into the future.

extra dividend: A sum paid in addition to the firm's regular dividend.

F

fallen angel: Investment-grade security whose quality has deteriorated.

federal agency bonds: Debt issued by an agency of the federal government.

federal funds rate: The rate of interest a bank charges another bank for borrowing reserves.

Federal Deposit Insurance Corporation (FDIC): Federal government agency that supervises commercial banks and insures commercial bank deposits.

Federal Reserve: The central bank of the United States.

financial futures: Contract for the future delivery of a financial asset.

financial intermediary: A financial institution, such as a commercial bank, that borrows from one group and lends to another.

financial leverage: The use of borrowed funds to acquire an asset.

financial life cycle: The stages of life during which individuals accumulate and subsequently use financial assets.

financial risk: The risk associated with a firm's sources of financing.

firm commitment: Agreement with an investment banker who guarantees a sale of securities by agreeing to purchase the entire issue at a specified price.

fiscal policy: Taxation, expenditures, and debt management of the federal government.

fixed asset turnover: Ratio of sales to fixed assets; tells how many fixed assets are needed to generate sales.

flat: A description of a bond that trades without accrued interest.

foreign exchange market: Market for the buying and selling of currencies.

full disclosure laws: The federal and state laws requiring publicly held firms to disclose financial and other information that may affect the value of their securities.

future sum of an annuity: Compound value of a series of equal annual payments.

futures contract: An agreement for the future delivery of a commodity at a specified date.

futures price: The price in a contract for the future delivery of a commodity.

G

general obligation bond: A bond whose interest does not depend on the revenue of a specific project; government bonds supported by the full faith and credit of the issuer (i.e., authority to tax).

Ginnie Mae: Mortgage pass-through bond issued by the Government National Mortgage Association.

global funds: Mutual funds whose portfolios include securities of firms with international operations that are located throughout the world.

good-till-canceled order: An order placed with a broker that remains in effect until it is executed by the broker or canceled.

gross domestic product (GDP): Total value of all final goods and services newly produced within a country by domestic factors of production.

gross profit margin: Percentage earned on sales after deducting the cost of goods sold.

H

head-and-shoulder pattern: A tool of technical analysis; a pattern of security prices that resembles a head and shoulders.

hedging: Taking opposite positions to reduce risk.

high-yield securities: Non-investment-grade securities offering a high return.

holding period return (HPR): Total return (income plus price appreciation during a specified time period) divided by the cost of the investment.

I

income: The flow of money or its equivalent produced by an asset; dividends and interest.

income bond: A bond whose interest is paid only if it is earned by the firm.

increasing rate bond: Bond whose coupon rises over time.

indenture: The document that specifies the terms of a bond issue.

index fund: A mutual fund whose portfolio duplicates an index of stock prices.

individual retirement account (IRA): An individual retirement plan that is available to workers.

inefficient portfolio: A portfolio whose return is not maximized given the level of risk.

inflation-indexed securities: Securities whose principal and interest payments are adjusted for changes in the Consumer Price Index.

initial public offering (IPO): The first sale of common stock to the general public.

inside information: Privileged information concerning a firm.

interest: Payment for the use of money.

interest rate risk: The uncertainty associated with changes in interest rates; the possibility of loss resulting from increases in interest rates.

internal rate of return: Percentage return that equates the present value of an investment's cash inflows with its cost.

international funds: American mutual funds whose portfolios are limited to non-American firms.

intrinsic value: What an option is worth as stock.

inventory turnover: The speed with which inventory is sold.

investment (in economics): The purchase of plant, equipment, or inventory.

investment (in lay terms): Acquisition of an asset such as a stock or a bond.

investment banker: An underwriter; a firm that sells new issues of securities to the general public.

investment value as debt: The value of a convertible as if it were nonconvertible debt.

irregular dividends: Dividend payments that either do not occur in regular intervals or vary in amount.

J

Jensen performance index: A measure of performance that compares the realized return with the return that should have been earned for the amount of risk borne by the investor.

K

Keogh account (HR-10 plan): A retirement plan that is available to self-employed individuals.

L

leverage: Magnification of the potential return on an investment.

limit order: An order placed with a broker to buy or sell at a specified price.

liquidity: Moneyness; the ease with which assets can be converted into cash with little risk of loss of principal.

load fee: Sales charge levied by mutual funds.

load fund: A mutual fund that charges a commission to purchase or sell its shares.

long position: Owning assets for their income and possible price appreciation.

M

M-1: Sum of demand deposits, coins, and currency.

M-2: Sum of demand deposits, coins, currency, and savings accounts at banks.

maintenance margin: The minimum equity required for a margin account. (The minimum level of funds required before a margin call.)

maintenance margin (futures): The minimum level of funds in a margin account that triggers a margin call.

margin: The amount that an investor must put down to buy securities on credit.

margin (futures): Good faith deposit made when purchasing or selling a futures contract.

margin call: A request by a broker for an investor to place additional funds or securities in an account as collateral against borrowed funds or as a good faith deposit.

margin requirement: The minimum percentage, established by the Federal Reserve, that the investor must put up in cash to buy securities.

marginal tax rate: The tax rate paid on an additional last dollar of taxable income; an individual's tax bracket.

market order: An order to buy or sell at the current market price or quote.

market risk: Systematic risk; the risk associated with the tendency of a stock's price to fluctuate with the market.

marketability: The ease with which an asset may be bought and sold.

maturity date: The time at which a debt issue becomes due and the principal must be repaid.

money market instruments: Short-term securities, such as Treasury bills, negotiable certificates of deposit, or commercial paper.

money market mutual funds: Mutual funds that specialize in short-term securities.

moral backing: Nonobligatory support for a debt issue.

mortgage bond: A bond that is secured by property, especially real estate.

mortgage trust: A real estate investment trust that specializes in loans secured by real estate.

moving average: An average in which the most recent observation is added and the most distant observation is deleted before the average is recomputed.

municipal (tax-exempt) bond: A bond issued by a state or one of its political subdivisions whose interest is not taxed by the federal government.

mutual fund: An open-end investment company.

N

naked option writing: The selling (i.e., writing) of an option without owning the underlying security.

Nasdaq: National Association of Securities Dealers Automatic Quotation system; quotation system for over-the-counter securities.

negotiable certificate of deposit: A certificate of deposit in which the rate and the term are individually negotiated by the bank and the lender and which may be bought and sold.

net asset value (NAV): The asset value of a share in an investment company; total assets minus total liabilities divided by the number of shares outstanding.

net profit margin: The ratio of earnings after interest and taxes to sales.

no-load mutual fund: A mutual fund that does not charge a commission for buying its shares.

noncumulative preferred stock: Preferred stock whose dividends do not accumulate if the firm misses a dividend payment.

NYSE composite index: New York Stock Exchange index; an index of prices of stocks listed on the New York Stock Exchange.

O

odd lot: A unit of trading, such as 22 shares, that is smaller than the general unit of sale.

open-end investment company: A mutual fund; an investment company from which investors buy shares and to which they resell them.

open interest (futures): The number of futures contracts in existence for a particular commodity with a specified price expiring in a specified month.

open interest (options): The number of call or put options in existence on a particular stock at a specified exercise price and a specified expiration date.

open market operations: The buying or selling of Treasury securities by the Federal Reserve.

operating profit margin: Percentage earned on sales before adjusting for nonrecurring items, interest, and taxes.

option: The right to buy or sell something at a specified price within a specified time period.

ordinary annuity: A series of equal annual payments in which the payments are made at the end of each year.

originating house: An investment banker that makes an agreement with a firm to sell a new issue of securities and forms the syndicate to market them.

over-the-counter (OTC) market: The informal secondary market for unlisted securities.

P

paper profits: Price appreciation that has not been realized.

partnership: An unincorporated business owned by two or more individuals.

payout ratio: The ratio of dividends to earnings.

PEG ratio: The price/earnings ratio divided by the growth rate of earnings.

point-and-figure chart (X-O chart): A chart composed of Xs and Os that is used in technical analysis to summarize price movements.

portfolio: An accumulation of assets owned by the investor and designed to transfer purchasing power to the future.

portfolio risk: The total risk associated with owning a portfolio; the sum of systematic and unsystematic risk.

preemptive rights: The right of current stockholders to maintain their proportionate ownership in the firm.

preferred stock: A class of equity whose claim is prior to that of common stock on the corporation's earnings, and on its assets in case of liquidation or reorganization.

preliminary prospectus (red herring): Initial document detailing the financial condition of a firm that must be filed with the SEC to register a new issue of securities.

premium: The market price of an option.

premium (of a bond): The extent to which a bond's price exceeds the face amount of the debt.

premium (over net asset value): The extent to which the price of a closed-end investment company's stock exceeds the share's net asset value.

present value: The current worth of an amount to be received in the future.

present value of an annuity: The present worth of a series of equal payments.

primary market: The initial sale of securities.

principal: The amount owed; the face value of a debt.

private placement: The nonpublic sale of securities.

programmed trading: Coordinated buying or selling of portfolios triggered by computers.

purchasing power risk: The uncertainty that future inflation will erode the purchasing power of assets and income.

put bond: A bond that the holder may redeem (i.e., sell back to the issuer) at a specified price and a specified time.

put option: An option to sell stock at a specified price within a specified time period.

Q

quick ratio (acid test): Current assets excluding inventory divided by current liabilities; a measure of liquidity.

R

rate of return: The annual percentage return realized on an investment.

rate of return (internal rate of return, or IRR): The discount rate that equates the cost of an investment with the cash flows generated by the investment.

real estate investment trust (REIT): Closed-end investment company that specializes in real estate or mortgage investments.

realized return: The sum of income and capital gains earned on an investment.

recapitalization: An alteration in a firm's sources of finance, such as the substitution of long-term debt for equity.

receivables turnover: The speed with which a firm collects its accounts receivable.

recession: A period of rising unemployment and declining national output.

refunding: The act of issuing new debt and using the proceeds to retire existing debt.

regional funds: Mutual funds that specialize in a particular geographical area.

registered bond: A bond whose ownership is registered with the commercial bank that distributes interest payments and principal repayments.

registered representative: A person who buys and sells securities for customers; a broker.

registration: Process of filing information with the SEC concerning a proposed sale of securities to the general public.

regular dividends: Steady dividend payments that are distributed at regular intervals.

reinvestment rate risk: The risk associated with reinvesting earnings or principal at a lower rate than was initially earned.

repurchase agreement (repo): Sale of a short-term security in which the seller agrees to buy back the security at a specified price.

required return: The return necessary to induce the investor to purchase an asset.

reserve requirement: The percentage of cash that banks must hold against their deposit liabilities.

reset bond: Bond whose coupon is periodically reset.

retention ratio: The ratio of earnings not distributed to earnings.

return: The sum of income plus capital gains earned on an investment in an asset.

return on assets: The ratio of earnings to total assets.

return on equity: The ratio of earnings to equity.

revaluation: An increase in the value of one currency relative to other currencies.

revenue bond: A bond whose interest is paid only if the debtor earns sufficient revenue.

rights offering: Sale of new securities to existing stockholders.

risk: The possibility of loss; the uncertainty of future returns.

round lot: The general unit of trading in a security, such as 100 shares.

S

secondary market: A market for buying and selling previously issued securities.

Securities and Exchange Commission (SEC): Government agency that enforces the federal securities laws.

Securities Investor Protection Corporation (SIPC): The agency that insures investors against failures by brokerage firms.

securitization: The process of converting an illiquid asset into a marketable security.

semiannual compounding: The payment of interest twice a year.

serial bond: A bond issue in which specified bonds mature each year.

Series EE bonds: Savings bonds issued in small denominations by the federal government.

share averaging: A system for the accumulation of shares in which the investor periodically buys the same number of shares.

Sharpe performance index: A risk-adjusted measure of performance that standardizes the return in excess of the risk-free rate by the standard deviation of the portfolio's return.

short position: Selling borrowed assets for possible price deterioration; being short in a security or a commodity.

short sale: The sale of borrowed securities in anticipation of a price decline; a contract for future delivery.

sinking fund: A series of periodic payments to retire a bond issue.

specialist: A market maker on the New York Stock Exchange who maintains an orderly market in a stock.

speculation: An investment that offers a potentially large return but is also very risky; a reasonable probability that the investment will produce a loss.

split coupon bond: Bond with a zero or low initial coupon followed by a period with a high coupon.

spot price: The current price of a commodity.

spread: The difference between the bid and the ask prices.

Standard & Poor's 500 stock index: A value-weighted index of 500 stocks.

statement of cash flows: An accounting statement that enumerates a firm's cash inflows and cash outflows.

stock: A security representing ownership in a corporation.

stock dividend: A dividend paid in stock.

stock index futures: A contract based on an index of securities prices.

stock index options: Rights to buy and sell based on an aggregate measure of stock prices.

stock repurchase: The buying of stock by the issuing corporation.

stock split: Recapitalization that affects the number of shares outstanding, their par value, the earnings per share, and the price of the stock.

stop order: A purchase or sell order designed to limit an investor's loss or to assure a profit on a position in a security.

straight-line depreciation: The allocation of the cost of plant and equipment by equal annual amounts over a period of time.

street name: The registration of securities in a brokerage firm's name instead of in the buyer's name.

surplus: Receipts exceeding disbursements.

swap: An agreement to exchange payments.

syndicate: A selling group assembled to market an issue of securities.

systematic risk: Risk from fluctuations in securities prices; e.g., market risk.

T

tax anticipation note: Short-term government security secured by expected tax revenues.

tax-deferred annuity: A contract sold by an insurance company in which the company guarantees a series of payments and whose earnings are not taxed until they are distributed.

tax-exempt bond: A bond whose interest is excluded from federal income taxation.

tax shelter: An asset or investment that defers, reduces, or avoids taxation.

technical analysis: An analysis of past volume and/or price behavior to identify which assets to purchase or sell and the best time to purchase or sell them.

10-K report: A required annual report filed with the SEC by publicly held firms.

10-Q report: A required quarterly report filed with the SEC by publicly held firms.

third market: Over-the-counter market for securities listed on an exchange.

13-D report: Document filed with the SEC by an individual who acquires 5 percent of a publicly held firm's stock.

time premium: The amount by which an option's price exceeds the option's intrinsic value.

time-series analysis: An analysis of a firm over a period of time.

time-weighted rate of return: Geometric average of individual holding period returns.

times-dividend-earned ratio: Earnings divided by preferred dividend requirements.

times-interest-earned: Ratio of earnings before interest and taxes divided by interest expense; a coverage ratio that measures the safety of debt.

total asset turnover: Ratio of sales to total assets; tells how many total assets are used to generate sales.

trader: An investor who frequently buys and sells.

tranche: Subdivision of a bond issue.

Treasury bills: Short-term federal government securities.

Treasury bonds: The long-term debt of the federal government.

Treasury notes: The intermediate-term debt of the federal government.

Treynor index: A risk-adjusted measure of performance that standardizes the return in excess of the risk-free rate by the portfolio's systematic risk.

trustee: An appointee, usually a commercial bank, responsible for upholding the terms of a bond's indenture.

12b-1 fees: Fees that a mutual fund may charge to cover marketing and advertising expenses.

U

undercapitalized: Having insufficient equity financing.

underwriting: The process by which securities are sold to the general public and in which the investment banker buys the securities from the issuing firm.

unit trust: A passive investment company with a fixed portfolio of assets that are self-liquidating.

unsystematic risk: The risk associated with individual events that affect a particular security.

U.S. Treasury bill: Short-term debt of the federal government.

V

valuation: The process of determining the current worth of an asset.

value: What something is worth; the present value of future benefits.

variable interest rate bond: A long-term bond with a coupon rate that varies with changes in short-term rates.

venture capitalist: Firm specializing in investing in the securities, especially stock, of small, emerging companies.

voting rights: The rights of stockholders to vote their shares.

W

warrant: An option issued by a company to buy its stock at a specified price within a specified time period.

Y

yield curve: The relationship between time to maturity and yields for debt in a given risk class.

yield to call: The yield earned on a bond from the time it is acquired until the time it is called and retired by the firm.

yield to maturity: The yield earned on a bond from the time it is acquired until the maturity date.

Z

zero coupon bond: A bond on which interest accrues and is paid at maturity, and is initially sold at a discount.

INDEX

The **bold** entries refer to the page on which the term is defined in the margin notes. Although the definition usually occurs the first time the word is used, there are instances in which a term is cross-referenced prior to the marginal definition.